ABC Thumb Index

With
Thum
page
letter
the Fr
French section of this dictionary.

You place your thumb on the letter you want at the edge of this
page, then flip through the dictionary till you come to the appropriate pages in the French-
English or English-French section.

Left-handed people should use
the ABC Thumb Index at the
end of the book.

A
B
C
D
E
F
G
H
I
J
K
L
M
N
O
P
Q
R
S
T
U
V
W
X
Y
Z

LANGENSCHEIDT'S
POCKET FRENCH
DICTIONARY

FRENCH-ENGLISH
ENGLISH-FRENCII

Edited by
THE LANGENSCHEIDT
EDITORIAL STAFF

Completely revised edition

LANGENSCHEIDT
NEW YORK · BERLIN · MUNICH

Neither the presence nor the absence of a designation that any entered word constitutes a trademark should be regarded as affecting the legal status of any trademark.

6 7 8 8 9 10 * 2001 2000 1999 98 97

© 1970, 1992 Langenscheidt KG, Berlin and Munich
Printed in Germany

Preface

This revised edition of the "Pocket French Dictionary" has two main goals: to retain all the tried and tested features of its predecessor while at the same time keeping the user up to date with the constant development of language. Thus many new words and phrases have been included in this dictionary, as well as – due to its ever-increasing importance – ample material from the sphere of colloquial and familiar language. To quote just a few random specimens: biocarburant biofuel, la vogue rétro nostalgia, télétravail telecommuting, avoir la pêche be feeling great, ficher en l'air chuck up, se mettre en rogne blow one's top; halfway house centre de réadaption, identikit portrait-robot, time lag décalage horaire, rumpus room salle de jeux, kick up a rumpus faire un scandale, and all that jazz et tout le bataclan.

This dictionary provides clear answers to questions on the conjugation of French verbs. The user is referred to a list of model verbs in the appendix by the reference number after each verb in the dictionary. Those forms of French irregular verbs from which tenses can be derived have separate entries.

The phonetic transcription has been given in square brackets after each French entry, using the system of the International Phonetic Association (IPA).

In addition to the vocabulary, this dictionary contains special quick-reference sections of proper names, abbreviations, numerals, and weights and measures.

Designed for the widest possible variety of uses, this Langenscheidt dictionary, with its more than 55 000 references and 100 000 translations, will be of great value to students, teachers, and tourists as well as in home and office libraries.

Contents

Arrangement of the Dictionary and Guide for the User 5

Symbols and Abbreviations Used in This Dictionary 6

The Phonetic Symbols of the International Phonetic Association 7

Numerals 9

French-English Dictionary 11

English-French Dictionary 325

French Proper Names 599

Common French Abbreviations 602

English Geographical Names 606

Common British and American Abbreviations 607

French Weights and Measures 608

Temperature Conversion Tables 609

Conjugations of French Verbs 611

Arrangement of the Dictionary and Guide for the User

1. Arrangement. Strict alphabetical order has been maintained throughout this dictionary. Those forms of French irregular verbs from which the various tenses can be derived have also been given in their proper alphabetical order. Irregular plural forms of English and French nouns have been entered immediately after the respective headwords. Letters in brackets indicate that the word may be spelt with or without the letter bracketed.

2. Vocabulary. Some of the numerous words formed with ...er, ...ing, ...ism, ...ist, ...ness, re..., in... or un... (English) and ...ago, ...ation, ...eur, ...ier, ...isme, in... or re... (French) have not been listed. In order to find out their meanings, look up the radical.

3. Pronunciation. Pronunciation is given in square brackets by means of the symbols of the International Phonetic Association (p. 10).

4. Explanatory additions have been printed in italics; e.g. **smooth** lisse (*surface*); régulier (*movement*).

5. Subject Labels. The field of knowledge from which a headword or some of its meanings are taken is, where possible, indicated by figurative or abbreviated labels or by other labels written out in full. A figurative or abbreviated label placed immediately after a headword (or, in the French-English part between headword and its phonetic transcription) applies to all translations. Any label preceding an individual translation refers to this only.

6. Translations of similar meanings have been subdivided by commas, the various senses by semicolons.

7. French homonyms of different etymologies have usually been subdivided by exponents;
e.g. **mousse**[1] ship's boy ...
   mousse[2] moss...
   mousse[3] blunt...

8. Grammatical Information. The **gender** of French nouns is always given. The **indication of the parts of speech** has been omitted where it is obvious. **French feminine forms** have generally been suppressed. They have, however, been retained.

a) in adjectives which serve at the same time as feminine nouns (e.g. **étendu, e**);

b) in nouns where the feminine is of equal importance (e.g. **amant, e**);

c) in nouns where the feminine has an additional meaning (e.g. **veilleur, -euse**).

Conjugation of verbs. The number given in round brackets after each French infinitive refers to the table of conjugations on pages 625–638.

Symbols and Abbreviations
Used in This Dictionary

Symbols

The **tilde** (~, ~) serves as a mark of repetition. The tilde in bold type (~) replaces either the headword or the part preceding the vertical bar; e.g. **vénér|able ...; ~ation** (= vénération) ...; **~er** (= vénérer) ...

The simple tilde (~) replaces:

a) The headword immediately preceding (which may itself contain a tilde in bold type);

b) within the phonetic transcription of French headwords, the whole of the pronunciation of the preceding headword, or of some part of it which remains unchanged;

e.g. **vénér|able** [vene'rabl] ...; **~ation** [~ra'sjɔ̃] = [venera'sjɔ̃] ...; **-er** [~'re] = [vene're].

The tilde with circle (ℒ, ℒ). When the first letter changes from capital to small or vice-versa, the usual tilde is replaced by a tilde with circle (ℒ, ℒ);

e.g. **saint** ...; **ℒ-Esprit** = Saint--Esprit;
croix ...; **ℒ-Rouge** = Croix--Rouge;

common ...; **ℒ Market** = Common Market; **independence** ...; **ℒ Day** = Independence Day.

F	*familier*, colloquial.	🚂	*chemin de fer*, railway, *Am.* railroad.
V	*vulgaire*, vulgar.	✈	*aviation*, aviation.
†	*vieilli*, obsolete.	♪	*musique*, music.
♣	*botanique*, botany.	△	*architecture*, architecture.
⊚	*technologie*, technology; *mécanique*, mechanics.	⚡	*électricité*, electricity.
⚒	*mines*, mining.	⚖	*droit*, law.
✕	*militaire*, military.	A͜	*mathématique*, mathematics.
⚓	*nautique*, nautical; *marine*, navy.	✗	*agriculture*, agriculture.
✝	*commerce*, commercial; *finances*, finance.	♠	*chimie*, chemistry.
		✸	*médecine*, medicine.
		⌀	*blason*, heraldry.

Abbreviations used in this directionary are listed at the end of the book.

The Phonetic Symbols of the International Phonetic Association

A. Vowels

Note: In French the vowels are "pure", i.e. there is no slackening off or diphthongization at the end of the sound. Thus, the [e] of *né* [ne] has no tail as in English *nay* [nei].

[ɑ] back vowel, mouth well open, tongue lowered, as in English *father*: long in *pâte* [pɑ:t], short in *cas* [kɑ]

[ɑ̃] [ɑ]-sound, but with some of the breath passing through the nose: long in *prendre* [prɑ̃:dr], short in *banc* [bɑ̃]

[a] clear front vowel, tongue further forward than for [ɑ] and corners of the mouth drawn further back: long in *page* [pa:ʒ], short in *rat* [ra]

[e] closed vowel, tongue raised and well forward, corners of the mouth drawn back, though not as far as for [i]; purer than the vowel in English *nay*, *clay*, etc.: *été* [e'te]

[ɛ] open vowel, tongue less raised and further back than for [e], corners of the mouth drawn back but slightly less than for [e]; purer than the sound in English *bed*: long in *mère* [mɛ:r], short in *après* [a'prɛ]

[ɛ̃] [ɛ]-sound, but with some of the breath passing through the nose: long in *plaindre* [plɛ̃:dr], short in *fin* [fɛ̃]

[ə] rounded sound, something like the **a** in English *about*: *je* [ʒə], *lever* [lə've]

[i] closed vowel, tongue very high, corners of the mouth well back, rather more closed than [i] in English *sea*: long in *dire* [di:r], short in *vie* [vi]

[o] closed vowel, tongue drawn back, lips rounded; no tailing off into [u] or [w] as in English *below*: long in *fosse* [fo:s], short in *peau* [po]

[ɔ] open **o** but closer than in English *cot*, with tongue lower, lips more rounded, mouth more open: long in *fort* [fɔ:r], short in *cotte* [kɔt]

[ɔ̃] [ɔ]-sound, but with some of the breath passing through the nose: long in *nombre* [nɔ̃:br], short in *mon* [mɔ̃]

[ø] a rounded [e], pronounced rather like the **ir** of English *birth* but closer and with lips well rounded and forward: long in *chanteuse* [ʃɑ̃'tø:z], short in *peu* [pø]

[œ] a rounded open **e** [ɛ], a little like the **ur** of English *turn* but with the tongue higher and the lips well rounded: long in *fleur* [flœ:r], short in *œuf* [œf]

[œ̃] [œ]-sound, but with some of the breath passing through the nose: long in *humble* [œ̃:bl], short in *parfum* [par'fœ̃]

[u] closed vowel with back of the tongue raised close to the soft palate and the front drawn back and down, and lips far forward and rounded; rather like the **oo** of English *root* but tighter and without the tailing off into the [w] sound: long in *tour* [tu:r], short in *route* [rut]

[y] an [i] pronounced with the lips well forward and rounded: long in *mur* [my:r], short in *vue* [vy]

B. Consonants

Note: the consonant sounds not listed below are similar to those of English, except that they are much more dry: thus the [p] is not a breathed sound and [t] and [d] are best pronounced with the tip of the tongue against the back of the top teeth, with no breath accompanying the sound.

[j] a rapidly pronounced sound like the **y** in English *yes*: *diable* [dja:bl], *dieu* [djø], *fille* [fi:j].

[l] usually more voiced than in English and does not have its 'hollow sound': *aller* [a'le].

[ɲ] the "n mouillé", an [n] followed by a rapid [j]: *cogner* [kɔ'ɲe].

[ŋ] not a true French sound; occurs in a few borrowed foreign words: *meeting* [mi'tiŋ].

[r] in some parts of France the [r] may be sounded like a slightly rolled English [r], but the uvular sound is more generally accepted. It has been described as sounding like a short and light gargle: *ronger* [rɔ̃'ʒe].

[ʃ] rather like the **sh** of English *shall*, never like the **ch** of English *cheat*: *chanter* [ʃɑ̃'te].

[ɥ] like a rapid [y], never a separate syllable: *muet* [mɥɛ].

[w] not as fully a consonant as the English [w]. It is half-way between the consonant [w] and the vowel [u]: *oui* [wi].

[ʒ] a voiced [ʃ]; it is like the second part of the sound of **di** in the English *soldier*, i.e. it does not have the [d] element: *j'ai* [ʒe]; *rouge* [ru:ʒ].

C. Use of the sign ' to mark stress

The stressed syllable is indicated by the use of ' before it. This is to some extent theoretical. Such stress as there is is not very marked and the presence of the ' may be considered a reminder that the word should not normally be stressed in any other syllable, especially if the word resembles an English one which *is* stressed elsewhere. Though a stress mark is shown for each word of more than one syllable, all the words in one breath group will not in fact carry the stress indicated: thus, though *mauvais* may be transcribed [mɔ've], in *mauvais ami* there is only one main stress, on the *-mi*.

In words of one syllable only, the stress mark is not given.

D. Use of the sign : to mark length

When the sign [:] appears after a vowel it indicates that the duration of the vowel sound is rather longer than for a vowel which appears without it. Thus the [œ] of *feuille* [fœ:j] is longer than the [œ] of *feuillet* [fœ'jɛ]. In unstressed syllables one frequently finds a semi-long vowel but this fine shade of duration has not been marked in the transcription.

Numerals

Cardinal Numbers

0	zéro *nought, zero, cipher*		60	soixante *sixty*
1	un, une *one*		70	soixante-dix *seventy*
2	deux *two*		71	soixante et onze *seventy-one*
3	trois *three*		72	soixante-douze *seventy-two*
4	quatre *four*		80	quatre-vingts *eighty*
5	cinq *five*		81	quatre-vingt-un *eighty-one*
6	six *six*		90	quatre-vingt-dix *ninety*
7	sept *seven*		91	quatre-vingt-onze *ninety-one*
8	huit *eight*		100	cent *a or one hundred*
9	neuf *nine*		101	cent un *one hundred and one*
10	dix *ten*		200	deux cents *two hundred*
11	onze *eleven*		211	deux cent onze *two hundred and eleven*
12	douze *twelve*		1000	mille *a or one thousand*
13	treize *thirteen*		1001	mille un *one thousand and one*
14	quatorze *fourteen*		1100	onze cents *eleven hundred*
15	quinze *fifteen*		1967	dix-neuf cent soixante-sept *nineteen hundred and sixty-seven*
16	seize *sixteen*			
17	dix-sept *seventeen*			
18	dix-huit *eighteen*		2000	deux mille *two thousand*
19	dix-neuf *nineteen*		1 000 000	un million *a or one million*
20	vingt *twenty*			
21	vingt et un *twenty-one*			
22	vingt-deux *twenty-two*		2 000 000	deux millions *two million*
30	trente *thirty*			
40	quarante *forty*		1 000 000 000	un milliard *one thousand millions, Am. one billion*
50	cinquante *fifty*			

Ordinal Numbers

1er	le premier, 1re la première *the first*		20e	vingtième *twentieth*
2e	le deuxième, la deuxième *the second*		21e	vingt et unième *twenty-first*
			22e	vingt-deuxième *twenty-second*
3e	le *or* la troisième *the third*		30e	trentième *thirtieth*
4e	quatrième *fourth*		31e	trente et unième *thirty-first*
5e	cinquième *fifth*		40e	quarantième *fortieth*
6e	sixième *sixth*		41e	quarante et unième *forty-first*
7e	septième *seventh*		50e	cinquantième *fiftieth*
8e	huitième *eighth*		51e	cinquante et unième *fifty-first*
9e	neuvième *ninth*		60e	soixantième *sixtieth*
10e	dixième *tenth*		61e	soixante et unième *sixty-first*
11e	onzième *eleventh*		70e	soixante-dixième *seventieth*
12e	douzième *twelfth*		71e	soixante et onzième *seventy-first*
13e	treizième *thirteenth*			
14e	quatorzième *fourteenth*		72e	soixante-douzième *seventy-second*
15e	quinzième *fifteenth*			
16e	seizième *sixteenth*		80e	quatre-vingtième *eightieth*
17e	dix-septième *seventeenth*		81e	quatre-vingt-unième *eighty-first*
18e	dix-huitième *eighteenth*			
19e	dix-neuvième *nineteenth*		90e	quatre-vingt-dixième *ninetieth*

91e quatre-vingt-onzième *ninety-first*
100e centième *hundredth*

101e cent unième *hundred and first*
200e deux centième *two hundredth*
1000e millième *thousandth*

Fractions

$^1/_2$ (un) demi *one half*; la moitié *(the) half*

1 $^1/_2$ un et demi *one and a half*

$^1/_3$ un tiers *one third*

$^2/_3$ (les) deux tiers *two thirds*

$^1/_4$ un quart *one quarter*

$^3/_4$ (les) trois quarts *three quarters*

$^1/_5$ un cinquième *one fifth*

$^5/_8$ (les) cinq huitièmes *five eighths*

$^9/_{10}$ (les) neuf dixièmes *nine tenths*

0,45 zéro, virgule, quarante-cinq *point four five*

17,38 dix-sept, virgule, trente-huit *seventeen point three eight*

French-English Dictionary

A

a [a] *3rd p. sg. pres. of* **avoir** 1.

à [~] *prp. place*: at (*table, Hastings*), in (*Edinburgh*), on (*the wall*); *direction*: to, into; *origin*: from, of; *time*: at (*7 o' clock, noon, his words*); in (*spring etc.*); *agent etc.*: with, by (means of); *manner*: in; on (*condition*), *price*: for (*two dollars*); *distribution, measurements*: by; *dative, possession*: **donner qch. à q.** give s.th to s.o., give s o s.th.; **grâce à Dieu!** thank God!; **c'est à moi** this is mine; **à terre** on *or* to the ground; **au secours!** help!; **emprunter à** borrow from; **c'est bien aimable à vous** that's very kind of you; **à la longue** in (1b) lower; **à le voir** seeing him; **à tout moment** constantly; **à partir de ...** from ... (on); **peu à peu** little by little; **bateau** *m* **à vapeur** steamer; **maison** *f* **à deux étages** two-storied house; **verre** *m* **à vin** wineglass; **fait à la main** handmade; **à voix basse** in a low voice; **à la nage** swimming; **peinture** *f* **à l'huile** painting in oil; **aux yeux bleus** blue-eyed; **à merveille** wonderfully; **à prix bas** at a low price; **à mes frais** at my expenses; **à louer** to let; **à vendre** for sale; **à la bonne heure** well done!; fine!

abaisse|ment [abɛs'mã] *m* lowering; *prices, temperature, etc.*: drop; *ground*: dip; *fig.* humbling, abasement; **~er** [abɛ'se] (1b) lower; *fig. a.* reduce; humble; **s'~** fall, drop, go down; *fig.* humble o.s.; *fig.* **s'~ à** descend *or* stoop to.

abandon [abã'dõ] *m* abandonment; desertion; neglect; destitution; *rights*: surrender; lack of restraint; *sp.* withdrawal; **à l'~** completely neglected; **~ner** [~dɔ'ne] (1a) abandon; leave; give up; renounce (*a claim*); **s'~** neglect o.s.; give way (to, **à**); give o.s. up (to, **à**).

abasourdir [abazur'diːr] (2a) stun.

abat [a'ba] *m*: **pluie** *f* **d'~** downpour.

abâtard|ir [abatar'diːr] (2a) debase; **s'~** degenerate; **~issement** [~dis'mã] *m* degeneration.

abat-jour [aba'ʒuːr] *m/inv.* lampshade; sun-blind; △ skylight.

abatt|age [aba'taːʒ] *m* knocking down; *tree*: felling; *animals*: slaughter; F dressing-down; **~ant** [~'tã] *m* table: flap; **~ement** [abat'mã] *m* dejection; **~ à la base** personal allowance, *Am.* exemption; **~is** [~'ti] *m cuis.* giblets *pl.*; *sl.* **~** *pl.* limbs; **~oir** [~'twaːr] *m* slaughterhouse; **~re** [a'batr] (4a) knock down; fell; **✠** shoot down; *fig.* depress, demoralize; *fig.* wear out; **~ de la besogne** get through a lot of work; **ne te laisse pas ~** don't let things get you down; **s'~** crash; fall; **s'~ sur** swoop down on; *fig.* hail down on; **~u** *fig.* [aba'ty] depressed.

abat-vent [aba'vã] *m/inv.* chimney cowl; wind screen.

abb|aye [abe'i] *f* abbey; **~é** [a'be] *m* abbot; priest; **~esse** [a'bɛs] *f* abbess.

abcès ✠ [ap'sɛ] *m* abscess.

abdi|cation [abdika'sjõ] *f* abdication; renunciation; **~quer** [abdi'ke] (1m) *v/t.* abdicate; *v/t.* renounce.

abc [abe'se] ABC (*a. fig.*); *school*: alphabet primer.

abdomen [abdɔ'mɛn] *m* abdomen.

abeille [a'bɛːj] *f* bee; **~ mâle** drone.

aberration [abɛra'sjõ] *f* aberration.

abêtir [abɛ'tiːr] (2a) make stupid, stupefy; **s'~** become stupid.

abhorrer [abɔ're] (1a) loathe, abhor.

abîm|e [a'biːm] *m* abyss, chasm; **~er** [abi'me] (1a) spoil, damage, ruin; *sl.* beat up, smash; **s'~** get spoilt *or* damaged *or* ruined; be plunged (in, **dans**).

abject [ab'ʒɛkt] despicable; **~ion** [~ʒɛk'sjõ] *f* abjectness.

abjurer [abʒy're] (1a) abjure.

ablation [abla'sjõ] *f* ablation, removal.

abnégation [abnega'sjõ] *f* abnegation, self-denial, self-sacrifice.

aboiement [abwa'mã] *m* bark(ing).

abois [a'bwa] *m/pl.*: **aux ~** at bay.

abol|ir [abɔ'liːr] (2a) abolish; **~ition** [~li'sjɔ̃] f abolition; *debt*: cancelling.

abomin|able [abɔmi'nabl] abominable; awful (*a. fig.* = *very big*); **~er** [~'ne] (1a) abominate, loathe.

abond|ance [abɔ̃'dɑ̃ːs] f abundance; *en* ~ plentiful(ly *adv.*); *parler d'~* extemporize; **~ant** [~'dɑ̃] abounding (in, *en*); **~er** [~'de] (1a) abound (in, *en*).

abonn|é *m*, **e** f [abɔ'ne] *paper, telephone*: subscriber; 🚇 *etc.* season ticket holder, *Am.* commuter; **~ement** [abɔn'mɑ̃] *m* subscription; *carte f d'~* season ticket, *Am.* commutation ticket; **~er** [abɔ'ne] (1a): *s'~ à* subscribe to.

abord [a'bɔːr] *m* approach, access (to, *de*); **~s** *pl.* outskirts; *d'~* (at) first; *au premier* ~, *de prime* ~ at first sight; *dès l'~* from the outset; *d'un* ~ *facile* easy to approach; **~able** [abɔr'dabl] reasonable (*price*); reasonably priced (*goods*); accessible (*place*); approachable (*person*); **~age** ⚓ [~'daːʒ] *m* boarding; collision; **~er** [~'de] (1a) *v/i.* land; *v/t.* reach; grapple (*a ship*); *fig.* approach (*s.o., a problem*).

aborigène [abɔri'ʒɛn] aboriginal; native.

abortif [abɔr'tif] abortive.

aboucher [abu'ʃe] (1a) join; *s'~ avec* make contact with.

abouter ⊙ [abu'te] (1a) join.

about|ir [abu'tiːr] (2a) lead ([in]to, *à*), end (in, *à*); burst (*abscess*); *fig.* succeed; **~issant** [~ti'sɑ̃] bordering; *see à.* **tenant**; **~issement** [~tis'mɑ̃] *m* issue; materialization; success.

aboyer [abwa'je] (1h) bark, bay.

abrasif [abra'zif] abrasive.

abrég|é [abre'ʒe] *m* summary, précis; **~er** [~] (1g) shorten, abbreviate.

abreuv|er [abrœ've] (1a) water; *fig.* swamp, shower (with, *de*); **~** drink (*animal*); **~oir** [~'vwaːr] *m* watering place.

abréviation [abrevja'sjɔ̃] f abbreviation; *par* ~ for short.

abri [a'bri] *m* shelter; *à l'~ de* sheltered from; *mettre à l'~* shelter (from, *de*).

abricot [abri'ko] *m* apricot; **~ier** [~kɔ'tje] *m* apricot tree.

abriter [abri'te] (1a) shelter (from *de*, *contre*); *s'~* take shelter.

abroger [abrɔ'ʒe] (1e) abrogate.

abrupt [a'brypt] abrupt; steep, sheer.

abrut|i [abry'ti] idiot; **~ir** [~'tiːr] (2a) make stupid; stupefy; *s'~* become sottish; **~issement** [~tis'mɑ̃] *m* stupefying.

absen|ce [ap'sɑ̃ːs] f absence; lack; 🚑 (mental) blanc, black-out; **~** *d'esprit* absent-mindedness; **~t** [~'sɑ̃] absent; *fig.* absent-minded; **~téisme** [~sɑ̃te'ism] *m* absenteeism; **~téiste** [~sɑ̃te'ist] *su.* absentee; **~ter** [~sɑ̃'te] (1a): *s'~* (*de*) go out (of), absent o.s. (from), stay away (from).

absolu [absɔ'ly] absolute; pure (*alcohol*); **~ment** [apsɔly'mɑ̃] *n* absolutely; by all means; **~** *pas!* certainly not!; **~tion** [~'sjɔ̃] f absolution (from, *de*); **~tisme** [~'tism] *m* absolutism.

absor|ber [apsɔr'be] (1a) *v/t.* absorb; take (*a medicine, food, etc.*); *fig.* take up (*time, energy, etc.*); *s'~* be absorbed (in, *dans*); **~ption** [~sɔrp'sjɔ̃] f absorption (*a. fig.*).

ab|soudre [ap'sudr] (4bb) *eccl., fig.* absolve; **~sous, -te** [~'su, ~'sut] *p.p.* of *absoudre.*

absten|ir [apstə'niːr] (2h): *s'~* refrain *or* abstain (from, *de*) (*a. fig.* from voting *de voter*); **~tion** [~tɑ̃'sjɔ̃] f abstention (from, *de*).

abstinen|ce [apsti'nɑ̃ːs] f abstinence; *faire* ~ *de* abstain from (*s.th.*); **~t** [~'nɑ̃] **1.** *adj.* abstemious; **2.** *su.* teetotaller.

abstraction [apstrak'sjɔ̃] f abstraction; ~ *faite de cela* apart from that; *faire* ~ *de qch.* leave s.th. out of account.

abstrai|re [aps'trɛːr] (4ff) abstract; *s'~* cut o.s. off (from, *de*); **~t** [~'trɛ] abstract.

abstrus [aps'try] obscure.

absurd|e [ɑp'syrd] **1.** *adj.* absurd; **2.** *su./m* absurdity; **~ité** [~syrdi'te] f absurdity; nonsense.

abus [a'by] *m* abuse (of, *de*); ~ *de confiance* breach of trust; *faire* ~ *de* abuse; overindulge in; **~er** [aby'ze] (1a) *v/t.* deceive; *s'~* be mistaken; *v/i.:* ~ *de* misuse; impose upon; **~if** [~'zif] excessive; improper.

acabit [aka'bi] *m* quality, nature.

académi|cien [akademi'sjɛ̃] *m* academician; **~e** [~'mi] f academy; learned society; school (*of art etc.*); educational district; **~que** [~'mik] academic.

acajou [aka'ʒu] *m* mahogany.

acariâtre [aka'rjɑːtr] peevish.

accabl|ement [akablə'mɑ̃] *m* depression, dejection; **~er** [~'ble] (1a) overwhelm (with, **de**); weigh down, crush.

accalmie [akal'mi] *f* lull; slackness.

accaparer [akapa're] (1a) hoard; *fig.* monopolize; engross; take up (*time, energy, etc.*); take up the time (and energy) of (*s.o.*).

accéder [akse'de] (1f): **~ à** reach; attain; have access to; accede to (*a request*).

accélér|ateur [akselera'tœːr] **1.** *adj.* accelerating; **2.** *su./m* accelerator; **~ation** [~ra'sjɔ̃] *f* acceleration; speeding up, *mot.* **pédale f d'~** accelerator; **~er** [~'re] (1f) accelerate; *v/t. a.* speed up.

accent [ak'sɑ̃] *m* accent; stress; tone; **mettre l'~ sur** emphasize; **~uation** [aksɑ̃tɥa'sjɔ̃] *f* stress(ing); **~uer** [~'tɥe] (1n) stress; accentuate; emphasize.

accept|able [aksɛp'tabl] acceptable; **~ation** [~ta'sjɔ̃] *f* acceptance (*a.* **♥**); **~er** [~'te] (1a) accept; agree to; **~ion** [~'sjɔ̃] *f* meaning, sense; **sans ~ de personne** without respect of persons; **dans toute l'~ du mot** in the full meaning *or* in every sense of the word.

accès [ak'sɛ] *m* access, approach; *fever etc.*: fit, attack, bout.

access|ible [aksɛ'sibl] accessible; get-at-able; **~ion** [~'sjɔ̃] *f* accession; adherence; **~oire** [~'swaːr] **1.** *adj.* secondary, **occupation** *f* **~** sideline; **2.** *su./m* subsidiary matter; **~s** *pl.* accessories.

accident [aksi'dɑ̃] *m* accident; **~ de (la) circulation** (*or* **de la route**) road accident; *fig.* **~ de personne** casualty; **~ de terrain** unevenness; **par ~** accidentally; **~é** [aksidɑ̃'te] **1.** *adj.* uneven (*ground*); chequered, *Am.* checkered (*life*); **2.** *su* injured person; **~el** [~'tɛl] accidental, casual; **~er** [~'te] (1a) give variety to; injure, damage; **s'~** have an accident.

acclam|ation [aklama'sjɔ̃] *f* acclamation; **~s** *pl.* cheers; **~er** [~'me] (1a) acclaim, hail, applaud, cheer.

acclimat|ation [aklimata'sjɔ̃] *f* acclimatization; **~er** [~'te] (1a) acclimatize (to, **à**).

accoint|ance [akwɛ̃'tɑ̃ːs] *f*: **avoir des ~s avec** have contacts *or* relations with.

accol|ade [akɔ'lad] *f* embrace; brace; **~er** [~'le] (1a) couple; bracket; tie up (*a plant*).

accommod|ant [akɔmɔ'dɑ̃] accommodating; obliging; **~ation** [~da'sjɔ̃] *f* adaptation; **~ement** [akɔmɔd'mɑ̃] *m* compromise; **~er** [~mɔ'de] (1a) prepare (*food*); adapt (to, **à**); **s'~ à** adapt o.s. to; **s'~ de** put up with.

accompagn|ateur *m*, **-trice** *f* [akɔ̃paɲa'tœːr, ~'tris] **♪** accompanist; escort, guide; *child:* accompanying adult; **~ement** [~paɲ'mɑ̃] *m* accompaniment (*a.* **♪**); **~er** [~pa'ɲe] (1a) accompany; come *or* go with.

accompl|i [akɔ̃'pli] accomplished; **~ir** [~'pliːr] carry out, perform, do; accomplish; fulfil (*a wish, request, etc.*); **s'~** be fulfilled; **~issement** [~plis'mɑ̃] *m* carrying out, accomplishment; fulfillment.

accord [a'kɔːr] *m* agreement; harmony; **♪** chord; *gramm.* concordance; *pol.* treaty; **~ commercial** trade agreement; **d'~** o.k.; **d'un commun ~** by common consent, by mutual agreement; **tomber d'~** reach an agreement; **~éon ♪** [~de'ɔ̃] *m* accordion; *fig.* **en ~** crumpled (up); **~er** [~'de] (1a) grant; match; **♪**, *radio:* tune; **s'~** agree (*a. gramm.*); harmonize (with, **avec**); **~eur** [~'dœːr] *m* tuner.

accort [a'kɔrt] pleasing, winsome.

accost|able [akɔs'tabl] approachable; **~age** [~'taːʒ] *m* approaching (of, **de**); **~er** [~'te] (1a) **♣** berth; **~ q.** accost s.o.

accot|ement [akɔt'mɑ̃] *m* road: shoulder, verge, **~ stabilisé** hard shoulder; **~ non stabilisé** no hard shoulder, *Br. a.* soft verges; **~er** [akɔ'te] (1a) lean, rest (against, **contre**; on, **sur**); **s'~** lean (against, **contre**).

accouch|ée [aku'ʃe] *f* woman in childbed; **~ement** [akuʃ'mɑ̃] *m* confinement; **~ sans douleur** painless delivery; **~er** [aku'ʃe] (1a) *v/i.* have a baby, be delivered (of, **de**); *v/t.* deliver (*a woman*); **~eur** [~'ʃœːr] *m* obstetrician; **~euse** [~'ʃøːz] *f* midwife.

accoud|er [aku'de] (1a): **s'~** lean (on one's elbows); **s'~ à** *or* **sur** *or* **contre** lean one's elbows on *or* against; **~oir** [~'dwaːr] *m* armrest.

accoupl|ement [akuplə'mɑ̃] *m* coupling; **⚡ ~ en série** series connection;

~**er** [~'ple] (1a) couple; switch; **s'**~ mate.

accourir [aku'ri:r] (2i) run up.

accoutr|ement [akutrə'mã] *m* getup; ~**er** [~'tre] (1a) rig (*s.o.*) out (in, *de*).

accoutum|ance [akuty'mã:s] *f* (to, **à**) habituation; addiction; ~**é** [~'me] accustomed (to, **à**); **à l'**~**e** usually; ~**er** [~'me] (1a) accustom (*s.o.*) (to, **à**).

accrédit|er [akredi'te] (1a) accredit (*an ambassador*) (to, **auprès de**); give substance to, substantiate (*news etc.*); **s'**~ gain credence; ~**eur** [~'tœ:r] *m* guarantor; ~**if** [~'tif] *m* ✝ (letter) of credit.

accroc [a'kro] *m clothes:* tear; *fig.* hitch; **sans** ~ smooth(ly *adv.*).

accroch|age [akrɔ'ʃa:ʒ] *m* hooking; *box.* clinch; *radio:* picking-up; F squabble; ~**er** [~'ʃe] (1a) *v/t.* hang (up) (on, from **à**); collide with (*a vehicle*); hook; ✗ engage; *radio:* pick up; *sl.* pawn (*a watch*); F buttonhole (*s.o.*); **s'**~ hang on (*a. fig.*); cling (to, **à**); get caught (on, **à**); *v/i.* stick, jam; *fig.* catch on (*song etc.*); ~**eur** [~'tœ:r] tenacious, persistent; eye-catching, catchy.

accroire [a'krwa:r] (4n): **en faire** ~ **à q.** take s.o. in, deceive s.o.

accroissement [akrwas'mã] *m* growth; increase; ✗ accretion.

accroître [a'krwa:tr] (4o) *v/t.* increase; *v/i.*, **s'**~ grow.

accroupir [akru'pi:r] (2a): **s'**~ crouch (down); squat (down).

accru [a'kry] *p.p. of* **accroître.**

accueil [a'kœj] *m* reception, welcome; **faire bon** ~ **à** welcome (*s.o.*); ~**lant** [akœ'jã] friendly; affable; ~**lir** [~'ji:r] (2c) welcome; receive; accommodate.

acculer [aky'le] (1a) corner (*s.o.*); *fig.* ~ **à** drive to.

accumul|ateur [akyza'tœ:r] **1.** *adj.* accusing; incriminating; **2.** *su.* accumulator; ~**er** [~'le] (1a) accumulate; pile up.

accus|ateur [akyza'tœ:r] **1.** *adj.* accusing; incriminating; **2.** *su.* accuser; ~**ation** [~za'sjɔ̃] *f* accusation; charge; ~**é** [~'ze] **1.** *adj.* marked; prominent (*feature*); **2.** *su./m* accused; ✝ ~ **de réception** acknowledgement (of receipt); ~**er** [~'ze] (1a) accuse; *fig.* emphasize; show; acknowledge; *fig.* **s'**~ stand out.

acerb|e [a'sɛrb] sharp, acerbic; ~**ité** [asɛrbi'te] *f* sharpness, acerbity.

acér|é [ase're] sharp, keen; ~**er** [~] (1f) steel; *fig.* sharpen, give edge to.

acétate ꭞ [ase'tat] *m* acetate; ~ **de cuivre** verdigris.

achalandé [aʃalã'de]: **bien** ~ well-stocked (*shop*).

acharn|é [aʃar'ne] fierce, relentless; ~**ement** [~nə'mã] *m* tenacity; fierceness; relentlessness; ~**er** [~'ne] (1a): **s'**~ **à** try desperately to; be intent on; **s'**~ **sur** (*or* **contre**) set o.s. against.

achat [a'ʃa] *m* purchase, buying; **faire des** ~**s** go shopping, do some shopping, shop; ✝ **pouvoir** *m* **d'**~ purchasing power.

achemin|ement [aʃmin'mã] *m* course (towards, **vers**); routing; ~**er** [~mi'ne] (1a) put on the way; forward (to **sur**, **vers**); **s'**~ make one's way (towards **vers, sur**).

achet|er [aʃ'te] (1d) buy (*a. fig.* = *bribe*); ~ **qch. à q.** buy s.th. from s.o.; buy s.th. for s.o., buy s.o. s.th.; ~ **cher** (**bon marché**) buy at a high price (cheap); ~**eur** *m,* **-euse** *f* [~'tœ:r, ~'tø:z] buyer.

achèvement [aʃɛv'mã] *m* completion; **achever** [aʃ've] (1d) *v/t.* finish; F do for; **s'**~ draw to a close; *v/i.:* ~ **de** (*inf.*) finish (*ger.*).

achopp|ement [aʃɔp'mã] *m* obstacle; **pierre** *f* **d'**~ stumbling-block; ~**er** [aʃɔ'pe] (1a): ~ **sur** stumble over (*a. fig.*).

acid|e ꭞ [a'sid] **1.** *adj.* sharp, acid; **2.** *su./m* acid; ~ **chlorhydrique** hydrochloric acid; ~ **sulfurique** sulphuric acid; ~**ifier** [asidi'fje] (*a.* **s'**~) acidify; ~**ité** [~'te] *f* acidity, sourness; ~**ulé** [asidy'le] slightly sour, sourish.

acier [a'sje] *m* steel; ~ **laminé** rolled steel; **d'**~ steel(y), of steel; **aciérie** [asje'ri] *f* steelworks *usu. sg.*

acompte [a'kɔ̃:t] *m* down payment, deposit, payment on account; instalment; F *fig.* foretaste; **par** ~**s** *pl.* by instalments.

à-côté [ako'te] *m* side-issue; *money:* extra, s.th. on the side.

à-coup [a'ku] *m* jerk; **par** ~**s** by fits and starts.

acoustique [akus'tik] **1.** *adj.* acoustic; **2.** *su./f* acoustics *pl.*

acqu|éreur [ake'rœːr] m purchaser; **~érir** [~'riːr] (21) acquire, obtain; win (*esteem*, *friends*), gain (*valour*); **~errai** [aker're] 1st p. sg. fut. of **acquérir**; **~êt** [a'kɛ] m acquisition; **~ièrent** [a'kjɛ:r] 3rd p. pl. pres. of **acquérir**; **~iers** [~] 1st p. sg. pres. of **acquérir**.

acquiesc|ement [akjɛs'mɑ̃] m consent; **~er** [akjɛ'se] (1k) agree; assent (to, **à**).

acquis [a'ki] **1.** 1st p. sg. p.s. of **acquérir**; **2.** p.p. of **acquérir**; **3.** su./m experience; **~ition** [akizi'sjɔ̃] f purchase; fig. **~s** pl. attainments.

acquit [a'ki] m ✝ receipt (for, **de**); **par ~ de conscience** for conscience sake; **pour ~** paid; **~tement** [akit'mɑ̃] m acquittal; **~ter** [aki'te] (1a) ✝ acquit; pay (*a debt*); ✝ receipt (*a bill*); fulfil (*an obligation*); **~ q. de qch.** release s.th. from s.th.; **s'~ de** discharge (*a debt*); fulfil (*a duty*).

acre ✝ [ukr] m acre.

âcre [ɑːkr] sharp; caustic (*remark*); **~té** [ɑkrə'te] f bitterness, acidity.

acrimoni|e [akrimɔ'ni] f acrimony; **~eux** [~'njø] acrimonious, bitter.

acrobat|e [akrɔ'bat] su. acrobat; **~ic** [~.ba'si] f acrobatics pl.; **~tique** [~'tik] acrobatic.

acte [akt] m act (a. thea.), action; deed (a. ✝✝); ✝✝ writ; **~s** pl. proceedings; **~ civil** civil marriage; **~ de décès** death certificate; **prendre ~ de** take note of.

acteur [ak'tœːr] m actor.

actif [ak'tif] **1.** adj. active; busy; **2.** su./m ✝ assets pl., credit (side), gramm. active voice; **avoir à son ~** have to one's credit or name.

action [ak'sjɔ̃] f action, act; effect; machine: working; ✝✝ lawsuit; ✝ share (certificate), Am. stock; **champ m d'~** sphere of action; **~naire** [aksjɔ'nɛːr] m/f shareholder, Am. stockholder; **~ner** [~'ne] (1a) ✪ set in motion; work, operate; ✝✝ sue.

activ|er [akti've] (1a) activate; speed up; **s'~** busy o.s., be busy (with, **à**); ⊦ get a move on; **~ité** [~vi'te] f activity.

actrice [ak'tris] f actress.

actualité [aktɥali'te] f topicality, topical question; **l'~** current events pl.; **~s** pl. news-reel sg., news sg.; **d'~** topical.

actuel [ak'tɥɛl] current, present, topical.

acuité [akɥi'te] f acuteness (a. ✿).

acuponcture, acupuncture [akypɔ̃k-'tyːr] f acupuncture.

adapt|ateur phot. [adapta'tœːr] m adapter; **~ation** [~ta'sjɔ̃] f adaptation; adjustment; **~er** [~'te] (1a) adapt, adjust (s.th. to s.th., qch. **à** qch.).

addition [adi'sjɔ̃] f addition; accretion; restaurant: bill, Am. check; **~nel** [adisjɔ'nɛl] additional; **~ner** [~'ne] (1a) add up; add (to, **à**); **~ un liquide de qch.** add s.th. to a liquid, additionné de sucre with sugar added.

adéno... [adenɔ] glandular, adeno...

adépte [a'dɛpt] su. follower.

adéquat [ade'kwa] adequate.

adhér|ence [ade'rɑ̃ːs] f adhesion (a. ✿, phys.), **~ent** [~'rɑ̃] adj. that sticks (to, **à**); su. member; **~er** [~'re] (1f): **~ à** cling to; support (*a party*) join (*a party*, *club*, etc.); be a member of.

adhésif [ade'zif] sticky; **emplâtre** m **~** adhesive plaster; **~ion** [~'zjɔ̃] f adhesion (a. fig.).

adieu [a'djø] **1.** int. goodbye!; **dire ~ à** say goodbye or farewell to; fig. give up, renounce (s.th.); **2.** su./m: **faire ses ~x** (**à**) say goodbye (to).

adipeux [adi'pø] adipose, fat.

adjacent [adʒa'sɑ̃] adjacent (to, **à**); **être ~ à** border on.

adjectif [adʒɛk'tif] m adjective.

adjoin|dre [ad'ʒwɛ̃ːdr] (4m) associate, appoint as assistant; add, attach (to, **à**); **~t** [~'ʒwɛ̃] adj., su./m assistant; **~ au maire** deputy-mayor.

adjudant [adʒy'dɑ̃] m warrant officer.

adjudicat|aire [adʒydika'tɛːr] m successful tenderer; auction: successful bidder, purchaser; **~ion** [~'sjɔ̃] f invitation to tender; sale by auction; contract: allocation; auction: knocking down; **mettre en ~** invite tenders for; put up for auction.

adjuger [adʒy'ʒe] (11) award; auction: knock down.

adjur|ation [adʒyra'sjɔ̃] f adjuration; plea, **~er** [~'re] (1a) adjure, implore.

admettre [ad'mɛtr] (4v) admit; let in; permit.

administr|ateur [administra'tœːr] m administrator; bank: director; **~atif** [~'tif] administrative; **~ation** [~'sjɔ̃] f administration; management; governing body; civil service; **~er** [~] (1a) administer; manage.

admir|able [admi'rabl] wonderful; **~ateur** [admira'tœːr] **1.** *adj.* admiring; **2.** *su.* admirer; **~ation** [~'sjɔ̃] *f* admiration; **~er** [admi're] (1a) admire.

admis [ad'mi] **1.** *p.p. of* ***admettre***; **2.** *adj.* accepted; conventional; **~sible** [admi'sibl] admissible; eligible (to, **à**); **~sion** [~'sjɔ̃] *f* admission; ⚙ inlet.

admon|estation [admɔnɛsta'sjɔ̃] *f*, **~ition** [~ni'sjɔ̃] *f* admonition; **~ester** [~nɛs'te] (1a) admonish.

adolescen|ce [adɔlɛ'sɑ̃ːs] *f* adolescence, youth; **~t** [~'sɑ̃] adolescent.

adonner [adɔ'ne] (1a): ***s'~ à*** devote o.s. to; take to (*drink etc.*), become addicted to.

adopt|er [adɔp'te] (1a) adopt; *parl.* pass (*a bill*); **~if** [~'tif] adoptive (*parent*); **~ion** [~'sjɔ̃] *f* adoption; ***fils*** *m* ***par ~*** adopted son; ***pays*** *m* ***d'~*** adopted country.

ador|able [adɔ'rabl] adorable; **~ation** [~ra'sjɔ̃] *f* adoration, worship; **~er** [~'re] (1a) adore (*a. fig.*); *fig. a.* love, be crazy about; worship (*God*); F dote on.

adosser [ado'se] (1a): **~ à** (*or* ***contre***) lean *or* stand (*s.th.*) against; ***s'~ à*** (*or* ***contre***) lean against.

adouc|ir [adu'siːr] (1a) sweeten; allay (*a pain*); polish (*metal*); ***s'~*** grow softer; **~issement** [~sis'mɑ̃] *m* softening; sweetening.

adress|e [a'drɛs] *f* address, skill, dexterity; **~er** [adrɛ'se] (1a) address; send; direct; ***~ la parole à q.*** address s.o.; ***s'~ à*** speak to; go and see; inquire at; be intended for.

adroit [a'drwa] dexterous.

adul|ateur *m*, **-trice** *f* [adyla'tœːr, ~'tris] flatterer; **~ation** [~la'sjɔ̃] *f* sycophancy; **~er** [~'le] (1a) fawn upon (*s.o.*).

adulte [a'dylt] adult, grown-up.

adult|ération [adyltera'sjɔ̃] *f* adulteration; **~ère** [adyl'tɛːr] *su.*/*m* adulterer; adultery; **~érin** [~te'rɛ̃] adulterine.

advenir [advə'niːr] (2h) happen; ***advienne que pourra*** come what may.

adventice [advɑ̃'tis] casual (*a.* ⚘).

adverbe [ad'vɛrb] *m* adverb.

advers|aire [advɛr'sɛːr] *m* adversary, opponent; **~e** [~'vɛrs] adverse, unfavo(u)rable; ⚖ opposing (*party*); **~ité** [~vɛrsi'te] *f* bad luck.

aér|age [ae'raːʒ] *m* aeration; airing; **~ation** [~ra'sjɔ̃] *f* airing, ventilation; **~é** [~'re] airy; **~er** [~'re] (1f) air, give (*s.th.*) an airing; aerate; ***s'~*** get some fresh air; **~ien** [~'rjɛ̃] aerial; air-...; ***ligne*** *f* ***~ne*** airline.

aéro... [aerɔ] flying-..., air-...; **~bus** [~'bys] *m* airbus; **~drome** [~droːm] *m* aerodrome, *Am.* airdrome; **~dynamique** [~dina'mik] **1.** *adj.* aerodynamic; streamlined; **2.** *su.*/*f* aerodynamics *sg.*; **~gare** [~'gaːr] *f* air terminal; **~gramme** [~'gram] *m* air letter; **~plane** [~'plan] *m* airplane, aircraft; **~port** [~'pɔːr] *m* airport; **~postal** [~pɔs'tal] airmail...; **~train** (*TM*) [~'trɛ̃] *m* hovertrain.

affab|ilité [afabili'te] *f* affability (to, ***envers***); **~le** [a'fabl] affable.

affad|ir [afa'diːr] (2a) make insipid; dull; **~issement** [~dis'mɑ̃] *m* loss of flavo(u)r; growing insipid.

affaibl|ir [afɛ'bliːr] (2a) weaken; ***s'~*** grow weaker; droop; **~issement** [~blis'mɑ̃] *m* weakening; reducing.

affair|e [a'fɛːr] *f* business; matter; ⚖ case; **~s** *pl. a.* belongings; **~s** *pl.* ***étrangères*** foreign affairs; ***avoir ~ à*** have to deal with; be faced with (*a problem etc.*); ***faire l'~*** do (nicely); do the trick; ***parler ~s*** talk business; ***son ~ est faite*** he is done for; ***voilà l'~*** that's it!; **~é** [afɛ're] busy; **~ement** [afɛr'mɑ̃] *m* bustle; **~er** [afɛ're] (1a): ***s'~*** busy oneself, be busy; **~isme** [afɛ'rism] *m* (political) racketeering.

affaiss|ement [afɛs'mɑ̃] *m* sinking; subsidence; depression; **~er** [afɛ'se] (1b) cause to sink; weigh down; ***s'~*** sink, subside; give way; cave in; collapse.

affaler [afa'le] (1a): ***s'~*** F drop.

affamer [afa'me] (1a) starve.

affect|ation [afɛkta'sjɔ̃] *f* mannerism; appropriation; assignment (*to a post*); **~é** [~'te] affected, F put-on; **~er** [~'te] (1a) assign; set apart; pretend; assume (*a shape*); affect (*a.* ⚕); have a predilection for; **~ion** [~'sjɔ̃] *f* affection (*a.* ⚕); fondness; **~ionner** [~sjɔ'ne] (1a) be fond of, have a liking for; **~ueux** [~'tɥø] affectionate.

afférent [afe'rɑ̃] relating, relative (to, **à**); accruing.

affermir [afɛr'miːr] (2a) consolidate, make firm; *fig.* strengthen.

affich|age [afi'ʃaːʒ] *m* bill-posting; *fig.* F show; **~e** [a'fiʃ] *f* poster; **~er** [afi'ʃe] (1a) post up; *fig.* parade; **s'~ pour** set up for; **~eur** [~'ʃœːr] *m* bill-sticker.

affidé [afi'de] *m* confederate; spy.

affilage ☉ [afi'laːʒ] *m* sharpening.

affilée [afi'le]: **d'~** at a stretch, on end.

affiler [afi'le] (1a) sharpen, whet.

affili|ation [afilja'sjɔ̃] *f* affiliation; **~é** [afi'lje] *m* (affiliated) member; associate; **~er** [afi'lje] (1o) affiliate (with, to à); **s'~ à** join (*a society etc.*).

affiloir [afi'lwaːr] *m* hone; *razor:* strop; *knife:* steel; whetstone.

affin|age [afi'naːʒ] *m* ☉ refining; *fig.* improvement; **~er** [~'ne] (1a) refine; improve; point (*needles*).

affinité [afini'te] *f* affinity (*a.* 🐾).

affirm|atif, ve [afirma'tif, ~'tiːv] **1.** *adj.* affirmative; **2.** *su./f* affirmative; *dans l'~ve* in the affirmative; if so; *répondre par l'~ve* answer yes *or* in the affirmative; **~ation** [~ma'sjɔ̃] *f* assertion; **~er** [~'me] (1a) assert.

affleurer [aflœ're] (1a) *v/t.* make *or* be level with; *v/i. fig.* emerge.

afflic|tion [aflik'sjɔ̃] *f* affliction; **~ger** [afli'ʒe] (1l) afflict (with, *de*).

afflu|ence [afly'ɑ̃ːs] *f* crowd(s *pl.*); throng; *heures f/pl. d'~* rush hours; **~ent** [~'ɑ̃] *m* tributary; **~er** [~'e] (1n) flow; *fig.* crowd throng, flock (*people*); **~x** [a'fly] *m* afflux, rush.

affol|ement [afɔl'mɑ̃] *m* panic; *engine:* racing; **~er** [afɔ'le] (1a) frighten, terrify; throw into a panic; madden; **s'~** (get in a) panic, go crazy, ☉ *etc.* (begin to) race (*engine etc.*).

affourager [afura'ʒe] (1l) fodder.

affranch|ir [afrɑ̃'ʃiːr] (2a) free; exempt; *post:* frank; **~issement** [~ʃis'mɑ̃] *m* release; exemption; *post:* franking.

affres [afr] *f/pl.* pangs, throes.

affréter ⚓ [afre'te] (1f) charter.

affreux [a'frø] frightful; ghastly.

affriander [afriɑ̃'de] (1a) allure.

affriolant enticing; exciting.

affront [a'frɔ̃] *m* insult; *faire un ~ à* insult; **~er** [~'te] (1a) face; *fig.* brave.

affubler *pej.* [afy'ble] (1a) rig out (in, *de*).

affût [a'fy] *m* hiding place; guncarriage; *être à l'~* be on the lookout (for, *de*); **~er** ☉ [afy'te] (1a) sharpen; grind.

afin [a'fɛ̃] **1.** *prp.:* **~ de** (*inf.*) (in order) to (*inf.*); **2.** *cj.:* **~ que** (*sbj.*) in order that, so that.

africain [afri'kɛ̃] *adj., su.* African.

aga|çant [aga'sɑ̃] irritating, annoying, aggravating; **~cer** [~'se] (1k) irritate, annoy.

âge [aːʒ] *m* age; period; generation; *d'~ à, en ~ de* of an age to; *entre deux ~s* middle-aged; *quel ~ avez-vous?, quel est votre ~?* how old are you?; *à ton ~* when I was your age; **âgé** [a'ʒe] old, aged; elderly; *~ de deux ans* aged 2.

agenc|e [a'ʒɑ̃ːs] *f* agency; bureau; *bank:* branch office; **~ de publicité** advertising agency; **~ de voyages** travel bureau; **~ement** [aʒɑ̃s'mɑ̃] *m* arrangement, lay-out; **~er** [~'se] (1k) arrange (down).

agenda [aʒɛ̃'da] *m* notebook, memorandum book; appointment book; diary.

agenouiller [aʒnu'je] (1a): **s'~** kneel (down).

agent [a'ʒɑ̃] *m* agent; middleman; (*a.* **~ de police**) policeman, (police) constable; **~ de brevet** patent agent; **~ de change** stockbroker; **~ de location** house agent; **~ de maîtrise** supervisor, foreman; **~ chimique** chemical agent.

agglomér|ation [aglɔmera'sjɔ̃] *f* agglomeration; built-up area, town; **~urbaine** urban districts; **~é** [~'re] *m* chipboard; **~er** [~'re] (1f) agglomerate; compress.

agglutiner [aglyti'ne] (1a) stick (together); agglutinate.

aggrav|ation [agrava'sjɔ̃] *f* worsening; *penalty:* increase; ⚖, ⚕ aggravation; **~er** [~'ve] (1a) aggravate; increase; **s'~** worsen.

agile [a'ʒil] agile, nimble; **~ité** [aʒili'te] *f* agility, nimbleness.

agi|r [a'ʒiːr] (2a) act; behave; **~ bien envers** (*or* **avec**) behave well towards; *il s'agit de* (*inf.*) it is necessary to (*inf.*), one (*etc.*) must; *... dont il s'agit* in question; *il s'agit de savoir si* the question is whether; *s'~ de* be a question of; **~tateur** *m*, **-trice** *f* [aʒita'tœːr, ~'tris] agitator; **~tation** [~ta'sjɔ̃] *f* agitation; excitement; **~té** [~'te] restless; excited; perturbed; choppy (*sea*); **~ter** [~'te] (1a) agitate, stir, shake; debate; **s'~** move (about); fidget.

agne|au [a'ɲo] *m* lamb; **~lin** [aɲɔ'lɛ̃] *m* fur: lambskin.

agon|ie [agɔ'ni] *f* death agony; **~ir** [~'niːr] (2a) *v/t.*: **~ q. d'injures** call s.o. names; **~iser** [~ni'ze] (1a) be dying.

agraf|e [a'graf] *f* hook; clasp; clip; **~er** [agra'fe] (1a) hook; fasten; *sl.* nab, pinch.

agraire [a'grɛːr] agrarian.

agrand|ir [agrã'diːr] (2a) make bigger; increase; enlarge; **~issement** [~dis'mã] *m* enlargement; increase; *phot.* blow-up; **~isseur** *phot.* [~di'sœːr] *m* enlarger.

agréable [agre'abl] agreeable.

agréé [agre'e] *m commercial court*: counsel, attorney; **~er** [~] (1a) *v/t.* accept; **veuillez ~, Monsieur, mes salutations distinguées** yours faithfully; *v/i.*: **~ à** be agreeable to, suit.

agrég|at ✪ [agre'ga] *m* aggregate; **~ation** [~ga'sjɔ̃] *f in France*: competitive State examination for appointment as teacher in a *lycée*; **~é** [~'ʒe] *m* one who has passed the *agrégation*; **~er** [~'ʒe] (1g) incorporate (into, **à**).

agrément [agre'mã] *m* consent; pleasure; charm; **~s** *pl.* ornaments; **voyage** *m* **d'~** pleasure-trip; **~er** [~mã'te] (1a) adorn, embellish.

agrès [a'grɛ] *m/pl.* ⊕ tackle *sg.*, gear *sg.*; *sp.* apparatus *sg.*, fittings.

agress|eur [agrɛ'sœːr] *m* aggressor; **~if** [~'sif] aggressive; **~ion** [~'sjɔ̃] *f* aggression; attack; ✪ *etc.*, *a. fig.* stress, strain; **~ivité** [agresivi'te] *f* aggressiveness.

agric|ole [agri'kɔl] agricultural (*products*); **~ulteur** [~kyl'tœːr] *m* farmer; **~ulture** [~kyl'tyːr] *f* agriculture; husbandry.

agripper [agri'pe] (1a) clutch; grab; **s'~** (**à**) clutch (at); hold on (to).

aguerrir [agɛ'riːr] (2a) harden, season; **s'~ à** become hardened to.

aguets [a'gɛ] *m/pl.*: **aux ~** on the watch or look-out.

aguicher *sl.* [agi'ʃe] (1a) excite; tantalize; *sl.* turn (*s.o.*) on.

ahuri|r [ay'riːr] (2a) bewilder, stun, stupefy; **~ssement** [~ris'mã] *m* bewilderment, stupefaction.

ai [e] *1st p. sg. pres. of* **avoir** 1.

aide [ɛːd] *su.* assistant; help; **~** *f* **ménagère** home help; *su./f.* help, assistance; *pol.* **~ économique** economic aid; **à l'~ de** by means of; **venir en ~ à q., venir à l'~ de q.** help s.o.; come to s.o.'s assistance; **~-mémoire** [~me'mwaːr] *m/inv.* reminder; memory aid; memorandum; **~r** [ɛ'de] (1b) *v/t.* help; **s'~ de** make use of; *v/i.*: **~ à qch.** help (towards) s.th., contribute to s.th.

aie [ɛ] *1st p. sg. pres. sbj. of* **avoir** 1.

aïeul [a'jœl] *m* grandfather; **aïeule** [~] *f* grandmother; **aïeuls** [~] *m/pl.* grandparents; grandfathers; **aïeux** [a'jø] *m/pl.* ancestors, forefathers.

aigle [ɛgl] *su./m* eagle; *fig.* genius.

aiglefin *icht.* [ɛglə'fɛ̃] *m* haddock.

aigr|e [ɛːgr] **1.** *adj.* sour; sharp; bitter (*tone*); shrill (*voice*); **2.** *su./m* sharpness; **~e-doux, ~e-douce** [ɛgrə'du, ~'dus] bitter-sweet; *fig.* subacid; **~efin** [~'fɛ̃] *m icht.* haddock; *fig.* swindler; **~elet** [~'lɛ] sourish; **~ette** [ɛ'grɛt] *f orn.* aigrette (*a. cost.*, ⚜), egret (*a.* ❀); **~eur** [ɛ'grœːr] *f* sourness (*a. fig.*); ranco(u)r; ✚ **~s** *pl.* acidity sg. (of the stomach); heartburn *sg.*; **~ir** [ɛ'griːr] (2a) *vt/i.* turn sour; *v/t. fig.* embitter.

aigu, -guë [e'gy] sharp, pointed; acute; *fig.* intense; bitter; piercing; high(-pitched).

aiguill|age 🚂 [egɥi'jaːʒ] *m* shunting, *Am.* switching; points *pl.*, *Am.* switch; **~e** [e'gɥiːj] *f* needle (*a.* pine, compass); *clock*: hand; *mountain*: point; *church-tower*: spire; 🚂 points *pl.*, *Am.* switch; **~er** [egɥi'je] (1a) 🚂 shunt, *Am.* switch; *fig.* direct, steer, orient(ate); **~on** [~'jɔ̃] *m* goad; sting; *fig.* spur, stimulus; **~onner** [~jɔ'ne] (1a) goad; *fig.* spur on.

aiguiser [eg(ɥ)i'ze] (1a) whet (*a. fig.*), sharpen; *fig.* excite.

ail *cuis.* [aːj] *m* garlic.

ail|e [ɛl] *f* wing (*a.* ✗, *sp.*); windmill: sail; ⊕ blade; **~é** [ɛ'le] winged; **~eron** [ɛl'rɔ̃] *m* pinion; small wing; *shark*: fin; *water-wheel*: float(-board); **~ette** ⊕ [ɛ'lɛt] *f* fin; blade; vane; **~ier** *sp.* [ɛ'lje] *m* wing(er).

aille [aj] *1st p. sg. pres. sbj. of* **aller** 1.

ailleurs [a'jœːr] *adv.* elsewhere; **d'~** moreover; **nulle part ~** nowhere else.

aimable [ɛ'mabl] agreeable, nice.

alimentaire A

aimant [ε'mɑ̃] m magnet (a. fig.); **~er** [εmɑ̃'te] (1a) magnetize.

aimer [ε'me] (1b) love; ~ (inf.) like (ger.) or to (inf.); **j'aimerais** I would like; **j'aimerais mieux** I would rather.

aîn|é [ε'ne] elder; eldest; **il est mon ~ de trois mois** he is 3 months older than I; **~esse** [ε'nεs] f: **droit** m **d'~** law of primogeniture.

ainsi [ε̃'si] **1.** adv. thus; so; in this way; ~ **soit-il!** so be it!; eccl., a. co. amen; **pour ~ dire** so to speak; **2.** cj. so; ~ **que** as well as; like.

air¹ [εːr] m air; atmosphere; **courant** m **d'~** draught, Am draft; **en l' ~** (up)into the air; **il y a qch. dans l'~** there is s.th. in the wind; fig. **être (mettre) en l'~** be in (throw into) confusion; fig. **flanquer** (or F **ficher**) **en l'~** throw away; F chuck up or out, knock over; fig. **paroles** f/pl. **en l'~** idle talk; fig. **projets** m/pl. **en l'~** castles in the air; fig. **vivre de l'~ du temps** live on air.

air² [~] m look, appearance; air, manner; **avoir l'~ de** look like; **avoir l'~ de** (inf.) seem to (inf.), **se donner des ~s** give o.s. airs.

air³ ♪ [~] m air, tune, melody; aria.

aire [~] f area; site; (threshing-)floor; area; eyrie; ~ **d'atterrissage** landing strip or patch; meteor. ~ **de haute (basse) pression** high (low) pressure (area).

airelle ♀ [ε'rεl] f blueberry.

aisance [ε'zɑ̃:s] f ease; comfort; easy circumstances; **cabinet** m **d'~s** water-closet; **aise** [εːz] **1.** adj.: **être bien ~** be very glad; **2.** su./f case, comfort; **à l'~, à son ~** comfortable; adv. comfortably; **mal à l'~** ill at ease; **aisé** [ε'ze] easy; well-to-do, well-off (for money).

aisselle anat. [ε'sεl] f armpit.

ajouré [aʒu're] perforated; open-work.

ajourn|ement [aʒurnə'mɑ̃] m postponement; adjournment; deferment; **~er** [~'ne] (1a) postpone; adjourn; defer.

ajouter [aʒu'te] (1a) v/t. add (to, à); (venir) **s'~** come on top of; **~ foi à** believe (s.th.); v/i.: ~ **à** add to.

ajust|age ⚙ [aʒys'ta:ʒ] m fitting; **~ement** [~tə'mɑ̃] m adjustment; **~er** [~'te] (1a) adjust, fit; adapt; arrange; aim at; ~ **une montre** put a watch right;

s'~ fit; tally; adapt o.s.; **~eur** [~'tœːr] m fitter.

ajutage [aʒy'ta:ʒ] m nozzle; jet.

alacrité [alakri'te] f alacrity.

alambi|c [alɑ̃'bik] m still; **~qué** [~bi'ke] oversubtle, strained.

alangui|r [alɑ̃'giːr] (2a) make languid; **s'~** grow languid; **~ssement** [~gis'mɑ̃] m languor.

alarm|e [a'larm] f alarm; **donner l'~** sound the alarm; **~er** [alar'me] (1a) alarm, startle; disquiet; worry; **s'~** be(come) alarmed; worry; **~iste** [~'mist] m alarmist.

albâtre [al'bɑːtr] m alabaster.

album [al'bɔm] m album.

albumine ♣ [alby'min] f albumin.

alcali [alka'li] m alkali; **~ volatil** ammonia, **~n** [~'lɛ̃] alkaline.

alcool [al'kɔl] m alcohol; ~ **dénaturé** methylated spirits pl.; **~ique** [alkɔ'lik] alcoholic; **~iser** [~li'ze] (1a) alcoholize; **~isme** [~'lism] m alcoholism.

alcootest [alkɔ'tεst] m breathalyser; breath test.

alcôve [al'koːv] f recess.

aléa [ale'a] m hazard; **~toire** [~a'twaːr] risky; problematic(al).

alêne ⚙ [a'lεn] f awl.

alentour [alɑ̃'tuːr] **1.** adv. around; **2.** su./m ~**s** pl. surroundings; **aux ~s de** in the neighbo(u)rhood of; fig. (round) about, around.

alert|e [a'lεrt] **1.** adj. agile; alert; brisk; **2.** su./f alarm, alert; **fausse ~** false alarm; **~er** [alεr'te] (1a) alert.

alés|age ⚙ [ale'za:ʒ] m boring; reaming; bore; **~er** ⚙ [~'ze] (1f) bore; ream.

alezan [al'zɑ̃] su./m, adj. chestnut (horse).

algarade [alga'rad] f quarrel, row; outburst (of anger).

algèbre [al'ʒεːbr] f algebra.

algue ♀ [alg] f alga; seaweed.

alibi [ali'bi] m alibi.

alién|able ⚖ [alje'nabl] alienable; **~ation** [~na'sjɔ̃] f alienation; ♣ insanity; **~é** [~'ne] lunatic; **~er** [~'ne] (1f) alienate; unhinge (s.o.'s mind).

align|ement [aliɲ'mɑ̃] m alignment; **~er** [ali'ɲe] (1a) align; **s'~** fall into line; toe the line; **non aligné** nonaligned.

aliment [ali'mɑ̃] m food; ~**s** pl. **naturels** health food sg.; **~aire** [alimɑ̃'tεːr] alimentary; (for) food; dietary; **~ation** [~ta'sjɔ̃] f feeding; food; supplying, supply; **~ défectueuse** malnutrition; **~ en essence** fuelling; **magasin** m **d'~** food shop, Am. store; **~er** [~'te] (1a) feed (a. ⚙); nourish (a. fig.); **~ en qch.** supply with s.th.

alinéa [aline'a] m paragraph; **nouvel ~** new line.

alit|é [ali'te] confined to bed; **~er** [~] (1a): **s'~** take to one's bed.

alizé [ali'ze] m trade wind.

allaiter [alɛ'te] (1b) breast-feed; suckle (animal).

allant [a'lɑ̃] m drive, go, energy.

allécher [ale'ʃe] (1f) entice, tempt.

allé, e [a'le] **1.** p.p. of **aller 1**; **2.** su./f (tree-lined) walk, path; avenue; bus etc: aisle; **~es** pl. et **venues** f/pl. comings and goings.

allégation [alega'sjɔ̃] f allegation.

allég|ement [alleʒ'mɑ̃] m alleviation (of, de), relief (from, de);✝ **~ fiscal** tax relief; **~er** [~le'ʒe] (1g) make lighter; lighten; fig. alleviate.

allégorie [allego'ri] f allegory.

allègre [al'lɛːgr] lively; cheerful; **allégresse** [~le'grɛs] f joy; liveliness.

alléguer [alle'ge] (1s) cite, quote; put forward (an excuse etc.).

allemand [al'mɑ̃] adj., su. German.

aller [a'le] **1.** (1q) go; **~** (inf.) be going to (inf.), go and ...; a. = fut. tense; **~ à q.** suit or fit s.o.; **~** (**bien**) **avec** go (well) with; **~** (**bien**) **ensemble** go (well) together; match; **~ à cheval** ride (a horse); **~ bien** be well; **~ chercher** see **chercher**; **~ en diminuant** grow steadily less; **~ en voiture** go by car; **~ se coucher** go to bed; **~ sur la cinquantaine** be getting on for fifty; **~ voir** go and see (s.o.); **allons!** let's go!; nonsense!; come along!; **comment allez-vous?** how are you?; **il va sans dire** it goes without saying; **il y va de ...** is at stake; **la clef va à la serrure** the key fits the lock; **n'allez pas croire ...!** don't be-lieve ...!; F **on y va!** coming!; **s'en ~** go away; **2.** su./m outward journey; 🚆 single ticket; **~ et retour** journey there and back; **à l'~** on the outward journey; **au pis ~** if the worst comes to the worst; **pis ~** make-shift.

allergie [alɛr'ʒi] f allergy; **~gique** [~'ʒik] allergic (to, **à**).

alli|age [a'lja:ʒ] m alloy; **~ance** [a'ljɑ̃:s] f alliance; marriage; wedding ring; **~é** [a'lje] su. ally; relation by marriage; **~ier** [~] (1o) ally; unite; alloy (metals); combine (with, **à**); go ally itself, be-come allied (with, **à**); fig. match, go together.

allô! [a'lo] int. hullo!, hello!

allocation [alɔka'sjɔ̃] f allocation; allowance; benefit; **~s** pl. **familiales** family allowances; **~ de chômage** unemployment benefit.

allocution [alɔky'sjɔ̃] f speech.

allogène [alɔ'ʒɛn] non-native; alien.

allong|e [a'lɔ̃:ʒ] f extension (piece); meat-hook; box. reach; **~er** [alɔ̃'ʒe] (1l) lengthen; prolong; sl. aim (a blow) (at, **à**); **s'~** stretch (out); lie down.

allouer [a'lwe] (1p) grant; allocate.

allum|age [aly'ma:ʒ] m lighting; ⚙ ignition; mot. **~ prématuré** backfire; **~ raté** misfire; **couper l'~** switch off the ignition; **~er** [aly'me] (1a) light, kindle; switch on (the light); **s'~** catch fire; light up; **~ette** [~'mɛt] f match; **~ de sûreté** safety match.

allure [a'lyːr] f gait; bearing; speed; pace; appearance; business: trend; **à toute ~** at full speed; **forcer l'~** increase (the) speed; fig. **prendre une bonne ~** take a promising turn.

alluvi|al [ally'vjal] alluvial; **~on** [~'vjɔ̃] f alluvial (deposit).

almanach [alma'na] m almanac.

aloi [a'lwa] m standard, quality (a. fig.); fig. **de bon ~** genuine; sterling.

alors [a'lɔːr] adv. then; at or by that time; in that case; well (then); **~ même que** even when or though; **~ que** at a time when; whereas; **d'~** of that time; **jusqu'~** until then; F **et ~?** and what then?; so what?

alouette orn. [a'lwɛt] f lark.

alourd|ir [alur'diːr] (2a) make heavy; dull; weigh down; **~issement** [~dis'mɑ̃] m heaviness.

aloyau [alwa'jo] m sirloin (of beef).

alpaga zo. [alpa'ga] m alpaca.

alpage [al'pa:ʒ] m mountain pasture; **alpe** [alp] f height; **les 2s** pl. the Alps; **alpestre** [al'pɛstr] alpine.

alphab|et [alfa'bɛ] m alphabet; primer; **~étique** [~be'tik] alphabetical.

alpin [al'pɛ̃] alpine; **~isme** [alpi'nism] *m* mountaineering; **~iste** [~'nist] *su.* mountaineer.

alsacien [alza'sjɛ̃] *adj.*, *su.* Alsatian.

altéra|ble [alte'rabl] liable to deterioration; **~tion** [~ra'sjɔ̃] *f* deterioration; *coinage:* debasing; *colour:* fading; *fig.* misrepresentation.

altercation [altɛrka'sjɔ̃] *f* dispute.

altérer¹ [alte're] (1f) change for the worse; debase; impair; distort; spoil; **s'~** deteriorate.

altérer² [~] (1f) make thirsty.

altern|ance [altɛr'nɑ̃:s] *f* alternation; **~ des cultures** crop rotation; **~atif** [~na'tif] alternate; alternative; **⚡ courant** *m* **~** alternating current; **~ative** [~na'ti:v] *f* alternation; alternative; **~er** [~tɛr'ne] (1a) alternate.

Altesse [al'tɛs] *f* title: Highness.

alti|er [al'tje] haughty, **~tude** [alti'tyd] *f* altitude; **✔ prendre de l'~** climb.

alto ♪ [al'to] *m* alto; viola.

altruis|me [altry'ism] *m* altruism; **~te** [~'ist] **1.** *adj.* altruistic; selfless; **2.** *su.* altruist.

alumin|e [aly'min] *f* alumina; **~ium** [~mi'njɔm] *m* alumin(i)um.

alun [a'lœ̃] *m* alum.

alunir [aly'ni:r] (2a) land on the moon.

alvéole [alve'ɔl] *m* cell of honeycomb; *a* ⊙ cell; *tooth:* socket; cavity.

amabilité [amabili'te] *f* amiability; kindness; **~s** *pl.* civilities.

amadou [ama'du] *m* tinder; **~er** [~'dwe] (1p) coax, wheedle.

amaigr|ir [ameˈɡriːr] (2a) make thin; reduce, **s'~** lose weight, grow thin; **~issement** [~ɡris'mɑ̃] *m* slimming; emaciation.

amalgam|ation [amalgama'sjɔ̃] *f* amalgamation; **✝** merger; **~e** [~'gam] *m* amalgam; *fig.* mixture; **~er** [~ga'me] (1a) amalgamate.

amand|e [a'mɑ̃:d] *f* almond; kernel; **~ier** [~'dje] *m* almond-tree.

amant *m*, *e* *f* [a'mɑ̃, ~'mɑ̃:t] lover.

amarr|e ⚓ [a'maːr] *f* mooring rope; **~er** [ama're] (1a) moor; secure.

amas [a'mɑ] *m* heap; crowd; **~ de neige** snowdrift; **~ser** [ama'se] (1a) (*a.* **s'~**) heap up; accumulate.

amateur [ama'tœ:r] *m* lover (*of music, sports, etc.*); amateur.

amatir [ama'tiːr] (2a) mat; dull.

amazone [ama'zo:n] *f* amazon.

ambages [ɑ̃m'ba:ʒ] *f/pl.* circumlocution *sg.*; **sans ~** forthrightly.

ambassad|e [ɑ̃mba'sad] *f* embassy; **~eur** [~sa'dœːr] *m* ambassador.

ambian|ce [ɑ̃'bjɑ̃:s] *f* environment; **~t** [ɑ̃'bjɑ̃] surrounding; **conditions** *f/pl.* **~es** environment *sg.*

ambidextre [ɑ̃bi'dɛkstr] **1.** *adj.* ambidextrous; **2.** *su.* ambidexter.

ambigu, -guë [ɑ̃mbi'gy] equivocal; **~ïté** [~gɥi'te] *f* ambiguity.

ambiti|eux [ɑ̃bi'sjø] **1.** *adj.* ambitious; affected (*style*); **2.** *su.* ambitious person; **~on** [~'sjɔ̃] *f* ambition; **~onner** [~sjɔ'ne] (1a) seek.

amble [ɑ̃:bl] *m* amble, easy pace.

ambre [ɑ̃:br] *m:* **~ jaune** amber.

ambulan|ce [ɑ̃by'lɑ̃:s] *f* ambulance (*a. mot.*); **✕** field hospital; **~cier** [~lɑ̃'sje] *m* ambulance man or driver; **~t** [~'lɑ̃] itinerant, travel(l)ing; **~toire** [~la'twa:r] ambulatory.

âme [ɑ:m] *f* soul; feeling; *cable etc.:* core; *fig.* **~s** *pl.* souls, inhabitants; *fig.* **~ damnée** *s.o.'s* slave; **rendre l'~** breathe one's last.

améliorat|ion [ameljora'sjɔ̃] *f* improvement; **~er** [~'re] (1a) improve.

amen [a'mɛn] *int.* amen.

aménag|ement [amenaʒ'mɑ̃] *m* arrangement; adjustment; development; **~ du territoire** town and country planning; **~ intérieur** interior decoration; **~er** [~na'ʒe] (1l) arrange; fit out; develop (*an area etc.*).

amend|e [a'mɑ̃:d] *f* fine; **sous peine d'~** on pain of a fine; **mettre q. à l'~** fine *s.o.*; **~er** [amɑ̃'de] (1a) amend; improve; **s'~** *a.* mend one's ways.

amen|ée ⊙ [am'ne] *f:* **~ d'air** air intake; **~er** [~] (1d) lead (to, **à**); bring (in, up, down, out); cause; throw (*a number*); **~ pavillon** strike one's flag; *sl.* **amène-toi!** come along!

aménit|é [ameni'te] *f* amenity.

amenuis|ement [amnɥiz'mɑ̃] *m* dwindling; decrease; **~er** [amnɥi'ze] (1a) thin down; diminish; **s'~** dwindle, decrease, diminish.

amer [a'mɛːr] bitter (*a. fig.*).

améric|ain [ameri'kɛ̃] *adj.*, *su.* American; **~aniser** [~kani'ze] (1a) Americanize.

amerrir ✓ [amɛ'riːr] (2a) alight on the water; splash down.

amertume [amɛr'tym] f bitterness.

ameubl|ement [amœblə'mɑ̃] m furnishing; furniture; **~ir** [~'bliːr] (2a) break up (the soil).

ameuter [amø'te] (1a) draw (a crowd of); incite (the mob) (against, **contre**); **s'~** (gather into a) mob.

ami [a'mi] **1.** su. friend; **2.** adj. friendly; **~able** [a'mjabl] friendly; **à l'~** amicably; **vendre à l'~** sell privately.

amiante min. [a'mjɑ̃:t] m asbestos.

amical [ami'kal] friendly; amicable.

amidon [ami'dɔ̃] m starch; **~ner** [~dɔ'ne] (1a) starch.

amincir [amɛ̃'siːr] (2a) make thinner; slim down.

amir|al [ami'ral] m admiral; **vaisseau** m ~ flagship; **~auté** [~ro'te] f admiralty.

amitié [ami'tje] f friendship; friendliness; **~s** pl. compliments; **faites-lui mes ~s** give him my compliments; **faites-moi l'~ de** (inf.) do me the favo(u)r of (ger.).

ammoniac [amɔ'njak]: **gaz** m ~ ammonia; **sel** m ~ sal ammoniac.

amnésie [amne'zi] f amnesia.

amnisti|e [amnis'ti] f amnesty; **~er** [~'tje] (1o) grant an amnesty to.

amocher sl. [amɔ'ʃe] (1a) make a mess of; bash up.

amoindr|ir [amwɛ̃'driːr] (2a) lessen, reduce; **s'~** diminish; **~issement** [~dris'mɑ̃] m lessening.

amoll|ir [amɔ'liːr] (2a) soften; weaken; **~issement** [~lis'mɑ̃] m softening; weakening.

amoncel|er [amɔ̃s'le] (1c) (a. **s'~**) pile up; accumulate; **~lement** [~sɛl'mɑ̃] m heap(ing); piling; pile.

amont [a'mɔ̃] m: **en** ~ upstream; beforehand, in advanve; **en** ~ **de** above; before, previous to.

amor|çage [amɔr'saːʒ] m pump: priming; starting; fish: baiting; **~ce** [a'mɔrs] f bait; priming; fuse; fig. beginning; **~cer** [amɔr'se] (1k) bait; prime (a pump); fig. begin, start.

amorphe [a'mɔrf] amorphous.

amort|ir [amɔr'tiːr] (2a) deaden (a noise, a pain); cushion, absorb (a shock); ✝ amortize, pay off; ✝ write off; **~isse-**

ment ✝ [~tis'mɑ̃] m redemption; paying-off; **~isseur** ⊘ [~ti'sœːr] m shock absorber.

amour [a'muːr] m love; passion; **~s** f/pl. amours; **l'~ du prochain** love of one's neighbo(u)r; iro. **pour l'~ de Dieu** for heaven's sake; **~acher** [amura'ʃe] (1a): **s'~ de** fall in love with; **~ette** [~'rɛt] f love affair; F crush; **~eux** [~'rø] loving; ~ **de** in love with; **~-propre** [amur'prɔpr] m self-respect; vanity.

amovible [amɔ'vibl] removable; detachable.

ampère ⚡ [ɑ̃'pɛːr] m ampere.

amphibie [ɑ̃fi'bi] **1.** adj. amphibious; **2.** su./m amphibian.

amphithéâtre [ɑ̃fite'ɑːtr] m amphitheatre; univ. lecture hall.

ampl|e [ɑ̃:pl] ample; complete; **~eur** [ɑ̃'plœːr] f width; extent; ~ **du son** volume of sound; **~iation** [ɑ̃plia'sjɔ̃] f certified copy; **~ificateur** [~fika'tœːr] m radio: amplifier, booster; phot. enlarger; **~ification** [~fika'sjɔ̃] f amplification (a. radio); development; fig. exaggeration; **~ifier** [~'fje] (1o) amplify (a. ⚡), develop; fig. exaggerate; **~itude** [~'tyd] f amplitude.

ampoul|e [ɑ̃'pul] f ⚗ flask; ⚡ bulb; blister; **~é** [ɑ̃pu'le] bombastic.

amput|ation [ɑ̃pyta'sjɔ̃] f amputation; book: curtailment; **~er** [~'te] (1a) ✂ amputate; fig. cut down.

amulette [amy'lɛt] f amulet, charm.

amus|ant [amy'zɑ̃] amusing; funny; **~e-gueule** F [amyz'gœl] m/inv. appetizer; **~ement** [amyz'mɑ̃] m amusement; pastime; **~er** [amy'ze] (1a) amuse, entertain; **s'~** a. have fun; **amusez-vous bien!** enjoy yourself!; **s'~ de** make fun of; **~ette** [~'zɛt] f diversion; plaything.

amygdal|e anat. [amig'dal] f tonsil; **~ite** [~da'lit] f tonsillitis.

an [ɑ̃] m year; **avoir dix ~s** be ten (years old); **jour** m **de l'**~ New Year's day; **par** ~ a year; **tous les trois ~s** every three years.

anachronisme [anakrɔ'nism] m anachronism.

analgésique [analʒe'zik] adj., su./m analgesic.

analog|ie [analɔ'ʒi] f analogy; **par** ~ by analogy (with, **avec**); **~ue** [~'lɔg] **1.** adj.

analogous (to, with **à**), similar (to, **à**);
2. *su./m* analogue.

analpha|bète [analfa'bɛt] illiterate;
~**bétisme** [~be'tism] *m* illiteracy.

analy|se [ana'liːz] *f* analysis; *⚕️* ~ *du*
sang bloodtest; ~**ser** [~li'ze] (1a) analyse; ~**tique** [~li'tik] analytic(al).

ananas [ana'na] *m* pineapple.

anarchie [anar'ʃi] *f* anarchy.

anathème [ana'tɛm] *m* anathema, curse.

anatomi|e [anatɔ'mi] *f* anatomy; F figure
(*woman*); ~**que** [~'mik] anatomical.

ancêtre [ɑ̃'sɛtr] *m* ancestor.

anchois [ɑ̃'ʃwa] *m* anchovy.

ancien [ɑ̃'sjɛ̃] ancient, old; past; former;
senior; ~ **élève** *m* old boy, *Am.* alum-
nus; ~ *combattant* ex-serviceman, *Am.*
veteran; ~**nement** [ɑ̃sjɛn'mɑ̃] *adv.* formerly, ~**nnuté** [~'te] *f* antiquity; length
of service.

ancr|age [ɑ̃'kra:ʒ] *m* anchorage; ~**e**
[ɑ̃:kr] *f* anchor; *être à l'* ~ ride at anchor; ~**er** [ɑ̃'kre] (1a) anchor; *fig.* fix
firmly.

andouille [ɑ̃'duːj] *f* chitterling sausage,
sl. duffer, sap.

âne [ɑːn] *m* ass; donkey (*a. fig.*).

anéant|ir [aneɑ̃'tiːr] (2a) destroy; *fig.*
overwhelm; ~**issement** [~tis'mɑ̃] *m* an-
nihilation; dejection.

anecdote [anɛk'dɔt] *f* anecdote.

anémi|e *⚕️* [ane'mi] *f* an(a)emia; ~**er**
[~'mje] (1a) weaken; ~**que** [~'mik] *m*
an(a)emic.

ânerie [ɑn'ri] *f* blunder; ignorance.

anesthési|e *⚕️* [anɛstɛ'zi] *f* an(a)esthe-
sia; an(a)esthetic; ~**er** [~'zje] (1a)
an(a)esthetize; ~**que** [~'zik] *adj., su./m*
an(a)esthetic.

anfractuosité [ɑ̃fraktɥozi'te] *f* irregularity; ~**s** *pl.* winding(s *pl.*) *sg.*

ang|e [ɑ̃:ʒ] *m* angel; ~ *gardien* guardian
angel; *fig. être aux* ~**s** be on cloud
seven; ~**élique** [ɑ̃ʒe'lik] **1.** *adj.* an-
gelic; **2.** *su./f.* ⚕️, *cuis.* angelica; ~**élus**
[~'lys] *m* angelus.

angin|e *⚕️* [ɑ̃'ʒin] *f* angina; tonsillitis;
~**eux** [ɑ̃'ʒi'nø] anginal.

anglais, e [ɑ̃'glɛ, ~'glɛːz] **1.** *adj., su./m*
ling. English; **2.** *su./m* ♂ Englishman;
les ♀ *m/pl.* the English; *su./f* ♀ English-
woman.

angle [ɑ̃:gl] *m* angle; corner; edge; ~
visuel angle of vision.

anglican [ɑ̃gli'kɑ̃] Anglican; *l'Église* *f*
~**e** the Church of England.

angli|ciser [ɑ̃glisi'ze] (1a) anglicize;
~**cisme** [~'sism] *m* anglicism; ~**ciste**
[~'sist] *su.* authority on English language and literature.

anglo... [ɑ̃glo] Anglo ...; ~**phile** [~'fil]
Anglophil(e); ~**phone** [~'fɔn] English-speaking (person); ~**saxon**,
-onne [~sak'sɔ̃, ~'sɔn] Anglo-Saxon.

angoiss|e [ɑ̃'gwas] *f* anguish, agony;
~**er** [ɑ̃gwa'se] (1a) anguish, distress.

anguille [ɑ̃'giːj] *f* eel; *il y a* ~ *sous roche*
there's a snake in the grass

angul|aire [ɑ̃gy'lɛːr] angular; *pierre* *f* ~
corner-stone; ~**eux** [~'lø] angular, rugged.

anicroche [ani'krɔʃ] *f* hitch, snag.

aniline *🧪* [ani'lin] *f* aniline.

animal [ani'mal] **1.** *su./m* animal; *fig.*
dolt; **2.** *adj.* animal, brutish; *règne* *m*
~ animal kingdom; ~**ité** [~'te] *f* animali-
ty; animal kingdom.

anim|ateur [anima'tœːr] **1.** *adj.* animat-
ing; **2.** *su.* enlivener, *Br. a.* compère; organ-
izer; *fig.* driving force (*person*); ~**ation**
[~'sjɔ̃] *f* animation; liveliness; ~**er**
[ani'me] (1a) liven up; animate; *TV*
etc.: emcee (*Br. a.* compère) (*a show*);
s'~ come to life; liven up.

animosité [animozi'te] *f* animosity.

anis ⚕️ [a'ni] *m* anise; aniseed.

annal, e [an'nal] **1.** *adj.* valid for one
year; **2.** *su./f:* ~**es** *pl.* annals.

anneau [a'no] *m* ring (*a.* ⊙, *sp.*); ⊙
chain; link; *hair:* ringlet.

année [a'ne] *f* year; ~ *bissextile* leap
year; ~ *civil* natural year; ~**lumière**,
pl. ~**s-lumière** [~ly'mjɛːr] *f* light year.

annex|e [an'nɛks] **1.** *su./f* annex(e); *let-*
ter: enclosure; *state:* dependency; **2.**
adj. annexed; *lettre* *f* ~ covering letter;
~**er** [annɛk'se] (1a) annex; ~**ion** [~'sjɔ̃]
f annexation.

annihiler [anni'le] (1a) destroy.

anniversaire [anivɛr'sɛːr] **1.** *adj.* anniversary; **2.** *su./m* birthday; anniversary; ~ *de mariage* wedding anniversary;
gâteau *m* *d'*~ birthday cake.

annonc|e [a'nɔ̃:s] *f* announcement; ad-
vertisement; *fig.* presage, sign; *journ.*
petites ~**s** *pl.* classified adverts; ~**er**
[anɔ̃'se] (1k) announce; foretell; *s'*~
promise (*well, ill*); ~**eur** [~'sœːr] *m* ad-

vertizer; ♀**iation** [~sja'sjɔ̃] f: **fête** f **de l'~**
Lady Day.

annot|ation [anɔta'sjɔ̃] f note, annotation; **~er** [~'te] (1a) annotate.

annu|aire [a'nɥɛːr] m yearbook; annual; *teleph.* directory; **~el** [a'nɥɛl] annual, yearly; **~ité** [anɥi'te] f annual instalment; annuity.

annulaire [any'lɛːr] **1.** *adj.* ringlike, annular; **2.** *su./m* ring finger.

annul|ation [anyla'sjɔ̃] f annulment; *judgment:* quashing; **~er** [~'le] (1a) annul; cancel; set aside (*a will*).

anoblir [anɔ'bliːr] (2a) ennoble.

anode ♀ [a'nɔd] f anode.

anodin [anɔ'dɛ̃] *adj.*, *su./m* anodyne.

anomalie [anɔma'li] f anomaly.

ânonner [anɔ'ne] (1a) stumble out.

anonym|at [anɔni'ma] m anonymity; **~e** [~'nim] **1.** *adj.* anonymous; unnamed; **société** f **~** limited company, *abbr.* Ltd., *Am.* Inc. Ltd.; **2.** *su./m* anonymous writer.

anormal [anɔr'mal] abnormal.

anse [ɑ̃ːs] f handle; loop; bay.

antagonis|me [ɑ̃tagɔ'nism] m antagonism; **~te** [~'nist] m opponent.

antan [ɑ̃'tɑ̃] *adj.*: **d'~** of yester year.

antarctique [ɑ̃tark'tik] **1.** *adj.* antarctic; **2.** *su./m* l'♀ the Antarctic.

anté... [ɑ̃te] pre..., ante...

antécédent [ɑ̃tese'dɑ̃] *adj.*, *su./m* antecedent; **~s** *pl.* (past) records; **sans ~s judiciaires** with a clean record.

antédiluvien [ɑ̃tedily'vjɛ̃] antediluvian (*a. fig.*).

antenne [ɑ̃'tɛn] f *zo.* antenna, F feeler; *radio:* aerial.

antérieur [ɑ̃te'rjœːr] anterior, prior, previous (to, **à**).

anthère ♀ [ɑ̃'tɛːr] f anther.

anthologie [ɑ̃tɔlɔ'ʒi] f anthology.

anthropo... [ɑ̃trɔpɔ] anthropo...; **~logie** [~lɔ'ʒi] f anthropology; **~morphe** *zo.* [~'mɔrf] m anthropoid (ape); **~phage** [~'faːʒ] **1.** *su./m* cannibal; **2.** *adj.* cannibalistic.

anti... [ɑ̃ti] anti...; ante...; **~aérien** [~ae'rjɛ̃] anti-aircraft (*fire etc.*); **~biotique** ♀ [~bjɔ'tik] m antibiotic; **~chambre** [~'ʃɑ̃ːbr] f waiting-room; **faire ~ chez** dance attendance on; **~choc** [~'ʃɔk] *adj./inv.* shockproof.

anticip|ation [ɑ̃tisipa'sjɔ̃] f anticipation;

par ~ in advance; **~ de paiement** advance payment; **~er** [~'pe] (1a) *v/t.*, *v/i.*: **~ sur** anticipate.

anti...: ~clérical [ɑ̃tikleri'kal] anticlerical; **~conceptionnel** [~kɔ̃sɛpsjɔ'nɛl] contraceptive; **~corps** [~'kɔːr] m antibody; **~dater** [~da'te] (1a) antedate; **~dépresseur** [~depre'sœːr] antidepressant; **~dérapant** [~dera'pɑ̃] m non-skid tyre (*Am.* tire); **~dote** ♀ [~'dɔt] m antidote (to, for, against **à**, **de**).

antienne [ɑ̃'tjɛn] f antiphon; *fig.* **chanter toujours la même ~** be always harping on the same string.

antigel [ɑ̃ti'ʒɛl] m antifreeze.

antilope *zo.* [ɑ̃ti'lɔp] f antelope.

anti...: ~pathie [ɑ̃tipa'ti] f antipathy (against, to **contre**); **~pathique** [~pa'tik] disagreeable; **~pode** [~'pɔd] m antipode; *fig. the* very opposite; **~polluant** [~pɔly'ɑ̃] non-polluting.

antiqu|aille [ɑ̃ti'kaːj] f lumber; junk; **~aire** [~'kɛːr] m antiquary, antique dealer; **~e** [ɑ̃'tik] ancient; antique; antiquated; **~ité** [ɑ̃tiki'te] f antiquity; **~s** *pl.* antiques.

anti...: ~rides [ɑ̃ti'rid] m anti-wrinkle cream; **~rouille** [~'ruːj] *adj./inv.* anti-rust; **~sémite** [~se'mit] **1.** *adj.* anti-semitic; **2.** *su.* anti-Semite; **~septique** ♀ [~sɛp'tik] *adj.*, *su./m* antiseptic; **~social** [~sɔ'sjal] antisocial; **~solaire** [~sɔ'lɛːr]: **crème** f **~** sun cream; **~spasmodique** ♀ [~spasmɔ'dik] antispasmodic; **~thèse** [~'tɛːz] f antithesis.

antre [ɑ̃ːtr] m cave; den, lair.

anxiété [ɑ̃ksje'te] f anxiety; **anxieux** [~'sjø] anxious, uneasy.

août [u] m August.

apache [a'paʃ] m hooligan, hoodlum.

apais|ement [apɛz'mɑ̃] m appeasement; calming; soothing; **~er** [apɛ'ze] (1b) appease (*a. one's hunger*), calm, soothe, slake (*one's thirst*); **s'~** calm down; die down.

apanage [apa'naːʒ] m portion.

aparté [apar'te] m *thea.* aside; F private conversation; **en ~** aside.

apathie [apa'ti] f apathy; **~que** [~'tik] apathetic, listless.

apatride [apa'trid] stateless (person).

aper|cevable [apɛrsə'vabl] perceivable; **~cevoir** [~sə'vwaːr] (3a) see; **s'~ de** notice; become aware of; **~çu** [~'sy] *m* glimpse; general idea *or* survey.

apéritif [aperi'tif] *m* aperitif.

apeuré [apœ're] frightened.

aphone ✶ [a'fɔn] voiceless.

aphorisme [afɔ'rism] *m* aphorism.

apht|e ✶ [aft] *m* aphtha; **~eux** *vet.*, ✶ [af'tø]: **fièvre** *f* **aphteuse** foot-and-mouth disease.

apicult|eur [apikyl'tœːr] *m* beekeeper; **~ure** [~'tyːr] *f* beekeeping.

apitoyer [apitwa'je] (1h) move (to pity); **s'~ sur** feel pity for (*s.o.*).

aplanir [apla'niːr] (2a) level; *fig.* smooth (away).

aplat|ir [apla'tiːr] (2a) flatten, *fig.* crush; **s'~** flatten o.s.; *fig.* grovel.

aplomb [a'plɔ̃] *m* perpendicularity; *fig.* balance; coolness; self-possession; *pej.* insolence; **d'~** vertical(ly *adv.*); steady (steadily *adv.*); F in good shape; △ **prendre l'~** take the plumb.

apo... [apɔ] apo...; **~calypse** [~ka'lips] *f* apocalypse; **~calyptique** [~kalip'tik] apocalyptic; *fig.* obscure (*style*); **~cryphe** [~'krif] apocryphal; **~dictique** [~dik'tik] indisputable; **~gée** [~'ʒe] *m* culminating point; *ast.* F apogee; **~logie** [apɔ'trɔf] *f* apology; **~plexie** [~plɛk'si] *f* apoplexy; **~stasie** [~sta'zi] *f* apostasy; *pol.* F ratting; **~stasier** [~sta'zje] (1o) apostatize; renounce one's faith *or* principles *or* party; **~stat** [~s'ta] apostate, F turncoat.

apostroph|e [apɔs'trɔf] *f* apostrophe, rude remark; **~er** [~trɔ'fe] (1a) apostrophize; address (*s.o.*) sharply.

apothéose [apɔte'oːz] *f* apotheosis; *fig. a.* pinnacle.

apothicaire [apɔti'kɛːr] *m*: **compte** *m* **d'~** exorbitant bill.

apôtre [a'poːtr] *m* apostle (*a. fig.*); **faire le bon ~** play the saint.

apparaître [apa'rɛːtr] (4k) appear; become evident.

apparat [apa'ra] *m* pomp, show.

appareil [apa'rɛːj] *m* apparatus (*a. fig., ✶, ⚘*); △ bond; *phot.* camera; ⚙ machinery; ⚙ device; *radio:* set; display; **~ de projection** projector; *teleph.* **qui est à l'~?** who is speaking?; **~lage** [~rɛ'laːʒ] *m* ⚓ getting under way; equipment; ⚙ fixture.

appareiller¹ [apare'je] (1a) match (up); pair.

appareiller² [apare'je] (1a) *v/t.* fit out (*a. ⚓*); *v/i.* ⚓ get under way.

appar|emment [apara'mɑ̃] apparently; evidently; **~ence** [~'rɑ̃ːs] *f* appearance, look; **en ~** seemingly; **sauver les ~s** save one's face; **~ent** [~'rɑ̃] apparent; evident.

apparenter [aparɑ̃'te] (1a): **s'~ à** marry into (*a family*); unite with.

apparier [apa'rje] (1o) mate.

apparition [apari'sjɔ̃] *f* appearance; apparition; spectre; vision.

appartement [apart'mɑ̃] *m* flat, *Am.* apartment

apparten|ance [apartə'nɑːs] *f*: **~ à** membership of, belonging to; **~ir** [~'niːr] (2h) *v/i.* belong (to, **à**); **il appartient à q. de faire qch.** it rests with s.o. to do s.th.; *v/t.:* **s'~** be one's own master.

appas [a'pɑ] *m/pl.* charms.

appât [a'pɑ] *m* bait; lure; **mordre à l'~** take the bait; **~er** [apa'te] (1a) lure, entice; fatten (up) (*poultry etc.*).

appauvr|ir [apo'vriːr] (2a) impoverish; **~s'~** grow poorer; **~issement** [~vris'mɑ̃] *m* impoverishment; deterioration.

appeau [a'po] *m* decoy; birdcall.

appel [a'pɛl] *m* call; appeal (*a. ✶*); **~ d'air** intake of air; *teleph.* **~ interurbain** trunk-call; **~ téléphonique** (tele)phone call; *✶* **cour** *f* **d'~** Court of Appeal; **faire ~ à** have recourse to; **~er** [ap'le] (1c) *v/t.* call; call to; call up; send for; **~ l'attention de q. sur qch.** call s.o.'s attention to s.th.; **s'~** be called; *v/i.* **~ d'un jugement** appeal against a sentence; **en ~ à** appeal to; **~lation** [apɛla'sjɔ̃] *f* appellation; trade name.

appendic|e [apɛ̃'dis] *m* appendix (*a. anat.*); **~ite** [~'dit] *f* appendicitis.

appentis [apɑ̃'ti] *m* lean-to (*roof*).

appert [a'pɛːr]: **il ~ de** it appears from.

appesant|ir [apəzɑ̃'tiːr] (2a) make heavy; weigh down; dull; **s'~ sur** insist upon; **~issement** [~tis'mɑ̃] *m* heaviness; dullness.

appét|issant [apeti'sɑ̃] appetizing, tempting (*a. fig.*); **~it** [~'ti] *m* appetite; craving.

applaud|ir [aplo'diːr] (2a) *vt/i.* applaud; clap; **s'~ de** congratulate o.s. on; *v/i.:* **~ à** approve (of); **~issements** [~dis'mɑ̃] *m/pl.* applause *sg.*

appli|cable [apli'kabl] applicable (to,

à); **~cation** [~ka'sjɔ̃] f application; fig. diligence; **~que** [a'plik] f applied ornament; (wall-)bracket; **~qué** [apli'ke] diligent; **~quer** [~] (1m) apply; F **~ une gifle à q.** fetch s.o. one; fig. **s'~ à** apply o.s. to.

appoint [a'pwɛ̃] m contribution; help, support; (a. **monnaie** f d'**~**) small change; d'**~** secondary; extra; **faire l'~** give the right change; **~ements** [apwɛt'mã] m/pl. salary sg; **~er** [apwɛ'te] (1a) pay a salary to.

appontement ⚓ [apɔ̃t'mã] m gangplank; landing stage.

apport [a'pɔːr] m contribution; **capital** m d'**~** initial capital; **~er** [apɔr'te] (1a) bring; provide.

appos|er [apo'ze] (1a) affix (to, à); put; set (a seal); **~ition** [~zi'sjɔ̃] f affixing; gramm. apposition.

appréci|able [apre'sjabl] appreciable; **~ation** [~sja'sjɔ̃] f estimate; appreciation; **~er** [~'sje] (1a) estimate; appreciate.

appréhen|der [apreã'de] (1a) dread; seize; **~sion** [~'sjɔ̃] f apprehension; 🕵 arrest.

apprenant [aprə'nã] m learner, student.

apprendre [a'prãːdr] (4aa) learn; teach (s.o. s.th., **qch. à q.**); **~ à q. à faire qch.** teach s.o. (how) to do s.th.

apprenti [aprã'ti] m apprentice; learner; **~ssage** [~ti'saːʒ] m apprenticeship.

apprêt [a'prɛ] m preparation; ⚙ finishing; cuis. seasoning; fig. affectation; **~é** [~'te] affected; **~er** [~'te] (1a) prepare; ⚙ finish; starch; **s'~** get ready; be imminent.

apprivoiser [aprivwa'ze] (1a) tame.

approbat|eur [aprɔba'tœːr], **~if** [~'tif] approving; **~ion** [~'sjɔ̃] f approval.

approch|e [a'prɔʃ] f approach; **les ~s de** the immediate surroundings of (a town etc.); **~er** [aprɔ'ʃe] (1a) v/t. bring (s.th.) near; **s' ~ de** come near (to); v/i. approach; come near.

approfond|ir [aprɔfɔ̃'diːr] (2a) deepen; fig. go deeper into; **~issement** [~dis'mã] m deepening; fig. thorough investigation.

appropri|ation [aprɔpria'sjɔ̃] f adaptation (to, à); **~ de fonds** embezzlement; **~er** [~pri'e] (1o) adapt (to, à); **s' ~ qch.** usurp s.th.

approuver [apru've] (1a) approve (of); consent to; confirm.

approvisionn|ement [aprɔvizjɔn'mã] m supply(ing); stock(ing); **~er** [~zjɔ'ne] (1a) supply (with, en).

approximat|if [aprɔksima'tif] approximate; **~ion** [~'sjɔ̃] f approximation.

appu|i [a'pɥi] m support; rest, prop, stay; **à l'~** in support of this; **à l'~ de** in support of; **~i(e)-tête**, pl. **~is-tête** [apɥi'tɛːt] m headrest; mot. head-restraint; **~yer** [apɥi'je] (1h) v/t. support; press; rest (against, **contre**); v/i.: **~ sur** rest on; press, push (a button etc.), press down; fig. emphasize, stress; **~ sur la** (or **~ à**) **droite** bear to the right; **s' ~ sur** rest on or against; fig. rely on.

âpre [ɑːpr] rough, harsh; biting; **~ à** eager for; **~ au gain** greedy.

après [a'prɛ] **1.** prp. space, time: after; behind; idea of attack: at, on, to; **~ quoi** after which; **~ tout** after all; **~ avoir lu ce livre** after reading this book; **d'~** according to; **2.** cj. **~ que** after, when; **3.** adv. after(wards), later; next; **~-demain** [aprɛdə'mɛ̃] adv. the day after tomorrow; **~-midi** [~mi'di] m/inv. afternoon; **~-vente** [~'vãːt]: **service** m **~** after-sales service.

âpreté [aprə'te] f roughness; sharpness; bitterness; keenness.

à-propos [aprɔ'po] m aptness, suitability; opportuneness.

apt|e [apt] fit(ted) (to, for à); apt; **~itude** [apti'tyd] f aptitude; fitness; 🕵 capacity, qualification.

apurer ♰ [apy're] (1a) audit.

aqua|relle [akwa'rɛl] f aquarelle, water-colo(u)r; **~tique** [~'tik] aquatic; marshy (land).

aqueduc [ak'dyk] m aqueduct.

aquilin [aki'lɛ̃] aquiline.

arab|e [a'rab] adj., su. Arabian; Arab; **chiffre** m **~** Arabic numeral; **~esque** [ara'bɛsk] adj., su./f arabesque; **~ique** [ara'bik] Arabic; Arabian; **gomme** f **~** gum arabic.

arable [a'rabl] arable (land).

arachide ♀ [ara'ʃid] f peanut.

araignée [arɛ'ɲe] f zo. spider; F **avoir une ~ au plafond** have bats in the belfry; **toile** f d'**~** cobweb.

aratoire [ara'twaːr] agricultural.

arbalète [arba'lɛt] f crossbow.

arbitr|age [arbi'tra:ʒ] *m* arbitration; **conseil** *m* **d'~** conciliation board; **~aire** [~'trɛ:r] arbitrary; **~e** [ar'bitr] *m* referee; umpire; *phls.* **libre ~** free will; **~er** [~bi'tre] (1a) arbitrate; *sp.* referee.
arbor|er [arbɔ're] (1a) hoist (*a flag*); *fig.* wear, display; sport (*a garment*); **~icul-ture** [~rikyl'ty:r] *m* arboriculture.
arbre [arbr] *m* tree; ⊙ shaft; **~ manivelle** crankshaft; **arbrisseau** [~bri'so] *m* shrub.
arbuste ♀ [ar'byst] *m* bush, shrub.
arc [ark] *m* bow; △ arch; ♈, ⊙ arc.
arcade [ar'kad] *f* archway; ⊙ arch.
arcanes [ar'kɑn] *m/pl.* mysteries.
arc-boutant, *pl.* **arcs-boutant** [arkbu'tɑ̃] *m* flying buttress; stay.
arceau [ar'so] *m* hoop; arch.
arc-en-ciel, *pl.* **arcs-en-ciel** [arkɑ̃'sjel] *m* rainbow.
archaïque [arka'ik] archaic.
archange [ar'kɑ̃:ʒ] *m* archangel.
arche¹ [arʃ] *f* arch; hoop.
arche² *bibl.* [~] *f* Ark.
archéolog|ie [arkeɔlɔ'ʒi] *f* arch(a)eolo-gy, **~ue** [~'lɔg] *m* arch(a)eologist.
archer [ar'ʃe] *m* archer.
archet [ar'ʃɛ] *m* bow.
archétype [arke'tip] **1.** *adj.* archetypal; **2.** *su./m* archetype.
archevê|ché [arʃəvɛ'ʃe] *m* archdiocese; **~que** [~'vɛk] *m* archbishop.
archi... [arʃi] arch...; extremely; to the hilt; **~bondé** [~bɔ̃'de], **~comble** [~'kɔ̃:bl] packed (full).
archipel [arʃi'pel] *m* archipelago.
architec|te [arʃi'tɛkt] *m* architect; **~ure** [~tɛk'ty:r] *f* architecture; **~ de paysage** landscape gardening *or* design.
archiv|es [ar'ʃi:v] *f/pl.* archives, records; **~iste** [~ʃi'vist] *su.* archivist.
arçon [ar'sɔ̃] *m* saddle bow.
ard|emment [arda'mɑ̃] *adv. of* **ardent**; **~ent** [~'dɑ̃] hot, burning; *fig.* passion-ate; *fig.* **être sur des charbons ~s** be on tenterhooks; **~eur** [~'dœ:r] *f* heat; *fig.* ardo(u)r.
ardillon [ardi'jɔ̃] *m* buckle: tongue.
ardoise [ar'dwa:z] *f* slate.
ardu [ar'dy] steep, abrupt; difficult.
arène [a'rɛn] *f* arena; *poet.* sand.
arête [a'rɛt] *f* (fish) bone; ⊙ edge; *mount.* ridge; ♀ awn; **à ~s vives** sharp-edged.

argent [ar'ʒɑ̃] *m* silver; money; **~ comp-tant** cash; **~ de poche** pocket-money; **en avoir pour son ~** have one's money's worth; **~an** [arʒɑ̃'tɑ̃] *m* nickel silver; **~é** [~'te] silver(ed); silvery; sil-ver-plated; **~er** [~'te] (1a) silver; **~erie** [~'tri] *f* silverware.
argentin¹ [arʒɑ̃'tɛ̃] silvery (*voice*).
argentin² [~] *adj., su.* Argentinian, Ar-gentine.
argenture [arʒɑ̃'ty:r] *f* mirror: silvering; silver plating.
argil|e [ar'ʒil] *f* clay; **~ réfractaire** fire-clay; **~eux** [arʒi'lø] clayey.
argot [ar'go] *m* slang; **~ique** [~gɔ'tik] slangy.
argu|er [ar'gɥe] (1e): **~ de** *put* (*s.th.*) forward (as a reason); **~ment** [urgy'mɑ̃] *m* argument; summary; **~mentation** [~mɑ̃ta'sjɔ̃] *f* argumenta-tion; **~menter** [~mɑ̃'te] (1a) argue (about, **à propos de**; against, **contre**); **~tie** [~'si] *f* quibble.
arid|e [a'rid] arid, dry; barren; **~ité** [ari-di'te] *f* aridity, barrenness.
aristo *sl.* [aris'to] *m* swell, toff.
aristocrat|e [aristɔ'krat] *su.* aristocrat; **~ie** [~kra'si] *f* aristocracy.
arithméti|cien [aritmeti'sjɛ̃] *m* arithme-tician; **~que** [~'tik] **1.** *adj.* arithmetical; **2.** *su./f* arithmetic.
arlequin [arlə'kɛ̃] *m* Harlequin.
armat|eur [arma'tœ:r] *m* shipowner; **~ure** [~'ty:r] *f* frame(work); ♪ arma-ture; ♪ key-signature.
arm|e [arm] *f* arm; weapon; ✕ branch of the service; **~ à feu** firearm; *sp.* **faire des ~s** fence; **~é** [ar'me] reinforced (*concrete*); **verre** *m* **~** wired glass; **~ée** [ar'me] *f* army; **~ de l'air** Air Force; **~ de mer** Navy; **~ de métier** regular army; ♀ **du salut** Salvation Army; **~ement** [armə'mɑ̃] *m* armament; arming; **~er** [ar'me] (1a) arm (with, **de**); equip; ♻ commission; cock (*a pistol*); set (*an ap-paratus*); **s'~ de patience** take patience.
armistice [armis'tis] *m* armistice.
armoire [ar'mwa:r] *f* cupboard; ward-robe; **~ à pharmacie** medicine-chest; **~ au linge** linen closet.
armoiries [armwa'ri] *f/pl.* (coat *sg.* of) arms; armorial bearings.
armur|e [ar'my:r] *f* armo(u)r; **~ier** [~'rje] *m* armo(u)rer; gunsmith.

arom|ate [arɔ'mat] *m* aromatic; **~atique** [arɔma'tik] aromatic; **~atiser** [~ti'ze] (1a) flavo(u)r.

arôme [a'ro:m] *m* aroma; *cuis.* flavo(u)ring.

arpent [ar'pɑ̃] *m* (*approx.*) acre; **~age** [arpɑ̃'ta:ʒ] *m* (land-)surveying; **~er** [~'te] (1a) pace (up and down); survey (*the land*); **~eur** [~'tœːr] *m* surveyor.

arqué [ar'ke] arched, curved; *jambes* **~es** bow legs, bandy legs; **arquer** [~] (1m) bend; arch.

arrach|é [ara'ʃe] *m sp.* snatch; *fig. à l'~* narrow (*victory etc.*); *fig. obtenir qch. à l'~* (just manage to) snatch s.th.; **~e-pied** [~'pje] *adv.: d'~* relentlessly; fiercely; *travailler d'~* F work flat out; **~er** [ara'ʃe] (1a) tear out *or* away (from, **à**); extract (*a tooth*); extort (*money*).

arrang|ement [arɑ̃ʒ'mɑ̃] *m* arrangement (*a. ♪*); settlement, agreement; **~er** [arɑ̃'ʒe] (1l) arrange (*a. ♪*); put in order; tidy; organize; settle (*a dispute*); suit (*s.o.*); *cela m'arrange* that suits me; F *cela s'arrangera* it'll turn out all right; *s'~* manage (with, *de*), make do (with *de*); come to an agreement (with, *avec*); *s'~ pour faire qch.* see to it that one can do s.th.

arrérages [arere'a:ʒ] *m/pl.* arrears.

arrestation [aresta'sjɔ̃] *f* arrest; *t/t* **~ préventive** preventive custody.

arrêt [a're] *m* stop (*a. ☉*); stopping; halt; interruption; *admin.* decree; *t/t* decision; *t/t* arrest; *lock:* tumbler; *bus etc.:* stop(ping place); **⚔ ~s** *pl.* arrest *sg.*; **~ de mort** death sentence; *cran* **m** *d'~* safety-catch; *t/t* **rendre un ~** deliver judgement; *robinet* **m** *d'~* stop-cock; *sans* **~** continually; *temps* **m** *d'~* pause, halt; **~é** [are'te] *m* order; decree; **~er** [~] (1a) *v/t.* stop; arrest; fasten; draw up; decide; close (*an account*); *s'~* stop; halt, pause; cease (*noise*); *sans s'~ a.* without (a) letup; *v/i.: ~ de faire qch.* stop doing s.th.; *ne pas ~ de faire qch. a.* keep doing s.th.

arrhes [a:r] *f/pl.* deposit *sg.*

arrière [a'rjɛːr] **1.** *adv.: en* **~** behind, back, backward(s); *in arrears*; **2.** *su./m* back (part), rear; *sp.* back; **⚙** */inv.* back; *mot.* **feu ~** rearlight; *roue* **f** **~** rearwheel; **~éré** [arje're] **1.** *adj.* late; in

arrears; backward (*child, country*); **2.** *su./m* arrears *pl.*

arrière...: **~boutique** [arjɛrbu'tik] *f* back shop; **~cour** [~'ku:r] *f* backyard; **~garde** ⚔ [~'gard] *f* rearguard; **~goût** [~'gu] *m* aftertaste; **~grand-pere** [~grɑ̃'pɛːr] *m* great-grandfather; **~main** [~'mɛ̃] *f* back of the hand; *horse:* hindquarters *pl.*; backhand stroke; **~pensée** [~pɑ̃'se] *f* ulterior motive; mental reservation; **~petit-fils**, *pl.* **~petits-fils** [~pəti'fis] *m* great-grandson; **~plan** [~'plɑ̃] *m* background.

arriérer [arje're] (1f) postpone; *s'~* fall behind; get into arrears.

arrière-saison [arjɛrsɛ'zɔ̃] *f* late season *or* autumn, *Am.* late fall.

arrimer ⚓ [ari'me] (1a) stow; trim (*a ship*); fasten.

arriv|ant *m, e f* [ari'vɑ̃, ~'vɑ̃:t] comer; **~ée** [~'ve] *f* arrival; ☉ intake; *sp.* finish; **~er** [~'ve] (1a) arrive (at, **à**), come; happen (to, **à**); **~ à** reach, come to; **~ à** (*inf.*) manage to (*inf.*), succeed in (*ger.*); *il m'arrive de ...* (*inf.*) I sometimes ... (*inf.*); **~iste** [~'vist] *su.* careerist.

arrogan|ce [arɔ'gɑ̃:s] *f* arrogance; **~t** [~'gɑ̃] arrogant; haughty.

arroger [arɔ'ʒe] (1l): *s'~* claim.

arrond|ir [arɔ̃'diːr] (2a) round (off) (*a. fig. a sum*); *s'~* fill out; become round; **~issement** *admin.* [~dis'mɑ̃] *m* district.

arros|age [aro'za:ʒ] *m* watering; **~er** [~'ze] (1a) water; wet; sprinkle; F wash down (*the food*); F celebrate (*s.th.*) with a drink; **~oir** [~'zwa:r] *m* watering can.

arsenal [arsə'nal] *m* arsenal (*a. fig.*).

arsenic 🜍 [arsə'nik] *m* arsenic.

art [a:r] *m* art; skill; **~s** *pl.* **et métiers** *m/pl.* arts and crafts.

artère [ar'tɛːr] *f* artery (*a. fig.*); **artériel** [arte'rjɛl] arterial.

arthrite 🜊 [ar'trit] *f* arthritis; gout.

artichaut *cuis.* [arti'ʃo] *m* artichoke.

article [ar'tikl] *m* article; item; *treaty:* clause; *journ.* **~ de fond** leader, editorial; *à l'~ de la mort* at the point of death.

articul|aire 🜊 [artiky'lɛːr] articular, of the joints; **~ation** [~la'sjɔ̃] *f anat.*, *speech:* articulation; joint; **~er** [~'le] (1a) articulate; link.

artific|e [arti'fis] *m* artifice; expedient;

feu m d'~ fireworks pl.; fig. flash of wit; ~iel [artifi'sjɛl] artificial; ~ier [~'sje] m pyrotechnist; ~ieux [~'sjø] artful, cunning.

artill|erie ✗ [artij'ri] f artillery, ordnance; ~ antiaérienne anti-aircraft artillery; ~eur [~ti'jœːr] m artilleryman.

artisan [arti'zɑ̃] m artisan; craftsman; fig. creator; ~at [~za'na] m handicraft; craftsmen pl.

artiste [ar'tist] su. artist; ♪, thea. performer; ~ique [~tis'tik] artistic.

as¹ [a] 2nd p. sg. pres. of avoir 1.

as² [ɑːs] m ace (a. fig.); sl. être plein aux ~ have stacks of money.

asbeste [as'bɛst] m asbestos.

ascendan|ce [asɑ̃'dɑ̃ːs] f ancestry; astr. ascendant; ~t [~'dɑ̃] 1. adj. upward (motion etc.); 2. su./m ascendency; influence; ~s pl. ancestry sg.

ascens|eur [asɑ̃'sœːr] m lift, Am. elevator; ~ion [~'sjɔ̃] f ascent; climb; l'2 Ascension (Day).

ascète [a'sɛt] su. ascetic; ascétisme [ase'tism] m asceticism.

asepsie ☞ [asɛp'si] f asepsis.

asexué [asɛksu'e] biol. asexual; sexless.

asiatique [azja'tik] adj., su. Asian.

asile [a'zil] m asylum; home, shelter; refuge; ~ d'aliénés mental hospital.

asocial [asɔ'sjal] antisocial.

aspect [as'pɛ] m aspect; sight; appearance, look; fig. viewpoint.

asperge ✿ [as'pɛrʒ] f asparagus.

asperger [aspɛr'ʒe] (1l) sprinkle.

aspérité [aspɛri'te] f asperity, roughness, harshness; unevenness.

asperseur [aspɛr'sœːr] m sprinkler.

asphalte [as'falt] m asphalt.

asphyxi|e [asfik'si] f asphyxia(tion), suffocation; ~er [~'sje] (1o) (a. s'~) asphyxiate, suffocate.

aspic [as'pik] m zo. asp; cuis. aspic.

aspir|ant [aspi'rɑ̃] 1. adj. sucking; ⊚ suction-...; 2. su. aspirant, candidate; ~ateur [~ra'tœːr] 1. adj. suction-...; 2. su./m vacuum cleaner; ~ation [~ra'sjɔ̃] f aspiration; inhaling; sucking up; ~er [~'re] (1a) v/t. breathe in; suck in or up; v/i.: ~ à aspire to, long for.

aspirine ☞ [aspi'rin] f aspirin.

assagir [asa'ʒiːr] (2a) make wiser; steady, sober (down).

assaillir [asa'jiːr] (2s) assail, attack; fig. beset (with, de).

assain|ir [asɛ'niːr] (2a) make healthier; cleanse; clean (up); clear; drain (marshes); stabilize (the economy etc.); reorganize (the finances etc.); ~issement [~nis'mɑ̃] m cleansing; cleaning (up); clearing; marshes: draining; economy: stabilization; finances: reorganization.

assaisonn|ement [asɛzɔn'mɑ̃] m seasoning; salad: dressing; ~er [~zɔ'ne] (1a) season (with, de).

assassin, e [asa'sɛ̃, ~'sin] 1. su./m assassin; murderer; à l'~! murder!; su./f murderess. 2. adj. murderous; ~at [~si'na] m murder; assassination; ~er [~si'ne] (1a) murder; assassinate.

assaut [a'so] m assault, attack; sp. match; faire ~ de bandy (words).

ass|èchement [asɛʃ'mɑ̃] m drying; ~écher [ase'ʃe] (1f) dry; drain.

assembl|age [asɑ̃'blaːʒ] m gathering, collection; ⊚ assembling; joint, connection; ~ée [~'ble] f assembly, meeting; gathering; ~ générale general meeting; ~er [~'ble] (1a) assemble (a. ⊚); gather; convene (a committee); connect; s'~ gather.

assener [asə'ne] (1d) strike.

assentiment [asɑ̃ti'mɑ̃] m agreement, consent; signe m d' ~ nod.

asseoir [a'swaːr] (3c) seat, place; pitch (a tent); establish (a tax); base (an opinion); on le fit ~ he was asked to take a seat; s'~ sit down; settle.

assermenté [asɛrmɑ̃'te] sworn.

assertion [asɛr'sjɔ̃] f assertion.

asserv|ir [asɛr'viːr] (2a) enslave (to, à); subdue; subject; ~issement [~vis'mɑ̃] m slavery, subjection.

asseyons [asɛ'jɔ̃] 1st p. pl. pres. of asseoir.

assez [a'se] adv. enough; rather; sufficiently; fairly; ~! that will do!; (en) avoir ~ de be sick (and tired) of; F j'en ai ~! a I'm fed up with it.

assidu|u [asi'dy] diligent; regular; attentive (to s.o., auprès de q.); ~ité [~dɥi'te] f diligence, assiduity; ~ments pl. constant attentions; ~ûment [~dy'mɑ̃] adv. of assidu.

assieds [a'sje] 1st p. sg. pres. of asseoir.

assiéger [asje'ʒe] (1g) besiege (a. fig.); fig. thought etc.: beset.

assiérai [asje're] *1st p. sg. fut. of as-seoir*.

assiett|e [a'sjɛt] *f* plate; *horse:* seat; ◎ *etc.* basis; *tax:* establishment; F *il n'est pas dans son* ~ he's out of sorts; ~**ée** [asje'te] *f* plate(ful).

assign|ation [asiɲa'sjɔ̃] *f* assignment; ⚖ summons, subpoena; ~**er** [~'ɲe] (1a) assign; allot; fix (*a time*); allocate, ♦ earmark (*a sum*); ⚖ summon, subpoena.

assimilation [asimila'sjɔ̃] *f* assimilation; **assimiler** [~'le] (1a) assimilate; compare; give equal status to.

assis¹ [a'si] *1st p. sg. p.s. of asseoir*.

assis², **e** [~, ~'si:z] **1.** *p.p. of asseoir; 2. adj.* seated, sitting; *être* ~ be sitting; ☷ *etc.* *place f* ~**e** seat; **3.** *su./f* foundation; stratum, layer; ⚖ *cour f d'*~**es** Assize Court.

assist|ance [asis'tɑ̃:s] *f* assistance, help; audience, spectators *pl.*; presence; ~ *judiciaire* (free) legal aid; ~ *sociale* (social) welfare work; ~**ant** [~'tɑ̃] *su.* assistant; ~**s** *pl.* spectators, audience *sg.*; ~**er** [~'te] (1a) *v/i.*: ~ *à* be present at; be at, see; witness; *v/t.* help (*s.o.*).

associ|ation [asɔsja'sjɔ̃] *f* association; ♦ partnership; society; union; ~ *de bienfaisance* charitable organization; ~**é** [asɔ'sje] *m* partner; associate; ~**er** [~] (1o) associate, unite; join up; *s'*~ (*à or avec*) join (in *s.th.*); keep company with; ♦ enter into partnership with.

assoiffé [aswa'fe] thirsty.

assoirai F [aswa're] *1st p. sg. fut. of asseoir; assois* F [a'swa] *1st p. sg. pres. of asseoir*.

assombrir [asɔ̃'bri:r] (2a) darken; make gloomy; cloud.

assomm|er [asɔ'me] (1a) knock out; kill; *fig.* bore; ~**oir** [~'mwa:r] *m: fig. coup m d'*~ staggering blow.

assomption [asɔ̃p'sjɔ̃] *f* assumption; *l'*⚜ the Assumption.

assort|i [asɔr'ti] assorted; (*well-,badly-*) matched; ♦ (*well-, badly-*) stocked; ~ *à* matching; ~**iment** [~ti'mɑ̃] *m* assortment, range; ◎ set; ~**ir** [~'ti:r] (2a) (*a. s'*~) match (with, *à qch.*).

assoup|ir [asu'pi:r] (2a) make drowsy; lull (*a pain etc.*); *s'*~ doze off; wear off; ~**issement** [~pis'mɑ̃] *m* drowsiness; doze; 🌿 torpor.

assouplir [asu'pli:r] (2a) make supple; break in (*a horse*).

assourdir [asur'di:r] (2a) deafen; deaden; damp; muffle (*a sound*).

assouvir [asu'vi:r] (2a) appease; gratify; glut (*the market*); *s'*~ gorge; become sated (with, *de*).

assoyons F [aswa'jɔ̃] *1st p. pl. pres. of asseoir*.

assujett|i [asyʒɛ'ti] subject, liable (to, *à*); ~ *aux droits de douane* liable to duty; ~**ir** [~'ti:r] (2a) subjugate, subdue; fasten; compel (to *inf.*, *à inf.*); ~**issement** [~tis'mɑ̃] *m* subjugation; securing.

assumer [asy'me] (1a) assume; take (*a responsibility*) upon o.s.

assur|ance [asy'rɑ̃:s] *f* assurance (*a.* ♦), self-confidence; security; ♦ insurance; ~**s** *pl. sociales* social security *sg.*; ~*automobile* car insurance; ~ *maladie* health-insurance; ~ *au tiers* third-party insurance; ~ *tous risques* comprehensive insurance; ~*-vie* life insurance; ~*-vieillesse* old-age insurance; *passer un contrat d'*~ take out an insurance policy; ~**é** [~'re] **1.** *adj.* sure; confident; **2.** *su.* ♦ the insured; ~**ément** [~re'mɑ̃] *adv.* assuredly; ~**er** [~'re] (1a) assure; fasten; make secure; ensure (*a result*); ♦ insure; provide, maintain (*a service etc.*); carry out, undertake, handle (*work etc.*); *s'*~ a. make sure (of, *de*; that, *que*); *s'*~ *de a.* ensure; ~**eur** ♦ [~'rœ:r] *m* insurers *pl.*; insurance agent.

asthm|atique 🌿 [asma'tik] asthmatic; ~**e** 🌿 [asm] *m* asthma.

asticot [asti'ko] *m* maggot; F *un drôle d'*~ a queer fellow; ~**er** F [~kɔ'te] (1a) plague, worry.

astiquer [asti'ke] (1m) polish.

astre [astr] *m* star (*a. fig.*).

astreindre [as'trɛ̃:dr] (4m) subject; force, compel (to, *à*); bind.

astringent [astrɛ̃'ʒɑ̃] *adj.*, *su./m* astringent.

astro... [astrɔ] astro...; ~**logie** [~lɔ'ʒi] *f* astrology; ~**logue** [~'lɔg] *m* astrologer; ~**naute** [~'no:t] *m* astronaut; ~**nautique** [~no'tik] *f* astronautics *sg.*; ~**nef** [~'nɛf] *m* spaceship; ~**nome** [~'nɔm] *m* astronomer; ~**nomie** [~nɔ'mi] *f* astronomy; ~**nomique** [~nɔ'mik] astronomical (*year, a.* F *price*).

astuc|e [as'tys] f craftiness; wile; **~ieux** [~ty'sjø] crafty, artful.

asymétrique [asime'trik] asymmetrical, unsymmetrical.

atavisme [ata'vism] m atavism.

atelier [atə'lje] m workshop; studio; staff; **~ de constructions mécaniques** engine works sg.; **~ de réparations** repair shop.

atermoyer [atɛrmwa'je] (1h) temporize, procrastinate.

athée [a'te] su. atheist; **athéisme** [ate'ism] m atheism.

athlète [at'lɛt] m (Am. track and field) athlete; **athlétism** [~le'tism] m (Am. track and field) athletics pl.

atlantique [atlɑ̃'tik] adj., su. Atlantic.

atlas [at'lɑs] m atlas; ♀ Atlas.

atmosphère [atmɔs'fɛːr] f atmosphere (a. fig.).

atoll [a'tɔl] m atoll, coral island.

atom|e [a'toːm] m atom (a. fig.); **~ique** [atɔ'mik] atomic; **bombe** f **~** atom(ic) bomb; **énergie** f **~** atomic energy; **~iser** [~mi'ze] atomize; pulverize; **~iseur** [~mi'zœːr] m spray, atomizer.

atout [a'tu] m trump; fig. asset, advantage.

atoxique [atɔk'sik] non-poisonous.

être [ɑːtr] m hearth.

atroc|e [a'trɔs] atrocious, dreadful; grim; **~ité** [atrɔsi'te] f atrocity.

atrophi|e [atrɔ'fi] f emaciation; **~er** [~'fje] (1o): **s'~** atrophy.

attabler [ata'ble] (1a): **s'~** sit down to table; fig. own up, come clean.

attach|e [a'taʃ] f tie, link; strap; ♂ brace; paper clip; **chien** m **d'~** house-dog; **~ement** [ataʃ'mɑ̃] m attachment (a. fig.); **~er** [ata'fe] (1a) v/t. tie (up), fasten; attach; attract; s'~ à attach o.s. to; cling to; apply o.s. to; s'~ **aux pas de q.** dog s.o.; v/i. stick.

attaqu|e [a'tak] f attack; ♂ a. fit; **être d'~** feel fit; **~er** [ata'ke] (1m) attack; ♂ sue (s.o.); F begin; **s'~ à** attack; fig. tackle.

attard|é [atar'de] belated; backward; old-fashioned; **~er** [~] (1a) delay; **s'~** linger (over, sur).

attein|dre [a'tɛ̃dr] (4m) v/t. reach; overtake; hit (a target); affect; v/i.: **~ à** attain (to); achieve; **~t, e** [a'tɛ̃, ~'tɛ̃ːt] 1. p.p. of **atteindre**; 2. su./f

reach; attack (a. ♂), blow; injury; **hors d'~e** out of reach.

attel|age [at'laːʒ] m harnessing; team (of oxen etc.); ♥ etc. coupling; **~er** [~'le] (1c) harness; connect; ♥ etc. couple; **s'~ à** get down to (a task); **~le** [a'tɛl] f splint.

attenant [at'nɑ̃] adjacent (to, **à**).

attend|ant [atɑ̃'dɑ̃]: **en ~** adv. meanwhile; prp. pending; **en ~ que** (sbj.) until, till (ind.); **~re** [a'tɑ̃dr] (4a) v/i. wait; v/t. wait for; expect (from, **de**); **attendez voir!** wait and see!; **faire ~ q.** keep s.o. waiting; **s'~ à** expect (s.th.), be prepared for.

attendr|ir [atɑ̃'driːr] (2a) make tender; tenderize (meat); fig. touch, move; **s'~ sur** feel sorry for; **~issement** [~dris'mɑ̃] m emotion; pity.

attendu [atɑ̃'dy] 1. p.p. of **attendre**; 2. prp. on account of; **~ que** seeing that ...; ♣♣ whereas; 3. su./m: **~s** pl. ♣♣ reasons adduced.

attentat [atɑ̃'ta] m assassination; attempt; attack; outrage.

attente [a'tɑ̃ːt] f wait(ing), expectation; **contre toute ~** contrary to expectations.

attenter [atɑ̃'te] (1a) make an attempt (on, **à**).

attenti|f [atɑ̃'tif] attentive (to, **à**); careful; **~on** [~'sjɔ̃] f attention, care; **~!** look out!; **faire ~ (à)** pay attention (to); take care (of); **faire ~ à** (inf.) make or be sure to (inf.), mind to (inf.).

atténu|ant [ate'nɥɑ̃] ♣♣ mitigating or extenuating (circumstances); **~er** [~'nɥe] (1n), mitigate; lessen; soften; **s'~** a. die down.

atterrer [ate're] (1a) stun; crush.

atterr|ir [ate'riːr] (2a) land; **~issage** [~ri'saːʒ] m landing; **~ forcé** forced landing; **train** m **d'~** = **~isseur** [ateri'sœːr] m undercarriage.

attest|ation [atɛsta'sjɔ̃] f attestation; **~er** [~'te] (1a) testify, certify.

attiéd|ir [atje'diːr] (2a) cool, take the chill off; **s'~** (grow) cool.

attifer [ati'fe] (1a) usu. pej. dress up.

attiger F [ati'ʒe] (1l) exaggerate, F lay it on.

attirail [ati'raːj] m outfit; gear; F pomp; pej. paraphernalia pl.

attir|ance [ati'rɑ̃ːs] f attraction; **~er**

[~'re] (1a) attract; (al)lure; **s'~** win (*s.th.*).

attiser [ati'ze] (1a) stir up (*a. fig.*).

attitré [ati'tre] appointed, regular.

attitude [ati'tyd] *f* attitude; bearing.

attouchement [atuʃ'mã] *m* touch(ing).

attract|if [atrak'tif] attractive; gravitational (*force*); **~ion** [~'sjõ] *f* attraction (*a. fig.*), pull.

attrait [a'trɛ] *m* attractiveness, charm; inclination (for, *pour*).

attrapage F [atra'pa:ʒ] *m* tiff, quarrel; blowing-up.

attrap|e [a'trap] *f* trick, hoax; joke (article); **~e-mouches** [atrap'muʃ] *m/inv.* fly-paper; **~er** [atra'pe] (1a) catch (*a. ♣*); trap (*a. fig.*); F scold; **se faire ~** be taken in.

attrayant [atrɛ'jã] attractive.

attribu|er [atri'bɥe] (1n) attribute (to, **à**); assign; **s'~** appropriate; **~t** [~'by] *m* attribute; **~tion** [~by'sjõ] *f* attribution; allocation; **~s** *pl.* competence *sg.*, powers.

attrister [atris'te] (1a) sadden; **s'~** become sad; cloud over (*sky*).

attrition [atri'sjõ] *f* attrition.

attroup|ement [atrup'mã] *m* unlawful assembly; mob; **~er** [atru'pe] (1a) gather together; **s'~** flock together; crowd.

atypique [ati'pik] atypical.

aubaine [o'bɛn] *f* godsend.

aube[1] [o:b] *f* dawn; *eccl.* alb.

aube[2] [~] *f* paddle, float; blade.

aubépine ♣ [obe'pin] *f* hawthorn.

auberge [o'bɛrʒ] *f* inn, tavern; **~ de la jeunesse** youth hostel.

aubergine ♣ [ober'ʒin] *f* egg-plant.

aubergiste [ober'ʒist] *su.* innkeeper; *su./m* landlord; *su./f* landlady.

aucun [o'kœ̃] **1.** *adj.* any; **2.** *pron.* any(one); *with* **ne** *or on its own:* none; **d'~s** some (people); **~ement** [okyn'mã] *adv.* by no means.

audac|e [o'das] *f* audacity (*a. fig.*); boldness; F **payer d'~** brazen it out; **~ieux** [oda'sjø] bold, daring.

au-dedans [odə'dã] *adv.* inside; **~ de** within; **au-dehors** [~'ɔ:r] *adv.* outside; **~ de** outside, beyond; **au-delà** [~'la] **1.** *adv.* beyond; **~ de** on the other side of; **2.** *su./m* beyond; **au-dessous** [~'su] *adv.* below; **~ de** under; beneath; **au-dessus** [~'sy] *adv.* above; on top; **~**

de over, above; *fig.* beyond; **au-devant** [~'vã] *adv.* ahead; **aller ~ de** go to meet; anticipate.

audi|ble [o'di:bl] audible; **~ence** [o'djã:s] *f* attention, interest; **⚖** hearing; audience; *radio etc.:* public; **~ovisuel** [odjovi'zɥɛl] audiovisual; **~teur, -trice** [odi'tœ:r, ~'tris] *su.* hearer, listener; **~teurs** *m/pl.* audience; **~tif** [~'tif] auditory; **appareil** *m* **~** hearing aid; **~tion** [~'sjõ] *f* hearing, recital; audition; (*musical*) recital; **~tionner** [~sjo'ne] (1a) *v/t.* audition (*s.o.*); *v/i.* (give an) audition; **~toire** [~'twa:r] *m* audience.

auge [o:ʒ] *f* trough (*a. ♥*); manger.

augment|ation [ogmãta'sjõ] *f* increase; prices, wages: rise; **~er** [~'te] (1a) *vt/i.* increase; *v/t.* raise (*a price, the wages*); *v/i.* rise; grow.

augur|e [o'gy:r] *m* augur(y); omen; **~er** [ogy're] (1a) augur; forecast.

auguste [o'gyst] **1.** *adj.* majestic; **2.** *su./m circus:* the funny man.

aujourd'hui [oʒur'dɥi] today; (**d'**) **~ en huit** today week.

aumôn|e [o'mo:n] *f* alms; charity; **~ier** [omo'nje] *m* chaplain (*a. ✗*).

aune [o:n] *m* alder.

auparavant [opara'vã] *adv.* before(hand); **d'~** preceding.

auprès [o'prɛ] *adv.* near; close by; **~ de** near, beside; compared with; in the opinion of, with (*s.o.*).

aurai [ɔ're] *1st p. sg. fut. of* **avoir 1.**

auréole [ɔre'ɔl] *f* halo; *phot.* halation.

auriculaire [ɔriky'lɛ:r] auricular; ear-...; **doigt** *m* **~** little finger.

aurifère [ɔri'fɛ:r] gold-bearing.

aurore [ɔ'rɔ:r] *f* dawn (*a. fig.*), daybreak; **~ boréale** northern lights *pl.*

auspice [ɔs'pis] *m* auspice; omen.

aussi [o'si] **1.** *adv.* also; too; **~ ... que** as ... as; **moi ~** so am (do, can) I, F me too; **2.** *cj.* therefore; and so; **~ bien** moreover; **~tôt** [osi'to] *adv.* immediately; **~ que** as soon as.

austère [ɔs'tɛ:r] austere, stern; **austérité** [~teri'te] *f* austerity.

austral [ɔs'tral] southern.

australien [ɔstra'ljɛ̃] *adj., su.* Australian.

autant [~] *adv.* as much, as many; so much, so many; **(pour) ~ que** as far as; **d'~ (plus) que** all the more as; **en faire ~** do the same.

autar|cie [otar'si] *f* autarky; **~cique**
[~'sik] autarkical.

autel [o'tɛl] *m* altar.

auteur [o'tœːr] *m* author (*a. fig.*); *crime*:
perpetrator; **droit** *m* **d'~** copyright;
femme *f* **~** authoress.

authenti|cité [otɑ̃tisi'te] *f* authenticity;
~que [~'tik] authentic.

auto F [o'to] *f* (motor-)car.

auto... [oto] auto-..., self-...; motor-...;
~bus [~'bys] *m* (motor) bus; **~car**
[~'kaːr] *m* motor coach.

autochtone [otɔk'tɔn] **1.** *adj.* aboriginal;
2. *su.* autochthon.

auto...: ~clave [otoˈklaːv] *m* sterilizer;
cuis. pressure cooker; **~collant** [~ɔ'lɑ̃]
1. *adj.* self-adhesive; **2.** *su./m* sticker;
~crate [~'krat] *m* autocrat, **~cratie**
[~kra'si] *f* autocracy; **~didacte**
[~di'dakt] self-taught (person);
~drome [~'droːm] *m* motor-racing
track; **~école** [~e'kɔl] *f* driving school;
~graphe [~'graf] *adj.*, *su./m* auto-
graph; **~mate** [~'mat] *m* automaton;
~mation [~ma'sjɔ̃] *f* automation; **~ma-
tique** [~ma'tik] automatic; **~matisa-
tion** ⊙ [~matisa'sjɔ̃] *f* automation;
~matiser [~mati'ze] (1a) automate.

automn|al [otɔm'nal] autumnal; **~e**
[o'tɔn] *m* autumn, *Am.* fall.

auto...: ~mobile [otɔmɔ'bil] **1.** *su./f* (mo-
tor-)car; **2.** *adj.* self-propelling; **canot**
m **~** motor boat; **~mobilisme**
[~mɔbi'lism] *m* motoring; **~mobiliste**
[~mɔbi'list] *su.* motorist; **~nome**
[~'nɔm] independent; self-governing;
~nomie [~nɔ'mi] *f* independence; **~por-
trait** [~pɔr'trɛ] *m* self-portrait; **~pro-
pulsé** [~prɔpyl'se] self-propelled.

autopsie [otɔp'si] *f* autopsy.

autorail 🚂 [otoˈraːj] *m* rail-car.

autori|sation [otɔriza'sjɔ̃] *f* authoriza-
tion; licence; **~exceptionnelle** special
permission; **~sé** [~'ze] authorized; au-
thoritative (*source*); **~ser** [~'ze] (1a) au-
thorize, permit, **~taire** [~'tɛːr] authori-
tarian; **~té** [~'te] *f* authority; (legal)
power; **faire ~** be an authority.

auto...: ~route [oto'rut] *f* motorway,
Am. superhighway; **~ de l'information**
information superhighway; **~stop**
[~'stɔp] *m* hitch-hiking; **faire de l'~**
hitch-hike; **~stoppeur** *m*, **-euse** *f*
[~sto'pœːr, ~'pøːz] hitchhiker.

autour¹ *orn.* [o'tuːr] goshawk.

autour² [~] *adv.* (a)round; about; **~ de**
(a)round, about (*s.th.*).

autre [oːtr] **1.** *adj.* other; different; further; **~ chose** something else; **d'~ part**
on the other hand; **l'~ jour** the other
day; **nous ~s Français** we Frenchmen;
tout ~ chose quite a different matter; **2.**
pron./indef. (an)other; **~s** *pl.* others; **à
d'~s!** tell that to the marines!; **de
temps à ~** now and then; **l'un l'~** each
other; **ni l'un ni l'~** neither; **tout ~** anybody else; **un(e) ~** another; another
(one), one more; **~fois** [otrə'fwa] *adv.*
formerly; **~ment** [~'mɑ̃] *adv.* otherwise;
(or) else.

autrichien [otri'ʃjɛ̃] *adj.*, *su.* Austrian.

autruche *orn.* [o'tryʃ] *f* ostrich; **pratiquer la politique de l'~** stick one's head
in the sand.

autrui [o'trɥi] *pron.* other people.

auvent [o'vɑ̃] *m* porch roof.

auxiliaire [oksi'ljɛːr] auxiliary.

avach|i [ava'ʃi] limp, flabby; **~ir** [~ʃiːr]
(2a) make limp or flabby or
sloppy; **s'~** lose shape; become sloppy.

aval¹, *pl.* **-s** ✝ [a'val] *m* endorsement.

aval² [~] *m*: **en ~** downstream; afterwards; **en ~ de** below; after.

avalanche [ava'lɑ̃ːʃ] *f* avalanche.

avaler [ava'le] (1a) swallow; gulp down;
inhale (*the cigarette smoke*).

avalis|er ✝ [avali'ze] (1a) endorse (*a
bill*); **~te** ✝ [~'list] *m* endorser.

à-valoir [ava'lwaːr] *m/inv.* advance (payment), down payment, deposit.

avanc|e [a'vɑ̃ːs] *f* advance (*a.* ✝); pro-
gress; lead; **à l'~**, **d'~** in advance; **être
en ~** be early or ahead; **faire des ~s à**
make up to (*so.*); **~ement** [avɑ̃s'mɑ̃] *m*
advancement; promotion; **~er** [avɑ̃'se]
(1k) *v/t.* advance (*a.* ✝); hasten (*s.th.*);
put on (*a watch*); promote; *fig.* be of
help to; **s' ~** advance; move forward;
fig. commit o.s., F stick one's neck out;
v/t. advancee; be fast (*watch*); be
ahead; △ project; **~ en âge** be getting
on (in years).

avanie [ava'ni] *f* affront, snub.

avant [a'vɑ̃] **1.** *prp.* before (*Easter, the
end*); in front of (*the house*); within
(*three days*); **~ peu** before long; **~ tout**
above all; **2.** *adv.* beforehand; pre-
viously; **d'~** before, previous; **peu de**

temps ~ shortly before; *plus* ~ further; **3.** *cj.:* ~ *que* (*sbj.*) before (*ind.*); ~ *de* (*inf.*) before (*ger.*); **4.** *adj./inv.* front ...; *roue f* ~ front wheel; **5.** *su./m* front; ⚓ bow; *en* ~*!* advance!; *mettre en* ~ advance (*an argument etc.*).

avant-... [avã] fore ...

avantag|e [avã'taːʒ] *m* advantage; benefit; *tennis:* vantage; *à l'* ~ *de* to the benefit of; ~*er* [~ta'ʒe] (1l) favo(u)r; flatter (*dress etc.*); ~*eux* [~ta'ʒø] attractive (*price*); profitable; conceited.

avant...: ~*bras* [avã'brɑ] *m/inv.* forearm; ~*centre sp.* [~'sãːtr] *m* centre forward; ~*coureur* [~ku'rœːr] **1.** *su./m* forerunner; **2.** *adj.* precursory; premonitory (*sign*); ~*dernier* [~dɛr'nje] last but one; ~*garde* [~'gard] *f* vanguard (*a. fig.*); ~*guerre* [~'gɛːr] *m or f* pre-war period; ~*hier* [~'tjɛːr] the day before yesterday; ~*poste* ✕ [~'pɔst] *m* outpost; ~*projet* [~prɔ'ʒɛ] *m* pilot study; ~*propos* [~prɔ'po] *m/inv.* preface; ~*scène* *thea.* [~'sɛn] *f* proscenium; stage-box.

avar|e [a'vaːr] miserly (person); ~*ice* [ava'ris] *f* avarice; stinginess; ~*icieux* [~ri'sjø] stingy.

avari|e [ava'ri] *f* ⚓ average; damage; ~*é* [~'rje] damaged; spoiled; rotting, bad; ~*er* [~'rje] (1o) spoil; damage; *s'* ~ go bad, rot.

avatar [ava'taːr] *m* avatar; ~*s pl.* ups and downs; vicissitudes.

avec [a'vɛk] **1.** *prp.* with; for, in spite of (*all his riches*); ~ *patience* patiently; ~ *l'âge* with age; ~ *ça* into the bargain; *et* ~ *ça, Madame?* anything else, Madam?; ~ *ce temps-là* in this weather; *divorcer d'* ~ *sa femme* divorce one's wife; **2.** *adv.* F with it *or* them, *or* him, *or* her.

avenant[1] [av'nã] pleasant; *à l'* ~ in keeping (with, *de*).

avenant[2] ⚖ [av'nã] *m* codicil, rider.

avènement [avɛn'mã] *m* arrival, coming; *king:* accession; **avenir** [av'niːr] *m* future; *à l'* ~ in (the) future; **avent** [a'vã] *m* Advent.

aventur|e [avã'tyːr] *f* adventure; love affair; *à l'* ~ at random; *dire la bonne* ~ tell fortunes; *parc m d'* ~ adventure playground; ~*er* [avãty're] (1a) risk; *s'* ~ venture; ~*eux* [~'rø] adventurous;

bold (*theory*); ~*ier* [~'rje] **1.** *adj.* adventurous; **2.** *su./m* adventurer.

avenue [av'ny] *f* avenue; drive.

avérer [ave're] (1f) *v/t.:* *s'* ~ ... turn out to be ..., prove (to be) ..., show oneself to be ...

averse [a'vɛrs] *f* shower, downpour.

aversion [avɛr'sjõ] *f* aversion (to, *pour*), dislike (of, for *pour*).

avert|ir [avɛr'tiːr] (2a) warn (of, *de*); notify; ~*issement* [~tis'mã] *m* warning; notification; foreword; ~*isseur* [~ti-'sœːr] *m* warner; warning signal; *mot.* horn; ~ *d'incendie* fire-alarm.

aveu [a'vø] *m* confession; *homme m sans* ~ disreputable character.

aveugl|e [a'vœgl] **1.** *adj.* blind; ~ *d'un œil* blind in one eye; **2.** *su.* blind person; *en* ~ blindfold; *les* ~*s pl.* the blind; ~*ément* [avœgle'mã] *adv.* blindly; ~*ement* [~glə'mã] *m* blindness; ~*e-né* [~glə'ne] (person) blind from birth; ~*er* [~'gle] (1a) blind; dazzle; stop (*a leak*); ~*ette* [~'glɛt] *adv.:* *à l'* ~ blindly.

aveulir [avœ'liːr] (2a) enfeeble.

avez [a've] *2nd p. pl. pres.* of **avoir 1.**

aviat|eur *m*, **-trice** *f* [avja'tœːr, ~'tris] aviator; ~*ion* [~'sjõ] *f* aviation; flying; air force; ~ *civile* civil aviation; ~ *de ligne* air traffic.

aviculteur [avikyl'tœːr] *m* bird fancier; poultry farmer.

avid|e [a'vid] greedy (for, *de*); ~*ité* [avidi'te] *f* greediness; eagerness.

avil|ir [avi'liːr] (2a) debase; lower; *s'* ~ lower o.s.; lose value, fall (*price etc.*); ~*issement* [~lis'mã] *m* debasement, depreciation.

aviné [avi'ne] drunk.

avion [a'vjõ] *m* aeroplane, *Am.* airplane, F plane; ~ *à décollage vertical* vertical takeoff aircraft; ~ *à réaction* jet (plane); ~ *de bombardement* bomber; ~ *de chasse* fighter; ~ *de ligne* airliner; ~ *de transport* transport plane; *par* ~ by airmail.

aviron [avi'rõ] *m* oar; rowing.

avis [a'vi] *m* opinion; notice; advice; warning; ~ *d'expert* expert opinion; *être d'* ~ *que* feel *or* think *or* be of the opinion that; *à mon* ~ in my opinion; *jusqu'à nouvel* ~ until further notice; *sans* ~ *préalable* without notice; *un* ~ a piece of advice; ~*é* [avi'se] shrewd;

prudent; **bien** (**mal**) ~ well-(ill-)advised; **~er** [~] (1a) *v/t.* catch sight of; inform; **s'~** realize, notice; **s'~ de** realize; dare (*inf.*); *v/i.:* ~ **à** see about.

avitaminose ♣ [avitami'no:z] *f* avitaminosis, vitamin deficiency.

aviver [avi've] (1a) revive, brighten; touch up (*a colour*); sharpen; burnish (*metal*); irritate (*a wound*).

avocat¹ [avɔ'ka] *m* barrister, counsel; *Am.* counsellor; advocate.

avocat² ♣ [~] *m* avocado (pear).

avoine [a'vwan] *f* oat(s. *pl.*).

avoir [a'vwa:r] (1) **1.** *v/t.* have; obtain; hold; ~ **en horreur** detest; ~ **faim** be hungry; ~ **froid** be cold; ~ **honte** be ashamed; ~ **lieu** take place; ~ **soif** be thirsty; **en** ~ **assez** be fed up; **en** ~ **contre** have a grudge against; **j'ai vingt ans** I am 22; **qu'avez vous?** what's the matter with you?; *v/impers.:* **il y a** there is, there are; **il y a un an** a year ago; **2.** *su./m* property; possession; ✝ credit; ~ **à l'étranger** deposits *pl.* abroad.

avoisiner [avwazi'ne] (1a) border on; be near to.

avons [a'võ] *1st p. pl. pres. of* **avoir 1.**

avort|ement [avɔrtə'mã] *m* ♣ miscarriage (*a. fig.*); abortion; **~er** [~'te] (1a) miscarry (*a. fig.*); **faire** ~ procure an abortion; **~on** [~'tõ] *m* abortion; F shrimp.

avou|able [a'vwabl] avowable; **~é** [a'vwe] *m* solicitor; attorney; **~er** [~] (1p) admit, confess; **s'~ coupable** plead guilty.

avril [a'vril] *m* April; **poisson** *m* **d'~** April fool.

axe [aks] *m* axis (*a. pol.*); ⊕ axle.

axiome [ak'sjo:m] *m* axiom.

ayant [ɛ'jã] *p.pr. of* **avoir 1;** ~ **droit,** *pl.* **~s droit** ⚖ *su./m* rightful claimant; **ayons** [ɛ'jõ] *1st p. pl. pres. sbj. of* **avoir 1.**

azot|ate [azɔ'tat] *m* nitrate; **~e** [a'zɔt] *m* nitrogen; **~ite** [azɔ'tit] *m* nitrite.

azur [a'zy:r] *m* azure, blue.

azyme [a'zim] unleavened (*bread*).

B

baba¹ [ba'ba] *m* rum cake.

baba² F [~] *adj./inv.* flabbergasted.

babeurre [ba'bœːr] *m* buttermilk.

babil [ba'bil] *m* prattle; babble; **~lage** [babi'ja:ʒ] *m* babbling; **~ler** [~'je] (1a) prattle; babble.

babines F [ba'bin] *f/pl.* chops.

babiole [ba'bjɔl] *f* bauble; trifle.

bâbord ⚓ [ba'bɔːr] *m* port (side).

babouin *zo.* [ba'bwɛ̃] *m* baboon.

bac¹ [bak] *m* ferry(-boat); container; **passer q. en** ~ ferry s.o. over.

bac² F [~] *see* **baccalauréat; baccalauréat** [bakalɔre'a] *m* school-leaving certificate.

bacchanale F [baka'nal] *f* orgy.

bâche [ba:ʃ] *f* tank, cistern; casing; canvas; ~ **goudronnée** tarpaulin.

bachelier, -ère *f* [baʃə'lje, ~'ljɛːr] holder of the **baccalauréat.**

bâcher [ba'ʃe] (1a) cover; case.

bachot¹ [ba'ʃo] *m* skiff, boat.

bachot² [~] *m see* **baccalauréat; ~er** F [baʃɔ'te] (1a) cram (for an exam).

bacille [ba'sil] *m* bacillus.

bâc|le [ha:kl] *f* bar; **~er** [ba'kle] (1a) bar; block; F scamp, botch.

bactérie [bakte'ri] *f* bacterium.

badaud [ba'do] *m* onlooker, gaper.

badigeon [badi'ʒõ] *m* whitewash; **~nage** [~ʒɔ'na:ʒ] *m* whitewashing; **~ner** [~ʒɔ'ne] (1a) whitewash; smear, daub; ♣ paint.

badin [ba'dɛ̃] playful; **~age** [badi'na:ʒ] *m* banter.

badine [ba'din] *f* cane, switch.

badiner [badi'ne] (1a) jest; toy.

baffe F [baf] *f* slap (in the face).

bafou|er [ba'fwe] (1p) scoff at; **~illage** [bafu'ja:ʒ] *m* stammering; **~iller** [~'je] (1a) splutter; *sl.* talk nonsense.

bâfrer *sl.* [ba'fre] (1a) guzzle.

B

bagage [ba'ga:ʒ] *m* luggage, *Am.* baggage; *plier* ~ decamp.

bagarr|e [ba'gar] *f* fight(ing); scuffle; brawl; riot; *~er* F [~ga're] (1a): **se** ~ quarrel.

bagatelle [baga'tɛl] *f* trifle; *~l* nonsense!; F *pour une* ~ for a song.

bagne ⚖ [baɲ] *m* convict prison.

bagnole F [ba'nɔl] *f* motor car.

bagou(t) F [ba'gu] *m* glibness.

bague [bag] *f* ring; band; ~ *d'arrêt* set collar; *~nauder* F [~no'de] (1a) *a.* **se** ~ go for a stroll; stroll about; *~tte* [ba'gɛt] *f* stick, rod; stick of bread; ♪ baton; ~ *magique* magic wand.

bahut [ba'y] *m* sideboard; *sl.* school.

bai [bɛ] *adj., su./m* bay.

baie¹ ⚘ [~] *f* berry.

baie² *geog.* [~] *f* bay, bight.

baie³ △ [~] *f* bay, embrasure.

baign|ade [bɛ'nad] *f* bathe, dip; *~er* [~'ne] (1b) *v/t.* bath(e); **se** ~ bathe; take a bath *v/i.* steep; F *ça baigne dans l'huile* things are going fine; *~eur m,* *-euse f* [~'nœːr, ~'nøːz] bather; *su./f machine:* bather; *~oire* [~'nwaːr] *f* bath (tub); *thea.* ground-floor box.

bail, *pl.* **baux** [ba:j, bo] *m* lease; *prendre à* ~ take a lease of, lease.

bâill|ement [baj'mɑ̃] *m* yawn; gaping; *~er* [ba'je] (1a) yawn; gape.

bailleur *m,* **-eresse** *f* [ba'jœːr, baj'rɛs] ⚖ lessor; ♥ ~ *de fonds* backer; sleeping *or* silent partner.

bâillon [ba'jɔ̃] *m* gag; muzzle; *~ner* [~jɔ'ne] (1a) gag; silence.

bain [bɛ̃] *m* bath(ing); F *fig. dans le* ~ in the picture, informed; implicated; involved; *~douche,* *pl.* *~s-douches* [~'duʃ] *m* shower-(bath).

baïonnette ✗ [bajɔ'nɛt] *f* bayonet.

bais|emain [bɛz'mɛ] *m* hand-kissing; *~er* [bɛ'ze] **1.** *su./m* kiss; **2.** (1b) *v/t.* V make love to (*s.o.*); ~ *q. à la joue* kiss s.o.'s cheek; *~oter* F [~zɔ'te] (1c) peck at.

baiss|e [bɛs] *f* fall (*a.* prices); subsidence; decline; *en* ~ falling (*stocks*); *~er* [bɛ'se] (1b) *v/t.* lower; turn down; drop; **se** ~ bend down; stoop; *v/i.* decline; fall; sink; ebb.

bajoue [ba'ʒu] *f* jowl.

bal, *pl.* **bals** [bal] *m* ball; dance; *~ade* F [ba'lad] *f* stroll; outing; *~ader* F [bala'de] (1a) take for a walk; carry about; **se** ~ (take a) stroll; *~adeuse* [~'døːz] *f* inspection lamp.

baladin [bala'dɛ̃] *m* mountebank.

balafr|e [ba'lafr] *f* gash, slash; scar; *~er* [~la'fre] (1a) slash; scar.

balai [ba'lɛ] *m* broom; brush; *coup m de* ~ sweep; *fig.* clean sweep.

balan|ce [ba'lɑ̃ːs] *f* balance (*a.* ♈); scales *pl.*; ♈ ~ *de(s) paiements* balance of payments; *fig.* **mettre en** ~ weigh up; *~cer* [balɑ̃'se] (1k) *v/t.* swing; throw, fling, F chuck; *sl.* chuck out; balance; ♥ weigh up; **se** ~ rock; sway; swing; *sl.* **se** ~ *de* not to care a damn about; *~cier* [~'sje] *m* balancing pole; *pump:* handle; ◉ beam; *~coire* [~'swaːr] *f* see-saw; swing.

balay|er [balɛ'je] (li) sweep out *or* up *or* away (*a. fig.*); *fig.* clear out; *telev.* scan; *~ette* [~'jɛt] *f* small brush; *~eur,* **-euse** [~'jœːr, ~'jøːz] *su. person:* sweeper; *su./f machine:* sweeper; *~ures* [~'jyːr] *f/pl.* sweepings.

balbuti|ement [balbysi'mɑ̃] *m* stammering; *~er* [~'sje] (1o) *v/t.* mumble; stammer; *v/t.* stammer out.

balcon [bal'kɔ̃] *m* △ balcony; *thea.* dress circle.

baldaquin [balda'kɛ̃] *m* canopy.

balein|e [ba'lɛn] *f* whale(bone); *~ier* [balɛ'nje] *m* whaler (*ship, man*); *~ière* [~'njɛːr] *f* whaleboat.

balis|e [ba'liːz] *f* ♄ beacon; ✈ runway light; sign, marker; *a.* ~ *flottante* buoy; *~er* [~li'ze] (1a) ♄ beacon; ♄ buoy; provide with runway lights *or* signs; mark out.

balistique [balis'tik] **1.** *adj.* ballistic; **2.** *su./f* ballstics *sg.*

baliverne F [bali'vɛrn] *f* mostly *~s pl.* nonsense *sg.*

ballade [ba'lad] *f* ballad.

ballant [ba'lɑ̃] **1.** *adj.* dangling; slack (*rope*); **2.** *su./m* swing.

ballast [ba'last] *m* ballast.

balle¹ [bal] *f* ball; bullet, shot; ♈ bale; pack; *sl.* head; *sl.* franc.

balle² [~] *f* husk, chaff; ♙ glume.

ballerine [bal'rin] *f* ballet dancer, ballerina; **ballet** [ba'lɛ] *m* ballet.

ballon [ba'lɔ̃] *m* balloon; (foot)ball; ~ *de plage* beach ball; *fig.* ~ *d'essai* feeler; *~nement* [~lɔn'mɑ̃] *m* distension; *~ner* [~lɔ'ne] (1a) distend; bloat.

ballot [ba'lo] *m* pack, bundle; F chump; **~tage** *pol.* [balɔ'taːʒ] *m* second ballot; **~ter** [~'te] (1a) *v/t.* toss (about), shake about; *fig. ballotté entre* tossed *or* torn between; *v/i.* shake.

bal(l)uchon F [baly'ʃɔ̃] *m* bundle.

balnéaire [balne'ɛːr] bath...; *station f* ~ spa; seaside resort.

balourd [ba'luːr] **1.** *adj.* awkward; **2.** *su.* awkward person; *su./m* ⊙ unbalance; **~ise** [~lur'diːz] *f* awkwardness; F bloomer.

baltique [bal'tik] Baltic.

balustr|ade [balys'trad] *f* halustrade; (hand)rail; **~e** [~'lystr] *m* baluster; banister.

bambin F [bã'bɛ̃] *su.* little child.

bamboch|e F [bã'bɔʃ] *f: faire* ~ = **~er** F [bãbɔ'ʃe] (1a) go on the spree.

bambou [bã'bu] *m* bamboo(-cane).

ban [bã] *m* † proclamation; F applause; *mettre au* ~ banish; *outlaw* (from, *de*); *publier les* **~s** publish the bans; *fig. le* ~ *et l'arrière-* ~ *de ses amis etc.* all his friends *etc.*

banal [ba'nal] commonplace; vulgar; **~iser** [~nali'ze] (1a) vulgarize.

banan|e [ba'nan] *f* banana; *sl.* medal; *sl.* helicopter; **~ier** [~na'nje] *m* banana tree.

banc [bã] *m* bench (*a.* ⊙); seat; pew; *oysters:* bed; *mud:* bank; *coral:* reef; *(witness-)box; fish:* school; ~ *d'épreuve* testing bench.

bancal [bã'kal] **1.** *adj.* bandy-legged; unsteady, rickety; **2.** *su.* bandy-legged person.

bandage [bã'daːʒ] *m* ⚕ bandaging; bandage; ⊙ hoop; ~ *herniaire* truss.

bande[1] [bãːd] *f* band, strip; stripe; tape; stretch (*of land*); ⚕ bandage; strap; *cin.* reel; *post:* wrapper; ⚓ list; ~ *dessinée* comic strip; strip cartoon; ~ *magnétique* recording tape; ⊙ ~ *transporteuse* conveyor belt.

bande[2] [~] *f* band; party; flock.

band|eau [bã'do] *m* headband; bandage; **elette** [bãd'lɛt] *f* strip; **~er** [bã'de] (1a) bandage, bind up; wind up, tighten; *fig.* ~ *les yeux à* blindfold (*s.o.*); **~erole** [~'drɔl] *f* streamer; *cartoon:* balloon.

bandit [bã'di] *m* gangster; crook.

bandoulière [bãdu'ljɛːr] *f* shoulder strap; *en* ~ slung over the shoulder.

banlieu|e [bã'ljø] *f* surburbs *pl.*, outskirts *pl.*; *de* ~ suburban; **~sard** [~ljø'zaːr] *su.* suburbanite.

banne [ban] *f* hamper; awning.

banni [ba'ni] *su.* outcast; exile.

bannière [ba'njɛːr] *f* banner.

bannir [ba'niːr] (2a) banish (from, *de*).

banque [bãːk] *f* bank; ~ *du sang* blood bank; ~ *par actions* joint-stock bank; *faire sauter la* ~ break the bank; **~route** ✝ [bã'krut] *f* bankruptcy; *faire* ~ go bankrupt.

banquet [bã'kɛ] *m* banquet, feast.

banquette [bã'kɛt] *f* bench, seat.

banquier [bã'kje] *m* banker.

banquise [bã'kiːz] *f* pack-ice.

baptê|me [ba'tɛːm] *m* baptism; *nom m de* ~ Christian name; **~iser** [bati'ze] (1a) baptize; ✝ *fig.* water (down); **~ismal** [batis'mal], **~istaire** [~'tɛːr] baptismal.

baquet [ba'kɛ] *m* tub, bucket.

bar [baːr] *m* (public) bar.

baragouin F [bara'gwɛ̃] *m* gibberish; **~er** F [~gwi'ne] (1a) jabber.

baraque [ba'rak] *f* hut, shed; F dump, joint, hole.

baratin F [bara'tɛ̃] *m* sweet talk; patter; **~er** F [~ti'ne] (1a) *vt/i.* sweet-talk; patter; *v/t.* chat (*s.o.*) up.

baratt|e [ba'rat] *f* churn; **~er** [~ra'te] (1a) churn.

barbacane [barba'kan] *f* draining channel; loophole.

barbar|e [bar'baːr] **1.** *adj.* barbaric, barbarous; **2.** *su./m* barbarian; **~ie** [barba'ri] *f* barbarism; barbarity, cruelty.

barbe [barb] *f* beard; F bore; ~ *à papa* candyfloss, *Am.* cotton candy; *se faire faire la* ~ get o.s. shaved; (*se*) *faire la* ~ shave.

barbeau [bar'bo] *m icht.* barbel; ♣ cornflower; *sl.* pimp; **barbelé** [~bə'le] barbed; *fil m de fer* ~ barbed wire.

barber *sl.* [bar'be] (1a) bore.

barbiche [bar'biʃ] *f* goatee.

barbi|er [bar'hje] *m* barber; **~fier** F [~bi'fje] (1o) shave.

barbot|age [barbɔ'taːʒ] *m* splashing; mess, mud; *sl.* filching; *sl.* mumbling; **~er** [~'te] (1a) splash (about); mumble; *sl.* filch; **~eur, -euse** [~'tœːr, ~'tøːz] *su.* F light-fingered person; *su./m* ⊙ stirrer; *su./f* rompers *pl.*

B

barbouill|age [barbu'ja:ʒ] *m* daubing; scrawl(ing); **~er** [~'je] (1a) daub; smear (with, *de*); scrawl; *fig.* botch; **~eur** F [~'jœːr] *m* dauber.

barbu [bar'by] bearded (*a.* ♃).

barbue *icht.* [~] *f* brill.

barda *sl.* [bar'da] *m* ✕ pack, kit; stuff, things *pl.*

bardane ♀ [bar'dan] *f* burdock.

barder¹ *sl.* [bar'de] (1a): *ça barde* sparks are flying.

barder² [~] (1a) bard (*with bacon*); laod (*a. fig.*); armo(u)r; cover.

bardot [bar'do] *m* packmule.

barème [ba'rɛm] *m* table, (price *etc.*) list; scale; schedule; graph.

baril [ba'ri] *m* cask(ful); **~let** [~ri'jɛ] *m* keg; cylinder; ⊚ barrel.

bariol|age [barjo'la:ʒ] *m* medley of colo(u)rs; **~er** [~'le] (1a) variegate; paint in gaudy colo(u)rs.

baromètre [baro'mɛtr] *m* barometer; F (weather-)glass.

baron [ba'rɔ̃] *m* baron; **~ne** [~'rɔn] *f* baroness.

baroque [ba'rɔk] **1.** *adj.* quaint; baroque; **2.** *su./m* baroque.

baroud F [ba'rud] *m* fight(ing).

barque ♭ [bark] *f* barge, boat.

barrage [ba'ra:ʒ] *m* barring; dam (-ming); *fig.* obstruction; ⊚ barrage (*a.* ✕); ♱ *cheque*: crossing.

barr|e [ba:r] *f* bar (*a.* ♬♬); ⊚ rod; *gold*: ingot; ♪ helm; stroke (*of the pen*); *tex.* stripe; ♪ bar(-line); (tidal) bore; *sp.* **~s** *pl.* **parallèles** parallel bars; ♬♬ **~ des témoins** witness-box; **~eau** [ba'ro] *m* bar (*a.* ♬♬); rail; rung; *être reçu au ~ be* called to the bar, *Am.* pass the bar; **~er** [ba're] (1a) bar; block (up); dam (*a stream*); close (*a road*); cross out (*a word*); ♪ steer; *route f barrée* no thoroughfare; *sl. se ~* make off.

barrette¹ [ba'rɛt] *f* biretta.

barrette² [~] *f* hairslide.

barreur ♪ [ba'rœːr] *m* helmsman.

barri|cader [barika'de] (1a) barricade; **~ère** [~'rjɛːr] *f* barrier (*a.* ♞, *a. fig.*); 🚗 *level-crossing*, *town*: gate; turnpike; *sp.* starting post.

barrique [ba'rik] *f* hogshead, cask.

bas, basse [ba, baːs] **1.** *adj.* low; mean; lower; *basse fréquence radio*: low frequency; *au ~ mot* at the lowest esti-

mate; *chapeaux ~!* hats off!; *en ~ âge* of tender years; **2.** *su./m* lower part; bottom; stocking; *fig.* low state; **3.** *adv.* low (down); *ici-~* here below; *à ~ ...!* down with ...!; *en ~* (down) below.

basaner F [baza'ne] (1a) tan.

bascul|e [bas'kyl] *f* weighing machine; seesaw; *cheval m à ~* rocking horse; *wagon m à ~* tipwaggon, *Am.* dump cart; **~er** [~ky'le] (1a) *vt/i.* rock; tip (up); topple over; *v/i. fig.* fluctuate; *fig. ~ dans* get into.

bas|e [ba:z] *f* base (*a.* ♞, ♣); *surv.* base(line); bottom; ⊚ bedplate; *fig.* basis, foundation; **~ aérienne** airbase; **~ de lancement** rocket launching site; **~ d'entente** working basis; **~er** [ba'ze] (1a) base (on, *sur*).

bas-fond [ba'fɔ̃] *m* low ground; *fig.* underworld; ♣ shallows *pl.*

basque¹ [bask] *f* coat: tail.

basque² [~] *adj., su.* Basque.

basse [ba:s] *f* ♪ bass; ♣ shoal; **~-cour**, *pl.* **~s-cours** [~'kuːr] *f* farm-yard; **~sse** [ba'sɛs] *f* baseness; mean action.

basset *zo.* [ba'sɛ] *m* basset hound.

bassin [ba'sɛ̃] *m* basin (*a. geog.*); artificial lake; bowl; ♣ dock; *anat.* pelvis; *sl.* bore; **~ de retenue** reservoir; **~e** [~'sin] *f* pan; **~ à confitures** preserving pan; **~er** [basi'ne] (1a) bathe, wet (warm (*a bed*); *sl.* bore; **~oire** [~'nwaːr] *f* warming pan; *sl.* bore.

basson ♪ [ba'sɔ̃] *m* bassoon(ist).

bastille ✕ [bas'ti:j] *f* small fortress.

bastingage ♣ [bastɛ̃'ga:ʒ] *m* bulwarks *pl.*; rails *pl.*

bastion ✕, *fig.* [bas'tjɔ̃] *m* bastion.

bastonnade [basto'nad] *f* bastinado; † flogging.

bastringue *sl.* [bas'trɛ̃:g] *m* dancing hall; shindy; honky-tonk.

bât [ba] *m* packsaddle; *c'est là que* (or *voilà où*) *le ~ blesse* that's where the shoe pinches.

batail|le [ba'ta:j] *f* battle (*a. fig.*); **~er** [bata'je] (1a) fight (against, *contre*); **~eur** [~'jœːr] quarrelsome (person); **~on** ✕, *a. fig.* [bata'jɔ̃] *m* battalion.

bâtard [bɑ'taːr] *adj., su.* bastard.

bateau ♣ [ba'to] *m* boat, ship; **~ à vapeur** steamer; **~ de sauvetage** lifeboat; F *monter un ~ à q.* pull s.o.'s leg; **~-citerne**, *pl.* **~x-citernes** [batosi'tɛrn] *m*

tanker; **~-feu,** pl. **~x-feux** [~'fø] m
lightship; **~-mouche,** pl. **~x-mouches**
[~'muʃ] m small passenger steamer.

bateleur m, **-euse** f [ba'tlœːr, ~'tløːz]
knock-about comedian; juggler.

batel|ier [batə'lje] m boatman; ferry-
man; **~erie** [batel'ri] f lighterage; inland water transport.

bâté [ba'te]: **âne ~** ass, fool.

bath sl. [bat] fab, great.

bâti [ba'ti] m frame(work); ⚙ bed, support.

batifoler F [batifɔ'le] (1a) frolic (about).

bâtiment [bati'mã] m building, edifice;
⚓ vessel.

bâtir¹ [ba'tiːr] (2a) build, erect; **terrain m
à ~** building site.

bâtir² [~] (2a) baste, tack.

bâtisse [ba'tis] f masonry; F house.

batiste tex. [ba'tist] f cambric.

bâton [ba'tõ] m stick; staff; truncheon; **~
d'encens** joss stick; **~ de rouge à
lèvres** lipstick; **~net** [batɔ'ne] m short
stick; cuis. **~s** pl. **de poisson** fish fingers, Am. fish sticks.

bat|s [ba] 1st p. sg. pres. of **battre; ~tage**
[ba'taːʒ] m beating; threshing; F plugging, boosting; **~tant** [~'tã] **1.** adj. pelt-
ing (rain); **porte** f **~e** swingdoor; F **~
neuf** brandnew; **2.** su./m door; leaf;
bell: clapper; F fig. fighter, go-getter;
~te [bat] f beetle, rammer; cricket: bat;
~tement [~'mã] m beating; palpitation;
pulsation; (gap etc.) interval ♪ ⚡ ✕ battery; ♪ drums pl.; **~ de cuisine** kitchen
utensils pl.; **~teur** [~'tœːr] m cricket:
batsman; cuis. beater; ♪ drummer;
~teuse [~'tøːz] f thresher; **~toir**
[~'twaːr] m beetle; bat (a. sp.); F fig.
(large) hand, paw.

battre [batr] (4a) v/t. beat, strike; thresh;
mint (money); defeat; scour (the countryside); shuffle (cards); **~ q. en brèche**
run s.o. down; **se ~** fight; v/i. throb;
clap; bang; **battu, e** [ba'ty] **1.** p.p. of
battre; 2. su./f hunt. beat.

baudet [bo'dɛ] m donkey, ass.

bauge [boːʒ] f wallow; fig. pigsty.

baume [boːm] m balsam; balm.

bauxite 🜛 [bok'sit] f bauxite.

bavard [ba'vaːr] **1.** adj. talkative; **2.** su.
chatterbox; F bore; **~age** [bavar'daːʒ]
m gossip; chatter; **~er** [~'de] (1a) gossip; chatter.

bav|e [baːv] f slobber; foam; fig. venom;
~er [ba've] (1a) dribble, slobber; F fig.
~ de be agape with (astonishment etc.);
F fig. **en ~** have a hard time (of it); fig. **~
sur** besmirch (s.o.'s reputation etc.);
~ette [ba'vɛt] f bib; F **tailler une ~** chew
the fat; **~eux, ~euse** [~'vø] slobbery; wet.

bavure [ba'vyːr] f burr; smudge.

bazar [ba'zaːr] m bazaar; sl. **tout le ~** the
whole caboodle; **~der** sl.[~zar'de] (1a)
sell off.

béant [be'ã] gaping, yawning.

béat [be'a] smug, complacent; **~itude**
[heati'tyd] f bliss.

beau (adj. before vowel or h mute **bel**) m,
belle f, m/pl. **beaux** [bo, bɛl, bo] **1.** adj.
beautiful; fine; handsome; **au ~ milieu
de** right in the middle of; **avoir ~** (inf.)
(inf.) in vain; **il fait ~** (temps) the
weather is fine; **2.** su /m **le ~** the beautiful; **être au ~** be set fair (weather); **faire
le ~** sit up and beg (dog); su./f beauty.

beaucoup [bo'ku] adv. much, many; **~
de** a lot of, much, many; **de ~** by far.

beau-fils, pl. **beaux-fils** [bo'fis] m step-
son; son-in-law; **beau-frère,** pl.
beaux-frères [~'frɛːr] m brother-
in-law; **beau-père,** pl. **beaux-pères**
[~'pɛːr] m father-in-law; stepfather.

beauté [bo'te] f beauty; fig. belle.

beaux-arts [bo'za:r] m/pl. fine arts;
beaux-parents [~.pa'rã] m/pl. par-
ents-in-law.

bébé [be'be] m baby; doll.

bec [bɛk] m bird: beak, bill; tool: nose;
spout; ♪ mouthpiece; pen: nib; F
mouth; **~ de gaz** lamppost; F fig. **tomber sur un ~ (de gaz)** be stymied.

bécane F [be'kan] f bike, bicycle.

bécarre ♪ [be'kaːr] m natural (sign).

bécasse orn. [be'kas] f woodcock.

bec-de-cane, pl. **becs-de-cane**
[bɛkdə'kan] m spring lock; door handle; flat-nosed pliers pl.; **bec-de-
-lièvre,** pl. **becs-de-lièvre** [~'ljɛːvr] m
harelip.

bêch|e [bɛʃ] f spade; **~er** [bɛ'ʃe] (1a) dig;
turn (the soil) over; F fig. run (s.o.)
down, pull (s.o., s.th.) to pieces; **~oir**
[~'fwaːr] m hoe.

bécot [be'ko] m snipe; F peck; **~er** F
[beko'te] (1a) give (s.o.) a peck.

becqueter [bɛk'te] (1c) peck at; pick up;
sl. eat; F kiss.

bedaine F [bə'dɛn] *f* belly; paunch.

bedeau *eccl.* [bə'do] *m* beadle.

bedon *f* [bə'dɔ̃] *m* paunch.

bée [be] *adj./f:* **bouche** *f* ~ gaping.

beffroi [bɛ'frwa] *m* belfry; gantry.

bégayer [bege'je] (1i) stammer.

bègue [bɛg] stuttering (person); *être* ~ stammer.

bégueter [beg'te] (1d) bleat (*goat*).

béguin [be'gɛ̃] *m* hood; bonnet; F infatuation; **~e** [~'gin] *f eccl.* beguine; F devout woman.

beige [bɛːʒ] beige; unbleached.

beigne *sl.* [bɛɲ] *f* blow; bruise.

beignet *cuis.* [be'nɛ] *m* doughnut.

bel [bɛl] *see* **beau 1**; ~ **esprit** *m* person: wit; *un* ~ **âge** a ripe old age.

bêle|ment [bɛl'mã] *m* bleating; **~r** [bɛ'le] (1a) bleat (*sheep*).

belette *zo.* [bə'lɛt] *f* weasel.

belge [bɛlʒ] *adj., su.* Belgian.

bélier *zo.* [be'lje] *m* ram (*a.* ⊙).

belinogramme [bəlinɔ'gram] *m* telephotograph.

bellâtre [bɛ'lɑːtr] *m* fop.

belle [bɛl] *see* **beau 1**; *à la* ~ **étoile** in the open; *iro.* **en faire de** ~**s** be up to s.th. pretty; *l'échapper* ~ have a narrow escape; **~fille**, *pl.* ~**s-filles** [~'fiːj] *f* stepdaughter; daughter-in-law; **~mère**, *pl.* ~**s-mères** [~'mɛːr] *f* stepmother; mother-in-law; **~s-lettres** [~'lɛtr] *f/pl.* belles-lettres, humanities; **~sœur**, *pl.* ~**s-sœurs** [~'sœːr] *f* sister-in-law.

belli|cisme [belli'sism] *m* warmongering; **~gérant** [~ʒe'rã] *adj., su./m* belligerent; **~queux** [~'kø] warlike.

bémol ♪ [be'mɔl] *m* flat.

bénédic|ité [benedisi'te] *m* grace; **~tion** [~dik'sjɔ̃] *f* blessing.

bénéfic|e ✝ [bene'fis] *m* profit; benefit; **~iaire** ✝ [~fi'sjɛːr] *m* payee; beneficiary; **~ier** [~fi'sje] (1o) profit (by, *de*).

benêt [bə'nɛ] stupid *or* silly (man).

bénévole [bene'vɔl] benevolent; gratuitous, unpaid; voluntary.

béni|gnité [beniɲi'te] *f* kindness; mildness (*a.* ✻); **~n, -igne** [be'nɛ̃, ~'niɲ] kind; benign (*a.* ✻).

béni|r [be'niːr] (2a) bless; **~t** [~'ni] consecrated; *eccl.* **eau** *f* ~**e** holy water; **~tier** [~ni'tje] *m* holy-water basin.

benne [bɛn] *f* hamper; *telpherway:* bucket seat; (**camion** *m* **à**) ~ **basculante** tipping wag(g)on.

benoît [bən'wa] sanctimonious; bland.

béquille [be'kij] *f* crutch; *bicycle:* stand; ⚓ shore, prop; **marcher avec des** ~**s** walk on crutches.

bercail [bɛr'kaːj] *m/sg.* sheepfold.

berc|eau [bɛr'so] *m* cradle (*a. fig., a.* △); ⊙ bed; arbo(u)r; **~er** [~'se] (1k) rock; lull; delude (with promises, **de promesses**); **~euse** [~'søːz] *f* rocking chair; ♪ lullaby.

béret [be'rɛ] *m* (*a.* ~ **Basque**) beret.

berge [bɛrʒ] *f* bank; flank; rampart.

berg|er [bɛr'ʒe] *m* shepherd; **~ère** [~'ʒɛːr] *f* shepherdess; easy chair; **~erie** [~ʒə'ri] *f* sheep pen; **~eronnette** *orn.* [~ʒərɔ'nɛt] *f* wagtail.

berline [bɛr'lin] *f* coach: Berlin; *mot.* saloon (car), *Am.* sedan.

berlue [bɛr'ly] *f* ✻ false vision; *fig.* **avoir la** ~ see things all wrong.

berner [bɛr'ne] (1a) fool (*s.o.*).

bernique! *sl.* [bɛr'nik] *int.* no go!

besicles *iro.* [bə'zikl] *f/pl.* glasses.

besogn|e [bə'zɔɲ] *f* work; job; **~eux** [~zɔ'ɲø] needy, hard-up.

besoin [bə'zwɛ̃] *m* need, want; poverty; *au* ~ if necessary; *avoir* ~ *de* need; *il est* ~ it is necessary.

besti|al [bɛs'tjal] brutish; **~alité** [~tjali'te] *f* brutishness; bestiality; **~aux** [~'tjo] *m/pl.* livestock *sg.*

bêta, -asse [bɛ'ta, ~'tas] **1.** *adj.* stupid; **2.** *su.* blockhead, ass.

bétail [be'taːj] *m/sg.* livestock.

bête [bɛːt] **1.** *su./f* animal; beast; fool; ~ **de trait** draught animal; ~ **fauve** deer; *fig.* **chercher la petite** ~ split hairs; *fig.* **ma** ~ **noire** my pet aversion; **2.** *adj.* silly; **bêtise** [bɛ'tiːz] *f* stupidity; blunder; nonsense.

béton [be'tɔ̃] *m* concrete; *fig.* **du** ~ absolutely safe *or* reliable; **~nière** [~tɔ'njɛːr] *f* cement mixer.

bette [bɛt] *f* beet; **~rave** [bɛ'trav] *f* beet (root); sugar-beet.

beugl|ant *sl.* [bø'glã] *m* cheap café-concert; **~ement** [~glə'mã] *m* lowing; **~er** [~'gle] (1a) low.

beurr|e [bœr] *m* butter; *sl.* **c'est du** ~ is child's play; *faire son* ~ feather one's nest; F **un œil au** ~ **noir** a black eye; **~er** [~'re] (1a) butter.

beuverie [bø'vri] f drinking bout.

bévue [be'vy] f blunder, slip; *commettre une* ~ drop a brick.

bezef sl. [be'zɛf] adv.: *pas* ~ not much.

biais [bjɛ] **1.** adj. oblique; **2.** su./m skew; slant; fig. expedient; *de (or en)* ~ slantwise; *regarder de* ~ look askance at; **~er** [bjɛ'ze] (1b) slant; fig. use evasions.

bibelot [bi'blo] m knick-knack.

biberon [bi'brɔ̃] m baby: feeding (Am. nursing) bottle; F tippler; **~ner** F [~brɔ'ne] (1a) tipple.

bibi sl. [bi'bi] m I, me, myself; hat.

Bible [bibl] f Bible.

biblio... [biblio] biblio...; **~bus** [~'bys] m mobile library, Am. bookmobile; **~graphie** [~gra'fi] f bibliography; **~thécaire** [~te'kɛːr] m librarian; **~thèque** [~'tɛk] f library; bookcase; ~ *de prêt* lending library.

biblique [bi'blik] Biblical.

biche [biʃ] f hind; *ma* ~ my darling.

bicher sl. [bi'ʃe] (1a): *ça biche?* how goes it?; things alright with you?

bichon [bi'ʃɔ̃] m lapdog; **~ner** [~ʃɔ'ne] (1a) spruce up, titivate.

bicolore [biko'loːr] of two colo(u)rs.

bicoque [bi'kɔk] f shanty; F dump.

bicorne [bi'kɔrn] m cocked hat.

bicyclette [bisi'klɛt] f (bi)cycle.

bide sl. [bid] m belly; flop, washout.

bidoche sl. [bi'dɔʃ] f meat.

bidon [bi'dɔ̃] m tin, can, drum; sl. belly; sl. rubbish, pack of lies; **~ville** [bidɔ̃'vil] m shanty town.

bidule ⊦ [bi'dyl] f thing(umabob).

bief [bjɛf] m canal reach; mill race.

bielle ⊕ [bjɛl] f connecting rod.

bien [bjɛ̃] **1.** adv. usu. well; right(ly), proper(ly); rather; indeed; adjectivally: good, nice, fine, all right; ~ *de la peine* much trouble; ~ *des gens* many people; ~ *que* (sbj.) (al)though; *aller* ~ be well; *eh* ~! well!; *être* ~ a. be on good terms (with, *avec*); *se porter* ~ be in good health; *tant* ~ *que mal* so so; *c'est* ~ *du lui!* that's just like him!; **2.** su./m good; welfare; property, wealth; goods pl.; ~ *public* common weal; ⊕ ~ *pl. de consommation* consumer goods; **~-aimé** [~nɛ'me] beloved; **~-être** [~'nɛːtr] m well-being; **~faisance** [~fɛzɑ̃ːs] f charity; *œuvre f ou société f ou association f de* ~ charitable organization, charity; **~faisant** [~fə'zɑ̃] beneficent; beneficial; **~fait** [~'fɛ] m benefit; service; **~faiteur, -trice** [~fɛ'tœːr, ~'tris] **1.** su./m benefactor; su./f benefactress; **2.** adj. beneficent; **~fondé** [~fɔ̃'de] m grounds pl. (for, *de*); **~heureux** [~nœ'røː] happy; blessed.

biennal [biɛ'nal] biennial.

bienséan|ce [bjɛ̃se'ɑ̃ːs] f propriety; **~t** [~'ɑ̃] seemly, decent.

bientôt [bjɛ̃'to] adv. soon, before long; *à* ~! so long!

bienveillan|ce [bjɛ̃vɛ'jɑ̃ːs] f kindness, goodwill; benevolence; **~t** [~'jɑ̃] kind(ly), benevolent.

bienvenu, e [bjɛ̃və'ny] **1.** adj. welcome (to, *à*); **2.** su. welcome person; *soyez le* ~! welcome!; su./f welcome; *souhaiter la* ~ *e à* welcome.

bière[1] [bjɛːr] f beer.

bière[2] [~] f coffin.

biffer [bi'fe] (1a) cancel (a word); ~ *les indications inutiles* strike out what does not apply.

bifteck [bif'tɛk] m beefsteak.

bifur|cation [bifyrka'sjɔ̃] f road etc.: fork; 🚋 junction; **~quer** [~'ke] (1m) fork, branch off.

bigam|e [bi'gam] **1.** adj. bigamous; **2.** su. bigamist; **~ie** [~ga'mi] f bigamy.

bigarr|er [biga're] (1a) variegate; **~ure** [~'ryːr] f variegation.

bigleux [bi'glø] shortsighted.

bigorner sl. [bigɔr'ne] (1a) smash up; *se* ~ fight.

bigot [bi'go] sanctimonious.

bigoudi [bigu'di] m (hair) curler.

bigre! sl. [bigr] int. gosh!; **~ment** sl. [~gmɑ̃] adv. darn (well).

bijou, pl. **-x** [bi'ʒu] m jewel, gem; **~terie** [biʒu'tri] f jewellery, Am. jewelry; jeweller's shop; **~tier** [~'tje] m jeweller.

bikini [biki'ni] m bikini.

bilan [bi'lɑ̃] m ✝ balance sheet; fig. outcome; fig. consequences pl. fig. toll; fig. *faire le* ~ (*de*) take stock (of).

bilatéral [bilate'ral] bilateral.

bil|e [bil] f bile, gall, **~er** sl. [bi'le] (1a) *ne te bile pas!* take it easy!; **~ieux** [~'ljø] bilious; fig. testy.

bilingue [bi'lɛ̃ːg] bilingual.

bill|ard [bi'jaːr] m billards pl.; billiard table or room; F operating table; **~e** [bij] f (billiard etc.) ball; marble; billet,

B

block; *sl.* mug (= *face*); *sl.* nut (= *head*).

billet [bi'jɛ] *m* note; ticket (*a.* 🎫, *thea.*); ✝ bill; **~ circulaire** tourist ticket; **~ de banque** bank-note, *Am. a.* bill; **~ de faire part** notice (*of wedding etc.*); **~ doux** love-letter.

billevesée [bilvə'ze] *f* crazy notion.

billion [bi'ljɔ̃] *m* billion; *Am.* trillion.

billot [bi'jo] *m* (chopping) block.

bimbeloterie [bɛ̃blɔ'tri] *f* toys *pl.*

bimensuel [bimɑ̃'sɥɛl] fortnightly.

binaire [bi'nɛːr] binary.

biner [bi'ne] (1a) hoe, dig; **binette** [~'nɛt] *f* hoe; *sl.* face.

biocarburant [biɔkarby'rɑ̃] *m* biofuel.

biochimie ⚗ [biɔʃi'mi] *f* biochemistry.

biographe [biɔ'graf] *m* biographer.

biophysique [biɔfi'zik] *f* biophysics *sg.*

bipartisme *pol.* [bipar'tism] *m* coalition government.

biplace [bi'plas] *adj., su.* two-seater.

bipolaire ⚡ [bipɔ'lɛːr] bipolar.

bique [bik] *f* nannygoat.

biréacteur ✈ [bireak'tœːr] **1.** *adj./m* twin jet; **2.** *su./m* twin-jet plane.

bis¹, bise [bi, biːz] greyish-brown.

bis² [bis] *adv.* twice; again; encore!; *no. 9 ~ 9A* (*house etc.*).

bisaïeul [biza'jœl] *m* great-grandfather; **~e** [~] *f* great-grandmother.

bisannuel [biza'nɥɛl] biennial.

bisbille F [bis'biːj] *f* bickering.

biscornu F [biskɔr'ny] queer.

biscotte [bis'kɔt] *f* rusk.

biscuit [bis'kɥi] *m* biscuit, *Am.* cookie.

bise¹ [biːz] *f* north wind.

bise² F [~] *f* (little) kiss; **faire une ~ à q.** give *s.o.* a little kiss.

biseau ⚙ [bi'zo] *m* bevel; **en ~** bevelled; **~ter** [~zo'te] (1a) bevel; *fig.* mark (*cards*).

bisque [bisk] *f* shellfish soup; **~er** F [bis'ke] (1m) **faire ~ q.** rile *s.o.*

bisser [bi'se] (1a) encore (*a singer*); repeat; **~extile** [biseks'til]: **année** *f* **~** leap year.

bistre [bistr] blackish-brown.

bistrot [bis'tro] *m* pub; café.

bitum|e [bi'tym] *m* asphalt; **~er** [~ty'me] (1a) tar; asphalt.

bizarre [bi'zaːr] odd, strange; **~rie** [~zar'ri] *f* oddness; whim.

bizut(h) *sl.* [bi'zy] *m* beginner.

blackbouler [blakbu'le] (1a) blackball, turn down.

blafard [bla'faːr] wan, pale.

blagu|e [blag] *f* tobacco pouch; F nonsense; F (practical) joke; **~ à part** joking apart; **~er** F [bla'ge] (1m) *v/i.* joke; *v/t.* make fun of, F kid.

blair *sl.* [blɛːr] *m* nose.

blaireau [blɛ'ro] *m zo.* badger; shaving brush; *paint.* brush.

blairer *sl.* [blɛ're] (1a): **je ne peux pas le ~** I can't stand him.

blâm|able [blɑ'mabl] blameworthy; **~e** [blɑːm] *m* blame; reprimand; **~er** [blɑ'me] (1a) blame; reprimand.

blanc, blanche [blɑ̃, blɑ̃ːʃ] **1.** *adj.* white; pure; blank (*paper, cartridge etc.*); **nuit** *f* **blanche** sleepless night; **2.** *su.* white (person); *su./m* blank; white wine; (egg) white; white meat; **chauffer à ~** make white-hot; *fig.* work (*s.o.*) up; **saigner à ~** bleed white; ✗ **tirer à ~** fire blanks; **chèque en ~** blank cheque; **~-bec**, *pl.* **~s-becs** F [blɑ̃'bɛk] *m* greenhorn.

blanch|âtre [blɑ̃'ʃɑːtr] whitish; **~e** ♪ [blɑ̃ːʃ] *f* half note; **~eur** [blɑ̃'ʃœːr] *f* whiteness; purity; **~ir** [~'ʃiːr] (2a) *v/t.* whiten; bleach; wash; *v/i.* turn white; **~issage** [~ʃi'saːʒ] *m* laundering; **~isserie** [~ʃis'ri] *f* laundry; **~isseuse** [~ʃi'søːz] *f* laundress.

blanc-seing, *pl.* **blancs-seings** [blɑ̃'sɛ̃] *m* blank signature.

blaser [bla'ze] (1a) blunt; surfeit; **se ~** become indifferent (to, *de*).

blason [bla'zɔ̃] *m* coat of arms.

blasph|émateur [blasfema'tœːr] **1.** *su.* blasphemer; **2.** *adj.* blasphemous; **~ème** [~'fɛm] *m* blasphemy; **~émer** [~fe'me] (1f) blaspheme.

blatte [blat] *f* cockroach.

blé [ble] *m* wheat; corn; grain.

blêm|e [blɛːm] wan, pale; livid; **~ir** [blɛ'miːr] (2a) grow pale.

bléser [ble'ze] (1f) lisp.

bless|er [blɛ'se] (1a) injure; wound; hurt; offend; **~ure** [~'syːr] *f* wound; injury.

blet, blette [blɛ, blɛt] over-ripe.

bleu, bleue *m/pl.* **bleus** [blø] **1.** *adj.* blue; *cuis.* underdone; **une peur** *f* **bleue** a blue funk; **zone** *f* **bleue** zone of parking restrictions in the centre of a town; **2.** *su./m* blue; **✗** bruise; F greenhorn; **~s** *pl.* overalls; **~âtre** [~'ɑ:tr] bluish; **~ir** [~'i:r] (2a) blue.

blind|age [blɛ̃'da:ʒ] *m* armo(u)r plating; **~é** [~'de] *adj.*, *su./m* armo(u)red (car); **~er** [~'de] (1a) armo(u)r-plate; *fig.* F *fig.* harden, make immune *or* indifferent (to, **contre**).

bloc [blɔk] *m* block (memo) pad; mass; *pol.* bloc; **☼** unit; *sl.* clink; **à ~** tight, hard, right home; **en ~** in the lump: wholesale; **~age** [blɔ'ka:ʒ] *m* blocking; **☼** jamming; **~ des prix** freezing of prices; **~ des salaires** pay freeze.

bloc-notes, *pl.* **blocs-notes** [blɔk'nɔt] *m* writing pad, tablet.

blocus [blɔ'kys] *m* blockade.

blond [blɔ̃] blond, fair; pale (*ale*).

bloquer [blɔ'ke] (1m) block (up); blockade; stop (*a cheque*); jam on (*the brake*); freeze (*prices*); F lock up; **se ~** get jammed.

blottir [blɔ'ti:r] (2a): **se ~** crouch, squat; nestle.

blouse [blu:z] *f* blouse; smock, overall; **blouson** [blu'zɔ̃] *m* lumber jacket, *Am.* windbreaker.

bluet ✤ [bly'ɛ] *m* cornflower.

bluff F [blœf] *m* bluff; **~er** F [blœ'fe] (1a) bluff.

blut|age [bly'ta:ʒ] *m* sifting; **~er** [~'te] (1a) sift (*flour*).

bobard Г [bɔ'ba:r] *m* tall story.

bobin|age ✦, **☼** [bɔbi'na:ʒ] *m* winding; **~e** [~'bin] *f* bobbin, reel, spool; roll, coil; *sl.* dial (= *face*); **~er** [bɔbi'ne] (1a) wind, spool.

bobo F [bɔ'bo] *m* hurt; sore; pain.

bocal [bɔ'kal] *m* jar; globe, fish bowl; *chemist:* show bottle.

bock [bɔk] *m* glass of beer.

bœuf [bœf, *pl.* bø] **1.** *su./m* ox; beef; **2.** *adj.* F terrific, tremendous.

boggie 🚃 [bɔ'ʒi] *m* bogie, *Am.* truck.

bohème [bɔ'ɛm] *adj.*, *su.* Bohemian; **bohémien** [~e'mjɛ̃] *adj.*, *su.* Bohemian; gypsy.

boire [bwa:r] (4b) **1.** *v/t.* drink; absorb; soak up *or* in; drink in (*s.o.'s words*); **~ un coup** have a drink; *v/i.* drink; be a drunkard; **~ comme un trou** drink like a fish; **2.** *su./m* drink(ing).

bois [bwa] *m* wood; timber; forest; **~** *pl. stag:* antlers; **~ contre-plaqué** ply-

wood; **~ de construction** timber; **~ de lit** bedstead; **♩ les ~** *pl.* the woodwind *sg.*; **touchez du ~** touch wood!; **~age** [bwa'za:ʒ] *m* timbering; **~er** [bwa'ze] (1a) panel; afforest; timber; **~erie** [bwaz'ri] *f* panelling; wainscoting; woodwork.

boisselier [bwasə'lje] *m* cooper.

boisson [bwa'sɔ̃] *f* drink; beverage.

boîte [bwat] *f* box; bin; tin, *Am.* can; **☼** case; F place, room; F joint, dump; F company, firm; *sl.* **~ à gants** glove compartment; **~ à outils** toolbox; **~ aux lettres** letterbox, *Am.* mailbox; **~ de conserves** tin, *Am.* can; *sl.* **~ de nuit** nightclub; *mot.* **~ de vitesses** gearbox, *Am.* transmission; **~ postale** post office box; **en ~** tinned, *Am.* canned; F **mettre q. en ~** pull s.o.'s leg.

boît|er [bwa'te] (1a) limp; **~eux** [~'tø] lame; rickety.

boîtier [bwa'tje] *m* watch: case.

boivent [bwa:v] *3rd p. pl. pres. of* **boire 1.**

bol [bɔl] *m* bowl; *sl.* (good) luck; *sl.* **en avoir ras le ~** be fed up (with it).

bolchevis|me [bɔlʃə'vism] *m* Bolshevism; **~te** [~'vist] Bolshevist.

bolide [bɔ'lid] *m* bolide; fireball.

bombance F [bɔ̃'bɑ̃:s] *f* feast(ing).

bombard|ement [bɔ̃bardə'mɑ̃] *m* shelling; bombing; bombardment; **~er** [~'de] (1a) bombard; pelt with (*de*) (*stones, questions*); **~ier** [~'dje] *m* bomber.

bombe [bɔ̃:b] *f* ✗ bomb; spray; F feast; **faire la ~** go on a spree; **~er** [bɔ̃'be] (1a) bulge; curve, arch; camber; stick out (*one's chest*).

bon, bonne [bɔ̃, bɔn] **1.** *adj. usu.* good; nice; right; fit (for, **à**); benevolent; dutiful (*son*); ✝ sound (*firm*); witty; **~ à manger** eatable; ready(ly); **~ marché** cheap(ly); **~** witticism; **à quoi ~?** what's the use?; **de bonne famille** of good family; **de bonne foi** truthful, honest; **de bonne heure** early; **prendre qch. en bonne part** take s.th. in good part; **tenir ~** stand firm *or* fast, hold out; **pour de ~** in earnest; really; **2. bon** *adv.* nice; good; **il fait ~** (*faire qch.*) it's good *or* nice (*to do s.th.*); **3.** *su./m* voucher, ticket, coupon; ✝ draft.

bonace [bɔ'nas] *f* lull (*before storm*).

bonasse [~] meek, soft.

bonbon [bɔ̃'bɔ̃] *m* sweet, *Am.* candy.

B

bonbonne [bõ'bɔn] f carboy; demijohn.
bonbonnière [bõbɔ'njɛːr] f sweet (meat)
box; fig. snug little dwelling.
bond [bõ] m jump; bound; leap; *faire
faux ~ à q.* let s.o. down; stand s.o. up.
bond|e [bõːd] f plug; bung(hole); sluice;
~é [bõ'de] packed, crammed.
bond|ir [bõ'diːr] (2a) jump; bounce; ca-
per; **~issement** [~dis'mã] m bounding,
leaping.
bonheur [bɔ'nœːr] m happiness; good
luck; success; *par ~* luckily; *porter ~*
bring good luck.
bonhomie [bɔnɔ'mi] f simple goodheart-
edness; *avec ~* good-naturedly; **bonhomme**, pl. **bonshommes** [bɔ'nɔm,
bõ'zɔm] m fellow, guy.
boni ✝ [bɔ'ni] m surplus; profit; **~fier**
[bɔni'fje] (1o) (*a. se ~*) improve; **~ment**
[~'mã] m *advertizing:* puff; *pej.* clap-
trap.
bonjour [bõ'ʒuːr] m good morning; good
afternoon.
bonne [bɔn] f maid; servant; waitress; ~
à tout faire maid of all work.
bonnement [bɔn'mã] adv.: (*tout*)~ simply; plainly.
bonnet [bɔ'nɛ] m cap; F *gros ~* bigwig,
Am. big shot; **~erie** [bɔn'tri] f hosiery;
~ier [~'tje] m hosier.
bonsoir [bõ'swaːr] m good evening;
good night.
bonté [bõ'te] f kindness; *ayez la ~ de*
(*inf.*) be so kind as to (*inf.*).
boom ✝ [bum] m boom.
bord [bɔːr] m edge, border; *road etc.:*
side; *cup etc.:* brim; *lake, river etc.:*
shore, bank; *fig.* verge, brink; ♣ *à ~* on
board; ♣ *par-dessus ~* overboard;
~age [bɔr'daːʒ] m hem(ming), bor-
der(ing); **~é** [~'de] m braid; ♣ plank-
ing; **~ée** [~'de] f broadside; *fig.* cou-
rir une ~ go on the spree.
bordel [bɔr'dɛl] m brothel.
bordelais [bɔrdə'lɛ] of Bordeaux.
border [bɔr'de] (1a) border; line (with,
de); tuck (*s.o.*) up or in; ~ *un lit* tuck in
the bed clothes.
bordereau ✝ [bɔrdə'ro] m memorandum; invoice; note, slip; list.
bordure [bɔr'dyːr] f border(ing); frame;
edge; rim; kerb, Am. curb.
bore 🜍 [bɔːr] m boron.
boréal [bɔre'al] north(ern).

borgne [bɔrɲ] one-eyed; *fig.* suspicious,
shady.
borique 🜍 [bɔ'rik] boric, boracic.
born|e [bɔrn] f limit; boundary(-stone);
~ *kilométrique* (*approx.*) milestone; **~é**
[bɔr'ne] limited; narrow; **~er** [~'ne] (1a)
limit; bound; *se ~ à* content o.s. with;
restrict or limit o.s. to (*doing s.th.*).
bosquet [bɔs'kɛ] m grove, thicket.
boss|e [bɔs] f hump; bump; knob; *fig.
avoir la ~ de* have a gift for; *en ~* in
relief; **~eler** [~'le] (1c) emboss; batter;
~er *sl.* [bɔ'se] (1a) plod; **~u** [~'sy] 1. *adj.*
hunchbacked; 2. *su.* hunchback; **~uer**
[~'sɥe] (1n) dent, batter.
bot [bo] *adj.:* *pied m ~* clubfoot.
botanique [bɔta'nik] 1. *adj.* botanical; 2.
su. f botany.
botte¹ [bɔt] f boot; **~s** *pl. à l'écuyère*
riding boots; *à propos de ~s* for or
about nothing.
botte² [bɔt] f bunch; bale; coil; **~ler**
[~'tle] (1c) bundle; bunch.
botter [bɔ'te] (1a) put boots on; F kick;
sl. ça me botte I like that; o.K.!
bottine [bɔ'tin] f (half-)boot.
bouc [buk] m he-goat; goatee.
boucan F [bu'kã] m hullabaloo.
boucan|er [buka'ne] (1a) cure (with
smoke); smoke; tan; *sl.* kick up a row;
~ier [~'nje] m buccaneer.
bouche [buʃ] f mouth; opening; nozzle;
cannon: muzzle; **~-à-~** m/inv.
mouth-to-mouth artificial respiration,
kiss of life; ~ *d'eau* hydrant; ~ *de
métro* underground (*Am.* subway) entrance; *sl. ta ~!* shut up!
bouché [bu'ʃe] choked; F stupid; F *à l'
éméri* absolutely blockheaded.
bouchée [~] f mouthful; *cuis.* patty.
boucher¹ [bu'ʃe] (1a) stop (up); shut up;
cork (*a bottle*).
boucher² [bu'ʃe] m butcher; **~ie** [buʃ'ri] f
butcher's shop or trade; slaughter (*a.
fig.*).
bouche-trou [buʃ'tru] m stopgap.
bouchon [bu'ʃõ] m cork, stopper, plug;
float; *mot.* (*a. ~ de circulation*) traffic
jam; **~ner** [buʃɔ'ne] (1a) rub down; F
fig. coddle, cosset.
boucl|e [bukl] f buckle; loop; ear-ring;
curl, lock; **~er** [bu'kle] (1a) *v/t.* buckle;
loop; curl (*one's hair*); F lock up; *v/i.*
curl (*hair*).

bouclier [bu'klje] m shield.

boud|er [bu'de] (1a) v/i. sulk; shirk; v/t. be sulky with; **~erie** [~'dri] f sulkiness; **~eur** [~'dœr] sulky.

boudin [bu'dɛ̃] m black pudding, Am. blood sausage; **ressort m à ~** spiral spring; **~er** [budi'ne] (1a): F **se ~ dans** squeeze o.s. into (a garment).

boue [bu] f mud; dirt; slush.

bouée ♣ [bu'e] f buoy.

boueu|r [bu'œr] m scavenger; dustman, Am. garbage collector; **~x** [bu'ø] muddy; dirty.

bouffa|nt [bu'fɑ̃] puffed (sleeve); baggy; **~rde** [~'fard] f pipe.

bouffe¹ [buf] comic.

bouffe² sl. [~] f food, F grub.

bouffée [bu'fe] f puff, whiff; waft; gust; flush; fig. fit; **bouffer** [~] (1u) puff out; F eat.

bouff|i [bu'fi] puffed (with, **de**), swollen; bloated; **~ir** [~'fir] (2a) swell; **~issure** [~fi'syr] f swelling; bombast.

bouffon [bu'fɔ̃] **1.** adj. farcical; comical; **2.** su./m clown; **~nerie** [~fɔn'ri] f buffoonery.

bouge [buʒ] m dump, hovel; bulge.

bougeoir [buʒ'war] m candlestick.

bouger [bu'ʒe] (1l) move, stir.

bougie [bu'ʒi] f candle(-power); mot. sparking plug, Am. spark plug.

bougon F [bu'gɔ̃] grumpy.

bougre [bugr] **1.** su./m fellow; **2.** int. gosh!; **~ment** sl. [bugrə'mɑ̃] adv. darn; **~sse** sl. [~'grɛs] f jade.

boui-boui, pl. **bouis-bouis** F [bwi'bwi] m penny gaff, honky-tonk.

bouillabaisse [buja'bɛs] f (Provençal) fish soup.

bouillant [bu'jɑ̃] boiling (a. fig with, **de**); hot; fig. hot-headed.

bouille sl. [bu:j] f face; head.

bouill|i, e [bu'ji] **1.** p.p. of **bouillir**; **2.** su./m boiled beef; su./f gruel; **~ir** [~'ji:r] (2e) boil; **faire ~ l'eau** boil the water; **~oire** [buj'wa:r] f kettle, Am. tea-kettle; **~on** [bu'jɔ̃] m broth (a. biol.); soup; restaurant; unsold copies pl.; fig. **boire un ~** suffer a loss; **~onner** [~jɔ'ne] (1a) bubble; seethe; foam (with, **de**); **~otte** [~'jɔt] f hot-water bottle; kettle; **~otter** [~jɔ'te] (1a) simmer.

boulang|er [bulɑ̃'ʒe] **1.** su./m baker; **2.** (1l) bake; **~ère** [~'ʒɛ:r] f baker's wife;

farmer's market van; **~erie** [bulɑ̃ʒ'ri] f baker's shop; baking.

boule [bul] f ball; bowl; sl. head; **~s** pl. **Quiès** (TM) earplugs.

bouleau ♣ [bu'lo] m birch(-wood).

bouledogue [bul'dɔg] m bulldog.

boule|r F [bu'le] (1a) roll; **envoyer ~** send (s.o.) packing; **~t** [~'lɛ] m ~ (de canon) cannonball; fig. drag; **~tte** [~'lɛt] f pellet; (~ de viande) meat ball; sl. blunder.

boulevard [bul'va:r] m boulevard.

boulevers|ement [bulvɛrsə'mɑ̃] m overthrow; confusion; **~er** [~'se] (1a) upset (a. fig.); bowl over.

boulon [bu'lɔ̃] m bolt; **~ner** [~lɔ'ne] (1a) v/t. bolt; v/i. sl. swot.

boulot [bu'lo] **1.** adj. dumpy; **2.** su./m work; job; **~ter** F [~lɔ'te] (1a) eat; **ça boulotte!** things are fine!

bouquet [bu'kɛ] m bunch, bouquet; **c'est le ~!** that takes the cake!; **~ière** [buk'tje:r] f flowergirl.

bouquin F [bu'kɛ̃] m book; **~er** [buki'ne] (1a) collect old books; F read; **~eur** [~'nœ:r] m book fancier; **~iste** [~'nist] m second-hand bookseller.

bourb|e [burb] f mud; mire; slime; **~eux** [bur'bø] muddy; **~ier** [~'bje] m mire; fig. mess.

bourde F [burd] f blunder, bloomer, howler.

bourdon [bur'dɔ̃] m great bell; zo. bumblebee; **faux ~** drone; **~ner** [~dɔ'ne] (1a) hum, buzz.

bourg [bu:r] m market town; **~ade** [bur'gad] f large village; **~eois** [~'ʒwa] **1.** adj. middle-class; pej. narrow-minded; **2.** su. citizen; middle-class person; F Philistine; **les petits ~** the petty bourgeoisie sg.; su./f **la ~e, ma ~e** my wife, F the missus; **~eoisie** [~ʒwa'zi] f middle class(es pl.), bourgeoisie.

bourgeon [bur'ʒɔ̃] m ♣ bud; ♣ pimple; **~ner** [~ʒɔ'ne] (1a) bud.

bourgogne [bur'gɔɲ] m burgundy; **bourguignon** [~gi'ɲɔ̃] adj., su. Burgundian.

bourlinguer [burlɛ̃'ge] (1m) ♣ strain; fig. knock about (the world).

bourra|de [bu'rad] f blow; thrust; **~ge** [~'ra:ʒ] m stuffing; cramming; F **~ de crâne** bluff, eyewash; media: brainwashing.

bourrasque [bu'rask] *f* squall; gust.

bourre [bu:r] *f* wad; stuffing; *sl.* cop (= *policeman*).

bourré [bu're] packed, crammed, stuffed (with, **de**); chockfull; *sl.* plastered (= *drunk*).

bourreau [bu'ro] *m* executioner.

bourr|eler [bur'le] (1c) torture; **~elet** [~'lɛ] *m* bulge; draught excluder; **~elier** [~ə'lje] *m* saddler; **~er** [bu're] (1a) stuff; cram; pad.

bourriche [bu'riʃ] *f* hamper(ful).

bourri|cot [buri'ko] *m* donkey; **~que** [~'rik] *f* she-ass; blockhead; *faire tourner q. en* **~** drive s.o. crazy.

bourru [bu'ry] **1.** *adj.* churlish; **2.** *su./m:* **~** *bienfaisant* rough diamond.

bours|e [burs] *f* purse (*a. fig.*); bag; *zo.* pouch; scholarship; ♥ ♀ Stock Exchange; **~icot** F [bursi'ko] *m* nest egg; **~ier** [~'sje] *m* scholarship holder; ♥ speculator.

boursouffl|er [bursu'fle] (1a) puff up; bloat; **~ure** [~'fly:r] *f* swelling; blister; *fig.* turgidity.

bous [bu] *1st p. sg. pres. of* **bouillir**.

bouscul|ade [busky'lad] *f* hustle; scrimmage; **~er** [~'le] (1a) knock (*s.th.*) over; jostle (*s.o.*).

bous|e [bu:z] *f* cowdung; **~iller** [buzi'je] (1a) botch, bungle; ruin, wreck, F bust up.

boussole [bu'sɔl] *f* compass; F *perdre la* **~** lose one's head.

boustifaille F [busti'fa:j] *f* grub.

bout [bu] *m* end; extremity; *cigarette:* tip; *pen:* nib; bit; *ground:* patch; *à* **~** worn out, F all in; *être à* **~** *de qch.* have run out of s.th.; *à* **~** *de forces* at the end of one's tether; *au* **~** *de* after; *au* **~** *du compte* after all; *de* **~** *en* **~** from beginning to end; *joindre les deux* **~***s* make both ends meet; *venir à* **~** *de* manage; (be able to) cope with.

boutade [bu'tad] *f* whim; sally.

boute-en-train [butã'trɛ̃] *m/inv.* life and soul (*of a party*).

bouteille [bu'tɛ:j] *f* bottle; **~** *isolante* Thermos bottle; *prendre de la* **~** age (*wine*); *fig.* grow old.

boutique [bu'tik] *f* shop; booth; ◎ set of tools; *parler* **~** talk shop; **~ier** [~ti'kje] *m* shopkeeper.

boutoir *zo.* [bu'twa:r] *m* snout; *fig.* **coup** *m de* **~** thrust; cutting remark.

bouton [bu'tõ] *m* button; ♣ bud; ✻ pimple; stud, link; knob; *tourner le* **~** switch on *or* off; **~-d'or,** *pl.* **~s-d'or** ♀ [~tõ'dɔ:r] *m* butter-cup; **~ner** [~tɔ'ne] (1a) button (up); **~nière** [~tɔ'njɛ:r] *f* buttonhole; ✻ incision; **~-poussoir,** *pl.* **~s-poussoirs** [~tõpu'swa:r] *m* push-button; **~-pression,** *pl.* **~s-pression** [~tõprɛ'sjõ] *m* press-stud.

bouture ✿ [bu'ty:r] *f* cutting.

bouv|erie [bu'vri] *f* cowshed; **~ier** [~'vje] cowherd.

bovin [bɔ'vɛ̃] bovine.

box, *pl.* **boxes** [bɔks] *m* horse-box; *mot.* lock-up; **~** *des accusés* dock.

box|e [bɔks] *f* boxing; **~er** [bɔk'se] (1a) box; **~eur** [~'sœ:r] *m* boxer.

boyau [bwa'jo] *m* hose-pipe; bowel; gut; ✕ trench; tube.

boycott|age [bɔjkɔ'ta:ʒ] *m* boycotting; **~er** [~'te] (1a) boycott.

bracelet [bras'lɛ] *m* bracelet; **~** *de montre* watch-strap; **~-montre,** *pl.* **~s-montres** [~lɛ'mõ:tr] *m* wrist-watch.

braconn|age [brakɔ'na:ʒ] *m* poaching; **~er** [~'ne] (1a) poach; **~ier** [~'nje] *m* poacher.

brader [bra'de] (1a) sell off cheap.

braguette [bra'gɛt] *f* trousers: flies *pl.*

brai [brɛ] *m* tar, pitch.

braill|ard [brɑ'ja:r] **1.** *adj.* bawling; **2.** *su.* bawler; **~er** [~'je] (1a) bawl.

braire [brɛ:r] (4c) bray (*donkey*); F cry.

brais|e [brɛz] *f* embers *pl.*; *sl.* cash; **~er** *cuis.* [brɛ'ze] (1b) braise.

brait [brɛ] *p.p. of* **braire**.

bramer [bra'me] (1o) bell (*stag*).

brancard [brɑ̃'ka:r] *m* stretcher; hand-barrow; *carriage:* shaft.

branch|age [brɑ̃'ʃa:ʒ] *m* branches *pl.*; **~e** [brɑ̃:ʃ] *f* branch (*a. fig.*, ♀, ✝); bough; *spectacles:* side; **~er** [brɑ̃'ʃe] (1a) ⚡ plug in(to, *sur*); ◎ *etc., fig.* connect *or* link (up) (with, *sur*).

branchies *zo.* [brɑ̃'ʃi] *f/pl.* gills.

brande ♀ [brɑ̃:d] *f* heather; heath.

brandiller [brɑ̃di'je] (1a) dangle.

brandir [brɑ̃'di:r] (2a) brandish.

branl|ant [brɑ̃'lɑ̃] shaky; loose (*tooth*); **~e** [brɑ̃:l] *m* shaking; impulse; *en* **~** in action; **~e-bas** [brɑ̃l'ba] *m/inv.* commotion; **~er** [brɑ̃'le] (1a) shake; move.

braqu|age [bra'ka:ʒ] *m car etc.*: steering; *gun*: aiming, pointing; *car*: **rayon de ~** turning circle; **~er** [bra'ke] (1m) aim, point; *mot.* change the direction of.

bras [bra] *m* arm; handle; jib; **~** *pl.* workmen; **~ dessus, ~ dessous** arm-in-arm; **à ~ tendus** at arm's length; **à tour de ~** with might and main; **en ~ de chemise** in shirt-sleeves.

braser ⚙ [bra'ze] (1a) solder.

brasier [bra'zje] *m* brazier; blaze; **brasiller** [~zi'je] (1a) *v/i.* sparkle; sizzle; *v/t.* grill.

brassage [bra'sa:ʒ] *m* brewing; *fig.* (inter)mixing.

brassard [bra'sa:r] *m* armband.

brasse [bras] *f* ✠ fathom; *swimming*: breast-stroke; **~ée** [bra'se] *f* armful; *swimming*: stroke.

brasser [bra'se] (1a) brew (*a. fig.*); stir (up); (inter)mix; F handle (*an affair*); **~ie** [bras'ri] *f* brewery; beer saloon; restaurant.

brassière [bra'sje:r] *f* strap; bodice; **~ de sauvetage** life jacket.

brav|ache [bra'vaʃ] *m* bully; swaggerer; **~ade** [~'vad] *f* bravado; **~e** [bra:v] brave; good, honest; **un ~ homme** a worthy man; **un homme ~** a brave man; **~er** [bra've] (1a) defy; brave; **~o** [~'vo] *int.* bravo!; well done!; **~oure** [~'vu:r] *f* bravery.

break *mot.* [brɛk] *m* estate (car), *Am.* station wagon.

brebis [brə'bi] *f* ewe; sheep.

brèche [brɛʃ] *f* breach; gap; notch; **~dent** [~'dɑ̃] gap-toothed (person).

bredouill|e [brə'du:j] empty-handed; **se coucher ~** go supperless to bed; **~er** [~du'je] (1a) mumble.

bref [brɛf] (**bref, brɛ:v**) **1.** *adj.* brief, short; **2.** *bref adv.* in short.

breloque [brə'lɔk] *f* (watch-)charm; **battre la ~** work irregularly (*watch*).

brésilien [brezi'ljɛ̃] *adj., su.* Brazilian.

bretelle [brə'tɛl] *f* strap; *mot.* link road; **~s** *pl.* braces, *Am.* suspenders; *mot.* **~ de contournement** bypass.

breton [brə'tɔ̃] *adj., su.* Breton.

breuvage [brœ'va:ʒ] *m* beverage.

brève [brɛ:v] *f* ♩ breve; *tel.* dot.

brevet [brə'vɛ] *m* patent; certificate, diploma; **~ de pilote** pilot's licence;

~é [brəv'te] certificated (*teacher etc.*), commissioned (*officer*); **~er** [~] (1c) patent; license.

bréviaire [bre'vjɛ:r] *m* breviary.

bribes [brib] *f/pl.* scraps; bits.

bric-à-brac [brika'brak] *m/inv.* odds *pl.* and ends *pl.*; curios *pl.*

bricoll|e [bri'kɔl] *f* strap, harness; trifle, small matter; **~er** F [~kɔ'le] (1a) do odd jobs; potter; **~eur** [~kɔ'lœ:r] *m* potterer.

brid|e [brid] *f* bridle; rein (*a. fig.*); strap; ⚙ flange; **~ de serrage** clamp; **à ~ abattue** at full speed; **lâcher la ~ à l'émotion** give free rein to one's feelings; **tenir la ~ haute à** be high-handed with; **~er** [bri'de] (1a) bridle; curb; flange; truss (*fowl*).

briève|ment [briɛv'mɑ̃] *adv.* briefly; **~té** [~'te] *f* brevity; concision.

brigad|e [bri'gad] *f* brigade; *workers*: gang; shift; **~ier** [~ga'dje] *m* ✕ corporal; ⚙ foreman.

brigand [bri'gɑ̃] *m* robber; ruffian; **~age** [~gɑ̃'da:ʒ] *m* robbery.

brigu|e [brig] *f* intrigue; **~er** [bri'ge] (1m) seek, aspire to *or* after.

brill|ant [bri'jɑ̃] **1.** *adj.* shining, bright; **2.** *su./m* brilliance; gloss; brilliant; **~er** [~'je] (1a) shine, glisten, sparkle; F **~ par son absence** be conspicuous for one's absence.

brimade [bri'mad] *f* vexation; rag, hazing.

brimbaler [brɛ̃ba'le] (1a) *v/t.* dangle, wobble; *v/t.* carry about.

brimborion [brɛ̃bɔ'rjɔ̃] *m* bauble.

brimer [bri'me] (1a) vex; rag, *Am.* haze.

brin [brɛ̃] *m* grass: blade; *rope*: strand; bit; **~dille** [~'di:j] *f* twig.

bringue[1] F [brɛ:g] *f* spree, F binge.

bringue[2] F [~] *f*: **grande ~** tall (and ugly) woman, F beanpole.

brioche [bri'ɔʃ] *f* brioche; bun.

brique [brik] *f* brick; *soap*: bar; **~t** [bri'kɛ] *m* lighter; **~ter** [brik'te] (1c) brick; **~terie** [~'tri] *f* brick-yard; **~tte** [bri'kɛt] *f* briquette.

brisant [bri'zɑ̃] **1.** *adj.* high-explosive; **2.** *su./m* reef, breaker.

brise ✠ [bri:z] *f* breeze.

brisées [bri'ze] *f/pl.*: **aller sur les ~ de q.** trespass on s.o.'s preserves.

brise...: **~glace** [briz'glas] *m/inv.* ice-breaker; **~lames** ✠ [~'lam] *m/inv.* breakwater; groyne.

B

bris|er [bri'ze] (1a) v/t. break; shatter; crush; v/i. break (with, **avec**); **~eur** [~'zœːr] m breaker, wrecker; **~ de grève** strikebreaker; **~ure** [~'zyːr] f break; joint.

britannique [brita'nik] **1.** adj. British; Britannic (*majesty*); **2.** su.: **les ~s** m/pl. the British.

broc [bro] m jug, pitcher.

brocant|er [brɔkã'te] (1a) deal in second-hand goods; barter; **~eur** [~'tœːr] m second-hand dealer.

brocart † [~] m brocade.

broch|e [brɔʃ] f spit; spindle; peg; brooch; **◎** etc. pin; **~er** [brɔ'ʃe] (1a) stitch; emboss; **livre broché** paper-bound book.

brochet icht. [brɔ'ʃɛ] m pike.

brochette [brɔ'ʃɛt] f skewer; pin.

brochure [brɔ'ʃyːr] f brochure; pamphlet; booklet.

brodequin [brɔd'kɛ̃] m half-boot.

brod|er [brɔ'de] (1a) embroider (a. fig.); **~erie** [~'dri] f embroidery.

bronche anat. [brɔ̃ːʃ] f windpipe.

broncher [brɔ̃'ʃe] (1a) stumble; move; falter; **sans ~** without flinching.

bronchite ✶ [brɔ̃'ʃit] f bronchitis.

bronz|e [brɔ̃ːz] m bronze; **~er** [brɔ̃'ze] (1a) bronze; tan.

bross|e [brɔs] f brush; **~s** pl. brushwood sg.; **cheveux m/pl. en ~** crewcut sg.; **~er** [brɔ'se] (1a) brush; scrub; F thrash; F **se ~** do without.

brou [bru] m husk (of *walnut*).

brouet [bru'ɛ] m (thin) gruel.

brouette [bru'ɛt] f wheelbarrow.

brouhaha [brua'a] m hubbub.

brouillage [bru'jaːʒ] m radio: jamming; interference.

brouilla|rd [bru'jaːr] m fog; smog; **~sser** [~ja'se] (1a) drizzle.

brouill|e F [bru:j] f quarrel; **être en ~ avec** have fallen out with; **~er** [bru'je] (1a) mix or muddle up; confuse; blur; *radio:* jam; scramble (*eggs*); *fig.* set at variance; **se ~** get mixed up, become muddled or confused or blurred; go cloudy, be breaking up (*weather*); quarrel, fall out (with, **avec**); **~eur** [~'jœːr] m radio: jammer.

brouillon¹ [bru'jɔ̃] unmethodical, muddleheaded (*person*); **avoir l'esprit ~** be muddleheaded.

brouillon² [bru'jɔ̃] m rough copy; scribbling paper; **~ner** [~jɔ'ne] (1a) make a rough copy of.

brouss|ailles [bru'saːj] f/pl. brushwood sg., scrub sg.; **en ~** shaggy (*hair*); **~e** [brus] f the bush.

brout|er [bru'te] (1a) v/t. browse (on), graze; v/i. **◎** jump; **~ille** [~'tiːj] f trifle.

broy|age [brwa'jaːʒ] m crushing; grinding; **~er** [~'je] (1h) crush; grind; **~eur** [~'jœːr] m grinder.

bru [bry] f daughter-in-law.

bruin|e [brɥin] f drizzle; **~er** [brɥi'ne] (1a) drizzle; **~eux** [~'nø] drizzly.

brui|re [brɥiːr] (4d) rustle; hum; **~ssement** [brɥis'mã] m rustling; humming; murmuring.

bruit [brɥi] m noise; clatter; din; clang; *fig.* rumo(u)r; **~ de fond** background noise; **~ sourd** thud; **le ~ court que** ... rumo(u)r has it that ...; **~tage thea.** [brɥi'taːʒ] m sound effects pl. **~eur** m, **-euse** f [~'tœːr, - 'øːz] sound-effects engineer.

brûl|é [bry'le] m smell of burning; **~e-gueule** F [bryl'gœl] m/inv. nose-warmer (= pipe); **~e-pourpoint** [~pur'pwɛ̃] adv.: **à ~** point-blank; **~er** [bry'le] (1a) v/t. burn; scorch; overrun (a signal); **✔** nip; v/i. burn, be on fire; be consumed; F be hot; **~ de** (inf.) be eager to (inf.); **~eur** [~'lœːr] m gas etc. burner; **~ot** [~'lo] m fire-brand; **~ure** [~'lyːr] f burn; scald; **✔** frost nip; **~s** pl. **d'estomac** heartburn sg.

brum|e [brym] f thick fog; **~eux** [bry'mø] foggy; fig. hazy.

brun, ~e [brœ̃, bryn] **1.** adj. brown; dark-haired; **2.** su./m brown; su./f brunette; nightfall; **~âtre** [bry'nɑːtr] brownish; **~ir** [~'niːr] (2a) v/t. brown; tan; v/t. polish.

brusqu|e [brysk] blunt, brusque, abrupt; sudden; **~er** [brys'ke] (1m) be blunt with (s.o.); precipitate (s.th.); **~erie** [~skə'ri] f abruptness.

brut [bryt] raw; crude (*oil*); unrefined; uncut; **poids m ~** gross weight; **~al** [bry'tal] brutal; fierce; harsh (*colour*); brute (*force*); unvarnished (*truth*); **~aliser** [~tali'ze] (1a) ill-treat; bully; **~alité** [~tali'te] f brutality; suddenness (of an event etc.); **~e** [bryt] f brute; lout.

bruyant [brɥi'jã] noisy, loud.

bruyère [brɥi'jɛːr] f heath(er); briar.
bu [by] p.p. of *boire 1*.
buanderie [bɥɑ̃'dri] f wash-house.
buccal [byk'kal] of the mouth.
bûche [byːʃ] f log; block; F blockhead; *ramasser une* ~ have a fall.
bûcher¹ [by'ʃe] m woodshed; wood-stack; stake.
bûcher² [~] (1a) rough-hew; sl. thrash; F grind (at), work hard (at).
bûcheron [byʃ'rɔ̃] m woodcutter.
bûcheur m, **-euse** f F [by'ʃœːr, ~'ʃøːz] plodder; eager beaver.
budget [byd'ʒɛ] m budget; F *boucler son* ~ make ends meet; ~**étaire** [~ʒe'tɛːr] budgetary.
buée [bɥe] f steam, vapo(u)r.
buffet [by'fɛ] m sideboard; buffet; 🚂 refreshment room.
buffle [byfl] m buffalo (hide).
buis [bɥi] m box-tree; ~**son** [bɥi'sɔ̃] m bush; thicket; ~**sonneux** [bɥiso'nø] bushy; ~**sonnier, ère** [~'nje, ~'njɛːr] adj.: *faire l'école* ~**ère** play truant, Am. play hooky.
bulbe ♀ [bylb] m bulb, **bulbeux** [byl'bø] bulbous, ♀ bulbed.
bulle [byl] f bubble; blister; *cartoon:* balloon; *faire des* ~**s** bubble; blow bubbles.
bulletin [byl'tɛ̃] m bulletin; form; report; 🚂 ~ *de bagages* luggage ticket, Am. baggage check; ~ *météorologique* weather forecast.
buraliste [byra'list] su. tax collector; tobacconist; clerk.
bureau [by'ro] m writing table, desk; office; department; ~ *de douane* customs house; *thea.* ~ *de location* box

office; ~ *de poste* post office; ~ *de renseignements* information bureau; ~ *de tabac* tobacconist's; *deuxième* ~ Intelligence (Department); ~**crate** [byro'krat] m bureaucrat, ~**cratie** [~kra'si] f bureaucracy.
burette [by'rɛt] f cruet; oilcan.
burin [by'rɛ̃] m etching needle; cold chisel; engraving; ~**er** [~ri'ne] (1a) engrave; chisel.
burlesque [byr'lɛsk] comical.
bus [by] *1st p. sg. p.s.* of *boire 1*.
buse¹ [byz] f orn. buzzard; F fool.
buse² [~] f pipe; nozzle; shaft.
busqué [bys'ke] arched; *nez* m ~ hook nose.
buste [byst] m bust.
but [by(t)] m target; aim; purpose; *avoir pour* ~ intend; *de* ~ *en blanc* bluntly; *marquer un* ~ score a goal; ~**é** [by'te] obstinate, mulish; ~**er** [~] (1a) v/i.: ~ *contre* stumble over; bump against or into, hit; *fig.* ~ *sur* or *contre* meet with, come up against (*a difficulty etc.*); v/t. prop (up); *fig.* make (*s.o.*) obstinate; *se* ~ be(come) obstinate; ~**eur** *foot.* [~'tœːr] m striker.
butin [by'tɛ̃] m booty, spoils pl.; ~**er** [~ti'ne] (1a) plunder; gather honey (*bee*).
butoir [by'twaːr] m catch, stop; buffer.
butte [byt] f hillock; *en* ~ *à* exposed to; ~**er** [by'te] (1a) earth up.
buvable [by'vabl] drinkable; sl. acceptable, ~**ard** [~'vaːr] m blotting-paper; ~**ette** [~'vɛt] f refreshment bar; ~**eur** [~'vœːr] m drinker; toper; ~**ons** [~'vɔ̃] *1st p. pl. pres.* of *boire 1*; ~**oter** F [~vɔ'te] (1a) sip; tipple.

C

ça [sa] F *abbr.* of *cela; c'est* ~! that's right! *et avec* ~? anything else?
çà [~] **1.** *adv.* here; ~ *et là* here and there; **2.** *int.* (*ah*) ~! now then!
cabale [ka'bal] f cabal; faction.
caban|e [ka'ban] f hut; kennel; ~**on**

[~ba'nɔ̃] m small hut; padded cell.
cabaret [kaba'rɛ] m night club; † pub, bar.
cabas [ka'bɑ] m basket.
cabestan [kabɛs'tɑ̃] m winch.
cabillau(d) [kabi'jo] m fresh cod.

cabine [ka'bin] f cabin; booth; ~ **telephonique** telephone booth; **~t** [~bi'nɛ] m small room; office; practice; # a. consulting room; ## chambers pl.; ministry; ~ **de toilette** dressing room; ~ (**de travail**) study.

câbl|e [kɑ:bl] m cable (a. = cablegram); ~ **de remorque** hawser; **~er** [kɑ'ble] (1a) cable (a message); twist; **~ogramme** [~blɔ'gram] m cablegram.

caboche [ka'bɔʃ] f nail; F pate (= head).

caboss|e F [ka'bɔs] f bump; **~er** F [~bɔ'se] (1a) bump, bruise.

cabot|age ⚓ [kabɔ'ta:ʒ] m coastal navigation; **~er** [~'te] (1a) coast; **~in** [~'tɛ̃] m ham actor; show-off; **~inage** [~ti'na:ʒ] m thea. hamming; fig. showing-off; playacting.

cabrer [ka'bre] (1a) ✈ elevate; **se** ~ rear; **se** ~ **contre** rebel against.

cabri zo. [ka'bri] m kid; **~ole** [kabri'ɔl] f caper, leap; **~oler** [~ɔ'le] (1a) caper; **~olet** [~ɔ'lɛ] m cab(riolet).

cacahouète [kaka'wɛt] f peanut.

cacao [kaka'o] m ♣ cacao; ♣ cocoa.

cacarder [kakar'de] (1a) cackle.

cacatoès [kakatɔ'ɛs] m cockatoo.

cachalot [kaʃa'lo] m sperm whale.

cache [kaʃ] su./f hiding place; **~-cache** [~'kaʃ] m hide-and-seek; **~-col** [~'kɔl] m/inv. scarf; **~-nez** [~'ne] m/inv. muffler.

cach|er [ka'ʃe] (1a) hide, conceal; **esprit** m **caché** sly person; **~e-sexe** [kaʃ'seks] m/inv. G-string; **~et** [ka'ʃɛ] m seal; stamp; mark; F fee; ✗ cachet; **courir le** ~ give private lessons; **~eter** [kaʃ'te] (1c) seal; **~ette** [ka'ʃɛt] f hiding place; **en** ~ secretly; **~ot** [~'ʃo] m prison; **~otterie** [~'tri] f mysterious ways pl.; **faire des** ~**s** act secretively.

caco... [kako] caco...; **~phonique** [~fɔ'nik] cacophonous, discordant.

cadastre [ka'dastr] m cadastre.

cadav|éreux [kadave'rø] deathlike; **~érique** [~'rik] cadaveric; **rigidité** f ~ rigor mortis; **~re** [ka'dɑ:vr] m dead body.

cadeau [ka'do] m present, gift.

cadenas [kad'na] m padlock; clasp.

cadenc|e [ka'dɑ̃:s] f cadence (a. ♪); rhythm; fig. rate; **à la** ~ **de** at the rate of; **en** ~ in time; rhythmically; **~é** [~dɑ̃'se] rhythmic(al).

cadet [ka'dɛ] **1.** adj. younger; **2.** su. (the) younger; **il est mon** ~ he is my junior (by 3 years, **de 3 ans**); su./m ✗ cadet; golf: caddie.

cadr|an [ka'drɑ̃] m dial; **~e** [kɑ:dr] m frame; fig. frame(work), context; fig. setting, surroundings pl.; fig. scope, limits pl.; **personnel** ~: executive, manager; **~er** [ka'dre] (1a) tally.

caduc, -que [ka'dyk] obsolete; ## null, lapsed; ♣ deciduous; **~ité** [~dysi'te] f ## nullity; ♣ caducity.

cafard [ka'fa:r] m zo. cockroach; F sneak; F **le** ~ the blues; **~er** F [~far'de] (1a) sneak (on); be feeling low.

café [ka'fe] m coffee; café; ~ **complet** continental breakfast; ~ **crème** white coffee; ~ **nature** black coffee; **~-concert**, pl. **~s-concerts** [~fekɔ̃'sɛ:r] m café with a cabaret show.

cafetier, -ère [kaf'tje, ~'tjɛ:r] su. café-owner; su./f coffee-pot.

cafouill|age F [kafu'ja:ʒ] m muddle; **~er** F [~'je] (1a) muddle things up, get into a muddle (person); not to work properly (machinery etc.).

cage [ka:ʒ] f cage; casing; lift: shaft; ~ **de l'escalier** stairwell.

cagn|eux [ka'nø] knock-kneed; **~otte** [~'nɔt] f pool, kitty.

cagot [ka'go] sanctimonious.

cahier [ka'je] m paper book; exercise book; notebook.

cahin-caha F [kaɛka'a] adv. so-so.

cahot [ka'o] m jolt; **~er** [kaɔ'te] (1a) jolt; **~eux** [~'tø] bumpy.

cahute [ka'yt] f hut; cabin; hovel.

caïd F [ka'id] m (big) boss, big chief.

caille orn. [kɑ:j] f quail.

caillebotis [kɑjbɔ'ti] m grating.

caill|ebotte [kaj'bɔt] f curds pl.; **~er** [ka'je] curdle, clot; sl. be cold; **~ot** [ka'jo] m clot.

caillou, pl. **-x** [ka'ju] m pebble; **~tage** [kaju'ta:ʒ] m rough-cast; gravel; pebble paving; **~ter** [~'te] (1a) ballast (a road); pave with pebbles; **~teux** [~'tø] stony; shingly; **~tis** [~'ti] m gravel; road metal.

caiss|e [kɛs] f case, box; ✝ cash-box; (pay-)desk; thea. pay-box; ✝ fund; ⚙ body; **~enregistreuse** cash-register; **argent** m **en** ~ cash in hand; **faire la** ~ balance the cash; **grosse** ~ instrument:

bass drum; **tenir la ~** be in charge of the cash; **~ier** m, **-ère** f [kɛˈsje, ~ˈsjɛːr] cashier; **~on** [~ˈsɔ̃] m ☉, ✗ caisson.

cajol|er [kaʒɔˈle] (1a) coax, wheedle; **~erie** [~ʒɔlˈri] f wheedling; **~eur** [~ʒɔˈlœːr] **1.** *adj.* wheedling; **2.** *su.* wheedler.

cal, *pl.* **cals** [kal] m callosity.

calamit|é [kalamiˈte] f disaster; **~eux** [~ˈtø] calamitous.

calandr|e [kaˈlɑ̃ːdr] f mangle; roller; *mot.* radiator grill; **~er** [~lɑ̃ˈdre] (1a) mangle; calender.

calcaire [kalˈkɛːr] **1.** *adj.* calcareous; chalky; **2.** *su./m* limestone.

calciner [kalsiˈne] (1a) char; burn (to cinders *or* ashes).

calcul [kalˈkyl] m calculation; ♣ calculus; ♣ arithmetic; ✼ calculus, stone; **~ateur** [kalkylaˈtœːr] **1.** *adj.* scheming; **2.** *su.* calculator; reckoner; **~atrice** [~ˈtris] f *machine:* calculator; **~er** [~ˈle] (1a) reckon, calculate; **~ de tête** work (*s.th.*) out in one's head; **~ette** [~ˈlɛt] f pocket or desk calculator.

cale¹ ♣ [kal] f hold; quay: slope, slip; **~ sèche** drydock.

cale² [kal] f wedge; prop.

calé F [kaˈle] clever, smart, bright; tough, difficult; **~ en** well up in, clever at.

calebasse [kalˈbɑːs] f gourd.

calèche [kaˈlɛʃ] f barouche, calash.

caleçon [kalˈsɔ̃] m (pair of) underpants *pl.;* **~ long** long johns *pl.;* **~ de bain** bathing trunks *pl.*

calembour [kalɑ̃ˈbuːr] m pun.

calembredaines [kalɑ̃brəˈdɛn] f/pl. nonsense *sg.*, balderdash *sg.*

calendrier [kalɑ̃ˈdrje] m calendar.

calepin [kalˈpɛ̃] m notebook.

caler [~] (1a) *v/t.* prop up; wedge; *mot.* stall; F **se les ~** have a good feed; *v/i.* *mot.* stall; F give up.

calfater [kalfaˈte] (1a) ca(u)lk.

calfeutrer [kalføˈtre] (1a) stop up.

calibr|e [kaˈlibr] m ✗ calibre (a. fig.); ☉ bore; grade, size; ☉ ga(u)ge; **~er** [~liˈbre] (1a) grade (*fruits, eggs, etc.*); ☉ ga(u)ge.

calice [kaˈlis] m chalice; calyx.

califourchon [kalifurˈʃɔ̃] *adv.:* **à ~** a-stride.

câlin [kɑˈlɛ̃] caressing; **~er** [~liˈne] (1a) wheedle; caress; pet.

calleux [kaˈlø] horny, callous.

callosité [kalɔziˈte] f callosity.

calmant [kalˈmɑ̃] **1.** *adj.* ✼ tranquillizing, sedative; *a. fig.* soothing; **2.** *su./m* ✼ tranquillizer, sedative; painkiller.

calme [kalm] **1.** *su./m* calm(ness); quietness; *fig.* peace; **~ plat** ♣ dead calm (*a. fig.*); **2.** *adj.* calm; quiet; **~r** [kalˈme] (1a) calm (down); quiet(en) down; soothe; **se ~** calm down.

calomni|ateur [kalɔmnjaˈtœːr] **1.** *adj.* slanderous; **2.** *su.* slanderer; **~e** [~ˈni] f calumny, slander; **~er** [~ˈnje] (1o) slander.

calori|e *phys.* [kalɔˈri] f caloric; **~fère** [kalɔriˈfɛːr] m stove; heating; **~fique** *phys.* [~ˈfik] heating; **~fuge** [~ˈfyːʒ] (heat-)insulating.

calot [kaˈlo] m (*child's*) marble; forage cap; **~te** [~ˈlɔt] f (skull)cap; dome; F slap, box on the ears; *fig.* clergy; **~ter** F [~ˈlɔte] (1a) cuff.

calque [kalk] m tracing; copy; **~r** [kalˈke] (1m) trace (from, **sur**); copy; *fig.* model (on, **sur**); **papier** m **à ~** tracing paper.

calvaire [kalˈvɛːr] m *eccl.* calvary; *fig.* martyrdom.

calvinis|me [kalviˈnism] m Calvinism; **~te** Calvinist.

calvitie [kalviˈsi] f baldness.

camarade [kamaˈrad] *su.* mate, friend, companion, *a. pol.* comrade; **~rie** [~raˈdri] f comradeship.

camard, e [kaˈmaːr, ~ˈmard] **1.** *adj.* snub-nosed; **2.** *su.:* **la ~e** Death.

cambr|é [kɑ̃ˈbre] arched; with high insteps *or* arches (*feet*); **~er** [~ˈbre] (1a) bend; arch; **se ~** throw out one's chest; arch one's back.

cambriol|age [kɑ̃briɔˈlaːʒ] m house breaking; burglary; **~er** [~ˈle] (1a) burgle; **~eur** [~ˈlœːr] m housebreaker; burglar.

cambrure [kɑ̃ˈbryːr] f curve; arch; *feet,* *shoes:* instep.

cambuse [kɑ̃ˈbyːz] f ♣ hovel; *sl.* hole, dump; ♣ storeroom.

cam|e *sl.* [kam] f drug; *sl.* junk; **~é** *sl.* [kaˈme] drug-addicted (person); *su.* *sl.* a. junkie.

caméléon *zo.* [kameleˈɔ̃] m chameleon.

camelot [kamˈlo] m street hawker; **~e** [~ˈlɔt] f junk, trash, rubbish.

caméra [kame'ra] *f* cine-camera, *Am.* movie camera.

camion [ka'mjɔ̃] *m* lorry, *Am.* truck; **~-citerne,** *pl.* **~s-citernes** [~mjɔ̃si'tɛrn] *m lorry:* tanker, *Am.* tank truck; **~-grue,** *pl.* **~s-grues** [~mjɔ̃'gry] *m* breakdown lorry, *Am.* wrecker; **~ner** [kamjɔ'ne] (1a) cart; truck; **~nette** [~'nɛt] *f* small lorry, *Am.* light truck; **~neur** [~'nœːr] *m* lorry (*Am.* truck) driver; haul(i)er.

camisole [kami'sɔl] *f woman:* dressing jacket; **~ de force** strait jacket.

camomille ♀ [kamɔ'miːj] *f* camomile.

camoufl|age [kamu'flaːʒ] *m* disguising; camouflage; **~er** [~'fle] (1a) disguise; **~et** [~'flɛ] *m* snub.

camp [kɑ̃] *m* camp; party; *fig.* side; **~ de vacances** holiday camp; F **ficher** (*or sl.* **fouter**) **le ~** clear out; **~agnard** [kɑ̃pa'naːr] **1.** *adj.* rustic; **2.** *su./m* countryman; **~agne** [~'paɲ] *f* countryside; campaign; **à la ~** in the country; **~agnol** [~pa'ɲɔl] *m* vole.

campan|ile [kɑ̃pa'nil] *m* belltower; **~ule** [~'nyl] *f* bellflower.

camp|ement ✕ [kɑ̃p'mɑ̃] *m* encampment; camp (party); **~er** [kɑ̃'pe] (1a) *v/i.* camp; *v/t.* F place; *fig.* arrange; **se ~ devant** plant o.s. in front of *etc.*; **~eur** [~'œːr] *m* camper; **~ing** [~'piŋ] *m* camping; (*a.* **terrain** *m* **de ~**) camping site; **faire du ~** go camping.

camus [ka'my] snub-nosed.

canadien, -enne [kana'djɛ̃, ~'djɛn] **1.** *adj.* Canadian; **2.** *su.* ♀ Canadian; *su./f* sheepskin jacket; canoe.

canaille F [ka'naːj] **1.** *adj.* low, base; **2.** *su./f* bastard; rascal; † rabble.

canal [ka'nal] *m* canal; channel; *fig. par le ~ de* through, via; **~isation** [~naliza'sjɔ̃] *f* canalization; ☉ mains *pl.*; **~iser** [~nali'ze] (1a) canalize; *fig.* channel.

canapé [kana'pe] *m* couch, sofa; *cuis.* fried slice of bread.

canard [ka'naːr] *m* duck; F false news; *pej.* newspaper, rag; F brandy-soaked lump of sugar; ♪ wrong note; **~er** [~'de] (1a) snipe at.

canari *orn.* [kana'ri] *m* canary.

canasson *sl.* [kana'sɔ̃] *m* horse; nag.

cancan¹ [kɑ̃'kɑ̃] *m* dance: cancan.

cancan² [kɑ̃'kɑ̃] *m* gossip; **~er** [kɑ̃ka'ne] (1a) gossip.

cancer ♐ [kɑ̃'sɛːr] *m* cancer; **~éreux** [kɑ̃se'rø] cancerous; **~érigène** [~ri'ʒɛn] carcinogenous; **~re** [kɑ̃:kr] *m* crab; F dunce.

candeur [kɑ̃'dœːr] *f* artlessness.

candi [kɑ̃'di] **1.** *adj./m* candied; **2.** *su./m:* **~s** *pl.* crystallized fruit.

candidat *m, e f* [kɑ̃di'da, ~'dat] candidate; **~ure** [~da'tyːr] *f* candidature; **poser sa ~ à** apply for.

candide [kɑ̃'did] artless, ingenuous.

can|e [kan] *f* (female) duck; **~er** *sl.* [ka'ne] (1a) chicken out, funk it; **~eton** [kan'tɔ̃] *m* duckling.

canette [~] *f* can; bottle; spool.

canevas [kan'va] *m* canvas; outline.

caniche *zo.* [ka'niʃ] *m* poodle.

canicul|aire [kaniky'lɛːr] scorching (*heat, day, etc.*); **~e** [~'kyl] *f* dog days *pl.*; scorching heat.

canif [ka'nif] *m* penknife.

canin [ka'nɛ̃] **1.** *adj.* canine; **dent** *f* **~e =** **2.** *su./f* canine (tooth).

caniveau [kani'vo] *m* gutter; ⚡ main.

canne [kan] *f* cane; reed; **~ à pêche** fishing rod; **~ier** △ [~'le] (1c) flute.

cannelle ♀ [ka'nɛl] *f* cinnamon.

cannelle² [~] *f* tap; spout; spigot.

cannelure △ [kan'lyːr] *f* fluting.

canon¹ [ka'nɔ̃] *m* ✕ gun; *rifle etc.:* barrel; *sl.* glass of wine.

canon² [ka'nɔ̃] *m, eccl.,* ♪ canon; *fig.* model, standard; **~ique** [~'nik] canonical; **âge** *m* **~** respectable age; **~iser** [~ni'ze] (1a) canonize.

canonn|ade [kanɔ'nad] *f* cannonade; **~ier** [~'nje] *m* gunner; **~ière** [~'njɛːr] *f* gunboat; pop-gun.

canot [ka'no] *m* boat; **~ automobile** motorboat; **~ de sauvetage** lifeboat; **~ pliable** folding boat; **~ pneumatique** rubber dinghy; **~age** [kanɔ'taːʒ] *m* boating; **~er** [~'te] (1a) go boating; **~ier** [~'tje] *m* boatman; *cost.* boater.

cantatrice [kɑ̃ta'tris] *f* (professional) singer, vocalist.

cantine [kɑ̃'tin] *f* canteen; equipment case.

cantique *eccl.* [kɑ̃'tik] *m* hymn.

canton [kɑ̃'tɔ̃] *m* canton, district.

cantonade *thea.* [kɑ̃tɔ'nad] *f* wings *pl.*; **à la ~** off-stage.

cantonn|er ✕ [kɑ̃tɔ'ne] (1a) billet; station; *fig.* confine; **~ier** [~'nje] *m* roadman.

canular [kany'la:r] *m* hoax.

canule [ka'nyl] *f ⚕* cannula; *sl.* bore.

caoutchouc [kau'tʃu] *m* rubber; rubber *or* elastic band; **~ mousse** foam rubber.

cap [kap] *m geog.* cape, headland; *♨* course; **de pied en ~** from head to foot; **mettre le ~ sur** head for.

capable [ka'pabl] capable, able.

capacité [kapasi'te] *f* capacity.

cape [kap] *f* cape, cloak; hood; **rire sous ~** laugh up one's sleeve.

capharnaüm [kafarna'om] *m* shambles *sg.*

capillaire [kapil'lɛ:r] capillary.

capilotade [kapilo'tad] *f cuis.* hash; *fig.* **en ~** smashed (to pieces); crushed (to a pulp).

capitaine [kapi'tɛn] *m* captain.

capital, e [kapi'tal] **1.** *adj.* capital; essential; deadly (*sin*); **peine f ~e** death penalty; **2.** *su./m ♱* capital; **~ d'exploitation** working capital; **~ et intérêt** principal and interest; *su./f geog.* capital; *typ.* capital (letter); **~iser** [~tali'ze] (1a) *v/t.* accumulate, amass; *v/i.* save; **~isme** [~ta'lism] *m* capitalism.

capiteux [kapi'tø] heady (*wine*).

capitonner [kapito'ne] (1a) pad; upholster.

capitul|ation [kapityla'sjɔ̃] *f* surrender; **~er** [~'le] (1a) surrender.

capon † [ka'pɔ̃] *m* coward.

caporal [kapo'ral] *m* corporal; *F tobacco:* shag; **~isme** [~ra'lism] *m* narrow militarism.

capot [ka'po] *m mot.* bonnet, *Am.* hood; companion hatch; **~age** [~po'ta:ʒ] *m* overturning; **~e** [~'pot] *f* greatcoat; *mot.* hood, *Am.* convertible top; **~er** [~po'te] (1a) capsize, overturn; *fig.* fail, founder.

câpre ♣ [kɑ:pr] *f* caper.

capric|e [ka'pris] *m* whim; impulse; **~ieux** [~pri'sjø] whimsical.

capsul|e [kap'syl] *f* capsule; *bottle:* cap; *✗* primer; **~er** [~sy'le] (1a) cap (*a bottle*).

capt|er [kap'te] (1a) win, gain; capture; *☉* harness (*a source*); catch (*water*); *radio:* pick up; *teleph.* tap; **~ieux** [~'sjø] fallacious, specious.

capt|if [kap'tif] captive; **~iver** [~ti've] (1a) captivate; fascinate; **~ivité** [~tivi'te] *f* captivity.

captur|e [kap'ty:r] *f* capture; catch; **~er** [~ty're] (1a) capture.

capuchon [kapy'ʃɔ̃] *m* hood; cowl; *pen:* cap.

caquet [ka'kɛ] *m*, **~age** [kak'ta:ʒ] *m* cackling; F gossip, yackety-yak; **rabattre le caquet à** (*or* **de**) *q.* make s.o. sing small; **~er** [~'te] (1c) cackle; F gossip, yackety-yak.

car¹ [ka:r] *m* car; bus.

car² [~] *cj.* for, because.

carabin|e [kara'bin] *f* rifle; carbine; **~é** [~bi'ne] sharp, violent; F **a whopper of...**

caracoler [karako'le] (1a) prance.

caract|ère [karak'tɛ:r] *m* character; nature; feature, characteristic; letter; **~érisé** [~teri'ze] clear(cut), downright; **~ériser** [~teri'ze] (1a) characterize; **se ~ par** be distinguished by; **~éristique** [~teris'tik] **1.** *adj.* characteristic (of, de); **2.** *su./f* characteristic.

caraf|e [ka'raf] *f* decanter; carafe; **rester en ~** be left stranded; **~on** [~ra'fɔ̃] *m* small decanter *or* carafe.

caramb|olage [karãbo'la:ʒ] *m billiards:* cannon, *Am.* carom; collision, crash; **~oler** [~bo'le] (1a) *v/i. billiards:* cannon, *Am.* carom; *v/t.* crash *or* bump into, hit; **se ~** collide.

carapater *sl.* [karapa'te] (1a): **se ~** decamp, scram

caravane [kara'van] *f* caravan (*a. mot.*); (house) trailer; F conducted party.

carbon|ate *♨* [karbo'nat] *m* carbonate; **~e** *♨* [~'bon] *m* carbon; *(a.* **papier m ~)** carbon paper; **~iser** [~boni'ze] (1a) carbonize; burn; char.

carbur|ant [karby'rɑ̃] *m* motor fuel; **~ateur** *mot.* [~byra'tœ:r] *m* carburet(t)or; **~e** *♨* [~'by:r] *m* carbide.

carcan [kar'kɑ̃] *m hist.* iron collar; *fig.* yoke, restraint.

carcasse [kar'kas] *f* carcass; frame.

carcinome *♱* [karsi'nom] *m* carcinoma.

cardan *☉* [kar'dɑ̃] *m* universal joint; **arbre m à ~** cardan shaft.

carder [kar'de] (1a) card, comb.

cardiaque *♱* [kar'djak] cardiac; **crise f ~** heart attack.

cardinal [kardi'nal] *adj., su./m* cardinal.

carême [kɑ'rɛm] *m* Lent; *comme mars en ~* without fail, inevitably.

carence [kɑ'rɑ̃ːs] *f* incompetence, inadequacy; deficiency; lack; *maladie f par ~* deficiency disease.

carène [kɑ'rɛn] *f* hull; **caréner** [~re'ne] (1f) ⚓ careen; streamline.

caress|e [kɑ'rɛs] *f* caress; **~er** [~rɛ'se] (1a) caress; stroke; *fig.* cherish.

cargaison ⚓ [kɑrgɛ'zɔ̃] *f* cargo; freight; **cargo** [~'go] *m* cargo boat.

caricature [karika'tyːr] *f* caricature; cartoon.

carie [kɑ'ri] *f* 𝑭 caries; *trees:* blight; 𝑭 *(a. ~ dentaire)* tooth decay; **carier** [~'rje] (1o): *se ~* decay.

carillon [kari'jɔ̃] *m* carillon, chime; **~ner** [~jɔ'ne] (1a) chime; sound.

carlin [kar'lɛ̃] *m* pug.

carlingue ✈ [kar'lɛ̃ːg] *f* cabin.

carmin [kar'mɛ̃] carmine.

carna|ge [kar'naːʒ] *m* slaughter; **~ssier**, **~ssière** [karna'sje, ~'sjɛːr] **1.** *adj.* carnivorous; **2.** *su./f* game bag; *su./m* carnivore; **~tion** [~'sjɔ̃] *f* flesh tint.

carnaval, *pl.* **-als** [karna'val] *m* carnival; King Carnival.

carne *sl.* [karn] *f* tough meat.

carnet [kar'nɛ] *m* notebook; *(cheque-, ticket-, etc.)* book; **~ de bal** card; **✝ ~ de commande** order book.

carnivore [karni'voːr] **1.** *adj.* carnivorous; **2.** *su./m* 𝑭 carnivore.

carott|e [kɑ'rɔt] *f* ♀, 🗡 carrot; *tobacco:* plug; *sl.* trick, swindle; **~er** F [~rɔ'te] (1a) steal, F pinch; cheat, F do.

carpe¹ *anat.* [karp] *m* carpus.

carpe² *icht.* [~] *f* carp.

carpette [kar'pɛt] *f* rug.

carquois [kar'kwa] *m* quiver.

carr|é, e [kɑ're] **1.** *adj.* square; plain, blunt; **2.** *su./m* square; 🗡 patch; *staircase:* landing; *cuis.* loin; *su./f sl.* digs *pl.*; **~eau** [~'ro] *m* small square; tile; floor; *(window)* pane; *cards:* diamonds *sg.*; *à ~x* checked; *se garder (or tenir) à ~* take every precaution; **~efour** [kar'fur] *m* crossroads *pl.*; square *(in town)*; **~elage** [kar'laːʒ] *m* tiling; **~eler** [~'le] (1c) tile; square.

carrément [kare'mɑ̃] *adv.* bluntly; straight (out); **carrer** [kɑ're] (1a) square; *se ~ dans* ensconce o.s. in.

carrier [kɑ'rje] *m* quarryman.

carrière¹ [kɑ'rjɛːr] *f* quarry.

carrière² [~] *f* career; course.

carriole [kɑ'rjɔl] *f* light cart.

carrossable [kɑrɔ'sabl] passable *(for vehicles)*; **carrosse** [~'rɔs] *m* ✝ coach; *fig.* **rouler ~** live in style; **carrosserie** *mot.* [~rɔs'ri] *f* body.

cartable [kar'tabl] *m* satchel; schoolbag.

carte [kart] *f* card; *restaurant:* menu; map; ticket; *~ blanche* a free hand; 🗡 *~ d'accès au bord* boarding pass; *~ d'identité* identity card; *mot. ~ grise* car licence; *~ perforée* punch(ed) card; *~ postale* postcard; *mot. ~ verte* insurance document, *Br.* green card; *jouer ~s sur table* be above-board.

cartel ✝, *pol.* [kar'tɛl] *m* cartel.

carte-lettre, *pl.* **cartes-lettres** [kartə'lɛtr] *f* letter-card.

carter ⚙ [kar'tɛːr] *m* casing; case; chain guard.

cartilage|e [karti'laːʒ] *m* cartilage, gristle; **~ineux** [~laʒi'nø] cartilaginous, gristly; 🦴 hard.

carto|graphe [kartɔ'graf] *m* map-maker; **~graphie** [~gra'fi] *f* mapping.

carto|n [kar'tɔ̃] *m* cardboard (box); *art:* cartoon; *phot.* mount; *... en ~ a.* paper... *(cup etc.)*; *~ bitumé* roofing felt; *fig.* **homme m de ~** man of straw; **~nner** [~tɔ'ne] (1a) bind in boards; **~nné** hardback *(book)*; **~thèque** [kartɔ'tɛk] *f* card index.

cartouche [kar'tuʃ] *m* cartridge; *pen:* refill; *cigarettes:* carton.

cas [kɑ] *m* case *(a. 𝑭 disease, patient; a. gramm.)*; circumstance; affair; *en ~ de ...* in case of ...; *au ~ où (cond.)*, *en ~ que (sbj.)* in case ... should *(inf.)*; *dans tous les ~*, *en tout ~* in any case; *en aucun ~* in no circumstances; *dans ce ~* if so; *faire grand ~ de* think highly of *(s.th.)*; *faire peu de ~ de* set little value on.

casanier [kaza'nje] *m* stay-at-home.

casaque [ka'zak] *f* coat, jacket.

cascad|e [kas'kad] *f* waterfall, cascade; **~eur** [~ka'dœːr] *m* stuntman; acrobat.

case [kɑːz] *f* hut; compartment; *~ postale* Post Office box.

caser [kɑ'ze] (1a) F put; marry off; find a job for; put *(s.o.)* up; *se ~* settle down.

caserne ✕ [ka'zɛrn] *f* barracks *pl.*; **~er** ✕ [~zɛr'ne] (1a) barrack.

casier [ka'zje] *m* compartment; locker; pigeonhole; filing cabinet; rack; ⚖ ~ **judiciaire** police record; ⚖ ~ **vierge** clean record.

casqu|e [kask] *m* helmet; ~**s** *pl.* **d'écoute** earphones; ~**er** F [~'ke] (1m) fork out (= *pay*); ~**ette** [~'kɛt] *f* cap.

cassa|ble [ka'sabl] breakable; ~**nt** [~'sɑ̃] brittle; crisp; curt, short; ~**tion** [~sa'sjɔ̃] *f* ⚖ quashing; ✕ reduction to the ranks; ⚖ **cour** *f* **de** ~ Supreme Court of Appeal.

casse [kɑːs] *f* breakage; F row.

casse... : ~**-cou** [kas'ku] *m/inv.* daredevil; *adj./inv.* risky, dangerous; ~**croûte** [~'krut] *m/inv.* snack; ~**noisettes** [~nwa'zɛt] *m/inv.*, ~**noix** [~'nwa] *m/inv.* nutcrackers *pl.*; ~**pieds** F [~'pje] *m/inv.* bore, F pain in the neck; ~**pipe(s)** F [~'pip] *m/inv.* war.

casser [ka'se] (1a) *v/t.* break; crack; ✕ reduce to the ranks; ⚖ quash; F ~ **sa pipe** kick the bucket; *v/i.* **se** ~ break.

casserole [kas'rɔl] *f* saucepan.

casse-tête [kas'tɛt] *m/inv.* club, truncheon; *fig* puzzle; noise, din.

cassette [ka'sɛt] *f* casket; cassette.

casseur [ka'sœːr] *m* breaker; *cars:* scrap dealer; *fig.* ~ **de vitres** troublemaker.

cassis[1] [ka'sis] *m* ♣ black currant; *sl.* nut (= *head*).

cassis[2] [ka'si] *m* road: bump.

cassure [ka'syːr] *f* break, fragment.

caste [kast] *f* caste; class.

castor *zo.*, ♦ [kas'tɔːr] *m* beaver.

casuel [ka'zɥɛl] **1.** *adj.* accidental, casual; **2.** *su./m* perquisites *pl.*

casuistique [kazɥis'tik] *f* casuistry.

cata|clysme [kata'klism] *m* disaster; ~**logue** [~'lɔg] *m* catalog(ue); **faire le** ~ **de** run over the list of; ~**loguer** [~lɔ'ge] (1m) list; ~**lyseur** [~li'zœːr] *m* catalyst; ~**phote** [~'fɔt] *m road:* cat's eye, *mot.* reflector; ~**racte** [~'rakt] *f* cataract.

catarrhe ♣ [ka'taːr] *m* catarrh.

catastroph|e [katas'trɔf] *f* disaster; ~**ique** [~trɔ'fik] catastrophic.

catch [katʃ] *m* catch-as-catch-can.

catéchiser [kateʃi'ze] (1a) *eccl.* catechize; *fig.* coach; lecture.

catégor|ie [katego'ri] *f* category; ~**ser** [~ri'ze] (1a) classify.

cathédrale [kate'dral] *f* cathedral.

cathode ⚡ [ka'tɔd] *f* cathode.

catholique [katɔ'lik] *adj., su.* Catholic; F **pas** ~ suspicious, fishy.

catimini F [katimi'ni] *adv.:* **en** ~ stealthily; on the sly.

catin F [ka'tɛ̃] *f* prostitute.

cauchemar [koʃ'maːr] *m* nightmare.

causal [ko'zal] causal, causative.

cause [koːz] *f* cause; reason; ⚖ case; **à** ~ **de** on account of; **en** ~ involved; **mettre en** ~ question (*s.th.*); **pour** ~ for a good reason.

causer[1] [ko'ze] (1a) cause.

caus|er[2] [~] (1a) chat, talk; ~**erie** [koz'ri] *f* chat, talk; ~**eur, -euse** [~'zœːr, ~'zøːz] **1.** *adj.* chatty; **2.** *su.* talker; *su./f* settee for two.

causti|cité [kostisi'te] *f* ♣, *fig.* causticity; ~**que** [~'tik] caustic.

cauteleux [kot'lø] cunning, wary.

cautère [ko'tɛːr] *m* cautery; **cautériser** [~teri'ze] (1a) cauterize.

caution [ko'sjɔ̃] *f* security, guarantee; bail; **se porter** ~ go bail; **sujet à** ~ unreliable; ~**nement** [~sjɔn'mɑ̃] *m* surety; ~**ner** [~sjɔ'ne] (1a) stand surety for (*s.o.*); *fig.* support.

caval|cade [kaval'kad] *f* cavalcade; procession; ~**er** *sl.* [~va'le] (1a) *v/i.* run; *v/t.* pester; ~**erie** [~val'ri] *f* cavalry; ~**ier, -ère** [~va'lje, ~'ljɛːr] **1.** *su.* rider; *su./m dancing:* partner; *chess:* knight; **2.** *adj.* haughty; jaunty.

cav|e [kaːv] **1.** *su./f* cellar; vault; **2.** *adj.* hollow; ~**eau** [ka'vo] *m* cellar; burial vault; ~**erne** [~'vɛrn] *f* cave; den; cavity; ~**erneux** [~vɛr'nø] cavernous; hollow (*voice*); ~**ité** [~vi'te] *f* cavity, hollow.

ce[1] [s(ə)] *dem./pron./n* it; this; that; these, those; **ce qui** (or **que**) what, which; **c'est pourquoi** therefore; **c'est moi** it is I, F it's me.

ce[2] (*before vowel or h mute* **cet**) *m*, **cette** *f*, **ces** *pl.* [sə, set, se] *dem./adj.* this, that, *pl.* these, those; **ce ...-ci** this; **ce ...-là** that.

céans [se'ɑ̃] *adv.* here(in).

ceci [sə'si] *dem./pron./n* this.

cécité [sesi'te] *f* blindness.

céder [se'de] (1f) give up (to, **à**); ~ **qch. à q.** *a.* let s.o. have s.th.; **le** ~ **à q.** be second to s.o. (in, **en**); *v/i.* give in, give way (to, **à**).

cédille *gramm.* [se'di:j] *f* cedilla.

cèdre [sɛ:dr] *m tree or wood:* cedar.

cégétiste [seʒe'tist] *m* trade-unionist (=*member of the C.G.T.*).

ceindre [sɛ̃:dr] (4m) (*de*, with) gird; bind; surround; wreathe.

ceintur|e [sɛ̃'ty:r] *f* belt; girdle; waist; circle; ~ **de sauvetage** lifebelt; ~ **de sécurité** seat *or* safety belt; **~er** [sɛ̃ty're] (1a) seize (*s.o.*) round the waist; *fig.* surround, encircle (with, *de*).

cela [s(ə)la] *dem./pron./n* that; ~ **fait** thereupon; **comment ~?** how?

célébration [selebra'sjɔ̃] *f* celebration; **célèbre** [~'lɛbr] famous; **célébrer** [sele'bre] (1f) celebrate.

celer [sə'le] (1d) conceal; hide.

célérité [seleri'te] *f* speed, rapidity.

céleste [se'lɛst] heavenly, celestial.

célibat [seli'ba] *m* celibacy; **~aire** [~ba'tɛ:r] **1.** *adj.* unmarried; **2.** *su./m* bachelor; *su./f* bachelor girl; unmarried woman.

celle [sɛl] *f see* **celui.**

cellier [sɛ'lje] *m* storeroom.

cellul|aire [sely'lɛ:r] cellular; *régime m* ~ solitary confinement; **~e** [~'lyl] *f* cell; ~ **photo-électrique** exposure meter; **~eux** [sely'lø] cell(at)ed; **~oïde** [~lo'id] *m* celluloid; **~ose** [~'lo:z] *f* cellulose.

celui *m*, **celle** *f*, **ceux** *m/pl.*, **celles** *f/pl.* [sə'lɥi, sɛl, sø, sɛl] *dem./pron.* he (*acc.* him); she (*acc.* her); the one, that; *pl.* they (*acc.* them); those; **~-ci** *etc.* [səlɥi'si *etc.*] the latter; this one; **~-là** *etc.* [səlɥi'la *etc.*] the former; that one.

cendr|e [sɑ̃:dr] *f* ash; *mercredi m des* ~*s* Ash Wednesday; **~é, e** [sɑ̃'dre] **1.** *adj.* ashy; **2.** *su./f sp.* cinders *pl.*; **~eux** [~'drø] ashy; gritty; **~ier** [~dri'e] *m* ashtray; **♀illon** [sɑ̃dri'jɔ̃] *f* Cinderella.

Cène [sɛn] *the* Last Supper.

cens|é [sɑ̃'se]: *être ~ faire qch.* be supposed to do s.th.; **~ément** [~se'mɑ̃] *adv.* supposedly; **~eur** [~'sœ:r] *m* censor; **~ure** [~'sy:r] *f* censorship; **~urer** [~sy're] (1a) censure; censor.

cent [sɑ̃] hundred; *cinq pour ~* five per cent; *trois ~ dix* three hundred and ten; *trois ~s ans* three hundred years; **~aine** [sɑ̃'tɛn] *f* (about) a hundred; **~enaire** [sɑ̃t'nɛːr] **1.** *adj.* a hundred

years old; venerable; **2.** *su./m* centenary; centenarian.

centi... [sɑ̃ti] centi...; **~ème** [~'tjɛm] hundredth; **~grade** [~ti'grad] centigrade; **~me** [~'tim] *m* ¹/₁₀₀ *of a franc*; **~mètre** [~ti'mɛtr] *m measure:* (*approx.*) ²/₅ inch; tape-measure.

centr|al, e [sɑ̃'tral] **1.** *adj.* central; **2.** *su./m* telephone exchange; *su./f* (~ *électrique etc.*) power station (*Am.* plant); **~aliser** [~trali'ze] (1a) centralize; **~e** [sɑ̃:tr] *m* centre, *Am.* center; middle; **~er** [sɑ̃'tre] (1a) centre, *Am.* center; adjust; **~ifuge** [sɑ̃tri'fy:ʒ] centrifugal.

centuple [sɑ̃'typl] *m* hundredfold.

cep ✎ [sep] *m* vinestock; vine.

cèpe ♀ [sɛp] *m* flap mushroom.

cependant [səpɑ̃'dɑ̃] *cj.* however, nevertheless, yet.

cérami|que [sera'mik] **1.** *adj.* ceramic; **2.** *su./f* ceramics *pl.*, pottery; **~ste** [~'mist] *su.* potter.

cerceau [sɛr'so] *m* hoop.

cercl|e [sɛrkl] *m* circle; ring (*a.* ⊙); *barrel:* hoop; dial; group; sphere; *faire ~* (*autour de*) gather (round); **~er** [sɛr'kle] (1a) encircle; ring; hoop.

cercueil [sɛr'kœːj] *m* coffin.

céréale ♀ [sere'al] *adj.*, *su./f* cereal.

cérébral [sere'bral] cerebral, brain...; *fatigue f* ~**e** brain-fag.

cérémoni|al, e *pl.* **-als** [seremɔ'njal] *m* ceremonial; **~e** [~'ni] *f* ceremony; formality; *sans ~* informal(ly *adv.*); **~eux** [~'njø] formal.

cerf *zo.* [sɛːr] *m* stag, hart; **~-volant**, *pl.* **~s-volants** [sɛrvɔ'lɑ̃] *m* kite.

ceris|e [sə'riːz] *f* cherry; **~ier** [səri'zje] *m* cherry tree.

cern|e [sɛrn] *m* ring (*round wound etc.*); **~er** [~'ne] (1a) encircle; surround; *fig.* delimit, define; shell (*nuts*); *avoir les yeux cernés* have rings under one's eyes.

cert|ain [sɛr'tɛ̃] certain, sure; positive, definite; (*before noun*) one; some; **~es** [sɛrt] *adv.* indeed; **~ificat** [sɛrtifi'ka] *m* certificate; testimonial; ~ **de bonne vie et mœurs** certificate of good character; **~ification** [~fika'sjɔ̃] *f* certification; witnessing; **~ifier** [~'fje] (1o) certify, witness (*a signature*); **~itude** [~'tyd] *f* certainty.

cérumen [sery'mɛn] *m* ear-wax.

cerveau [sɛr'vo] *m* brain; *fig.* mind; *fuite f de ~x* brain drain; **cervelle** [~'vɛl] *f* brains *pl.*; *brûler la ~ à q.* blow s.o.'s brains out; *se creuser la ~* rack one's brains.

ces [se] *pl.* of **ce²**.

césarienne ⚕ [seza'rjɛn] *adj./f: opération f ~* Caesarean (operation).

cess|ation [sesa'sjɔ̃] *f* cessation; suspension; stoppage; *~e* [sɛs] *f: n'avoir pas de ~ que* not to rest until; *sans~* constantely; continuously; *~er* [sɛ'se] (1a) stop, end, cease; *~ez-le-feu* [ˌsela'fø] *m/inv.* ceasefire; *~ion* [~'sjɔ̃] *f* transfer.

c'est-à-dire [sɛta'diːr] *cj.* that is to say, i.e.; in other words.

césure [se'zyːr] *f* caesura.

cet *m*, **cette** *f* [sɛt] *see* **ce²**.

ceux [sø] *m/pl. see* **celui**.

chacal, *pl.* **-als** *zo.* [ʃa'kal] *m* jackal.

chacun [ʃa'kœ̃] *pron./indef.* each (one); everybody.

chafouin [ʃa'fwɛ̃] *adj.* sly(-looking).

chagrin¹ [ʃa'grɛ̃] **1.** *su./m* grief; sorrow; trouble; annoyance; **2.** *adj.* sorry; sad; troubled (at, *de*).

chagrin² [~] *m* shagreen.

chagriner [ʃagri'ne] (1a) grieve, distress; annoy; *se ~* fret.

chahut ⊢ [ʃa'y] *m* row, rag; *~er* ⊢ [~y'te] (1a) *v/i.* kick up a row; *sl.* boo; *v/t.* rag (*s.o.*); **boo** (*s.o.*).

chai [ʃɛ] *m* wine and spirit store.

chaîn|e [ʃɛn] *f* chain; link(s *pl.*); train (*of ideas*); *tex.* warp; *mountains*: range; *travail m à la ~* assembly line work; *~er* [ʃɛ'ne] (1b) chain; *~ette* [~'nɛt] *f* small chain; *~on* [~'nɔ̃] *m* link.

chair [ʃɛːr] *f* flesh; meat; pulp.

chaire [~] *f eccl.*, *a. univ.* chair; pulpit; rostrum, tribune.

chaise [ʃɛːz] *f* chair; *~ longue* couch.

chaland [ʃa'lɑ̃] *m* lighter, barge.

châle [ʃɑːl] *m* shawl.

chalet [ʃa'lɛ] *m* chalet; cottage.

chaleur [ʃa'lœːr] *f* heat (*a. of animals*), warmth; ardo(u)r; zeal; *~eux* [~lœ'rø] warm; ardent; hearty.

châlit [ʃa'li] *m* bedstead.

chaloupe ⚓ [ʃa'lup] *f* launch.

chalumeau [ʃaly'mo] *m* drinking straw; ♩, ⚙ pipe; ⚙ blowlamp.

chalut [ʃa'ly] *m* trawl; drag-net; *~ier* ⚓ [~ly'tje] *m* trawler.

chamailler F [ʃama'je] (1a): *se ~* squabble (with, *avec*).

chamarr|er [ʃama're] (1a) adorn; *~ure* [~'ryːr] *f* (*tawdry*) decoration.

chambard F [ʃɑ̃'bar] *m*, *~ement* [~bardə'mɑ̃] *m* upheaval; *~er* F [~bar'de] (1a) upset (*a. fig.*).

chambranle ⌂ [ʃɑ̃'brɑ̃:l] *m* frame.

chambr|e [ʃɑ̃:br] *f* (bed) room; chamber (*a. pol.*, ♈, ⚙); *mot.* *~ à air* inner tube; *~ à un lit* single room; ♌ *des députés* Chamber of Deputies; *phot.* *~ noire* dark room; *~ sur la cour (rue)* back (front) room; *musique f de ~* chamber music; *~ée* [ʃɑ̃'bre] *f* roomful; *~er* [~'bre] (1a) lock up; bring (*wine*) to room temperature.

chameau [ʃa'mo] *m zo.* camel; 🚂 shunting engine; *~lier* [~mə'lje] *m* camel-driver.

chamois [ʃa'mwa] *m* chamois.

champ [ʃɑ̃] *m* field (*a. fig.*); ground; space; range; *~ d'activité* scope of activity; *sp.* *~ de courses* racetrack; *à tout bout de ~* at every end and turn; *à travers ~s* across country; *sur-le-~* on the spot.

champ|agne [ʃɑ̃'paɲ] *su./m* champagne; *su./f: fine ~* liqueur brandy; *~enois* [ʃɑ̃pə'nwa] of Champagne.

champêtre [ʃɑ̃'pɛːtr] rural, rustic.

champignon [ʃɑ̃pi'nɔ̃] *m* 🍄 mushroom; F *mot.* accelerator pedal.

champion *m*, **-onne** *f* [ʃɑ̃'pjɔ̃, ~'pjɔn] *sp.*, *fig.* champion; *~nat* [~pjɔ'na] *m* championship.

chançard [ʃɑ̃'saːr] *m* lucky (person).

chance [ʃɑ̃:s] *f* luck; chance; *avoir de la ~* be lucky; *avoir la ~ de* (*inf.*) be lucky enough to (*inf.*); *c'est une ~ que* it's lucky that; *bonne ~!* good luck!; *pas de ~!* hard luck!

chanceler [ʃɑ̃s'le] (1c) reel, stagger, totter; falter.

chancelier [ʃɑ̃sə'lje] *m* chancellor.

chanceux [ʃɑ̃'sø] lucky, fortunate.

chancir [ʃɑ̃'siːr] (2a) go mo(u)ldy.

chandail [ʃɑ̃'daːj] *m* sweater.

Chandel|eur [ʃɑ̃d'lœːr] *f: la ~* Candlemas; *2ier* [~ʃɑ̃də'lje] *m* candlestick; *2le* [~'dɛl] *f* candle; *tennis:* lob; ⚙ prop; *à la ~* by candlelight; *devoir une fière ~ à* *q.* owe s.o. a debt of gratitude; *en voir trente-six ~s* see stars.

chanfrein [ʃɑ̃'frɛ̃] *m* bevelled edge.

chang|e [ʃɑ̃:ʒ] *m* ✝ exchange; *hunt.* wrong scent; *donner le ~ à q.* sidetrack s.o.; *~eable* [ʃɑ̃'ʒabl] changeable; exchangeable; *~eant* [~'ʒɑ̃] changeable, variable; *~ement* [ʃɑ̃ʒ'mɑ̃] *m* change; *mot. ~ de vitesse* gear-change, *Am.* gearshift; *~er* [ʃɑ̃'ʒe] (1l) *v/t.* change; exchange (for, *contre*); alter; *se ~* change (one's clothes); *se ~ en* change *or* turn into; *v/i.* change, alter (s.th., *de qch.*); *~ de train* change (trains); *~eur* [~'ʒœ:r] *m* changer.

chanoine *eccl.* [ʃa'nwan] *m* canon.

chanson [ʃɑ̃'sɔ̃] *f* song; *~ner* [ʃɑ̃so'ne] (1a) lampoon; *~nier, -ère* [~'nje, ~'njɛ:r] *su.* singer; *su./m* song book.

chant [ʃɑ̃] *m* singing; song; chant; canto; *au ~ du coq* at cock-crow.

chantage [ʃɑ̃'ta:ʒ] *m* blackmail.

chant|epleure [ʃɑ̃tə'plœːr] *f* colander; funnel; tap; spout; *~er* [ʃɑ̃'te] (1a) *v/t.* sing; celebrate; *~ victoire sur* crow over; *v/i.* sing; crow (*cock*); *faire ~ q.* blackmail s.o.; F *si ça vous chante* if it suits you.

chanteur *m*, **-euse** *f* [ʃɑ̃'tœːr, ~'tøːz] singer; F *maître m ~* blackmailer.

chantier [ʃɑ̃'tje] *m* building site; (*timber-, work- etc.*) yard; *traffic sign:* roadworks; *sur le ~* in hand.

chantonner [ʃɑ̃to'ne] (1a) hum.

chanvre [ʃɑ̃:vr] *m* hemp; cannabis.

chaos [ka'o] *m* chaos, confusion.

chaparder F [ʃapar'de] (1a) filch.

chape [ʃap] *f eccl.* cope; cover(ing); *mot.* tread.

chapeau [ʃa'po] *m* hat; *chimney:* cowl; ⊙ cap; *~!* hats off!, well done!; *~ haut de forme* top hat; *~ melon* bowler.

chapelain [ʃap'lɛ̃] *m* chaplain.

chapel|et [ʃa'plɛ] *m* rosary; *onions:* string; *fig.* string, series; *~ier* [~ʃpə'lje] *m* hatter.

chapelle [ʃa'pɛl] *f* chapel; *~ ardente* chapel of rest.

chapellerie [ʃapɛl'ri] *f* hat-shop.

chaperon [ʃa'prɔ̃] *m* hood; △ coping; chaperon; *~ner* [~prɔ'ne] (1a) hood; chaperon; cope (*a wall*).

chapiteau [ʃapi'to] *m* △ capital; ⊙ *etc.* cap; *circus:* big top.

chapitr|e [ʃa'pitr] *m* chapter; subject; *~er* [~pi'tre] (1a) lecture.

chapon [ʃa'pɔ̃] *m* capon.

chaque [ʃak] *adj.* each, every.

char [ʃar] *m* wag(g)on; cart; ✗ tank; *~ funèbre* hearse.

charabia [ʃara'bja] *m* gibberish.

charbon [ʃar'bɔ̃] *m* coal; *~ de bois* charcoal; *fig. sur des ~ ardentes* on tenterhooks; *~nage* [~bɔ'na:ʒ] *m* coal mine; *~ner* [~bɔ'ne] (1a) char; *cuis.* burn; *~nerie* [~bɔn'ri] *f* coal depot; *~nier* [~bɔ'nje] **1.** *adj.* coal-...; **2.** *su./m* coalman; charcoal burner; *~ est maître chez lui* a man's home is his castle.

charcut|er [ʃarky'te] (1a) cut (*meat*); ✗ F butcher (*a patient*); *~erie* [~'tri] *f* pork-butcher's shop *or* meat; *~ier* [~'tje] *m* pork-butcher.

chardon [ʃar'dɔ̃] *m* thistle.

charg|e [ʃarʒ] *f* load, burden; loading; ⊙, ⚡, ♪, ✗ charge; cost; office; responsibility; exaggeration; *~ payante* pay load; *à ~ de revanche* on condition of reciprocity; *être à la ~ de* be dependent on *or* depending upon; *femme f de ~* housekeeper; *~é* [ʃar'ʒe] **1.** *adj.* loaded, laden (with, *de*); full (of, *de*); heavy (with, *de*); full, busy (*day, schedule*); ♪ coated, furry (*tongue*); overladen (*a. fig.*); *~ de* in charge of; **2.** *su./m:* *univ. ~ de cours* lecturer; *~ement* [~ʒə'mɑ̃] *m* load; lading; cargo; charging; *~er* [~'ʒe] (1l) (*de*, with) load, burden; charge (*a.* ✗, ♪, ⚡); put in charge (of, *de*); *thea.* overact; *~ q. de coups* drub s.o.; *se ~* become overcast (*sky*); fur (*tongue*); *se ~ de* take care of, charge of; *se ~ de* (*inf.*) undertake to (*inf.*).

chariot [ʃa'rjo] *m* wag(g)on; cart; *typewriter:* carriage.

charit|able [ʃari'tabl] charitable (to, *envers*); *~é* [~'te] *f* charity; alms *sg.*

charivari [ʃariva'ri] *m* din, noise.

charlatan [ʃarla'tɑ̃] *m* charlatan; quack; *~isme* [~ta'nism] *m* charlatanism.

charm|ant [ʃar'mɑ̃] charming; *~e* [ʃarm] *m* charm; spell; *~er* [ʃar'me] (1a) charm; delight; *~eur* [~'mœːr] **1.** *adj.* charming; **2.** *su.* charmer.

charmille [ʃar'mij] *f* arbo(u)r.

charnel [ʃar'nɛl] carnal; sensual.

charnière [ʃar'njɛːr] *f* hinge.

charnu [ʃar'ny] fleshy.

charogne [ʃa'rɔɲ] f carrion.

charpent|e [ʃar'pɑ̃:t] f framework; **~er** [ʃarpɑ̃'te] (1a) frame; shape; cut; **~erie** [~'tri] f carpentry; timber-yard; **~ier** [~'tje] m carpenter.

charpie ♂ [ʃar'pi] f lint.

char|retée [ʃar'te] f cartload; F *fig.* **une ~ de** loads of; **~retier** [~'tje] m carter; **~rette** [ʃa'rɛt] f cart; **~ à bras** handcart, pushcart, barrow; **~riage** [~'rja:ʒ] m cartage; **~rier** [~'rje] (1o) cart, carry; *sl.* kid; **~ron** [~'rɔ̃] m cartwright.

charrue [ʃa'ry] f plough, *Am.* plow; *fig.* **mettre la ~ devant les bœufs** put the cart before the horse.

charte [ʃart] f charter; *la Grande* ♀ Magna C(h)arta.

charter [ʃar'tɛ:r] m charter flight.

chas [ʃa] m needle: eye.

chasse [ʃas] f hunt(ing); game, bag; shooting season; hunting ground; *wheels:* play; ☉ flush.

châsse [ʃɑ:s] f shrine; frame.

chasse...: ~-mouches [ʃas'muʃ] m/inv. fly swatter; **~-neige** [~'nɛ:ʒ] m/inv. snow-plough, *Am.* snowplow; *ski:* stem.

chass|er [ʃa'se] (1a) hunt, pursue; drive away; drive (*a nail*); v/i. (*usu.* **~ à courre**) go hunting (s.th., **à qch.**); drive; skid; **~eur** [ʃa'sœːr] m hunter; *hotel:* page boy, *Am.* bell-hop; ✈ fighter.

chassieux [ʃa'sjø] bleary-eyed.

châssis [ʃɑ'si] m frame (*a. mot.*, 🚗); *mot.* chassis; window-sash; ✈ undercarriage; ⚘ hotbed.

chaste [ʃast] chaste, pure; **~té** [~ə'te] f chastity, purity.

chat *zo.* [ʃa] m (tom-)cat.

châtai|gne [ʃa'tɛɲ] f chestnut; **~gnier** [ʃatɛ'ɲe] m chestnut-tree; **~n** [ʃa'tɛ̃] *adj., su./m* chestnut, brown.

château [ʃa'to] m castle; *fig.* **~ de cartes** house of cards; *fig.* **~x** *pl.* **en Espagne** castles in the air.

chateaubriand, châteaubriant *cuis.* [ʃatobri'ã] m grilled steak.

châtelain [ʃat'lɛ̃] m castellan; lord (*of the manor*).

châtier [ʃɑ'tje] (1o) punish, chastise; *fig.* refine (*one's style*).

chatière [ʃa'tjɛːr] f cat-hole; ventilation hole; secret entrance.

châtiment [ʃati'mɑ̃] m punishment.

chatoiement [ʃatwa'mɑ̃] m sheen.

chaton¹ [ʃa'tɔ̃] m jewel: setting.

chaton² [~] m *zo.* kitten; ⚘ catkin.

chatouill|ement [ʃatuj'mɑ̃] m tickling; **~er** [ʃatu'je] (1a) tickle; F thrash; **~eux** [~'jø] ticklish; sensitive; delicate (*question*).

chatoyer [ʃatwa'je] (1h) shimmer.

châtrer [ʃa'tre] (1a) castrate, geld.

chatte [ʃat] f (she-)cat; **~mite** F [~'mit] f toady; **~rie** [ʃa'tri] f wheedling.

chatterton ⚡ [ʃatɛr'tɔn] m insulating or adhesive tape.

chaud [ʃo] **1.** *adj.* warm; hot; *fig.* keen, ardent; bitter (*tears*); **avoir ~** be or feel warm or hot, **il fait ~** it is warm or hot; **2.** *adv.* warm *etc.*; **3.** *su./m* heat; warmth, tenth (*qch.*); **au ~** keep warm; **~froid**, *pl.* **~s-froids** [ʃo'frwa] m: *cuis.* **~ de ...** cold jellied...; **~ière** [ʃo'djɛːr] f boiler; **~ron** [~'drɔ̃] m ca(u)ldron.

chauff|age [ʃo'faːʒ] m heating; **~ au pétrole** oil heating; **~ central** central heating; **~ard** F [~'faːr] m road hog; **~e** [ʃoːf] f heating.

chauffe...: ~-bain [ʃof'bɛ̃] m geyser, **~-eau** [ʃo'fo] m/inv. water-heater; **~-plats** [ʃof'pla] m/inv. dish-warmer.

chauff|er [ʃo'fe] (1a) v/t. heat; warm (up), heat (up); *sl.* pinch; v/i. get warm or hot; ☉ overheat; **~ au pétrole** use oil for heating; F **ça va ~** sparks will fly; **~erette** [~'frɛt] f footwarmer; dish-warmer; **~eur, -euse** [~'fœːr, ~'føːz] *su. mot.* driver; *su./m* ♣ stoker; *su.* coach (*for examination*); *su./f* fireside chair.

chauss|ée [ʃo'se] f road; causeway; **~e-pied** [ʃos'pje] m shoehorn; **~er** [ʃo'se] (1a) v/t. put on (*shoes etc.*); put shoes on (*s.o.*); fit (*shoe*); **~ large** be wide-fitting (*shoe*); **~ du 40** take size 40 (in shoes); **se ~** put on (one's) shoes; **~e-trape** [ʃos'trap] f trap; trick; **~ette** [ʃo'sɛt] f sock; **~on** [~'sɔ̃] m slipper; ballet shoe; gym shoe; **~ure** [~'syːr] f shoe, boot.

chauve [ʃoːv] bald (person); **~-souris**, *pl.* **~s-souris** *zo.* [ʃovsu'ri] f bat.

chauvin [ʃo'vɛ̃] *adj., su./m* chauvinist; **~isme** [~vi'nism] m jingoism.

chaux [ʃo] f lime; ~ *éteinte* slaked lime; *blanchir à la* ~ whitewash.

chavirer ⚓ [ʃavi'reː] (1a) capsize.

chef [ʃɛf] m head, principal; chieftain; master; leader; *cuis.* chef; ♪ conductor; *fig.* heading; ⚙ ~ *d'atelier* shop foreman; ~ *de bande* ringleader; *sp.* ~ *d'équipe* captain; ~ *d'État* chief of State; 🚂 ~ *de train* guard, *Am.* conductor; *au premier* ~ in the first place; *de mon* ~ on my own authority; ... *en* ~ ... in chief; ~*d'œuvre*, *pl.* ~*s-d'œuvre* [ʃɛ'dœːvr] m masterpiece; ~*lieu*, *pl.* ~*s-lieux* [ʃɛf'ljø] m chief town.

chemin [ʃə'mɛ̃] m way; road; path; ~ *de fer* railway, *Am.* railroad; ~ *faisant* on the way; *faire son* ~ make one's way; ~*eau* [ʃəmi'no] m tramp; ~*ée* [~'ne] f chimney; ⚓ funnel; fireplace; mantelpiece; ~*er* [~'ne] (1a) tramp, plod on; ~*ot* [~'no] m railwayman.

chemis|e [ʃə'miːz] f shirt; chemise; wrapper; folder; *boiler etc.*: jacket; ~*erie* [~miz'ri] f haberdashery; ~*ette* *cost.* [ʃəmi'zɛt] f jumper; chemisette (*of women*); ~*ier*, -*ère* [~'zje, ~'zjɛːr] *su.* shirtmaker; *su./f* shirt-blouse.

chenal [ʃə'nal] m channel, fairway.

chêne 🌳 [ʃɛːn] m oak.

chéneau [ʃe'no] m gutter.

chenil [ʃə'ni] m dog kennel.

chenille [ʃə'niːj] f caterpillar (*a.* ⚙).

chenu [ʃə'ny] hoary (*hair*); snowy.

cheptel [ʃɛp'tɛl] m (live-)stock.

chèque [ʃɛk] m cheque, *Am.* check; ~ *barré* crossed cheque; ~ *de voyage* traveller's cheque; ~ *sans provision* cheque without cover; **chéquier** [ʃe'kje] m cheque book.

cher, chère [ʃɛːr] **1.** *adj.* dear, beloved; expensive; *moins* ~ cheaper; *peu* ~ cheap; **2.** *su./m: mon* ~ my dear friend; *su./f: ma chère* my dear; **3.** *cher adv.*: *coûter* ~ be expensive; *vendre* ~ sell dear.

cherch|er [ʃɛr'ʃe] (1a) look for; seek; ~ *à* (*inf.*) try to, seek to (*inf.*); *aller* ~ (*a* go and) get *or* fetch; go for; *envoyer* ~ send for; *venir* ~ call for; come for; fetch; ~*eur* [~'ʃœːr] m seeker; researcher; finder.

chère [ʃɛːr] f: (*la*) *bonne* ~ good food.

chér|i m, e f [ʃe'ri] darling; ~*ir* [~'riːr]

(2a) cherish; ~*ot* F [~'ro] F (too) expensive.

cherté [ʃɛr'te] f dearness; high price(s *pl.*).

chétif [ʃe'tif] puny, wretched.

cheval [ʃə'val] m horse; *mot.* horsepower; *sp.* ~ *de bois* vaulting horse; ~ *de course* race-horse; *à* ~ on horseback; *aller à* ~ ride on horseback; *être à* ~ *sur* straddle, be *or* sit astride (*s.th.*); *fig.* be a stickler for; ~*er* [~va'le] (1a) shore up; ~*eresque* [ʃəval'rɛsk] chivalrous; ~*erie* [~'ri] f knighthood; chivalrousness; ~*et* [ʃəva'lɛ] m trestle; *violin etc.*: bridge; ⚙ rest; easel; sawhorse; ~*ier* [~'lje] m knight; *fig.* ~ *d'industrie* swindler; ~*ière* [~'ljɛːr] f signet-ring; ~*in* [~'lɛ̃] equine; ~*vapeur*, *pl.* *chevaux-vapeur* [ʃəvalva'pœːr, ~vova'pœːr] m horsepower.

chevauch|é [ʃəvo'ʃe] ride; ~*er* [~] (1a) ride; be *or* sit astride, straddle (*s.th.*); (*a. se* ~) overlap (each other).

chevelu [ʃə'vly] long-haired; ~*re* [~'vlyːr] f hair; *comet*: tail.

chevet [ʃə'vɛ] m bedhead; *au* ~ *de q.* at *s.o.*'s bedside; *lampe f de* ~ bedside lamp; *livre m de* ~ favo(u)rite reading.

cheveu, *pl.* ~*x* [ʃə'vø] m hair *sg.*; *avoir mal aux* ~*x* have a hang over; *couper les* ~*x en quatre* split hairs; F *se prendre aux* ~*x* have a real set-to; *tiré par les* ~*x* far-fetched.

chevill|e [ʃə'viːj] f peg (*a. violin*); pin; bolt; *anat.* ankle; ~*er* [~'vi:je] (1a) peg.

chèvre [ʃɛːvr] f zo. goat; ⚙ trestle.

chevr|eau zo. [ʃə'vro] m kid; ~*ette* [ʃə'vrɛt] f zo. kid; roe-doe; ~*euil* [~'vrœːj] m roebuck; ~*on* [~'vrɔ̃] m ⚒ rafter; ✗ stripe; ~*onné* [~vrɔ'ne] *fig.* experienced; ~*oter* [ʃəvrɔ'te] (1a) tremble (*voice*); bleat (*goat*).

chez [ʃe] *prp. direction:* to; *place:* at (*s.o.'s house*); with (*my aunt*); in (*a. fig.*); *post:* care of; *fig.* among (*the English*); ~ *Zola* in Zola; ~ *soi* at home; *être* (*aller*) ~ *soi* be at (go) home; *faire comme* ~ *soi* make o.s. at home; *de q.* from *s.o.*'s (house); *de* ~ *soi* from home; ~*moi* (*etc.*) [~'mwa] m/*inv.*: *mon* ~ my home.

chiasse [ʃjas] f *fly etc.*: dirt; *sl. avoir la* ~ have the runs; be in a blue funk.

chic [ʃik] **1.** *su./m* chic, style; **2.** *adj.*

smart, stylish; first-rate, F classy, posh; F decent.

chican|e [ʃi'kan] f quibbling; chicanery; **~er** [ʃika'ne] (1a) v/i. quibble, cavil; v/t. wrangle with (*s.o.*); haggle over (*s.th.*); **~eur** [~'nœːr] argumentative.

chiche [ʃiʃ] scanty; niggardly, mean.

chichis F [ʃi'ʃi] m/pl. frills (a. fig.).

chicorée ⚕ [ʃiko're] f chicory.

chicot [ʃi'ko] m tooth; tree: stump.

chien [ʃjɛ̃] m dog; gun: hammer; **~ d'aveugle** guide dog; **~ méchant!** beware of the dog!; **entre ~ et loup** in the twilight.

chier V [ʃje] (1o) shit.

chiffe [ʃif] f rag; fig. (a. **~ molle**) spineless individual.

chiffon [ʃi'fɔ̃] m rag; scrap; F **parler ~s** talk dress; fig. annoy; **~ner** [ʃifɔ'ne] (1a) crumple, crease; fig. annoy; **~nier** [~'nje] m rag-picker; dresser.

chiffr|e [ʃifr] m figure, number, numeral; code; amount; mark; monogram; **~ d'affaires** turnover; **~er** [ʃi'fre] (1a) v/i. calculate; reach a high figure; v/t. number, express in figures; write in code, encode.

chignon [ʃi'ɲɔ̃] m coil of hair.

chimère [ʃi'mɛːr] f chimera; **chimérique** [~me'rik] illusory.

chimi|e [ʃi'mi] f chemistry; **~que** [~'mik] chemical; **~ste** [~'mist] su. chemist (*not pharmacist*).

chiner F [ʃi'ne] (1a) kid, rag.

chinois, e [ʃi'nwa, ~'nwaːz] 1. adj., su./m ling. Chinese; fig. **c'est du ~** that's all double-dutch or Greek (to me); 2. su./m ♀ Chinaman; **les ♀** m/pl. the Chinese; su./f ♀**e** Chinese woman; **~erie** [~nwaz'ri] f Chinese curio; F trick; **~s** pl. **administratives** red tape sg.

chiper sl. [ʃi'pe] (1a) pinch.

chipoter F [ʃipo'te] (1a) nibble at one's food; quibble; haggle.

chique [ʃik] f tobacco: quid.

chiqué sl. [ʃi'ke] m fake, pretence.

chiquenaude [ʃik'noːd] f flick; flip.

chiquer [ʃi'ke] (1m) chew (*tobacco*).

chiromancie [kiromɑ̃'si] f palmistry.

chirurgi|cal [ʃiryrʒi'kal] surgical; **~e** [~'ʒi] f surgery; **~en** [~'ʒjɛ̃] m surgeon.

chlor|ate [klɔ'rat] m chlorate; **~e** [klɔːr] m chlorine; **~hydrique** [klɔri'drik] adj.: **acide** m **~** hydrochloric acid.

choc [ʃɔk] m shock; impact; clash.

chocolat [ʃoko'la] m chocolate.

chœur [kœːr] m choir; chorus.

choir [ʃwaːr] (3d) fall.

choi|sir [ʃwa'ziːr] choice, select; **~sir** [~'ziːr] (2a) choose, pick, select (from **entre**, **parmi**); **~x** [ʃwa] m choice; option; selection; **au ~** as you wish; **de ~** choice; **de premier ~** best quality...

chôm|age [ʃo'maːʒ] m unemployment; stoppage; **en ~** out of work; **~er** [~'me] (1a) take a day off; be idle; be unemployed; **jour m chômé** day off; holiday; **~eur** [~'mœːr] m unemployed worker; **les ~s** the unemployed.

chope [ʃɔp] f beer mug, stein.

choper F [ʃo'pe] (1a) steal, F pinch; catch; arrest, F nab.

chopin|e [ʃo'pin] f half-litre mug; **~er** [~pi'ne] (1a) booze.

choqu|ant, e [ʃo'kɑ̃] shocking; gross; **~er** [~'ke] (1m) shock; bump against; clink (*glasses*); **se ~** collide (with, **contre**); take offence (at, **de**).

choral, e [kɔ'ral] 1. adj. choral; 2. su./m chorale; su./f choral society.

chorus [kɔ'rys] m chorus, **faire ~** chorus one's agreement.

chose [ʃoːz] 1. su./f thing; matter; **autre ~** something else; **peu de ~** very little; **quelque ~** something; **quelque ~ de bon** something good; 2. adj./inv. F: **tout ~** queer, out-of-sorts.

chou, -x [ʃu] m cabbage; **~x pl. de Bruxelles** Brussels sprouts; **~ frisé** kale, **être bête comme ~** be simplicity itself; **mon ~!** darling!

choucas orn. [ʃu'ka] m jackdaw.

chouchou, -oute f [ʃu'ʃu, ~'ʃut] darling, pet; **~ter** [~ʃu'te] (1a) pamper, pet.

choucroute [ʃu'krut] f sauerkraut.

chouette [ʃwɛt] 1. su./f orn. owl; 2. F adj. fine, splendid.

chou...: ~-fleur, pl. **~x-fleurs** [ʃu'flœːr] m cauliflower.

choyer [ʃwa'je] (1h) pamper.

chrétien [kre'tjɛ̃] adj., su. Christian; **~té** [~tjɛ̃'te] f Christendom.

Christ [krist] m Christ; ♀ crucifix.

christianis|er [kristjani'ze] (1a) christianize; **~me** [~'nism] m Christianity.

chrome [kroːm] m chromium; chrome.

chromo... [krɔmo] chromo..., colo(u)r-...

chroniqu|e [krɔ'nik] **1.** adj. chronic; **2.** su./f chronicle; news sg.; **~eur** m, **-euse** f [~ni'kœːr, ~'kø:z] chronicler; reporter.

chrono... [krɔnɔ] chrono...; **~logie** [~lɔ'ʒi] f chronology; **~logique** [~lɔ'ʒik] chronological; **~mètre** [~'mɛtr] m chronometer; sp. **~ à déclic** stopwatch; **~métrer** sp. [~me'tre] (1f) time; **~métreur** sp. [~me'trœːr] m timekeeper.

chrysalide zo. [kriza'lid] f pupa.

chuchote|ment [ʃyʃɔt'mɑ̃] m whisper(ing); **~r** [~'te] (1a) whisper.

chut! [ʃyt] int. ssh!; hush!

chute [~] f fall; overthrow, ruin; drop; **~ d'eau** waterfall; **~ des reins** small of the back.

chuter¹ [ʃy'te] (1a) hush; hiss.

chuter² [~] (1a) fall; decrease; thea. (be a) flop.

ci [si] **1.** adv. here; **cet homme-~** this man; **2.** dem./pron. see **ceci**; **comme ~ comme ça** so so.

cible [sibl] f target (a. fig.); ✝ etc. target group.

ciboulette ♣ [sibu'lɛt] f chive.

cicatri|ce [sika'tris] f scar; **~ser** [~tri'ze] (1a): **se ~** heal (up), scar over.

ci...: **~contre** [si'kɔ̃tr] adv. opposite; **~dessous** [~'dsu] adv. below; **~dessus** [~'dsy] adv. above(-mentioned); **~devant** [~'dvɑ̃] adv. formerly.

cidre [sidr] m cider.

ciel [sjɛl] **1.** su./m (pl. **cieux** [sjø]) sky, heaven; clime.

cierge [sjɛrʒ] m candle, taper.

cigale zo. [si'gal] f cicada.

cigare [si'gaːr] m cigar; **~tte** [~ga'rɛt] f cigarette.

cigogne [si'gɔɲ] f orn. stork; ⊙ crank brace.

ciguë ♣, ♣ [si'gy] f hemlock.

ci-inclus [siɛ̃'kly], **ci-joint** [~'ʒwɛ̃] letter etc.: enclosed.

cil [sil] m (eye)lash.

ciller [si'je] (1a) blink; wink.

cime [sim] f top, summit; peak.

ciment [si'mɑ̃] m cement; **~ armé** reinforced concrete; **~er** [simɑ̃'te] (1a) cement (a. fig.).

cimetière [sim'tjɛːr] m cemetery.

cinabre [si'naːbr] m cinnabar.

ciné F [si'ne] m films pl., Am. movies pl.; **~aste** [sine'ast] m cinematographer;

film producer; scenario writer; **~journal** [~ʒur'nal] m news-reel; **~ma** [~'ma] m cinema, Am. movie; **~matographique** [~'fik] film-...

ciné-roman [sinerɔ'mɑ̃] m film story.

cinétique phys. [sine'tik] **1.** adj. kinetic; **2.** su./f kinetics pl.

cingl|ant [sɛ̃'glɑ̃] lashing (rain); biting (cold); fig. scathing; **~é** F [~'gle] nuts (= mad); **~er** [~'gle] (1a) v/t. lash; ♣ v/i. steer a course.

cinoche F [si'nɔʃ] flicks pl., Am. movies pl.

cinq [sɛ̃:k; before consonant sɛ̃] five; date, title: fifth; **~uantaine** [sɛ̃kɑ̃'ten] f (about) fifty; **la ~** the age of fifty; **~uante** [~'kɑ̃:t] fifty; **~uantième** [~kɑ̃'tjɛm] fiftieth; **~uième** [~'kjɛm] **1.** adj./num., su. fifth; **2.** su./m fifth, Am. sixth floor.

cintr|e [sɛ̃:tr] m △ arch; coat or clothes hanger; thea. **~s** pl. flies; **~é** [sɛ̃'tre] arched; cost. waisted, slim-fitting; sl. nuts (= mad); **~er** [~] (1a) bend, curve; arch.

cirage [si'ra:ʒ] m waxing; polish.

circon... [sirkɔ̃] circum...; **~cire** [~'si:r] (4e) circumcise; **~cis** [~'si] p.p. of **circoncire**; **~férence** [~fe'rɑ̃:s] f circumference; **~flexe** gramm. [~'flɛks] m circumflex (accent); **~locution** [~lɔky'sjɔ̃] f circumlocution; **~scription** [~skrip-'sjɔ̃] f admin. district; **~ électorale** constituency; **~scrire** [~s'kri:r] (4e) circumscribe; limit; locate (a fault); **~spect, e** [~s'pɛ, ~s'pɛkt] circumspect; **~spection** [~spɛk'sjɔ̃] f circumspection; **~stance** [~s'tɑ̃:s] f circumstance; event; **de ~** occasional; improvised; **~stancié** [~stɑ̃'sje] detailed; **~stanciel** [~stɑ̃'sjɛl] due to circumstances; **~venir** [~v'ni:r] (2h) circumvent.

circuit [sir'kɥi] m circuit; roundabout way; ✝ **court ~** short-circuit.

circul|aire [sirky'lɛ:r] adj., su./f circular; **~ation** [~la'sjɔ̃] f circulation; (road etc.) traffic; **~ interdite** no thoroughfare; **~atoire** [~la'twa:r] circulatory; **~er** [~'le] (1a) circulate, flow; run; **circulez!** move along!

cire [si:r] f wax; taper; **~ d'abeille** beeswax; **~ à parquet** floor polish; **ciré** [si're] m oilskins pl.; **cirer** [~'re] (1a) wax; polish.

cirque [sirk] m circus.

cis|ailles [si'zɑːj] f/pl. shears; wire-cut *sg.*; **~ailler** [~zɑ'je] (1a) clip; cut; *fig.* cripple; **~eau** [~'zo] m chisel; **~eaux** m/pl. scissors; shears; **~eller** [siz'le] (1d) chisel; chase (*silver*); **~eleur** [~'lœːr] m chiseler; engraver; **~elure** [~'lyːr] f chiseling.

citad|elle [sita'dɛl] f citadel, stronghold; **~in, e** [~'dɛ̃, ~'din] su./m townsman; su./f townswoman.

oitation [sita'sjɔ̃] f quotation; ⚖ summons *sg.*; ⚖ subpoena.

cité [si'te] f city; housing estate; *Paris*: the Cité; **~ universitaire** students' residential blocks *pl.*; *fig.* **avoir droit de ~** be accepted.

citer [si'te] (1a) quote, cite; ⚖ summon; ⚖ subpoena (*a witness*).

citerne [si'tɛrn] f cistern, tank(-car).

citoyen m, **-enne** f [sitwa'jɛ̃, ~'jɛn] citizen.

citron [si'trɔ̃] m lemon; **~ pressé** lemon squash; **~nade** [sitrɔ'nad] f lemonade; **~nier** [~'nje] m lemon-tree.

citrouille 🌿 [si'truːj] f pumpkin.

civet *cuis.* [si've] m stew.

civière [si'vjɛːr] f stretcher.

civil [si'vil] **1.** su./m civilian; civil status or dress; **en ~** in civilian clothes; *dans le* **~** in civilian life; **2.** *adj.* civil; ✗ civilian; polite (to, towards **à**, **envers**); ⚖ **droit** m **~** common law; **état** m **~** civil status; register office; **~isateur** [siviliza'tœːr] **1.** *adj.* civilizing; **2.** *su.* civilizer; **~isation** [~za'sjɔ̃] f civilization; **~iser** [~'ze] (1a) civilize; **~ité** [~'te] f courtesy; **~ités** f/pl. compliments; **faire des ~ à** pay one's compliments to.

civique [si'vik] civic; civil (*rights*); **civisme** [~'vism] m good citizenship.

clabaud|age [klabo'daːʒ] m spiteful gossip; **~er** [~bo'de] (1a) talk scandal.

claie [klɛ] f grid; screen.

clair [klɛːr] **1.** *adj.* clear; bright; **2.** *adv.* clearly, plainly; thinly; **3.** *su./m* light; *garment*: thin place; **tirer au ~** decant (*wine*); *fig.* bring to light; **~et** [klɛ'rɛ] **1.** *adj.* pale, light; **2.** *su./m* red wine; **~e-voie**, *pl.* **~es-voies** [klɛr'vwa] f open-work; △ skylight; **~ière** [klɛ'rjɛːr] f clearing.

clairon ♪ [klɛ'rɔ̃] m bugle(r); **~ner** [~rɔ'ne] (1a) v/i. sound the bugle; v/t. *fig.* trumpet abroad.

clairsemé [klɛrsə'me] thinly-sown; sparse; thin (*hair, beard*).

clairvoyan|ce [klɛrvwa'jɑ̃ːs] f perceptiveness; clear-sightedness; **~t** [~'jɑ̃] perceptive; clear-sighted.

clamer [kla'me] (1a) cry (*s.th.*) out; **clameur** [~'mœːr] f clamo(u)r.

clan [klɑ̃] m clan; *fig.* clique.

clandestin [klɑ̃dɛs'tɛ̃] clandestine, secret; stealthy; **passager m ~** stowaway.

clapet [kla'pɛ] m valve.

clapier [kla'pje] m rabbit hutch; F *fig.* dump, hole.

clapot|ement [klapɔt'mɑ̃] m, **~is** [klapɔ'ti] m *waves*: lapping; **~er** [~'te] (1a) lap; ripple; **~eux** [~'tø] choppy (*sea*).

clapper [kla'pe] (1a) click.

claque [klak] su./f slap; *thea.* claque; *sl.* death; F *prendre ses cliques et ses* **~s** clear off; su./m opera-hat, crush-hat; **~dent** ⊢ [~'dɑ̃] m starveling; **~ment** [~'mɑ̃] m smack; slam; clapping; chattering.

claqué F [kla'ke] all in, dead beat.

claquemurer [klakmy're] (1a) immure; **se ~** shut o.s. up.

claqu|er [kla'ke] (1m) v/i. clap; crack (*whip*), slam (*door*); break; snap (*string etc.*); burn out (*lamp*); F kick the bucket (= *die*); F go bust; **~ des doigts** snap one's fingers; **~ des mains** clap; v/t. slap; bang; *thea.* applaud; F blue (*money*); F **se ~** tire o.s. out; **~eter** [klak'te] (1c) cackle (*hen*), clapper (*stork*); **~eur** *thea.* [~'kœːr] m hired clapper.

clarifier [klari'fje] (1o) clarify.

clarinette [klari'nɛt] f clarinet(tist).

clarté [klar'te] f clearness; brightness; gleam; *fig.* lucidity.

class|e [klɑːs] f class (*a. sociology*; *a.* 🐾 *etc.*); category; school: form, *Am.* grade; classroom; lessons *pl.*; **aller en ~** go to school; **faire la ~** teach; **~ement** [klɑs'mɑ̃] m classification; 📁 filing; grading; **~er** [klɑ'se] (1a) classify; 📁 file; grade; **~eur** [~'sœːr] m 📁 file; ⚙ sorter; filing cabinet; **~ification** [klɑsifika'sjɔ̃] f classification; **~ifier** [~'fje] (1o) classify.

classique [kla'sik] **1.** *adj.* classical (*music etc.*); classic; standard; **2.** *su./m* classic; classicist.

clause ⚖ [kloːz] f clause.

claustral [klos'tral] monastic.

clavecin ♪ [klav'sɛ̃] *m* harpsichord.

clavette ⊛ [kla'vɛt] *f* pin, key, peg.

clavicule [klavi'kyl] *f* collar-bone.

clavier ♪ *etc.* [kla'vje] *m* piano, *type-writer*: keyboard; *voice*: range.

clé, clef [kle] *f* key (*a. fig., a.* ♪); ⊛ spanner, wrench; **~ à molette** adjustable spanner; **~ anglaise** monkey wrench; △, *fig.* **de voûte** keystone; **fausse ~** skeleton key; **mettre sous ~** lock up.

clémen|ce [kle'mã:s] *f* clemency; leniency; mercy; **~t** [~'mã] lenient; merciful; mild (*disease etc.*).

clenche [klã:ʃ] *f* (door-)latch.

clerc [klɛ:r] *m* clergyman; ♛ clerk; *fig.* expert; **faire un pas de ~** blunder; **cler-gé** [klɛr'ʒe] *m* clergy *pl.*; **clérical** [kleri'kal] *adj.*, *su./m* clerical.

clich|é [kli'ʃe] *m typ.* plate; *illustration*: block; *phot.* negative; *fig.* cliché, stock phrase; **~er** [~'ʃe] (1a) stereotype.

client *m,* **e** *f* [kli'ã, ~'ã:t] client; *customer*; ♣ patient; *hotel*: guest; **~èle** [~ã'tɛl] *f* customers *pl.*; ♣ practice; **donner sa ~ à** patronize.

clign|er [kli'ɲe] wink; blink; **~otant** *mot.* [kliɲɔ'tã] *m* indicator; *fig.* warning light; blinker; **~oter** [~'te] (1a) blink; flicker; twinkle.

climat [kli'ma] *m* climate; region; *fig.* atmosphere; **~érique** [klimate'rik] **1.** *su./f* climacteric; **2.** *adj.* climacteric; *a.* = **~ique** [~'tik] climatic (*conditions*); **station f ~** health resort; **~isation** [~tiza'sjɔ̃] *f* air conditioning; **~iser** [~ti'ze] (1a) air-condition.

clin [klɛ̃] *m:* **~ d'œil** wink; **en un ~ d'œil** in the twinkling of an eye.

clini|cien ♣ [klini'sjɛ̃] *su./m, adj./m* clinician; **~que** ♣ [~'nik] **1.** *adj.* clinical; **2.** *su./f* clinic; hospital.

clinquant [klɛ̃'kã] *m* tinsel; *fig.* showiness; tawdriness.

clip [klip] *m* jewellery: clip.

clique F [klik] *f* set, clique; **~t** ⊛ [kli'kɛ] *m* catch; ratchet; **~ter** [klik'te] (1c) rattle; clink; jingle; *mot.* pink; **~tis** [~'ti] *m* rattle; clinking; jingling; *mot.* pinking.

cliv|age [kli'va:ʒ] *m* cleavage; gap, split; **~er** [~i've] (1a) split, cleave.

cloaque [klɔ'ak] *m* cesspool (*a. fig.*).

clochard F [klɔ'ʃa:r] *m* tramp.

cloche [klɔʃ] *f* bell; bell-jar; ✶ blister; dish-cover; *sl.* idiot; **~-pied** [~'pje] *adv.*: **sauter à ~** hop.

clocher¹ [klɔ'ʃe] *m* church tower; steeple; **de ~** parochial; **esprit m de ~** parochialism.

clocher² [~] (1a) F be *or* go wrong; limp, hobble.

clochette [klɔ'ʃɛt] *f* handbell; ❦ bellflower; **~ d'hiver** snowdrop.

cloison [klwa'zɔ̃] *f* partition; ⚓ bulkhead; *fig.* barrier; **~ner** [~zɔ'ne] (1a) partition; compartmentalize.

cloître [klwa:tr] *m* cloister; monastery; **~er** [klwa'tre] (1a) cloister.

clopin|-clopant F [klɔpɛ̃klɔ'pã] *adv.* hobbling; **~er** [~pi'ne] (1a) limp.

cloque ✶ [klɔk] *f* lump, swelling.

clore [klɔ:r] (4f) *vt/i.* enclose (*land*); **clos, close** [klo, klo:z] **1.** *p.p. of* **clore; 2.** *adj.* closed; shut in; finished; **3.** *su./m* enclosure; vineyard.

clôt [klo] *3rd p. sg. pres. of* **clore; ~ure** [~'ty:r] *f* fence; closing, closure; **~urer** [~ty're] (1a) fence (in) *or* enclose (*land*); conclude, close.

clou [klu] *m* nail; *fig.* hit, highlight; ✶ boil; *sl.* pawnshop; *sl.* clink; **~s** *pl.* pedestrian crossing *sg.*; *cuis.* **~ de girofle** clove; **~er** [klu'e] (1a) nail; pin down; *fig.* tie; **~ter** [~'te] (1a) stud.

clown [klun] *m* clown; buffoon; **~erie** [~'ri] *f* clownish trick.

coagul|ation [koagyla'sjɔ̃] *f* coagulation, congealing; **~er** [~'le] (1a) coagulate, clot; curdle.

coali|ser *pol.* [koali'ze] (1a) unite; **~tion** [~'sjɔ̃] *f* coalition.

coasser [koa'se] (1a) croak.

coassocié *m,* **e** *f* [koasɔ'sje] co-partner.

cocagne [kɔ'kaɲ] *f*: **pays m de ~** land of plenty.

cocaïne [kɔka'in] *f* cocaine.

cocasse F [kɔ'kas] comical, droll.

coccinelle *zo.* [kɔksi'nɛl] *f* ladybird.

coche¹ [kɔʃ] *m* † stage-coach; **faire la mouche du ~** be a busy-body; F **manquer le ~** miss the boat.

coche² [~] *f* nick, notch.

cocher¹ [kɔ'ʃe] (1a) nick, notch; check off, tick off.

cocher² [kɔ'ʃe] *m* coachman, F cabby; **cochère** [~'ʃɛ:r] *adj./f*: **porte f ~** carriage-entrance.

cochon [kɔ'ʃɔ̃] **1.** *su./m* pig, hog; *fig.* swine; ~ *de lait* sucking-pig; ~ *d'Inde* guinea-pig; **2.** *adj. sl.* filthy; **~ner** [~ʃɔ'ne] (1a) *v/i.* farrow; *v/t.* F botch; **~nerie** [~ʃɔn'ri] *f* filth, smut; foul trick; rubbish, trash; **~net** [~ʃɔ'nɛ] *m* young pig; *bowls:* jack.

coco [kɔ'ko] *su./m* (*a. noix f de* ~) coco(a)nut; *sl.* head; F guy; F darling; F stomach; *su./f* F snow, coke (= *cocaine*).

cocon [kɔ'kɔ̃] *m* cocoon.

cocotte¹ [kɔ'kɔt] *f* chuck-chuck (= *hen*); F *darling*; *pej.* tart.

cocotte² *cuis.* [~] *f* stew-pan.

cocu F [kɔ'ky] *m* cuckold; **~fier** F [~ky'fje] (1o) cuckold.

cod|e [kɔd] *m* code (*a. 🏛, a. tel.*); ~ *postal* postcode, *Am.* zip code; *mot.* **se mettre en** ~ dip or dim the headlights, *Am. a.* put on the low beams; **~er** [kɔ'de] (1a) (en)code; **~ifier** [~di'fje] (1o) codify.

coéducation [koedyka'sjɔ̃] *f* coeducation.

coefficient [koefi'sjɑ̃] *m* coefficient; ~ *de sécurité* safety factor.

cœur [kœːr] *m* heart (*a. fig.*); *cards:* heart(s *pl.*); 🏥 **~poumon** *m* **artificiel** heart-lung machine; *à* ~ *joie* to one's heart's content; *avoir à* ~ *de* (*inf.*) feel like (*ger.*); *avoir à* ~ *de* (*inf.*) make a point of (*ger.*); *avoir mal au* ~ feel sick; *par* ~ by heart; *prendre qch. à* ~ take s.th. to heart; *tenir au* ~ *à q.* mean a great deal to s.o.

coexistence [kɔɛgzis'tɑ̃ːs] *f* coexistence (*a. pol.*).

coffr|age [kɔ'fraːʒ] *m* 🔺 lining; shuttering; **~e** [kɔfr] *m* chest, box; *mot.* boot, *Am.* trunk; **~e-fort**, *pl.* **~es-forts** [~ɔ'fɔːr] *m* safe; strong-box; **~er** [kɔ'fre] (1a) F imprison; 🔨 line; **~et** [~'frɛ] *m* small box.

cogérance [kɔʒe'rɑ̃ːs] *f* co-administration; joint management.

cognac [kɔ'ɲak] *m* cognac, brandy

cognée [kɔ'ɲe] *f* axe, hatchet; **cogner** [~] (1a) knock; bang.

cohabiter [kɔabi'te] (1a) cohabit.

cohé|rence [kɔe'rɑ̃ːs] *f* coherence; *avec* ~ coherently; **~rent** [~'rɑ̃] coherent; **~sion** [~'zjɔ̃] *f* cohesion.

cohue [kɔ'y] *f* crowd, throng.

coi, coite [kwa, kwat] quiet; *se tenir* ~ keep quiet; F lie doggo.

coiff|e [kwaf] *f* head-dress; cap; **~é** [kwa'fe] *adj.: être* ~ *de* be wearing a hat; have done one's hair; *fig.* be infatuated (with, *de*); *né* ~ born lucky; **~er** [~'fe] (1a) *v/t.* cover (*one's head*); *hat:* suit; put on (*a hat*); do (*one's hair*); *sp., fig.* beat (*an opponent*); *fig.* control; *de combien êtes coiffez-vous?* what size in hats do you take?; **~eur, -euse** [~'fœːr, ~'føːz] *su.* hairdresser; *su./f* dressing-table; **~ure** [~'fyːr] *f* head-dress; hairstyle; hairdressing.

coin [kwɛ̃] *m* corner; nook; *ground:* patch; *coins:* die; 🔩 wedge; *fig.* stamp; ~ *du feu* fireside.

coinc|ement 🔩 [kwɛ̃s'mɑ̃] *m* jamming; **~er** [kwɛ̃'se] (1k) wedge; *fig. sl.* corner; arrest; *v/i.,* **se** ~ jam, stick.

coincid|ence [kɔɛ̃si'dɑ̃ːs] *f* coincidence; **~er** [~'de] (1a) coincide.

coing 🌿 [kwɛ̃] *m* quince.

coït [kɔ'it] *m* coitus.

coke [kɔk] *m* coke; *coll.* coke.

col [kɔl] *m* neck; collar; *geog.* pass; *fig.* ~ *blanc* (*bleu*) white- (blue-)collar worker.

colchique 🌿 [kɔl'ʃik] *m* colchicum.

colère [kɔ'lɛːr] **1.** *su./f* anger; *se mettre en* ~ become angry; **2.** *adj.* irascible; **coléreux** [kɔle'rø], **colérique** [~'rik] choleric, hot tempered.

colifichet [kɔlifi'ʃɛ] *m* trinket.

colimaçon *zo.* [kɔlima'sɔ̃] *m* snail.

colin-maillard [kɔlɛ̃ma'jaːr] *m* game: blind-man's buff.

colique 🏥 [kɔ'lik] *f* diarrhoea; colic.

colis [kɔ'li] *m* packet, parcel; luggage; *par* ~ *postal* by parcel post.

collabor|ateur *m*, **-trice** *f* [kɔllabora'tœːr, ~'tris] collaborator; *review:* contributor; **~ation** [~ra'sjɔ̃] *f* collaboration; contribute; **~er** [~'re] (1a) collaborate; *journ.* contribute.

coll|age [kɔ'laːʒ] *m* pasting; gluing; F cohabitation; **~ant** [~'lɑ̃] sticky; close-fitting; (skin)tight; *pej.* clinging.

collatéral [kɔllate'ral] collateral.

collation [kɔlla'sjɔ̃] *f* 🏛 conferment; *typ.* proof-reading; *documents:* collation; light meal; **~ner** [~sjo'ne] (1a) *v/t.* collate; check; *v/i.* have a snack.

colle [kɔl] *f* paste, glue; F *fig.* poser; *school:* detention; F fib.

collect|e [kɔlˈlɛkt] *f eccl. etc.* collection; **~eur** [kɔllɛkˈtœːr] *m* collector; ⚙ sewer; *mot.* manifold; **~if** [~ˈtif] collective; **~ion** [~ˈsjɔ̃] *f* collection; **~ionner** [~sjɔˈne] (1a) collect; **~ivité** [~tiviˈte] *f* community; group; common ownership.

collège [kɔˈlɛːʒ] *m* college; school; secondary grammar school; **~ électoral** electorate.

collégien, -enne [kɔleˈʒjɛ̃, ~ˈʒjɛn] *su.* college-student; *su./m* schoolboy; *su./f* schoolgirl.

collègue [kɔlˈlɛg] *su.* colleague.

coller [kɔˈle] (1a) *v/t.* stick, paste, glue (on, *sur*); stick up (*or* on *or* together); press; F stick with, cling to (*s.o.*); F stick *s.th.* in a *place*; F plough (a *candidate*); **se ~ à** (*or* **contre**) press *or* flatten o.s. against; F **se ~ qch.** (**sur le dos**) get landed with s.th.; *v/i.* stick; cling (to, *à*); *sl.* **ça colle?** things all-right?

collet [kɔˈlɛ] *m* collar; cape; *cuis.*, tooth, violin, ⚙ neck; ⚙ flange; snare; *fig.* **~ monté** strait-laced (*person*); **~er** [kɔlˈte] (1c) *v/t.* collar; **se ~** come to grips; *v/i.* set snares.

colleur *m*, **-euse** *f* [kɔlˈlœːr, ~ˈløːz] (*bill-*)sticker; examiner; *sl.* liar.

collier [kɔlˈlje] *m* necklace; collar (a. ⚙); **coup de ~** big effort.

colline [kɔˈlin] *f* hill.

collision [kɔlliˈzjɔ̃] *f* collision; **entrer en ~** collide (with, **de**).

colloque [kɔlˈlɔk] *m* conference; conversation.

collus|ion ⚖ [kɔllyˈzjɔ̃] *f* collusion; **~oire** ⚖ [~ˈzwaːr] collusive.

colmater [kɔlmaˈte] (1a) seal (up *or* off); plug (up); fill in (*holes*).

colocataire [kɔlɔkaˈtɛːr] *su.* joint tenant; co-tenant.

colomb|e *orn.* [kɔˈlɔ̃ːb] *f* dove; **~ier** [kɔlɔ̃ˈbje] *m* dovecot(e).

colon [kɔˈlɔ̃] *m* colonist, settler.

colonel ✕ [kɔlɔˈnɛl] *m* colonel.

colon|ial [kɔlɔˈnjal] *adj.*, *su./m* colonial; **~alisme** [~njaˈlism] *m* colonialism; **~e** [~ˈni] *f* colony, settlement; **~ de vacances** holiday camp; **~sateur** [kɔlɔnizaˈtœːr] **1.** *adj.* colonizing; **2.** *su.* colonizer; **~sation** [~zaˈsjɔ̃] *f* colonization; **~ser** [~ˈze] (1a) colonize.

colonne [kɔˈlɔn] *f* column; **~ Morris** advertizing column *or* pillar.

color|ant [kɔlɔˈrɑ̃] *adj.*, *su./m* colo(u)ring; **~er** [~ˈre] (1a), **~ier** [~ˈrje] (1o) colo(u)r; **~is** [~ˈri] *m* colo(u)r(ing); hue.

colossal [kɔlɔˈsal] gigantic; **colosse** [~ˈlɔs] *m* colossus; F giant.

colport|age [kɔlpɔrˈtaːʒ] *m* peddling; **~er** [~ˈte] (1a) peddle; spread (*news*); **~eur** [~ˈtœːr] *m* pedlar, *Am.* peddler; *fig.* newsmonger.

coltiner [kɔltiˈne] (1a) carry (on one's back); F *fig.* **se ~** saddle o.s. with (*s.th.*, *s.o.*).

coma ⚕ [kɔˈma] *m* coma.

combat [kɔ̃ˈba] *m* ✕ battle, engagement; struggle (a. *fig.*); **hors de ~** out of action; **~if** [kɔ̃baˈtif] pugnacious; **~tant** [~ˈtɑ̃] *m* fighter; **~tre** [kɔ̃ˈbatr] (4a) fight.

combien [kɔ̃ˈbjɛ̃] *adv.* how (many *or* much); **~ de temps** how long; F **le ~ sommes-nous?** what day of the month is it?

combin|aison [kɔ̃binɛˈzɔ̃] *f* combination, plan; *cost.* overalls *pl.*; *woman:* slip; **~e** F [kɔ̃ˈbin] *f* plan, scheme; **~er** [~biˈne] (1a) combine; devise, concoct.

comble [kɔ̃ːbl] **1.** *su./m fig.* height, summit; △ roof(ing); **au ~ de la joie** overjoyed; **c'est le ~** *or* **un ~!** that beats all!; **pour ~** to cap it all; **de fond en ~** from top to bottom; *fig.* **mettre le ~ à** crown; **2.** *adj.* heaped up; packed; **~er** [kɔ̃ˈble] (1a) fill (up); make good (a *deficit*); fulfill; gratify; **~ q. de qch.** shower s.th. on s.o.

combusti|ble [kɔ̃bysˈtibl] **1.** *adj.* combustible; **2.** *su./m* fuel; **~on** [~ˈtjɔ̃] *f* burning; combustion.

comédie [kɔmeˈdi] *f* comedy; *fig.* playacting; **~n** [~ˈdjɛ̃] **1.** *su.* comedian; **2.** *adj.* theatrical.

comestible [kɔmɛsˈtibl] **1.** *adj.* edible; **2.** *su./m* article of food.

comète *astr.* [kɔˈmɛt] *f* comet.

comique [kɔˈmik] **1.** *adj.* comic (*author*); comical, funny; **2.** *su./m* comedian; comedy-writer; comedy.

comité [kɔmiˈte] *m* committee; **~ d'arbitrage** arbitration board.

command|ant ✕, ⚓ [kɔmɑ̃ˈdɑ̃] *m* commanding officer, commander; **~e**

[~'maːd] *f* ✝ order; ✪, ✓ control; ✪ lever; *mot.* drive; **de ~** feigned, affected; ✪ **~ à distance** remote control; **sur ~** to order; **~ement** [~mãd'mã] *m* command; ⚖ summons *sg.*; *eccl.* commandment; **~er** [~mã'de] (1a) *v/t.* command; order (s.th. from s.o., *qch. à q.*); dominate; **se ~** control o.s.; *v/i.* give orders; **~ à** control.

commandit|aire ✝ [kɔmãdi'tɛːr] *m* sleeping *or Am.* silent partner; **~e** [~'dit] *f* (*a.* **société *f* en ~**) limited partnership; **~er** ✝ [~'te] (1a) finance (*an enterprise*).

comme [kɔm] **1.** *adv.* as, like; how; in the way of; **~ ça** like that; **c'est tout ~** it comes to the same thing; **~ il faut** proper(ly *adv.*); **2.** *cj.* as, seeing that; just as.

commémor|atif [kɔmemɔra'tif] commemorative (of, **de**); memorial (*service*); **~ation** [~ra'sjɔ̃] *f* commemoration; **~er** [~'re] (1a) commemorate.

commen|çant [kɔmã'sã] *m* beginner; **~cement** [~mãs'mã] *m* beginning, start, outset; **~cer** [~mã'se] (1k) begin; start.

commensal *m*, **e** [kɔmã'sal] table companion; regular guest.

commensurable [kɔmãsy'rabl] commensurable (with, to **avec**).

comment [kɔ'mã] **1.** *adv.* how; why; **2.** *int.* **~?** (I beg your) pardon?, sorry?; F **et ~!** and how.

comment|aire [kɔmã'tɛːr] *m* commentary; comment; **~ateur** *m*, **-trice** *f* [~ta'tœːr, ~'tris] commentator; **~er** [~'te] (1a) comment upon.

commérage [kɔme'raːʒ] *m* gossip.

commer|çant [kɔmɛr'sã] **1.** *adj.* commercial; business...; busy, shopping (*street*); businesslike (*person*). **2.** *su./m* merchant; **~ce** [~'mɛrs] *m* trade, commerce; **~ de détail** retail trade; **registre** *m* **du ~** Commercial Register; **~cer** [kɔmɛr'se] (1k) trade (with, **avec**) trade; *fig.* have dealings; **~cial** [~'sjal] commercial.

commère [kɔ'mɛːr] *f* gossip.

commett|ant [kɔmɛ'tã] *m* ⚖, ✝ principal; **~re** [~'mɛtr] (4v) commit.

commis [kɔ'mi] **1.** *p.p. of* **commettre**; **2.** *su./m* clerk; agent; assistant.

commisération [kɔmizera'sjɔ̃] *f* pity; commiseration.

commissa|ire [kɔmi'sɛːr] *m* commis-

sioner; *police:* superintendent; **~riat** [~sa'rja] *m* commissioner's office; police station.

commission [kɔmi'sjɔ̃] *f* commission; *admin.* board; errand; **faire la ~ à q.** give s.o. the message; **~naire** [~sjɔ'nɛːr] *m* delivery boy *or* man; messenger; ✝ commission agent; **~ de transport** forwarding agent; **~ner** [~sjɔ'ne] (1a) commission.

commissure [kɔmi'syːr] *f:* **~ des lèvres** corner of the mouth.

commod|e [kɔ'mɔd] **1.** *adj.* convenient, comfortable; handy; good-natured; **2.** *su./f* chest of drawers; **~ité** [kɔmɔdi'te] *f* convenience; comfort.

commotion [kɔmɔ'sjɔ̃] *f* commotion; ⚡, ⚕ shock; ⚕ concussion.

commuer ⚖ [kɔ'mɥe] (1p) commute (to, **en**).

commun, e [kɔ'mœ̃, ~'myn] **1.** *adj.* common; joint; vulgar; ✝ average; **chose *f* ~e** common cause; **faire bourse ~e** pool resources; **2.** *su./m* common run; common funds *pl.*; **~s** *pl.* outbuildings; **en ~** in common; *su./f admin.* parish; **Chambre *f* des ~es** House of Commons; ⚖ **al** [kɔmy'nal] communal, parish...; **~auté** [~no'te] *f* community; *pol.* ⚑ French Community.

communi|ant *m*, **e** *f eccl.* [kɔmy'njã, ~'njãt] communicant; **~cable** [kɔmyni'kabl] communicable; **~catif** [~ka'tif] communicative; infectious (*laughter*); **~cation** [~ka'sjɔ̃] *f* communication; (telephone) call; *teleph.* **~ locale** (*interurbaine*) local (long-distance) call; **~er** *eccl.* [kɔmy'nje] (1o) communicate; **~on** [~'njɔ̃] *f* communion (*a. eccl.*); **~qué** [kɔmyni'ke] *m* communiqué; **~ de presse** press release; **~quer** [~] (1m) *v/t.* communicate; impart (*s.th.*); **se ~** spread (to, **à**); *v/i.* communicate; be in connection; (**faire**) **~** connect.

communis|ant [kɔmyni'zã] **1.** *adj.* communistic; **2.** *su.* communist sympathizer; **~me** [~'nism] *m* communism; **~te** [~'nist] *su., adj.* communist.

commutateur ⚡ [kɔmyta'tœːr] *m* switch, commutator.

compac|ité [kɔ̃pasi'te] *f* compactness; **~t** [~'pakt] compact.

compagn|e [kɔ̃'paɲ] *f* companion;

mate; **~ie** [kɔ̃paˈɲi] f company (a. ✝, ✕, a. person); **de** or **en ~** together; **tenir ~ à q.** keep s.o. company; **~on** [~ˈnɔ̃] m companion; mate; **~ de route** fellow traveller.

compar|able [kɔ̃paˈrabl] comparable; **~aison** [~rɛˈzɔ̃] f comparison.

comparaitre ⚎ [kɔ̃paˈrɛːtr] (4k) appear.

compar|atif [kɔ̃paraˈtif] adj., su./m comparative; **~er** [~ˈre] (1a) compare (to, with, **à, avec**).

comparse [kɔ̃ˈpars] m thea. supernumerary, F super; fig. person of no significance.

compartiment [kɔ̃partiˈmɑ̃] m compartment; partition; division; chess etc.: square.

comparution ⚎ [kɔ̃paryˈsjɔ̃] f appearance.

compas [kɔ̃ˈpa] m compass(es pl.); **~sé** [kɔ̃paˈse] formal, stiff.

compassion [kɔ̃paˈsjɔ̃] f pity.

compatible [kɔ̃paˈtibl] compatible.

compati|r [kɔ̃paˈtiːr] (2a): **~ à** sympathize with; **~ssant** [~tiˈsɑ̃] (**pour,** to(wards)) compassionate; sympathetic.

compatriote [kɔ̃patriˈɔt] su. compatriot.

compens|ateur [kɔ̃pɑ̃saˈtœːr] 1. adj. compensating; equalizing; 2. su./m compensator; ✗ trimmer; **~ation** [~saˈsjɔ̃] f compensation; balancing; ✝ **accord m de ~** barter agreement; ✝ **chambre f de ~** clearing-house; **~er** [~ˈse] (1a) compensate, make up for; ⊙ balance.

compère [kɔ̃ˈpɛːr] m eccl. godfather; fig. accomplice; F comrade, pal.

compét|ence [kɔ̃peˈtɑ̃ːs] f competence (a. ⚎); skill; **~ent** [~ˈtɑ̃] competent (a. ⚎).

compétit|eur m, **-trice** f [kɔ̃petiˈtœːr, ~ˈtris] competitor, rival (for, **à**); **~if** [~ˈtif] competitive (prices); rival; **~ion** [~ˈsjɔ̃] f competition; sp. event.

compiler [kɔ̃piˈle] (1a) compile.

complai|re [kɔ̃ˈplɛːr] (4z) v/i. please (s.o., **à q.**); v/t.: **se ~** take pleasure (in ger., **à** inf.; in s.th., **dans** or **en qch.**); **~sance** [kɔ̃plɛˈzɑ̃ːs] f kindness, complaisance; complacency; **~sant** [~ˈzɑ̃] obliging, complaisant; complacent.

complément [kɔ̃pleˈmɑ̃] m complement; **~aire** [~mɑ̃ˈtɛːr] complementary; further (information).

compl|et [kɔ̃ˈplɛ] 1. adj. complete; **~!** full up; hotel: no vacancies; thea. full house; 2. su./m (a. **~-veston**) suit; **au (grand) ~** whole, entire, in its entirety; **~éter** [~pleˈte] (1f) complete, fill up.

complexe [kɔ̃ˈplɛks] 1. adj. complicated; 2. su./m complex; **~é** [~plɛkˈse] (person) suffering from a complex.

complexion [kɔ̃plɛkˈsjɔ̃] f constitution; temperament.

complication [kɔ̃plikaˈsjɔ̃] f complication (a. ⚕); complexity.

complic|e [kɔ̃ˈplis] 1. su. accomplice (of, **de**); 2. adj. conniving; knowing, understanding (look); **~ité** [~plisiˈte] f complicity.

compliment [kɔ̃pliˈmɑ̃] m compliment; congratulation; **~er** [~mɑ̃ˈte] (1a) compliment (on **de, sur**).

compliqu|é [kɔ̃pliˈke] complicated; ⚕ compound (fracture); **~er** [~] (1m) complicate.

complot [kɔ̃ˈplo] m plot, conspiracy; **~er** [~plɔˈte] (1a) plot, scheme (to inf., **de** inf.).

componction [kɔ̃pɔ̃kˈsjɔ̃] f: **avec ~** solemnly.

comport|ement [kɔ̃pɔrtəˈmɑ̃] m behavio(u)r; psych. etc. **de ~** behavio(u)ral; **~er** [~ˈte] (1a) be composed of, consist of; include; involve; **se ~** behave.

compos|ant [kɔ̃poˈzɑ̃] m component; **~é** [~ˈze] 1. adj. compound; **être ~ de** consist of; fig. studied; 2. su./m compound; **~er** [~ˈze] (1a) v/t. make up; form; set up; compose; typ set; **se ~ de** consist of; v/i. compose music etc.; come to terms (with, **avec**); **~iteur** [~ziˈtœːr] m composer; type-setter; **~ition** [~ziˈsjɔ̃] f making-up; formation; setting-up; composition; school: essay; examination (paper); **venir à ~** come to terms.

composter [kɔ̃pɔsˈte] (1a) punch (a ticket).

compote [kɔ̃ˈpɔt] f stewed fruit; **en ~** stewed; fig. to or in a pulp.

compréhensi|ble [kɔ̃preãˈsibl] understandable; **~on** [~ˈsjɔ̃] f understanding.

comprendre [kɔ̃ˈprɑ̃ːdr] (4aa) understand; include; F **je comprends!** I see!

compress|e ⚕ [kɔ̃ˈprɛs] f compress; **~er** [kɔ̃prɛˈse] (1a) press; **~eur** [~ˈsœːr] m compressor; mot. **~** supercharger;

road-roller; **~ion** [~'sjɔ] f compression;
🔘 crushing; repression; ✝ restriction.
comprim|é 💊 [kɔ̃pri'me] m tablet; **~er**
[~] (1a) compress; repress.
compris [kɔ̃'pri] **1.** p.p. of **comprendre**;
2. adj. (inv. before su.): **non ~** exclusive
of; **service m ~** service included; **tout ~**
all in; **y ~** including.
compro|mettre [kɔ̃prɔ'mɛtr] (4v) com-
promise (s.o.); endanger; implicate;
~mis [.'mi] m compromise (a, 🏛).
compt|abilité ✝ [kɔ̃tabili'te] f book
keeping; **~ en partie double** double
entry book keeping; **~able** [~'tabl] **1.**
adj. responsible; **2.** su. book keeper;
~ant [~'tɑ̃] **1.** adj./m ready (cash); **2.**
su./m cash; **au ~** cash down; **3.** adv. in
cash; **~e** [kɔ̃t] m account; reckoning;
fig. profit; **~ à rebours** rocket countdown, **~ de chèques postaux** postal
cheque account; **~ d'épargne** savings
account; **~ rendu** report; book etc.:
review; **à ~** on account; fig. **à bon ~**
cheap; **en fin de ~, au bout du ~** after
all; **se rendre ~ de** realize; **tenir ~ de**
qch. take s.th. into account; **~e-gout-
tes** [kɔ̃t'gut] m/inv. dropper; 🔘
drip-feed lubricator; **~er** [kɔ̃'te] (1a)
v/t. count (up); value; expect; v/i. reckon; **~ sur** rely on, count on; fig. **~ avec**
reckon with; date: **à ~ du ...** from ...
(on); **~eur** [~'tœr] m meter; counter;
~ à gaz gas-meter; **~ de courant** elec-
tricity meter; **~ de Geiger** Geiger counter; **~ de stationnement** parking meter;
~ de vitesse speedometer; **~oir**
[~'twa:r] m ✝ counter; cashier's desk;
bar; ✝ bank.
compulser [kɔ̃pyl'se] (1a) examine,
check (documents).
computer [kɔ̃py'te] (1a) compute.
comte [kɔ̃t] m earl; count; **comtesse**
[~'tɛs] f countess.
concass|er [kɔ̃ka'se] (1a) crush; **~eur**
[~'sœr] m crushing mill.
concave [kɔ̃'ka:v] concave.
concéder [kɔ̃se'de] (1f) (con)cede.
concentr|ation [kɔ̃sɑ̃tra'sjɔ̃] f concen-
tration; **camp m de ~** concentration
camp; **~é** [~'tre] adj. condensed (milk);
fig. reserved; **~er** [~'tre] (1a) concentrate; focus; **se ~** concentrate (on, **sur**).

concept [kɔ̃'sɛpt] m concept; **~ible**
[kɔ̃sɛp'tibl] conceivable; **~ion** [~'sjɔ̃] f
conception; idea.
concern|ant [kɔ̃sɛr'nɑ̃] prp. concerning;
~er [~'ne] (1a) concern; **en ce qui concerne ...** as far as ... is concerned.
concert [kɔ̃'sɛːr] m concert; fig. agreement; fig. **de ~** (**avec**) together (with);
in unison (with); **~er** [kɔ̃sɛr'te] (1a)
(pre)arrange; plan; **se ~** work together.
concession [kɔ̃se'sjɔ̃] f concession,
grant; **~naire** [~sjo'nɛːr] m ✝ agent,
dealer; licence-holder.
concev|able [kɔ̃s'vabl] conceivable;
~oir [~'vwaːr] (3a) conceive; understand; imagine; word.
concierge [kɔ̃'sjɛrʒ] su. door keeper;
caretaker, Am. janitor; **~rie** [~sjɛrʒə'ri]
f door-keeper's lodge.
concili|able [kɔ̃sili'jabl] reconcilable;
~abule [~lja'byl] m secret meeting;
~ant [~'ljɑ̃] conciliatory; **~ateur** m, **-tri-
ce** f [~lja'tœːr, ~'tris] peace-maker;
~ation [~lja'sjɔ̃] f conciliation; **~er**
[~'lje] (1o) reconcile; fig. win, gain ([for]
s.o., **à q.**).
concis [kɔ̃'si] concise, terse; **~ion** [~si'sjɔ̃]
f concision, terseness.
concitoyen m, **-enne** f [kɔ̃sitwa'jɛ̃, ~'jɛn]
fellow-citizen.
conclu|ant [kɔ̃kly'ɑ̃] conclusive; **~re**
[~'klyːr] (4g) conclude (a. a treaty, a.
fig.); finish; infer (from, **de**); **~sion**
[~kly'zjɔ̃] f conclusion.
concombre 🍀 [kɔ̃'kɔ̃bːr] m cucumber.
concorda|nce [kɔ̃kɔr'dɑːs] f concord-
ance; agreement; **~t** [~'da] m con-
cordat.
concord|e [kɔ̃'kɔrd] f harmony; **~er**
[~kɔr'de] (1a) agree; tally.
concour|ant [kɔ̃ku'rɑ̃] 𝒜 etc. conver-
gent; concerted (efforts etc.); **~ir**
[~'riːr] (2i) compete; **~ à** contribute to,
work towards; **~s** [~'kuːr] m assistance,
help; competition; **hors ~** not competing (for prize); fig. outstanding, unequalled.
concr|et [kɔ̃'krɛ] concrete; **~éter**
[kɔ̃kre'te] (1f) solidify; **~étion** [~'sjɔ̃] f
concretion (a. 💊).
concupiscen|ce [kɔ̃kypi'sɑːs] f concu-
piscence; **~t** [~'sɑ̃] concupiscent.
concurre|ment [kɔ̃kyra'mɑ̃] adv. joint-

ly; ✝ in competition; **~nce** [~'rɑ̃:s] *f* competition; **~ déloyale** unfair competition; **faire ~ à** compete with; ✝ **jusqu'à ~ de** to the amount of; **~nt** [~'rɑ̃] **1.** *adj.* co(-)operating; competing; **2.** *su.* competitor.

concussion [kɔ̃ky'sjɔ̃] *f* embezzlement.

condamn|able [kɔ̃dɑ'nabl] blameworthy; **~ation** [~na'sjɔ̃] *f* condemnation; 🜨 sentence; 🜨 **à vie** life sentence; **~er** [~'ne] (1a) condemn; 🜨 sentence; *fig.* blame; board up, block up.

condens|ateur ⚡ [kɔ̃dɑ̃sa'tœːr] *m* condenser; **~é** [~'se] *m journ.* digest; précis; sum-up; **~er** [~'se] (1a) condense.

condescend|ance [kɔ̃dɛsɑ̃'dɑ̃:s] *f* condescension; **~re** [~'sɑ̃:dr] (4a) condescend (to *inf.*, **à** *inf.*).

condiment [kɔ̃di'mɑ̃] *m* seasoning.

condisciple [kɔ̃di'sipl] *m* school-fellow; fellow-student.

condition [kɔ̃di'sjɔ̃] *f* condition (*a. sp. etc.*); circumstances *pl.*; **~s** *pl.* **de travail** working conditions; **à ~** on condition, ✝ on approval; **à ~ que** provided *or* providing (that); **~nel** [kɔ̃disjɔ'nɛl] *adj., su./m* conditional; **~ner** [~'ne] (1a) condition; ✝ package.

condoléance [kɔ̃dɔle'ɑ̃:s] *f* condolence.

conduct|ance ⚡ [kɔ̃dyk'tɑ̃:s] *f* conductivity; **~eur** [~'tœːr] **1.** *adj.* ⚡ conducting; ⚙ driving; **2.** *su.* leader; *mot.* driver; 🜨 guard, *Am.* conductor; **~ible** [~'tibl] conductive; **~ion** [~'sjɔ̃] *f* conduction.

condui|re [kɔ̃'dɥiːr] (4h) conduct (*a.* ♪, ⚙); lead (to, **à**); *mot.* steer, drive; ✝ run; *mot.* **permis** *m* **de ~** driving licence, *Am.* driver's license; **se ~** behave; **~sis** [dɥi'zi] *1st p. sg. p.s. of* **conduire**; **~sons** [~dɥi'zɔ̃] *1st p. pl. pres. of* **conduire**; **~t, e** [~'dɥi, ~'dɥit] **1.** *p.p. of* **conduire**; **2.** *su./m* conduit, pipe; *anat.* duct; **~ principal** main; **~ souterrain** drain; *su./f* guidance; *vehicle:* driving; management; ⚙ pipe; *fig.* behavio(u)r; *mot.* **~ à gauche (à droite)** left-hand (right-hand) drive; *mot.* **~ en état d'ivresse** drunken driving.

cône [koːn] *m* cone; **en ~** tapering.

confection [kɔ̃fɛk'sjɔ̃] *f* making; ready-made clothes *pl.*; *cost.* **de ~** ready-made; **~ner** [~sjɔ'ne] (1a) make (up); manufacture.

confédér|ation [kɔ̃federa'sjɔ̃] *f* (con)federation; **~é** [~'re] confederate; **~er** [~'re] (1f) confederate.

confér|ence [kɔ̃fe'rɑ̃:s] *f* conference; *univ.* lecture; **~ avec projections** lantern lecture; **~ de presse** press conference; **~encier** *m*, **-ère** *f* [~'rɑ̃'sje, ~'sjɛːr] lecturer, speaker; **~er** [~'re] (1f) *v/t.* compare (*text*); confer (a *degree*); *v/i.* confer (with, **avec**).

confess|e *eccl.* [kɔ̃'fɛs] *f* confession; **~er** [kɔ̃fɛ'se] (1a) confess (*a. eccl.*); admit; *eccl.* **se ~** confess, go to confession; **~eur** [~'sœːr] *m* confessor; **~ion** [~'sjɔ̃] *f* confession; **~ionnal** *eccl.* [~sjɔ'nal] *m* confessional; **~ionnel** [~sjɔ'nɛl] denominational.

confian|ce [kɔ̃'fjɑ̃:s] *f* confidence, trust, reliance; **~ en soi** self-confidence; **avoir ~ en, faire ~ à** a. trust; **homme** *m* **de ~** reliable man; **~t** [~'fjɑ̃] confident.

confiden|ce [kɔ̃fi'dɑ̃:s] *f* confidence, (little) secret; **~t** [~'dɑ̃] *m* confidant; **~tiel** [~dɑ̃'sjɛl] confidential.

confier [kɔ̃'fje] (1o) (to, **à**); entrust; confide; **se ~ à** confide in.

configuration [kɔ̃figyra'sjɔ̃] *f* configuration (*a. astr.*); lie (of the land).

confin|er [kɔ̃fi'ne] (1a) *v/i.* border (on, **à**); *v/t.* shut (*s.o.*) up; **~s** [~'fɛ̃] *m/pl.* limits.

confirm|atif [kɔ̃firma'tif] confirmative; **~ation** [~ma'sjɔ̃] *f* confirmation (*a.* 🜨, *eccl., etc.*); **~er** [~'me] (1a) confirm (*a eccl.*); corroborate.

confis [kɔ̃'fi] *1st p. sg. pres. and p.s. of* **confire.**

confiscation [kɔ̃fiska'sjɔ̃] *f* confiscation; seizure, forfeiture.

confis|erie [kɔ̃fiz'ri] *f* confectionery; confectioner's; **~eur** [~'zœːr] *m* confectioner; **~ons** [~fi'zɔ̃] *1st p. pl. pres. of* **confire.**

confisquer [kɔ̃fis'ke] (1m) confiscate, seize; take away.

confit [kɔ̃'fi] *p.p. of* **confire; ~ure** [~fi'tyːr] *f* jam, preserve; F soft soap.

conflit [kɔ̃'fli] *m* conflict; clash; ✝ **~ salarial** wages dispute.

confluent [kɔ̃fly'ɑ̃] **1.** *adj.* confluent; **2.** *su./m* confluence, meeting.

confondre [kɔ̃'fɔ̃:dr] (4a) confuse, mix

up; (inter)mingle; confound (*s.o.*); **se ~** become confused; merge, (inter-)mingle; **se ~ en excuses** apologize profusely.

conform|ation [kɔ̃fɔrma'sjɔ̃] *f* conformation; **~e** [~'fɔrm] conformable; consistent (with, **à**); **~ément** [~'formemɑ̃]: **~ à** in accordance with; **~er** [~me] (1a) conform (to, **à**); **se ~ à** comply with; **~ité** [~mi'te] *f* conformity (with, **avec**; to, **à**).

confort [kɔ̃'fɔːr] *m* comfort; **~able** [~fɔr'tabl] comfortable; **~er** [~fɔr'te] (1a) strengthen; confirm.

con|fraternité [kɔ̃fraterni'te] *f* (good) fellowship; **~frère** [~'frɛːr] *m* colleague; fellow(-doctor *etc.*); **~frérie** [~fre'ri] *f* confraternity.

confront|ation [kɔ̃frɔ̃ta'sjɔ̃] *f* confrontation; *text:* collation; **~er** [~'te] (1a) confront; compare.

confus [kɔ̃'fy] confused; indistinct (*noise*); obscure (*style*); *fig.* ashamed; **~ion** [kɔ̃fy'zjɔ̃] *f* confusion; embarrassment; *dates etc.*: mistake.

congé [kɔ̃'ʒe] *m* leave; holiday; notice (to quit); ⚔ discharge; *admin.* permit; **~ payé** paid holidays *pl.* (*Am.* vacation); **deux jours** *m/pl.* **de ~** two days off; **donner (son) ~ à** q. give s.o. notice; **prendre ~ de** take leave of; **~dier** [kɔ̃ʒe'dje] (1o) dismiss; ⚔ discharge.

congélation [kɔ̃ʒela'sjɔ̃] *f* freezing; frost-bite; **congeler** [kɔ̃ʒ'le] (1d) freeze (*a.* ♣ credits); congeal.

congénère [kɔ̃ʒe'nɛːr] *su.* congener; F **mes ~s** my likes.

congénital [kɔ̃ʒeni'tal] congenital.

congestion ❀ [kɔ̃ʒɛs'tjɔ̃] *f* congestion; **~ cérébrale** stroke; **~ner** [~tjɔ'ne] (1a) congest.

conglomér|at [kɔ̃glɔme'ra] *m* conglomerate; **~er** [~'re] (1f) conglomerate.

congratuler [kɔ̃graty'le] (1a) congratulate.

congrégation *eccl.* [kɔ̃grega'sjɔ̃] *f* community; brotherhood.

congr|ès [kɔ̃'grɛ] *m* congress; **~essiste** [~grɛ'sist] *su.* member of a congress.

congru [kɔ̃'gry] adequate; suitable; **portion** *f* **~e** bare living; **~ent** [~gry'ɑ̃] congruent (with, **à**).

coni|cité [kɔnisi'te] *f* conical shape; **~fère** ♀ [~'fɛːr] **1.** *adj.* coniferous; **2.**

su./m: **~s** *pl.* conifers; **~que** [kɔ'nik] conic(al); tapering.

conjectur|e [kɔ̃ʒɛk'tyːr] *f* surmise, guess; **~er** [ty're] (1a) guess.

conjoint [kɔ̃'ʒwɛ̃] **1.** *adj.* joint; married; A **règle** *f* **~e** chain-rule; **2.** *su./m* spouse; **~s** *pl.* husband and wife.

conjonct|ion [kɔ̃ʒɔ̃k'sjɔ̃] *f* conjunction (*a. gramm., astr.*); union; **~ure** [~'tyːr] *f* conjuncture; **~ (économique)** economic situation; **haute ~** boom.

conjugaison [kɔ̃ʒygɛ'zɔ̃] *f* gramm. biol., etc. conjugation; pairing.

conjugal [kɔ̃ʒy'gal] conjugal.

conjuguer [kɔ̃ʒy'ge] (1m) gramm. conjugate; pair; combine, join.

conjungo F [kɔ̃ʒyˈgo] *m* marriage.

conjur|ateur [kɔ̃ʒyra'tœːr] *m* magician; **~ation** [~'sjɔ̃] *f* conspiracy; exorcism; F **~s** *pl.* entreaties; **~é** *m*, **e** [kɔ̃ʒy're] conspirator; **~er** [~] (1a) conspire; avert (*danger*); exorcise (*spirits*); entreat (s.o. to *inf.*, **q. de** *inf.*); **se ~** conspire.

connais [kɔ'nɛ] *1st p. sg. pres.* of **connaître**; **~sable** [kɔnɛ'sabl] recognizable (by, **à**); **~sance** [~'sɑ̃ːs] *f* knowledge; acquaintance (*a. person*); ❀ consciousness; **en (pleine) ~ de cause** with full knowledge of the facts, advisedly; **~sement** ♣ [kɔnɛs'mɑ̃] *m* bill of lading; **~seur** [~nɛ'sœːr] **1.** *adj.* expert; **2.** *su.* connoisseur, expert; **~sons** [~nɛ'sɔ̃] *1st p. pl. pres.* of **connaître**.

connaître [kɔ'nɛːtr] (4k) know; be aware of, understand; experience; **s'y ~ en qch.** be an expert in s.th.; **faire ~ q. à** introduce s.o. to.

connecter ⚡ [kɔnɛk'te] (1a) connect (to, with **avec**).

connexe [kɔ'nɛks] connected; **~ion** [kɔnɛk'sjɔ̃] *f* connection (*a.* ⚡).

connivence [kɔni'vɑ̃ːs] *f* connivance.

connu [kɔ'ny] *p.p.* of **connaître**; **connus** [~] *1st p. sg. p.s.* of **connaître**.

conqué|rant [kɔ̃ke'rɑ̃] *m* conqueror; **~rir** [~'riːr] (21) conquer; *fig.* win; **~ête** [kɔ̃'kɛːt] *f* conquest; **~is** [~'ki] *p.p.* of **conquérir**.

consacrer [kɔ̃sa'kre] (1a) consecrate (*a.* fig.); devote (*energies*); **expression** *f* **consacrée** stock phrase.

consanguinité [kɔ̃sɑ̃gini'te] *f* ⚕ consanguinity; inbreeding.

conscien|ce [kõ'sjã:s] *f* consciousness; conscience; *avoir bonne (mauvaise)* ~ have a clear (bad) conscience; *avoir* ~ *de* be aware of; **~cieux** [~sjã'sjø] conscientious; **~t** [~'sjã] aware (of, *de*).

conscri|ption ✕ [kõskrip'sjõ] *f* conscription, *Am.* draft; **~t** ✕ [~'kri] *m* conscript, *Am.* draftee.

consécration [kõsekra'sjõ] *f* consecration; dedication.

consécutif [kõseky'tif] consecutive; ~ *à* following upon, due to.

conseil [kõ'sɛːj] *m* advice; committee; ⚖ counsel; ✝ *d'administration* board of directors; ~ *de guerre* council of war; court-martial; ~ *d'employés* works committee; ~ *des ministres* Cabinet; ⚖ *judiciaire* guardian; *président m du* ♀ Prime Minister; **~ler** [~sɛ'je] **1.** (1a) advise; **2.** *su./m* adviser; councillor; ~ *d'orientation professionnelle* vocational guidance counsellor; ~ *municipal* town councillor.

consent|ement [kõsãt'mã] *m* consent; **~ir** [~sã'tiːr] (2b) *v/i.* consent, agree (to, *à*); *v/t.* allow, grant (to, *à*).

conséquen|ce [kõse'kã:s] *f* consequence; *de* ~ important; *en* ~ consequently; *ne pas tirer à* ~ be of no consequence; **~t** [~'kã] **1.** *adj.* consistent; logical; F important, seizeable; **2.** *su./m* ⅄ consequent; *par* ~ consequently.

conserva|ble [kõsɛr'vabl] that will keep *(food)*; **~teur** [~va'tœːr] **1.** *adj.* preservative; *pol.* Conservative; **2.** *su.* keeper, curator; **~tion** [~va'sjõ] *f* preservation; **~toire** [~va'twaːr] *m* academy *(of music etc.).*

conserv|e [kõ'sɛrv] *f* preserved food; **~er** [~sɛr've] (1a) preserve, keep.

considér|able [kõside'rabl] considerable; important; **~ation** [~ra'sjõ] *f* consideration; respect; **~er** [~'re] (1f) consider; regard (as, *comme*). respect.

consigne [kõ'siɲ] *f* order, instructions *pl.*; password; ✕ confinement; *school:* detention; ✕ guardroom; 🛄 left-luggage office, *Am.* checkroom; 🛄 deposit (on *a bottle etc. sur*); **~er** [~si'ɲe] (1a) ⚖ deposit; ✝ consign; ✕ confine to barracks; *school:* detain *(a pupil)*; ✝ put a deposit on *(a bottle etc.)*; 🛄 put in the left-luggage office, *Am.* check *(bag-*

gage); ~ *(par écrit)* register; ~ *sa porte à q.* not to be at home to s.o.

consist|ance [kõsis'tã:s] *f* consistency; **~er** [~'te] (1a) consist (of, in *en, dans*; in *ger.*, *à inf.*).

consol|ateur [kõsola'tœːr] **1.** *adj.* consoling; **2.** *su.* consoler; **~ation** [~la'sjõ] *f* consolation; **~er** [kõso'le] (1a) console; *se* ~ *de* be consoled for, get over *(s.th.).*

consolider [kõsoli'de] (1a) strengthen, consolidate *(a. se ~).*

consomm|ateur *m*, **-trice** *f* [kõsoma'tœːr, ~'tris] consumer; *café etc.:* customer; **~ation** [~ma'sjõ] *f* consumption; consummation *(a. of marriage)*; *café:* drink; ✝ *biens m/pl. de* ~ consumer goods; **~é** [~'me] **1.** *adj.* consummate *(skill)*; **2.** *su./m cuis.* clear soup; **~er** [~'me] (1a) consume, use up; consummate.

conson|ance [kõso'nã:s] *f* consonance; *aux* ~ *...*, *de* ~ *... (+ adj.)* ...-sounding; **~ne** [kõ'son] *f* consonant.

consort [kõ'soːr] *m* consort; ~ *s pl.* associates, confederates; **~ium** [~sor'sjom] *m* consortium.

conspir|ateur [kõspira'tœːr] conspirator; **~ation** [~ra'sjõ] *f* conspiracy; **~er** [~'re] (1a) conspire, plot.

conspuer [kõs'pɥe] (1a) decry; boo.

consta|mment [kõsta'mã] constantly; **~nce** [~'tã:s] *f* constancy; steadiness; **~nt, e** [~'tã, ~'tã:t] **1.** *adj.* constant; steadfast; **2.** *su./f* ♪, *phys.* constant.

constat [kõs'ta] *m* report; official statement; **~ation** [kõstata'sjõ] *f* not(ic)ing; statement; certifying; **~er** [~'te] (1a) notice; note; state; record, certify.

constell|ation [kõstɛlla'sjõ] *f* constellation; **~é** [~'le] studded, spangled, spotted (with, *de*); ~ *d'étoiles* star-spangled.

constern|ation [kõstɛrna'sjõ] *f* dismay; **~er** [~'ne] (1a) dismay.

constip|ation ✦ [kõstipa'sjõ] *f* constipation; **~é** [~'pe] ✦ constipated; *fig.* stiff, awkward, strained; **~er** [~'pe] constipate.

constitu|ant [kõsti'tɥã] constituent; **~er** [~'tɥe] (1n) form, make (up); constitute; appoint; set up *(a committee)*; **~tif** [~ty'tif] constituent; **~tion** [~ty'sjõ] *f* ✦, *pol.* constitution; formation; composition, make-up; setting up; **~tionnel** constitutional.

construct|eur [kɔ̃stryk'tœːr] *m* builder, constructor; **~ion** [~'sjɔ̃] *f* construction; building; *de ~ française* French-built.

construi|re [kɔ̃s'trɥiːr] (4h) construct; build; **~sis** [~trɥi'zi] *1st p. sg. p. s. of* **construire**; **~sons** [~trɥi'zɔ̃] *1st p. pl. pres. of* **construire**; **~t** [~'trɥi] *p.p. of* **construire**.

consul [kɔ̃'syl] *m* consul; **~aire** [kɔ̃sy'lɛːr] consular; **~at** [~'la] *m* consulate.

consult|ant [kɔ̃syl'tɑ̃] consulting; consultant; **~atif** [~ta'tif] advisory; **~ation** [~ta'sjɔ̃] *f* consultation; *✝* opinion, advice; *✝* surgery, doctor's office; *heures f/pl. de ~* consulting (*Br. a.* surgery hours; *se* ~ [~'te] (1a) *v/t.* consult; *se* ~ confer; *v/i.* be in the office, hold surgery (*doctor*).

consumer [kɔ̃sy'me] (1a) consume; devour, wear out; *se* ~ waste away.

contact [kɔ̃'takt] *m* contact; switch; *✝* ~ *à fiche* plug; *mot.* *clef f de* ~ ignition key; *entrer en* ~ *avec* get in touch with; **~er** [~tak'te] (1a) contact.

contagi|eux [kɔ̃ta'ʒjø] contagious; infectious; **~on** [~'ʒjɔ̃] *f* contagion.

contaminer [kɔ̃tami'ne] (1a) *✝* infect; contaminate.

conte [kɔ̃ːt] *m* story, tale.

contempl|atif [kɔ̃tɑ̃pla'tif] contemplative; **~er** [~'ple] (1a) contemplate; meditate upon.

contemporain [kɔ̃tɑ̃pɔ'rɛ̃] *adj.*, *su.* contemporary.

conten|ance [kɔ̃t'nɑ̃ːs] *f* capacity; *fig.* bearing, attitude; countenance; *faire bonne* ~ put on a bold front; *perdre* ~ lose one's composure; **~eur** ✝ [~'nœːr] *m* container; **~ir** [~'niːr] (2h) contain (*a. fig.* = control), hold.

content [kɔ̃'tɑ̃] **1.** *adj.* content(ed); pleased, happy (about, *de*); **2.** *su./m* F fill; **~ement** [~tɑ̃t'mɑ̃] *m* contentment; **~er** [~tɑ̃'te] (1a) content; *se* ~ make do, be content (with, *de*).

contentieux [kɔ̃tɑ̃'sjø] *m* ✝ matters *pl.* in dispute; ✝ legal department.

contenu [kɔ̃t'ny] *m* content(s *pl.*).

conter [kɔ̃'te] (1a) tell, relate; *en* ~ *à q.* pull s.o.'s leg.

contest|able [kɔ̃tɛs'table] debatable, questionable; **~ation** [~ta'sjɔ̃] *f* dispute; **~er** [~'te] (1a) dispute; contest, question; protest.

conteur *m*, **-euse** *f* [kɔ̃'tœːr, ~'tøːz] narrator; story-teller; romancer.

contexte [kɔ̃'tɛkst] *m* context.

contigu, -guë [kɔ̃ti'gy] adjoining.

continen|ce [kɔ̃ti'nɑ̃ːs] *f* continence; **~t** [~'nɑ̃] **1.** *adj.* chaste; *✝* unintermitting (*fever*); **2.** *su./m geog.* continent; **~tal** [~nɑ̃'tal] continental.

contingent [kɔ̃tɛ̃'ʒɑ̃] **1.** *adj.* contingent; **2.** *su./m* quota; allowance; **~ement** [~ʒɑ̃t'mɑ̃] *m* quota system; **~er** [~ʒɑ̃'te] (1a) fix quotas for.

continu [kɔ̃ti'ny] continuous; continual; unbroken; *✝* direct (*current*); *A* continued; **~ation** [~nɥa'sjɔ̃] *f* continuation; *weather:* long spell; **~el** [~'nɥɛl] continual; continuous; **~er** [~'nɥe] *v/t.* continue, continue with, go on with; *se* ~ continue, go on; *v/i.* ~ *à or de* (*inf.*) go on (*ger.*), continue (*ger.*) or to (*inf.*); **~ité** [~nɥi'te] *f* continuity; continuation.

contorsion [kɔ̃tɔr'sjɔ̃] *f* contortion.

contour [kɔ̃'tuːr] *m* outline; *town:* circuit; **~ner** [~tur'ne] (1a) outline; by-pass (*a town*); distort (*one's face*); F get round (*the law*).

contract|ant [kɔ̃trak'tɑ̃] **1.** *adj.* contracting; **2.** *su.* contracting party; **~er** [~'te] (1a) contract (*debt, habit, illness, marriage, etc.*); **~ion** [~'sjɔ̃] *f* contraction; narrowing; **~uel** *m*, **~uelle** *f* traffic warden, *f a.* F meter maid.

contradict|eur [kɔ̃tradik'tœːr] *m* opponent; **~ion** [~'sjɔ̃] *f* contradiction; **~oire** [~'twaːr] contradictory; inconsistent (with, *à*).

contrain|dre [kɔ̃'trɛ̃ːdr] (4m) compel, force; restrain; **~t, e** [~'trɛ̃, ~'trɛ̃ːt] **1.** *adj.* cramped (*style*); forced (*smile*); **2.** *su./f* compulsion; constraint; restraint.

contra|ire [kɔ̃'trɛːr] **1.** *adj.* opposite; contrary (to, *à*); *en sens* ~ in the opposite direction; **2.** *su./m* contrary; *au* ~ on the contrary; **~rier** [kɔ̃tra'rje] (1o) thwart, oppose, vex; **~riété** [~rie'te] *f* annoyance.

contrast|e [kɔ̃'trast] *m* contrast; **~er** [~tras'te] (1a) contrast.

contrat [kɔ̃'tra] *m* contract; *passer un* ~ enter into an agreement.

contravention [kɔ̃travɑ̃'sjɔ̃] *f* infringement; *mot.* parking ticket *or* fine.

contre [kɔ̃ːtr] **1.** *prp.* against; contrary

to; (in exchange) for; ⇄, *sp.* versus; **dix ~ un** ten to one; **2.** *adv.* against *or* on it.

contre... [kõtr(ə)] counter...; anti...; contra...; back...; **~allée** [~a'le] *f* side-lane; **~amiral** ⚓ [~ami'ral] *m* rear-admiral; **~assurance** [~asy'rãːs] *f* reinsurance; **~balancer** [kõtrəbalã'se] (1k) counterbalance; **~bande** [~'bãːd] *f* contraband; **~bandier** [~bã'dje] *m* smuggler; **~bas** [~'ba] *adv.:* **en ~** lower down (than, *de*); **~basse** ♪ [~'baːs] *f* doublebass; **~bouter** [~bu'te], **~buter** [~by'te] (1a) buttress; **~carrer** [~ka're] (1a) thwart; **~cœur** [~'kœːr] *adv.:* **à ~** reluctantly; **~coup** [~'ku] *m* rebound; repercussion; **par ~** as a (indirect) result; **~courant** [~ku'rã] *m:* **à ~** against the current; **~dire** [~'diːr] (4p) contradict; **~dit** [~'di] *adv.:* **sans ~** unquestionably.

contrée [kõ'tre] *f* region.

contre...: **~écrou** ⊙ [kõtre'kru] *m* counter-nut; **~épreuve** [~e'prœːv] *f* crosscheck; **~espionnage** [~espjo'naːʒ] *m* counter-espionage; **~façon** [kõtrafa'sõ] *f* forgery; **~facteur** [~fak'tœːr] *m* forger; **~faction** [~fak'sjõ] *f* forgery; **~faire** [~'fɛːr] (4r) imitate, mimic; forge; counterfeit (*money etc.*); disguise (*one's voice etc.*); deform; **~ficher** *sl.:* **se ~ de** not to care a rap about; **~fort** [~'fɔːr] *m* △ buttress; *boot:* stiffening; **~s** *pl.* foot-hills; **~haut** [~'o] *adv.:* **en ~** higher up; **~jour** [~'ʒuːr] *m:* **à ~** against the light; **~maître** [~'mɛːtr] *m* foreman; **~mesure** [~mə'zyːr] *f* countermeasure; **~partie** [~par'ti] *f* opposite view; *fig.* compensation; **en ~** in compensation; in return; **~pied** *fig.* [~'pje] *m* opposite (of, *de*); **prendre le ~ (de)** take the opposite view (of); take the opposite course (to); **~plaqué** [~pla'ke] *m* plywood; **~poids** [~'pwa] *m* counterweight; **~poil** [~'pwal] *adv.:* **à ~** the wrong way; **~point** ♪ [~'pwɛ̃] *m* counterpoint; **~poison** [~pwa'zõ] *m* antidote (to, *de*).

contrer [kõ'tre] (1a) *box.* counter; *cards:* double; *fig.* cross, thwart.

contre...: **~seing** [kõtrə'sɛ̃] *m* counter-signature; **~sens** [~'sãːs] *m* misinterpretation; nonsense; **à ~** the wrong way; **~signer** [~si'ɲe] (1a) countersign; **~temps** [~'tã] *m* mishap; hitch, snag;

inconvenience; **à ~** at the wrong moment; out of time; **~venant** *m*, e *f* ⇄ [~və'nã, ~'nãːt] offender; **~venir** [~və'niːr] (2h): **~ à** contravene; **~vent** [~'vã] *m* outside shutter; **~vérité** [~veri'te] *f* ironical statement; untruth.

contribu|able [kõtri'bɥabl] *su.* taxpayer; **~er** [~'bɥe] (1n) contribute (towards, à); **~tion** [~by'sjõ] *f* contribution; tax; **mettre à ~** have recourse to.

contrit [kõ'tri] contrite; **~ion** [~tri'sjõ] *f* penitence, contrition.

contrôl|e [kõ'troːl] *m* check(ing), inspection; supervision; verification; ✝ auditing; hallmark(ing); assaying; **~ des naissances** birth control; **coupon de ~** *ticket:* stub; **~er** [kõtro'le] (1a) check; verify; examine (*a passport etc.*); **~eur** *m*, **-euse** *f* [~'lœːr, ~'løːz] inspector; supervisor; ticket collector.

contrordre [kõ'trɔrdr] *m* countermand; **sauf ~** unless countermanded.

controuvé [kõtru've] invented, fabricated.

controvers|e [kõtrɔ'vɛrs] *f* controversy; **~er** [~vɛr'se] (1a) debate; controvert.

contumace ⇄ [kõty'mas]: **par ~** in absentia.

contusion [kõty'zjõ] *f* bruise; **~ionner** [~zjɔ'ne] (1a) bruise.

conurbation [kɔnyrba'sjõ] *f* conurbation.

convaincre [kõ'vɛ̃ːkr] (4gg) convince; prove (*s.o.*) guilty of (*de*).

convalescen|ce [kõvale'sãːs] *f* convalescence; **être en ~** convalesce; **~t** [~'sã] *adj., su.* convalescent.

conven|able [kõv'nabl] suitable; decent; **~ance** [~'nãːs] *f* fitness; conformity; decency; convenience; **à la ~ de q.** to s.o.'s liking; **~ir** [~'niːr] (2h): **~ à** suit, fit; **~ de** agree upon; admit, acknowledge (*s.th.*); **c'est convenu!** agreed!; **il convient de** (*inf.*) it is advisable *or* fitting to (*inf.*).

convention [kõvã'sjõ] *f* convention; agreement; **~s** *pl.* clauses; **~ collective** collective bargaining; **~nel** [~sjo'nɛl] conventional.

converg|ence [kõver'ʒãːs] *f* convergence; **~er** [~'ʒe] (1l) converge.

convers|ation [kõversa'sjõ] *f* conversation, talk; *teleph.* call; **~er** [~'se] (1a) converse, talk.

conver|sion [kɔ̃vɛr'sjɔ̃] *f* conversion (*a.* ✞); **~ti** *m*, **e** *f* [~'ti] convert; **~tible** [~'tibl] convertible (into, *en*); **~tir** [~'tiːr] (2a) convert (to, **à**; into, *en*); **~tisseur** [~ti'sœːr] *m* ⚙ ⚡ converter.

convexe [kɔ̃'vɛks] convex.

conviction [kɔ̃vik'sjɔ̃] *f* conviction.

convier [kɔ̃'vje] (1o) invite (to, **à**); *fig. a.* urge (to *inf.*, **à** *inf.*).

convive [kɔ̃'viːv] *su.* table companion.

convocation [kɔ̃vɔka'sjɔ̃] *f* convocation; ✕ calling-up, *Am.* draft.

convoi [kɔ̃'vwa] *m* convoy; 🚂 train.

convoit|er [kɔ̃vwa'te] (1a) covet; **~ise** [~'tiːz] *f* covetousness; lust.

convoler *iro.* [kɔ̃vɔ'le] (1a) (re)marry.

convoquer [kɔ̃vɔ'ke] (1m) summon; ✕ call up, *Am.* draft.

convoy|er ⚓ [kɔ̃vwa'je] (1h) escort; **~eur** [~'jœːr] *m* escort.

convuls|er [kɔ̃vyl'se] (1a) convulse; **~if** [~'sif] convulsive; **~ion** [~'sjɔ̃] *f* convulsion; spasm.

coopérat|eur *m*, **-trice** *f* [kɔɔpera'tœːr, ~'tris] co(-)operator; **~if, -ve** [~'tif, ~'tiːv] **1.** *adj.* co(-)operative; **2.** **~tive** *su.* f co(-)operative stores *pl.*; **~ immobilière** building society; **~ion** [~'sjɔ̃] *f* co(-)operation.

coopérer [kɔɔpe're] (1f) co(-)operate.

coordination [kɔɔrdina'sjɔ̃] *f* coordination.

coordonn|ées Ⓐ [kɔɔrdɔ'ne] *f/pl.* coordinates; **~er** [~] (1a) coordinate (with, **à**); arrange.

copain F [kɔ'pɛ̃] *m* pal, *Am.* buddy.

copeau ⚙ [kɔ'po] *m* (wood) shaving.

copi|e [kɔ'pi] *f* (carbon) copy, transcript; *typ.* imitation; *phot.* print; *school.* paper; **~or** [~'pje] (1o) copy; *school:* crib (from, **sur**).

copieux [kɔ'pjø] copious; hearty.

copilote ✈ [kɔpi'lɔt] *m* co-pilot.

copine F [kɔ'pin] *f* girl: pal, chum; **~r** F [kɔpi'ne] (1a) be pally; be pals.

copiste [kɔ'pist] *su.* copier, copyist.

copropriétaire [kɔprɔprije'tɛːr] *m* joint owner, co-owner.

coq¹ ⚓ [kɔk] *m* ship's cook.

coq² *orn.* [kɔk] *m* cock, *Am.* rooster; **~ de bruyère** wood-grouse; **être comme un ~ en pâte** be in clover; **le ~ du village** cock of the walk.

coque [kɔk] *f* egg: shell; ⚓ hull; **œuf** *m* **à la ~** boiled egg.

coquelicot ♣ [kɔkli'ko] *m* red poppy.

coqueluche [kɔk'lyʃ] *f* 🏥 whooping-cough; *fig.* darling, favo(u)rite.

coqueriquer [kɔkri'ke] (1m) crow.

coquet, -ette [kɔ'kɛ, ~'kɛt] **1.** *adj.* coquettish; smart (*hat*); trim (*garden*); tidy (*sum*); **2.** *su./f* flirt; **~er** [kɔk'te] (1c) flirt (with, **avec**).

coquetier [kɔk'tje] *m* egg-cup.

coquetterie [kɔkɛ'tri] *f* coquetry; affectation; smartness, daintiness.

coquill|age [kɔki'jaːʒ] *m* shellfish; shell; **~e** [~'kiːj] *f* egg, nut, snail: shell; *typ.* misprint; ⚙ casing; *cuis.* (*a.* **~ Saint-Jaques**) scallop; *fig.* **sortir de sa ~** come out of one's shell.

coquin, e [kɔ'kɛ̃, ~'kin] **1.** *adj.* roguish; **2.** *su.* rogue; *su./f* hussy.

cor¹ [kɔːr] *m* ♪ horn(-player); **à ~ et à cri** insistently; **sonner** (*or* **donner**) **du ~** sound the horn.

cor² 🏥 [~] *m* corn.

corail, *pl.* **-aux** [kɔ'raːj, ~'ro] *m* coral; **corallin** [kɔra'lɛ̃] coral-red.

corbeau [kɔr'bo] *m* *orn.* raven; △ corbel; F person of ill omen.

corbeille [kɔr'bɛːj] *f* basket; *thea.* dress circle.

corbillard [kɔrbi'jaːr] *m* hearse.

cord|age [kɔr'daːʒ] *m* rope; stringing; **~e** [kɔrd] *f* rope, thread; ♪ string; **~ à linge** clothes line; **~ raide** tight-rope; **~ à sauter** skipping rope; **~s** *pl.* **vocales** vocal cords; **~eau** [kɔr'do] *m* string, line; fuse; *fig.* **au ~** perfectly straight; **~ée** [~'de] *f* mount. rope (*of climbers*); cord (*of wood*); **~elière** [~də'ljɛːr] *f* girdle; *typ.* ornamental border; **~er** [kɔr'de] (1a) twist (into rope); string (*a racket*); cord (*a trunk*).

cordial [kɔr'djal] **1.** *adj.* hearty, warm, cordial; **2.** *su./m* cordial; **~ité** [~djali'te] *f* cordiality.

cordon [kɔr'dɔ̃] *m* cord; string; tape; *cordon:* *anat.* **~ ombilical** navel string; **~-bleu**, *pl.* **~s-bleus** F *fig.* [~də'blø] *m* first-rate cook; **~ner** [~dɔ'ne] (1a) twist (*hemp*).

cordonn|erie [kɔrdɔn'ri] *f* shoemaking; shoemaker's shop; **~ier** [kɔrdɔ'nje] *m* shoemaker.

coriace [kɔ'rjas] tough.

corn|e [kɔrn] *f* horn; *stag etc.*: antler; ⚡ hard skin, calluses *pl.*; *book*: dog's-ear; **~ à chaussures** shoehorn; **bêtes** *f/pl.* **à ~s** horned cattle; **~é, e** [kɔr'ne] **1.** *adj.* horny; **2.** *su./f anat.* cornea.

corneille *orn.* [kɔr'nɛːj] *f* crow.

cornemus|e ♪ [kɔrnə'myːz] *f* bagpipe; **~eur** [~my'zœːr] *m* piper.

corne|r [kɔr'ne] (1a) dog's-ear (*a page*); **~t** [~'nɛ] *m* ♪ (*~ à pistons*) cornet; *pastry:* horn; *icecream:* cone; screw of paper.

corniche [kɔr'niʃ] *f rock:* ledge; *coast* road; △ cornice.

cornichon [kɔrni'ʃɔ̃] *m* gherkin; F nitwit.

cornu [kɔr'ny] horned; *fig.* absurd.

cornue [kɔr'ny] **~** *etc.* [~] *f* retort.

coroll|aire [kɔrɔl'lɛːr] *m* corollary; **~e** ♀ [~'rɔl] *f* corolla.

coron [kɔ'rɔ̃] *m* miner's quarters *pl.*

corporat|if [kɔrpɔra'tif] corporat(iv)e; **~ion** [~'sjɔ̃] *f* corporate body; guild.

corporel [kɔrpɔ'rɛl] of the body, bodily; corporal (*punishment*).

corps [kɔr] *m* body; *diplomatic etc.* corps; **~ à ~** hand to hand; **~ de bâtiment** main building; **~ de logis** housing unit; **~ de métier** trade association; ⚡ *etc.*, *fig.* **~ étranger** foreign body; **~ in a body; faire ~ avec** be an integral part of; ⚓ **perdu ~ et biens** lost with all hands.

corpulen|ce [kɔrpy'lɑ̃ːs] *f* stoutness, corpulence; **~t** [~'lɑ̃] stout.

corpuscule [kɔrpys'kyl] *m* corpuscle; particle.

correct [kɔ'rɛkt] correct; right; accurate; **~eur** *m*, **-trice** *f* [kɔrɛk'tœːr, ~'tris] corrector; proof reader; **~if** [~'tif] *m* corrective; **~ion** [~'sjɔ̃] *f* correction; correctness; punishment; thrashing; **~ionnel, -elle** ⚖ [~sjɔ'nɛl] **1.** *adj.* correctional; **délit** *m* **~** minor offence; **tribunal** *m* **~** = **2.** *su./f* court of petty sessions, *Am.* police court.

correspond|ance [kɔrɛspɔ̃'dɑ̃ːs] *f* correspondence; ⚞ *etc.* connection; *par* **~** by letter; by post; **~ancier** *m*, **-ère** *f* ♱ [~dɑ̃'sje, ~'sjɛːr] correspondence clerk; **~ant** [~dɑ̃] *su.* ♱, *journ.* correspondent; penfriend; **~re** [kɔrɛs'pɔ̃ːdr] (4a): **~ à** correspond to *or* with, suit; fit, tally with; **~ avec q.** be in correspondence with s.o.

corridor [kɔri'dɔːr] *m* corridor.

corrig|é [kɔri'ʒe] *m* fair copy; right version *or* solution; **~er** [~'ʒe] (1l) correct; put right; punish; cure (of, *de*); **~ible** [~'ʒibl] corrigible.

corroborer [kɔrrɔbɔ're] (1a) corroborate, confirm.

corroder [kɔrrɔ'de] (1a) corrode.

corrompre [kɔ'rɔ̃ːpr] (4a) corrupt; spoil; bribe; taint (*meat*).

corrosi|f [kɔrrɔ'zif] *adj.*, *su./m* corrosive; **~on** [~'zjɔ̃] *f* corrosion.

corroyer [kɔrwa'je] (1h) curry (*leather*); trim (*wood*); weld (*metal*).

corrupt|eur [kɔryp'tœːr] **1.** *adj.* corrupting; **2.** *su.* corrupter; briber; **~ible** [~'tibl] corruptible; open to bribery; **~ion** [~'sjɔ̃] *f* corruption; bribery; decomposition.

corsage [kɔr'saːʒ] *m* bodice.

corsaire [kɔr'sɛːr] *m* corsair, pirate.

corse [kɔrs] *adj.*, *su.* Corsican.

corsé [kɔr'se] strong; full-bodied (*wine*); spicy (*story*); F substantial.

corselet [kɔrsə'lɛ] *m* bodice.

corser [kɔr'se] (1a) add spice to; pep up; intensify.

corset [kɔr'sɛ] *m* corset; **~ière** [~sə'tjɛːr] *f* corsetmaker.

cortège [kɔr'tɛːʒ] *m* procession.

corvée [kɔr've] *f* ✗ fatigue; *fig.* drudgery, chore; thankless job.

coryphée [kɔri'fe] *m* leader, chief.

cosmétique [kɔsme'tik] **1.** *adj.* cosmetic; **2.** *su./m* hair oil.

cosmique [kɔs'mik] cosmic.

cosmo... [kɔsmɔ] cosmo...; **~naute** [~'noːt] *su.* cosmonaut; **~polite** [~pɔ'lit] *adj.*, *su.* cosmopolitan.

coss|ard *sl.* [kɔ'saːr] lazy(bones); **~e** [kɔs] *f* pod, husk; shell; *sl.* laziness **~u** [kɔ'sy] rich.

costaud F [kɔs'to] strong, sturdy.

costum|e [kɔs'tym] *m* (men's) suit; costume, dress; **~er** [~ty'me] (1a) dress up (as, *en*); **bal** *m* **costumé** fancy-dress ball.

cot|ation ♱ [kɔta'sjɔ̃] *f* quotation; **~e** [kɔt] *f* quota; *admin.* assessment; number; mark; *sp.* odds *pl.*; classification; ♱ quotation; *fig.* rating, standing; popularity; **~ d'alerte** danger mark; F **avoir la ~ (d'amour)** be (very) popular; **~é** [kɔ'te]: **bien (mal) ~** (not) highly considered *or* thought of.

côte [ko:t] *f* rib; slope; hill; coast; **~ à ~** side by side.

côté [ko'te] *m* side; direction, way; **à ~ de** beside; **de ~** sideways; **de mon ~** for my part; **du ~ de** near, in the vicinity of; from; to(wards); **d'un ~ ..., de l'autre ~** on the one hand ..., on the other hand; **la maison d'à ~** next door.

coteau [ko'to] *m* slope, hill(side).

côtelé [kot'le] ribbed; **~ette** [~'lɛt] *f* veal. cutlet; mutton, pork: chop; F **~s** *pl.* whiskers: mutton chops.

coter [ko'te] (1a) mark; number (*a document*); ♣ class (*a ship*); quote (*prices*); *admin.* assess.

coterie [ko'tri] *f* set, circle, clique.

côtier [ko'tje] coastal.

cotillon [koti'jɔ̃] *m* † petticoat.

cotis|ation [kotiza'sjɔ̃] *f* contribution; fee; quota; **~er** [~'ze] (1a) pay one's share; **se ~** club together.

coton [ko'tɔ̃] *m* cotton; *a.* **~ hydrophile** cotton wool, *Am.* absorbent cotton; **élever dans du ~** coddle; **~nades** [kotɔ'nad] *f/pl.* cotton goods; **~neux** [~tɔ'nø] fluffy; woolly (*fruit, style*); **~nier** [~tɔ'nje] 1. *adj.* cotton-...; 2. *su./m* ♣ cotton-plant.

côtoyer [kotwa'je] (1h) keep close to; skirt; border on (*a. fig.*); *fig.* rub shoulders with (*a. fig.*).

cotte [kot] *f* workman's overalls *pl.*

cou [ku] *m* neck.

oouac [kwak] *m* squawk (*a. ♪, fig.*).

couard [kwa:r] 1. *adj.* cowardly; 2. *su.* coward; **~ise** [kwar'di:z] *f* cowardice.

couch|ant [ku'ʃɑ̃] 1. *su./m* sunset; west; 2. *adj.*: **chien m ~** setter; *fig.* fawner; **soleil m ~** setting sun; **~e** [kuʃ] *f* layer; paint *etc.*: coat; *geol. etc.* (*a. social*) stratum; (*baby's*) nappy, *Am.* diaper; **~s** *pl.* childbirth *sg.*; **fausse ~** miscarriage; F **il en a une ~!** what a fathead!; **~er** [ku'ʃe] 1. (1a) *v/t.* put to bed; lay down; beat down; write (*s.th.*) down (**on**, **sur**), mention (*s.o.*) (in one's will, **sur son testament**); **~ en joue** (take) aim at; **se ~** go to bed; lie down; set (*sun*); *v/i.* sleep; 2. *su./m* going to bed; sun: setting; **~erie** *sl.* [ku'ʃri] *f* oft. *pl.* love-making; **~ette** [~'ʃɛt] *f* cot; berth; **~eur** [~'ʃœːr] *m*: **mauvais ~** awkward customer, nasty fellow.

couci-couça [kusiku'sa] *adv.* so-so.

coucou [ku'ku] *m* cuckoo(-clock).

coud|e [kud] *m* elbow; bend; **coup m de ~** nudge; **jouer des ~s** elbow one's way; **~ée** [ku'de] *f* cubit; **avoir les ~s franches** have elbow room; **~er** [ku'de] (1a) bend (*a pipe*); **~oyer** [~dwa'je] (1h) rub shoulders with; *fig.* be *or* come close to.

coudre [kudr] (4l) sew; stitch; **machine f à ~** sewing-machine.

coudrier ♣ [ku'drje] *m* hazel(-tree).

couenne [kwan] *f* pork: rind.

couiner [kwi'ne] (1a) squeal.

coula|ge [ku'la:ʒ] *m* pouring (*a. metall.*); leaking; ♣ scuttling; *fig.* leakage; **~nt** [~'lɑ̃] 1. *adj.* flowing; *fig. a.* smooth, easy; 2. *su./m* sliding ring.

coule [kul] *adv.*: **être à la ~** be with it, know the ropes, know all the tricks

coul|ée [ku'le] *f* flow; ⊙ casting; **~er** [~] (1a) *v/t.* pour; sink (*a ship*); *fig.* slip; F ruin; **se ~** slide, slip; *v/i.* flow, run; ♣ sink; ⊙ run; leak (*pen, vat*); *fig.* slip by (*time*).

couleur [ku'lœːr] *f* colo(u)r (*a. fig.*); complexion; *cards:* suit.

couleuvre [ku'lœːvr] *f* snake; F **avaler des ~s** pocket an insult.

coulis [ku'li] 1. *adj./m:* **vent m ~** insidious draught; 2. *su./m* ⊙ filling; *cuis.* purée.

coulisse [ku'lis] *f* ⊙ slide; *thea.* wing; backstage; *fig.* background; ♦ outside market; **dans les ~s** backstage (*a. fig.*); **porte f à ~** sliding door; *fig.* **regard m en ~** sideglance; **~er** [kuli'se] (1a) *v/t.* fit with slides; *v/i.* slide.

couloir [ku'lwa:r] *m* corridor (*a. 🚂, geog.*), passage; *parl.* lobby; ⊙ shoot; *cin. film:* track; *water:* gully.

coup [ku] *m* blow, knock; hit, thrust; stab, stroke; sound; beat; shot; *wind:* gust; turn; trick; knack; F drink; *fig.* influence; **🌡 ~ de chaleur** heat-stroke; **~ de maître** master stroke; **~ de poing** blow (with the fist); **~ de téléphone** (telephone) call; **à ~s de** with (the help of), by; **à ~ sûr** certainly, definitely; **après ~** after the event; **donner un ~ de brosse** give a brush(-down); **donner un ~ de main à** give a helping hand to; **~ d'œil** glance; **~ de pied** kick; **~ de poing** punch; **du ~** this time; at that; at the same time; therefore; **du même ~ at**

the same time; *d'un* (*seul*) ~ at one go; *au or du premier* ~ at the first attempt; F *être dans le* ~ be with it; F *monter le* ~ *à q.* deceive s.o.; *pour le* ~ for the moment; *saluer d'un* ~ *de chapeau* raise one's hat to; *sous le* ~ *de* under the influence or effect of; *tenir le* ~ take it; *tout à* ~ suddenly; *tout d'un* ~ (all) at once.

coupable [ku'pabl] **1.** *adj.* guilty; **2.** *su.* culprit; 🏛 delinquent.

coupa|ge [ku'pa:ʒ] *m* cutting; *wine*: blending; **~nt** [~'pɑ̃] *m* edge.

coup-de-poing, *pl.* **coups-de-poing** [kud'pwɛ̃] *m* (~ *américain*) knuckle-duster, *Am.* brass knuckles.

coupe[1] [kup] *f* cutting; felling; cut; section; ~ *des cheveux* haircut; *fig.* *sous la* ~ *de q.* under s.o.'s thumb or control.

coupe[2] [~] (drinking) cup; *sp.* cup.

coupe...: **~cigares** [kupsi'ga:r] *m/inv.* cigar-cutter; **~circuit** 🔌 [~sir'kɥi] *m/inv.* circuit-breaker; **~faim** [~'fɛ̃] *m/inv.* appetite suppressant; **~jarret** [~ʒa'rɛ] *m* cut-throat.

couper [ku'pe] (1a) *v/t.* cut (*a.* tennis); cut off or down; chop; interrupt; water down (*wine*); 🔌 switch off; *cards*: trump; *teleph.* ~ *la communication* ring off; *se* ~ intersect; F *fig.* give o.s. away; *v/i.:* *sl.* ~ *à* dodge (*s.th.*); ~ *dans le vif* cut to the quick; *teleph.* *ne coupez pas!* hold the line!

couperet [ku'prɛ] *m* chopper.

coupeur, -euse [ku'pœ:r, ~'pø:z] *su.* cutter; *su./f* cutting machine.

coupl|age [ku'pla:ʒ] *m* coupling; **~e** [kupl] *su./f.* two, couple; *su./m* pair, couple; ⚙ torque; **~er** [ku'ple] (1a) couple; 🔌 connect; **~et** [~'plɛ] *m* verse.

coupole [ku'pɔl] *f* cupola, dome.

coup|on [ku'pɔ̃] *m* ✝ coupon; ticket; *material*: remnant; **~réponse** *post*: reply coupon; **~ure** [~'py:r] *f* cut (*a.* ⚡, *thea.*); gash; (newspaper-)cutting; paper money.

cour [ku:r] *f* court (*a.* 🏛); (court-)yard; *thea.* *côté* ~ O.P.; *faire la* ~ *à* court, woo.

courag|e [ku'ra:ʒ] *m* courage; **~eux** [~ra'ʒø] brave, courageous.

coura|mment [kura'mɑ̃] *adv.* fluently; usually; **~nt** [~'rɑ̃] **1.** *adj.* running; current; ✝ standard (*make*); **2.** *su./m* ⚡,

water: current; stream; present month; *au* ~ (*de*) well informed (of or about), acquainted (with); *être au* ~ *de a.* know all about; *mettre q. au* ~ (*de*) inform s.o. (about or of); *dans le* ~ *de* in the course of; *fin* ~ at the end of this month; ⚡ ... (*pour*) *tous* ~**s** A.C./D.C. ...

courbatu [kurba'ty] stiff, aching; **~re** [~'ty:r] *f* stiffness; aching; **~s** *pl.* aches and pains.

courb|e [kurb] **1.** *adj.* curved; **2.** *su./f* curve; sweep; **~er** [kur'be] (1a) bend; **~ette** [~'bɛt] *f:* *faire des* ~**s** *à* kowtow to; **~ure** [~'by:r] *f* curve; camber; curvature.

coureur, -euse [ku'rœ:r, ~'rø:z] *su.* runner (*a.* *sp.*); *frequenter* (*of cafés etc.*); hunter (*of prizes*); *Am.:* *sp.* ~ *de fond* stayer; ~ *de jupons* skirt-chaser; *su./f* street-walker.

courge [kurʒ] *f* gourd; *Am.* squash.

courir [ku'ri:r] (2i) *v/i.* run; race; flow; *fig.* be current; ⚓ sail; *v/t.* run after; pursue; hunt; run (*a race*); frequent; haunt; ~ *le monde* travel widely.

couronn|e [ku'rɔn] *f* crown; wreath; ⚙ rim; **~ement** [~rɔn'mɑ̃] *m* crowning; coronation; **~er** [~rɔ'ne] (1a) crown (*a. fig.*); *fig.* award a prize to.

courrai [ku're] *1st sg. fut. of courir.*

courri|er [ku'rje] *m* courier; mail; letters *pl.*; *journ.* column; ~ *électronique* electronic mail; **~ériste** *journ.* [~rje'rist] *su.* columnist.

courroie [ku'rwa] *f* strap; ⚙ belt.

courrou|cer [kuru'se] (1k) anger; *poet.* ~**x** [~'ru] *m* anger.

cours [ku:r] *m* course (*a.* △, *univ.*); *money*: circulation; ✝ quotation; *school*: class(es *pl.*); ~ *d'eau* stream; ✝ ~ *des changes* rate of exchange; *au* ~ *de* in the course of; *en* ~ in progress.

course [kurs] *f* run(ning); race; trip; ⚓ cruise; ⚙ stroke; errand; ~ *aux armements* armaments race; ~ *de chevaux* horse-race; *faire des* ~**s** go shopping.

coursier [kur'sje] *m* messenger.

court[1] [ku:r] *m* (tennis-)court.

court[2] [ku:r] **1.** *adj.* short, brief; *à* ~ (*de*) short (of); *sl.* *avoir la peau* ~*e* be lazy; **2.** *adv.* short; *couper* ~ cut short; *tout* ~ simply.

courtage ✝ [kur'ta:ʒ] *m* brokerage.

courtaud [kur'to] stocky (person).

court-circuit, pl. **courts-circuits** ⚡ [kursir'kɥi] m short circuit; **~er** [~kɥi'te] (1a) ⚡, fig. short-circuit.

courtier [kur'tje] m broker.

courtis|an [kurti'zɑ̃] m courtier; **~ane** [~'zan] f courtesan; **~er** [~'ze] (1a) court; woo; toady to.

courtois [kur'twa] polite (to[wards], **envers**); **~ie** [~twa'zi] f courtesy.

couru 1. p.p. of **courir**; 2. adj. sought after; popular; † accrued; **~s** [~] 1st p. sg. p.s. of **courir**.

cous|euse [ku'zø:z] f seamstress, stitcher; stitching machine; **~is** [~'zi] 1st p. sg. p.s. of **coudre**, **~ons** [~'zɔ̃] 1st p. pl. pres. of **coudre**.

cousin¹ [ku'vl] m midge, gnat.

cousin² m, e f [ku'zɛ̃, ~'zin] cousin; **~age** F [~zi'na:ʒ] m cousinship; cousinry; (poor) relations pl.

coussin [ku'sɛ̃] m cushion; pad; **~et** [~si'nɛ] m small cushion; ⚙ bearing.

cousu [ku'zy] 1. p.p of **coudre**; 2. adj. sewn; fig. **~ d'or** rolling in money; **~ main** hand-sewn; fig. excellent, first-rate; fig. solid, reliable.

coût [ku] m cost; **~s** pl. expenses; **~ de la vie** cost of living; **~ant** [ku'tɑ̃] adj.: **prix** m **~** cost price.

coute|au [ku'to] m knife; ⚡ blade; **être à ~x tirés** be at daggers drawn; **~las** [kut'la] m cutlass; cook's knife; **~lier** [kutə'lje] m cutler; **~llerie** [~tel'ri] f cutlery.

coûter [ku'te] (1a) cost; **coûte que coûte** at all costs; **coûteux** [~'tø] expensive, costly.

coutil tex. [ku'ti] m twill; ticking.

coutum|e [ku'tym] f custom, habit; **avoir ~ de** be accustomed to; **comme de ~** as usual; **~ier** [~ty'mje] customary; unwritten (law).

coutur|e [ku'ty:r] f sewing; dressmaking; seam (a. ⚙); **haute ~** high-class dressmaking; F **battre q. à plate(s) ~(s)** beat s.o. hollow, demolish s.o.; fig. sur (or sous) **toutes les ~s** from every angle, from all sides; **~ier, -ère** [~ty'rje, ~'rjɛ:r] su. dressmaker; su./f: thea. **répétition f des ~ères** dress rehearsal.

couvaison [kuvɛ'zɔ̃] f brooding time; **couvée** [~'ve] f eggs: clutch; chicks: brood.

couvent [ku'vɑ̃] m nuns: convent; monks: monastery.

couver [ku've] (1a) v/t. hatch (a. a plot); be sickening for; (molly) coddle; fig. **~ des yeux** look fondly at; v/i. smo(u)lder; fig. be brewing, develop.

couvercle [ku'vɛrkl] m lid, cover.

couvert, e [ku'vɛːr, ~'vɛrt] 1. p.p. of **couvrir**; 2. adj. hidden; overcast (sky); wooded (country); **rester ~** keep one's hat on; 3. su./m cover; charge; cover(ing); **être à ~** be sheltered (from, **de**); a. fig. be safe (from, **do**); **le vivre et le ~** board and lodging; **mettre (ôter) le ~** lay (clear) the table; **sous le ~ de** under the pretext of; su./f pottery: glaze; **~ure** [~vɛr'ty:r] f cover; coverage (a. journ.); roofing; blanket; † security; fig. **sous ~ de** under cover of.

couveuse [ku'vø:z] f sitting hen; incubator.

couvi [ku'vi] adj./m addled (egg).

couvre [ku:vr] 1st p. sg. pres. of **couvrir**; **~chef** [ku:vrə'ʃɛf] m headgear; **~feu** [~'fø] m curfew; **~lit** [~'li] m bedspread; **~pied(s)** [~'pje] m quilt.

couvr|eur [ku'vrœːr] m roofer; **~ir** [~'vri:r] (2f) cover (with, **de**) (a. journ., †); cover up; conceal; **se ~** cover o.s. (a. with honour etc.); put one's hat on; clothe o.s., become overcast (sky etc.)

crabe [kra:b] m crab.

crach|at [kra'ʃa] m spit; ⚡ sputum; **~é** [~'ʃe] adj.: **ce garçon est son père tout ~** this boy is the dead spit of his father; **~er** [~'ʃe] (1a) vt/i. spit; v/t. F cough up (money); v/i. splutter (pen); **~oir** [~'ʃwa:r] m spittoon; F **tenir le ~** hold the floor; **~oter** [~ʃɔ'te] (1a) sputter.

craie [krɛ] f chalk.

crain|dre [krɛ̃:dr] (4m) fear, be afraid or scared of; † **craint l'humidité** keep dry; **je crains qu'il (ne) vienne** I am afraid he will come; **je crains qu'il ne vienne pas** I am afraid he will not come; **~gnis** [krɛ'ɲi] 1st p. sg. p.s. of **craindre**; **~gnons** [~'ɲɔ̃] 1st p. pl. pres. of **craindre**; **~ns** [krɛ̃] 1st p. sg. pres. of **craindre**; **~nt, e** [krɛ̃, krɛ̃:t] 1. p.p. of **craindre**; 2. su./f fear; **de ~ que ... (ne)** (sbj.) lest; **~ntif** [krɛ̃'tif] fearful.

cramoisi [kramwa'zi] crimson.

cramp|e ⚡ [krɑ̃:p] f cramp; **~on** [krɑ̃'pɔ̃]

m cramp, staple; calk; ⚓ tendril; F bore; **~onner** [~pɔ'ne] (1a) clamp; F pester; **se ~ à** cling to.

cran [krɑ̃] *m* notch; *ratchet:* catch; *wheel:* cog; peg; F pluck, guts *pl.*; F **être à ~** be on edge.

crâne¹ [krɑːn] *m* cranium, skull.

crâne² F [krɑːn] plucky; jaunty.

crapaud [kra'po] *m* toad; tub easy-chair; ♪ baby-grand; F urchin.

crapul|e [kra'pyl] *f* lewdness; blackguard; mob; **~eux** [~py'lø] lewd; foul.

craque [krak] *f* tall story; lie.

craquelé [kra'kle] crackled (*glass*).

craquelure [kra'kly:r] *f* crack.

craqu|ement [krak'mɑ̃] *m* crackling; creaking; **~er** [kra'ke] (1m) *v/i.* crack; crackle; crunch (*snow*); squeak (*shoes etc.*); split; *fig.* give way; F *fig.* break down; *v/t.* strike (*a match*); **~eter** [krak'te] (1c) crackle; chirp.

crash ✈ [kraʃ] crash-landing.

crass|e [kras] **1.** *adj./f* crass (*ignorance*); **2.** *su./f* dirt, filth; F dirty trick; **~eux** [kra'sø] filthy.

cratère [kra'tɛːr] *m* crater.

cravache [kra'vaʃ] *f* riding-whip.

cravat|e [kra'vat] *f* (neck)tie; ◎ collar; **~er** [~va'te] (1a) put a tie on; *sp.* collar; *sl.* take *s.o.* for a ride.

cray|eux [krɛ'jø] chalky; **~on** [~'jɔ̃] *m* pencil; **~ à cils** eyebrow pencil; **~-lèvres** lip-pencil; **~onnage** [~jɔ'naːʒ] *m* pencil sketch; **~onner** [~jɔ'ne] (1a) sketch; pencil.

créance [kre'ɑ̃ːs] *f* belief, credence; claim; ✝ credit; **créancier** *m*, **-ère** *f* [~ɑ̃'sje, ~'sjɛːr] creditor.

créat|eur [krea'tœːr] **1.** *adj.* creative; **2.** *su.* creator; ✝ issuer; **~ion** [~'sjɔ̃] *f* creation; establishment; **~ure** [~'tyːr] *f* creature; F person.

crécelle [kre'sɛl] *f* rattle; F chatterbox.

crèche [krɛʃ] *f* manger; crib (*a. eccl.*); crèche, day nursery; *sl.* pad (= home, house, room).

crédence [kre'dɑ̃ːs] *f* sideboard.

crédibilité [kredibili'te] *f* credibility.

crédit [kre'di] *m* credit (*a.* ✝, *a. fig.*); **~ municipal** pawn-office; **à ~** on credit; **faire ~ à** give credit to; **~er** [~di'te] (1a): **~ q. de** credit s.o. with; give s.o. credit for; **~eur** [~di'tœːr] **1.** *su.* creditor; **2.** *adj.* credit-...

credo [kre'do] *m/inv.* creed (*a. fig.*).

crédul|e [kre'dyl] credulous; **~ité** [~dyli'te] *f* credulity.

créer [kre'e] (1a) create; issue (*a bill*); appoint (*s.o. magistrate*).

crémaillère [krema'jɛːr] *f* pot-hook; ◎ rack; rack-railway; F **pendre la ~** give a house-warming (party).

crémation [krema'sjɔ̃] *f* cremation; **crématoire** [~'twaːr] crematory; **four** *m* **~** crematorium.

crème [krɛm] *f* cream (*a. fig.*); *cuis. a.* custard; *fig. the* best.

crém|er [kre'me] (1f) cream; **~erie** [krɛm'ri] *f* dairy; small restaurant; **~eux** [kre'mø] creamy; **~ier, -ère** [~'mje, ~'mjɛːr] *su./m* dairyman; *su./f* dairymaid; cream-jug.

crén|eau [kre'no] *m* loophole; slot; *fig.* gap; *mot.* parking space; *mot.* **faire un ~** get into the *or* a parking space; **~ler** [krɛn'le] (1c) crenel(l)ate (*a wall*); ◎ tooth.

crêpe¹ [krɛp] *m tex.* crape; crêpe (rubber); mourning band.

crêpe² *cuis.* [~] *f* pancake.

crêper [krɛ'pe] (1a) frizz, crimp; F **se ~ le chignon** fight (*woman*).

crép|i △ [kre'pi] *m* roughcast; **~ir** [~'piːr] (2a) roughcast.

crépit|ation [krepita'sjɔ̃] *f* crackle; **~er** [~'te] (1a) crackle; sputter.

crép|on [kre'pɔ̃] *m tex.* crépon; hairpad; **~u** [~'py] fuzzy; crinkled.

crépuscule [krepys'kyl] *m* twilight.

cresson [krɛ'sɔ̃] *m* (water)cress.

crête [krɛːt] *f* crest; *zo.* comb.

crétin *m*, **e** *f* [kre'tɛ̃, ~'tin] 🝙 cretin.

creuser [krø'ze] (1a) hollow out; dig; furrow; groove; *fig.* wrinkle; **se ~ la tête** rack one's brains.

creuset [krø'zɛ] *m* crucible (*a. fig.*).

creux, creuse [krø, krøːz] **1.** *adj.* hollow, sunken (*cheeks*); slack (*period*); **assiette** *f* **creuse** soup plate; **heures** *f/pl.* **creuses** off-peak hours; **2.** *su./m* hollow; *stomach:* pit; F bass voice; **~ de la main** hollow of the hand.

crevaison [krəvɛ'zɔ̃] *f* bursting (*a.* ◎); *mot.* puncture; *sl.* death.

crevant F [krə'vɑ̃] boring; funny.

crevass|e [krə'vas] *f* crack; crevice; crevace; chap; flaw; **~er** [~va'se] (1a) crack; chap.

crève F [krɛːv] *f* death; **~-cœur** [krɛv'kœːr] *m/inv.* heartache, grief.

crever [krə've] (1d) *vt/i.* burst; *v/i.* F die; F *mot.* have a puncture; F **~ de faim** starve; F **~ de rire** split one's sides with laughter; *v/t.* burst; puncture; *fig.* overwork (*s.o.*); **~ le cœur à q.** break s.o.'s heart; *ça crève les yeux* it stares you in the face; *se ~ de travail* work o.s. to death.

crevette *zo.* [krə'vɛt] *f* shrimp.

cri [kri] *m* cry; shriek (*of horror etc.*); *hinge:* creak; *bird:* chirp; *mouse:* squeak; F slogan; *... dernier ~* the latest thing in ...; *pousser un ~* scream; **~ailler** [~ɑ'je] (1a) bawl; whine, F grouse; **~ contre** rail at; **~aillerie** [~ɑj'ri] *f* bawling; whining; scolding; **~ant** [~'ɑ̃] glaring, crying; **~ard** [~'aːr] **1.** *adj.* shrill; pressing (*debt*); loud (*colour*); **2.** *su.* bawler.

crible [kribl] *m* sieve; ⚙ screen; **~er** [kri'ble] (1a) sift, screen, *a. fig.* riddle; *fig.* **criblé de dettes** up to the ears in debt.

cric ⚙ [krik] *m* jack.

cri|ée [kri'e] *f* auction; **~er** [~'e] (1a) *v/i.* cry; scream; squeak; *v/t.* proclaim; hawk (*wares*); shout.

crim|e [krim] *m* crime; **~ d'État** treason; **~ d'incendie** arson; **~inalité** [~inali'te] *f* criminal nature (*of an act*); **~ juvénile** juvenile delinquency; **~inel** [krimi'nɛl] **1.** *adj.* criminal; guilty; **2.** *su.* criminal.

crin [krɛ̃] *m* horsehair; *fig.* **à tous ~s** out and out; F *être comme un ~* be very touchy.

crincrin F [krɛ̃'krɛ̃] *m* fiddle(r).

crinière [kri'njɛːr] *f* mane.

crique [krik] *f* cove; ⚙ flaw.

criquet [kri'kɛ] *m zo.* locust; *zo.* F cricket; *sl.* person: shrimp.

crise [kriːz] *f* crisis; ⚕ attack; **~ du logement** housing shortage; **~ économique** slump.

crisp|ation [krispa'sjɔ̃] *f* contraction; contortion; tensing; twitch(ing); **~é** [~'pe] tense, strained; uptight; **~er** [~'pe] (1a) contract; contort; tense (up); clench (*one's fists*); F irritate (*s.o.*); **se ~** a. tighten.

crisser [kri'se] (1a) grate, rasp; squeak; **~ des dents** grind one's teeth.

cristal [kris'tal] *m* crystal(glass); **~lin** [~ta'lɛ̃] crystalline; clear as crystal; **~liser** [~tali'ze] (1a) crystallize.

critère [kri'tɛːr] *m* criterion, test; **critérium** *sp.* [~te'rjɔm] *m* selection match *or* race.

critiqu|e [kri'tik] **1.** *adj.* critical; **2.** *su./m* critic; *su./f* criticism; **~er** [~ti'ke] (1m) criticize; find fault with; review (*a book*).

croasser [krɔa'se] (1a) croak; caw.

croc [kro] *m* hook; *zo.* fang; **~-en-jambe,** *pl.* **~s-en-jambe** [krɔkɑ̃'ʒɑ̃:b] *m* trip; *faire un ~* trip s.o. up.

croche ♪ [krɔʃ] *f* quaver, *Am.* eighth.

croch|et [krɔ'ʃɛ] *m* hook, crochet-hook; skeleton key; *typ.* square bracket; *zo.* fang, *faire un ~* swerve; make a detour; *fig.* *vive aux ~s de q.* live off s.o.; **~eter** [krɔʃ'te] (1d) pick (*a lock*); **~u** [krɔ'ʃy] hooked; crooked; *fig.* *avoir les doigts ~es* be light-fingered (*thief*); be close-fisted.

crocodile [krɔkɔ'dil] *m zo.* crocodile; *larmes f/pl. de ~* crocodile tears.

croire [krwaːr] (4n) *v/i.* believe (in, **à**; in God, *en Dieu*); **~ en** *a.* have confidence in; *v/t.* believe; think; **~ q. intelligent** believe s.o. to be intelligent; *à l'en ~* according to him (her); *faire ~ qch. à q.* lead s.o. to believe s.th.; *s'en ~* be conceited.

crois [krwa] *1st p. sg. pres. of croire.*

croîs [~] *1st p. sg. pres. of croître.*

crois|ade [krwa'zad] *f* crusade; **~é, e** [~'ze] **1.** *adj.* crossed; *mots m/pl.* **~s** crossword puzzle; **2.** *su./m* crusader; *tex.* twill; *su./f* crossing; casement window; **~ement** [krwaz'mɑ̃] *m* crossing; intersection; *animals:* cross(breed); **~er** [krwa'ze] (1a) *v/t.* cross (*a. biol.*); fold (*one's arms*); *v/i.* ♣ cruise; **~eur** ♣ [~'zœːr] *m* cruiser; **~ière** [~'zjɛːr] *f* cruise; *vitesse f de ~* cruising speed; *fig.* pace.

crois|sance [krwa'sɑ̃s] *f* growth; **~ant** [~'sɑ̃] **1.** *adj.* waxing; **2.** *su./m* moon: crescent; *cuis.* croissant; **~ons** [~'sɔ̃] *1st p. pl. pres. of croître.*

croître [krwaːtr] (4o) grow; increase; wax (*moon*); lengthen (*days*).

croix [krwa] *f* cross; *la* ♀ *Rouge* the Red Cross; *en ~* crosswise.

croquant¹ [krɔ'kɑ̃] crisp.

croquant² [krɔ'kɑ̃] *m* F clodhopper.

croque au sel [krɔko'sɛl] *adv.*: **manger à la ~** eat with salt only.

croque...: ~-madame [krɔkma'dam] *m/inv.* toasted ham and cheese sandwich with fried egg; **~-mitaine** F [~mi'tɛn] *m* bog(e)y; **~-monsieur** [~ma'sjø] *m/inv.* toasted ham and cheese sandwich.

croquer [krɔ'ke] (1m) munch; sketch; *fig.* gobble up; leave out.

croquette *cuis.* [krɔ'kɛt] *f* rissole.

croquis [krɔ'ki] *m* sketch; outline.

crosse [krɔs] *f* crozier; *gun*: butt; *piston*: crosshead; *golf*: club.

crotale [krɔ'tal] *m* rattlesnake.

crott|e [krɔt] *f* droppings *pl.* **~in** [~'tɛ̃] *m* horse dung.

crouler [kru'le] (1a) totter, crumble; collapse; fall.

croup|e [krup] *f animal*: croup, rump; *hill*: crest; **en ~** behind (the rider); on the pillion; **monter en ~** *a.* ride pillion; **~etons** [~tɔ̃] *adv.*: **à ~** squatting; **~ier** [~'pje] *m* croupier; **~ière** [~'pjɛːr] *f* crupper; *fig.* **tailler des ~s à** make things difficult for; **~ion** [~'pjɔ̃] *m bird*: rump; **~ir** [~'piːr] (2a) stagnate; *fig.* **~ dans** wallow in.

croust|ade *cuis.* [krus'tad] *f* pie; **~illant** [krusti'jɑ̃] crisp; crusty; *fig.* spicy; attractive (*woman*).

croût|e [krut] *f* crust; rind; ✄ scab; F daub; **F casser la ~** have a snack; **~er** F [kru'te] (1a) eat; **~eux** [~'tø] scabby; **~on** [~'tɔ̃] *m* piece of crust; *sl.* dauber; *sl.* old fossil.

croy|able [krwa'jabl] believable; trustworthy; **~ance** [~'jɑ̃ːs] *f* belief; faith; **~ant** [~'jɑ̃] 1. *adj.* believing; 2. *su.* believer; **les ~s** *m/pl.* the faithful; **~ons** [~'jɔ̃] *1st p. pl. pres. of* **croire.**

cru¹ [kry] raw; coarse.

cru² [~] *m* wine region; vineyard; F locality; **de mon ~** of my own (invention); **(vin de) grand ~** great wine.

cru³ [~] *p.p. of* **croire.**

crû, crue, *m/pl.* **crus** [~] *p.p. of* **croître.**

cruauté [kryo'te] *f* cruelty.

cruch|e [kryʃ] *f* jug; *sl.* dolt; **~on** [kry'ʃɔ̃] *m* small jug; mug.

crucial [kry'sjal] crucial; **~fier** [~'fje] (1o) crucify; **~fix** [~'fi] *m* crucifix; **~forme** [~'form] cross-shaped.

crudité [krydi'te] *f* crudity; coarseness;

indigestibility; **~s** *pl.* gross words; *cuis.* raw vegetables.

crue [kry] *f water*: rise; flood.

cruel [kry'ɛl] cruel (to, **envers**).

crûment [kry'mɑ̃] *adv. of* **cru¹.**

crus [kry] *1st p. sg. p.s. of* **croire.**

crûs [~] *1st p. sg. p.s. of* **croître.**

crusse¹ [krys] *1st p. sg. impf. sbj. of* **croire.**

crusse² [~] *1st p. sg. impf. sbj. of* **croître.**

crustacé [krysta'se] *m* shellfish.

crypte △, ✄, *anat.* [kript] *f* crypt.

cubage [ky'baːʒ] *m* cubic content.

cube [kyb] 1. *su./m* cube; **~s** *pl. toy*: building blocks; 2. *adj.* cubic; **cuber** ✄ [ky'be] (1a) cube.

cubi|que [ky'bik] cubic; ✄ **racine** *f* **~** cube root; **~sme** *paint.* [~'bism] *m* cubism.

cueille [kœːj] *1st p. sg. pres. of* **cueillir; ~erai** [kœj're] *1st p. sg. fut. of* **cueillir; ~ette** [kœ'jɛt] *f* picking, gathering; **~ir** [~'jiːr] (2c) gather, pick; *fig.* win; *fig.* snatch (*a kiss*); F pick (*s.o.*) up; F catch, nab.

cuill|er, ~ère [kɥi'jɛːr] *f* spoon; **~ à café** coffee spoon; *cuis.* teaspoonful; **~ à pot** ladle; **~erée** [kɥij're] *f* spoonful.

cuir [kɥiːr] *m* leather; hide; **~ chevelu** scalp; **~asse** [kɥi'ras] *f* armo(u)r; **~assé** [kɥira'se] *m* battleship; **~asser** [~'se] (1a) armo(u)r-plate; *fig.* harden.

cui|re [kɥiːr] (4h) *v/t.* cook; fire (*bricks*); **~ à l'eau** boil; **~ au four** bake, roast; *v/i.* cook; be boiling (*a. fig.*); smart (*eyes*); **faire ~** cook (*s.th.*); **~sant** [kɥi'zɑ̃] burning, stinging; smarting; *fig.* bitter (*cold*); burning (*desire*).

cuisin|e [kɥi'zin] *f* kitchen; ⚓ galley; cookery; cooking; **faire la ~** do the cooking; **~er** [zi'~ne] (1a) *v/t.* cook; *v/t. fig.* F grill (*s.o.*); F cook (*accounts*); **~ier, -ère** [~zi'nje, ~'njɛːr] *su.* cook; *su./f* cooker, Am. range.

cuis|is [kɥis] *1st p. sg. p.s. of* **cuire; ~ons** [~'zɔ̃] *1st p. pl. pres. of* **cuire.**

cuisse [kɥis] *f* thigh; *cuis.* leg.

cuisson [kɥi'sɔ̃] *f* cooking; baking; boiling; *bricks, fig.*: burning.

cuissot [kɥi'so] *m venison*: haunch.

cuistre [kɥistr] *m* pedant; F cad.

cuit, e [kɥi, kɥit] 1. *p.p. of* **cuire;** 2. *su./f bricks*: baking; boiling; **F pendre une ~**

get tight; **~er** sl. [kчi'te] (1a): **se ~** get drunk.

cuivr|e [kчi:vr] m copper; **~ jaune** brass; ♪ **~s** pl. brass sg.; **~é** [kчi'vre] coppery; bronzed; metallic (voice); **~eux** [~'vrø] coppery; 🜍 cuprous.

cul V [ky] m arse, Am. ass; bottom; **~asse** [ky'las] f ✕ breech; ⚡ yoke; ⊙ cylinderhead.

cubut|e [ky'byt] f somersault; tumble; F **faire la ~** ✈ fail; pol. fall; **~er** [~by'te] (1a) v/i. turn a somersault; topple over; F ✈ fail; F pol. fall; v/t. overthrow (a. pol.); upset; tip; **~eur** [~by'tœːr] m ⊙ tipper; ⚡ tumbler.

cul...: ~-de-jatte, pl. **~s-de-jatte** [kyd'ʒat] m legless cripple; **~-de-sac**, pl. **~s-de-sac** [~'sak] m dead end (street).

culée [ky'le] f abutment; **culer** [~'le] (1a) go backwards.

culinaire [kyli'nɛːr] culinary.

culmin|ant [kylmi'nɑ̃] culminating; **point** m **~** highest point; **~ation** astr. [~na'sjɔ̃] f culmination; **~er** [~'ne] (1a) culminate, reach the highest point

culot [ky'lo] m bottle etc.: bottom; ⊙ base; F cheek, nerve; tobacco pipe: dottle; **~te** [~'lɔt] f pants pl.; knickers pl.; panties pl.; breeches pl.; beef: rump; **~té** seasoned (pipe); F cheeky.

culpabilité [kylpabili'te] f guilt.

culte [kylt] m worship; cult; religion; (church) service.

cultiv|able [kylti'vabl] arable; **~ateur** [~va'tœːr] **1.** su. cultivator; farmer; **2.** adj. farming; **~é** [~'ve] cultivated; fig. cultured; **~er** [~'ve] (1a) cultivate (a. fig.); till.

cultur|e [kyl'tyːr] f cultivation (a. fig.), growing; fish etc.: breeding; **~s** pl. cultivated land sg.; **la ~** culture; **~el** [~ty'rɛl] cultural; **~isme** [~ty'rism] m bodybuilding.

cumin ♣ [ky'mɛ̃] m cum(m)in.

cumul [ky'myl] m plurality (of offices); **~er** [~'le] (1a) hold (offices) or draw (salaries) simultaneously.

cupid|e [ky'pid] greedy, covetous; **~ité** [~pidi'te] f greed, cupidity.

cura|ble [ky'rabl] curable; **~ge** [~'raːʒ] m clearing or cleaning (out); **~telle** ⚖

[kyra'tɛl] f guardianship; **~teur** m, **-trice** f [~'tœːr, ~'tris] trustee; guardian; **~tif** [~'tif] adj., su./m curative.

cure [kyːr] f care; ⚕, eccl. cure.

curé [ky're] m parish priest.

cure-dent [kyr'dɑ̃] m toothpick.

curée [ky're] f hunt. quarry; rush (for the spoils).

cure...: ~-ongles [ky'rɔ̃ːgl] m/inv. nail-cleaner; **~-pipe** [kyr'pip] m pipe-cleaner.

cur|er [ky're] (1a) clean; pick (one's teeth); dredge; **~etage** [kyra'taːʒ] m ⚕ curetting.

curi|eux [ky'rjø] **1.** adj. curious; interested (in, de); strange, odd; **curieusement** a. oddly enough; **2.** su./m the odd thing (about, de); **~osité** [~rjozi'te] f curiosity; **~s** sights (of a town).

curiste [ky'rist] su. patient taking a cure.

curseur ⊙ [kyr'sœːr] m slide(r).

cursif, -ve [kyr'sif, ~'siːv] **1.** adj. cursive; cursory; **2.** su./f cursive.

cutané [kyta'ne] cutaneous.

cuv|age [ky'vaːʒ] m, **~aison** [~vɛ'zɔ̃] f fermenting in vats; **~e** [kyːv] f vat; ⊙ tank; **~ée** [~'ve] f vatful; vintage; **~er** [~'ve] (1a) ferment; **~ette** [~'vɛt] f (wash)basin; bowl; watch: cap.

cyanure 🜍 [sja'nyːr] m cyanide.

cybernétique [sibɛrne'tik] **1.** su./f cybernetics sg.; **2.** adj. cybernetic.

cyclable [si'klabl] for cyclists; **piste** f **~** cycle path.

cycl|e [sikl] m cycle (a. fig); **~ique** [si'klik] cyclic(al); **~isme** sp. [~'klism] m cycling; **~iste** [~'klist] **1.** su. cyclist; **2.** adj. cycling; **~omoteur** [siklɔmɔ'tœːr] m moped.

cyclone meteor. [si'klon] m cyclone.

cygne orn. [siɲ] m swan.

cylindr|e ⊙ [si'lɛ̃ːdr] m cylinder; roller; **~ée** mot. [silɛ̃'dre] f (cubic) capacity; **~er** [~'dre] (1a) ⊙ roll; **~ique** [~'drik] cylindrical.

cymbale ♪ [sɛ̃'bal] f cymbal.

cyni|que [si'nik] cynical; cynic; fig. shameless; **~sme** [~'nism] m cynicism; fig. effrontery.

cyprès ♣ [si'prɛ] m cypress; **cyprière** [~pri'ɛːr] f cypress-grove.

D

da [da]: *oui-da!* yes indeed!

d'ac *sl.* [dak] okay, OK.

dactylo F [dakti'lo] *su.* typist; *su./f* typing; **~graphe** [daktilɔ'graf] *su.* typist; **~graphie** [~gra'fi] *f* typing; **~graphier** [~gra'fje] (1o) type.

dada [da'da] *m* hobby(-horse), fad; *fig.* **enfourcher son ~** get on to one's pet subject.

dadais F [da'dɛ] *m* simpleton.

dague [dag] *f* dagger; ♣ dirk.

daigner [dɛ'ɲe] (1b) deign.

daim [dɛ̃] *m zo.* deer; buck; † buckskin; **en ~** suède (*gloves*).

dall|age [da'la:ʒ] *m* paving; tiled floor; **~e** [dal] *f* flagstone; *sl.* throat; **~er** [da'le] (1a) pave; tile.

daltoni|en ♣ [daltɔ'njɛ̃] colo(u)r-blind (person); **~sme** ♣ [~'nism] *m* colo(u)r-blindness.

damas [da'mɑ] *m tex.* damask; ♀ damson; **~quiner** [~maski'ne] (1a) damascene.

dame [dam] **1.** *su./f* lady; *cards, chess*: queen; ⊚ rammer; **~ du vestiaire** cloakroom (*Am.* checkroom) attendant; *jeu m de* **~s** draughts, *Am.* checkers; **2.** *int.* indeed!; of course!; **~-jeanne**, *pl.* **~s-jeannes** [~'ʒan] *f* demijohn; **damer** [da'me] (1a) *draughts, checkers*: crown (*a piece*); ⊚ ram; *fig.* **~ le pion à** outwit (*s.o.*).

damier [da'mje] *m* draught-board, *Am.* checker-board; *tex.* **à ~** chequered, checked.

damn|able [dɑ'nabl] *fig.* detestable, damnable; **~ation** [~na'sjɔ̃] *f* damnation; **~er** [~'ne] (1a) damn; F *faire* **~ q.** drive s.o. crazy.

dancing [dɑ̃'siŋ] *m* public dance.

dandiner [dɑ̃di'ne] (1a) dandle; *se* **~** waddle; strut; sway.

danger [dɑ̃'ʒe] *m* danger; **~ de mort!** danger of death!; **~eux** [dɑ̃ʒ'rø] dangerous (to, *pour*).

danois [da'nwa] **1.** *adj., su./m ling.* Danish; **2.** *su* ♀ Dane; *les* ♀ *m/pl.* the Danes.

dans [dɑ̃] *prp. usu.* in (*the street, a month, the morning, the past*); *place:* within

(*the limits*); among (*the crowd*); *direction:* into; *time:* within (*an hour*), during; *condition:* in; with; under (*these circumstances*); *origin:* out of, from; *entrer* **~** *une pièce* enter a room; **~ Racine** in Racine; **~ l'intention de** (*inf.*) with the intention of (*ger.*); *boire* **~** drink from; *prendre* **~** take from *or* out of.

dans|ant [dɑ̃'sɑ̃] springy; lively; *thé m* **~** tea-dance; **~e** [dɑ̃:s] *f* dance; dancing; *fig.* F battle; *sl.* thrashing; **~ macabre** Dance of Death; *salle f de* **~** ball-room; **~er** [dɑ̃'se] (1a); prance (*horse*); **~eur, -euse** [~'sœr, ~'sø:z] *su.* dancer; (dance-)partner; **~ de corde** tight-rope dancer; *su./f* ballerina; **~otter** F [~sɔ'te] (1a) hop, skip.

dard [da:r] *m* † dart; *zo.* sting (*a. fig.*); piercing ray; ♀ pistil; **~er** [dar'de] (1a) shoot forth; spear; *fig.* flash (*a glance*) (at, *sur*).

dare-dare F [dar'da:r] *adv.* post-haste, at top speed.

darne *cuis.* [darn] *f fish:* slice, steak.

dartr|e ♣ [dartr] *f* dartre; scurf; **~eux** [dar'trø] scabby.

date [dat] *f* date; **~ limite** deadline; target date; *de longue* **~** of long standing; *en* **~ de ...** dated ...; *faire* **~** mark an epoch; *jusqu'à une* **~ récente** until recently.

dater [da'te] (1a) *v/i.* date (from, *de*); **à ~ de ce jour** from that day; *v/t.* date (*a letter*).

datt|e ♀, † [dat] *f* date; *sl.* **des ~s!** not on your life!, *Am.* no dice!; **~ier** ♀ [da'tje] *m* date-palm.

daube *cuis.* [do:b] *f* stew.

dauber[1] † [do'be] (1a) *a.* **~ sur** backbite (*s.o.*); jeer at (*s.o.*).

dauber[2] *cuis.* [do'be] (1a) stew.

dauphin [do'fɛ̃] *m zo.* dolphin; *hist.* Dauphin (= *eldest son of French king*); △ gargoyle.

davantage [davɑ̃'ta:ʒ] *adv.* more (and more); longer (*space, time*).

de [də] *prp. usu.* of; *material:* (made) of (*wood*), in (*velvet*); *cause:* of (*hunger*), from (*exhaustion*); with, for (*joy*); *origin:* from, out of; *distance:* of, from;

direction: to (*a side*); *place*: at, in; on (*a side*); *time*: by (*day*); by (*name*); *manner*: in (*this way*); *measure, comparison*: by; *partitive article*: **du pain** (some) bread; **~ la viande** (some) meat; **des légumes** vegetables; **un litre ~ vin** a litre of wine; **la ville ~ Paris** (the city of) Paris; **le mois ~ janvier** January; **assez ~** enough; **beaucoup ~** much, many; **moins ~** less; **pas ~** no; **peu ~** few; **plus ~** more; **tant ~** so much, so many; **trop ~** too much, too many; **qch. ~ rouge** s.th. red; *genitive, possession*: **mon père** of my father, my father's; **le journal d'hier** yesterday's paper; **les œuvres ~ Molière** Molière's works; **matériaux ~ construction** building materials; **membre du Parlement** Member of Parliament; **souvenirs d'enfance** childhood memories; **amour ~** love of; **chapeau ~ paille** straw hat; **mourir ~ cancer** die of cancer; **~ haut en bas** from top to bottom; **saigner du nez** bleed from the nose; **à trois miles ~ distance** at a distance of three miles; **~ ... à ...** from ... to ...; **la route (le train) ~ Bordeaux** the Bordeaux road (train); **~ ce côté** on this side; **~ nos jours** in our times; **du temps ~ Henri IV** in the days of Henry IV; **à 2 heures ~ l'après-midi** at 2 p.m.; **avancer ~ 5 minutes** be 5 minutes fast (*watch*); **se nourrir ~** feed on; **frapper ~** strike with; **montrer du doigt** point at; **précédé ~** preceded by; **trois mètres ~ long, long ~ trois mètres** three metres long; **âgé ~ 5 ans** 5 years old *or* of age; **plus âgé ~ 2 ans** older by 2 years; **plus ~ 6** more than 6; **d'un œil curieux** with an inquiring look or eye; **des marchandises ~ 20 F.** 20 F. worth of goods; **digne ~ ...**-worthy, worthy of; **un jour ~ libre** a day off.

dé¹ [de] *m gaming*: die; **~s** *pl*. dice; **le ~ est jeté** the die is cast; *cooking*: **couper en ~s** dice.

dé² [~] (*a*. **~ à coudre**) thimble.

dé-...³ [de], **de-**... [də] un ..., dis ...

déambuler F [deãby'le] (1a) stroll about, saunter.

débâcle [de'bɑːkl] *f ice*: breaking up; *fig*. disaster; collapse; F *pol*. landslide; **~er** [~bɑ'kle] (1a) *v/t*. clear (*a harbour*); *v/i*. break up (*ice*).

déball|age [deba'laːʒ] *m* unpacking; F *fig*. outpouring, effusion; **~er** [~'le] (1a) unpack; F *fig*. let out, air, display.

déband|ade [debã'dad] *f* stampede; rout; **à la ~** in disorder; **~er** [~'de] (1a) unbend; unbandage; **se ~** slacken; scatter, disperse.

débaptiser [debati'ze] (1a) rename.

débarbouiller [debarbu'je] (1a) wash (*s.o.'s*) face; **se ~** *fig*. get out of difficulties as best one can.

débarcadère [debarka'dɛːr] *m* ♨ landing-stage; 🚉 arrival platform.

débard|age ♨ [debar'daːʒ] *m* unloading; **~er** [~'de] (1a) unload; **~eur** [~'dœːr] *m* ♨ stevedore, docker; *garment*: slipover.

débarqu|ement [debarkə'mã] *m* ♨ unloading; 🚉 F arrival; **~er** [~'ke] (1m) *vt/i.* ♨ disembark; *v/t*. bus etc.: set down; F dismiss (*s.o.*); *v/i.* 🚉 alight.

débarras [deba'rɑ] *m* lumber or junk room; **bon ~!** good riddance!; **~ser** [~ra'se] (1a) clear (of, **de**); **se ~ de** get rid of.

débat [de'ba] *m* discussion; debate; dispute; ⚖ **~s** *pl*. proceedings.

débâtir [debɑ'tiːr] (2a) demolish.

débattre [de'batr] (4a) debate, discuss; **se ~** struggle; flounder about.

débauch|age [debo'ʃaːʒ] *m* laying off, dismissal; **~e** [de'boːʃ] *f* debauch(ery); *fig*. profusion; **~é** [debo'ʃe] 1. *adj*. debauched; 2. *su*. debauchee; **~er** [~] (1a) entice away (*a workman*); F tempt away; lay off (*workmen*).

débil|e [de'bil] weak, feeble; **~ité** [debili'te] *f* weakness; **~iter** [~] (1a) weaken, undermine (*the health*).

débin|e *sl*. [de'bin] *f* poverty; **~er** *sl*. [~bi'ne] (1a) run (*s.o.*) down; **se ~** make o.s. scarce.

débit [de'bi] *m* retail shop; ♥ turnover, sales *pl*.; ⊚ output; ♥ debit; *river*: flow; **~ de tabac** tobacconist's; **avoir un ~ facile** have the gift of the gab; **portez ... au ~ de mon compte** debit me with ...; **~ant** *m*, **e** *f* [debi'tɑ̃, ~'tãːt] dealer; **~er** [~'te] (1a) sell; cut up (*logs*); ⊚ yield; reel of (*a poem*); *pej*. deliver (*a speech*); ♥ debit (s.o. with s.th. **qch. à q., q. de qch.**).

débiteur¹, **-trice** [debi'tœːr, ~'tris] 1. *su*. debtor; 2. *adj*. debit...

débiteur² *m*, **-euse** *f* [debi'tœːr, ~'tøːz] retailer; *usu. pej.* utterer; **~ de calomnies** scandal-monger.

déblai [de'blɛ] *m* clearing; excavation; excavated material; **~ement** [~blɛ'mɑ̃] *m* digging out; removal.

déblatérer [deblate're] (1f) rail (against, *contre*); drivel, twaddle.

déblayer [deblɛ'je] (1h) clear away, remove; clear (*a. fig.*).

déblo|cage [deblɔ'kaːʒ] *m* clearing; ✝, ⚙ releasing; **~quer** [~'ke] (1m) unblock; ✝, ⚙ release; free, clear.

débobiner [debɔbi'ne] (1a) unwind, unreel.

déboires [de'bwaːr] *m/pl.* disappointments; setbacks; troubles.

déboiser [debwa'ze] (1a) deforest.

déboîter [debwa'te] (1a) *v/t.* ✝ dislocate; ⚙ disconnect; *v/i. mot.* filter; haul out of the line.

débonder [debɔ̃'de] (1a) unbung (*a cask*); *fig.* **~ son cœur**, **se ~** pour out one's heart.

débonnaire [debɔ'nɛːr] meek; **~té** [~nɛr'te] *f* good nature.

débord|é [debɔr'de] *fig.* overwhelmed (with work, *de travail*); dissipated (*life*); **~ement** [~də'mɑ̃] *m* overflowing; *fig.* outburst; **~ements** *m/pl.* dissipation *sg.*; **~er** [~'de] (1a) *vt/i.* overflow, run over; *v/t.* stick out beyond.

débotter [debɔ'te] (1a) take off (*s.o.'s*) boots; *fig.* **au débotté** immediately on arrival.

débouch|é [debu'ʃe] *m* outlet; opening; ✝ market; **~er** [~] (1a) *v/t.* clear; uncork; *v/i.* emerge; open (**on**, *sur*); **~ sur** *a.* lead to; end up in.

déboucler [debu'kle] (1a) unbuckle.

débouler [debu'le] (1a) roll down, tumble down; *hunt.* bolt.

déboulonner [debulɔ'ne] (1a) unrivet, unbolt; F debunk; oust.

débourber [debur'be] (1a) clean (out); get (*s.o.*) out of a mess.

débourrer [debu're] (1a) break in (*a horse*); clean out (*a pipe*); *fig.* smarten (*s.o.*) up.

débours [de'buːr] *m* (*usu. pl.*) disbursement; outlay; **~er** [~bur'se] (1a) spend; disburse.

déboussoler F [debusɔ'le] (1a) disorient(ate); disconcert.

debout [də'bu] *adv.* upright; standing (up); **~!** get up!; *être* ~ be up; *fig.* **ne pas tenir ~** not to stand up; *4 places* **~** 4 standing; *se tenir* **~** stand.

déboutonner [debutɔ'ne] (1a) unbutton; *manger (rire) à ventre déboutonné* eat (laugh) immoderately; *fig.* **se ~** unbosom o.s.

débraillé [debra'je] untidy; free (*conversation*); loose (*morals*).

débranch|ement [debrɑ̃ʃ'mɑ̃] *m* disconnecting; **~er** ⚡ [~brɑ̃'ʃe] (1a) disconnect, unplug; cut (off).

débray|age [debrɛ'jaːʒ] *m mot.* declutching; F strike, *Am.* walkout; **~er** [~'je] (li) *vt/i.* ⚙, *mot.* declutch; *v/i.* F knock off work.

débrider [debri'de] (1a) unbridle; halt; ✝ incise; *sans* **~** on end.

débris [de'bri] *m/pl.* debris *sg.*; remains; wreckage *sg.*; rubbish *sg.*

débrouill|ard F [debru'jaːr] smart, resourceful; **~er** [~'je] (1a) disentangle; *a. fig.* unravel; *se* **~** find a way out of difficulties; manage (to *inf.*, *pour inf.*); cope.

débusquer [debys'ke] (1m) drive *or* chase out.

début [de'by] *m* beginning, start; coming out; *thea.* debut; *de* **~** starting (*salary etc.*); *faire ses* **~** make a first appearance; **~ant** *m*, **e** *f* [deby'tɑ̃, ~'tɑ̃ːt] beginner; new performer; **~er** [~'te] (1a) begin; appear for the first time.

déc(a)... [dek(a)] dec(a)...

deçà [də'sa] *adv.* on this side; **~ delà** here and there; to and fro; on all sides; *en* **~ de** on this side of.

décacheter [dekaʃ'te] (1c) unseal.

décade [de'kad] *f* decade.

décaden|ce [deka'dɑ̃ːs] *f* decadence, decay; **~t** [~'dɑ̃] decadent.

décaféiné [dekafei'ne] caffeine-free.

décaisser [dekɛ'se] (1b) unpack, unbox; ✝ pay out; ✔ plant out.

décal|age [deka'laːʒ] *m* shifting; *fig.* gap, discrepancy; **~er** [~'le] (1a) shift (forward *or* back); move forward; put back.

décalqu|age [dekal'kaːʒ] *m*, **~e** [~'kalk] *m* transfer(ring); tracing (off); **~er** [~kal'ke] (1m) trace off.

décamper [dekɑ̃'pe] (1a) decamp.

décanat [deka'na] *m* deanship.

décanter [dekã'te] (1a) decant.

décap|age [deka'pa:ʒ] *m*, **~ement** [~kap'mã] *m* scouring; *metal*: pickling; **~er** [~ka'pe] (1a) scour.

décapiter [dekapi'te] (1a) behead.

décapotable *mot.* [dekapɔ'tabl] convertible; drop-head (*coupé*).

décapsulateur [dekapsyla'tœːr] *m* (crown-cork) opener.

décatir [deka'tiːr] (2a) *tex.* take the gloss off; F **se ~** age.

décav|é F [deka'vc] broke; worn-out; **~er** F [~] (1a) clean (*s.o.*) out.

décéder [dese'dɔ] (1f) die, decease.

déceler [desə'le] (1d) reveal, disclose; betray; divulge.

décembre [de'sã:br] *m* December.

décemment [desa'mã] *adv.* of **décent**; **décence** [~'sãːs] *f* decency.

décent [de'sã] decent; modest.

décentralisor *admin.* [desãtrali'ze] (1a) decentralize.

décentrer [desã'tre] (1a) throw off centre.

déception [desep'sjɔ̃] *f* disappointment.

décerner [dcser'ne] (1a) award (*a prize* to, **à**), confer (*an honour*) (on, **à**); ⚖ issue (*a writ etc.*).

décès [de'sɛ] *m* decease, death.

décev|ant [desə'vã] deceptive; disappointing; **~oir** [~'vwaːr] (3a) deceive, disappoint.

déchaîn|ement [deʃɛn'mã] *m* unchaining; *fig.* outburst; **~er** [~ʃɛ'ne] (1b) let loose (*a. fig.*); **se ~** break loose; **se ~ contre** storm at.

déchanter F [deʃã'te] (1a) change one's tune; sing small

décharg|e [de'ʃarʒ] *f* ⚡, ✕, ⚖, ⚙ discharge; ✕ volley; ⚖ acquittal; ✝ receipt; ✝ credit; **~ (publique or municipale)** rubbish (*Am.* garbage) dump; **tuyau m de ~** outlet; **~eoir** ⚙ [deʃar'ʒwaːr] *m* outlet; waste pipe; **~er** [~'ʒe] (1l) unload (*a cart, a gun*); ⚓ unlade; discharge (*a. ⚡, ⚙, ⚖, a gun*) (at **sur, contre**); empty; exempt (*from,* **de**); ⚖ acquit; *fig.* relieve; *fig.* vent; **se ~ de** pass off (*a responsibility etc.*) (onto, **sur**).

décharné [deʃar'ne] lean; gaunt.

déchausser [deʃo'se] (1a) take off (*s.o.'s*) shoes; bare (*a tooth*).

dèche *sl.* [dɛʃ] *f*: **dans la ~, dans une ~ noire** broke.

déchéance [deʃe'ãːs] *f* downfall; decline; ⚖ expiration; forfeiture.

déchets [de'ʃɛ] *m/pl.* scraps; waste *sg.*; trash *sg.*; *fig.* dregs, scum.

déchiffr|er [deʃi'fre] (1a) decipher; decode; ♪ read at sight.

déchiqueter [deʃik'te] (1c) hack, slash, tear to shreds (*a. fig.*).

déchir|ant [deʃi'rã] heart-rending; agonizing; racking (*cough*); **~ement** [~ʃir'mã] *m* tearing (*a. ⚡*); laceration; **~ de cœur** heartbreak; **~er** [deʃi're] (1a) tear (up); *fig.* rend; **~ure** [~'yːr] *f* tear, rent; ⚡ laceration.

déchoir [de'ʃwaːr] (3d) decline.

déchu [de'ʃy] **1.** *p.p. of* **déchoir; 2.** *adj.* fallen; expired; forfeited.

déci... [desi] deci...

décid|é [desi'de] decided; resolute, confident; **~ément** [~de'mã] *adv.* certainly, positively, really; **~er** [~'de] (1a) *v/t.* decide, settle; decide on; **~ q. à** (*inf.*) persuade s.o. to (*inf.*); *v/i.:* **~ de** (*inf.*) decide to (*inf.*), make up one's mind to (*inf.*); **~ de qch.** determine s.th.

décim|al, e [desi'mal] *adj., su./f* decimal; **~er** [~'me] (1a) decimate; thin out; deplete.

décisi|f [desi'sif] decisive; conclusive (*proof*), positive (*tones*); F cock-sure (*person*); **~on** [~'sjɔ̃] *f* decision; resolution.

déclam|ateur [deklama'tœːr] **1.** *su./m* declaimer; **2.** *adj. see* **déclamatoire**; **~ation** [~ma'sjɔ̃] *f* declamation; ranting; **~atoire** [~ma'twaːr] declamatory; ranting; turgid (*style*); **~er** [~'me] (1a) declaim; rant.

déclar|ation [deklara'sjɔ̃] *f* declaration; statement; *admin.* registration, notification; **~ de revenu** income tax return; **~er** [~'re] (1a) declare (*a. ✝*); ⚖ **coupable** find guilty; **avez-vous qch. à ~?** have you anything to declare?; **se ~** declare (for, **pour;** against, **contre**); speak one's mind; declare one's love; break out (*fire etc.*).

déclasser [deklɑ'se] (1a) bring (*s.o.*) down in the world; declare obsolete; *sp.* penalize (*a runner*).

déclench|er [deklã'ʃe] (1a) unlatch (*a door*); ⚙ release (*a. phot.*), disengage; trigger; F start; **~eur** [~'ʃœːr] *m* release (*a. phot.*); *phot.* **~ automatique** self-timer.

déclic ⊙ [de'klik] *m* catch, pawl; trigger; **montre** *f* **à** ~ stop-watch.

déclin [de'klɛ̃] *m* decline, decay; waning; fall; **au** ~ **du jour** at the close of day; **~aison** [dekline'zɔ̃] *f astr.* declination; ♃ variation; *gramm.* declension; **~er** [~'ne] (1a) *v/i.* deviate; decline; *fig.* fade, fail, wane; *v/t.* decline (*a. gramm.*); refuse; state (*one's name*).

déclive [de'kli:v] **1.** *adj.* sloping; **2.** *su./f.* slope; **~ité** [~klivi'te] *f* slope, gradient, incline.

décocher [dekɔ'ʃe] (1a) shoot, let fly; let off; discharge.

décoder [dekɔ'de] (1a) decode; decipher.

décoiffer [dekwa'fe] (1a) remove (*s.o.'s*) hat; ruffle (*s.o.'s*) hair.

décoll|age [dekɔ'la:ʒ] *m* unsticking; ✈ takeoff; **~er** [~'le] (1a) *v/t.* unstick; loosen; *v/i.* ✈ take off; F budge; *sp.* fall behind.

décolleté [dekɔl'te] **1.** *adj.* low-necked (*dress*); wearing a low-necked dress; **2.** *su./m* low neckline.

décolorer [dekɔlɔ're] (1a) discolo(u)r; fade; **se** ~ grow pale.

décombres [de'kɔ̃:br] *m/pl.* rubbish *sg.*; debris *sg.*, *buildings:* rubble *sg.*

décommander [dekɔmɑ̃'de] (1a) cancel; ✝ countermand; **se** ~ excuse o.s. from an invitation; cancel an appointment.

décompos|er [dekɔ̃po'ze] (1a) decompose; split up; distort (*the features*); **se** ~ decay; **~ition** [~zi'sjɔ̃] *f* decomposition; rotting.

décompt|e [de'kɔ̃:t] *m* ✝ deduction; balance due; detailed account; **~er** [~kɔ̃'te] (1a) deduct; calculate (*the interest*); reckon off.

déconcerter [dekɔ̃sɛr'te] (1a) disconcert; upset (*plans*); baffle.

déconfit [dekɔ̃'fi] crestfallen; nonplussed; **~ure** [~fi'ty:r] *f* ruin; insolvency; defeat.

décongeler [dekɔ̃'ʒle] (1d) thaw (out); defreeze.

décongestionner [dekɔ̃ʒɛstjɔ'ne] (1a) relieve congestion in; clear.

déconseiller [dekɔ̃sɛ'je] (1a) advise (s.o. against s.th., *qch. à q.*; *q. de inf.* s.o. against *ger.*).

déconsidérer [dekɔ̃side're] (1f) discredit, slur, run down.

décontenancer [dekɔ̃tnɑ̃'se] (1k) put out of countenance, abash.

déconvenue [dekɔ̃v'ny] *f* disappointment; discomfiture; *fig.* blow.

décor [de'kɔ:r] *m house:* decoration; *thea.* set(ting); *thea.* **~s** *pl.* scenery *sg.*; *mot. sl.* **rentrer dans le** ~ run into a wall *etc.*; **~ateur** *m*, **-trice** *f* [dekɔra'tœ:r, ~'tris] decorator; stage-designer; **~ation** [~ra'sjɔ̃] *f* decoration (*a. medal*); **~er** [~'re] (1a) decorate.

décortiquer [dekɔrti'ke] (1m) husk (*rice*); shell (*nuts*); peel (*fruit*).

décorum [dekɔ'rɔm] *m* propriety.

découcher [deku'ʃe] (1a) sleep out.

découdre [de'kudr] (4l) rip open.

découler [deku'le] (1a): ~ **de** follow or result from.

découp|age [deku'pa:ʒ] *m* cutting up or out; carving; cut-out (*figure*); **~er** [~'pe] (1a) carve (*a chicken*); cut up or out; ⊙ punch; *fig.* **se** ~ stand out (against, *sur*).

découplé [deku'ple]: **bien** ~ well-built.

décourag|ement [dekuraʒ'mɑ̃] *m* discouragement, despondency; **~er** [~ra'ʒe] (1l) discourage; dissuade (from, *de*); **se** ~ lose heart.

décousu [deku'zy] **1.** *p.p.* of **découdre**; **2.** *adj.* unsewn; *fig.* disjointed; rambling; *su./m* disconnectedness; **~re** [~'zy:r] *f* rip.

découv|ert, e [deku'vɛ:r, ~'vɛrt] **1.** *p.p.* of **découvrir**; **2.** *adj.* exposed; ✝ overdrawn; **3.** *su./m* ✝ overdraft; open ground; **à** ~ openly; exposed; ✝ unsecure (*credit*), short (*sale*); *su./f* uncovering; discovery (*a. fig.*); **aller à la ~e** explore; **~eur** [~'vœ:r] *m* discoverer; **~rir** [~'vri:r] (2f) uncover; discover; find out; **se** ~ take off one's hat; clear up (*sky*).

décrasser [dekra'se] (1a) clean, scrape; *fig.* polish (*s.o.*) up.

décrép|ir △ [dekre'pi:r] (2a) strip the rough-cast off; **~it** [~'pi] decrepit; **~itude** [~pi'tyd] *f* decrepitude; decay.

décret [de'krɛ] *m* decree; **~er** [~kre'te] (1f) order; declare; decree; **~loi**, *pl.* **~s-lois** [~kre'lwa] *m* order in council, *Am.* executive decree.

décrire [de'kri:r] (4q) describe.

décroch|er [dekrɔ'ʃe] (1a) *v/t.* unhook; *teleph.* lift (*the receiver*); uncouple; F get, land (o.s.) (s.th.); v/i. teleph. lift the receiver; F fig. switch off; **~ez-moi-ça** sl. [~.[emwa'sa] m/inv. second-hand clothes' shop.

décroiss|ance [dekrwa'sɑ̃:s] f, **~ement** [~krwas'mɑ̃] m decrease; decline; wane. **décroître** [de'krwa:tr] (4o) decrease; wane.

décrott|er [dekrɔ'te] (1a) get the mud off; F fig. polish (s.o.) up; **~oir** [~'twa:r] m door-scraper.

décru, e [de'kry] 1. p.p. of **décroître**; 2. su./f water: fall, subsidence.

déçu [de'sy] p.p. of **décevoir**.

décupl|e [de'kypl] adj., su./m tenfold; **~er** [~.ky'ple] (1a) increase tenfold.

dédai|gner [dedɛ'ɲe] (1b) scorn, disdain; **~gneux** [~'ɲø] scornful; **~n** [de'dɛ̃] m disdain, scorn (of, **de**); disregard (of, **de**; for, **pour**).

dédalu [de'dal] m labyrinth (a. fig.).

dedans [də'dɑ̃] 1. adv. in, inside, within; **en ~ de** within; F **mettre q. ~** take s.o. in; 2. su./m inside.

dédi|cace [dedi'kas] f dedication (a. fig.); **~er** [~'dje] (1o) dedicate.

dédire [de'di:r] (4p): **se ~ de** go back upon, retract; break (a promise); **dédit** [~'di] m withdrawal; promise: breaking; ṛ penalty.

dédommag|ement [dedɔmaʒ'mɑ̃] m indemnity; damages pl.; **~er** [~ma'ʒe] (1l) compensate (for, **de**).

dédouaner [dedwa'ne] (1a) clear (s.th.) through the customs.

dédoubler [dedu'ble] (1a) divide into two; unfold; unline (a coat).

déduction [dedyk'sjɔ̃] f ✝, phls. deduction; ✝ allowance; discount.

déduire [de'dɥi:r] (4h) infer, deduce; ✝ deduct.

déesse [de'ɛs] f goddess.

défaill|ance [defa'jɑ̃:s] f failure; ✿ faint, weakness; ṛ default; **~ir** [~'ji:r] (2t) fail; falter; sink (heart); faint (person); ṛ fail to appear.

défai|re [de'fɛ:r] (4r) undo; ◉ etc. take down, disassemble; unpack, distort (the face); upset; ✗ defeat (an army etc.); **se ~** come undone; undo one's coat; get rid (of, **de**); **~te** [~'fɛt] f defeat; fig. lame excuse; failure; **~tisme** [defɛ'tism] m defeatism.

défalquer [defal'ke] (1m) deduct.

défausser [defo'se] (1a): **se ~** discard.

défaut [de'fo] m defect; want, lack; fault; flaw; ṛ default; **✝ ~ de provision** no funds; **à ~ de** for want of; **en ~** at fault; **faire ~** fail; be missing.

défav|eur [defa'vœr] m disfavo(u)r (with, **auprès de**); **~orable** [~vɔ'rabl] unfavo(u)rable; **~oriser** put at a disadvantage.

défect|ion [defɛk'sjɔ̃] f defection (from, **de**); **faire ~** fall away, defect; **~ueux** [~'tɥø] faulty, **~uosité** [~tɥozi'te] f defect; flaw.

défend|able [defɑ̃'dabl] defensible; **~eur** m, **-eresse** f ṛ [~'dœr, ~'drɛs] defendant; respondent; **~re** [de'fɑ̃:dr] (4a) defend (a. ṛ, a. ✗), forbid; **à son corps défendant** reluctantly; F fig. **se ~ de** (inf.) refrain from (ger.), help (ger.); F fig. **se ~ bien en qch.** be good at s.th.

défens|e [de'fɑ̃:s] f defence, Am. defense (a. ṛ); prohibition; elephant: tusk; **~ de fumer** no smoking; ṛ **légitime ~** self-defence; **~eur** [defɑ̃'sœːr] m defender; ṛ counsel for the defense, Am defense attorney; **~if, -ve** [~'sif, ~'si:v] adj., su./f defensive.

défér|ence [defe'rɑ̃:s] f deference; **par ~ pour** out of or in deference to; **~er** [~'re] (1f) v/t. ṛ **~ q. à la justice** hand s.o. over to the law; v/i.: **~ à** defer to.

déferler [defɛr'le] (1a) v/t. unfurl (a flag, sails); v/i. break (waves).

défeuiller [defœ'je] (1a) strip the leaves off; **se ~** shed its leaves.

défi [de'fi] m challenge; **lancer un ~ à** challenge, **mettre q. au ~** dare or defy s.o. (to inf., de inf.).

défian|ce [de'fjɑ̃:s] f distrust; **~ de soi-même** diffidence; **vote m de ~** vote of no confidence; **~t** [~'fjɑ̃] distrustful; cautious.

déficit [defi'si] m deficit; shortage; **~aire** [~si'tɛ:r] showing a deficit.

défier [de'fje] (1o) challenge; dare; brave, defy; **se ~ de** distrust.

défigurer [defigy're] (1a) disfigure.

défil|ade F [defi'lad] f procession; **~é** [~'le] m geog. gorge; march past; parade; **~er** [~'le] (1a) v/i. march or move (past); v/t. unthread, undo; F **se ~** back out, slip out of it, dodge it.

défin|i [defi'ni] definite (a. gramm.); défined; **~ir** [~'niːr] (2a) define; *fig.* describe; **se ~** become clear; **~issable** [defini'sabl] definable; **~itif, e** [~'tif, ~'tiːv] **1.** *adj.* definitive; **à titre ~** permanently; **2.** *su./f:* **en ~ve** finally; **~ition** [~'sjɔ̃] *f* definition; *cross-words:* clue.

déflation [defla'sjɔ̃] deflation.

défleurir [deflœ'riːr] (2a) *v/t.* strip (*a plant*) of its bloom; *v/i.*, **se ~** lose its blossom.

déflorer [deflɔ're] (1a) strip (*s.th.*) of its bloom; deflower (*a virgin*).

défoncer [defɔ̃'se] (1k) stave in; smash in; break up (*a road*); *fig.* destroy; *sl.* **se ~** get high (*on drugs*).

déform|ation [defɔrma'sjɔ̃] *f* deformation; warping; distortion; **~er** [~'me] (1a) put out of shape; deform; warp; **se ~** lose its shape.

défouler F [defu'le] (1a): **se ~** let off steam.

défraichir [defre'ʃiːr] (2a): **se ~** become shopsoiled (*Am.* shopworn); fade.

défrayer [defre'je] (1i) defray (*s.o.'s*) expenses; **~ la conversation** be the topic of conversation; be the life of the conversation.

défricher [defri'ʃe] (1a) reclaim (*land*); *fig.* break new ground in.

défroncer [defrɔ̃'se] (1k) smooth out.

défroque *fig.* [de'frɔk] *f usu.* **~s** *pl.* cast-off clothing *sg.*

défunt [de'fœ̃] **1.** *adj.* deceased; late; **2.** *su.* deceased, *Am.* decedent.

dégag|é [dega'ʒe] clear; unconstrained; off-hand (*manner, tone*); **~ement** [~gaʒ'mɑ̃] *m* clearing; freeing; relief; emission; passage; **~er** [~ga'ʒe] (1l) clear; free; extricate; relieve; release; emanate, give off; *fig.* isolate, bring out; **se ~** free o.s.; clear; emanate, be given off; emerge, come out.

dégain|e F [de'gɛːn] *f* (awkward) way of carrying o.s.; **~er** [~gɛ'ne] (1b) unsheathe.

déganter [degɑ̃'te] (1a) unglove.

dégarnir [degar'niːr] (2a) strip; dismantle; ♻ unrig; thin out (*a tree*); **se ~** empty (*room*); become bald; lose its leaves (*tree*).

dégât [de'gɑ] *m* food etc.: waste; **~s** *pl.* damage *sg.*; havoc *sg.*

dégauchir [dego'ʃiːr] (2a) rough-plane

(*wood*); straighten; *fig.* knock the corners off (*s.o.*).

dégel [de'ʒɛl] *m* thaw; **~ée** F [deʒɔ'le] *f* shower of blows; **~er** [~] (1d) thaw (*a. fig.*).

dégénére|r [deʒene're] (1f) degenerate (from, **de**; into, **en**); **~scence** [~rɛ'sɑ̃ːs] *f* degeneration.

dégingandé [deʒɛ̃gɑ̃'de] lanky.

dégivrer [deʒi'vre] (1a) de-ice.

déglacer [degla'se] (1k) defrost.

dégobiller *sl.* [degɔbi'je] (1a) puke.

dégommer F [degɔ'me] (1a) fire (*s.o.*).

dégonfl|e *sl.* [deʒɔ̃'fle] *m* funk; **~er** [~] (1a) deflate; reduce; *fig.* debunk (*s.o.*); **se ~ mot.** go flat; F back out, F chicken out.

dégorg|eoir [degɔr'ʒwaːr] *m* outlet, spout; **~er** [~'ʒe] (1l) *v/t.* cleanse; unstop (*a pipe etc.*); disgorge (*a. fig.*); *v/i.* flow out; overflow.

dégot(t)er *sl.* [degɔ'te] (1a) find, F unearth.

dégouliner F [deguli'ne] (1a) roll (down); trickle.

dégourd|i [degur'di] smart (person); **~ir** [~'diːr] (2a) warm (up), take the stiffness from (*one's legs etc.*); take the chill off (*a liquid*); *fig.* F lick (*s.o.*) into shape; **se ~ les jambes** stretch one's legs; **se ~** become more alert.

dégoût [de'gu] *m* disgust, loathing (for, **pour**); **~er** [degu'te] (1a) disgust, repel; **se ~ de** take a dislike to, grow sick of.

dégoutter [degu'te] (1a) drip, trickle (from, with **de**).

dégrad|ation [degrada'sjɔ̃] *f* degradation; *rock:* weathering; *colours:* shading off; ⚖ **~ civique** loss of civil rights; **~er** [~'de] (1a) degrade; shade off (*colours*); damage; **se ~** deteriorate.

dégrafer [degra'fe] (1a) unhook.

dégraisser [degrɛ'se] (1a) remove the fat from; skim; take the grease marks out of.

degré [də'gre] *m* degree; *stairway:* step; **~ centésimal** degree centigrade; **~ de congélation** freezing point; **par ~s** by degrees.

dégrèvement [degrɛv'mɑ̃] *m* tax reduction; **dégrever** [~grə've] (1d) reduce the tax(es) on (*s.th.*); grant (*s.o.*) a tax relief.

dégringol|ade F [degrɛ̃gɔ'lad] f tumble, fall; *currency:* collapse; **~er** F [~'le] (1a) tumble down.

dégriser [degri'ze] (1a) sober (*s.o.*).

dégrossir [degro'si:r] (2a) rough-hew; rough-plane; rough out; F lick (*s.o.*) into shape.

dégrouiller *sl.* [degru'je] (1a): **se ~** hurry up, F get a move on.

déguenillé [degəni'je] **1.** *adj.* ragged, tattered; **2.** *su.* ragamuffin.

déguerpir [degɛr'pi:r] (2a) F clear off, beat it; **faire ~** drive off.

déguis|ement [degiz'mɑ̃] *m* disguise; *fig.* concealment; fancy dress; **~er** [~gi'ze] (1a) disguise; conceal; **se ~** disguise o.s.; dress up (as [a], **en**).

dégust|ateur [degysta'tœ:r] *m* taster; **~ation** [~ta'sjɔ̃] f tasting; **~er** [~'te] (1a) taste; F sip; enjoy.

déhancher [deɑ̃'ʃe] (1a): **se ~** sway one's hips.

dehors [də'ɔ:r] **1.** *adv.* outside, out; *diner ~* dine out; **en ~** outside; outwards; **en ~ de** outside; apart from; **en ~ de moi** without my knowledge *or* participation; **mettre q. ~** turn s.o. out; **2.** *su./m* outside, exterior; **~** *pl.* appearances.

déifier [dei'fje] (1o) deify; *fig.* make a god of; **déité** [~'te] f deity.

déjà [de'ʒa] *adv.* already, before.

déjection [deʒɛk'sjɔ̃] f 💊 evacuation; **~s** *pl. a.* ejecta (*of a volcano*).

déjeter ⊙ [deʒə'te] (1c) twist; warp (*wood*); buckle (*metal*).

déjeuner [deʒœ'ne] **1.** (1a) *v/i.* have breakfast; (have) lunch; **2.** *su./m* lunch; **petit ~** breakfast.

déjouer [de'ʒwe] (1p) *v/t.* thwart; foil; outwit; elude; baffle.

déjuger [deʒy'ʒe] (1l): **se ~** reverse one's opinion.

delà [də'la] *adv., prp.* beyond.

délabrer [dela'bre] (1a) dilapidate; wreck; ruin (*a. one's health*).

délacer [dela'se] (1k) unlace.

délai [de'lɛ] *m* (period *or* extension of) time; time limit; deadline; **à bref ~** shortly, soon; at short notice; **dans un ~ de ...** within ...; **dans le ~ fixé, dans les ~s** within the period prescribed; **sans ~** without delay.

délaisser [delɛ'se] (1b) forsake; desert; abandon; give up.

délass|ement [delas'mɑ̃] *m* rest, relaxation; recreation; **~er** [~la'se] (1a) rest, refresh; **se ~** relax.

délat|eur *m*, **-trice** f [dela'tœ:r, ~'tris] informer; **~ion** [~'sjɔ̃] f informing, denunciation, squealing.

délavé [dela've] washed out; faded.

délayer [delɛ'je] (1i) dilute; thin down; *fig.* spin out (*a speech*).

délect|able [delɛk'tabl] delightful; **~er** [~'te] (1a): **se ~ à** delight in.

délég|ation [delega'sjɔ̃] f delegation; **~ué** [dele'ge] **1.** *adj.* delegated; **2.** *su.* delegate; **~uer** [~] (1s) delegate.

délester [delɛs'te] (1a) unballast; unload; *fig.* relieve (of, **de**).

délétère [dele'tɛ:r] deleterious.

délibér|atif [delibera'tif] deliberative; **~ation** [~ra'sjɔ̃] f deliberation, debate (on, **sur**); reflection; resolution; **~é** [~'re] **1.** *adj.* deliberate; determined; **de propos ~** deliberately; **2.** *su./m* 🏛 consultation; **~er** [~'re] (1f) deliberate; ponder (on **de, sur**).

délicat [deli'ka] **1.** *adj.* delicate; fragile; dainty; nice, tricky (*situation, question*); fastidious (*eater*); sensitive (*skin*); scrupulous; **2.** *su./m*: **faire le ~** be squeamish; **~esse** [~ka'tɛs] f delicacy; **avec ~** tactfully.

délic|e [de'lis] *m* delight; **~es** f/pl. pleasure *sg.*; **~ieux** [~li'sjø] delicious; delightful.

délictueux [delik'tɥø] unlawful.

délié [de'lje] slim, thin, slender; glib (*tongue*); nimble; **délier** [~] (1o) undo; release; absolve; **sans bourse ~** without spending a penny.

délimiter [delimi'te] (1a) delimit; fix the boundaries of; demarcate; define.

délinquance 🏛 [delɛ̃'kɑ̃:s] f delinquency; **~ juvénile** juvenile delinquency; **délinquant** *m*, **e** f 🏛 [~'kɑ̃, ~'kɑ̃:t] delinquent, offender.

délir|ant [deli'rɑ̃] delirious; **~e** [~'li:r] *m* 💊 delirium; *fig.* frenzy; **~er** [~li're] (1a) be delirious; rave.

délit 🏛 [de'li] *m* misdemeano(u)r, offence; **en flagrant ~** red-handed.

délivr|ance [deli'vrɑ̃:s] f deliverance; release; rescue; 💊 confinement; delivery; *certificate etc.:* issue; **~er** [~'vre] (1a) (set) free; deliver (*a.* 💊, *a certificate*); release; issue (*a certificate*).

déloger [delɔ'ʒe] (1l) v/i. remove; go away; v/t. turn or drive out.

déloy|al [delwa'jal] false; ♣ unfair (*competition*); sp. foul; **~auté** [~jo'te] f disloyalty, treachery.

déluge [de'ly:ʒ] m deluge, flood.

déluré [dely're] smart, sharp, knowing; forward, cheeky.

démailler [demɑ'je] (1a): **se ~** ladder (*stocking*).

demain [dᵊ'mɛ̃] adv., su./m tomorrow; **à ~!** see you tomorrow!; **~ en huit** tomorrow week.

démancher [demɑ̃'ʃe] (1a) unhaft (a *tool*); F dislocate; **~** upset.

demand|e [dᵊ'mɑ̃:d] f request (for, **de**); demand (a. ♣); admin. etc. application; ⚖ claim; **~ d'emploi** application for a job; **~ en mariage** proposal (of marriage); **à la ~ générale** by general request; **sur ~** on request; **~er** [~mɑ̃'de] (1a) ask (for); beg, request; demand, require; wish, want; apply for; **~ q.** ask for s.o.; **~ qch. à q.** ask s.o. for s.th.; **se ~** wonder; **~eur** m, **~eresse** f [~mɑ̃-'dœːr, ~'drɛs] applicant; ⚖ plaintiff; teleph. caller; **~ d'emploi** job seeker.

démang|eaison [demɑ̃ʒɛ'zɔ̃] f itching; fig. F itch, longing; **~er** [~'ʒe] (1l): **~ à q.** itch (*arm, leg, etc.*).

démant|èlement [demɑ̃tɛl'mɑ̃] m dismantling; **~eler** [~mɑ̃t'le] (1d) dismantle; break up (a *gang*).

démantibuler [demɑ̃tiby'le] (1a) ruin, break up, smash up.

démaquill|age [demaki'jaːʒ] m: **crème m de ~** cleansing cream; **~ant** [~'jɑ̃] m make-up remover; **~er** [~'je] (1a) remove the make-up.

démarcation [demarka'sjɔ̃] f demarcation, boundary.

démarche [de'marʃ] f step (a. fig.); gait; **faire des ~s pour** take steps to.

démarquer [demar'ke] (1m) remove the marks from; ♣ mark down (*prices*); fig. plagiarize; **se ~** dissociate or differentiate o.s. (from, **de**).

démarr|age [dema'raːʒ] m start; **~er** [~'re] (1a) start; fig. get moving, get off the ground; **faire ~ mot.** start; set in motion; **~eur** mot. [~'rœːr] m starter.

démasquer [demas'ke] (1m) unmask; show (a *light etc*).

démêl|é [deme'le] m dispute; **~er** [~'le]

(1a) unravel; clear up; **avoir qch. à ~ avec q.** have a bone to pick with s.o.

démembrer [demɑ̃'bre] (1a) dismember; break up.

déménag|ement [demenaʒ'mɑ̃] m moving (house); **~er** [~na'ʒe] (1l) v/t. (re)move; move everything out of (a *room, house, etc.*); v/i. move house; fig. go out of one's mind; **~eur** [~na'ʒœːr] m furniture remover.

démence [de'mɑ̃:s] f madness.

démener [dem'ne] (1d): **se ~** struggle, thrash about; fig. make an effort.

dément [de'mɑ̃] m lunatic.

dément|i [demɑ̃'ti] m denial; failure; **~ir** [~'tiːr] (2b) contradict; deny; belie; **se ~** fail.

démérit|e [deme'rit] m demerit; **~er** [~'rite] (1a) be blameworthy; **~ auprès de q.** forfeit s.o.'s esteem.

démesuré [deməzy're] inordinate, beyond measure; excessive.

démettre [de'metr] (4v) dislocate; **se ~ de** give up; abandon; resign from.

demeur|ant [dᵊmœ'rɑ̃] m: **au ~** after all; **~e** [~'mœːr] f dwelling, residence; **à ~** permanent(ly); ♣ **en ~** in arrears; **mettre q. en ~ de** (*inf.*) call upon s.o. to (*inf.*); **mise f en ~** summons; **~é** [~mœ're] mentally retarded; **~er** [~mœ're] (1a) live, reside; stay, stop; **~ court** stop short; **en ~ là** leave off.

demi [dᵊ'mi] **1.** adj. (*inv. before su.*) half, demi-..., semi-...; **une demi-heure** half an hour; **une heure et demie** an hour and a half; **dix heures et demie** half past ten; **2.** su./m half; sp. half-back; **~-cercle** [dᵊmi'sɛrkl] m semicircle; **~-fond** sp. [~'fɔ̃] m medium distance; **~-frère** [~'frɛːr] m half-brother; **~-jour** [~'ʒuːr] m/inv. half-light; **~-journée** [~ʒur'ne] f part-time work; half-day.

démilitariser [demilitari'ze] (1a) demilitarize.

demi-...: ~-mot [dᵊmi'mo] adv.: **à ~** without many words; **~-pension** [~pɑ̃'sjɔ̃] f part board; **~-saison** [~sɛ'zɔ̃] f mid-season; **~-sec** [~'sɛk] medium dry (*wine*); **~-sœur** [~'sœːr] f half-sister; **~-sommeil** [~sɔ'mɛːj] m somnolence.

démission [demi'sjɔ̃] f resignation; **~naire** [~sjɔ'nɛːr] **1.** adj. resigning; **2.** su. resigner; **~ner** [~sjɔ'ne] (1a) resign; fig. give up.

demi...: **~-tarif** [dəmita'rif] *m*: (**à ~** at) half-price *or* half-fare; **~ton** ♪ [~'tɔ̃] *m* semitone; **~-tour** [~'tuːr] *m* half-turn, *mot.* U-turn; **faire ~** turn back.

démobiliser [demɔbili'ze] (1a) ⚔ demobilize; *fig* demoralize.

démocrat|e [demɔ'krat] **1.** *adj.* democratic; **2.** *su.* democrat; **~ie** [~kra'si] *f* democracy.

démod|é [demɔ'de] old-fashioned; **~er** [~] (1a): **se ~** go out of fashion.

demoiselle [dəmwa'zɛl] *f* young lady; spinster; shop-girl; *zo.* dragon-fly; **~ d'honneur** bridesmaid.

démoli|r [demɔ'liːr] (2a) demolish (*a an argument*), pull down; *fig.* ruin; **~sseur** [~li'sœːr] *m* demolition worker *or* contractor, *Am.* wrecker; *fig.* demolisher; **~tion** [~li'sjɔ̃] *f* demolition; **~s** *pl.* rubbish *sg.*, rubble *sg.*

démon [de'mɔ̃] *m* demon, devil.

démonstrati|f [demɔ̃stra'tif] demonstrative (*a. gramm.*); **~on** [~'sjɔ̃] *f* demonstration.

démont|able ⚙ [demɔ̃'tabl] dismountable; collapsible; **~age** [~'taːʒ] *m* dismantling; removal; **~er** [~'te] (1a) unseat; ⚙ dismantle; unmount; *fig.* upset, take aback, fluster.

démontrer [demɔ̃'tre] (1a) demonstrate, show; prove.

démoraliser [demɔrali'ze] (1a) demoralize; *fig.* dishearten.

démordre [de'mɔrdr] (4a) let go; give in: **ne pas ~ de** stick to.

démunir [demy'niːr] (2a) deprive (of, **de**); **se ~ de** part with; **démuni de** without, out of.

démythifier [demiti'fje] (1a) demystify; debunk.

dénationaliser [denasjɔnali'ze] denationalize.

dénatur|é [denaty're] unnatural; 🜍 methylated, *Am.* denatured; **~er** [~] (1a) adulterate; *fig.* misrepresent, distort; pervert.

dénégation [denega'sjɔ̃] *f* denial.

déni 🜨 [de'ni] *m* denial, refusal.

déniaiser F [denjɛ'ze] (1a) wise (*s.o.*) up; smarten (*s.o.'s*) wits; *fig.* initiate (*s.o.*) sexually.

dénicher [deni'ʃe] (1a) *v/t.* find, get; drive out; track down; *v/i.* fly away; F clear out.

denier [də'nje] *m* small coin; money; **les ~s** *pl.* **publics** public funds.

dénier [de'nje] (1o) deny; disclaim.

dénigrer [deni'gre] (1a) disparage, run (*s.o.*) down; backbite.

dénivell|ation [denivɛla'sjɔ̃] *f*, **~ement** [~vɛl'mɑ̃] *m* uneavenness; difference in level.

dénombr|ement [denɔ̃brə'mɑ̃] *m* counting; census; **~er** [~'bre] (1a) count; take a census of.

dénominat|eur 𝔄 [denɔmina'tœːr] *m* denominator; **~if** [~'tif] denominative; **~ion** [~'sjɔ̃] *f* denomination.

dénommer [denɔ'me] (1a) name.

dénonc|er [denɔ̃'se] (1k) denounce (*a. a treaty*); betray, indicate; expose; **~q.** (*à la police*) inform against s.o.; **~iateur** [~sja'tœːr] **1.** *su.* informer; **2.** *adj.* accusatory; **~iation** [~sja'sjɔ̃] *f* denunciation.

dénoter [denɔ'te] (1a) denote, show.

dénou|ement [denu'mɑ̃] *m* untying; outcome; solution; **~er** [~'nwe] (1p) untie; unravel; *fig.* resolve, clear up; **~ come undone;** *fig.* be resolved.

denrée [dɑ̃'re] *f usu.* **~s** *pl.* commodity *sg.*; produce *sg.*; **~s** *pl.* **alimentaires** food-stuffs.

dense [dɑ̃:s] dense (*a. phys.*); thick; **densité** [dɑ̃si'te] *f* density; *phys.* specific weight.

dent [dɑ̃] *f* tooth (*a.* ⚙); *elephant:* tusk; ⚙ *a.* cog; *fork:* prong; **~ de lait** (*de sagesse*) milk tooth (wisdom tooth); **~s** *pl.* **artificielles** denture *sg.*; *sl.* **avoir la ~ be** hungry; **avoir une ~ contre** have a grudge against; **en ~s de scie** jagged, serrated; **être sur les ~s** be worn out, be overworked; be under pressure; **faire ses ~s** cut (one's) teeth; **mal aux ~s** toothache; **sans ~s** toothless; **~aire** [dɑ̃'tɛːr], **~al** [~'tal] dental; **~-de-lion,** *pl.* **~s-de-lion** [dɑ̃d'ljɔ̃] *f* dandelion; **~é:** ⚙ **roue** *f* **~é** cog wheel; **~eler** [dɑ̃t'le] (1c) notch; indent (*a. fig.*); **~elle** [dɑ̃'tɛl] *f* lace; wrought ironwork; **~elure** [dɑ̃t'lyːr] *f* indentation; **~er** [dɑ̃'te] (1a) cog (*a wheel*); **~ier** [~'tje] *m* set of false teeth; **~ifrice** [~ti'fris] *m* tooth-paste; **~iste** [~'tist] *m* dentist; **~ition** [~ti'sjɔ̃] *f* teething; **~ure** [~'tyːr] *f* set of (*natural*) teeth; ⚙ cogs *pl.*

dénucléarisé [denykleari'ze] atom-free (*zone*).

dénu|der [deny'de] (1a) lay bare; strip; **~ement** [~ny'mã] *m* destitution; bareness; **~er** [~'nɥe] (1n) strip (of, *de*); **dénué de** ...less.

dépann|age [depa'na:ʒ] *m* repairing, *fig.* helping (out), help, relief; *mot.* (*a. service m de* ~) breakdown service; **~er** [~'ne] (1a) repair, fix; *fig.* help (out), tide over, relieve; **~euse** *mot.* [~'øːz] *f* breakdown van, *Am.* wrecker.

dépareillé [depare'je] odd, unmatched; *articles m/pl.* **~s** oddments.

déparer [depa're] (1a) strip (*of ornaments*); *fig.* spoil, mar.

déparié [depa'rje]: *gant m* **~** odd glove.

départ [de'paːr] *m* departure (*a.* ✍); start; ♻; sailing; *sp.* **~ lancé** flying start; *point m de* **~** starting point; *fig.* start, beginning.

départager [departa'ʒe] (1l) decide between; separate; **~ les voix** give the casting vote.

département [depart'mã] *m* department (*a. pol. Am., a. admin.*); Ministry; *fig.* province.

départir [depar'tiːr] (2b): *se* **~ de** give up, abandon.

dépass|ement [depas'mã] *m* exceeding; *mot.* passing, overtaking; **~er** [~pa'se] (1a) *v/t.* pass, go beyond; exceed (*a. a speed*); *mot.* pass, overtake (*a car etc.*); project beyond; *fig.* outshine, surpass; *F cela me dépasse* it's beyond me; *sp.* **~ à la course** outrun; *v/i.* stick out, show; *mot.* pass, overtake; *,défense de* **~'** no passing.

dépayser [depei'ze] (1a) take (*s.o.*) out of his element; mislead.

dépecer [depǝ'se] (1d *a.* 1k) cut up; dismember; break up.

dépêch|e [de'pɛːʃ] *f* dispatch; telegram; **~er** [depe'ʃe] (1a) dispatch; *se* **~** hurry up (to *inf., de inf.*).

dépeigner [depɛ'ɲe] (1a) ruffle.

dépeindre [de'pɛ̃ːdr] (4m) depict.

dépenaillé [depǝnɑ'je] ragged.

dépendance [depã'dãːs] *f* dependence; dependency (*of a country*); domination; **~s** *pl.* outbuildings.

dépendre¹ [de'pãːdr] (4a) depend (on, *de*); *cela dépend* that depends; *il*

dépend de vous de (*inf.*) it lies with you to (*inf.*).

dépendre² [~] (4a) unhang.

dépens [de'pã] *m/pl.* ✍ costs; *fig.* **aux** ~ **de** at the expense of.

dépens|e [de'pãːs] *f* expenditure, spending, expense; *gas etc.*: consumption; **~er** [depã'se] (1a) spend; *se* **~** exert o.s.; **~ier** [~'sje] *adj., su./m* spendthrift.

déperdition [deperdi'sjɔ̃] *f* waste; loss; *gas:* escape; leakage.

dépéri|r [depe'riːr] (2a) decline, dwindle; **~ssement** [~ris'mã] *m* declining, dwindling, decay.

dépêtrer [depɛ'tre] (1a) extricate, free; *se* **~ de q.** shake s.o. off.

dépeupler [depœ'ple] (1a) depopulate; thin (*a forest*).

dépil|ation [depila'sjɔ̃] *f* depilation; **~atoire** [~la'twaːr] *adj., su./m* depilatory; **~er** [~'le] (1a) remove the hair from.

dépister [depis'te] (1a) track down; put off the scent; *fig.* detect, discover.

dépit [de'pi] *m* vexation; **en** **~ de** in spite of; **~er** [~pi'te] (1a) vex, annoy; *se* **~** be vexed (at, *de*).

déplac|é [depla'se] out of place; **~ement** [~plas'mã] *m* moving, shifting; movement; relocation, transfer; displacement (*a.* ♻); travel(ling); *frais m/pl. de* **~** travelling expenses; **~er** [~pla'se] (1k) shift; move; dislodge; displace; transfer (*s.o.o.*); *se* **~** move; move *or* get around; travel.

déplai|re [de'plɛːr] (4z) *v/i.*: **~ à** displease; *v/t.*: *se* **~** be unhappy; **~sant** [deple'zã] unpleasant; **~sir** [~'ziːr] *m* displeasure.

déplanter [deplã'te] (1a) displant.

dépli|ant [depli'ã] *m* folding album; folder; **~er** [~'e] (1a) unfold.

déploiement [deplwa'mã] *m* unfolding; *goods, courage, etc.*: display; stretching; deployment.

déplor|able [deplɔ'rabl] deplorable; **~er** [~'re] (1a) deplore; mourn.

déployer [deplwa'je] (1h) unfold; display (*goods, patience*); deploy.

déplumer [deply'me] (1a) pluck; *se* **~** mo(u)lt; *F* grow bald.

dépopulation [depɔpyla'sjɔ̃] *f* depopulation; falling population.

déport|ation [depɔrta'sjɔ̃] *f* deportation; **~ements** [depɔrtǝ'mã] *m/pl.* misconduct *sg.*; **~er** [~'te] (1a) deport; carry off course.

dépos|ant m, e f [depo'zã, ~'zãːt] ✝ depositor; ⚖ witness; **~er** [~'ze] (1o) *v*/*t*. put (*or* set, lay) down; drop (*a passenger*) (off); deposit (*money, a sediment, etc.*); depose (*a king etc.*); *parl.* introduce (*a bill*); file (*an application, petition etc.*); lodge (*a complaint*); register (*a trademark*); **se ~** settle; *v*/*i.* settle (*wine*); ⚖ give evidence (against, **contre**); depose (that, **que**); **~itaire** [~zi'tɛːr] *su.* trustee; ✝ agent (for, **de**); **~ition** [~zi'sjɔ̃] f ⚖, *king:* deposition.

déposs|éder [deposse'de] (1f) (**de**) dispossess (from), deprive (of); **~ession** [~sɛ'sjɔ̃] f dispossession.

dépôt [de'po] m deposit; ⚖ bailment; handing in; ✝ warehouse; *customs:* bond; sediment; 🚂 shed; police station; ♣ accumulation; *trade-mark:* registration; **~ de marchandises** goods depot, freight yard; **~oir** [depo'twaːr] m rubbish (*Am.* garbage) dump; junk room *or* yard.

dépouill|e [de'puːj] f skin; slough; **~s** *pl.* spoils; **~ mortelle** mortal remains *pl.*, **~ement** [~puj'mã] m despoiling; flaying; examination; *votes:* count; **~er** [~pu'je] (1a) skin; strip; plunder; rob; examine; open (*letters*); count (*votes*).

dépourv|oir [depur'vwaːr] (3m) deprive (of s.th., **de qch.**); **~u** [~'vy] **1.** *adj.*: **~ de** lacking, short of; **2.** *adv.*: **au ~** unawares.

dépoussiérer [depusje're] (1a) dust down, dust off.

déprav|ation [deprava'sjɔ̃] f depravation; depravity; **~er** [~'ve] (1a) deprave, corrupt.

dépréci|ation [depresja'sjɔ̃] f depreciation, wear and tear; **~er** [~'e] (10) depreciate; belittle, F run down; **se ~** lose value.

déprédat|eur [depreda'tœːr] **1.** *su.* depredator; embezzler; **2.** *adj.* depredatory; **~ion** [~'sjɔ̃] f plundering; embezzlement.

dépr|essif [depre'sif] depressing; **~ession** [~'sjɔ̃] f depression; ♣ **~ nerveuse** nervous breakdown; **~imer** [~pri'me] (1a) depress; lower.

depuis [də'pɥi] **1.** *prp.* since, for; from; **~ quand?** since when?; **je suis ici ~ cinq**

jours I have been here for five days; **~ ... jusqu'à** from ... (down) to; **2.** *adv.* since (then); afterwards; **3.** *cj.*: **~ que** since.

dépurer [depy're] (1a) purify.

député|ation [depyta'sjɔ̃] f deputation; membership of Parliament; **~é** [~'te] m deputy, M.P., *Am.* Representative; **~er** [~'te] (1a) depute; delegate (to **à, vers**).

déraciner [derasi'ne] (1a) uproot; *fig.* eradicate.

déraidir [derɛ'diːr] (2a) take the stiffness out of; *fig.* relax.

dérailler [derɑ'je] (1a) 🚂 go off the rails; ┼ talk wildly; ┼ behave weirdly.

déraison [derɛ'zɔ̃] f unreasonableness; folly; **~nable** [~zɔ'nabl] unreasonable, foolish; **~ner** [~zɔ'ne] (1a) talk nonsense; rave.

dérang|ement [derãʒ'mã] m disturbance; disarrangement; trouble; **~er** [~rã'ʒe] (1l) disturb; upset, disarrange; trouble, bother; **se ~** go *or* come out; move; *fig.* put o.s. out (on account of, **pour**; to *inf.*, **pour** *inf.*).

dérap|age [dera'paːʒ] m mot. skid(ding); **~er** [~'pe] (1a) skid.

dératé F [dera'te] m: **courir comme un ~** run like a hare.

derechef [dərə'ʃef] *adv.* once more.

déréglé [dere'gle] out of order; immoderate; **dérèglement** [~rɛglə'mã] m disorder; irregularity; profligacy; **dérégler** [~re'gle] (1f) upset, disarrange.

dérider [deri'de] (1a) smooth; unwrinkle; *fig.* cheer (*s.o.*) up.

déris|ion [deri'zjɔ̃] f derision; **tourner en ~** ridicule, laugh at; **~oire** [~'zwaːr] ridiculous, laughable.

dériv|atif [deriva'tif] *adj., su./m* derivative, **~ation** [~'sjɔ̃] f derivation; *watercourse:* diversion; shunt(ing); ⚓ drift; **~e** [de'riːv] f ✈ leeway; **aller à la ~** drift; ✈ drift; **2** su./f leeway; **aller à la ~** drift; ✈ leeway; **~é** [deri've] m derivative.

dériver¹ [deri've] (1a) drift.

dériver² [~] (1a) *v*/*t.* divert; shunt; derive; *v*/*i.*: **~ de** derive from.

derni|er, -ère [dɛr'nje, ~'njɛːr] **1.** *adj.* last, latest; utmost (*importance etc.*); ✝ closing (*price*); least (*trouble*); vilest (*of men*); **mettre la ~ère main à** give the finishing touch to; **2.** *su.* last, latest; **~èrement** [~njɛr'mã] *adv.* recently.

dérob|ade [dero'bad] f side-stepping, evasion; **~é** [~'be] secret, hidden; **~ée** [~'be] adv.: **à la ~** secretly, furtively, on the sly; **~er** [~'be] (1a) steal; hide; **se ~** hide (o.s.); slip away; give way (under, **sous**); fig. dodge the issue; fig. **se ~ à** shirk, shy away from; sidestep.

déroger [dero'ʒe] (1l) deviate (from, **à**); fig. lower o.s., stoop (to inf., **jusqu'à** inf.).

dérouiller [deru'je] (1a) remove the rust from; fig. polish up.

dérouler [deru'le] (1a) unroll; unreel; unfold (one's plan); **se ~** unfold (scene); fig. take place, go off; develop.

dérout|e [de'rut] f rout; **~er** [~ru'te] (1a) re-route; fig. baffle.

derrière [dɛ'rjɛːr] **1.** adv. behind, in the rear; **par ~** from the rear; **2.** prp. behind, in the rear of, Am. back of; **être ~ q.** back s.o. up; **3.** su./m back, rear; F backside; **de ~** rear..., hind...

dès [dɛ] prp. from, since; upon (arrival); as early as; **~ lors** from then on; **~ que** as soon as.

désabonner [dezabɔ'ne] (1a): **se ~** cancel one's subscription (to, **à**).

désabuser [dezaby'ze] (1a) disabuse, disillusion; undeceive.

désaccord [deza'kɔːr] m discord; disagreement; **en ~** at variance; **~er** [~kɔr'de] (1a) ♪ put out of tune; fig. set at variance.

désaccoutumer [dezakuty'me] (1a): **~ q.de** (inf.) break s.o. of the habit of (ger.).

désaffecté [dezafɛk'te] disused; abandoned.

désagréable [dezagre'abl] disagreeable; unpleasant; nasty.

désagréger [dezagre'ʒe] (1a) disintegrate; geol. weather (rock).

désagrément [dezagre'mã] m unpleasantness; nuisance; discomfort.

désajuster [dezaʒys'te] (1a) disarrange; ⚙ throw out of gear.

désaltérer [dezalte're] (1f) quench (s.o.'s) thirst; water (a plant).

désamorcer [dezamɔr'se] (1k) unprime; defuse (a. fig.).

désappoint|ement [dezapwɛt'mã] m disappointment; **~er** [~pwɛ̃'te] (1a) disappoint.

désapprendre [deza'prãːdr] (4aa) unlearn; forget (a subject).

désappr|obateur [dezaprɔba'tœːr] disapproving; **~ouver** [~pru've] (1a) disapprove (of), object to.

désarçonner [dezarsɔ'ne] (1a) unseat (a rider); fig. dumbfound.

désarm|ement [dezarmə'mã] m disarmament; **~er** [~'me] (1a) disarm (a fig.); ♣ lay up (a ship).

désarroi [deza'rwa] m disorder.

désarticuler [dezartiky'le] (1a) dislocate; ✂ disarticulate.

désassembler [dezasã'ble] (1a) disassemble; disconnect (joints).

désastr|e [de'zastr] m disaster; **~eux** [~zas'trø] disastrous.

désavantag|e [dezavã'taːʒ] m disadvantage; **~er** [~ta'ʒe] (1l) disadvantage; **~eux** [~ta'ʒø] unfavo(u)rable.

désaveu [deza'vø] m disavowal, denial; repudiation; disclaimer; **désavouer** [~'vwe] (1p) disown; disavow; repudiate; disclaim.

désaxé [dezak'se] ⊙ out of true; a. fig. eccentric; fig. unbalanced.

desceller [desɛ'le] (1a) unseal, break the seal of; loosen; force (a safe).

descen|dance [desã'dãːs] f descent; coll. descendants pl.; **~dant** [~'dã] **1.** adj. downward; ⚕ decreasing; 🚂 up-...(platform, train); **2.** su. descendant; **~dre** [dɛ'sãːdr] (4a) v/i. go or come down; fall, drop (temperature etc.); get out, get off, alight (passenger); descend; stay (at a hotel); be descended; **~ chez q.** stay with s.o.; v/t. go or come down; take (s.th.) down; lower; bring or shoot down; F drop (s.o.) (at an address); **~te** [~'sãːt] f way down; descent; slope; decline; police: raid; alighting; landing; taking down; piston: downstroke; △ down-pipe; radio: down-lead; ✝ drop; **de lit** (bed-side) rug.

descripti|f [dɛskrip'tif] descriptive; **~on** [~'sjõ] f description.

désempar|é [dezãpa're] helpless; crippled (vehicle etc.); **~er** [~]: **sans ~** without stopping.

désemplir [dezã'pliːr] (2a) v/t. half-empty; v/i.: **ne pas ~** be always full.

désenchant|é [dezãʃã'te] (1a) disenchant; fig. disillusion.

désencombrer [dezãkõ'bre] (1a) clear; disencumber.

dessein

désenfler [dezã'fle] (1a) *swelling etc.*: go down.

désengager [dezãga'ʒe] (1l) free from an engagement *or* an obligation.

désenivrer [dezãni'vre] (1a) sober.

désennuyer [dezãnɥi'je] (1h) amuse (*s.o.*); divert (*s.o.*).

désensibiliser [desãsibili'ze] (1a) desensitize.

déséquilibr|e [dezeki'libr] *m* lack of balance; unbalance; **~er** [~li'bre] (1a) throw off balance; unbalance.

désert [de'zɛːr] **1.** *adj.* deserted; desert (*island*); wild (*country*); **2.** *su./m* desert; **~er** [dezɛr'te] (1a) *v/t.* forsake, abandon; *v/i.* ✕ desert; **~eur** [~'tœːr] *m* deserter; **~ion** [~'sjõ] *f* desertion.

déses|pérant [dezespe'rã] heart-breaking; disheartening; **~péré** [~'re] desperate (*a.* ✕); hopeless (*a.* ✗); **~pérer** [~'re] (1f) *v/i.* despair (of, **de**); lose hope; lose heart; *v/t.* drive (*s.o.*) to despair; **~poir** [dezɛs'pwaːr] *m* despair; desperation; **en ~ de cause** as a last resource.

désétatiser [dezetati'ze] (1a) denationalize; ✝ *etc.* decontrol.

déshabill|é [dezabi'je] *m* undress, **~er** [~] (1a) undress, strip.

déshabituer [dezabi'tɥe] (1n): **~ q. de** (*inf.*) break s.o. of the habit of (*ger.*); **se ~** grow unused (to, **de**).

déshériter [dezeri'te] (1a) disinherit; deprive; *les déshérites* the underprivileged.

déshon|nête [dezɔ'nɛt] immodest; **~neur** [~'nœːr] *m* dishono(u)r; **~orer** [~nɔ're] (1a) dishono(u)r.

désign|ation [dezinɑ'sjõ] *f* designation; appointment (as, **au poste de**); **~er** [~'ne] (1a) designate; appoint.

désillusionner [dezillyzjɔ'ne] (1a) disillusion, undeceive.

désinfecter [dezɛ̃fɛk'te] (1a) disinfect; decontaminate.

désintégration [dezɛ̃tegra'sjõ] *f* disintegration; *atom:* splitting.

désintér|essé [dezɛ̃terɛ'se] unselfish; unbiased; **~essement** [~rɛs'mã] *m* impartiality; unselfishness; ✝ paying off; **~esser** [~rɛ'se] (1a) ✝ pay off; **se ~ de** lose interest in; **~êt** [~'rɛ] *m* disinterest, indifference.

désinvolt|e [dezɛ̃'vɔlt] unconstrained;

off-hand; F cheeky; **~ure** [~vɔl'tyːr] *f* ease (*of bearing*); F cheek.

désir [de'ziːr] *m* desire, wish; **~able** [dezi'rabl] desirable; **~er** [~'re] (1a) desire, wish, want; *laisser à ~* leave much to be desired; **~eux** [~'rø] eager (to, **de**).

désister [dezis'te] (1a): **se ~** withdraw, renounce.

désobéi|r [dezɔbe'iːr] (2a): **~ à** disobey; **~ssance** [~i'sãːs] *f* disobedience (to, **à**); **~ssant** [~i'sã] disobedient.

désoblig|eant [dezɔbli'ʒã] disobliging, unfriendly, **~er** [~'ʒe] (1l) disoblige (*s.o.*); offend (*s.o.*).

désodorisant [dezɔdori'zã] *m* deodorant.

désœuvr|é [dezœ'vre] **1.** *adj.* idle; at a loose end; **2.** *su.* idler; **~ement** [~vrə'mã] *m* idleness; leisure.

désol|ation [dezɔla'sjõ] *f* desolation; grief; **~é** [~'le] very sorry; **~er** [~'le] (1a) desolate; distress; grieve; **se ~** be upset.

désolidariser [desolidari'ze] (1a): **se ~ (de)** dissociate o.s. (from).

désopil|ant ⊢ [dezopi'lã] side-splitting, screaming; **~er** *fig.* [~'le] (1a): **se ~** shake with laughter.

désord|onné [dezordɔ'ne] disorderly, untidy; excessive; **~re** [~'zordr] *m* disorder (*a.* ✗); dissoluteness; **~res** *m/pl.* disturbances, riots.

désorganisation [dezorganiza'sjõ] *f* disorganization.

désorienter [dezorjã'te] (1a) mislead; *fig.* bewilder, confuse, puzzle; *fig.* **tout désorienté** *a.* at a loss.

désormais [dezor'mɛ] *adv.* from now on, henceforth.

désoss|é [dezo'se] boneless, flabby; **~er** [~] (1a) bone; *fig.* take to pieces.

despot|e [dɛs'pɔt] *m* despot; **~ique** [~po'tik] despotic; **~isme** [~po'tism] *m* despotism.

dessaisir [desɛ'ziːr] (2a) ⚖ dispossess, **se ~ de** part with, give up.

dessal|é *fig.* [desa'le] knowing, sharp (*person*); **~er** [~] (1a) desalinate; soak (*fish*); *fig.* put (*s.o.*) up to a thing or two; *fig.* **se ~** learn a thing or two.

dessécher [dese'ʃe] (1f) dry (up); wither (*a plant*); drain; parch.

dessein [de'sɛ̃] *m* design; scheme, plan; intention; **à ~** on purpose.

desseller [desɛ'le] (1a) unsaddle.

desserrer [desɛ're] (1a) loosen; release; unclench.

dessert [de'sɛːr] *m* dessert; **~e** [~'sɛrt] *f* sideboard; *public transport:* service, servicing.

desservir[1] [desɛr'viːr] (2b) clear away; (*a.* **~ la table**) clear the table.

desservir[2] [~] (2b) *public transport:* serve; call at (*a port,* 🚂 *a station*).

desservir[3] [~] (2b) put (*s.o.*) at a disadvantage.

dessiller [desi'je]: F **~ les yeux à q.** open s.o.'s eyes (*to the truth*).

dessin [de'sɛ̃] *m* drawing; sketch; △ plan; pattern, design; **~ à main levée** free-hand drawing; *cin.* **~ animé** (animated) cartoon; **~ateur** *m,* **-trice** *f* [desina'tœːr, ~'tris] drawer; designer; cartoonist; **~er** [~'ne] (1a) draw; design; lay out (*a garden*); outline; **se ~** stand out; appear; *fig.* take shape.

dessouler [desu'le] (1a) sober (up).

dessous [də'su] **1.** *adv.* under(neath), below; **de ~** underneath; from under; **en ~** underneath; *fig.* in an underhand way; **de ~** from under; **2.** *su./m* underside, lower part; **~** *pl.* (*women's*) underclothing *sg.;* *fig.* seamy side *sg.;* **avoir le ~** get the worst of it.

dessus [də'sy] **1.** *adv.* on top (of it *etc.*); above; **en ~** at the top, above; **sens ~ dessous** topsy-turvy; **de ~** from, (from) off; **2.** *su./m* top, upper side or part; **avoir** (**prendre**) **le ~** have (get) the upper hand; *fig.* **le ~ du panier** the pick of the basket; **~-de-lit** [dəsyd'li] *m/inv.* bedspread.

destin [des'tɛ̃] *m* destiny; **~ataire** [destina'tɛːr] *su.* addressee; 🕂 payee; **~ation** [~na'sjɔ̃] *f* destination; **à ~ de** 🚂 for, to; 🚢 bound for; *post:* addressed to; **~ée** [~'ne] *f* destiny; **~er** [~'ne] (1a) intend (for, **à**); **se ~ à** enter (*a profession*).

destitu|er [dɛsti'tɥe] (1n) dismiss; **~tion** [~ty'sjɔ̃] *f* dismissal.

destruct|eur [dɛstryk'tœːr] **1.** *adj.* destructive; destroying; **2.** *su.* destroyer; **~if** [~'tif] destructive (of, **de**); **~ion** [~'sjɔ̃] *f* destruction.

désu|et, -ète [de'sɥɛ, ~'sɥɛt] out-of-date; **~étude** [~sɥe'tyd] *f* disuse.

désun|ion [dezy'njɔ̃] *f* separation; *fig.*

dissension; **~ir** [~'niːr] (2a) divide; take apart; *fig.* set at variance.

détachant [deta'ʃɑ̃] *m* stain remover.

détachement [detaʃ'mɑ̃] *m* detachment (*a.* ✕); indifference.

détacher[1] [~'ʃe] (1a) untie; undo; remove; take off, detach; send, detach, dispatch; **se ~** come off or out or undone or loose; get loose, free o.s.; pull or break away (from, **de**); *fig.* grow away (from, **de**); stand out (against, **sur**).

détacher[2] [~] (1a) clean, remove stains from.

détail [de'taj] *m* detail; particular; 🕂 retail; **vendre au ~** retail; **~lant** *m,* **e** *f* [deta'jɑ̃, ~'jɑ̃ːt] retailer; **~ler** [~'je] (1a) enumerate; itemize; detail; cut up; 🕂 retail.

détaler F [deta'le] (1a) decamp.

détaxe [de'taks] *f* tax reduction or removal or refund.

détective [detɛk'tiːv] *m* detective.

déteindre [de'tɛ̃dr] (4m) *v/t.* remove the colo(u)r from; *v/i.* fade, run; **~ sur q.** influence s.o.

dételer [det'le] (1c) *v/t.* unharness; 🚂 uncouple; *v/i.* F stop (working).

détendre [de'tɑ̃dr] (4a) loosen, slacken; relax; steady (*one's nerves*); unhang (*curtains*); **se ~** slacken; relax.

détenir [det'niːr] (2h) hold; detain (*goods, s.o., a.* 🏛️).

détente [de'tɑ̃ːt] *f* relaxation; slackening; *gun:* trigger; *fig.* improvement (*of relations*); *mot.* power stroke; *fig.* **dur à la ~** close-fisted.

déten|teur *m,* **-trice** *f* [detɑ̃'tœːr, ~'tris] holder (*a. sp.*); **~tion** [~'sjɔ̃] *f* detention, (with)holding; possession; custody; 🏛️ **maison** *f* **de ~** house of detention; **~u** [det'ny] **1.** *p.p.* of **détenir; 2.** *su.* prisoner.

déterger [detɛr'ʒe] (1l) cleanse.

détériorer [deterjo're] (1a) make worse; spoil; impair, damage.

détermin|ant 🅰 [detɛrmi'nɑ̃] *m* determinant; **~ation** [~na'sjɔ̃] *f* determination; **~é** [~'ne] definite; *fig.* resolute; **~er** [~'ne] (1a) determine; cause; **~ q. à** induce s.o. to; **~ de** (*inf.*) resolve to (*inf.*); **se ~** make up one's mind (to *inf.,* **à** *inf.*); resolve (upon s.th., **à qch.**).

déterrer [detɛ're] (1a) unearth.

détersif [detɛr'sif] detergent.

détest|able [detɛs'tabl] detestable; **~er** [~'te] (1a) hate; detest.

déton|ateur [detɔna'tœːr] *m* detonator; *fig.* trigger; **~ation** [~na'sjɔ̃] *f* detonation; *gun:* report; **~er** [~'ne] (1a) detonate, explode.

détonner [detɔ'ne] (1a) sing out of tune; *fig.* clash (*colours*).

détor|dre [de'tɔrdr] (4a) untwist, unravel; unlay (*a rope*); **~s** [~'tɔːr] untwisted; **~tiller** [~tɔrti'je] (1a) untwist; disentangle.

détour [de'tuːr] *m* detour, roundabout way; **~s** *pl.* curves, turns; *tours et ~s* ins and outs (*u. fig.*).

détourn|é [detur'ne] roundabout (*way*); indirect; *fig.* distorted; **~ement** [~na'mɑ̃] *m* diversion; embezzlement; **½** abduction; **~** *d'avion* highjacking; **~er** [~'ne] (1a) divert; turn away; embezzle; entice; **½** abduct; highjack (*an airplane*); *se ~ de* turn aside from.

détracteur *m*, **-trice** *f* [detrak'tœːr, ~'tris] detractor, disparager.

détraquer [detra'ke] (1m) put out of order or of action; *fig.* upset.

détremp|e [de'trɑ̃ːp] *f* distemper; **~er** [~trɑ̃'pe] (1a) soak; dilute.

détresse [de'trɛs] *f* distress.

détriment [detri'mɑ̃] *m* detriment, injury; *au ~ de* to the prejudice of.

détritus [detri'tys] *m* rubbish.

détroit *geog.* [de'trwa] *m* strait(s *pl.*).

détromper [detrɔ̃'pe] (1a) undeceive, enlighten; F *détrompez-vous!* don't you believe it!

détrôner [detro'ne] (1a) dethrone; *fig.* replace, supersede.

détrousser [detru'se] (1a) rob.

détruire [de'trɥiːr] (4h) destroy.

dette [dɛt] *f* debt (*a fig.*); **~s** *pl. actives* assets; **~s** *pl. passives* liabilities.

deuil [dœːj] *m* mourning (*a. clothes*); loss; bereavement; *en faire son ~* do without it; *porter le ~ de q.* mourn for s.o.

deux [dø] two; *date, title:* second; *~ fois* twice; *à nous ~* between us; *tous les ~ jours* every other day; *en ~* in two (*pieces*); *nous ~* the two of us; *tous (les) ~* both; **~ième** [dø'zjɛm] **1.** *adj./num., su.* second; **2.** *su./m* second, *Am.* third floor.

deux...: ~-pièces [dø'pjɛs] *m* (woman's) two-piece suit; **~-points** [~'pwɛ̃] *m/inv.* colon; **~-roues** [~'ru] *m/inv.* two--wheeled vehicle.

dévaler [deva'le] (1a) rush down.

dévaliser [devali'ze] (1a) rob.

dévaloris|ation ✝ [devalɔriza'sjɔ̃] *f* fall in value; **~er** ✝ [~'ze] (1a) devaluate (*the currency*).

dévalu|ation ✝ [devalɥa'sjɔ̃] *f* devaluation; **~er** ✝ [~'lɥe] (1n) devaluate.

devan|cer [dəvɑ̃'se] (1k) precede, outstrip (*s.o.*); forestall; **~cier** *m*, **-ère** *f* [~'sje, ~'sjɛːr] precursor; predecessor; **~t** [də'vɑ̃] **1.** *adv.* in front, ahead; **2.** *prp.* in front of; ahead of; in the presence of; *fig.* in the eyes of; **3.** *su./m* front, forepart; *de ~* fore...; *prendre les ~s* make the first move, forestall the others *etc.*; **~ture** [~vɑ̃'tyr] *f* shop window.

dévast|ateur [devasta'tœːr] devastating, destructive; **~er** [~'te] (1a) devastate.

dévein|ard [deve'naːr] unlucky (person); **~e** F [~'vɛn] *f* bad luck.

développ|ement [devlɔp'mɑ̃] *m* development; *pays m en voie de ~* developing country; **~er** [~lɔ'pe] (1a) develop; expand (*a. ♣*).

devenir [dəv'niːr] (2h) become; grow (*tall, sad, etc.*).

dévergondé [devɛrgɔ̃'de] shameless; licentious.

dévers|er [devɛr'se] (1a) pour off; dump; tip (out); unload; *fig.* discharge, empty; **~oir** [~'swaːr] *m* overflow; *fig.* outlet.

dévêtir [deve'tiːr] (2g) undress; take off; *se ~ de* divest o.s. of.

déviation [devja'sjɔ̃] *f* deviation; *road:* diversion; **⊘** deflection.

dévider [devi'de] (1a) reel off.

dévier [de'vje] (1o) *v/i.* deviate; *faire ~* divert; *v/t.* deflect; turn aside.

devin [də'vɛ̃] *m* soothsayer; **~er** [~vi'ne] (1a) guess; foresee; see through (*s.o.*); **~eresse** [~vin'rɛs] *f* fortune teller; **~ette** [dəvi'nɛt] *f* riddle.

devis [də'vi] *m* estimate; tender.

dévisager [deviza'ʒe] (1l) stare at (*s.o.*); scan (*s.o.*); disfigure.

devis|e [də'viːz] *f* motto; ✝ currency; **~s** *pl. étrangères* foreign currency; **~er** [~vi'ze] (1a) chat.

dévisser ⊙ [devi'se] (1a) unscrew.

dévoiler [devwa'le] (1a) unveil.

devoir [də'vwaːr] **1.** (3a) v/t. owe; v/aux. have to, must; should, ought to, be to; *j'aurais dû le faire* I should have done it; *je devrais le faire* I ought to do it; **2.** su./m duty; *school:* home-work; exercise; ✝ debit; ~**s** pl. respects; *rendre ses* ~ *s* à pay one's respect to (s.o.).

dévolu [devɔ'ly] **1.** adj. (à) devolved (upon); lapsing (to); **2.** su./m: *jeter son* ~ *sur* have designs on.

dévor|ant [devɔ'rɑ̃] ravenous; ~**er** [~'re] (1a) devour; consume; squander; F ~ *l'espace* eat up the miles.

dévot [de'vo] devout; pej. sanctimonious; ~**ion** [~vo'sjɔ̃] f devotion.

dévou|é [de'vwe] devoted; ~**ement** [~vu'mɑ̃] m devotion (to, à), self-abnegation; ~**er** [~'vwe] (1p) devote.

dévoy|é [devwa'je] delinquant; (1h) lead (s.o.) astray; *se* ~ go astray.

devrai [də'vre] *1st p. sg. fut.* of *devoir 1.*

dextérité [dɛksteri'te] f dexterity.

diabète ✳ [dja'bɛt] m diabetes; **diabétique** [~be'tik] adj., su. diabetic.

diab|le [dja:bl] m devil; trolley; *comment* ~ how the devil; *au* ~ *vauvert* at the back of beyond; *bon* ~ not a bad fellow; *tirer le* ~ *par la queue* be hard up; ~**lement** F [djablə'mɑ̃] adv. devilish; ~**lerie** [~blə'ri] f devilry; F fun; mischievousness; ~**lotin** [~blɔ'tɛ̃] m imp; ~**olique** [bɔ'lik] diabolic(al).

diacre eccl. [djakr] m deacon.

diadème [dja'dɛm] m diadem.

diagnosti|c ✳ [djagnɔs'tik] m diagnosis; *faire le* ~ *de* diagnose; ~**que** ✳ [~'tik] diagnostic; ~**quer** [~ti'ke] (1m) diagnose.

diagonal, e [djagɔ'nal] adj., su./f diagonal.

diagramme [dja'gram] m diagram.

dialecte [dja'lɛkt] m dialect.

dialectique [djalɛk'tik] f dialectics pl.

dialogu|e [dja'lɔg] m dialog(ue); ~**er** [~lɔ'ge] (1m) converse, talk.

diamant [dja'mɑ̃] m diamond.

diamètre Ⱥ [dja'mɛtr] m diameter.

diapason ♪ [djapa'zɔ̃] m diapason; pitch; tuning-fork; *voice:* range; *fig. au* ~ *(de)* in harmony or tune (with).

diaphane [dja'fan] transparent.

diaphragme [dja'fragm] m diaphragm; *phot.* diaphragm stop.

diapositive *phot.* [djapɔzi'tiːv] f transparency, slide.

diapré [dja'pre] variegated.

diarrhée ✳ [dja're] f diarrhoea.

dict|ateur [dikta'tœːr] m dictator; ~**ature** [~'tyːr] f dictatorship; ~**ée** [~'te] f dictation; ~**er** [~'te] (1a) dictate (a. fig.); ~**ion** [~'sjɔ̃] f diction; ~**ionnaire** [~sjɔ'nɛːr] m dictionary; ~**on** [~'tɔ̃] m saying.

dièse ♪ [djɛːz] m sharp.

diesel ⊙ [di'zɛl] m diesel engine.

diète [djɛt] f diet; regimen; **diététique** [djete'tik] dietary.

dieu [djø] m god; ♀ God; *mon* ♀! dear me!; *pour l'amour de* ♀ for Christ's sake.

diffam|ateur m, -**trice** f ⚖ [difama'tœːr, ~'tris] defamer; ~**ation** ⚖ [~'sjɔ̃] f defamation; ~ *écrite* libel; ~ *orale* slander; ~**atoire** [~'twaːr] defamatory; ~**er** [difa'me] (1a) defame.

différ|emment [difera'mɑ̃] differently; ~**ence** [~'rɑ̃s] f difference; *à la* ~ *de* unlike; ~**encier** [~rɑ̃'sje] (1o) differentiate (a. Ⱥ) (from de, d'avec); distinguish (between, entre); ~**end** [~'rɑ̃] m dispute; quarrel; ~**ent** [~'rɑ̃] different; ~**entiel, -elle** [~rɑ̃'sjɛl] adj., mot. su./m, Ⱥ su./f differential; ~**er** [~'re] (1f) v/t. postpone, put off, defer; delay; v/i. differ (from, de).

diffic|ile [difi'sil] difficult; *fig.* hard to please; ~**ulté** [~kyl'te] f difficulty.

difform|e [di'fɔrm] misshapen; ~**ité** [~fɔrmi'te] f malformation.

diffus [di'fy] diffused (*light*); diffuse (*style etc.*); ~**er** [dify'ze] (1a) diffuse; *radio:* broadcast; ~**eur** [~'zœːr] m ⊙ spray nozzle; broadcaster (*person*); ~**ion** [~'zjɔ̃] f heat, light: diffusion; *news:* spreading; *radio:* broadcasting; *germs:* spread; *style:* diffuseness.

digérer [diʒe're] (1f) digest (*food, news*); F *fig.* put up with; **digestible** [diʒɛs'tibl] digestible; **digestif** [~'tif] adj., su./m digestive; **digestion** [~'tjɔ̃] f digestion.

digital [diʒi'tal] digital; *empreinte* f ~ *e* fingerprint.

dign|e [diɲ] worthy, deserving; dignified (*air*); ~**itaire** [diɲi'tɛːr] m dignitary; ~**ité** [~'te] f dignity.

digression [digrɛ'sjɔ̃] f digression.

digue [dig] f dike, dam; barrier.

dilapider [dilapi'de] (1a) squander; misappropriate (*trust funds*).

dilat|ation [dilata'sjɔ̃] f eye: dilation; expansion; ♂ distension; **~er** [~'te] (1a) dilate, expand; distend, fig. **~ le cœur** gladden the heart; **~oire** [~'twaːr] dilatory.

dilection [dilɛk'sjɔ̃] f dilection.

dilemme [di'lɛm] m dilemma.

dilettante [dilet'tɑ̃ːt] su. amateur.

diligence [dili'ʒɑ̃ːs] f diligence; stage-coach; † haste; **~t** [~'ʒɑ̃] diligent; speedy; prompt.

dilu|er [di'lɥe] (1a) dilute (with, **de**); **~tion** [~ly'sjɔ̃] f dilution.

diluvien [dily'vjɛ̃] diluvial (clay), diluvian (*fossil*); torrential (*rain*).

dimanche [di'mɑ̃ːʃ] m Sunday.

dîme [dim] f tithe.

dimension [dimɑ̃'sjɔ̃] f dimension, size; **prendre les ~s de** measure out; fig. understand; fig. become, grow into.

diminu|er [dimi'nɥe] (1n) diminish; decrease; lessen; **~tion** [~ny'sjɔ̃] f diminution; decrease; lessening.

dind|e [dɛ̃ːd] f turkey-hen; stupid woman; **~on** [dɛ̃'dɔ̃] m turkey; fool.

dîn|er [di'ne] 1. (1a) dine; 2. su./m dinner; **~-débat** working dinner; **~ette** [~'nɛt] f snack; **~eur** m, **-euse** f [~'nœːr, ~'nøːz] diner.

dingo F [dɛ̃'go], **dingue** F [dɛ̃g] crazy, sl. nuts.

dinguer F [dɛ̃'ge] (1m): **aller ~** crash down; go sprawling; **envoyer ~** send (*s.o.*) packing; send (*s.th.*) flying.

diocèse eccl. [djɔ'sɛːz] m diocese.

dioptrie opt. [djɔp'tri] f diopter.

diphtérie ♂ [difte'ri] f diphtheria.

diphtongue gramm. [dif'tɔ̃ːg] f diphthong.

diplomat|e [diplɔ'mat] m diplomat; **~ie** [~ma'si] f diplomacy; **~ique** [~ma'tik] 1. adj. diplomatic; 2. su./f diplomatics pl.

diplôm|e [di'ploːm] m diploma, certificate; **~é** [~plo'me] 1. adj. certificated; **ingénieur** m **~** qualified engineer; 2. su. graduate.

dire [diːr] 1. (4p) say; tell; recite (*a poem*); show, reveal; **~ à q. de** (*inf.*) tell s.o. to (*inf.*); **~ du mal de** speak ill of; **~ que oui (non)** say yes (no); F **à qui**

le dites-vous? don't I know it!; **à vrai ~** to tell the truth; **cela ne me dit rien** that doesn't mean a thing to me; it doesn't appeal to me; I don't like it; **cela va sans ~** it goes without saying; **c'est-à-~** i.e.; in other words; **on dirait que** one would think that, it seems (or looks) as though; **on dirait qu'elle est triste** she looks sad; **on dirait un Américain** he looks like an American; **on le dit riche** he is said to be rich; **on dit** people say, **pour tout ~** in a word; **que dites-vous de ...?** what do you think of ...?; **que diriez-vous de ...?** what about ...?; **se ~** claim to be; be used (*word*); **vouloir ~** mean; 2. su./m statement; **au ~ de** according to.

direct [di'rɛkt] 1. adj. direct; ╦ through (*train*); 2. su./m through or express train; radio, telev.: live broadcast; **en ~** live (*broadcast, a. fig.*); box. **~ du droit** straight right.

direct|eur, -trice [dirɛk'tœːr, ~'tris] 1. su./m director, manager; school: headmaster; principal; prison: warden; Journ. editor; † **~ gérant** managing director; su./f directress; manageress; school: headmistress; 2. adj. controlling; guiding (*principle*); ⊕ driving; ⊕ steering; **~ion** [~'sjɔ̃] f direction; † management; † manager's office; † board of directors; school: headship; ⊕ driving; ⊕ steering; **en ~ de** a. bound or heading for, ...bound; **train m en ~ de** train for; **~ive** [~'tiːv] f directive; **~oire** [~'twaːr] m eccl. directory; hist. ⊊ Directory.

dirig|er [diri'ʒe] (1l) direct; manage, F run; mot. drive; steer; ♪ conduct; be in charge of; aim, level (at, **sur**) (*an arm*, fig. criticism etc.); **se ~ vers** head or make for; **~isme** [~'rism] m state intervention (in economical matters).

dis [di] 1st p. sg. pres. and p.s. of **dire** 1.

discern|ement [disɛrnə'mɑ̃] m discernment; discrimination (between ... and, **de ... et de**); **~er** [~'ne] (1a) discern; distinguish (between s.th. and s.th., **qch. de qch.**).

discipl|e [di'sipl] m disciple; **~ine** [disi'plin] f discipline; **~iner** [~pli'ne] (1a) discipline; control.

discontinu [diskɔ̃ti'ny] discontinuous; intermittent; broken (*line etc.*); **~er** [~'nɥe] (1n) stop.

disconven|ance [diskɔ̃v'nã:s] *f* unsuitability; disparity; **~ir** [~'niːr] (2h): **~ de** deny; **~ que** (*sbj.*) deny that (*ind.*).

discord|ance [diskɔr'dãːs] *f* discordance; disagreement; **~e** [dis'kɔrd] *f* discord; **~er** [~kɔr'de] (1a) ♪ be discordant; clash (*colours*); disagree.

discothèque [diskɔ'tɛk] *f* record library; disco(thèque).

discour|eur *m*, **-euse** *f* [disku'rœːr, ~'røːz] speechifier, *Am.* spieler; **~ir** [~'riːr] (2i) discourse; **~s** [~'kuːr] *m* speech (*a. gramm.*); talk(ing).

discourtois [diskur'twa] rude.

discrédit [diskre'di] *m* discredit; **~er** [~di'te] (1a) disparage.

discret, -ète [dis'krɛ, ~'krɛt] discreet; unobtrusive, quiet; ♣, ♬ discrete; *sous pli ~* under plain cover; **discrétion** [~kre'sjɔ̃] *f* discretion; *à ~* as much as one wants; unlimited; *être à la ~ de* be at the mercy of.

discriminat|ion [diskrimina'sjɔ̃] *f* discrimination; *sans ~* indiscriminately; **~oire** [~'twaːr] discriminatory.

disculper [diskyl'pe] (1a) clear (s.o. of s.th., *q. de qch.*).

discu|ssion [disky'sjɔ̃] *f* discussion; argument; **~ter** [~'te] (1a) discuss; question; argue (about).

disert [di'zɛːr] eloquent; fluent.

disette [di'zɛt] *f* scarcity, dearth.

diseur, -euse [di'zœːr, ~'zøːz] *su.* speaker; talker; *su./f thea.* diseuse.

disgrâce [dis'grɑːs] *f* disfavo(u)r; misfortune; **disgracier** [disgra'sje] (1o) dismiss from favo(u)r; **disgracieux** [~'sjø] awkward; rude.

disjoindre [dis'ʒwɛ̃ːdr] (4m) separate; *se ~* come apart; **disjoncteur** *∮* [disʒɔ̃k'tœːr] *m* circuit-breaker; **disjonction** [~'sjɔ̃] *f* separation.

dislo|cation [dislɔka'sjɔ̃] *f* breaking up; ♣ dislocation; *fig.* dismemberment; **~quer** [~'ke] (1m) break up; ♣ dislocate; dismember; disperse.

disons [di'zɔ̃] *1st p. pl. pres. of dire 1.*

disparaître [dispa'rɛːtr] (4k) disappear; vanish.

dispar|ate [dispa'rat] **1.** *adj.* ill-matched; dissimilar; **2.** *su./f* disparity; **~ité** [~ri'te] *f* disparity.

disparition [dispari'sjɔ̃] *f* disappearance.

dispendieux [dispã'djø] expensive.

dispens|aire ♣ [dispã'sɛːr] *m* community clinic; out-patients' department; **~e** [~'pãːs] *f* exemption; *eccl.* dispensation; **~er** [~pã'se] (1a) dispense; excuse (from, *de*); *se ~ de* avoid, get out of.

dispers|er [disper'se] (1a) disperse, scatter; **~ion** [~'sjɔ̃] *f* dispersion; breaking up; ♭ dissipation.

disponib|ilité [disponibili'te] *f* availability; **~s** *pl.* available means *sg.*; *en ~* unattached; **~le** [~'nibl] available; spare (*time*).

dispos [dis'po] in good form; alert.

dispos|er [dispo'ze] (1a) *v/t.* dispose; arrange; *se ~* (*à*) prepare (for *s.th.*; to *inf.*); *v/i.*: **~ de** have at one's disposal; *vous pouvez ~* you may go; **~itif** [~zi'tif] *m* ◎ device; system; plan; **~ition** [~zi'sjɔ̃] *f* disposition; arrangement; disposal; tendency (to, *à*); **~s** *pl.* talent *sg.*; *à la ~ de q.* at s.o.'s disposal.

disproportion [disprɔpɔr'sjɔ̃] *f* disproportion; **~né** [~sjɔ̃'ne] disproportionate.

disput|e [dis'pyt] *f* debate; quarrel; *chercher ~ à* pick a quarrel with; **~er** [~py'te] (1a) *v/i.* argue; debate; *v/t. sp.* play; **~ qch. à q.** contend with s.o. for s.th.; F **~ q.** tell s.o.; F *se ~* argue, quarrel, have an argument; **~eur** [~py'tœːr] **1.** *adj.* quarrelsome; **2.** *su.* arguer.

disquaire [dis'kɛːr] *m* record dealer.

disqualifier *sp.* [diskali'fje] (1o) disqualify.

disque [disk] *m* disk; *sp.* discus; 📻 signal; ◎ plate; (gramophone) record; *teleph. ~ d'appel* dial; *~ de longue durée*, *~ microsillon* long-playing record; *mot. ~ de stationnement* parking disc.

dissection [disɛk'sjɔ̃] *f* dissection.

dissembla|ble [disã'blabl] *adj.*: *~ à* (*or de*) dissimilar to (*s.th.*); **~nce** [~'blãːs] *f* dissimilarity.

disséminer [disemi'ne] (1a) spread; scatter; disseminate.

dissen|sion [disã'sjɔ̃] *f* dissension; **~timent** [~ti'mã] *m* dissent.

disséquer [dise'ke] (1s) dissect.

dissert|ation [disɛrta'sjɔ̃] *f* dissertation; essay; **~er** [~'te] (1a) discourse (on, *sur*), F hold forth.

dissiden|ce [disi'dãːs] *f* dissidence; dis-

sent; **~t** [~'dã] **1.** *adj.* dissident; **2.** *su.*
dissenter.

dissimilitude [disimili'tyd] *f* dissimilar-
ity.

dissimul|ation [disimyla'sjõ] *f* dissem-
bling, dissimulation; concealment,
cover-up; **~é** [~'le] hidden; secretive;
~er [~'le] (1a) conceal, hide; cover.

dissip|ateur [disipa'tœ:r] spendthrift;
~ation [~pa'sjõ] *f* dissipation (*a. fig.*);
waste; inattention; **~er** [~'pe] (1a)
dissipate; waste; disperse, dispel; clear
up (*a misunderstanding*); divert.

dissocier [diso'sje] (1o) dissociate.

dissol|u [diso'ly] dissolute; **~uble** [~'lybl]
soluble; **~ution** [~ly'sjõ] *f* 🍎 solution;
⚖ *a. parl.* dissolution; disintegration;
dissoluteness; **~vant** [disol'vã] *adj.*,
su./m solvent.

dissonan|ce [diso'nã:s] *f* dissonance; **~t**
[~'nã] dissonant, discordant; clashing,
jarring.

dissou|dre [di'sudr] (4bb) dissolve, an-
nul (*a marriage*); **~s, -te** [~'su, ~'sut]
p.p. of **dissoudre**.

dissua|der [disqa'de] (1a) dissuade
(*from* [*doing*] s.th., *de* [*faire*] *qch.*); **~ q.
de faire qch.** talk s.o. out of doing
s.th.; **~sion** [~'zjõ] *f* dissuasion; ✗ *ar-
mo f de* ~ deterrent weapon.

distan|ce [dis'tã:s] *f* distance; *à* ~ at *or*
from a distance; *à une* ~ *de ...* at a
distance of ...; ... away; *mot.* ~ *d'arrêt*
braking distance; ⊙ *commande f à* ~
remote control; *garder ses* ~*s* keep
one's distance; *fig. prendre ses* ~*s*
keep o.s. aloof; *tenir à* ~ keep (*s.o.*) at
arm's length; **~cer** [~tã'se] (1k) outdis-
tance; outrun; **~t** [~'tã] distant; aloof;
far away (from, *de*); **~** (*l'un de l'autre*)
de ,,, ... away (from one another).

disten|dre [dis'tã:dr] (4a) distend; strain
(*a muscle*); stretch; **~sion** [~tã'sjõ] *f* distension.

distiller [disti'le] (1a) distil; **~ie** [~til'ri]
f distillery.

distinct [dis'tẽ(:kt)] distinct; separate;
clear; **~if** [~tẽk'tif] distinctive; **~ion**
[~tẽk'sjõ] *f* distinction; discrimination;
refinement.

distingu|é [distẽ'ge] eminent; refined;
sentiments m/pl. ~s yours truly; **~er** [~]
(1m) distinguish; single out; hono(u)r;
fig. se ~ stand out.

distorsion [distor'sjõ] *f* distortion; ✚ im-
balance.

distraction [distrak'sjõ] *f* absent-
-mindedness; amusement; severance;
embezzlement.

distrai|re [dis'tre:r] (4ff) separate;
embezzle; amuse; distract; **~t** [~'trɛ]
inattentive.

distribu|er [distri'bɥe] (1n) distribute;
give out; hand out; deal out; deliver
(*letters*); deal (*cards*); **~teur** [~by'tœ:r]
m 🔧 distributor; ticket clerk; ~ *automatique* slot *or* vending machine;
~tion [~by'sjõ] *f* distribution; giving *etc.*
out; *post.* delivery; *thea.* cast(ing).

district [dis'trik(t)] *m* district.

dit [di] **1.** *p.p. of* **dire 1; 2.** *adj.* so-called;
autrement ~ in other words; **~es** [dit]
2nd p. pl. pres. of **dire 1.**

diurne [djyrn] diurnal; day-(*bird*).

divag|ation [divaga'sjõ] *f* wandering; rav-
ing; **~uer** [~'ge] (1m) wander, rave.

diverg|ence [diver'ʒã:s] *f* divergence;
fig. difference; **~er** [~'ʒe] (1l) diverge;
branch off.

divers [di'vɛr] diverse; various; **~ifler**
[diversi'fje] (1o) vary; **~ion** [~'sjõ] *f*
diversion; **~ité** [~si'te] *f* diversity,
variety.

diverti|r [diver'ti:r] (2a) divert; ✚ misap-
propriate; **~ssement** [~tis'mã] *m*
amusement; ✚ misappropriation.

dividende [divi'dã:d] *m* dividend.

divin [di'vẽ] divine (*a. fig.*); **~ateur** [divina-
'tœ:r] prophetic; **~ation** [~'sjõ] *f*
divination (*a. fig.*); **~atoire** [~'twa:r]
divining-...; *baguette f* ~ dowsing rod;
~iser [divini'ze] (1a) deify; *fig.* glorify;
~ité [~'te] *f* divinity.

divis|er [divi'ze] (1a) divide (into, *en*);
split (up); **~eur** [~'zœ:r] *m* divider; ⚙
divisor; **~ible** [~'zibl] divisible; **~ion**
[~'sjõ] *f* division; split(-up).

divorce [di'vors] *m* divorce (*a. fig.*); **~er**
[~vor'se] (1k) divorce (s.o., *d'*) *avec q.*);
break (with, *d')* *avec*).

divulg|ation [divylga'sjõ] *f* divulgence;
~uer [~'ge] (1m) divulge.

dix [dis; *before consonant* di; *before
vowel and h mute* diz] ten; *date, title:*
tenth; **~-huit** [di'zɥit; *before consonant*
~'zɥi] eighteen; *date, title:* eighteenth;
~-huitième [~zɥi'tjɛm] eighteenth;
~ième [~'zjɛm] tenth; **~-neuf** [diz'nœf;

before vowel and h mute ~'nœv] nineteen; *date*, *title*: nineteenth; **~neu-vième** [~nœ'vjɛm] nineteenth; **~sept** [dis'sɛt] seventeen; *date*, *title*: seventeenth; **~septième** [~sɛ'tjɛm] seventeenth.

dizaine [di'zɛn] *f* (about) ten.

do ♪ [do] *m/inv.* do, *note*: C.

docile [dɔ'sil] docile; amenable; **~ité** [~sili'te] *f* docility; obedience.

dock [dɔk] *m* ⚓ dock; ♏ warehouse.

docte [dɔkt] learned (*a. iro.*).

docteur [dɔk'tœːr] *m* doctor; **~oral** [dɔktɔ'ral] doctoral; *fig.* pedantic; **~orat** [~'ra] *m* doctor's degree; **~oresse** [~'rɛs] *f* (lady) doctor.

doctrine [dɔk'trin] *f* doctrine, tenet.

document [dɔky'mã] *m* document; **~aire** [~mã'tɛːr] *adj.*, *su./m* documentary; **~er** [~mã'te] (1a) document.

dodeliner [dɔdli'ne] (1a): ~ *de la tête* wag one's head.

dodo *ch.sp.* [do'do] *m* bye-byes, sleep; bed; *faire* ~ (go to) sleep.

dodu [dɔ'dy] plump, chubby.

dogme [dɔgm] *m* dogma, tenet.

dogue *zo.* [dɔg] *m*: ~ *anglais* mastiff.

doigt [dwa] *m* finger; ~ *de pied* toe; *à deux ~s de* within an ace of; *montrer du* ~ point at; **~é** [dwa'te] *m* ♪ fingering; *fig.* tact, adroitness, diplomacy.

dois [dwa] *1st p. sg. pres. of* **devoir 1**; **doit** ♏ [~] *m* liability; **doivent** [dwa:v] *3rd p. pl. pres. of* **devoir 1**.

doléances [dɔle'ãːs] *f/pl.* complaints; grievances; **dolent** [~'lã] painful (*limb*); plaintive (*voice etc.*).

domaine [dɔ'mɛn] *m* domain; realm; property; *fig.* sphere, field.

dôme [doːm] *m* dome; *fig.* vault.

domesticité [dɔmɛsti'te] *f* domestic service; *animal*: domesticity; staff (of servants); **~que** [~'tik] **1.** *adj.* domestic; menial; **2.** *su.* servant; **~quer** [~ti'ke] (1m) domesticate; tame.

domicile [dɔmi'sil] *m* residence; ⚖ domicile; *travail à* ~ home-work; **~iaire** [dɔmisi'ljɛːr] domiciliary; **~ier** [~'lje] (1o) domicile; *se* ~ *à* take up residence at.

dominateur [dɔmina'tœːr] **1.** *adj.* dominant; domineering; **2.** *su.* ruler; **~ation** [~na'sjɔ̃] *f* domination; control; **~er** [~'ne] (1a) *v/t.* dominate; master;

control; overlook; *v/i.* rule; predominate; prevail (*opinion*); ~ *sur* rule over.

dominical [dɔmini'kal] Sunday-...; *oraison f* ~ Lord's Prayer.

dommage [dɔ'maːʒ] *m* damage, injury; **~s** *pl.* damage *sg.* (*to property*); **~s** *pl. de guerre* war damage (compensation) *sg.*; ⚖ **~s** *pl.* **-intérêts** *m/pl.* damages; *c'est* ~, *quel* ~! what a pity!; *c'est* ~ *que* it's a pity (that); **~able** [dɔma'ʒabl] harmful.

domptable [dɔ̃'tabl] tamable; **~er** [~'te] (1a) tame; break in (*a horse*); *fig.* subdue; **~eur** *m*, **-euse** *f* [~'tœːr, ~'tøːz] tamer.

don [dɔ̃] *m* gift (*a. fig.*) (for, *de*); present; *faire* ~ *à q. de qch.* make a present of s.th. to s.o.; **~ataire** ⚖ [dɔna'tɛːr] *su.* donee; **~ateur, -trice** [~'tœːr, ~'tris] *su.* giver; *su./m* doner; *su./f* donatrix; **~ation** [~'sjɔ̃] *f* donation.

donc [dɔ̃k; dɔ̃] **1.** *adv.* then; just ...; *allons* ~! come along!; nonsense!; *pourquoi* ~? (but) why?; **2.** *cj.* therefore, so, thus, then; hence.

donjon [dɔ̃'ʒɔ̃] *m* castle: keep.

donnant † [dɔ'nã] generous; ~ ~ give and take; **~e** [dɔn] *f* cards: deal; **~é** [dɔ'ne] (*étant*) ~ (*que*) given (that); **~ée** [~'ne] *f* datum (*pl. data*); fundamental idea *or* theme; fact; *traitement m des* ~s data processing; **~er** [~'ne] (1a) *v/t.* give; give away; deal (out), hand *or* give out; yield (*a profit, a result*); ⚡ donate (*blood*); confer (*a title*) upon; ♏ ~ *avis* give notice; *teleph.*: ~ *à q. la communication avec* put s.o. through to; ~ *q. pour perdu* give s.o. up for lost; *elle lui donna un enfant* she bore him a child; *se* ~ *à* abandon o.s. to; *v/i.* give; yield; ⚔ attack, fire; ~ *à entendre* give to understand; ~ *contre* run against; ~ *dans* run into; *sun*: shine into; *fig.* have a tendency to(wards); ~ *sur* look out on; lead to; **~eur** *m*, **-euse** *f* [~'nœːr, ~'nøːz] giver, donor; *cards*: dealer; ♏ seller; ~ *de sang* blood donor.

dont [dɔ̃] *pron.* whose, of whom (which); by *or* from *or* among *or* about whom (which).

donzelle F [dɔ̃'zɛl] *f* hussy.

doper *sp.* [dɔ'pe] (1a) dope; **~ing** *sp.* [dɔ'piŋ] *m* doping; dope.

doré [dɔ're] guilt, guilded; golden.

dorénavant [dɔrena'vɑ̃] *adv.* henceforth.

dorer [dɔ're] (1a) gild; brown (*meat*).

dorloter [dɔrlɔ'te] (1a) pamper.

dorm|ant [dɔr'mɑ̃] 1. *adj.* sleeping; dormant; still (*water*); 2. *su.* sleeper; ~casing, frame; **~eur, -euse** [~'mœːr, ~'møːz] *su.* sleeper; *fig.* sluggard; *su./f* stud earring; **~ir** [~'miːr] (2b) sleep; be asleep; ✝ lie idle; *fig.* be latent; **~ comme une souche** (*or* **un loir**) sleep like a log; **~ trop longtemps** oversleep; **histoire f à ~ debout** incredible story; **~itif** [~mi'tif] *adj.*, *su./m* soporific.

dortoir [dɔr'twaːr] *m* dormitory.

dorure [dɔ'ryːr] *f* gilding; glazing.

dos [do] *m* back (*a. of a chair, page*, etc.); nose; bridge; book; spine; ridge; **en ~ d'âne** ridged; **en avoir plein le ~** be fed up with it; **tourner le ~ à** turn one's back on; **voir au ~** see over.

dos|age [do'zaːʒ] *m* dosage; **~e** [doz] *f* 🌡 dose; *fig.* share; **~er** [do'ze] (1a) determine the dose of; 🌡 titrate; 🌡 measure out.

dossier [do'sje] *m* chair etc.: back; 🌡 record; file, documents *pl.*; 🌡 case history.

dot [dɔt] *f* dowry; **~al** [dɔ'tal] dotal; **~ation** [~ta'sjɔ̃] *f* endowment; ⚙ equipment; **~er** [~'te] (1a) dower; endow, ⚙ equip (with, *de*).

douair|e [dwɛːr] *m* dower; jointure; **~ière** [dwɛ'rjɛːr] *f* dowager.

douan|e [dwan] *f* customs *pl.*; **~ier** [dwa'nje] 1. *adj.* customs...; 2. *su./m* customs officer.

doubl|age [du'blaːʒ] *m* cost. lining; cin. dubbing; **~e** [dubl] 1. *adj.* double; **à ~ face** two-faced (*person*); **à ~ sens** ambiguous; **partie f ~** golf: foursome; 2. *su./m* double; **en ~** in duplicate; **plier en ~** fold in two; **~s** *pl.* **messieurs** tennis: men's doubles; **~é** [du'ble] *m* rolled gold; plated ware; **~er** [~'ble] (1a) double (*a.* ⚓ *a cape*); fold in two; cost. linc; metal: plate; cin. dub; pass; thea. understudy; mot. **défense de ~** no overtaking!; **~ une classe** repeat a class; **~ure** [~'blyːr] *f* lining; understudy.

douc|eâtre [du'sɑːtr] sweetish; sickly; **~ment** [dus'mɑ̃] gently; softly; smooth-

ly; carefully; **~ereux** [dus'rø] sweetish, cloying; *fig.* smooth-tongued; **~et** [du'sɛ] meek; mild; **~eur** [~'sœːr] *f* sweetness; gentleness; mildness; **~s** *pl.* sweets, Am. candies; *fig.* **en~** soft(ly); gentle (gently); smooth(ly), careful(ly).

douch|e [duʃ] *f* shower(-bath); 🌡 douche; **~er** [du'ʃe] (1a) give a shower-bath; F cool off.

douer [dwe] (1p) endow (with, *de*); **être doué pour** have a gift for.

douille [duːj] *f* socket; ⚙ sleeve.

douillet [du'jɛ] cosy; effeminate.

doul|eur [du'lœːr] *f* pain; suffering; grief, ┼ **~oureux** [~lu'rø] painful; aching; *fig.* sad; *fig.* sorrowful.

dout|e [dut] *m* doubt; suspicion; **mettre** (*or* **révoquer**) **en ~** (call in) question (whether, **que**); **sans ~** no doubt; probably; **sans aucun ~** for sure; **~er** [du'te] (1a) *v/t.* doubt (that, if, whether **que**); **se ~ de** think, suspect; **je m'en doutais** I thought as much; *v/i.:* **~ de** doubt, be doubtful of, have one's doubts about; **~eur** [~'tœːr] 1. *su.* doubter; 2. *adj.* doubting; **~eux** [~'tø] doubtful; dubious.

douve [duːv] *f* moat; *tub:* stave.

doux, douce [du, dus] 1. *adj.* soft; sweet; mild (*a.* steel); gentle; smooth; **eau f douce** fresh water; **vin m ~** must; 2. *adv.:* F **filer doux** sing small; **tout doux!** take it easy!; *sl.* **en douce** on the quiet.

douz|aine [du'zɛn] *f* dozen; **à la ~** by the dozen; **~e** [duːz] twelve; *date, title:* twelfth; **~ième** [du'zjɛm] twelfth.

doyen *m*, **-enne** *f* [dwa'jɛ̃, ~'jɛn] dean; diplomat: doyen; **~ d'âge** senior; **~né** [~jɛ'ne] *m* deanery.

dragage [dra'gaːʒ] *m* dredging.

dragée [dra'ʒe] *f* sugared almond; pill; *sl.* bullet; small shot; **tenir la ~ haute à** make (*s.o.*) pay dearly.

dragon [dra'gɔ̃] *m* dragon; flying lizard; **~ne** [~'gɔn] *f* tassel.

dragu|e [drag] *f* ⚙ dredger; drag-net; **~er** [dra'ge] (1m) dredge (*a.* for s.th.); drag (*a pond*); sweep for (*mines*); *sl.* (try and) pick up (*a girl* etc.).

drain [drɛ̃] *m* drain(-pipe); **~age** [drɛ'naːʒ] *m* drain(age); **~er** [~'ne] (1a) drain; *fig.* attract.

dram|atique [drama'tik] 1. *adj.* dramatic; 2. *su./m* drama; **~atiser** [~ti'ze] (1a) dramatize; **~aturge** [~'tyrʒ] m playwright; **~e** [dram] m drama; play.

drap [dra] m cloth; sheet; F **être dans de beaux ~s** be in a pretty mess; **~eau** [dra'po] m flag; *telev.* irregular synchronism; **sous les ~x** ✗ in the services; on the side of, **de**); **~er** [~'pe] (1a) drape; cover with cloth; **~erie** [~'pri] f drapery; curtains *pl.*; **~ier** [~'pje] m draper.

dress|age [drɛ'saːʒ] m training; putting up; **~er** [drɛ'se] (1a) put up; erect (*a monument etc.*); fix up (*a bed*); raise; prick up (*one's ears*); lay, set (*the table, a trap*); draw up (*a list*); pitch (*a tent*); establish; lodge (*a complaint*); train (*an animal, a person*); drill (*recruits*); trim (*a hedge*); dress (*wood*); straighten out (*a wire*); **se ~** draw o.s. up, rise; stand; stand on end (*hair*); **~eur, -euse** f [~'sœːr, ~'søːz] trainer (*of animals*); adjuster; **~oir** [~'swaːr] m sideboard.

dribbler *sp.* [dri'ble] (1a) dribble.

drille F [driːj] m fellow, chap.

drogue [drɔg] f drug; *coll.* drugs *pl.*; **~é** [drɔ'ge] 1. high (on drugs); 2. *su.* drug addict; **~er** [drɔ'ge] (1m) drug (up); dose up; **se ~** be on *or* take drugs; **~erie** [~'gri] f chemist's, *Am.* drugstore.

droit, e [drwa, drwat] 1. *adj.* straight (*a line*); right (*angle, side*); upright (*a. fig.*); vertical; stand-up (*collar*); **au ~ de** at right angles with; 2. *adv.* straight; **tout ~** straight ahead *or* on; 3. *su./m* right; privilege; law; fee, charge; **~s** *pl.* **d'auteur** royalties; **~s** *pl.* **civiques** civil rights; **~ de douane** (customs) duty; **~ des gens** law of nations; **~ du plus fort** right of the strongest; **à qui de ~** to the proper quarter; **avoir ~ à** be entitled to; be eligible for; **de (bon) ~** by right; **être en ~ de** (*inf.*) have a right to (*inf.*); **faire son ~** study law; *su./f* right hand; straight line; **de ~e** on the right; *direction:* to the right; **tenir la ~e** keep to the right; *pol.* **la ~e** the Right, the Conservatives *pl.*; **~ier** [drwa'tje] 1. *adj.* right-handed; *pol.* right-wing; 2. *su.* right-handed person; *pol.* conservative; **~iste** [~'tist] rightist; **~ure** [~'tyːr] f uprightness.

drôle [droːl] funny; **un(e) ~ de** a funny; **drôlerie** [droːl'ri] f fun.

dromadaire *zo.* [drɔma'dɛːr] m dromedary.

dru [dry] 1. *adj.* thick; close; dense; vigorous; 2. *adv.:* **tomber ~** fall thick and fast.

dû, due, *m/pl.* **dus** [dy] 1. *p.p. of* **devoir** 1; 2. *adj., su./m* due.

duc [dyk] m duke; *orn.* horned owl; **~al** [dy'kal] ducal; ... of a duke.

duch|é [dy'ʃe] m dukedom; **~esse** [~'ʃɛs] f duchess; duchess satin.

ductil|e [dyk'til] ductile; **~ité** [~tili'te] f malleability; *fig.* docility.

duel [dɥɛl] m duel; **duelliste** [dɥɛ'list] m duellist.

dûment [dy'mã] *adv.* in due form.

dune [dyn] f dune; **~s** *pl.* downs.

duo ♪ [dɥo] m duet.

dup|e [dyp] f dupe; **être ~ de** be taken in by; **prendre q. pour ~** make a cat's-paw of s.o.; **~er** [dy'pe] (1a) dupe; take (*s.o.*) in; **~erie** [~'pri] f trickery; take-in; **~eur** [~'pœːr] m cheat; hoaxer.

duplic|ata [dyplika'ta] *m/inv.* duplicate; **~ité** [~si'te] f double-dealing.

dur, e [dyːr] 1. *adj.* hard (*a. fig.*); stiff; tough; harsh; **avoir le sommeil ~** be a heavy sleeper; **avoir l'oreille ~e,** **être ~ d'oreille** be hard of hearing; **être ~ avec** (*or* **pour**) **q.** be hard on *or* rough with s.o.; 2. *adv.* hard; 3. *su./m* F tough guy; hard-liner; *su./f* **coucher sur la dure** sleep on the bare ground.

durab|ilité [dyrabili'te] f durability; **~le** [~'rabl] lasting; solid.

durant [dy'rã] *prp.* during; **~ des années** for years; **sa vie ~** his life long; **des heures ~** for hours (and hours).

durci|r [dyr'siːr] (2a) *v/t.* harden; hard-boil; *v/i.* harden; set (*concrete*); **~ssement** [~sis'mã] m hardening, toughening; stiffening.

durée [dy're] f length (of time); duration; ⊙ wear, life; **de courte ~** short-lived; **durer** [~] (1a) last; wear (*goods*); hold out (*person*); **le temps me dure** time hangs heavy on my hands.

dur|eté [dyr'te] f hardness (*a. fig.*); toughness; *fig.* harshness; austerity; severity; **~ d'oreille** hardness of hearing; **~illon** [dyri'jõ] m foot: corn; callosity.

dus [dy] *1st p. sg. p.s. of* **devoir** 1.

duvet [dy'vɛ] *m* down; *tex.* fluff, nap; F down quilt; **~é** [dyv'te], **~eux** [~'tø] downy, fluffy.

dynam|ique [dina'mik] **1.** *adj.* dynamic; **2.** *su./f* dynamics *sg.*; **~ite** [~'mit] *f* dy-namite; **~o** ⚡, ⚙ [~'mo] *f* dynamo.

dynastie [dinas'ti] *f* dynasty.

dysenterie ✱ [disā'tri] *f* dysentery.

dyspepsi|e ✱ [dispɛp'si] *f* indigestion; **~que** [~pɛp'sik] dyspeptic.

E

eau [o] *f* water; **~ de toilette** lotion; **~ du robinet** tap water; **~ potable** drinking water; **~ vive** running water; **aller aux ~x** go to a spa; **faire ~** (spring a) leak; **jeux** *m/pl.* **d'~x** ornamental fountains; **nager entre deux ~x** swim under wa-ter; *fig.* **l'~ m'en vient à la bouche** it makes my mouth water; **ville f d'~** spa; **~-de-vie**, *pl.* **~x-de-vie** [od'vi] *f* bran-dy; spirits *pl.*; **~-forte**, *pl.* **~x-fortes** [o'fɔrt] *f* nitric acid; etching.

ébah|ir [eba'iːr] (2a) stupefy; flabber-gast; **~ssement** [~is'mã] *m* stupefac-tion.

ébarber [ebar'be] (1a) trim; clip.

ébat|s [e'ba] *m/pl.* frolics, gambols; **prendre ses ~** gambol; **~tre** [e'batr] (4a): **s'~** frolic, frisk about.

ébaubi [ebo'bi] astounded.

ébauch|e [e'boːʃ] *f* sketch, outline; rough draft; *fig.* ghost (*of a smile*); **~er** [ebo'ʃe] (1a) sketch (out); *fig.* give a hint of; **s'~** take shape.

ébène [e'bɛn] *f* ebony; **ébéniste** [ebe'nist] *m* cabinetmaker.

éberlué [ebɛrly'e] flabbergasted.

éblou|ir [eblu'iːr] (2a) dazzle (*a. fig.*); **~ssement** [~is'mã] *m* dazzle; glare; dizziness.

éborgner [ebɔr'ɲe] (1a) blind in one eye; ✂ disbud.

ébouillanter [ebuja'te] (1a) scald.

éboul|ement [ebul'mã] *m* collapsing; fall of stone; landslide; **~er** [ebu'le] (1a) bring down; **s'~** cave in; slip (*land*); **~is** [~'li] *m* debris; fallen earth; scree.

ébouriffer [eburi'fe] (1a) ruffle (*a. fig.*), dishevel; *fig.* amaze.

ébrancher ✂ [ebrã'ʃe] (1a) prune.

ébranl|ement [ebrãl'mã] *m* shaking; *fig.*

disturbance; **~er** [ebrã'le] (1a) shake (*a. fig.*); *fig. a.* undermine, weaken; **s'~** start, set off.

ébrécher [ebre'ʃe] (1f) notch; chip (*a plate*); jag (*a knife*); make a hole in (*one's fortune*); *fig.* damage.

ébriété [ebrie'te] *f* drunkenness.

ébrou|ement [ebru'mã] *m* snort(ing); **~er** [~'e] (1a): **s'~** snort; splash about; shake o.s.

ébruiter [ebrɥi'te] (1a) noise abroad; di-vulge; blab out (*a secret*).

ébullition [ebyli'sjɔ̃] *f* boiling; turmoil; **point** *m* **d'~** boiling point.

écaill|e [e'kaːj] *f* ✱, ⚙, fish, *etc.*: scale; paint: flake; shellfish: shell; tortoise-shell; **~er** [eka'je] (1a) scale (*fish*); open (*oysters*); **s'~** flake or peel off; **~eux** [eka'jø] scaly; flaky.

écal|e [e'kal] *f* pea: pod; nut: husk; **~er** [eka'le] (1a) shell (*peas*); hull.

écarlate [ekar'lat] *adj., su./f* scarlet.

écarquiller [ekarki'je] (1a) open wide (*one's eyes*); straddle.

écart [e'kaːr] *m* gap; divergence; differ-ence; separation; *cards:* discard(ing); margin (*of prices*); *fig.* digression; *fan-cy:* flight; **~ (de conduite)** misdemean-o(u)r; **à l'~** apart; aloof; out of the way; **faire un ~** swerve; shy (*horse*); *gymn.* **grand ~** splits *pl.*; **se tenir à l'~** stand aside or aloof; **~é** [ekar'te] remote; isolated; lonely.

écarteler [ekartə'le] (1d) ⚔ *hist.* quar-ter; *fig.* tear apart; **écartelé entre** torn between.

écart|ement [ekartə'mã] *m* gap, space (between, **de**); 🚂 ga(u)ge; *mot.* wheel-base; ⚙ deflection; **~er** [~'te] (1a) sep-arate; spread; remove; avert; push aside (*a. proposals*); divert (*suspicion etc.*); **s'~** move aside; diverge; deviate (from, **de**).

ecclésiastique [ɛklezjas'tik] **1.** *adj.* ecclesiastical; clerical (*hat etc.*); **2.** *su./m* clergyman; **~s** *pl.* clergy.

écervelé [esɛrvə'le] **1.** *adj.* scatter--brained, flighty; **2.** *su.* scatter-brain.

échafaud [eʃa'fo] *m* scaffolding; platform; ⚖ scaffold; **~age** [~ʃo'da:ʒ] *m* scaffolding; *fig.* structure; *fig.* piling up; **~er** [~ʃo'de] (1a) construct.

échalas [eʃa'la] *m* vineprop; hop-pole; *fig.* spindleshanks.

échalier [eʃa'lje] *m* stile; gate.

échalote ♀ [eʃa'lɔt] *f* shallot.

échancr|er [eʃɑ̃'kre] (1a) indent, notch; **~ure** [~'kry:r] *f* indentation; cut; *dress:* neckline; notch.

échange [e'ʃɑ̃:ʒ] *m* exchange (*a.* ✝); ✝ barter; **libre ~** free trade; **en ~ de** in exchange *or* return for; **~er** [eʃɑ̃'ʒe] (1l) exchange (for *pour, contre*); **~eur** *mot.* [~'ʒœːr] *m* interchange.

échantillon [eʃɑ̃ti'jɔ̃] *m* sample (*a. fig.*); specimen; pattern; **~ner** [~jɔ'ne] (1a) sample.

échapp|atoire [eʃapa'twa:r] *f* way out, loop-hole; **~é, e** [~'pe] **1.** *adj.* runaway; **2.** *su.* fugitive; *su./f* escape; (free) space; *sp.* spurt; **~e de lumière** burst of light; **par ~es** by fits and starts; **~ement** [eʃap'mɑ̃] *m gas etc.:* escape; ⚙ outlet; *mot.* **tuyau** *m* (**pot** *m*) **d'~** exhaust-pipe (silencer); **~er** [eʃa'pe] (1a) escape; **~ à** escape (from), get away from; run out on; *fig.* escape, avoid, dodge (*s.th., s.o.*); defy; **laisser ~** let slip; set free; **~ des mains à q.** slip out of s.o.'s hands; **le mot m'a échappé** the word has slipped my memory; **l'~ belle** have a narrow escape; **s'~** escape (from, **de**); slip out; disappear.

écharde [e'ʃard] *f* splinter.

écharpe [e'ʃarp] *f* sash; scarf; ✈ sling; **en ~** slantwise; **~er** [eʃar'pe] (1a) slash; cut up; card (*wool*).

échasse [e'ʃɑːs] *f* stilt.

échaud|er [eʃo'de] (1a) scald; *fig.* **se faire ~** burn one's fingers.

échauff|ement [eʃof'mɑ̃] *m* ⚙ heating; overheating; *fig.* over-excitement; **~er** [eʃo'fe] (1a) overheat; ⚙ heat; *fig.* warm; **s'~** warm up; *fig.* become heated; run hot.

échéan|ce ✝ [eʃe'ɑ̃:s] *f* falling due; date; *tenancy:* expiration; **à longue ~** long-dated; **~t** [~'ɑ̃] ✝ falling due; **le cas ~** if necessary.

échec [e'ʃɛk] *m* failure; setback, defeat; *chess:* check (*a. fig.*); **~s** *pl.* chess(-board) *sg.*; **voué à l'~** doomed to failure.

échel|le [e'ʃɛl] *f* cart etc.: rack; **~le** [e'ʃɛl] *f* ladder (*a. fig., a. of a stocking*); *colours, drawing, map, prices, wages, etc.:* scale; **~ double** pair of steps; **~ mobile** (**des salaires**) sliding scale (of wages); **~ sociale** social scale; **faire la courte ~ à q.** give s.o. a helping hand; **sur une grande ~** on a large scale; **~on** [eʃ'lɔ̃] *m* ladder: rung; *admin.* grade; *fig.* step; ✗ echelon; ♪ degree; *pol. etc.* **à l'~ le plus élevé** at the highest level; **en ~** stepped (*gearing*); **~onnement** [eʃlɔn'mɑ̃] *m* placing at intervals; spreading (*over a period*); *holidays:* staggering; **~onner** [eʃlɔ'ne] (1a) place at intervals; space out; spread (*over a period*); stagger (*a. holidays etc.*); grade.

échev|eau [eʃ'vo] *m* skein; *fig.* maze; **~eler** [eʃə'vle] (1c) dishevel.

échin|e *anat.* [e'ʃin] *f* backbone; **~er** [eʃi'ne] (1a) break (*s.o.'s*) back; *fig.* tire (*s.o.*); *sl.* ruin; **s'~** (**à** *inf.*) wear o.s. out (*ger.*).

échiquier [eʃi'kje] *m* chessboard; checker pattern; *Br.* ♀ Exchequer; **en ~** chequerwise.

écho [e'ko] *m* echo; **faire ~** echo.

échoir [e'ʃwa:r] (3d) fall due; ⚖ expire; fall (*to s.o.'s lot*); *fig.* befall.

échouer [e'ʃwe] (1p) *v/i.* ♣ ground; *fig.* fail; *fig.* land, end up (in **dans**); *v/t.* run (*a ship*) aground; *fig* **faire ~** fail, thwart; ruin.

échu [e'ʃy] ✝ due; expired.

éclabouss|er [eklabu'se] (1a) splash (with, **de**); **~ure** [~'sy:r] *f* splash.

éclair [e'klɛːr] *m* flash (of lightning); **~s** *pl.* **de chaleur** heat lightning *sg*; **visite** *f* **~** lightning visit; **~age** [ekle'ra:ʒ] *m* light(ing); ✗ scouting; **~ par projecteurs** flood-lighting; **~agiste** [~ra'ʒist] *m* lighting engineer; **~cie** [ekler'si] *f* fair period (*a. fig.*); break (*of clouds*); clearing (*in a forest*); **~cir** [~'si:r] (2a) clear (up); brighten; thin (*a forest*); clarify (*a liquid*); thin out (*a sauce*); *fig.* solve, explain; **~er** [eklɛˈre] (1b) *v/t.* light, illuminate; *fig.* enlighten; ✗ reconnoitre; **~ au néon** light by neon; *v/i.* give light, shine; *il éclaire* it is lightening; **~eur** [⁓ˈrœːr] *m* scout; *mot.* **~ de tablier** dashboard light.

éclat [eˈkla] *m* splinter, chip, burst (*of laughter, of thunder*); explosion; flash (*of gun, light*); brightness, brilliance (*a. fig.*); *fig* glamo(u)r; **~ de rire** burst of laughter; *faire* **~** create a stir; *faux* **~** tawdriness; *rire aux* **~s** roar with laughter; **~ant** [eklaˈtɑ̃] brilliant, sparkling; magnificent; loud (*noise*); *fig.* obvious; **~er** [⁓ˈte] (1a) burst, explode; shatter; break up; split up; flash (*a. fig.*); shine out *or* forth; clap (*thunder*), break out (*fire, laughter, war*), spread, be scattered; **~ de rire** burst out laughing; F **s'~** have a great time, have a ball.

éclips|e [eˈklips] *f* eclipse; *fig.* disappearance; **~er** [eklipˈse] (1a) eclipse (*a. fig.*); obscure; **s'~** vanish.

éclisse ✶ [eˈklis] *f* splint; **~r** [ekliˈse] (1a) splint, put in splints.

éclopé [ekloˈpe] lame (person).

éclo|re [eˈkloːr] (4f) hatch (*bird*); ⚘ bloom; *fig.* come to light; **~sion** [eklɔˈzjɔ̃] *f* eggs: hatching; ⚘ blooming; *fig.* birth, dawning.

éclus|e [eˈklyːz] *f* lock; flood gate; **~ier** [eklyˈzje] *m* lock keeper.

écœurer [ekœˈre] (1a) disgust, sicken, nauseate; *fig.* dishearten.

écol|e [eˈkɔl] *f* school; **~ de commerce** commercial school; **~ des arts et métiers** industrial school; engineering college; **~ libre** private school; **~ mixte** mixed school, *Am.* co-educational school; **~ primaire supérieure** central school; **~ professionnelle** training school; **~ secondaire** secondary school; **~ supérieure** college, academy; *faire* **~** attract followers; *faire l'~* (**à**) teach; **~ier, -ère** [ekɔˈlje, ⁓ˈljɛːr] *su.* pupil; *su./m* schoolboy; *su./f* schoolgirl.

écolo|gie [ekɔlɔˈʒi] *f* ecology; **~gique** [⁓ˈʒik] ecological; **~gisme** [⁓ˈʒism] *m* ecology movement.

éconduire [ekɔ̃ˈdɥiːr] (4h) show out; get rid of; reject (*a suitor*).

économ|e [ekɔˈnɔm] **1.** *adj.* economical, thrifty; sparing; **2.** *su.* treasurer; **~ie** [ekɔnɔˈmi] *f* economy; economics *sg.*; saving; thrift; management; **~s** *pl.* savings; **~ dirigée** controlled economy; **~ domestique** domestic economy; housekeeping; **~ politique** political economy; economics *sg*; *faire des* **~s** save (up); **~ique** [⁓ˈmik] **1.** *adj.* economic (*doctrine, system*); economical, cheap, **2.** *su./f* economics *sg.*; **~iser** [⁓miˈze] (1a) save (on, **sur**); **~iste** [⁓ˈmist] *m* (political) economist.

écoper [ekɔˈpe] (1a) *v/t.* ⚓ bail out; F *vt/i.*: **~** (**de**) get; *v/i.* get it, take the rap.

écorc|e [eˈkɔrs] *f* bark; peel; crust; **~er** [ekɔrˈse] (1k) bark; peel.

écorch|er [ekɔrˈʃe] (1a) skin; chafe (*the skin*), scrape, murder (*a language*), grate on (*the ear*); burn (*one's throat*); fleece (*a client*); **~ure** ✶ [⁓ˈʃyːr] *f* abrasion, F scratch.

écorn|er [ekɔrˈne] (1a) chip the corner(s) off (*s.th.*); dog-ear (*a book*); *fig.* make a hole in (*one's fortune*); **~ifler** F [⁓niˈfle] (1a) sponge, *Am.* bum.

écossais [ekɔˈsɛ] **1.** *adj.* Scottish; **2.** *su./m ling.* Scots; *su.* ♀ Scot; *les* **2** *m/pl.* the Scots.

écossor [ekɔˈse] (1a) shell, hull.

écot [eˈko] *m* share of the bill); *payer chacun son* **~** go Dutch.

écoul|ement [ekulˈmɑ̃] *m* (out)flow; ⚙ waste-pipe; *crowd:* dispersal; ✝ sale; **~or** [ekuˈle] (1a) ✝ sell off; *s'~* flow out; pass (*time*).

écourter [ekurˈte] (1a) shorten, F cut short; clip; *fig.* curtail.

écoute [eˈkut] *f* listening(-in); *être aux* **~s** listen (in); *fig.* keep one's ears open (for, **de**); *heures f/pl. de grande* **~** *radio* (*TV*): peak listening (viewing) hours; *mettre q. sur* **~(s)** tap s.o.'s telephone.

écout|er [ekuˈte] (1a) *v/t.* listen to; pay attention to; *v/i.* listen (in); **~eur, -euse** [⁓ˈtœːr, ⁓ˈtøːz] *su.* person, *a. radio:* listener; *su./m teleph.* receiver; *radio:* ear-phone.

écoutille ⚓ [ekuˈtiːj] *f* hatchway.

écran [eˈkrɑ̃] *m* screen; *phot.* filter; *faire* **~ à** screen; *fig.* be *or* get in the way of; *le petit* **~** television; *porter à l'~* film (*a play*).

écraser [ekrɑ'ze] (1a) crush; *mot.* run over; F glut (*the market*); *fig.* overwhelm; *fig.* ruin; *mot.* F ~ **le champignon** step on the gas; *mot.* ~ **le frein** slam on the brakes; ✔, *mot.* **s'~** crash (into, *contre*); *sl.* keep one's mouth shut.

écrémer [ekre'me] (1f) cream, skim (*milk, a. fig.*); ◎ dross.

écrevisse *zo.* [ekrə'vis] *f* crayfish.

écrier [ekri'e] (1a): **s'~** cry (out).

écrin [e'krɛ̃] *m* (jewel-)case.

écri|re [e'kri:r] (4q) write (down); spell (*a word*); **~vis** [ekri'vi] *1st p. sg. p.s. of* **écrire;** **~vons** [~'vɔ̃] *1st p. pl. pres of* **écrire;** **~t** [e'kri] **1.** *p.p. of* **écrire; 2.** *su./m* writing; document; *univ. etc.* written examination; *par* ~ in writing; **~teau** [ekri'to] *m* placard; notice; **~toire** [~'twa:r] *m* inkstand; writing-desk; **~ture** [~'ty:r] *f* (hand)writing; script; ✝ entry; ♀ **sainte** Holy Scripture; ✝ **~s** accounts, books; **~vailler** [~va'je] (1a) scribble; be a hack-writer; **~vain** [~'vɛ̃] *m* writer; **femme** *f* ~ woman writer; **~vasser** F [~va'sje] *m* hack-writer.

écrou¹ ◎ [e'kru] *m* (screw-)nut.

écrou² [e'kru] *m* committal to jail; **levée** *f* **d'~** release from prison.

écrouer [ekru'e] (1a) imprison.

écroul|ement [ekrul'mɑ̃] *m* collapse; crumbling; fall (*a. fig.*); *fig.* ruin; **~er** [ekru'le] (1a): **s'~** collapse (*a. fig.*); fall (down); crumble; break up; give way; come to nothing.

écu [e'ky] *m* shield; **~s** *pl.* money.

écueil [e'kœ:j] *m* reef; *fig.* danger.

écuelle [e'kɥɛl] *f* bowl, basin; pan.

éculé [eky'le] (1a) down-at-heel (*shoe*); *fig.* hackneyed.

écum|e [e'kym] *f* froth; foam; lather; scum; ~ **de mer** meerschaum; **~er** [eky'me] (1a) *v/t.* skim; *v/i.* foam, froth (*a. fig.*); **~eux** [~'mø] foamy, frothy; scummy.

écur|age [eky'ra:ʒ] *m* cleansing; cleaning (out); **~er** [~'re] (1a) scour; clean (out); pick (*one's teeth*).

écureuil *zo.* [eky'rœ:j] *m* sqirrel.

écurie [eky'ri] *f* stable; *fig.* team.

écusson [eky'sɔ̃] *m* ⊘ shield; ◎ keyplate; ✗ badge; ♣ shield-bud.

écuyer, -ère [ekɥi'je, ~'jɛ:r] *su.* rider; *su./m* riding-master; **bottes** *f/pl.* **à l'~ère** riding boots.

édent|é [edɑ̃'te] toothless; *zo.* edentate; **~er** [~] (1a) break the teeth of; **s'~** lose one's teeth.

édicter [edik'te] (1a) enact (*a law*).

édifi|cation [edifika'sjɔ̃] *f* construction; (moral) edification; **~ce** [edi'fis] *m* building; **~er** [~'fje] (1o) build; edify (morally); *fig.* F enlighten.

édit [e'di] *m* edict.

édit|er [edi'te] (1a) edit; publish (*a book etc.*); **~eur** [~'tœ:r] *m* text: editor; *book etc.*: publisher; **~ion** [~'sjɔ̃] *f* edition; publishing (trade); **~orial** [~tɔ'rjal] *adj.*, *su./m* editorial.

édredon [edrə'dɔ̃] *m* eiderdown.

éduca|ble [edy'kabl] educable; trainable (*animal*); **~tif** [~ka'tif] educational; educative; **~tion** [~ka'sjɔ̃] *f* education; upbringing; rearing; training (*a. animals*).

édulcorer [edylkɔ're] (1a) sweeten.

éduquer [edy'ke] (1m) educate; bring up (*a child*); train (*an animal, a faculty*); **mal éduqué** ill-bred.

effac|é [efa'se] faded; inconspicuous; retiring (*person, manners*), retired (*life*); receding (*chin*); **~er** [~] (1k) efface, blot out; erase (*a. a tape*); *fig.* outshine; **s'~** wear away; fade away; stand aside; keep in the background.

effar|ement [efar'mɑ̃] *m* alarm; dismay; **~er** [efa're] (1a) frighten; **s'~** be scared (at, by *de*).

effaroucher [efaru'ʃe] (1a) startle; scare away; alarm; shock.

effect|if [efɛk'tif] **1.** *adj.* effective; ✝ real; **2.** *su./m* manpower; ✗ total strength; ♣ complement; ◎ stock; **~uer** [~'tɥe] (1n) effect, carry out, execute; accomplish.

efféminer [efemi'ne] (1a) effeminate.

effervescen|ce [efɛrvɛ'sɑ̃:s] *f* effervescence; *fig.* exitement; **~t** [~'sɑ̃] effervescent; *fig.* in a turmoil.

effet [e'fɛ] *m* effect, result; impression; ✝ bill; **~s** *pl.* things, clothes; ~ **secondaire** side effect; **à cet** ~ for this purpose; **en** ~ indeed; **mettre à l'**~ put (*s.th.*) into operation; **prendre** ~ become operative; **produire son** ~ operate, act.

effeuiller [efœ'je] (1a) strip of petals or leaves; **s'~** shed its petals or leaves.

efficac|e [efi'kas] effective; efficient; **~ité** [~kasi'te] *f* efficacy; efficiency.

effigie [efiˈʒi] f effigy.

effil|é [efiˈle] slender; pointed; **~er** [~ˈle] (1a) unravel; taper; **~ocher** [~lɔˈʃe] (1a) ravel out; fray.

efflanqué [eflɑ̃ˈke] lean, F skinny.

effleurer [efloeˈre] (1a) graze, touch lightly (*a. on a subject*); brush.

efflorescence [eflɔrɛˈsɑ̃ːs] f 🌹 flowering; 🌹 efflorescence; 🌹 rash.

effluent [eflyˈɑ̃] adj., su./m effluent; **effluve** [eˈflyːv] m effluvium; exhalation; fig. breath.

effondr|ement [efɔ̃drəˈmɑ̃] m collapse; breakdown; 🌹 slump; **~er** [~ˈdre] (1a): **s'~** collapse; cave in; break down.

efforcer [efɔrˈse] (1k): **s'~ de** (inf.) do one's best to (inf.), try hard to (inf.).

effort [eˈfɔːr] m effort.

effraction 🌹 [efrakˈsjɔ̃] f breaking open; **vol** m **avec ~** house-breaking (by day), burglary (by night).

effrayer [efrɛˈje] (1i) scare, terrify; **s'~** be frightened (at, **de**).

effréné [efreˈne] unbridled.

effriter [efriˈte] (1a) crumble; cause to crumble; **s'~** crumble.

effroi [eˈfrwa] m terror, fear, fright.

effront|é [efrɔ̃ˈte] impudent; **~erie** [~ˈtri] f effrontery, impudence.

effroyable [efrwaˈjabl] frightful.

effusion [efyˈzjɔ̃] f effusion (*a. fig.*); out-pouring; **~ de sang** bloodshed.

égailler [egaˈje] (1a) scatter.

égal [eˈɡal] **1.** adj. equal, level, smooth, even (*a. fig.*), regular; steady (*pace*); **cela m'est ~** I don't care, it's all the same to me; I don't mind; **c'est ~** all the same; **2.** su. equal; su./m: **à l'~ de** (just) like, as much as; **d'~ à ~** as equals; **sans ~** unequalled; matchless; **~ement** equally; as well, also, too; **~er** [eɡaˈle] (1a) equal, fig. compare with, **~iser** [eɡaliˈze] (1a) equalize (*a. sp.*); level; make even; 🌹 equate; **~itaire** [~ˈtɛːr] egalitarian; **~ité** [~ˈte] f equality; evenness; sp. **à ~** equal on points.

égard [eˈɡaːr] m regard, consideration; **~s** pl. respect sg.; attentions (to, **pour**); **à cet ~** in this respect; **à l'~ de** with respect to; as regards; **à mon ~** concerning me; **à tous ~s** in every respect; **manque** m **d'~** lack of consideration; **par ~ pour** out of respect for; **sans ~ pour** without regard for.

égar|ement [eɡarˈmɑ̃] m (mental) aberration; distraction; **~er** [eɡaˈre] (1a) mislay; fig. lead astray, mislead; **avoir l'air égaré** look distraught; **s'~** lose one's way, get lost; go astray (*a. fig.*); fig. wander (from the point).

égayer [eɡɛˈje] (1i) cheer up; enliven; **s'~** make merry (about, **de**).

églant|ier 🌹 [eɡlɑ̃ˈtje] m wild rose-bush; **~ine** 🌹 [~ˈtin] f wild rose.

église [eˈɡliːz] f church.

égoïs|me [eɡɔˈism] m egoism; **~te** [~ˈist] **1.** su. egoist; **2.** adj. selfish, egoistic.

égorg|er [eɡɔrˈʒe] (1l) cut the throat of; slaughter; fig. fleece; **~eur** [~ˈʒœːr] m cut-throat.

égosiller [eɡoziˈje] (1a): **s'~** shout o.s. hoarse.

égout [eˈɡu] m sewer; **~ter** [eɡuˈte] (1a) drain; **s'~** drain; drip; **~toir** [~ˈtwaːr] m drainer.

égratign|er [eɡratiˈɲe] (1a) scratch (*a.* 🌹); fig. gibe at; **~ure** [~ˈnyːr] f scratch; fig. gibe.

égrener [eɡrəˈne] (1d) pick off (*grapes*); shell (*peas*); fig. mark out or deal with one by one; **~ son chapelet** say the rosary; **s'~** drop (away), scatter.

égrillard [eɡriˈjaːr] lewd, F dirty.

eh! [e] int. hey!; hi!; **~ bien!** well!

éhonté [eɔ̃ˈte] shameless.

éjaculer [eʒakyˈle] (1a) ejaculate.

éjection [eʒɛkˈsjɔ̃] f ejection.

élaborer [elabɔˈre] (1a) elaborate.

élaguer [elaˈɡe] (1m) prune (*a. fig.*).

élan[1] [eˈlɑ̃] m spring, dash, bound; impetus; fig. impulse; fig. outburst.

élan[2] zo. [~] m elk, moose.

élanc|é [elɑ̃ˈse] slim, slender; **~ement** [elɑ̃sˈmɑ̃] m fig. yearning (towards, **vers**); 🌹 twinge; **~er** [elɑ̃ˈse] (1k) v/i. twinge, throb, v/t.: **s'~** rush, hurl or fling o.s.

élargi|r [elarˈʒiːr] (2a) widen; broaden; cost. let out (*a garment*); 🌹 release; **s'~** widen; broaden; cost. stretch (*garment*); **~ssement** [~ʒisˈmɑ̃] m widening; broadening; 🌹 release.

élasti|cité [elastisiˈte] f elasticity; springiness; **~que** [~ˈtik] **1.** adj. elastic; flexible; **2.** su./m rubber (band).

élect|eur [elɛkˈtœːr] m pol. voter; elector (*a. hist.*); **~ion** [~ˈsjɔ̃] f election (*a. fig.*); fig. choice; **~s** pl. **partielles** by-election *sg.*; **~oral** [~tɔ'ral] electoral, election...; **~orat** [~tɔ'ra] *m coll., hist.* electorate.

électri|cien [elɛktri'sjɛ̃] *m* electrician; **~cité** [~si'te] *f* electricity; **~fier** [~'fje] (1o) electrify; **~que** [elɛk'trik] electric(al); **~ser** [~tri'ze] (1a) electrify; *fig.* thrill; *fil m* **électrisé** live wire.

électro... [elɛktro] electro...; **~aimant** [~ɛ'mɑ̃] *m* electro-magnet; **~cardio-gramme** ⚕ [~kardjɔ'gram] *m* electro-cardiogram; **~choc** ⚕ [~'ʃɔk] *m* electric shock; **~magnétique** [~maɲe'tik] electromagnetic; **~ménager** [~mena'ʒe]: *appareils m/pl.* **~s** domestic electrical equipment *sg.*

électron *phys.* [elɛk'trɔ̃] *m* electron; **~icien** [~trɔni'sjɛ̃] *m* electronics engineer; **~ique** [~trɔ'nik] **1.** *adj.* electronic; **2.** *su./f* electronics *sg.*

électrophone [elɛktro'fɔn] *m* record player.

éléga|mment [elega'mɑ̃] *adv.* elegantly; **~nce** [~'gɑ̃:s] *f* elegance; **~nt** [~'gɑ̃] elegant; smart.

élément [ele'mɑ̃] *m* element; ingredient; ⚡ cell; **~s** *pl. a.* rudiments; **~aire** [~mɑ̃'tɛːr] elementary.

éléphant *zo.* [ele'fɑ̃] *m* elephant.

élevage [el'vaːʒ] *m* rearing; ranch.

élévation [eleva'sjɔ̃] *f* elevation; lifting; rise; height; altitude.

élève [e'lɛːv] *su.* pupil; student.

élev|é [el've] high; *fig.* lofty; **~er** [~'ve] (1d) raise; put up, erect, set up; breed (*cattle etc.*); keep (*bees, hens*); bring up (*a child*); *fig.* elevate (*the spirit etc.*); ⚡ **~ au carré** (*au cube*) square (cube); *s'~* rise; go up; *fig.* arise (*difficulties etc.*); *s'~ à* amount to; *fig.* *s'~ contre* rise up *or* protest against; **~eur** [~'vœːr] *m* breeder (*of cattle*).

éligible [eli'ʒibl] eligible.

élimer [eli'me] (1a) wear out.

éliminer [elimi'ne] (1a) eliminate (*a.* ⚡); get rid of; ⚡ *s'~* cancel out.

élire [e'liːr] (4t) elect, choose.

élit|aire [eli'tɛːr] elitist; **~e** [e'lit] *f* elite.

elle [el] *pron./pers./f subject:* she, it; **~s** *pl.* they; *object:* her, it; (to) her, (to) it; **~s** *pl.* them; (to) her, (to) it; hers, its; *à* **~s** *pl.* to them; theirs; *c'est* it is she, it's her; *ce sont* **~s** *pl.*, F *c'est* **~s** *pl.* it is they, it's them.

elle-même [ɛl'mɛːm] *pron./rfl.* herself; *elles-mêmes pl.* themselves.

ellip|se [e'lips] *f gramm.* ellipsis; ⚡ ellipse; **~tique** [elip'tik] elliptic(al).

élocution [elɔky'sjɔ̃] *f* elocution.

éloge [e'lɔːʒ] *m* praise; eulogy.

éloign|é [elwa'ɲe] remote; far; far-off, faraway; **~ement** [elwaɲ'mɑ̃] *m* distance; remoteness; removal; *fig.* estrangement; **~er** [elwa'ɲe] (1a) remove; move (*s.th.*) away; dismiss (*a thought*); avert (*a danger*); estrange (*s.o.*); *s'~* go *or* move away; *s'~ du sujet* wander from the subject.

éloquence [elɔ'kɑ̃ːs] *f* eloquence; **éloquent** [~'kɑ̃] eloquent.

élucider [elysi'de] (1a) elucidate.

élucubrations [elykybra'sjɔ̃] *f/pl. pej.* wild imaginings.

éluder [ely'de] (1a) evade; shirk.

Élysée [eli'ze] *m myth.* Elysium; *pol.* Élysée (*= Paris residence of the President of the French Republic*).

émacier [ema'sje] (1o): *s'~* waste away, become emaciated.

émail, *pl.* **-aux** [e'maːj, ~'mo] *m* enamel; *phot.* glaze; **~ler** [ema'je] (1a) enamel; glaze (*porcelain, phot.*); *fig.* spangle (with, *de*).

émanation [emana'sjɔ̃] *f* emanation.

émancip|ation [emɑ̃sipa'sjɔ̃] *f* emancipation; **~er** [~'pe] (1a) emancipate; liberate.

émaner [ema'ne] (1a) emanate, issue, originate.

emball|age [ɑ̃ba'laːʒ] *m* packing; package; *sp.* spurt; **~er** [~'le] (1a) *v/t.* pack (up); *mot.* race (*the engine*); F thrill, excite; F blow (*s.o.*) up; *sl.* arrest; *s'~* bolt (*horse*); race (*engine*); F get worked up (*person*); **~eur** *m*, **-euse** *f* [~'lœːr, ~'løːz] packer.

embarbouiller F [ɑ̃barbu'je] (1a) dirty; *fig.* muddle (*s.o.*).

embarca|dère [ɑ̃barka'dɛːr] *m* ⚓ landing-stage; wharf; 🚋 platform; **~tion** [~'sjɔ̃] *f* craft; boat.

embardée [ɑ̃bar'de] *f* swerve.

embargo [ɑ̃bar'go] *m* embargo.

embarqu|ement [ɑ̃barkə'mɑ̃] *m* embarkation; shipment; **~er** [~'ke] (1m) *v/t.* embark; ship; *v/i.* embark (*a. fig.* upon, *dans*).

embarras [ɑ̃ba'ra] *m* hindrance, obstacle; impediment; trouble; embarrassment; **~** *pl.* **d'argent** money difficulties; F **faire des ~** make a fuss; **~ser** [~ra'se] (1a) clutter (up); hinder; bother; put in an awkward position; puzzle; **s'~ de** burden o.s. with.

embauch|age [ãbo'ʃaːʒ] *m*, **~e** [ã'boːʃ] *f* hiring; **pas d'embauche** no vacancies; **~er** [ãbo'ʃe] (1a) hire.

embaumer [ãbo'me] (1a) *v/t.* embalm (*a corpse, the garden*); perfume; smell of; *v/i.* smell sweet.

embell|ie [ãbɛ'li] *f* fair period; **~ir** [~'liːr] (2a) *v/t.* make (look) more attractive; embellish; *v/i.* improve in looks; **~issement** [~lis'mã] *m* embellishment.

emberlificoter F [ãbɛrlifiko'te] (1a) get (s.o.) round; **s'~** get tangled.

embêt|ement [ãbɛt'mã] *m* nuisance, trouble, annoyance; F bother; **~er** F [ãbɛ'te] (1a) annoy; bore.

emblée [ã'ble] *adv.*: **d'~** right away.

emblème [ã'blɛːm] *m* emblem.

embob(el)iner F [ãbɔb(l)i'ne] (1a) get round, coax.

emboîter [ãbwa'te] (1a) fit together, joint; fit, put (into, **dans**); enclose, encase; *fig.* **~ le pas à q.** dog s.o.'s footsteps; **s'~** fit together.

embolie 🎾 [ãbɔ'li] *f* embolism.

embonpoint [ãbɔ̃'pwɛ̃] *m* stoutness.

embouché [ãbu'ʃe]: **mal ~** foul-mouthed; **~ure** [~'ʃyːr] *f* river: mouth; ♪ mouthpiece.

embourber [ãbur'be] (1a): **s'~** get stuck (in the mud).

embourgeoiser [ãburʒwa'ze] (1a): **s'~** become conventional.

embouteill|age [ãbutɛ'jaːʒ] *m* bottling; *fig.* traffic jam, holdup; ✆ bottleneck; **~er** [~'je] (1a) bottle; block up; jam (*the traffic*).

emboutir [ãbu'tiːr] (2a) press (*metal*); emboss; tip; *mot.* crash into.

embranch|ement [ãbrãʃ'mã] *m* branching (off); junction; *fig.* branch; **~er** [ãbrã'ʃe] (1a) join up; **s'~** connect up (with, **sur**).

embras|ement [ãbraz'mã] *m* conflagration; *fig.* burning passion; **~er** [ãbra'ze] (1a) set on fire; *fig.* fire; *fig.* set aglow.

embrass|ade [ãbra'sad] *f* hug; kissing;

~er [~'se] (1a) kiss; *fig.* embrace; *fig.* take up (*a career*).

embrasure [ãbra'zyːr] *f* embrasure; window-recess; doorway.

embray|age [ãbrɛ'jaːʒ] *m* ⚙ connecting; putting into gear; *mot.* clutch; *mot.* **~ à disques** disc clutch; **~er** [~'je] (1i) *v/t.* ⚙ couple; throw into gear; F *fig.* start; *v/i. mot.* let in the clutch; F *fig.* start.

embrocher [ãbrɔ'ʃe] (1a) *cuis.* put on the spit; F run (*s.o.*) through.

embrouiller [ãbru'je] (1a) tangle; muddle (up); confuse; **s'~** get tangled up.

embroussaillé [ãbrusɑ'je] bushy; *fig.* tousled; F complicated.

embrumer [ãbry'me] (1a) shroud with mist or fog; *fig.* cloud.

embruns [ã'brœ̃] *m/pl.* sea spray *sg.*

embrunir [ãbry'niːr] (2a) darken.

embryon [ãbri'jɔ̃] *m* embryo.

embûche [ã'byːʃ] *f* trap, pitfall.

embuer [ã'bɥe] (1n) dim (*a. fig.*).

embus|cade [ãbys'kad] *f* ambush; **se tenir** (or **être**) **en ~** lie in ambush; **~quer** [~'ke] (1m) place in ambush; **s'~** lie in wait; take cover; F shirk.

éméché F [eme'ʃe] slightly the worse for drink or F for wear.

émeraude [em'roːd] *su./f, adj./inv.* emerald.

émerger [emɛr'ʒe] (1l) emerge.

émeri [em'ri] *m* emery(-powder).

émérite [eme'rit] emeritus (*professor*); experienced, practised.

émersion [emɛr'sjɔ̃] *f* emergence.

émerveiller [emɛrvɛ'je] (1a) amaze; **s'~** marvel (at, **de**).

émett|eur [emɛ'tœːr] **1.** *adj.* issuing; *radio:* transmitting; **2.** *su./m* ✆ issuer; *radio:* transmitter; **~-récepteur** *radio:* F walkie-talkie; **~re** [e'mɛtr] (4v) emit, send out; ✆ issue; utter (*a sound*); express (*an opinion*); *radio:* broadcast, put forward (*a claim*).

émeute [e'møːt] *f* riot, disturbance.

émietter [emjɛ'te] (1a) crumble; *fig.* waste, fritter away.

émigr|ation [emigra'sjɔ̃] *f* emigration; **~é** [~'gre] expatriate; **~er** [~'gre] (1a) emigrate.

émin|emment [emina'mã] *adv.* to a high degree; **~ence** [~'nãːs] *f* eminence (*a. fig.*, *title*); **~ent** [~'nɑ̃] eminent; high, elevated.

émiss|aire [emi'sɛːr] **1.** *su./m* messenger; ☻ outlet; **2.** *adj.*: **bouc** *m* **~** scapegoat; **~ion** [~'sjɔ̃] *f* emission; ✝ issue; uttering (*of sound, of counterfeit coins*); *heat*: radiation; *radio*, *TV*: program(me), broadcast(ing).

emmagasiner [ɑ̃magazi'ne] (1a) ✝ warehouse, store; *fig.* store up.

emmailloter [ɑ̃majo'te] (1a) swaddle (*a baby*); swathe (*one's leg*).

emmancher [ɑ̃mɑ̃'ʃe] (1a) put a handle on (*s.th.*); *fig.* get (*s.th.*) going, start.

emmêler [ɑ̃mɛ'le] (1a) tangle; *fig.* mix up, get in a tangle.

emménager [ɑ̃mena'ʒe] (1l) *v/i.* move in; *v/t.* move (*s.o., s.th.*) in.

emmener [ɑ̃m'ne] (1d) take (*s.o.*) away, lead (*s.o.*) away *or* out.

emmerd|ant V [ɑ̃mɛr'dɑ̃] boring; annoying; **~er** [~'de] (1a) bore (*s.o.*) (stiff); bug, give (*s.o.*) a pain in the neck; **s'~** be bored.

emmitoufler [ɑ̃mitu'fle] (1a) muffle up (in *dans, de*).

émoi [e'mwa] *m* turmoil; anxiety.

émoluments [emoly'mɑ̃] *m/pl.* emoluments, pay *sg.*, salary *sg.*

émonder [emɔ̃'de] (1a) ✎ prune (*a. fig. a book*), trim; *fig.* clean.

émotion [emo'sjɔ̃] *f* emotion; *fig.* agitation; **~nable** [~sjo'nabl] emotional; excitable; **~ner** F [~sjo'ne] (1a) affect; thrill.

émotivité [emotivi'te] *f* emotivity.

émou|dre ☻ [e'mudr] (4w) sharpen; **~lu** [emu'ly] sharp; *fig.* **frais ~ de** fresh from (*school etc.*).

émousser [emu'se] (1a) ☻ blunt (*a. fig.*); *fig. a.* dull, take the edge off.

émoustiller F [emusti'je] (1a) cheer up, exhilarate, F ginger up.

émouv|ant [emu'vɑ̃] moving, touching; **~oir** [~'vwaːr] (3f) move; affect, touch; stir up, rouse.

empailler [ɑ̃pa'je] (1a) stuff.

empan [ɑ̃'pɑ̃] *m* span.

empaqueter [ɑ̃pak'te] (1c) pack up.

emparer [ɑ̃pa're] (1a): **s' ~ de** seize, lay hands on; take possession of.

empât|é [ɑ̃pɑ'te] coated (*tongue*); thick (*voice*); bloated (*face*); **~er** [~] (1a) make thick; bloat (up); **s'~** put on flesh.

empêch|ement [ɑ̃pɛʃ'mɑ̃] *m* obstacle, hindrance, hitch; **~er** [ɑ̃pɛ'ʃe] (1a) prevent (from *ger.*, *de inf.*); stop; hinder; **s'~ de** stop o.s. (from (*doing*); **on ne peut s'~ de** *a.* one cannot help (*doing*).

empennage ✈ [ɑ̃pe'naːʒ] *m* tail unit; stabilizer(s *pl.*).

empereur [ɑ̃'prœːr] *m* emperor.

empes|é F [ɑ̃pə'ze] stiff (*manner*); **~er** [~] (1a) starch; stiffen.

empester [ɑ̃pɛs'te] (1a) stink out (*a room*); stink (of).

empêtrer [ɑ̃pɛ'tre] (1a) hobble (*an animal*); entangle; *fig.* involve (in, *dans*); *fig.* embarrass (*s.o.*).

empha|se [ɑ̃'faːz] *f* bombast, pomposity; emphasis; **~tique** [ɑ̃fa'tik] bombastic; grandiloquent.

empiéter [ɑ̃pje'te] (1f) *v/i.*: **~ sur** encroach upon.

empiffrer F [ɑ̃pi'fre] (1a): **s'~** stuff o.s. (with, *de*).

empiler [ɑ̃pi'le] (1a) pile (up); crowd (*people*); F cheat (out of, *de*).

empire [ɑ̃'piːr] *m* empire; influence; **~ sur soi-même** self-control.

empirer [ɑ̃pi're] (1a) worsen.

empiri|que [ɑ̃pi'rik] empirical, rule-of-thumb; **~sme** [~'rism] *m* empiricism; *fig.* guess-work.

emplacement [ɑ̃plas'mɑ̃] *m buildings etc.*: site; place, spot; ⚓ berth.

emplâtre [ɑ̃'plaːtr] *m* ✚ plaster; patch; F lout, clot.

emplette [ɑ̃'plɛt] *f* shopping.

empl|oi [ɑ̃'plwa] *m* employment; use; post, job, situation; **~** *du temps* schedule, time-table; **mode** *m* **d'~** directions *pl.* for use; **plein ~** full employment; **sans ~** unemployed, jobless; **~oyé** *m*, **e** *f* [ɑ̃plwa'je] employee; **~oyer** [~'je] (1h) employ; use; spend (*time*); **s'~ à** apply *or* devote o.s. to ([*doing*] *s.th.*); **~oyeur** *m*, **-euse** *f* [~'jœːr, ~'jøːz] employer.

empocher [ɑ̃pɔ'ʃe] (1a) pocket (*a. fig.*); *fig.* receive, F get.

empoigner [ɑ̃pwa'ɲe] (1a) grip (*a. fig.*); grasp, seize; catch, arrest.

empois [ɑ̃'pwa] *m* starch.

empoisonn|er [ɑ̃pwazɔ'ne] (1a) poison; *fig.* corrupt; *fig.* bore (*s.o.*) to death; reek of; infect; **~eur** [~'nœːr] **1.** *su.* poisoner; **2.** *adj.* poisonous.

emport|é [ãpɔr'te] hot-headed *or* quick-tempered; angry; **~ement** [~tə'mã] *m* (fit of) anger; **avec ~** angrily; **~e-pièce** [~tə'pjɛs] *m/inv.* punch; *fig.* **à l'~** sarcastic; **~er** [~'te] (1a) carry away, take away; remove; ✗ carry; **plats** *m/pl.* **à ~** take-away meals, *Am.* meals to go; **l'~** win, get the upper hand (of, *sur*); prevail (over, *sur*); **s'~** lose one's temper, flare up; bolt (*horse*).

empoté [ãpɔ'te] clumsy (person).

empourprer [ãpur'pre] (1a) crimson; purple; **s'~** flush (*person*).

emprein|dre [ã'prɛːdr] (4m) imprint, stamp, impress; **~te** [ã'prɛːt] *f* impress, stamp, impression.

empress|é [ãprɛ'se] eager; willing; fussy; **~ement** [ãprɛs'mã] *m* eagerness, promptness; hurry; **avec ~** readily; **~er** [ãprɛ'se] (1a) **s'~** bustle about; fuss about; **s'~ de** (*inf.*) hasten to (*inf.*).

emprise [ã'priːz] *f* hold (on, *sur*); mastery; 𝕥𝕥𝕤 expropriation.

emprisonner [ãprizɔ'ne] (1a) imprison; confine (*s.o. to his room*).

emprunt [ã'prœ̃] *m* loan; borrowing; *gramm.* loanword; **nom** *m* **d'~** assumed name; ✝ **souscrire à un ~** subscribe to a loan; **~é** [ãprœ̃'te] sham; derived; awkward; **~er** [~'te] (1a) borrow (from, *of* à); assume (*a name*); take (*a road*); **~eur** *m*, **-euse** *f* [~'tœːr, ~'tøːz] borrower.

empuantir [ãpɥã'tiːr] (2a) make (*s.th.*) stink; infect (*the air*).

ému [e'my] *p.p. of* **émouvoir**.

émul|ateur [emyla'tœːr] rival; **~ation** [~'sjõ] *f* emulation; **~e** [e'myl] *su.* imitator; equal.

en[1] [ã] *prp.* place: in (*France*); at; *direction*: into (*town*); to (*France, town*); *time*: in (*summer*); (with)in (*an hour*); *state*: in (*mourning, English*); on (*leave, strike, sale*); at (*war*); as, like (*a friend*); *change*: into (*decay, English*); to (*dust, pieces*); *material*: of; get: **~ dansant** (*while*) dancing; **~ attendant** in the meantime; **~ tête** at the head (of, *de*); **~ voiture** by car; **~ avion** by air; **~ avant** in front; *direction*: forward, on; **~ (l'an) 1789** in 1789; **~ colère** angry; **~ fait** in fact; **~ vie** alive, living; **changer des livres ~ francs** change pounds into francs; **... ~ bois** wooden ...; **fertile**

(*riche*) **~** fertile (rich) in; **de mal ~ pis** from bad to worse; **de moins ~ moins** less and less; **de plus ~ plus** more and more.

en[2] [ã] **1.** *adv.* from there; on that account, for it; **j'~ viens** I have just come from there; **2.** *pron. genitive*: of *or* about *or* by *or* from *or* with him (her, it, them); *quantity*: of it *or* them; *partitive use*: some, any, negative: not any, none; *sometimes untranslated*: **qu'~ pensez-vous?** what is your opinion?; **qu'~ dira-t-on?** what will people say (about it)?; **il ~ mourut** he died of it; **j'~ ai cinq** I have five (of them); **je vous ~ offre la moitié** I offer you (a) half of it; **j'~ ai besoin** I need it *or* some; **je n'~ ai pas** I haven't any; **prenez-~** take some; **c'~ est fait de moi** I am done for; **s'~ aller** go away.

enamourer [ãnamu're] (1a): **s'~** fall in love with (**de**).

encadr|ement [ãkadrə'mã] *m* framing; frame(work); setting; **~er** [~'dre] (1a) frame; enclose.

encaiss|e [ã'kɛs] *f* ✝ cash (in hand); *box.* punishment; **~é** *fig.* [ãkɛ'se] deep (*valley*), sunken (*road*); **~er** [~'se] (1b) ✝ encase; 🎵 plant in tubs; collect (*money*); cash (*a bill*); embank (*a river*); *fig.* swallow (*an insult*); *fig.* stand, bear.

encan [ã'kã] *m* (public) auction.

en-cas *cuis.* [ã'ka] *m/inv.* snack.

encastrer ⊙ [ãkas'tre] (1a): **~ dans** fit *or* sink *or* embed into; **s'~ dans** fit into.

encaustiqu|e [ãkos'tik] *f* encaustic; wax polish; **~er** [~'tị'ke] (1m) wax.

enceindre [ã'sɛːdr] (4m) surround.

enceinte[1] [ã'sɛːt] *f* enclosure; *box.* ring; surrounding wall(*s pl.*).

enceinte[2] [ã'sɛːt] *adj./f* pregnant.

encens [ã'sã] *m* incense; *fig.* flattery; **~er** [ãsã'se] (1a) *eccl.* cense; burn incense to; *fig.* flatter.

encercler [ãsɛr'kle] (1a) encircle.

enchaîn|ement [ãʃɛn'mã] *m* chaining (up); *fig.* sequence, chain; **~er** [ãʃɛ'ne] (1b) *v/t.* chain (up); *fig.* link up (*a. ideas*); *v/i.* go on, continue.

enchant|é [ãʃã'te] enchanted; delightful (*place*); *fig.* delighted (at, with **de**); **~ de vous voir** pleased to meet you; **~ement** [ãʃãt'mã] *m* spell; *fig.* charm; *fig.* delight; **~er** [ãʃã'te] (1a) bewitch; delight;

enchanteur, -eresse ['tœːr, ~trɛs] **1.** *su. fig.* charmer; **2.** *adj.* enchanting; delightful.

enchâss|er [ɑ̃ʃɑ'se] (1a) set (*jewels etc.*); insert; **~ure** [~'syːr] *f* setting.

enchère [ɑ̃'ʃɛːr] *f* bid(ding); **dernière ~** highest bid; **mettre** (*or* **vendre**) **aux ~s** put up for auction.

enchéri|r [ɑ̃ʃe'riːr] (2a) *v/t.* bid for; raise the price of; *v/i.* go up (*in price*); **~ sur** outbid (*s.o.*); *fig.* outdo, go beyond; **~ssement** † [~ris'mɑ̃] *m* rise; **~sseur** [~ri'sœːr] *m* bidder.

enchevêtrer [ɑ̃ʃve'tre] (1a) halter (*a horse*); *fig.* entangle; △ join.

enclav|e *pol.* [ɑ̃'klaːv] *f* enclave; **~er** [ɑ̃kla've] (1a) enclave (*a territory*); *fig.* hem in, enclose.

enclencher [ɑ̃klɑ̃'ʃe] (1a) ⚙ engage; ⚡ switch on; *fig.* set going.

enclin [ɑ̃'klɛ̃] inclined (to, **à**).

enclo|re [ɑ̃'kloːr] (4f) enclose; wall in, fence in; **~s** [ɑ̃'klo] *m* enclosure.

enclume [ɑ̃'klym] *f* anvil (*a. anat.*).

encoche [ɑ̃'kɔʃ] *f* notch; slot.

encoffrer [ɑ̃kɔ'fre] (1a) lock up (*a. fig.*); *fig.* hoard (*money*).

encoignure [ɑ̃kɔ'ɲyːr] *f* corner.

encoller [ɑ̃kɔ'le] (1a) glue; size.

encolure [ɑ̃kɔ'lyːr] *f* neck (*a. of horse*); size in collars; neck-line.

encombr|ant [ɑ̃kɔ̃'brɑ̃] cumbersome; bulky; **~e** [ɑ̃'kɔ̃ːbr] *m:* **sans ~** without difficulty; **~ement** [ɑ̃kɔ̃brə'mɑ̃] *m* obstruction; congestion; bulk(iness); **~er** [~'bre] (1a) clutter *or* block (up); **s'~ de** burden o.s. with.

encontre [ɑ̃'kɔ̃ːtr] *prp.:* **à l'~ de** against; **aller à l'~ de** run counter to.

encore [ɑ̃'kɔːr] **1.** *adv.* still; yet; too; more; once again; **~ un** another one; **~ une fois** once more; **non seulement ... mais ~** not only ... but also; **pas ~** not yet; **quoi ~?** what else?; **2.** *cj.:* **~ que** (*sbj. or cond.*) although (*ind.*).

encorner [ɑ̃kɔr'ne] (1a) bull: gore.

encourager [ɑ̃kura'ʒe] (1l) encourage; cheer up.

encourir [ɑ̃ku'riːr] (2i) incur.

encrasser [ɑ̃kra'se] (1a) soil; choke (*a machine*); soot up (*a plug*).

encr|e [ɑ̃ːkr] *f* ink; **~ de Chine** Indian ink; **~er** *typ.* [ɑ̃'kre] (1a) ink; **~ier** [ɑ̃kri'e] *m* ink-well.

encroûter [ɑ̃kru'te] (1a) encrust; rough-cast; *fig.* **s'~** get into a rut.

encyclopédie [ɑ̃siklɔpe'di] *f* encyclop(a)edia.

endetter [ɑ̃de'te] (1a) get into debt.

endeuiller [ɑ̃dœ'je] (1a) plunge into mourning; shroud in gloom.

endiablé [ɑ̃dja'ble] possessed; *fig.* wild; reckless; *fig.* mischievous.

endiguer [ɑ̃di'ge] (1m) dam up (*a river*); dike (*land*); *fig.* stem, check.

endimanché [ɑ̃dimɑ̃'ʃe] in one's Sunday best.

endoctriner [ɑ̃dɔktri'ne] (1a) indoctrinate, instruct; F win over.

endolori [ɑ̃dɔlɔ'ri] sore; tender.

endommager [ɑ̃dɔma'ʒe] (1l) damage; injure.

endormi [ɑ̃dɔr'mi] sleeping (*a. fig.*), asleep; numb (*limb*); dormant (*faculty etc.*); sleepy, drowsy; **~ir** [~'miːr] (2b) send to sleep; numb (*the leg etc.*); deaden (*a pain*); *fig.* bore; lull (*a suspicion*); *fig.* hoodwink (*s.o.*); **s'~** go to sleep (*a. fig.*); **~issement** [~mis'mɑ̃] *m* going to sleep; sleepiness.

endos † [ɑ̃'do] *m*, **~sement** † [ɑ̃dos'mɑ̃] *m* endorsement; **~ser** [~'se] (1a) † endorse; † back; put on (*clothes*); *fig.* assume; **~ qch. à q.** saddle s.o. with s.th.; **~seur** † [~'sœːr] *m* endorser.

endroit [ɑ̃'drwa] *m* place; spot; site; side; *tex.* right side; **à l'~ de** towards, regarding; **par ~s** in places.

endui|re [ɑ̃'dɥiːr] (4h) △ coat (with, **de**) (*a. fig.*); smear (with, **de**); **~t** [ɑ̃'dɥi] *m* tar *etc.*: coat(ing).

enduran|ce [ɑ̃dy'rɑ̃ːs] *f* endurance; *fig.* patience; **~t** [~'rɑ̃] patient.

endurcir [ɑ̃dyr'siːr] (2a) harden (*a. fig.* the heart); *fig.* inure (to, **à**).

endurer [ɑ̃dy're] (1a) endure, bear.

énerg|étique [enɛrʒe'tik] ⚡ energizing; ⚙ of energy; **~ie** [~'ʒi] *f* energy; ⚙ fuel and power; ⚙ **~ consommée** power consumption; **~ique** [~'ʒik] energetic; drastic.

énerv|ement [enɛrvə'mɑ̃] *m* exasperation; F state of nerves; **~er** [~'ve] (1a) enervate; irritate, annoy; F get on (*s.o.'s*) nerves.

enfan|ce [ɑ̃'fɑ̃ːs] *f* childhood; infancy; dotage; **~t** [ɑ̃'fɑ̃] *su.* child; ⚖ infant; **~**

trouvé foundling; **d'~** childlike; childish; *su./m* boy; *su./f* girl; **~ter** [ãfã'te] (1a) give birth to; father (*an idea*); **~tillage** [~ti'jaːʒ] *m* childishness; *fig.* **~s** *pl.* baby tricks; **~tin** [~'tẽ] childish; infantile.

enfer [ã'fɛːr] *m* hell.

enfermer [ãfɛr'me] (1a) shut up; lock up; shut in, enclose.

enferrer [ãfɛ're] (1a) pierce.

enfiévrer [ãfje'vre] (1f) make (*s.o.*) feverish; *fig.* excite, stir up.

enfil|ade [ãfi'lad] *f* series; suite; row; *fig.* string; **~er** [~'le] (1a) thread (*a needle*); string (*pearls etc.*); slip on (*clothes*); take (*a road*); F *fig.* (a. **s'~**) eat, F get through; drink, F knock back.

enfin [ã'fẽ] **1.** *adv.* at last, finally; in short; **2.** *int.* at last!; still!

enflammer [ãfla'me] (1a) inflame; set on fire; strike (*a match*); *fig.* stir up; **s'~** *fig.* flare up; *fig.* inflame.

enfler [ã'fle] (1a) *vt/i.* swell; *v/t.* puff out (*one's cheeks*); *fig.* inflate; *fig.* puff up; **enflure** [ã'flyːr] *f* swelling; *style:* turgidity.

enfon|cement [ãfõs'mã] *m* breaking open; *nail:* driving in; sinking; *ground:* hollow; △ recess; ⚓ bay; **~cer** [ãfõ'se] (1k) *v/t.* break in or open; drive (*a nail etc.*) in; thrust; break through; F get the better of; **s'~** plunge; sink; subside; go in; *v/t.* sink; **~cure** [~'syːr] *f* hollow.

enfouir [ã'fwiːr] (2a) bury; hide.

enfourcher [ãfur'ʃe] (1a) mount, get astride (*a bicycle etc.*).

enfourner [ãfur'ne] (1a) put in the oven; F **~ dans** stick or shove or stuff into.

enfreindre [ã'frẽːdr] (4m) transgress (*the law*); violate (*a treaty*).

enfuir [ã'fɥiːr] (2d): **s'~** flee; escape (from, **de**); leak (*liquid*).

enfumer [ãfy'me] (1a) fill or blacken with smoke; smoke out.

engag|é [ãga'ʒe] **1.** *adj. fig.* committed (*literature*); **2.** *su./m* ✕ volunteer; **~ement** [ãgaʒ'mã] *m* obligation, promise; commitment; *employee:* taking on, *artist etc.:* engagement; entry, insertion, introduction; *negotiations etc.:* opening; start; ✕ engagement; **~er** [ãga'ʒe] (1l) *v/t.* commit; take on (*an employee*), engage (*an artist*); insert, introduce, engage; invest; in-

volve (*s.o.*); encourage, advise (to *inf.*), à *inf.*); pawn (*a watch etc.*); pledge (*one's word*); ⚖ institute (*proceedings*); *fig.* begin, open; **s'~** commit o.s.; take a job, get taken on; **s'~ à** (*inf.*) undertake or promise to (*inf.*), commit o.s. to (*ger.*); start (up), begin (*negotiations etc.*); **s'~ dans** ⚙ fit into; enter (*a road*); *fig.* enter into.

engeance [ã'ʒãːs] *f* bunch, lot.

engelure 🌿 [ãʒ'lyːr] *f* chilblain.

engendrer [ãʒã'dre] (1a) beget; *fig.* engender; generate; breed.

engin [ã'ʒẽ] *m* machine; tool; ✕ ballistic missile; F gadget, contraption.

englober [ãglɔ'be] (1a) include.

engloutir [ãglu'tiːr] (2a) swallow (up) (a. *fig.*); gulp; engulf; *fig.* sink.

engluer [ãgly'e] (1a) lime (*a bird, twigs*); *fig.* trap, ensnare (*s.o.*).

engorger [ãgɔr'ʒe] (1l) block, choke up; ⚙ obstruct; 🌿 congest.

engou|ement [ãgu'mã] *m* 🌿 obstruction; *fig.* infatuation (with, **pour**); **~er** [~'e] (1a) 🌿 obstruct; **s'~** *fig.* be crazy (about, **de**).

engouffrer [ãgu'fre] (1a) engulf; F devour (*food*); *fig.* swallow up; **s'~** rush (into, **dans**) (*wind*).

engourdi|r [ãgur'diːr] (2a) (be)numb; *fig.* dull (the mind); **~ssement** [~dis'mã] *m* numbness; *fig.* dullness; *market:* slackness.

engrais 🌿 [ã'grɛ] *m* manure; fattening pasture or food; **~ser** [ãgrɛ'se] (1a) *v/t.* fatten (*animals*), cram (*poultry*); make (*s.o.*) fat; 🌿 manure, fertilize; *v/i.* grow fat; thrive.

engranger 🌿 [ãgrã'ʒe] (1l) garner.

engrenage [ãgrə'naːʒ] *m* ⚙ gear(ing); ⚙ engaging; *fig.* network.

engueuler *sl.* [ãgœ'le] (1a) tell *s.o.* off, blow (*s.o.*) up.

enguirlander [ãgirlã'de] (1a) wreathe (with, **de**); F tell (*s.o.*) off.

enhardir [ãar'diːr] (2a) embolden; **s'~** venture (to, **à**).

énigm|atique [enigma'tik] enigmatic; **~e** [e'nigm] *f* enigma; **parler par ~s** speak in riddles.

enivr|ement [ãnivrə'mã] *m* elation; intoxication; **~er** [~'vre] (1a) intoxicate; make (*s.o.*) drunk; **s'~** get drunk.

enjamb|ée [ãʒã'be] *f* stride; **~er** [ãʒã'be]

(1a) stride over (*an object*); span, straddle.

enjeu [ã'ʒø] *m* gaming, *fig.*: stake.

enjoindre [ã'ʒwɛ̃:dr] (4m) enjoin.

enjôl|er [ãʒo'le] (1a) wheedle, coax; cajole; **~eur** [~'lœ:r] **1.** *su.* coaxer; cajoler; **2.** *adj.* coaxing; cajoling.

enjoliv|er [ãʒɔli've] (1a) embellish; **~eur** *mot.* [~'vœ:r] *m* hub cap.

enjou|é [ã'ʒwe] jaunty, sprightly; playful, lively; **~ement** [ãʒu'mã] *m* sprightliness; playfulness.

enlacer [ãla'se] (1k) entwine; interlace; embrace, clasp; ⊚ dowel.

enlaidir [ãlɛ'di:r] (2a) *v/t.* disfigure; make ugly; *v/i.* grow ugly.

enlèvement [ãlɛv'mã] *m* removal; carrying off; kidnapping, abduction; *garbage etc.*: collection; ✕ storming; **enlever** [ãl've] (1d) remove; take off; take away (from, **à**); carry off (*a. fig. a prize*), *fig.* win; kidnap, abduct; collect (*garbage etc.*); ✕ take; *fig.* do (*s.th.*) brilliantly; **~ en arrachant (grattant)** snatch (rub) away; **s'~** come off or out (*stain etc.*); take off (*balloon etc.*); peel off (*bark, paint, skin, etc.*); F **s'~ comme des petits pains** sell like hot cakes.

enliser [ãli'ze] (1a): **s'~** sink; get stuck; *fig.* get bogged down.

enneig|é [ãnɛ'ʒe] snow-clad; **~ement** [ãnɛʒ'mã] *m* condition of the snow; **bulletin** *m* **d'~** snow report.

ennemi [ɛn'mi] *su.*, *adj.* enemy.

ennoblir [ãnɔ'bli:r] (2a) ennoble.

ennu|i [ã'nɥi] *m* annoyance; boredom; trouble; **~s** *pl.* worries; **~yer** [ãnɥi'je] (1h) bore; annoy; **s'~** be bored (with, **de**); long (for, **de**); **~yeux** [~'jø] boring; vexing.

énonc|é [enɔ̃'se] *m* statement; wording; **~er** [~'se] (1k) state, set forth; express; **~iation** [~sja'sjɔ̃] *f* stating, declaring; expressing.

enorgueillir [ãnɔrgœ'ji:r] (2a) make proud; **s'~** be proud o.s. on.

énorm|e [e'nɔrm] enormous, huge; *pej.* shocking; **~ément** [enɔrme'mã] *adv.* enormously; *fig.* very; **~** (**de**) a lot (of); **~ité** [~mi'te] *f* hugeness; *fig.* enormity; gross blunder; *fig.* shocking thing.

enquérir [ãke'ri:r] (2l): **s'~ de** inquire about; **~ête** [ã'kɛ:t] *f* inquiry; investigation; **~ par sondage** sample survey;

~êter [ãkɛ'te] (1a) hold an inquiry; investigate.

enquiquiner F [ãkiki'ne] (1a) get on (*s.o.'s*) nerves.

enracin|ement [ãrasin'mã] *m* taking root; deep-rootedness; **~er** [~si'ne] (1a) dig in; implant; **s'~** take root; *fig.* become rooted.

enrag|é [ãra'ʒe] **1.** *adj.* mad; rabid; *fig.* keen (on, **de**); **2.** *su.* enthusiast; **~er** [~] (1l) be mad (*a. fig.*); fume; **faire ~ q.** drive s.o. wild.

enrayer [ãrɛ'je] (1i) check, stem; **s'~** ⊚ jam.

enregistr|ement [ãrəʒistrə'mã] *m* registration; recording (*a.* ♪); **~er** [~ʒis'tre] (1a) register, *Am.* check (*a.* 🚗); record (*a. music*); *sp.* score (*a goal*); **~eur** [~'trœ:r] **1.** *adj.* recording; registering; **2.** *su./m* (*tape- etc.*) recorder.

enrhumer [ãry'me] (1a) give (*s.o.*) a cold; **s'~** catch (a) cold.

enrichir [ãri'ʃi:r] (2a) enrich (*a. fig.*; *a.* ⊚); make (*s.o.*) wealthy.

enrober [ãrɔ'be] (1a) coat (with, **de**); imbed (in, **de**).

enrôl|er [ãro'le] (1a) enrol(l), recruit; enlist; **s'~** enrol(l) (in, **dans**).

enrou|é [ã'rwe] hoarse; **~ement** [ãru'mã] *m* hoarseness.

enrouiller [ãru'je] (1a) rust.

enrouler [ãru'le] (1a) wind (around, **autour de**); roll or wind or coil up.

enroutiné [ãruti'ne] routine-minded; stick-in-the-mud.

ensabler [ãsa'ble] (1a) ♣ strand; cover with sand; silt up; **s'~** get stranded; silt up.

ensanglanter [ãsãglã'te] (1a) stain or cover with blood.

enseigne [ã'sɛɲ] *f* (shop) sign; ♣ ensign; *fig.* **logés à la même ~** all in the same boat.

enseign|ement [ãsɛɲ'mã] *m* teaching; education; *fig.* lesson; **~ primaire (secondaire, supérieur)** primary (secondary, higher) education; **~er** [ãsɛ'ɲe] (1a) teach (s.o. s.th., **qch. à q.**).

ensembl|e [ã'sã:bl] **1.** *adv.* together; **2.** *su./m* whole; unity; *cost.* ensemble, suit; 🏛 block (of buildings); ⊚ set; **dans l'~** on the whole; **vue** *f* **d'~** general view; **~ier** [ãsãbli'e] *m* (interior) decorator.

enserrer [ãse're] (1a) squeeze; hem in.

ensevelir [ãsə'vliːr] (2a) bury.

ensoleillé [ãsɔlɛ'je] sunny, sunlit.

ensommeillé [ãsɔmɛ'je] drowsy.

ensorcel|er [ãsɔrsə'le] (1c) bewitch (a. fig.); **~eur, -euse** [~sə'lœːr, ~'løːz] **1.** su. fig. charmer; su./m sorcerer; su./f sorceress; **2.** adj. bewitching (a. fig.); **~lement** [~sɛl'mã] m witchcraft; spell.

ensuite [ã'sɥit] adv. then, after(wards); next; **et ~?** what then?

ensuivre [ã'sɥiːvr] (4ee): **s'~** follow, ensue, result (from, **de**).

entacher [ãta'ʃe] (1a) taint, sully.

entaill|e [ãta:j] f notch; groove; chin etc.: gash; **~er** [~ta'je] (1a) notch; groove; gash (s.o.'s chin).

entam|e [ã'tãm] f loaf: first slice; **~er** [ãtɑ̃'me] (1a) cut into (a loaf); open, start (a bottle etc., a. fig.); start (a discussion etc.); broach (a cask, a subject); damage, harm (a. fig.); wear down, weaken (s.o.'s resistance etc.).

entasser [ãta'se] (1a) pile up; accumulate; crowd together (people).

enten|dement [ãtãd'mã] m understanding; **~dre** [ã'tãːdr] (4a) hear; understand; intend, mean; attend (a lecture); **~ dire que** hear that; **~ parler de** hear of; **~ raison** listen to reason; **laisser ~** hint; **s'~** agree; get on (with, **avec**); get on (together); **s'~ à** be good or an expert at; **~du** [ãtã'dy] **1.** adj. agreed, knowing (smile etc.); **2.** int. all right; O.K.; **bien ~!** of course!; **~te** [ã'tãːt] f understanding; agreement; meaning.

enter [ã'te] (1a) ✍ graft (a. ☉).

enterr|ement [ãtɛr'mã] m burial; **~er** [ãtɛ're] (1a) bury; fig. outlive; fig. shelve (a question).

en-tête [ã'tɛːt] m letterhead; heading; **entêté** [ãtɛ'te] stubborn; **entetement** [ãtɛt'mã] m stubbornness; **entêter** [ãtɛ'te] (1a) go to (s.o.'s) head; **s'~** be obstinate; **s'~ à** (inf.) persist in (ger.).

enthousias|me [ãtu'zjasm] m enthusiasm; **~mer** [~zjas'me] (1a) fill with enthusiasm; **s'~** enthuse (over, **pour**); **~te** [~'zjast] **1.** adj. enthusiastic; **2.** su. enthusiast (for, **de**).

entich|ement [ãtiʃ'mã] m infatuation (for **de, pour**); **~er** [ãti'ʃe] (1a): **s'~ de** become infatuated with.

entier [ã'tje] **1.** adj. whole (a. number);

entire, complete; total; full (control, fare, etc.); fig. headstrong; **cheval** m **~** stallion; **2.** su./m entirety; **en ~** in full; completely.

entité [ãti'te] f entity.

entôler sl. [ãto'le] (1a) con.

entonner¹ [ãto'ne] (1a) barrel.

entonner² [~] (1a) strike up (a tune); eccl. intone.

entonnoir [ãtɔ'nwaːr] m funnel.

entorse ✍ [ã'tɔrs] f sprain, wrench.

entortiller [ãtɔrti'je] (1a) twist, wind, wrap; wrap up; fig. complicate, muddle (up); F fig. get a(round) (s.o.), hoodwink.

entour|age [ãtu'raːʒ] m surroundings pl.; circle (of friends etc.), entourage; surround, frame; **~er** [~'re] (1a) surround (with, **de**); encircle (a. ✗).

entracte [ã'trakt] m thea. interval, Am intermission; ♪ interlude.

entraide [ã'trɛːd] f mutual aid; **entraider** [ãtrɛ'de] (1b): **s'~** help one another.

entrailles [ã'trɑːj] f/pl. guts; bowels; fig. pity sg.; compassion sg

entrain [ã'trɛ̃] m spirit, go, mettle.

entraîn|ement [ãtrɛn'mã] m impulse, impetus; fig. heat (of discussion); ☉ drive; sp. training; **~er** [ãtrɛ'ne] (1a) carry away; drag along; fig. lead (s.o.); ☉ drive; fig. involve; fig. entail; sp. train, coach; **~eur** [~'nœːr] m sp. trainer; team: coach; pacemaker; **~euse** [~'nøːz] f dance hostess.

entrave [ã'traːv] f fetter, shackle; fig. hindrance; **entraver** [ãtra've] (1a) fetter, shackle; fig. hinder.

entre [ã:tr] prp. between; in (s.o.'s hands); among (others, other things); out of (a number); **~ autres** among other things; among others; **soit dit ~ nous** between ourselves; **~ amis** among friends; **moi ~ autres** I for one; **d'~** (out) of, (from) among; **l'un (ceux) d'~ eux** one (these) of them.

entre...: ~bâillé [ãtrəba'je] half-open; **~chats** [~'ʃa] m/pl. capers; **~choquer** [~ʃɔ'ke] (1m) clink (glasses); **s'~** collide; clash; **~côte** cuis. [~'koːt] f rib of beef; **~couper** [~ku'pe] (1a) interrupt; **~croiser** [~krwa'ze] (1a) cross.

entrée [ã'tre] f entry; entrance; admission (a. ☉), access; admission charge; entrance ticket; ✝ receipt; cuis. first course; *fig.* beginning, outset; **d'~** (*de jeu*) right from the beginning.

entre...: ~faites [ɑ̃trə'fɛt] *f/pl.*: **sur ces ~** meanwhile; **~gent** [~'ʒɑ̃] *m* tact; wordly wisdom; **~lacer** [~la'se] (1k) interlace; intertwine; **~lacs** [~'la] *m* △ knotwork; *fig.* tangle; **~lardé** [~lar'de] streaky; **~larder** [~lar'de] (1a) lard; interlard (*a speech*) (with, *de*); **~mêler** [~mɛ'le] (1a) intermingle; blend; intersperse (*a speech*) (with, *de*); *fig.* **s'~ dans** meddle with; **~mets** *cuis.* [~'mɛ] *m* sweet; **~metteur, -euse** [~mɛ'tœːr, ~'tøːz] *su.* go-between; *su./m* ✝ middleman; procurer; *su./f* procuress; **~mettre** [~'mɛtr] (4v): **s'~** intervene; act as go-between; **~mise** [~'miːz] *f* intervention; mediation; **~pont** ♣ [~'pɔ̃] *m* between-decks; **d'~** steerage (*passenger*); **~poser** ✝ [~po'ze] (1a) warehouse; *customs*: bond; **~poseur** ✝ [~po'zœːr] *m* warehouseman; **~positaire** ✝ [~pozi'tɛːr] *m* warehouseman; *customs*: bonder; **~pôt** [~'po] *m* ✝ warehouse; ✗ depot; **~ frigorifique** cold store; **en ~** in bond; **~prenant** [~prə'nɑ̃] enterprising; **~prendre** [~'prɑ̃ːdr] (4aa) undertake; contract for (*work*); **~preneur** (*s.o.*); **~preneur** [~prə'nœːr] *m* contractor; **~prise** [~'priːz] *f* enterprise; ✝ firm, concern; **~ de transport** carriers *pl.*

entrer [ɑ̃'tre] (1a) *v/i.* go or come in, enter; **~ dans** go or come into, enter (*a room etc.*, *fig. a. career etc.*); *fig.* enter into or (up)on; *fig.* form part of; *fig.* understand, share (*s.o.'s feelings etc.*); **~ en** enter upon (*s.th.*) or into (*competition*); *fig.* **en jeu** come into play; *faire* **~** show (*s.o.*) in; get or fit or insert (*s.th.* into, *dans*); *v/t.* bring in, introduce.

entre...: ~rail 🛤 [ɑ̃trə'rɑːj] *m* ga(u)ge; **~sol** △ [~'sɔl] *m floor*: mezzanine; **~temps** [~'tɑ̃] **1.** *m/inv.* interval; **2.** *adv.* meanwhile; **~teneur** [~tə'nœːr] *m* maintainer; **~tenir** [~tə'niːr] (2h) maintain; keep up; talk to (*s.o.*) (about, *de*); entertain; **s'~** talk (with, *avec*); *sp.* keep o.s. fit; **~tien** [~'tjɛ̃] *m* maintenance, upkeep; conversation; **~toise** △ [~'twaːz] *f* strut; **~voir** [~'vwaːr] (3m) catch a glimpse of; *fig.* foresee, have an inkling of; *laisser* **~** disclose; hint; **~vue** [~'vy] *f* interview.

entrouvrir [ɑ̃tru'vriːr] (2f) half-open; *fig.* **s'~** yawn (*chasm*).

énumér|ation [enymera'sjɔ̃] *f* enumeration; **~er** [~'re] (1f) enumerate.

envahi|r [ɑ̃va'iːr] (2a) overrun; invade; *fig.* feeling: steal over (*s.o.*); **~sseur** [~i'sœːr] *m* invader.

envelopp|e [ɑ̃'vlɔp] *f* envelope; wrapping; ✪ casing, lagging; *fig.* exterior; **~ement** [ɑ̃vlɔp'mɑ̃] *m* wrapping; **✽ ~ humide** wet pack; **~er** [ɑ̃vlɔ'pe] (1a) envelop (*a. fig.*); wrap (up); cover; ✗ encircle.

envenimer [ɑ̃vəni'me] (1a) poison; aggravate; *fig.* embitter (*s.o.*).

envergure [ɑ̃vɛr'gyːr] *f* (wing)span; spread, breadth; *fig.* calibre; *fig.* scope; *fig.* **de grande ~** *a.* large-scale.

enverrai [ɑ̃vɛ're] *1st p. sg. fut.* of **envoyer.**

envers¹ [ɑ̃'vɛːr] *prp.* to(wards).

envers² [~] *m tex.* reverse (*a. fig.*, *of medal*), back; *fig.* seamy side; **à l'~** inside out; *fig.* topsy-turvy.

envi [ɑ̃'vi] *adv.*: **à l'~** vying with each other; in emulation.

envi|able [ɑ̃'vjabl] enviable; **~e** [ɑ̃'vi] *f* envy; wish, desire; need; longing, fancy; **✽** hangnail; **✽** birthmark; *avoir* **~ de qch.** want s.th.; *avoir* **~ de** (*inf.*) want to (*inf.*), feel like (*inf.*); *avoir* **~ que** wish or want that; *donner* **~ à q. de** (*inf.*) make s.o. want to (*inf.*) or feel like (*ger.*); *faire* **~ à q.** make s.o. envious; **~er** [ɑ̃'vje] (1o) envy (s.o. s.th., *qch. à q.*); long for; **~eux** [ɑ̃'vjø] envious.

environ [ɑ̃vi'rɔ̃] *adv.* about, approximately; **~s** [~'rɔ̃] *m/pl.* vicinity *sg.*; surroundings; *aux* **~ de** about (*fifty*), towards (*Christmas*); **~nement** [~rɔn'mɑ̃] *m* surroundings *pl.*; environment; **~ner** [~rɔ'ne] (1a) surround; encompass.

envisager [ɑ̃viza'ʒe] (1l) envisage; consider, view; **~ de** (*inf.*) think of (*ger.*); consider (*ger.*).

envoi [ɑ̃'vwa] *m* sending; dispatch; consignment, parcel; shipment; *coup m* **d'~** *foot.* kickoff; *fig.* (starting) signal.

envol [ɑ̃'vɔl] *m* (taking) flight; **✈** takeoff; **~er** [ɑ̃vɔ'le] (1a): **s'~** fly (away) (*a. fig.*); **✈** take off.

envoûter [ɑ̃vu'te] (1a) bewitch.

envoy|é [ɑ̃vwa'je] **1.** *p.p.* of **envoyer; 2.** *su.* messenger; *su./m: journ.* **~ spécial**

special correspondent; **~er** [~] (1r) send; forward; fling, hurl; shoot; **~ chercher** send for; *sl.* **s'~** get saddled with; gulp down.

épagneul *m*, **e** *f* [epa'nœl] spaniel.

epais, se [e'pɛ, ~'pɛːs] thick; dense (*a. mind*); stout (*glass*); **~seur** [epe'sœːr] *f* thickness; depth; denseness; **~sir** [~'siːr] (2a) *v/t.* thicken; *v/i.*, **s'~** get thicker; thicken; *cuis. a.* jell; grow stout (*person*).

épanch|ement [epɑ̃ʃ'mɑ̃] *m* effusion (*a. fig.*); outpouring; **~er** [epɑ̃'ʃe] (1a) *fig.* pour out; **s'~** pour (out); *fig.* open one's heart.

épandre [e'pɑ̃:dr] (4a) spread.

épanouir [epa'nwiːr] (2a) **&** open (out); **s'~** bloom; open up; *fig.* light up (*face*).

épargn|e [e'parɲ] *f* thrift; saving; **♥ caisse** *f d'~* savings bank; **~er** [epar'ɲe] (1a) save (up), economize; be sparing with; *fig.* spare (*s.o.*).

éparpiller [eparpi'je] (1a) scatter.

épars [e'paːr] scattered; sparse.

épat|ant F [epa'tɑ̃] marvel(l)ous, F fab, great; **~er** [~'te] (1a) F flabbergast; *nez m* **épaté** flat nose; F **~ le bourgeois** shock conventional people; **~eur** *m*, **-euse** *f* F [~'tœːr, ~'tøːz] bluffer.

épaul|e [e'poːl] *f* shoulder; *un coup d'~* a shove; *fig.* a leg-up; *par-dessus l'~* disduinfully; **~ement** [epol'mɑ̃] *m* geog., **⊕** revetment wall; **△** buttress; **~er** [epo'le] (1a) support (*a.* △); help, back (*s.o.*) up; bring (*a gun*) to the shoulder; **~ette** [~'lɛt] *f* epaulette; shoulder strap.

épave [e'paːv] *f* wreck (*a. fig.*).

épée [e'pe] *f* sword; rapier; *coup m d'~ dans l'eau* wasted effort.

épeler [e'ple] (1c) spell (out).

éperdu [eper'dy] distraught, frantic; **~ment** [~dy'mɑ̃] desperately; **~ amoureux** madly in love; *je m'en moque* **~** I couldn't care less.

éperon [e'prɔ̃] *m* spur; *bridge:* cutwater; **△** buttress; *eyes:* crow's-foot, **~né** [epro'ne] spurred; crow footed (*eyes*); **~ner** [~] (1a) spur.

épervier [eper'vje] *m* *orn.* sparrow-hawk; *fishing:* cast-net.

éphémère [efe'mɛːr] **1.** *adj.* ephemeral, fleeting; **2.** *su./m zo.* may-fly.

épi [e'pi] *m* grain: ear; **&** spike.

épic|e [e'pis] *f* spice; *pain m d'~* ginger-

bread; **~er** [epi'se] (1k) spice (*a. a story*); **~erie** [epis'ri] *f* grocer's (shop), *Am.* grocery; **~ier** *m*, **-ère** *f* [epi'sje, ~'sjɛːr] grocer.

épidémie **⚕** [epide'mi] *f* epidemic.

épiderme [epi'dɛrm] *m* epidermis.

épier [e'pje] (1o) watch (*s.o.*); spy on (*s.o.*); watch *or* look out for.

épilat|ion [epila'sjɔ̃] *f* depilation; *eyebrows:* plucking; **~oire** [~'twaːr] *adj.*, *su./m* depilatory.

épilepsie **⚕** [epilɛp'si] *f* epilepsy.

épiler [epi'le] (1a) depilate; remove hairs; pluck (*one's eyebrows*).

épilogu|e [epi'lɔg] *m* epilog(ue); **~er** [~lɔ'ge] (1m) comment (lengthily) (on, *sur*).

épiloir [epi'lwaːr] *m* tweezers *pl.*

épinard **&** [epi'naːr] *m* spinach.

épine [e'pin] *f* **&** thorn (*a. fig.*), prickle; *anat.* **~ dorsale** spine.

épineux [epi'nø] thorny (*a. fig.*); prickly (*a. fig. person*); *fig.* knotty.

épingl|e [e'pɛ̃gl] *f* pin; **~ à chapeau** hatpin; **~ à linge** clothes-peg; **~ de nourrice** safety-pin; *fig.* **coup** *m d'~* pin-prick; *tiré à quatre* **~s** spick and span; *mot.* **virage** *m en* **~ à cheveux** hairpin bend; **~er** [epɛ̃'gle] (1a) pin (up); Γ catch, nab (*s.o.*).

épinière [epi'njɛːr] *adj./f:* **moelle** *f* **~** spinal cord.

épisode [epi'zɔd] *m* episode; *cin.* **film** *m* **à ~s** serial film.

épitaphe [epi'taf] *f* epitaph.

épithète [epi'tɛt] *f* epithet.

épître [e'pitr] *f* epistle; *fig.* letter.

éploré [eplɔ're] tearful, in tears.

épluch|er [eply'ʃe] (1a) peel (*a fruit*); clean (*salad etc.*); *fig.* examine closely, sift; **~ures** [~'ʃyr] *f/pl.* peelings; *fig.* refuse *sg.*

époint|é [epwɛ̃'te] blunt; **~er** [~] (1a) blunt (*s.th.*).

épong|e [e'pɔ̃:ʒ] *f* sponge; *fig.* **passer l'~ sur** say no more about (*s.th.*); Γ *fig.* **jeter l'~** throw in the towel *or* sponge; **~er** [epɔ̃'ʒe] (1l) sponge (up); mop (*one's brow*); *a. fig.* soak up, absorb.

épopée [epo'pe] *f* epic (poem).

époque [e'pɔk] *f* epoch, age, era; period; time; **à l'~** at the time of (**de**); at that time, then; *la Belle* **⍾** *that up to 1914*; *faire* **~** mark an epoch.

époumoner [epumɔ'ne] (1a) put (s.o.) out of breath; **s'~** pant.

épous|ailles [epu'zɑ:j] f/pl. wedding sg.; **~e** [e'pu:z] f wife; **~ée** [epu'ze] f bride; **~er** [~'ze] (1a) marry; fig. take up (a cause); fig. embrace (an idea); fig. make (s.th.) one's own; fig. fit; fig. **~ son temps** move with the times.

épousset|er [epus'te] (1c) dust; beat (a carpet); rub down (a horse); **~te** [epu'sɛt] f duster, whisk.

époustouflant F [epustu'flɑ̃] amazing, extraordinary.

épouvant|able [epuvɑ̃'tabl] horrible; appalling; **~ail** [~vɑ̃'ta:j] m scarecrow; fig. bogy; **~e** [~'vɑ̃:t] f fright; **~er** [~vɑ̃'te] (1a) scare.

époux [e'pu] m husband; ⚭ a. spouse; **les ~** pl. ... the ... couple sg.

éprendre [e'prɑ̃:dr] (4aa): **s'~ de** fall in love with; take a fancy to.

épreuve [e'prœ:v] f test (a. ⊙, a. school examination); proof (a. typ.); phot. print; fig. trial; sp. event; **à l'~ de** proof against (s.th.); **à toute ~** never-failing; ⊙ fool-proof; **mettre à l'~** put to the test.

épris [e'pri] in love (with, **de**).

éprouv|er [epru've] (1a) feel, experience; meet with (difficulties); suffer (a loss); experience, learn; test, try; put to the test; fig. afflict, try; **~ette** [~'vɛt] f 🧪 test-tube; probe.

épuis|é [epɥi'ze] exhausted; run down; ♣ sold out; out of print; **~ement** [epɥiz'mɑ̃] m exhaustion; draining; depletion; **~er** [epɥi'ze] (1a) exhaust; use up; wear (s.o.) out; **s'~** run out (provisions etc.), run dry, dry up (source); wear o.s. out.

épurer [epy're] (1a) purify; refine; filter; pol. purge; fig. expurgate.

équateur [ekwa'tœ:r] m equator.

équation [ekwa'sjɔ̃] f equation.

équerre [e'kɛ:r] f square; right angle; angle-iron; **d'~, en ~** square.

équestre [e'kɛstr] equestrian.

équilibr|e [eki'libr] m balance (a. fig.); equilibrium; **~ politique** balance of power; **~er** [ekili'bre] (1a) balance; counterbalance.

équinoxe [eki'nɔks] m equinox.

équip|age [eki'pa:ʒ] m ⚓, ✈ crew; retinue; **~e** [e'kip] f workmen: gang; sp. team; **~ de nuit** night shift; **esprit m d'~**

team spirit; **~ement** [ekip'mɑ̃] m equipment; gear; outfit; **~er** [eki'pe] (1a) equip; fit out; ⚓ man.

équitable [eki'tabl] equitable, just.

équitation [ekita'sjɔ̃] f horsemanship; **école f d'~** riding-school.

équité [eki'te] f equity; fairness.

équival|ent [ekiva'lɑ̃] adj., su./m equivalent; **~oir** [~'lwa:r] (3l) be equivalent (to, **à**; amount (to, **à**).

équivoqu|e [eki'vɔk] **1.** adj. equivocal; fig. dubious; **2.** su./f ambiguity; **~er** [~vɔ'ke] (1m) equivocate.

érable 🌿 [e'rabl] m maple.

érafl|er [era'fle] (1a) scratch; **~ure** [~'fly:r] f graze, scratch.

éraillé [era'je] m hoarse, rasp.

ère [ɛ:r] f era, epoch.

érection [erɛk'sjɔ̃] f erection (a. biol.); position: establishment.

éreint|ement F [erɛt'mɑ̃] m exhaustion; fig. slashing; **~er** [erɛ'te] (1a) break the back of; F exhaust, wear (s.o.) out; fig. slash, cut to pieces; **s'~ à** (inf.) wear o.s. out (ger.).

ergot [ɛr'go] m zo. spur; 🌿 ergot; ⊙ catch; **~age** F [ɛrgɔ'ta:ʒ] m quibbling; **~é** [~'te] spurred (cock); ergoted (corn); **~er** F [~'te] (1a) quibble (about, **sur**; **~eur** [~'tœ:r] **1.** adj. quibbling; **2.** su. quibbler.

ergothérapie [ɛrgɔtera'pi] f occupational therapy; work therapy.

ériger [eri'ʒe] (1l) erect; establish (an office); fig. exalt, raise (to, **en**); **~ qch. en principe** lay s.th. down as a principle; **s'~ en** pose as.

ermitage [ɛrmi'ta:ʒ] m hermitage; **ermite** [~'mit] m hermit; recluse.

éro|der geol. [erɔ'de] (1a) erode; wear away; **~sif** [~'zif] erosive; **~sion** [~'zjɔ̃] f erosion; eating away.

érotique [erɔ'tik] erotic; **érotisme** [~'tism] m eroticism; ✦ erotism.

err|ements [ɛr'mɑ̃] m/pl. bad habits; **anciens ~** bad old ways; **~er** [ɛ're] (1b) wander, roam; flit (smile); **~eur** [ɛ'rœ:r] f error; mistake; **faire ~** be mistaken, be wrong.

erroné [ɛrɔ'ne] erroneous; wrong.

éructation [erykta'sjɔ̃] f F belch(ing).

érudit [ery'di] **1.** adj. erudite, learned; **2.** su. scholar; **~ion** [~di'sjɔ̃] f erudition, learning.

érupti|f [eryp'tif] eruptive; **~on** [~'sjɔ̃] *f* eruption; *teeth*: cutting.

es [ɛ] *2nd p. sg. pres. of* **être 1.**

ès [ɛs] *prp.*: **docteur** *m* **~ sciences** doctor of science.

esbroufe F [ɛs'bruf] *f* bluff(ing); showing off; **faire de l'~** bluff; show off; **✠ à l'~** snatch-and-grab.

escabe|au [ɛska'bo] *m* stool; step-ladder; **~lle** [~'bɛl] *f* stool.

escadr|e [ɛs'kadr] ✕ squadron; **~ille** [ɛska'drij] *f* ✠ flotilla; ✈ flight; **~on** [~'drɔ̃] *m* squadron.

escalad|e [ɛska'lad] *f* climb(ing); escalation; **~er** [~la'de] (1a) climb.

escalator [ɛskala'tɔːr] *m* escalator.

escale [ɛs'kal] *f* ✠ port of call; ✈ stop; call, **faire ~** (**à**) call (at), stop over (at).

escalier [ɛska'lje] *m* staircase; stairs *pl.*; **~ roulant** escalator; **~ tournant** (*or* **en colimaçon**) spiral staircase.

escalope *cuis.* [ɛska'lɔp] *f* cutlet.

escamot|able [ɛskamɔ'tabl] pull-down (*arm-rest*); ✈ retractable; **~er** [~'te] (1a) conjure away; *fig.* dodge, get round; pinch, filch; **~eur** [~'tœːr] *m* conjuror.

escampette F [ɛskã'pɛt] *f*: **prendre la poudre d'~** skedaddle, vamoose.

escapade [ɛska'pad] *f* escapade.

escarbille [ɛskar'bij] *f* bit of cinder.

escargot [ɛskar'go] *m* snail.

escarmouche [ɛskar'muʃ] *f* skirmish.

escarp|é [ɛskar'pe] steep, **~ement** [~pə'mã] *m* steep slope.

escarpin [ɛskar'pɛ̃] *m* light shoe.

escarpolette [ɛskarpɔ'lɛt] *f* swing.

escient [ɛ'sjã] *m*: **à bon ~** advisedly.

esclaffer [ɛskla'fe] (1a): **s'~** burst out laughing, guffaw.

esclandre [ɛs'klãdr] *m* scandal.

esclav|age [ɛskla'vaːʒ] *m* slavery; drudgery; **~e** [~'klaːv] *su.* slave.

escompt|e ✞ [ɛs'kɔ̃t] *m* discount; rebate; **~er** [~kɔ̃'te] (1a) ✞ discount; *fig.* reckon on, hope for.

escort|e [ɛs'kɔrt] *f* ✕ *etc.* escort; ✠ convoy; **~er** [~kɔr'te] (1a) escort.

escrim|e [ɛs'krim] *f* fencing; **~er** [ɛskri'me] (1a): **s'~** fight (with, **contre**); **s'~ à** work hard at; **~eur** [~'mœːr] *m* fencer.

escro|c [ɛs'kro] *m* swindler; **~quer** [~krɔ'ke] (1m) swindle; **~ qch. à q.** cheat s.o. out of s.th.

espac|e [ɛs'paːs] *m* space; interval; room; **dans** (*or* **en**) **l'~ de** within; **~ement** [~pas'mã] *m* spacing; **~er** [~pa'se] (1k) space (out); **s'~** become less frequent.

espadrille [ɛspa'drij] *f* sandal.

espagnol [ɛspa'ɲɔl] **1.** *adj.*, *su./m ling.* Spanish; **2.** *su.* ♀ Spaniard.

espèce [ɛs'pɛs] *f* kind, sort; ✞ case; ♀, *zo.* species; **~s** *pl.* cash *sg.*; **~ de...!** silly ...!; **~ humaine** mankind.

espér|ance [ɛspe'rãːs] *f* hope; expectation; **~ de vie** life expectancy; **~er** [~'re] (1f) *v/t.* hope for; **~** *j'espère, j'espère* I hope so; *v/i.* trust (in, **en**).

espiègle [ɛs'pjɛgl] **1.** *adj.* mischievous, roguish; **2.** *su.* imp; **~rie** [~pjɛglə'ri] *f* mischief; prank.

espion, -onne [ɛs'pjɔ̃, ~'pjɔn] *su.* spy; secret agent; *su./m* concealed microphone; window-mirror; **~nage** [ɛspjɔ'naːʒ] *m* espionage, spying; **~ner** [~'ne] (1a) spy (upon).

espoir [ɛs'pwaːr] *m* hope; expectation.

esprit [ɛs'pri] *m* spirit; mind; wit; disposition; **~-de-vin** spirit(s *pl*) of wine; **le Saint-♀** the Holy Ghost; **plein d'~** witty; **faire de l'~** (try to) be witty; **rendre l'~** give up the ghost; **venir à** (*sortir de*) **l'~ de q.** cross (slip) s.o.'s mind.

esquif [ɛs'kif] *m* small boat, skiff.

esquimau [ɛski'mo] *adj.*, *su.* Eskimo; *su./m cuis.* choc-ice.

esquint|er F [ɛskɛ̃'te] (1a) tire (*s.o.*) out; *fig.* ruin; run (*s.o.*) down.

esquiss|e [ɛs'kis] *f* sketch; draft; **~er** [~ki'se] (1a) sketch, outline.

esquiver [ɛski've] (1a) avoid, evade; dodge; *fig.* **s'~** steal away.

essai [e'sɛ] *m* ⊘ trial; essay; test; *sp.* try; attempt (to, **pour**); **~ nucléaire** atomic test; **à l'~** on trial; **coup** *m* **d'~** first attempt; **faire l'~ de** try (*s.th.*); **pilote** *m* **d'~** test pilot.

essaim [e'sɛ̃] *m* swarm *m*; **~age** [esɛ'maːʒ] *m* excessive growth; **~er** [~'me] (1a) swarm.

essay|age [esɛ'jaːʒ] *m* testing; *cost.* trying on; **~er** [~'je] (1i) try (on [*à to inf.*, **de** *inf.*]); test; *cost.* try on; taste; **~** try one's hand at.

essen|ce [e'sãːs] f essence; *trees:* species; 🌳 oil; petrol, *Am.* gasoline; extract (*of beef etc.*); *fig.* pith; *poste m d'~* filling station, *Am.* service station; **~tiel** [esã'sjɛl] **1.** *adj.* essential; **2.** *su./m* main thing.

essieu [e'sjø] m axle.

essor [e'sɔːr] m flight, soaring; *fig.* upswing, boom; **~er** [esɔ're] (1a) dry; wring (*linen*); **~euse** [~'røːz] f ⚙ drainer; *laundry:* wringer.

essouffler [esu'fle] (1a) make (*s.o.*) breathless, wind; *s'~* get out of breath; *fig.* exhaust o.s.

essuie...: **~-glace** *mot.* [esɥi'glas] m windscreen wiper, *Am.* windshield wiper; **~-mains** [~'mjɛ̃] m/inv. (hand-)towel; **~-pieds** [~'pje] m/inv. door-mat.

essuyer [esɥi'je] (1h) wipe; dry; mop up; dust; *fig.* suffer (*defeat etc.*); *fig.* meet with (*a refusal*).

est¹ [ɛst] **1.** *su./m* east; *de l'~* east(ern); *d'~* easterly (*wind*); *l'🧭 de* the east of; *vers l'~* eastward(s); **2.** *adj./inv.* east(ern); esterly.

est² [ɛ] *3rd p. sg. pres. of* **être 1.**

estafette [esta'fɛt] f courier.

estafilade [estafi'lad] f gash; slash.

estamp|e [ɛs'tãːp] f print, engraving; ⚙ stamp, punch, die; **~er** [estã'pe] (1a) stamp, emboss; *fig.* fleece (*s.o.*); **~ille** [~'piːj] f stamp; ♱ trade-mark; **~iller** [~pi'je] (1a) stamp; ♱ mark.

esth|ète [ɛs'tɛt] su. (a)esthete; **~éticien** m, **-enne** f [esteti'sjɛ̃, ~'sjɛn] (a)esthetician; beautician; **~étique** [~'tik] **1.** adj. (a)esthetic; **2.** *su./f* (a)esthetics pl.

estim|able [ɛsti'mabl] estimable; assessable; **~atif** [~'tif] estimated (*cost etc.*); *devis m ~* estimate; **~ation** [~'sjõ] f estimation; valuation; **~e** [ɛs'tim] f esteem; *à l'~* by guesswork; *tenir q. en haute (petite) ~* hold s.o. in high (low) esteem; **~er** [~ti'me] (1a) estimate; value, appraise, assess; *fig.* (hold in) esteem (*s'~*) consider (*o.s.*).

estival [ɛsti'val] summer...; **~nt** m, e f [~'vã, ~'vãːt] summer visitor.

estoc [ɛs'tɔk] m: *frapper d'~ et de taille* cut and thrust; **~ade** [ɛstɔ'kad] f (finishing) blow.

estoma|c [ɛstɔ'ma] m stomach; *avoir l'~ dans les talons* be faint with hunger;

~quer F [~ma'ke] (1m) flabbergast (*s.o.*).

estomp|e [ɛs'tõːp] f stump (drawing); **~er** [estõ'pe] (1a) shade off; *fig.* blur, dim; *s'~* become blurred.

estrade [ɛs'trad] f platform, stage.

estragon 💐 [ɛstra'gõ] m tarragon.

estropi|é m, e f [ɛstrɔ'pje] cripple; **~er** [~] (1o) cripple, lame, maim, *fig.* distort; *fig.* mangle (*a word*), murder (*a language*).

estuaire [ɛs'tɥɛːr] m estuary.

estudiantin [ɛstydjã'tɛ̃] student...

esturgeon [ɛstyr'ʒõ] m sturgeon.

et [e] and; *et ... et* both ... and.

étable [e'tabl] f cattleshed; pigsty.

établi¹ [eta'bli] m workbench.

établi|² [eta'bli] established (*fact*); determined (*limit*); **~ir** [~'bliːr] (2a) establish; set up (*a business etc., sp. a record*); construct; ascertain (*facts*); prove (*a charge*); draw up (*a list, an account, a plan*); institute (*a tax, a post*); *⚡ ~ le contact* make contact; *s'~* set (o.s.) up, establish o.s.; settle (o.s.); become established; **~issement** [~blis'mã] m establishment; institution; settlement; ♱ firm; factory.

étag|e [e'taːʒ] m stor(e)y, floor; *fig.* degree, rank; stage (*a. of rocket*); *geol.* layer; *fig. de bas ~* low(-class); under[eta'ʒe] (1l) (ar)range in tiers; *fig.* grade, stagger, spread (out); **~ère** [~'ʒɛːr] f shelves pl.

étai [e'tɛ] m prop (*a. fig.*), strut.

étain [e'tɛ̃] m tin; pewter.

étal, *pl.* **~s** [e'tal] m *market:* stall; **~age** [eta'laːʒ] m ♱, *fig.* display, show; shop window; **~agiste** [~la'ʒist] window dresser; **~er** [~'le] (1a) ♱ *fig.* display; *fig.* show, disclose; stagger (*holidays*); spread (out); *s'~* sprawl; spread *or* stretch out.

étalon¹ [eta'lõ] m stallion.

étalon² [eta'lõ] m standard; **~-or** gold standard; *poids-~* troy weight; **~nage** [~lɔ'naːʒ] m standardization; ga(u)ging; **~ner** [~lɔ'ne] (1a) standardize; calibrate; ga(u)ge.

étamine¹ [eta'min] f butter-muslin, cheesecloth; bolting cloth; *passer qch. par l'~* sift s.th. (*a. fig.*).

étamine² 💐 [~] f stamen).

étanch|e [e'tãːʃ] (water-, air)tight; **~éité**

[etɑ̃ʃei'te] f watertightness; **~er** [~'ʃe] (1a) sta(u)nch (blood); stem (a liquid); quench (one's thirst); stop (a leak); make watertight.

étang [e'tɑ̃] m pond, pool.

étant [e'tɑ̃] p. pr. of être 1.

étape [e'tap] f ✗, a. fig. stage; halting-place; fig. step (towards, **vers**).

état [e'ta] m state (a. pol., a. fig.); condition; fig. position; profession, trade; status; **~civil** civil status; **bureau de l'~ civil** register office; **~ d'esprit** frame of mind; **en toute ~ de cause** in any case; **~ transitoire** transition stage; **réduit à l'~ de** reduced to; **être en ~ de** (inf.) be in a position to (inf.); **faire ~ de** put forward; **homme m d'~** statesman; **hors d'~** useless; **remettre en ~** put in order; **~isation** [etatiza'sjɔ̃] f nationalisation (of industries); **~isme** [~'tism] m state control; **~-major**, pl. **~s-majors** ✗ [~ma'ʒɔːr] m staff.

étau ⚙ [e'to] m vice, Am. vise.

étay|age [etε'jaːʒ] m propping (up); **~er** [~'je] (1i) prop (up) (a. fig.).

été¹ [e'te] p.p. of être 1.

été² [~] m summer; F **~ de la Saint-Martin** Indian summer.

éteignoir [etε'ɲwaːr] m candle: snuffer; fig. wet blanket; **éteindre** [e'tɛ̃ːdr] (4m) put out (a fire); ⚡, ⚙ etc. turn or switch off; extinguish (the light, a race, etc.); quench (one's thirst); pay off (a debt); abolish (a right); fig. put an end to (s.o.'s hope); fig. dim (the light); allay (fears); slake (lime); **s'~** go out (light etc.); fade; die; die out (family, race); die down (noise, fig. passions etc.).

étend|age [etɑ̃'daːʒ] m hanging out; **~ard** [~'daːr] m flag; **~oir** [~'dwaːr] m clothes-line; drying-yard; **~re** [e'tɑ̃ːdr] (4a) extend; stretch; spread (out); lay (a tablecloth); dilute (with, **de**); lay (s.o.) down; hang (linen); roll out (pastry); widen; **s'~** spread; stretch (out); extend; stretch out, lie down; **~u, e** [etɑ̃'dy] 1. adj. extensive; wide-spread; 2. su. f extent; expanse; voice, knowledge: range; length.

étern|el [eter'nɛl] (1a) eternal; **~iser** [eterni'ze] (1a) eternalize; **s'~** drag on; **~ité** [~'te] f eternity.

éternuer [eter'nɥe] (1n) sneeze.

êtes [ɛt] 2nd p. p. pres. of être 1.

éther [e'tɛːr] m ether; **~é** [ete're] etherial; fig. skyey.

éthique [e'tik] adj. ethical; 2. su./f ethics pl.; moral philosophy.

étincel|er [etɛ̃s'le] (1c) sparkle (a. fig.); gleam (anger.); twinkle (star); **~le** [etɛ̃'sɛl] f spark; **~lement** [~sɛl'mɑ̃] m sparkling; twinkling.

étioler [etjo'le] (1a): **s'~** droop, wilt (plant); waste away.

étique [e'tik] emaciated, skinny.

étiquet|er [etik'te] (1c) label; **~te** [eti'kɛt] f label, tag; etiquette.

étirer [eti're] (1a) stretch; draw out.

étoffe [e'tɔf] f material, cloth; fig. quality, makings pl., stuff; **~é** [etɔ'fe] plump (person); meaty (style); **~er** [etɔ'fe] (1a) stuff; fig. fill out.

étoil|e [e'twal] f astr. star; typ. asterisk; **~ du berger** evening star; zo. **~ de mer** starfish; **~ filante** falling star; **à la belle ~** in the open; **~er** [etwa'le] (1a) spangle; **étoilé** starry; star-spangled.

étonn|ement [etɔn'mɑ̃] m astonishment; **~er** [etɔne] (1a) astonish, amaze; **s'~** be surprised (at s.th., **de qch**; at ger., **de** inf.).

étouff|ée [etu'fe] f: **cuire à l'~** braise; **~ement** [etuf'mɑ̃] m stifling; suffocation; fig. hushing up; **~er** [etu'fe] (1a) vt/i. suffocate, choke; stifle; v/t. damp (a sound); hush up (an affair).

étourd|erie [eturdə'ri] f inadvertence; blunder; **~i** [~'di] 1. adj. thoughtless; 2. su. scatterbrain; **~ir** [~'diːr] (2a) stun, daze; make dizzy; deaden (a pain etc.); **~issement** [~dis'mɑ̃] m giddiness; dizzy spell; pain etc.: deadening.

étourneau orn. [etur'no] m starling.

étrange [e'trɑ̃ːʒ] strange; **~r** [etrɑ̃'ʒe] 1. adj. foreign (a. fig.); unknown; irrelevant (to, **à**); **~ à** unacquainted with; 2. su. foreigner; stranger; **à l'~** abroad; **~té** [etrɑ̃ʒ'te] f strangeness.

étrangl|ement [etrɑ̃glə'mɑ̃] m strangulation; ⚙ etc. narrowing; fig. **goulet** m (or **goulot** m) **d'~** bottleneck; **~er** [~'gle] (1a) v/t. strangle, choke, throttle; ⚙ strangulate; v/i.: **~ de colère** choke with rage.

étrave ⚓ [e'traːv] f stem(post).

être [ɛːtr] 1. (1) be, exist; belong (to, **à**); lie, stand; F go; passive voice: be (seen);

si cela est if so; *ça y est* it is done; *c'est ça* that's it; *c'est moi* it is me; *c'en est assez!* enough (of it)!; *lequel sommes-nous?* what is the date today?; *c'est à lui de* (*inf.*) it rests with him to (*inf.*); ~ *de* come *or* be from (*a town, country, etc.*); *elle s'est blessée* she has hurt herself; *elle s'est blessé le doigt* she has hurt her finger; *en* ~ join in, take part; *où en sommes-nous?* how far have we got?; ~ *pour quelque chose (beaucoup) dans* play a(n important) part in; *il est* it is (*2 o'clock*); there is *or* are; *il était une fois* once upon a time there was; *est-ce qu'il travaille?* does he work?, is he working?; *elle est venue, n'est-ce pas?* she has come, hasn't she?; **2.** *su./m* being; existence.

étrein|dre [e'trɛ̃:dr] (4m) clasp; grasp; embrace, hug; *fig.* grip; **~te** [e'trɛ̃t] *f* embrace; grasp; grip.

étrenn|e [e'trɛn] *f*: ~*s pl.* New Year's gift *sg.*; Christmas box *sg.*; *avoir l'*~ *de* = ~*er* [etrɛ'ne] (1a) wear (*a garment*) *or* use (*s.th.*) for the first time.

êtres [ɛ:tr] *m/pl.*: *les* ~ *d'une maison* the ins and outs of a house.

étrier [etri'je] *m* stirrup (*a. anat.*).

étrill|e [e'tri:j] *f* currycomb; ~*er* [etri'je] (1a) curry.

étriqué [etri'ke] (1m) make too narrow *or* tight; curtail (*a speech*).

étroit [e'trwa] narrow (*a. mind*); tight; close (*relations*); limited; strict (*sense*); *à l'*~ cramped for room; (*live*) economically; ~*esse* [etrwa'tɛs] *f* narrowness; tightness.

étud|e [e'tyd] *f* study (*a.* ♪); office; prep room; research; ~ *du marché* marketing research; *à l'*~ under consideration; *thea.* under rehearsal; *faire ses* ~*s* study; ~*iant, m, e f* [ety'djɑ̃, ~'djɑ̃:t] student; ~*ier* [~'dje] (1o) study; examine, go into, investigate; design, device.

étui [e'tɥi] *m* case, cover; *hat*: box.

eu, e [y] *p.p.* of *avoir 1*.

eucharistie *eccl.* [økaris'ti] *f* Eucharist; Lord's Supper.

eunuque [ø'nyk] *m* eunuch.

euphémi|que [øfe'mik] euphemistic; ~*sme* [~'mism] *m* euphemism.

euphori|e [øfɔ'ri] *f* euphoria; ~*ser* [~ri'ze] (1a) put into a euphoric mood.

européen [ørɔpe'ɛ̃] *adj., su.* European.

eus [y] *1st p. sg. p.s.* of *avoir 1*.

euthanasie [øtana'zi] *f* euthanasia.

eux [ø] *pron./pers. m/pl. subject*: they; *object*: them; *à* ~ to them; theirs; *ce sont* ~ it is they, F it's them; ~-*mêmes* [~'mɛm] *pron./rfl.* themselves.

évacu|ation [evakɥa'sjɔ̃] *f* evacuation; draining, emptying; ~*er* [~'kɥe] (1n) evacuate; drain, empty; clear.

évad|é [eva'de] fugitive; ~*er* [~] (1a): *s'*~ escape, run away.

évalu|ation [evalɥa'sjɔ̃] *f* valuation; estimate; assessment; ~*er* [~'lɥe] (1n) value; estimate; assess.

évangélique [evɑ̃ʒe'lik] evangelical; **Évangile** [~'ʒil] *m* Gospel.

évanoui|r [eva'nwi:r] (2a): *s'*~ ♣ faint; *fig.* vanish; fade; ~*ssement* [~nwis'mɑ̃] *m* ♣ faint; *fig.* disappearance; *radio*: fading.

évapor|ation [evapɔra'sjɔ̃] *f* evaporation; ~*é* [~'re] flighty (person); ~*er* [~'re] (1a): *s'*~ evaporate.

évas|er [eva'ze] (1a) widen (*the opening of*); flare (*a skirt*); Δ splay; ~*if* [~'zif] evasive; ~*ion* [~'zjɔ̃] *f* escape; evasion; distraction; ✝ ~ *des capitaux* exodus of capital.

évêché [eve'ʃe] *m* bishopric, see; diocese; bishop's palace.

éveil [e'vɛ:j] *m* awakening; alertness; *en* ~ on the alert; ~*lé* [eve'je] awake; alert; ~*ler* [~] (1a) awaken; *fig.* arouse; *s'*~ wake up.

événement [evɛn'mɑ̃] *m* event.

évent [e'vɑ̃] *m* open air; vent(-hole); *whale*: spout; staleness, flatness.

éventail [evɑ̃'ta:j] *m* fan; *fig. salaries*: range; *en* ~ fan-wise.

éventaire [evɑ̃'tɛ:r] *m* street stall.

éventé [evɑ̃'te] stale; ~*er* [~] (1a) air; fan; *fig.* get wind of, discover; *fig.* divulge; *s'*~ go stale.

éventrer [evɑ̃'tre] (1a) disembowel; *fig.* rip open; gut (*a fish*).

éventu|alité [evɑ̃tɥali'te] *f* possibility; ~*el* [~'tɥɛl] possible.

évêque [e'vɛ:k] *m* bishop.

évertuer [ever'tɥe] (1n): *s'*~ do one's utmost (to *inf.*, *à inf.*).

évid|emment [evida'mɑ̃] of course, certainly; obviously; ~*ence* [~'dɑ̃:s] *f* obviousness, evidence; obvious fact; *à l'*~, *de toute* ~ (quite) obviously; *en* ~ in a prominent *or* conspicuous position; **~ent** [~'dɑ̃] obvious, evident.

évider [evi'de] (1a) hollow out; groove; pink (*leather*); cut away.

évier [e'vje] *m* scullery: sink.

évincer [evɛ̃'se] (1k) evict; oust.

évit|able [evi'tabl] avoidable; **~ement** [evit'mɑ̃] *m* avoidance; *route* *f* *d'*~ by-pass (road); **~er** [evi'te] (1a) *v/t.* avoid; *fig.* spare (*trouble*); *v/i.*: ~ *de* (*inf.*) avoid (*ger.*).

évocat|eur [evɔka'tœːr] evocative (of, *de*); **~ion** [~'sjɔ̃] *f* evocation (🕸 *a.* spirits, *a.* past); conjuring up.

évolu|er [evɔ'lɥe] (1n) develop, evolve; ✗ manœuvre; move; **~tion** [~ly'sjɔ̃] *f* ✗ manœuvre; evolution; *fig.* development.

évoquer [evɔ'ke] (1m) evoke (*a.* 🕸), bring to mind; conjure up.

ex... [ɛks] former; ex-...; late.

exact [ɛg'zakt] exact; punctual.

exaction [ɛgzak'sjɔ̃] *f* exaction.

exactitude [ɛgzakti'tyd] *f* exactness; accuracy; *time:* punctuality.

exagér|ation [ɛgzaʒera'sjɔ̃] *f* exaggeration; **~er** [~ʒe're] (1f) *vt/i.* exaggerate; *v/i. a.* go too far.

exalt|ation [ɛgzalta'sjɔ̃] *f* extolling; exaltation; (over-)excitement; **~é** [~'te] **1.** *adj.* overstrung; **2.** *su.* fanatic; **~er** [~'te] (1a) exalt, praise; excite; *s'*~ enthuse.

exam|en [ɛgza'mɛ̃] *m* examination; ⚙ test; ⚙ overhaul; survey; investigation; *à l'*~ under consideration; ~ *d'entrée* entrance examination; **~inateur** *m*, **-trice** *f* [~mina'tœːr, ~'tris] examiner; **~iner** [~mi'ne] (1a) examine; scrutinize; investigate; ⚙ overhaul; *fig.* scan.

exaspér|ation [ɛgzaspera'sjɔ̃] *f* aggravation; *fig.* exasperation; **~er** [~'re] (1f) exasperate; aggravate.

exaucer [ɛgzo'se] (1k) grant, fulfill (*a* wish); hear (*a prayer*).

excavateur *m*, **-trice** *f* ⚙ [ɛkskava'tœːr, ~'tris] excavator, grub.

excéd|ant [ɛkse'dɑ̃] excess (*luggage*); **~ent** [~'dɑ̃] *m* surplus; ~ *de poids* excess weight; **~er** [~'de] (1f) exceed; *fig.* exasperate, irritate.

excell|ence [ɛksɛ'lɑ̃ːs] *f* excellence; ♀ Excellency; *par* ~ particularly, above all; **~ent** [~'lɑ̃] excellent, delicious; **~er** [~'le] (1a) excel (in, *en*; in *ger.*, *à* *inf.*).

excentrique [ɛksɑ̃'trik] **1.** *adj.* eccentric; outlying, remote; **2.** *su.* eccentric.

except|é [ɛksɛp'te] *prp.* except(ing), save; **~er** [~'te] (1a) except, exclude (from, *de*); **~ion** [~'sjɔ̃] *f* exception (*a.* 🕸); ~ *faite de, à l'*~ *de* with the exception of; *pol.* *état* *m* *d'*~ state of emergency; *sauf* ~ with certain exceptions; **~ionnel** [~sjɔ'nɛl] exceptional.

excès [ɛk'sɛ] *m* excess; exceeding; *à l'*~, *avec* ~ excessively, to excess; **excessif** [~sɛ'sif] excessive; unreasonable.

exciser ⚕ [ɛksi'ze] (1a) excise.

excit|able [ɛksi'tabl] excitable; **~ant** [~'tɑ̃] **1.** *su./m* stimulant; **2.** *adj.* exciting; **~er** [~'te] (1a) excite; cause; *s'*~ get excited; get worked up.

exclam|ation [ɛksklama'sjɔ̃] *f* exclamation; *point* *m* *d'*~ exclamation mark; **~er** [~'me] (1a) *s'*~ exclaim; protest; make an outcry.

exclu|re [ɛks'klyːr] (4g) exclude (from, *de*); **~sif** [ɛkskly'zif] exclusive; sole (*agent, right*); **~sion** [~'zjɔ̃] *f* exclusion; *pupil:* expulsion; *à l'*~ *de* excluding; **~sivité** [~zivi'te] *f* exclusiveness; sole right (in, *de*).

excommunier *eccl.* [ɛkskɔmy'nje] (1o) excommunicate.

excré|ment [ɛkskre'mɑ̃] *m* excrement; **~ter** [~'te] (1f) excrete.

excroissance [ɛkskrwa'sɑ̃ːs] *f* excrescence.

excursion [ɛkskyr'sjɔ̃] *f* excursion, trip; hike; **~niste** [~sjɔ'nist] *su.* tripper; hiker.

excus|e [ɛks'kyːz] *f* excuse; **~s** *pl.* apology *sg.*; **~er** [~ky'ze] (1a) excuse; *s'*~ apologize (for, *de*).

exécr|able [ɛgze'krabl] abominable; disgraceful; **~ation** [~kra'sjɔ̃] *f* execration; **~er** [~'kre] (1f) detest.

exécut|er [ɛgzeky'te] (1a) execute (*a.* ♱, *a.* 🕸 *a murderer, etc.*); perform (*a.* ♪); carry out; *s'*~ comply; *fig.* pay up; **~eur, -trice** [~'tœːr, ~'tris] *su.*: 🕸 ~ *testamentaire* executor; su./m executioner; **~if** [~'tif] *adj., su./m* executive; **~ion** [~'sjɔ̃] *f* execution (*a.* ♱, *a.* 🕸 *of a murderer*); performance (*a.* ♪).

exempl|aire [ɛgzɑ̃'plɛːr] **1.** *adj.* exemplary; **2.** *su./m* sample; *book:* copy; *en double* ~ in duplicate; **~e** [~'zɑ̃ːpl] *m* example; *par* ~ for instance; *par* ~! well I never!

exempt [ɛg'zɑ̃] exempt (from, *de*); free; immune; ~ **d'impôts** tax-free; ~**er** [ɛgzɑ̃'te] (1a) exempt; ~**ion** [~'sjɔ̃] *f* exemption.

exerc|er [ɛgzɛr'se] (1k) exercise; ✗ *etc.* train, drill; exert (*one's influence*); practise (*a trade*); **s'~** practise (s.th., *à qch.*); *fig.* make itself felt, work, operate; ~**ice** [~'sis] *m* exercise; ✗ drill, training; *power*: use; practice; ✝ ~ **fiscal** financial year; (*year's*) trading.

exhal|aison [ɛgzalɛ'zɔ̃] *f* exhalation; ~**s** *pl.* fumes; ~**ation** [~la'sjɔ̃] *f* exhaling; ~**er** [~'le](1a) exhale; breathe out, emit; *fig.* express, utter, give vent to.

exhausser [ɛgzo'se] (1a) raise (by, *de*), heighten.

exhib|er [ɛgzi'be] (1a) 🏛 produce; show; display; *pej.* show off; ~**ition** [~bi'sjɔ̃] *f* exhibition; show(ing).

exhorter [ɛgzɔr'te] (1a) exhort.

exhumer [ɛgzy'me] (1a) exhume; *fig.* unearth, bring to light.

exig|eant [ɛgzi'ʒɑ̃] exacting; ~**ence** [~'ʒɑ̃:s] *f* demand, requirement; exactingness; ✝ ~**s** *pl.* conditions; ~**er** [~'ʒe] (1l) demand, require; ~**ible** [~'ʒibl] due (*payment*).

exigu, -guë [ɛgzi'gy] exiguous; scanty; slender (*means*); ~**ité** [~gɥi'te] *f* tininess; slenderness.

exil [ɛg'zil] *m* exile; ~**é** *m*, **e** *f* [ɛgzi'le] exile; ~**er** [~] (1a) exile.

exist|ence [ɛgzis'tɑ̃:s] *f* existence; life; ~**er** [~'te] (1a) exist, be; be extant.

exode [ɛg'zɔd] *m* exodus (*a. fig.*); ~ **rural** *sociology:* urban drift.

exonérer [ɛgzɔne're] (1f) exempt; free; exonerate.

exorbitant [ɛgzɔrbi'tɑ̃] exorbitant.

exorciser *eccl.* [ɛgzɔrsi'ze] (1a) exorcize; lay (*a ghost*).

exotique [ɛgzɔ'tik] exotic.

expansi|bilité [ɛkspɑ̃sibili'te] *f* expansibility; *fig.* expansiveness; ~**f** [~'sif] expansive; *fig.* effusive; ~**on** [~'sjɔ̃] *f* expansion; *fig.* expansiveness; *culture:* spread.

expatrier [ɛkspatri'e] (1a) expatriate; exile, banish.

expecta|nt [ɛkspɛk'tɑ̃] expectant; ~**tive** [~ta'ti:v] *f* expectancy.

expédient [ɛkspe'djɑ̃] 1. *adj.* expedient (to, *de*); 2. *su./m* expedient, shift.

expédi|er [ɛkspe'dje] (1o) dispatch; send; hurry through; forward (*mail etc.*); ~**teur** *m*, -**trice** *f* [ɛkspedi'tœ:r, ~'tris] sender; ✝ shipper; forwarding agent; ~**tif** [~'tif] prompt; ~**tion** [~'sjɔ̃] *f* expedition; dispatch; ✝ shipping.

expérience [ɛkspe'rjɑ̃:s] *f* experience; 🏛 *etc.* experiment, test; *par* ~ from experience.

expériment|é [ɛksperimɑ̃'te] experienced; skilled; ~**er** [~] (1a) *v/t.* test; *v/i.* experiment (on, *sur*).

expert [ɛks'pɛ:r] 1. *adj.* expert, skilled (in *en, dans*); able; 2. *su./m* expert (in, at *en*) (*a.* 🏛); ✝ valuer; ~**ise** [ɛkspɛr'ti:z] *f* expert appraisal *or* opinion.

expi|able [ɛks'pjabl] expiable; ~**ation** [~pja'sjɔ̃] *f* expiation; *eccl.* atonement (for, *de*); ~**atoire** [~pja'twa:r] expiatory; ~**er** [~'pje] (1o) expiate, atone for.

expir|ation [ɛkspira'sjɔ̃] *f* expiration, breathing out; termination, expiry; ~**er** [~'re](1a) *v/t.* breathe out; *v/i.* expire (*a.* 🏛), die.

explica|ble [ɛkspli'kabl] explicable; ~**tif** [~ka'tif] explanatory; ~**tion** [~ka'sjɔ̃] *f* explanation.

explicite [ɛkspli'sit] explicit; plain.

expliquer [ɛkspli'ke] (1m) explain; comment upon (*a text*); account for; **s'~** be understandable; **s'~ avec** have it out with.

exploit [ɛks'plwa] *m* exploit, feat; 🏛 writ; ~**able** [ɛksplwa'tabl] workable; exploitable; ~**ation** [~ta'sjɔ̃] *f* exploitation (*a. fig.*); ✝ *etc.* running, working, operating; ~**er** [~'te] (1a) exploit (*a. fig.*); ✝ *etc.* run, work, operate; *fig.* take advantage of.

explor|ateur [ɛksplɔra'tœ:r] 1. *adj.* exploratory; 2. *su.* explorer; ~**ation** [~ra'sjɔ̃] *f* exploration; ~**er** [~re] (1a) explore.

explos|er [ɛksplo'ze] (1a) explode; *faire* ~ blow up; ~**ible** [~'zibl] explosive; ~**if** [~'zif] *adj.*, *su./m* explosive; ~**ion** [~'zjɔ̃] *f* explosion; bursting; ~ **démographique** population explosion; ⊙ *à* ~ internal combustion (*engine*).

exportation ✝ [ɛkspɔrta'sjɔ̃] *f* export(ation); ~**s** *pl.* exports.

expos|ant, e [ɛkspo'zɑ̃, ~'zɑ̃:t] *su.* exhibitor; *su./m* A exponent; ~**é** [~'ze] *m* report; outline; account; talk; ~**er**

129 **exulter**

[~'ze] (1a) display, show; exhibit; expose (*a. phot.*), jeopardize; explain, expound, put forward (*plans, facts, ideas, etc.*); **~ition** [~zi'sjɔ̃] *f* display(ing); exhibition; exposition; exposure (*to danger; of a baby*); statement.

exprès, expresse [ɛks'prɛ, ~'prɛs] 1. *adj.* explicit; 2. **exprès** *adv.* on purpose; 3. *su./m* express messenger; *lettre f* **exprès** express letter.

express 🚂 [ɛks'prɛs] *m* express.

expressément [ɛksprɛse'mɑ̃] expressly.

expressi|f [ɛksprɛ'sif] expressive; **~on** [~'sjɔ̃] *f* expression.

exprimer [ɛkspri'me] (1a) express; put into words, voice.

expropri|ation [ɛksprɔpria'sjɔ̃] *f* expropriation; **~er** [~'e] (1a) expropriate.

expulser [ɛkspyl'se] (1a) expel (*a. an electron, a pupil*); eject (*s.o.*).

expurger [ɛkspyr'ʒe] (1l) expurgate, bowdlerize (*a book*).

exquis [ɛks'ki] exquisite; **~ément** [~kize'mɑ̃] *adv.* of **exquis**.

exsangue [ɛk'sɑ̃:g] bloodless.

extas|e [ɛks'tɑ:z] *f* ecstasy; **~ié** [~ta'zje] enraptured; **~ier** [~ta'zje] (1o): *s'*~ go into raptures (*over devant, sur*).

extens|eur [ɛkstɑ̃'sœːr] *m muscle:* extensor; *sp.* chest-expander; *trousers:* stretcher; ✈ shock-absorber; **~ible** [~'sibl] extensible; **~ion** [~'sjɔ̃] *f* extent; extension (*a.* ♥); stretching; ⊕ tension; *gramm. par* ~ in a wider sense.

exténuer [ɛkste'nɥe] (1n) exhaust, tire; † extenuate.

extérieur [ɛkste'rjœːr] 1. *adj.* exterior, external, outer; *affaires f/pl.* ~es foreign affairs; 2. *su./m* exterior (*a. cin.*); outside; *fig.* appearance.

extermin|ateur [ɛkstɛrmina'tœːr] 1. *adj.* exterminating; 2. *su.* exterminator; **~er** [~'ne] (1a) exterminate, destroy, wipe out.

extern|at [ɛkstɛr'na] *m* day-school; **~e**

[~'tɛrn] 1. *adj.* outer, 🌡 out(*patient*); 🌡 *usage m* ~ external application; 2. *su.* day-pupil.

extinct|eur [ɛkstɛ̃k'tœːr] 1. *adj.* extinguishing; 2. *su./m* fire-extinguisher; **~ion** [~'sjɔ̃] *f* extinction; extinguishing; suppression; termination; *race:* dying out; *voice:* loss.

extirper [ɛkstir'pe] (1a) eradicate (*a. fig.*), extirpate, root out.

extorquer [ɛkstɔr'ke] (1m) extort (from, out of **à**); **extorsion** [~tɔr'sjɔ̃] *f* extortion; blackmail.

extra [ɛks'tra] 1. *su./m/inv.* extra; hired waiter; temporary job; 2. *adj./inv.* extra-special; 3. *adv.* extra-...

extraction [ɛkstrak'sjɔ̃] *f* extraction, *gold:* winning; *fig.* origin, descent.

extrad|er [ɛkstra'de] (1a) extradite; **~ition** [~di'sjɔ̃] *f* extradition.

extrai|re [ɛks'trɛːr] (4ff) extract; pull (*a tooth*); quarry (*stone*); win (*gold*); copy out (*a passage*); **~t** [~'trɛ] *m* extract; excerpt.

extraordinaire [ɛkstraɔrdi'nɛːr] 1. *adj.* extraordinary; uncommon; 2. *su./m* extraordinary thing.

extravag|ance [ɛkstrava'gɑ̃:s] *f* absurdity; *fig.* ~s *pl.* nonsense *sg.*; **~ant** [~'gɑ̃] absurd; exorbitant (*price*); **~uer** [~'ge] (1m) rave; talk nonsense.

extrême [ɛks'trɛːm] 1. *adj.* extreme; furthest; drastic (*measures*); intense; 2. *su./m* extreme; *pousser à l'*~ carry to extremes; **~-onction** *eccl.* [ɛkstremɔ̃k'sjɔ̃] *f* extreme unction; **2-Orient** [~mɔ'rjɑ̃] *m* the Far East.

extrémi|ste [ɛkstre'mist] *su.* extremist; **~té** [~mi'te] *f* extremity; very end, tip; extreme; plight, straits *pl.*; point of death.

extrinsèque [ɛkstrɛ̃'sɛk] extrinsic.

exubéran|ce [ɛgzybe'rɑ̃:s] *f* exuberance; **~t** [~'rɑ̃] immoderate.

exult|ation [ɛgzylta'sjɔ̃] *f* exultation; **~er** [~'te] (1a) exult, rejoice.

F

fa ♪ [fa] *m/inv.* F; **~ dièse** F sharp.

fabl|e [faːbl] *f* fable; story; *fig.* talk *or* laughing stock (*of the town*).

fabri|cant [fabriˈkɑ̃] *m* manufacturer; maker; **~cation** [~kaˈsjɔ̃] *f* manufacture; *document:* forging; *fig.* fabrication; **~ en série** mass production; **~que** [faˈbrik] *f* manufacture; factory; *paper:* mill; make; church council; **~quer** [~briˈke] (1m) ⊕ manufacture; *fig.* make, do; *fig.* fabricate (*lies, a document*).

fabul|er [fabyˈle] (1a) fantasize; make up stories; **~eux** [~ˈlø] fabulous.

façade [faˈsad] *f* façade; front(age).

face [fas] *f* face; countenance; aspect; front; ♪ *record:* side; surface; **de ~** full-face (*photo*); **d'en~** opposite; **en ~ de** in front of; in the presence of; opposite; **~ à** facing; **faire ~ à** face; *fig.* meet; cope with; deal with; **pile ou ~** heads *or* tails.

facéti|e [faseˈsi] *f* facetious remark; prank; **~eux** [~ˈsjø] facetious.

facette [faˈsɛt] *f* facet (*a. zo.*).

fâch|é [faˈʃe] sorry; angry, cross (about **de**; with s.o. **avec q.**); annoyed; **~er** [~] (1a) make angry; offend; grieve; **se ~** get angry (with, **contre**); over, **pour**); fall out (with, **avec**); **~eux** [faˈʃø] annoying; regrettable; awkward (*situation*).

facial [faˈsjal] facial, face-...

facil|e [faˈsil] easy; simple; facile; *fig.* pliable; fluent (*tongue*); **~ité** [fasiliˈte] *f* easiness; ease; readiness; aptitude; complaisance; ♰ **~s** *pl.* **de paiement** easy terms; **~iter** [~] (1a) facilitate (for s.o., **à q.**).

façon [faˈsɔ̃] *f* make; fashioning; way, manner; **~s** *pl.* manners, behavio(u)r *sg.*; ceremony *pl.*, fuss *sg.*; affectation *sg.*; **à la ~ de** like; **de ~ à** so as to; **de ~ que** so that; **de la bonne ~** properly; **de ma ~** of my own composition; **de toute ~** in any case; **en quelque ~** in a way; **sans ~(s)** simple; simply; without further ado.

faconde [faˈkɔ̃d] *f* loquaciousness.

façonn|er [fasoˈne] (1a) shape; fashion; make; **~ier** [~ˈnje] fussy, ceremonious.

facteur [fakˈtœːr] *m* postman, *Am.* mailman; (*instrument*) maker; ⅍, *fig.* factor.

factice [fakˈtis] artificial, factitious.

facti|eux [fakˈsjø] **1.** *adj.* factious, seditious; **2.** *su.* sedition-monger; **~on** [~ˈsjɔ̃] *f* ⚔ guard; *fig.* faction.

factotum [faktoˈtɔm] *m* handyman.

factuel [faktyˈɛl] factual, objective.

factur|e [fakˈtyːr] *f* make (*of an article*); ♰ invoice; ♪ manufacturing; **~er** ♰ [~tyˈre] (1a) invoice.

facult|atif [fakyltaˈtif] optional; **arrêt** *m* **~** request stop; **~é** [~ˈte] *f* faculty (*a. univ, a. fig*); ability; power(s *pl.*); option.

fada F [faˈda] *m* fool; **fadaise** [faˈdɛːz] *f* nonsense; silliness.

fade [fad] flat, tasteless; washed-out (*colour*); **fadeur** [faˈdœːr] *f* insipidity; *fig.* pointlessness.

fagot [faˈɡo] *m* bundle of sticks; *fig.* **sentir le~** smack of heresy; **~er** [~ˈte] F (1a) dress up, get up.

faibl|e [fɛbl] **1.** *adj.* weak; feeble; faint; slight; gentle (*slope*); low, poor (*performance, yields, etc.*); lame (*excuse*); slender (*means*); **2.** *su./m* weakness, foible; *person:* weakling; **les économiquement ~s** *pl.* the under-privileged; **~esse** [fɛˈblɛs] *f* weakness, feebleness; frailty; ⚓ weakness, dizzy spell; *fig.* weak point; *number:* smallness; **~ir** [~ˈbliːr] (2a) weaken; ⊕ lose power.

faïenc|e [faˈjɑ̃ːs] *f*, **~erie** [~jɑ̃sˈri] *f* earthenware.

faille [faj] *3rd p. sg. pres. sbj. of* **falloir**.

faill|i *m, e* ♰ [faˈji] bankrupt; **~ible** [~ˈjibl] fallible; **~ir** [~ˈjiːr] (2n): **~ faire qch.** almost *or* nearly do s.th.; **j'ai failli tomber** I nearly fell; **~ à un devoir** fail in a duty; **~ite** [~ˈjit] *f* bankruptcy; **faire ~** go bankrupt; *fig.* collapse.

faim [fɛ̃] *f* hunger; **avoir (très) ~** be (very) hungry.

fainéant [fɛneˈɑ̃] **1.** *adj.* idle, lazy; **2.** *su.* idler; sluggard; **~er** [~ɑ̃ˈte] (1a) idle, loaf; **~ise** [~ɑ̃ˈtiːz] *f* idleness, laziness.

faire [fɛːr] (4r) **1.** *v/t.* make; do; perform; pack (*a trunk*); cover (*a distance*); work (*miracles*); play (*a.* ♪); feign; matter; ♯ run (*a temperature*); *thea.* act (*a part*); *followed by an inf.*: make, cause, have; **~ attention** pay attention; take care; **~ de la peinture** paint; **~ de q. son héritier** make s.o. one's heir; **~ du bien à** do (*s.o.*) good; *mot.* **~ 150 kilomètres** *or* **du 150 à l'heure** do 150 kilometres per hour; **~ du sport** go in for sports; **~ entrer** show (*s.o.*) in; **~ faire** have (*s.th.*) done *or* made (by s.o., **à q.**); **~ fortune** make a fortune; **† ~ le commerce de** deal in; **~ venir** send for; **en ~ trop** overdo; **ne ~ que** (*inf.*) do nothing but (*inf.*); **trois et six font neuf** three and six are *or* make nine; **se ~** be done, become, happen; **se ~ à** get used to; **ça ne fait rien!** it doesn't matter!; never mind!; **ça ne me fait rien** I don't care; **comment se fait-il que?** how is it that?; **il peut se ~ que** it may happen that; **ne vous en faites pas!** don't worry!; **se ~ entendre** make o.s. heard; be heard; **2.** *v/i.* do, act; manage; make (with, **de**); last; say, remark; *plus adjective*: look; **~ bien de** (*inf.*) do well *or* right to (*inf.*); **~ bien sur dress**: look well on (*s.o.*); **~ de son mieux** do one's best (to *inf.*, **pour** *inf.*); *time*: **ça fait ... que** it's ... since; **elle fait très jeune** she looks quite young; **fit-il** he said, said he; **je ne peux ~ autrement que de** (*inf.*) I cannot but (*inf.*); **laisser ~ q.** let s.o. alone; **qu'y ~?** what can be done about it?; **3.** *v/impers.* be; **il fait chaud (beau, nuit)** it is hot (fine, dark); **~-part** [fɛrˈpaːr] *m/inv.* notice, announcement.

faisable [fəˈzabl] feasible.

faisan [fəˈzɑ̃] *m* pheasant.

faisceau [fɛˈso] *m* bundle; stack; *rays*: pencil, beam; **~x** *pl.* fasces.

faiseur *m*, **-euse** *f* [fəˈzœːr, ~ˈzøːz] maker, doer; *fig.* bluffer; **faisons** [fəˈzɔ̃] *1st p. pl. pres. of* **faire**; **fait** [fɛ] **1.** *p.p. of* **faire**; **c'en est ~ de** it's all up with; **2.** *su./m* fact; deed; act; achievement; happening; case; matter, point; **au ~** by the way; after all; **au ~ de** informed about, familiar with; **de** (*or* **en**) **~** as a matter of fact; actually; **~s** *pl.* **divers** news in brief; **du ~ de** on account of; **en ~ de** as regards; in the way of; **en venir au ~** come to the point.

faît|age △ [fɛˈtaːʒ] *m* roof-tree; **~e** [fɛːt] *m* top; △ ridge; crest.

faites [fɛt] *2nd p. pl. pres. of* **faire**.

falaise [faˈlɛːz] *f* cliff.

fallacieux [falaˈsjø] fallacious.

fall|oir [faˈlwaːr] (3e) be necessary, be lacking; **il faut que je** (*sbj.*) I must (*inf.*); **il me faut** (*inf.*) I must (*inf.*); **il me faut qch.** I want s.th.; I need s.th.; **comme il faut** proper(ly *adv.*); **peu s'en faut** very nearly; **tant s'en faut** not by a long way; **~u** [~ˈly] *p.p. of* **falloir**; **~ut** [~ˈly] *3rd p. sg. p.s. of* **falloir**.

falot¹ [faˈlo] *m* lantern; lamp.

falot² [faˈlo] wan; dull, colo(u)rless.

falsifi|cateur *m*, **-trice** *f* [falsifikaˈtœːr, ~ˈtris] forger (*of papers*); adulterator; **~cation** [~ˈsjɔ̃] *f* forgery; adulteration; **~er** [falsiˈfje] (1a) falsify; forge; adulterate.

famé [faˈme] *adj.*: **bien** (**mal**) **~** of good (evil) repute.

famélique [fameˈlik] **1.** *adj.* starving, famished; **2.** *su.* starveling.

fameux [faˈmø] famous; excellent.

famil|ial [famiˈljal] family...; domestic; **~iariser** [familjariˈze] (1a) familiarize; **se ~ avec** grow familiar with; **~iarité** [~ˈte] *f* familiarity; *fig.* **~s** *pl.* liberties; **~ier** [famiˈlje] **1.** *adj.* family..., domestic; familiar; **2.** *su.* inimate; **~le** [~ˈmiːj] *f* family.

famine [faˈmin] *f* famine.

fanal [faˈnal] *m* lantern; lamp.

fana F [faˈna] enthusiast(ic); **~tique** [fanaˈtik] fanatic; **~tisme** [~ˈtism] *m* fanaticism.

fan|e [fan] *f* haulm; *carrots*: top; dead leaves *pl.*; **~er** [faˈne] (1a) toss (*the hay*); *fig.* fade; **se ~** wither; fade.

fanfar|e [fɑ̃ˈfaːr] *f* trumpets: flourish; fanfare; brass band; **~on** [fɑ̃faˈrɔ̃] **1.** *adj.* bragging; **2.** *su.* braggart, boaster; **faire le ~** brag; **~onnade** [~rɔˈnad] *f* boasting.

fanfreluche [fɑ̃frəˈlyʃ] *f* bauble.

fang|e [fɑ̃ːʒ] *f* mud; filth, Γ muck; **~eux** [fɑ̃ˈʒø] muddy; dirty, filthy.

fantaisi|e [fɑ̃teˈzi] *f* imagination; fancy (*a. fig.*); *fig.* whim; ♪ fantasia; **de ~** imaginary; **† fancy-...**; **~ste** [~ˈzist] **1.** *adj.* fantastic, freakish; **2.** *su.* fanciful person.

fantasmagorie [fɑ̃tasmagɔˈri] *f* phantasmagoria; weird spectacle.

fantasque [fɑ̃'task] odd; whimsical.

fantassin [fɑ̃ta'sɛ̃] *m* infantryman.

fantastique [fɑ̃tas'tik] fantastic; weird; *fig.* incredible.

fantoche [fɑ̃'tɔʃ] *m* puppet (*a. fig.*).

fantôme [fɑ̃'to:m] *m* phantom, ghost, spectre; illusion.

faon [fɑ̃] *m* fawn; roe calf.

faquin [fa'kɛ̃] *m* scoundrel; rascal.

faraud F [fa'ro] *su.*: *faire le ~* show off, brag, boast.

farce [fars] *f* joke; trick; *thea.*, *fig.* farce; *cuis.* stuffing; **~eur** *m*, **-euse** *f* [far'sœːr, ~'søːz] joker; **~ir** *cuis.*, *fig.* [far'siːr] (2a) stuff.

fard [faːr] *m* make-up; rouge; *fig.* artifice; *parler sans ~* speak plainly or candidly; *sl.* *piquer un ~* blush.

fardeau [far'do] *m* burden, load.

farder [far'de] (1a) make (*s.o.*) up; paint; *fig.* disguise; *se ~* make up.

farfelu F [farfə'ly] eccentric.

farfouiller [farfu'je] (1a) *v/i.* rummage (in, among *dans*); *v/t.* explore.

faribole [fari'bɔl] *f* nonsense.

farin|e [fa'rin] *f* flour, meal; *fig.* type; **~er** *cuis.* [fari'ne] (1a) flour.

farouche [fa'ruʃ] wild; fierce; shy, timid; unapproachable.

fart [faːr] *m* ski wax; **~er** [far'te] (1a) wax (*one's skis*).

fascicule [fasi'kyl] *m* part, section.

fascinat|eur [fasina'tœːr] fascinating; **~ion** [~'sjɔ̃] *f* fascination.

fasciner [fasi'ne] (1a) fascinate; *fig.* entrance; bewitch.

fascisme *pol.* [fa'ʃism] *m* fascism; **fasciste** [~'ʃist] *adj.*, *su.* fascist.

fasse [fas] *1st p. sg. pres. sbj.* of *faire.*

faste [fast] *m* pomp, display.

fastidieux [fasti'djø] dull; irksome.

fastueux [fas'tɥø] showy; sumptuous.

fat [fat] **1.** *adj./m* foppish; conceited; **2.** *su./m* conceited idiot.

fatal, e [fa'tal] *m/pl.* **-als** fatal; *fig.* inevitable; *femme f ~e* vamp; **~iste** [fata'list] **1.** *adj.* fatalistic; **2.** *su.* fatalist; **~ité** [~li'te] *f* fatality.

fatigu|e [fa'tig] *f* fatigue (*a.* ⊗); tiredness, weariness; overwork; *tomber de ~* be worn out; **~é** [fati'ge] tired, weary; **~er** [~] (1m) *v/t.* tire, make (*s.o.*) tired; overwork; ⊗ *etc.* strain; *fig.* bore (*s.o.*);

v/i. ⊗ labo(u)r, strain (*engine*); *se ~* get tired; tire o.s.

fatras [fa'trɑ] *m* jumble; lumber.

fatuité [fatɥi'te] *f* conceit.

faubour|g [fo'buːr] *m* suburb; outskirts *pl.*; *fig.* **~s** *pl.* working classes; **~ien** [~bu'rjɛ̃] **1.** *adj.* suburban; *fig.* common; **2.** *su.* suburbanite.

fauch|age [fo'ʃaːʒ] *m*, **~aison** [~ʃɛ'zɔ̃] *f* mowing (time); **~é, e** [fo'ʃe] **1.** *adj.* F broke; **2.** *su./f* swath; **~er** [~'ʃe] (1a) mow (down) (*a. fig.*); cut; reap (*corn*); *sl.* steal; **~eur, -euse** [~'ʃœːr, ~'ʃøːz] *su. person:* reaper; *su./f machine:* reaper; **~eux** *zo.* [~'ʃø] *m* harvest spider, *Am.* daddy-longlegs.

faucille [fo'siːj] *f* sickle.

faucon *orn.* [fo'kɔ̃] *m* falcon, hawk.

faudra [fo'dra] *3rd p. sg. fut.* of *falloir.*

faufiler [fofi'le] (1a) tack, baste; *se ~* thread *or* worm one's way (into, *dans*).

faune [foːn] *su./m myth.* faun; *su./f zo.* fauna.

fauss|aire [fo'sɛːr] *m* forger, falsifier; **~er** [~'se] (1a) falsify; distort (*facts, ideas, words*); ⊗ force (*a lock etc.*); ⊗ buckle, bend, warp, strain; *fig.* **~ compagnie à q.** give s.o. the slip.

fausset ♪ [fo'sɛ] *m* falsetto.

fausseté [fos'te] *f* falseness, falsity; falsehood; *fig.* treachery, duplicity.

faut [fo] *3rd p. sg. pres.* of *falloir.*

faut|e [foːt] *f* fault; error; mistake; *foot. etc.* foul; **~ de** for want of; *faire ~* be lacking; *sans ~* without fail.

fauteuil [fo'tœːj] *m* arm-chair; easy chair; *meeting:* chair; *thea.* stall; **~ à bascule** see *rocking-chair*; 𝆑𝆑 **~ électrique** electric chair; **~ roulant** wheel chair; Bath chair.

fauteur *m*, **-trice** *f* [fo'tœːr, ~'tris] instigator; 𝆑𝆑 abettor.

fautif [fo'tif] faulty; offending.

fauve [foːv] **1.** *adj.* tawny; musky (*smell*); lurid (*sky*); **2.** *su./m* fawn; **~s** *pl.* wild beasts; deer *pl.*; **~tte** *orn.* [fo'vɛt] *f* warbler.

faux¹ ♪ [fo] *f* scythe.

faux², fausse [fo, foːs] **1.** *adj.* false; untrue, wrong; imitation...; fraudulent; forged (*document*); ♪ out of tune; **~ col** *m* detachable collar; **~ frais** *m/pl.* incidental expenses; **~ mouvement** awkward movement; *teleph.* **~ numéro**

m wrong number; *fig.* **~ pas** *m* blunder; **fausse monnaie** *f* counterfeit coin(s *pl.*); **2. faux** *adv.* falsely; ♩ out of tune; **3.** *su./m:* **le ~** falsehood; *the untrue;* 🕳 forgery; **~fuyant** *fig.* [~fɥi'jɑ̃] *m* subterfuge; **~monnayeur** [~monɛ'jœːr] *m* counterfeiter.

fav|eur [fa'vœːr] *f* favo(u)r; **à la ~ de** thanks to; under cover of (*darkness etc*); **de ~** complimentary (*ticket*); preferential (*treatment*); **en ~** in favo(u)r (of, *de*); **~orable** [favɔ'rabl] favo(u)r-able; **~ori, -te** [~'ri, ~'rit] **1.** *adj.* favo(u)rite; **2.** *su.* favo(u)rite; **~oris** *m/pl* side whiskers; **~oriser** [~ri'ze] (1a) favo(u)r; promote.

fébrile [fe'bril] feverish, febril.

fécal [fe'kal] f(a)ecal; **matières** *f/pl.* **~es** = **fèces** [fɛs] *f/pl.* f(a)ecces; 🕳 precipitate *sg.*; 🔬 stool *sg.*

fécond [fe'kɔ̃] fertile; productive (of, *en*); prolific; **~ation** [fekɔ̃da'sjɔ̃] *f* fertilisation; **~ artificielle** artificial insemination; **~er** [fekɔ̃'de] (1a) fecundate; fertilize; **~ité** [~di'te] *f* fertility; fecundity.

fédér|al [fede'ral] *adj., su./m* federal; **~atif** [~ra'tif] federative; **~ation** [ra'sjɔ̃] *f* federation; **~é** [~'re] *adj., su./m* federate.

fée [fe] *f* fairy; **conte** *m* **de ~** fairytale; **vieille ~** old hag; **~rie** [~'ri] *f* fairyland; fairy scene; *fig.* enchantment, *thea.* fairy-play; **~rique** [~'rik] fairy; magic.

fein|dre [fɛ̃ːdr] (4m) feign, pretend (to *inf.*, **de** *inf.*); **~te** [fɛ̃ːt] *f* sham; make-believe; *sp.* feint; slight limp.

fêler [fɛ'le] (1a) (*a.* **se ~**) crack.

félicit|ation [felisita'sjɔ̃] *f* congratulation; **~é** [~'te] *f* bliss, joy; **~er** [~'te] (1a): **~ q. de** congratulate s.o. on; **se ~ (de)** congratulate o.s. (on); be glad (about)

félin [fe'lɛ̃] **1.** *adj. zo.* feline, cat-...; cat-like; **2.** *su./m zo.* feline, cat.

félon [fe'lɔ̃] **1.** *adj.* disloyal; **2.** *su./m* traitor; **~ie** [~lɔ'ni] *f* disloyalty.

fêlure [fɛ'lyːr] *f* crack; split.

femelle *zo.* [fə'mɛl] *adj., su./f* female.

fémini|n [femi'nɛ̃] **1.** *adj.* feminine; female; woman's...; womanly; **2.** *su./m gramm.* feminine; **~ser** [~ni'ze] (1a) make (look) feminine.

femme [fam] *f* woman; wife; woman ..., lady ...; **~ de chambre** housemaid; **~ de**

charge housekeeper; **~lette** F [~'lɛt] *f* little woman; weakling.

fémur [fe'myːr] *m* thigh-bone.

fenaison 🖊 [fənɛ'zɔ̃] *f* haymaking.

fend|iller [~di'je] (1a) crack(le); chap; craze (*glaze*); **~re** [fɑ̃ːdr] (4a) split, cleave; slit; crack; chop; cut through; **se ~** crack; split; F **se ~ la gueule** split one's sides; F **se ~ de** shell out (*money*), stand (*a drink*).

fenêtre [fə'nɛːtr] *f* window; **~ à bascule** balance window; **~ à coulisse** (*or* **guil-lotine**) sash-window.

fenil [fə'ni] *m* hayloft.

fente [fɑ̃ːt] *f* crack, split; slit; chink; gap; crevice; opening; ⚙ slot.

féodal [feɔ'dal] feudal.

fer [fɛːr] *m* iron; **~ à cheval** horseshoe; **~ à repasser** (flat-)iron; ⚙ **~ à souder** soldering iron; **~ de lance** spearhead (*a. fig.*); **de ~** iron; **donner un coup de ~ à** press, iron; **fil m de ~** wire.

ferai [fə're] *1st p. sg. fut.* of **faire**.

fer-blanc, *pl.* **fers-blancs** [fɛr'blɑ̃ *m* tin(-plate); **ferblanterie** [fɛrblɑ̃'tri] *f* tinware; ⚙ tin-shop; **ferblantier** [~'tje] *m* tinsmith.

férié [fe'rje] *adj./m:* **jour** *m* **~** public holiday; *eccl.* holy day.

férir † [fe'riːr] (2u) strike; **sans coup ~** without striking a blow.

ferme¹ [fɛrm] **1.** *adj.* firm; fixed; **2.** *adv.* firmly; **frapper ~** hit hard.

ferme² [~] *f* farm; farmhouse.

ferment [fɛr'mɑ̃] *m* ferment (*a. fig.*); **~ation** [~mɑ̃ta'sjɔ̃] *f* fermentation; *fig.* unrest; **~er** [~mɑ̃'te] (1a) ferment (*a. fig.*).

fermer [fɛr'me] (1a) *vt/i.* shut (up), close (up); shut *or* close down (*company etc.*); *vt/i.* turn *or* switch off; fasten; **se ~** shut (up), close (up); **~ à clef** lock; **~ au verrou** bolt; **~ à vis** screw down; *sl.* **ferme ça!**, **la ferme!** shut up!

fermeté [fɛrmə'te] *f* firmness; steadfastness.

fermeture [fɛrmə'tyːr] *f* shutting, closing; *company etc.*; shutting *or* closing down; fastening; **~ éclair** (*or* **à glissière**) zip fastener; zipper.

fermier, -ère [fɛr'mje, ~'mjɛːr] *su.* farmer; *su./f.* farmer's wife.

fermoir [fɛr'mwaːr] *m* snap; clasp.

féroc|e [fe'rɔs] ferocious (*a. fig.*); **~ité** [~rɔsi'te] *f* fierceness; ferocity.

ferr|aille [fɛˈrɑːj] f scrap iron; scrap heap; *mettre à la ~* scrap; **~ailleur** [~rɑˈjœːr] m scrap merchant; **~é** [~ˈre] fitted with iron; hobnailed, studded (*boots*); F well up (in, *en*); **~er** [~ˈre] (1a) shoe (*a horse*); **~eux** [~ˈrø] ferrous; **~onnerie** [~rɔnˈri] f ironwork; ironmongery.

ferroviaire [fɛrɔˈvjɛːr] railway-...

ferrure [fɛˈryːr] f iron-fittings pl.

ferry-boat [feriˈboːt] m train ferry.

fertil|e [fɛrˈtil] rich (in, *en*); **~iser** [fɛrtiliˈze] (1a) fertilize; **~ité** [~ˈte] f fertility; richness.

féru [feˈry]: ~ *de* obsessed by.

férule [feˈryl] f: *être sous la ~ de* be under (*s.o.'s*) (iron) rule.

ferv|ent [fɛrˈvɑ̃] **1.** *adj.* fervent, earnest, ardent; **2.** *su.* devotee, ... fan; **~eur** [~ˈvœːr] f fervo(u)r.

fess|e [fɛs] f buttock; **~ée** [fɛˈse] f spanking; **~e-mathieu** [fɛsmaˈtjø] m skinflint; **~er** [fɛˈse] (1a) spank.

festin [fɛsˈtɛ̃] m feast.

festival, pl. **-als** [fɛstiˈval] m festival; **festivité** [~viˈte] f festivity.

feston [fɛsˈtɔ̃] m festoon; *needlework:* scallop.

festoyer [fɛstwaˈje] (1h) feast.

fêt|ard m, e f F [fɛˈtaːr, ~ˈtard] reveller; **~e** [fɛːt] f feast, festival; holiday; festivity; fête; party; name day; *~ foraine* fun fair; *des Mères* Mother's day; *faire ~ à* welcome; **~e-Dieu**, pl. **~es-Dieu** *eccl.* [fɛtˈdjø] f Corpus Christi; **~er** [fɛˈte] (1a) fête (*s.o.*); celebrate.

fétiche [feˈtiʃ] m fetish; *mot.* mascot.

fétid|e [feˈtid] fetid, stinking, rank; **~ité** [~tidiˈte] f fetidness, foulness.

fétu [feˈty] m wisp of straw.

feu¹ [fø] m fire (*a. of a gun, a. fig.*); *mot. etc.* light; *~ de joie* bonfire; *~ follet* will-o'-the-wisp; **~x** pl. *de signalisation,* F *~ rouge* traffic lights pl.; *mot. ~ vert (rouge)* green (red) light (*a. fig.*); *à petit ~* on a slow fire; *fig.* by inches; *au ~!* fire!; *au coin du ~* by the fireside; *coup m de ~* shot; *donner du ~ à q.* give s.o. a light; *fig. donner le ~ vert (à q.)* give (s.o.) the green light; *fig. entrer dans le ~ pour q.* go through fire and water for s.o.; *faire ~* fire (at, *sur*); *fig. faire long ~* fail; *ne pas faire long ~* be

short-lived; *mettre le ~ à qch.* set fire to s.th.; *par le fer et le ~* by fire and sword; *prendre ~* catch fire; *fig.* flare up.

feu² [fø] *adj. (inv. before article and poss. adj.)* late, deceased; *la feue reine, feu la reine* the late queen.

feuill|age [fœˈjaːʒ] m foliage; **~e** [fœːj] f 🌞 leaf; *paper:* sheet; *admin.* form; 🎵 chart; 🛒 list; F *journ.* paper; *~ de chou* rag; *~ de paie* wage-sheet; *~ de route* ✈ way-bill; ✗ marching orders pl.; *~ volante* fly-sheet; **~e-morte** [fœjˈmɔrt] *adj./inv.* dead-leaf (*colour*); **~et** [fœˈje] m book: leaf; *admin.* form; sheet; ⊙ plate; **~etage** *cuis.* [fœjˈtaːʒ] m, **~eté** *cuis.* [~ˈte] m puff paste; **~eter** [~ˈte] (1c) skim through (*a book*); *cuis.* roll and fold; ⊙ divide into sheets; **~eton** [~ˈtɔ̃] m *journ.* serial (story); **~u** [fœˈjy] leafy.

feutr|e [føːtr] m felt (*hat*); stuffing; **~er** [føˈtre] (1a) felt; pad.

fève 🌱 [fɛːv] f bean.

février [fevriˈe] m February.

fi! [fi] *int.* fie!; for shame!; *faire ~ de* scorn, turn up one's nose at.

fiab|ilité [fjabiliˈte] f reliability; **~le** [fjabl] reliable.

fiacre [fjakr] m horse-drawn cab.

fianç|ailles [fjɑ̃ˈsɑːj] f/pl. engagement sg., betrothal sg. (to, *avec*); **fiancé** [~ˈse] m fiancé; **fiancée** [~ˈse] f fiancée; **fiancer** [~ˈse] (1k) betroth; *se ~* become engaged (to, *à*).

fibr|e [fibr] f fibre; *wood:* grain; *~ de verre* glass-wool; *avoir la ~ sensible* be impressionable; **~eux** [fiˈbrø] fibrous, stringy.

ficel|er [fisˈle] (1c) tie up; *sl.* dress (*s.o.*) badly; **~le** [fiˈsɛl] **1.** *su./f* string; *sl.* **connaitre toutes les ~s** know the ropes; **2.** *adj.* wily.

fich|e [fiʃ] f ⊙ peg; *paper:* form, voucher; sheet, slip (*of paper*); label; index card; 🔌 plug; *fig.* scrap; 🔌 *femelle* jack; *~ de paye* wages slip; **~er** [fiˈʃe] (1a) stick in, drive in; *sl.* do; *sl.* put; *sl.* give; *sl. ~ q. à la porte* throw s.o. out; *sl. fichez-moi la paix!* leave me alone!; *sl. fichez(-moi) le camp!* clear off!; *sl. se ~* make fun of; not to care (a hang) about; **~ier** [~ˈʃje] m file (*case*).

fichoir [fiˈʃwaːr] m clothes-peg.

fichu¹ [fiˈʃy] m scarf; shawl.

fichu² *sl.* [~] **1.** *p.p.* of **ficher; 2.** *adj.* lost, done for, *sl.* bust; rotten, *sl.* lousy; *mal* ~ wretched; out of sorts.

ficti|f [fik'tif] fictitious; sham; **~on** [~'sjɔ̃] *f* fiction, invention.

fidèle [fi'dɛl] **1.** *adj.* faithful, true; exact; **2.** *su. eccl.* **les ~s** *pl.* the congregation *sg.*; **fidélité** [~deli'te] *f* fidelity; integrity; *de haute* ~ hi-fi.

fiduciaire [fidy'sjɛːr] fiduciary; trust ...; *monnaie f* ~ paper money.

fief [fjɛf] *m hist.* fief; *fig.* preserve, (private) kingdom; **~fé** [fjɛ'fe] out and out.

fiel [fjɛl] gall; bile; *fig.* bitterness.

fiente [fjɑ̃ːt] *f* dung; droppings *pl.*

fier¹ [fje] (1o). *se* ~ *à* trust (*s.o.*); *fiez-vous à moi!* leave it to me!

fier², fière [fjɛːr] proud; haughty.

fierté [fjɛr'te] *f* pride; haughtiness.

fièvre ⚕ [fjɛːvr] *f* fever; **fiévreux** [fje'vrø] **1.** *adj.* feverish (*a. fig.*); fever-ridden; **2.** *su.* fever patient.

figer [fi'ʒe] (1l) congeal, coagulate; *fig.* **se ~** freeze (*smile*).

fignoler [fiɲɔ'le] (1a) fiddle-faddle (over *s.th.*).

figu|e ⚘ [fig] *f* fig.; F *mi-~, mi-raisin* so-so; **~ier** [fi'gje] *m* fig-tree.

figur|ant *m, e f* [figy'rɑ̃, ~'rɑ̃ːt] *thea.* extra; walker-on; **~atif** [~ra'tif] figurative; **~ation** [~ra'sjɔ̃] *f* figuration, representation; *thea.* extras *pl.*; **~e** [fi'gyːr] *f* ◬, person: figure; shape, form; face; appearance; court-card; **~é** [figy're] **1.** *adj.* figured (*cloth etc.*); *fig.* figurative; **2.** *su. au* ~ figuratively; **~er** [~'re] (1a) *v/t.* represent (*a. thea.*); paint (*a. fig.*), draw; *se* ~ imagine; *v/i.* figure; appear; *thea.* ~ *sur la scène* walk on; **~ine** [~'rin] *f* statuette; ✝ model.

fil [fil] *m* thread (*a. fig.*); yarn; string; wire, ◉ line; strand; *water:* current; *blade:* edge; *meat, wood:* grain; *wool:* ply; ◬ ~ *à plomb* plumbline; ~ *de la Vierge* gossamer; F *coup de* ~ phone call; *au* ~ *de l'eau* with the current; *au* ~ *des jours* as the days go (*or* went) by; *de* ~ *en aiguille* gradually; *donner du* ~ *à retordre à* give a lot of trouble to; ⚡ *sans* ~ wireless; **~age** [fi'laːʒ] *m* spinning; yarn; *metall.* drawing; **~ament** [~la'mɑ̃] *m* ⚡, ⚘ filament; *silk:* thread; **~amenteux** [~lamɑ̃'tø] fibrous; *fig.* stringy; **~andre** [~'lɑ̃ːdr] *f*

meat etc.: string; **~andreux** [~lɑ̃'drø] stringy; streaked; *fig.* complicated; **~asse** [~'las] *f* tow; oakum; *sl.* stringy meat; **~ateur, -trice** *f* [~la'tœːr, ~'tris] *tex.* spinner; shadower; **~ature** [~la'tyːr] *f* spinning (mill); *police:* shadowing.

file [fil] *f* line, file; (~ *d'attente*) queue, *Am.* line; *à la* ~ in file; *fig.* on end, without a break; *chef m de* ~ leader; *en* ~ *indienne* in single file; **filer** [fi'le] (1a) *v/t. tex.* spin; draw (*metal*); play out (*cards*); pay out (*a cable*); shadow (*s.o.*); *v/i.* flow smoothly; run (*oil*); rope (*wine*); smoke (*lamp*); *fig* slip by, go by; go, travel; F make off; ~ *doux* sing small.

fil|et [fi'le] *m* net; *screw:* thread; *cuis.* fillet, tenderloin; *water:* trickle; dash (*of lemon*); 🚂 *etc.* baggage rack; ~ *à provisions* string bag; ~ *de voix* thin voice; *coup m de* ~ *fish:* haul; **~etage** [fil'taːʒ] *m screw:* thread(ing); **~eter** [~'te] (1d) ◉ draw; thread (*a bolt*); **~eur** *m*, **-euse** *f tex.* [fi'lœːr, ~'løːz] spinner.

filia|l, e [fi'ljal] **1.** *adj.* filial; **2.** *su./f* ✝ branch; **~tion** [~lja'sjɔ̃] *f* filiation; descendants *pl.*; *fig.* relationship.

filière [fi'ljɛr] *f* usual channels *pl.*; *fig. passer par la* ~ work one's way up from the bottom.

filigrane [fili'gran] *m* filigree (work); *paper:* watermark.

fil|le [fiːj] *f* daughter; girl; maid; ~ *publique* prostitute; ~ *de salle* waitress; *jeune* ~ girl; *vieille* ~ old maid; **~e-mère**, *pl.* **~es-mères** [fij'mɛːr] *f* unmarried mother; **~ette** [fi'jɛt] *f* little girl; **~eul, e** [~'jœl] *su.* godchild; *su./m* godson; *su./f* goddaughter.

film [film] *m* film (*a. cin.*); ~ *en couleurs* colo(u)r film; ~ *muet (parlant)* silent film (sound-film); *tourner un* ~ make a film; **~er** [fil'me] (1a) film.

filon [fi'lɔ̃] *m* ⚒ vein, still; *sl.* good fortune; *sl.* cushy job, *Am.* bonanza.

fil|ou [fi'lu] *m* thief; swindler; **~ter** [filu'te] (1a) swindle (*s.o.* out of *s.th.* ❡, *de qch*); rob (*s.o.* of *s.th.*, *qch. à q.*); **~terie** [~'tri] *f* swindle.

fils [fis] *m* son.

filtr|age [fil'traːʒ] *m liquid:* filtering; ~ *à interférences radio:* interference elimination; **~e** [filtr] *m* filter; *coffee:* percolator; **bout** m ~ **cigarette**: filter-tip; **~er** [fil'tre] (1a) filter.

fin¹ [fɛ̃] f end, termination, close, conclusion; aim, object; **à la** ~ at last; **à toutes ~s** for all purposes; **en ~ de compte** after all, in the end; **mettre ~ à** put an end to; **prendre** ~ come to an end; **tirer à sa** ~ draw to a close.

fin² [fɛ̃] fine; pure; choice; slender; sly; small; subtle; keen (*ear*).

final, e, m/pl. **-als** [fi'nal] **1.** adj. final; last; **2.** su./f end syllable; ♩ keynote; ♩ finale; sp. finals pl.

financ|e [fi'nɑ̃:s] f finance; ready money; **ministère ~ des ~s** Exchequer, Treasury (a. Am.); **~er** [finɑ̃'se] (1k) finance; **~ier** [~'sje] **1.** adj. financial; stock (*market*); **2.** su./m financier.

finass|er F [fina'se] (1a) use trickery; **~erie** [~nas'ri] f trickery; cunning.

finaud [fi'no] cunning (person).

fine [fin] f liqueur brandy.

finesse [fi'nɛs] f fineness; slenderness; cunning; telev.: sharpness.

fin|i [fi'ni] **1.** adj. finished (a fig.); over; ꭤ, gramm., etc. finite; fig. pej. absolute, complete; **2.** su./m phls. etc. finite; **~ir** [~'ni:r] (2a) vt/i. finish; end; end up; ~ **de faire qch.** stop doing s.th.; ~ **par faire qch.** finally or eventually do s.th.; **en** ~ **avec** get over (and done) with; **à n'en plus** ~ endless(ly); **~ition** ⊕ [~ni'sjɔ̃] finishing.

finlandais [fɛ̃lɑ̃'dɛ] **1.** adj. Finnish; **2.** su. ♀ Finn; **finnois** [fi'nwa] **1.** adj., su./m ling. Finnish; **2.** su. ♀ Finn.

fiole [fjɔl] f phial; flask; sl. nut (= head).

fioritures [fjɔri'ty:r] f/pl. writing, style: flourishes; ♩ grace-notes.

firmament [firma'mɑ̃] m firmament, sky, heavens pl.

firme [firm] f firm; ✝ imprint.

fis [fi] *1st p. sg. p.s. of* **faire.**

fisc [fisk] m Inland; (Am. Internal) Revenue; **~al** [fis'kal] fiscal, tax...

fiss|ile [fi'sil] fissile; **~ion** [~'sjɔ̃] f (phys. nuclear) fission; **~ure** [~'sy:r] f fissure (a. ✖), crack, split; **~urer** [~sy're] (1a) crack, fissure.

fiston sl. [fis'tɔ̃] m son, youngster.

fix|age [fik'sa:ʒ] m fixing; **~ateur** [~sa'tœ:r] m hair cream; phot. fixer; **~ation** [~sa'sjɔ̃] f fixing; fastening; settling; ski: binding; psych. fixation; **~e**

fixe [fiks] **1.** adj. fixed; steady, regular (*jobs*); set (*date etc.*); permanent, fast (*colour*); **à heure** ~ at set hours or times; **jour** ~ regular day; **menu m à prix** ~ set menu; **~é** [fik'se] fixed; set; appointed (*time*); fig. decided (*person*); fig. ~ **sur** (**le compte de**) informed about, in the picture about; **au jour** ~ on the appointed day; **2.** su./m fixed salary; **~er** [fik'se] (1a) fix (a. phot., ♛, ✝, value, time); fasten; set (a time, date, etc.), arrange; hold (s.o.'s attention); focus (one's attention) (on, **sur**); determine, lay down (rules etc.); look hard at; ~ **son choix sur** decide or settle on; ~ **son regard sur** fix one's eyes on; **se** ~ settle (down); fig. focus (on, **sur**); **~ité** [~si'te] f fixity.

flacon [fla'kɔ̃] m bottle; flask.

flageller [flaʒɛl'le] (1a) scourge.

flageoler [flaʒɔ'le] (1o) tremble.

flagorner [flagɔr'ne] (1a) toady to.

flagrant [fla'grɑ̃] flagrant; striking.

flair [flɛ:r] m sense of smell; fig. nose; fig. flair; **~er** [fle're] (1b) smell at; smell, scent (a fig.).

flamand [fla'mɑ̃] **1.** adj., su./m ling. Flemish; **2.** su. ♀ Fleming.

flamant orn. [fla'mɑ̃] m flamingo.

flamb|ant [flɑ̃'bɑ̃]: ~ **neuf** brandnew; **~eau** [~'bo] m torch; **~ée** [~'be] f blaze; flare-up; fig. outburst; **~er** [~'be] (1a) v/i. blaze; burn; v/t. singe; **~oyer** [~bwa'je] (1h) blaze (a. fig.).

flamme [flɑm] f flame; fig. love.

flammèche [fla'mɛʃ] f spark.

flan [flɑ̃] m cuis. custard tart; sl. **c'est du** ~! it's a load of hooey!

flanc [flɑ̃] m flank, side; ~ **de coteau** hillside; F **sur le** ~ laid up; exhausted; sl. **tirer au** ~ malinger.

flancher F [flɑ̃'ʃe] (1a) flinch; give in; F quit, chicken out; ⊕ etc. break down.

flandrin F [flɑ̃'drɛ̃] m lanky fellow.

flanelle tex. [fla'nɛl] f flannel.

flân|er [flɑ̃'ne] (1a) stroll; lounge about; loaf; **~eur** m, **-euse** f [~'nœ:r, ~'nø:z] stroller; loafer.

flanquer¹ F [flɑ̃'ke] (1m) chuck, fling; put; give.

flanquer² [flɑ̃'ke] (1m) flank.

flapi F [fla'pi] tired out, done up.

flaque [flak] f puddle, pool.

flash, pl. **~es** [flaʃ] m flash-light.

flasque [flask] flabby, limp.

flatt|er [fla'te] (1a) flatter (s.o. on s.th., *q. sur qch.*; s.o. by or in ger., *q. de inf.*); caress, stroke; **~erie** [~'tri] *f* flattery; **~eur** [~'tœːr] **1.** *adj.* flattering; pleasing; **2.** *su.* flatterer.

flatu|lence ♂ [flaty'lɑ̃ːs] *f* flatulence, F wind; **~lent** [~ty'lɑ̃] flatulent.

fléau [fle'o] *m* flail; *balance:* beam; *fig.* scourge; pest, curse; plague.

flèche¹ [flɛ:ʃ] *f* arrow; *balance etc.:* pointer; *church:* spire; ♣ *etc.* pole; *crane:* jib; **monter en ~** rocket *or* zoom up; *fig.* **faire ~ de tout bois** use all means.

flèche² [~] *f* bacon: flitch.

fléchi|r [tle'ʃiːr] (2a) *vt/i.* bend; *v/t. fig.* move, sway (*s.o.*); *v/i.* give way; sag (*cable*, ♣); weaken, *fig.* flag; go down (*prices*); **~ssement** [~ʃis'mɑ̃] *m* bending *etc.*; *see* **fléchir**.

fleg|matique [flɛgma'tik] phlegmatic; **~me** [flɛgm] *m* imperturbability, coolness.

flemm|ard *sl.* [flɛ'maːr] **1.** *adj.* lazy; **2.** *su.* slacker; **~e** *sl.* [flɛm] *f* laziness; *tirer sa ~* laze about.

flet *icht.* [flɛ] *m* flounder.

flétri|r [fle'triːr] (2a) (*a.* **se ~**) fade; wilt; wither.

flétri|r [~] (2a) condemn; stain, blemish; *hist.* brand.

flétrissure¹ [fletri'syːr] *f* fading.

flétrissure² [~] *f* blemish.

fleur [flœːr] *f* flower (*a. fig.*); blossom; *fig.* prime; **à ~ de** level with; just above; **à ~ de peau** skin-deep; **en ~** in bloom; **~aison** [flœrɛ'zɔ̃] *f* blooming.

fleurer [flœ'rc] (1a) smell (of).

fleur|et [flœ'rɛ] *m* fencing: foil; *tex.* floss silk; ✂ borer; **~ette** [~'rɛt] *f* small flower; *conter ~* à flirt with; **~ir** [~'riːr] (2o) *v/i.* bloom; *fig.* flourish; *v/t.* decorate with flowers; **~iste** [~'rist] *su.* florist; **~on** [~'rɔ̃] *m* ♣ floret; rosette; *fig.* **un ~ à sa couronne** a feather in one's cap.

fleuve [flœːv] *m* river.

flex|ible [flɛk'sibl] flexible; **~ion** [~'sjɔ̃] *f* bending; flexion; *gramm.* inflexion; **~ueux** [~'syø] winding.

flic *sl.* [flik] *m* cop, policeman; **~aille** *sl.* [fli'kaj] *f:* **la ~** the police, *sl.* the fuzz.

flipper [flipœːr] *m* pin-ball machine.

flirt [flœrt] *m* flirt(ation); **flirter** [flœr'te] (1a) flirt.

flocon [flɔ'kɔ̃] *m snow:* flake; *wool:* flock; **~neux** [~kɔ'nø] fleecy.

flonflons [flɔ̃'flɔ̃] *m/pl.* blare *sg.*

flora|ison [flɔre'zɔ̃] *f* flowering, blooming; **~l** [~'ral] floral.

flore [flɔːr] *f* ♣ flora; *myth.* ♀ Flora.

florès [flɔ'rɛːs] *m:* **faire ~** be in vogue; be a success.

floriculture [flɔrikyl'tyːr] *f* flower growing.

florissant *fig.* [flɔri'sɑ̃] *f* flourishing.

flot [flo] *m* wave; stream; crowd; *fig.* flood; **à ~** afloat; **~tant** [~'tɑ̃] floating (*a.* ♣); flowing (*hair*); loose (*garment*); *fig.* irresolute.

flotte [flɔt] *f* ♣ fleet; Γ water; F rain.

flott|ement [flɔt'mɑ̃] *m* wavering; **~er** [flɔ'te] (1a) float, flow (*hair*); *fig.* waver; **~eur** [~'tœːr] *m* ⊙ float; ♣ buoy.

flottille ♣ [flɔ'tiːj] *f* flotilla.

flou [flu] **1.** *adj.* blurred; soft (*hair*); loose-fitting; **2.** *su./m* haziness.

flouer F [flu'e] (1a) swindle, do.

fluctu|ation [flyktɥa'sjɔ̃] *f* fluctuation; **~er** [~'tɥe] (1n) fluctuate.

fluet [fly'ɛ] thin; slender.

fluid|e [flɥid] **1.** *adj.* fluid; *fig. a.* flowing; **2.** *su./m* fluid; **~ifier** [flɥidi'fje] (1o) fluidify.

flût|e [flyːt] *f* ♪ flute; tall champagne glass; *bread:* long thin roll; F **~s** *pl.* legs; *sl.* **~!** bother!; *sl.* **jouer des ~s** make off; **~er** [fly'te] (1a) ♪ play the flute; *sl.* drink; **voix flûtée** soft *or* piping voice.

fluvial [fly'vjal] river...; water...

flux [fly] *m* flow; **le ~ et le reflux** the ebb and flow; **~ion** ♂ [flyk'sjɔ̃] *f* inflammation.

foc ♣ [fɔk] *m* jib.

focal [fɔ'kal] focal; **~isation** [~kaliza'sjɔ̃] *f* focussing; **~iser** [~kali'ze] (1a) focus.

foi [fwa] *f* faith; belief; confidence (in, *dans*); **ajouter ~ à** believe (in); **avoir ~ en** have faith in; **de bonne (mauvaise) ~** *adv.* in good (bad) faith; *adj.* honest (dishonest); **digne de ~** reliable; **faire ~ de** prove, attest; **ma ~!** upon my word!; **mauvaise ~** insincerity; unfairness; **sous la ~ du serment** on oath.

foie [~] *m* liver; *sl.* **avoir les ~s** be scared (stiff).

foin [fwɛ̃] **1.** *su./m* hay; *sl.* row; F **avoir**

du ~ dans ses bottes have feathered one's nest.

foire [fwaːr] *f* fair; F *fig.* ~ *d'empoigne* free-for-all.

fois [fwa] *f* time, occasion; *une ~* once; *à la ~* at once; at the same time; *encore une ~* once more; *une ~ que* when.

foison [fwaˈzɔ̃] *f* abundance, plenty; *à ~* in abundance; **~ner** [~zɔˈne] (1a) abound (in, with *de*), teem (with, *de*); swell, ⚙ buckle.

fol [fɔl] *see* **fou**.

fol|âtre [fɔˈlɑːtr] frisky; **~âtrer** [~lɑˈtre] (1a) frolic; F act the fool; **~âtrerie** [~lɑtrəˈri] *f* frolic; **~ichon** [~liˈʃɔ̃] playful; funny; **~ie** [~ˈli] *f* madness; folly; *~ des grandeurs* megalomania.

folle [fɔl] *f*; **~ment** madly; **~t** [fɔˈle] scatterbrained; *poil m ~* down; *see* **feu**.

foment|ateur *m*, **-trice** *f* [fɔmɑtaˈtœːr, ~ˈtris] fomenter; **~ation** [~taˈsjɔ̃] *f* fomentation); **~er** [~ˈte] (1a) 🩺 foment (*a. fig.*).

fon|cé [fɔ̃ˈse] dark, deep (*colour*); **~cer** [~ˈse] (1k) *v/t.* make darker; *v/i.* turn darker; F charge, rush, dash (at, *sur*).

foncier [fɔ̃ˈsje] real (*property*); ground (*rent*); *fig.* fundamental.

fonction [fɔ̃kˈsjɔ̃] *f* function (*a.* 🅰, 🩺); *fig.* *en ~ de* in step with; *être ~ de* depend on; *faire ~ de* act as; **~naire** [fɔ̃ksjɔˈnɛːr] *m* official; civil servant; **~nel** [~ˈnɛl] functional; **~ner** [~ˈne] (1a) function; ⚙ work.

fond [fɔ̃] *m* bottom; △, *fig.* basis; *paint.* background; back, far end; *fig.* gist; *à ~* thoroughly; *à ~ de train* at top speed; *au ~*, *dans le ~* after all; at bottom; **~amental** [fɔ̃damɑ̃ˈtal] fundamental; essential.

fond|ateur *m*, **-trice** *f* [fɔ̃daˈtœːr, ~ˈtris] founder; **~ation** [~ˈsjɔ̃] *f* foundation (*a.* △); **~é** [fɔ̃ˈde] **1.** *adj.* authorized; *être ~ à* (*inf.*) have reason to (*inf.*); **2.** *su./m*: *~ de pouvoir* ⚖ proxy; ✝ managing director; ✝ chief clerk; **~ement** [fɔ̃dˈmɑ̃] *m* base; F bottom; *sans ~* unfounded; **~er** [fɔ̃ˈde] (1a) found (*a.* ✝, *a. fig.*); fund (*a debt*); *fig.* justify.

fond|erie ⚙ [fɔ̃ˈdri] *f* foundry; founding; **~eur** [~ˈdœːr] *m* founder; smelter; **~re** [fɔ̃ːdr] (4a) *vt/i.* melt; dissolve; blend; *v/t.* smelt; cast (*a bell*); ✝ amalgamate;

v/i. fig. melt away; thin down; *~ sur* swoop down on.

fondrière [fɔ̃driˈɛːr] *f* bog, quagmire; hollow (*in the ground*).

fonds [fɔ̃] *m* land, estate; fund; *~ pl.* cash *sg.*, capital *sg.*; ✝ public funds; *~ de commerce* business, goodwill; ✝ *~ pl. de roulement* working capital *sg.*; *~ perdu* life annuity; F *à ~perdu* without security.

fondue [fɔ̃ˈdy] *f* melted cheese.

font [fɔ̃] *3rd p. pl. pres. of* **faire**.

fontaine [fɔ̃ˈtɛn] *f* fountain; spring.

fonte [fɔ̃ːt] *f* melting; smelting; *metal:* casting; cast iron.

fonts *eccl.* [fɔ̃] *m/pl.* (*a.* ~ *baptismaux*) font *sg.*

football *sp.* [futˈbɔl] *m* soccer; **~eur** [~bɔˈlœːr] *m* footballer.

for [fɔːr] *m*: *~ intérieur* conscience; *dans mon ~ intérieur* in my heart (of hearts).

forage [fɔˈraːʒ] *m* boring, drilling.

forain [fɔˈrɛ̃] **1.** *adj.* itinerant; *fête f ~e* fun fair; **2.** *su.* itinerant; hawker.

forban [fɔrˈbɑ̃] *m* crook, swindler.

forçat [fɔrˈsa] *m* convict.

forc|e [fɔrs] *f* strength; force (*a.* ✕, *a.* ⚙); power (*a.* ⚙); *~ aérienne* (*tactique*) (tactical) air force; *~ de frappe* ✕ strike force; *fig.* force(fulness); ⚖ *majeure* overpowering circumstances *pl.*; *à ~ de* by means of, by dint of; *à toute ~* at all costs; *de première ~* first-class ...; *de vive ~* by sheer force; *un cas de ~ majeure* an act of God; **~ément** [fɔrseˈmɑ̃] *adv.* inevitably.

forcené, e [fɔrsəˈne] **1.** *adj.* mad; **2.** *su./m* madman; *su./f* madwoman.

forcer [fɔrˈse] (1k) force (to *inf.* à *inf.*); run (*a blockade*); break open, force (*a lock etc.*); ✕, ⚙ strain; increase (*one's pace, speed*).

forer ⚙ [fɔˈre] (1a) bore, drill.

forestier [fɔresˈtje] **1.** *adj.* forest-...; forest-clad; **2.** *su./m* forester.

foret ⚙ [fɔˈre] *m* drill; bit; gimlet.

forêt [~] *f* forest; *fig. hair:* shock.

forfaire [fɔrˈfɛːr] (4r) be false (to, **à**); *~ à* fail in (*one's duty*).

forfait¹ [fɔrˈfɛ] *m* heinous crime.

forfait² [~] *m sp. etc.* withdrawal; *declarer ~* withdraw (from the competition).

forfait³ [fɔrˈfɛ] *m* contract; *à ~* for a fixed

sum; job-(*work*); (*buy*, *sell*) as a job lot; ~**aire** [~fɛ'tɛːr] lump (*sum*).

forfanterie [fɔrfɑ̃'tri] *f* bragging.

forge [fɔrʒ] *f* smithy; ~**er** [~'ʒe] (1l) forge; *fig.* invent; ~**eron** [~ʒə'rɔ̃] *m* smith; ~**eur** [~'ʒœːr] *m* forger.

form|aliser [fɔrmali'ze] (1a): **se** ~ take offence (at, **de**); ~**aliste** [~'list] **1.** *adj.* formal, stiff; **2.** *su.* formalist (*a. phls.*); ~**alité** [~li'te] *f* form(ality); **une simple** ~ a pure formality; ~**at** [fɔr'ma] *m* size (*a. phot.*); ~**ateur** [~ma'tœːr] formative; ~**ation** [~ma'sjɔ̃] *f* formation (*a.* ✗, ♪); ~ (**professionnelle** vocational) training; ~**e** [fɔrm] *f* form (*a. sp.*, *fig.*, *typ.*); shape; pattern; mo(u)ld; formality, ♣ dock; ~**s** *pl.* manners; **en** ~ fit, up to scratch; **en** ~ **de** ... ...-shaped; **par** ~ **d'avertissement** by way of warning; **pour la** ~ for form's sake, **prendre** ~ take shape; **coue** ~ **de** in the form of; ~**el** [fɔr'mɛl] formal; strict; categorical; ~**er** [~'me] (1a) form; shape; *fig.* train (*s.o.*).

formidable [fɔrmi'dabl] formidable, dreadful; *fig.* tremendous.

formul|aire [fɔrmy'lɛːr] *m admin.* form; formulary; ~**e** [~'myl] *f* ✗, 🏛, *a. fig.* formula; *post:* form; ~**er** [~my'le] (1a) formulate; express.

fort [fɔːr] **1.** *adj.* strong; robust; good (at, **en**); large (*sum*); *fig.* big; ample (*resources*); thick; stout; heavy (*rain*, *sea*); steep; high (*fever*, *wind*); *fig.* difficult; *fig.* severe; **à plus** ~**e raison** all the more; **c'est** (**un peu**) ~!, **c'est trop** ~ that's a bit much!; **se faire** ~ **de** undertake to, claim to be able to; **2.** *adv.* very; strongly; loud(ly); **avoir** ~ **à faire pour** (*inf.*) have a hard time doing (*ger.*); **3.** *su./m* strong part; strong man; *fig.* strong point; *fig.* height (*of fever*, *season*); ✗ stronghold, fort.

forteresse [frtə'rɛs] *f* stronghold.

fortifi|ant [fɔrti'fjɑ̃] **1.** *adj.* invigorating; **2.** *su./m* tonic; ~**cation** [~fika'sjɔ̃] *f* fortification; ~**er** [~'tje] (1o) fortify; strengthen (*a. fig.*).

fortuit [fɔr'tɥi] chance..., casual.

fortun|e [fɔr'tyn] *f* fortune; **de** ~ emergency ..., makeshift ...; **bonne** (**mauvaise**) ~ good (bad) luck; **dîner à la** ~ **du pot** take pot-luck; ~**é** [~ty'ne] well-off, rich.

foss|e [foːs] *f* pit, hole; trench; grave; ~**é** [fo'se] *m* ditch, trench; moat; ~**ette** [~'sɛt] *f* dimple.

fossile [fo'sil] **1.** *adj.* fossilized (*a. fig.*); **2.** *su./m* fossil (*a. fig.*).

fossoyeur [foswa'jœːr] *m* grave-digger.

fou (*adj. before vowel or h mute* **fol**) *m*, **folle** *f*, *m/pl.* **fous** [fu, fɔl, fu] **1.** *adj.* mad, crazy (about, **de**); in love (with, **de**); *fig.* tremendous; silly, foolish; **2.** *su.* lunatic; *su./m* fool; *chess:* bishop.

foudre¹ [fudr] *m* tun.

foudr|e² [fudr] *f* thunderbolt (*a. fig.*); lightning; *fig.* **coup** *m* **de** ~ love at first sight; **la** ~ **est tombée** lightning struck (at, **à**); ~**oyer** [fudrwa'je] (1h) strike (by lightning); *fig.* dumbfound, crush; *fig.* ~ **du regard** look daggers at.

fouet [fwɛ] *m* whip, ~ (**à oeufs**) (cgg) whisk; ~**ter** [fwɛ'te] (1a) whip; flog; whisk (*eggs*); *rain:* lash against.

fougère ♣ [fu'ʒɛːr] *f* fern.

fougu|e [fug] *f* fire, spirit, ardo(u)r; ~**eux** [fu'gø] fiery, ardent.

fouill|e [fuːj] *f* excavation; *fig.* search; ~**er** [fu'je] (1a) *v/t.* dig, excavate; search (*s.o.*); *v/i.* rummage; ~**is** [~'ji] *m* jumble, mess.

fouin|ard ⊢ [fwi'naːr] inquisitive; ~**e** *zo.* [fwin] *f* stone marten; ~**er** ⊢ [fwi'ne] (1a) nose *or* ferret about.

foui|r [fwiːr] (2a) dig; ~**sseur** [fwi'sœːr] burrowing (*animal*).

foulard [fu'laːr] *m* scarf, foulard.

foul|e [ful] *f* crowd; throng; mob; **la** ~ the masses; **une** ~ **de** masses of, ⊢ heaps of; **en** ~ in masses; ~**ée** *f* stride; **dans la** ~ **de q.** close behind s.o.; ⊢ **dans la** ~ on the same occasion, at the same time; ~**er** [fu'le] (1a) tread; press, crush; *tex.* full; *fig.* ~ **aux pieds** trample down; **se** ~ **la cheville** sprain one's ankle; ⊢ **se la rate** work o.s. to death; ⊢ **ne pas se** (**la**) ~ take it easy, not to overwork o.s.; ~**ure** 🩹 [~'lyːr] *f* sprain.

four [fuːr] *m* oven; kiln; *thea.*, *a.* ⊢ flop; **petits** ~ *pl.* pastry *sg.*, cookies.

fourbe [furb] **1.** *adj.* rascally; double-dealing; **2.** *su.* cheat; ~**rie** [furbə'ri] *f* swindle; deceit.

fourbi ⊢ [fur'bi] *m* things *pl.*, gear; caboodle.

fourbir [fur'biːr] (2a) furbish, polish.

fourbu [fur'by] tired out.

fourch|e [furʃ] f fork; **en ~** forked; **~er** [fur'ʃe] (1a) fork; fig. **la langue m'a fourché** I made a slip of the tongue; **~ette** [~'ʃɛt] f (table)fork; **~on** [~'ʃɔ̃] m prong; bough: fork; **~u** [~'ʃy] forked; cloven (hoof).

fourgon [fur'gɔ̃] m van, waggon; 🚂 luggage van, Am. baggage car.

fourgonner F [furgɔ'ne] (1a) poke about (in, dans).

fourmi zo. [fur'mi] f ant; **~ blanche** termite; fig. **avoir des ~s** have pins and needles; **~lier** zo. [furmi'lje] m ant-eater; **~lière** [~'ljɛːr] f ant-hill; fig. nest; **~ller** [~'je] (1a) teem (with, de); fig. tingle.

fourn|aise fig. [fur'nɛːz] f furnace; **~eau** [~'no] m 🔥 cooker, stove; pipe: bowl; sl. idiot; **haut ~** blast-furnace; **~ée** [~'ne] f ovenful; ⚙ charge; batch (a. fig.).

fourni [fur'ni] thick, bushy.

fourn|iment [furni'mɑ̃] m kit; gear; **~ir** [~'niːr] (2a) v/t. furnish, supply (with, de); 🏭 produce; v/i. provide (for, à); **~isseur** [~ni'sœːr] m supplier; **~iture** [~'tyːr] f supplying; **~s** pl. supplies; equipment sg.

fourrag|e [fu'raːʒ] m fodder; ✕ foraging; **~er** [fura'ʒe] (1l) forage.

fourré [fu're] **1.** adj. furry; lined; filled (with, de); **coup ~** backhanded blow; **paix f ~e** sham peace; **2.** su./m thicket.

fourreau [fu'ro] m sheath; case.

fourr|er F [fu're] (1a) line with fur: stuff, thrust; cram; F stick, poke; **se ~** wrap o.s. up; hide o.s.; **~eur** [~'rœːr] m furrier.

fourrière mot. [fu'rjɛːr] f pound; **emmener une voiture à la ~** tow a car away.

fourrure [fu'ryːr] f fur; lining.

fourvoyer F [furvwa'je] (1h) lead astray, mislead; **se ~** be mistaken.

foutaise F [fu'tɛːz] f rubbish, rot.

fout|re F [futr] **1.** (4a) throw; give; do; **~ la paix à q.** leave s.o. alone; **~ le camp** clear out; **~ q. dedans** do s.o.; **je m'en fous** I don't care; **2.** int. damn it!; **~u** F [fu'ty] damned; done for, sl. bust(ed).

fox zo. F [fɔks] m foxterrier.

foyer [fwa'je] m hearth; fig. home; ⚙ fire-box; boiler: furnace; ⚡, phys. focus; hotel: lounge; fig. seat, centre, Am. center.

frac [frak] m dress-coat.

fracas [fra'ka] m crash; din; **~sant** [~ka'sɑ̃] deafening (noise); fig. sensational; **~ser** [~ka'se] (1a) shatter; smash.

fraction [frak'sjɔ̃] f fraction (a. ℝ), portion; pol. group; **~naire** [fraksjo'nɛːr] fractional; **nombre m ~** improper fraction; **~ner** [~'ne] (1a) split up; fractionate.

fractur|e [frak'tyːr] f breaking open; lock: forcing; ✝, geol. fracture; **~er** [~'tyre] (1a) break open; force (a lock); ✝ fracture, break.

fragile [fra'ʒil] fragile; fig. weak; **~ité** [~ʒili'te] f fragility; frailty.

fragment [frag'mɑ̃] m fragment, bit; snatch (of a song etc.); **~aire** [~mɑ̃'tɛːr] fragmentary.

fraîch|eur [frɛ'ʃœːr] f freshness (a. fig.); fig. bloom; **~ir** [~'ʃiːr] (2a) grow colder; freshen (wind).

frais¹, fraîche [frɛ, frɛʃ] **1.** adj. fresh; cool; recent; wet (paint); **2.** adv.: **il fait ~** it is cool; cuis. **servir ~** serve chilled; **~ arrivé** just arrived; **fleur f ~ or fraîche cueillie** freshly picked flower; **3.** su./m fresh air; **au ~** in a cool place; **de ~** freshly.

frais² [frɛ] m/pl. cost sg., expenses, charges; **~ d'entretien** maintenance costs, upkeep sg.; ✝ **~ de port en plus** carriage sg. extra; **aux ~** at the expense of; **faire les ~ de** bear the cost of; fig. provide the topic(s) of (a conversation).

fraise¹ [frɛːz] f strawberry.

fraise² [~] f cuis. coul; collar: ruff.

fraiser ⚙ [frɛ'ze] (1a) mill; countersink.

frambois|e [frɑ̃'bwaːz] f raspberry; **~ier** 🌿 [~'zje] m raspberry-bush.

franc¹, franche [frɑ̃, frɑ̃ːʃ] **1.** adj. frank; free; fair; fig. clear; **~ de port** carriage paid; post-free; foot. **coup m ~** free kick; **2.** franc adv. frankly; **pour parler ~** to be frank.

franc² [frɑ̃] m coin: franc.

français, e [frɑ̃'sɛ, ~'sɛːz] **1.** adj., su./m ling. French; **2.** su./m Frenchman; **les ♀** m/pl. the French; su./f. ♀ Frenchwoman.

franchement [frɑ̃ʃ'mɑ̃] adv. frankly; openly; straight (out); F really.

franchi|r [frɑ̃'ʃiːr] (2a) jump over, clear; cross; pass through; fig. overcome; **~se**

[~'ʃiːz] *f* frankness; *admin.* exemption; **~ de bagages** baggage (*Am.* luggage) allowance; **en ~** duty-free; **~ssable** [~ʃi'sabl] passable.

franc-maçon, *pl.* **francs-maçons** [frɑ̃ma'sɔ̃] *m* freemason; **~nerie** [~sɔn'ri] *f* freemasonry.

franco ✝ [frɑ̃'ko] *adv.* free, postpaid.

francophone [frɑ̃ko'fɔn] French-speaking (person).

franc-tireur, *pl.* **francs-tireurs** [frɑ̃ti-'rœːr] *m* sniper; *fig.* free lance.

frange [frɑ̃ːʒ] *f* fringe.

frangin *sl.* [frɑ̃'ʒɛ̃] *m* brother; **frangine** *sl.* [~'ʒin] *f* sister.

franquette ⌐ [frɑ̃'kɛt] *adv.*: **à la bonne ~** without ceremony.

frapp|e [frap] *f typing, piano etc.*: touch; *box.* punch; *mint:* stamp(ing); *sl.* tough guy, thug; **~er** [~'pe] (1a) *vt/i.* strike (*a. fig.*), hit, *v/t.* mint (*money*); ice (*a drink*); *fig.* dumbfound (*s.o.*); **se ~** get worked up; worry; *v/i.* knock (at the door, **à la porte**); **~ du pied** stamp one's foot; **~ juste** strike home.

frasque [frask] *f* escapade.

fratern|el [frater'nɛl] brotherly; **~iser** [~ni'ze] (1a) fraternize (with, **avec**); **~ité** [~ni'te] *f* fraternity, brotherhood.

fratricide [fratri'sid] *su., su./m* fratricide.

fraud|e [froːd] *f* fraud; **~ fiscale** tax evasion; **faire entrer en ~** smuggle in; **~er** [fro'de] (1a) cheat, swindle; **~eur** [~'dœːr] *m* defrauder; **~ fiscal** tax evader.

frayer [frɛ'je] (1i) *v/t.* rub; clear (*a path, a way*); **se ~ un chemin** make a way for o.s.; *v/t.* spawn (*fish*); **~ avec** associate with.

frayeur [frɛ'jœːr] *f* fright, terror.

tredaine [frə'dɛn] *f* escapade; prank.

fredonner [frədɔ'ne] (1a) hum.

frégate ⚓ [fre'gat] *f* frigate.

frein [frɛ̃] *m mot. etc.*, *a. fig.* brake; *horse:* bit; **~ à air comprimé** air brake; **~ de secours** emergency brake; **~s** *pl.* **à disque** disc brakes; **mettre un ~ à** check; **ronger son ~** chump the bit; **~er** [frɛ'ne] (1a) *vt/i.* brake; *v/t. fig.* slow down or up; check.

frelater [frəla'te] (1a) adulterate.

frêle [frɛl] frail, weak.

frelon *zo.* [frə'lɔ̃] *m* hornet.

freluquet F [frəly'kɛ] *m* whippersnapper.

frémi|r [fre'miːr] (2a) shudder; rustle; quiver (*a. fig.* with, **de**); **~ssement** [~mis'mɑ̃] *m* quiver; shudder; rustle; *wind:* sighing.

frêne ⚘ [frɛːn] *m* ash(tree).

fréné|sie [frene'zi] *f* frenzy; **~tique** [~'tik] frantic; frenzied.

fréqu|emment [freka'mɑ̃] *adv.* of **fréquent**; **~ence** [fre'kɑ̃ːs] *f* ♪ ⚡, etc. frequency; **~ent** [~'kɑ̃] frequent; **~entation** [~kɑ̃ta'sjɔ̃] *f* frequenting; association (with, **de**); (*a. ~s pl.*) company (*sg.*); **~enté** [~kɑ̃'te]: (**très ~** very) busy (*place*); **bien** (**mal**) **~** of good (ill) repute; **~enter** [~kɑ̃'te] (1a) frequent; see (*s.o.*) (frequently).

frère [frɛːr] *m* brother; *eccl.* monk.

trérot F [fre'ro] *m* little brother.

fresque [frɛsk] *f* fresco.

frut ⚓ [frɛ] *m* freight; cargo; **prendre à ~** charter; **fréter** [fre'te] (1f) freight; charter; fit out (*a ship*); F hire (*a car etc.*).

frétiller [freti'je] (1a) wriggle; wag.

fretin [frə'tɛ̃] *m* (small) fry.

friable [fri'abl] crumbly.

friand [fri'ɑ̃] dainty; **~ de fond of**; **~ise** [~ɑ̃'diːz] *f* titbit, delicacy.

fric *sl.* [frik] *m sl.* bread, cash (= *money*).

frica|ndeau *cuis.* [frikɑ̃'do] *m* larded veal; **~ssée** *cuis.* [frika'se] *f* hash; **~sser** [~'se] (1a) fricassee.

fric-frac *sl.* [frik'frak] *m/inv.* burglary.

friche ⚘ [friʃ] *f* fallow land; waste land; **en ~** fallow; *fig.* undeveloped.

fricoter F [friko'te] (1a) cook; *fig.* cook up, be up to (*s.th.*).

friction [frik'sjɔ̃] *f* ⊙ friction; *scalp:* massage; ⚘ rubbing; *sp.* rub-down; **frictionner** [~sjɔ'ne] (1a) rub; give (*s.o.*) a rub-down; massage.

frigidaire (*TM*) [friʒi'dɛːr] *m* refrigerator.

frigidité ⚘ [friʒidi'te] *f* frigidity.

frigo F [fri'go] *m* refrigerator; **~rifier** [frigɔri'fje] (1o) refrigerate; freeze; **~rifique** [~'fik] refrigerating.

frileux [fri'lø] chilly, shivery.

frimas F [fri'ma] *m* hoar-frost.

frime F [frim] *f* sham, make-believe.

frimousse F [fri'mus] *f* little face.

fringale F [frɛ̃'gal] *f* keen appetite.

fringant [frɛ̃'gɑ̃] frisky; dashing.

fringues F [frɛ̃g] *f/pl.* togs.

frip|er [fri'pe] (1a) crease; crumple;

~erie [~'pri] f old clothes (shop); fig. rubbish; **~ier** m, **-ère** f [~'pje, ~'pjɛːr] second-hand dealer.

fripon [fri'põ] **1.** adj. roguish; **2.** su. rascal; **~nerie** [~pɔn'ri] f prank.

fripouille F [fri'puːj] f bad lot, cad.

frire [friːr] (4s) (a. **faire ~**) fry.

frise △ [friːz] f frieze.

friser [fri'ze] (1a) vt/i. curl; wave; v/t. skim, graze; fig. border on.

frison [fri'zõ] m curl, ringlet.

frisquet F [fris'kɛ] chilly.

frisson [fri'sõ] m shiver, shudder; thrill; **~ner** [~sɔ'ne] (1a) (with, **de**) shiver; quiver; be thrilled.

frit [fri] p.p. of **frire**; **~erie** [fri'tri] f fried-fish shop; **~es** f [frit] f/pl. F chips, Am. French fries; **~ure** [~'tyːr] f frying (fat); fried fish; radio: crackling.

frivol|e [fri'vɔl] frivolous; **~ité** [~vɔli'te] f frivolity; **~s** pl. fancy goods.

froc eccl. [frɔk] m cowl; frock.

froid [frwa] **1.** adj. cold (a. fig. smile, reception); chilly; **à ~** when cold (a. cuis.); **avoir ~** be cold (person); **battre ~ à** cold-shoulder (s.o.); **faire ~** be cold (weather); **prendre ~** catch a cold or chill; **2.** su./m cold; fig. coldness; **être en ~** (**avec**) be on bad terms (with); **~eur** [frwa'dœːr] f coldness; chilliness; indifference; fig. chill; ⚕ frigidity.

froiss|ement [frwas'mɑ̃] m crumpling etc., see **froisser**; **~er** [frwa'se] (1a) crumple, crease; fig. offend, hurt, ruffle (s.o.); **se ~** take offence (at, **de**).

frôl|ement [frol'mɑ̃] m light brushing; **~er** [fro'le] (1a) brush against or past, graze; fig. come near to.

fromage [fro'maːʒ] m cheese; fig. soft job; **~ de tête** pork brawn; **~r** [~ma'ʒe] **1.** adj. cheese ...; **2.** su./m cheesemonger; **~rie** [~maʒ'ri] f cheesemonger's (shop); cheese dairy.

froment ♪ [fro'mɑ̃] m wheat.

fronc|e [frõːs] f crease; dress etc.: gather; **~ement** [frõs'mɑ̃] m puckering; **~ des sourcils** frown; **~er** [frõ'se] (1k) pucker, wrinkle; **~ les sourcils** frown; scowl; **~is** [~'si] m dress: gathering.

frondaison [frõdɛ'zõ] f foliation.

frond|e [frõːd] f sling; (toy) catapult; **~er** [frõ'de] (1a) catapult; (a. **~ contre**) scoff at; **~eur** [~'dœːr] **1.** su./m slinger; fig. scoffer; **2.** adj. bantering; irreverent.

front [frõ] m front (a. ✕); forehead; brow; face; fig. impudence, cheek; **de ~** abreast; front-...; head-on (collision); at once, at one time, together; **faire ~ à** face (s.th.); **~al** [frõ'tal] frontal, front-...; head-on (collision); **~ière** [~'tjɛːr] f frontier; border; **~ispice** [~tis'pis] m frontispiece.

frott|ement [frɔt'mɑ̃] m rubbing; scraping; ☉, fig. friction; **~er** [frɔ'te] (1a) vt/i. rub; scrape; v/t. rub down; scour; strike (a. match); fig. **~é à** rub shoulders with; cross swords with.

frou-frou [fru'fru] m gown: rustle.

frouss|ard sl. [fru'saːr] **1.** adj. cowardly; **2.** su. coward; **~e** sl. [frus] f funk; **avoir la ~** be scared.

fruct|ifier [frykti'fje] (1o) bear fruit; **~ueux** [~'tɥø] profitable.

frugal [fry'gal] frugal; **~ité** [~gali'te] f frugality.

fruit [frɥi] m fruit; fig. profit; fig. result; **~s** pl. **de mer** sea-food sg.; **~ sec** dried fruit; fig. person: failure; **~é** [frɥi'te] fruity; **~ier** [~'tje] **1.** adj. fruit(-tree); **2.** su./m fruit dealer.

frusques sl. [frysk] f/pl. togs (= clothes).

fruste [fryst] rough (a. fig.).

frustrer [frys'tre] (1a) frustrate; **~ q. de qch.** deprive s.o. of s.th.

fugace [fy'gas] fleeting, passing.

fugitif [fyʒi'tif] fugitive.

fugue [fyg] f ♪ fugue; running away; **faire une ~** run away.

fui|r [fɥiːr] (2d) v/i. flee; leak (barrel); recede (forehead); v/t. avoid, shun; **~s** [fɥi] 1st p. sg. pres. and p.s. of **fuir**; **~te** [fɥit] f flight; escape; liquid, a. fig. leak(age); avoiding; **mettre en ~** put to flight; **prendre la ~** take to flight.

fulgur|ation [fylgyra'sjõ] f flashing; ⚕ fulguration; **~er** [~'re] (1a) flash, fulgurate.

fuligineux [fyliʒi'nø] smoky; murky.

fulminer [fylmi'ne] (1a) fulminate.

fume-cigare(tte) [fymsi'gaːr, ~ga'rɛt] m/inv. cigar(ette)-holder.

fumé [fy'me] smoked; glass: tinted; **~e** [~] f smoke; soup: steam; vapo(u)rs pl.

fumer¹ [~] (1a) vt/i. smoke (cigarettes, fish, meat); v/i. steam; fig. be fuming (with anger etc.).

fumer² ♪ [~] (1a) manure.

fum|erie [fym'ri] f opium: den; **~et**

[fy'mɛ] *m* aroma; **~eur** *m*, **-euse** *f* [~'mœːr, ~'møːz] *su.* smoker; **~eux** [~'møɔ] smoky; *fig.* hazy, woolly.
fumier [fy'mje] *m* dung (hill).
fumiste [fy'mist] *m* stovesetter; F unreliable individual, phoney; **~rie** F [fymistə'riː] *f* eyewash; farce; phoney.
fun|èbre [fy'nɛbr] funeral; gloomy; **~érailles** [fyne'raːj] *f/pl.* funeral *sg.*; **~éraire** [~'rɛːr] funeral.
funeste [fy'nɛst] fatal, deadly.
funiculaire [fyniky'lɛːr] **1.** *adj.* funicular; **2.** *su./m* funicular railway.
fur [fyːr] *m*: **au ~ et à mesure que** (in proportion) as.
furet [fy'rɛ] *m zo.* ferret; *fig.* pry; **~er** [fyr'te] (1d) ferret about; nose about; **~eur** [~'tœːr] **1.** *adj.* prying; **2.** *su.* ferreter, *fig.* rummager.
fur|eur [fy'rœːr] *f* fury; **aimer avec** (*or* **à la**) **~** be passionately fond of; *fig.* **faire ~** be all the rage; **~ibond** [~ri'bɔ̃] furious (person); **~ie** [~'ri] *f* fury, rage; **mettre q. en ~** make s.o. furious; **~ieux** [~'rjø] furious.
furoncle [fy'rɔ̃kl] *m* furuncle.
furtif [fyr'tif] furtive, stealthy.
fus [fy] *1st p. sg. p.s. of* **être 1.**
fusain [fy'zɛ̃] *m* charcoal (sketch); **fuseau** [~'zo] *m tex.* spindle; **~ horaire** time zone; *cost.* **pantalon** *m* **~** tapering trou-

sers *pl.*; **en ~** tapering (at both ends).
fusée [fy'ze] *f* rocket; **~ éclairante** flare; **~ engin** booster.
fusel|age ✈ [fyz'laːʒ] *m* fuselage; **~er** [~'le] (1c) taper; streamline.
fuser [fy'ze] (1a) burst out (*laughter etc*); **fusible** [~'zibl] **1.** *adj.* fusible; **2.** *su./m* ⚡ fuse(-wire).
fusil [fy'zi] *m* rifle, gun; **coup** *m* **de ~** shot; *fig. sl.* gross overcharging; **~lade** [fyzi'jad] *f* rifle-fire; (execution by) shooting; **~ler** [~'je] (1a) ⚔ shoot; *sl.* smash up.
fusion [fy'zjɔ̃] *f* fusion; ✝ merger; **~ner** [~zjo'ne] (1a) merge; blend.
fustiger [fysti'ʒe] (1l) censure.
fût [fy] *m* gun: stock; *tools etc.:* handle; △ shaft; △ barrel, cask.
futaie [fy'tɛ] *f* forest; **arbre** *m* **de haute ~** full-grown tree, timber tree; **futaille** [~'taːj] *f* cask, tun.
futé F [fy'te] sharp, cunning.
futil|e [fy'til] futile; trifling; **~ité** [~tili'te] *f* futility; **~s** *pl.* trifles.
futur, e [fy'tyːr] **1.** *adj.* future; **2.** *su./m* intended (husband); *gramm.* future; *su./f* intended (wife).
fuy|ant [fɥi'jɑ̃] fleeing; vanishing (*perspective*); shifty (*eyes*); *fig.* receding (*forehead, line*); **~ard** [~'jaːr] *su.* fugitive; **~ons** [~'jɔ̃] *1st p. pl. pres. of* **fuir.**

G

gabare ⚓ [ga'baːr] *f* barge.
gabarit [gaba'ri] *m* size; *fig.* calibre; *fig.* sort, kind.
gabelou *pej.* [ga'blu] *m* customs officer; tax collector.
gâcher [ga'ʃe] (1a) mix (*mortar*); slake (*lime*); *fig.* spoil.
gâchette [ga'ʃɛt] *f* gun: trigger.
gâch|eur *m*, **-euse** *f* [gɑ'ʃœːr, ~'ʃøːz] bungler; **~is** [~'ʃi] *m* △ wet mortar; mud; F *fig.* mess.
gaff|e [gaf] *f* boat-hook; F *fig.* blunder; F **faire une ~** put one's foot in it; *sl.* **faire ~** be careful; **~er** F

[ga'fe] (1a) blunder, drop a brick.
gaga *sl.* [ga'ga] **1.** *su./m* dodderer; **2.** *adj.* doddering, senile.
gag|e [gaːʒ] *m* ✝ pledge, pawn; *fig.* token; forfeit; **~s** *pl.* wages; **mettre en ~** pawn; **~er** [ga'ʒe] (1l) pay wages to (*s.o.*); hire (*a servant*); F bet; **~eur** *m*, **-euse** *f* [~'ʒœːr, ~'ʒøːz] wagerer; **~eure** [~'ʒyːr] *f* (almost) impossible undertaking.
gagn|e-pain [gaɲ'pɛ] *m/inv.* livelihood; job; **~-petit** [~pə'ti] low wage earner; **~er** [ga'ɲe] (1a) *v/t.* win (*a. fig.*); gain; earn; reach, arrive at; **~ de la place**

save space; ~ *du temps* gain time; ~ *sa vie* earn one's livelihood; *v/i.* improve; profit (*by*, **à**); spread (*fire*); **~eur** *m*, **-euse** *f* [~'nœːr, 'nøːz] earner; gainer; winner.

gai [ge] gay, jolly, cheerful; lively; ☉ easy (*bolt*); F *un peu* ~ a bit merry; **~eté** [~'te] *f* cheerfulness; mirth; **~s** *pl.* frolics; broad jokes; ~ *de cœur* wantonness.

gaillard, e [ga'jaːr, ~'jard] 1. *adj.* jolly, merry; strong, well; ribald (*story*); 2. *su./m* fellow; *su./f* strapping girl; **~ise** [~jar'diːz] *f* jollity; **~s** *pl.* risky stories.

gain [gɛ̃] *m* gain, profit; earning; *cards etc.*: winnings *pl.*

gaine [gɛn] *f* sheath; casing; girdle; △ shaft; **~er** [gɛ'ne] (1b) sheathe, cover.

gala [ga'la] *m* gala; *en grand* ~ in state; *habits m/pl. de* ~ full dress *sg.*

gala|mment [gala'mɑ̃] *adv. of galant 1*; **~nt** [~'lɑ̃] 1. *adj.* courteous, gallant; *aventure f* ~*e* (love) affair; 2. *su./m* ladies' man; lover; **~nterie** [~lɑ̃'tri] *f* attentiveness; love affair; **~s** *pl.* compliments.

galaxie [galak'si] *f* Milky Way.

galbe [galb] *m* curve; contour; line(s *pl.*) (*of a car*); shapeliness.

gale [gal] *f* scabies, the itch.

galère [ga'lɛːr] *f* galley; *fig.* labo(u)r; *vogue la* ~*!* let's risk it!

galerie [gal'ri] *f* ✗, *thea., etc.* gallery; arcade; *mot.* roof rack.

galet [ga'lɛ] *m* pebble; ☉ roller; ☉ pulley; **~s** *pl.* shingle *sg.*

galetas [gal'ta] *m* garret; hovel.

galette [ga'lɛt] *f* flat cake; *sl.* money.

galeux [ga'lø] mangy (*dog*); ♀ scurfy (*tree*); with the itch (*person*); F *fig.* *brebis f galeuse* black sheep.

galimatias [galima'tja] *m* farrago; gibberish.

gallicisme [gali'sism] *m* gallicism, French turn of phrase.

gallois, e [ga'lwa, ~'lwaːz] 1. *adj., su./m ling.* Welsh; 2. *su./m* ♀ Welshman; *les* ♀ *m/pl.* the Welsh; *su./f* ♀ Welshwoman.

galoche [ga'lɔʃ] *f* clog; overshoe.

galon [ga'lɔ̃] *m* braid; ✗ stripe.

galop [ga'lo] *m* gallop; ~ *d'essay* trial run; *fig. au* ~ quickly; *au grand* ~ at full gallop; **~er** [galo'pe] (1a) gallop; **~in** [~'pɛ̃] *m* urchin.

galvan|iser [galvani'ze] (1a) ☉ galvanize (*a. fig.*); **~oplastie** [~nɔplas'ti] *f* electroplating.

galvauder [galvo'de] (1a) tarnish, sully; debase.

gamb|ade [gɑ̃'bad] *f* caper; **~ader** [~ba'de] (1a) caper, gambol.

gamelle [ga'mɛl] *f* ✗ mess tin; billy (can).

gamin, e [ga'mɛ̃, ~'min] *su.* urchin; *su./m* little boy; *su./f* little girl.

gamma *phys.* [ga'ma] *m*: *rayons m/pl.* ~ gamma rays.

gamme [gam] *f* ♪ scale; *fig.* range.

gammé [ga'me] *adj.*: *croix f* ~*e* swastika.

gangrène [gɑ̃'grɛn] *f* gangrene; ♀, *a. fig.* canker; **~ener** [gɑ̃grə'ne] (1d) ♂ gangrene; *fig.* corrupt.

gant [gɑ̃] *m* glove; ~ *de boxe* boxing--glove; ~ *de toilette* washing-glove; *jeter* (*relever*) *le* ~ throw down (take up) the gauntlet; **~elet** [gɑ̃t'lɛ] *m* gauntlet; **~er** [gɑ̃'te] (1a) glove; *fig.* suit (*s.o.*); **~erie** [~'tri] *f* glove-shop or counter.

garag|e [ga'raːʒ] *m mot.* garage; 🚂 shunting; **~iste** [~ra'ʒist] *m* garage owner *or* mechanic.

garant [ga'rɑ̃] *su.* surety, bail; security; *se porter* ~ vouch (for, **de**); *su./m* guarantee; **~ie** [garɑ̃'ti] *f* safeguard; guarantee (*a.* ✝); ✝ warranty; pledge; **~ir** [~'tiːr] (2a) guarantee (*a.* ✝); ✝ underwrite; vouch for; *fig.* protect.

garce *sl.* [gars] *f* bitch, strumpet.

garçon [gar'sɔ̃] *m* boy; young man; (*a. vieux* ~) bachelor; *café etc.*: waiter; ~ *d'honneur* best man; **~ne** [~'sɔn] *f* bachelor girl; **~net** [~sɔ'nɛ] *m* little boy; **~nière** [~sɔ'njɛːr] *f* bachelor apartment.

garde [gard] *su./f* looking after, guarding, care; 🚂 *etc.* custody; ✗, *sp. etc.* guard; watch; nurse; *book:* fly leaf; *book:* end paper; *sword:* hilt; ~ *d'enfants* child minder; ~ *à vous!* look out!; *de* ~ on duty; *faire la* ~ keep watch; *mettre en* ~ warn; *monter la* ~ stand guard; *prendre* ~ beware, be careful (*of,* **à**); *être sur ses* ~*s* be on one's guard; *su./m* guardian, watchman; keeper; warden; **~-barrière**, *pl.* **~s-barrière(s)** 🚂 [gardaba'rjɛːr] *m* gate-keeper; **~-bébé** [~be'be] *su.* babysitter; **~-boue** [~'bu] *m/inv.* mudguard, fender; **~-corps** [~'kɔːr] *m/inv.* life-line; **~-feu** [~'fø] *m/inv.* fender; **~-fou** [~'fu] *m* parapet; handrail; **~-malade,** *pl.* **~s-malades** [~ma'lad] *su./m* male nurse; *su./f* nurse; **~-manger** [~mã'ʒe] *m/inv.* pantry; meat safe; **~-nappe,** *pl.* **~s-nappe(s)** [~'nap] *m* tablemat.

gard|er [gar'de] (1a) keep; preserve; retain; protect; watch over, look after; **se ~** refrain (from *ger.,* **de** *inf.*); take care (not to *inf.,* **de** *inf.*); beware (of, **de**); **~erie** [~'dri] *f* day nursery; **~e robe** [~də'rɔb] *f* wardrobe, clothes; **~e-vue** [~də'vy] *m/inv.* eye-shade; lampshade; **~ien** [~'djɛ̃] 1. *su.* guardian; keeper; *prison.* guard; *foot.* **~ de but** goalkeeper; **~ de la paix** policeman; 2. *adj.:* **ange m ~** guardian angel.

gare¹ [gaːr] *f* siding; 🚉 station; **~ maritime** harbo(u)r-station.

gare²! [~] *int.* look out!; **sans crier ~** without warning.

garenne [ga'rɛn] *su./f* warren; fishing preserve; *su./m* (*a.* **lapin m de ~**) wild rabbit.

garer [ga're] (1a) *mot.* park; dock (*a vessel*); **~ un** *mot.* pull to one side; **F** *mot.* park; get out of the way; take cover (from, **de**).

gargaris|er [gargari'ze] (1a): **se ~** gargle; **F** revel (in, **de**); **~me** [~'rism] *m* gargle; gargling.

gargote [gar'gɔt] *f* (third-rate) eating house; cook-shop.

gargouill|e △ [gar'guːj] *f* gargoyle; **~er** [~gu'je] (1a) gurgle; rumble; **~is** [~gu'ji] *m* gurgling.

garnement F [garnə'mã] *m* scamp.

garn|i [gar'ni] † *m* furnished room; **~ir** [~'niːr] (2a) (with, **de**) cover, ⚙ *etc. a.* line, fit; fill, 💧 *etc. a.* stock; decorate, *a. cuis.* trim, garnish; **~ison** ✗ [~ni'zõ] *f* garrison; **~iture** [~ni'tyːr] *f* cover(ing), ⚙ lining, fitting(s *pl.*); filling; trimming(s *pl.*), trim, garnishing; *cuis.* vegetables *pl.*

garrot [ga'ro] *m* ⚙ tongue (*of saw*); 💧 tourniquet; **~ter** [~rɔ'te] (1a) bind (*s.o.*) hand and foot; tie, strap; *fig.* muzzle.

gars F [gɑ] *m* lad, young fellow, boy.

gascon [gas'kõ] *adj., su.* Gascon; **~nade** [~kɔ'nad] *f* bragging; tall story.

gas(-)oil [ga'zɔjl] *m* fuel *or* diesel oil.

gaspiller [gaspi'je] (1a) waste, squander; dissipate; fritter away.

gastrite 💉 [gas'trit] *f* gastritis.

gastro... [gastro] gastro...; **~nome** [~'nɔm] *m* gastronome(r).

gâteau [gɑ'to] *m* cake; tart; pudding; honeycomb; lump; *fig.* profit; *fig.* **partager le ~** split the profit.

gât|er [gɑ'te] (1a) spoil (*a. fig.*); **se ~** go bad (*food etc.*); change for the worse, deteriorate; **~erie** [~'tri] *f* spoiling (*of a child*); **~s** *pl.* goodies; **~eux** [~'tø] 1. *su./m* old dotard; 2. *adj.* senile.

gauch|e [goːʃ] 1. *adj.* left; crooked; clumsy, ✗ on *or* to the left; **tourner à ~** turn left; 2. *su./f* left hand; left-hand side; **tenir sa ~** keep to the left; **~er** [go'ʃe] 1. *adj.* left-handed; 2. *su.* left-hander; **~erie** [goʃ'ri] *f* clumsiness; **~ir** [go'ʃiːr] (2a) (*a.* **se ~**) warp; *fig.* distort; **~isme** *pol.* [~'ʃism] *m* leftism; **~issement** [~ʃis'mã] *m* warping; **~iste** *pol.* [~'ʃist] leftist.

gaudriole F [godri'ɔl] *f* broad joke.

gaufr|e *cuis.* [go'fr] *f* waffle; **~ de miel** honeycomb; **~ette** [go'frɛt] *f* wafer biscuit.

gaule [goːl] *f* long pole; fishing rod.

gaulois [go'lwa] 1. *adj.* of Gaul; *fig.* spicy; 2. *su./m ling.* Gaulish; *su.* 2 Gaul; **~erie** [~lwaz'ri] *f* broad joke.

gausser [go'se] (1a): **se ~ de** make fun of.

gave [gaːv] *m* mountain-torrent

gaver [ga've] (1a) cram (*a. fig. a. pupil*); 🐦 force-feed; **se ~** gorge.

gaz [gɑːz] *m* gas; **~ d'échappement** exhaust gas; **~ hilarant** laughing gas; *mot.* **couper les ~** throttle back; *mot.* **F mettre les ~** step on the gas; *mot.* **pédale f de ~** accelerator.

gaze [~] *f* gauze; *fig.* **sans ~** bluntly.

gazer [gɑ'ze] (1a) *v/t.* gas; *v/i. mot. sl.* speed (along); **F** be all right.

gazette [ga'zɛt] *f* gazette; *person:* gossip(er).

gaz|eux [go'zø] gaseous; 💧 aerated, fizzy, **~ier** [~'zje] *m* gasman.

gazon [ga'zõ] *m* grass; turf; lawn.

gazouill|ement [gazuj'mã] *m* chirping, warbling, twittering; babbling; **~er** [gazu'je] (1a) warble, chirp, twitter; babble; **~is** [~'ji] *m* see **gazouillement.**

géant, e [ʒeˈɑ̃, ~ˈɑ̃t] **1.** *su./m* giant; *su./f* giantess; **2.** *adj.* gigantic.

geindre [ʒɛ̃ːdr] (4m) whine; moan.

gel [ʒɛl] *m* frost; freezing (*a.* ✝, *fig.*).

gélatine [ʒelaˈtin] *f* gelatine.

gel|ée [ʒəˈle] *f* frost; *cuis.* jelly; **~ blanche** hoar-frost; **~er** [~] (1d) *vt/i.* freeze (*a.* credits); *v/t.* frostbite; **se ~** freeze, get frozen stiff (*person*); *v/i.* become frozen; *avoir gelé* be frozen (*river*); *on gèle ici* it is freezing (in) here.

gélivure [ʒeliˈvyːr] *f* frost-crack.

Gémeaux *astr.* [ʒeˈmo] *m/pl.:* **les ~** Gemini; **géminé** [~miˈne] twin.

gémi|r [ʒeˈmiːr] (2a) groan, moan; lament; **~ssement** [~misˈmɑ̃] *m* groan(ing), moan(ing).

gemme [ʒɛm] *f min.* gem; ✿ (leaf)bud; resin; *sel m* ~ rock-salt.

gênant [ʒɛˈnɑ̃] inconvenient, in the way; *fig.* awkward (silence).

gencive *anat.* [ʒɑ̃ˈsiːv] *f* gum.

gendarm|e [ʒɑ̃ˈdarm] *m* gendarme, constable; F virago; **~er** [ʒɑ̃darˈme] (1a): **se ~** flare up; **~erie** [~məˈri] *f* constabulary; headquarters *pl.* of the gendarmes.

gendre [ʒɑ̃ːdr] *m* son-in-law.

gêne [ʒɛːn] *f* embarrassment, uneasiness; trouble, bother; discomfort; financial straits *pl.*; *sans ~* unconstrained; **gêner** [ʒɛˈne] (1a) bother; hamper; embarrass; inconvenience; hinder; *cela vous gêne-t-il?* is that troubling you?; *la robe me gêne* the dress is too tight for me; *fig.* **se ~** put o.s. out; be shy; squeeze up; *sourire m gêné* embarrassed smile.

général, e [ʒeneˈral] **1.** *adj.* general; *d'une façon ~e* broadly speaking; *en ~* generally; **2.** *su./m* general; *su./f.* ✗ alarm; *thea.* dress-rehearsal; **~iser** [~raliˈze] (1a) generalize; **~iste** ✚ [~raˈlist] *m* (*a. médecin m ~*) general practitioner, G.P.; **~ité** [~raliˈte] *f* generality.

générat|eur, -trice [ʒeneraˈtœːr, ~ˈtris] **1.** *adj.* generating; **2.** *su./f* generator; dynamo; *su./m* ⊕ boiler; **~ion** [~ˈsjɔ̃] *f* generation.

génér|eux [ʒeneˈrø] generous; liberal; abundant; **~osité** [~roziˈte] *f* generosity; liberality.

genèse [ʒəˈnɛːz] *f* genesis.

genêt ✿ [ʒəˈnɛ] *m* broom.

génétique [ʒeneˈtik] **1.** *adj.* genetic; **2.** *su./f* genetics *pl.*

gêneur *m*, **-euse** *f* [ʒɛˈnœːr, ~ˈnøːz] intruder; nuisance; spoil-sport.

genévrier ✿ [ʒənevriˈe] *m* juniper.

géni|al [ʒeˈnjal] inspired, of genius; **~e** [~ˈni] *m* spirit, *person:* genius; spirit, characteristic; ✗ engineers *pl.*; **~ civil** civil engineering.

genièvre [ʒəˈnjɛːvr] *m* ✿ juniper-berry; juniper(-tree); gin.

génisse [ʒeˈnis] *f* heifer.

génital [ʒeniˈtal] genital; *anat.* *organes m/pl.* **génitaux** genitals.

genou, *pl.* **-x** [ʒəˈnu] *m* knee; ⊕ elbow-joint; *se mettre à ~x* kneel down; **~illère** [~nuˈjɛːr] *f* knee-pad; ⊕ *articulation f à ~* ball-and-socket joint.

genre [ʒɑ̃ːr] *m* kind, type, sort; *gramm.* gender; *art:* genre; *zo. etc.* genus; **se donner un ~** put on airs; **le ~ humain** mankind.

gens [ʒɑ̃] *m/pl.* people, folk *sg.*; *tous les ~ intéressés* all people interested; *petites ~* small fry; *vieilles ~* old folks; *~ d'église* clergy *pl.*; *~ de lettres* men of letters; *~ de mer* sailors.

genti|l, -ille [ʒɑ̃ˈti, ~ˈtiːj] nice; kind; pretty; **soi ~!** be good!; **~lhomme**, *pl.* **~ls-hommes** [ʒɑ̃tiˈjɔm, ~tiˈzɔm] *m* nobleman; **~llesse** [~ˈjɛs] *f* politeness; *avoir la ~ de* (*inf.*) be so kind as to (*inf.*); **~ment** [~ˈmɑ̃] *adv.* of *gentil.*

génuflexion *eccl.* [ʒenyflɛkˈsjɔ̃] *f* genuflexion; *faire une ~* genuflect.

géograph|e [ʒeoˈgraf] *m* geographer; **~ie** [~graˈfi] *f* geography; **~ique** [~graˈfik] geographic(al).

geôlier [ʒoˈlje] *m* jailer.

géologie [ʒeolɔˈʒi] *f* geology.

géométrie [ʒeomeˈtri] *f* geometry.

géran|ce [ʒeˈrɑ̃ːs] *f* management; board of directors; **~t** [~ˈrɑ̃] *m* (managing) director; manager; *journ.* **rédacteur-~** managing editor.

gerbe [ʒɛrb] *f* sheaf; *water, flowers:* spray; *sparks etc.:* shower, flurry; *fig.* bundle, collection.

gercer [ʒɛrˈse] (1k) (*a.* **se ~**) chap (*skin*); crack; **gerçé** chapped (*skin*); **gerçure** [~ˈsyːr] *f* crack, fissure; *skin:* chap; flaw.

gérer [ʒeˈre] (1f) manage, run.

germain [ʒɛrˈmɛ̃] first (*cousin*).

germanique [ʒɛrma'nik] Germanic.

germ|e [ʒɛrm] m germ (a. fig.); **~er** [ʒɛr'me] (1a) germinate; sprout; fig. develop; **~ination** [~mina'sjɔ̃] f germination.

gérondif gramm. [ʒerɔ̃'dif] m gerund.

gésir [ʒe'zi:r] (2q) lie; **ci-gît** here lies.

gestation [ʒɛsta'sjɔ̃] f gestation.

geste¹ [ʒɛst] f: **faits** m/pl. **et ~s** pl. doings.

gest|e² [ʒɛst] m gesture; *hand etc.*: wave, waving; **~iculation** [ʒɛstikyla'sjɔ̃] f gesticulation.

gestion [ʒɛs'tjɔ̃] f management.

gestique [ʒɛs'tik] f gestures pl.

gibbosité [ʒibozi'te] f hump.

gibecière [ʒib'sjɛːr] f game-bag.

gibet [ʒi'bɛ] m gibbet, gallows sg.

gibier [ʒi'bje] m game.

giboulée [ʒibu'le] f sudden shower.

giboy|er [ʒibwa'je] (1h) go shooting; **~eux** [~'jø] abounding in game.

gibus [ʒi'bys] m opera-hat.

gicl|er [ʒi'kle] (1a) squirt; splash; **~eur** mot. [~'klœːr] m jet; nozzle.

gifle [ʒifl] f slap in the face; box on the ear; **~r** [ʒi'fle] (1a). **~ q.** slap s.o.'s face; box s.o.'s ears.

gigantesque [ʒigɑ̃'tɛsk] gigantic.

gigogne [ʒi'gɔɲ] **poupée** f (**table** f) **~** nest of dolls (tables).

gigot [ʒi'go] m cuis. leg of mutton; **~er** F [~go'te] (1a) kick; fidget.

gigue [ʒig] f haunch of venison; gawky girl; F **~s** pl. legs.

gilet [ʒi'lɛ] m waistcoat, vest; cardigan; **~ de sauvetage** life-jacket.

gingembre ♣ [ʒɛ̃'ʒɑ̃:br] m ginger.

girafe zo. [ʒi'raf] f giraffe.

girandole [ʒirɑ̃'dɔl] f chandelier, jewels: girandole; *flowers*: cluster.

giratoire [ʒira'twaːr] gyratory (*traffic*); **sens** m **~** roundabout.

girofle ♣ [ʒi'rɔfl] m clove.

girolle ♣ [ʒi'rɔl] f chanterelle.

giron [ʒi'rɔ̃] m lap; fig. bosom.

girouette [ʒi'rwɛt] f weathercock.

gisant [ʒi'zɑ̃] m univ. recumbent effigy.

gisement [ʒiz'mɑ̃] m geol. deposit; **~s** pl. **houillers** coalfields; **gisons** [ʒi'zɔ̃] 1st p. pl. pres. of **gésir**; **gît** [ʒi] 3rd p. sg. pres. of **gésir**.

gitan m, e f [ʒi'tɑ̃, ~'tan] gipsy.

gîte [ʒit] su./m resting-place, lodging;

hare: form; geol. vein; su./f ♣ list; **gîter** [ʒi'te] (1a) lodge; lie.

givr|age ✓ [ʒi'vraːʒ] m icing; **~e** [ʒiːvr] m hoar-frost; **~er** [ʒi'vre] (1a) frost (*s.th.*) over; ice up.

glabre [glɑːbr] clean-shaven.

gla|ce [glas] f ice; ice cream; mirror; (plate)glass; mot. etc. window; **~cé** [gla'se] icy (a. fig. stare, politeness); cuis. etc. iced; **~cer** [~] (1k) freeze; glaze; fig. chill; cuis. frost, ice; **~ciaire** geol. [~'sjɛːr] glacial; ice-(age)...; glacial, e, m/pl. **-als** [~'sjal] icy (a. fig.); frosty (*air*); ice-...; frigid; **~cier** [~'sje] m geol. glacier; ice-cream man; **~cière** [~'sjɛːr] f icebox; cold-room; **~cis** [~'si] m slope; **~çon** [~'sɔ̃] m icicle (a. fig. person); ice cube; ice floe; **~cure** [~'syːr] f glazing.

glaïeul ♣ [gla'jœl] m gladiolus.

glair|e [glɛːr] f white of egg; mucus, phlegm; ❀ flaw; **~eux** [glɛ'rø] glaireous; full of phlegm (*throat*.)

glaise [glɛːz] f clay, loam.

glaive [glɛːv] m sword.

gland [glɑ̃] m ♣ acorn; tex. tassel.

glande ♣, anat. [glɑ̃:d] f gland.

gland|er [glɑ̃'de], **~ouiller** sl. [~du'je] (1a) hang around.

glan|e [glan] f gleaning; pears: cluster; onions: rope; **~er** [gla'ne] (1a) glean (a. fig.); **~eur** m, **-euse** f [~'nœːr, ~'nøːz] gleaner; **~ure** [~'nyːr] f gleanings pl. (a. fig.)

glapi|r [gla'piːr] (2a) yelp, bark; **~ssement** [~pis'mɑ̃] m yelping.

glas [glɑ] m knell; ✗ salvo of guns.

glauque [glɔːk] bluish green.

glèbe [glɛb] f earth, sod; † land; **attaché à la ~** bound to the soil.

gliss|ade [gli'sad] f slip; sliding; slide; **~ant** [~'sɑ̃] sliding (a. ❀ joint); slippery (a. fig.); **~ement** [glis'mɑ̃] m sliding, slipping; gliding; geol. landslide; **~er** [gli'se] (1a) v/i. slip; slide; glide; mot. skid; **~ sur** glance off (s.th., s.o.); fig. not to dwell upon, let pass; v/t. slip (s.th. into s.th., a. stitch, etc.); **se ~** slip; creep (a. fig.); **~ière** [~'sjɛːr] f slide; mot. **~ de sécurité** crash barrier; **~oir** [gli'swaːr] m ❀ slide; chute; **~oire** [~] f slide (on ice etc.).

glob|al [glɔ'bal] total; overall; global; **~e** [glɔb] m globe; **~ de l'œil**, **~ oculaire** eyeball; **~ulaire** [glɔby'lɛːr] globular;

~ule [~'byl] *m* globule; *blood*: corpuscle; **~uleux** [~by'lø] globular.

gloire [glwaːr] *f* glory; **se faire ~ de** glory in; **~ria** [glɔ'rja] *m* F coffee with brandy; **~riette** [~'rjɛt] *f* arbo(u)r; **~rieux** [~'rjø] glorious; proud, vain (about, **de**); **~rification** [~rifika'sjɔ̃] *f* glorification; **~rifier** [~ri'fje] (1o) glorify; **se ~ de** glory in; **~riole** [~'rjɔl] *f* vainglory.

glos|e [gloːz] *f* gloss, commentary; criticism; **~er** [glo'ze] (1a) *v/t.* gloss; *v/i.*: **~ sur** find fault with.

glossaire [glɔ'sɛːr] *m* glossary.

glouglou [glu'glu] *m* gurgle; *turkey*: gobble; **~ter** [~glu'te] (1a) gurgle.

glouton [glu'tɔ̃] 1. *adj.* greedy; 2. *su./m* glutton; *zo.* wolverine; **~nerie** [~tɔn'ri] *f* gluttony.

glu [gly] *f* bird-lime; glue; **~ant** [~'ã] sticky; **il est ~** he's a sticker.

glycine ♀ [gli'sin] *f* wistaria.

gnangnan [nã'nã] peevish (person).

gn(i)ole, gnôle *sl.* [nɔl] *f* brandy.

go F [go] *adv.*: **tout de ~** immediately.

goal *sp.* [gol] *m* goal(keeper).

gobelet [gɔ'blɛ] *m* goblet; cup.

gobe-mouches [gɔb'muʃ] *m/inv.* *orn.* fly-catcher; F simpleton.

gober [gɔ'be] (1a) swallow (*a.* F *fig.*); F *fig.* like (*s.o.*) very much; *sl.* catch; F **se ~** think no end of o.s.

goberger [gɔbɛr'ʒe] (1l): **se ~** guzzle; feed well.

godailler [gɔda'je] (1a) *see* **goder.**

godasses *sl.* [gɔ'das] *f/pl.* boots.

godelureau [gɔdly'ro] *m* dandy.

gode|r [gɔ'de] (1a) pucker; bag (*trousers*); **~t** [~'dɛ] *m* cup; bowl; ⚙ bucket; *cost.* flare; pucker.

godich|e F [gɔ'diʃ], **~on** [~di'ʃɔ̃] 1. *adj.* awkward; 2. *su./m* simpleton.

godillot [gɔdi'jo] *m* (military) boot.

goémon [gɔe'mɔ̃] *m* seaweed.

gogo [gɔ'go] *m* sucker, mug; **à ~** galore; (*money*) to burn.

gogue|nard [gɔg'naːr] 1. *adj.* mocking; 2. *su.* mocker, chaffer; **~tte** F [gɔ'gɛt] *f*: **en ~** on the spree.

goinfr|e [gwɛ̃ːfr] *m* glutton, F pig; **~er** [gwɛ̃'fre] (1a): **se ~** guzzle.

goitr|e ♂ [gwaːtr] *m* goitre; **~eux** [gwa'trø] goitrous (person).

golfe *geog.* [gɔlf] *m* gulf, bay.

gomm|e [gɔm] *f* gum; india-rubber; **~er** [gɔ'me] (1a) erase; *fig.* suppress; *fig.* blur; **~eux** [~'mø] sticky.

gond [gɔ̃] *m* (door-)hinge; F **sortir de ses ~s** blow one's top.

gondol|e [gɔ̃'dɔl] *f* gondola; ♂ eye-bath; **~er** [~dɔ'le] (1a) *v/i.* (*a.* **se ~**) warp; buckle; blister; *v/t.* *sl.* **se ~** split one's sides with laughter.

gonfl|age [gɔ̃'flaːʒ] *m* inflation; *mot.* blowing-up; **~é** [~'fle] swollen; bloated; *fig.* puffed-up; F *a.* **~ à bloc** *pej.* cocksure; **~ement** [~flə'mã] *m* inflation; swelling; bulging; ♂ distension; **~er** [~'fle] (1a) swell (up); inflate; blow up; ♂ distend; **~eur** *mot.* [~'flœːr] *m* air-pump.

gordien [gɔr'djɛ̃] *adj./m*: **nœud** *m* **~** Gordian knot.

goret [gɔ'rɛ] *m* piglet; F dirty pig.

gorg|e [gɔrʒ] *f* throat, neck; *woman*: breast, bosom; *geog.*, *a.* *hunt.* gorge; ♂ groove; *axle*: neck; *lock*: tumbler; **à pleine ~** at the top of one's voice; **mal m à la ~** sore throat; *fig.* **rendre ~** make restitution; **~ée** [gɔr'ʒe] *f* draught; gulp; **~er** [~'ʒe] (1l) gorge; cram.

gorille [gɔ'riːj] *m* *zo.* gorilla; F *fig.* bodyguard.

gosier [go'zje] *m* throat; gullet; **à plein ~** loudly.

gosse F [gɔs] *su.* kid, youngster.

gothique [gɔ'tik] *adj., su./m* *art*: Gothic; *su./f* *typ.* Old English.

gouaill|er [gwa'je] (1a) chaff; **~erie** [gwaj'ri] *f* banter; **~eur** [gwa'jœːr] mocking, facetious.

gouape F [gwap] *f* blackguard.

goudron [gu'drɔ̃] *m* tar; **~nage** [~drɔ'naːʒ] *m* tarring; **~ner** [~drɔ'ne] (1a) tar; **~neux** [~drɔ'nø] tarry.

gouffre [gufr] *m* gulf, pit, abyss.

goujat [gu'ʒa] *m* lout, boor.

goujon *icht.* [gu'ʒɔ̃] *m* gudgeon.

goujon[2] [gu'ʒɔ̃] *m* ♂ gudgeon; △ stud; ♂ tenon; bolt.

goul|ée [gu'le] *f* ♂ channel; F mouthful; **~et** [~'lɛ] *m* neck; ⚓ narrows *pl.*; **~ot** [~'lo] *m* bottle: neck; spout; **~u** [~'ly] greedy.

goupill|e ♂ [gu'piːj] *f* pin; (*stop*)bolt; gudgeon; cotter; **~er** [~pi'je] (1a) ♂ pin, key; *sl.* wangle.

goupillon [gupi'jɔ̃] *m eccl.* aspergillum; *bottle, gun, lamp:* brush.

gourbi [gur'bi] *m* (Arab) hut; shack.

gourd [gu:r] benumbed; stiff.

gourde [gurd] *f ⚘* gourd, calabash; flask; *sl.* blockhead.

gourdin [gur'dɛ̃] *m* club, bludgeon.

gourmand [gur'mã] **1.** *adj.* greedy; **2.** *su.* gourmand, glutton; **~er** [~mã'de] (1a) rebuke; **~ise** [~mã'di:z] *f* greediness; **~s** *pl.* sweetmeats.

gourm|e [gurm] *f vet.* strangles *pl.*; *⚕* impetigo; *jeter sa ~* F sow one's wild oats; **~é** [gur'me] stiff, formal.

gousse [gus] *f* pod; *garlic:* clove; **~t** [gu'sɛ] *m* vest pocket; ⊙ bracket.

goût [gu] *m* taste (*a. fig.*); flavo(u)r; .... style; *avoir bon ~* taste nice; *mauvais ~* bad taste; **~er** [gu'te] **1.** (1a) *v/t.* taste; *fig.* enjoy, appreciate; *v/i.* take a snack; **~ à** try (*s.th.*); **~ de** taste (for the first time); **2.** *su./m* snack.

goutte¹ *⚕* [gut] *f* gout.

goutt|e² [gut] *f* drop; F sip; **~ à ~** drop by drop; *f ne ... ~* not ... at all; **~e-à-goutte** *⚕* *m/inv.* drip; **~elette** [~'lɛt] *f* droplet; **~er** [gu'te] (1a) drip.

gouttière △ [gu'tjɛ:r] *f* gutter.

gouvern|ail [guver'na:j] *m ⚓* rudder; helm; *✈ ~ de direction* vertical rudder; *✈ ~ de profondeur* elevator; **~ant, e** [~'nɑ̃, ~'nɑ̃:t] **1.** *adj.* ruling; **2.** *su./f* housekeeper; governess; **~e** [gu'vɛrn] *f* guidance; *✈ ~s* *pl.* controls; **~ement** [guvɛrnə'mã] *m* government; **~emental** [~nəmɑ̃'tal] Government-...; **~er** [~'ne] (1a) govern, rule; control; ⚓ steer; **~eur** [~'nœ:r] *m* governor.

grabat [gra'ba] *m* pallet; wretched bed; *fig. sur un ~* in abject poverty.

grabuge F [gra'by:ʒ] *m* squabble.

grâce [grɑ:s] *f* grace (*a. eccl., a. ✝*); gracefulness; favo(u)r; mercy; *⚖* pardon; *~!* for pity's sake; *~ à* thanks to; *coup m de ~* finishing stroke; *de mauvaise ~* unwillingly; *faire ~ de qch. à q.* spare s.o. s.th.; *rendre ~(s)* give thanks (to s.o. for s.th., *à q. de qch.*); **gracier** [gra'sje] (1o) pardon.

graci|euseté [grasjøz'te] *f* graciousness; kindness; **~eux** [~'sjø] graceful, pleasing; gracious; courteous; *à titre ~* free (of charge).

gracile [gra'sil] slender, slim; thin.

grad|ation [grada'sjɔ̃] *f* gradual process; *par ~* gradually; **~e** [grad] *m* rank (*a.* ✖), grade (*a.* ♚); *univ.* degree; ⚓ rating; **~é** [gra'de] *m* ✖ non-commissioned officer; **~in** [~'dɛ̃] *m* step; *en ~s* in tiers; **~uation** *phys.* [~dɥa'sjɔ̃] *f* graduating; scale; **~uel** [~'dɥɛl] gradual; **~uer** [~'dɥe] (1n) graduate; increase gradually.

graillon [grɑ'jɔ̃] *m* smell of burnt fat; F clot of phlegm; **~ner** [~jɔ'ne] (1a) bring up phlegm, hawk.

grain [grɛ̃] *m* grain (*a. of sand, powder, salt*); seed; *coffee:* bean; berry; bead; texture; speck (*a. fig.*); ⚓ squall; ⊙ lining; *~ de beauté* beauty spot; *~ de raisin* grape; F *avoir un ~* be a bit cracked.

graine [grɛn] *f* seed; *monter en ~* run to seed; F *de la mauvaise ~* a bad lot.

graiss|age [grɛ'sa:ʒ] *m* greasing, oiling; **~e** [grɛs] *f* grease (*a.* ⊙); fat; *sl.* money; **~er** [grɛ'se] (1a) grease, lubricate; make greasy; F *~ la patte à q.* grease s.o.'s palm; **~eux** [~'sø] greasy; fatty.

gramm|aire [gram'mɛ:r] *f* grammar; **~airien** *m*, **-enne** *f* [~mɛ'rjɛ̃, ~'rjɛn] grammarian; **~atical** [~mati'kal] grammatical.

gramme [gram] *m measure:* gram.

gramophone [gramɔ'fɔn] *m* gramophone, *Am.* phonograph.

grand [grã] **1.** *adj.* great, big, large; tall; high (*building, explosives, wind*); wide, extensive; grown-up; noble, high class (*wines*); chief; main (*road*); *~ public m* general public; *au ~ jour* in broad daylight; *en ~* on a large scale; *un ~ homme* a great man; *un homme ~* a tall man; **2.** *su./m* great man; grown-up.

grand| chose [grɑ̃'ʃo:z] *su./inv.: ne ... pas ~* not much; **~eur** [~'dœ:r] *f* size; greatness; magnitude; **~ir** [~'di:r] (2a) *v/i.* grow; grow up (*child*); increase; *v/t.* make look taller or bigger; magnify (*a. fig.*); enlarge.

grand... **~-livre**, *pl.* **~s-livres** [grɑ̃'li:vr] *m* ledger; **~-mère**, *pl.* **~(s)-mères** [~'mɛ:r] *f* grandmother; **~-messe** *eccl.* [~'mɛs] *f* high mass; **~-peine** [~'pɛn] *adv.: à ~* with great difficulty *or* much trouble; **~-père**, *pl.* **~s-pères** [~'pɛ:r] *m* grandfather; **~-route** [~'rut] *f* highway;

~rue [~'ry] f main street; **~s-parents** [~pa'rɑ̃] m/pl. grandparents.

grange [grɑ̃:ʒ] f barn; garner.

granit [gra'ni] m granite.

granul|aire [grany'lɛːr] granular; **~ation** [~la'sjɔ̃] f granulation (a. ♣); **~e** [gra'nyl] m, **~é** [grany'le] m granule; **~er** [~'le] (1a) granulate; stipple (an engraving); **~eux** [~'lø] granular.

graphique [gra'fik] **1.** adj. graphic; **2.** su./m graph; diagram.

grapp|e [grap] f bunch; cluster; onions: string; **~iller** [grapi'je] (1a) glean (in vineyards); F pilfer.

grappin [gra'pɛ̃] m ♣ grapnel; ⊚ grab; **~s** pl. climbing-irons; F **mettre le ~ sur** get hold of.

gras, ~se [grɑ, grɑ:s] **1.** adj. fat; fatted (animal); fatty (acid, tissue); oily (rag, voice); stout; thick (beam, mud, weather etc.); rich (food, coal); soft (outline, stone); typ. bold(-faced); fig. coarse: **fromage** m **~** cream cheese; **2.** su./m fat; ⊚ thickness; **~ de la jambe** calf of the leg); **faire ~** eat meat; **~-double** cuis. [grɑ'dubl] m tripe.

grassouillet [grasu'jɛ] chubby.

gratifi|ant [grati'fjɑ̃] gratifying; satisfying; **~cation** [~fika'sjɔ̃] f bonus; **~er** [~'fje] (1o): **~ q. de qch.** present or favo(u)r or hono(u)r s.o. with s.th.

gratin [gra'tɛ̃] m cuis. cheese-topped dish; F fig. the upper crust; cuis. **au ~** with cheese topping; **~é** [~ti'ne] cuis. with a cheese topping; F a hell of a ...

gratis [gra'tis] adv. free (of charge).

gratitude [grati'tyd] f gratitude.

gratt|e [grat] f ⊚ scraper; F rake-off, graft; ♣ F itch; **~e-ciel** [~'sjɛl] m/inv. sky-scraper; **~e-cul** [~'ky] m/inv. dog-rose: hip; **~e-papier** F [~pa'pje] m/inv. penpusher; **~e-pieds** [~'pje] m/inv. shoe-scraper; **~er** [gra'te] (1a) scrape; scratch; scrape off; sp. overtake (a rival); sl. make (s.th.) on the side; **se ~** scratch (o.s.); **~oir** [~'twaːr] m scraper; **~ures** [~'tyːr] f/pl. scrapings.

gratuit, ~e [gra'tɥi] gratuitous; unmotivated; **à titre ~** free of charge; **~é** [~tɥi'te] f gratuitousness.

gravats [gra'va] m/pl. debris.

grave [graːv] **1.** adj. grave; solemn; bad, serious; important; ♪ deep; **2.** su./m ♪ etc. low register.

grav|eler [grav'le] (1c) gravel; **~eux** [~'lø] gravelly (soil); gritty; ♣ suffering from gravel; fig. smutty; ♣ **~le** ♣ [gra'vɛl] f gravel; **~ure** [grav'lyːr] f smutty story.

grav|er [gra've] (1a) engrave, carve; **~eur** [~'vœːr] m engraver.

gravier [gra'vje] m gravel, grit.

gravir [gra'viːr] (2a) climb; mount.

gravit|ation [gravita'sjɔ̃] f gravitation(al pull); **~é** [~'te] f phys., a. fig. gravity; **~er** [~'te] (1a) revolve (round, **autour de**); move; gravitate (towards, **vers**).

gravure [gra'vyːr] f engraving; etching; print; **~ en taille-douce, ~ sur cuivre** copper-plate engraving.

gré [gre] m will, wish; liking; **à mon ~** as I please; to my liking; **au ~ de ...** wherever ... carries; **bon ~, mal ~** willy-nilly; **contre le ~ de** against s.o.'s will; **de bon ~** willingly; **de mon plein ~** of my own accord; **savoir ~ à q. de qch.** be grateful to s.o. for s.th.

grec, ~que [grɛk] adj., su. Greek.

gréement ♣, ✈ [gre'mɑ̃] m rigging; **gréer** ♣, ✈ [~'e] (1a) rig.

greff|age ✗ [grɛ'faːʒ] m grafting; **~e** [grɛf] su./m ♣♣ office, registry; su./f ✗, ♣ graft(ing); ♣ **~ du cœur** heart transplant; **~er** ✗, ♣ [grɛ'fe] (1a) graft; **~ier** [~'fje] m clerk of the court; **~on** ✗ [~'fɔ̃] m graft, slip.

grège [grɛːʒ] adj./f raw (silk).

grêle¹ [grɛːl] thin (a. fig. voice); spindly; anat. small (intestine).

grêl|e² [grɛːl] f hail; **~é** ♣ [grɛ'le] pock-marked; **~er** [~'le] (1a) v/impers. hail; v/t. damage by hail; **~on** [~'lɔ̃] m hail-stone.

grelot [grə'lo] m small bell; F (tele)phone; F **avoir les ~s** shake (with fear); **~ter** [~lɔ'te] (1a) shake, tremble (with, **de**); tinkle.

grenad|e [grə'nad] f ♣ pomegranate; ✗ grenade; **~ier** [grəna'dje] m ♣ pomegranate(-tree); ✗ grenadier; F **woman:** amazon.

grenat [grə'na] adj., su/m garnet.

greneler ⊚ [grən'le] (1c) grain.

grener [grə'ne] (1d) v/i. seed (cereals); v/t. grain (salt, leather).

grenier [grə'nje] m granary; (hay-, corn-)loft; △ attic, garret.

grenouill|age [grənu'jaːʒ] m (shady)

dealings *pl.*; **~e** [grə'nuːj] *f* frog; F club money, funds *pl.*; F *manger la* **~** run off with the funds.

grès [grɛ] *m* sandstone; stoneware.

grésil [gre'zi] *m* (fine) hail.

grésiller [grezi'je] (1a) crackle; sizzle.

grève [grɛːv] *f* strand; ⊙ strike, walkout; **~ bouchon** selective action; **~ de la faim** hunger strike; **~ perlée** go-slow strike, *Am.* slow-down strike; **~ sauvage** wildcat strike; **~ sur le tas** sit-down strike; *faire* **~** be on strike, *se mettre en* **~** go on strike, walk out; *faire la* **~** *du zèle* work to rule.

grever [grə've] (1d) burden (*an estate*) (with, *de*); ⚖ entail.

gréviste [gre'vist] *su.* striker.

gribouiller [gribu'je] (1a) scrawl, scribble.

grief [gri'ɛf] *m* grievance; *faire* **~** *à q. de qch.* hold s.th. against s.o.

grièvement [griɛv'mã]: **~** *blessé* seriously injured.

griff|ade [gri'fad] *f* scratch (*of claw*); **~e** [grif] *f* claw (*a.* ⊙); ⚓ maker's label; *a. fig.* stamp; **~er** [~'fe] (1a) scratch, claw.

griffonn|age [grifɔ'naːʒ] *m* scrawl; **~er** [~'ne] (1a) scrawl, scribble.

grignoter [griɲɔ'te] (1a) nibble (at); *fig.* wear down or away.

grigou F [gri'gu] *m* miser, skinflint.

gril [gril] *m cuis.* grill; grid (*a.* ⊙); *fig. être sur le* **~** be on tenterhooks.

grillade *cuis.* [gri'jad] *f* grilled meat.

grillage[1] [gri'jaːʒ] *m cuis.* grilling; roasting (*a.* ⊙), ⚡ burning-out.

grill|age[2] [gri'jaːʒ] *m* lattice; (*wire*) netting *or* fencing; **~ager** [~ja'ʒe] (1l) lattice; surround with wire netting; **~e** [griːj] *f* grate (*a.* ⊙); grating; iron gate, railing; ⚡, *radio, fig.* grid; *mot.* grille; *fig.* schedule.

griller[1] [gri'je] (1a) *v/t. cuis.* grill; toast; roast; singe; scorch; ⚡, ⊙ burn out; *fig.* race past, cut out; jump (*a stop etc.*); F smoke (*a cigarette*); *v/i.* ⚡ burn out; *fig.* be burning (with s.th., *de qch.*); *to inf., de inf.*).

griller[2] [~] (1a) rail in; bar.

grillon *zo.* [gri'jõ] *m* cricket.

grimac|e [gri'mas] *f* grimace; **~er** [~ma'se] (1k) grimace; screw one's face up.

grimer *thea.* [gri'me] (1a) make up.

grimoire [gri'mwaːr] *m* (unintelligible) gibberish; scribble, scrawl.

grimp|er [grɛ̃'pe] (1a) *vt/i.* climb (up); *v/i.* ⚓ climb, creep, trail; **~ereau** *orn.* [~'pro] *m* tree-creeper; **~eur** [~'pœːr] climbing.

grinc|ement [grɛ̃s'mã] *m see* **grincer**; **~er** [grɛ̃'se] (1a) grind; gnash (*teeth*); creak (*door*); scratch (*pen*).

grincheux [grɛ̃'ʃø] **1.** *adj.* grumpy; testy; touchy; **2.** *su.* grumbler.

gringalet F [grɛ̃ga'le] *m* little fellow.

griotte ⚓ [gri'ɔt] *f* morello cherry.

gripp|e [grip] *f* dislike; ⚕ influenza, flu; *prendre q. en* **~** take a dislike to s.o.; **~é** ⚕ [gri'pe] *adj.*: *être* **~** have the flu; **~er** [~] (1a) *v/t.*, *a. se* **~** ⊙ jam; wrinkle, pucker; **~e-sou,** *pl.* **~e-sou(s)** F [grip'su] *m* miser.

gris [gri] grey, *Am.* gray; *a. fig.* dull; tipsy; *faire grise mine* make a sour face, **~aille** [gri'zaːj] greyness; *a. fig.* dullness; **~âtre** [~'zaːtr] greyish.

grisbi *sl.* [gris'bi] *m* dough (= *money*).

griser [gri'ze] (1a) F make tipsy; *se* **~** F get tipsy.

grisonner [grizɔ'ne] (1a) turn grey (*hair*).

grisou ⚒ [gri'zu] *m* fire-damp; gas; *coup m de* **~** fire-damp explosion.

grive *orn.* [griːv] *f* thrush.

grivois [gri'vwa] risqué, spicy (*joke*); **~erie** [~vwaz'ri] *f* smutty joke.

grogn|ement [grɔɲ'mã] *m* grunt; growl; snarl; grumbling; **~er** [grɔ'ɲe] (1a) *v/i.* grunt; grumble; *v/t.* growl out (*s.th.*); **~eur** [~'ɲœːr], **~on** [~'ɲõ] **1.** *adj.* grumbling; peevish; **2.** *su./m* grumbler; cross-patch; **~onner** F [~ɲɔ'ne] (1a) grunt; grumble; be peevish.

groin [grwɛ̃] *m* pig: snout.

grol(l)e *sl.* [grɔl] *f* shoe.

grommeler [grɔm'le] (1c) mutter.

grond|ement [grɔ̃d'mã] *m* rumbling; roar(ing); growl; **~er** [grɔ̃'de] (1a) *v/i.* growl (*dog*); grumble (at, *contre*); rumble (*thunder*); roar (*sea, storm*); *v/t.* scold; **~erie** [~'dri] *f* scolding; **~eur,** **-euse** [~'dœːr, ~'døːz] **1.** *adj.* scolding; **2.** *su.* grumbler; *su./f* shrew.

gros, ~se [gro, groːs] **1.** *adj.* big, large, stout, fat; thick; broad (*humour etc.*); foul (*word*); heavy (*rain, sea*); swollen (*river*); *fig.* teeming (with, *de*); *fig.* fraught (with, *de*); **~ bétail** *m* cattle; **~ doigt** *m du pied* big toe; F *grosse*

légume f big shot; **avoir le cœur ~** be heavy-hearted; **2. gros** adv. a great deal, a lot; (*write*) in large letters; **3.** su./m bulk, main part; thickest part; *winter etc.*: heart; **✝ de ~** wholesale (*price, business, firm, etc.*); **en ~** rough, broad (*estimate etc.*); (*describe etc.*) roughly, broadly, **✝,** *fig.* wholesale; (*write*) in large letters; su./f gross, twelve dozen.

groseille [gro'zɛːj] f (red) currant; **~ à maquereau** gooseberry; **~ier ♀** [~zɛˈje] m currant-bush.

gross|esse ♀ [gro'sɛs] f pregnancy; **~eur** [~'sœːr] f size, bulk; *lips*: thickness; ♀ swelling; **~ier** [~'sje] coarse, gross, crude, rude, crass (*ignorance etc.*); **~ièreté** [~sjɛrˈte] f coarseness; rudeness; grossness; **dire des ~s** be offensive; **~ir** [~'siːr] (2a) v/t. enlarge, magnify (a. opt., a. fig.); swell; v/i. grow bigger, increase; put on weight (*person*); **~issement** [~sisˈmã] m magnification; enlargement; increase, swelling; **~iste ✝** [~'sist] m wholesaler.

grotesque [grɔ'tɛsk] **1.** adj. grotesque; **2.** su./m freak.

grotte [grɔt] f grotto; cave.

grouiller [gru'je] (1a) v/i. swarm, teem, be alive (with, **de**); rumble (*belly*); v/t.: *sl.* **se ~** hurry up.

group|e [grup] m group; *trees etc.*: a. cluster; ♀ **~ sanguin** blood group; **~ement** [~'mã] m group(ing); **~er** [gru'pe] (1a) group; **se ~** form a group or groups; gather, cluster (round, **autour de**).

grue [gry] f orn., ⊙ crane; F prostitute; F **faire le pied de ~** cool one's heels.

grume|au [gry'mo] m clot; *salt, sauce etc.*: lump; **~ler** [grym'le] (1c): **se ~** clot, curdle; go lumpy; **~leux** [~'lø] curdled; gritty; lumpy.

grutier [gry'tje] m crane-driver.

gué [ge] m ford.

guenille [gə'niːj] f rag; F trollop.

guêp|e zo. [gɛːp] f wasp; **~ier** [gɛ'pje] m wasps' nest; bee-eater.

guère [gɛːr] adv.: **ne ... ~** hardly, little, scarcely, not much or many.

guéret [ge'rɛ] m fallow land.

guéridon [geri'dõ] m pedestal table.

guérill|a [geri'ja] f guerilla (war); **~ero** [~je'ro] m person: guerilla.

guéri|r [ge'riːr] (2a) v/t. cure; heal (*a wound etc.*); v/i. get better, be cured; heal (*wound*); **~son** [geri'zõ] f cure; *wound*: healing; recovery; **~ssable** [~'sabl] curable; healable; **~sseur** m, **-euse** f [~'sœːr, ~'søːz] healer; quack.

guérite [ge'rit] f sentry box; hut.

guerr|e [gɛːr] f war(fare); *fig.* quarrel; **Grande ♀** World War I; **faire la ~** make war (on, **à**); **de bonne ~** fair; **~ier** [gɛ'rje] **1.** adj. warlike; **2.** su./m warrior; **~oyer** [~rwa'je] (1h) wage war.

guet [gɛ] m watch; patrol; **faire le ~** be on the look-out; **~apens**, pl. **~s-apens** [geta'pã] m ambush.

guêtre [gɛːtr] f gaiter; mot. patch.

guett|er [gɛ'te] (1a) lie in wait for, watch for (a. fig.); **~eur** ✗, ♫ [~'tœːr] m person: look-out.

gueul|ard, e F [gœ'laːr, ~'lard] **1.** adj. loud-mouthed (*person*); noisy; **2.** su. loudmouth; **~e** [gœl] f animal, sl. person: mouth; opening; sl. face; F look, appearance; F **avoir de la ~** look great; **avoir la ~ de bois** have a hangover; sl. **casser la ~ à q.** sock s.o.; sl. **ta ~!** shut up!; **~e-de-loup**, pl. **~es-de-loup ♀** [~də'lu] snapdragon; **~er** sl. [gœ'le] (1a) bawl; **~eton** F [gœl'tõ] m blow-out, spread.

gui ♀ [gi] m mistletoe.

guibolle sl. [gi'bɔl] f leg.

guichet [gi'fɛ] m post office, bank etc.: counter, window; wicket, hatch; 🚂 ticket window; thea. box office.

guide¹ [gid] m guide (a. ✗, a. ⊙).

guide² [~] f rein; girl guide.

guid|e-âne [gi'dɑːn] m standing instructions pl.; *paper*: ruled guide; **~er** [~'de] (1a) conduct, direct; drive (a car etc.); steer.

guidon [gi'dõ] m handlebars pl.

guigne [giɲ] f heart-cherry; F fig. bad luck.

guigner F [gi'ɲe] (1a) steal a glance at; eye, ogle; have one's eyes on.

guignol [gi'ɲɔl] m Punch.

guignon [gi'ɲõ] m bad luck.

guillemets [gij'mɛ] m/pl. inverted commas, quotation marks.

guilleret [gij'rɛ] gay; broad (*joke*).

guillotine [gijɔ'tin] f guillotine.

guimpe [gɛ̃p] f chemisette.

guind|age ☼ [gɛ̃'daːʒ] *m* hoist(ing);
~**é** [~'de] stiff; strained; stilted
(*style*).

guinguette [gɛ̃'gɛt] *f* suburban tavern;
out-of-town inn.

guirlande [gir'lɑ̃ːd] *f* garland.

guise [giːz] *f* manner, way; **à votre ~!** as
you like!; **en ~ de** by way of.

guitare ♪ [gi'taːr] *f* guitar.

gustati|f [gysta'tif] gustative; gustatory;
~**on** [~ta'sjɔ̃] *f* tasting.

guttural [gyty'ral] *f* throaty (*voice*).

gymnas|e [ʒim'naːz] *m* gymnasium; ~**te**
[~'nast] *su.* gymnast; ~**tique** [~nas'tik] *f*
gymnastics *sg.*; fitness exercises *pl.*

gynécolog|iste ❊ [ʒinekɔlɔ'ʒist], ~**ue** ❊
[~'lɔg] *su.* gyn(a)ecologist.

gypse [ʒips] *m* gypsum.

H

(Before the so-called aspirate *h*, marked
*h, there is neither elision nor liaison.)

habil|e [a'bil] clever, skil(l)ful; clever;
~**eté** [abil'te] *f* skill, ability; cleverness;
(clever) trick; ~**ité** ⚖ [~'te] (1a) entitle (s.o. to
inf., **q. à** *inf.*).

habill|age [abiːja:ʒ] *m* dressing; ☼
assembling; ✝ get-up; ~**ement** [abij'mɑ̃]
m clothing; clothes *pl.*; ~**er** [abi'je] (1a)
dress; clothe; ✝ get up (*an article*);
cover; *dress*: suit (s.o.); **s'~** dress (o.s.),
get dressed; dress up (*us*, **en**).

habit [a'bi] *m* (full-dress) suit; dress coat;
dress; coat; *eccl.* frock.

habit|able [abi'tabl] habitable; ~**acle**
[~'takl] *m* ⚓ binnacle; ✈ cockpit; *poet.*
dwelling; ~**ant** *m*, **e** *f* [~'tɑ̃, ~'tɑ̃ːt] inhabitant; resident; ~**at** ❊, *zo.*, *etc.* [~'ta]
m habitat; ~**ation** [~ta'sjɔ̃] *f* habitation;
dwelling; housing; ~**er** [~'te] (1a) *v/t.*
inhabit, live in; *v/i.* live, reside.

habitu|de [abi'tyd] *f* habit; **avoir l'~ de**
be used to (s.th., doing s.th.); **avoir l'~
de** (*inf.*) *a.* be in the habit of (*ger.*); **j'ai
l'~, j'en ai l'~** I am used to it; **d'~** usually; **par ~** out of habit; ~**é** *m*, **e** *f* [~'tɥe]
regular customer; **el** [~'tɥɛl] usual;
customary; ~**er** [~'tɥe] (1n): **~ q. à** accustom s.o. *or* get s.o. used to (s.th.,
doing s.th.); **s'~ à** get used to.

***hâbl|erie** [ɑblə'ri] *f* boasting; *~**eur**
[ɑ'blœːr] *m* boaster.

***hach|e** [aʃ] *f* axe; *~**e-légumes**
[~le'gym] *m/inv.* vegetable-cutter; *~**er**

[a'ʃe] (1a) chop (up); hash (*meat*), hack
up; hatch (*a drawing etc.*); *~**ereau**
[aʃ'ro] *m*, *~**ette** [a'ʃɛt] *f* hatchet; *~**is**
[a'ʃi] *m* hash.

***hagard** [a'gaːr] wild, distraught.

***haï** [a'i] *p.p.* of **haïr.**

***haie** [ɛ] *f* hedge(row); *people*: line; *sp.*
hurdle; *sp.* **course** *f* **de ~s** hurdle-race;
faire la ~ be lined up.

***haillon** [a'jɔ̃] *m* rag, tatter.

***hain|e** [ɛn] *f* hate, hatred; *~**eux** [ɛ'nø]
full of hatred.

***haïr** [a'iːr] (2m) hate, loathe; ***hais** [ɛ]
1st p. sg. pres. of **haïr; *haïs** [a'i] *1st p.
sg. p.s. of* **haïr; *haïssable** [ai'sabl]
hateful, odious; ***haïssent** [a'is] *3rd p.
pl. pres. of* **haïr.**

***halage** [a'laːʒ] *m* hauling; towing.

***hâle** [ɑːl] *m* tan; sunburn; ***hâlé** ❊
[a'le] (sun)tanned.

haleine [a'lɛn] *f* breath; *fig.* wind; **à perte d'~** until out of breath; **avoir l'~
courte** be short-winded; **de longue ~** of
long duration; long-term (*plans*); **hors
d'~** out of breath; **tenir en ~** keep
breathless.

***haler** [a'le] (1a) ⚓ haul; tow.

***hal|ètement** [alɛt'mɑ̃] *m* panting;
*~**eter** [al'te] (1d) pant; puff.

***hall** [ɔl] *m* hall; *hotel*: lounge; ☼ shop;
*~**e** [al] *f* (covered) market.

***hallebarde** [al'bard] *f* halberd.

***hallier** [a'lje] *m* thicket, copse.

hallucina|nt [alysi'nɑ̃] hallucinating; *fig.*
incredible, staggering; ~**tion** [~na'sjɔ̃] *f*
hallucination.

*halo [a'lo] *m* meteor. halo; *phot.* halation; *opt.* blurring.

*halte [alt] *f* halt (*a.* 🚋), stop; stopping-place; *faire* ~ stop, halt.

haltère [al'tɛːr] *m* dumbbell.

*hamac [a'mak] *m* hammock.

*hameau [a'mo] *m* hamlet.

hameçon [am'sɔ̃] *m* (fish)hook; *fig.* bait; *fig. mordre à l'*~ take the bait.

*hampe [ɑ̃ːp] *f* pole; shaft.

*hanche [ɑ̃ːʃ] *f* hip; *horse:* haunch.

*handicap [ɑ̃di'kap] *m* handicap; ***~er** [~ka'pe] (1a) handicap; *les handicapés* (*mentaux or physiques*) the (mentally *or* physically) handicapped.

*hangar [ɑ̃'gaːr] *m* shed; lean-to; boathouse; ✈ hangar.

*hanneton [an'tɔ̃] *m* cockchafer.

*hant|er [ɑ̃'te] (1a) haunt; *maison f hantée* haunted house; ***~ise** [ɑ̃'tiːz] *f* obsession.

*happer [a'pe] (1a) *v/t.* snap (up); catch, snatch, seize, grab.

*harangu|e [a'rɑ̃ːg] *f* harangue; ***~er** [arɑ̃'ge] (1m) harangue.

*haras [a'rɑ] *m* stud-farm; stud.

*harasser [ara'se] (1a) wear out.

*harc|èlement [arsɛl'mɑ̃] *m* harassing; ***~eler** [~sɔ'le] (1d) harass, harry (*a.* ✕); badger; nag at.

*harde [ard] *f* herd; *orn.* flock.

*hardes [ard] *f/pl.* old clothes.

*hardi [ar'di] bold; daring; rash; impudent; ***~esse** [~'djɛs] *f* boldness; daring; rashness; effrontery.

*hareng [a'rɑ̃] *m* herring.

*hargn|e [arɲ] *f* aggressiveness; ***~eux** [ar'nø] surly; nagging (*wife*).

*haricot¹ 🍲 [ari'ko] *m* bean; ~ *blanc* haricot bean; ~ *rouge* kidney bean; ~ *vert* French bean.

*haricot² *cuis.* [~] *m* stew, haricot.

*haridelle F [ari'dɛl] *f* jade, nag.

harmoni|e [armɔ'ni] *f* ♪ harmony (*a. fig.*); ♪ brass and reed band; **~eux** [~'njø] harmonious; **~que** [~'nik] harmonic; **~ser** [~ni'ze] (1a) harmonize.

*harnacher [arna'ʃe] (1a) harness; rig (*s.o.*) out.

*harnais [ar'nɛ] *m* harness.

*haro [a'ro] *m*: *crier* ~ *sur* denounce.

harpagon [arpa'gɔ̃] *m* skinflint.

*harpe ♪ [arp] *f* harp.

*harpon [ar'pɔ̃] *m* harpoon; 🔺 wall-sta-

ple; ***~ner** [~pɔ'ne] (1a) harpoon; *fig.* buttonhole (*s.o.*).

*hasard [a'zaːr] *m* chance, luck; stroke *or* piece of luck; hazard; *à tout* ~ (just) in case; on the off chance; *au* ~ at random; aimlessly; *... de* ~ chance ...; *par* ~ by chance; ***~é** [azar'de] risky; bold; ***~er** [~'de] (1a) risk, hazard (*one's life, fortune, etc.*); venture, hazard (*a question etc.*); *se* ~ *dans etc.* venture into *etc.* (*a place*); *se* ~ *à* (*inf.*) venture to (*inf.*), risk (*ger.*); ***~eux** [~'dø] hazardous, risky; daring.

*hât|e [ɑːt] *f* haste, hurry; *à la* ~ in a hurry; hurriedly; *avoir* ~ *de* (*inf.*) be in a hurry to (*inf.*); long to (*inf.*); *en* (*toute*) ~ with all possible speed; ***~er** [ɑ'te] (1a) hasten, hurry; ***~if** [ɑ'tif] hasty; premature; early (*fruit etc.*).

*hauss|e [oːs] *f* rise (*a.* ✝, *Am.* raise); ⚙ block, prop; *à la* ~ on the rise; ***~ement** [os'mɑ̃] *m* raising; ~ *d'épaules* shrug; ***~er** [o'se] (1a) *v/t.* raise (*a.* ♪; *a. a house, the price, one's voice*); lift; shrug (*one's shoulders*); *v/i.* rise; heave in sight; ***~ier** ✝ [o'sje] *m* bull.

*haut, e [o, oːt] **1.** *adj.* high; tall; loud (*voice*); upper (*floor etc.*); *la haute mer* the open sea; *la mer haute* high tide; **2.** *adv.* high (up); aloud; haughtily; back (*in time*); *la* ~ *main* easily; ~ *les mains!* hands up!; *d'en* ~ *adj.* upstairs; upper; *en* ~ *adv.* above; upstairs; **3.** *su./m* height; top; *tomber de son* ~ fall flat; fall down; *fig.* be taken aback; *vingt pieds de* ~ 20 feet high; **~ement** highly; loudly, *fig.* openly.

*hautain [o'tɛ̃] proud; haughty.

*haut...: ***~bois** ♪ [o'bwa] *m* oboe; (*a.* ***~boïste** [obo'ist] *m*) oboist; ***~-de-forme,** *pl.* ***~s-de-forme** [od'fɔrm] *m* top hat.

*hautement [ot'mɑ̃] *adv.* highly; loudly; loftily; frankly.

*Hautesse [o'tɛs] *f title:* Highness.

*hauteur [o'tœːr] *f* height; hill(-top); level; 🔺, *astr.* altitude; ♪ pitch; *fig.* loftiness; *fig. a.* haughtiness; *à* (*la*) ~ *de* level with; as high as; *fig. à la* ~ *de* equal to, up to (*a job*); *être à la* ~ be up to it; ✈ *prendre de la* ~ gain height; *tomber de toute sa* ~ fall flat; F *fig.* be taken aback; *sp. saut en* ~ high jump.

*haut...: ***~-fond,** *pl.* ***~s-fonds** [o'fɔ̃] *m* shallows *pl.*; ***~-le-cœur** [ɔl'kœːr] *m/ inv.* nausea; ***~-le-corps** [~'kɔːr] *m/inv.* sudden start; ***~-parleur** [oparˈlœːr] *m* loudspeaker.

*hâve [ɑːv] haggard, gaunt; wan.

*havre ⚓ [ɑːvr] *m* harbo(u)r, haven.

*hayon *mot.* [ɛ'jɔ̃] *m* rear door; *car:* hatchback.

*hé! [e] *int.* hi!; I say!; what!

hebdomadaire [ɛbdɔmaˈdɛːr] *adj., su./m* weekly (paper *or* publication).

héberger [ebɛrˈʒe] (1l) accommodate, put up, take in.

hébét|er [ebeˈte] (1f) stupefy; daze; *fig.* stun; **~ude** [~'tyd] *f fig.* daze, dazed condition; ♣ hebetude.

hébraïque [ebraˈik] Hebrew; **~eu** [e'brø] *adj., su./m lng.* Hebrew.

hécatombe [ekaˈtɔ̃b] *f* hecatomb; F *fig. persons:* (great) slaughter.

hectare [ɛkˈtaːr] *m* hectare (2.47 acres).

hectique [ɛkˈtik] hectic.

*hein? F [ɛ̃] *int.* what?; isn't it?

hélas! [e'lɑːs] *int.* alas!

héler [e'le] (1f) hail (*a taxi*).

hélice [e'lis] *f* ✈, *anat.* helix; spiral; ⚓ screw; ♣, ✈ propeller.

hélicoptère [elikɔp'tɛːr] *m* helicopter.

héliport ✈ [eli'pɔːr] *m* heliport.

helvéti|en [ɛlveˈsjɛ̃] *adj., su.* Swiss; **~que** [~'tik] Helvetic, Swiss.

hémi... [emi] hemi...; **~sphère** [emisˈfɛːr] *m* hemisphere.

hémo... [emɔ] h(a)em(o)..., **~globine** [~glɔ'bin] *f* h(a)emoglobin; **~rragie** ♂ [~ra'ʒi] *f* h(a)emorrhage; **~rroïdes** ♂ [~rɔ'id] *f/pl.* h(a)emorrhoids.

*henné ♣ [ɛn'ne] *m* henna.

henni|r [ɛ'niːr] (2a) whinny, neigh; ***~ssement** [ɛnisˈmɑ̃] *m* neigh(ing).

héraldique [eralˈdik] heraldic.

*héraut [e'ro] *m* herald (*a. fig.*).

herb|acé ♣ [ɛrbaˈse] herbaceous; **~age** [~'baːʒ] *m* pasture; grass; *cuis.* green stuff; **~e** [ɛrb] *f* grass; herb; weed; **~s** *pl. potagères* pot herbs; **en ~** unripe; *fig.* budding; *fines* **~s** *pl.* herbs for seasoning; *mauvaise* **~** weed; *fig.* bad lot; **~eux** [~'bø] grassy; **~icide** [~biˈsid] *m* weed killer; **~ivore** *zo.* [~biˈvɔːr] **1.** *adj.* herbivorous; **2.** *su./m* herbivore; **~ori-ser** [~bɔriˈze] (1a) botanize; **~u** [~'by] grassy.

*hère [ɛːr] *m*: *pauvre* **~** poor devil.

hérédit|aire [erediˈtɛːr] hereditary; **~é** [~'te] *f* heredity; inheritance.

héré|sie [ereˈzi] *f* heresy; **~tique** [~'tik] **1.** *adj.* heretical; **2.** *su.* heretic.

*hériss|é [eriˈse] bristling (with, *de*); bristly; prickly; spiked (with, *de*); ***~er** [~'se] (1a) bristle (up); ruffle; **se ~** bristle (up) (*a. fig.*); ***~on** [~'sɔ̃] *m zo.* hedge-hog; ✿ brush.

hérit|age [eriˈtaːʒ] *m* inheritance, heritage; **~er** [~'te] (1a): **~** (*de*) *qch.* inherit s.th. (from s.o., *de q.*); **~ier, -ère** [~'tje, ~'tjɛːr] *su.* heir; su./f heiress.

hermétique [ɛrmeˈtik] hermetic; (air-, water)tight; impenetrable.

hermine [ɛr'min] *f* ermine.

*horniaire ♂ [ɛr'njɛːr] hernial; *bandage m* **~** truss; ***hernie** ♂ [~'ni] *f* hernia, rupture.

héroïne [erɔ'in] *f* heroine; 💊 heroin; **~que** [~'ik] heroic; **~sme** [~'ism] *m* heroism.

*héron *orn.* [e'rɔ̃] *m* heron.

*héros [e'ro] *m* hero.

*herse ⚒ [ɛrs] *f* harrow.

hésit|ation [ezitaˈsjɔ̃] *f* hesitation; **~er** [~'te] (1a) hesitate; falter.

hétéro... [eterɔ] hetero...; **~clite** [~'klit] irregular; odd; **~doxe** [~'dɔks] hetero-dox; **~gène** [~'ʒɛn] heterogeneous; *fig.* incongruous.

*hêtre ♣ [ɛːtr] *m* beech.

*heu! [ø] *int.* ah!; h'm!; pooh!

heure [œːr] *f* hour; time; moment; ... o'clock; *six* **~s** *pl.* 6 o'clock; **~** *d'été* summer time; ✕ **~** *H* zero hour; **~** *légale* standard time; *à l'***~** on time; *à l'***~** (*de*) ... in the ... age; in the ... fashion; *à la bonne* **~!** fine!; *à tout à l'***~!** see you later!; F *c'est l'***~** time's up!; *de bonne* **~** early; *quelle* **~** *est-il?* what time is it? *pour l'***~** at present, at the moment.

heureu|sement [œrøzˈmɑ̃] luckily, fortunately; thank goodness; **~** que it's lucky or fortunate that; **~x** [œ'rø] happy; lucky; successful; fortunate; apt (*reply*).

*heurt [œːr] *m* blow, shock; *fig. sans* **~** smoothly; ***~é** [œr'te] clashing; jerky; ***~er** [~'te] (1a) *v/t.* knock, hit; collide (with); jostle; *v/t.* run into; *fig.* offend (*feelings*); **se ~** collide (with, *à*); clash; *fig. se* **~** *à a.* meet with, come up against (*difficulties etc.*); *~oir [~'twa:r] *m* knocker; ☉ stop; 🜨 buffer.

hexagone [ɛgza'gɔn] *m* ♣ hexagon; *fig. l'~* France.

hiberner [iber'ne] (1a) hibernate.

*hibou orn. [i'bu] *m* owl.

*hic [ik] *m* snag, hitch, catch.

*hideux [i'dø] hideous.

hiémal [je'mal] winter-...

hier [jɛ:r] *adv.* yesterday; *~ soir* last night; F *fig. né d'~* born yesterday.

*hiérarchie [jerar'ʃi] *f* hierarchy; *~que* [~'ʃik] hierarchical; *voie f ~* official channels *pl.*

hiéroglyphe [jerɔ'glif] *m* hieroglyph; *fig.* scrawl.

hilar|ant [ila'rɑ̃] mirth-provoking, *~ité* [~ri'te] *f* hilarity, laughter.

hippi|que [ip'pik] equine, horse-...; *con-cours m ~* horse-show *or* race; *~sme* [~'pism] *m* horse-racing.

hippo... [ipɔ] horse-...; *~campe zo.* [~'kɑ̃:p] *m* sea horse; *~drome* [~'drɔ:m] *m* race track; *~mobile* [~mɔ'bil] horse-drawn; *~potame zo.* [~pɔ'tam] *m* hippopotamus.

hirondelle *orn.* [irɔ̃'dɛl] *f* swallow.

hirsute [ir'syt] shaggy; *fig.* boorish.

hispanique [ispa'nik] Spanish.

*hisser [i'se] (1a) hoist, pull up.

histo|ire [is'twa:r] *f* history; story; F fib; F *~ de (faire qch.)* just to (*do s.th.*); *faire des ~s* make a fuss; *~rien* [istɔ'rjɛ̃] *m* historian; *~riette* [~'rjɛt] *f* anecdote; *~rique* [~'rik] **1.** *adj.* historic(al); **2.** *su./m* historical account.

histrion [istri'ɔ̃] *m* ham (actor).

hiver [i'vɛ:r] *m* winter; *~nal* [iver'nal] winter-...; wintry (*weather*); *~ner* [~'ne] (1a) winter; hibernate.

*hobereau [ɔ'bro] *m orn.* hobby; F small country squire, squireen.

*hoch|ement [ɔʃ'mɑ̃] *m* shake *or* nod (*of the head*); *~er [ɔ'ʃe] (1a): ~ la tête* shake *or* nod one's head; *~et [ɔ'ʃɛ] *m* rattle; *fig.* toy.

*holà [ɔ'la] **1.** *int.* hallo!; stop!; **2.** *m/inv.-* F *mettre le ~ à qch.* put a stop to s.th.

*holding 🜨 [ɔl'diŋ] *m* holding company.

*hold-up [ɔl'dœp] *m/inv.* hold-up.

hollandais, e [ɔlɑ̃'dɛ, ~'dɛ:z] **1.** *adj., su./m ling.* Dutch; **2.** *su./m* ♀ Dutchman; *les* ♀ *m/pl.* the Dutch; *su./f* ♀ Dutchwoman.

holocauste [ɔlɔ'ko:st] *m* holocaust; *fig.* sacrifice.

*homard zo. [ɔ'ma:r] *m* lobster.

homélie [ɔme'li] *f* homily (*a. fig.*).

homicide [ɔmi'sid] **1.** *su./m* homicide (*person or crime*); *~ par imprudence* (*or involontaire*) manslaughter; *~ prémédité* murder; **2.** *adj.* homicidal.

homm|age [ɔ'ma:ʒ] *m* homage, tribute; token of esteem; *~s pl.* compliments; *rendre ~* pay tribute (to, *à*); *~asse* F [ɔ'mas] *f* mannish.

homme [ɔm] *m* man; *~ d'affaires* businessman; *~ de métier* craftsman; *~ d'État* statesman; *~-grenouille, pl. ~s-grenouilles* [~grə'nu:j] *m* frogman.

homo... [ɔmɔ] homo...; *~gène* [~'ʒɛn] homogeneous; *~généiser* [~ʒenei'ze] (1a) homogenize; *~logue* [~'lɔg] **1.** *adj.* homologous; **2.** *su./m* homologue; *person:* counterpart, opposite number; *~loguer* [~lɔ'ge] (1m) 🜨 confirm; prove (*a will*); *sp.* recognize.

*hongre [ɔ̃:gr] *m* gelding.

*hongrois [ɔ̃'grwa] *adj., su.* Hungarian.

honnête [ɔ'nɛ:t] honest; upright; respectable; well-bred; reasonable (*price*); *~s gens m/pl.* decent people; *~té* [ɔnɛt'te] *f* honesty.

honneur [ɔ'nœr] *m* hono(u)r; *avoir l'~* have the hono(u)r (of *ger.*, *de inf.*); *faire ~ à* hono(u)r, 🜨 a. meet (*an obligation*); *rendre ~ à* pay tribute to.

*honnir † [ɔ'ni:r] (2a) disgrace; spurn; *honni soit qui mal y pense* evil be to him who evil thinks.

honor|abilité [ɔnɔrabili'te] *f* respectability; *~able* [~'rabl] hono(u)rable; respectable; 🜨 reputable; *~aire* [~'rɛ:r] **1.** *adj.* honorary; **2.** *su./m: ~s pl.* fee(s *pl.*) *sg.*; *~er* [~'re] (1a) hono(u)r; respect; 🜨 meet; *s'~ de* pride o.s. on; *~ifique* [~ri'fik] honorary.

*hont|e [ɔ̃:t] *f* (sense of) shame; disgrace; *avoir ~* be ashamed (of, *de*); *faire ~ à* put to shame; *~eux* [ɔ̃'tø] ashamed; disgraceful; shameful.

hôpital [ɔpi'tal] *m* hospital.

*hoquet [ɔ'kɛ] *m* hiccup; gasp; *~er* [ɔk'te] (1c) have the hiccups.

horaire [ɔ'rɛ:r] **1.** *adj.* hour-...; per hour; **2.** *su./m* timetable; *~ souple* flexible working hours *pl.*

*horde [ɔrd] *f* horde.

horizon [ɔri'zɔ̃] *m* horizon (*a. fig.*); panorama, view; **~tal** [~zɔ̃'tal] horizontal.

horloge [ɔr'lɔːʒ] *f* clock; **~** *normande* grandfather clock; *teleph.* **~** *parlante* speaking clock; **~r** [~lɔ'ʒe] *m* watch- or clockmaker; **~rie** [~lɔʒ'ri] *f* watchmaker's (shop).

hormis [ɔr'mi] *prp.* except.

hormone [ɔr'mɔn] *f* hormone.

horoscope [ɔrɔs'kɔp] *m* horoscope; *faire* (*or tirer*) *un* **~** cast a horoscope.

horr|eur [ɔ'rœːr] *f* horror; *avoir* **~** *de*, *avoir en* **~** hate, detest; *faire* **~** *à* disgust, fill with horror; **~ible** [ɔ'ribl] horrible, awful; **~ipiler** [ɔripi'le] (1a) F make (*s.o.'s*) flesh creep; F *fig.* exasperate.

*****hors** [ɔːr] *prp.* except (for); (*a.* **~** *de*) out of; outside; beyond, but, save; **~** *d'atteinte* out of reach (of, *de*); *fig.* beyond reach; **~** *du commun* out of the common; **⚡ ~** *circuit* cut off; **~** *concours* hors concours; *sp.* **~** *jeu* offside; **~** *ligne* (*or classe*) outstanding; **✝ ~** *vente* no longer on sale; **~** (*de*) *pair* peerless; **~** *de sens* out of one's senses; **~** *de soi* beside o.s. (with rage); **~** *d'ici!* get out!

*****hors...:** *****~-bord** [ɔr'bɔːr] *m/inv.* outboard motor boat; *****~-d'œuvre** [~'dœːvr] *m/inv. cuis.* first course; *fig.* irrelevant matter; *****~-jeu** *sp.* [~'ʒø] *m/ inv.* off side; *****~-la-loi** [~la'lwa] *m/inv.* outlaw; ***** **~-saison** [~sɛ'zɔ̃] off-season (*tariff etc.*) *book:* plate.

hortensia ⚘ [ɔrtɑ̃'sja] *m* hydrangea.

horti|cole [ɔrti'kɔl] horticultural; **~culture** [~kyl'tyːr] *f* gardening.

hospi|ce [ɔs'pis] *m* hospice; alms-house; (*orphan's*) home; **~talier, -ère** [ɔspi-ta'lje, ~'ljɛːr] hospitable; hospital-...; **~taliser** [~li'ze] (1a) hospitalize; **~talité** [~li'te] *f* hospitality; *donner* (*or offrir*) *l'~* *à* put s.o. up.

hostie *eccl.* [ɔs'ti] *f* host.

hostile [ɔs'til] hostile (to, *à*); **hostilité** [~tili'te] *f* hostility.

hôte [oːt] *m* host; landlord; *su.* guest; **~esse** [o'tɛs] *su./f* hostess; *hôtesse de l'air* air hostess.

hôtel [o'tɛl] *m* hotel; **~** (*particulier* private) mansion; **~** *de ville* town hall, city hall; **~** *garni* residential hotel; *maître m d'~* head waiter; butler; **~-Dieu**, *pl.*

~s-Dieu [otɛl'djø] *m* principal hospital; **~ier** [otɛ'lje] *m* innkeeper; hotel-keeper; **~lerie** [otɛl'ri] *f* inn; hotel trade.

*****hotte** [ɔt] *f* basket; hod, ⚙ hood.

*****houblon** ⚘ *etc.* [u'blɔ̃] *m* hop(s *pl.*).

*****hou|e** ⚒ [u] *f* hoe; **~er** [u'e] (1a) hoe.

*****houill|e** [uj] *f* coal; *fig.* **~** *blanche* water-power; *****~er, -ère** [u'je, ~'jɛːr] **1.** *adj.* coal-...; *production f* **~ère** output of coal; **2.** *su./f* coal mine; *****~eux** [u'jø] coal-bearing.

*****houle** [ul] *f* swell, surge, billows *pl.*

*****houlette** [u'lɛt] *f* (*shepherd's etc.*) crook; ⚒ trowel; ⚙ hand-ladle.

*****houleux** [u'lø] surging; stormy.

*****houp!** [up] *int.* up!; off you go!

*****houppe** [up] *f* tuft; tassel, bob; pompon; *zo.* crest; (powder-)puff.

*****hourd|age** ⚙ [ur'daːʒ] *m*, *****~is** [ur'di] *m* rough masonry.

*****houspiller** [uspi'je] (1a) tell (*s.o.*) off; rag (*audience etc.*).

*****house** [us] *f* (dust) cover.

*****houx** ⚘ [u] *m* holly.

*****hublot** ⚓ [y'blo] *m* port-hole.

*****huche** [yʃ] *f* trough; bin; hopper.

*****hue!** [y] *int.* gee up!; *tirer à* **~** *et à dia* pull in opposite directions.

*****hu|ée** [y'e] *f* boo, hoot; **~s** *pl.* booing *sg.*; *****~er** [y'e] (1a) *v/t.* boo, jeer (*s.o.*); *v/i.* hoot (*owl*).

huil|age [ɥi'laːʒ] *m* oiling, lubrication; **~e** [ɥil] *f* oil; **~** *de foie de morue* cod-liver oil; **~** *minérale* petroleum; *fig. faire tache d'~* spread; F *les* **~s** *pl.* the big shots; **~é** *huilé* working *or* running smoothly; **~eux** [ɥi'lø] oily; **~ier** [~'lje] *m* cruet stand.

huis [ɥi] *m:* ⚖ *à* **~***-clos* in camera; F *à* **~** *clos* in private; **~serie** ⚙ [ɥis'ri] *f* door-frame; **~sier** [ɥi'sje] *m* usher; ⚖ bailiff.

*****huit** [ɥit; *before consonant* ɥi] eight; *date, title:* eighth; *d'aujourd'hui en* **~** today week; *tous les* **~** *jours* once a week, every week; *****~aine** [~'tɛn] *f* (about) eight; week; *****~ième** [~'tjɛm] eighth.

huître [ɥiːtr] *f* oyster.

huma|in [y'mɛ̃] **1.** *adj.* human; humane; **2.** *su./m: les* **~s** *pl.* human beings; **~niser** [ymani'ze] (1a) humanize; *fig. s'~* become more sociable; **~nitaire** [~'tɛːr]

humanitarian; **~nité** [~'te] f humanity; mankind; **~s** pl. the humanities.
humble [œ̃:bl] humble; lowly.
humecter [ymɛk'te] (1a) moisten.
***humer** [y'me] (1a) breathe in (the air, a perfume); sip; swallow.
humeur [y'mœːr] f mood; disposition; temper; ill humo(u)r, bad temper; **avec ~** crossly; peevishly; **de bonne (mauvaise) ~** in a good (bad) mood.
humid|e [y'mid] humid; **~ité** [ymidi'te] f moisture; humidity.
humili|er [ymi'lje] (1o) humiliate, humble; **~té** [~li'te] f humility.
humoriste [ymɔ'rist] **1.** adj. humorous (writer); **2.** su. humorist; **humoristique** [~ris'tik] humorous.
humour [y'muːr] m (sense of) humo(u)r.
humus [y'mys] m humus.
***hupp|e** [yp] f orn. hoopoe; bird: crest; **~é** [y'pe] orn. tufted; F smart; F **les gens** m/pl. **~s** the swells.
***hurl|ement** [yrlə'mɑ̃] m howl(ing); roar; bellow; ***~er** [~'le] (1a) howl; roar; bawl (out).
hurluberlu [yrlybɛr'ly] m scatterbrain; harum-scarum.
***huron** F [y'rɔ̃] m boor.
***hussard** ⚔ [y'saːr] m hussar; **~e** [y'sard] f: **à la ~** cavalierly.
***hutte** [yt] f hut, cabin, shanty.
hybrid|e [i'brid] adj., su./m hybrid; **~ité** [ibridi'te] f hybridity.
hydraulique [idro'lik] **1.** adj. hydraulic; **2.** su./f hydraulics sg.

hydravion [idra'vjɔ̃] m seaplane.
hydro... [idrɔ] water-...; **~carbure** 🜊 [~kar'byːr] m hydrocarbon; **~céphalie** [~sefa'li] f water on the brain; **~fuge** [~'fyːʒ] waterproof; **~gène** 🜊 [~'ʒɛn] m hydrogen; **~glisseur** 🜊 [~gli'sœːr] m hovercraft; **~phobie** 🜊 [~fɔ'bi] f rabies; **~pisie** 🜊 [~pi'zi] f dropsy; **~thérapie** 🜊 [~tera'pi] f water-cure.
hyène zo. [jɛn] f hyena.
hygi|ène [i'ʒjɛn] f hygiene; admin. health; **~énique** [iʒje'nik] hygienic, sanitary; **papier** m **~** toilet paper.
hym|en [i'mɛn] m anat. hymen; poet. = **~énée** [ime'ne] m marriage.
hymne [imn] su./m patriotic song; national anthem; su./f eccl. hymn.
hyper... [ipɛr] hyper...; **~bole** ⚆ [~'bɔl] f hyperbola; **~métrope** 🜊 [~me'trɔp] longsighted; **~tension** [~tɑ̃'sjɔ̃] f a. **artérielle** high blood pressure; **~trophie** [~trɔ'fi] f hypertrophy.
hypno|se [ip'noːz] f hypnosis; **~tiser** [ipnɔti'ze] (1a) hypnotize; **~tiseur** [~ti'zœːr] m hypnotist.
hypo... [ipɔ] hypo...; **~crisie** [-kri'zi] f hypocrisy; **~crite** [~'krit] **1.** adj. hypocritical; **2.** su. hypocrite; **~thécaire** [~te'kɛːr] mortgage-...; **créancier** m **~** mortgagee; **~thèque** [~'tɛk] f mortgage; **prendre une ~** raise a mortgage; **~théquer** [~te'ke] (1f) mortgage; **~thèse** [~'tɛːz] f hypothesis.
hystérie [iste'ri] f hysteria; **hystérique** 🜊 [~'rik] hysteric(al).

I

I, i [i] m I, i; **i grec** y.
ibérique geog. [ibe'rik] Iberian.
iceberg [is'bɛrg] m iceberg.
ichtyo... [iktjɔ] ichthyo..., fish-...; **~saure** [~'soːr] m ichthyosaurus.
ici [i'si] adv. here; now; teleph. **~ Jean** John speaking; **~ Londres** radio: London calling; this is London; **d'~ (à) lundi** by Monday; **d'~ (à) trois jours** within the next three days; **d'~**

demain by tomorrow; **d'~ là** by that time, by then; in the meantime; **d'~ peu** before long; **jusqu'~** place: as far as here; time: up to now; **par ~** here(abouts); this way; **près d'~** nearby.
iconoclaste [ikɔnɔ'klast] **1.** adj. iconoclastic; **2.** su. iconoclast.
ictère 🜊 [ik'tɛːr] m jaundice; **ictérique** [~te'rik] jaundiced (eyes).

idéal, e, *m/pl.* **-als, -aux** [ide'al, ~'o] **1.** *adj.* ideal; **2.** *su./m* ideal.

idée [i'de] *f* idea; notion; mind, head; intention, purpose; suggestion; **~ fixe** obsession.

identifier [idãti'fje] (1o) identify; **s'~ à** identify o.s. with; **identique** [~'tik] identical (with, **à**); **identité** [~ti'te] *f* identity.

idéologie [ideɔlɔ'ʒi] *f* ideology.

idiom|atique [idjɔma'tik] idiomatic; **~e** [i'djɔːm] *m* idiom; language.

idiot [i'djo] **1.** *adj.* idiotic; **2.** *su.* idiot; **~ie** [idjɔ'si] *f* idiocy; **~isme** [~'tism] *m* idiom(atic expression).

idoine [i'dwan] appropriate.

idol|âtre [idɔ'lɑːtr] **1.** *adj.* idolatrous, *fig.* **être ~ de** worship; **2.** *su./m* idolater; *su./f* idolatress; **~âtrer** [~lɑ'tre] (1a) *v/i.* worship idols; *v/t. fig.* idolize; **~âtrie** [~lɑ'tri] *f* idolatry; **~e** [i'dɔl] *f* idol.

if **Ꝗ** [if] *m* yew (tree).

ignare [i'naːr] illiterate, ignorant.

igné [ig'ne] igneous; **~ifuge** [igni'fyːʒ] **1.** *adj.* non inflammable; **2.** *su./m* fireproof(ing) material; **~ition** [~'sjɔ̃] *f* ignition.

ignoble [i'nɔbl] ignoble, base; vile.

ignomini|e [inɔmi'ni] *f* ignominy, shame; **~eux** [~'njø] ignominious.

ignor|ance [inɔ'rɑ̃ːs] *f* ignorance; **~ant** [~'rɑ̃] **1.** *adj.* ignorant (of, **de**); **2.** *su.* ignoramus; **~er** [~'re] (1a) not to know; not to know about (*s.th.*); be unaware of; ignore (*s.o.*); **ne pas ~ que** know quite well that.

Il [il] **1.** *pron./pers./m* he, it; **~s** *pl.* they; **2.** *pron./impers.* it; **il vint deux hommes** two men came.

île [iːl] *f* island; isle.

illégal [ille'gal] illegal, unlawful.

illégitim|e [illeʒi'tim] illegitimate (*child*); unlawful; *fig.* spurious; **~ité** [~timi'te] *f* illegitimacy.

illettré [ille'tre] illiterate.

illicite [illi'sit] illicit; *sp.* foul.

illico **F** [illi'ko] *adv.* at once.

illimité [illimi'te] unlimited.

illisible [illi'zibl] illegible.

illogique [illɔ'ʒik] illogical.

illuminer [illymi'ne] (1a) illuminate, light up; *fig.* enlighten (*s.o.*).

illus|ion [illy'zjɔ̃] *f* illusion; delusion; **~ d'optique** optical illusion; **~ionner**

[~zjɔ'ne] (1a) delude; deceive; **~oire** [~'zwaːr] illusory.

illustr|ation [illystra'sjɔ̃] *f* illustration; **~e** [~'lystr] illustrious, renowned; **~é** [illys'tre] *m* magazine; **~er** [~] (1a); illustrate; **s'~** win fame.

îlot [i'lo] *m* islet; *houses:* block.

imag|e [i'maːʒ] *f* image; picture; **~é** [ima'ʒe] colo(u)rful (*style*); **~erie** [imaʒ'ri] *f* imagery; **~inable** [imaʒi'nabl] imaginable; **~inaire** [~'nɛːr] imaginary (*a.* **A**); **~inatif** [~na'tif] imaginative; **~ination** [~na'sjɔ̃] *f* imagination; fancy; **~iner** [~'ne] (1a) imagine, picture; think up; **s'~** imagine *or* picture o.s.

imbécil|e [ɛ̃be'sil] imbecile; **~ité** [~sili'te] *f* imbecility; stupidity.

imbiber [ɛ̃bi'be] (1a) impregnate (with, **de**); **s'~ de** soak up, **F** drink.

imbu [ɛ̃'by]: **~ de** full of.

imbuvable [ɛ̃by'vabl] undrinkable.

imit|able [imi'tabl] imitable; worthy of imitation; **~ateur** [imita'tœːr] **1.** *adj.* imitative; **2.** *su./m* imitator; **~ation** [~'sjɔ̃] *f* imitation; counterfeiting; forgery; **à l'~ de** in imitation of; **~er** [imi'te] (1a) imitate.

immaculé [immaky'le] immaculate.

immanent [imma'nɑ̃] immanent.

immangeable [ɛ̃mɑ̃'ʒabl] uneatable.

immanquable [ɛ̃mɑ̃'kabl] infallible; inevitable; which cannot be missed.

immatériel [immate'rjɛl] immaterial; **†** intangible.

immatricul|ation [immatrikyla'sjɔ̃] *f* registration; enrol(l)ment; *mot.* **numéro** *m* **d'~** registration (*Am.* license) number.

immaturité [immatyri'te] *f* immaturity.

immédiat [imme'dja] immediate; **dans l'~** for the moment.

immémorial [immemɔ'rjal] immemorial.

immens|e [im'mɑ̃ːs] immense, vast; **~ité** [~mɑ̃si'te] *f* immensity.

immerger [immɛr'ʒe] (1l) immerse.

immersion [immɛr'sjɔ̃] *f* immersion; **⚓** *submarine:* submergence.

immeuble [im'mœbl] **1.** *adj.* **🏛** real; **2.** *su./m* real estate; house, building; **~ tour** tower block.

immigr|ant [immi'grɑ̃] *adj., su.* immigrant; **~ation** [~gra'sjɔ̃] *f* immigration;

~é *m,* **e** *f* [~'gre] immigrant; **~er** [~'gre] (1a) immigrate.

imminen|ce [immi'nɑ̃:s] *f* imminence; **~t** [~'nɑ̃] imminent.

immi|scer [immi'se] (1k): **s'~ dans** interfere with; **~xtion** [immik'sjɔ̃] *f* interference.

immobil|e [immɔ'bil] motionless; *fig.* steadfast; **~ier, ère** ♣ [immɔbi'lje, ~'ljɛːr] real; estate (*agent*); **~iser** [~li'ze] (1a) immobilize; **s'~** stop; come to a standstill; **~ité** [~li'te] *f* immobility.

immodéré [immɔde're] excessive.

immodeste [immɔ'dɛst] immodest.

immond|e [im'mɔ̃d] foul; unclean; **~ices** [~mɔ̃'dis] *f/pl.* rubbish *sg., Am.* garbage; filth.

immoral [immɔ'ral] immoral; **~ité** [~rali'te] *f* immorality.

immort|aliser [immɔrtali'ze] (1a) immortalize; **~alité** [~tali'te] *f* immortality; **~el** [~'tɛl] immortal; everlasting.

immotivé [immɔti've] unmotivated.

immuable [im'myabl] immutable.

immuniser ♣ [immyni'ze] (1a) immunize; **immunité** [~'te] *f* immunity (from, **contre**); *admin.* exemption from tax.

immu(t)abilité [immyabili'te, ~mytabili'te] *f* immutability, fixity.

impair [ɛ̃'pɛːr] **1.** *adj.* ♣ odd; **2.** *su./m* F blunder.

impardonnable [ɛ̃pardɔ'nabl] unpardonable; unforgivable.

imparfait [ɛ̃par'fɛ] **1.** *adj.* imperfect; unfinished; **2.** *su./m gramm.* imperfect (tense).

imparité [ɛ̃pari'te] *f* inequality.

impartial [ɛ̃par'sjal] impartial.

impasse [ɛ̃'pɑːs] *f* dead end, blind alley; *fig.* deadlock.

impassib|ilité [ɛ̃pasibili'te] *f* impassibility; **~le** [~'sibl] unmoved; unimpressionable.

impatien|ce [ɛ̃pa'sjɑ̃:s] *f* impatience; **~t** [~'sjɑ̃] impatient; eager (to *inf.,* **de** *inf.*); **~ter** [~sjɑ̃'te] (1a) irritate, annoy; **s'~** lose patience.

impay|able F [ɛ̃pɛ'jabl] screamingly funny; **~é** ♣ [~'je] unpaid (*debt*); dishono(u)red (*bill*).

impeccable [ɛ̃pe'kabl] impeccable.

impénétrable [ɛ̃pene'trabl] impenetrable (by, **à**); *fig.* inscrutable.

impéniten|ce [ɛ̃peni'tɑ̃:s] *f* impenitence; **~t** [~'tɑ̃] impenitent.

imper F [ɛ̃'per] *m* raincoat.

impératif [ɛ̃pera'tif] *adj., su./m* imperative.

impératrice [ɛ̃pera'tris] *f* empress.

imperceptible [ɛ̃pɛrsɛp'tibl] imperceptible, undiscernible.

imperfection [ɛ̃pɛrfɛk'sjɔ̃] *f* imperfection; incompleteness; defect.

impéri|al, e [ɛ̃pe'rjal] **1.** *adj.* imperial; **2.** *su./f; bus:* top-deck; *beard:* imperial; **~alisme** [~rja'lism] *m* imperialism; **~eux** [~'rjø] imperious; urgent.

impérissable [ɛ̃peri'sabl] imperishable, undying.

imperméable [ɛ̃pɛrme'abl] **1.** *adj.* impermeable; **2.** *su./m* raincoat.

impersonnel [ɛ̃pɛrsɔ'nɛl] impersonal.

impertinen|ce [ɛ̃pɛrti'nɑ̃:s] *f* impertinence; *♣* irrelevance; **~t** [~'nɑ̃] impertinent; *♣* irrelevant.

impétu|eux [ɛ̃pe'tɥø] impetuous; hot-headed; impulsive; **~osité** [~tɥozi'te] *f* impulsiveness.

impitoyable [ɛ̃pitwa'jabl] pitiless (towards **à, envers**); merciless.

implacable [ɛ̃pla'kabl] implacable, (towards **à, à l'égard de, pour**).

implanter [ɛ̃plɑ̃'te] (1a) plant; *fig.* implant; *♣* graft; **s'~** take root.

impli|cation [ɛ̃plika'sjɔ̃] *f* implication; **~s** *pl.* consequences; **~cite** [~'sit] implicit; implied, tacit; **~quer** [~'ke] (1m) involve; imply; implicate.

implorer [ɛ̃plɔ're] (1a) implore.

imploser [ɛ̃plɔ'ze] (1a) implode.

impoli [ɛ̃pɔ'li] impolite; rude (to **envers, avec**); **~tesse** [~li'tɛs] *f* impoliteness; rudeness.

impolitique [ɛ̃pɔli'tik] ill-advised.

impondérable [ɛ̃pɔ̃de'rabl] *adj., su./m* imponderable.

impopula|ire [ɛ̃pɔpy'lɛːr] unpopular; **~rité** [~lari'te] *f* unpopularity.

importan|ce [ɛ̃pɔr'tɑ̃:s] *f* importance; size, extent; **~t** [~'tɑ̃] **1.** *adj.* important; considerable, big; weighty; **2.** *su.:* F **faire l'~** act important; *su./m* essential point; **l'~** the important thing.

importa|teur ♣ [ɛ̃pɔrta'tœːr] **1.** *su.* importer; **2.** *adj.* importing; **~ion** ♣ [~'sjɔ̃] *f* import(ation).

importer¹ [ɛ̃pɔr'te] (1a) import.

importer² [~] (1a) matter; be important; *n'importe!* never mind!; *n'importe quoi* anything; *qu'importe?* what does it matter?

importun [ɛ̃pɔr'tœ̃] importunate; troublesome; unwelcome; untimely; **~ément** [ɛ̃pɔrtyne'mɑ̃] *adv. of importun 1*; **~er** [~'ne] (1a) bother (with, *de*); **~ité** [~ni'te] *f* importunity.

impos|able [ɛ̃po'zabl] taxable; **~ant** [~'zɑ̃] impressive; **~er** [~'ze] (1a) *v/t.* prescribe, impose; force (*an opinion*) (upon, **à**); admin. tax, eccl. lay on (*hands*); **~ le respect** command respect; **~ silence à q.** enjoin silence on s.o.; *s'~* be essential; *v/i.: en ~ à q.* impress s.o.; **~ition** [~zi'sjɔ̃] *f* taxation.

impossib|ilité [ɛ̃posibili'te] *f* impossibility; **~le** [~'sibl] impossible; ⊢ fantastic.

impost|eur [ɛ̃pos'tœːr] *m* impostor; **~ure** [~'tyːr] *f* imposture.

impôt [ɛ̃'po] *m* tax, duty; taxation.

impoten|ce [ɛ̃po'tɑ̃ːs] *f* lameness; helplessness; **~t** [~'tɑ̃] **1.** *adj.* crippled, helpless; **2.** *su.* invalid.

impraticable [ɛ̃prati'kabl] impracticable; impassable (*road*).

imprécation [ɛ̃preka'sjɔ̃] *f* curse.

imprécis [ɛ̃pre'si] vague; unprecise.

imprégner [ɛ̃pre'ɲe] (1f) impregnate (*a. fig.*) (with, *de*).

imprenable ✕ [ɛ̃prə'nabl] impregnable.

imprescriptible ⚖ [ɛ̃preskrip'tibl] indefeasible; imprescriptible.

impression [ɛ̃prɛ'sjɔ̃] *f* *fig.*, *book*, *seal*: impression; print(ing); *coins*: stamping; *paint*. priming, **envoyer à l'~** send to press; **~nable** [ɛ̃presjo'nabl] sensitive; **~ner** [~'ne] (1a) impress; **~nisme** [~'nism] *m* impressionism.

imprévisible [ɛ̃previ'zibl] unforeseeable, unpredictable; **imprévision** [~'zjɔ̃] *f* lack of foresight.

imprévoyance [ɛ̃prevwa'jɑ̃ːs] *f* lack of foresight; improvidence; **~u** [~'vy] unexpected.

imprim|é [ɛ̃pri'me] *m* printed paper; **~s** *pl. post*: printed matter *sg.*; **~er** [~'me] (1a) print; impress; impart (*a movement*); *paint*. prime; **~erie** [ɛ̃prim'ri] *f* printing(-house); **~eur** [ɛ̃pri'mœːr] *m* printer.

improba|ble [ɛ̃prɔ'babl] improbable, unlikely; **~tion** [~ba'sjɔ̃] *f* strong disapproval.

improbité [ɛ̃prɔbi'te] *f* dishonesty.

improductif [ɛ̃prɔdyk'tif] unproductive; ⊢ idle (*assets*, *money*).

impromptu [ɛ̃prɔ̃p'ty] **1.** *adj.* extempore; impromptu; **2.** *adv.* off the cuff; out of the blue.

impropr|e [ɛ̃prɔpr] wrong; unfit (for, **à**); **~iété** [ɛ̃proprie'te] *f* impropriety; incorrectness.

improuvable [ɛ̃pru'vabl] unprovable.

improvis|er [ɛ̃provi'ze] (1a) improvise, extemporize; **~te** [~'vist] *adv.*: **à l'~** unexpectedly; unawares.

impruden|ce [ɛ̃pry'dɑ̃ːs] *f* imprudence; rashness; **~t** [~'dɑ̃] imprudent, rash; unwise.

impud|ence [ɛ̃py'dɑ̃ːs] *f* impudence; **~ent** [~'dɑ̃] impudent (person), **~eur** [~'dœːr] *f* shamelessness; **~icité** [~disi'te] *f* indecency; **~ique** [~'dik] indecent; shameless.

impuissan|ce [ɛ̃pɥi'sɑ̃ːs] *f* powerlessness; impotence (*a. ⚕*); **~t** [~'sɑ̃] powerless, helpless; ineffectual; ⚕ impotent.

impulsi|f [ɛ̃pyl'sif] impulsive; **~on** [~'sjɔ̃] *f* ⚡, ⚙, *a. fig.* impulse; ⊢ stimulus; *fig.* prompting.

impun|ément [ɛ̃pyne'mɑ̃] *adv.* with impunity; **~i** [~'ni] unpunished; **~ité** [~ni'te] *f* impunity.

impur [ɛ̃'pyːr] impure; **~eté** [ɛ̃pyr'te] *f* impurity, unchastity.

imput|able [ɛ̃py'tabl] imputable (to, **à**); ⊢ chargeable (to, **sur**); **~er** [~'te] (1a) impute (to, **à**); ⊢ charge (*a sum*) (to **à**, **sur**).

imputrescible [ɛ̃pytrɛ'sibl] rot-proof.

inabordable [inabor'dabl] unapproachable; prohibitive (*price*).

inacceptable [inaksɛp'tabl] unacceptable.

inaccessible [inakse'sibl] inaccessible; impervious (to, **à**).

inaccompli [inakɔ̃'pli] unaccomplished, unfulfilled.

inaccoutumé [inakuty'me] unaccustomed (to, **à**); unusual.

inachevé [inaʃ've] unfinished.

inacti|f [inak'tif] inactive; ⊢ dull; inert; **~on** [~'sjɔ̃] *f* idleness; ⊢ dullness; **~vité** [~tivi'te] *f* inactivity; ⊢ dullness; inertness.

inadapté [inadap'te] not adapted (to, **à**); maladjusted (person).

inadvertance [inadvɛr'tãːs] f inadvertence; **par ~** inadvertently.

inaltérable [inalte'rabl] unvarying; which does not deteriorate.

inamovible [inamo'vibl] irremovable; for life (*post*); built in; fixed.

inanimé [inani'me] inanimate, lifeless; unconscious.

inanité [inani'te] f futility.

inanition [inani'sjɔ̃] f starvation.

inaperçu [inaper'sy] unnoticed.

inappréciable [inapre'sjabl] inappreciable (*quantity*); fig. invaluable.

inapte [i'napt] unfit (for, **à**); unsuited (to, **à**); uncapable (of *ger.*, **à** *inf.*).

inassouvi [inasu'vi] unappeased; unquenched; fig. unsatisfied.

inattaquable [inata'kabl] unattackable; irrefutable; irreproachable.

inattendu [inatã'dy] unexpected.

inattentif [inatã'tif] inattentive (to, **à**); heedless (of, **à**).

inaugurer [inogy're] (1a) inaugurate (*a. fig.*); open; unveil (*a monument*).

inavoué [ina'vwe] unacknowledged.

incalculable [ɛ̃kalky'labl] countless, incalculable.

incandescence [ɛ̃kɑ̃dɛ'sãːs] f incandescence; **⚡ à ~** glow (*lamp*).

incapable [ɛ̃ka'pabl] incapable (of *ger.*, **de** *inf.*); **~cité** [~pasi'te] f incapacity (*a.* ⚖); unfitness.

incarnat [ɛ̃kar'na] flesh-colo(u)red; **~ation** [~na'sjɔ̃] f incarnation; **~é** [~'ne] ingrown (*nail*); **~er** [~'ne] (1a) incarnate.

incartade [ɛ̃kar'tad] f prank; insult.

incassable [ɛ̃ka'sabl] unbreakable.

incend|iaire [ɛ̃sã'djɛːr] *adj.*, *su.* incendiary; **~ie** [~'di] *m* fire; ⚖ **~ volontaire** arson; **~ié** *m*, **e** f [~'dje] person rendered homeless by fire; **~ier** [~'dje] (1o) set (*s.th.*) on fire.

incert|ain [ɛ̃sɛr'tɛ̃] uncertain, doubtful; unreliable; undecided (about, **de**); **~itude** [~ti'tyd] f uncertainty, doubt; fig. indecision.

incessa|mment [ɛ̃sɛsa'mã] *adv.* incessantly; at any moment; without delay; **~nt** [~'sã] ceaseless.

incest|e [ɛ̃'sɛst] **1.** *adj.* incestuous; **2.** *su./m* incest; **~ueux** [ɛ̃sɛs'tɥø] incestuous.

inchiffrable [ɛ̃ʃi'frabl] immeasurable; fig. invaluable.

incide|mment [ɛ̃sida'mã] incidentally; **~nce** [~'dãːs] f incidence; effect, consequence; **~nt** [~'dã] **1.** *adj.* incident(al); **2.** *su./m* incident; difficulty, hitch; **~ de parcours** mishap, (minor) setback.

incis|er [ɛ̃si'ze] (1a) make an incision in; ⚕ lance (*an abscess*); **~if, -ve** [~'zif, ~'ziːv] **1.** *adj.* incisive; **dent** f **~ve = 2.** *su./f* incisor; **~ion** [~'zjɔ̃] f incision.

inciter [ɛ̃si'te] (1a) incite, prompt.

incivil [ɛ̃si'vil] uncivil, rude.

inclin|aison [ɛ̃kline'zɔ̃] f incline, slope; ⚓ ship: list; **~ation** [~na'sjɔ̃] f inclination (*a. fig.*); *body:* bending; *head:* nod; **~er** [~'ne] (1a) incline (*a. fig.*), slope; bend; **s'~** fig. yield (to, **devant**); ⚓ heel; ✈ bank.

inclu|re [ɛ̃'klyːr] (4g) include; *letter:* enclose; **~s** [ɛ̃'kly] enclosed; *la lettre ci-~e* enclosed letter; **~sif** [ɛ̃kly'zif] inclusive.

incohérent [ɛ̃kɔe'rã] incoherent.

incolore [ɛ̃kɔ'lɔːr] colo(u)rless.

incomber [ɛ̃kɔ̃'be] (1a): **~ à** be incumbent upon; devolve upon.

incommensurable [ɛ̃kɔmãsy'rabl] ⚖ incommensurable; irrational (*root*); incommensurate; fig. immeasurable.

incommod|ant [ɛ̃kɔmɔ'dã] annoying; troublesome; offensive (*smell etc.*); **~e** [ɛ̃kɔ'mɔd] inconvenient; uncomfortable; troublesome; unwieldy; **~ément** [ɛ̃kɔmɔde'mã] *adv.* inconveniently; **~er** [~'de] (1a) bother, annoy; inconvenience; disturb; make (*s.o.*) feel ill at ease; **~ité** [~di'te] f inconvenience.

incomparable [ɛ̃kɔ̃pa'rabl] incomparable, unrivalled.

incompatible [ɛ̃kɔ̃pa'tibl] incompatible.

incomplet, -ète [ɛ̃kɔ̃'plɛ, ~'plɛt] incomplete, unfinished.

incompréhensi|ble [ɛ̃kɔ̃preã'sibl] incomprehensible; **~f** [~'sif] uncomprehending.

inconcevable [ɛ̃kɔ̃sə'vabl] unimaginable, unthinkable.

inconciliable [ɛ̃kɔ̃si'ljabl] irreconcilable.

inconditionnel [ɛ̃kɔ̃disjɔ'nɛl] unconditional; unquestioning.

inconduite [ɛ̃kɔ̃'dɥit] f misbehavio(u)r; loose living; ⚖ misconduct.

incongelable [ɛ̃kɔ̃ʒ'labl] unfreezable; non-freezing.

incongr|u [ɛ̃kɔ̃'gry] incongruous; improper; **~uité** [~grɥi'te] *f* incongruity; unseemliness; **~ûment** [~gry'mɑ̃] *adv.* of *incongru*.

inconnu,e [ɛ̃kɔ'ny] **1.** *adj.* unknown (to **à**, **de**); **2.** *su.* unknown; *su./f* **~** unknown (quantity).

inconscien|ce [ɛ̃kɔ̃'sjɑ̃:s] *f* unconsciousness; ignorance (of, **de**); **~t** [~'sjɑ̃] **1.** *adj.* unconscious; **2.** *su.* unconscious person; *su./m psych.* the unconscious.

inconséquence [ɛ̃kɔ̃se'kɑ̃:s] *f* inconsequence; thoughtlessness.

inconsidéré [ɛ̃kɔ̃side're] inconsiderate (*person*); ill considered.

inconsistant [ɛ̃kɔ̃sis'tɑ̃] unsubstantial; weak, flabby; inconsistent.

inconsolable [ɛ̃kɔ̃sɔ'labl] unconsolable; disconsolate (*person*).

inconstan|ce [ɛ̃kɔ̃s'tɑ̃:s] *f* inconstancy, fickleness; changeableness (*of weather*); **~t** [~'tɑ̃] inconstant, fickle; changeable (*weather*).

inconstitutionnel [ɛ̃kɔ̃stitysjɔ'nɛl] unconstitutional.

incontest|able [ɛ̃kɔ̃tɛs'tabl] incontestable; **~é** [~'te] undisputed.

incontinen|ce [ɛ̃kɔ̃ti'nɑ̃:s] *f* incontinence (*a.* ♋); **~t** [~'nɑ̃] **1.** *adj.* incontinent; **2.** *adv.* † forthwith.

inconvenan|ce [ɛ̃kɔ̃v'nɑ̃s] *f* unseemliness; unsuitableness; impropriety; **~t** [~'nɑ̃:t] unseemly; unsuitable; improper.

inconvénient [ɛ̃kɔ̃ve'njɑ̃] *m* disadvantage, drawback; *fig.* objection, **si vous n'y voyez pas d'~** if you don't mind.

inconverti|ble [ɛ̃kɔ̃vɛr'tibl] inconvertible (*a.* ♥); **~ssable** [~ti'sabl] *fig.* incorrigible; ♥ inconvertible.

incorpor|ation [ɛ̃kɔrpɔra'sjɔ̃] *f* incorporation; ✗ enlistment; **~el** [~'rɛl] incorporeal; intangible (*property*); **~er** [~'re] (1a) incorporate; mix (with **à**, **avec**, **dans**).

incorrect [ɛ̃kɔ'rɛkt] incorrect; **~ion** [~rɛk'sjɔ̃] *f* incorrectness.

incorrigible [ɛ̃kɔri'ʒibl] incorrigible, *fig.* F hopeless.

incorruptible [ɛ̃kɔryp'tibl] incorruptible.

incréd|ibilité [ɛ̃kredibili'te] *f* incredibility; **~ule** [~'dyl] incredulous; sceptical (about, of **à l'égard de**); *eccl.* unbelieving; **~ulité** [~dyli'te] *f* incredulity; *eccl.* unbelief.

incrimin|ation [ɛ̃krimina'sjɔ̃] *f* (in)crimi-

nation; indictment; **~er** [~'ne] (1a) incriminate; accuse.

incroya|ble [ɛ̃krwa'jabl] incredible; **~nce** [~'jɑ̃:s] *f* unbelief.

incrust|ation [ɛ̃krysta'sjɔ̃] *f* ◎ inlaid work; *boiler:* fur(ring), scale; **~er** [~'te] (1a) ◎ inlay (with, **de**); **s'~** fur or scale up; F take root (*guest*).

incubat|eur [ɛ̃kyba'tœːr] *m* incubator; **~ion** [~'sjɔ̃] incubation.

incube [ɛ̃'kyb] *m* nightmare.

inculper [ɛ̃kyl'pe] (1a) indict.

inculquer [ɛ̃kyl'ke] (1m) inculcate.

inculte [ɛ̃'kylt] uncultivated; wild.

incur|able [ɛ̃ky'rabl] incurable; **~ie** [~'ri] *f* carelessness, negligence.

incursion [ɛ̃kyr'sjɔ̃] *f* inroad, foray.

indébrouillable [ɛ̃debru'jabl] impossible to disentangle; tangled.

indécen|ce [ɛ̃de'sɑ̃:s] *f* indecency, **~t** [~'sɑ̃] indecent; improper.

indéchiffrable [ɛ̃deʃi'frabl] undecipherable; illegible; unintelligible.

indécis [ɛ̃de'si] undecided; irresolute; blurred; doubtful; **~ion** [~si'zjɔ̃] *f* indecision; uncertainty.

indéfini [ɛ̃defi'ni] indefinite; **~ssable** [~ni'sabl] indefinable.

indéfrisable [ɛ̃defri'zabl] *f* permanent wave.

indélébile [ɛ̃dele'bil] indelible; kiss-proof (*lipstick*).

indélicat [ɛ̃deli'ka] indelicate, coarse; tactless (*act*); dishonest.

indémaillable [ɛ̃dema'jabl] ladder-proof, non-run (*stocking*).

indemn|e [ɛ̃'dɛmn] undamaged; unhurt; **~isation** [ɛ̃dɛmniza'sjɔ̃] *f* indemnification; **~iser** [~'ze] (1a) indemnify (for, **de**); **~ité** [~'te] *f* indemnity; allowance; **~ de déplacement** travel allowance; **~ de maladie** sick pay.

indéniable [ɛ̃de'njabl] undeniable.

indépenda|mment [ɛ̃depɑ̃da'mɑ̃] *adv.* of *indépendant*; **~nce** [~'dɑ̃:s] *f* independence (of **de**, **à l'égard de**); **~nt** [~'dɑ̃] independent (of, **de**); self-contained (*flat etc.*).

indescriptible [ɛ̃dɛskrip'tibl] indescribable (F *a. fig.*).

indéterminé [ɛ̃detɛrmi'ne] undetermined; indeterminate (♋, *fig.*).

index [ɛ̃'dɛks] *m* forefinger; index; pointer; *the* Index; *fig.* black list.

indicat|eur [ɛ̃dika'tœːr] **1.** *adj.* indicatory; **~ de** indicating (*s.th.*); **2.** *su./m* ⊚ indicator, ga(u)ge; 🚆 time-table; directory; informer; **~ de vitesse** speedometer; **~if** [~'tif] **1.** *adj.* indicative; **2.** *su./m radio etc.*: station-signal; signature-tune; *gramm.* indicative; **~ion** [~'sjɔ̃] *f* indication; information; sign, token; **~s** *pl.* instructions; directions.

indice [ɛ̃'dis] *m* indication, sign; *opt.*, ⅍ index; *fig.* clue; rating, grading.

indicible [ɛ̃di'sibl] unspeakable.

indien, -enne [ɛ̃'djɛ̃, ~'djɛn] *adj.*, *su.* Indian.

indifféren|ce [ɛ̃dife'rɑ̃ːs] *f* indifference (towards, *pour*); **~t** [~'rɑ̃] indifferent (*a.* 🐜) (to, *à*); unconcerned; unimportant.

indigence [ɛ̃di'ʒɑ̃ːs] *f* poverty (*a. fig.*).

indigène [ɛ̃di'ʒɛn] *adj.*, *su.* native.

indigent [ɛ̃di'ʒɑ̃] **1.** *adj.* poor; **2.** *su.* pauper; *su./m:* **les ~s** *pl.* the poor.

indigest|e [ɛ̃di'ʒɛst] indigestible; **~ion** [~ʒɛs'tjɔ̃] *f* indigestion.

indignation [ɛ̃diɲa'sjɔ̃] *f* indignation.

indigne [ɛ̃'diɲ] unworthy (of, *de*).

indigner [ɛ̃di'ɲe] (1a) shock; **s'~** be indignant (with, at *contre, de*).

indiquer [ɛ̃di'ke] (1m) indicate; point out; recommend; show; direct to; tell (of); state, give (*details, data etc*).

indirect [ɛ̃di'rɛkt] indirect.

indiscipliné [ɛ̃disipli'ne] undisciplined; unmanageable; unruly.

indiscret, -ète [ɛ̃dis'krɛ, -'krɛt] indiscreet; tactless; *fig.* prying (*look*).

indiscutable [ɛ̃disky'tabl] indisputable, unquestionable.

indispensable [ɛ̃dispɑ̃'sabl] indispensable (to, for *à*); essential.

indisponible [ɛ̃dispo'nibl] unavailable; ⅍ inalienable.

indispos|é [ɛ̃dispo'ze] unwell, indisposed; **~er** [~'ze] (1a) make (*s.o.*) unwell; *fig.* antagonize, irritate, annoy; *fig.* **~ q. contre** make s.o. hostile to; **~ition** [~zi'sjɔ̃] *f* indisposition.

indisputable [ɛ̃dispy'tabl] unquestionable.

indissociable [ɛ̃diso'sjabl] inseparable.

indissoluble [ɛ̃diso'lybl] 🐜 insoluble; *fig.* indissoluble.

indistinct [ɛ̃dis'tɛ̃(ːkt)] indistinct.

individu [ɛ̃divi'dy] *m* individual (*a. pej.*); **~aliser** [~dɥali'ze] (1a) individualize;

~aliste [~dɥa'list] **1.** *adj.* individualistic; **2.** *su.* individualist; **~alité** [~dɥali'te] *f* individuality; **~el** [~'dɥɛl] individual.

indivis ⅍ [ɛ̃di'vi] joint; *par* **~** jointly; **~ible** [~vi'zibl] indivisible.

indocil|e [ɛ̃do'sil] intractable; **~ité** [~sili'te] *f* intractability.

indolen|ce [ɛ̃do'lɑ̃ːs] *f* 🎨, *fig.* indolence; **~t** [~'lɑ̃] **1.** 🎨, *fig.* indolent; *fig.* apathetic; **2.** *su.* idler.

indolore 🎨 [ɛ̃do'loːr] painless.

indomptable [ɛ̃dɔ̃'tabl] unconquerable; indomitable; uncontrollable.

indu [ɛ̃'dy] undue; ungodly (*hour*).

indubitable [ɛ̃dybi'tabl] unquestionable, undeniable.

induction [ɛ̃dyk'sjɔ̃] *f* induction.

induire [ɛ̃'dɥiːr] (4h) infer, induce; *fig.* **~ en** lead into; **~ en erreur** mislead.

indulgen|ce [ɛ̃dyl'ʒɑ̃ːs] *f* indulgence (*a. eccl.*); forbearance; **~t** [~'ʒɑ̃] **~ pour** indulgent to, lenient with.

indûment [ɛ̃dy'mɑ̃] *adv.* unduly.

industri|aliser [ɛ̃dystriali'ze] (1a) industrialize; **~e** [~'tri] *f* industry; **~-clef** key-industry; **~el** [~tri'ɛl] **1.** *adj.* industrial; **2.** *su./m* industrialist; **~eux** [~tri'ø] industrious.

inébranlable [inebrɑ̃'labl] unshakable.

inédit [ine'di] unpublished; new.

ineffable [ine'fabl] ineffable.

inefficac|e [inefi'kas] ineffective; **~ité** [~kasi'te] *f* inefficacy.

inégal [ine'gal] unequal; irregular (*pulse etc.*); uneven; changeable; **~ité** [~gali'te] *f* inequality (*a.* ⅍); irregularity; unevenness.

inéluctable [inelyk'tabl] inescapable.

inemployé [inɑ̃plwa'je] unused.

inept|e [i'nɛpt] inept, stupid; **~ie** [linɛp'si] *f* ineptitude; stupidity.

inépuisable [inepɥi'zabl] inexhaustible.

inert|e [i'nɛrt] inert; passive; inactive; **~ie** [inɛr'si] *f* inertia; inactivity.

inespéré [inɛspe're] unhoped-for.

inestimable [inɛsti'mabl] invaluable; priceless.

inévitable [inevi'tabl] inevitable.

inexact [inɛg'zakt] inexact; unpunctual; **~itude** [~zakti'tyd] *f* inexactitude; unpunctuality.

inexcusable [inɛksky'zabl] inexcusable.

inexistant [inɛgzi'stɑ̃] non-existent.

inexorable [inɛgzɔ'rabl] inexorable.

inexpéri|ence [inɛkspe'rjɑ̃:s] f lack of experience; **~menté** [~rimɑ̃'te] untested; inexperienced.

inexplicable [inɛkspli'kabl] inexplicable.

inexprimable [inɛkspri'mabl] inexpressible; unspeakable.

inextinguible [inɛkstɛ̃'gibl] inextinguishable; *fig.* uncontrollable (*laughter*).

inextirpable [inɛkstir'pabl] ineradicable.

inextricable [inɛkstri'kabl] inextricable.

infaillible [ɛ̃fa'jibl] infallible.

infaisable [ɛ̃fə'zabl] unfeasible.

infamant [ɛ̃fa'mɑ̃] defamatory; ignominious; **infâme** [ɛ̃'fɑːm] infamous; vile, foul; **infamie** [ɛ̃fa'mi] f infamy.

infant [ɛ̃'fɑ̃] m infante; **~e** [ɛ̃'fɑ̃:t] f infanta; **~erie** ✕ [ɛ̃fɑ̃'tri] f infantry; **~icide** [~ti'sid] su., su./m infanticide; **~ile** [~'til] infantile (*disease*); *fig.* childish.

infarctus ⚕ [ɛ̃fark'tys] m infarct(ion); ~ **du myocarde** coronary (thrombosis).

infatigable [ɛ̃fati'gabl] untiring.

infatuer [ɛ̃fa'tɥe] (1n) infatuate.

infécond [ɛ̃fe'kɔ̃] barren; sterile.

infect [ɛ̃'fɛkt] foul; stinking; filthy; **~er** [ɛ̃fɛk'te] (1a) infect; pollute; stink of; **~ion** [~'sjɔ̃] f infection; stench.

inférer [ɛ̃fe're] (1f) infer (from, **de**).

inféri|eur [ɛ̃fe'rjœːr] 1. *adj.* inferior (to, **à**); lower; ~ **à** a. lower than, below; 2. *su.* subordinate; **~orité** [~rjori'te] f inferiority.

infernal [ɛ̃fer'nal] infernal; devilish; ⚕ **pierre** f **~e** lunar caustic.

infertile [ɛ̃fer'til] infertile, barren.

infester [ɛ̃fɛs'te] (1a) infest (with, **de**).

infid|èle [ɛ̃fi'dɛl] 1. *adj.* unfaithful; inaccurate; infidel; 2. *su.* unbeliever; **~elité** [~deli'te] f infidelity (to, **envers**); inaccuracy; unbelief.

infiltr|ation [ɛ̃filtra'sjɔ̃] f infiltration; **~er** [~'te] (1a); **s'~** infiltrate; seep in; filter (through).

infime [ɛ̃'fim] lowly; least; F tiny.

infini [ɛ̃fi'ni] *adj.* infinite; *su./m* infinity; **à l'~** endless(ly); **~ment** [~ni'mɑ̃] *adv.* infinitely; **~té** [~ni'te] f infinity; *fig.* great *or* endless number.

infirm|e [ɛ̃'firm] 1. *adj.* infirm; crippled; *fig.* weak; 2. *su.* invalid; **~er** [ɛ̃fir'me]

(1a) disprove; ⚖ quash; **~erie** [~mə'ri] f infirmary; sick-room; **~ier** [~'mje] m (hospital-)attendant; male nurse; **~ière** [~'mjɛːr] f nurse; **~ité** [~mi'te] f infirmity; *fig.* weakness.

inflamma|ble [ɛ̃fla'mabl] inflammable, flammable; **~tion** [~ma'sjɔ̃] f inflammation; **~toire** [~ma'twaːr] inflammatory.

inflation ✝ *etc.* [ɛ̃fla'sjɔ̃] inflation.

infléch|ir [ɛ̃fle'fiːr] (2a) bend; **~issement** [~'fis'mɑ̃] m modification.

inflexi|ble [ɛ̃flɛk'sibl] inflexible; **~on** [~'sjɔ̃] f inflection, inflexion.

infliger [ɛ̃fli'ʒe] (1l) inflict.

influ|ence [ɛ̃fly'ɑ̃:s] f influence; **~encer** [~ɑ̃'se] (1k) influence; **~ent** [~'ɑ̃] influential; **~er** [~'e] (1a): ~ **sur** influence.

informati|cien [ɛ̃fɔrmati'sjɛ̃] m computer scientist; **~on** [ɛ̃fɔrma'sjɔ̃] f information; inquiry; **~s** *pl.* radio: news; **~que** [~'tik] f computer science; data processing; **~sation** [~tiza'sjɔ̃] f computerization; **~ser** [~ti'ze] (1a) computerize.

informe [ɛ̃'fɔrm] formless; shapeless; unshapely.

informel [ɛ̃fɔr'mɛl] informal; casual.

informer [ɛ̃fɔr'me] (1a) v/t. inform; **s'~** inquire (about, **de**).

infortun|e [ɛ̃fɔr'tyn] f misfortune; adversity; **~é** [~ty'ne] unlucky.

infraction [ɛ̃frak'sjɔ̃] f infringement; ⚖ offence; breach (of, **à**).

infranchissable [ɛ̃frɑ̃ʃi'sabl] impassable; insuperable (*difficulty*).

infrarouge [ɛ̃fra'ruːʒ] infra-red.

infrastructure [ɛ̃frastryk'tyːr] f infrastructure; ⚙ substructure.

infroissable [ɛ̃frwa'sabl] crease-resistant.

infructueux [ɛ̃fryk'tɥø] unfruitful, barren; *fig.* unavailing, fruitless.

infus [ɛ̃'fy] innate, intuitive; **~er** [ɛ̃fy'ze] (1a) v/t. infuse (a. *fig*), brew (*tea*); v/i. a. draw (*tea*); **~ion** [~'zjɔ̃] f infusion; herb tea.

ingéni|er [ɛ̃ʒe'nje] (1o): **s'~ à** try hard to; **~eur** [~'njœːr] m engineer; ~ **du son** sound engineer; ~ **mécanicien** mechanical engineer; **~eux** [~'njø] ingenious; clever; **~osité** [~njozi'te] f ingenuity; cleverness.

ingénu, e [ɛ̃ʒe'ny] 1. *adj.* ingenuous, artless; 2. *su./f thea.* ingénue; **~ité** [~nɥi'te] f ingenuousness.

ingér|ence [ɛ̃ʒe'rãːs] f interference; **~er** [~'re] (1f) ingest; **s'~ dans** interfere in.

ingrat [ɛ̃'gra] ungrateful (to[wards], **envers**; for, **à**); thankless (*task*), ✍, *fig.* unproductive; awkward (*age*).

ingrédient [ɛ̃gre'djã] m ingredient.

inguérissable [ɛ̃geri'sabl] incurable.

ingurgiter [ɛ̃gyrʒi'te] (1a) ✍ ingurgitate; F swallow.

inhabil|e [ina'bil] unskil(l)ful; clumsy; **~eté** [~bil'te] f lack of skill (in, **à**); clumsiness.

inhabit|able [inabi'tabl] uninhabitable; **~é** [~'te] uninhabited.

inhal|ateur ✍ [inala'tœːr] m inhaler; **~ation** [~'sjõ] f inhalation; **~er** [~'le] (1a) inhale.

inhéren|ce [ine'rãːs] f inherence (in, **à**); **~t** [~'rã] inherent (in, **à**).

inhib|er [ini'be] (1a) inhibit; **~ition** *psych.* [~bi'sjõ] f inhibition.

inhumain [iny'mɛ̃] inhuman; cruel.

inhumer [iny'me] (1a) bury, inter.

inimaginable [inimaʒi'nabl] unimaginable.

inimitable [inimi'tabl] inimitable.

inimitié [inimi'tje] f enmity.

ininflammable [inɛ̃fla'mabl] non-inflammable, uninflammable.

inintellig|ence [inɛ̃teli'ʒãːs] f lack of intelligence; **~ent** [~'ʒã] unintelligent; obtuse; **~ible** [~'ʒibl] unintelligible.

inique [i'nik] iniquitous; **iniquité** [iniki'te] f iniquity.

initi|al, e [ini'sjal] *adj.*, *su./f* initial; *adj. a.* starting ...; first; **~ateur** [inisja'tœːr] initiator; originator; **~ative** [~sja'tiːv] f initiative; **~er** [~'sje] (1o) initiate (**à**, *fig.*).

inject|er [ɛ̃ʒɛk'te] (1a) inject (with **de**, **avec**); impregnate (*wood*); **injecté de sang** bloodshot (*eye*); **~ion** [~'sjõ] f injection; impregnation.

injonction [ɛ̃ʒõk'sjõ] f injunction.

injur|e [ɛ̃'ʒyːr] f insult, abuse; ravages *pl.* (*of time*); **~ier** [ɛ̃ʒy'rje] (1o) insult, abuse; **~ieux** [~'rjø] abusive.

injust|e [ɛ̃'ʒyst] **1.** *adj.* unjust, unfair (to, **envers**); unrighteous; **2.** *su./m* wrong; **~ice** [ɛ̃ʒys'tis] f injustice; **~ifiable** [~ti'fjabl] unjustifiable.

inlassable [ɛ̃la'sabl] tireless.

inné [in'ne] innate.

innoce|mment [inɔsa'mã] *adv.* of *inno-*

cent 1; **~nce** [~'sãːs] f innocence; **~nt** [~'sã] innocent; artless; **~nter** [~sã'te] (1a) clear (*s.o.*), prove (*s.o.*) innocent; justify.

innocuité [innɔkɥi'te] f harmlessness.

innombrable [innõ'brabl] innumerable, countless.

innov|ation [innɔva'sjõ] f innovation; **~er** [~'ve] (1a) innovate.

inoccupé [inɔky'pe] unoccupied.

inoculer [inɔky'le] (1a) inoculate, infect (*s.o.* with *s.th.*, **qch. à q.**).

inodore [inɔ'dɔːr] odo(u)rless.

inoffensif [inɔfã'sif] harmless.

inond|ation [inõda'sjõ] f inundation; flood(ing); **~er** [~'de] (1a) inundate; flood, swamp.

inopérant ✍ [inɔpe'rã] inoperative.

inopiné [inɔpi'ne] unexpected, unforeseen.

inopportun [inɔpɔr'tœ̃] inopportune; untimely.

inorganisation [inɔrganiza'sjõ] f disorganization, lack of organization.

inoubliable [inubli'abl] unforgettable.

inouï [i'nwi] unheard of.

inoxydable [inɔksi'dabl] rust-proof; rustless; stainless (**steel**).

inqualifiable [ɛ̃kali'fjabl] beyond words; indescribable; scandalous.

inqui|et, -ète [ɛ̃'kjɛ, ~'kjɛt] anxious; worried; uneasy; **~étant** [ɛ̃kje'tã] worrying, disquieting; **~éter** [~'te] worry; make uneasy; disturb; **s'~** worry (about, **de qch.; pour q.**); **s'~ de** (*inf.*) take the trouble to (*inf.*), bother to (*inf.*); **s'~ de savoir si** be anxious to know whether; **~étude** [~'tyd] f anxiety; worry; **se faire des ~s** worry.

insaisissable [ɛ̃sɛzi'sabl] unseizable; elusive; ✍ not attachable.

insalissable [ɛ̃sali'sabl] dirt-proof.

insalubr|e [ɛ̃sa'lybr] insanitary; **~ité** [~lybri'te] f unhealthiness.

insanité [ɛ̃sani'te] f insanity.

insatiable [ɛ̃sa'sjabl] insatiable.

insciemment [ɛ̃sja'mã] *adv.* unconsciously.

inscri|ption [ɛ̃skrip'sjõ] f inscription; registration, enrol(l)ment; *univ.* matriculation; **~re** [~'kriːr] (4q) inscribe; register; enroll.

insect|e [ɛ̃'sɛkt] m insect; **~icide** [ɛ̃sɛkti'sid] m insecticide.

insécuriser [ɛsekyri'ze] (1a) give (s.o.) a feeling of insecurity.

insensé [ɛsɑ̃'se] insane; weird.

insensib|ilisation ✻ [ɛsɑ̃sibiliza'sjɔ̃] f an(a)esthetization; **~iliser** ✻ [~'ze] (1a) an(a)esthetize; **~ilité** [~'te] f insensibility (a. fig.); insensitiveness; indifference; **~le** [ɛsɑ̃'sibl] insensible; insensitive.

inséparable [ɛsepa'rabl] inseparable (companion).

insérer [ɛse're] (1f) insert; **insertion** [ɛsɛr'sjɔ̃] f insertion.

insidieux [ɛsi'djø] insidious.

insigne¹ [ɛ̃'siɲ] distinguished; remarkable; signal (favour).

insigne² [~] m ✕, sp., etc. badge.

insignifiant [ɛsiɲi'fjɑ̃] insignificant.

insinuer [ɛ̃si'nɥe] (1n) insinuate, imply; **s'~** steal or creep (into, dans).

insipide [ɛsi'pid] insipid; tasteless.

insist|ance [ɛsis'tɑ̃:s] f insistence; **~er** [~'te] (1a) insist (on ger. à, pour inf.); **~ sur** stress; persist in.

insociable [ɛsɔ'sjabl] unsociable.

insolation [ɛsɔla'sjɔ̃] f insolation; sunstroke; phot. daylight printing.

insolen|ce [ɛsɔ'lɑ̃:s] f insolence; **~t** [~'lɑ̃] insolent; overbearing.

insolite [ɛsɔ'lit] unusual; strange.

insoluble [ɛsɔ'lybl] insoluble.

insolvable ✝ [ɛsɔl'vabl] insolvent.

insomnie [ɛsɔm'ni] f insomnia.

insonoriser [ɛsɔnɔri'ze] (1a) soundproof.

insouc|iance [ɛsu'sjɑ̃:s] f unconcern; **~ant** [~'sjɑ̃] unconcerned, carefree, thoughtless; **~eux** [~'sjø] carefree; unconcerned (about, de).

insoumis [ɛsu'mi] unsubdued; unruly; insubordinate.

insoutenable [ɛsut'nabl] untenable, indefensible; unbearable (pain).

inspect|er [ɛspɛk'te] (1a) inspect; ✝ etc. examine; **~eur** [~'tœːr] m inspector; examiner; shop-walker, Am. floor-walker; **~ion** [~'sjɔ̃] f inspection; examination.

inspir|ation [ɛspira'sjɔ̃] f inspiration (a. fig.); **~er** [~'re] (1a) inspire (s.o. with s.th., qch. à q.) (a. fig.).

instab|ilité [ɛstabili'te] f instability; **~le** [~'tabl] unstable; unreliable.

install|ation [ɛstala'sjɔ̃] f installation; putting in; settling (in); moving in; setting up; ⊚ equipment; ⊚ plant; **~er** [~'le] (1a) install; put in or up; ⊚ etc. fit up; fit out; settle; **s'~** settle down; settle in; set up.

instamment [ɛstA'mɑ̃] adv. earnestly; urgently.

instan|ce [ɛs'tɑ̃:s] f ✝✝ authority; **~s** pl. entreaties; **en ~ de** on the point of; **~t** [~'tɑ̃] **1.** adj. pressing; imminent; **2.** su./m instant, moment; **à l'~** this instant; **~tané** [~tɑ̃ta'ne] **1.** adj. instantaneous; instant (coffee etc.); **2.** su./m phot. snapshot.

instar [ɛs'taːr] m: **à l'~ de** like.

instaur|ation [ɛstɔra'sjɔ̃] f founding, institution; **~er** [~'re] (1a) establish, found, institute.

instiga|teur m, **-trice** f [ɛstiga'tœːr, ~'tris] instigator (of, de); inciter (to, de); **~ion** [~'sjɔ̃] f instigation.

instiller [ɛsti'le] (1a) instil (a. fig.).

instinct [ɛs'tɛ̃] m instinct; **d'~** instinctively; **~if** [~tɛk'tif] instinctive.

institu|er [ɛsti'tɥe] (1n) institute; set up; **~t** [~'ty] m institute; **~teur, -trice** [~ty'tœːr, ~'tris] su. school-teacher; **~tion** [~ty'sjɔ̃] f institution.

instru|cteur [ɛstryk'tœːr] m instructor (a. ✕), teacher; **~ctif** [~'tif] instructive; **~ction** [~'sjɔ̃] f instruction; education; ✕ training; ✝✝ preliminary investigation; **~s** pl. directions; **~ civique** civics sg.; **~ publique** state education; **avoir de l'~** be well educated; **~ire** [ɛstrɥiːr] (4h) inform; educate; teach; ✕ train; ✝✝ investigate; **~it** [ɛstry'i] educated; learned.

instrument [ɛstry'mɑ̃] m instrument (a. ♪, ✝✝, fig.); **~ de musique** musical instrument.

inou [ɛ̃'oy] m: **à l'~ de** unknown to.

insubordination [ɛsybɔrdina'sjɔ̃] f insubordination; **insubordonné** [~dɔ-'ne] insubordinate.

insuccès [ɛsyk'sɛ] m failure.

insuffisan|ce [ɛsyfi'zɑ̃:s] f insufficiency; fig. unsatisfactoriness; **~t** [~'zɑ̃] insufficient; inadequate.

insuffler [ɛsy'fle] (1a) inflate; ✻ spray (one's throat); fig. inspire.

insulaire [ɛsy'lɛːr] **1.** adj. insular; **2.** su. islander.

insuline ✻ [ɛsy'lin] f insulin.

insult|e [ɛ̃'sylt] f insult; **~er** [ɛ̃syl'te] (1a) vt/i. insult; v/i. † **~ à** jeer at.

insupportable [ɛ̃sypɔr'tabl] unbearable; insufferable; intolerable.

insurg|é [ɛ̃syr'ʒe] adj., su. rebel; **~er** [~] (1l): **s'~** rebel (against, **contre**).

insurmontable [ɛ̃syrmɔ̃'tabl] insurmountable, insuperable.

insurrection [ɛ̃syrɛk'sjɔ̃] f insurrection, rebellion, rising.

intact [ɛ̃'takt] intact; undamaged.

intarissable [ɛ̃tari'sabl] inexhaustible; never-failing; long-winded.

intégral, e [ɛ̃te'gral] **1.** adj. integral (a. Å), full; **2.** su./f Å integral; ♪ etc. complete works pl. or series; **~ement** [~gral'mɑ̃] fully, in full; **intégrant** [~'grɑ̃] integral; **intégration** [~gra'sjɔ̃] f integration; **intègre** [ɛ̃'tɛgr] honest; incorruptible; **intégrer** [ɛ̃te'gre] (1f) integrate; **intégrité** [ɛ̃tegri'te] f integrity.

intellect [ɛ̃te'lɛkt] m intellect; **~uel** [~lɛk'tɥɛl] intellectual.

intellig|ence [ɛ̃teli'ʒɑ̃s] f intelligence; understanding; **d'~ avec** in agreement or collusion; **en bonne (mauvaise)** ~ on good (bad) terms; **~ent** [~'ʒɑ̃] intelligent; **~ible** [~'ʒibl] intelligible.

intempér|ance [ɛ̃tɑ̃pe'rɑ̃s] f intemperance; **~ant** [~'rɑ̃] intemperate; **~ie** [~'ri] f weather; inclemency; **~s** pl. bad weather sg.

intempestif [ɛ̃tɑ̃pɛs'tif] untimely.

intens|e [ɛ̃'tɑ̃s] intense; severe (cold, pain); powerful; deep (colour); heavy (flow); high (fever); bitter (cold); **~if** [ɛ̃tɑ̃'sif] intensive; **~ifier** [~si'fje] (1a) (a. **s'~**) intensify; **~ité** [ɛ̃tɑ̃si'te] f intensity etc.; see **intense**.

intenter t͡s [ɛ̃tɑ̃'te] (1a) bring (an action); institute (proceedings).

intention [ɛ̃tɑ̃'sjɔ̃] f intention; purpose, aim; **à ton ~** for you; **~né** [~sjɔ'ne] ...intentioned; **~nel** [~sjɔ'nɛl] intentional.

inter... [ɛ̃tɛr] inter...; **~allié** [~a'lje] interallied; **~calaire** [~ka'lɛːr] intercalary; **~caler** [~ka'le] (1a) intercalate; ≠ cut in; **~céder** [~se'de] (1f) intercede for s.o.'s behalf, **pour q.**; with s.o., **auprès de q.**); **~cepter** [~sɛp'te] (1a) intercept; ☼ shut off; **~changeable** [~ʃɑ̃ʒabl] interchangeable; **~continental** [~kɔ̃tinɑ̃-'tal] intercontinental; **~dépendance**

~dépendance [~depɑ̃'dɑ̃ːs] f interdependence; **~diction** [~dik'sjɔ̃] f interdiction; **~dire** [~'diːr] (4p) prohibit, forbid; fig. bewilder; admin. suspend; **~dit** [~'di] **1.** adj. forbidden; bewildered, taken aback; perplexed; **2.** su./m eccl. interdict.

intér|essé [ɛ̃tere'se] interested (party); selfish; **~esser** [~re'se] (1b) interest; concern; **s'~** take an interest (in, **à**); **~êt** [~'rɛ] m interest (a. ✝); advantage; ✝ **à ~ fixe** fixed-interest.

interférence [ɛ̃tɛrfe'rɑ̃ːs] f interference.

intérieur [ɛ̃te'rjœːr] **1.** adj. interior, inner; inward; geog. inland ...; pol. domestic, home ...; **2.** su./m interior; inside (a. sp.); home.

intérim [ɛ̃te'rim] m/inv. interim; **~aire** [~ri'mɛːr] **1.** adj. temporary, acting; **2.** su. deputy; F temp.

inter...: **~jection** [ɛ̃tɛrʒɛk'sjɔ̃] f interjection; **~jeter** [~ʒə'te] (1c) interject; t͡s **~ appel** appeal; **~ligne** [~'liɲ] su./m space (between two lines); **~ligner** [~li'ɲe] (1a) interline; **~linéaire** [~line'ɛːr] interlinear; **~locuteur** m, **-trice** f [~lɔky'tœːr, ~'tris] interlocutor; **~lope** [~'lɔp] shady, dubious; **~loquer** fig. [~lɔ'ke] (1m) nonplus; **~mède** [~'mɛd] m medium; thea. interlude; **~médiaire** [~me'djɛːr] **1.** adj. intermediate; **2.** su./m intermediary; ✝ middleman; **par l'~ de** through.

interminable [ɛ̃tɛrmi'nabl] never-ending, interminable.

intermitten|ce [ɛ̃tɛrmi'tɑ̃ːs] f intermittence; **par ~** intermittently; **~t** [~'tɑ̃] intermittent; irregular.

internat [ɛ̃tɛr'na] m living-in; boarding-school; ✇ internship.

international, e [ɛ̃tɛrnasjɔ'nal] adj., su. sp. international; su./f Internationale (hymn).

intern|e [ɛ̃'tɛrn] **1.** adj. internal; inner; Å interior; resident; **2.** su. school: boarder; ✇ intern; **~ement** [ɛ̃tɛrnə'mɑ̃] m internment; confinement; **~er** [~'ne] (1a) intern.

inter...: **~pellation** [ɛ̃tɛrpɛla'sjɔ̃] f question(ing); interpellation; **~peller** [~pe'le] (1a) interpellate; arrest; **~phone** [~'fɔn] m intercom; **~planétaire** [~plane'tɛːr] interplanetary; **~polateur** m, **-trice** f [~pɔla'tœːr, ~'tris] interpolator; **~poler** [~pɔ'le] (1a) interpolate;

~poser [~po'ze] (1a) interpose; **s'~** *a.* intervene; *par ... interposé* through..., by..., with the help of ...; **~position** [~pozi'sjɔ̃] *f* interposition; *fig.* intervention; **~prétation** [~preta'sjɔ̃] *f* interpretation (*a. thea.*, *♪*, *etc.*); **~prète** [~'prɛt] *su.* interpreter; *fig.* exponent; **~préter** [~pre'te] (1f) interpret; **~rogateur** [ɛ̃teroga'tœːr] **1.** *adj.* questioning, inquiring; **2.** *su./m* questioner; *school:* examiner; **~rogation** [~roga'sjɔ̃] *f* question(ing); *point m d'~* question-mark; **~rogatoire** [~roga'twaːr] *m* ♣ examination; questioning; **~roger** [~rɔ'ʒe] (1l) question; examine; *fig.* consult; **rompre** [~'rɔ̃ːpr] (4a) interrupt; break (*a journey, a. ♪*); stop; **~rupteur** *⚡* [~ryp'tœːr] *m* switch; **~ruption** [~ryp'sjɔ̃] *f* interruption; stopping; **~section** [~sɛk'sjɔ̃] *f* ♣ *etc.* intersection; *road:* crossing; **~stellaire** [~stɛlˈlɛːr] interstellar; **~stice** [ɛ̃tɛrsˈtis] *m* interstice; chink; **~urbain** [ɛ̃teryr'bɛ̃] interurban; **~valle** [~'val] *m* interval (*a. ♪*); *dans l'~* in the meantime; *par ~s* off and on; **~venir** [~vəˈniːr] (2h) intervene; *fig.* happen; **~vention** [~vɑ̃'sjɔ̃] *f* intervention; *⚕* operation; **~vertir** [ver'tiːr] (2a) invert (*an order, a. ♣*); **~view** [~'vju] *f* interview(ing); **~viewer 1.** [~'vju] *v/t.* interview; **2.** *su./m* [~vju'vœːr] interviewer.

intestin [ɛ̃tɛs'tɛ̃] **1.** *adj.* internal; **2.** *su./m* bowel; **~ grêle** small intestine; **gros ~** large intestine; **~al** [~ti'nal] intestinal.

intim|ation [ɛ̃tima'sjɔ̃] *f* intimation; *admin.* notice; **~e** [ɛ̃'tim] intimate; inner; private; **♣** *er* [ɛ̃ti'me] (1a) intimate; notify; **♣** summon.

intimider [ɛ̃timi'de] (1a) intimidate; threaten; F bully.

intimité [ɛ̃timi'te] *f* intimacy; privacy; *fig.* depths *pl.*; *dans l'~* privately.

intitul|é [ɛ̃tity'le] *m* title; heading; **~er** [~] (1a) entitle, call.

intoléra|ble [ɛ̃tɔleˈrabl] intolerable, unbearable; **~nce** [~'rɑ̃ːs] *f* intolerance; **~nt** [~'rɑ̃] intolerant.

intonation [ɛ̃tɔnaˈsjɔ̃] *f* speech: intonation; *voice:* modulation, pitch.

intoxi|cation [ɛ̃tɔksikaˈsjɔ̃] *f* poisoning; **~ alimentaire** food poisoning; **~quer** *⚕* [~'ke] (1m) poison.

intraitable [ɛ̃trɛ'tabl] unmanageable; *⚕* beyond treatment.

intramusculaire *⚕* [ɛ̃tramyskyˈlɛːr] *adj.* (*su./f*) intramuscular (injection).

intransigeant [ɛ̃trɑ̃ziˈʒɑ̃] **1.** *adj.* intransigent; **2.** *su. pol.* die-hard.

intransitif [ɛ̃trɑ̃zi'tif] intransitive.

intraveineux, -euse [ɛ̃travɛ'nø, ~'nøːz] *adj.* (*su./f.*) intravenous (injection).

intrépide [ɛ̃tre'pid] intrepid.

intrig|ant [ɛ̃tri'gɑ̃] **1.** *adj.* scheming; **2.** *su./m* intriguer; **~ue** [~'trig] *f* intrigue; plot (*a. thea. etc.*); love-affair; **~uer** [ɛ̃tri'ge] (1m) *v/t.* intrigue; *v/t.* puzzle.

intrinsèque [ɛ̃trɛ̃'sɛk] intrinsic

introdu|ction [ɛ̃trɔdyk'sjɔ̃] *f* introduction; **~ire** [~'dɥiːr] (4h) introduce; show in; **s'~** get in, enter.

introniser [ɛ̃trɔni'ze] (1a) enthrone.

introuvable [ɛ̃tru'vabl] undiscoverable; incomparable.

intrus [ɛ̃try] *su.* intruder; **~ion** [ɛ̃try'zjɔ̃] *f* intrusion.

intuitif [ɛ̃ɥi'tif] intuitive; **~on** [~'sjɔ̃] *f* intuition, insight.

inusable [iny'zabl] everlasting.

inutil|e [iny'til] useless; pointless; unnecessary; superfluous; **~isable** [inytili'zabl] unusable; **~isé** [~'ze] unused; **~ité** [~'te] *f* uselessness.

invaincu [ɛ̃vɛ̃'ky] unbeaten; unvanquished; unconquered.

invalid|e [ɛ̃va'lid] **1.** *adj.* invalid (*a. ♣*); **✕** disabled; rickety; **2.** *su.* invalid; *su./m* disabled soldier; **~er** [ɛ̃vali'de] (1a) **♣** invalidate; **~ité** [~di'te] *f* infirmity; disablement; **♣** invalidity.

invariable [ɛ̃va'rjabl] invariable.

invasion [ɛ̃va'zjɔ̃] *f* invasion.

invective [ɛ̃vɛk'tiːv] *f* invective; **~er** [~ti've] (1a) *v/t.* abuse (*s.o.*); *v/i.:* **~ contre** rail at, inveigh against.

invendable *♣* [ɛ̃vɑ̃'dabl] unsaleable, unmerchantable.

invent|aire [ɛ̃vɑ̃'tɛːr] *m* inventory; *faire son ~* take stock; **~er** [~'te] (1a) invent; **~eur** [~'tœːr] **1.** *adj.* inventive; **2.** *su.* inventor; **♣** finder; **~ion** [~'sjɔ̃] *f* invention; inventiveness; **~orier** ♣ [~tɔ'rje] (1o) make an inventory of, take stock of.

inver|se [ɛ̃'vɛrs] *adj.*, *su./m* opposite; inverse; reverse; **en ~** reverse; **~ser** [ɛ̃vɛr'se] (1a) reverse; **~sible** [~'sibl] reversible; **~sion** [~'sjɔ̃] *f* inversion; *⚡* reversal.

J

investigat|eur [ɛ̃vɛstiga'tœ:r] **1.** adj. investigating; **2.** su./m investigator; **~ion** [~'sjɔ̃] f investigation.

invest|ir [ɛ̃vɛs'ti:r] (2a) invest; **~issement** [~tis'mɑ̃] m investment; **~isseur** [~ti'sœ:r] m investor.

invétérer [ɛ̃vete're] (1f): **s'~** become inveterate.

invincible [ɛ̃vɛ̃'sibl] invincible.

inviolable [ɛ̃vjɔ'labl] inviolable; burglar-proof; *parl.* immune.

invisible [ɛ̃vi'zibl] invisible.

invit|ation [ɛ̃vita'sjɔ̃] f invitation; *sans* ~ uninvited; **~é** m, e f [ɛ̃vi'te] guest; **~er** [~] (1a) invite (to *inf.*, *à inf.*); ask, request; *fig.* tempt.

invivable F [ɛ̃vi'vabl] unlivable-with; impossible to live in.

invocation [ɛ̃vɔka'sjɔ̃] f invocation.

involontaire [ɛ̃vɔlɔ̃'tɛ:r] involuntary.

invoquer [ɛ̃vɔ'ke] (1m) invoke, call upon; put forward (*an excuse*); refer to (*a law etc.*).

invraisembla|ble [ɛ̃vrɛsɑ̃'blabl] unlikely; **~nce** [~'blɑ̃:s] f unlikelihood, improbability.

iode 🜍, ⚚ [jɔd] m iodine.

ion 🜍, ⚡, *phys.* [jɔ̃] m ion.

ioni|que *phys.* [jɔ'nik] ionic; **~sation** *phys.* [~niza'sjɔ̃] f ionization.

irai [i're] *1st p. sg. fut. of aller 1.*

irascible [ira'sibl] irritable, testy; quick-tempered.

iris [i'ris] m ⚚, *anat.*, *phot.* iris; **~é** [~'ze] iridescent.

irlandais, e [irlɑ̃'dɛ, ~'dɛ:z] **1.** adj., su./m ling. Irish; **2.** su./m ⚥ Irishman; *les* ⚥ *pl.* the Irish; *su./f* ⚥ Irishwoman.

ironie [irɔ'ni] f irony; **ironique** [~'nik] ironic(al); **ironiser** [~ni'ze] (1a) speak ironically.

irradiation [irradja'sjɔ̃] f ⚚, *phys.* irradiation; *phot.* halation; **irradier** [~'dje] (1o) *v/t.* irradiate; *v/i.* radiate, spread (*pain etc.*).

irraisonnable [irrɛzɔ'nabl] irrational.

irréali|sable [irreali'zabl] unrealizable (*a.* ♱); **~té** [~'te] f unreality.

irrécusable [irreky'zabl] unimpeachable; unchallengeable.

irréductible [irredyk'tibl] ♱, ⚚ irreducible; *fig.* unshakable; indomitable.

irréel [irre'ɛl] unreal.

irréfléchi [irrefle'ʃi] thoughtless.

irrégul|arité [irregylari'te] f irregularity; unevenness; **~ier** [~'lje] irregular; uneven.

irrémédiable [irreme'djabl] incurable; *fig.* irreparable.

irréparable [irrepa'rabl] irreparable; *fig.* irretrievable.

irrépréhensible [irrepreɑ̃'sibl] blameless.

irrépressible [irrepre'sibl] uncontrollable, irrepressible.

irréprochable [irrepro'ʃabl] irreproachable; ⚖ unimpeachable.

irrésistible [irrezis'tibl] irresistible.

irrésolu [irrezɔ'ly] irresolute; unsolved (*problem*); **irrésolution** [~ly'sjɔ̃] f indecision, irresolution.

irrespectueux [irrɛspɛk'tɥø] disrespectful (to *pour, envers*).

irresponsabilité [irrɛspɔ̃sabili'te] f irresponsibility; **irresponsable** [~'sabl] irresponsible.

irrétrécissable *tex.* [irretresi'sabl] unshrinkable; *rendre* ~ sanforize.

irrévocable [irrevɔ'kabl] irrevocable; absolute (*decree*).

irrig|ation [irriga'sjɔ̃] f irrigation; **~uer** [~'ge] (1m) irrigate.

irrit|able [irri'tabl] irritable, touchy; **~er** [~'te] (1a) irritate; ♱ inflame; *s'~* become angry (at, with s.o. *contre q.*; at s.th., *de qch.*).

irruption [irryp'sjɔ̃] f irruption; inrush; *river:* flood; *faire* ~ burst in (on, *chez*).

islamique [isla'mik] Islamic; **islamisme** [~'mism] m Islam(ism).

islandais [islɑ̃'dɛ] **1.** adj., su./m ling. Icelandic; **2.** su. Icelander.

isobare *meteor.* [izɔ'ba:r] f isobar.

isol|ateur ⚡ [isɔla'tœ:r] m insulator; **~é** [iso'le] isolated; lonely; lone; remote, out-of-the-way; **~ement** [izɔl'mɑ̃] m isolation; ⚡ insulation; **~ément** [izole'mɑ̃] *adv.* separately; **~er** [~'le] (1a) isolate; ⚡ insulate; **~oir** [~'lwa:r] m polling booth.

isotope *phys.* [izɔ'tɔp] m isotope.

israéli|en [israe'ljɛ̃] adj., su. Israeli; **~te** [~'lit] **1.** adj. Jewish, of the Israelites; **2.** su. ⚥ Israelite, Jew.

issu, e [i'sy] **1.** adj.: ~ *de* descended from; born of; **2.** f issue, end; result; outlet; *à l'~e de* at the end of; after; *sans ~e* blind (*alley*).

isthme *geog.*, *anat.* [ism] *m* isthmus.

itali|en [ita'ljɛ̃] *adj.*, *su.* Italian; **~que** *typ.* [~'lik] *adj.*, *su./m* italic.

itinéra|ire [itine'rɛːr] **1.** *adj.* road-...; **2.** *su./m* itinerary; route; guide-book; **~nt** [~'rɑ̃] itinerant.

ivoire [i'vwaːr] *m* ivory.

ivr|e [iːvr] drunk (with, *de*); *fig.* ~ **de** wild with (*anger*, *joy*, *etc.*); **~esse** [i'vrɛs] *f* drunkenness; *fig.* ecstasy; **~ogne, -esse** [i'vrɔɲ, ivrɔ'ɲɛs] **1.** *adj.* drunken; **2.** *su.* drunkard.

J

jabot [ʒa'bo] *m bird*: crop; *cost.* frill, jabot.

jacass|e *zo.* [ʒa'kas] *f* magpie; **~or** [~ka'se] (1a) chatter, gossip; **~erie** [~kas'ri] *f* gossip.

jachère ✓ [ʒa'ʃɛːr] *f* fallow (land); (*être*) **en** ~ (lie) fallow.

jacinthe ♀ [ʒa'sɛ̃ːt] *f* hyacinth.

jacobin [ʒako'bɛ̃] *m* sympathizer with radical democracy.

ja(c)quot *orn.* [ʒa'ko] *m* Poll(y).

jactance [ʒak'tɑ̃ːs] *f* boast(ing).

jade *min.* [ʒad] *m* jade.

jadis [ʒa'dis] *adv.* formerly, long ago; *de* ~ *a.* of old.

jaill|ir [ʒa'jiːr] (2a) gush, spurt out; shoot or burst forth; flash; **~ssement** [~jis'mɑ̃] *m* gushing *etc.*

jais *min.* [ʒɛ] *m* jet.

jalon [ʒa'lɔ̃] *m* surveying staff; pole; *fig.* **poser** (*or* **planter**) **des** ~**s** prepare the ground for (*de*, *pour*); **~ner** [~lɔ'ne] (1a) stake out; *fig.* mark.

jalou|ser [ʒalu'ze] (1a) be jealous of; **~sie** [~'zi] *f* jealousy; Venetian blind; **~x** [ʒa'lu] jealous (of, *de*); eager (for, *de*).

jamais [ʒa'mɛ] *adv.* ever; never; ~ **plus** never again; **à** (*or* **pour**) ~ for ever; **ne** ... ~ never.

jamb|age [ʒɑ̃'baːʒ] *m* △ jamb; post; **~e** [ʒɑ̃ːb] *f* leg; *glass*: stem; **à toutes** ~**s** at top speed; **prendre ses** ~**s à son cou** take to one's heels; **~é** [ʒɑ̃'be]: **bien** ~ with shapely legs; **~ière** [~'bjɛːr] *f* legging; *sp.* shinguard; **~on** [~'bɔ̃] *m* ham; **œufs** *m/pl.* **au** ~ ham and eggs; **~onneau** [~bɔ'no] *m* knuckle of ham.

jante [ʒɑ̃ːt] *f* wheel: felloe; rim.

janvier [ʒɑ̃'vje] *m* January.

japon [ʒa'pɔ̃] *m* Japan porcelain; **~ais** [~pɔ'nɛ] *adj.*, *su.* Japanese.

japper [ʒa'pe] (1a) yelp.

jaquette [ʒa'kɛt] *f man*: morning coat; *woman*: jacket; *book etc.*: (dust) cover.

jardin [ʒar'dɛ̃] *m* garden; ~ **d'enfants** kindergarten; **~age** [ʒardi'naːʒ] *m* gardening; *diamond*: flaw, ~ **paysagiste** landscape gardening; **~er** [~'ne] (1a) garden; **~et** [~'nɛ] *m* small garden; **~ier, -ère** [~'nje, ~'njɛːr] **1.** *adj.* garden...; **2.** *su.* gardener; **~ paysagiste** landscape gardener; *su./f* flower stand; **~ère d'enfants** kindergarten teacher; *cuis.* **à la** ~**ère** garnished with vegetables.

jargon [ʒar'gɔ̃] *m* jargon; slang.

jarre [ʒaːr] *f* (earthenware) jar.

jarret [ʒa'rɛ] *m* back of the knee; *cuis.* shin; *veal*: knuckle; ⚙ elbow; **~elle** [ʒar'tɛl] *f* suspender, *Am.* garter; **~ière** [~'tjɛːr] *f* garter.

jars *orn.* [ʒaːr] *m* gander.

jas|er [ʒa'ze] (1a) chatter, talk; gossip; **~eur** [~'zœːr] **1.** *adj.* talkative; **2.** *su.* chatterbox; gossip.

jasmin ♀ [ʒas'mɛ̃] *m* jasmine.

jaspe [ʒasp] *m* jasper; **~ sanguin** bloodstone; **~é** [ʒas'pe] marbled.

jatte [ʒat] *f* bowl; *milk*: pan, basin.

jauge [ʒoːʒ] *f* ga(u)ge (*a.* ⚙); ⚓ tonnage; *mot.* ~ (**d'huile**) dipstick; **~er** [ʒo'ʒe] (1l) ga(u)ge (*a. fig.*).

jaun|âtre [ʒo'naːtr] yellowish; **~e** [ʒoːn] **1.** *adj.* yellow; **2.** *adv.*: **rire** ~ give a sickly smile; **3.** *su./m* yellow; yolk; F strike-breaker; **~et** [ʒo'nɛ] yellowish; **~ir** [~'niːr] (2a) yellow; **~isse** 🐛 [~'nis] *f* jaundice.

javel [ʒa'vɛl] *m*: *eau f de ~* bleach.

javelot [ʒav'lo] *m* javelin.

je [ʒə] *pron./pers.* I.

je-m'en-fichisme F [ʒəmɑ̃fi'ʃism] *m/inv.* couldn't-care-less attitude.

jet [ʒɛ] *m* throw, cast(ing) (*a. metall.*); jet (*a. ☼, ✓*); *liquid*: gush; *light*: flash; ⚓ jetsam; ♀ sprout; ☼ blast; *du premier ~* at the first attempt *or* try *or* go; *~ée* [~'te] *f* jetty; breakwater; *~er* [~'te] (1c) cast, fling, hurl; throw away; ⚓ drop (*anchor*); lay (*the foundations*); utter (*a cry*); give off (*sparks*); *se ~ river*: flow (into, *dans*); *se ~ sur* pounce on; *se ~ vers* rush towards; *~on* [~'tɔ̃] *m* counter, chip; *teleph.* *~ de téléphone* telephone token.

jeu [ʒø] *m* game; play (*a. ☼*); gambling; *thea.* acting; *tools etc.*: set; *machine etc.*, *a. fig.*: working; ☼ clearance; *fig.* action; *fig.* interaction; *cards*: pack; *~ de mots* pun; *~d'esprit* witticism; *ca-cher son ~* hide one's cards; *être en ~* be at stake; *entrer en ~* come into play; *mettre en ~* stake; *il a beau ~ de* (*or* *pour*) (*inf.*) it's easy for him to (*inf.*).

jeudi [ʒø'di] *m* Thursday; *~ saint* Maundy Thursday.

jeun [ʒœ̃] *adv.*: *à ~* on an empty stomach, fasting; sober.

jeune [ʒœn] **1.** *adj.* young; youthful; younger; *fig.* new; early (*fruit*); **2.** *su.* young person *or* animal; *su./m les ~s* pl. the young *pl.*

jeûn|e [ʒøn] *m* fast(ing), abstinence; *~er* [ʒø'ne] (1a) fast (from, *de*).

jeunesse [ʒœ'nɛs] *f* youth; boyhood; girlhood; *fig.* youthfulness, freshness; *pl.* the young *pl.*
jeunet F [~'nɛ] very young.

joaill|erie [ʒɔaj'ri] *f* jewel(le)ry; *~ier* *m* [ʒɔa'je] jeweller.

job F [ʒɔb] *m* job, employment.
jobard F [ʒɔ'ba:r] *m* dupe, F mug; *~er* [ʒɔbar'de] (1a) fool, dupe.

jocrisse [ʒɔ'kris] *m* fool; clown.

joie [ʒwa] *f* joy; delight; pleasure.

joi|gnable [ʒwa'ɲabl] available (*person*); *~gnis* [~'ɲi] *1st p. sg. p.s. of joindre*; *~gnons* [~'ɲɔ̃] *1st p. pl. pres. of joindre*; *~ndre* [ʒwɛ̃:dr] (4m) *v/t.* join (*a. ☼ etc.*), put together; attach to, *à*) *in a letter etc.*: enclose (with, *à*); combine (with, *à*); get in touch with, contact (*s.o.*); ✝ *pièces f/pl. jointes* enclosures; *se ~ à*

join; *v/i.* meet; *~ns* [ʒwɛ̃] *1st p. sg. pres. of joindre*; *~nt* [ʒwɛ̃] **1.** *p.p. of joindre*; **2.** *su./m* joint (*a. ☼*); join; *metall.* seam; *trouver le ~* find a way to *inf.*, *pour inf.*; *of ger.*, *de inf.*); *~nté* [ʒwɛ̃'te] jointed; *~nture* [~'ty:r] *f* joint; knuckle.

joli [ʒɔ'li] pretty; nice; *~et* [ʒɔ'ljɛ] rather pretty; *~ment* [ʒɔli'mɑ̃] *adv.* prettily; well; F awfully; F pretty.

jon|c Ḳ [ʒɔ̃] *m* rush; cane; *~cher* [~'ʃe] (1a) strew (with, *de*).

jonction [ʒɔ̃k'sjɔ̃] *f* junction.

jongl|er [ʒɔ̃'gle] (1a) juggle (*a. fig.*); *~erie* [ʒɔ̃glə'ri] *f* juggling; *fig.* trick; *~eur* [~'glœ:r] *m* juggler.

jouable [ʒwabl] playable.

joue [ʒu] *f* cheek; *~ contre ~* check by jowl; *mettre en ~* take aim at.

jou|er [ʒwe] (1p) *v/t./i.* play (*a. ♩, thea.*); *v/t.* back (*a horse*); stake, bet; pretend to be; feign; F fool (*s.o.*); *se ~ de* take (*s.th.*) in one's stride; make light of; *v/i.* gamble; ☼ warp; ☼ run well; ☼ have too much play; *~ à* play (*a play, cards, football, at soldiers, etc.*); *~ de ♩* play (*an instrument*); *fig.* use, make use of; *à qui de ~?* *cards*: whose turn is it?; *faire ~* set in motion; bring into play; *~et* [ʒwɛ] *m* toy (*a. fig.*); *~eur* [ʒwœ:r] **1.** *su./m* player; gambler; **2.** *adj.* fond of playing.

joufflu [ʒu'fly] chubby.

joug [ʒu] *m* yoke; *balance*: beam.

joui|r [ʒwi:r] (2a) enjoy o.s.; F be thrilled; *~ de* enjoy (*s.th.*); F *faire ~* thrill, delight; *~ssance* [ʒwi'sɑ̃:s] *f* enjoyment; use; ✝ right to interest.

joujou, *pl.* *-x* F [ʒu'ʒu] *m* toy.

jour [ʒu:r] *m* day; daytime; daylight; light (*a. fig.*); opening, gap; *fig.* aspect; *~ de fête* holiday; *~ ouvrable* workday; *à ~ sewing*: open-work ...; up to date; *au grand ~*, *en plein ~* in broad daylight; *fig.* publicly; *au ~ le ~* from day to day; *de ~* by day; *de nos ~s* nowadays; *donner le ~ à* give birth to; *du ~ au lendemain* overnight; at a moment's notice; *il fait ~* it is getting light; it is (day)light; *fig.* *demain il fera ~* tomorrow is another day; *fig.* *se faire ~* appear; come to the front; *l'autre ~* the other day; *mettre à ~* bring up to date, update; *mettre au ~* disclose, uncover,

reveal; **par** ~ per *or* a *or* each day; *cuis.*
plat *m* **du** ~ today's special dish; **petit** ~
morning twilight; *fig.* **sous un autre** ~
in a different light; *fig.* **sous son vrai** ~
in its true light *or* colo(u)rs; **tous les**
(deux) ~s every (other) day; **un** ~ one
day; some day; **un** ~ **ou l'autre** sooner
or later; **vivre au** ~ **le** ~ live from hand
to mouth; **voir le** ~ be born.

journal [ʒur'nal] *m* diary; journal (*a.*
♱); log-book; newspaper; ~ **parlé** *ra-*
dio: news; **~ier** [ʒurna'lje] **1.** *adj.* daily;
2. *su./m* day-labo(u)rer; **~isme** [~'lism]
m journalism; **~iste** [~'list] *su.* journal-
ist.

journ|ée [ʒur'ne] *f* day; day's work *or*
journey; daily wage; **à la** ~ by the day;
~ellement [~ncl'mɑ̃] *adv.* daily

jovial, e, *m/pl* **-als, -aux** [ʒɔ'vjal, ~'vjo]
jolly, jovial; good-natured; **~ité** [~vja-
li'te] *f* joviality, jollity.

joyau [ʒwa'jo] *m* jewel (*a. fig.*).

joyeux [ʒwa'jø] merry, joyful.

jubil|aire [ʒybi'lɛːr] jubilee-...; **~é** [~'le]
m jubilee; golden anniversary; **~er**
[~'le] (1a) rejoice; gloat.

juch|er [ʒy'ʃe] (1a) perch; roost; **~oir**
[~'ʃwaːr] *m* perch.

judic|ature [ʒydika'tyːr] *f* judgeship;
~iaire [~'sjɛːr] judicial, legal; **~ieux**
[~'sjø] judicious.

jug|e [ʒyːʒ] *m* judge (*a. fig.*); *sp.* umpire;
~ **d'instruction** examining magistrate;
~ement [ʒyʒ'mɑ̃] *m* judgment; ♱ sentence, award; *fig. a.* opinion; ♱ **passer**
en ~ stand trial; **~eote** F [ʒy'ʒɔt] *f* common sense; **~er** [~ʒe] (1l) *v/t.* judge; ♱
pass sentence on; ♱ try (for, **pour**); *fig.*
think, consider; ~ **bon de** (*inf.*) think fit
to (*inf.*); *v/i.*: ~ **de** judge, appreciate.

jugul|aire [ʒygy'lɛːr] *f* jugular (vein);
chin strap; **~er** [~'le] (1a) check; stop;
stifle; put down.

juif, juive [ʒɥif, ʒɥiːv] **1.** *adj.* Jewish; **2.**
su./m Jew; **petit** ~ funny bone; *su./f* ♀
Jewess.

juillet [ʒɥi'jɛ] *m* July.

juin [ʒɥɛ̃] *m* June.

julienne [ʒy'ljɛn] *f* vegetable soup.

jum|eau, -elle [ʒy'mo, ~'mɛl] *adj.*, *su.*
twin; *su./f:* **~elles** *pl.* binoculars; ◉
cheeks; **~elage** [ʒym'laːʒ] *m* twinning
(of towns); **~elé** [~'le] twin.

jument [ʒy'mɑ̃] *f* mare.

jungle [ʒɔ̃ːgl] *f* jungle.

jupe [ʒyp] *f* skirt; **jupon** [ʒy'pɔ̃] *m* petticoat; *fig.* women *pl.*

jur|é [ʒy're] *m* juror, juryman; **~s** *pl.*
jury; **~er** [ʒy're] (1a) *v/t.* swear; vow;
v/i. curse; *fig.* clash (*colours*); **~eur**
[~'rœːr] *m* swearer.

jurid|iction [ʒyridik'sjɔ̃] *f* jurisdiction;
~que [~'dik] judicial.

juriste ♱ [ʒy'rist] *m* jurist.

juron [ʒy'rɔ̃] *m* oath, swear-word.

jury [ʒy'ri] *m* jury, board, panel.

jus [ʒy] *m* juice; *cuis.* gravy.

jusant ♱ [ʒy'zɑ̃] *m* ebb(-tide).

jusqua'au-boutis|me *pol. etc.* [ʒysko-
bu'tism] *m* extremism, hard-line attitude; **~te** hard-liner.

jusque [ʒysk(ə)] *prp.* (*usu.* **jusqu'à**) until,
till; as far as (to), up *or* down to; **jus-**
qu'à ce que (*sbj.*) until; **jusqu'au bout**
to the (bitter) end; **jusqu'ici** thus *or* so
far.

just|e [ʒyst] **1.** *adj.* just, fair; exact; tight
(*garment, fit*); right (*time, watch,*
word); **~-milieu** *m* golden mean; **au** ~
exactly; **2.** *adv.* rightly; just; precisely;
scarcely; **~ement** [ʒysta'mɑ̃] *adv.* right
ly; precisely; **~esse** [~'tɛs] *f* exactness;
accuracy; **de** ~ just, barely, by a hair's
breadth; **~ice** [~'tis] *f* justice; equity;
aller en ~ go to law; **se faire** ~ revenge
o.s.; commit suicide; **~iciable**
[~li'sjabl] *adj.:* ~ **de** amenable to (*a.*
fig.).

justifi|cation [ʒystifika'sjɔ̃] *f* justifica-
tion; **~er** [~'fje] (1o) *v/t.* justify; *v/i.:* ~
de give proof of.

juteux [ʒy'tø] juicy, F lucrative.

juvénil|e [ʒyve'nil] juvenile; youthful;
~ité [~nili'te] *f* youthfulness.

juxtaposer [ʒykstapo'ze] (1a) juxtapose,
place side by side.

K

kakatoès [kakatɔˈɛs] *m* cockatoo.
kangourou [kɑ̃guˈru] *m* kangaroo.
kaolin [kaɔˈlɛ̃] *m* china clay, kaolin.
képi [keˈpi] *m* peaked cap, kepi.
kermesse [kɛrˈmɛs] *f* village fair.
kérosène [kerɔˈzɛn] *m* kerosene.
kidnapp|er [kidnaˈpe] (1a) kidnap; **~eur**
[~ˈpœːr] *m* kidnapper.
kif kif *sl.* [kifˈkif] all the same.
kilo... [kilɔ] kilo...; **~(gramme)** [~(ˈgram)]
m measure: kilogram(me); **~mètre**
[~ˈmɛtr] *m measure*: kilometer;

~métrage [~meˈtraːʒ] *m* number of
kilometers; **~watt** ⚡ [~ˈwat] *m* kilowatt;
~heure kilowatt-hour.
kinésithéra|peute [kineziteraˈpøːt] *su.*
physiotherapist; **~pie** [~ˈpi] *f* physio-
therapy.
kiosque [kjɔsk] *m* kiosk; *newspaper*:
stall; ⚓ conning-tower.
klaxon *mot.* [klakˈsɔ̃] *m* horn; **~ner**
[~sɔˈne] (1a) sound the horn.
krach ♣ [krak] *m* crash.
kyrielle F [kiˈrjɛl] *f* string (of, **de**).

L

la¹ [la] *see* **le**.
la² ♪ [~] *m/inv.* la, *note*: A.
là [la] *adv. place*: there; *time*: then; **~ où**
where; **ce livre-~** that book; **c'est ~**
que that is where; **de ~** hence; **~-bas**
[~ˈba] *adv.* over there.
labeur [laˈbœːr] *m* labo(u)r, toil.
labor|antine [labɔrɑ̃ˈtin] *f* female labor-
atory assistant; **~atoire** [~raˈtwaːr] *m* laboratory; **~ieux** [~ˈrjø] (hard)working.
labour [laˈbuːr] *m* ploughing, *Am.* plow-
ing; **~able** [labuˈrabl] *arable*; **~er** [~ˈre]
(1a) plough, *Am.* plow; *fig.* furrow,
gash, slash (into); **~eur** [~ˈrœːr] *m*
ploughman, *Am.* plowman.
lac [lak] *m* lake; F **dans le ~** in a fix.
lacer [laˈse] (1k) lace (up).
lacérer [laseˈre] (1f) lacerate; tear.
lacet [laˈsɛ] *m* (*shoe-etc.*) lace; *hunt.*
snare (*a. fig.*); *road*: hairpin bend.
lâch|age [lɑˈʃaːʒ] *m* release; F *friends*:
dropping; **~e** [lɑːʃ] **1.** *adj.* loose, slack,
lax; cowardly; **2.** *su./m* coward; **~er**
[lɑˈʃe] (1a) *v/t.* release, loosen; slacken;
let go of; *fig.* give up, *a. friend*: drop; let
out; *fig.* **~ pied** give way; *v/i.* become
loose; give way; snap (*rope etc.*); **~eté**
[lɑʃˈte] *f* cowardice; **~eur** *m*, **-euse** *f* F
[lɑˈʃœːr, ~ˈʃøːz] quitter.

lacis *anat.*, *etc.* [laˈsi] *m* network.
laconique [lakɔˈnik] laconic.
lacrymogène [lakrimɔˈʒɛn] tear-excit-
ing; *gaz m* ~ tear-gas.
lacs [lɑ] *m* noose; snare (*a. fig.*).
lacté [lakˈte] milky; milk-(*diet*); lacteal;
voie *f* **~e** Milky Way.
lacune [laˈkyn] *f* gap, blank.
là-dessous [latˈsu] *adv.* underneath,
under there; **là-dessus** [~ˈsy] *adv.*
thereupon (*places, time*); on that.
ladite [laˈdit] *see* **ledit**.
ladre [lɑːdr] **1.** *adj.* stingy; **2.** *su./m*
miser; **~rie** [lɑdrəˈri] *f* stinginess.
lai [lɛ] **1.** *adj. eccl.* lay-...; **2.** *su./m eccl.*
layman; lay; **laïc** [laˈik] *see* **laïque**.
laïcisation [laisizaˈsjɔ̃] *f* secularisation;
laïcité [~ˈte] *f* secularity.
laid [lɛ] ugly; mean (*deed*); **~eron**
[lɛˈdrɔ̃] *mf* ugly woman; **~eur** [~ˈdœːr] *f*
ugliness.
laie¹ [lɛ] *f* wild sow.
laie² [~] *f* forest path.
lain|age [lɛˈnaːʒ] *m* wool(l)en article; **~e**
[lɛn] *f* wool; **~ peignée** worsted; **~eux**
[~ˈnø] woolly.
laïque [laˈik] **1.** *adj.* secular; undenominational; **2.** *su./m* layman.
laisse [lɛs] *f* leash, lead; *fig.* **tenir q.**

large

en ~ keep s.o. in leading-strings.

laissé(e)-pour-compte, *pl.* **laissé(e)s-pour-compte** ✝, *fig.* [lesepur'kɔ̃t] **1.** *adj.* rejected; **2.** *su.* reject.

laiss|er [le'se] (1b) *v/t.* leave; let, allow, permit; ~ *là qch.* give s.th. up; *v/i.:* ~ *à penser* give food for thought; ~**er-aller** [lɛsea'le] *m/inv.* unconstraint; ~**er-faire** [~'fɛːr] *m* inaction; ~**ez-passer** [~pɑ'se] *m/inv.* pass, permit.

lait [lɛ] *m* milk; ~ *de chaux* whitewash; ~ *en poudre* powdered milk; ~**age** [lɛ'taːʒ] *m* dairy products *pl.*; ~**erie** [~'tri] *f* dairy; creamery; ~**eux** [~'tø] milky; milk-...; ~**ier, -ère** [~'tje, ~'tjɛːr] **1.** *adj.* milk-...; **2.** *su./m* milk-man; ⊚ slag; *su./f* milk-woman; milk-cart.

laiton [lɛ'tɔ̃] *m* (yellow) brass.

laitue ♀ [lɛ'ty] *f* lettuce.

laïus ⊢ [la'jys] *m* speech.

lambeau [lã'bo] *m* shred, bit, rag.

lambin [lã'bɛ̃] **1.** *adj.* dawdling, slow; **2.** *su./m* dawdler; ~**er** ⊢ [~bi'ne] (1a) dawdle.

lambris ⚠ [lã'bri] *m* wainscoting; wall-lining.

lame [lam] *f* thin plate; *razor etc.:* blade; ♣ wave; *blind:* slat; ~**lle** [la'mɛl] *f* lamella; flake; thin sheet.

lament|able [lamã'tabl] lamentable; pitiful; ~**ation** [~ta'sjɔ̃] *f* lamentation; ~**er** [~'te] (1a): *se* ~ lament (s.th., *de qch*).

lamette [la'mɛt] *f* small blade.

lamin|er [lami'ne] (1a) ⊚ laminate; *fig.* reduce, curtail; ~**oir** [~'nwaːr] *m* rolling mill; *fig. passer au* ~ put (s.o.) or go through the mill.

lampadaire [lãpa'dɛːr] *m* street lamp *or* light; standard (*Am.* floor) lamp; lamp post.

lampe [lãːp] *f* lamp; *radio:* valve; *telev.* tube; ~ *à arc* arc-light; ~ *de poche* flash-lamp, electric torch.

lamp|ée [lã'pe] *f* water etc.: draught, *Am.* draft; ~**er** [~] (1a) gulp down.

lampion [lã'pjɔ̃] *m* Chinese lantern; **ste** [~'pist] *m* underling.

lamproie *icht.* [lã'prwa] *f* lamprey.

lampyre *zo.* [lã'piːr] *m* fire-fly.

lance [lãːs] *f* spear; lance; ⊚ nozzle; hose; *fig. rompre une* ~ (*or des* ~**s**) *avec* cross swords with.

lanc|ement [lãs'mã] *m* throwing; *baseball:* pitch; ♣ launching (*a rocket, a*

fig.); ~**er** [lã'se] (1k) throw, fling, hurl; launch (♣, ✝ *an article, a rocket, fig. an attack, a. fig. a person*); ✝ fire (*a torpedo*); utter (*an oath*); emit (*smoke, steam*); *mot., fig.* start; ⊚, *fig.* set going; *se* ~ rush, dart; *fig. se* ~ *dans* go or launch into.

lancinant [lãsi'nã] shooting (*pain*).

landau, *pl.* **-s** [lã'do] *m* pram, *Am.* baby carriage.

lande [lãːd] *f* heath, moor.

langage [lã'gaːʒ] *m* language; speech; ~ *chiffré* coded text.

lange [lãːʒ] *m* swaddling-cloth.

langoureux [lãgu'rø] languishing.

langouste *zo.* [lã'gust] *f* lobster.

langue [lãːg] *f* tongue; language; ~ *d'arrivée* target language; ~ *de départ* source language; ~ *maternelle* native language; *avoir la* ~ *bien pendue* have a glib tongue; *de* ~ *anglaise* English-speaking; ~**tte** [lã'gɛt] *f* metal, shoe: (small) tongue; ⊚ feather.

langueur [lã'gœːr] *f* languor; listlessness.

langui|r [lã'giːr] (2a) languish, pine; *thea.* drag; *fig.* be dull, ~**ssant** [~gi'sã] languid.

lanière [la'njɛːr] *f* thong, lash.

lantern|e [lã'tɛrn] *f* lantern; *opt.* ~ *à projections* slide projector; ~ *rouge* rear light; *fig.* tail-ender; ~ *vénitienne* Chinese lantern; ~**eau** [lãtɛr'no] *m* skylight; ~**er** [~'ne] (1a) dawdle; *faire q.* ~ make s.o. wait.

lapalissade [lapali'sad] *f* truism.

laper [la'pe] (1a) lap (up).

lapid|aire [lapi'dɛːr] terse, lapidary; ~**er** [~'de] (1a) stone.

lapin [la'pɛ̃] *m* rabbit; ⊢ fellow; ⊢ *poser un* ~ *à q.* stand s.o. up.

laps [laps] *m:* ~ *de temps* lapse *or* space of time; **lapsus** [la'psys] *m* pen, tongue: slip; *memory:* lapse.

laqu|e [lak] *su./f* lac; hair spray; *su./m* lacquer; ~**er** [la'ke] (1m) lacquer.

laquelle [la'kɛl] *see* **lequel**.

larcin ⚖ [lar'sɛ̃] *m* larceny, theft.

lard [laːr] *m* bacon; back-fat; ⊢ *faire du* ~ grow fat; ~**er** [lar'de] (1a) *cuis.* lard (*a. fig.*); *fig.* assail (with, *de*); ~**on** [~'dɔ̃] *m* *cuis.* piece of larding bacon; ⊢ kid, baby.

large [larʒ] **1.** *adj.* broad; wide; ample;

generous, liberal; **2.** *adv.* broadly; **~ ouvert** wide open; *calculer* **~** allow extra; *voir* **~** think big; **3.** *su./m* breadth, width; space; ⚓ open sea; *3 mètres de* **~** 3 metres wide *or* in width; *être au* **~** have plenty of space *or* room; be well off; ⚓ *au* **~** *de* off (*Calais, Dover, etc.*); F *prendre le* **~** run away, F clear off; **~ement** widely; generously; considerably, greatly; at least, easily; more than enough; **~esse** [lar'ʒɛs] *f* generosity, liberality; **~eur** [~'ʒœːr] *f* breadth, width; **~ d'esprit** broadness of mind.

larguer [lar'ge] (1m) ⚓ let go *or* cast off (*a rope*); release (*bombs etc.*); drop (*a. fig.*); F *fig.* chuck (up *or* out).

larm|e [larm] *f* tear; *fig.* drop; **~oyant** [larmwa'jɑ̃] tearful; *pej.* maudlin; **~oyer** [~mwa'je] (1h) *fig. pej.* weep.

larron [la'rɔ̃] *m* † thief; *s'entendre comme* **~** *s en foire* be as thick as thieves.

larve *biol.* [larv] *f* larva, grub.

laryngite ✶ [larɛ̃'ʒit] *f* laryngitis.

las, lasse [lɑ, lɑːs] tired, weary.

lascar [las'kaːr] *m* lascar; F fellow.

lasci|f [la'sif] lascivious, lewd; **~veté** [~siv'te] *f* lasciviousness.

lasser [lɑ'se] (1a) tire; *fig.* exhaust; *se* **~** grow weary (of, *de*); **lassitude** [~si'tyd] *f* weariness.

latent [la'tɑ̃] latent.

latéral [late'ral] lateral; side-...

latin [la'tɛ̃] *adj., su./m ling.* Latin.

latitude [lati'tyd] *f* latitude.

latt|e [lat] *f* lath; board; **~is** [~'ti] *m* lath-work.

laudatif [loda'tif] laudatory.

laurier ♀, *fig.* [lɔ'rje] *m* laurel.

lava|ble [la'vabl] washable; **~bo** [~va'bo] *m* wash-stand; lavatory; **~ge** [~'vaːʒ] *m* washing; *pol.* **~ de cerveau** brainwashing.

lavande ♀ [la'vɑ̃ːd] *f* lavender.

lava|ndière [lava'djɛːr] *f* washer-woman; **~sse** F [~'vas] *f* slops *pl.*

lave *geol.* [laːv] *f* lava.

lav|e-glace, *pl.* **~e-glaces** *mot.* [lav'glas] *m* windscreen (*Am.* windshield) washer; **~e-mains** [~'mɛ̃] *m/inv.* hand-basin; **~ement** ✶ [~'mɑ̃] enema; **~er** [la've] (1a) wash; scrub (*a.* 🔧, ⚙); bathe (*a wound*); *fig.* clear; F *la tête à* tell (*s.o.*) off; **~erie** [lav'ri] *f* launderet-

te; **~ette** [~'vɛt] *f* dish cloth; **~eur, -euse** [~'vœːr, ~'vøːz] *su.* washer; *su./f* washing machine; **~e-vaisselle** [lavvɛ'sɛl] *m/inv.* dish washer; **~oir** [la'vwaːr] *m* wash house; **~ure** [~'vyːr] *f*: **~** (*de vaisselle*) dishwater.

lax|atif ✶ [laksa'tif] *adj., su./m* laxative; **~ité** [laksi'te] *f* laxity.

layette [lɛ'jɛt] *f* baby-linen.

lazaret ⚓ [laza're] *m* lazaret(to).

le *m,* **la** *f,* **les** *pl.* [lə, la, le] **1.** *art./def.* the; **2.** *pron./pers.* him, her, it; *pl.* them.

leader *pol., sp.* [li'dœːr] *m* leader.

lèche [lɛʃ] *f: sl. faire de la* **~ à** suck up to; **~cul** V [~'ky] *m/inv.* arse-crawler.

lécher [le'ʃe] (1f) lick; *fig.* elaborate (*one's style*); **lécheur** *m,* **-euse** *f* [~'ʃœːr, ~'ʃøːz] *pej.* toady; **lèche-vitrines** F [lɛʃvi'trin] *m/inv.* windowshopping.

leçon [lə'sɔ̃] *f* reading; lesson (*a. fig.*); **~ particulière** private lesson.

lect|eur *m,* **-trice** *f* [lɛk'tœːr, ~'tris] reader; *univ.* foreign assistant; **~ure** [~'tyːr] *f* reading (*a. parl.*); *faire la* **~ à** read to s.o.

ledit *m,* **ladite** *f,* **lesdits** *m/pl.,* **lesdites** *f/pl.* [lə'di, la'dit, le'di, le'dit] *adj.* the above-mentioned.

légal [le'gal] legal; forensic (*medicine*); **monnaie** *f* **~e** legal tender; **~iser** [legali'ze] (1a) legalize; certify; **~ité** [~'te] *f* legality.

légat|aire [lega'tɛːr] *su.* legatee; heir; **~ion** [~'sjɔ̃] *f* legation.

légend|aire [leʒɑ̃'dɛːr] legendary; F epic (*fight*); **~e** [~'ʒɑ̃:d] *f* legend (*a. coins, illustrations, maps*).

léger [le'ʒe] light (*a. wine*); slight; weak (*tea*); *fig.* flighty; *fig.* frivolous; *à la légère* lightly; *prendre à la* **~** *a.* make light of (*s.th.*); **légèreté** [leʒɛr'te] *f* lightness *etc.*; *see* **léger.**

légion [le'ʒjɔ̃] *f* legion; *fig.* large number; **~ d'Honneur** Legion of Hono(u)r; **~ étrangère** Foreign Legion; **~naire** [~ʒjɔ'nɛːr] *m hist.* legionary; ✗ soldier of the Foreign Legion; member of the Legion of Hono(u)r.

légis|lateur [leʒisla'tœːr] *m* legislator; **~latif** [~'tif] legislative; **~lation** [~'sjɔ̃] *f* legislation; **~lature** [~'tyːr] *f* legislature; term of office.

légitim|ation [leʒitima'sjɔ̃] *f* child; legiti-

mation; official recognition; ~e [~'tim]
1. *adj.* legitimate; **2.** *su./f sl.* wife; ~er
[~ti'me] (1a) legitimate; justify; recognize; ~ité [~timi'te] *f* legitimacy; lawful-
ness.

legs [lɛ] *m* legacy; bequest; **léguer**
[le'ge] (1s) bequeath, leave.

légum|e [le'gym] *m* vegetable; ⚥ pod;
~ineux, -euse ⚥ [legymi'nø, ~nøːz] **1.**
adj. leguminous; **2.** *su./f* leguminous
plant.

lendemain [lɑ̃d'mɛ̃] *m* day after; *fig.* future; *le ~ matin* the next morning; *fig.*
sans ~ short-lived.

léni|fier ⚥ [leni'fje] (1o) soothe; ~tif ⚥
[~'tif] *adj., su./m* lenitive.

lent [lɑ̃] slow; ~teur [lɑ̃'tœːr] *f* slowness.

lentille [lɑ̃'tiːj] *f* ⚥ lentil; *opt.* lens; ~s *pl.*
cornéennes contact lenses.

léonin [leɔ'nɛ̃] leonine; *fig.* **part** *f* ~e
lion's share.

léopard *zo.* [leɔ'paːr] *m* leopard.

lèpre ⚥ [lɛpr] *f* leprosy (*a. fig.*); **lépreux**
[le'prø] **1.** *adj.* leprous; **2.** *su.* leper.

lequel *m,* **laquelle** *f,* **lesquels** *m/pl.,*
lesquelles *f/pl.* [lə'kɛl, la'kɛl, le'kɛl]
1. *pron./rel.* who, whom, which; **2.** *pron./
interr.* which (one)?; **3.** *adj* which.

les [le] *see* **le.**

lès [le] *prp.* near ...

lèse-majesté ⚥ [lɛzmaʒɛs'te] *f* high
treason; **léser** [le'ze] (1f) wrong (*s.o.*);
injure; damage.

lésiner [lezi'ne] (1a) skimp (on, *sur*);
~erie [~zin'ri] *f* stinginess.

lésion [le'zjɔ̃] *f* injury; ⚥ lesion.

lessiv|age [lesi'vaːʒ] *m* washing; ~e
[~'siːv] *f* wash(ing); washing powder;
faire la ~ do the laundry; (1a) wash; scrub; clean; *sl.* clean (*s.o.*)
out; F *fig.* **lessivé** washed out, all
in.

lest ⚓ [lɛst] *m* ballast.

leste [~] light (*a. fig.*); nimble, agile.

lester [lɛs'te] (1a) ballast; weight.

léthargie [letar'ʒi] *f* lethargy; **léthargi-
que** [~'ʒik] lethargic.

lettr|e [lɛtr] *f* letter; ~s *pl.* literature *sg.,*
letters; ~ **recommandée** *post:* regis-
tered letter; ✝ ~ **de change** bill of exchange; ~ **de commerce** business letter; *pol.* ~ **de créance** credentials *pl.;* ~
de crédit letter of credit; **au pied de la
~, à la ~** literally; **en toutes ~s** in full;

homme *m* (**femme** *f*) **de** ~s man (woman) of letters; ~é [le'tre] literate.

leu [lø] *m:* **à la queue** ~ ~ in single file.

leur [lœːr] **1.** *adj./poss.* their; **2.** *pron./
pers.* them; (to) them; **3.** *pron./poss.:* **le**
(**la**) ~, **les** ~**s** *pl.* theirs, their own; **les**
~**s** *pl.* theirs, their own; **les** ~**s** *pl.* their
people.

leurr|e [lœːr] *m* bait (*a. fig.*); *fig.* illusion,
deception; ~er [lœ're] (1a) decoy; al-
lure; deceive, delude, take in; **se** ~ delude o.s.

levage [lə'vaːʒ] *m* raising; rising.

levain [lə'vɛ̃] *m* yeast; leaven (*a. fig.*).

levant [lə'vɑ̃] *m* east; **levantin** [~vɑ̃'tɛ̃]
adj., su Levantine.

lev|é [lə've] *m* ♪ upbeat; *surv.* survey;
~ée [~'ve] *f* raising; closing; ⚔
levy(ing); embankment; *post:* collection, *sea:* swell; removal; *piston:* travel;
valve: lift; *cards:* trick; ~er [~'ve] (1d)
v/t. lift; raise (*a.* ⚔); adjourn, close (*a.
meeting*); levy (⚔, *a. taxes*); *post:* collect; *post:* clear (*a letter-box*); strike (*a.
camp*); ⚓ weigh (*anchor*); remove (*a
bandage, a doubt*); **se** ~ get up, rise;
stand up; come up; lift; break (*day*);
clear (*weather*); *v/i.* ⚥ shoot; *cuis.* rise
(*dough*). **2.** *su./m* getting up, rising;
thea. curtain: rise; *surv.* surveying; **au** ~
on getting up; ~ **du jour** daybreak; ~ **du
soleil** sunrise.

levier [lə'vje] 🜨 *m* lever.

lèvre [lɛːvr] *f* lip; *crater:* rim.

lévrier [le'vrje] *m* greyhound.

levure [lə'vyːr] *f* yeast; ~ **artificielle** bak-
ing-powder.

lez [le] *see* **lès.**

lézard [le'zaːr] *m zo.* lizard; *fig.* idler; ~e
[~'zard] *f* chink, crack; ~er [~zar'de]
(1a) *v/t.* crack, split; *v/i.* F bask in the
sun; loaf.

liage [lja:ʒ] *m* binding; **liaison** [lje'zɔ̃] *f*
connection (*a.* ✝), relationship; con-
tact; *fig.* link; *gramm. etc.* liaison; ♪
slur; **liant; liait** [ljɑ̃] **1.** *adj.* sociable; **2.** *su./m*
sociability; flexibility; 🜨 binding
agent.

liasse [ljas] *f* bundle, packet; wad.

libell|e [li'bɛl] *m* lampoon; ~er [libɛl'le]
(1a) draw up (*a document*); make out (*a
cheque*); word (*a letter, petition, etc.*).

libellule *zo.* [libɛl'lyl] *f* dragon-fly.

lib|éral [libe'ral] *adj., su./m* liberal;

K
L

~**éralisme** [libera'lism] *m* liberalism;
~**éralité** [~li'te] *f* liberality; ~**érateur**
[~'tœːr] **1.** *adj.* liberating; **2.** *su./m* liberator; ~**ération** [~'sjɔ̃] *f* liberation; ✵
discharge (*a.* ✗, ⚕); ~**érer** [libe're] (1f)
free; liberate; set free; release; ✗,
discharge; ✗ exempt; **se** ~ free *etc.*
o.s.; take (*a day etc.*) off, (try and) be
free; ~**erté** [liber'te] *f* liberty, freedom;
⚙ clearance; **prendre des** ~**s avec** take
liberties with; **prendre la** ~ **de** (*inf.*)
take the liberty of (*ger.*); ~**ertin** [~'tɛ̃]
dissolute; licentious; ~**ertinage**
[~ti'naːʒ] *m* dissolute ways *pl.*; licentiousness.

libid|ineux [libidi'nø] lewd, lustful; ~**o**
psych. [~'do] *f* libido.

libraire [li'brɛːr] *su.* bookseller; **librairie**
[~brɛ'ri] *f* bookshop; book-trade; publishing house.

libre [libr] free; clear (*passage etc.*); independent; ~ **à vous de** (*inf.*) you are
welcome to (*inf.*); *teleph.* **pas** ~ line
engaged (*Am.* busy); **temps** *m* ~ spare
time; ~**échange** [libre'ʃãːʒ] *m*
free(-)trade; ~**service**, *pl.* ~**s-services** [librasɛr'vis] *m* self-service;
self-service store *or* restaurant, *etc.*

licenc|e [li'sãːs] *f* fig., *admin.* licence; ~
poétique poetic licence; **prendre des**
~**s avec** take liberties with; ~**ié** *m*, **e** *f*
[lisã'sje] *univ.* bachelor; ⚕ licensee; ~**iement** ✗ *etc.* [~sjã'mã] *m* disbanding;
~**ier** [~'sje] (1o) disband; lay off (*workmen*); ~**ieux** [~'sjø] licentious.

licher *sl.* [li'ʃe] (1a) lick; drink.

licite [li'sit] licit, lawful.

licou [li'ku] *m* halter.

lie [li] *f* lees *pl.*; dregs *pl.* (*a. fig.*).

liège [ljɛːʒ] *m* 🌿 cork (oak); float.

lien [ljɛ̃] *m* tie (*a.* ⚙), bond; link; **lier** [lje]
(1o) tie (up); bind (*a.* ✍); link (*ideas*);
cuis. thicken; ~ **connaissance avec**
strike up an acquaintance with; **se** ~
avec make friends with.

lierre 🌿 [ljɛːr] *m* ivy.

liesse [ljɛs] *f*: **en** ~ rejoicing.

lieu [ljø] *m* locality, spot; site; *fig.*
reason, cause (for, to, **de**, **à**); ~**x** *pl.*
premises; ~ **commun** commonplace;
au ~ **de** instead of; **au** ~ **que** whereas;
avoir ~ take place; **avoir** ~ **de** (*inf.*)
have good reason for (*ger.*); **donner** ~ **à**
give rise to, give cause for; **en premier**

~ first of all; **en dernier** ~ lastly; **il y a**
(**tout**) ~ **de** (*inf.*) there is (every) reason
for (*ger.*); **tenir** ~ **de** take the place of;
serve *or* act as.

lieue [ljø] *f measure*: league.

lièvre *zo.* [ljɛːvr] *m* hare.

liftier [lif'tje] *m* lift boy, *Am.* elevator
operator.

liga|ment *anat.* [liga'mã] *m* ligament;
~**ture** [~'tyːr] *f* tying; ✍, *typ.* ligature; ⚡
splice; ~**turer** [~ty're] (1a) bind; ✍ ligature.

lign|e [liɲ] *f* line (*a.* ✎); row; *geog. the*
equator; **à la** ~! new paragraph!; F **elle**
a de la ~ she has a good figure; 🚂
grande ~ main line; **hors** ~ incomparable; **pêcher à la** ~ angle; ~**ée** [li'ɲe] *f*
line(age); descendants *pl.*

ligoter [ligo'te] (1a) tie up.

ligu|e [lig] *f* league; ~**er** [li'ge] (1m) (*a. se*
~) form into a league; unite, *a. fig.*
combine; ~**eur** [~'gœːr] *m* leaguer.

lilas 🌿 [li'la] *su./m, adj./inv.* lilac.

lima|ce *zo.* [li'mas] *f* slug; ~**çon** [~ma'sɔ̃]
m zo. snail; *anat.* cochlea; **escalier** *m*
en ~ spiral staircase.

limbe [lɛːb] *m astr.* rim; *fig. dans les* ~**s**
rather vague.

lim|e ⚙ [lim] *f* file; ~ **à ongles** nail-file;
~**er** [li'me] (1a) file; polish.

limier *zo.* [li'mje] *m* bloodhound.

limit|atif [limita'tif] limiting, restrictive;
~**ation** [~'sjɔ̃] *f* limitation; ~ **des naissances** birth-control; ~**e** [li'mit] **1.** *su./f*
limit; boundary (*a. sp.*); ~ **d'élasticité**
tensile strength; **2.** *adj.*: **cas** *m* ~ border-line case; **date** *f* ~ deadline; **vitesse**
f ~ speed limit; ~**er** [limi'te] (1a) (to, **à**)
limit; restrict; border, bound; **se** ~ **à** be
limited to (*thing*); **se** ~ **à** (*inf.*) limit *or*
confine o.s. to (*ger.*); ~**rophe** [~'trɔf]
bordering (on, **de**).

limoger [limo'ʒe] (1l) dismiss.

limon[1] [li'mɔ̃] *m* mud, slime, silt.

limon[2] 🌿 [li'mɔ̃] *m* sour lime; **limonade**
[limo'nad] *f* lemon soda.

limoneux [limo'nø] muddy; bog-...

limpid|e [lɛ̃'pid] clear, limpid; ~**ité**
[~pidi'te] *f* limpidity; clarity.

lin [lɛ̃] *m* 🌿 flax; *tex.* linen; **linceul**
[lɛ̃'sœl] *m* shroud.

linéa|ire [line'ɛːr] linear; **mesure** *f* ~
measure of length; ~**ment** [~a'mã] *m*
feature (*a. fig.*).

linge [lɛ̃:ʒ] *m* linen; **~ de corps** underwear; **~ de table** table linen; **~ sale** dirty linen (*a. fig.*); **~rie** [lɛ̃ʒ'ri] *f* underwear.
lingot *metall.* [lɛ̃'go] *m* ingot.
lingu|al [lɛ̃'gwal] lingual; **~istique** [~gɥis'tik] **1.** *adj.* linguistic; **2.** *su./f* linguistics *sg.*
linoléum [linɔle'ɔm] *m* oilcloth.
linon *tex.* [li'nɔ̃] *m* lawn; batiste.
linotte *orn.* [li'nɔt] *f* linnet; red poll; F **tête** *f* **de ~** feather-brain.
linteau ⚠ [lɛ̃'to] *m* lintel.
lion [ljɔ̃] *m* lion (*a.* F); *fig.* **part** *f* **du ~** lions's share; **~ceau** [ljɔ̃'so] *m* lion cub; **~ne** [ljɔn] *f* lioness.
lipp|e [lip] *f* thick lower lip; F **faire la ~** pout; **~u** [~'py] thick-lipped.
liqué|faction [likefak'sjɔ̃] *f* liquefaction; **~fier** [~'fje] (1o) (*a.* **se ~**) liquefy.
liqueur [li'kœ:r] *f* liqueur.
liquidat|ion [likida'sjɔ̃] *f* liquidation; ✝ settlement; clearance sale.
liquid|e [li'kid] **1.** *adj.* liquid (*a. gramm.*, ✝ *debt.*); ready (*money*); **2.** *su./m* liquid; **~er** [~ki'de] (1a) liquidate (*a. fig.*); settle (*an account, fig. a question*); ✝ sell off (*goods*); *fig.* get rid of; *fig.* finish off.
lire [li:r] (4t) *v/i.* read (about, **sur**); *v/t.* read; **cela se lit sur votre visage** it shows in your face; **je vous lis difficilement** I have difficulty with your handwriting.
lis ❀ [lis] *m* lily.
liseron ❀ [liz'rɔ̃] *m* bindweed.
lis|eur, -euse [li'zœ:r, ~'zø:z] *su.* reader; *su./f* book-wrapper; reading-lamp; *cost.* bed jacket; **~ibilité** [~zibili'te] *f* legibility; **~ible** [~'zibl] legible; readable.
lisière [li'zjɛ:r] *f tex.* list; *forest*: edge; border; *fig.* leading-strings *pl.*
lisons [li'zɔ̃] *1st p. pl. pres. of* **lire**.
lisse [lis] smooth, polished; glossy.
lisser [li'se] (1a) smooth, polish.
liste [list] *f* list; roll; register.
lit [li] bed (*a.* ⚠, ⚙, *river, etc.*); **~ de mort** death-bed; **~ de plume** feather bed; **enfant** *mf* **du second ~** child of the second marriage; **faire ~ à part** sleep apart; **garder le ~** be confined to one's bed.
litanie [lita'ni] *f* F litany; *eccl.* **~s** *pl.* litany *sg.*
liteau [li'to] *m* ⚠ rail; *tex.* stripe.
literie [li'tri] *f* bedding.
litière [li'tjɛ:r] *f* litter.
litig|e [li'ti:ʒ] *m* dispute; (law)suit; **~ieux** [~ti'ʒjø] litigious.
litre [litr] *m measure*: litre, liter.
littéra|ire [lite'rɛ:r] literary; **~l** [~'ral] literal; ⚖ documentary; **~ture** [~ra'ty:r] *f* literature.
littoral [litɔ'ral] **1.** *adj.* coastal, littoral; **2.** *su./m* coast-line; shore.
liturgie *eccl.* [lityr'ʒi] *f* liturgy.
livid|e [li'vid] livid; ghastly; **~ité** [~vidi'te] *f* lividness; ghastliness.
livraison ✝ [livrɛ'zɔ̃] *f* delivery; **~ à domicile** home delivery.
livre¹ [li:vr] *m* book; **~ de cuisine** cookery (*Am.* cook) book.
livre² [~] *f money, weight*: pound.
livrée [li'vre] *f* livery, servants *pl.*
livrer [~] (1a) deliver; **~ à** give or hand over to, deliver up to; **se ~ à** give o.s. up to; confide in; indulge in; engage in; carry out.
livret [li'vrɛ] *m* booklet; ♪ libretto; (*bank-*)book; (*student's*) handbook.
livreur [li'vrœ:r] *m* delivery man.
lobe [lɔb] *m* ❀, *anat.* lobe; **~ de l'oreille** ear lobe.
loca|l [lɔ'kal] **1.** *adj.* local; **2.** *su./m* premises *pl.*; room; **~liser** [lɔkali'ze] (1a) locate; localize; **~lité** [~li'te] *f* place; **~taire** [~'tɛ:r] *su.* tenant, occupier; hirer; **~tif** [~'tif] rental; tenant's ...; **~tion** [~'sjɔ̃] *f* hiring; letting, renting; tenancy; booking; **~ de livres** lending library; **bureau** *m* **de ~** box-office; **~tion-vente**, *pl.* **~tions-ventes** [~sjɔ̃-'vɑ̃:t] *f* hire purchase system.
loch ⚓ [lɔk] *m* log.
lock-out ⚙ [lɔ'kaut] *m/inv.* lock-out.
locomo|bile [lɔkɔmɔ'bil] travelling; **~tif, -ve** [~'tif, ~'ti:v] **1.** *adj.* transportable; **2.** *su./f* locomotive, engine; *fig.* dynamic element; **~tion** [~'sjɔ̃] *f* locomotion.
locution [lɔky'sjɔ̃] *f* idiom.
lof ⚓ [lɔf] *m* windward side.
log|e [lɔ:ʒ] *f* hut; cabin; lodge; *thea.* box; *thea.* (*artist's*) dressing-room; **~eable** [lɔ'ʒabl] habitable; **~ement** [lɔʒ'mɑ̃] *m* lodging, housing; accommodation; ⚙ seating, housing; **~er** [lɔ'ʒe] (1l) *v/t.* lodge, house; ⚔ billet; put; ⚙ fix, set; *v/i.* live; reside; **~ en garni** live in lodg-

ings; **~ette** [~'ʒɛt] f small lodge; **~eur** [~'ʒœːr] m landlord; **~euse** [~'ʒøːz] f landlady.

logi|ciel [lɔʒi'sjɛl] m computer: software; **~cien** [~'sjɛ̃] m logician; **~que** [~'ʒik] **1.** adj. logical; **2.** su./f logic.

logis [lɔ'ʒi] m home, dwelling.

logistique(s) [lɔʒis'tik] f/(pl.) logistics sg.

loi [lwa] f law; **faire la ~** lay down the law; **mettre hors la ~** outlaw; parl. **projet m de ~** bill; **se faire une ~ de** make a point of.

loin [lwɛ̃] adv. far, a long way (from, **de**; a. fig.); past: a long time ago; future: a long way off; **au ~** far off, in the distance; **de ~** from a distance; **come** etc. a long way; fig. by far; **de ~ en ~** now and then; here and there; **plus ~** further (on); **~ des yeux, ~ du cœur** out of sight, out of mind; **~tain** [~'tɛ̃] **1.** adj. far-away; distant; remote; **2.** su./m **au ~, dans le ~** in the distance.

loir [lwaːr] m dormouse.

loisi|ble [lwa'zibl]: **il lui est ~ de** (inf.) he is at liberty to (inf.); **~r** [~'ziːr] m leisure; spare time; **~s** pl. leisure activities; **à ~** at leisure.

lombes anat. [lɔ̃ːb] m/pl. loins.

londonien [lɔ̃dɔ'njɛ̃] **1.** adj. London ...; **2.** su. ♀ Londoner.

long [lɔ̃], **~ue** [lɔ̃ːg] **1.** adj. long; thin (sauce); ✝ **à ~ terme** long-dated (bill); **de longue main** well in advance; **être ~ à** (inf.) be long in (ger.); **2. long** adv.: fig. **en dire ~** speak volumes; **en savoir ~** know quite a lot (about, **sur**); **3.** su./m length; **de ~ en large** to and fro; **deux pieds de ~** two feet long; **le ~ de** (all) along; **tomber de tout son ~** fall full length; su./f gramm. long syllable; **à la longue** in the long run.

longanimité [lɔ̃ganimi'te] f forbearance; long-suffering.

longe [lɔ̃ːʒ] f tether; cuis. loin.

longer [lɔ̃'ʒe] (1l) go along, skirt; **~on** [lɔ̃'rɔ̃] m △ crossbeam.

longévité [lɔ̃ʒevi'te] f longevity.

longitud|e [lɔ̃ʒi'tyd] f longitude; **~inal** [~tydi'nal] lengthwise.

longtemps [lɔ̃'tɑ̃] adv. long, a long time; **il y a ~** long ago.

longueur [lɔ̃'gœːr] f length (a. sp.); fig.

tedious passage; phys., fig. **~ d'onde(s)** wavelength; **à ~ de ...** all ... long, for ...

lopin [lɔ'pɛ̃] m ground: patch, plot.

loquac|e [lɔ'kwas] talkative; **~ité** [~kwasi'te] f talkativeness.

loque [lɔk] f rag; (human) wreck.

loquet [lɔ'kɛ] m latch; knife: clasp.

loqueteux [lɔk'tø] ragged, tattered.

lorgn|er [lɔr'ɲe] (1a) ogle, leer at; covet; **~ette** [~'nɛt] f opera-glasses pl.; **~on** [~'nɔ̃] m pince-nez.

lorrain [lɔ'rɛ̃] **1.** adj. of or from Lorraine; **2.** su. ♀ Lorrainer.

lors [lɔːr] adv.: **~ de** at the time of, at; **~ de son mariage** when he was married; **~ même que** even when; **dès ~** since that time; consequently; **lorsque** [lɔrsk(ə)] cj. when.

losange △ [lɔ'zɑ̃ːʒ] m rhomb(us); **en ~** diamond-shaped.

lot [lo] m portion, share, lot (a. fig.); **gros ~** first prize, jackpot; **~erie** [lɔ'tri] f lottery (a. fig.); raffle.

lotion [lɔ'sjɔ̃] f ✝, ◎ washing; ♣ lotion; **~ capillaire** hairwash.

loti|r [lɔ'tiːr] (2a) divide up (into plots); **~ q. de qch.** allot s.th. to s.o.; **bien (mal) loti** well- (badly-)off; **~ssement** [~tis'mɑ̃] m lot, plot; (housing) development.

loto [lɔ'to] m lotto; lotto set.

louable [lwabl] praiseworthy.

louage [lwa:ʒ] m hiring out; hire.

louang|e [lwɑ̃:ʒ] f praise; **~er** [lwɑ̃'ʒe] (1l) praise; **~eur** [~'ʒœːr] **1.** adj. adulatory; **2.** su./m adulator.

louche¹ [luʃ] dubious, shady, fishy.

louche² [~] f ladle; ◎ reamer.

loucher [lu'ʃe] (1a) squint; **~ie** [luʃ'ri] f squint.

louer¹ [lwe] (1p) rent, hire; book; **à ~** to let.

louer² [~] (1p) praise; commend (s.o. for s.th., **q. de qch.**); **se ~ de** be very pleased with (s.o., s.th.); congratulate o.s. on (ger., de inf.).

loueur m, **-euse** f [lwœːr, lwøːz] hirer out.

loufoque F [lu'fɔk] cranky, daft.

loulou zo. [lu'lu] m Pomeranian.

loup [lu] m zo. wolf; (eye) mask; **à pas de ~** stealthily; **hurler avec les ~s** do in Rome as the Romans do.

loupe [lup] f ♣ wen; ♀ excrescence; opt. lens, magnifying-glass.

louper F [lu'pe] (1a) mess up; botch, bungle; miss (*one's train; a. fig.*).

lourd [lu:r] heavy; clumsy; *fig.* dull; sultry; **~aud** [lur'do] clumsy (fellow); **~eur** [~'dœr] f heaviness; clumsiness.

loustic F [lus'tik] *m* wag.

loutre zo. [lutr] f otter.

louve zo. [lu:v] f she-wolf; **~eteau** [luv'to] *m* wolf-cub (*a. Scouts*).

louvoyer [luvwa'je] (1h) ♣ tack; *fig.* manœuvre; *fig.* hedge.

loyal [lwa'jal] fair, sincere, faithful; ⚖ true; **~auté** [~jo'te] f fairness; honesty; loyalty (to, *envers*).

loyer [lwa'je] *m* rent(al); ♥ price.

lu [ly] *p.p. of* **lire.**

luble [ly'bi] f whim, fad.

lubri|cité [lybrisi'te] f lechery; **~fiant** ⊙ [~'fjɑ̃] **1.** *adj* lubricating; **2.** *su./m* lubricant; **~fication** [~fika'sjɔ̃] f lubrication; **~fier** [~'tje] (1o) lubricate; **~que** [ly'brik] lustful, lewd.

lucarne [ly'karn] f dormer window.

lucid|e [ly'sid] lucid (*a. ✱*); clear-minded *or* -headed *or* -sighted; **~ité** [~sidi'te] f lucidity (*a. ✱*).

lucratif [lykra'tif] lucrative, **lucre** [lykr] *m* lucre; profit.

luette *anat.* [lɥɛt] f uvula.

lueur [lɥœr] f glimmer; flash.

lug|e [ly:ʒ] f toboggan; **~er** [ly'ʒe] (1l) toboggan.

lugubre [ly'gybr] dismal, gloomy.

lui¹ [lɥi] *p.p. of* **luire.**

lui² [~] *pron./pers. subject:* he; *object:* him, her, it; (to) him, (to) her, (to) it; **à ~** to him, to her, to it; his, hers, its; *c'est ~* it is he, F it's him; **~-même** [~'mɛm] *pron./rfl./m* himself, itself.

luire [lɥi:r] (4u) shine, gleam; *fig.* dawn (hope); **luisis** [lɥ'zi] *1st p. sg. p.s. of luire*, **luisons** [~'zɔ̃] *1st p. pl. pres. of luire.*

lumi|ère [ly'mjɛr] f light; *fig.* (*a. pl.* **~s**) knowledge; **à la ~ de** by (*fig.* in) the light of; **~gnon** [lymi'nɔ̃] *m* candle-end; poor light, **~naire** [~'nɛr] *m coll.* lighting; **~nescence** [~nɛ'sɑ̃s] f luminescence; **~neux** [~'nø] luminous; bright (*a. fig.* idea); illuminated (*advertisement*).

luna|ire [ly'nɛ:r] lunar; **~ison** *astr.* [~ne'zɔ̃] f lunation; **~tique** [~na'tik] whimsical, capricious.

lunch [lœ̃:ʃ] *m* lunch(eon); snack; **~er** [lœ̃'ʃe] (1a) have lunch.

lundi [lœ̃'di] *m* Monday; F **faire le ~** take Monday off.

lun|e [lyn] f moon; **~ de miel** honeymoon; **clair** *m* **de ~** moonlight; **être dans la ~** be in the clouds; **~é** [ly'ne]: **bien (mal) ~** in a good (bad) mood.

lunet|ier [lyn'tje] *m* optician; **~te** [ly'nɛt] f telescope; **~s** *pl.* spectacles; goggles; **~s** *pl.* **de soleil** sunglasses.

lunule [ly'nyl] f *anat. a.* & lunule, lunula; *finger-nail:* half-moon.

lupanar [lypa'na:r] *m* brothel.

lurette F [ly'rɛt] f: **il y a belle ~** a long time ago.

luron [ly'rɔ̃] *m* (jolly) fellow; **~ne** [~'rɔn] f (lively) lass.

lus [ly] *1st p. sg. p.s. of lire¹*.

lustr|e [lystr] *m* lustre (*a. fig.*), gloss; chandelier; **~er** [lys'tre] (1a) glaze, gloss; F make shiny (*with wear*).

luth ♪ [lyt] *m* lute.

luthérien [lyte'rjɛ̃] *adj., su.* Lutheran.

lutin [ly'tɛ̃] **1.** *adj.* impish; **2.** *su./m* imp; **~er** [~ti'ne] (1a) take liberties with (*a woman*).

lutt|e [lyt] f fight; struggle; conflict; *sp.* wrestling; *sp.:* **à la corde** tug-of-war; **~er** [ly'te] (1a) fight; struggle; *sp., fig.* wrestle; **~eur** *m*, **-euse** f [~'tœ:r, ~'tø:z] wrestler; *fig.* fighter.

luxe [lyks] *m* luxury; abundance.

luxer ✱ [lyk'se] (1a) dislocate.

luxueux [lyk'sɥø] luxurious; showy.

luxur|e [lyk'sy:r] f lewdness, lechery; **~iant** [~sy'rjɑ̃] luxuriant; **~ieux** [~sy'rjø] lecherous, lewd.

luzerne ♀ [ly'zɛrn] f alfalfa.

lycée [li'se] *m* (state) secondary school; **lycéen** *m*, **-enne** f [~se'ɛ̃, ~se'ɛn] pupil at a *lycée*.

lyncher [lɛ̃'ʃe] (1a) lynch.

lynx zo. [lɛ̃ks] *m* lynx.

lyr|e [li:r] f ♪ lyre; **ique** [li'rik] **1.** *adj.* lyric(al); **2.** *su./m* lyric poet; **~isme** [~'rism] *m* lyricism.

M

ma [ma] *see* **mon.**

maboul F [ma'bul] crazy.

macabre [ma'kɑːbr] gruesome.

macaron *cuis.* [maka'rɔ̃] *m* macaroon; **~i** [~rɔ'ni] *m/inv. cuis.* macaroni; F wop (*Italian*).

macédoine [mase'dwan] *f* **~ (de fruits)** fruit salad.

macérer [mase're] (1f) soak, steep; *fig.* mortify (*the flesh*).

Mach *phys.* [mak] *npr.*: **nombre** *m* **de ~** mach (number).

mâche ♀ [mɑːʃ] *f* corn-salad.

mâcher [mɑ'ʃe] (1a) chew; munch; **~ à q. la besogne** half-do s.o.'s work for him; **ne pas ~ ses mots** not to mince matters.

machin F [ma'ʃɛ̃] *m* thing, gadget.

machin|al [maʃi'nal] mechanical; **~ation** [~na'sjɔ̃] *f* plot; **~e** [ma'ʃin] *f* machine; engine (*a.* 😊); *fig.* machinery; **~ à calculer** calculating machine, calculator; **~ à écrire** typewriter; **~ à photocopier** photocopier; **~ à sous** slot machine; **~er** [~ʃi'ne] (1a) plot; **~erie** [~ʃin'ri] *f* machinery; ⚓ engine-room; **~iste** [~ʃi'nist] *m thea.* scene shifter; bus driver.

mâch|oire [mɑ'ʃwaːr] *f* jaw (*a.* 😊); **~onner** [~ʃɔ'ne] (1a) mumble; mutter; chew, munch; **~urer** [~ʃy're] (1a) soil, stain; chew.

macis ♀, *cuis.* [ma'si] *m* mace.

maçon [ma'sɔ̃] *m* mason.

maçonner [masɔ'ne] (1a) 🔺 build; 🔺 face; brick up; **~ie** [~sɔn'ri] *f* 🔺 masonry; freemasonry.

macul|e [ma'kyl] *f* spot, stain; **~er** [~ky'le] (1a) stain; *v/i.* blur.

madame, *pl.* **mesdames** [ma'dam, me'dam] *f* Mrs.; madam; F lady.

madeleine [mad'lɛn] *f* ♀ (*sort of*) pear; *cuis.* sponge-cake.

mademoiselle, *pl.* **mesdemoiselles** [madmwa'zɛl, medmwa'zɛl] *f* Miss; young lady.

madère [ma'dɛːr] *m* Madeira (wine).

Madone [ma'dɔn] *f* Madonna.

madrier 🔺 [madri'e] *m* beam.

madrilène [madri'lɛn] **1.** *adj.* of Madrid; **2.** *su.* ♀ inhabitant of Madrid.

maestria [maestri'ja] *f* skill.

magasin [maga'zɛ̃] *m* shop, *Am.* store; warehouse; *camera, gun:* magazine; ✝ **grand ~** department store; ✝ **en ~** in stock; **~ier** [~zi'nje] *m* warehouseman.

magazine [maga'zin] *m* magazine.

mag|e [ma:ʒ] **1.** *su./m* magus; **2.** *adj.*: *bibl.* **les Rois** *m/pl.* **2s** the Magi; **~icien** *m,* **-enne** *f* [maʒi'sjɛ̃, ~'sjɛn] magician; **~ie** [~'ʒi] *f* magic; **~ique** [~'ʒik] *f* magic(al).

magistra|l [maʒis'tral] magisterial; *fig.* pompous; *fig.* masterly; **~t** [~'tra] *m* magistrate; magistracy; **~ture** [~tra'tyːr] *f* magistrature; magistracy; **~ assise** Bench, judges *pl.*; **~ debout** public prosecutors *pl.*

magma [mag'ma] *m* magma; *fig.* muddle.

magnanim|e [maɲa'nim] magnanimous; **~ité** [~nimi'te] *f* magnanimity.

magnat [mag'na] *m* magnate.

magnési|e [maɲe'zi] *f* magnesia; **~um** [maɲe'zjɔm] *m* magnesium.

magnét|ique [maɲe'tik] magnetic; **~isme** [~'tism] *m* magnetism; **~ophone** [~tɔ'fɔn] *m* tape recorder; **~ à cassettes** cassette recorder; **~oscope** [~tɔ'skɔp] *m* video(-tape) recorder; **~oscoper** [~tɔskɔ'pe] video-tape.

magnifi|cence [maɲifi'sãːs] *f* magnificence, splendo(u)r; **~que** [~'fik] magnificent; *fig.* marvellous.

magot¹ *zo.* [ma'go] *m* barbary ape.

magot² F [~] *m* savings *pl.*, hoard.

mahomét|an [maɔme'tã] *adj., su.* Moslem; **~isme** [~'tism] *m* Mohammedanism.

mai [mɛ] *m* May; may-pole.

maigr|e [mɛːgr] **1.** *adj.* thin, lean; meagre (*meal, a. fig.*); **2,** *su./m* meat: lean; **faire ~** fast; **~elet** [mɛgrə'le] rather thin; **~eur** [~'grœːr] *f* thinness; *fig.* meagreness; **~ir** [~'griːr] (2a) *v/i.* grow thin; lose weight; *v/t.* make thinner.

mail [ma:j] *m* 😊 maul; avenue.

maille¹ [ma:j] *f* stitch; *chain:* link; (chain-)mail; *net:* mesh.

maille² [~] *f*: **avoir ~ à partir avec q.** have a bone to pick with s.o.

maillechort [maj'ʃɔːr] *m* nickel *or* German silver.

maillet [ma'jɛ] *m* mallet.

maillo|n [ma'jɔ̃] *m* chain: link; **~t** [ma'jo] *m* swaddling clothes *pl.*; *sp.* jersey, vest; **~ de bain** swimsuit; bathing trunks *pl.*

main [mɛ̃] *f* hand (*a.* cards; *a.* handwriting); **~ courante** handrail; **à la ~** in one's hand; (*do s.th.*) by hand; **à ~ levée** free-hand; **à pleines ~s** lavishly; **bas (haut) les ~s!** hands off (up)!; **battre des ~s** clap (one's hands); *fig.* **de bonnes ~s** on good authority; **en ~** under control, in hand; **en un tour de ~** straight off; **en venir aux ~s** come to blows; **la ~ dans la ~** hand in hand; **mettre la ~ sur** lay hands on; **prêter la ~** lend a hand; **serrer la ~ à q.** shake hands with s.o.; **sous la ~** to hand, at hand, handy; **sous ~** underhanded(ly *adv.*); **~-d'œuvre**, *pl.* **~s-d'œuvres** ⚙ [~'dœːvr] *f* labo(u)r; manpower; **~forte** [~'fɔrt] *f*: **prêter ~** give assistance.

maint [mɛ̃] many a; **~es fois** often.

maintenant [mɛ̃t'nɑ̃] *adv.* now; **dès ~** from now on, henceforth.

main|tenir [mɛ̃t'niːr] (2h) keep; maintain (*a. fig.*); support; uphold; **se ~** continue; hold one's own; **~tien** [mɛ̃'tjɛ̃] *m* maintenance; upholding; bearing.

maire [mɛːr] *m* mayor; **mairie** [mɛ'ri] *f* town hall; mayoralty.

mais [mɛ] but; **~ oui!** sure!, of course!; **~ non!** no indeed!; not at all!

maïs ♀ [ma'is] *m* maize, *Am.* corn.

maison [mɛ'zɔ̃] *f* house, home, household; family; ✝ (*a.* **~ de commerce**) firm, company; **~ close** brothel; **~ de rapport** apartment house; **~ de santé** nursing home; mental hospital; ✝ **~ mère** head office; **~née** [mɛzo'ne] *f* household.

maîtr|e, -esse [mɛːtr, mɛ'trɛs] **1.** *su./m* master (*a. fig.*); *fig.* ruler; owner; *school:* teacher; 🏛 *lawyer's title*; *univ.* **~ de conférences** lecturer; **être ~ de** be in control of; have at one's disposal; **être passé ~ en** be a past master of or in; *su./f* mistress; **2.** *adj.* main, principal; **~e-autel**, *pl.* **~es-autels** [mɛtro'tɛl] *m* high altar; **~isable**

[~tri'zabl] controllable; **~ise** [~'triːz] *f* mastership; *fig.* mastery; *fig.* command, control; **~iser** [~tri'ze] (1a) master; control.

majest|é [maʒɛs'te] *f* majesty; **~ueux** [~'tɥø] majestic, stately.

majeur [ma'ʒœːr] **1.** *adj.* major (*a.* 🏛, ♪, *phls.*), greater; *fig.* main, chief; **devenir ~** come of age; **2.** *su./m* 🏛 major; middle finger.

major ✗ [ma'ʒɔːr] *m* regimental adjutant; **~ général** chief of staff; **~ation** [~ʒɔra'sjɔ̃] *f* (excessive) increase; **~dome** [~ʒɔr'dɔm] *m* major-domo, steward; **~or** [maʒo're] (1a) increase (excessively); **~ité** [~ri'te] *f* majority.

majuscule [maʒys'kyl] **1.** *adj.* capital (*letter*); **2.** *su./f* capital letter.

mal [mal] **1.** *su./m* evil; hurt, harm; pain; 🩺 disease; wrong; **~ de cœur** nausea; **~ de l'air** air sickness; **~ de mer** seasickness; **~ de tête** headache; **~ du pays** homesickness; **avoir ~ au ventre** have a stomach ache; **avoir du ~ à** (*inf.*) find it difficult to (*inf.*); **faire ~** (**à q.**) hurt (s.o.); **faire du ~ à q.** harm s.o.; **prendre ~** be taken ill; **prendre ~ qch.** take s.th. amiss; **se donner du ~** take pains; **2.** *adv.* badly; uncomfortably; **~ à l'aise** ill at ease; **~ à propos** at the wrong time; **~ fait** badly made; **être ~** be uncomfortable; be wrong; **pas ~** presentable; F **pas ~ de** a lot of; **se sentir ~** feel ill; **se trouver ~** faint.

malad|e [ma'lad] **1.** *adj.* ill, sick; **2.** *su.* patient; sick person; **~ie** [mala'di] *f* disease; illness, sickness; ailment; **~ de la vache folle** mad cow disease; **~if** [~'dif] sickly.

maladr|esse [mala'drɛs] *f* clumsiness; blunder; **~oit** [~'drwa] **1.** *adj.* awkward; **2.** *su./m* blunderer.

malais|e [ma'lɛːz] *f* discomfort; *fig.* uneasiness, unrest; **~é** [~lɛ'ze] difficult.

malappris [mala'pri] ill-mannered (person).

malavisé [malavi'ze] ill-advised.

malaxer [malak'se] (1a) mix; knead (*dough*).

malchanc|e [mal'ʃɑ̃ːs] *f* bad luck; mishap; **~eux** [~ʃɑ̃'sø] unlucky.

maldonne [mal'dɔn] *f* cards: misdeal; error, misunderstanding.

mâle [mɑːl] **1.** *adj.* male (♀, screw, person); zo. buck, bull, cock; fig. virile; manly; 2. su./m male.

malédiction [maledik'sjɔ̃] f curse.

maléfi|ce [male'fis] m evil spell; ~que [~'fik] evil; maleficent.

malencontreux [malɑ̃kɔ̃'trø] unfortunate, awkward.

malentendu [malɑ̃tɑ̃'dy] m misunderstanding.

mal-être [mal'ɛtr] m (feeling of) discomfort; uneasiness.

malfai|sance [malfɛ'zɑ̃s] f harm(fulness); ~sant [~fə'zɑ̃] harmful; evil-minded (person); ~teur m, -trice f [~fɛ'tœːr, ~'tris] malefactor.

malfamé [malfa'me] ill-famed.

malgré [mal'gre] prp. despite, in spite of; ~ **moi** against my will; ~ **tout** still.

malhabile [mala'bil] clumsy.

malheur [ma'lœːr] m bad luck; misfortune; unhappiness; **quel ~!** what a pity!; ~**eux** [~lœ'rø] unlucky; unhappy; unfortunate.

malhonnête [malɔ'nɛt] dishonest; fig. rude; indecent; ~**té** [~nɛt'te] f dishonesty; fig. rudeness.

malic|e [ma'lis] f malice; trick; **ne pas voir ~ à** not to see any harm in; ~**ieux** [~li'sjø] mischievous; sly.

mal|ignité [malini'te] f malignity (a. ✱); ~**in, -igne** [~'lɛ̃, ~'liɲ] smart, clever; cunning; fig. difficult; ✱ malignant.

malingre [ma'lɛ̃ːgr] sickly, weakly.

malintentionné [malɛ̃tɑ̃sjɔ'ne] evil-minded (person).

malle [mal] f trunk; mot. boot, Am. trunk.

malmener [malmə'ne] (1d) ill-treat, maltreat, handle roughly.

malotru [malɔ'try] uncouth; vulgar.

malpeigné [malpɛ'ɲe] unkempt.

malpropre [mal'prɔpr] dirty (a. fig.); slovenly; ~**té** [~prɔprə'te] f dirt(iness) (a. fig.); slovenliness.

malsain [mal'sɛ̃] unhealthy; unwholesome; dangerous.

malséant [malse'ɑ̃] unseemly.

malsonnant [malsɔ'nɑ̃] offensive.

maltraiter [maltrɛ'te] (1a) ill-treat, maltreat; handle roughly; batter.

malveillan|ce [malvɛ'jɑ̃ːs] f ill will, spite; ~**t** [~'jɑ̃] spiteful.

malversation ✍ [malvɛrsa'sjɔ̃] f embezzlement; breach of trust.

maman [ma'mɑ̃] f mam(m)a.

mamel|le [ma'mɛl] f teat; ~**on** [mam'lɔ̃] m nipple; geog. hillock.

mammifère zo. [mami'fɛːr] 1. adj. mammalian; 2. su./m mammal.

mamours [ma'muːr] m/pl. caresses.

manant [ma'nɑ̃] m boor; yokel.

manche¹ [mɑ̃ːʃ] m handle; haft; ♪ violin: neck; ~ **à balai** broomstick; ✈ control stick; **jeter le ~ après la cognée** give up.

manche² [~] f sleeve; hose; shaft; sp. set; ✈ ~ **à air** wind sock; **la ≗** the Channel.

manch|eron [mɑ̃ʃ'rɔ̃] m handle; ~**ette** [mɑ̃'ʃɛt] f cuff; journ. headline; ~**on** [~'ʃɔ̃] m muff; ⊕ casing.

manchot [mɑ̃'ʃo] 1. adj. one-armed; fig. clumsy; 2. su./m orn. penguin.

mandant ✍ [mɑ̃'dɑ̃] m principal.

mandarine ♀ [mɑ̃da'rin] f mandarin(e), tangerine.

mandat [mɑ̃'da] m mandate; commission; ✍ power of attorney; ✍ warrant; ✝ money or postal order; ~**aire** [mɑ̃da'tɛːr] su. agent; proxy; pol. mandatory; ~**er** [~'te] (1a) give a mandate to; write a money order for (a sum); ~**poste**, pl. ~**s-poste** [~'pɔst] m postal or money order.

mander [mɑ̃'de] (1a) instruct (s.o.); † summon (s.o.); journ. **on mande ...** it is reported ...

manège [ma'nɛːʒ] m riding school; fig. trick; (a. ~ **de chevaux de bois**) roundabout, merry-go-round.

manette ⊕ [ma'nɛt] f lever.

mang|eable [mɑ̃'ʒabl] eatable; ~**eaille** F [~'ʒɑːj] f food, F grub; ~**eoire** [~'ʒwaːr] f manger; ~**er** [mɑ̃'ʒe] 1. (1l) vt/i. eat; v/t. corrode (metal); squander (money); mumble (words); fig. use up, consume; 2. su./m food; ~**e-tout** [mɑ̃ʒ'tu] m/inv. French bean; ~**eur** m, -**euse** f [mɑ̃'ʒœːr, ~'ʒøːz] eater; fig. devourer.

maniab|ilité [manjabili'te] f handiness; manageableness; ~**le** [~'njabl] manageable; handy (tool).

mani|aque [ma'njak] 1. adj. finicky, fussy; fanatic; 2. su. ✱ maniac; ~**e** [~'ni] f mania; funny habit.

mani|ement [mani'mɑ̃] m handling; ~**er** [~'nje] (1o) manage; handle.

mani|ère [ma'njɛːr] f manner (a. paint.

etc.), way; *fig.* mannerisms *pl.*; **à la ~ de** after the manner of; **de ~ à** so as to; **de ~ que** (*sbj.*), **de ~ à** (*inf.*) so that; **d'une ~ ou d'une autre** somehow or other; **en aucune ~** in no way; **faire des ~s** be affected; **~éré** [manje're] affected; *paint. etc.* mannered; **~érisme** [~'rism] *m* mannerism.

manif F [ma'nif] *f* demo.

manifest|ation [manifesta'sjɔ̃] *f* manifestation; *pol.* demonstration; **~e** [~'fɛst] **1.** *adj.* manifest; **2.** *su./m* manifesto; **~er** [~fɛs'te] (1a) *v/t.* show, manifest; *v/i. pol.* demonstrate; **manifestant** demonstrator.

manigance F [mani'gã:s] *f* trick, scheme; F monkey business; dealings *pl.*; **~er** [~gã'se] (1k) plot, scheme.

manipul|ateur [manipyla'tœ:r] *m* handler; *tel.* sending key, **~ation** [~la'sjɔ̃] *f* manipulation; **~er** [~'le] (1a) manipulate (*a.fig.*); operate.

manitou F [mani'tu] *m* big shot.

manivelle ⊙ [mani'vɛl] *f* crank.

manne [man] *f bibl.* manna; *fig.* godsend.

mannequin [man'kɛ̃] *m* fashion model; lay figure; dummy; puppet.

manœuvr|able [manœ'vrabl] manœuvrable, manageable; **~e** [ma'nœ:vr] *su./f* manœuvre, *Am.* maneuver (*a.* ✕); *su./m* labo(u)rer; **~er** [manœ'vre] (1a) *v/t.* work (*a machine etc.*); 🚂 shunt; *vt/i.* manœuvre (*a.* ✕).

manoir [ma'nwa:r] *m* country-house; *hist.* manor.

manqu|e [mã:k] *m* lack, want, shortage; *fig.* emptiness; ⚕, *fig.* withdrawal symptom; **~ de** for want of; F **à la ~** poor, second-rate; **~é** [mã'ke] unsuccessful; **~ement** [mãk'mã] *m* failure; **~ à qch.** breach of; **~er** [mã'ke] (1m) *v/t.* miss (*a. fig.*); spoil; *v/i.* lack; be absent; be missing; fail; **~ à q.** be missed by s.ô.; **~ à qch.** fail in s.th.; commit a breach of s.th.; **~ de qch.** lack s.th., not to have s.th.; **j'ai manqué (de) tomber** I nearly fell; **ne pas ~ de** (*inf.*) not to fail to (*inf.*).

mansarde △ [mã'sard] *f* attic, garret(-window); *roof:* mansard.

mansuétude [mãsɥe'tyd] *f* gentleness, meekness.

mante [mã:t] *f* sleeveless cloak; *zo.* (*a.* ~ **religieuse**) praying mantis.

mant|eau [mã'to] *m* coat; cloak (*a. fig.*); mantle; ⊙ casing; **sous le ~** secretly; **~elet** [mãt'lɛ] *m* mantlet.

manucur|e [many'ky:r] *su.* manicurist; **~er** [~ky're] (1a) manicure.

manuel [ma'nɥɛl] **1.** *adj.* manual; **2.** *su./m* manual, handbook.

manufactur|e [manyfak'ty:r] *f* manufacture; ⊙ plant; **~er** [~ty're] (1a) manufacture; **~ier** [~ty'rje] manufacturing.

manuscrit [manys'kri] **1.** *adj.* hand-written; **2.** *su./m* manuscript.

manutention [manytã'sjɔ̃] *f* handling, storehouse; **~ner** [~sjɔ'ne] (1a) handle; store; pack (up).

mappemonde [map'mɔ̃:d] *f* map of the world.

maquereau [ma'kro] *m icht.* mackerel; V pimp.

maquette [ma'kɛt] *f* model (*a. thea.*); ⊙ mock-up; *book:* dummy.

maquignon [maki'ɲɔ̃] *m* horse-dealer; *pej.* shady dealer; **~nage** [~ɲo'na:ʒ] *m* horse dealing; *pej.* (underhand) dealings *pl.*

maquill|age [maki'ja:ʒ] *m* make-up; **~er** [~'je] (1a) make up; *phot.* work up; *fig.* disguise, fake.

maquis [ma'ki] *m* scrub; *fig.* maze; *pol.* **prendre le ~** go underground.

maraîcher [mare'ʃe] **1.** *m* market gardener, *Am.* truck farmer; **2.** *adj.* **culture f maraîchère** market gardening, *Am.* truck farming.

marais [ma'rɛ] *m* marsh; bog; swamp.

marasme [ma'rasm] *m* ⚕ marasmus, wasting; *fig.* depression (*a.* ♰).

marâtre [ma'ra:tr] *f* step-mother; cruel *or* unnatural mother.

maraud|age [maro'da:ʒ] *m*, **~e** [ma'ro:d] *f* pilfering, thieving; **en maraude** cruising (*taxi*); **~er** [~ro'de] (1a) cruise (*taxi*).

marbr|e [marbr] *m* marble; *typ.* press-stone; **~er** [mar'bre] (1a) marble; *fig.* mottle.

marc [ma:r] *m* grapes *etc.*: marc; (*tea-*)leaves *pl.*, (*coffee-*)grounds *pl.*

marchand [mar'ʃã] **1.** *adj.* marketable; trade (*name, price*); commercial (*town*); ♣ merchant (*navy, ship*); **2.** *su./m* merchant, dealer, shop-keeper; **~ de journaux** news agent; **~ de légumes** greengrocer; **~ des qua-**

tre-saisons costermonger, *Am.* huckster; ~ **en** (*or* **au**) **détail** retailer; ~ **en gros** wholesaler; **~age** [marʃɑ̃'da:ʒ] *m* bargaining; **~er** [~'de] (1a) bargain (over), haggle (over); *fig.* **ne pas** ~ not to spare, not to be sparing with; **~ise** [~'di:z] merchandise, goods *pl.*

marche [marʃ] *f* walk; march; tread; step, stair; ☉, ✺ running; *fig. events, stars, time, etc.:* course; *fig.* (rate of) progress; ~ **arrière** *mot.* reversing; **en** ~ moving, running; **mettre en** ~ start, set going, set in motion.

marché [mar'ʃe] *m* market (*a. financial*); deal, bargain; ~ **commun** Common Market; ~ **des changes** exchange market; ~ **du travail** labo(u)r market; ~ **noir** black market; (**à**) **bon** ~ cheap(ly); (**à**) **meilleur** ~ more cheaply, cheaper; **le bon** ~ the cheapness (of, **de**); (**aller**) **faire son** ~ go shopping; *fig.* **par-dessus le** ~ into the bargain.

marchepied [marʃə'pje] *m vehicle:* footboard; *mot.* running-board; step-ladder; *fig.* stepping-stone.

march|er [mar'ʃe] (1a) walk, go; step; ✕ *etc.* march; ☉ *etc.* run, function, work; move; go well; F agree, go along; F be taken in, swallow it; F **faire** ~ **q.** take s.o. in, fool s.o.; ☉ ~ **à vide** run idle; ~ **sur les pieds de q.** tread on s.o.'s feet; **faire** ~ (*a business*); F **faire** ~ **q.** fool s.o.; **~eur** [~'ʃœ:r] *su.* walker.

mardi [mar'di] *m* Tuesday; ~ **gras** Shrove Tuesday.

mare [ma:r] *f* pond; pool (*a. fig.*).

marécag|e [mare'ka:ʒ] *m* bog, fen; **~eux** [~ka'ʒø] boggy, marshy.

maréchal [mare'ʃal] *m* marshal; **~ferrant** *m* blacksmith.

marée [ma're] *f* tide; ✝ fresh fish; *fig.* flood, wave, surge; ~ **basse** (**haute**) low (high) tide, low (high) water; **grande** ~ spring tide; **la** ~ **descend** (**monte**) the tide is going out (coming in).

mareyeur *m*, **-euse** *f* [mare'jœ:r, ~'jø:z] fishmonger.

marg|e [marʒ] *f* border, edge; margin (*a. fig., a.* ✝); *fig.* scope; ~ **bénéficiaire** profit margin; **être en** ~ (**de**) on the fringe (of); **~inal** [~ʒi'nal] marginal.

margouillis F [margu'ji] *m* mud.

margoulin F [margu'lɛ̃] *m* (small-time) crook.

marguerite ✿ [margə'rit] *f* marguerite, daisy.

mari [ma'ri] *m* husband; **~able** [~'rjabl] marriageable; **~age** [~'rja:ʒ] *m* marriage; wedding; ~ **d'amour** love match; **~é, e** [~'rje] **1.** *adj.* married; **2.** *su./m* bridegroom; *su./f* bride; **~er** [~'rje] (1o) marry off; *fig.* join, blend; **se** ~ get married (to, **avec**); *fig.* harmonize (with, **à**); **~eur** *m*, **-euse** *f* [~'rjœ:r, ~'rjø:z] matchmaker.

marin [ma'rɛ̃] **1.** *adj.* marine; sea...; nautical; **2.** *su./m* sailor.

marinade [mari'nad] *f* pickle; brine; *cuis.* marinade.

marine [ma'rin] **1.** *adj./inv.* navy (-blue); **2.** *su./f* ⚓ navy.

mariner *cuis.* [mari'ne] (1a) pickle.

marinier [mari'nje] bargee.

marionette [marjo'nɛt] *f* puppet.

marital [mari'tal] marital; **~ement** [~tal'mɑ̃] *adv.* maritally; **vivre** ~ live together as husband and wife.

maritime [mari'tim] maritime (⚓, *law, power*); shipping (*agent*); naval (*dockyard*); marine (*insurance*); seaborne; seaside (*town*).

marivaudage [marivo'da:ʒ] *m* sophisticated flirting.

marjolaine ✿ [marʒo'lɛn] *f* marjoram.

marmaille F [mar'ma:j] *f* kids *pl.*

marmelade [marmə'lad] *f* compote (*of fruit*); (*orange*) marmelade; F mess; *fig.* **en** ~ pounded to a jelly.

marmit|e [mar'mit] *f* pot; F **faire bouillir la** ~ keep the pot boiling; **~on** [~mi'tɔ̃] *m* cook's boy.

marmonner [marmɔ'ne] (1a) mumble, mutter.

marmoréen [marmɔre'ɛ̃] marble...

marmot F [mar'mo] *m* kid.

marmott|e [mar'mɔt] *f zo.* marmot; ✝ case of samples; **~er** [marmɔ'te] (1a) mumble, mutter.

marocain [marɔ'kɛ̃] *adj., su.* Moroccan.

maronner [marɔ'ne] (1a) growl.

maroquin [marɔ'kɛ̃] *m* morocco (-leather); F minister's portfolio; **~erie** [~kin'ri] *f* leather goods *pl.*

marotte [ma'rɔt] *f* (*fool's*) cap and bells *pl.*; dummy head; F fad.

marqu|ant [mar'kɑ̃] outstanding; **~e** [mark] *f* mark (*a.* ✝, *a. fig.*); ✝ brand, make (*a. mot.*); *sp.* score; *fig.* token; ~

déposée registered trademark; **de ~** distinguished (*person*), † F choice; **~er** [mar'ke] (1m) *v/t.* mark; stamp; brand; *sp.* score (*goals*); ind. indicate; *fig.* show (*one's age etc.*); *fig.* watch (*one's opponent etc.*); *v/i.* be outstanding; F **~ mal** make a bad impression; **~eterie** [~kə'tri] *f* inlaid work.

marquis [mar'ki] *m* marquis; **~e** [~'ki:z] *f* title: marchioness; marquee; awning, canopy.

marraine [ma'rɛn] *f* godmother; *eccl., a. fig.* sponsor.

marr|ant *sl.* [ma'rɑ̃] funny; odd; **~e** *sl.* [ma:r] *f:* **en avoir ~** be fed up (with, **de**); **~er** *sl.* [ma're] (1a): **se ~** langh; split one's sides; have fun.

marron[1] [ma'rɔ̃] **1.** *su./m* **♣** chestnut; F blow; **2.** *adj./inv.* brown.

marron[2] [ma'rɔ̃] unqualified; unlicensed.

maronnier **♣** [marɔ'nje] *m* chestnut (-tree).

mars [mars] *m* March; *astr.* Mars.

marsouin *zo.* [mar'swɛ̃] *m* porpoise.

marteau [mar'to] *m* hammer (*a.* ♪, *a. anat.*); (*door-*)knocker; **~ pneumatique** pneumatic drill.

martel [mar'tɛl] *m* † hammer; *fig.* **se mettre ~ en tête** worry; **~er** [~tə'le] (1d) hammer; pound; *fig.* **~ ses mots** speak each word with emphasis.

martial [mar'sjal] martial (*a. law*).

martinet[1] [marti'nɛ] *m* tilt hammer; (small) whip.

martinet[2] *orn.* [~] *m* swift, martlet.

martre *zo.* [martr] *f* marten.

martyr *m,* **e** *f* [mar'ti:r] martyr; **enfant** *m* **~** battered child; **~e** [~'ti:r] *m* martyrdom; *fig.* agonies *pl.;* **~iser** [~tiri'ze] (1a) martyr(ize); *fig.* torture; batter (*a child etc*).

marxis|me [mark'sism] *m* Marxism; **~te** [~'sist] *adj., su.* Marxist.

mas [mɑs] *m* small farmhouse.

mascarade [maska'rad] *f* masquerade (*a. fig.*).

mascaret [maska'rɛ] *m* tidal wave.

mascotte [mas'kɔt] *f* mascot, charm.

masculin [masky'lɛ̃] **1.** *adj.* masculine; male; **2.** *su./m gramm.* masculine.

masqu|e [mask] *m* mask; *thea.* masque; **~ à gaz** gas mask; **~er** [mas'ke] (1m) mask; conceal; hide.

massacr|ant [masa'krɑ̃]: **humeur** *f* **~e** bad temper; **~e** [~'sakr] *m* slaughter (*a. fig.*); **~er** [masa'kre] (1a) massacre; *fig.* make a hash of; murder (*music*); kill (*a ball*); *fig.* watch; **~eur** *m,* **-euse** *f* [~'krœ:r, ~'krø:z] slaughterer; *fig.* bungler.

massage **♪** [ma'sa:ʒ] *m* massage.

masse[1] **☉** [mas] *f* sledgehammer.

masse[2] [~] *f* mass; bulk; † fund; ⚡ earth; *fig.* crowd, heap; *phys.* **~ critique** critical mass; **en ~** in a body; as a whole; *fig.* mass...

massepain [mas'pɛ̃] *m* marzipan.

masser[1] [ma'se] (1a) mass, crowd.

masser[2] [ma'se] (1a) massage.

massicot [masi'ko] *m* books: guillotine, trimmer.

massif [ma'sif] **1.** *adj.* massive, bulky; heavy; solid (*gold*); **2.** *su./m* clump; *geog.* mountain mass.

massue [ma'sy] *f* club; *fig.* **en coup de ~** sledge-hammer (*arguments*).

mastic [mas'tik] *m* mastic; cement; putty; *tooth:* filling, stopping.

mastiquer[1] [masti'ke] (1m) masticate; chew.

mastiquer[2] [~] (1m) **☉** cement; stop (*a hole, a tooth*); putty.

mastroquet F † [mastrɔ'kɛ] *m* pub(keeper).

masure [ma'zy:r] *f* hovel, shack.

mat[1] [mat] *adj./inv.* dull, flat, lustreless.

mat[2] [~] *adj./inv.* checkmated; **être ~** be checkmate; **faire ~** checkmate (*s.o.*).

mât [mɑ] *m* **♣** mast; pole; ✈ strut; **☎ ~ de signaux** signal post.

matador [mata'dɔ:r] *m* matador; *fig.* magnate; *fig.* bigwig.

matamore [mata'mɔ:r] *m* braggart.

match, *pl. a.* **matches** *sp.* [matʃ] *m* match; **~ retour** return match.

matelas [mat'la] *m* mattress; **☉ ~ d'air** air-cushion; **~ pneumatique** air mattress; **~er** [matla'se] (1a) pad; **~sure** [~'sy:r] *f* padding.

matelot [mat'lo] *m* sailor; **~e** [~'lɔt] *f* fish stew.

mater[1] [ma'te] (1a) mat, dull.

mater[2] [~] (1a) (check)mate (*at chess*); *fig.* subdue, curb; *fig.* bring under control.

matéri|aliser [materjali'ze] (1a) materialize; **~aliste** [~'list] **1.** *adj.* materialistic; **2.** *su.* materialist; **~au** △ [~'rjo] *m* material; **~aux** ⊙, △, *fig.* [~'rjo] *m/pl.* materials; **~el** [~'rjɛl] **1.** *adj.* material; **2.** *su./m* ⊙ plant; equipment; *war:* material; *data processing:* hardware; **~ humain** manpower; men *pl.*

matern|el [matɛr'nɛl] maternal; mother (*tongue*); **école f ~le** infant school; **~ité** [~ni'te] *f* maternity, motherhood; lying-in hospital.

mathémati|cien *m*, **-enne** *f* [matemati'sjɛ̃, ~'sjɛn] mathematician; **~que** [~'tik] **1.** *adj.* mathematical; **2.** *su./f*, **~s** *pl.* mathematics.

matière [ma'tjɛːr] *f* material; matter, substance; *fig.* subject; **~s premières** raw material *sg.*; ⊙ **~s** *pl.* **plastiques** plastics; **en ~ de** as regards; in matters of; **table f des ~s** table of contents.

matin [ma'tɛ̃] **1.** *su./m* morning; **de bon** (*or* **grand**) **~**, **au petit ~** early in the morning; **2.** *adv.* early; **~al** [~ti'nal] morning...; early; **être ~** be an early riser; **~ée** [~ti'ne] *f* morning; *thea.* afternoon performance; **faire la grasse ~** sleep late; **~ière** [~ti'njɛːr]: **l'etoile f ~** the morning star.

matir [ma'tiːr] (2a) mat, dull.

matois [ma'twa] sly (person).

matou *zo.* [ma'tu] *m* tom-cat.

matraqu|e [ma'trak] *f* bludgeon; **~er** [~tra'ke] (1a) beat (*s.o.*) up; bombard (*a. fig.*); *fig.* overcharge, overburden.

matras 🔬 [ma'tra] *m* matrass.

matri|arcat [matriar'ka] *m* matriarchy; **~ce** [~'tris] *su./f* matrix; ⊙ die; ♂ master record; *anat.* uterus; **~cule** [~'kyl] *su./f* register, roll; *su./m* registration *or* reference number; ✕ regimental number.

matrone [ma'trɔn] *f* matron.

maturation [matyra'sjɔ̃] *f* ripening.

mâture ♻ [ma'tyːr] *f* masting.

maturité [matyri'te] *f* maturity; ripeness.

maudi|re [mo'diːr] (4p) curse; *fig.* grumble about; **~t** [~'di] **1.** *p.p. of* **maudire**; **2.** *adj.* (ac)cursed; *fig.* execrable, damnable.

maugréer [mogre'e] (1a) curse; *fig.* grumble (about, at **contre**).

maure [moːr] Moorish.

mausolée [mozo'le] *m* mausoleum.

maussade [mo'sad] surly, sullen; *fig.* depressing (*weather*); irritable.

mauvais [mo've] **1.** *adj.* bad; evil, wick-

ed; wrong; ill; nasty, unpleasant; **de ~e humeur** in a bad temper; **2.** *adv.*: **il fait ~** the weather is bad; **sentir ~** smell bad.

mauve [moːv] *su./f* 🌿 mallow; *su./m, adj.* mauve, purple.

maxillaire *anat.* [maksil'lɛːr] *m* jaw-bone; **~ supérieur** maxilla.

maxime [mak'sim] *f* maxim; **maximum**, *pl. a.* **maxima** [~si'mɔm, ~'ma] *su./m, adj.* maximum; **porter au ~** maximize.

mazout [ma'zut] *m* fuel oil.

me [mə] **1.** *pron./pers.* me; to me; **~ voici!** here I am!; **2.** *pron./rfl.* myself, to myself.

méandre [me'ɑ̃ːdr] *m* wind(ing), bend; **faire des ~s** meander, wind.

mec F [mɛk] *m* guy, fellow.

mécani|cien [mekani'sjɛ̃] *m* mechanic; engineer; 🚂 engine driver, *Am.* engineer; **~que** [~'nik] **1.** *adj.* mechanical; **2.** *su./f* mechanics *sg.*; mechanism; engineering; **~ser** [~ni'ze] (1a) mechanize; **~sme** [~'nism] *m* mechanism.

mécano ⊙ F [meka'no] *m* mechanic.

mécha|mment [meʃa'mɑ̃] *adv. of* **méchant**; **~nceté** [~ʃɑ̃s'te] *f* nastiness; meanness; malice, spite; spiteful remark *or* action; **~nt** [~'ʃɑ̃] **1.** *adj.* nasty, mean, bad; spiteful.

mèche[1] [mɛʃ] *f lamp:* wick; ⚡ match fuse; *whip:* lash; *hair:* lock; ⊙ bit, drill; **éventer la ~** discover a secret; **vendre la ~** blab out.

mèche[2] [~] *f:* **de ~ avec** in collusion with; hand in glove with; **il n'y a pas ~!** nothing doing!

mécompte [me'kɔ̃ːt] *m* miscalculation, error; *fig.* disappointment.

méconn|aissable [mekɔne'sabl] unrecognizable; **~aissance** [~ne'sɑ̃ːs] *f* failure to recognize; **~aître** [~'nɛːtr] (4k) misjudge; not to appreciate; be unaware of, not to know.

mécontent [mekɔ̃'tɑ̃] dissatisfied *or* discontented *or* displeased (with, **de**); annoyed (at, **de**; that, **que**); **~ement** [~tɑ̃t'mɑ̃] *m* dissatisfaction (with, **de**); displeasure (at, **de**); **~er** [~tɑ̃'te] (1a) dissatisfy; displease, annoy.

médaill|e [me'daːj] *f* medal; **~é** [meda'je] **1.** *adj.* holding a medal; **2.** *su.* medal-winner; **~on** [~'jɔ̃] *m* medallion; locket; *journ.* inset.

médecin [met'sɛ̃] *m* doctor, physician;

⚓ ~ **du bord** ship's doctor; ~ **légiste** *approx.* coroner, *Am.* legal examiner; **femme** *f* ~ lady doctor; ~**e** [~'sin] *f* medicine.

media, média [me'dja] *m/pl.* (mass) media.

média|n [me'djɑ̃] median; middle...; ~**t** [~'dja] mediate; ~**teur** [medja'tœːr] **1.** *adj.* mediatory; **2.** *su./m* mediator; ~**tion** [~'sjɔ̃] *f* mediation.

médic|al [medi'kal] medical; ~**ament** [medika'mɑ̃] *m* medicament; ~**ment|er** [~mɑ̃'te] (1a) dose (*s.o.*); ~**amenteux** [~mɑ̃'tø] medicinal; ~**astre** [medi'kastr] *m* quack; ~**ation** [~ka'sjɔ̃] *f* medical treatment; ~**inal** [~si'nal] medicinal.

médiéval [medje'val] medi(a)eval.

médiocr|e [me'djɔkr] mediocre; poor, second-rate, indifferent; ~**ité** [~djɔkri'te] *f* mediocrity; **F** *person:* second-rater.

médi|re [me'diːr] (4p): ~ **de q.** slander *s.o.*; ~**sance** [medi'zɑ̃ːs] *f* slander, scandal; ~**sant** [~'zɑ̃] **1.** *adj.* slanderous; **2.** *su.* slanderer.

médit|atif [medita'tif] meditative; ~**ation** [~ta'sjɔ̃] *f* meditation; ~**er** [~'te] (1a) *v/i.* meditate; *v/t.* meditate (on) (*s.th.*); ~ **de** (*inf.*) think of (*ger.*), contemplate (*ger.*).

Méditerranée *geog.* [meditɛra'ne]: **La** ~ the Mediterranean (Sea).

médium [me'djɔm] *m* medium.

médius [me'djys] *m* middle finger.

médus|e [me'dyːz] *f* jellyfish; ~**er** [~dy'ze] (1a) dumbfound; petrify.

méfait [me'fɛ] *m* misdeed; ill or damaging effect; *ravages pl.*

méfi|ance [me'fjɑ̃ːs] *f* distrust; ~**ant** [~'fjɑ̃] distrustful; ~**er** [~'fje] (1o): **se** ~ be on one's guard; **se** ~ **de** be suspicious of, distrust; look out for, watch.

mégarde [me'gard] *f*: **par** ~ inadvertently; accidentally.

mégère [me'ʒɛːr] *f* shrew, scold.

mégot F [me'go] *m* *cigarette:* fag end, *Am.* butt; *cigar:* stump; ~**er F** [~go'te] (1a) skimp (on, *sur*).

meilleur [mɛ'jœːr] **1.** *adj.* better; **le** ~ the better (*of two*), the best (*of several*); **2.** *su./m* best.

méjuger [meʒy'ʒe] (1l): ~ **de** misjudge.

mélancoli|e [melɑ̃kɔ'li] *f* melancholy; ~**que** [~'lik] melancholy.

mélang|e [me'lɑ̃ːʒ] *m* mixture, blend; *cards:* shuffling; ~**s** *pl.* miscellany *sg.*; ~**er** [melɑ̃'ʒe] (1l) mix; blend; **F** mix up (*a. fig.*); ~**eur** [~'ʒœːr] *m* mixer.

mélasse [me'las] *f* molasses *pl.*, treacle; **F** **dans la** ~ in the soup.

mêlée [mɛ'le] *f* × fray; scuffle; scramble; ~**er** [~] (1a) mix; blend; ~ **q. à** (or **dans**) involve *s.o.* in; **se** ~ **à** join; mix with; **se** ~ **de** meddle in, interfere in or with.

mélèze ♣ [me'lɛːz] *m* larch.

méli-mélo, *pl.* **mélis-mélos F** [melime'lo] *m* jumble; clutter; mess.

mélo|die ♪ [melɔ'di] *f* melody, tune; ~**dieux** [~'djø] melodious; ~**drame** [~'dram] *m* melodrama.

melon [mə'lɔ̃] *m* ♣ melon; bowler (hat), *Am.* derby (hat).

membrane [mɑ̃'bran] *f* ♣, *anat.*, ⊕ membrane; *zo. duck etc.:* web.

membr|e [mɑ̃ːbr] *m* member; *body:* limb; ~**ure** [~'bryːr] *f* limbs *pl.*

même [mɛːm] **1.** *adj.* same; *after noun:* self, very; **ce** ~ **soir** the same evening; **ce soir** ~ this very evening; **en** ~ **temps** at the same time; **la bonté** ~ kindness itself; **les** ~**s personnes** the same persons; *see* **vous-même**; **2.** *adv.* even; **à** ~ **de** (*inf.*) able to, in a position to (*inf.*); **boire à** ~ **la bouteille** drink out of the bottle; **de** ~ **que** like, as; as well as; **tout de** ~ all the same.

mémère F [me'mɛːr] *f* mother, **F** mum(my); grandmother, **F** granny.

mémoire¹ [me'mwaːr] *f* memory; **de** ~ by heart, from memory; **de** ~ **d'homme** within living memory; **en** ~ **de** in memory of.

mémoire² [~] *m* memorandum; memorial; record; dissertation; ✝ bill; ✠ statement; **~s** *pl.* memoirs.

mémor|able [memɔ'rabl] noteworthy; ~**ial** [~'rjal] *m* memorial.

menac|e [mə'nas] *f* threat; ~**er** [~na'se] (1k) threaten (with, **de**).

ménage [me'naːʒ] *m* housekeeping; housework; *fig.* household; family; *fig.* married couple; **faire bon** (**avec**) ~ get on well (with); **femme** *f* **de** ~ cleaner; **être heureux en** ~ be happily married; **monter son** ~ set up house; ~**ment** [~naʒ'mɑ̃] *m* care; consideration, caution.

M

ménager[1] [mena'ʒe] (1l) spare (*s.o.*, *s.th.*; *fig.* s.o. s.th., **qch. à q.**); treat with care, treat gently, go easy on; use sparingly *or* economically; be sparing with; arrange; ◉ *etc.* make, put in; *fig.* reserve, have in store (for, **à**).

ménager[2], **-ère** [mena'ʒe, ~'ʒɛːr] **1.** *adj.* domestic; *fig.* thrifty, sparing (of, **de**); **2.** *su./f* housewife; canteen of cutlery; cruet-stand; **~ie** [~naʒ'ri] *f* menagerie.

mendi|ant [mɑ̃'djɑ̃] **1.** *adj.* mendicant; **2.** *su.* beggar; **~cité** [~disi'te] *f* begging; beggary; **~er** [~'dje] (1o) beg (for); **~ des compliments** fish for compliments.

menées [mə'ne] *f/pl.* intrigues.

mener [~] (1d) *v/t.* lead; take, get (to, **à**); *fig.* run, manage; **~ qch. à bien** (*or* **à bonne fin**) see s.th. through; **cela peut le ~ loin** that may take him a long way; *v/i.* lead (to, **à**).

meneur [mə'nœːr] *m* leader; *pej.* agitator; **~ de jeu** emcee.

méninges F [me'nɛ̃ʒ] *m/pl.* brains.

ménisque [me'nisk] *m* meniscus.

menotte [mə'nɔt] *f* ◉ handle; link; F little hand; **~s** *pl.* handcuffs.

mensonge [mɑ̃'sɔ̃ʒ] *m* lie; **~ officieux** (*or* **pieux**) white lie; **~r** [~sɔ̃'ʒe] untrue; false; illusory.

mensu|alité [mɑ̃suali'te] *f* monthly payment *or* instalment; monthly salary; **~el** [~'sɥɛl] monthly.

mensurations [mɑ̃syra'sjɔ̃] *f/pl.* measurements.

mental [mɑ̃'tal] mental; **~ité** [~tali'te] *f* mentality.

menteur [mɑ̃'tœːr] **1.** *adj.* lying; deceptive; false; **2.** *su.* liar.

menthe ♧ [mɑ̃:t] *f* mint.

mention [mɑ̃'sjɔ̃] *f* mention; **faire ~ de** = **~ner** [~sjɔ'ne] (1a) mention.

mentir [mɑ̃'tiːr] (2b) lie (to, **à**).

menton [mɑ̃'tɔ̃] *m* chin; **~net** [mɑ̃tɔ'nɛ] *m* ◉ catch; ⚙ flange.

menu [mə'ny] **1.** *adj.* small; fine; minute; slim; petty; **2.** *adv.* small, fine; **hacher ~** mince; **3.** *su./m* detail; *meal:* menu; **par le ~** in detail.

menuis|erie [mənɥiz'ri] *f* woodwork; joinery, carpentry; joiner's workshop; **~ier** [~ɥi'zje] *m* joiner; carpenter.

méphitique [mefi'tik] noxious.

méplat [me'pla] *m* flat part.

méprendre [me'prɑ̃:dr] (4aa): **se ~ sur** be mistaken about, misjudge.

mépris [me'pri] *m* contempt, scorn; **au ~ de** in defiance of, contrary to; **~able** [mepri'zabl] contemptible; **~ant** [~'zɑ̃] scornful.

méprise [me'priːz] *f* mistake.

mépriser [mepri'ze] (1a) despise.

mer [mɛr] *f* sea; tide; **~ haute** high tide; **haute ~** open sea.

mercanti F [mɛrkɑ̃'ti] *m* profiteer; **~le** [~'til] mercenary.

mercenaire [mɛrsə'nɛːr] *adj.*, *su./m* mercenary.

mercerie [mɛrsə'ri] *f* haberdashery; haberdasher's, *Am.* notions shop.

merci [mɛr'si] **1.** *adv.* thank you, thanks (for, **de**); **~ bien, ~ beaucoup** many thanks; **2.** *su./m* thanks *pl.*; *su./f* mercy; **crier ~** beg for mercy; **sans ~** pitiless(ly *adv.*).

mercredi [mɛrkrə'di] *m* Wednesday.

mercure ⚥ [mɛr'kyːr] *m* mercury.

merde V [mɛrd] *su./f.*, *int.* shit.

mère [mɛr] *f* mother (*a. fig.*); ◉ die, mo(u)ld; **~(-)célibataire** unmarried mother.

méridi|en, -enne [meri'djɛ̃, ~'djɛn] **1.** *adj.* meridian; midday; **2.** *su./m* meridian; *su./f* meridian line; midday nap; sofa; **~onal** [~djɔ'nal] **1.** *adj.* south(ern); **2.** *su.* southerner.

mérinos zo. [meri'nos] *m* merino.

mérit|e [me'rit] *m* merit; quality; ability; **sans ~** undeserving; **~er** [meri'te] (1a) deserve, merit; **~oire** [~'twaːr] praiseworthy.

merlan [mɛr'lɑ̃] *m* icht. whiting; *sl.* hairdresser.

merle [mɛrl] *m* orn. blackbird; F *fig.* **~ blanc** white crow.

merluche icht. [mɛr'lyʃ] *f* cod, stockfish.

merveill|e [mɛr'vɛːj] *f* marvel, wonder; **à ~** wonderfully, excellently; **~eux** [~vɛ'jø] marvellous, wonderful.

mes [me] *see* **mon**.

més... [mez] mis...; **~alliance** [meza-'ljɑ̃:s] *f* misalliance.

mésange orn. [me'zɑ̃:ʒ] *f* tit(mouse).

mésaventure [mezavɑ̃'tyːr] *f* misadventure, mishap, mischance.

mesdames [me'dam] *pl.* of **madame**; **mesdemoiselles** [medmwa'zɛl] *pl.* of **mademoiselle**.

mésentente [mezɑ̃'tɑ̃:t] f misunderstanding, disagreement.

mésestimer [mezɛsti'me] (1a) underestimate; hold in low esteem.

mesquin [mɛs'kɛ̃] mean, stingy; **~erie** [~kin'ri] f meanness.

mess ✕ [mɛs] m mess.

messag|e [me'sa:ʒ] m message (a. fig.); **~er** m, **-ère** [~sa'ʒe, ~'ʒɛːr] messenger; **~eries** [~saʒ'ri] f/pl. shipping (company) sg.; delivery service sg.

messe eccl., a. ♪ [mɛs] f mass.

messieurs [mɛ'sjø] pl. of **monsieur**.

mesur|able [məzy'rabl] measurable; **~age** [~'ra:ʒ] m measurement; **~e** [mə'zy:r] f measure; extent, degree; step; fig. moderation; verse: metre; ♪ time; à bar; à ~ que (in proportion) as; **donner sa ~** show what one is capable of; **en ~ de** in a position to, **outre ~** excessively; overly, unduly; **poids** m/pl. **et ~s** pl. weights and measures; **prendre des ~s contre** take measures against; **prendre les ~s de q.** take s.o.'s measurements; fig. **sans ~** boundless; **sur ~** to order; **~er** [məzy're] (1a) measure; calculate; estimate; **se ~ avec** pit o.s. against; **~eur** [~'rœːr] m gauge.

métairie [mete'ri] f small farm.

métal [me'tal] m metal; **~lifère** [metalli'fɛːr] metalliferous; **~lique** [~'lik] metallic; ✦ **encaisse** f **~** gold reserve; **~lo** F [~'lo] m metal-worker; **~lurgie** [~lyr'ʒi] f metallurgy; **~lurgiste** [~lyr'ʒist] m metallurgist; metal-worker.

méta...: **~morphose** [metamɔr'foːz] f transformation; **~morphoser** [~mɔrfo'ze] (1a) transform; **~stase** ✶ [~'staːz] f metastasis.

métayer [mete'je] m tenant farmer.

météo [mete'o] su./m meteorologist; **~re** [~'ɔːr] m meteor; **~rologie** [~ɔrɔlɔ'ʒi] f meteorology.

méthod|e [me'tɔd] f method, system, way; **~ique** [~tɔ'dik] methodical.

méticuleux [metiky'lø] meticulous.

métier [me'tje] m job; trade; craft; profession; tex. loom.

métis, -isse [me'tis] half-breed.

métrage [me'tra:ʒ] m measurement; metric length; cin. **court** (**long**) **~** short (full-length) film; **mètre** [mɛtr] m

metre, Am. meter; rule, yardstick; **~ à ruban** tape measure; **~ carré** square metre; **~ cube** cubic metre; **~ pliant** folding rule; **métrique** [~'trik] **1.** adj. metric; **2.** su./f metrics sg.

métro F [me'tro] m underground railway, tube, Am. subway.

métropol|e [metrɔ'pɔl] f metropolis; capital; mother country; **~itain** [~pɔli'tɛ̃] **1.** adj. metropolitan; **2.** su./m metropolitan; underground railway.

mets¹ [mɛ] m food; dish; **~ tout préparé** ready-to-serve meal.

mets² [~] 1st p. sg. pres. of **mettre**.

mett|able [me'tabl] wearable; **~eur** [~'tœːr] m ✦ setter; **~ en scène** thea. producer; cin. director.

mettre [mɛtr] (4v) put; place; set; lay (a. the table); put on (clothes); wear (clothes); ✦ etc. put in, install; fig. suppose; **~ à l'aise** put (s.o.) at his ease; **~ au point** adjust; ✦ tune; opt. focus; develop, create; fig. clarify (an affair); zo.: **~ bas** drop young; **~ de côté** save; **~ deux heures à** (inf.) take two hours to (inf.); **~ en colère** make angry; **~ en jeu** bring into play or discussion; thea. **~ en scène** stage; **mettons que ce soit vrai** let us suppose this is true; **se ~** place o.s., stand; **se ~ à** (inf.) begin (ger., to inf.); **se ~ à l'œuvre** set to work; **se ~ en route** start out; **se ~ ensemble** live together; **se ~ en tête de** (inf.) take it into one's head to (inf.); **s'y ~** set about it.

meubl|ant [mœ'blɑ̃] decorative, effective, nice; **~e** [mœbl] **1.** adj. loose (ground); 🛐 **biens** m/pl. **~s** movables; **2.** su./m piece of furniture; **~s** pl. furniture sg.; **~é** [mœ'ble] m furnished room; **~er** [~] (1a) furnish; fig. fill (with, de).

meule¹ [mœːl] f haystack; pile.

meul|e² [mœːl] f ✦ millstone; grindstone; **~ de fromage** large round cheese.

meun|erie [mœn'ri] f flour; milling; **~ier** [mœ'nje] m miller.

meurent [mœːr] 3rd p. pl. pres. of **mourir**; **meurs** [~] 1st p. sg. pres. of **mourir**; **meurt-de-faim** F [mœrdə'fɛ̃] m/inv. starveling; **de ~** starvation (wage).

meurtr|e [mœrtr] m murder; **~ier, -ère** [mœrtri'e, ~'ɛːr] **1.** adj. murderous; **2.**

M

su./m murderer; su./f murderess; ⚠ loophole.

meurtrir [mœr'tri:r] (2a) bruise; **~ssure** [~tri'sy:r] f bruise.

meus [mø] *1st p. sg. pres. of* **mouvoir.**

meute [mø:t] f pack; *fig.* mob.

meuvent [mœ:v] *3rd p. pl. pres. of* **mouvoir.**

mi ♩ [mi] m/inv. mi, *note:* E.

mi... [mi] adv. half, mid, semi-; **~clos** half open; **à ~chemin** half-way; **la ~janvier** mid-January.

miauler [mjo'le] (1a) mew, meow.

miche [miʃ] f round loaf.

micheline 🚆 [miʃ'lin] f rail-car.

micmac F [mik'mak] m funny business or things pl.

micro F [mi'kro] m radio: mike.

microbe [mi'krɔb] m microbe.

micro...: **~phone** [mikrɔ'fɔn] m microphone; **~processeur** [~prɔsɛ'sœ:r] m microprocessor; **~scope** [~krɔs'kɔp] m microscope; **~sillon** [~krɔsi'jɔ̃] m microgroove; long-playing record.

midi [mi'di] m noon; **~ et demi** half past twelve; *geog.* **le ♌ the** South of France; **~nette** F [~di'nɛt] f dressmaker's assistant; shopgirl; office girl.

M

mie [mi] f bread: soft part, crumb.

miel [mjɛl] m honey; **~lé** [mjɛ'le] honeyed; honey-like; **~leux** [~'lø] like honey; *fig.* honeyed.

mien, mienne [mjɛ̃, mjɛn] **1.** *pron./poss.:* **le ~, la ~ne, les ~s** m/pl. **les ~nes** f/pl. mine; **2.** su./m mine, my own; **les ~s** pl. my (own) people.

miette [mjɛt] f crumb; *fig.* bit.

mieux [mjø] **1.** adv. better; rather; **aimer ~** prefer; **♯ aller ~** feel or be better; **à qui ~ ~** one trying to outdo the other; **de ~ en ~** better and better; **je ne demande pas ~ que de** (inf.) I shall be delighted to (inf.); **le ~** (the) best; **tant ~** all the better; **valoir ~** be better; **vous feriez ~ de** (inf.) you had better (inf.); **2.** su./m best; change for the better; **au ~** at best; **de son** etc. **~** as best he etc. can (or could).

mièvre [mjɛːvr] delicate; affected.

mignard [mi'na:r] affected, mincing; dainty; **~ardise** [~nar'di:z] f affectation; **~on** [~'nɔ̃] **1.** adj. dainty, nice, sweet; **péché** m **~** besetting sin; **2.** su. darling, pet.

migraine [mi'grɛn] f headache.

migrat|eur [migra'tœːr] migratory; migrant; **~ion** [~'sjɔ̃] f migration.

mijaurée [miʒo're] f pretentious or affected woman.

mijoter [miʒo'te] (1a) vt/i. simmer; v/t. hatch (a plot); **se ~** be brewing.

mil [mil] thousand (only in dates).

mildiou ♀, ✗ [mil'dju] m mildew.

milice ✗ [mi'lis] f militia.

milieu [mi'ljø] m middle; *fig.* environment; *fig.* (social) background; *fig.* middle course; *the* underworld; **au ~ de** in the middle of.

milit|aire [mili'tɛːr] **1.** adj. military; **2.** su./m soldier; **~ant** [~'tɑ̃] **1.** adj. militant; **2.** su./m fighter (for, de); **~ariser** [~tari'ze] (1a) militarize; **~arisme** [~ta'rism] m militarism; **~er** [~'te] (1a) be a militant; *fig.* **~ en faveur de** (contre) militate in favo(u)r of (against).

mille [mil] **1.** adj./num./inv., su./m/inv. thousand; **mettre dans le ~** hit the bull's eye; F *fig.* on target; **2.** su./m mile.

mille...: **~pattes** zo. [mil'pat] m/inv. centipede, millepede.

millésime [mille'zim] m date.

millet ♀ [mi'jɛ] m millet.

milli|aire [mil'jɛːr]: **borne** f **~** milestone; **~ard** [~'ljaːr] m milliard, Am. billion; **~ème** [~'ljɛm] thousandth; **~er** [~'lje] m (about) a thousand; **~on** [~'ljɔ̃] m million.

mim|e [mim] m/f mimic; mime; **~er** [mi'me] (1a) mime; mimic (s.o.); **~ique** [~'mik] mimic.

minable *fig.* [mi'nabl] shabby.

minauder [mino'de] (1a) simper, smirk; **~ie** [~'dri] f simpering.

mince [mɛ̃s] thin; slender, slight.

mine¹ [min] f appearance, look; **~s** pl. simperings; **avoir bonne** (mauvaise) **~** look well (ill); look good (bad); **faire ~ de** (inf.) make as if to (inf.); **ne pas payer de ~** not to look much.

min|e² [min] f ✗, ✗, ⚓, *fig.* mine; *pencil:* lead; *fig.* store; **~ de houille** coal-mine; **~er** [mi'ne] (1a) ✗ mine; *fig.* undermine, consume; **~erai** ✗ [min'rɛ] m ore.

minéral [mine'ral] adj., su./m mineral; **~ogique** [~ralɔ'ʒik] mineralogical; mot.

numéro m ~ registration (Am. license) number; mot. **plaque** f ~ number plate.
minet m, **-ette** f [mi'nɛ, ~'nɛt] puss(ycat); young trendy.
mineur[1] [mi'nœːr] adj., su. minor.
mineur[2] [~] m ⚒ miner; ✕ sapper.
miniature [minja'tyːr] f miniature.
minier, -ère [mi'nje, ~'njɛːr] 1. adj. mining; 2. su./f open-cast mine.
mini-jupe [mini'ʒyp] f miniskirt.
minim|al [mini'mal] minimal; **~e** [~'nim] tiny; fig. trivial; **~iser** [~nimi'ze] (1a) play down; **~um**, pl. a. **~a** [~ni'mɔm, ~'ma] 1. su./m minimum; ~ **vital** minimum living wage; 2. adj. minimum.
minist|ère [minis'tɛːr] m ministry; pol. a. office, government department; ⚹ **de la Défense nationale** Ministry of Defence, Am. Department of Defense; ⚹ **des Affaires étrangères** Foreign Office, Am. State Department; ⚹ **public** Public Prosecutor; **~re** [~'nistr] m pol., eccl. minister; ⚹ **de la Défense nationale** Minister of Defence, Am. Secretary of Defense; ⚹ **des Affaires étrangères** Foreign Secretary, Am. Secretary of State; ⚹ **des Finances** France: Minister of Finance, Britain: Chancellor of the Exchequer, Am. Secretary of the Treasury.
minois F [mi'nwa] m pretty face.
minorité [minɔri'te] f minority (a. ⚖); **mettre en** ~ defeat, outvote.
minuit [mi'nɥi] m midnight.
minuscule [minys'kyl] 1. adj. tiny; small (letter); 2. su./f small letter.
minut|e [mi'nyt] 1. su./f minute; ⚖ draft; **à la** ~ this instant; to the minute; 2. int. wait a bit!; **~er** [miny'te] (1a) time; **~erie** [~'tri] f ⚡ time switch.
minuti|e [miny'si] f (attention to) minute detail; **~eux** [~'sjø] detailed, painstaking, thorough.
mioche F [mjɔʃ] su. urchin; kid(die).
mirac|le [mi'raːkl] m miracle (a. fig.); **~uleux** [~raky'lø] miraculous.
mir|age [mi'raːʒ] m mirage; fig. illusion; **~e** [miːr] f ✕ aiming; ✕ head; surv pole; **~er** [mi're] (1a) aim at; candle (an egg); scrutinize; **se** ~ look at o.s.; be reflected.
mirifique F [miri'fik] wonderful.
mirobolant F [mirobɔ'lɑ̃] terrific.
miroi|r [mi'rwaːr] m mirror, look-

ing-glass; **~tement** [~rwat'mɑ̃] m flash; gleam; shimmer; **~ter** [mirwa'te] (1a) flash; glitter; sparkle; fig. **faire** ~ paint in glowing colo(u)rs.
miroton [mirɔ'tõ] m onion-stew.
mis[1] [mi] 1st p. sg. p.s. of **mettre.**
mis[2] [mi] p.p. of **mettre.**
misanthrope [mizã'trɔp] 1. su./m misanthropist; 2. adj. misanthropic.
mise [miːz] f placing, putting; auction: bid; gamble: stake; dress, attire; ✝ outlay; ⚡ ~ **à la terre** earthing, Am. grounding; ⚓ ~ **à l'eau** launching; ~ **à pied** sacking; ~ **au point** adjustment; phot. focussing; creation; fig. development; ~ **en liberté** release; ~ **en marche** starting; ~ **en plis** hair: setting; mot. ~ **en route** starting up; thea. ~ **en scène** staging; ~ **en service** commencement of service; ~ **en train** start(ing); ✝ ~ **en vente** putting up for sale; **ne pas être de** ~ be out of place; **miser** [mi'ze] (1a) v/t. bid; stake; v/i. count (on, **sur**).
misérable [mize'rabl] 1. adj. miserable; wretched; mean; 2. su. wretch; **misère** [~'zɛːr] f misery.
miséricord|e [mizeri'kɔrd] 1. su./f mercy, forgiveness; 2. int. mercy!; **~ieux** [~kɔr'djø] merciful.
missile ✕ [mi'sil] m missile; ~ **de croisière** cruise missile.
mission [mi'sjõ] f mission; **~naire** [~sjɔ'nɛːr] m missionary.
mistral [mis'tral] m mistral (cold north-east wind in Provence).
mitaine [mi'tɛn] f mitten.
mite [mit] f moth; cheese: mite; **mité** [mi'te] moth-eaten; shabby; fig. spoilt (countryside).
mi-temps [mi'tɑ̃] f sp. half-time, interval; ✝ **à** ~ half-time (work).
miteux F [mi'tø] shabby; seedy.
mitiger [miti'ʒe] (11) mitigate.
mitonner [mitɔ'ne] (1a) v/i. simmer; v/t. let simmer; fig. hatch.
mitoyen [mitwa'jɛ̃] common (to two things), △ party (wall).
mitraill|e [mi'traːj] ✕ grape-shot; shell fire; **~er** ✕ [mitra'je] (1a) machine-gun, strafe; fig. pelt (with, **de**); **~ette** ✕ [~'jɛt] f tommy gun; **~eur** ✕ [~'jœːr] m machine gunner; **~euse** ✕ [~'jøːz] f machine gun.
mixt|e [mikst] mixed; joint; ~ **double** m

M

tennis: mixed doubles *pl.*; *enseigne-ment m* ~ co-education; **~ure** [~'ty:r] *f* mixture.

mobil|e [mɔ'bil] **1.** *adj.* mobile; movable (*a. feast*); moving; detachable; *fig.* inconstant; **2.** *su./m* moving body or part; *fig.* motive, spring; **~ier** [~bi'lje] **1.** *adj.* 🏛 movable; ✝ transferable; **2.** *su./m* furniture.

mobilis|ation [mɔbiliza'sjɔ̃] *f* mobilization; **~er** [~'ze] (1a) mobilize.

mobilité [mɔbili'te] *f* mobility.

mobylette (*TM*) [mɔbi'lɛt] *f* moped.

moche F [mɔʃ] ugly; F lousy.

modal [mɔ'dal] modal; **~ité** [~dali'te] *f* modality; ♪ form of scale; ✝ **~s** *pl.* terms and conditions.

mode [mɔd] *su./m gramm.* mood; method; *su./f* fashion; **à la ~** fashionable, F in; **à la ~ de** in the style of; *cuis.* ... fashion; **à la dernière ~** in the latest fashion.

modèle [mɔ'dɛl] **1.** *su./m* model (*a. fig.*), pattern; **prendre q. pour ~** model o.s. on s.o.; **2.** *adj.* model...

model|é [mɔd'le] *m* relief; contours *pl.*; **~er** [~'le] (1d) model (on, *sur*); mo(u)ld; shape.

modér|ateur [mɔdera'tœːr] **1.** *su./m* moderator; ⚙ control; **2.** *adj.* moderating; **~ation** [~ra'sjɔ̃] *f* moderation; **~é** [~'re] moderate; sober; **~er** [~'re] (1f) moderate; restrain.

modern|e [mɔ'dɛrn] modern; **~iser** [mɔdɛrni'ze] (1a) modernize; **~ité** [~ni'te] *f* modernity.

modest|e [mɔ'dɛst] modest; **~ie** [~dɛs'ti] *f* modesty.

modicité [mɔdisi'te] *f* means: modesty; prices: reasonableness.

modifi|able [mɔdi'fjabl] modifiable; **~er** [~'fje] (1o) modify, alter.

modique [mɔ'dik] reasonable, moderate (*price*); modest (*means*).

modiste [mɔ'dist] *f* milliner.

modul|ateur ⚡ [mɔdyla'tœːr] *m* modulator; **~ation** [~'sjɔ̃] *f* modulation (♪, *a. voice*); *voice*: inflexion; **~e** [mɔ'dyl] *m* ⚡ modulus; △ module; unit; size; **~ lunaire** lunar module; **~er** [~dy'le] (1a) modulate.

moell|e [mwal] *f* marrow; ♣ pith (*a. fig.*); **~eux** [mwa'lø] marrowy; *fig.* soft; *fig.* mellow (*light, voice*).

mœurs [mœrs] *f/pl.* morals; manners, customs; *animals*: habits.

moi [mwa] **1.** *pron./pers. subject*: I; *object*: me; (to) me; **à ~** to me; mine; **c'est ~** it is I, F it's me; **de vous à ~** between you and me; **2.** *su./m* ego, self.

moignon 🖐 *m* stump.

moi-même [mwa'mɛːm] *pron./rfl.* myself.

moindre [mwɛ̃dr] less(er); **le** (**la**) ~ least; the slightest; **moindrement** [mwɛ̃drə'mɑ̃] *adv.*: **pas le ~** not in the least.

moine [mwan] *m* monk; **~au** [mwa'no] *m orn.* sparrow; *sl.* fellow.

moins [mwɛ̃] **1.** *adv.* less (than, *que*); fewer; **~ de deux** less than two; **à ~ de** (*inf.*), **à ~ que ... (ne)** (*sbj.*) unless; **au ~** at least; **de ~ en ~** less and less; **du ~** at least; at all events; **le ~** (the) least; **2.** *prp.* minus, less; **cinq heures ~ dix** ten minutes to five; **~-value** ✝ [~va'ly] *f* depreciation.

moire *tex.* [mwaːr] *f* watered silk.

mois [mwa] *m* month; month's pay; **double, treizième ~** extra month's pay.

mois|i [mwa'zi] **1.** *adj.* mo(u)ldy; musty; **2.** *su./m* mo(u)ld, mildew; **~ir** [~'ziːr] (2a) *v/i.* go mo(u)ldy; F *fig.* rot (*person*); *v/t.* make mo(u)ldy; **~issure** [~zi'syːr] *f* mo(u)ld(iness).

moisson [mwa'sɔ̃] *f* harvest(-time); **~ner** [mwasɔ'ne] (1a) harvest; reap; *fig.* gather; **~neur** [~'nœːr] *m* harvester; **~neuse** [~'nøːz] *f* harvester (*a. machine*); **~batteuse** combine harvester.

moite [mwat] moist, damp; clammy; **moiteur** [mwa'tœːr] *f* moistness.

moitié [mwa'tje] **1.** *su./f* half; F better half; **à ~ chemin** half-way; **à ~ prix** half-price; **2.** *adv.* half.

mol [mɔl] *see* **mou 1.**

molaire [mɔ'lɛːr] *adj., su./f* molar.

môle [moːl] *m* mole; pier.

molécul|aire [mɔleky'lɛːr] molecular; **~e** [~'kyl] *f* molecule.

molester [mɔlɛs'te] (1a) molest.

moll|asse F [mɔ'las] soft, flabby; **~e** [mɔl] *see* **mou 1;** **~esse** [mɔ'lɛs] *f* softness; flabbiness; slackness; **~et** [~'le] **1.** *adj.* softish; soft-boiled (*egg*); **2.** *su./m leg*: calf; **~etière** [mɔl'tjɛːr] *f* puttee; **~ir** [mɔ'liːr] (2a) soften; slacken; give way.

mollusque *zo.* [mɔ'lysk] *m* mollusc.

M

môme *sl.* [moːm] *su.* child: kid, brat.

moment [mɔˈmɑ̃] *m* moment (*a. phys.*); **au ~ où** (*or* **que**) just when; **par ~s** now and again; **pour le ~** for the time being; **~ané** [~mɑ̃taˈne] momentary; temporary.

momeries [mɔmˈri] *f/pl.* mumbo-jumbo.

momi|e [mɔˈmi] *f* mummy; **~fier** [~miˈfje] (1o) mummify.

mon *m*, **ma** *f*, *pl.* **mes** [mɔ̃, ma, me] *adj./poss.* my.

monacal *eccl.* [mɔnaˈkal] monastic.

monar|chie [mɔnarˈʃi] *f* monarchy; **~que** [mɔˈnark] *m* monarch.

monastère [mɔnasˈtɛːr] *m* monastery; *nuns*: convent.

monceau [mɔ̃ˈso] *m* heap, pile.

mond|ain [mɔ̃ˈdɛ̃] **1.** *adj.* mundane, wordly; fashionable; **la police ~e, la ☿** the vice squad; **2.** *su.* socialite; **~anité** [~daniˈte] *f* worldliness; **~e** [mɔ̃d] *m* world (*a. fig.*); people; *fig.* society; **au bout du ~** at the back of beyond; **dans le ~ entier** all over the world; **homme *m* du ~** man of good breeding; **il y a du ~** there is a crowd; **recevoir du ~** entertain (guests); **tout le ~** everyone; *fig.* **un ~ de** lots *pl.* of; **~ial** [mɔ̃ˈdjal] world-wide; world (*war*).

monétaire [mɔneˈtɛːr] monetary.

moniteur [mɔniˈtœːr] *m* school, *telev.*: monitor; *sp.* coach.

monn|aie [mɔˈnɛ] *f* money; (small) change; currency; **~ forte** hard currency; **donner la ~ de** give change for; **~ayer** [~nɛˈje] (li) coin; **~ayeur** [~nɛˈjœːr] *m*: **faux ~** forger, counterfeiter.

monobloc [mɔnɔˈblɔk] in one piece.

mono...: ~gramme [mɔnɔˈgram] *m* monogram; initials *pl.*; **~logue** [~ˈlɔg] *m* monolog(ue); **~loguer** [~lɔˈge] (1m) soliloquize.

mono...: ~phonie [mɔnɔfɔˈni] *f* monaural reproduction; **en ~** (in) mono; **~pole** [~ˈpɔl] *m* monopoly; **~poliser** [~pɔliˈze] (1a) monopolize; **~tone** [~ˈtɔn] monotonous; **~tonie** [~tɔˈni] *f* monotony.

monseigneur, *pl.* **messeigneurs** [mɔ̃sɛˈɲœːr, mɛsɛˈɲœːr] *m* My Lord; Your Grace; **monsieur**, *pl.* **messieurs** [məˈsjø, meˈsjø] *m* Mr.; sir; gentleman; *in letters*: Dear Sir.

monstr|e [mɔ̃ːstr] *adj.*, *su./m* monster; **~ueux** [mɔ̃stryˈø] monstrous; huge; **~uosité** [~oziˈte] *f* monstrosity.

mont [mɔ̃] *m* mount(ain).

montage [mɔ̃ˈtaːʒ] *m* putting up; hoisting; ⊕ assembling; *gun*, *phot.*, *etc.*: mounting; ⚡ wiring; *mot. tire*: fitting (on); *cin. film*: editing; ⊕ **chaîne *f* de ~** assembly line.

montagn|ard [mɔ̃taˈɲaːr] **1.** *adj.* mountain...; **2.** *su.* mountaineer, highlander; **~e** [~ˈtaɲ] *f* mountain; **la ~** the mountains *pl.*; **~eux** [~taˈnø] mountainous, hilly.

montant [mɔ̃ˈtɑ̃] **1.** *adj.* rising; uphill; ⛴ up (*train*, *platform*); *cost.* high necked; **2.** *su./m* ♱ amount, total; *ladder*, *window*: upright; (*tent-*)pole; *stair*: riser; (*lamp-*)post; *cuis.* strong taste, tang.

mont-de-piété, *pl.* **monts-de-piété** [mɔ̃dəpjeˈte] *m* pawnshop.

monte...: ~charge [mɔ̃tˈʃarʒ] *m/inv.* hoist; good lift; **~pente** [~ˈpɑ̃ːt] *m* ski lift.

mont|é, e [mɔ̃ˈte] **1.** *adj.* mounted (*a. police*); equipped; F *fig.* **coup *m* ~** put-up job; *fig.* **être ~** be worked up; **être ~ contre** be dead set against (*s.o.*); **2.** *su./f* going up; climb(ing); rise, rising; ascent; slope, hill(side); **~er** [~ˈte] (1a) *v/t.* climb (up), ascend; go upstairs; rise; amount (to, **à**); boil up (*milk*); **~ à** (*or* **sur**) **un arbre** climb a tree; **~ dans un train** get on a train, *Am.* board a train; **~ en avion** get into a plane; **~ sur un navire** get aboard a ship; **faire ~** raise (*prices*); *v/t.* mount (*a. phot.*, ✗ *guard*), climb, go up (*the stairs, a hill*); ride (*a horse*); set up; put up; raise; ⊕ *etc.* assemble; take up, carry up; turn up (*a lamp etc.*); equip; wind up (*a watch*); ⊕ assemble; *thea.* stage (*a play*); *fig.* plan, plot; F **~ la tête à q.** work s.o. up (against, **contre**); F **se ~ la tête** get worked up; **se ~** amount (to, **à**).

montr|e [mɔ̃ːtr] *f* watch; *sp. etc.* clock; show, display; **course *f* contre la ~** race against the clock; **faire ~ de** display; **~er** [mɔ̃ˈtre] (1a) show; display; indicate, point out; **se ~** *fig.* prove (o.s.); turn out; appear.

monture [mɔ̃ˈtyːr] *f* ⊕, *horse*, *picture*, *gem*: mount(ing); *spectacles*: frame;

M

gun etc.: stock; *sans* ~ rimless (*spectacles*).

monument [mɔny'mɑ̃] *m* monument; ~s *pl. town*: sights; **~al** [~mɑ̃'tal] monumental; F huge.

moquer [mɔ'ke] (1m): *se* ~ *de* make fun of; F *s'en* ~ not to care (a damn); **~ie** [mɔk'ri] *f* mockery.

moquette [mɔ'kɛt] *f* fitted carpet.

moqueur [mɔ'kœːr] **1.** *adj.* mocking; derisive; **2.** *su.* mocker.

moral, e [mɔ'ral] *adj. fig.* mental; **2,** *su./m* morale; (moral) nature; *su./f* morals *pl.*; *fables etc.*; moral; *faire la* ~ *à* preach at, lecture (*s.o.*); **~isateur** [mɔraliza'tœːr] moralizing (*person*); edifying; **~iser** [~li'ze] *vt/i.* moralize; *v/t.* preach at, lecture (*s.o.*); **~iste** [~'list] *su.* moralist; **~ité** [~li'te] *f* morality; morals *pl.*; *story*: moral.

moratoire [mɔra'twaːr] ⚖ moratory; ✝ *intérêts m/pl.* ~s interest *sg.* on over-due payments.

morbide [mɔr'bid] morbid, sickly.

morc|eau [mɔr'so] *m* piece; bit; scrap; **~eler** [~sə'le] (1c) cut up; divide (*land*); **~ellement** [~sɛl'mɑ̃] *m* cutting up; *land*: parcelling out.

mord|ant [mɔr'dɑ̃] biting; scathing, caustic; **~icus** [~mɔrdi'kys] *adv.* doggedly.

mordiller [mɔrdi'je] (1a) nibble.

mordoré [mɔrdɔ're] bronze.

mord|re [mɔrdr] (4a) *vt/i.* bite; ⚙ catch; ~ *sur* go over into; *v/t.* corrode (*metal*); *se* ~ *les lèvres* bite one's lips; *v/i. fig.* ~ *à* get one's teeth into; take to (*a subject*); **~u** F [mɔr'dy] crazy (about, *de*); *un* ~ *de ... à ...* fan.

morfondre [mɔr'fɔ̃dr] (4a): *se* ~ wait; *fig.* be bored.

morgue[1] [mɔrg] *f* haughtiness.

morgue[2] [~] *f* mortuary, morgue.

moribond [mɔri'bɔ̃] dying (person).

moricaud [mɔri'ko] dark-skinned.

morigéner [mɔriʒe'ne] (1f) scold.

morille 🍴 [mɔ'riːj] *f fungus*: moral.

morne [mɔrn] gloomy; dismal.

moros|e [mɔ'roːz] morose, surly; **~ité** [~rozi'te] *f* moroseness.

morphin|e 💉 [mɔr'fin] *f* morphine; **~omane** [~fino'man] morphia addict.

mors [mɔːr] *m harness*: bit; ⚙ jaw; *prendre le* ~ *aux dents* lose one's temper, get mad.

morse *zo.* [mɔrs] *f* walrus.

morsure [mɔr'syːr] *f* bite; *fig.* sting.

mort[1] [mɔːr] *f* death; *à* ~ deadly; *mourir de sa belle* ~ die in bed.

mort[2] [mɔːr] **1.** *p.p. of mourir*; **2.** *adj.* dead; stagnant (*water*); *paint. nature f* ~*e* still life; *poids m* ~ dead weight; *point m* ~ *mot.* neutral (*gear*); *fig.* dead-lock; **3.** *su.* dead person; *su./m* dummy (*at cards*); *fig. faire le* ~ sham dead.

mortaise ⚙ [mɔr'tɛːz] *f* mortise.

mort|alité [mɔrtali'te] *f* mortality; **~el** [mɔr'tɛl] **1.** *adj.* mortal; fatal (*accident etc.*); *fig.* boring; **2.** *su.* mortal; **~e-saison, ~es-saisons** ✝ mɔrtsɛ'zɔ̃] *f* slack season.

mortier △, ✗ [mɔr'tje] *m* mortar.

mort|ification [mɔrtifika'sjɔ̃] *f* mortification; **~ifier** [~'fje] (1o) mortify; **~né** [mɔr'ne] still-born (baby); **~uaire** [mɔr'tɥɛːr] mortuary; death ...; *drap m* ~ pall.

morue [mɔ'ry] *f icht.* cod; F slut.

morv|e [mɔrv] *f* mucus, V snot; **~eux** [mɔr'vo] **1.** *adj. vet.* glandered; F snotty; **2.** *su.* F greenhorn.

mosaïque [mɔza'ik] *f* mosaic.

mosquée [mɔs'ke] *f* mosque.

mot [mo] *m* word; note, line; saying; ~ *à* ~ word for word; ~ *d'ordre* watchword; *à* ~*s couverts* by hints; *avoir des* ~*s avec q.* fall out with s.o.; *en un* ~ in a word; *prendre q. au* ~ take s.o. at his word; *ne pas souffler* ~ keep one's mouth shut; *sans* ~ *dire* without a word.

motard F [mɔ'taːr] *m* motor cyclist; speed cop.

motel [mɔ'tɛl] *m* motel.

moteur, -trice [mɔ'tœːr, ~'tris] **1.** *adj.* motive, driving; *anat.* motory; **2.** *su./m* ⚙ motor; engine; *fig.* mover, driving force; ~ *à combustion interne*, ~ *à explosion* internal combustion engine; ~ *à deux temps* two-stroke engine; ~ *à réaction* jet engine.

motif [mɔ'tif] **1.** *adj.* motive; **2.** *su./m* motive; *fig.* grounds *pl.*; ♪ theme; *needlework*: pattern.

motion [mɔ'sjɔ̃] *f* motion; *parl.* ~ *de confiance* (*censure*) motion of confidence (no-confidence).

motiv|ation [mɔtiva'sjɔ̃] *f* motivation;

~er [~'ve] (1a) motivate; cause; ⚖ give the reasons for.

moto F [mɔ'to] *f* motor bike.

moto... [mɔtɔ] motor...; **~cyclette** [~si'klɛt] *f* motor cycle; **~cycliste** [~si'klist] *su.* motor cyclist; **~riser** [mɔtɔri'ze] (1a) motorize.

motte [mɔt] *f* clod; sod; (**~ de beurre**) butter pat.

motus! [mɔ'tys] *int.* keep it quiet!

mou (*adj. before vowel or h mute* **mol**) *m*, **molle** *f*, *m/pl.* **mous** [mu, mɔl, mu] **1.** *adj.* soft; weak; flabby; slack; close (*weather*); calm (*sea*); **2.** *su./m* slack; *cuis.* lights *pl.*

mouchard *pej.* [mu'ʃaːr] *m* (police) informer; **~er** [~ʃar'de] (1a) spy (on s.o.); *sl.* squeal (on s.o.).

mouche [muʃ] *f* fly; *target:* bull's-eye; spot, speck; patch (*on face*); **faire ~** hit the bull's-eye; **faire d'une ~ un éléphant** make a mountain out of a molehill; **prendre la ~** get angry; F **quelle ~ le pique?** what is biting him?

moucher [mu'ʃe] (1a) wipe (s.o.'s) nose; snuff (*a candle*); *fig.* snub (s.o.); **se ~** blow one's nose.

mouchet|er [muʃ'te] (1c) spot, fleck; **~ure** [muʃ'tyːr] *f* spot.

mouch|oir [mu'ʃwaːr] *m* handkerchief; **~ure** [~'ʃyːr] *f* (nasal) mucus.

moudre [mudr] (4w) grind.

moue [mu] *f* pout; **faire la ~** pout.

mouette *orn.* [mwɛt] *f* gull.

moufle [mufl] *f* mitt(en).

mouill|age [mu'jaːʒ] *m* wetting, moistening; *wine:* watering; ⚓ anchoring; **~er** [~'je] (1a) wet, soak; water (*wine etc.*); ⚓ drop (*the anchor*); **~ure** [~'jyːr] *f* wetting.

moulant [mu'lɑ̃] skintight (*dress*).

moule¹ [~'ly] *f* mussel.

moul|e² [mul] *m* ⊚ mo(u)ld; matrix; cast; **~er** [mu'le] (1a) ⊚ cast; mo(u)ld; *fig.* show the shape of, fit tightly (round); *fig.* **~ sur** model (*s.th.*) on; **écriture moulée** block letters *pl.*

moulin [mu'lɛ̃] *m* mill (*a.* ⊚); **~ à café** coffee-mill; **~ à vent** windmill.

moul|ons [mu'lɔ̃] *1st p. pl. pres. of* **moudre**; **~u** [~'ly] **1.** *adj. fig.* dead-beat, aching; **2.** *p.p. of* **moudre**.

moulure [mu'lyːr] *f* mo(u)lding.

moulus [mu'ly] *1st p. sg. p.s. of* **moudre**.

mour|ant [mu'rɑ̃] **1.** *adj.* dying; faint (*voice*); F screamingly funny; **2.** *su.* dying person; **~ir** [~'riːr] (2k) die; die out; fade; **~ avant l'âge** come to an untimely end; **être à ~ de rire** be screamingly funny; **~rai** [mur'rɛ] *1st p. sg. fut. of* **mourir**; **~us** [mu'ry] *1st p. sg. p.s. of* **mourir**.

mousse¹ [mus] *m* ship's boy.

mousse² [~] *f* ♣ moss; froth; foam; *soap:* lather; *cuis.* mousse.

mousse³ [~] blunt.

mousseline [mus'lin] **1.** *su./f tex.* muslin; **2.** *adj./inv.: cuis.* **pommes** *f/pl.* **~** mashed potatoes.

mouss|er [mu'se] (1a) froth; lather (*soap*); fizz; **~eux** [~'sø] mossy; foaming; sparkling (*wine*).

moussu [mu'sy] mossy.

moustach|e [mus'taʃ] *f* moustache; **~u** [~ta'ʃy] moustached.

moustiqu|aire [musti'kɛːr] *f* mosquito-net; **~e** [~'tik] *m* mosquito.

moût [mu] *m* grapes; must.

moutard|e [mu'tard] *f* mustard; **~ier** [~tar'dje] *m* mustard-pot.

mouton [mu'tɔ̃] *m* sheep; *cuis.* mutton; **~s** *pl.* fleecy clouds; *sea:* whitecaps; **revenons à nos ~s** let us get back to the subject; **~ner** [~to'ne] foam (*sea*); **ciel** *m* **moutonné** mackerel sky; **~neux** [muto'nø] fleecy (*sky*); frothy (*sea*); **~nier** [~'nje] sheeplike.

mouv|ance [mu'vɑ̃s] *f* domain, sphere (of influence); mobility, instability; **~ant** [~'vɑ̃] moving; shifting; loose (*ground*); **~ement** [muv'mɑ̃] *m* movement; motion (*a. phys.*); ⊕, *fig.* change; *roads etc.:* traffic; ⊚ *machine:* works *pl.; fig.* impulse; *fig.* outburst; ⊚ **~ perdu** idle motion; **~ populaire** popular uprising; **~ syndical** trade-unionism; ⚒ **faire un faux ~** strain o.s.; **~ementé** [~mɑ̃'te] lively; busy; eventful (*life*); undulating (*ground*).

mouv|oir [mu'vwaːr] (3f) ⊚ *etc.*, *fig.* drive, move, propel; *fig.* prompt; **~rai** [~'vrɛ] *1st p. sg. fut. of* **mouvoir**.

moyen, -enne [mwa'jɛ̃, ~'jɛn] **1.** *adj.* middle; average; medium (*size, quality*); ♀ **Âge** Middle Ages *pl.;* **2.** *su./m* means *sg.*, way; medium; ℞ mean; **~s** *pl.* resources; **au ~ de** by means of; **il (n')y a (pas) ~ de** (*inf.*) it is (im)possible to (*inf.*); **pas ~!** nothing doing!; *su./f* average, mean; **en ~enne** on average; **~âgeux** [~jɛnɑ'ʒø] (*pej.* sham-)medi-(a)eval, historic; *fig.* antiquated; **~nant** [~jɛ'nɑ̃] *prp.* for (*money etc.*); **~ quoi** in return for which.

moyeu [mwa'jø] *m* wheel: hub.

mû, mue, *m/pl.* **mus** [my] *p.p. of* **mouvoir.**

mucosité [mykozi'te] *f* mucus.

mue [my] *f* mo(u)lt(ing) (season) *etc.*; *see* **muer; muer** [mɥe] (1n) mo(u)lt (*birds*); slough (*snake*); shed its coat *etc.* (*animal*); break (*voice*); cast its antlers (*stag*).

muet [mɥɛ] dumb *or* mute (person).

mufl|e [myfl] *m* muzzle, nose; *fig.* F boor, lout; **~erie** F [myflə'ri] *f* boorishness.

mugi|r [my'ʒi:r] (2a) bellow; low (*cow*); howl; roar (*sea, a. fig.*); **~ssement** [~ʒis'mɑ̃] *m* bellowing *etc.*

muguet [my'gɛ] *m* ❀ lily of the valley; ✚ thrush.

mulâtre *m*, **-tresse** *f* [my'lɑ:tr, ~la'trɛs] mulatto.

mule¹ [myl] *f* mule, slipper.

mule² *zo.* [~] *f* (she-)mule.

mulet¹ *zo.* [my'lɛ] *m* mule.

mulet² *icht.* [~] *m* grey mullet.

mulot *zo.* [my'lo] *m* field mouse.

multi [mylti] many...; **~colore** [~kɔ'lɔ:r] multi-colo(u)red; **~latéral** [~late'ral] multilateral.

multipl|e [myl'tipl] *adj., su./m* multiple; **~ication** [~tiplika'sjɔ̃] *f* multiplication; ⚙ gear(-ratio); increase; **~ier** [~tipli'e] (1a) multiply.

multitude [mylti'tyd] *f* multitude; mass; crowd.

municipal [mynisi'pal] municipal; local, town...; bye-(*law*); **~ité** [~pali'te] *f* municipality.

muni|r [my'ni:r] (2a) equip, provide (with, *de*); **~tions** [myni'sjɔ̃] *f/pl.* ✗ ammunition *sg.*; **~ de bouche** provisions *pl.*

mûr [my:r] ripe; mature (*age etc.*).

mur [my:r] *m* wall; ✗ **~ du son** sound barrier; **~aille** [~'ra:j] *f* high *or* thick wall; ⚓ *ship*: side.

mûre ❀ [my:r] *f* blackberry.

murer [my're] (1a) wall in *or* up.

mûrier ❀ [my'rje] *m* mulberry (-bush *or* -tree); **~ sauvage** bramble.

mûrir [my'ri:r] (2a) *vt/i.* ripen, mature.

murmur|e [myr'my:r] *m* murmur; whisper; **~er** [~my're] (1a) murmur; whisper; babble; growl.

mus [my] *1st p. sg. p.s. of* **mouvoir.**

musard [my'za:r] **1.** *adj.* idling; **2.** *su.* idler; **~er** [~zar'de] (1a) dawdle.

muscade ❀ [mys'kad] *f* nutmeg.

muscat [mys'ka] *m* muscat (grape *or* wine); musk-pear.

musc|le [myskl] *m* muscle; *fig.* brawn; **~lé** [mys'kle] muscular; brawny; sinewy (*a. fig.*); *fig.* powerful; *fig.* strong-arm (*politics etc.*); **~ler** [~] (1a) strengthen; **~ulaire** [~ky'lɛ:r] muscular; **~uleux** [~ky'lø] muscular.

museau [my'zo] *m* muzzle, snout.

musée [my'ze] *m* museum.

musel|er [myz'le] (1c) muzzle (*a. fig.*); **~ière** [~zə'lje:r] *f* muzzle.

muser [my'ze] (1a) dawdle; loaf.

musette [my'zɛt] *f* bag; ♪ country bagpipe; **bal** *m* **~** popular dance.

musi|cal [myzi'kal] musical; **~c-hall** [myzi'ko:l] *m* variety, *Am.* vaudeville; **~cien** [myzi'sjɛ̃] **1.** *adj.* musical; **2.** *su.* musician; **~que** [my'zik] *f* music; band.

musulman [myzyl'mɑ̃] *adj., su.* Moslem.

mut|abilité [mytabili'te] *m* instability; **~ation** [~ta'sjɔ̃] *f* change; ♪, *biol.* mutation; *personnel, property:* transfer; **~er** [~'te] (1a) transfer.

muti|lation [mytila'sjɔ̃] *f* mutilation; maiming; **~é** [~'le] *m*: **~ de guerre** disabled ex-serviceman; **~ du travail** disabled workman; **~er** [~'le] (1a) mutilate; maim; deface.

mutin [my'tɛ̃] **1.** *adj.* mischievous; **2.** *su./m* mutineer; **~er** [~ti'ne] (1a): **se ~** rebel; ✗ mutiny; **~erie** [~tin'ri] *f* rebellion; ✗ mutiny.

mutisme [my'tism] *m fig.* silence; mutism.

mutu|alité [mytɥali'te] *f* mutuality; **~el, -elle** [my'tɥɛl] **1.** *adj.* mutual; **2.** *su./f* mutual insurance company.

myop|e [mjɔp] near-sighted (person); **~ie** [mjɔ'pi] *f* near-sightedness.

myrte ❀ [mirt] *m* myrtle; **myrtille** ❀ [mir'til] *f* blueberry, bilberry.

myst|ère [mis'tɛ:r] *m* mystery; secrecy; **~érieux** [~te'rjø] mysterious; **~icisme** [~ti'sism] *m* mysticism; **~ifier** [~ti'fje]

(1o) hoax; **~ique** [~'tik] adj., su. mystic; su./f mystical theology.
myth|e [mit] m myth (a. fig.); legend;

~ique [mi'tik] mythical; **~ologie** [mitɔlɔ'ʒi] f mythology; **~ologique** [~lɔ'ʒik] mythological.

N

nabot [na'bo] dwarf(ish).
nacelle [na'sɛl] f ⚓ skiff, wherry; ✈ cockpit; balloon: basket.
nacre [nakr] f mother of pearl; **nacré** [na'kre] pearly.
nag|e [naʒ] f swimming; rowing; stroke; **~ sur le dos** backstroke; **à la ~** by swimming; F (tout) en **~** bathed in perspiration; **~eoire** [na'ʒwaːr] f icht. fin; **~er** [~'ʒe] (1l) swim; float; **~ dans l'opulence** be rolling in money; **~eur** m, **-euse** f [~'ʒœːr, ~'ʒøːz] swimmer.
naguère [na'gɛːr] adv. lately.
naïf [na'if] naive, artless, simple.
nain [nɛ̃] m dwarf.
nais [nɛ] 1st p. sg. pres. of naître; **~sance** [nɛ'sãːs] f birth; fig. origin; fig. root, **acte m de ~** birth certificate; **Français de ~** French-born; fig. **prendre ~** originate; **~sant**, **~sã**] dawning; incipient; **~sent** [nɛs] 3rd p. pl. pres. of naître.
naître [nɛːtr] (4x) be born; dawn; begin; **faire ~** give rise to, cause.
naïveté [naiv'te] f ingenuousness.
nana sl. [na'na] f chick (= girl).
nantir [nã'tiːr] (2a) provide (with, de).
nanti [nã'ti] well-to-do.
napalm ✺, ✗ [na'palm] m napalm.
nappe [nap] f (table)cloth; cover; sheet; **~ de pétrole** oil slick; **~ron** [na'prɔ̃] m (table)mat.
naquis [na'ki] 1st p. sg. p.s. of naître.
narcisse ♀ [nar'sis] m narcissus.
narco|se ✷ [nar'koːz] f narcosis; **~tique** [~kɔ'tik] adj., su./m narcotic.
narguer [nar'ge] (1m) flout, scoff at.
narine [na'rin] f anat. nostril.
narquois [nar'kwa] mocking.
narr|ateur m, **-trice** f [nara'tœːr, ~'tris] narrator; **~atif** [~'tif] narrative; **~ation** [~'sjɔ̃] f narration; **~er** [na're] (1a) narrate, relate.

nas|al, **e** [na'zal] adj., su./f gramm. nasal; **~aliser** gramm. [~zali'ze] (1a) nasalize; **~eau** [~'zo] m nostril; **~iller** [nazi'jaːr] nasal, twanging; **~iller** [~'je] (1a) v/i. speak with a twang; v/t. twang (out).
natal, **e**, m/pl. **-als** [na'tal] native; **~ité** [~tali'te] f birth rate; natality.
natation [nata'sjɔ̃] f swimming.
natif [na'tif] adj., su. native.
nation [na'sjɔ̃] f nation; **~al**, **e**, m/pl. **-aux** [~sjo'nal, ~'no] 1. adj. national; 2. su./m: **~aux** pl. nationals; su./f (a. **route** f **~e**) highway; main road; **~alisation** [nasjɔnaliza'sjɔ̃] f nationalization; **~aliser** nationalize; **~alisme** pol. [~'lism] m nationalism; **~aliste** pol. [~'list] 1. su. nationalist; 2. adj. nationalistic; **~alité** [~li'te] f nationality; nation.
nativité [nativi'te] f nativity.
natt|e [nat] f mat(ting); hair: braid, **~er** [na'te] (1a) braid, plait (one's hair, straw).
naturali|sation [natyraliza'sjɔ̃] f pol. naturalization; ✷, zo. acclimatizing; **~ser** [~li'ze] (1a) naturalize (a. ✷, zo.); stuff (an animal); **~sme** paint. etc. [~'lism] m naturalism; **~ste** [~'list] 1. su. naturalist; taxidermist; 2. adj. naturalistic; **~té** [~li'te] f naturalness;
natur|e [na'tyːr] 1. su./f nature; paint. **d'après ~** from nature; **de ~ à** (inf.) likely to (inf.), such as to (inf.); **de ~ par ~** by nature, naturally; **payer en ~** pay in kind; 2. adj./inv. cuis. etc. plain; **~el** [naty'rɛl] 1. adj. natural; 2. su./m disposition, nature; naturalness; cuis. **au ~** plain.
naufrag|e [no'fraːʒ] m shipwreck (a. fig.); **faire ~** be shipwrecked; **~é** [nofra'ʒe] shipwrecked (person).
nausé|abond [nozea'bɔ̃] nauseous;

evil-smelling; **~e** [~'ze] *f* nausea; sea-sickness; *fig.* loathing; **avoir la ~** feel sick; **~eux** [~ze'ø] nauseous; loathsome.

nautique [no'tik] ⚓ nautical; sea...; aquatic, water... (*sports*).

naval, e, *m/pl.* **-als** [na'val] naval, nautical; **constructions** *f/pl.* **~es** ship-building *sg.*

navet [na'vɛ] *m* turnip; F tripe, rubbish.

navette [na'vɛt] *f* shuttle (service); **~ spatiale** space shuttle; **faire la ~** ⚓ *etc.* ply; commute; come and go, shuttle.

navig|abilité [naviɡabili'te] *f* navigability; **~able** [~'ɡabl] navigable; **~ateur** [~ɡa'tœːr] **1.** *adj./m* seafaring; **2.** *su./m* navigator; sailor; **~ation** [~ɡa'sjɔ̃] *f* navigation, sailing; **~uer** [~'ɡe] (1m) navigate.

naviplane ⚓ [navi'plan] *m* hovercraft.

navire ⚓ [na'viːr] *m* ship, vessel; **~ de commerce** merchantman.

navrer [na'vre] (1a) grieve (*s.o.*) deeply; **j'en suis navré!** I am awfully *or* F terribly sorry!

ne [nə] *adv.*: **ne ... pas** not; **ne ... plus jamais** never again.

né [ne] **1.** *p.p. of* **naître; 2.** *adj.* born; **bien ~** of a good family.

néanmoins [neɑ̃'mwɛ̃] *adv.* nevertheless, however; yet.

néant [ne'ɑ̃] *m* nothing(ness); none; **réduire à ~** annihilate, dash.

nébul|eux, -euse [neby'lø, ~'løːz] **1.** *adj.* nebulous; cloudy; misty; F *fig.* obscure; **2.** *su./f astr.* nebula; **~osité** [~lozi'te] *f* haziness.

nécess|aire [nesɛ'sɛːr] **1.** *adj.* necessary (to, for **à**); **2.** *su./m* necessaries *pl.*; kit, set; **~ de toilette** toilet bag; **~ité** [~si'te] *f* necessity; indigence; **~iter** [~si'te] (1a) necessitate; **~iteux** [~si'tø] needy.

nécro|loge [nekrɔ'lɔːʒ] *m* obituary list; **~logie** [~lɔ'ʒi] *f* obituary.

néerlandais(e) [neɛrlɑ̃'dɛ[z]] **1.** *adj.* Dutch; **2.** *su.* ♀ Netherlander.

nef [nɛf] *f church:* nave; *poet.* ship.

néfaste [ne'fast] ill-fated; fatal.

négati|f [neɡa'tif] **1.** *adj.* negative; **2.** *su./m phot.* negative; **~on** [~'sjɔ̃] *f* negation; **~ve** [~'tiːv] *f:* **dans la ~** in the negative, if not; **répondre par la ~** say no.

néglig|é [negli'ʒe] **1.** *adj.* careless (*ap-

pearance, dress*); **2.** *su./m* undress; informal dress; dishabille; **~eable** [~'ʒabl] negligible; trifling; **~ence** [~'ʒɑ̃ːs] *f* negligence, neglect; oversight; **~ent** [~'ʒɑ̃] negligent, careless; **~er** [~'ʒe] (1l) neglect; be careless about; pay no heed to; overlook; disregard; **~ de** (*inf.*) neglect *or* fail to (*inf.*).

négoc|e [ne'ɡɔs] *m* trade, business; **~iable** ✝ [neɡo'sjabl] negotiable; **~iant** [~'sjɑ̃] *m* merchant; trader; **~iateur,** *m* **-trice** *f* [~sja'tœːr, ~'tris] negotiator; **~iation** [~sja'sjɔ̃] *f* negotiation; **~ier** [~'sje] (1o) *vt/i.* negotiate.

nègre [nɛːɡr] *m* negro; F ghost writer; **négresse** [ne'ɡrɛs] *f* negress.

neig|e [nɛːʒ] *f* snow (*a. sl. cocaine*); **~s** *pl.* **éternelles** perpetual snow *sg.*; **~ 🐾 carbonique** dry ice; **boule** *f* **de ~** snowball; **~er** [nɛ'ʒe] (1l) *v/impers.* snow; **~eux** [~'ʒø] snowy.

nénuphar [neny'faːr] *m* water-lily.

néo... [neo] neo-...; **~logisme** [~lɔ'ʒism] *m* neologism.

néon 🐾 [ne'ɔ̃] *m* neon; **éclairage** *m* **au ~** neon lighting.

nerf [nɛːr] *m anat.* nerve; *fig.* vigo(u)r, F guts *pl.*; *fig.* **avoir du ~** be vigorous; **avoir ses ~s** be on edge; **porter** (*or* **donner** *or* **F taper**) **sur les ~s à q.** get on s.o.'s nerves.

nerv|eux [nɛr'vø] nervous; sinewy; high-strung; *fig.* virile (*style etc.*); **~osité** [~vozi'te] *f* nervousness; irritability; irritation; **~ure** [~'vyːr] *f* vein; △ rib.

net, -te [nɛt] **1.** *adj.* clean; neat; clear; clear-cut, distinct; ✝ net; **2.** *net adv.* plainly, flatly; clearly; **refuser ~** refuse point-blank; **3.** *su./m:* **copie** *f* **au ~** fair copy; **mettre qch. au ~** make a fair copy of s.th.; **~teté** [nɛtə'te] *f* cleanness; clarity; distinctness; *fig.* decidedness; **~toiement** [nɛtwa'mɑ̃] *m* cleaning; clearing; **~toyage** [~'ja:ʒ] *m* cleaning; **~ à sec** dry-cleaning; **~toyer** [~'je] (1h) clean; clear; ⚙ scale; F clean out; **~ à sec** dry-clean.

neuf¹ [nœf; *before vowel or h mute* nœv] nine; *date, title:* ninth.

neuf², neuve [nœf, nœːv] **1.** *adj.* new; *fig.* inexperienced; **2.** *su./m* new; **quoi de ~?** what's new?; **remettre à ~** do up (like new).

neur|asthénie 🏥 [nøraste'ni] *f* neurasthenia; **~asthénique** [~'nik] neurasthenic; **~ologue** [nørɔ'lɔg] *m* neurologist.

neutr|aliser [nøtrali'ze] (1a) neutralize; **~alité** [~li'te] *f* neutrality; **~e** [nø:tr] neuter; neutral.

neutron *phys.* [nø'trɔ̃] *m* neutron.

neuvième [nœ'vjɛm] ninth.

neveu [nə'vø] *m* nephew.

név|ralgie [nevral'ʒi] *f* neuralgia; **~ralgique** [~'ʒik] neuralgic; *fig.* **point** *m* **~** sore spot; **~rose** [ne'vro:z] *f* neurosis; **~rosé** [nevro'ze] neurotic; **~rotique** [~'tik] neurotic.

nez [ne] *m* nose; *animal:* snout; ♪, ♫ bow, nose; scent; F **~ à ~** face to face; **au ~ de q.** under s.o.'s nose; F **avoir q. dans le ~** bear s.o. a grudge; **mener par le bout du ~** lead by the nose; **mettre le ~ dans** poke one's nose into.

ni [ni] *cj.* nor, or; **ni ... ni** neither ... nor; **ni moi non plus** nor I.

niable [njabl] deniable.

niais [njɛ] **1** *adj.* simple, silly; **2.** *su.* fool, simpleton; **~erie** [njɛz'ri] *f* foolishness, silliness.

niche [niʃ] *f* trick, practical joke.

niche² [niʃ] *f* niche, recess; **~ à chien** kennel; **~ée** [ni'ʃe] *f* nestful; brood; **~er** [~] *v/i.* nest; F *fig.* live, hang out; *v/t.:* **se ~** nest; *fig.* nestle; *fig.* lodge or put o.s.

nickel [ni'kɛl] *m* nickel; **~age** ◎ [ni'kla:ʒ] *m* nickel-plating.

nicotine [niko'tin] *f* nicotine.

nid [ni] *m* nest; **~ de poule** pothole; **~ifier** [nidi'fje] (1a) nest.

nièce [njɛs] *f* niece.

nier [nje] (1o) deny; repudiate (*a debt*); **on ne saurait ~ que** there can be no denying that.

nigaud [ni'go] **1.** *adj.* simple, silly; **2.** *su.* simpleton.

nimbe [nɛ̃:b] *m* nimbus, halo; **nimbé** [nɛ̃'be] haloed.

nipp|er F [ni'pe] (1a) rig (*s.o.*) out; **~es** F [nip] *f/pl.* old clothes; togs.

nique F [nik] *f:* **faire la ~ à** cock a snook at (*s.o.*); make fun of (*s.o.*).

nitouche [ni'tuʃ] *f:* **sainte ~** (little) hypocrite, goody-goody.

nitr|ate [ni'trat] *m* nitrate; **~e** [nitr] *m* saltpetre, *Am.* saltpeter.

nive|au [ni'vo] *m* level (*a.* ◎); *fig.* standard; ◎ ga(u)ge; *mot.* **~ d'essence** petrol gauge, *Am.* gasoline level gage; **~ de vie** standard of living; *pol.* **~ le plus élevé** highest level; **de ~** level (with, *avec*); ⬛ **passage** *m* **à ~** level (*Am.* grade) crossing; **~ler** [niv'le] (1c) level; ◎ true up; survey (*the ground*); **~llement** [nivel'mã] *m* land: surveying; levelling.

nob|iliaire [nɔbi'ljɛ:r] nobiliary; **~le** [nɔbl] **1.** *adj.* noble; lofty (*style*); **2.** *su.* person of noble birth; **~lesse** [nɔ'blɛs] *f* nobility (*a. fig.*).

noce [nɔs] *f* wedding; wedding party; **~s** *pl* **d'argent (d'or)** silver (golden) wedding *sg.*; F **faire la ~** go on the spree, live it up; **voyage** *m* **de ~s** honeymoon (trip); **noceur** *m*, **-euse** *f* F [nɔ'sœːr, ~'søːz] reveller; fast liver.

nocif [nɔ'sif] harmful, noxious; **nocivité** [~sivi'te] *f* harmfulness.

noct|ambule [nɔktã'byl] *su.* night bird, late-nighter; **~urne** [~'tyrn] **1.** *adj.* nocturnal; by night; **2.** *su./m* ♪ nocturne.

Noël [nɔ'ɛl] *m* Christmas; **le Père** (or **Bonhomme**) **~** Santa Claus; **joyeux ~!** merry Christmas!

nœud [nø] *m* knot (*a.* ⚓); *band:* bow; *fig.* tie, bond; *fig. question etc.*: crux; ♀, ☿, ♃ node; ⬛ junction.

noir, e [nwa:r] **1.** *adj.* black; dark; *fig.* gloomy (*thoughts*); *fig.*: illegal, illicit; *sl.* dead drunk; **2.** *su./m* black; negro; dark(ness); *fig.* **~ sur blanc** in black and white; **au ~** illegally, illicitly; **travailler au ~** moonlight; **broyer du ~** be in the dumps; **prendre le ~** go into mourning; **voir tout en ~** look on the black side of things; *su./f* black woman, negress; ♪ crotchet; **~âtre** [nwa'ra:tr] blackish, darkish; **~aud** [~'ro] swarthy (*person*); **~eur** [nwar'sœːr] *f* blackness; darkness; *fig.* gloominess; *fig.* foulness; **~oir** [~'si:r] (2a) *v/t.i.* blacken (*a. fig.*); **se ~** darken; **~cissure** [~si'sy:r] *f* smudge.

noise [nwa:z] *f:* **chercher ~ à** pick a quarrel with, *Am.* pick on.

noisetier ♀ [nwaz'tje] *m* hazel (tree); **noisette** [nwa'zɛt] **1.** *su./f* ♀ hazel-nut; **2.** *adj./inf.* (nut)brown; hazel (*eyes*); **noix** [nwa] *f* ♀ (wal)nut; *cuis.* **~ de veau** shoulder of veal.

nom [nɔ̃] *m* name; *gramm.* noun; reputation; ~ *de famille* surname; ~ *de guerre* assumed name; ~ *de jeune fille* maiden name; ~ *de plume* pen-name; ✝ ~ *déposé* registered trade name; *de* ~ by name; *du* ~ *de* called; *petit* ~ Christian name, *Am.* given name.

nomade [nɔ'mad] **1.** *adj.* wandering; nomadic; **2.** *su.* nomad.

nombr|able [nɔ̃'brabl] countable; ~*e* [nɔ̃:br] *m* number (*a. gramm.*); ~ *impair* (*pair, premier*) odd (even, prime) number; *bon* ~ *de* a good many ...; *au or du* ~ *de* one of; *sans* ~ countless; ~*er* [nɔ̃'bre] (1a) count; ~*reux* [~'brø] numerous.

nombril *anat.* [nɔ̃'bri] *m* navel.

nomina|l [nɔmi'nal] nominal; of names; ✝ *valeur f* ~*e* face value; ~*tif*,[~na'tif] *m* nominative; ~*tion* [~na'sjɔ̃] *f* nomination; appointment (to, *à*).

nomm|é [nɔ'me] **1.** *adj.* appointed (*day*); *à point* ~ at the right moment; **2.** *su.*: *un* ~ *Jean* one John; ~*ément* [~me'mɑ̃] *adv.* by name; especially; ~*er* [~'me] (1a) name; appoint; *se* ~ be called.

non [nɔ̃] *adv.* no; not; ~ *pas!* not at all!; ~ (*pas*) *que* (*sbj.*) not that (*ind.*); *dire que* ~ say no; *ne ... pas* ~ *plus* not ... either.

non-agression [nɔnagrε'sjɔ̃] *f*: *pacte m de* ~ non-aggression pact.

nonce [nɔ̃:s] *m* nuncio; ~ *apostolique* papal nuncio.

nonchalan|ce [nɔ̃ʃa'lɑ̃:s] *f* nonchalance; ~*t* [~'lɑ̃] nonchalant.

non...: ~*combattant* ⚔ [nɔ̃kɔba'tɑ̃] *m* non-combattant; ~*conformisme* [~kɔ̃fɔr'mism] *m* nonconformity; ~*engagé* [~ɑ̃ga'ʒe] non-aligned (country).

nonne [nɔn] *f* nun.

nonobstant [nɔnɔp'stɑ̃] **1.** *prp.* notwithstanding; **2.** *adv.* ✝ for all that.

nonpareil, -eille [nɔ̃pa'rε:j] matchless, unparalleled.

non...: ~*retour* [nɔ̃rə'tu:r] *m*: *point m de* ~ point of no return; ~*réussite* [~rey'sit] *f* failure; ~*sens* [~'sɑ̃:s] *m* meaningless act *or* expression; ~*valeur* [~va'lœ:r] *f* worthless object *or* person.

nord [nɔ:r] **1.** *su./m* north; *du* ~ north(ern); *fig.* *perdre le* ~ lose one's bearings; **2.** *adj./inv.* northern; ~*est* [nɔ'rεst] **1.** *su./m* north-east; **2.** *adj./inv.* north-eastern; ~*ouest* [nɔ'rwεst] **1.**

su./m north-west; **2.** *adj./inv.* north-western.

normal, e [nɔr'mal] **1.** *adj.* normal; usual; standard (*measures etc.*); natural; *Ecole f* ~*e* (teachers') training college; **2.** *su./f* norm; *au-desous de la* ~ above average; *revenir à la* ~ get back to normal; ~*isation* [nɔrmaliza'sjɔ̃] *f* standardization; ~*iser* [~li'ze] (1a) standardize; normalize.

normand [nɔr'mɑ̃] **1.** *adj.* Norman; *F réponse f* ~*e* non-committal answer; **2.** *su.* 2 Norman.

norme [nɔrm] *f* norm, standard.

norvégien [nɔrve'ʒjɛ̃] *adj.,* *su.* Norwegian.

nos [no] *pl.* of *notre.*

nostalgi|e [nɔstal'ʒi] *f* nostalgia; *fig.* homesickness; *fig.* yearning; ~*que* [~'ʒik] nostalgic; homesick.

notab|ilité [nɔtabili'te] *f* notability (*a. person*); *fig.* prominent person; ~*le* [nɔ'tabl] *adj.,* *su./m* notable.

notaire [nɔ'tε:r] *m* notary (public).

notamment [nɔta'mɑ̃] *adv.* particularly, especially.

not|e [nɔt] *f* note (*a.* ♪, *pol., fig.*); memo(randum); *school:* mark; *journ.* notice; ✝ account, bill; *prendre* ~ *de* note; *prendre des* ~*s* jot down notes; ~*er* [nɔ'te] (1a) note; note down, write down.

notice [nɔ'tis] *f* note, notice.

notifi|cation [nɔtifika'sjɔ̃] *f* notification, notice; ~*er* [~'fje] (1o) notify (s.o. of s.th., *qch. à q.*).

not|ion [nɔ'sjɔ̃] *f* notion, idea; ~*s pl.* smattering *sg.*; ~*oire* [~'twa:r] well-known; *pej.* notorious; ~*oriété* [~tɔrje'te] *f* notoriety; repute.

notre, *pl.* **nos** [nɔtr, no] *adj./poss.* our.

nôtre, *pl.* **nos** **1.** *pron./poss.*: *le* (*la*) ~, *les* ~*s pl.* ours; **2.** *su./m* ours, our own; *les* ~*s pl.* our (own) people.

nou|er [nwe] (1p) *v/t.* tie (up); knot; *fig.* enter into (*conversation, relations*); *v/i.* set (*fruit*); ~*eux* [nwø] knotty; ✿ arthritic; gnarled.

nouille [nu:j] *f cuis.* noodle; *F* spineless individual, drip, idiot.

nourr|ice [nu'ris] *f* wet nurse; ⊚ service *or* feed tank; ~*icier* [~ri'sje] nutritious; foster-(*father, mother*); ~*ir* [~'ri:r] (2a) *v/t.* feed, nourish; nurse (*a baby*); *fig.*

harbo(u)r (*hope, thoughts*); foster (*hatred*); strengthen; support (*a family*); **se ~ de** live on; *v/i.* be nourishing; **~issant** [~'sɑ̃] nourishing; **~isseur** [~'sœːr] *m* dairyman; **~isson** [~'sɔ̃] *m* baby at the breast; **~iture** [~'tyːr] *f* feeding; food; **la ~ et le logement** board and lodging.

nous [nu] **1.** *pron./pers. subject*: we; *object*: us; (to) us; **à ~** to us; ours; **ce sont ~,** F **c'est ~** it is we, F it's us; **2.** *pron./rfl.* ourselves; **3.** *pron./recip.* one another; **~mêmes** [~'mɛːm] *pron./rfl.* ourselves.

nouv|eau (*adj. before vowel or h mute* **-el**) *m*, **-elle** [nu'vo, ~'vɛl] **1.** *adj.* new; recent, fresh; another, further; novel; **~eaux riches** *m/pl.* newly rich; **le plus ~** latest; **qch. (rien) de ~** s.th. (nothing) new, **quoi de ~?** what's the news?; **~ venu** *m*, **nouvelle venue** *f* newcomer; **2. nouveau** *adv.*: **à ~, de ~** again; **~eau-né** [nuvo'ne] **1.** *adj.* new-born; **2.** *su./m* new-born child; **~eauté** [~'te] *f* newness, novelty; latest model; **✝ ~s** *pl.* fancy goods; **~el** [nu'vɛl] **1.** *adj. see* **nouveau; ~ an** *m* New Year; **~elle** [nu'vɛl] **1.** *adj. see* **nouveau**; **2.** *su./f* news *sg.*; short story; **avoir des ~s de q.** hear from *or* of s.o.; **~elliste** [~ɛ'list] *su.* short-story writer.

novateur [nɔva'tœːr] **1.** *adj.* innovating; **2.** *su.* innovator.

novembre [nɔ'vɑ̃ːbr] *m* November.

novic|e [nɔ'vis] **1.** *adj.* inexperienced (in **à, dans**); **2.** *su.* novice.

noyade [nwa'jad] *f* drowning.

noyau [nwa'jo] *m fruit*: stone, pit, kernel; *phys., biol., fig.* nucleus; ⚡ core; *fig.* group; *pol.* cell; *fig.* **~ dur** hard core; **~tage** [~jo'taːʒ] *m pol.* infiltration (into, **de**).

noyer¹ [nwa'je] (1h) drown (*a. fig.*); flood (*a. mot.*), immerse; **se ~** drown o.s.; be drowned, drown.

noyer² ⚘ [~] *m* walnut(-tree).

nu [ny] **1.** *adj.* naked, nude, bare; **pieds ~s** barefoot(ed); **2.** *su./m* nude; nudity;

3. *adv.*: **à nu** bare; **mettre à nu** lay bare; denude.

nuag|e [nɥa:ʒ] *m* cloud; **sans ~s** *fig.* perfect (*bliss*); **~eux** [nɥa'ʒø] cloudy, overcast; *fig.* hazy (*idea*).

nuance [nɥɑ̃:s] *f* shade (*a. fig.*), hue; *fig.* tinge; *fig.* nuance.

nubile [ny'bil] marriageable.

nucléaire *phys.* [nykle'ɛːr] nuclear.

nudi|sme [ny'dism] *m* nudism; **~té** [~di'te] *f* nakedness; bareness.

nue [ny] *f* high cloud; *fig.* **porter aux ~s** praise to the skies; *fig.* **tomber des ~s** be thunderstruck; **nuée** [nɥe] *f* storm-cloud; *fig.* swarm.

nuire [nɥiːr] (4u *a.* h): **~ à** harm, hurt; be injurious to; **nuisance** [nɥi'zɑ̃:s] *f environment*: nuisance; **nuisant** [~'zɑ̃] harmful, polluting, **nuisibilité** [~zibili'te] *f* harmfulness; **nuisible** [~'zibl] harmful, injurious.

nuit [nɥi] *f* night; dark(ness); **de ~** by night; **Il fait ~** it is *or* it's getting dark; **la ~ tombe** night is falling; **à la ~ tombante** at nightfall; **passer la ~** stay overnight (with, **chez**); **~ée** [nɥi'te] *f* night's work; overnight stay.

nul, ~le [nyl] **1.** *adj.* no, not one; void, null; *sp.* drawn (*game*); non-existent; *t͗t* invalid; **2.** *pron./indef.* no(t) one, nobody; **~lement** [nyl'mɑ̃] *adv.* not at all; **~lité** [nyli'te] *f t͗t* nullity, invalidity; *person*: nonentity; *fig.* incapacity.

numér|aire [nyme'rɛːr] *m* cash; metal currency; **~al** [~'ral] numeral, **~ation** ⵜ [~ra'sjɔ̃] *f* numeration; number system; **~ique** [~'rik] numerical; **~o** [~'ro] *m* number; *periodical*: issue, copy; F fellow; **~otage** [~rɔ'taːʒ] *m* numbering; *book*: paging; **~oter** [~rɔ'te] (1a) number; page (*a book*).

nuptial [nyp'sjal] bridal; wedding...

nuque [nyk] *f* nape of the neck.

nutriti|f [nytri'tif] nourishing; food...; **~on** [~'sjɔ̃] *f* nutrition.

nylon *tex.* [ni'lɔ̃] *m* nylon.

nymph|e *myth., zo.* [nɛ̃f] *f* nymph; **~éa** ⚘ [nɛ̃fe'a] *m* water-lily.

O

oasis [ɔa'zis] f oasis.

obédience [ɔbe'djã:s] f obedience; (*religious*) persuasion; *pol. etc.* allegiance.

obéi|r [ɔbe'i:r] (2a): ~ **à** obey; comply with (*s.th.*); *mot. etc., a. fig.* respond to; **se faire** ~ compel obedience (from, *par*); ~**ssance** [~i'sã:s] f obedience; ~**ssant** [~i'sã] obedient.

obélisque [ɔbe'lisk] m obelisk.

obéré [ɔbe're] (1f) (*a.* ~ **de dettes**) burdened with debt.

obèse [ɔ'bɛ:z] stout (person); **obésité** [ɔbezi'te] f obesity, corpulence.

obier ♀ [ɔ'bje] m guelder rose.

object|er [ɔbʒɛk'te] (1a) put forward, raise as an objection (to, **à**); plead, pretext; ~**eur** [~'tœ:r] m: ✕ ~ **de conscience** conscientious objector; ~**if** [~'tif] **1.** *adj.* objective; **2.** *su./m opt.* objective, lens; ✕, *fig.* objective, target; ~**ion** [~'sjõ] f objection; ✕ ~ **de conscience** conscientious objection; ~**ivité** [~tivi'te] f objectivity.

objet [ɔb'ʒɛ] m object; subject; item; *fig.* purpose, object(ive); ~**s** *pl.* **trouvés** lost property *sg.*

obligation [ɔbliga'sjõ] f obligation, duty; ♰ bond; ~**oire** [~'twa:r] obligatory; binding; **enseignement** m ~ compulsory education; ✕ **service** m **militaire** ~ compulsory military service.

oblig|é [ɔbli'ʒe] obliged, bound, compelled (to *inf.*, **de** *inf.*); indispensable; inevitable; *fig.* obliged, grateful; **être** ~ **de** (*inf.*) *a.* have to (*inf.*); ~**eamment** [~ʒa'mã] *adv.* of **obligeant**; ~**eance** [~'ʒã:s] f kindness; ~**eant** [~'ʒã] obliging; kind; ~**er** [~'ʒe] (1l) oblige (to, **à**); compel (to, **de**); do (*s.o.*) a favo(u)r; **s'**~ **à** bind o.s. to.

obliqu|e [ɔ'blik] **1.** *adj.* oblique; slanting; *fig.* **regard** m ~ sidelong glance; **2.** *su./f* oblique line; ~**er** [ɔbli'ke] (1m) turn off; ~**ité** [~ki'te] f obliqueness.

oblitér|ation [ɔblitera'sjõ] f cancellation; ~**er** [~'re] (1f) cancel (*a stamp*).

oblong [ɔ'blõ] oblong.

obnubiler [ɔbnybi'le] (1a) obsess.

obole [ɔ'bɔl] f (small) contribution; **apporter son** ~ **à** contribute one's mite to.

obscène [ɔp'sɛn] obscene; smutty; **obscénité** [~seni'te] f obscenity.

obscur [ɔps'ky:r] dark; gloomy; obscure; dim; humble (*person*); ~**cir** [~kyr'si:r] (2a) obscure; darken; dim; **s'**~ grow dark; become obscure *or* dim; ~**cissement** [~kyrsis'mã] m obscuring; darkening; ~**ité** [~kyri'te] f darkness; obscurity.

obséder [ɔpse'de] (1f) obsess; beset.

obsèques [ɔp'sɛk] f/pl. funeral *sg.*

obséqui|eux [ɔpse'kjø] obsequious; ~**osité** [~kjozi'te] f obsequiousness.

observ|able [ɔpsɛr'vabl] observable; ~**ance** [~'vã:s] f observance (*a. eccl.*); ~**ateur** [~va'tœ:r] **1.** *adj./m* observant; **2.** *su.* observer; ~**ation** [~va'sjõ] f observation; *rule:* observance; reproof, reprimand; ~**atoire** [~va'twa:r] m *astr.* observatory; observation post; ~**er** [~'ve] (1a) observe; keep (*a rule etc.*); watch; **faire** ~ **qch. à q.** draw s.o.'s attention to s.th.; **s'**~ be careful (doing s.th., **pour faire qch.**).

obsessi|f [ɔpsɛ'sif] obsessive; ~**on** [~'sjõ] f obsession.

obstacle [ɔps'takl] m obstacle; *sp.* hurdle; *sp.* **course** f **d'**~**s** obstacle *or* hurdle race; **faire** ~ **à** stand in the way of; hinder; obstruct.

obstin|ation [ɔpstina'sjõ] f obstinacy; ~**é** [~'ne] obstinate; ~**er** [~'ne] (1a): **s'**~ show obstinacy; insist (on *ger.*, **à** *inf.*); **s'**~ **à** (*inf.*) persist in (*ger.*).

obstru|ctif [ɔpstryk'tif] obstructive; ~**ction** [~'sjõ] f obstruction; ~**ctionnisme** *pol.* [~sjɔ'nism] m filibustering; ~**er** [ɔpstry'e] (1a) obstruct, block.

obtempérer [ɔptãpe're] (1f): ~ **à** comply with, obey.

obten|ir [ɔptə'ni:r] (2h) obtain, get; ~ **de** (*inf.*) be allowed to (*inf.*); ~ **de q. que** (*sbj.*) get s.o. to (*inf.*); ~**tion** [~tã'sjõ] f obtaining.

obtur|ateur [ɔptyra'tœ:r] *phot.* shutter; *mot.* throttle; ~**ation** [~ra'sjõ] f obturation; closing; filling; ~**er** [~'re] (1a) seal (up); stop,fill (*a tooth*).

obtus [ɔp'ty] obtuse; *fig. a.* dull.

obus ✕ [ɔ'by] m shell.

obvier [ɔb'vje] (1o): ~ **à** obviate.

oc [ɔk] *adv. langue f d'~* Langue d'oc, Old Provençal.

occasion [ɔka'zjɔ̃] *f* opportunity; occasion; ✝ bargain; ✝ secondhand buy; *à l'~ de* on the occasion of; *d'~* casual; ✝ second-hand; *par ~* occasionally; ~**ner** [~zjo'ne] (1a) cause; bring about.

occident [ɔksi'dɑ̃] *m* west; ~**al** [~dɑ'tal] **1.** *adj.* west(ern), occidental; **2.** *su.* occidental, westerner.

occire ✝ [ɔk'siːr] (4y) kill, slay; **occis** [~'si] *p.p.* of *occire.*

occlusion [ɔkly'zjɔ̃] *f* obstruction.

occulte [ɔ'kylt] occult; secret.

occup|ant [ɔky'pɑ̃] *m* occupant; 🏠, ✗ occupier; ~**ation** [~pa'sjɔ̃] *f* occupation (*a.* ✗); employment; *sans ~* unemployed; ~**er** [~'pe] (1a) occupy (*a.* ✗); employ (*workers etc.*); *s'~ à* be busy with; *s'~ de* see to; take care of; deal with; be in charge of; look after; attend to; take an interest in.

occurrence [ɔky'rɑ̃ːs] *f* case; *en l'~* in this (special) case.

océan [ɔse'ɑ̃] *m* ocean, sea (*a. fig.*); ~**ique** [~a'nik] oceanic, ocean...

ocre [ɔkr] *f* ochre.

octane 🔥 [ɔk'tan] *m* octane.

octobre [ɔk'tɔbr] *m* October.

octogone ▲ [ɔktɔ'gɔn] *m* octagon.

octro|i [ɔk'trwa] *m* grant(ing); *hist.* city toll; ~**yer** [~trwa'je] (1h) grant.

ocul|aire [ɔky'lɛːr] **1.** *adj.* ocular, eye ...; **2.** *su./m opt.* eyepiece; ~**iste** [~'list] *su.* oculist.

odeur [ɔ'dœːr] *f* smell; scent.

odieux [ɔ'djø] odious; hateful.

odor|ant [ɔdɔ'rɑ̃] fragrant; scented; ~**at** [~'ra] *m* (sense of) smell; ~**iférant** [~rife'rɑ̃] fragrant.

Oedipe [e'dip] *m*: (*complexe m d'~*) Oedipus complex.

œil, *pl.* **yeux** [œj, jø] *m* eye; *bread, cheese:* hole; notice, attention; *à l'~* by the eye; *sl.* free, gratis; *à l'~ nu* with the naked eye; *aux yeux de* in the opinion of; *à mes yeux* in my opinion, as I see it, *avoir l'~ à qch.* see to s.th.; *avoir l'~ sur* keep an eye on; *coup m d'~* glance; *entre quatre yeux* in confidence; *être tout yeux* be all eyes; F *faire l'~ à q.* make eyes at s.o.; *fermer les yeux sur*

shut one's eyes to; *perdre des yeux* lose sight of; F *pour vos beaux yeux* for love; *risquer un ~* take a peep; *sauter aux yeux* be obvious; *sous mes yeux* before my face; ~**-de-bœuf** [œjdə'bœf] *m* bull's-eye window; ~**-de-perdrix** 🌶 [~pɛr'dri] *m* soft corn; ~**lade** [œ'jad] *f* wink, glance.

œill|ère [œ'jɛːr] *f* blinker; ~**et** [œ'jɛ] *m* eyelet; ♣ carnation.

œsophage *anat.* [ezɔ'faːʒ] *m* gullet.

œuf [œf, *pl.* ø] *m* egg; ~**s** *pl.* **brouillés** scrambled eggs; ~**s** *pl.* **sur le** (*au* **ou**) **plat** fried eggs; ~ **dur** hard-boiled egg; *blanc m d'~* white of egg.

œuvr|e [œvr] *su./f* work; task; product(ion); (*welfare*) society; ~**s** *pl.* works (*a. eccl.*); *à l'~* at work; *mettre en l'~* make use of; try, do; *se mettre à l'~* set to work; *su./m* △ main work; *writer:* complete works *pl.*; ♪ opus; *grand ~* philosopher's stone; △ *gros ~* foundations *pl.* and walls *pl.*; ~**er** [œ'vre] (1a) work.

offens|e [ɔ'fɑ̃ːs] *f* insult; *eccl.* sin; ~**er** [ɔlɑ̃'se] (1a) offend; offend against; *s'~* take offence, *Am.* offense (at, *de*); ~**eur** [~'sœːr] *m* offender; ~**if, -ve** [~'sif, ~'siːv] *adj.*, ✗ *su./f* offensive.

offert [ɔ'fɛːr] *p.p.* of *offrir.*

offic|e [ɔ'fis] *su./m* office; agency; service (*a. eccl., a. fig.* = *turn*); *d'~* officially; automatically; *faire ~ de* act as; *su./f* pantry; ~**iel** [~'sjɛl] official; formal (*call*).

offici|er [ɔfi'sje] **1.** (1o) officiate; **2.** *su./m* officer; ~**eux** [~'sjø] unofficial; *à titre ~* unofficially.

offr|ande [ɔ'frɑ̃ːd] *f* offering; ~**ant** [ɔ'frɑ̃] *m*: *au plus ~* to the highest bidder; ~**e** [ɔfr] **1.** *1st p. sg. pres.* of *offrir;* **2.** *su./f* offer; ✝ tender; bid; *journ.* ~**s** *pl. d'emploi* situations vacant; *l'~ et la demande* supply and demand; ~**ir** [ɔ'friːr] (2f) offer; give (to, *à*); expose (to, *à*); *s'~ à:* present itself (*occasion etc.*); *s'~ qch.* treat o.s. to s.th., *s'~ à faire* offer to do.

offusquer [ɔfys'ke] (1m) offend; *s'~* take offence (at, *de*).

ogiv|al ▲ [ɔʒi'val] Gothic; ~**e** [ɔ'ʒiːv] *f* ▲ Gothic arch; ✗ warhead.

ogre [ɔgr] *m* ogre.

oie *zo.* [wa] *f* goose.

oignon [ɔ'nɔ̃] *m* onion; **&** bulb; **&** bunion; **en rang d'~s** in a row.

oindre [wɛ̃:dr] (4m) anoint.

oiseau [wa'zo] *m* bird (*a.* F = *guy*); ~ *chanteur* songbird; ~ *de passage* migratory bird; ~ *de proie* bird of prey; **à vol d'~** as the crow flies; **vue f à vol d'~** bird's-eye view; **~-mouche** humming-bird.

ois|eux [wa'zø] idle; pointless, useless; **~if** [~'zif] idle; unemployed; **~iveté** [~ziv'te] *f* idleness.

olé|agineux [ɔleaʒi'nø] oliagenous; oil-yielding; **~oduc** [ɔleɔ'dyk] oil pipeline.

olfactif [ɔlfak'tif] olfactory.

oliv|âtre [ɔli'vɑ:tr] olive (*colour*); sallow (*complexion*); **~e** [ɔ'li:v] **1.** *su.*/*f* **&** olive; **2.** *adj.*/*inv.* olive-green; **~ier** **&** [~'vje] *m* olive tree.

olympi|ade [ɔlɛ̃'pjad] *f* Olympiad; **~en** [~'pjɛ̃] Olympian; **~que** [~'pik] Olympic; *Jeux m/pl.* **~s** Olympic games.

ombelle **&** [ɔ̃'bɛl] *f* umbel.

ombilical [ɔ̃bili'kal] umbilical.

ombr|age [ɔ̃'bra:ʒ] *m* shade; *fig.* umbrage; **~ager** [ɔ̃bra'ʒe] (1l) (give) shade; **~ageux** [~'ʒø] shy (*horse*); touchy, sensitive (*person*); **~e** [ɔ̃:br] *f* shadow (*a. fig.*); shade; *fig.* dark; *fig.* obscurity; **~ à paupières** eyeshadow; **à l'~ de** in the shade of; *fig.* under cover of; *sl.* **à l'~** in jail; **~elle** [ɔ̃'brɛl] *f* parasol; **~er** [ɔ̃'bre] (1a) shade.

omelette *cuis.* [ɔm'lɛt] *f* omelet(te).

omettre [ɔ'mɛtr] (4v) omit, leave out; ~ **de** (*inf.*) fail to (*inf.*); **omission** [ɔmi'sjɔ̃] *f* omission.

omnibus [ɔmni'bys] *m* (omni)bus; **🚋** (*a.* **train** *m* ~) local train.

omni|potence [ɔmnipɔ'tɑ̃:s] *f* omnipotence; **~potent** [~pɔ'tɑ̃] omnipotent; **~présence** [~pre'zɑ̃s] *f* omnipresence; **~présent** [~pre'zɑ̃] omnipresent; **~science** [~'sjɑ̃s] *f* omniscience; **~scient** [~'sjɑ̃] omniscient.

on [ɔ̃] *pron.* one, people *pl.*, you; somebody; F we; **~ dit que** it is said that.

once [ɔ̃:s] *f* ounce; F *fig.* scrap, bit.

oncle [ɔ̃:kl] *m* uncle.

onct|ion [ɔ̃k'sjɔ̃] *f* unction; **~ueux** [~'tɥø] creamy, rich; *fig.* unctuous.

onde [ɔ̃:d] *f* wave (*a. hair, a. radio*); **~s** *pl.* **moyennes** *radio*: medium waves; *phys.*

~ *sonore* sound wave; **longueur f d'~** wavelenght (*a. fig.*); **~é, e** [ɔ̃'de] **1.** *adj.* wavy; *tex.* watered; **2.** *su.*/*f* (heavy) shower.

on-dit [ɔ̃'di] *m*/*inv.* rumo(u)r.

ondo|iement [ɔ̃dwa'mɑ̃] *m* undulation; *eccl.* emergency baptism; **~yer** [~'je] (1h) *v/i.* undulate, wave; billow; *v/t.* baptize.

ondul|ant [ɔ̃dy'lɑ̃] undulating; swaying (*gait*); uneven; **~ation** [~la'sjɔ̃] *f* undulation; *hair*: wave; **~atoire** [~la'twa:r] undulatory; wave-(*motion*); **~é** [~'le] undulating; wavy; *tôle f* **~e** corrugated iron; **~er** [~'le] (1a) *v/i.* undulate; wave; ripple; *v/t.* wave (*one's hair*); **~eux** [~'lø] wavy; sinuous.

onéreux [ɔne'rø] costly; **à titre ~** subject to payment.

ongl|e [ɔ̃:gl] *m* (finger)nail; *zo.* claw; ~ *des pieds* toenail; **~ée** [ɔ̃'gle] *f* numbness of the fingertips; **~et** [ɔ̃'glɛ] *m* thimble; *book:* tab; **~ier** [ɔ̃gli'e] *m* manicure set; **~s** *pl.* nail-scissors.

ont [ɔ̃] *3rd. p. pl. pres. of* **avoir 1.**

onz|e [ɔ̃:z] eleven; *date, title:* eleventh; **~ième** [ɔ̃'zjɛm] eleventh.

opacité [ɔpasi'te] *f* opacity.

opal|e [ɔ'pal] *f* opal; **~in, e** [ɔpa'lɛ, ~'lin] *adj.*, *su.*/*f* opaline.

opaque [ɔ'pak] opaque.

opéra [ɔpe'ra] *m* opera(house); **~-comique** [~rakɔ'mik] *m* light opera.

opérat|eur [ɔpera'tœ:r] *m* operator; *cin.* cameraman; **~ion** [~'sjɔ̃] *f* **𝄞**, ➗, ✕, *fig.* operation; **✝** transaction; **♂ salle f d'~** operating theatre; **~ionnel** [~sjɔ'nɛl] operational; **~oire** **♂** [~'twa:r] operating; post-operative.

opérer [ɔpe're] (1f) *v/t.* effect; make; do; carry out; **♂** operate on (*s.o.*) (for, **de**); **s'~** take place; *v/i.* act; work.

opérette ♪ [ɔpe'rɛt] *f* operetta.

opin|er [ɔpi'ne] (1a): ~ *de la tête*, F ~ *du bonnet* nod assent; **~iâtre** [~'nja:tr] obstinate, stubborn; **~iâtreté** [~njatrə'te] *f* obstinacy, stubbornness; **~ion** [~'njɔ̃] *f* opinion; **avoir bonne (mauvaise) ~ de** think highly (poorly) of.

opiomane [ɔpjɔ'man] *su.* opium addict; **opium** [ɔ'pjɔm] *m* opium.

opportun [ɔpɔr'tœ̃] opportune, timely; appropriate (*time, moment*); **~isme** [~'nism] *m* opportunism; **~iste** [~'nist]

organiser

adj., su. opportunist; **~ité** [~ni'te] *f* timeliness; opportuneness.

oppos|ant [opo'zã] **1.** *adj.* opposing; **2.** *su.* opponent; **~é** [~'ze] **1.** *adj.* opposite (*a.* ♃); opposing; *fig.* contrary; **2.** *su./m* opposite (of, *de*); **à l'~** on the other side; **à l'~ de** contrary to; **~er** [~'ze] (1a) put *or* place opposite one another; set against one another, set in opposition, oppose; contrast (with, **à**); **~ qch. à** set s.th. against; put s.th. up against; *fig.* match s.th. with; *fig.* put s.th. forward against (*another argument etc.*); **s'~** confront one another; conflict, clash; **~s'~ à** oppose; be opposed to; be the opposite of; **~ition** [~zi'sjõ] *f* opposition (*a. parl.*); contrast; **en ~ à** in conflict; at variance; **par ~ à** as opposed to; in contrast with.

oppress|ant [ɔprɛ'sã] oppressive; **~er** [~'se] (1a) oppress; suffocate; weigh down; **~eur** [~'sœ:r] *m* oppressor; **~if** [~'sif] oppressive; **~ion** [~'sjõ] *f* oppression (*a. fig.*); difficulty in breathing.

opprimer [ɔpri'me] (1a) oppress; crush; stifle.

opprobre [ɔ'prɔbr] *m* disgrace.

opter [ɔp'te] (1a) opt.; choose; **~ pour** decide in favo(u)r of.

opticien [ɔpti'sjɛ̃] *m* optician.

optimis|me [ɔpti'mism] *m* optimism; **~te** [~'mist] **1.** *adj.* optimistic; sanguine; **2.** *su.* optimist.

option [ɔp'sjõ] *f* option (on, *sur*).

optique [ɔp'tik] **1.** *adj.* optic(al); **2.** *su./f* optics *sg.*(*a lense etc.*); *fig.* perspective, angle.

opulen|ce [ɔpy'lã:s] *f* affluence; wealth; **~t** [~'lã] opulent, wealthy.

opuscule [ɔpys'kyl] *m* pamphlet.

or[1] [ɔ:r] *m* gold; **en ~** gold(en).

or[2] [ɔ:r] *cj.* now; well (now).

orag|e [ɔ'ra:ʒ] *m* thunderstorm, *a. fig.* storm; **~eux** [ɔra'ʒø] stormy.

oraison [ɔrɛ'zõ] *f* prayer; oration; **~ dominicale** Lord's Prayer.

oral [ɔ'ral] oral.

orang|e [ɔ'rã:ʒ] **1.** *su./f* ♀ orange; *su./m* colour: orange; **2.** *adj./inv.* orange (*colour*); **~é** [ɔrã'ʒe] *adj., su./m* orange(y); **~eade** [~'ʒad] *f* orange squash; **~er** [~'ʒe] orange tree.

orat|eur [ɔra'tœ:r] *m* orator, speaker;

spokesman; **~oire** [~'twa:r] **1.** *adj.* oratorical; **2.** *su./m* chapel.

orbe[1] [ɔrb] *m* **mur m ~** blind wall.

orb|e[2] [ɔrb] *m* orb; globe, sphere; **~ite** [ɔr'bit] *f* orbit; *anat.* eye: socket; **~iter** [~bi'te] (1a) orbit.

orchestr|e ♩ [ɔr'kɛstr] *m* orchestra; **chef m d'~** conductor; **~er** [~kɛs'tre] (1a) ♩ orchestrate; *fig.* mount (*a campaign etc.*).

orchidée ♀ [ɔrki'de] *f* orchid.

ordinaire [ɔrdi'nɛ:r] **1.** *adj.* ordinary, usual, customary; average; regular (*petrol, gas*); ⚖ **tribunal m ~** civil court; **vin m ~** table wine; **2.** *su./m* daily fare; **à l'~, d'~** usually; **sortir de l'~** be out of the ordinary.

ordinateur [ɔrdina'tœ:r] *m* computer.

ordonn|ance [ɔrdɔ'nã:s] *f* arrangement, layout, organisation; 🩺 prescription; ⚖ order; ✗ orderly; **~é** [~'ne] orderly; well-ordered; **~er** [~'ne] (1a) organize, arrange, put in order; 🩺 prescribe; ⚖ order; *eccl.* ordain; **~ à** (*inf.*) order to (*inf.*); **s'~** organize itself *or* themselves.

ordre [ɔrdr] *m* order; orderliness, tidiness; category, class, sort, nature; *eccl.* **~s** *pl.* Holy Orders; **~ du jour** agenda; *pol.* **~ public** law and order; **avoir de l'~** be orderly; **de premier ~** first-class, outstanding; **jusqu'à nouvel ~** until further notice; **mettre en ~, mettre de l'~ dans** put in order; tidy up; sort out.

ordur|e [ɔr'dy:r] *f* dirt, filth, **~s** *pl.* refuse *sg.*, garbage *sg.*; **~ier** [~dy'rje] filthy; scurrilous, lewd.

oreill|e [ɔ'rɛːj] *f* ear; *vase:* handle; *book:* dog's ear; *fig.* hearing; **être tout ~s** be all ears; **tirer les ~s à** (*or de*) pull (*s.o.'s*) ears; **~er** [ɔrɛ'je] *m* pillow; **~ette** [~'jɛt] *f* anat. auricle; *cap.* ear-flap; **~ons** 🩺 [~'jõ] *m/pl.* mumps *sg.*

ores [ɔ:r] *adv.:* **d'~ et déjà** already.

orfèvre [ɔr'fɛ:vr] *m* goldsmith; **~rie** [~fɛvrə'ri] *f* goldsmith's trade *or* shop; gold *or* silver plate.

organ|e [ɔr'gan] *m* anat., *fig.* organ; ⚙ **~s de commande** controls; **~igramme** flow chart *or* diagram; organization chart; **~ique** [ɔrga'nik] organic; **~isateur** [~niza'tœ:r] **1.** *su.* organizer; **2.** *adj.* organizing; **~isation** [~niza'sjõ] *f* organization; setting up; setup; **~iser** [~ni'ze] (1a) organize; arrange; set up;

~isme [~'nism] *m* organism; **~iste** ♩ [~'nist] *su.* organist.

orgasme [ɔr'gasm] *m* orgasm.

orge ♩ [ɔrʒ] *f* barley; **~let** ♣ [~ʒə'lɛ] *m* eyelid: stye.

orgie [ɔr'ʒi] *f* orgy; *fig.* profusion.

orgue [ɔrg] *su./m* organ; **~ de Barbarie** barrel-organ; *su./f:* **les grandes ~s** *pl.* the grand organ *sg.*

orgueil [ɔr'gœj] *m* pride; *pej.* arrogance; **~leux** [~gœ'jø] proud.

orient [ɔ'rjɑ̃] *m* Orient, East; *pearl:* water; **~al** [ɔrjɑ̃'tal] oriental; **~ation** [~ta'sjɔ̃] *f* orientation; positioning; direction; guidance; *fig.* leaning, trend; **~ professionnelle** vocational *or* careers guidance; **~er** [~'te] (1a) orientate; position; turn (towards, *vers*); direct; guide; **s'~** find one's bearings; *fig.* **s'~ vers** turn towards; **~eur** careers advisory officer.

orifice [ɔri'fis] *m* opening; ⊕ port.

origan [ɔri'gɑ̃] *m* oregano.

origin|aire [ɔriʒi'nɛːr] original; **~ de** originating from; native to; **~al** [~'nal] **1.** *adj.* original; novel; *fig.* eccentric; **2.** *su.* eccentric; *su./m text etc.:* original; **~alité** [~nali'te] *f* originality; *fig.* eccentricity; **~e** [ɔri'ʒin] *f* origin; **à l'~** originally; at first; **être à l'~ de** be the cause of; **dès l'~** from the outset; **~el** [~ʒi'nɛl] *eccl.* original (*sin*); fundamental.

oripeaux [ɔri'po] *m/pl.* rags.

orme ♣ [ɔrm] *m* elm.

orn|é [ɔr'ne] ornate; **~ement** [~nə'mɑ̃] *m* ornament; adornment; **~emental** [~nemɑ̃'tal] ornamental; **~ementer** [~nəmɑ̃'te] (1a) ornament; **~er** [~'ne] (1a) decorate; adorn.

ornière [ɔr'njɛːr] *f* rut; ⊕ groove.

ornitholog|ie [ɔrnitɔlɔ'ʒi] ornithology; **~ue** [~'lɔg], **~iste** [~lɔ'ʒist] *su.* ornithologist.

orphelin [ɔrfə'lɛ̃] **1.** *adj.* orphan(ed); **~ de père (mère)** fatherless (motherless); **2.** *su.* orphan; **~at** [~li'na] *m* orphanage.

orteil [ɔr'tɛːj] *m* (big) toe.

ortho... [ɔrtɔ] orth(o)...; **~doxe** [~'dɔks] orthodox; **~graphe** [~'graf] *f* spelling, orthography; **~graphier** [~gra'fje] (1o) spell (*a word*) (correctly); **mal ~** mis-spell; **~pédie** [~pe'di] *f* orthop(a)edy; **~phonie** [~fɔ'ni] *f* correct pronunciation; ♣ speech therapy.

ortie ♣ [ɔr'ti] *f* nettle.

orvet *zo.* [ɔr'vɛ] *m* slow-worm.

os [ɔs, *pl.* o] *m* bone; F difficulty, hitch; *fig.* **trempé jusqu'aux ~** soaked to the skin; F **tomber sur un ~** come up against a snag.

oscill|ation [ɔsilla'sjɔ̃] *f* oscillation; *pendulum:* swing; *fig.* fluctuation; **~er** [~'le] (1a) oscillate, sway; swing (*pendulum*); ♣ fluctuate; *fig.* waver.

osé [o'ze] bold, daring.

oseille ♣ [ɔ'zɛːj] *f* sorrel.

oser [o'ze] (1a) dare.

osier ♣ [ɔ'zje] *m* willow; wicker.

oss|ature *anat.*, ⊕, *fig.* [ɔsa'tyːr] *f* (skeletal *or* bone) structure; frame(work); **~elet** [ɔs'lɛ] *m* little bone; **~ements** [~'mɑ̃] *m/pl.* bones; **~eux** [ɔ'sø] bony; **~ifier** [ɔsi'fje] (1o) ossify.

osten|sible [ɔstɑ̃'sibl] conspicuous; patent; **~soir** *eccl.* [~'swaːr] *m* monstrance; **~tation** [~ta'sjɔ̃] ostentation; **faire ~ de** make a display of, parade; **~tatoire** [~ta'twaːr] ostentatious.

ostréiculture [ɔstreikyl'tyːr] *f* oyster breeding.

otage [ɔ'taːʒ] *m* hostage; **prendre q. en ~** take s.o. hostage.

otarie *zo.* [ɔta'ri] *f* sea-lion.

ôter [o'te] (1a) remove; take away (from s.o., **à q.**); s.th. from, **qch. de**); take off (*one's gloves etc.*).

oto-rhino ♣ [ɔtɔri'no], **oto-rhino-laryngologiste** [ɔtɔrinɔlarɛ̃gɔlɔ'ʒist] *su.* ear nose and throat specialist.

ottomane [ɔtɔ'man] *f* divan.

ou [u] *cj.* or; **ou ... ou** either ... or; **ou bien** or else.

où [u] **1.** *adv.* place, direction: where; time: when; **2.** *pron./rel.* place, direction: where; time: when, on which; *fig.* at *or* in which; **d'où** where ... from; hence, therefore; **par où?** which way?

ouat|e [wat] *f* wadding; cotton wool; **~é** [wa'te] quilted; *fig.* muffled.

oubli [u'bli] *m* forgetfulness; forgetting; oblivion; oversight.

oubli|er [ubli'e] (1a) forget; forget about; **faire ~** live down; **s'~** forget o.s.; **~ettes** [~'ɛt] *f/pl.* dungeon *sg.*; *fig.* oblivion; **~eux** [~'ø] forgetful, unmindful (of, **de**).

ouest [wɛst] **1.** *su./m* west; **de l'~**

west(ern); **d'~** westerly (wind); **2.** adj./
inv. west(ern).

oui [wi] **1.** adv. yes; **dire que ~** say yes;
mais ~! certainly!; yes indeed!; **2.**
su./m/inv. yes.

ouï-dire [wi'di:r] m/inv. hearsay; **par ~**
by hearsay; **ouïe** [wi] f (sense of) hearing; **~s** pl. ♪ sound-holes; icht. gills;
ouïr [wi:r] (2r) hear.

ouragan [ura'gɑ̃] m hurricane.

ourdir [ur'di:r] (2a) hatch (a plot).

ourle|r [ur'le] (1a) hem; rim; **~t** [~'lɛ] m
hem; rim.

ours [urs] m bear (a. fig.); **~ blanc** polar
bear; **~ en peluche** Teddy bear; **~e** [~] f
zo. she-bear; astr. **la Grande ♀** the
Great Bear; **~in** [ur'sɛ̃] m sea urchin;
~on [~'sɔ̃] m bear cub.

oust(e)! F [ust] int. get a move on!

outil [u'ti] m tool; **~lage** [uti'laːʒ] m tool
set; ☻ equipment; **~ler** [~'je] (1a) equip
(with tools); ☻ fit out.

outrag|e [u'traːʒ] m insult; outrage; **⚖ ~
à magistrat** contempt of court; **~eant**
[utra'ʒɑ̃] offensive; **~er** [~'ʒe] (1l)
insult, offend; outrage; **~eusement**
[~ʒøz'mɑ̃] outrageously.

outranc|e [u'trɑ̃:s] f excess; **à ~** to excess;
~ier [utrɑ̃'sje] extreme.

outre [u:tr] **1.** prp. besides; in addition
to; **2.** adv.: **~ que** in addition to the fact
that; **en ~** moreover; **passer ~** not
to take notice of, **à)**; **~cuidance**
[utrakɥi'dɑ̃:s] f bumptiousness; **~cui-
dant** [~'dɑ̃] bumptious; **~mer** [~'mɛːr]
m lapis lazuli; ultramarine; **~-mer**
[~'mɛːr] adv. overseas...; **~passer**
[~pa'se] (1a) exceed; go beyond.

outr|é [u'tre] exaggerated; outraged;

~er [~] (1a) exaggerate; outrage.

ouvert [u'vɛːr] **1.** p.p. of **ouvrir**; **2.** adj.
open; fig. **à bras ~s** with open arms;
~ure [uvɛr'tyːr] f opening; ♪ overture.

ouvra|ble [u'vrabl] workable; **jour** m **~**
working day; **~ge** [u'vraːʒ] m work;
workmanship; **~gé** [uvra'ʒe] finely
worked; elaborate.

ouvre [u:vr] 1st p. sg. pres. of **ouvrir**.

ouvré [u'vre] ☻ finished (product);
worked; **jour** m **~** working day.

ouvre-|boîtes [uvrə'bwat] m/inv. tin
(Am. can) opener; **~bouteilles**
[~bu'tɛːj] m/inv. bottle-opener; **~lettres**
[~'lɛtr] m/inv. letter-opener.

ouvreuse [u'vrøːz] f usherette.

ouvrier, -ère [uvri'e, ~'ɛːr] **1.** su. worker;
su./m: **~ qualifié** skilled worker; su./f
factory girl; zo. worker (bee or ant); **2.**
adj. working (class); labo(u)r ...

ouvrir [u'vriːr] (2f) v/t. open; a. fig. open
up; turn on, switch on; **~ l'appetit à q.**
whet s.o.'s appetite; **s'~** open (up); fig.
s'~ à q. open one's heart to s.o.; confide in s.o.; **s'~ les veines** cut one's
wrists; v/i. open; be open (shop etc.); **~
sur** open onto (door etc.).

ovaire ♀, anat. [ɔ'vɛːr] m ovary.

ovale [ɔ'val] adj., su./m oval.

ovation [ɔva'sjɔ̃] f ovation; **faire une ~ à
=** **~ner** [~sjɔ'ne] (1a) give (s.o.) an ovation.

oxyd|able [ɔksi'dabl] oxidizable, **~ation**
[~da'sjɔ̃] f oxidization; **~e** [ɔk'sid] m
oxide; **~er** [~si'de] (1a) oxidize; **s'~** become oxidized.

oxygène [ɔksi'ʒɛn] oxygen; **oxygéné**
[~ʒe'ne] oxygenated; **eau** f **~e** hydrogen peroxide.

P

P

pacage [pa'kaːʒ] m pasture.

pacifi|cateur [pasifika'tœːr] **1.** adj. paci-
fying; **2.** su. peacemaker; **~cation**
[~'sjɔ̃] f pacification; **~er** [pasi'fje] (1o)
pacify; **~que** [~'fik] **1.** adj. peaceable,
peace-loving (person, people etc.),

peaceful; **l'océan** m ♀ **= 2.** su./m: **le ♀**
the Pacific (Ocean).

pacotille [pako'tiːj] f trash; **de ~** cheap.

pact|e [pakt] m pact, agreement; **~iser**
[pakti'ze] (1a) come to terms.

paf F [paf] tight (drunk).

pagaie [pa'gɛ] f paddle.

pagaïe F, **pagaille** F [pa'ga:j] f mess, shambles; lots pl., loads pl.; **en ~** in a mess; loads of ...; **mettre** (or **semer**) **la ~ dans** make a shambles of, mess up.

pagayer [page'je] (1i) paddle.

page [pa:ʒ] f page; **à la ~** up to date.

pagne [paɲ] m loincloth.

paie [pɛ] f pay(ment), wages pl.; **jour m de ~** payday; **~ment** [~'mɑ̃] m payment; **~ contre livraison** cash on delivery; **~ partiel** part payment.

païen [pa'jɛ̃] adj., su. pagan, heathen.

paillard [pa'ja:r] bawdy; **~ise** [~jar'di:z] f bawdiness; lewd talk.

paill|asse [pa'jas] f straw mattress; **~son** [~ja'sɔ̃] m doormat; mat(ting); **~e** [paɪj] f straw; gem, fig.: flaw; **~ de fer** steel wool; fig. **homme m de ~** man of straw; **tirer à la courte ~** draw lots; **~é** [pɑ'je] flawy; **~er** [~'je] (1a) (cover with) straw; **~et** [~'jɛ] m pale red wine; **~eté** [paj'te] sequined; **~ette** [pa'jɛt] f spangle, sequin; soap etc.: flake.

pain [pɛ̃] m bread; loaf; soap: cake, tablet; butter: pat; sugar: lump; **~ d'épice** gingerbread; **petit ~** roll.

pair [pɛːr] **1.** adj. equal; ♈ even (number); **2.** su./m equality; ♈ par; parl. peer; person: equal; **au ~** au pair; **de ~** together, hand in hand (with, **avec**); **hors (de) ~** peerless, unrivalled.

paire [pɛːr] f pair; birds etc.: brace; **faire la ~** be two of a kind.

paisible [pɛ'zibl] peaceful, quiet.

paître [pɛːtr] (4k) graze; F **envoyer q. ~** send s.o. packing.

paix [pɛ] f peace; quiet, peacefulness; **faire la ~** make peace; **avoir la ~** have peace (and quiet); **laisser q. en ~**, **laisser la ~ à q.** leave s.o. alone.

pal, pl. **pals** [pal] m pale, stake.

palabr|er [pala'bre] (1a) palaver; **~es** [~'labr] m or f/pl. palaver.

palais¹ [pa'lɛ] m palace; coll. lawyers pl.; **~ de justice** law-courts pl.

palais² anat., fig. [~] m palate.

palan [pa'lɑ̃] m pulley block; hoist.

pale¹ eccl. [pal] f chalice-cover, pall.

pale² [~] f ♈ blade; vane; sluice.

pâle [pɑːl] pale, pallid; wan; ashen.

palefrenier [palfrə'nje] m groom.

paletot [pal'to] m overcoat.

palette [pa'lɛt] f paint., fig. palette;

cuis. shoulder; ☉ paddle; for goods: pallet.

pâleur [pɑ'lœːr] f pallor, paleness.

pali|er [pa'lje] m stairs: landing; fig. level; **par ~s** in stages; **sur le même ~** on the same floor; **~ère** [~'ljɛːr]: **porte f ~** landing door.

palinodie [palinɔ'di] f recantation.

pâlir [pɑ'liːr] (2a) v/i. grow or go pale; fade; v/t. make pale.

palissad|e [pali'sad] f palisade, fence; ✗ stockade.

palissandre [pali'sɑ̃:dr] m rosewood.

palliatif [pallja'tif] adj., su./m palliative; makeshift.

pallier [pal'lje] (1o) (a. **~ à**) palliate.

palm|arès [palma'rɛːs] m prize list; list of winners; **~e** [palm] f palm leaf or branch; fig. palm; skin diving etc.: flipper; **~é** [pal'me] ♃ palmate; orn. webfooted; **~eraie** [palmə'rɛ] f palmgrove; **~ier** [~'mje] m palm tree; **~pède** [~mi'pɛd] adj. (su./m) webfooted (bird).

palombe orn. [pa'lɔ̃:b] f ringdove.

pâlot, -otte [pɑ'lo, ~'lɔt] palish.

palp|able [pal'pabl] palpable; **~er** [pal'pe] (1a) feel, touch, finger; ♃ palpate; F make, pocket (money).

palpit|ation [palpita'sjɔ̃] f palpitation; **~ant** fig. [~'tɑ̃] exciting, thrilling; **~er** [~'te] (1a) palpitate; throb, beat (heart); flutter, quiver; fig. thrill (with, **de**).

palu|déen [palyde'ɛ̃] marsh...; ♃ malarial (fever); **~disme** [~'dism] m malaria.

pâm|er [pɑ'me] (1a): **se ~ de**, **être pâmé de** be overcome with; **se ~ de joie** be in raptures; **se ~ de rire** split one's sides with laughter; **~oison** [~mwa'zɔ̃] f swoon.

pamphl|et [pã'flɛ] m lampoon; **~étaire** [~fle'tɛːr] m lampoonist.

pamplemousse [pãplə'mus] m grapefruit.

pan [pã] m cost. flap; wall: piece; building, prism, nut: side; sky: patch.

panacée [pana'se] f panacea.

panach|e [pana'naʃ] m plume, tuft; smoke: wreath; mot. etc. **faire ~** turn over; **~é** [pana'ʃe] **1.** adj. mixed; **2.** su./m shandy; **~er** [~] (1a) variegate; election: split (one's votes).

panade [pa'nad] f cuis. bread soup; F **dans la ~** in need; in the soup.

panama [pana'ma] m panama hat.

pancarte [pɑ̃'kart] *f* sign, notice; placard, bill.

pancréas [pɑ̃kre'as] *m* pancreas.

pané *cuis.* [pa'ne] breaded.

panier [pa'nje] *m* basket; ~ **à salade** salad washer; *fig.* prison van; *fig.* ~ **percé** spendthrift; F **le dessus du ~** the pick of the bunch.

panification [panifika'sjɔ̃] *f* bread-making.

paniqu|e [pa'nik] *adj., su./f* panic; ~**er** [~ni'ke] (1a) panic.

panne[1] [pan] *f* breakdown, failure; **en ~** broken down, stuck; **être en ~ de ...** have run out of ...; **laisser en ~** leave (*s.o.*) in the lurch; **tomber en ~** have a breakdown.

panne[2] [~] *f* fat; *tex.* plush.

panneau [pa'no] *m* panel; board; sign; ~ **d'affichage** notice (*Am.* bulletin) board; ~ **de signalisation** roadsign; △ ~ **préfabriqué** prefabricated section; *fig.* **donner** (*or* **marcher**) **dans le ~** walk into the trap.

panoplie [pano'pli] *m* outfit; set, range.

panoram|a [panɔra'ma] *m* panorama; ~**ique** panoramic.

panse [pɑ̃s] *f* paunch.

pans|ement [pɑ̃s'mɑ̃] *m* dressing, bandage; ~**er** [pɑ̃'se] (1a) dress, bandage (*a wound*); groom (*a horse*).

pansu [pɑ̃'sy] *f* potbellied.

pantalon [pɑ̃ta'lɔ̃] *m* trousers *pl., Am.* pants *pl.*; slacks *pl.*

pantelant [pɑ̃t'lɑ̃] panting; twitching (*flesh etc.*).

panthère *zo.* [pɑ̃'tɛːr] *f* panther.

pantin [pɑ̃'tɛ̃] *m* toy: jumping jack; *fig.* puppet.

pantois [pɑ̃'twa] flabbergasted.

pantomime [pɑ̃tɔ'mim] *f* dumb show; pantomime.

pantoufl|ard [pɑ̃tu'flaːr] *m* stay-at-home type; ~**e** [~'tufl] *f* slipper.

paon [pɑ̃] *m* peacock.

papa F [pa'pa] *m* papa, dad(dy); **de ~** old(-fashioned), antiquated; **fils m à ~** professional son.

pap|al [pa'pal] papal; ~**auté** [~po'te] *f* papacy; ~**e** [pap] *m* pope.

papelard [pa'plaːr] smarmy.

paperass|e [pa'pras] *f* red tape; useless paper(s *pl.*); ~**erie** [~pras'ri] *f* old papers; *fig.* red tape; *fig.* (annoying) pa-

perwork; ~**ier** [~pra'sje] *m* bureaucrat.

papet|erie [pap'tri] *f* paper mill; stationery; stationer's (shop); ~**ier** [~'tje] *m* stationer; paper-manufacturer.

papier [pa'pje] *m* paper; document; ♰ bill(s *pl.*); ~ **à lettres** writing paper; ~ **à musique** music paper; ~ **couché** art paper; ~ **d'emballage** brown paper; ~ **de verre** sand paper, glass paper; ~ **peint** wallpaper; ~**-monnaie** [~pjemɔ'nɛ] *m* paper money.

papille [pa'piːj] *f* papilla; ~**s** *pl.* **gustatives** taste buds.

papillo|n [papi'jɔ̃] *m zo.* butterfly; *cost.* (*a.* **nœud m ~**) bow tie; *mot.* parking ticket; ⚙ wing nut; ~ **de nuit** moth; ~**nner** [~jɔ'ne] (1a) flutter; flit; ~**te** [~'jɔt] *f* curlpaper; ~**ter** [~jɔ'te] (1a) blink (*eyes, light*); twinkle, flicker.

paprika ♀ [papri'ka] *m* red pepper.

pâque [pɑːk] *f* (*Jewish*) Passover.

paquebot ⚓ [pak'bo] *m* (passenger) liner.

pâquerette ♀ [pɑ'krɛt] *f* daisy.

Pâques [pɑːk] *su./m* Easter; *su./f.* ~ *pl.* **fleuries** Palm Sunday *sg.*

paquet [pa'kɛ] *m* parcel; package; pack; bundle; ⚓ ~ **de mer** heavy sea; **faire ses ~s** pack one's bags; ~**er** [pak'te] (1c) parcel.

par [par] *prp.* cause, *agent, author*: by; *place*: by (*sea*), through (*the door*); via (*Calais*); *time*: on (*a fine evening*); in (*the rain*); *motive*: from, through; out of (*curiosity*); *instrument, means*: by (*mail, train, etc.*); *distribution*: per (*annum*), each, a (*week etc.*); in (*hundreds, numerical order*); ~ **eau et ~ terre** by land and sea; ~ **où?** which way?; ~ **ici** this way; round here; ~ **la fenêtre** out of the window; ~ **bonheur** (*malheur*) (un)fortunately; ~ **avion** *post:* via airmail; **prendre ~ la main** take by the hand; **jour ~ jour** day by day; **deux ~ deux** two by two; **commencer ~** (*inf.*) begin by (*ger.*); **finir par faire qch.** eventually do s.th.; **de ~** by, in conformity with (*the conditions, nature, etc.*); **de ~ le roi** in the King's name; ~**-ci** here; ~**-là** there; ~**-ci ~-là** now and then; ~ **derrière** from behind; ~**-dessous** under, beneath; ~**-delà** beyond; ~**-dessus** over; on top (of); ⚏ ~**-devant** before.

parabol|e [para'bɔl] *f bible*: parable; *A* parabola; **~ique** [~bɔ'lik] parabolic.

parachever [paraʃ've] (1d) perfect.

parachut|e [para'ʃyt] *m* parachute; **~er** [~ʃy'te] (1a) parachute; drop; **~iste** [~ʃy'tist] *m* parachutist.

parad|e [pa'rad] *f sp.* parry; *horse*: checking; *fig.* reply, repartee; *X* parade; *fig.* show; **faire ~ de** show off; display; **~er** [~ra'de] (1a) strut (about).

paradis [para'di] *m* paradise; *thea.* gallery, F the gods *pl.*; **~iaque** [~di-'zjak] paradisiac; **~ier** *orn.* [~di'zje] *m* bird of paradise.

paradox|al [paradɔk'sal] paradoxical; **~e** [~'dɔks] *m* paradox.

parafe(r) *see* **paraphe(r)**.

paraffine [para'fin] *f* paraffin (wax).

parage [pa'raːʒ] *m*: **~s** *pl.* *♃* latitudes; regions; vicinity *sg.*, quarters; *dans les* **~s** (around) here.

paragraphe [para'graf] *m* paragraph.

parais [pa'rɛ] *1st p. sg. pres. of* **paraître**;
paraissons [~rɛ'sɔ̃] *1st p. pl. pres. of* **paraître**; **paraître** [~'rɛːtr] (4k) appear; seem, look; be visible; come out (*book etc.*); **vient de ~** just out (*book*); *v/impers.*: *à ce qu'il paraît* apparently; *il paraît que* (*ind.*) it seems that, they say that; *il paraît que oui* (*non*) it appears so (not).

parall|èle [para'lɛl] **1.** *adj.* parallel; *fig.* unofficial (*institution etc.*); alternative (*medicine etc.*); **2.** *su./f A etc.* parallel (line); *su./m geog., fig.* parallel; *établir* (*or faire*) *un ~* (*entre*) draw a parallel (between); *mettre en ~* compare; **~élisme** [~le'lism] *m* parallelism (between ... and *de* ... *à*, *entre* ... *et*).

paraly|ser [parali'ze] (1a) paralyse (*a. fig.*); cripple; **~sie** [~'zi] *f* paralysis; **~tique** [~'tik] paralytic.

parangon [parɑ̃'gɔ̃] *m* paragon.

parapet [para'pɛ] *m* parapet.

paraph|e [pa'raf] *m* flourish; initials *pl.*; **~er** [~ra'fe] (1a) initial.

para...: **~phrase** [para'fraːz] *f* paraphrase; **~phraser** [~fra'ze] (1a) paraphrase; **~pluie** [~'plɥi] *m* umbrella; **~site** [~'zit] **1.** *adj.* parasitic; **2.** *su./m* parasite; **~s** *pl.* *radio etc.*: interference *sg.*; **~sol** [~'sɔl] *m* sunshade; **~tonnerre** [~tɔ'nɛːr] *m* lightning rod; **~vent** [~'vɑ̃] *m* folding screen.

parbleu! [par'blø] *int.* you bet!

parc [park] *m* park; *cattle etc.* pen; *oisters*: bed; *👕*, *X* depot; *child*: play-pen; *mot.*: **~ de stationnement** car park, *Am.* parking lot.

parcell|e [par'sɛl] *f land*: lot, plot; small fragment; *fig.* bit, scrap, grain; **~iser** [~sɛli'ze] (1a) divide *or* split up.

parce que ['parskə] *cj.* because.

parchemin [parʃə'mɛ̃] *m* parchment; diplomas; **~é** [parʃəmi'ne] parchment-like, wizened.

parcimoni|e [parsimo'ni] *f* parsimony; **~eux** [~'njø] parsimonious.

parc(o)mètre [park(ɔ)'mɛtr] *m* parking meter.

parcour|ir [parku'riːr] (2i) travel through; cover (*a distance*); go *or* run through; go all over (*a place*); (*a. ~ du regard*, *~ des yeux*) glance through; run one's eyes over; **~s** [~'kuːr] *m* distance; journey, run, trip; course (*a. sp.*); route; *prix m du ~* fare.

pardessus [pardə'sy] *m* overcoat.

pardi! [par'di] *int.* of course!

pardon [par'dɔ̃] **1.** *su./m* forgiveness; pardon; **~!** pardon (me)!, I beg your pardon!; sorry!; **demander ~ à q.** ask s.o.'s pardon, apologize to s.o. (for *ger.*, *de inf.*); **~nable** [~dɔ'nabl] excusable; **~ner** [~dɔ'ne] (1a) forgive (s.o. for s.th., *qch. à q.*); pardon.

paré [pa're] prepared (for, *contre*).

pare...: **~balles** [par'bal] *adj./inv.* bullet-proof; **~boue** *mot.* [~'bu] *m/inv.* mudguard; **~brise** *mot.* [~'briːz] *m/inv.* windscreen, *Am.* windshield; **~chocs** *mot.* [~'ʃɔk] *m/inv.* bumper.

pareil, -eille [pa'rɛːj] **1.** *adj.* the same, alike; similar (to, *à*); such (a), like this *or* that; *sans* **~** unrivalled; **2.** *su.* equal, like; *su./f*: *rendre la* **~eille à** pay (*s.o.*) back in his own coin.

parent [pa'rɑ̃] *su.* relative, relation; *su./m*: **~s** *pl.* parents; **~é** [~rɑ̃'te] *f* relationship, relations *pl.*, relatives *pl.*

parenthèse [parɑ̃'tɛːz] *f* parenthesis; *typ.* bracket; *entre* **~s** in brackets; *fig.* incidentally.

parer [pa're] (1a) *v/t.* adorn, deck; *cuis.* dress; ward off, parry; avoid; **~** deck o.s. out (in, *de*); *se* **~ de** (*or contre*) protect o.s. from *or* against; *v/i.*: **~ à**

provide against *or* for; deal with, attend to; avert (*an accident*).

pare-soleil [parsɔ'lɛːj] *m/inv.* sun visor.

paress|e [pa'rɛs] *f* laziness; sluggishness; **~er** [~ɛ'se] (1a) laze (about); **~eux** [~ɛ'sø] lazy; sluggish.

par|faire [par'fɛːr] (4r) complete; perfect; **~fait** [~'fɛ] **1.** *adj.* perfect; complete; utter; **~!** splendid!; **2.** *su./m gramm.* perfect; *cuis.* icecream; **~faitement** [~fɛt'mɑ̃] *adv.* perfectly; **~!** exactly!

parfois [par'fwa] *adv.* sometimes.

parfum [par'fœ̃] *m* perfume, scent; fragrance; *cuis.* flavo(u)r; **~er** [~ty'me] (1a) perfume, scent (*flowers etc.*); put perfume *or* scent on; **se ~** use perfume *or* scent; **parfumé à ...** ~-scented, *cuis.* ...-flavo(u)red; **~erie** [~fyri'ri] *f* perfumery; perfume shop.

pari [pa'ri] *m* bet; wager; **~er** [~'rje] (1o) bet; **~eur** [~'rjœːr] *m* punter.

Parigot *m, e* f F [pari'go, ~'gɔt] Parisian.

parisien [~'zjɛ̃] *adj., su.* Parisian.

parit|aire [pari'tɛːr] *adj* joint (*commission*); **~é** [~'te] *f* parity.

parjur|e [par'ʒyːr] **1.** *adj.* perjured; **2.** *su.* perjurer; *su./m* perjury; **~er** [~ʒy're] (1a): **se ~** perjure o.s.

parking *mot.* [par'kiŋ] *m* parking; car park, *Am.* parking lot.

parl|ant [par'lɑ̃] speaking (*a. fig.*); *fig.* talkative; *fig.* expressive; *fig.* eloquent, that speaks for itself; *cin.* sound (*film*); **~é** [~'le] spoken (*language*).

parlement [parlə'mɑ̃] *m* parliament; **~aire** [~lamɑ̃'tɛːr] **1.** *adj.* parliamentary; **drapeau** *m* ~ flag of truce; **2.** *su./m* member of parliament; negotiator; **~arisme** [~ta'rism] *m* parliamentary government; **~ter** [~'te] (1a) parley.

parl|er [par'le] **1.** (1a) *v/i.* speak, talk (to, **à**; of, about **de**); be on speaking terms (with, **à**); **on m'a parlé de** I was told about; **sans ~ de** let alone ...; *v/t.* speak (*a language*); F **~ boutique** (**politique**, **raison**) talk shop (about politics, sense); **se ~** be spoken (*language*); be on speaking terms (*people*); **2.** *su./m* speech; way of speaking; **~eur, -euse** [~'lœːr, ~'løːz] *su.* talker; **~oir** [~'lwaːr] *m* parlo(u)r; **~ote** [~'lɔt] *f* chitchat.

parmi [par'mi] *prp.* among; amid.

parodi|e [parɔ'di] *f* parody; **~er** [~'dje] (1o) parody, burlesque.

paroi [pa'rwa] *f* (inner) wall; party wall; (inner) surface *or* side; **~ rocheuse** rock face.

paroiss|e [pa'rwas] *f* parish; **~ial** [parwa'sjal] parochial; parish-...; **~ien** [~'sjɛ̃] *su.* parishioner; *su./m* prayer-book.

parole [pa'rɔl] *f* word (*a.* = *promise*); **avoir la ~** have the floor; **donner la ~ à q.** call upon s.o. to speak; **prendre la ~** take the floor, speak; **tenir ~** keep one's word.

paroxysme [parɔk'sism] *m* paroxysm, height, climax.

parqu|er [par'ke] (1m) *vt/i.* park; *v/t.* pen up (*livestock*); **~et** [~'kɛ] *m* ⚠ floor(ing); *☆* public prosecutor's department; *bourse:* Ring.

parrain [pa'rɛ̃] *m* godfather; sponsor; **~er** [parɛ'ne] (1a) sponsor.

parsemer [parsə'me] (1d) strew, sprinkle (with, **de**); *fig.* spangle; be scattered over.

part [paːr] *f* share; part; portion; *food:* helping, *cake:* piece; **à ~** separately; apart from; apart from that; except for that; **à ~ cela** apart from that; **à ~ entière** full (*member etc.*); entirely, fully; **à ~ soi** to o.s.; **autre ~** elsewhere; **d'autre ~** moreover; **de la ~ de** on behalf of; from; **de ~ en ~** through and through; **de ~ et d'autre** on both sides; **d'une ~ ..., d'autre ~** on the one hand ... on the other hand; **faire ~ de qch. à q.** inform s.o. of s.th.; **faire la ~ de** take into account; **nulle ~** nowhere; **pour ma ~** I for one; **prendre ~ à** take part in; **quelque ~** somewhere; **~age** [par'taːʒ] *m* division, sharing; *☆, pol.* partition; share, portion, lot (*a. fig.*); **~ager** [~ta'ʒe] (1l) divide (up); share (*a. fig.*); **se ~** be divided; differ; **être bien partagé** be well endowed.

partance ⚓, ✈ [par'tɑ̃ːs] *f* departure; **en ~ pour** (bound) for.

partant [par'tɑ̃] *cj.* therefore.

partenaire [partə'nɛːr] *su.* partner.

parterre [par'tɛːr] *m* ✔ flower-bed; *thea.* pit.

parti[1] [par'ti] away; gone; F tipsy.

parti[2] [par'ti] *m* ✗, *pol., fig.* party; *fig.* side; *marriage:* match; *fig.* option, decision; **~ pris** prejudice; **prendre ~ (pour)** take sides (with); **prendre le ~ de** (*inf.*) decide to (*inf.*); **prendre un ~** come to a decision; **prendre son ~ de** resign o.s. to; **tirer ~ de** turn (*s.th.*) to account; utilize; use; **~al** [~'sjal] biased; partial (to, **envers**); **~alité** [~sjali'te] *f* partiality (for, to **envers**); bias.

particip|ation [partisipa'sjɔ̃] *f* taking part, participation (in, **à**); contribution (to, **à**); † interest; **~e** *gramm.* [~'sip] *m* participle; **~er** [~si'pe] (1a) take part, participate (in, **à**); contribute (to, **à**); share (in, **à**); **~ de** partake of.

particulari|ser [partikylari'ze] (1a) specify; **se ~ (par)** be distinguished (by); **~té** [~'te] *f* particularity (distinctive) feature.

particule [parti'kyl] *f* particle.

particul|ier [partiky'lje] **1.** *adj.* particular; private; exceptional; **2.** *su.* private individual; private life; **en ~** privately; **= ~ièrement** particularly.

parti|e [par'ti] *f* part (*a.* ♪); *hunt.*, ⚖ party; *sp.* match; † line of business; ⚖ **~ civile** plaintiff; **en grande ~** largely, for the most part; **en ~** in part, partly; **faire ~ de** be one of, belong to; **prendre q. à ~** go for s.o.; **~el** [~'sjɛl] partial, incomplete.

partir [par'tiːr] (2b) go (away); start; leave (for, **pour**); set out; go off (*a. gun etc.*); *hunt.* rise; come off (*button etc.*); **à ~ de** (starting) from.

partisan [parti'zɑ̃] **1.** *su.* follower; supporter, advocate; *su./m* ✗ partisan; **2.** *adj.*: **être ~ de** be in favo(u)r of, believe in, be all for.

partition ♪ [parti'sjɔ̃] *f* score.

partout [par'tu] *adv.* everywhere.

partouze *sl.* [par'tuz] *f* orgy.

paru [pa'ry] *p.p.* of **paraître**.

parure [pa'ryːr] *f* finery; *jewels etc.*: set; ⊚ parings *pl.*

parus [pa'ry] *1st p. sg. p.s.* of **paraître**.

parution [pary'sjɔ̃] *f book*: publication, appearance.

parven|ir [parvə'niːr] (2h): **~ à** arrive; reach; succeed in (doing s.th., **faire qch.**); **~u** *m*, **~ue** *f* [~'ny] upstart.

pas [pɑ] **1.** *su./m* step; tread; pace; footstep; footprint; *geog.* pass(age); ✆ , ⚙ *screw*: thread; distance (*between seats, rows, etc.*); *fig.* prece-

dence; *fig.* move; **~ de la porte** doorstep; *fig.* **~ de porte** key money; **~ à ~** step by step; **à grands ~** apace, quickly; *mot.* **aller au ~** go dead slow; **au ~** at a walking pace; **de ce ~** at once, immediately; *geog.* **le ~ de Calais** the Straits *pl.* of Dover; **faire les cent ~** pace up and down; ✗, *sp.* **marquer le ~** mark time; **2.** *adv.* not; **ne ... pas** not; **ne ... pas de** no; **ne ... pas un** not a (single) one; **ne ... pas non plus** nor *or* not ... either.

pas-d'âne ♀ [pɑ'dɑːn] *m/inv.* coltsfoot.

passa|ble [pɑ'sabl] passable, fair; **~de** F [~'sad] *f* brief love affair; **~ge** [~'saːʒ] *m* passage (*a. in a book*); ✆ , *river, etc.*: crossing; way; *mountain*: pass; △ arcade; ⚡ flow; *fig.* transition; **~ clouté** pedestrian crossing, *Am.* crosswalk; **~ souterrain** subway, *Am.* underground passage; **de ~** migratory (*bird*); *fig.* passing, casual; **être de ~** be passing through (*a town*), be in (*a town*) at the moment; **~ger** [~sa'ʒe] **1.** *adj.* passing (*a. fig.*); **2.** *su.* ✆ , ✈ *passenger*; **~gèrement** [~saʒɛr'mɑ̃] temporarily; **~nt** [~'sɑ̃] **1.** *su.* passer-by; *su./m belt*: loop; **2.** *adj.* busy, frequented (*road*); **~vant** [~sa'vɑ̃] *m* ⚓ gangway; *admin.* permit; transire.

passe [pɑːs] *f* ♣ , ✆ , *fencing, foot.*: pass; **bonne (mauvaise) ~** good (bad) position; **en ~ de** (*inf.*) in a fair way to (*inf.*), on the point of (*ger.*); **mot** *m* **de ~** password.

passé [pɑ'se] **1.** *su./m* past; *gramm.* past (*tense*); **2.** *adj.* past; over; faded (*colour*); last (*week etc.*); **3.** *prp.* after; **2 heures ~es (de 5 minutes)** (5 minutes) past 2 o'clock.

passe-droit [pɑs'drwa] *m* (special) privilege.

passéis|me [pase'ism] *m* attachment to the past; **~te** [~'ist] *adj.* (*su.* person) attached to the past.

passementerie [pasmɑ̃'tri] *f* trimmings *pl.*

passe...: **~-partout** [pɑspar'tu] **1.** *su./m/inv.* master key; *phot.* slip-in mount; **2.** *adj.* all-purpose...; *pej.* non-descript; **~-passe** *m/inv.*: **tour de ~** sleight of hand; trick; **~port** [~'pɔːr] *m* passport.

passer [pɑ'se] (1a) **1.** *v/i.* go; pass (by); go *or* come through; get through; go by; go away; call (by *or* in); become; be on (*film, show etc.*), be broadcast (*program, show*); go up to the next class (*student*); be handed down (*tradition*); **~ chez q.** call at s.o.'s *or* on s.o.; *mot.*: **en seconde** change into second gear; **~ par** go through; *road:* go over (*a mountain*); **~ pour** be thought to be, seem; **~ sur** overlook (*a fault*); **faire ~** pass (*s.th.*) on (to, **à**); while away (*the time*); get rid of; **laisser ~** let (*s.o.*) pass; miss (*an opportunity*); **passons!** no more about it!; **se faire ~ pour** pose as; **2.** *v/t.* pass; cross, go *or* come past; hand (over) (to, **à**); slip (*s.th. into a pocket*); slip on, put on (*a garment*); leave out, skip; overlook (*a mistake*); spend (*time*); sit for (*an examination*); vent (*one's anger*) (on, **sur**); *cuis* strain, sift; ✝ place (*an order*); *parl.* pass (*a bill*); **~ en fraude** smuggle (in), **se ~** happen; take place; *by* (*time*); pass off, be over; **se ~ de** do without (*s.th., qch., ger., inf.*).

passerelle [pasˈrɛl] *f* footbridge; gangway; *fig.* (inter)link.

passetemps [pasˈtɑ̃] *m/inv.* pastime; hobby.

passeur [paˈsœːr] *m* smuggler.

passible [paˈsibl] liable (to, **de**).

passif [paˈsif] **1.** *adj.* passive; *fig.* blind (*obedience*); **2.** *su./f gramm.* passive (*voice*); ✝ liabilities *pl.*

passion [paˈsjɔ̃] *f* passion (for, **de**) (*a. eccl.*); **~nant** [pasjoˈnɑ̃] thrilling; fascinating; **~né** [~ˈne] **1.** *adj.* passionate (for, **pour**); enthusiastic (about, **de**); **2.** *su.* enthusiast; **~nel** 🇫🇷 [~ˈnɛl]: *crime* **~** crime of jealousy; **~ner** [~ˈne] (1a) fascinate, grip, thrill, inflame (*a debate etc.*); **se ~ pour** have *or* develop a passion for; be a ... fan.

passivité [pasiviˈte] *f* passivity.

passoire [paˈswaːr] *f* strainer; sieve; colander.

pastel [pasˈtɛl] *su./m, adj.* pastel.

pasteur [pasˈtœːr] *m eccl.* pastor; **~iser** [~tœriˈze] (1a) pasteurize (*milk*).

pastiche [pasˈtiʃ] *m* pastiche, **~er** [~tiˈʃe] (1a) pastiche, parody.

pastille [pasˈtiːj] *f* pastille, lozenge.

pastis [pasˈtis] *m* aniseed aperitif; F muddle, mess.

pat [pat] *su./m adj./m* stalemate.

patate F [paˈtat] *f* potato.

patati! [pataˈti] *int.*: **et ~ et patata** and so forth and so on.

patatras! [pataˈtrɑ] *int.* crash!

pataud [paˈto] clumsy (person).

patauger [patoˈʒe] (1l) splash (about); wade (about); flounder (*a. fig.*).

pâte [pɑːt] *f* paste; dough; *paper:* pulp; **~s** *pl.* **alimentaires** Italien pastes; **~ dentifrice** tooth paste; F **une bonne ~** a good sort; F **une ~ molle** a spineless individual; **~é** [pɑˈte] *m cuis.* pie, pâté; *trees:* clump; *ink:* blot; **~ (de maisons)** block (of houses); **~ (de sable)** sandcastle.

pâtée [pɑˈte] *f* mash.

patelin F [patˈlɛ̃] *m* (native) village.

patent, e [paˈtɑ̃, ~ˈtɑ̃ːt] **1.** *adj.* patent; obvious; **2.** *su./f* trading dues *pl.*; trading licenses; **~é** [~tɑ̃ˈte] **1.** *adj.* licensed; **2.** *su.* licensee.

pater [paˈtɛːr] *m/inv.* Lord's prayer.

patère [paˈtɛːr] *f* coat peg.

patern|e [paˈtɛrn] avuncular; **~el** [patɛrˈnɛl] paternal; fatherly; **~ité** [~niˈte] *f* paternity, fatherhood.

pâteux [pɑˈtø] pasty; doughy (*bread*); thick (*voice*), coated (*tongue*).

pathétique [pateˈtik] **1.** *adj.* pathetic (*a. anat.*); **2.** *su./m* pathos.

patho|logie [patɔlɔˈʒi] *f* pathology; **~logique** [~lɔˈʒik] pathological.

pathos [paˈtɔs] *m* pathos.

patibulaire [patibyˈlɛːr] sinister.

patien|ce [paˈsjɑ̃ːs] *f* patience; **prendre ~** be patient; **~t** [~ˈsjɑ̃] *adj., su.* patient; **~ter** [~sjɑ̃ˈte] (1a) be patient; wait patiently.

patin [paˈtɛ̃] *m* skate; *sledge:* runner; ⚙ brake shoe; **~s** *pl.* **(à glace** ice) skates; **~s** *pl.* **à roulettes** roller skates; **~age** [~tiˈnaːʒ] *m* skating; *wheel, belt:* slipping; **~er** [patiˈne] (1a) skate; slip (*wheel, belt*); skid (*wheel*); *fig.* make no progress; **~ette** [~ˈnɛt] *f* scooter; **~eur** *m*, **-euse** *f* [~ˈnœːr, ~ˈnøːz] skater; **~oire** [~ˈnwaːr] *f* skating rink.

pâtir [pɑˈtiːr] (2a) suffer (from, **de**).

pâtiss|erie [patisˈri] *f* pastry; pastry shop; **~ier** [~tiˈsje] *m* pastrycook.

patois [paˈtwa] *m* dialect; jargon.

patouiller F [patuˈje] (1a) flounder.

patraque F [paˈtrak] seedy.

patriar|cal [patriarˈkal] patriarchal; **~che** [~ˈarʃ] *m* patriarch.

patrie [pa'tri] f native country.

patrimoine [patri'mwan] m patrimony, inheritance.

patriot|e [patri'ɔt] **1.** adj. patriotic; **2.** su. patriot; **~ique** [~ɔ'tik] patriotic; **~isme** [~ɔ'tism] m patriotism.

patron [pa'trɔ̃] m boss; head (of a firm); hotel etc.: owner, proprietor; protector; eccl. patron; cost. pattern; ✝ model; **~age** [patrɔ̃'na:ʒ] m patronage; eccl. young people's club; **~al** [~'nal] eccl. patronal; ✝ employers' ...; **~at** [~'na] m protection; ✝ coll. employers pl.; **~ne** [pa'trɔn] f mistress; protectress; eccl. patroness; **~ner** [patrɔ'ne] (1a) patronize, sponsor.

patrouill|e ✗ [pa'tru:j] f patrol; **~er** ✗ [patru'je] (1a) patrol.

patte [pat] f zo. paw; orn. foot; F leg; envelope, pocket: flap; F **~s** pl. **de mouche** writing: scrawl; **~-d'oie**, pl. **~s-d'oie** [~'dwa] f crossroads pl.; wrinkle: crow's foot.

pâtur|age [pɑty'ra:ʒ] m grazing; pasture; **~e** [~'ty:r] f fodder; food (a. fig.); pasture; **~er** [~ty're] (1a) graze.

paume [po:m] f palm of hand.

paum|é F [po'me] miserable, wretched; down-and-out; fig. lost; **~er** F [~] (1a) lose; catch, nab.

paupière [po'pjɛ:r] f eyelid.

paus|e [po:z] f pause, break; foot. half-time; ♪ rest; **~-café** coffee break; **~er** [po'ze] (1a) pause.

pauvre [po:vr] **1.** adj. poor; fig. **~** en lacking (in), short of; **2.** su.: **les ~s** pl. the poor; **~té** [~vrə'te] f poverty.

pavage [pa'va:ʒ] m paving.

pavaner [pava'ne] (1a): **se ~** strut (around).

pav|é [pa've] m paving stone; pavement; fig. the street(s pl.); **~er** [pa've] (1a) pave.

pavillon [pavi'jɔ̃] m pavilion; lodge, cabin; (small) house; ♪ bell; ⚓ flag; anat. external ear.

pavois [pa'vwa] m ⚓ bulwark; coll. flags pl.; fig. **élever sur le ~** extol; **~er** [~vwa'ze] (1a) v/t. deck with flags; v/i. put out the flags.

pavot [pa'vo] m poppy.

pay|able [pɛ'jabl] payable; **~ant** [~'jɑ̃] **1.** adj. with a charge for admission; fig. profitable; **~e** [pɛ:j] f see **paie**; **~ement**

[pɛj'mɑ̃] m see **paiement**; **~er** [pe'je] (1i) v/t. pay; pay for; fig. reward (for, **de**); **~ qch. à q.** buy or stand s.o. s.th., treat s.o. to s.th.; **~ cher** pay dear, fig. be sorry for; **~ de retour** reciprocate; **il me l'a fait ~ 100 F** he charged me 100 francs for it; **trop payé** overpaid; **se ~ qch.** treat o.s. to s.th.; **se ~ d'illusions** delude o.s.; v/i. pay (a. fig. = be worthwhile); suffer for, **pour**); be well-paid (job etc.); fig. **~ de sa personne** sacrifice o.s.; **~eur** [~'jœ:r] su. payer; bank: teller.

pays [pe'i] m country; land; region; village; **~age** [pei'za:ʒ] m landscape; **~agiste** [~za'ʒist] m landscape painter; landscape gardener; **~an, -anne** [~'zɑ̃, ~'zan] **1.** adj. farming, farmers'; **2.** su. countryman or -woman; peasant; **~annerie** [~zan'ri] f peasantry.

péage [pe'a:ʒ] m toll; tollhouse; **autoroute** f **à ~** toll motorway, Am. turnpike (road).

peau [po] f skin; ✝ pelt; ✝ leather; fruit: peel; fig. **faire ~ neuve** turn over a new leaf; **≗-Rouge**, pl. **≗x-Rouges** [~'ru:ʒ] m Red Indian.

peccadille [peka'di:j] f peccadillo.

pêche¹ ♀ [pɛ:ʃ] f peach; F **avoir la ~** be feeling great.

pêche² [~] f fishing; catch; **~ à la ligne** angling; **aller à la ~** go fishing.

péch|é [pe'ʃe] m sin; **~er** [~] (1f) sin; fig. err; fig. **~ contre** offend against.

pêcher¹ [pɛ'ʃe] m peach tree.

pêcher² [pɛ'ʃe] (1a) fish for; drag up (a corpse); fig. find, pick up; **~ie** [pɛʃ'ri] f fishing ground.

pécheur, -eresse [pe'ʃœ:r, peʃ'rɛs] **1.** adj. sinning; sinful; **2.** su. sinner.

pêcheur, -euse [pɛ'ʃœ:r, ~'ʃø:z] **1.** adj. fishing; **2.** su./m fisherman.

péculat [peky'la] m embezzlement.

pécule [pe'kyl] m savings pl.

pécuniaire [peky'njɛ:r] pecuniary.

pédagog|ie [pedagɔ'ʒi] f teaching; **~ique** [~'ʒik] teaching...; **~ue** [~'gɔg] su. teacher; educationist.

pédal|e [pe'dal] f pedal; F **perdre les ~s** get all mixed up; **~er** [peda'le] (1a) pedal; F cycle.

pédant [pe'dɑ̃] **1.** adj. pedantic; **2.** su. pedant; **~erie** [pedɑ̃'tri] f, **~isme** [~'tism] m pedantry.

pédé F [pe'de] *m* gay, queer; **~raste** [~de'rast] F homosexual.

pédestre [pe'dɛstr] on foot.

pédiatr|e [pe'dja:tr] *m* p(a)ediatrist; **~ie** [~dja'tri] *f* p(a)ediatrics *pl.*

pédicure [pedi'ky:r] *su.* chiropodist.

pègre [pɛ:gr] *f coll.* underworld.

peigne [pɛɲ] *m* comb; **se donner un coup de ~** run a comb through one's hair; *fig.* **passer au ~ fin** go over *s.th.* with a fine-tooth comb; **~é, e** [pe'ɲe] **1.** *adj. fig.* affected (*style*); **2.** *su./f* ⚒ *fig.* thrashing; **~er** [~'ɲe] (1a) comb; card (*wool*); hackle (*hemp*); polish (*one's style*); **~oir** [~'ɲwa:r] *m* dressing gown; **~ de bain** bathrobe.

peinard F [pɛ'naːr] quiet; cushy (*job etc.*); **se tenir ~, rester ~** keep quiet.

peindre [pɛ̃:dr] (4m) paint; *fig.* **~ en beau** paint (*things*) in rosy colo(u)rs; F **se ~** make up.

peine [pɛn] *f* sorrow; trouble, difficulty; effort; punishment; ⚖ sentence; pain; **à ~** hardly; **en valoir la ~** be worth while; **être en ~ de** be at a loss to; **faire de la ~ à** hurt, grieve; ☺ **homme m de ~** labo(u)rer; **se donner de la ~** take pains; **se donner** (*or* **prendre**) **la ~ de** (*inf.*) go to the trouble of (*ger.*); **sous ~ de** under pain of; for fear of; **ce n'est pas la ~ de** (*inf.*) it's no use (*ger.*), there's no point in (*ger.*); **~er** [pɛ'ne] (1a) *v/t.* hurt, grieve; *v/i.* toil; labo(u)r (*a. engine*).

peint|re [pɛ̃:tr] *m* painter; **~ en bâtiments** house painter; **~ure** [pɛ̃'ty:r] *f* painting, paint(work); **prenez garde à la ~!** wet paint!

péjoratif [peʒɔra'tif] pejorative.

pelage [pə'la:ʒ] *m* pelt, fur; **pelé** [pə'le] **1.** *adj.* peeled; bald (*person*); **2.** *su.* F baldpate.

pêle-mêle [pɛl'mɛl] **1.** *adv.* higgledy-piggledy; **2.** *su./m/inv.* jumble.

peler [pə'le] (1d) peel.

pèlerin [pɛl'rɛ̃, ~'rɛ̃] *su.* pilgrim; *su./f cost.* cape; **~age** [~ri'na:ʒ] *m* (place of) pilgrimage.

pelisse [pə'lis] *f* fur-lined coat.

pelle [pɛl] *f* shovel; spade; scoop; **~ mécanique** mechanical digger; F *fig.* **ramasser une ~** fall down.

pellet|erie [pɛl'tri] *f* fur making; fur trade; **~ier** [~'tje] *m* furrier.

pellicul|aire [pɛlliky'lɛ:r] pellicular; **~e** [~'kyl] *f* (thin) skin; *phot.*, *ice*, *oil*: film; **~s** *pl.* dandruff.

pelot|age [pəlɔ'ta:ʒ] *m wool etc.*: winding into balls; F petting; **~e** [~'lɔt] *f* string, wool: ball; cottonwool: wad; (pin)cushion; *game*: pelota; *fig.* **faire sa ~** feather one's nest; **~er** [pəlɔ'te] (1a) F pet, paw; F **se ~** pet, neck; **~on** [~'tɔ̃] *m* string, wool: ball; ✕ platoon; *sp.* bunch; **~ de tête** leaders *pl.*; **~ d'exécution** firing squad; **~onner** [~tɔ'ne] (1a) wind (*s.th.*) into a ball; **se ~** curl up, roll o.s. up.

pelouse [pə'lu:z] *f* lawn; grass plot.

peluch|e *tex.* [pə'lyʃ] *f* plush; **ours *m* en ~** teddy bear; **~er** [pəly'ʃe] (1a) become fluffy; **~eux** [~'ʃø] fluffy.

pelure [pə'ly:r] *f* peel; *onion*: skin; *cheese*: rind; F overcoat.

pénal [pe'nal] penal; **~ité** [~'te] *f* penalty.

penaud [pə'no] sheepish.

pench|able [pɑ̃'ʃabl] **1.** *adj.* sloping, leaning; *fig.* declining; **2.** *su./m* slope; *fig.* inclination (to, **for à**), tendency; *fig.* fondness (for s.o., **pour q.**); **~er** [~'ʃe] (1a) *v/t.* tip, tilt (*s.th.*); **se ~** lean (over); bend (down); *fig.* **se ~ sur** study, look into; *v/i.* tilt, lean (over), be slanting; *fig.* incline (to, **vers**).

pend|able [pɑ̃'dabl] outrageous; **~aison** [~dɛ'zɔ̃] *f death*: hanging; **~ant** [~'dɑ̃] **1.** *adj.* hanging; ⚖ pending; **2.** *su./m* pendant; *fig.* counterpart; ✕ *prp.* during; for (*2 days, 3 miles*); **~ que** while.

pendiller [pɑ̃di'je] (1a) dangle.

pend|re [pɑ̃:dr] (4a) hang (on, from **à**); **~u** [pɑ̃'dy] **1.** *p.p.* of **pendre**; hanged; hanging (on, from **à**).

pendul|aire [pɑ̃dy'lɛ:r] swinging, pendular (*motion*); **~e** [~'dyl] *su./m phys.* pendulum; *su./f* clock.

pêne [pɛ:n] *m lock*: bolt; latch.

pénétr|able [pene'trabl] penetrable; **~ant** [~'trɑ̃] penetrating; piercing; biting; *fig.* counterpart; ✕ *prp.* penetration (*a. fig*); **~é** [~'tre] *fig.* **~ de** full of, convinced of; **~er** [~'tre] (1f) *vt/i.* penetrate; *v/i.*: **~ dans** go or get or come into, enter; *v/t.* fathom (*a secret*); permeate (with, **de**); **se ~ de** become permeated with; *fig.* become convinced of, convince o.s. of.

pénible [pe'nibl] hard, difficult; painful;

P

F tiresome; **~ment** with difficulty; painfully; *reach etc.*: only just.

péniche ⚓ [pe'niʃ] f barge; lighter.

pénicilline [penisil'lin] f penicillin.

péninsul|aire [penɛ̃sy'lɛːr] peninsular; **~e** [~'syl] f peninsula.

péniten|ce [peni'tãːs] f penitence, repentance; *eccl.* penance; punishment; **~cier** [~tã'sje] m *eccl.*, ⚖ penitentiary; **~t** [~'tã] *adj.*, *su.* penitent.

penne [pɛn] f quillfeather.

pénombre [pe'nɔ̃ːbr] f half-light; penumbra; *obscurity (a. fig.)*.

pensant [pã'sã] thinking; **bien ~** right-thinking; conservative; **mal ~** heretical.

pensée¹ 🌸 [pã'se] f pansy.

pens|ée² [pã'se] f thought; idea; *fig.* mind; intention; **~er** [~'se] (1a) *v/i.* think (of, **à**); **~ faire qch.** intend to do s.th.; **faire ~** remind (s.o. of s.th., *q.* **à qch.**); **pensez à faire cela** don't forget to do this, remember doing this; **sans ~** thoughtlessly; *v/t.* think, believe; consider; **elle pense venir** she means to come; **~eur** [~'sœːr] m thinker; **~if** [~'sif] thoughtful.

pension [pã'sjɔ̃] f pension, allowance; boarding house; boarding school; (charge for) board and lodging; **~naire** [pãsjo'nɛːr] *su. boarding house, school*: boarder; *hôtel*: resident; 🏥 inmate; **~nat** [~'na] m boarding school; **~ner** [~'ne] (1a) pension off.

pensum [pɛ̃'sɔm] m chore.

pentagone [pɛ̃ta'gɔn] m pentagon.

pente [pãːt] f slope, incline; gradient; *river*: fall; *fig.* bent; **en ~** sloping.

Pentecôte [pãt'koːt] f Whitsun(tide); Pentecost; **dimanche m de la ~** Whitsunday.

pénultième [penyl'tjɛm] penultimate, last but one.

pénurie [peny'ri] f shortage.

pépère F [pe'pɛːr] m granddad.

pépie [pe'pi] f *vet.* pip; F *fig.* **avoir la ~** have a terrible thirst.

pépiement [pepi'mã] m chirp(ing); **pépier** [~'pje] (1o) chirp, cheep.

pépin [pe'pɛ̃] m *fruit*: pip, seed; F snag, hitch, trouble; F umbrella; *sl.* **avoir un ~ pour** have a crush on; **~ière** [~'njɛːr] f nursery.

perçant [pɛr'sã] piercing; keen (*cold, mind, etc.*); shrill (*voice*); **percée**

[pɛr'se] f opening; ✗, *fig.* breakthrough; **perce-neige** 🌸 [pɛrs'nɛːʒ] f/inv. snowdrop.

percept|eur [pɛrsɛp'tœːr] m tax collector; **~ibilité** [~tibili'te] f perceptibility; **~ible** [~'tibl] perceptible; collectable (*tax*); **~ion** [~'sjɔ̃] f perception; *taxes etc.*: collection.

perc|er [pɛr'se] (1k) *vt/i.* pierce; *fig.* penetrate; break through; *v/t.* make a hole in; perforate; broach (*a cask*); make (*a hole etc.*), cut (*an opening*), drill, bore; **~ une dent** cut a tooth; *fig.* **~ à jour** see through s.o.; *v/i.* come through; **~eur, -euse** [~'sœːr, ~'søːz] *su.* borer; driller; *su./f* drill.

percev|able [pɛrsə'vabl] perceivable; **~oir** [~'vwaːr] (3a) perceive; collect (*taxes etc.*).

perche¹ *icht.* [pɛrʃ] f perch.

perch|e² [pɛrʃ] f pole; F lanky individual; **tendre la ~ à** *q.* give s.o. a helping hand; *sp.* **saut m à la ~** pole vault; **~er** [pɛr'ʃe] (1a) *v/i.*, **se ~** perch, roost; F *fig.* live, F hang out; *v/t.* F put, stick; **~oir** [~'ʃwaːr] m perch, roost.

perclus [pɛr'kly] paralyzed.

percolateur [pɛrkɔla'tœːr] m coffee: percolator.

percu|ssion [pɛrky'sjɔ̃] f percussion; **~tant** [~'tã] percussive; *fig.* that strikes home; **~ter** [~'te] (1a) *v/t.* strike; hit; *v/i.*: **~ contre** crash into, hit.

perd|ant [pɛr'dã] **1.** *adj.* losing; **billet m ~ ticket**: blank; **2.** *su.* loser; **~ition** [~di'sjɔ̃] f *eccl.* perdition; ⚓ **en ~** in distress; **lieu m de ~** den of vice; **~re** [pɛrdr] (4a) *v/t.* lose; waste (*time, pains*); get rid of; be the ruin of; **~ q. de vue** lose sight of s.o.; **se ~** be lost; disappear; lose one's way, get lost; be wasted; go bad; be wrecked; *v/i.* lose; leak.

perdr|eau [pɛr'dro] m young partridge; **~ix** [~'dri] f partridge.

perdu [pɛr'dy] **1.** *p.p. of* **perdre**; **2.** *adj.* lost; waisted; *fig.* ruined; ⊙ sunk; *phys.* idle (*motion*); god-forsaken (*place*); spare (*time*).

père [pɛːr] m father; F **le ~ ...** old ...; **ses ~ et mère** his parents.

péremptoire [perãp'twaːr] peremptory.

pérenni|té [perɛnni'te] f everlastingness; **~ser** [~'ze] (1a) perpetuate.

perfection [pɛrfɛk'sjɔ̃] f perfection; **à la ~** to perfection; **~nement** [~sjɔn'mɑ̃] m improvement; perfecting; **~ner** [~sjɔ'ne] (1a) improve; perfect.

perfid|e [pɛr'fid] false; perfidious; **~ie** [~fi'di] f perfidy, treachery.

perfor|age [pɛrfɔ'raːʒ] m see **perforation**; **~ateur, -trice** [~ra'tœːr, ~'tris] **1.** adj. perforating; **2.** su./m perforator; su./f ⚙ boring or drilling machine; card punch; **~ation** [~ra'sjɔ̃] f perforation (a. ♣); punching; hole; **~er** [~'re] (1a) perforate; punch; make holes or a hole in; **~euse** [~'røːz] f see **perforatrice**.

péricliter [perikli'te] (1a) go downhill, go to ruin.

péril [pe'ril] m peril; **au ~ de** at the risk of; **~leux** [~ri'jø] perilous.

périm|é [peri'me] out-of-date, outdated; expired (ticket etc.); **~er** [~] (1a): **laisser ~** let expire.

périmètre [peri'mɛtr] m ⚕ perimeter; fig. area.

périod|e [pe'rjɔd] f period; **~icité** [perjodisi'te] f periodicity; **~ique** [~'dik] adj., su./m periodical.

péri...: **~pétie** [peripe'si] f sudden change; **~** pl. vicissitudes; **~phérie** [~fe'ri] f ⚕ circumference; town: outskirts pl.; **~phérique** [~fe'rik] **1.** adj. peripheral; outlying (district etc.); **boulevard** m **~ 2.** su./m ring road, circular route.

périr [pe'riːr] (2a) perish, die.

périscope [peris'kɔp] m periscope.

périssable [peri'sabl] perishable.

perl|e [pɛrl] f pearl; bead drop(let); fig. maid, wife, etc.; jewel; F howler; **~é** [pɛr'le] pearly; fig. perfect; **grève** m **~** go-slow (strike); **~er** [~'le] (1a) v/t. do or perform or execute with meticulous care; v/i. form or stand in beads (sweat); bead.

permanen|ce [pɛrma'nɑ̃s] f permanence; office etc. always open to the public; **de ~** on duty, on call, **en ~** permanently; **~t, e** [~'nɑ̃, ~'nɑ̃t] **1.** adj. permanent; **2.** su./f perm(anent wave).

perméable phys. [pɛrme'abl] permeable, pervious.

perm|ettre [pɛr'mɛtr] (4v) permit, allow; make (s.th.) possible; make it possible (to inf., **de** inf.); **~ à q. de faire qch.** enable s.o. to do s.th., make it

possible for s.o. to do s.th.; **se ~ de** (inf.) venture to (inf.); **~is** [~'mi] **1.** p.p. of **permettre**; **2.** adj. permitted, lawful; **3.** su./m permit; licence; (**a. ~ de conduire**) (driving) licence, Am. driver's license; **~ission** [~mi'sjɔ̃] f permission; ✗ leave; **~issionnaire** [~misjɔ'nɛːr] m soldier on leave.

pernicieux [pɛrni'sjø] pernicious.

permut|ation [pɛrmyta'sjɔ̃] f permutation; **~er** [~'te] (1a) change (round); permute.

péronnelle F [perɔ'nɛl] f silly goose.

pérorer [perɔ're] (1a) hold forth.

perpendiculaire [pɛrpɑ̃diky'lɛːr] upright; perpendicular (to, **à**).

perpétr|ation [pɛrpetra'sjɔ̃] f perpetration; **~er** [~'tre] (1f) commit.

perpétu|el [pɛrpe'tɥɛl] perpetual; for life; **~er** [~'tɥe] (1n) perpetuate; **~ité** [~tɥi'te] f perpetuity; **à ~** in perpetuity; ﷼ for life.

perplex|e [pɛr'plɛks] perplexed; **~ité** [~plɛksi'te] f perplexity.

perquisition ﷼ [pɛrkizi'sjɔ̃] f search; **~ domiciliaire** search of a house; **~ner** [~sjɔ'ne] (1a) (carry out a) search.

perron [pɛ'rɔ̃] m front steps pl.

perr|oquet [pɛrɔ'kɛ] m parrot; **~uche** [~'ryʃ] f parakeet; **~** (**ondulée**) budgerigar.

perruque [pɛ'ryk] f wig.

persan [pɛr'sɑ̃] adj., su. Persian.

persécut|er [pɛrseky'te] (1a) persecute; fig. harass; **~cur** [~'tœːr] m persecutor; **~ion** [~'sjɔ̃] f persecution.

persévér|ance [pɛrseve'rɑ̃s] f perseverance (in ger., **à** inf.); **~er** [~'re] (1f) persevere.

persienne [pɛr'sjɛn] f Venetian blind; slatted shutter.

persifl|age [pɛrsi'flaːʒ] m mockery; **~er** [~'fle] (1a) make fun of.

persil [pɛr'si] m parsley; **~lé** [~si'je] blue (-moulded) (cheese).

persist|ance [pɛrsis'tɑ̃s] f persistence (in ger., **à** inf.); continuance; **~ant** [~'tɑ̃] persistent; **~er** [~'te] (1a) persist (in s.th., **dans qch.**, in ger., **à** inf.); **la pluie persiste** it keeps on raining.

personn|age [pɛrsɔ'naːʒ] m personage; thea. character; pej. individual; **~aliser** [~nali'ze] (1a) personalize; give a personal touch to; **~alité** [~nali'te] f personality; *fig.* ~s *pl.* personal remarks; ~e [pɛr'sɔn] **1.** *su./f* person (*a. gramm.*); ɪ̈ɫ̈ ~ *morale* corporate body; *en* ~ in person; *jeune* ~ young lady; **2.** *pron./indef./m/inv.* anybody; (*with negative*) nobody; *qui l'a vu?* ~! who saw him? no one!; ~el [pɛrsɔ'nɛl] **1.** *adj.* personal; self-(*interest etc.*); not transferable (*ticket*); **2.** *su./m* staff, personnel; ✈ ~ *à terre* (*or rampant*) ground crew; ~ifier [~ni'fje] (1o) personify.

perspectif, -ve [pɛrspɛk'tif, ~'tiːv] **1.** *adj.* perspective; **2.** *su./f* perspective; *fig.* prospect; *fig.* viewpoint, angle; *fig. en* ~ in prospect.

perspicace [pɛrspi'kas] clear-sighted, perspicacious; ~ité [~kasi'te] *f* clear-sightedness, perspicacity.

persuader [pɛrsɥa'de] (1a) persuade; convince; (of, *de*; to *inf.*, *de inf.*); ~sif [~'zif] persuasive; ~sion [~'zjɔ̃] *f* persuasion; conviction.

perte [pɛrt] *f* loss, ruin; waste; leakage; ✗ ~s *pl.* casualties; ~ *sèche* dead loss; ✝ *à* ~ at a loss; *à* ~ *de vue* as far as the eye can see; *en pure* ~ to no purpose.

pertinence [pɛrti'nɑ̃ːs] *f* pertinence; ~t [~'nɑ̃] pertinent, relevant, apt; judicious.

perturbateur [pɛrtyrba'tœːr] **1.** *adj.* disruptive; disturbing; **2.** *su.* disturber; ~er [~'be] (1a) disrupt; disturb; upset; ~ation [~'sjɔ̃] *f* disruption; disturbance.

pervers [pɛr'vɛːr] **1.** *adj.* perverse; perverted; **2.** *su.* ✿ pervert; ~sion [~ver'sjɔ̃] *f* perversion; ~sité [~vɛrsi'te] *f* perversity; ~tir [~ver'tiːr] (2a) pervert.

pesage [pə'zaːʒ] *m* weighing; *turf:* weighing-in; ~mment [~za'mɑ̃] heavily; ~nt [~'zɑ̃] **1.** *adj.* heavy; weighty; **2.** *su./m: valoir son* ~ *d'or* be worth one's weight in gold; ~nteur [~zɑ̃'tœːr] *f* heaviness.

pèse... [pɛz] ...ometer; ...-scales *pl.*; ~-bébé [~be'be] *m* baby scales *pl.*

pesée [pə'ze] *f* weighing; leverage; *faire la* ~ *de* weigh (*s.th.*); **pèse-lettre** [pɛz-'lɛtr] *m* letter-scales *pl.*; **pèse-personne** [~pɛr'sɔn] *m* (bathroom) scales *pl.*; **peser** [pə'ze] (1d) *v/t.* weigh; consider; *v/i.* fig. lie *or* weigh heavy (on *sur*, *à*); ~ *sur* a. press hard on; **peson** [~'zɔ̃] *m* balance.

pessimisme [pɛsi'mism] *m* pessimism;

~te [~'mist] **1.** *adj.* pessimistic; **2.** *su.* pessimist.

pestle [pɛst] *f* plague (*a. fig.*); F *fig.* pest; ✿ ~ *noire* bubonic plague, *hist.* Black Death; ~er [pɛs'te] (1a): (*a.* ~ *contre*) curse (*s.o.*, *s.th.*); ~iféré [~tife're] pest-ridden; ~ilence [~ti'lɑ̃ːs] *f* stench; ~ilentiel [~tilɑ̃'sjɛl] foul(-smelling).

pet [pɛ] *m* V fart; *cuis.* ~-*de-nonne* doughnut, fritter.

pétale ✿ [pe'tal] *m* petal.

pétarade [peta'rad] *f* crackle; *mot.* backfire; ~arader [~ra'de] (1a) backfire; ~ard [~'taːr] *m* cracker; F row, racket; F gun; F *être en* ~ be (raging) mad (at, *contre*); F *faire du* ~ raise a stink; ~er F [~'te] (1f) V fart; *fig.* bust; burst; go off; ~illant [~ti'jɑ̃] sparkling; bubbly, fizzy; ~iller [~ti'je] (1a) crackle; bubble; sparkle; *fig.* scintillate.

petiot F [pə'tjo] tiny, little.

petit [pə'ti] **1.** *adj.* small, little; slight; minor (*nobility*, *subject*); tight (*shoes*); short; young (*a. zo.*); trifling; *pej.* mean; ~ *à* ~ little by little; (*v.*) *ami*(*e*) boyfriend (girlfriend); ~es *gens pl.* humble people; **2.** *su.* child, kid; *zo.* young; ~-*déjeuner* [~tideʒø'ne] (1a) (have) breakfast; ~e-fille, *pl.* ~es-filles [~tit'fiːj] *f* granddaughter; ~ement [~tit'mɑ̃] poorly; pettily; meanly; ~esse [~ti'tɛs] *f* smallness, littleness; *pej.* meanness; ~fils [~ti'fis] *m* grandson.

pétition [peti'sjɔ̃] *f* petition; ~naire [~sjɔ'nɛːr] *su.* petitioner.

petits-enfants [pətizɑ̃'fɑ̃] *m/pl.* grandchildren.

pétoche F [pe'tɔʃ] *f* fear; *avoir la* ~ be scared (stiff).

pétrification [petrifika'sjɔ̃] *f* petrification; ~er [~'fje] (1o) petrify.

pétrin [pe'trɛ̃] *m* kneading trough; F *fig.* mess, fix; ~ir [~'triːr] (2a) knead; mo(u)ld.

pétrole [pe'trɔl] *m* petroleum; mineral oil; paraffin, *Am.* kerosene; ~ier [petrɔ'lje] **1.** *adj.* oil-...; **2.** *su./m* tanker; ~ifère [~li'fɛːr] oil-bearing; oil-(*belt*, *field*, *well*).

pétulance [pety'lɑ̃ːs] *f* liveliness; ~t [~'lɑ̃] lively; frisky.

peu [pø] **1.** *adv.* little; few; *before adj.:* un-..., not very; ~ *à* ~ bit by bit; ~ *avant*

picoter

(après) shortly before (afterwards); ~
de little *(bread etc.)*, few *(people, things,
etc.)*; ~ **de chose** nothing much; ~
d'entre eux few of them; **à ~ près** near-
ly; more or less; *depuis* ~ of late; *pour ~
que (sbj.)* if ever *(ind.)*; *sous* ~ before
long; *viens un ~!* come here!; **2.** *su./m*
little, bit; want, lack; *le ~ de ...* the little
...; the lack of ...; *un ~ de* a bit of.

peupl|ade [pœ'plad] *f* (small) tribe,
people; ~**e** [pœpl] *m* people; nation;
~**er** [pœ'ple] (1a) populate (with, *de*);
stock *(with animals etc.)*; inhabit, live in
or on; *fig.* fill; *se* ~ fill up with people.

peuplier ♀ [pœpli'e] *m* poplar.

peur [pœ:r] *f* fear, dread; *avoir* ~ **be**
afraid (of, *de*), be scared (of, *de*); *de* ~
de *(faire)* **qch.** for fear of (doing) s.th.;
de ~ *que ... (ne) (sbj.)* for fear of *(ger.)*;
faire **à** frighten *(s.o.)*; ~**eux** [pœ'rø]
fearful; timid.

peut-être [pø'tɛːtr] *adv.* perhaps,
maybe; *peuvent* [pœːv] *3rd p. pl. pres.
of pouvoir 1*; *peux* [pø] *1st p. sg. pres.
of pouvoir 1*.

phalange [fa'lɑ̃ːʒ] *f anat.*, ⚔ phalanx.

phalène [fa'lɛn] *f* moth.

phare [faːr] *m* lighthouse; beacon; *mot.*
headlight; *baisser les* ~**s** dim or dip the
headlights; *en pleins* ~**s** on full beam,
Am. on high beams; *se mettre en* ~**s**
put on the full beam *(Am.* high beams).

pharis|aïque [fariza'ik] pharisaic(al);
~**aïsme** [~za'ism] *m* pharisaism; ~**ien**
[~'zjɛ̃] *m* pharisee.

pharma|ceutique [farmasø'tik] **1.** *adj.*
pharmaceutic(al); **2.** *su./f* pharmaceu-
tics *sg.*; ~**cie** [~'si] *f* pharmacy; chemist's (shop), *Am.* drugstore; medicine
chest, ~**cien** *m*, -**enne** *f* [~'sjɛ̃,
~'sjɛn] chemist, *Am.* druggist.

phase [faːz] *f* phase.

phénomène [feno'mɛn] *m* phenomenon; *fig.* wonder; *fig.* freak.

philanthrop|e [filɑ̃'trop] *su.* philanthro-
pist; ~**ie** [~trɔ'pi] *f* philanthropy.

philatéli|e [filate'li] *f* stamp collecting;
~**ste** [~'list] *su.* stamp collector.

philo...: ~**logie** [filɔlɔ'ʒi] *f* philology;
~**logue** [~'lɔg] *su.* philologist; ~**sophe**
[~'zɔf] **1.** *su.* philosopher; **2.** *adj.* philo-
sophical; ~**sophie** [~zɔ'fi] *f* philosophy;
~**sophique** [~zɔ'fik] philosophic(al).

phobie [fɔ'bi] *f* phobia.

phonétique [fɔne'tik] **1.** *adj.* phonetic; **2.**
su./f phonetics *pl.*

phonographe [fɔnɔ'graf] *m* gramophone; phonograph.

phoque [fɔk] *m zo.* seal; ♥ sealskin.

phosphate [fɔs'fat] *m* phosphate.

phosphore [fɔs'fɔːr] *m* phosphorus;
~**scent** [~fɔre'sɑ̃] phosphorescent.

photo [fɔ'to] *f* photo; *faire de la* ~ go in
for photography.

photo... [fɔto] photo...; ~**chromie**
[~krɔ'mi] *f* colo(u)r photography;
~**copie** [~kɔ'pi] *f* photocopy; ~**copier**
[~kɔ'pje] (1a) photocopy; ~**graphe**
[~'graf] *m* photographer; ~**graphie**
[~gra'fi] *f* photograph(y); ~**graphier**
[~gra'fje] (1o) photograph; *se faire* ~
have one's photo(graph) taken; ~**graphique** [~gra'fik] photographic; *appareil m* ~ camera.

phras|e [fraːz] *f* sentence; phrase *(a. ♪)*;
~ *toute faite* stock phrase; *sans* ~**s**
without mincing matters; ~**er** [fra'ze]
(1a) phrase.

physicien [fizi'sjɛ̃] *m* physicist.

physiolog|ie [fizjɔlɔ'ʒi] *f* physiology;
~**que** [~lɔ'ʒik] physiological.

physionomie [fizjɔnɔ'mi] *f* physiogno-
my; face, features; *fig.* aspect.

physique [fi'zik] **1.** *adj.* physical; bodily;
2. *su./f* physics *sg.*; *su./m* physique;
appearance, looks *pl.*; *au* ~ physically.

piaffer [pja'fe] (1a) paw the ground
(*horse*); stamp (the ground); *fig.* ~
d'impatience fidget.

piailler [pja'je] (1a) squawk.

pian|iste [pja'nist] *su.* pianist; ~**o**
[~'no] **1.** *adv.* ♪ piano, softly; F gently,
easy; **2.** *su./m* piano(forte); ~ *à queue*
grand piano; ~ *droit* upright piano;
~**oter** [~nɔ'te] (1a) ♪ tinkle (on the piano); *fig.* ~ *sur* drum one's fingers on.

piaule *sl.* [pjol] *f* pad.

piauler [pjo'le] (1a) cheep *(bird)*; whimper.

pic¹ [pik] *m* pick(axe), *geog.*, ♣ peak;
cards: pique; **à** ~ vertically, straight
down; *fig.* just at the right moment.

pic² *orn.* [~] *m* woodpecker.

picorer [pikɔ're] (1a) peck (at).

picot|é [pikɔ'te] pitted; ~**ement** [~'tmɑ̃]
m smarting (sensation); prickling; ~**er**
[~'te] (1a) (make) smart; prickle; peck
(at) *(bird)*.

pie¹ [pi] **1.** *su./f orn.* magpie; F chatterbox; **2.** *adj./inv.* piebald.

pie² [~] *œuvre f* ~ good work.

pièce [pjɛs] *f* piece; room (*in a house*); part (*a.* ⚙); coin; *cost.* patch; *thea.* play; ⚖ document; ⚙ ~s *pl. de rechange* spare parts; ~ *d'eau* ornamental lake; ~ *de résistance cuis.* principal dish; *fig.* principal feature; ~ *d'identité* identification (card); **à la** ~ separately; **5 F (la)** ~ 5 F each; **de toutes** ~s completely, entirely; **en** ~s in or to pieces; **mettre en** ~s smash or pull or tear (*s.th.*) to pieces; **tout d'une** ~ all of a piece.

pied [pje] *m* foot; base; *furniture:* leg; ⚘ stalk; *wineglass:* stem; *camera etc.:* stand; *lettuce etc.:* head; ~ *plat* flatfoot; **à** ~ on foot; walking; **au** ~ **de la lettre** literal(ly *adv.*); **au** ~ **levé** off the cuff; **avoir** ~ have a footing; **coup** *m* **de** ~ kick; **en** ~ full-length (*portrait*); *sl.* **c'est le** ~**!** that's great!; F **mettre q. à** ~ sack s.o.; **mettre sur** ~ establish, set up; **prendre** (*perdre*) ~ gain a (lose one's) foothold; ~**-à-terre** [~ta'tɛːr] *m/inv.* pied-à-terre; ~**-de-poule** [~d'pul] *adj.,* *su./m inv.* hound's-tooth; ~**-bot,** *pl.* ~**s-bots** [~'bo] *m* club-footed person.

piédestal [pjedɛs'tal] *m* pedestal.

pied-noir, *pl.* **pieds-noirs** [pje'nwaːr] *m* French settler in Algeria.

piège [pjɛːʒ] *m* trap; **prendre au** ~ trap; **tendre un** ~ **à** set a trap for; **piéger** [pje'ʒe] (1g) trap; booby-trap.

pierr|aille [pjɛ'raːj] *f* (loose) stones *pl.*; ~**e** [pjɛːr] *f* stone; ~ **à briquet** flint; *sl.* *fine* semi-precious stone; ~ *précieuse* gem; ~**eries** [pjɛrə'ri] *f/pl.* jewels; ~**eux** [~'rø] stony; ⚕ calculous.

piété [pje'te] *f* piety; devotion.

piétiner [pjeti'ne] (1a) *v/t.* trample on; *v/i.* stamp; (*a.* ~ *sur place*) mark time.

piéton [pje'tɔ̃] *m* pedestrian; ~**nier** [~tɔ'nje] pedestrian, for pedestrians.

piètre [pjɛtr] poor; mediocre; lame (*excuse*); **faire** ~ **figure** cut a sorry figure.

pieu [pjø] *m* stake, pile, post; *sl.* bed; ~**ter** *sl.* [~'te] (1a): **se** ~ hit the sack.

pieuvre *zo.* [pjœːvr] *f* octopus.

pieux [pjø] pious, devout; dutiful (*child*); ⚖ charitable (*bequest*).

pif F [pif] *m* nose; ~**ometre** F [~ɔ'mɛtr]: **au** ~ by guesswork.

pige [piːʒ] *f* measuring rod; *journ.* **à la** ~ (*paid*) by the line; *sl.* **faire la** ~ **à** do better than, outdo.

pigeon [pi'ʒɔ̃] *m* pigeon (*a.* F *fig.*); ~ *voyageur* homing pigeon.

piger *sl.* [pi'ʒe] (1l) understand, get (it); look (at).

pignocher F [piɲɔ'ʃe] (1a) pick (at one's food).

pignon [pi'ɲɔ̃] *m* △ gable; ⚙ cogwheel; ⚘ pine seed; *fig.* **avoir** ~ **sur rue** be well set up.

pile¹ [pil] *f* pile, heap; △ *bridge:* pier; *phys.* (atomic) pile; ⚡ battery; *phys.* ~ *couveuse* breeder reactor.

pile² [~] *f coin:* reverse; ~ **ou face** heads *pl.* or tails *pl.*; **jouer à** ~ **ou face** toss up; F exactly, right, just; F **s'arrêter** ~ stop short.

piler [pi'le] (1a) crush, grind.

pilier △ [pi'lje] *m* pillar (*a. fig.*).

pill|age [pi'jaːʒ] *m* looting, pillaging; ~**ard** [~'jaːr] *su.* loot, plunder; ~**er** [~'je] (1a) loot, plunder; *fig.* plagiarize; ~**eur** [~'jœːr] **1.** *adj.* looting; **2.** *su.* plunderer.

pilon [pi'lɔ̃] *m* pestle; F wooden leg; *cuis.* *fowl:* drumstick; ~**ner** [~lɔ'ne] (1a) pound, crush; ✕, *fig.* bombard.

pilori [pilɔ'ri] *m* pillory.

pilot|age [pilɔ'taːʒ] *m* piloting; ✈ flying; ✈ ~ *sans visibilité* blind flying; ~**e** [~'lɔt] **1.** *su./m* ⚓, ✈, *etc.* pilot; *fig.* guide; **2.** *adj.* pilot (*project etc.*), experimental; ⚓ low-priced (*drink etc.*); ~**er** [pilɔ'te] (1a) pilot; ✈ fly; drive; guide (round Paris, **dans Paris**).

pilule ⚕, *a. fig.* [pi'lyl] *f* pill.

pimbêche [pɛ̃'bɛʃ] *f* stuck-up girl.

piment [pi'mɑ̃] *m cuis.* red pepper; *fig.* spice; ~**er** [~mɑ̃'te] (1a) season with red pepper; *fig.* spice.

pimpant [pɛ̃'pɑ̃] trim and fresh.

pin ⚘ [pɛ̃] *m* pine(-tree), fir(-tree); **pomme** *f* **de** ~ fir-cone, pine-cone.

pinacle [pi'nakl] *m* pinnacle; F **porter au** ~ praise (*s.o.*) to the skies.

pinard F [pi'naːr] *m* wine.

pince [pɛ̃ːs] *f* ⚙ pincers *pl.*, pliers *pl.*; tongs *pl.*; tweezers *pl.*; clip; ⚙ crowbar; *crab:* claw; *sl.* hand; *cost.* pleat; ~ **à linge** clothes peg (*Am.* pin); ~ **à ongles** nail clippers *pl.*

pincé [pɛ̃'se] prim, affected, stiff.

pinceau [pɛ̃'so] *m* (paint) brush; *opt. light*: pencil; *sl.* foot.

pin|cer [pɛ̃'se] (1k) pinch; nip; grip; purse (*one's lips*); ♪ pluck; *cost.* put darts in; F catch, nab; *en ~ pour* have a crush on (*s.o.*); **~cettes** [~'sɛt] *f/pl.* tweezers; (fire) tongs; **~çon** [~'sɔ̃] *m* pinch(-mark).

pineraie ♀ [pin'rɛ] *f*, **pinède** ♀ [pi'nɛd] *f* pine forest.

pingouin [pɛ̃'gwɛ̃] *m* penguin.

pingre [pɛ̃:gr] miserly, stingy.

pinson [pɛ̃'sɔ̃] *m* finch.

pintade [pɛ̃'tad] *f* guinea-fowl.

pinter *sl.* [pɛ̃'te] (1a) booze.

ploch|e ♀ [pjɔʃ] *f* pick(axe); **~er** [pjɔ'ʃe] (1a) dig (*with a pick*); F *fig.* swot (at), grind (at); *fig.* **~ dans** dig *or* dip into (*one's savings etc.*); **~eur** [~'ʃœ:r] *su.* F swot, grind; *su./m* ⊕ navvy.

pion [pjɔ̃] *m* chess: pawn; *draughts*: man; F *school*: supervisor.

pioncer *sl.* [pjɔ̃'se] (1k) sleep.

pionnier [pjɔ'nje] *m* pioneer.

pipe [pip] *f* pipe; F cigarette; F *casser sa ~* die, F kick the bucket; F *par tête de ~* per head; F *se fendre la ~* split ones sides laughing.

piper [pi'pe] (1a) load (*a dice*); mark (*a card*); *ne pas ~ (mot)* not to breathe a word.

pipi *ch.sp.* [pi'pi] *m*: *faire ~* wee.

piqu|ant [pi'kɑ̃] **1.** *adj.* pricking; biting (*remark, wind*); tart (*wine*); pungent; *fig.* piquant; *cuis.* hot (*spice*); **2.** *su./m* ✗ sting; *zo.* quill; *cuis., a. fig.* bite; *fig.* piquancy; *fig.* point; **~e** [pik] *su./f* ✗ ✝ pike; pointed tip; pique; *su./m cards*: spade(s *pl.*); **~é 1.** *adj.* sour (*wine*); ♪ staccato; ✗ nose-(dive); F dotty; *see piquer*; **2.** *su./m* quilting; ✗ nosedive; **~e-assiette** F [pika'sjɛt] *m* sponger, scrounger; **~e-nique** [~'nik] *m* picnic; **~er** [pi'ke] (1m) *vt/i.* prick; sting (*a. fig.*); *v/t.* arouse, stir up (*s.o.'s interest etc.*); moths, worms: eat into; *tex.* quilt; stick (into, *dans*); arouse (*s.o.'s curiosity*); *cuis., fig.* lard; F steal, pinch; ✗ *~ q. à qch.* give an injection of s.th. to s.o.; F *un soleil* blush; *se ~* get mildewy; turn sour; *fig.* get offended; *se ~ de* pride o.s. on; *v/i.* swoop (down); (go into a) dive; fall (headfirst); rush, charge, dart.

piquet [pi'kɛ] *m* stake, post; picket; *~ de grève* strike picket; **~é** [pik'te] dotted, studded (with, *de*).

piquette [pi'kɛt] *f* poor wine; F defeat, thrashing.

piqûre [pi'ky:r] *f* sting, prick; bite; ✗ injection, shot; puncture; spot, stain; quilting, stitching, sewing.

pirat|e [pi'rat] *m* pirate; *~ de l'air* highjacker; **~erie** [~'tri] *f* piracy; *~ aérienne* highjacking.

pire [pi:r] worse; *le ~* (the) worst.

pis¹ [pi] *m* udder.

pis² [pi] *adv.* worse; *le ~* (the) worst; *au ~ aller* if the worst comes to the worst; **~-aller** [piza'le] *m/inv.* stopgap.

piscicult|eur [pisikyl'tœ:r] *m* pisciculturist; **~ure** [~kyl'ty:r] *f* pisciculture, fish-breeding.

piscine [pi'sin] *f* swimming pool.

piss|e [pis] *f* urine; **~enlit** ♀ [~sɑ̃'li] *m* dandelion; **~er** V [~'se] (1a) piss; **~oir** [~'swa:r] *m* urinal; **~otière** V [~so'tjɛ:r] *f* urinal.

pistache [pis'taʃ] *f* pistachio nut.

pist|e [pist] *f* (race)track; *circus*: ring; *hunt., a. fig.* trail, track; *police*: lead; ✈ *~ d'atterrissage* landing-strip; ✈ *~ d'envoi* runway; *cin.* ✗ **sonore** sound-track; **~er** [pis'te] *hunt.* track; tail (*s.o.*).

pistolet [pisto'lɛ] *m* pistol; (*a. ~ pulvérisateur*) spray gun.

piston [pis'tɔ̃] *m* ⊕ piston; ♪ cornet; *fig.* influence, pull; **~ner** F [~tɔ'ne] (1a) pull strings for (*s.o.*).

pit|ance [pi'tɑ̃:s] *f* (allowance of) food; **~eux** [~'tø] piteous, sorry, woeful.

pitié [pi'tje] *f* pity (on, *de*); *à faire ~* pitiful(ly); *avoir ~ de q., prendre q. en ~* have *or* take pity on s.o.; *faire ~ (à q.)* inspire pity (in s.o.); *ils me font ~* I feel sorry for them, I pity them; *(par) ~!* for pity's sake!; *sans ~* pitiless.

piton [pi'tɔ̃] *m* ⊕ ringbolt; F nose; *geog.* peak; *~ à vis* ✗ screw eye.

pitoyable [pitwa'jabl] pitiable.

pitre [pitr] *m* clown; **~rie** [~ə'ri] *f* tomfoolery; **~s** *pl. a.* antics.

pittoresque [pito'rɛsk] **1.** *adj.* picturesque; **2.** *su./m* picturesqueness.

pivoine [pi'vwan] *f* peony.

pivot [pi'vo] *m* pivot; **~er** [~vo'te] (1a) pivot; spin, swivel (round).

placa|ge [pla'ka:ʒ] *m* veneer(ing); **~rd** [~'ka:r] *m* cupboard; poster; **~rder** [~kar'de] (1a) post (*a bill*).

place [plas] *f* place, position; space, room; seat (*a.* 🚢, *thea.*, *etc.*); square; job, employment; **à la ~ de** instead of; **à votre ~** if I were you; **à sa ~,** **en ~** be, put etc. in it's (proper) place, where it belongs; **de ~ en ~, par ~s** here and there; **faire ~ à, laisser la ~ à** give way to; **sa ~ est dans …** he etc. belongs in …; **sur ~** on the spot; **~ment** [plas'mã] *m* placing; ✝ investment.

placer [pla'se] (1k) place; put; set; seat (*guests etc.*); find a job *or* place for (*s.o.*); get *or* put in (*a. fig. a remark etc.*); ✝ invest, place; **se ~** stand; sit (down); be placed.

placeur, -euse [pla'sœr, ~'sø:z] *su.* employment agent; *su./f thea.* usherette.

placid|e [pla'sid] placid, calm; **~ité** [~sidi'te] *f* placidity, calmness.

plafon|d [pla'fɔ̃] *m* ceiling (*a. fig., a.* ✈); *mot.* maximum speed; **~ner** [~fɔ'ne] (1a) reach a maximum; ✈, ✝ reach the ceiling (of, à).

plage [pla:ʒ] *f* beach; seaside resort; surface; place, area, zone; period (*of time*); section; range.

plagi|aire [pla'ʒjɛ:r] *m* plagiarist (from, de); **~at** [~'ʒja] *m* plagiarism; **~er** [~'ʒje] (1o) plagiarize.

plaid|er [plɛ'de] (1a) *vt/i.* plead; *v/i.* litigate; **~eur** *m*, **-euse** *f* 🛱 [~'dœ:r, ~'dø:z] litigant; **~oirie** 🛱 [~dwa'ri] *f* counsel's speech; **~oyer** [~dwa'je] *m* 🛱 defence speech; *fig.* plea (for, **en faveur de**).

plaie [plɛ] *f* wound; sore (*a. fig.*).

plaignant 🛱 [plɛ'ɲã] *su.* plaintiff.

plaindre [plɛ̃:dr] (4m) pity, be sorry for; **se ~** complain (about, of **de**; to **à**); moan.

plaine [plɛn] *f* plain.

plain-pied [plɛ̃'pje]: **de ~** at street level; *fig.* straight, directly; **de ~ avec** on a level with.

plaint|e [plɛ̃:t] *f* complaint (*a.* 🛱); moan; **porter ~** lodge a complaint; **~if** [plɛ̃'tif] plaintive.

plai|re [plɛ:r] (4z) *v/i.:* **à** please; *v/impers.:* **cela lui plaît** he likes that; **s'il vous** (*or* **te**) **plaît** please; *v/t.:* **se ~** delight (in, **à**); enjoy o.s.; **~samment** [plɛza'mã] *adv.* of *plaisant 1*.

plaisance [plɛ'zã:s] *f*: **de ~** pleasure(*boat, ground*); ⚓ yachting.

plaisant [plɛ'zã] **1.** *adj.* pleasant; amusing; **~er** [plɛzã'te] (1a) *v/i.* joke; **pour ~** for fun, for a joke; *v/t.* chaff (*s.o.*); **~erie** [~'tri] *f* joke; **par ~** for a joke; **~in** [~'tɛ̃] *m* joker.

plais|ir [plɛ'zi:r] *m* pleasure; delight; amusement; favo(u)r; **à ~** at will; without cause; **avec ~** willingly; **de ~** pleasure-…; **faire ~ à** delight; please; be nice to (*s.o.*); **menus ~s** *pl.* little luxuries; **~ons** [plɛ'zɔ̃] *1st p. pl. pres.* of *plaire*.

plaît [plɛ] *3rd p. sg. pres.* of *plaire*.

plan [plã] **1.** *adj.* plane (*a.* 🅰), level, flat; **2.** *su./m* 🅰, △, ✔, 🗲, *opt.* plane; *fig.* level, sphere; *fig.* rank, importance; △ *etc., fig.* plan; map; schedule; program(me); *cin.* **gros ~** close-up; **premier ~** foreground, *fig.* first importance; **second ~** background, *fig.* second rank; *fig.* **en ~** abandoned; stranded; **laisser en ~** drop (*s.th.*); leave (*s.o.*) high and dry; **sur le ~ de …** as far as … is concerned; **sur le ~** (+ *adj.*) from the … point of view, … speaking.

planch|e [plã:ʃ] *f* board; plank; ✔ bed; *thea.* **~s** *pl.* stage *sg.*; ⚓ **de débarquement** gangplank; **~er** [~'ʃe] **1.** *su./m* floor; **2.** bottom, minimum (*price etc.*); **~ette** [~'ʃɛt] *f* small board.

plané [pla'ne] gliding; **vol** *m* **~** glide.

planer [pla'ne] (1a) glide; soar; hover; float.

planét|aire [plane'tɛ:r] **1.** *adj.* planetary; **2.** *su./m* planetarium; **planète** *astr.* [~'nɛt] *f* planet.

planeur ✈ [pla'nœ:r] *m* glider.

planifi|cation [planifika'sjɔ̃] *f* planning; **~er** [~'fje] (1o) plan.

planning [pla'niŋ] *m* schedule, program(me); **~ familial** family planning.

planqu|e *sl.* [plã:k] hideaway; cushy job; **~er** *sl.* [plã'ke] (1m) hide (away) (*a.* **se ~**).

plant [plã] *m* sapling; plantation; **~age** [plã'ta:ʒ] *m* plantating.

plant|ation [plãta'sjɔ̃] *f* planting; plantation; **~e** [plã:t] *f* ✿ plant; *foot.* sole; **~ d'appartement** indoor plant; **~er** [plã'te] (1a) plant; stick, put; fix, set up; F **~ là** walk out on (*s.o.*); jilt (*s.o.*); chuck up, dump (*s.th.*); **se ~** (take a)

stand; get stuck; F *fig.* be all wrong;
~eur [~'tœ:r] *m* planter.
planton ✗ [plɑ̃'tɔ̃] *m* orderly.
plantureux [plɑ̃ty'rø] plentiful, copious,
rich; *fig.* buxom.
plaqu|e [plak] *f* sheet; *metal, phot.*:
plate; *marble*: slab; plaque; badge; ~
commémorative (votive) tablet; *mot.*
de police number plate; **~ de porte
(rue)** name plate (street plate); **~
tournante** turntable; **~é** ⊙ [pla'ke]
plated metal; electro-plate; veneered
wood; **~er** [~'ke] (1m) ⊙ plate; ⊙
veneer; *foot.* tackle; ♪ strike (*a chord*),
F run out on (*s.o.*); jilt (*s.o.*); chuck
(up); **~ette** [~'kɛt] *f* small plate; thin
slab; brochure.
plasma [plas'ma] *m* plasma.
plastic [plas'tik] *m* plastic explosive.
plastiqu|e [plas'tik] **1.** *adj.* plastic; **2.**
su./m plastic; *su./f* plastic art; *fig.* figure.
plat [pla] **1.** *adj.* flat (*a. fig.*); level;
smooth (*sea*); straight (*hair*); low-
heeled (*shoes*); empty (*purse*); *fig.* dull;
fig. poor, paltry; **2.** *su./m* flat part (*of
s.th.*); oar, *tongue*: blade; *cuis.* dish; **à ~**
flat; F *fig.* washed out, all in; F **mettre
les pieds dans le ~** put one's foot in it;
tomber à ~ fall flat.
platane ♣ [pla'tan] *m* plane tree.
plateau [pla'to] *m* tray; *geog.* plateau;
thea. stage; *record player*: turntable;
cuis. **~ de fromages** (choice of) cheeses
pl.
plate-bande, *pl.* **plates-bandes**
[plat'bɑ̃:d] *f* flower bed; border; F *fig.*
marches sur les platesbandes de q.
trespass on *s.o.*'s preserves.
platée [pla'te] *f* plate(ful).
plate-forme, *pl.* **plates-formes**
[plat'fɔrm] *f bus, a. fig.*; platform
platin|e [pla'tin] *su./f* lock, watch: plate;
record player: turntable; *su./m min.*
platinum.
platitude [plati'tyd] *f* platitude; dullness; *fig.* servility.
plâtr|age [plɑ'tra:ʒ] *m* plastering; plas-
ter-work; **~as** [~'tra] *m* rubble; lump
(of plaster *etc.*); **~e** [plɑ:tr] *m* plaster;
plaster statue; ✂ plaster cast; **battre
comme ~** beat to a jelly; **~er** [plɑ'tre]
(1a) plaster; ✂ put in plaster, put in a
plaster cast.

plausible [plo'zibl] plausible.
plébiscite [plebi'sit] *m* plebiscite.
plein [plɛ̃] **1.** *adj.* full; open (*country,
sea*); big with young (*animal*); solid
(*wood, wire*); **~ de** full of; F **~ de** (*choses
etc.*) a lot of, loads of (*things etc.*); **à ~**
full(y); at maximum; **pleine saison** the
height of the season; **en ~** right, exactly, directly; **en ~ air** in the open; **en ~
milieu** right in the middle; **en pleine
rue** in the open street; **2.** *su./m* full part;
building: solid part; fill(ing), *fig.* **battre
son ~** be in full swing (*carnival, season,
etc.*); *mot.* **faire le ~** fill up; **~emploi**
[plenɑ̃'plwa] *m* full employment;
~-temps [plɛ̃'tɑ̃] full-time (job).
pléni|er [ple'nje] plenary; **~potentiaire**
[plenipotɑ̃'sjɛːr] *adj.*, *su./m* plenipotentiary; **~tude** [~'tyd] *f* fullness.
pleur [plœːr] *f* tear; **~ard** [plœ'raːr] **1.** *adj.*
whimpering; tearful; **2.** *su.* whiner; **~er**
[plœ're] (1a) *v/i.* weep; cry (for, **de**;
over, **sur**) (*a. fig.*); water, run (*eyes*); ⊙
drip; *v/t.* weep for, mourn (for).
pleurésie ✗ [plœre'zi] *f* pleurisy
pleureur [plœ'rœːr] **1.** *adj.* tearful; weep-
ing (*a. willow*); **2.** *su.* weeper.
pleurnich|er [plœrni'ʃe] (1a) whine,
snivel, **~erie** [~niʃ'ri] *f* whining; **~eur**
[~ni'fœːr] **1.** *adj.* whining; **2.** *su.* whiner.
pleut [plø] *3rd p. sg. pres. of* **pleuvoir.**
pleutre [pløːtr] *m* **1.** *adj.* cowardly; **2.** *su.*
coward.
plouv|oir [plœ'vwaːr] (3g) *v/impers.* rain;
il pleut à verse it is pouring (with
rain); *v/i. fig.* rain *or* shower down, be
showered; **~ra** [~'vra] *3rd p. sg. fut. of*
pleuvoir.
pli [pli] *m* fold, pleat; wrinkle; (*a. faux ~*)
crease; ✝ cover; *arm, leg*: bend; *fig.*
habit; *ground*: undulation; **faire des ~s**
crease (up); **✝ cela ne fait pas un ~**
that's for sure; *fig.* **prendre un ~** acquire a habit; **✝ sous ce ~** enclosed;
~able [~'abl] folding; pliable; **~ant**
[~'ɑ̃] **1.** *adj.* folding; *fig.* docile; **2.** *su./m*
folding stool.
plie *ich.* [pli] *f* plaice.
plier [pli'e] (1a) *v/t.* fold (up); bend;
bow; **se ~ à** submit to; *fig.* give o.s. up
to; *v/i.* bend; yield.
pliss|é [pli'se] **1.** pleated *etc.* (*see* **plis-
ser**); **2.** *su./m cost.* pleats *pl.*; **~ement**
[plis'mɑ̃] folding; fold (*a. geol.*); puck-

er(ing); **~er** [pli'se] (1a) pleat; *cost.* put pleats in; fold (over); pucker (up) (*one's mouth*); screw up (*one's eyes*); crease, crumple.

plomb [plɔ̃] *m* lead; △ lead sink; ⚡ fuse; ♣ plummet; *hunt. etc.* shot; *fig.* weight; **à ~** vertically; upright; straight down; ✝ **mettre à ~** plumb (*a wall*); **mine** *f* **de ~** graphite; **sommeil** *m* **de ~** heavy sleep; **~age** [plɔ̃'ba:ʒ] *m* leading; ✝ sealing; *teeth*: filling; **~agine** [~ba'ʒin] *f* graphite; **~é** [~'be] leaded; leaden (*sky*); livid (*complexion*); **~er** [~'be] (1a) cover *or* weight with lead; ✝ stop, fill (*a tooth*); △ plumb; ✝ seal, put a lead seal on; **~erie** [~'bri] *f* plumbing; plumber's (*shop*); **~ier** [~'bje] *m* plumber.

plong|e [plɔ̃ʒ] *f* dishwashing; **faire la ~** be a dishwasher; **~eant** [plɔ̃'ʒɑ̃] plunging; from above (*view*); **~ée** [~'ʒe] *f* plunge, dive; *subm. diving*; (*skin*) diving; **~eoir** [~'ʒwa:r] *m* diving-board; **~eon** [~'ʒɔ̃] *m* dive; **~er** [~'ʒe] (1l) *vt/i.* plunge; dip; *fig.* **être plongé dans** be absorbed in; *v/i.* dive; ♣ submerge (*submarine*); *v/t.* stick, thrust, stab (into, *dans*); **1.** *adj.* diving; **2.** *su.* diver (*a. orn*); dish-washer.

plouc F [pluk] *m* country bumpkin.

ploy|able [plwa'jabl] pliable; **~er** [~'je] (1h) *vt/i.* bend; *v/i.* give way, sag.

plu¹ [ply] *p.p. of plaire.*

plu² [~] *p.p. of pleuvoir.*

pluie [plɥi] *f* rain; *fig.* shower; **craint la ~!** keep dry!; *fig.* **faire la ~ et le beau temps** rule the roost; **sous la ~** in the rain.

plum|age [ply'ma:ʒ] *m* plumage; **~ard** *sl.* [~'ma:r] *m* bed; **~e** [plym] *f* feather; pen; **homme** *m* **de ~** man of letters; **~er** [~'me] (1a) pluck (*poultry*); F fleece (*s.o.*).

plupart [ply'pa:r] *f*: **la ~** most, the greater part; **la ~ des gens** most people; **la ~ du temps** most of the time; mostly; **pour la ~** mostly; most of them.

pluriel *gramm.* [ply'rjɛl] **1.** *adj.* plural; **2.** *su./m* plural; **au ~** in the plural.

plus¹ [ply]; *oft.* plys *at end of wordgroup*; *before vowel* plyz] **1.** *adv.* more; ⚚ plus; **~ ... ~ ...** the more ... the more ...; **~ confortable** more comfortable; **~ de** more than (*2 days*); **~ de soucis!** no more worries!; **~ grand** bigger; **~ haut!**

speak up!; **~ que** more than (*he*); **~ rien** nothing more; **de ~** moreover; further(more); **de ~ en ~** more and more; **en ~** moreover; in addition (to, *de*); extra; **le ~ confortable** most comfortable; **le ~ grand** biggest; **moi non ~** nor I, F me neither; **ne ... ~** no more, no longer; not again; **non ~** (not) either; **rien de ~** nothing else *or* more; **tant et ~** plenty; **2.** *su./m*: **le ~** the most, the best; **au ~** at most.

plus² [ply] *1st p. sg. p.s. of plaire.*

plusieurs [ply'zjœ:r] *adj./pl., pron./ indef./pl.* several.

plus-que-parfait *gramm.* [plyskəpar'fɛ] *m* pluperfect.

plus-value [plyva'ly] *f* increase in value, appreciation; surplus.

plut [ply] *3rd p. sg. p.s. of pleuvoir.*

plutôt [ply'to] *adv.* rather, sooner (than, *que*); somewhat, quite.

pluvi|al [ply'vjal] rain-...; **~er** *orn.* [~'vje] *m* plover; **~eux** [~'vjø] rainy; wet; of rain.

pneu, *pl.* **~s** [pnø] *m mot.* tyre, *Am.* tire; express letter; **~matique** [~ma'tik] **1.** *adj.* air-..., pneumatic; **2.** *su./m* express letter.

pneumoni|e [pnømɔ'ni] *f* pneumonia; **~que** [~'nik] pneumonic.

pochade [pɔ'ʃad] *f* sketch.

pochard [pɔ'ʃa:r] *adj., su.* drunk.

poch|e [pɔʃ] *f* pocket; pouch; bag; **~er** [~'ʃe] (1a) *cuis.* poach; *fig.* black (*s.o.'s eye*); **~ette** [pɔ'ʃɛt] *f* breast pocket; bag; *matches*: book; fancy handkerchief.

poêle¹ [pwa:l] *m* (funeral) pall.

poêle² [pwa:l] *m* stove, cooker.

poêle³ [pwa:l] *f* frying pan.

poème [pɔ'ɛ:m] *m* poem; **poésie** [~e'zi] *f* poetry; poem; **poète** [~'ɛt] *m* poet; **femme** *f* **~** poetess; **poétique** [~e'tik] **1.** *adj.* poetic(al); **2.** *su./f* poetics *sg.*

poids [pwa] *m* weight; heaviness; *fig.* importance; load; *fig.* burden; *box.* **~ coq** bantam weight; *box.* **~ léger** light weight; *box.* **~ (mi-)lourd** (light) heavy weight; *box.* **~ mort** dead weight; *box.* **~ mouche** fly weight; *box.* **~ moyen** middle weight; 🏋 **~ spécifique** specific gravity; **~ utile** payload; *box.* **~ vif** live weight; *sp.* **lancer** *m* (*or* **lancement** *m*) **du ~** shot put; **prendre du ~** put on weight.

police

poignant [pwa'nɑ̃] poignant; keen.
poign|ard [pwa'naːr] m dagger; **~arder** [~ɲar'de] (1a) stab; **~e** [pwaɲ] f (strong) grip; **~ée** [pwa'ɲe] f handful; *door etc.*: handle; *sword*: hilt; *tool*: haft; **~ de main** handshake; **~et** [~'ɲɛ] m wrist; *cost.* cuff, wristband.

poil [pwal] m hair; coat, fur; *tex.* nap; ♦ down; *brush*: bristle; F **à ~** naked; F **au ~** great, fantastic; perfectly, fine; F **de bon (mauvais) ~** in a good (bad) mood; **~ant** F [pwa'lɑ̃] killing(ly funny); **~er** F [~'le] (1a): **se ~** split ones sides (laughing); **~u** [~'ly] hairy.

poinçon ⚙ [pwɛ̃'sɔ̃] m awl; punch; stamp; hallmark; pricker; **~ner** [pwɛ̃so'ne] (1a) prick; punch; stamp; **~neuse** ⚙ [~'nøːz] f punch.

poindre [pwɛ̃:dr] (4m) v/t. † sting; v/i. dawn, *fig.* appear; ♦ sprout.

poing [pwɛ̃] m fist.

point¹ [pwɛ̃] m point; *gramm.* full stop, *Am.* period; stitch (*a.* ✷); *opt.* focus; *sp.* score; *school*: mark; speck; dot; *dice*: pip; *fig.* extent, degree; *fig.* state, condition; *cost.* lace; *fig.* **~ chaud** hot spot; trouble spot; **~ d'arrêt** stopping place; **~ de vue** point of view; *fig.* **~ noir** problem; difficulty; weak spot or link; **~-virgule** semicolon; **à ~** in the right condition; on time; medium-cooked (*meat*); **à ce ~, à tel ~** so (much); **à quel ~** how (much); **à ce (or tel) ~ que, au ~ que** so (much) that; **au ~ de** (*inf.*) so (much) that; **au ~ mort** *mot.* in neutral; *fig.* at a standstill; *sp.* **battre aux ~s** beat (*s.o.*) on points; **deux ~s** colon; **en tout ~** on all points; **être sur le ~ de** (*inf.*) be about to (*inf.*); **faire le ~** take a bearing; get *or* find one's bearings; **faire le ~ de** take stock of; **mettre au ~** see **mettre**; **sur ce ~** on that score.

point² [~] adv.: **ne ... ~** not ... at all; **~ du tout!** not at all.

pointe [pwɛ̃:t] f point; tip; *spire, tree*: top; *geog.* headland; *day*: break; *fig.* hint, touch; *fig.* sally, witticism; *fig.* peak, maximum; **~ des pieds** tiptoe; *fig.* **de ~** top, leading; maximum; latest (*developments etc.*); **en ~** pointed, tapering; **heures** f/pl. **de ~** rush hours.

pointer¹ [pwɛ̃'te] (1a) v/t. prick up (*one's ears*); sharpen (*a pencil*); ♪ dot (*a note*); v/i. sprout, come up; soar (*bird, spire*).

point|er² [pwɛ̃'te] (1a) v/t. aim (*a gun etc.*); check (off); prick; F **se ~** turn up, show up; v/i. clock (*Am.* punch) in *or* out (*worker*); **~illé** [pwɛ̃ti'je] m dotted line; stippling; **~iller** [~'je] (1a) stipple; **~illeux** [~'jø] particular (about, **sur**); touchy.

pointu [pwɛ̃'ty] pointed; sharp; *fig.* shrill (*voice*); *fig.* touchy, peevish.

pointure [pwɛ̃'tyːr] f *shoes etc.*: size.

poire [pwaːr] f ♦ pear; *sl.* sucker; F head; **garder une ~ pour la soif** put s.th. by for a rainy day.

poireau [pwa'ro] m ♦ leek; F **faire le ~** = **~ter** [~rɔ'te] (1a) cool one's heels.

poirier [pwa'rje] m pear tree.

pois [pwa] m ♦ pea; *tex.* polka dot; *tex.* **à ~** spotted, dotted, polka-dot ...; *cuis.* **petits ~** pl. green peas.

poison [pwa'zɔ̃] m poison.

poissard, e [pwa'saːr, ~'sard] **1.** adj. vulgar; **2.** su.f fishwife.

poisse F [pwas] f bad luck; **~er** [pwa'se] (1a) make sticky; F nab (*s.o.*); **~eux** [~'sø] sticky.

poisson [pwa'sɔ̃] m fish; **~ d'avril** April Fool trick; **~ rouge** goldfish; **~nerie** [~sɔn'ri] f fish shop; **~neux** [~sɔ'nø] teeming with fish; **~nier** m, **~nière** f [~sɔ'nje, -'njɛːr] fishmonger.

poitrine [pwa'trin] f chest, breast; *woman*: bust.

poivr|e [pwaːvr] m pepper; F **~ et sel** gray-haired; **~é** [pwa'vre] peppery; *fig.* spicy (*story etc.*); **~er** [~'vre] (1a) pepper; F **se ~ (la gueule)** get drunk; **~ier** [~vri'e] m pepper plant; = **~ière** [~vri'ɛːr] f pepperpot; **~on** [~'vrɔ̃] m: (**~ vert, rouge**) (green, red) pepper; **~ot** F [~'vro] m drunkard.

poix [pwa] f pitch; cobbler's wax.

polaire [pɔ'lɛːr] adj. polar.

polar F [pɔ'laːr] m detective novel.

polaris|ation [pɔlariza'sjɔ̃] f *phys.* polarization; *fig.* focusing, cent(e)ring; **~er** *phys.* polarize; *fig.* attract, be the focus of (*interest etc.*); **se ~ (sur)** focus (on), centre (on, around), F (**complètement**) **polarisé** (completely) obsessed.

pôle [poːl] m pole; *geog.* **~ Nord (Sud)** North (South) Pole.

poli [pɔ'li] **1.** adj. polished (*a. fig.*); *fig.* polite; **2.** su./m polish.

police¹ [pɔ'lis] f police; **~ de la circula-**

tion traffic police; **~ judiciaire** (*approx.*) C.I.D., *Am.* F.B.I.; **agent** *m* **de ~** policeman; **fiche** *f* **de ~** registration form (*at a hotel*); **faire** (*or* **assurer**) **la ~** keep order.

police² [~] *f* insurance policy.

polichinelle [poliʃiˈnɛl] *m* Punch; buffoon; **secret** *m* **de ~** open secret.

policier [poliˈsje] **1.** *adj.* police...; detective (*film, novel*); **2.** *su./m* policeman; detective.

policlinique [polikliˈnik] *f* (municipal) clinic; outpatients' department.

poliment [poliˈmɑ̃] politely.

poliomyélite ✽ [poljɔmjeˈlit] *f* poliomyelitis; infantile paralysis.

poli|r [poˈliːr] (2a) polish (*a. fig.*); make glossy; burnish (*metal*).

polisson [poliˈsɔ̃] **1.** *adj.* naughty; *pej.* indecent; saucy; **2.** *su.* naughty child; dissolute person; **~ner** [~sɔˈne] (1a) run the streets (*child*); behave *or* talk lewdly; **~nerie** [~sɔnˈri] *f* mischievousness; indecent act *or* story.

politesse [poliˈtɛs] *f* politeness, courtesy; **~s** *pl.* civilities.

politi|card [politikaˈr] *m pej.* (unscrupulous) politician; **~cien(ne)** [~ˈsjɛ̃, ~ˈsjɛn] *m/f* politician; **~que** [~ˈtik] **1.** *adj.* political; *fig.* wary; *fig.* diplomatic; **homme** *m* **~** politician; **2.** *su./m* politician; *su./f* politics; policy; **~ de clocher** parish-pump politics; **~ de la porte ouverte** open-door policy; **~ extérieure** (**intérieure**) foreign (home) policy; **~ser** [~tiˈze] politicize.

pollu|ant [polˈlɥɑ̃] **1.** *adj.* polluting; **2.** *su./m* pollutant; **~er** [~ˈlɥe] (1n) pollute; **~tion** [~lyˈsjɔ̃] *f* pollution.

polo [poˈlo] *m sp.* polo; *cost.* T-shirt; polo shirt.

polonais [polɔˈnɛ] **1.** *adj., su./m ling.* Polish; **2.** *su.* ♀ Pole.

poltron [polˈtrɔ̃] **1.** *adj.* timid; cowardly; **2.** *su.* coward; **~nerie** [~trɔnˈri] *f* cowardice.

poly... [poli] poly...; **~copier** [~kɔˈpje] (1o) duplicate, *Am.* mimeograph; **~game** [~ˈgam] **1.** *adj.* polygamous; **2.** *su.* polygamist; **~glotte** [~ˈglɔt] *adj., su.* polyglot; **~gone** [~ˈgɔn] *m* polygon; ✕ shooting-range; **~technique** [~tɛkˈnik]: ♀ *f or* **École** *f* **~** Academy of Engineering.

pommade [pɔˈmad] *f* ointment, cream; **passer de la ~ à** soft-soap (*s.o.*).

pomm|e [pɔm] *f* apple; knob; F head; **~ de discorde** bone of contention; **~ de terre** potato; **~s** *pl.* **frites** *Br.* chips, *Am.* French fries; **~s** *pl.* **mousseline** mashed potatoes; F **tomber dans les ~s** pass out, faint; **~é** [pɔˈme] (round and) firm (*cabbage etc.*); *fig.* utter, downright.

pommeau [pɔˈmo] *m* pommel; knob.

pomm|elé [pɔmˈle] dappled; **ciel** *m* **~** mackerel sky; **~ette** [~ˈmɛt] *f* cheekbone; **~ier** [~ˈmje] *m* apple tree.

pompe¹ [pɔ̃ːp] *f* pomp, ceremony; **entrepreneur** *m* **de ~s funèbres** funeral director, *Am.* mortician.

pomp|e² [pɔ̃ːp] *f* ☉ pump; *sl.* shoe, boot; *sp.* F push-up; **~ à incendie** fire engine; F **à toute ~** at top speed, as fast as possible; **~er** [pɔ̃ˈpe] (1a) pump; pump out *or* up; absorb, suck up *or* in; F tire out, wear out; F copy, crib; *sl.* drink, gulp (down); **~ette** F [~ˈpɛt] tipsy.

pompeux [pɔ̃ˈpø] pompous; stately.

pompi|er [pɔ̃ˈpje] **1.** *su./m* fireman; **2.** *adj.* pompous, affected; **~ste** *mot.* [~ˈpist] *m* pump attendant.

pompon [pɔ̃ˈpɔ̃] *m* pompon; bobble; **~ner** [~pɔˈne] (1a) dress up.

ponc|e [pɔ̃ːs] *f*: (**pierre** *f*) **~** pumice (stone); **~er** [pɔ̃ˈse] sand (down); rub down; pumice.

poncif [pɔ̃ˈsif] *m* cliché, commonplace.

ponction ✽ [pɔ̃kˈsjɔ̃] *f* puncture; pricking; **~ner** [~sjɔˈne] (1a) puncture; tap; prick (*a blister*).

ponctu|alité [pɔ̃ktɥaliˈte] *f* punctuality; **~ation** *gramm.* [~ˈsjɔ̃] *f* punctuation; **~el** [pɔ̃kˈtɥɛl] punctual; punctual, isolated, individual; selective; **~er** [~ˈtɥe] (1n) punctuate.

pondér|ateur [pɔ̃deraˈtœːr] stabilizing; **~ation** [~raˈsjɔ̃] *f* balance (*a. fig.*); *fig.* level-headedness; **~é** [~ˈre] level-headed.

pond|eur, -euse [pɔ̃ˈdœːr, ~ˈdøːz] **1.** *adj.* (egg-)laying; **2.** *su. fig.* prolific producer; *su./f hen:* layer; **~re** [pɔ̃ːdr] (4a) lay (*an egg*); F *fig.* produce, bring forth.

poney *zo.* [pɔˈnɛ] *m* pony.

pongiste [pɔ̃ˈʒist] *su.* table tennis player.

pont [pɔ̃] *m* bridge; ☉, *mot.* axle; ♣ deck; *garage etc.:* ramp; *admin.* ♀s (**et chaus-**

sées) *m/pl.* highways department; ◎ ~ **à bascule** weigh bridge; *mot.* ~ **élévateur** repair ramp, grease rack; *fig.* **faire le** ~ take a day off (*between two holidays*).

ponte¹ [pɔ̃t] *f* eggs: laying; clutch, eggs *pl.*; *physiol.* ovulation.

ponte² F [~] big shot, big noise.

pontif|e [pɔ̃tif] *m* pontiff; *fig.* pundit; **~ical** [pɔ̃tifi'kal] *adj.*, *su./m* pontifical; **~icat** [~fi'ka] *m* pontificate; **~ier** [~'fje] (1o) pontificate.

pont-levis, *pl.* **ponts-levis** [pɔ̃lə'vi] *m* drawbridge.

popote F [pɔ'pɔt] **1.** *su./f* cooking; ╳ mess; **2.** *adj.* stay-at-home.

populace *pej.* [pɔpy'las] *f* populace, rabble; **~ier** F [~la'sje] vulgar.

popul|aire [pɔpy'lɛːr] popular (with, *auprès de*); people's, of the people; working-class ...; **~ariser** [~pylari'ze] (1a) popularize; **~arité** [~'te] *f* popularity; **~ation** [pɔpyla'sjɔ̃] *f* population; ~ **active** working population; **~eux** [~'lø] populous; **~o** F [~'lo] *m* (common *or* ordinary) people.

porc [pɔːr] *m* pig, hog; *cuis.* pork, pigskin.

porcelaine [pɔrsə'lɛn] *f* china(ware); porcelain.

porcelet [pɔrs'lɛ] *m* piglet.

porc-épic, *pl.* **porcs-épics** *zo.* [pɔrke'pik] *m* porcupine, *Am.* hedgehog.

porche △ [pɔrʃ] *m* porch, portal.

porch|er [pɔr'ʃe] *m* swineherd; **~ie** [~ʃə'ri] *f* pig farm; pigsty.

porcin [pɔr'sɛ̃] piglike; pig...

pore [pɔːr] *m* pore; **poreux** [pɔ'rø] porous; unglazed (*pottery etc.*).

port¹ [pɔːr] *m* port; harbo(u)r; haven (*a. fig.*); ~ **d'attache** port of registry; ~ **de mer** seaport; ~ **franc** free port; **arriver à bon** ~ arrive safely.

port² [pɔːr] *m* carrying; *goods etc.*: carriage; *letter*, *parcel*: postage; *uniform*: wearing; *person*: bearing; ~ **dû** carriage forward; ~ **payé** carriage *or* postage paid; **~able** [pɔr'tabl] portable; *cost.* wearable.

portail [pɔr'taːj] *m* archit.; *church*: portal.

porta|nt [pɔr'tɑ̃] **1.** *adj.* ◎ bearing; *fig.* **bien** (**mal**) ~ in good (bad) health; **à bout** ~ point-blanc; **2.** *su./m* ◎ stay,

strut; *trunk*: handle; **~tif** [~ta'tif] portable.

porte [pɔrt] *f* door; gate; entrance; pass; ~ **vitrée** glass door; **écouter aux** ~**s** eaves-drop; **mettre** (*or* F **flanquer**) **q. à la** ~ turn s.o. out; give s.o. the sack.

porte...: **~à-faux** [pɔrta'fo] *m*: **en** ~ in an unstable position; **~aiguilles** [~e'gɥiːj] *m/inv.* needle case; **~avions** ⚓ [~a'vjɔ̃] *m/inv.* aircraft carrier; **~bagages** [~ba'gaːʒ] *m/inv.* luggage rack, *Am.* baggage rack; **~billets** [~bi'jɛ] *m/inv.* note case, *Am.* billfold; **~bonheur** [~bɔ'nœːr] *m/inv.* talisman; **~cigarettes** [~siga'rɛt] *m/inv.* cigarette case; **~clefs** [~'kle] *m/inv.* key ring.

portée [pɔr'te] *f* bearing; △ span; *gun*: range; *voice*: compass; *arm*: reach; ♪ staff; *animals*: litter; *fig.* consequences *pl.*, implications *pl.*, meaning; **à** (**la**) ~ (**de**) within reach (of); **hors de** (**la**) ~ (**de**) out of reach (of); **à** (**hors de**) ~ **de voix** within (out of) earshot; **être à la** ~ **de** *q.* be within the understanding of (*s.o.*).

porte-fenêtre, *pl.* **portes-fenêtres** [pɔrtəf'nɛːtr] *f* French window.

porte...: **~feuille** [pɔrtə'fœːj] *m* portfolio; wallet; **~malheur** [pɔrtma'lœːr] *m/inv.* bringer of bad luck; **~manteau** [~mɑ̃'to] *m* coat rack, hat stand; **~mine** [~'min] *m/inv.* propelling pencil; **~monnaie** [~mɔ'nɛ] *m/inv.* purse; **~parapluies** [~para'plɥi] *m/inv.* umbrella-stand; **~parole** [~pa'rɔl] *m/inv.* spokesman; **~plume** [pɔrtə'plym] *m/inv.* penholder.

porter [pɔr'te] (1a) *v/t.* carry; bear; wear (*clothing, a beard, a ring etc.*); take; deal (*a blow*); bring (*a.* ⚖ *a charge, a complaint*); ♰ charge; ♰ place (*to s.o.'s credit*); produce (*fruit etc.*); *fig.* lead (*s.o.*) (to, **à**); *fig.* have (*an affection, an interest*); **se** ~ **bien** (**mal**) be well (unwell); be in good (bad) health; *pol.* **se** ~ **candidat** run (for, **à**); *v/i.* bear (*a. fig.*), rest (on, **sur**); deal (with, **sur**); carry (*sound etc.*); strike home (*shot, a. fig.* insult, *etc.*); ♂ be pregnant; *fig.* ~ **à la tête** go to the head (*wine*).

porte-serviettes [pɔrtsɛr'vjɛt] *m/inv.* towel rail.

porteur [pɔr'tœːr] **1.** *su.* porter; *letter, news, etc.*: bearer; ♂ (*germ-*)carrier;

su./m ✝ bearer, payee; *au* ~ (*payable*) to bearer; **2.** *adj.* pack-(*animal*); ⊙ bearing; carrier (*wave*, *vehicle*).

porte-voix [pɔrtə'vwa] *m/inv.* megaphone.

portier, -ère [pɔr'tje, ~'tjɛːr] *su.* doorman; gatekeeper; porter; *su./f mot.,* 🚗 door.

portion [pɔr'sjɔ̃] *f* portion; share.

porto [pɔr'to] *m* wine: port.

portrait [pɔr'trɛ] *m* portrait; ~ *robot* identikit (picture); **~iste** [pɔrtrɛ'tist] *su.* portrait painter; **~urer** [~ty're] (1a) portray.

portugais [pɔrty'gɛ] *adj., su.* Portuguese; *les* ⌕ *m/pl.* the Portuguese.

pos|e [poːz] *f* ⊙ fitting, placing, fixing; *bricks, pipes:* laying; *phot.* exposure; pose, posture; *pej.* pose, posing, pretention; *prendre une* ~ strike a pose; **~é** *fig.* [po'ze] sedate, staid, steady; **~ment** calmly (but firmly); unhurriedly; **~emètre** *phot.* [poz'mɛtr] *m* exposure meter; **~er** [po'ze] (1a) *v/t.* place, put; lay (*a. bricks, pipes, carpets*); lay down (*an object, fig. a principle*); ask (*a question*), set (*a problem*); ⊙ fix, fit; *posons le cas que* let us suppose that; *se* ~ settle; (come to) rest; alight, land; *fig.* come up, arise, present itself (*question, problem, etc.*); *se* ~ *comme* pass o.s. off as; *v/i.* rest, lie; *paint.* pose (*a. fig.*); *fig.* ~ *à* a claim to be; **~eur** [~'zœːr] *su.* affected person; *su./m pipes, mines:* layer; *adj.* affected, pretentious.

positif [pozi'tif] **1.** *adj.* positive; real, actual; matter-of-fact; **2.** *su./m phot.,* *gramm.* positive; concrete.

position [pozi'sjɔ̃] *f* position; *feux m/pl. de* ~ ✈ navigation lights; ⚓ riding lights; *mot.* parking lights; *prendre* ~ *sur* take a stand about.

posologie ⚕ [pozɔlɔ'ʒi] *f* dosage.

possédé [pɔse'de] possessed (by, *de; fig.* with, *pour*); **~er** [~] (1f) possess (*a. fig.*); own; have; have a thorough knowledge of; *fig. se* ~ control o.s.

possess|eur [pɔse'sœːr] *m* owner, possessor; **~if** *gramm.* [~'sif] *adj., su./m* possessive; **~ion** [~'sjɔ̃] *f* possession; *fig.* thorough knowledge (*of a subject*); ~ *de soi* self-control; *entrer en* ~ *de* take possession of.

possib|ilité [pɔsibili'te] *f* possibility;

avoir la ~ *de* (*inf.*) be in a position to (*inf.*); **~le** [~'sibl] **1.** *adj.* possible; *le plus* ~ as far as possible; as many or much as possible; *le plus* (*moins*) *de ...* ~ as many or much (few or little) ... as possible; *le plus vite* ~ as quickly as possible; **2.** *su./m au* ~ extremely; *dans la mesure du* ~ as far as possible; *faire tout son* ~ do all one can (to *inf.*, *pour inf.*).

postal [pɔs'tal] postal.

poste¹ [pɔst] *f* post (office); mail; postal service; **~ aérienne** air-mail; **~ restante** to be called for, *Am.* general delivery; *mettre à la* ~ post, *Am.* mail; *par la* ~ by post.

poste² [~] *m* post; job, position; ✂, ⊙, ⚡, police, fire, radio, tel. etc.: station; *radio, teleph.:* set; *teleph.* extension; ✝ entry; ✝ item; *mot.* (filling) station; ✈ ~ *de contrôle* control tower; ~ *de secours* first-aid post; ~ *de télévision* television set, F T.V.; ~ *de T.S.F.* radio.

poster [pɔs'te] (1a) post, *Am.* mail; post (*a sentry*).

postérieur [pɔste'rjœːr] **1.** *adj.* posterior; **2.** F *su./m* posterior, backside.

postérité [pɔsteri'te] *f* posterity.

posthume [pɔs'tym] posthumous.

postiche [pɔs'tiʃ] **1.** *adj.* false (*hair etc.*); imitation; **2.** *su./m* hairpiece.

postier *m*, **-ère** *f* [pɔs'tje, ~'tjɛːr] post office employee.

postillon [pɔsti'jɔ̃] *hist.* postilion; splutter; *envoyer des* ~*s* = **~ner** [~jɔ'ne] splutter.

post...: ~scolaire [pɔstskɔ'lɛːr] after-school; *school:* continuation ...; postgraduate; **~scriptum** [~skrip'tɔm] *m/inv.* postscript, P.S.

postul|ant *m*, **e** *f* [pɔsty'lɑ̃, ~'lɑ̃ːt] applicant; **~at** [~'la] *m* postulate; **~er** [~'le] (1a) apply for (*a post*); postulate.

posture [pɔs'tyːr] *f* posture.

pot [po] *m* pot; jar, jug, can; 🜃 crucible; ~ *à eau* water jug; ~ *à fleurs* flower pot; ~ *de fleurs* pot of flowers; F *boire un* ~ have a drink; *fig. découvrir le* ~ *aux roses* smell out the secret; F *fig. tourner autour du* ~ beat about the bush.

potable [pɔ'tabl] drinkable, F fair, acceptable; *eau f* ~ drinking water.

potage [pɔ'taːʒ] *m* soup; **~r** [~ta'ʒe] **1.**

231

pourrir

adj. pot-(*herbs*); kitchen (*garden*); **2.**
su./m kitchen *or* vegetable garden.

potasser F [pɔta'se] cram (for).

pot-au-feu [pɔto'fø] **1.** *su./m/inv.* boiled
beef and vegetables; **2.** *adj.* stay-at-
-home; **pot-de-vin**, *pl.* **pots-de-vin** F
[pod've] *m* bribe.

pote *sl.* [pɔt] *m* pal, *Am.* buddy.

poteau [pɔ'to] *m* post (*a. sp.*), stake; *sl.* †
pal; **~ indicateur** sign-post; **~ télégraphique** telegraph pole.

potelé [pɔt'le] *plump*, chubby.

potence [pɔ'tɑ̃s] *f* gallows *sg.*

potenti|aliser [pɔtɑ̃sjali'ze] (1a) potenti-
ate, increase the effect of; **~iel** [~'sjɛl]
adj., su./m potential.

poterie [pɔ'tri] *f* pottery; earthenware; **~
d'étain** pewter; **potier** [~'tje] *m* potter;
potiche [~'tiʃ] *f* (large) vase; F *fig.* fig-
urehead.

potin F [pɔ'tɛ̃] *m* noise, din; **~s** *pl.* gossip
sg.; **~er** F [pɔti'ne] (1a) gossip.

potiron ♣ [pɔti'rɔ̃] *m* pumpkin.

pot-pourri, *pl.* **pots-pourris** [pupu'ri] *m
cuis.* meat-stew; *♪* medley.

pou, *pl.* **poux** [pu] *m* louse; tick.

poubelle [pu'bɛl] *f* refuse bin, *Am.* garbage can; dustbin.

pouce [pus] *m* thumb; † *measure:* inch
(*a. fig.*); big toe; **manger sur le ~** have a
snack; **mettre les ~s** knuckle under,
give in; **s'en mordre les ~s** regret it
bitterly; **se tourner les ~s** twiddle
one's thumbs.

pouding *cuis.* [pu'diŋ] *m* pudding.

poudr|e [puːdr] *f* powder (*a.* ✗); dust;
café m en ~ instant coffee; *fig.* **jeter de
la ~ aux yeux de q.** throw dust in s.o.'s
eyes; **sucre m en ~** castor sugar; **~er**
[pu'dre] (1a) powder; **~eux** [~'drø]
dusty; powdery; **neige f poudreuse**
powder snow; **~ier** [~dri'e] *m,* **~ière**
[~dri'jɛːr] *f esp. fig.* powder keg; **~oie-
ment** [~drwa'mɑ̃] *m* haze; glitter, gleam,
glint; **~oyer** [~drwa'je] (1h) form clouds
of dust; send up (clouds of) dust; rise in
a flurry; glitter, gleam, glint.

pout [put] **1.** *int.* plop!, phew!; **2.** *su./m*
pouf(fe); **~fant** F [pu'fɑ̃] screamingly
funny; **~fer** [~'fe] (1a) (*a.* **~ de rire**)
burst out laughing; **~fiasse** *sl.* [puf'jas]
f (fat) woman *or* girl, *sl.* broad.

pouilleux [pu'jø] flea-ridden; *fig.* lousy;
wretched.

poulailler [pula'je] *m* henhouse; F *thea.*
peanut gallery, *the gods pl.*

poulain *zo.* [pu'lɛ̃] *m* foal, colt.

poul|arde *cuis.* [pu'lard] *f* fat pullet; **~e**
[pul] *f* hen; *cuis.* chicken; F girl; F tart; **~
d'Inde** turkey-hen; *fig.* **chair f de ~**
goose-flesh; **~et** [pu'lɛ] *m* chicken; *sl.*
cop; **~ette** [pu'lɛt] *f zo.* pullet; F girl.

poulie ⚙ [pu'li] *f* pulley; block.

poulpe *zo.* [pulp] *m* octopus.

pouls [pu] *m* pulse; **prendre le ~ de q.**
feel s.o.'s pulse; *fig.* **prendre** (*or* **tâter**)
le ~ be sound out.

poumon [pu'mɔ̃] *m* lung.

poupe ⚓ [pup] *f* stern, poop, *fig.* **avoir
le vent en ~** be on the road to success.

poupée [pu'pe] *f* doll (*a.* F *fig. – girl*);
bandaged finger.

poupin [pu'pɛ̃] chubby.

poupon *m,* **-onne** *f* F [pu'pɔ̃, ~'pɔn]
baby; **~ner** F [pupɔ'ne] (1a) coddle;
~nière [~'njɛːr] *f* day nursery.

pour [puːr] **1.** *prp. usu.* for; as for; in spite
of; † per (*cent*); **~ le plaisir** (**la vie**) for
fun (life); **~ moi** in my opinion; **~ cela**
as far as that goes; **~ être riche il ...**
though he is rich he ...; **~ de bon** in
earnest; **~ le moins** at least; **~ ainsi dire**
as it were; **~ que** (*sbj.*) so *or* in order
that; **être ~ quelque chose** (**beaucoup, rien**) **dans qch.** play a (big, no)
part in s.th.; **être ~** be in favo(u)r of;
sévère ~ hard on, strict with; **2.** *su./m:*
le ~ et le contre the pros *pl.* and cons
pl.

pourboire [pur'bwaːr] *m money:* tip.

pourceau [pur'so] *m* pig, hog.

pour-cent † [pur'sɑ̃] *m/inv.* per cent;
pourcentage † [~sɑ̃'taːʒ] *m* percentage; rate (of interest).

pourchasser [purʃa'se] (1a) pursue.

pourlécher [purle'ʃe] (1f): **se ~** lick.

pourparlers [purpar'le] *m/pl.* talks,
negotiations; parley *sg.*

pourpr|e [purpr] **1.** *su./f* dye, robe:
purple; **2.** *su./m, adj.* crimson.

pourquoi [pur'kwa] **1.** *adv., cj.* why;
c'est ~ therefore; that's why; **2.** *su./m/
inv.:* **le ~** the reason (for, **de**).

pourrai [pu're] *1st p. sg. fut. of* **pouvoir
1.**

pourr|i [pu'ri] **1.** *adj.* rotten, bad; addled
(*egg*); dank (*air*); **2.** *su./m* rotten part,
bad patch; **~ir** [~'riːr] (2a) *vt/i.* rot; *v/i.*

a. **se ~** go bad *or* rotten; *v/t.* spoil; **~iture** [~ri'ty:r] *f* rot(ting); rottenness.

poursui|te [pur'sɥit] *f* pursuit (*a. fig.*); chase; **~s** *pl.* legal action *sg.*; **~vant** [~sɥi'vã] *m* pursuer; ⚖ plaintiff; **~vre** [~'sɥi:vr] (4ee) pursue (*a. fig.*); chase (after), *fig. a.* seek (after); *fig.* hound (*s.o.*); *fig.* haunt (*s.o.*) (*idea, memory, etc.*); *fig.* continue, go on with; ⚖ prosecute, sue; **se ~** = *v/i.* go on, continue.

pourtant [pur'tã] *cj.* nevertheless, (and) yet.

pour|voi ⚖ [pur'vwa] *m* appeal; **~voir** [~'vwa:r] (3m) *v/t.* provide, supply, furnish (with, *de*); **~** *à* appeal; *v/i.*: **~ à** provide for; **~ à un emploi** provide for a post; **~voyeur** [~vwa'jœ:r] *m* supplier; provider.

pourvu [pur'vy] *cj.*: **~ que** provided (that).

poussah [pu'sa] *m* toy: tumbler; *fig.* potbellied man.

pouss|e [pus] *f* growth; 🌱 shoot; **~café** F [~ka'fe] *m/inv.* chaser (*after coffee*); **~é** [pu'se] advanced; extensive, thorough (*studies etc.*); highly developed; exaggerated; **~ée** [pu'se] *f* thrust; pressure (*a. business*); push; shove; 🌱 growth; **~er** (1a) *v/t.* push; shove; jostle (*s.o.*); *fig.* carry (to, *jusqu'à*); *fig.* urge on (*a crowd, a horse*); *fig.* utter (*a cry*), heave (*a sigh*); extend (*one's studies*); 🌱 put forth (*roots, leaves*); **se ~** push o.s. to the fore; *v/i.* push; 🌱 grow (*a. hair etc.*); **~ette** [~'sɛt] *f* push chair.

poussi|ère [pu'sjɛ:r] *f* dust; *fig.* **... et des ~s** ... and a bit; **~éreux** [~sje'rø] dusty.

poussif [pu'sif] short-winded, wheezy.

poussin [pu'sɛ̃] *m* chick.

poussoir [pu'swa:r] *m* push-button.

poutr|age ⚠ [pu'tra:ʒ] *m* framework; **~e** [pu:tr] *f* beam; girder; **~elle** [pu'trɛl] *f* girder.

pouvoir [pu'vwa:r] **1.** (3h) be able; can; be possible; *cela se peut bien* it is quite possible; *il se peut que* (*sbj.*) it is possible that (*ind.*); *puis-je?* may I?; *n'en ~ plus* be exhausted; be at the end of one's tether; *je n'en peux plus* I can't take any more; **2.** *su./m* power; *en mon etc. ~* (with)in my etc. power.

prairie [prɛ'ri] *f* meadow.

prati|cable [prati'kabl] practicable; feasible; passable (*road etc.*); **~cien** [~sjɛ̃]

m 🩺, ⚖ practitioner; practician; **~quant** *eccl.* [~'kã] church-going; **~que** [pra'tik] **1.** *adj.* practical; convenient; useful; **2.** *su./f* practice; *mettre en ~* put into practice; **~quer** [~ti'ke] (1m) *vt/i.* practise, *Am.* practice (🩺, ⚖, *eccl.*); *v/t.* exercise (*a profession*); put into practice (*a rule etc.*); ⚠ *etc.* make, cut (*a path etc.*); **se ~** be the practice.

pré [pre] *m* (small) meadow.

préalable [prea'labl] **1.** *adj.* previous; preliminary; **2.** *su./m* prerequisite, (pre)condition; *au ~* = **~ment** [~lable'mã] first, beforehand.

préambule [preã'byl] *m* preamble (to, *de*); *fig.* introduction; *sans ~* straight away.

préau [pre'o] *m* yard; playground.

préavis [prea'vi] *m* previous notice; *donner son ~* give (ones) notice.

préca|ire [pre'kɛ:r] precarious; **~rité** [~kari'te] *f* precariousness.

précaution [preko'sjõ] *f* (pre)caution; care; *avec ~* cautiously, carefully; **~ner** [~sjo'ne] (1a): **se ~ contre** take precautions against.

précéd|emment [preseda'mã] *adv.* previously, before; **~ent** [~'dã] **1.** *adj.* preceding, previous; earlier; **2.** *su./m* precedent; ⚖ *pl.* case-law *sg.*; *sans ~* unprecedented; **~er** [~'de] (1f) precede; go before; get *or* arrive ahead of (*s.o.*).

précept|e [pre'sɛpt] *m* precept; **~eur** *m*, **-trice** *f* [presɛp'tœ:r, ~'tris] tutor; teacher.

prêch|e [prɛ:ʃ] *m* sermon; **~er** [prɛ'ʃe] (1a) *v/t.* preach (to *s.o.*); *v/i.* preach; **~ d'exemple** (*or par l'exemple*) set an example; **~eur** *m*, **-euse** *f fig.* [~'ʃœ:r, ~'ʃø:z] sermonizer.

préci|eux [pre'sjø] precious; invaluable; *fig.* affected; **~osité** [~sjozi'te] *f* preciosity; affectation.

précipice [presi'pis] *m* precipice, chasm, *esp. fig.* abyss.

précipit|amment [presipita'mã] *adv.* hastily, hurriedly; in a hurry, headlong; **~ation** [~ta'sjõ] *f* (violent) haste, hurry; 🌧, *meteor.* precipitation (*rain etc.*); **~é** [~'te] hasty, hurried, (too) fast, precipitate; **~er** [~'te] (1a) throw, hurl (down); quicken, hasten; precipitate (*events, a.* 🧪); **se ~** rush (at, upon *sur*).

précis [pre'si] **1.** *adj.* precise, exact;

accurate; definite; **à dix heures ~es** at ten (o'clock) sharp; **2.** *su./m* summary; **~ément** [preizе'mã] precisely, exactly; *see* **précis**; **~er** [~'ze] (1a) *v/t.* specify; state (precisely), give (*a date, details, etc.*); be (more) specific or precise or explicit about; **~ que** a. make it clear that, point out that; **se ~** become clear(er); *v/i.* be more specific (about it); **~ion** [~'zjõ] *f* precision, accuracy; **~s** *pl.* (further) details, particulars.

précité [presi'te] above-mentioned.

précoc|e [pre'kɔs] early; precocious; premature; **~ité** [~kɔsi'te] *f* earliness; precocity.

préconçu [prekõ'sy] preconceived.

préconiser [prekɔni'ze] (1a) advocate; recommend.

précontraint ⊙ [prekõ'trɛ̃] prestressed (*concrete*).

précurseur [prekyr'sœːr] **1.** *su./m* forerunner precursor; **2.** *adj.* precursory; premonitory (*sign*).

prédécesseur [predese'sœːr] *m* predecessor.

prédestin|ation [predɛstina'sjõ] *f* predestination; **~er** [~'ne] (1a) predestine (for, **à**; to *inf.*, **à** *inf.*).

prédicat|eur [predika'tœːr] *m* preacher; **~ion** [~'sjõ] *f* preaching.

prédiction [predik'sjõ] *f* prediction.

prédilection [predilɛk'sjõ] *f* predilection, partiality, special liking; **de ~** favo(u)rite.

prédire [~'diːr] (4p) predict, foretell.

prédispos|er [predispo'ze] (1a) predispose; **~ition** [~zi'sjõ] *f* predisposition.

prédomin|ance [predɔmi'nãːs] *f* predominance, prevalence; **~ant** [~'nã] predominant; **~er** [~'ne] (1a) predominate; prevail (over, **sur**).

prééminen|ce [preemi'nãːs] *f* pre-eminence (over, **sur**); **~t** [~'nã] pre-eminent.

préfabriqu|é [prefabri'ke] prefabricated; **maison** *f* **~e** prefab (house); **~er** [~] (1m) prefabricate.

préfac|e [pre'fas] *f* preface (to **à**, **de**), **~er** [~fa'se] (1a) preface.

préfect|ure [prefɛk'tyːr] *f* prefecture; Paris police headquarters *pl.*

préfér|able [prefe'rabl] preferable (to, **à**), better (than, **à**); **~ence** [~'rãs] *f* preference (a. ✝); **de ~** preferably; in

preference (to, **à**); preferential (*tariff*); **de ~ à** a. rather than; **~er** [~'re] (1f) prefer (to, **à**; to do s.th., **faire qch.**).

préfet [pre'fɛ] *m* prefect.

préfixe *gramm.* [pre'fiks] prefix.

préhisto|ire [preis'twaːr] *f* prehistory; **~rique** [~tɔ'rik] prehistoric.

préjudic|e [preʒy'dis] *m* harm; wrong; damage; loss; **~ à** tort; **au ~ de** to the detriment of; **porter ~ à** do (*s.o., s.th.*) harm, be detrimental to; **sans ~ de** without prejudice to; **~iable** [preʒydi'sjabl] detrimental, harmful (to, **à**).

préjug|é [preʒy'ze] *m* prejudice; **~er** [~] (1l) (*a. ~ de*) prejudge.

prélasser [prela'se] (1a): **se ~** lounge, loll (*in a chair etc.*), sprawl.

prélèvement [prelɛv'mã] *m* previous deduction; *blood, gas, ore, etc.*: sample; **prélever** [prel've] (1d) deduct in advance; levy; take (*a sample* [*a.* ✚ *of blood*]) (*from*, **à**).

préliminaire [prelimi'nɛːr] *adj., su./m* preliminary (to, **de**).

prélud|e [pre'lyd] *m* prelude (*a. fig.*); **~er** [~ly'de] (1a) prelude.

prématuré [prematy're] premature; (too) early; untimely; **retraite** *f* **~é** early retirement.

préméditat|ion [premedita'sjõ] *f* premeditation; **avec ~** premeditated (*murder*); with intent; **~er** [~'te] (1a) premeditate.

premi|er, ~ère [prə'mje, ~'mjɛːr] **1.** *adj.* first; *fig.* leading, best; *title:* the first; ✚ prime (*number*); *admin. etc.* principal, head (*clerk*); former (*of two*); *pol.* **~ ministre** *m* Prime Minister; **le ~ venu** the first comer; **les cinq ~s** *pl.* the first five; **partir le ~** be the first to leave; **2.** *su./m* first, Am. second floor; **en ~** in the first place; *su./f thea.* first performance; *cin., fig.* première; *mot.* first (gear); F **de ~ère** first-class, first-rate; **~èrement** [~mjer'mã] *adv.* first; in the first place.

prémunir [premy'niːr] (2a) forewarn (*s.o.*) (against, **contre**); **se ~** protect o.s., take precautions (against, **contre**).

prena|ble [prə'nabl] pregnable; **~nt** [~'nã] captivating; absorbing.

prénatal, e, *m/pl.* **-als** *or* **-aux** [prena'tal, ~'to] prenatal, antenatal.

pren|dre [prã:dr] (4aa) **1.** v/t. take (a. lessons, time, the train, a road, etc.); (go and) get or fetch; collect; pick up, call for; catch (a. fire, a cold, the train); eat (a meal), have (tea, a meal); take on (an employee; a taste etc.); put on (weight, an attitude etc.); take in (tenants, boarders); fig. handle, treat; buy (a ticket); **~ a faire qch.** catch s.o. doing s.th.; **en amitié** take to (s.o.); ♣ **le large** put to sea; **~ mal** misunderstand; take (s.th.) badly; **~ plaisir à** take pleasure in; **~ pour** take (s.o.) for; **~ q. dans sa voiture** give s.o. a lift (Am. ride); **~ rendez-vous avec** make an appointment with; **~ sur soi** take (s.th.) upon o.s.; **pour qui me prenez-vous?** what do you take me for?; **se ~** get caught (in, **dans**); **se laisser ~** let o.s. be taken in; **se ~** be caught; set (liquid); **se ~ à** begin; **se ~ pour** think one is; fig. **s'en à** find fault with (s.o.); fig. **s'y ~** go about things, manage, cope; **2.** v/i. set (jelly, concrete, etc.), congeal, freeze; curdle (milk); cuis. thicken; cuis. catch (milk in pan); take root (tree); take (fire); fig. be successful, catch on; **~eur** m, **~euse** f [prə'nœːr, ~'nøːz] taker; ✝ lessee; ✝ buyer, purchaser; **~nent** [prɛn] 3rd p. pl. pres. of **prendre**.

prénom [pre'nɔ̃] m first name; **~mé** [pren'me] above-named; **le ~ X.** the said X; **~mer** [~] (1a): **se ~** be called.

prenons [prə'nɔ̃] 1st p. pl. pres. of **prendre**.

préoccup|ation [preɔkypa'sjɔ̃] f preoccupation; concern; **~er** [~'pe] (1a) preoccupy; worry; **se ~ de** concern o.s. with; be concerned about, worry or care about.

prépar|ateur m, **-trice** f [prepara'tœːr, ~'tris] preparer; assistant; **~atifs** [~'tif] m/pl. preparations; **~ation** [~'sjɔ̃] f preparation (for, à); preparing; ⊚ dressing; **~atoire** [~'twaːr] preparatory; **~er** [prepa're] (1a) prepare (for, à); coach (a pupil); prepare for (an examination); draw up (a speech); ⊚ dress; make (tea etc.); **se ~** prepare (o.s.); get ready; fig. be brewing.

prépondéran|ce [prepɔ̃de'rã:s] f preponderance; supremacy; **~t** [~'rã] dominating; preponderant; casting (vote).

prépos|é m, e f [prepo'ze] official in charge (of, à); employee; attendant; postman, Am. mailman.

préposition gramm. [prepozi'sjɔ̃] f preposition.

prérogative [preroga'tiːv] f prerogative; parl. privilege.

près [prɛ] **1.** adv. near, close (at hand); **à beaucoup ~** by far; **à cela ~** except for that; **de ~** closely; at close range; from close to; **ici ~** near by; **regarder de plus ~** take a closer look; **tout ~** very near; **~ de** near (to); close to; nearly; almost; **il était ~ de tomber** he (very) nearly fell. **présag|e** [pre'zaːʒ] m presage; **~er** [~za'ʒe] (1l) be a sign of; foresee.

presbyt|e ✟ [prɛz'bit] long-sighted; **~ie** ✟ [~'si] f long-sightedness.

prescience [prɛ'sjãːs] f prescience.

prescri|ptible ⚖ [prɛskrip'tibl] prescriptible; **~ption** [~'sjɔ̃] f ⊚, admin. regulation(s pl.); ✟, ✟ prescription; **~re** [prɛs'kriːr] (4q) prescribe (a. ✟, ✟); lay down; stipulate (for); ✟ bar (by statute of limitations etc.); ✟ **se ~ par** be barred at the end of (5 years).

préséance [prese'ãːs] f precedence.

présence [pre'zãːs] f presence (at, à); school, office, etc.: attendance; **~ d'esprit** presence of mind; **en ~ de** in the presence of; fig. in the face of (these facts etc.).

présent¹, e [pre'zã, ~'zãːt] **1.** adj. present (at, à); **2.** su./m present (time or gramm. tense); **à ~** at present; su./f: **la ~e** this letter.

présent² [pre'zã] m present, gift; **faire ~ de qch. à q.** present s.o. with s.th.; **~able** F [prezã'tabl] presentable; **~ateur** m, **-trice** f [~tã'tœːr, ~'tris] presenter; host, emcee; **~ation** [~ta'sjɔ̃] f presentation; introduction (to s.o., à q.); ✟ **à ~** at sight.

présenter [prezã'te] (1a) v/t. present; offer; show; introduce (formally); nominate (a candidate) submit; table (a bill); **je vous présente ma femme** may I introduce my wife; **se ~** appear; arise (problem, question); occur; **se ~ bien** (mal) look good (not too good); **se ~ chez q.** call on s.o.; v/i.: **~ bien** (mal) have a pleasant (an unattractive) appearance.

préserv|atif ✟ [prezerva'tif] m condom; **~er** [~'ve] (1a) protect or save (from, **de**).

présid|ence [prezi'dã:s] *f* presidency; ✝ board; chairmanship; **~ent** *m*, **e** *f* [~'dã, ~'dã:t] president; *admin.* chairman; **~directeur général** (P.D.G.) managing director, *Am. a.* chief executive officer (CEO); **~entiel** [~dã'sjɛl] presidential; **~er** [~'de] (1a) *v/t.* preside over *or* at, chair (*s.th.*); *v/i.:* **~ à** be in charge of; rule over, govern.

présompt|if [prezɔp'tif]: ⚖ **héritier** *m* **~** heir apparent; **~ion** [~'sjɔ̃] *f* presumption; **~ueux** [~'tɥø] presumptuous; self-conceited.

presqu|e [presk(ə)] *adv.* almost, nearly; **~'île** [pres'kil] *f* peninsula.

press|ant [prɛ'sã] urgent; **~e** [prɛs] *f* ☉, *journ., typ.* press; crowd, throng; **heures** *f/pl.* **de ~** rush hours; **sous ~** in the press (*book*); **~é** [prɛ'se] hurried (*style, words*); in a hurry (*person*); crowded, close; ☉ pressed; urgent (*letter, task*); **citron** *m* ☉ (fresh) lemon squash; **~e-citron** [prɛsi'trɔ̃] *m/inv.* lemon-squeezer.

pressent|iment [prɛsãti'mã] *m* presentiment; **~ir** [~'ti:r] (2b) have a presentiment *or* foreboding of, sense; sound (*s.o.*) out; foreshadow; hint at.

presse-papiers [prɛspa'pje] *m/inv.* paperweight.

presser [prɛ'se] (1a) *v/t.* press; squeeze; push (*a button*); speed up, hasten; urge on; **se ~** crowd; hurry (up); *v/i.* press; be urgent, **rien ne presse** there is no hurry.

press|ion [prɛ'sjɔ̃] *f* pressure (*a. fig.*); *cost.* snap fastener; ✦ **~ artérielle** blood pressure; **bière** *f* **à la ~** draught (*Am.* draft) beer; **faire ~ sur** press (*s.th.*); *fig.* put pressure on (*s.o.*); **~oir** [~'swa:r] *m* (*wine- etc.*) press; **~urer** [~'re] (1a) press (out); ✝ *fig.* extort money from, **~uriser** [~ri'ze] (1a) pressurize.

prestance [prɛs'tãs] *f* (fine *or* imposing) presence.

prestat|aire [prɛsta'tɛ:r] *su.* person receiving benefits; **~ion** [prɛsta'sjɔ̃] *f* (*insurance*) benefit; allowance; service, *sp., thea., fig.* performance.

preste [prɛst] nimble; quick.

prestidigitateur [prɛstidiʒita'tœ:r] *m* conjurer; juggler.

prestig|e [prɛs'ti:ʒ] *m* prestige; **~ieux** [~ti'ʒjø] prestigious.

présum|able [prezy'mabl] presumable; **~er** [~'me] (1a) presume; assume; (*trop*) **~** overestimate.

prêt¹ [prɛ] *m* loan; *wages:* advance.

prêt² [prɛ] ready (for s.th., **à qch.**; to *inf.*, **à** *inf.*); prepared.

prêt-à-porter [prɛtapɔr'te] *m* ready-to-wear clothes *pl.*

prétend|ant [pretã'dã] *m* pretender (*to throne*); suitor; **~re** [~'tã:dr] (4a) *v/t.* claim; assert, affirm, maintain; intend; *v/i.* lay claim (to, **à**); aspire (to, **à**); **~u** [~tã'dy] alleged; *pej.* so-called.

prête-nom *usu. pej.* [prɛt'nɔ̃] *m* man of straw, front.

prétent|ieux [pretã'sjø] pretentious; **~on** [~'sjɔ̃] *f* pretension, claim; pretentiousness.

prêter [prɛ'te] (1a) *v/t.* lend; loan; pay (*attention*); take (*an oath*); attribute, *fig.* credit (s.o. with s.th., **qch. à q.**); **~ à** impart to; **se ~ à** lend o.s. to; be a party to; *v/i.* give, stretch (*gloves etc.*); **~ à** give rise to.

prétérit [prete'rit] *m* preterite.

prêteur *m*, **-euse** *f* [prɛ'tœ:r, ~'tø:z] lender; **~ sur gages** pawnbroker.

prétext|e [pre'tɛkst] *m* pretext; excuse; **prendre ~ que** put forward as a pretext that; **sous ~ de** (**que**) on the pretext of (that); **sous aucun ~** on no account; **~er** [~tɛks'te] (1a) (give as a) pretext; plead.

prêtre [prɛ:tr] *m* priest; **~ise** [~'tri:z] *f* priesthood.

preuve [prœ:v] *f* proof; evidence; **faire ~ de** show, display; **faire ses ~s** prove o.s. *or* itself.

prévaloir [preva'lwa:r] (3l) *v/i.* prevail (against, **sur**); **faire ~** make good (*a claim etc.*); *v/t.:* **se ~ de** avail o.s. of; take advantage of; pride o.s. on.

préven|ance [prev'nã:s] *f* consideration, thoughtfulness; (kind) attention; **~ant** [~'nã] considerate, thoughtful; **~ir** [~'ni:r] (2h) inform (about, **de**); warn (about, **de**); forestall; prevent (*an accident, illness*); anticipate (*a wish*); **q en faveur** (**contre**) bias s.o. in favo(u)r of (against); **~tif** [prevã'tif] ✦, ⚖ preventive; deterrent; ⚖ **détention** *f* **préventive** detention awaiting trial; **~tion** [~'sjɔ̃] *f* prevention; ⚖ custody; **~ routière** road safety; **~u** [prev'ny] **1.**

p.p. of **prévenir**; **2.** *adj.* ⚖ accused, charged (of, *de*); **3.** *su.* defendant, accused.

prévis|ible [previ'zibl] foreseeable; **~ion** [~'zjɔ̃] *f* forecast (*a.* meteor.); anticipation; expectation.

prévoir [pre'vwaːr] (3m) foresee, anticipate, forecast (*the weather*); reckon on, expect; provide for, arrange for; plan, *in time*; *a.* schedule (for, *pour*); allow, provide; *comme prévu* as planned; as expected; *avez-vous qch. de prévu?* do you have any plans?; *rien de prévu* no plans.

prévoyan|ce [prevwa'jɑ̃ːs] *f* foresight; precaution; *société f de ~* provident society; **~t** [~'jɑ̃] provident; far-sighted.

prie-Dieu [pri'djø] *m/inv.* praying desk; **prier** [~'e] (1a) *v/t.* pray to; ask, entreat, beg; invite (*to dinner etc.*); *je vous (en) prie!* please (do)!; don't mention it!; *sans se faire ~* willingly, readily; *v/i.* pray; **prière** [~'ɛːr] *f* prayer; request; *~ de (ne pas)* (*inf.*) please (do not) (*inf.*).

prieur *eccl.* [pri'œːr] *m* prior.

primaire [pri'mɛːr] primary; simplistic; simple-minded (*person*).

prim|at [pri'ma] *m eccl.* primate; *fig.* primacy; **~auté** [~mo'te] *f* primacy.

prime¹ [prim] *f* premium; allowance, subsidy; bonus; free gift; *en ~* ✟ as a free gift; *fig.* moreover, besides; *fig. faire ~* be highly appreciated.

prime² [prim] prime, *fig.* first; *~ jeunesse* earliest youth; *de ~ abord* at first (sight).

primer¹ [pri'me] (1a) *v/i. (v/t.)* prevail (over).

primer² [~] (1a) award a prize to.

primesautier [primso'tje] impulsive.

primeurs [pri'mœːr] *f/pl.* early vegetables or fruit.

primevère ♀ [prim'vɛːr] *f* primrose.

primitif [primi'tif] primitive; first, early; original; primary.

primordial [primɔr'djal] (most) essential; primordial.

princ|e [prɛ̃ːs] *m* prince **~esse** [prɛ̃'sɛs] *f* princess; **~ier** [~'sje] princely.

princip|al [prɛ̃si'pal] **1.** *adj.* principal, chief, main; **2.** *su./m school:* head(master); chief clerk; ✟ principal; *fig.* main thing; **~auté** [~po'te] *f* principality.

principe [prɛ̃'sip] *m* principle; *en ~* in principle; *par ~* on principle; *sans ~s* unprincipled (*person*).

prin|tanier [prɛ̃ta'nje] spring...; **~temps** [~'tɑ̃] *m* spring(time).

prioritaire [priɔri'tɛːr] having priority, priority...; **priorité** [~'te] *f* priority; *mot.* right of way.

pris¹ [pri] *1st p. sg. p.s.* of **prendre**.

pris² [pri] **1.** *p.p.* of **prendre**; **2.** *adj.* taken (*seat etc.*); sold (out) (*tickets*); busy (*person, day, etc.*); 🐟 stuffed-up (*nose*), hoarse (*throat*); *fig. ~ de* seized by, stricken with (*fear etc.*); *bien ~* well-proportioned (*figure*).

prise [priːz] *f* hold, grip (*a. fig.*), grasp, taking; ✗ capture; ⚓ prize; ⚙ *machine:* engagement; cement *etc.:* setting; *snuff:* pinch; *fish:* catch; ⚙ sample; ⚙ *air, steam, etc.:* intake; *~ d'eau* intake of water; tap, cock; hydrant; F *~ de bec* squabble; *⚡ ~ de courant* wall plug; socket; *~ de sang* blood specimen; *⚡ ~ de terre* earth-connection; *~ de vues* taking of photographs; *avoir ~ sur* have a hold over or on; *fig. donner ~ à* lay o.s. open to; *⚙ en ~* in gear; *être aux ~s avec* be at grips with; *lâcher ~* let go; F *fig.* give in.

priser¹ [pri'ze] (1a) *v/t.* take, inhale, snuff; *v/i.* take snuff.

priser² [~] (1a) value, appreciate.

prisme [prism] *m* prism.

prison [pri'zɔ̃] *f* prison; **~nier** [~zɔ'nje] **1.** *su.* prisoner; *se constituer ~* give o.s. up (to the police); **2.** *adj.* ✗ captive.

privation [priva'sjɔ̃] *f* deprivation, loss; *fig.* privation, hardship.

privautés *pej.* [privo'te] *f/pl.* familiarity *sg.*, liberties.

privé [pri've] **1.** *adj.* private; **2.** *su./m* private life; *en ~* privately.

priver [pri've] (1a) deprive (of, *de*); *se ~ de* do or go without (s.th., *qch.*); refrain from (doing s.th., *faire qch*).

privil|ège [privi'lɛːʒ] *m* privilege; **~légier** [~le'ʒje] (1o) privilege; favo(u)r, give preference to.

prix [pri] *m* price, cost; value (*a. fig.*); prize; reward; *sp.* prize race; ✟ *exchange:* rate; *~ courant* current price; price list; *~ d'achat* purchasing price; *~ de revient* cost price; *~ de vente* selling price; *~ fait (or fixe)* fixed price; *~ uni-*

profond

que one-price store; **~ unitaire** unit-price; **à ~ d'ami** cheap; **à aucun ~** not at any price; **à tout ~** at all costs; **à vil ~** at a low price; **dernier ~** rock-bottom price; **faire un ~** quote a price (to, **à**); **hors de ~** exorbitantly expensive, prohibitive; **~ fixe** F [~'fiks] *m* restaurant with fixed-price meal.

probab|ilité [probabili'te] *f* probability (*a. &*); **selon toute ~** in all probability; **~le** [~'babl] likely, probable; **~ment** probably.

prob|ant [pro'bã] convincing; **~ation** [~ba'sjõ] *f* probation; **~atoire** [~ba'twa:r] trial ...; test ...; **~e** [prob] honest; **~ité** [probi'te] *f* integrity.

probl|ématique [problema'tik] problematical; questionable; **~ème** [~'blɛm] *m* problem; puzzle.

procéd|é [prose'de] *m* proceeding; conduct, behavio(u)r; ⊙ process; **~er** [~'de] (1f) proceed (from, **de**; to, **à**); **~ à** *a.* carry out, do, make; **~ure** [~'dy:r] *f* procedure.

procès [pro'sɛ] *m* (legal) proceedings *pl.*; trial; **~ civil** (law)suit; **~ criminel** (criminal) trial; *see a.* **procès-verbal**.

procession [prose'sjõ] *f* procession; parade; *fig.* cars etc.; string.

processus [prose'sys] *m* process.

procès-verbal [prosɛvɛr'bal] *m* report, statement; *mot.* parking ticket; **dresser (un) ~ contre** make a report on; take (*s.o.'s*) name and address, *mot.* book (*a motorist*).

proch|ain [pro'ʃɛ̃] **1.** *adj.* next (*in a series*); nearest; near; imminent; **2.** *su./m* fellow creature; **~ainement** [~ʃɛn'mã] *adv.* shortly, soon; **~e** [proʃ] **1.** *adj.* near, close; **2.** *su./m:* **~s** *pl.* relatives.

proclam|ation [proklama'sjõ] *f* proclamation; **~er** [~'me] (1a) proclaim; declare, announce.

procur|ation [prokyra'sjõ] *f* ✝, ✞ procuration, power of attorney; **par ~** by proxy; **~er** [~'re] (1a) get, obtain, procure; **se ~** get (o.s.); **~eur** [~'rœ:r] *m* ✞ **de la République** (*approx.*) Public Prosecutor, *Am.* district attorney.

prodigalité [prodigali'te] *f* prodigality; extravagance, lavishness.

prodig|e [pro'di:ʒ] *m* prodigy (*a. person*); wonder, marvel; **enfant** *mf* **~** infant

prodigy; **~ieux** [~di'ʒjø] prodigious, marvellous.

prodigu|e [pro'dig] prodigal; spendthrift; *fig.* **~ de** lavish with; free with; **l'enfant** *m* **~** the Prodigal Son; **~er** [~di'ge] (1m) lavish (on, **à**); be lavish with; not to spare; squander.

product|eur [prodyk'tœ:r] **1.** *adj.* producing; **2.** *su.* producer; ✓ *a.* grower; **~ible** [~'tibl] producible; **~if** [~'tif] productive; **~ion** [~'sjõ] *f* production; ⊙ output; product; **~ivité** [~tivi'te] *f* productivity.

produi|re [pro'dɥi:r] (4h) produce; **se ~** take place, happen, occur; *thea.* appear, perform; **~t** [~'dɥi] *m* product; ✓ produce; ✝ yield; ✝ **~ national brut** gross national product.

proéminen|ce [proemi'nã:s] *f* prominence; protuberance; **~t** [~'nã] prominent; projecting.

profan|ateur *m,* **-trice** *f* [profana'tœ:r, ~'tris] desecrator; **~ation** [~'sjõ] *f* desecration; **~e** [pro'fan] **1.** *adj.* profane; secular (*history, theatre, etc.*); **2.** *su.* layman; **~er** [~fa'ne] (1a) profane, desecrate.

proférer [profe're] (1f) utter.

profess|er [profe'se] (1a) profess; teach; **~eur** [~sœ:r] *m* teacher, master, professor (*a. fig. of a faith*); **~ion** [~'sjõ] *f* profession; occupation; **de ~** by profession; **~ionnel** [~sjo'nɛl] **1.** *adj.* professional; ⊙ occupational (*disease*); **enseignement** *m* **~** vocational training; **2.** *su. usu. sp.* professional; **~orat** [~so'ra] *m* teaching profession.

profil [pro'fil] *m* profile; outline; **de ~** in profile; **~er** [~fi'le] (1a) make stand out, silhouette; profile; *mot.* streamline; **se ~** be outlined, stand out, be silhouetted (against **contre, sur, à**); *fig.* become clear(er).

profit [pro'fi] *m* profit (*a. fig.*); advantage; **mettre qch. à ~** turn s.th. to account; **~able** [profi'tabl] profitable; **~er** [~'te] (1a) profit (by, **de**); *fig.* grow, thrive; *fig.* be economical, wear well (*material etc.*); **~ à q.** benefit s.o.; be profitable to s.o.; **~ de** take advantage of; **~eur** [~'tœ:r] *m* profiteer.

profond [pro'fõ] **1.** *adj.* deep; *fig.* profound; *fig.* deep-seated (*prejudice etc.*); **2.** *adv.* deep; **3.** *su./m* depth; bottom;

P

au plus ~ de in the depths of; at dead of (*night*); **~eur** [~fɔ̃'dœːr] *f* depth.

profus [prɔ'fy] profuse; **~ion** [~fy'zjɔ̃] *f* profusion; **à ~** lavishly.

progéniture [prɔʒeni'tyːr] *f* progeny, offspring.

prognose ✻ [prɔg'noːz] *f* prognosis.

programm|e [prɔ'gram] *m* program(me) (*a. radio, data processing*); *pol. a.* platform; (*a. ~ d'études*) syllabus, curriculum; **~ateur, -trice** [prɔgrama'tœːr, ~'tris] *su. radio, su./m data processing:* programmer; **~ation** [~maˈsjɔ̃] *f* programming; **~er** [~'me] (1a) program(me); *F fig. a.* plan; *radio, TV.:* bill, put on (*a programme*); **~eur** *m*, **-euse** *f* [~'mœːr, ~'møːz] *data processing:* programmer.

progrès [prɔ'grɛ] *m* progress; advancement; **faire des ~** make progress.

progress|er [prɔgrɛ'se] (1a) progress, advance; make headway or progress; **~if** [~'sif] progressive; graduated (*tax*); **~ion** [~'sjɔ̃] *f* progress(ion) (*a. Ⓐ*); advance(ment).

prohib|er [prɔi'be] (1a) prohibit, forbid; ban; *hunt.* **temps m prohibé** close season; **~itif** [prɔibi'tif] prohibitive (*price etc.*); prohibitory (*law*); **~ition** [~'sjɔ̃] *f* prohibition.

proie [prwa] *f* prey (*a. fig.*); **être en ~ à** be a prey to, be tortured by.

project|eur [prɔʒɛk'tœːr] *m* projector; floodlight; spot(light); **~ile** [~'til] *adj., su./m* projectile; missile; **~ion** [~'sjɔ̃] *f* projection; △ plan; (lantern) slide.

projet [prɔ'ʒɛ] *m* plan; project; scheme; *parl.* **~ de loi** government bill; **état m de ~** blueprint stage; **~er** [prɔʒ'te] (1c) plan ([to do] s.th., **[de faire] qch.**); throw, cast; throw up or out; project.

proléta|ire [prɔle'tɛːr] *m* proletarian; **~riat** [~ta'rja] *m* proletariate; **~rien** [~ta'rjɛ̃] proletarian.

prolif|ération [prɔlifera'sjɔ̃] *f* proliferation; **~érer** [~fe're] (1f) proliferate; **~ique** [~'fik] prolific.

prolixe [prɔ'liks] prolix, verbose.

prologue [prɔ'lɔg] *m* prolog(ue).

prolong|ation [prɔlɔ̃ga'sjɔ̃] *f time:* prolongation; *stay, ticket:* extension; *sp.* extra time; **~ement** [~lɔ̃ʒ'mɑ̃] *m* continuation; prolongation; extension; *fig.* effect; **~er** [~lɔ̃'ʒe] (1l) prolong; extend;

be a prolongation or extension of; **se ~** continue.

promen|ade [prɔm'nad] *f* walk(ing); stroll; drive (*in a car*), sail (*in a boat*), ride (*on a bicycle*); trip; *place:* avenue; **faire une ~** go for or take a walk; **~er** [~'ne] (1d) take (*s.o.*) for a walk or a drive *etc.*; walk (*a dog*); carry (*s.th.*) around; *fig.* run (*one's hand, one's eyes*) (over), cast (*one's mind*) (over, **sur**); **envoyer ~ q.** send s.o. about his business; **se ~** go or be out for a walk or ride *etc.*; *fig.* wander (*eyes, gaze*); **va te ~!** get away with you!; **~eur** *m*, **-euse** *f* [~'nœːr, ~'nøːz] stroller, walker; **~oir** [~'nwaːr] *m* promenade, (covered) walk.

pro|messe [prɔ'mɛs] *f* promise; **manquer à sa ~** break one's promise; **~metteur** [~mɛ'tœːr] **1.** *adj.* promising; **2.** *su.* (ready) promiser; **~mettre** [~'mɛtr] (4v) *v/t.* promise; *fig.* bid fair to; *fig.* **se ~ de** (*inf.*) resolve to (*inf.*); *v/i.* look or be promising; **se ~** [~'mi] **1.** *p.p. of* **promettre; 2.** *adj.* promised; **3.** *su.* fiancé.

promontoire [prɔmɔ̃'twaːr] *m* promontory; headland.

pro|moteur [prɔmɔ'tœːr] *su.* promoter; **~** (**de construction**) property developer; **~motion** [~mɔ'sjɔ̃] *f* promotion; ✝ (**en ~** on) special offer; **~mouvoir** [~mu'vwaːr] (3f) promote.

prompt [prɔ̃] quick; swift (*movement*); speedy (*recovery*); ready (*answer*); **~ à se décider** quick to make up one's mind; **~itude** [prɔ̃ti'tyd] *f* quickness; swiftness; readiness.

promu [prɔ'my] *p.p. of* **promouvoir.**

promulg|ation [prɔmylga'sjɔ̃] *f* promulgation; **~uer** [~'ge] (1m) promulgate (*a law*); issue (*a decree*).

prôn|e [proːn] *m* sermon; **~er** [pro'ne] (1a) praise, extol; recommend; preach (*moderation etc.*).

pronom [prɔ'nɔ̃] *m* pronoun; **~inal 1.** *adj.* pronominal; reflexive (*verb*); **verbe** *m* **~ = 2.** *su./m* reflexive verb.

pronon|çable [prɔnɔ̃'sabl] pronounceable; **~cé** [~'se] **1.** *adj. fig.* marked; **2.** *su./m* 🛠 decision; **~cer** [~'se] (1k) *v/t.* pronounce; 🛠 pass (*sentence*); order; deliver, make (*a speech*); *fig.* utter; **se ~** give one's opinion or decision (on, about **sur**); **se ~ pour** or **en faveur de**

(**contre**) decide for *or* in favo(u)r of (against) (*s.o., s.th.*); *v/i.* ⚖ give a verdict; **~ sur** adjudicate upon (*a question*); **~ciation** [~sja'sjɔ̃] *f* pronunciation.

pronosti|c [prɔnɔs'tik] *m* ⚕, *fig.* prognosis; forecast; **~quer** [~ti'ke] (1m) foretell; ⚕, *fig.* prognose; forecast.

propagand|e [prɔpa'gɑ̃d] *f* propaganda; publicity; advertising; **~iste** [~gɑ̃'dist] *su.* propagandist.

propag|ateur [prɔpaga'tœːr] **1.** *adj.* propagating; **2.** *su.* propagator; spreader; **~ation** [~ga'sjɔ̃] *f* propagation, spread(ing); **~er** [~'ʒe] (1l) propagate; spread; *fig.* popularize.

propane ⚗ [prɔ'pan] *m* propanc.

propension [prɔpɑ̃'sjɔ̃] *f* propensity.

proph|ète [prɔ'fɛt] *m* prophet; **~étie** [prɔfe'si] *f* prophecy; **~étique** [~'tik] prophetic; **~étiser** [~ti'ze] (1a) prophesy, foretell.

prophyla|ctique ⚕ [prɔfilak'tik] prophylactic; **~xie** [~'si] *f* prophylaxis; prevention of disease.

propice [prɔ'pis] propitious (to, for **à**); favo(u)rable (to, **à**).

proportion [prɔpɔr'sjɔ̃] *f* proportion (to, **à**), ratio; *fig.* **~s** *pl.* dimensions; **à ~** accordingly; **à ~ que** in proportion as; **en ~ de** in proportion *or* relation to; **~nel, -elle** [~sjɔ'nɛl] *adj., su./f* proportional; **~ner** [~sjɔ'ne] (1a): **~ à** proportion *or* adjust to.

propos [prɔ'po] *m* purpose; topic; remark; convenience; **~** *pl.* talk *sg.*; **à ~** relevant, timely; **à ~!** by the way!; **à ~ de** about; regarding, concerning, in connection with; **à ~ de rien** for no reason at all; **à ce ~** in this connection; **à tout ~** at every turn; **changer de ~** change the subject; **hors de ~** irrelevant (*comment*); ill-timed; **juger à ~** think fit; **mal à ~** inopportune(ly); out of place; **~er** [prɔpo'ze] (1a) propose; suggest; offer (*a solution, money*); put forward; **se ~ de** (*inf.*) propose *or* intend to (*inf.*); **se ~ pour** (*inf.*) offer to (*inf.*); **~ition** [~zi'sjɔ̃] *f* offer, proposal; ♫, *phls.*, ♪ proposition; *gramm.* clause.

propre¹ [prɔpr] **1.** *adj.*: *before the noun:* own; *after the noun:* proper, right (*word etc.*); literal (*sense*); **~ à** appropriate *or* suitable for; peculiar to, characteristic

of; **être ~ à** (*inf.*) be likely *or* fit *or* calculated to (*inf.*); **à rien** good for nothing; **à ... ment parler** strictly speaking; **le (la, les) ... ment dit(es)** the actual ..., the ... itself (themselves); **2.** *su./m* peculiarity, characteristic; *gramm.* **au ~** in the literal sense; **~ à rien** good-for-nothing.

propre² [~] **1.** *adj.* clean; neat; tidy; cleanly; *fig.* decent, honest; **2.** *su./m*: **mettre au ~** make a fair copy of; **c'est du ~ !** that's a fine thing!; **~té** [prɔp're'te] *f* cleanness; neatness; tidiness; cleanliness.

propriét|aire [prɔprie'tɛːr] *su.* proprietor, owner; *su./m* landlord; *su./f* landlady; **~é** [~'te] *f* property (*a. phys.*); estate; ownership; characteristic; appropriateness, suitability; *language etc.*: correctness; **~ littéraire** copyright.

proprio F [prɔpri'o] *m* proprietor.

propuls|er [prɔpyl'se] (1a) propel; fling; hurl; F **se ~** move, walk; **~eur** [~'sœːr] **1.** *adj./m* propelling; **2.** *su./m* propeller; **~ion** [~'sjɔ̃] *f* propulsion; **~ par reaction** rocket propulsion.

prorata [prɔra'ta] *m/inv.* share; **au ~ de** in proportion to.

prorog|ation [prɔrɔga'sjɔ̃] *f parl.* prorogation; ⚖ extension of time; **~er** [~'ʒe] (1l) adjourn, prorogue; ⚖, † extend (*a time-limit*).

prosa|ïque [prɔza'ik] prosaic; **~ïsme** [~'ism] *m* prosaicness.

proscri|ption [prɔskrip'sjɔ̃] *f* proscription, ban; banishment; **~re** [~'kriːr] (4q) proscribe; ban; banish; **~t** *m, e f* [~'kri, ~'krit] outlaw.

prose [proːz] *f* prose.

prospect|er [prɔspɛk'te] (1a) ✗ prospect; † canvass; **~ion** [~'sjɔ̃] *f* ✗ prospection; † canvassing; **~us** [~'tys] *m* prospectus; † leaflet; brochure.

prosp|ère [prɔs'pɛːr] prosperous; thriving; **~érer** [~pe're] (1f) prosper, thrive; **~érité** [~peri'te] *f* prosperity.

prosterner [prɔstɛr'ne] (1a): **se ~** prostrate o.s.; bow down (before, to **devant**); kowtow (to, **devant**).

prostitu|ée [prɔsti'tɥe] *f* prostitute; **~er** [~'tɥe] (1a) prostitute; **~tion** [~ty'sjɔ̃] *f* prostitution.

prostr|ation [prɔstra'sjɔ̃] *f* prostration; **~é** [~'tre] prostrate.

protagoniste [prɔtagɔ'nist] *m* protagonist.

protect|eur [prɔtɛk'tœːr] **1.** *adj.* ⊙, *pol.* protective; protecting; *pej.* patronizing; **2.** *su.* protector; **~ion** [~'sjɔ̃] *f* protection; patronage, wire-pulling.

protégé [prɔte'ʒe] *m* favo(u)rite; protégé; **~er** [~te'ʒe] (1g) protect (from, **de**; against, **contre**).

protest|ant [prɔtɛs'tɑ̃] *adj., su.* Protestant; **~antisme** [~tɑ̃'tism] *m* Protestantism; **~ataire** [~ta'tɛːr] *su.* objector; **~ation** [~ta'sjɔ̃] *f* protest (against, **contre**); protestation (*of friendship, innocence, etc.*), (*a.* ✝ *a bill*) *v/i.*: **~ contre** protest (against); **~ de qch.** protest s.th.

protêt [prɔ'tɛ] *m* protest.

prothèse ✻ [prɔ'tɛːz] *f* prosthesis; artificial limb; **~ (dentaire)** denture, false teeth *pl.*

protocol|aire [prɔtɔkɔ'lɛːr] formal; **~e** [~'kɔl] *m* protocol; etiquette.

prototype [prɔtɔ'tip] *m* prototype.

protubéran|ce [prɔtybe'rɑ̃ːs] *f* protuberance, bulge; **~t** [~'rɑ̃] protruding, bulging, protuberant.

prou [pru]: **peu ou ~** more or less.

proue ⚓ [~] *f* prow, bows *pl.*

prouesse [pru'ɛs] *f* prowess; feat.

prouvable [pru'vabl] provable; **prouver** [~'ve] (1a) prove.

proven|ance [prɔv'nɑ̃ːs] *f* (place of) origin, provenance; **en ~ de** from; **~ir** [~'niːr] (2h): **~ de** come from; originate in; result from.

proverbe [prɔ'vɛrb] *m* proverb; **~ial** [~vɛr'bjal] proverbial.

providen|ce [prɔvi'dɑ̃ːs] *f* providence; *fig.* guardian angel; salvation; **~tiel** [~dɑ̃'sjɛl] providential.

provinc|e [prɔ'vɛ̃ːs] *f* provinces *pl.*; *fig.* **de ~** provincial, *pej.* countrified; **~ial** [~vɛ̃'sjal] provincial.

provis|eur [prɔvi'zœːr] *m* lycee: headmaster, principal; **~ion** [~'zjɔ̃] *f* provision, stock, supply; *finance:* funds *pl.*; ✝ deposit; 💰 retaining fee; **faire ses ~s** go shopping; **sac** *m* **à ~s** shopping bag; **~oire** [~'zwaːr] provisional; temporary.

provo|cant [prɔvɔ'kɑ̃] provocative; **~cateur** [~ka'tœːr] **1.** *adj.* provocative; **2.** *su.* instigator; provoker; **~cation**

[~ka'sjɔ̃] *f* provocation; incitement; **~quer** [~'ke] (1m) provoke; incite (to, **à**); bring about, cause; create; arouse (*suspicion etc.*).

proxénète [prɔkse'nɛt] *su./m* procurer; *su./f* procuress.

proximité [prɔksimi'te] *f* closeness; nearness, proximity; **à ~** near (by); **à ~ de** close to.

prude [pryd] **1.** *adj.* prudish; **2.** *su./f* prude.

prude|mment [pryda'mɑ̃] *adv.* of **prudent**; **~nce** [~'dɑ̃ːs] *f* care(fulness); cautiousness; prudence; discretion; **~nt** [~'dɑ̃] careful, cautious; prudent; discreet; wise, advisable (to *inf.*, **de** *inf.*).

prud|erie [pry'dri] *f* prudery; **~'homme** [~'dɔm] *m*: **conseil** *m* **des ~s** conciliation board.

prune [pryn] *f* plum; F **pour des ~s** for nothing; **~au** [pry'no] *m* prune; F bullet; **~elle** [pry'nɛl] *f* ♀ sloe; *eye:* pupil; *fig.* apple of the eye; **~ier** [~'nje] *m* plum tree.

prurit ✻ [pry'ri(t)] *m* itching.

psalmodi|e [psalmɔ'di] *f* psalmody; *fig.* drone; **~er** [~mɔ'dje] (1o) *vt/i.* intone; *v/t.* drone (*s.th.*) out.

psaume [psoːm] *m* psalm.

pseudonyme [psødɔ'nim] *m* pseudonym; nom de plume; stage name.

ps(it)t! [ps(i)t] *int.* psst!; I say!

psychanaly|se [psikana'liːz] *f* psychoanalysis; **~ser** [~li'ze] (1a) psychoanalyze; **~ste** [~'list] *m* psychoanalyst; **~tique** [~li'tik] psychoanalytic(al).

psyché [psi'ʃe] *f* psyche; swing mirror.

psychiatr|e [psi'kjaːtr] *m* psychiatrist; **~ie** [psikja'tri] *f* psychiatry.

psychique [psi'ʃik] psychic.

psycho... [psiko] psycho...; **~logie** [~lɔ'ʒi] *f* psychology; **~ des enfants (foules)** child (mass) psychology; **~logique** [~lɔ'ʒik] psychological; **~logue** [~'lɔg] *su.* psychologist.

psychose [psi'koːz] *f* ✻ psychosis; obsessive fear; **~ de guerre** war scare.

psycho... [psiko:] **~somatique** [~sɔma'tik] psychosomatic; **~thérapeute** [~tera'pøt] psychotherapist; **~thérapie** [~tera'pi] *f* psychotherapy.

pu [py] *p.p. of* **pouvoir 1**.

puant [pɥɑ̃] stinking; F bumptious; **~eur** [pɥɑ̃'tœːr] f stench, stink.

pubère [py'bɛːr] pubescent; **puberté** [~bɛr'te] f puberty.

publi|able [pybli'able] publishable; **~c, -que** [~'blik] **1.** adj. public; state...; **2.** su./m public; audience; **en ~** in public; **le grand ~** the general public; **~cation** [pyblika'sjɔ̃] f publication; **~ciste** [~'sist] su. adman; **~citaire** [~si'tɛːr] **1.** adj. publicity-...; advertising...; **2.** su./m publicity man; **~cité** [~si'te] f publicity; advertising; ad(vertisement); **bureau** m **de ~** advertising agency; **~er** [~'e] (1a) publish.

puce [pys] f flea; **marché** m **aux ~s** flea market.

pucelle [py'sɛl] f maiden, virgin; **la ♀ (d'Orléans)** Joan of Arc.

pud|eur [py'dœːr] f modesty; decency; **sans ~** shameless(ly adv.), **~ibond** [~di'bɔ̃] prudish; **~icité** [~disi'te] f modesty; chastity; **~ique** [~'dik] modest; chaste.

puer [pɥe] (1n) stink (of); reek (of).

puéri|culture [pɥerikyl'tyːr] f rearing of children, infant care; **~l** [~'ril] puerile, childish; **~lité** [~rili'te] f puerility.

puîné † [pɥi'ne] younger.

puis¹ [pɥi] adv. then; next, **et ~** and then; moreover; **et ~ après?** what then?; so what?

puis² [~] *1st p. sg. pres. of* **pouvoir 1.**

puiser [pɥi'ze] (1a) draw (water etc.) (from, **dans**) (a. fig.); dip (into, **dans**).

puisque [pɥisk(ə)] cj. since, as.

puiss|amment [pɥisa'mɑ̃] adv. powerfully; fig. extremely; **~ance** [~'sɑ̃ːs] f power; force; fig. authority, control; pol. **~ mondiale** world(-)power; **~ant** [~'sɑ̃] powerful.

puisse [pɥis] *1st p. sg. pres. sbj. of* **pouvoir 1.**

puits [pɥi] m well; △ shaft.

pull-(over) [pyl(ɔ'vœːr)] m sweater.

pulluler [pyly'le] (1a) swarm, teem; pullulate; multiply rapidly.

pulpe [pylp] f pulp; finger etc.: pad; **~eux** [pyl'pø] pulpy, pulpous.

pulsation [pylsa'sjɔ̃] f pulsation; heart: beat, throb(bing).

pulsion psych. [pyl'sjɔ̃] urge, drive.

pulvér|isateur [pylveriza'tœːr] m pulverizer; atomizer; **~iser** [~'ze] (1a) pulverize (a. fig. s.o.); F sp. smash (a record); atomize (liquids); **~ulent** [~'lɑ̃] powdery.

puma zo. [py'ma] m puma, cougar.

punaise [py'nɛːz] f zo. bug; drawing pin, Am. thumbtack.

puni|r [py'niːr] (2a) punish (with, **de**); **~ssable** [pyni'sabl] punishable; **~tion** [~'sjɔ̃] f punishment.

pupille¹ 🕱🕱 [py'pil] su. ward.

pupille² anat. [~] f eye: pupil.

pupitre [py'pitr] m desk; ♪ music stand; ♪ (conductor's) rostrum; eccl. lectern.

pur [pyːr] pure; clear; neat, undiluted (drink etc.); fig. a. sheer (folly etc.).

purée [py're] f cuis. purée; (a. **~ de pommes de terre**) mashed potatoes; F **être dans la ~** be in a pretty mess.

pureté [pyr'te] f purity; pureness.

purg|atif 💊 [pyrga'tif] adj., su./m purgative; **~atoire** eccl. [~'twaːr] m purgatory (a. fig.); **~e** [pyrʒ] f 💊 purge (a. pol.); 🜨 bleeding, draining; **~er** [~'ʒe] (11) purge (fig., a. 💊), cleanse; 🕱🕱 serve (a sentence); 🜨 fig. clear (of, **de**); 🜨 a. bleed (a radiator etc.), drain (a pipe).

purifi|cation [pyrifika'sjɔ̃] f purification; **~er** [~'fje] (1o) purify; 🜨, fig. a. refine.

puris|me [py'rism] m purism; **~te** [~'rist] **1.** su. purist; **2.** adj. puristic.

purita|in [pyri'tɛ̃] **1.** su. Puritan; **2.** adj. puritan(ical) (a. fig.); **~nisme** [~ta'nism] m puritanism.

purpurin [pyrpy'rɛ̃] purplish, crimson.

pur-sang [pyr'sɑ̃] m/inv. purebred, thoroughbred.

pus¹ 💊 [py] m pus, matter.

pus² [~] *1st p. sg. pres. p.s. of* **pouvoir 1.**

pusillanim|e [pyzilla'nim] pusillanimous; faint-hearted; **~ité** [~nimi'te] f faint-heartedness.

putain V [py'tɛ̃] f whore; **~!** goddamn it!

putatif [pyta'tif] supposed.

putois zo. [py'twa] m polecat.

putr|éfaction [pytrefak'sjɔ̃] f putrefaction; **~éfier** [~'fje] (1o) (a. **se ~**) putrefy.

puzzle [pœzl] m jigsaw puzzle.

pygmée [pig'me] m pygmy.

pyjama [piʒa'ma] *m* (pair of) pyjamas *pl.*, *Am.* pajamas *pl.*

pylône [pi'lon] pylon.

pyramid|al [pirami'dal] pyramidal; **~e** △, ⚶ [~'mid] *f* pyramid.

pyroman|e [pirɔ'man] *su.* pyromaniac, arsonist; **~ie** [~ma'ni] pyromania.

Pyrrhus [pi'rys] *npr./m*: **victoire** *f* **à la ~** Pyrrhic victory.

python *zo. etc.* [pi'tɔ̃] *m* python.

Q

quadragénaire [kwadraʒe'nɛːr] *adj.* (*su.* man *or* woman) in his (her) forties.

quadrangulaire [kwadrɑ̃gy'lɛːr] quadrangular; four-cornered.

quadra|nt [ka'drɑ̃] *m* quadrant; **~ture** [kwadra'tyːr] *f* quadrature; *circle*: squaring (*a. fig.*).

quadrilatère [kwadrila'tɛːr] *su./m, adj.* quadrilateral.

quadrill|é [kadri'je] squared (*paper etc.*); grid (*map*); **~er** [~] (1a) square; *fig.* cover (*an area etc.*); *fig.* (bring under) control.

quadrimoteur ✈ [kwadrimɔ'tœːr] four-engined (plane).

quadriphonie [kwadrifɔ'ni] *f* quadrophony; **en ~** in quadrophonic sound.

quadrupède [kwadry'pɛd] **1.** *adj.* four-footed; **2.** *su./m* quadruped.

quadrupl|e [kwa'drypl] *adj., su./m* fourfold; **~er** [~dry'ple] (1a) quadruple, increase fourfold; **~é(e)s** *m(f)/pl.* quadruplets, quads.

quai [ke] *m* quay, wharf; 🚋 platform; *river*: embankment.

quali|ficatif [kalifika'tif] qualifying; **~fication** [~fika'sjɔ̃] *f* qualification; description, designation; **~fié** [~'fje] qualified (to, *pour*); skilled (*workman*); 🏴 aggravated; **~fier** [~'fje] (1o) call, style (by, *de*; s.o. s.th., *q. de qch.*); qualify; **se ~** qualify (for, *pour*); **se ~ de ...** call o.s. ...; **~tatif** [~ta'tif] qualitative; **~té** [~'te] *f* quality, property; nature; qualification; *fig.* capacity (as, *de*), authority; **avoir ~ pour** be qualified to; **de première ~** first-rate; **en (sa) ~ de** in his capacity as.

quand [kɑ̃] **1.** *adv.* when; **depuis ~?** how

long?; **2.** *cj.* when; **~ même** nevertheless, all the same; even though.

quant à [kɑ̃'ta] *prp.* as for, as to; **quant-à-soi** [kɑ̃ta'swa] *m/inv.* reserve; dignity; **rester sur son ~** keep aloof.

quantième [kɑ̃'tjɛm] *m* day of the month, date.

quantique *phys.* [kwɑ̃'tik]: **mécanique** *f* **~** quantum mechanics.

quantifier [kɑ̃ti'fje] (1o) quantify.

quantit|atif [kɑ̃tita'tif] quantitative; **~é** [~'te] *f* quantity; amount; (*une*) **~ de, des ~s de** a great deal of; **en (grande) ~** in large amounts; a lot of ...

quantum, *pl.* **-ta** [kwɑ̃'tɔm, ~'ta] *m* quantum; *phys.* **théorie** *f* **des quanta** quantum theory.

quarant|aine [karɑ̃'tɛn] *f* ✚ quarantine; **une ~ (de ...)** about forty (...); **la ~** the age of forty, the forties *pl.*; *fig.* **mettre** (*or* **laisser**) **q. en ~** send s.o. to Coventry; **~e** [~'rɑ̃ːt] forty; **~-cinq tours** *m record*: single; **~ième** [~rɑ̃'tjɛm] fortieth.

quart [kaːr] *m* ⚶ *etc.* quarter; ⚓ watch; **~ d'heure** quarter of an hour; **deux heures moins le ~** a quarter to two; *fig.* **un mauvais ~ d'heure** a hard time; **~e** [kart] *f* ♪ fourth.

quartier [kar'tje] *m* quarter; (fourth) part; piece, portion; *stone*: block; district, neighbo(u)rhood, area, quarter; *fig.* mercy; ✕ quarters *pl.*; ✕ **~ général** headquarters *pl.*; ✕ **faire ~** give quarter; **~-maître,** *pl.* **~s-maîtres** [~tje-'mɛːtr] *m* ⚓ leading seaman.

quarto [kwar'to] *adv.* fourthly.

quartz [kwarts] *m* quartz.

quasi [ka'zi] *adv.* almost, practically; **~ment** F [~zi'mɑ̃] *adv.* = **quasi.**

quatorz|e [ka'tɔrz] fourteen; *date, title:* fourteenth; **~ième** [~tɔr'zjɛm] fourteenth.

quatre [katr] four; *date, title:* fourth; **à ~ four** at a time; **à ~ pas d'ici** close by; **à ~ pattes** on all fours; *entre ~ yeux* between you and me; F *faire les ~ cent coups* live it up; *ne pas y aller par ~ chemins* not to beat about the bush; *se mettre en ~* put o.s. out; *un de ces (matins)* one of these days; **~-mâts** ♎ [katrə'ma] *m/inv.* four-master; **~-vingt-dix** [~vɛ̃'dis; *before consonant* ~'di; *before vowel or h mute* ~'diz] ninety; **~-vingt-dixième** [~vɛ̃di'zjɛm] ninetieth; **~-vingtième** [~vɛ̃'tjɛm] eightieth; **~-vingts** [~'vɛ̃] (*loses its -s when followed by another number*) eighty; *quatre-vingt-un* eighty-one; **quatrième** [katri'ɛm] **1.** *adj./num., su.* fourth. **2.** *su./m* fourth, *Am.* fifth floor.

quatuor ♩ [kwa'tɥɔr] *m* quartet; **à ~ cordes** string quartet.

que [kə] **1.** *pron./interr.* what?; how (many)!; **~ cherchez-vous?, qu'est-ce que vous cherchez?** what are you looking for?; **~ de monde!** what a lot of people!; **~ faire?** what can (could) be done?; **qu'est-ce ~ c'est ~ cela?** what's that?; **qu'est-ce ~ la littérature?** what is literature?; **2.** *pron./rel.* whom, that; which; what; *je ne sais ~ dire* I don't know what to say; *le jour qu'il vint* the day (when) he came; *l'homme ~ j'aime* the man (that) I love; **3.** *cj.* that; so that; when; whether; *replacing another cj. to avoid its repetition:* **puisque vous le dites et ~ nous le croyons** since you say so and we believe it; **~** (*sbj.*) **... ~** (*sbj.*) whether (*ind.*) ... or (*ind*); **~ le diable l'emporte!** to hell with him!; *aussi ... ~* as ...; *il y a ... ~* since ...; *je crois ~ oui* I think so; *ne ... ~* only, but; *non* (*pas*) **~** (*sbj.*) not that (*ind.*); *plus ~* more than.

quel *m,* **~le** *f,* **~s** *m/pl.,* **~les** *f/pl.* [kɛl] **1.** *adj/interr.* what; who; which; what (a)!; *quelle bonté!* how kind!; **~ que** (*sbj.*) whatever (*ind.*); **~s que soient ces messieurs** whoever these gentlemen may be; **2.** *adj/indef.* whatever; whoever; whichever.

quelconque [kɛl'kɔ̃:k] *adj./indef.* any, whatever; commonplace, ordinary; poor, indifferent.

quelque [kɛlk(ə)] **1.** *adj.* some, any; **~s** *pl.* some, (a) few; **~ peu** something; **~ ... qui** (*or* **que**) (*sbj.*) whatever (*ind.*); **2.** *adv.* some, about; **~ peu** somewhat, a little; **~ ... que** (*sbj.*) however (*adj.*); **~fois** [kɛlkə'fwa] *adv.* sometimes, now and then.

quelqu'un *m, e f, m/pl.* **quelques-uns** [kɛl'kœ̃, ~'kyn, ~kə'zœ̃] *pron./indef.* someone, anyone; somebody, anybody; *pl.* some, any; **~ d'autre** someone *or* somebody else; *être ~* be s.o. (important).

quémand|er [kemɑ̃'de] (1a) beg for; **~eur,** *m* **-euse** *f* [~'dœːr, ~'døːz] beggar.

qu'en-dira-t-on [kɑ̃dira'tɔ̃] *m/inv.:* **le ~** what people will say.

quenelle [kə'nɛl] *f* (fish-, meat-)ball.

quenouille [kə'nuːj] *f* distaff.

querell|e [kə'rɛl] *f* quarrel; **~er** [karɛ'le] (1a): *se ~* quarrel; **~eur,** *m* **-euse** *f* [~'lœːr] quarrelsome (person).

quérir [ke'riːr] (2v): *aller ~* go for; *envoyer ~* send for; *venir ~* come for.

question [kɛs'tjɔ̃] *f* question; matter; **~ d'actualité** topic of the day; *ce n'est pas la ~* that is not the point; *il est de ~* it is a question of; there is talk of; **... en ~ ...** in question; *hors de ~* out of the question; *il n'en est pas ~* no question of it; *(re)mettre qch. en ~* question s.th.; **... ne fait pas ~** there is no doubt about ...; **~naire** [kɛstjɔ'nɛːr] *m* questionnaire; **~ner** [~'ne] (1a) question (*s.o.*).

quête [kɛːt] *f* quest, search; *eccl. etc.* collection; *en ~ de* in search of; *faire la ~ eccl.* take the collection; pass the hat round; *fig.* seek (for); **~eur** *m,* **-euse** *f* [~'tœːr, ~'tøːz] collector (*of alms*).

quetsche [kwɛtʃ] *f* damson.

queue [kø] *f* tail; *pan, tool:* handle; ♎ stalk; *fig.* bottom, (tail) end; rear; *people:* queue, line; *faire (la)* **~** queue up, *Am.* line up; *mot.* *faire une* **~ de poisson** cut in (on, à); *fig.* *finir en* **~ de poisson** fizzle out.

qui [ki] **1.** *pron./ interr. subject: persons:* who, *two persons:* which; *things:* which; what; *object: persons:* whom; *things:* which; **~ est-ce ~ chante?** who is singing?; **~ est-ce que tu as vu?** who(m) did you see?; *à ~* to whom? *à ~ est ce*

livre? whose book is this?; **de ~** whose?; *of or from whom?*; **2.** *pron./rel. subject: persons:* who, that; (he *or* anyone) who; *things:* which, that; what; *after prp.: persons:* whom; *things:* which; **~pis est** what is worse; **~que ce soit** whoever it is; anyone; **ce ~** what; which; **n'avoir ~ tromper** have no one to deceive; **3.** *pron./indef.* some; **~ ..., ~ ...** some ..., some *or* others ...

quiconque [ki'kɔ̃:k] *pron./indef.* whoever, anyone who; anybody.

quidam *co.* [ki'dam] *m* individual.

quiétude [kɥie'tyd] *f* tranquillity, quiet, quietude; peace (of mind); **en toute ~** calmly.

quille¹ ⚓ [ki:j] *f* keel.

quille² [ki:j] *f sp.* skittle, ninepin; *sl.* leg; **jeu m de ~s** bowling.

quincaill|erie [kɛ̃kaj'ri] *f* hardware; hardware shop (*Am.* store); **~ier** [~ka'je] *m* hardware dealer.

quinconce [kɛ̃'kɔ̃:s]: **en ~** in fives; zigzag.

quinine 🌿, ⚕ [ki'nin] *f* quinine.

quinquagénaire [kɥɛ̃kwaʒe'nɛ:r] *adj.* (*su.* man *or* woman) in his (her) fifties.

quinquennal [kɥɛ̃kɥɛn'nal] five-year (*plan etc.*).

quint [kɛ̃]: **Charles ♀ Charles** V.

quintal † [kɛ̃'tal] *m* hundredweight.

quinte [kɛ̃:t] *f* ♪ fifth; ⚕ **~ (de toux)** coughing fit.

quintessenc|e [kɛ̃tɛ'sɑ̃:s] *f* quintessence; **~ié** [~sɑ̃'sje] (1o) refined.

quinteux † [kɛ̃'tø] *f* crotchety.

quintupl|e [kɛ̃'typl] *adj., su./m* fivefold; **~er** [~ty'ple] (1a) quintuple, increase fivefold; **~é(e)s** *m(f)/pl.* quintuplets, quins.

quinz|aine [kɛ̃'zɛn] *f* two weeks, *Br. a.*

fortnight; **une ~ (de ...)** about fifteen (...); **~e** [kɛ̃:z] fifteen; *date, title:* fifteenth; **~ jours** two weeks, *Br. a.* a fortnight; **~ième** [kɛ̃'zjɛm] fifteenth.

quiproquo [kiprɔ'ko] *m* mistake, misunderstanding.

quittanc|e † [ki'tɑ̃:s] *f* receipt; bill; **~er** [~tɑ̃'se] (1k) receipt.

quitte [kit] *adj.* free, clear (of, **de**); **être ~** be quits; **en être ~ pour qch.** get *or* come off with s.th.; **jouer (au) ~ ou double** play double or nothing; *adj./ inv.:* **~ à** (*inf.*) even if (*ind.*); **il le fera ~ à perdre son argent** he will do it even if he loses his money.

quitter [ki'te] (1a) leave (*s.o., s.th.*); give up (*a post, business, a. fig.*); take off (*one's coat, hat etc.*); *teleph.* **ne quittez pas!** hold the line!; **se ~** part (*couple, friends, etc.*).

qui-vive [ki'vi:v] *m/inv.:* **être sur le ~** be on the alert.

quoi [kwa] **1.** *pron./interr. things:* what; **~ donc!** what!; **2.** *pron./rel. what:* ~ **que** (*sbj.*) whatever (*ind.*); **~ qu'il en soit** be that as it may; **avoir de ~ vivre** have enough to live on; **(il n'y a) pas de ~!** don't mention it!; you're welcome!; **sans ~ ...** otherwise, or else!; **un je-ne-sais-~** a(n indescribable) something.

quoique [kwak(ə)] *cj.* (al)though.

quolibet [kɔli'bɛ] *m* jeer, gibe.

quorum [k(w)ɔ'rɔm] *m* quorum.

quota [k(w)ɔ'ta] *m* quota.

quote-part [kɔt'pa:r] *f* share.

quotidien [kɔti'djɛ̃] **1.** *adj.* daily; everyday; **2.** *su./m* daily (paper).

quotient [kɔ'sjɑ̃] *m* quotient; **~ intellectuel** (**QI**) intelligence quotient (IQ).

quotité [kɔti'te] *f* quota.

R

rabâcher [raba'ʃe] (1a) repeat (the same thing) over and over again.

rabais [ra'bɛ] *m* † *price:* reduction, discount; **au ~** at a reduced price, at a

discount; **~ser** [~bɛ'se] (1a) lower; reduce; *fig.* belittle; humble (*s.o., s.o.'s pride*).

rabat [ra'ba] *m handbag etc.:* flap; **~joie**

[~ba'ʒwa] *m/inv.* spoil-sport; **~teur** [~ba'tœːr] *m* tout; *hunt.* beater; **~tre** [~'batr] (4a) *v/t.* fold back *or* down; lower (*a. fig.*); *fig.* reduce; ✗ cut back; *hunt.* beat up (*game*); **~ qch. de** take s.th. off (*the price etc.*); *fig.* **en ~** climb down; *mot.* **se ~** get back into the inside lane; *fig.* **se ~ sur** fall back on.

rabbin [ra'bɛ̃] *m* rabbi.

rabibocher F [rabibɔ'ʃe] (1a) patch up; *fig.* reconcile.

rabiot *sl.* [ra'bjo] *m* food: extra; over-time; extra time.

rabique ♣ [ra'bik] rabic.

râbl|e [raːbl] *m* zo. back; *cuis.* saddle; **~é** [ra'ble] broad-backed.

rabot ☉ [ra'bo] *m* plane; **~er** [rabɔ'te] (1a) planc (down); scrape, graze; **~eux** [~'tø] rough, uneven, rugged.

rabougr|i [rabu'gri] stunted; **~ir** [~'griːr] (2a): **se ~** become stunted; shrivel (up).

rabrouer [rabru'e] (1a) scold; snub.

racaille [ra'kaːj] *f* rabble, riff-raff, scum.

raccommod|age [rakɔmɔ'daːʒ] *m* mending, repair(ing); darn(ing); **~er** [~mɔ'de] (1a) mend, repair; darn (*socks*); F *fig.* reconcile; **se ~ avec** make it up with (*s.o.*).

raccord [ra'kɔːr] *m* ☉ joint, connection; link; join; linking up; touch-up; **~ement** [rakɔrdə'mɑ̃] *m* joining, linking, connection; **~er** [~'de] (1a) join, link (up), connect.

raccourc|i [rakur'si] *m* short cut; *fig.* summary; **en ~** in brief, in a nutshell, abridged; **~ir** [~'siːr] (2a) *v/t.* shorten; cut short; *v/i.* grow shorter; *tex.* shrink; **~issement** [~sis'mɑ̃] *m* shortening.

raccro|c [ra'kro] *m:* **par ~** by chance; **~cher** [rakrɔ'ʃe] (1a) *v/t.* hang up again; F get hold of (*s.o., s.th.*); F accost; *v/i.* (at, **à**); *fig.* link, tie (with, **à**); *v/i.* teleph. hang up.

race [ras] *f* race; *zo.* species, breed; **racé** [ra'se] thoroughbred (*a. fig.*).

rach|at [ra'ʃa] *m* (re)purchase; ✝, *eccl.* redemption; *fig.* ransom(ing); *fig.* a-tonement, expiation; **~etable** [raʃ-'tabl] ✝ redeemable; *eccl.* atonable (*sin*); **~eter** [~'te] (1d) buy some more, buy another; buy back; *eccl.* buy in; buy (s.th. from s.o., *qch. à q.*), ✝, *eccl.* redeem (*a loan etc.; a sinner*); *fig.* ran-som (*a prisoner etc.*); *fig.* make up for

(*an error, misbehaviour, etc.*), atone for, expiate (*one's sins*); **se ~** make up for it; make amends.

rachiti|que ♣ [raʃi'tik] rachitic, rickety; **~sme** [~'tism] *m* rickets.

racine [ra'sin] *f* root; **&~ carrée** (**cubique**) square (cube) root; **prendre ~** take root.

rac|isme [ra'sism] *m* rac(ial)ism; **~te** [~'sist] *adj., su.* rac(ial)ist.

racl|ée F [ra'kle] *f* hiding, thrashing, licking; **~er** [~'kle] (1a) scrape; scrape out *or* away *or* off; **se ~ la gorge** clear one's throat; **~ette** [~'klet] *f* scraper; *cuis.* raclette (*cheese dish*); **~oir** [~'klwaːr] *m* scraper; **~ure** [~'klyːr] *f* scrapings *pl.*

racoler [rakɔ'le] (1a) solicit; tout for.

raconter [rakɔ̃'te] (1a) tell, relate; tell (s.o., **à q.**).

racornir [rakɔr'niːr] (2a) harden, toughen; make callous; shrivel.

radar [ra'daːr] *m* radar (set); **~iste** [~da'rist] *m* radar operator.

rade ⚓ [rad] *f* roads *pl.*, roadstead.

radeau [ra'do] *m* raft.

radia|ire [ra'djeːr] radiate(d); **~l** [~'djal] radial; **~nce** [~'djɑ̃ːs] *f* radiance; **~nt** [~'djɑ̃] radiant; **~teur** [~dja'tœːr] *m* radiator; heater.

radiation[1] [radja'sjɔ̃] *f* radiation.

radiation[2] [~] *f* striking out; *debt etc.:* cancellation, ⚖ disbarment.

radical [radi'kal] *adj., su./m* radical.

radié [ra'dje] radiate(d), rayed.

radier [ra'dje] (1o) strike out, cancel.

radieux [ra'djø] radiant (with joy).

radio F [ra'djo] *su./f* radio; ✗ X-ray pho-tograph; *su./m* radio(tele)gram; radio operator.

radin *sl.* [ra'dɛ̃] stingy.

radio... [radjo] radio...; **~actif** *phys.* [~ak'tif] radioactive; **~activité** [~aktivi-'te] *f* radioactivity; **~diffuser** [~dify'ze] (1a) broadcast; **~diffusion** [~dify-'zjɔ̃] *f* broadcasting; **~élément** *phys.* [~ele'mɑ̃] *m* radioactive element; **~ goniométrie** [~gɔnjɔme'tri] *f* direction finding; **~gramme** [~'gram] *m* ✗ radio-gram; ✗ X-ray photograph; **~graphie** ♣ [~gra'fi] *f* X-ray photograph(y); **~graphier** [~gra'fje] (1o) X-ray; **~ guidé** [~gi'de] radio-controlled; **~jour-nal** [~ʒur'nal] *m* radio: news bulletin;

~logue ⚕ [~'lɔg] m, **~logiste** ⚕ [~lɔ'ʒist] m radiologist; **~phonique** [~fɔ'nik] wireless ...; radio...; **~phono** [~fɔ'no] m instrument, furniture: radiogram; **~reportage** [~rəpɔr'ta:ʒ] m radio report; **~reporter** [~rəpɔr'tɛːr] m (radio) commentator; **~scopie** [~skɔ'pi] f radioscopy; **~télégramme** ⚡ [~tele'gram] m radio(tele)gram; **~téléphonie** [~telefɔ'ni] f radiotelephony; **~télévisé** [~televi'ze] broadcast on (both) radio and television; **~thérapie** [~tera'pi] f radiotherapy.

radis ♣ [ra'di] m radish; F **ne pas avoir un ~** be penniless, be broke.

radium ☊ [ra'djɔm] m radium.

radot|age [radɔ'ta:ʒ] m drivel; **~er** [~'te] (1a) drivel (on); **~eur** m, **-euse** f [~'tœːr, ~'tøːz] drivel(l)er.

radoub ⚓ [ra'du] m repair; **bassin ~ de** ~ dry dock; **~er** ⚓ [~du'be] (1a) repair.

radoucir [radu'siːr] (2a) make milder; **se ~** become milder (weather); fig. calm down.

rafale [ra'fal] f squall; gust; ✕ volley; **~ de pluie** cloudburst.

raffermi|r [rafɛr'miːr] (2a) (a. **se ~**) harden; firm (up); fig. strengthen; **se ~** a. become steady (voice, fig. trend etc.); **~ssement** [~mis'mã] m hardening; fig. strengthening.

raffin|age [rafi'na:ʒ] m refining; **~é** [~'fi'ne] refined; fig. subtle; **~ement** [~fin'mã] m (over-)refinement; subtlety; **~er** [~fi'ne] (1a) v/t. refine (☉, a. fig.); v/i. be (over-)meticulous (about, sur); **~erie** ☉ [~fin'ri] f refinery.

raffoler F [rafɔ'le] (1a): **~ de** be mad about.

raffut F [ra'fy] m row, din.

rafistoler F [rafistɔ'le] (1a) patch (s.th.) up; botch (s.th.) up.

rafle¹ ♣ [ra:fl] f stalk; cob.

rafle² [ra:fl] f police etc.: raid, roundup; **rafler** [ra'fle] (1a) swipe.

rafraîchi|r [rafrɛ'ʃiːr] (2a) v/t. cool; cool down; freshen up; refresh (a. one's memory); fig. brush up (a subject); fig. brighten up; **se ~** become cool(er); freshen; refresh o.s.; v/i. cool (down); cuis. **mettre (qch.) à ~** chill; **~ssement** [~ʃis'mã] m cooling etc.; see **rafraîchir**; **~s** pl. refreshments.

ragaillardir F [ragajar'diːr] (2a) buck (s.o.) up.

rag|e [ra:ʒ] f rage, fury; fig. mania; violent pain; ⚕ rabies; fig. **faire ~** rage, be raging; **~er** [ra'ʒe] (1l) rage, fume; **~eur** [~'ʒœːr] hot-tempered; angry.

ragot¹ [ra'go] squat; stocky.

ragot² F [ra'go] m gossip, talk.

ragoût cuis. [ra'gu] stew; **~ant** [ragu'tã]: **peu ~** unsavo(u)ry; unpleasant, unpalatable.

rai [rɛ] m light: ray; wheel: spoke.

raid [rɛd] m mot. long-distance run or ✈ flight; ✕, ✈ raid.

raid|e [rɛd] **1.** adj. stiff (a. manner); tight, taut (rope); straight; steep; F fig. unyielding; **2.** adv. steep(ly); hard; **tomber ~ mort** drop stone dead; **~eur** [rɛ'dœːr] f stiffness; rigidity; rope: tautness; steepness; **avec ~** violently; stubbornly; **~ir** [~'diːr] (2a) stiffen; tighten, pull tight or taut; **se ~** stiffen, tighten, tauten; tense (up); fig. harden (positions etc.); fig. take a hard line; **se ~ (contre)** brace o.s. (against); **~issement** [~dis'mã] m stiffening; tautening; fig. hardening.

raie¹ [rɛ] f line; streak; stripe; scratch; hair: parting; ⚲ furrow.

raie² icht. [~] f skate, ray.

raifort ♣ [rɛ'fɔːr] m horseradish.

rail [ra:j] m rail; railway, Am. railroad.

raill|er [ra'je] (1a) (a. **se ~ de**) mock at; **~erie** [raj'ri] f mockery; mocking remark; **~eur** [ra'jœːr] mocking.

rainure ☉ [rɛ'nyːr] f groove; slot.

raire [rɛːr] (4ff) bell (stag).

rais [rɛ] m see **rai**.

raisin [rɛ'zɛ̃] m grape(s pl.); **~s** pl. **de Corinthe** currants; **~s** pl. **de Smyrne** sultanas; **~s** pl. **secs** raisins.

raison [rɛ'zɔ̃] f reason; ⚕ ratio; ✞ **~ sociale** name (of a firm); **à ~ de** at the rate of; **à plus forte ~** all the more; **avoir ~** be right; **avoir ~ de** get the better of, get the upper hand of; **en ~ de** because of; **parler ~** talk sense; **~nable** [~zɔ'nabl] sensible, reasonable; rational; **~né** [~zɔ'ne] reasoned; **~nement** [~zɔn'mã] m reasoning; argument; **~ner** [~zɔ'ne] (1a) v/i. reason, argue (about, sur); v/t. reason with (s.o.).

rajeuni|r [raʒœ'niːr] (2a) v/t. make (look) younger; rejuvenate; renovate;

v/i. become *or* feel *or* look younger;
~ssement [~nis'mã] *m* rejuvenation;
renovation.

rajouter [raʒu'te] (1a) add.

rajust|ement [raʒystə'mã] *m* readjustment; **~er** [~'te] (1a) (re)adjust; straighten (out *or* up), tidy; rearrange.

râle¹ ♫ [ɽɑːl] *m* rattle; **~ d'agonie** death rattle.

râle² *orn.* [~] *m* rail.

ralent|i [ralã'ti] *m* slow motion; **au ~** slow(ly); **tourner au ~** tick over, idle; **~ir** [~'tiːr] (2a) slow down; relax; **~issement** [~tis'mã] *m* slowing down; slackening.

râler [rɑ'le] (1a) groan; be in agony; give the death rattle; F grouse.

ralli|ement [rali'mã] *m* rally(ing); **~er** [~'lje] (1o) rally; rejoin; **se ~** rally; **se ~ à** join; *fig.* come round to.

rallong|e [ra'lɔ̃ʒ] *f* ⊚ extension piece, *table:* extension leaf; ♣ additional sum *or* payment; **~ement** [~lɔ̃ʒ'mã] *m* extension; **~er** [~lɔ̃'ʒe] (1l) lengthen; thin (*a sauce*).

rallumer [raly'me] (1a) light up again, relight; rekindle (*a. ftg.*); **se ~** go on again (*light, fire*); *fig.* flare up again.

rallye *mot. etc.* [ra'li] *m* rally.

ramage [ra'maːʒ] *m orn.* song, warbling; *tex.* (*usu.* **~s** *pl.*) floral design *or* pattern.

ramas [ra'ma] *m* pile; collection; *pej.* set (*of robbers*), rabble.

ramass|é [rama'se] stocky; compact; **~er** [rama'se] (1a) gather (together); pick up; **se ~** pick o.s. up; *fig.* crouch (*animal*); **~is** [~'si] *m* pile; F pack.

rame¹ ♧ [~] *f* oar.

rame² [~] *f* ♣ *paper:* ream; ♖ *coaches, barges etc.:* string.

rameau [ra'mo] *m* ♣ twig, branch; *zo.* **~x** *pl.* antlers; *eccl.* **dimanche** *m* **des ~x** Palm Sunday.

ramener [ram'ne] (1d) bring *or* take back; ♣, *a. fig.* reduce (to, *à*); draw *or* pull (down, back, *etc.*); *fig.* restore (*peace*); *fig.* win (*s.o.*) over (to, *à*), **se ~** F turn up, come (back); *fig.* **se ~ à** come *or* boil down to.

ram|er [ra'me] (1a) row; **~eur** [~'mœːr] *m* rower.

~mi'fje (1o): **se ~** branch out; ramify; **~ille** [~'miːj] *f* twig.

ramolli|r [ramɔ'liːr] (2a) soften; **se ~** get soft(er); **~ssement** [~lis'mã] *m* softening.

ramon|er [ramɔ'ne] (1a) sweep (*the chimney*); ⊚ scour, clear; **~eur** [~'nœːr] *m* (chimney) sweep.

rampe [rɑ̃ːp] *f* slope, incline; ramp; *stairs:* handrail, banister(s *pl.*); *thea.* footlights *pl.*; **~ de lancement** launching pad.

ramper [rɑ̃'pe] (1a) creep; crawl; *fig.* fawn, grovel; ♣ trail; *fig.* lurk.

ramponneau F [rɑ̃pɔ'no] *m* blow.

ramure [ra'myːr] *f* branches *pl.*; *zo.* antlers *pl.*

rancard *sl.* [rɑ̃'kaːr] *m* tip-off, info; meeting, date; **~er** *sl.* [~kar'de] (1a) inform, tip (*s.o.*) off.

rancart F [rɑ̃'kaːr] *m:* **mettre au ~** discard; throw on the scrap-heap; F chuck out; *admin.* retire (*s.o.*).

ranc|e [rɑ̃ːs] rancid; **se ~** become rancid; **~issure** [~si'syːr] *f* rancidness.

rancœur [rɑ̃'kœːr] *f* ranco(u)r.

rançon [rɑ̃'sɔ̃] *f* ransom; *fig.* price; **~ner** [rɑ̃so'ne] (1a) hold to *or* for ransom; exact money from; ransom (*s.o.*); ♣ fleece.

rancun|e [rɑ̃'kyn] *f* grudge; **garder (de la) ~ à q.** bear s.o. a grudge (for, *de*); **sans ~!** no offence!; **~ier** [~ky'nje] spiteful (person).

randonnée [rɑ̃do'ne] *f* tour, excursion, (long) trip; outing; hike.

rang [rɑ̃] *m* row, line; order, class; tier; ✗, *a. fig.* rank; F *fig.* **de premier ~** first-rate; **~é, e** [rɑ̃'ʒe] **1.** *adj.* tidy; steady (*person*); orderly; (*bien*) ~ well-ordered; **2.** *su./f* row, line; array; **~er** [~] (1l) (ar)range; ✗ draw up; put (*s.th.*) away; tidy (*objects, a room*); *fig.* rank (among, *parmi*); ♪ hug (*the coast*); *fig.* steady (*s.o.*); keep back (*a crowd*); *mot.* park (*one's car*); **se ~** line up, get into line; *fig.* settle down (*in life, behaviour, etc.*); *mot.* pull over; *fig.* make way (*person*); *fig.* **se ~ à** fall in with, come round to.

ranimer [rani'me] (1a) revive; bring back to life; bring to (*a fainted person*); *a. fig.* rekindle; *fig.* restore, renew; **se ~**

revive; come back to life; come to (*person*); *a. fig.* rekindle.

rapac|e [ra'pas] **1.** *adj.* rapacious; **2.** *su./m* bird of prey; **~ité** [~pasi'te] *f* rapacity.

rapatri|ement [rapatri'mã] *m* repatriation; **~er** [~'e] (1a) repatriate; bring back (home) (again).

râpe [rɑ:p] *f* ⚙ rasp; *cuis.* grater; **râper** [rɑ'pe] (1a) ⚙ rasp; *cuis.* grate; **râpé** [~] **1.** *adj. cuis.* grated; threadbare (*clothes*); F **c'est ~** we've had it; **2.** *su./m* grated cheese.

rapetasser F [rapta'se] (1a) patch up; cobble (*shoes*); *fig.* botch up.

rapetisser [rapti'se] (1a) *v/t.* make (look) smaller; shorten (*clothes*); *v/i.* become smaller; shrink.

râpeux [rɑ'pø] rough; harsh.

rapiat F [ra'pja] stingy (person).

rapid|e [ra'pid] **1.** *adj.* fast, quick, swift, rapid; **2.** *su./m river:* rapid; 🚂 express (train); **~ité** [~pidi'te] *f* speed; *slope:* steepness.

rapié|çage [rapje'sa:ʒ] *m* patching (-up); **~cer** [~'se] (1f *a.* 1k) patch (up); mend.

rappel [ra'pɛl] *m pol. etc.* recall; reminder; *thea.* curtain call; ⚙ back-motion; ♱ back pay; ♒ booster shot; **~ à l'ordre** call to order; **~er** [~'ple] (1c) *pol., fig.* recall; call back; remind (s.o. of s.th., *qch. à q.*); *teleph.* ring back; *fig.* restore (*s.o. to health*); *parl.* **~ à l'ordre** call to order; **se ~** recall, remember (*s.th.*).

rappliquer [rapli'ke] (1m) *v/i.* F come *or* go back; *v/t.* re-apply.

rapport [ra'pɔ:r] *m* ♱, ⚙ return, yield; report; ♒, *mot.* ratio; relationship; connection (with, *avec*); relation; **~s** *pl.* intercourse *sg.*; *fig.* **en ~ avec** in keeping *or* touch with; **maison** *f* **de ~** apartment house; **mettre q. en ~ avec** put s.o. in touch with; **par ~ à** in relation to; compared with; **sous tous les ~s** in every respect; **~er** [rapɔr'te] *v/t.* bring back; *hunt.* retrieve; *admin.* revoke; ⚙ join, add; ♱ yield, produce; *fig.* get; report (*a fact etc.*); *fig.* **~ à** relate to; ascribe to; **se ~ à** relate to; **s'en ~ à** rely on; *v/i.* pay, be profitable; F tell tales; report (on, about *sur*); **~eur** [~'tœ:r] *su.* 🐝 *etc.* reporter; ♒ protractor; telltale.

rapprendre [ra'prã:dr] (4aa) learn *or* teach (*s.th.*) again.

rapproch|ement [raprɔʃ'mã] *m* bringing together; comparison; closeness; *fig.* reconciliation; **~er** [~prɔ'ʃe] (1a) bring (closer) together; put nearer (to, *de*); compare; *fig.* reconcile; **se ~** get closer *or* draw near (to, *de*); *fig.* become reconciled (with, *de*); *fig.* **se ~ de** be close to.

rapt [rapt] *m* abduction.

raquette [ra'kɛt] *f sp.* racket, ping-pong: bat; snowshoe.

rar|e [ra:r] rare; *fig.* singular, uncommon; 🌸 slow (*pulse*); sparse (*hair etc.*); **~éfaction** [rarefak'sjɔ̃] *f phys.* rarefaction; ♱ growing scarcity; **~éfier** [~'fje] (1o) *phys.* rarefy; **se ~** become scarce; **~eté** [rar'te] *f* rarity; scarcity; singularity.

ras¹ [rɑ] **1.** *adj.* close-cropped, close-shaven; open (*country*); **à ~ bord** to the brim, brim-full; **faire table rase** make a clean sweep; **coupé ~** cut short; **2.** *prp.:* **à** (*or* **au**) **~ de** level *or* flush with.

ras² [rɑ] *m see* **raz**.

ras|ade [rɑ'zad] *f* brim-full glass; **~age** [~'za:ʒ] *m* shaving; *tex.* shearing; **~er** [rɑ'ze] (1a) shave; *tex.* shear; F bore (*s.o.*); ✗ raze; *fig.* graze, skim; **crème** *f* **à ~** shaving cream; **rasé de près** close-shaven; **~ibus** F [~zi'bys] *adv.* very close; **~oir** [~'zwa:r] *m* razor; *fig.* **au ~** perfectly.

rassasier [rasa'zje] (1o) satisfy; satisfy (*s.o.'s*) hunger; **être rassasié** have eaten one's fill; *fig.* **(en) être rassasié de** have had enough of.

rassembl|ement [rasãblə'mã] *m* gathering; crowd; **~er** [~'ble] (1a) (re)assemble; gather (together).

rasseoir [ra'swa:r] (3c) **se ~** sit down again.

rasséréner [rasere'ne] (1f) **se ~** become serene again.

rassis [ra'si] sedate; stale (*bread*).

rassurer [rasy're] (1a) reassure; **rassuré** *a.* at ease, easy; **rassurez-vous!** don't worry!

rat [ra] *m zo.* rat; F *fig.* miser; **~ d'hôtel** hotel thief.

ratage [ra'ta:ʒ] *m* failure, F flop; messing-up.

ratatiner [ratati'ne] (1a) wreck, smash

up; **se** ~ shrivel (up); get wrinkled; **ra-tatiné** shrivel(l)ed (up); wrinkled.

ratatouille *cuis.* [rata'tu:j] *f* stew.

rate [rat] *f anat.* spleen; F **ne pas se fouler la** ~ take things easy.

raté [ra'te] *su. person:* failure, F wash-out; *su./m mot.* misfire.

râte|au [ra'to] *m* 🖊 rake; F large comb; **~ler** [rat'le] (1c) 🖊 rake; **~lier** [ratə'lje] *m* rack; F (set of) false teeth (*pl.*).

rater [ra'te] (1a) *v/i. mot., gun:* misfire (*a. fig.*); *fig.* fail; *v/t.* miss; mess up, spoil, *fig.* fail in (*an examination etc.*).

ratiboiser *sl.* [ratibwa'ze] (1a) pinch (= *steal*); ruin (*s.o.*).

ratifi|cation [ratifika'sjɔ̃] *f* ratification; **~er** [~'fje] (1o) ratify.

ration [ra'sjɔ̃] *f* ration, allowance.

rationali|ser [rasjonali'ze] (1a) rationalize; **~sme** *phls.* [~'lism] *m* rationalism; **~ste** [~'list] *adj., su.* rationalist; **~té** [~li'te] *f* rationality.

rationnel [rasjo'nɛl] rational.

rationn|ement [rasjɔn'mɑ̃] *m* rationing; **~er** [~sjɔ'ne] (1a) ration.

ratisser [rati'se] (1a) 🖊 rake; *fig.* comb (*police etc.*); F clean (*s.o.*) out, fleece, F rake (it) in.

rattach|ement [rataʃ'mɑ̃] *m* linking up; *pol.* union; **~er** [~ta'ʃe] (1a) fasten or tie up (again); *pol.* incorporate; *fig.* connect, link (with, **à**), tie (to, **à**)

rattraper [ratra'pe] (1a) catch again; recover (*one's health etc.*); make up for (*time, an error etc.*); catch up with; **se** ~ catch o.s.; stop o.s. falling; *fig.* make up for it, make good; catch up; **se** ~ **à** a. catch hold of.

ratur|e [ra'ty:r] deletion, erasure; **~er** [~ty're] (1a) erase, delete.

rauque [ro:k] hoarse, raucous.

ravag|e [ra'va:ʒ] *m* ravages *pl.*; havoc; **~er** [~va'ʒe] (1l) ravage; *fig. a.* harrow.

ravaler [rava'le] (1a) swallow (again or down); *fig.* choke back (*one's tears etc.*); F *fig.* take back (*a statement*); *fig.* reduce (to, **à**); *fig.* lower, 🔺 re-surface, refurbish.

ravauder [ravo'de] (1a) mend, patch (up); darn.

rave 🔩 [ra:v] *f* rape.

ravi [ra'vi] enraptured; delighted (with s.th., **de qch.**; to *inf.*, **de** *inf.*); **être** ~ **de** (*inf.*) *a.* be glad to (*inf.*).

ravigoter F [ravigo'te] (1a) buck up.

ravilir [ravi'li:r] (2a) degrade.

ravin [ra'vɛ̃] *m*, **~e** [~'vin] *f* ravine, gully; **~er** [~] (1a) furrow.

ravir [ra'vi:r] (2a) charm, delight; rob, ravish; **à** ~ marvel(l)ously.

raviser [ravi'ze] (1a): **se** ~ change one's mind; think again.

raviss|ant [ravi'sɑ̃] ravishing; delightful; lovely; **~ement** [~vis'mɑ̃] *m* rapture(s *pl.*); **~eur** [~vi'sœ:r] *m* abductor; kidnapper.

ravitaill|ement [ravitaj'mɑ̃] *m* supplying (with, **en**); ⊙ refuel(l)ing; **~er** [~ta'je] (1a) supply (with, **en**); *mot.* refuel; **se** ~ get fresh supplies.

raviver [ravi've] (1a) revive; brighten up; **se** ~ break out again.

ravoir [ra'vwa:r] *occurs only in inf.* get back again; have again.

ray|é [rɛ'je] striped; ~ (**de**) **rouge** red striped; **~er** [~] (1i) scratch (*a surface*); stripe (*cloth etc.*); groove (*a cylinder*); rule (*paper*); cross out.

rayon¹ [rɛ'jɔ̃] *m bookcase:* shelf; *store:* department; *fig.* speciality, line, field; ~ **de miel** honeycomb.

rayon² [rɛ'jɔ̃] *m* ray (*a. fig.*); *light:* beam; radius; *wheel:* spoke; 🖊 row; 🔩 **~s** *pl.* X X-rays; ~ **d'action** range; **~nage** [rɛjɔ'na:ʒ] *m* set of shelves; **~nant** [~jɔ'nɑ̃] radiant, beaming; *phys.* radio-active.

rayonne *tex.* [rɛ'jɔn] *f* rayon.

rayonn|ement [rɛjɔn'mɑ̃] *m* radiation; radiance; *fig.* influence; **~er** [~jɔ'ne] (1a) shine forth; radiate; *fig.* beam (with, **de**); tour, go touring.

rayure [rɛ'jy:r] *f tex.* stripe; *glass etc.:* scratch; ⊙ groove; *gun:* rifling.

raz [ra] *m* strong current; race; ~ **de marée** tidal wave (*a. fig.*).

razzi|a [ra(d)'zja] *f* raid, foray; F **faire** (**une**) ~ **dans** (*or* **sur**) = **~er** [~'zje] (1a) plunder.

ré 🎵 [re] *m/inv.* re, *note:* D.

réact|eur [reak'tœ:r] *m* 🔩, *phys.* reactor; 🖊 jet engine; **~if** 🧪 [~'tif] *m* reagent; **~ion** [~'sjɔ̃] *f* reaction; *rifle:* kick; 🔩 test; *phys.* ~ **en chaîne** chain reaction; **avion** *m* **à** ~ jet (*plane*); **~ionnaire** *pol.* [~sjɔ'nɛ:r] *adj., su.* reactionary.

réagir [rea'ʒi:r] (2a) react (to, **à**).

réali|sable [reali'zabl] realizable; avail-

able (*assets*); feasible; **~sateur, -trice**
[~za'tœːr, ~'tris] *su.* realizer; *su./m cin.*
director; **~sation** [~za'sjɔ̃] *f* realization;
carrying out; fulfil(l)ment; *cin.* production; **~ser** [~'ze] (1a) realize; achieve;
fulfil(l); *cin.* produce; carry out (*a plan*);
se ~ be realized; be fulfil(l)ed, come true;
fulfil(l) o.s. (*person*); **~sme** [rea'lism] *m*
realism; **~ste** [~'list] **1.** *adj.* realist(ic); **2.**
su. realist; **~té** [~li'te] *f* reality; **~s** *pl.*
facts; **en ~** really; actually.

réanimer [reani'me] (1a) resuscitate, revive.

réapparaître [reapa'rɛːtr] (4k) reappear.

rearm|ement [rearmə'mã] *m* rearma-
ment; **~er** [~'me] (1a) rearm; reload (*a
gun*).

réassortir ✝ [reasɔr'tiːr] (2a) restock;
match up.

réassurer [reasy're] (1a) reinsure.

rébarbatif [rebarba'tif] forbidding.

rebâtir [rəba'tiːr] (2a) rebuild.

rebattre [rə'batr] (4a) beat again; re-
shuffle (*cards*); **~ les oreilles à q. de** (*or
avec*) **qch.** tell s.o. about s.th. over and
over again; *rebattu* hackneyed; trite.

rebell|e [rə'bɛl] **1.** *adj.* rebellious; *fig. a.*
unruly; stubborn; **~ à** unamenable to;
resistant to; unable to understand; **2.**
su. rebel; **~er** [~bɛ'le] (1a): **se ~** rebel;
rébellion [rebɛ'ljɔ̃] *f* rebellion.

rebiffer F [rəbi'fe] (1a): **se ~** rebel, jib.

reboiser [rəbwa'ze] (1a) reafforest.

rebond [rə'bɔ̃] *m* bounce; rebound; **~i**
[rəbɔ̃'di] chubby; plump; **~ir** [~'diːr]
(2a) bounce; rebound; *fig.* get going
again; **faire ~** set *or* get (*s.th.*) going
again; **~issement** [~dis'mã] *m* new development.

rebord [rə'bɔːr] *m* edge, rim, border;
(*window*) sill; *cost.* hem.

rebours [rə'buːr] *m:* **à ~** against the
grain; *fig.* the wrong way.

rebouter ✶ [rəbu'te] (1a) set (*a broken
leg*).

rebrouss|e-poil [rəbrus'pwal] *adv.:* **à ~**
the wrong way; **~er** [~bru'se] (1a) brush
back; **~ chemin** turn back.

rebuffade [rəby'fad] *f* rebuff, snub.

rébus [re'bys] *m* rebus.

rebut [rə'by] *m* rejection; ✝ reject, trash;
⊕ waste; *fig.* scum; dead letter; *mettre
au ~* put on the scrap-heap; throw out;

~ant [rəby'tã] repellent; discouraging;
~er [~'te] (1a) repel; discourage.

récalcitrant [rekalsi'trã] recalcitrant.

recaler [rəka'le] (1a) fail (*s.o.*).

récapituler [rekapity'le] (1a) recapitulate, sum up, summarize.

recel ⚖ [rə'sɛl] *m stolen goods:* receiving; *criminal:* harbo(u)ring; **~er** [rəs'le]
(1d) ⚖ receive (*stolen goods*); har-
bo(u)r (*a criminal*); *fig.* conceal, contain; **receleur** *m*, **-euse** *f* ⚖ [~'lœːr,
~'løːz] receiver (of stolen goods).

récemment [resa'mã] *adv.* recently.

recens|ement [rəsãs'mã] *m admin.*
census; ✝(new) inventory; *fig.* review;
~er [rəsã'se] (1a) *admin.* take a census
of; list; ✝ inventory.

récent [re'sã] recent, fresh, new.

récépissé ✝ [resepi'se] *m* receipt.

récept|acle [resɛp'takl] *m* receptacle (*a.*
♣); **~eur** [~'tœːr] **1.** *adj.* receiving; *appareil m ~* = **2.** *su./m* ⊕, radio, *telev. a.*
teleph. receiver; *telev.* set; **~if** [~'tif] receptive; **~ion** [~'sjɔ̃] *f* reception (*a. telev.,
hotel, etc.*); welcome; *sp.* landing; **~ion-
ner** ✝ [~sjo'ne] (1a) check and sign for;
~ionniste [~sjo'nist] *su.* receptionist;
~ivité [~tivi'te] *f* receptivity.

récession [resɛ'sjɔ̃] *f* recession.

recette [rə'sɛt] *f* ✝ receipts *pl.*, returns
pl.; *thea. etc.* takings *pl.*; ✝ receipt;
admin. collectorship; *cuis., fig.* recipe;
✝ collection; *thea. etc.* **faire ~** be a
(box-office) hit.

recev|able [rəsə'vabl] admissible; **~eur,
-euse** [~'vœːr, ~'vøːz] *su.* receiver;
admin. collector; *tel.* addressee; *su./m
bus, tram:* conductor; (post-)master;
su./f thea. usherette; *bus, tram:* conduc-
tress; **~oir** [~'vwaːr] (3a) *v/t.* receive;
get; see (*a. visitor, client etc.*); admit
(*students, a. fig. customs*); promote (*to
a higher class*); accept (*an excuse*); **être
reçu à un examen** pass an examination; **être reçu avocat** qualify as a barrister; *v/i.* hold a reception; receive visi-
tors *etc.*; **~rai** [~'vre] *1st p. sg. fut. of
recevoir*.

rechange [rə'ʃãːʒ] *m:* **de ~** spare (*part
etc.*); alternative (*plan etc.*).

rechaper *mot.* [rəʃa'pe] (1a) retread (*a
tire*).

réchapper [reʃa'pe] (1a): **~ de** escape
from, come through (*s.th.*).

recharger [rəʃar'ʒe] (1l) reload; ⚡ recharge; refill.

réchaud [re'ʃo] m (portable) stove.

réchauff|é [reʃo'fe] m **1.** *adj.* stale, rehashed; **2.** *su./m* rehash; **~er** [~'fe] (1a) (re)heat; warm up (*Am.* over) (*food*); *fig.* warm (*s.o.'s heart*); **se ~** warm s.o. up; get warmer, warm up (*weather*).

rêche [rɛʃ] rough; difficult (*person*).

recherch|e [rə'ʃɛrʃ] f search (for, *de*); ⚖ enquiry; *fig.* studied elegance; **la ~** research; **~s** *pl.* ⚖ investigations; (scientific) research *sg.*; **à la ~ de** in search of; *fig.* **sans ~** unaffected; **~é** [rəʃɛr'ʃe] sought after; in demand; studied, elaborate (*elegance, style*); *fig.* far-fetched; affected; **~er** [~] (1a) look for; search for; seek; look for again; **aller ~ qch.** (go and get) s.th. again.

rechign|é [rəʃi'ɲe] sour (*look etc.*); surly (*person*); **~er** [~] (1a) balk (at, *devant*; at *ger.*, **à** *inf.*); look sour.

rechut|e 🜨, *eccl.* [rə'ʃyt] f relapse; **avoir** (*or* **faire**) **une ~ — ~er** [rəʃy'te] (1a) have a relapse.

récidiv|e [resi'diːv] f 🜨 recurrence; ⚖ repetition of an offence (*Am.* offense); **~er** [~di've] (1a) 🜨recur; ⚖ relapse into crime; **~iste** [~di'vist] *su.* recidivist.

récif [re'sif] m reef.

récipient [resi'pjɑ̃] m container.

récipro|cité [resiprɔsi'te] f reciprocity; interchange; **~que** [~'prɔk] **1.** *adj.* reciprocal (*a.* ⅄, *phls., gramm*), mutual; **et ~ment** andvice versa; **2.** *su./f:* **la ~** the same; the opposite, the reverse; **rendre la ~ à q.** pay s.o. back.

récit [re'si] m account; narrative; ♪ recitative; **~al,** *pl* **-als** ♪ [resi'tal] m recital; **~ant** m, **~ante** f [~tɑ̃, ~'tɑ̃t] *radio, telev. etc.*: narrator; host; **~ateur** m, **-trice** f [~ta'tœːr, ~'tris] reciter; **~ation** [~ta'sjɔ̃] f recitation; **~er** [~'te] (1a) recite.

réclam|ant(e) f) m [rekla'mɑ̃, ~'mɑ̃t] ⚖ claimant; **~ation** [~ma'sjɔ̃] f complaint; objection; ⚖ claim; **~e** [re'klaːm] f advertising; advertisement; ♥ **en ~** on offer; **~er** [~kla'me] (1a) *v/t.* ask for; require, call for, demand; ⚖ claim; **se ~ de** use s.o.'s name (as a reference); give s.th. as one's authority; *v/i.* complain.

reclass|ement [rəklas'mɑ̃] m reclas-

sification; *person*: rehabilitation; *civil servant*: regrading; **~er** [~kla'se] (1a) reclassify; rehabilitate (*s.o.*); find a new place for (*s.o.*); regrade *a* (*civil servant*).

reclus m, **e** f [rə'kly, ~'klyːz] recluse.

réclusion [rekly'zjɔ̃] f (*a.* **~ criminelle**) imprisonment.

récognition *phls.* [rekɔgni'sjɔ̃] f recognition.

recoiffer [rəkwa'fe] (1a) do (*s.o.'s*) hair (again).

recoin [rə'kwɛ̃] m nook, cranny.

reçois [rə'swa] *1st p. sg. pres. of* **recevoir**; **reçoivent** [~'swaːv] *3rd p. pl. pres. of* **recevoir**.

recoller [rəkɔ'le] (1a) stick together *or* on *or* down (again); *a. fig.* patch up.

récolt|e [re'kɔlt] f harvest(ing); crop; *fig.* profits *pl.*; **~er** [~kɔl'te] (1a) harvest; gather in; *fig.* collect; *fig.* get.

recommand|able [rəkɔmɑ̃'dabl] commendable; estimable; *fig.* advisable; **~ation** [~dɑ'sjɔ̃] f recommendation; *fig.* advice; *post:* registration; **~er** [~'de] (1a) recommend; *fig.* advise; *post:* register; **se ~ à** commend o.s. to; **se ~ de** give (*s.o.*) as a reference; *post:* **en recommandé** by registered post (*Am.* mail).

recommenc|er [rəkɔmɑ̃'se] (1k) *vt/i* start *or* begin (over) again; *v/t. a.* do *or* make (*s.th.*) again; *v/i. a.* do it again.

récompens|e [rekɔ̃'pɑ̃ːs] f reward (for, *de*); **en ~** as a reward, in return (for, *de*); **~er** [~pɑ̃'se] (1a) reward (for, *de*).

recompter [rəkɔ̃'te] (1a) recount.

réconcili|able [rekɔ̃si'ljabl] reconcilable; **~ateur** m, **-trice** f [~lja'tœːr, ~'tris] reconciler; **~ation** [~lja'sjɔ̃] f reconciliation; **~er** [~'lje] (1o) reconcile; **se ~** be(come) reconciled (with, *avec*).

recon|duction [rəkɔ̃dyk'sjɔ̃] f renewal; continuation; **~duire** [~'dɥiːr] (4h) lead back; see (*s.o.*) home; show (*s.o.*) to the door; ⚖ renew; extend, continue.

réconfort [rekɔ̃'fɔːr] m comfort; **~er** [~fɔr'te] (1a) comfort; fortify (*s.o.*).

reconnaissa|ble [rəkɔnɛ'sabl] recognizable (by, from **à**); **~nce** [~'sɑ̃ːs] f recognition; ⚔ reconnaissance; ♥ I.O.U.; acknowledgment; gratefulness, gratitude; **~nt** [~'sɑ̃] grateful (for, *de*; to, *envers*).

reconnaître [rəkɔ'nɛːtr] (4k) recognize

(by, **à**) (*a.* ⚖️, *a. a government*); know again; *fig.* acknowledge; ✗ reconnoitre; identify (*s.th.*); *fig.* be grateful for; **se ~** find one's way around; find one's bearings; **ne plus s'y ~** be (completely) lost; **se ~ à** be recognizable by.

reconquérir [rəkõke'ri:r] (2l) reconquer; win back (*a. fig.*); **reconquête** [~'kɛ:t] *f* reconquest.

reconstitu|ant 💊 [rəkõsti'tɥã] *adj., su./m* tonic, restorative; **~er** [~'tɥe] (1n) reconstitute; reconstruct (*a. an accident, a crime etc.*); rebuild, re-form, build up again; restore.

reconstru|ction [rəkõstryk'sjõ] *f* reconstruction, rebuilding; **~ire** [~'trɥi:r] (4h) rebuild.

recoquiller [rəkɔki'je] (1a) curl.

record [rə'kɔ:r] *su./m, adj./inv.* record.

recoudre [rə'kudr] (4l) sew up *or* on again; *fig.* link up.

recoup|e [rə'kup] *f* chips *pl.*, scraps *pl.*; **~ement** [~kup'mã] *m* crosscheck(ing); **~er** [~ku'pe] (1a) cut (again); *fig.* confirm, support; **se ~** match up, tally; intersect, overlap.

recourb|é [rəkur'be] hooked; curved; bent; **nez ~** hooknose; **~er** [~] bend (up *or* over).

recour|ir [rəku'ri:r] (2i) run back; **~ à** turn to (*s.o.*); resort to; **~s** [~'ku:r] *m* recourse; resort.

recouvrement¹ [rəkuvrə'mã] *m* covering; coating.

recouvr|ement² [rəkuvrə'mã] *m debt, health, etc.*: recovery; **~s** *pl.* outstanding debts; **~er** [~'vre] (1a) recover, regain; ✝ collect.

recouvrir [rəku'vri:r] (2f) cover (with, **de**); cover again, re-cover, put a new cover on; *fig.* cover up, hide, conceal; **se ~** become covered (with, **de**); overlap.

récréati|f [rekrea'tif] recreational; entertaining; **~on** [~'sjõ] *f* recreation; *school*: break.

recréer [rəkre'e] (1a) re-create.

récréer [rekre'e] (1a) amuse; refresh; **se ~** take some recreation.

récrier [rekri'e] (1a): **se ~** cry out, exclaim; *fig.* protest.

récrimin|ation [rekrimina'sjõ] *f* remonstration; **~er** [~'ne] (1a) remonstrate (against, **contre**).

récrire [re'kri:r] (4q) *v/t.* rewrite; *v/i.* reply by letter.

recroître 💠 [rə'krwa:tr] (4o) grow again.

recroqueviller [rəkrɔkvi'je] (1a): **se ~** curl *or* shrivel up (*leaf etc.*); curl *or* huddle o.s. up (*person*).

recru [rə'kry]: (*usu. ~ de fatigue*) tired out.

recrudescence [rəkrydɛ'sã:s] *f* recrudescence; fresh outbreak.

recru|e [rə'kry] *f* recruit; **~ter** [rəkry'te] (1a) recruit.

rectang|le [rɛk'tãgl] 1. *adj.* right-angled; 2. *su./m* rectangle; **~ulaire** [~tãgy'lɛ:r] rectangular.

recteur [rɛk'tœ:r] 1. *adj.* guiding; 2. *su./m univ.* rector.

rectifi|catif [rɛktifika'tif] 1. *adj.* rectifying; 2. *su./m* corrigendum; **~cation** [~'sjõ] *f* rectification; *fig.* correction; **~er** [rɛkti'fje] (1o) straighten, put right; correct; rectify.

rectiligne [rɛkti'liɲ] rectilinear; straight.

rectitude [rɛkti'tyd] *f* straightness; *fig.* rectitude; *fig.* correctness.

recto [rɛk'to] *m page*: recto.

reçu [rə'sy] 1. *su./m* receipt; 2. *adj.* accepted, recognized; 3. *p.p. of* **recevoir**.

recueil [rə'kœj] *m* collection; compendium; **~lement** [~kœj'mã] *m* meditation, contemplation; **~lir** [~kœ'ji:r] (2c) gather; collect; 🖋, *a. fig.* reap; *fig.* give shelter to, take in (*refugees etc.*); get, obtain (*information*); **se ~** gather one's thoughts; meditate.

recul [rə'kyl] *m* backward movement; recession, decline; retreat; ✗ kick, recoil; *fig.* distance; *fig.* setback; **avoir un mouvement de ~** start back; **avec le ~** from a distance, *fig.* with the passing of time; **prendre du ~** stand back (*a. fig.*); **~ade** [rəky'lad] *f* withdrawal; climb-down; **~é** [~'le] remote, distant; **~er** [~'le] (1a) *v/i.* move *or* draw *or* step back; back (up *or* away); *a. fig.* shrink back, recoil (from, **devant**); *fig.* decline, subside, go back, lose ground; *v/t.* move *or* push back; back (up); *fig.* extend; *fig.* postpone, put off; *fig.* start *or* shrink back; **~ons** [~'lõ] *adv.*: **à ~** backwards.

récupér|ation [rekypera'sjõ] *f loss*: recoupment; ⚙, 🔧 recovery; ⚙ reprocessing; rehabilitation; **~er** [~'re] (1f) get back; recover; recoup (*a loss*); ⊕ reprocess, salvage; rehabilitate (*persons*).

récurer [reky're] (1a) scour; clean.

reçus [rə'sy] *1st p. sg. p.s. of* **recevoir**.

récuser [reky'ze] (1a) challenge (*a witness, s.o.'s evidence*); **se ~** declare o.s. incompetent.

recycl|age [rəsi'kla:ʒ] *m* retraining; ⊕ recycling, reprocessing; **~er** [~'kle] (1a) retrain; ⊕ recycle, reprocess.

rédact|eur, -trice [redak'tœ:r, ~'tris] *su.* writer; drafter; *journ.* sub-editor; *su./m:* **~ en chef** editor; **~ion** [~'sjɔ̃] *f* drafting; *journ.* editorial staff; *journ.* editing; *journ.* (newspaper) office, *school:* essay, composition.

reddition [redi'sjɔ̃] *f* surrender.

redécouvrir [rədeku'vri:r] (2f) rediscover.

redemander [rədmã'de] (1a) ask for (*s.th.*) again *or* back; ask for more (*of s.th.*).

rédempt|eur [redãp'tœ:r] **1.** *adj.* redeeming; **2.** *su.* redeemer; **~ion** [~'sjɔ̃] *f* redemption (*a. eccl.*).

redescendre [rədɛ'sã:dr] (4a) *v/i.* go *or* come down again; *v/t.* bring *or* take down again; **~ l'escalier** go downstairs again.

redev|able [rəd'vabl] indebted (for, *de*), **être ~ de qch. à q.** owe s.o. s.th.; **~ance** [~'vã:s] *f* charge, fee; tax; **~oir** [~'vwa:r] (3a) owe still.

rédiger [redi'ʒe] (1l) write; draw up; *journ.* edit.

redingote [redɛ̃'gɔt] *f* frock coat.

redi|re [rə'di:r] (4p) *v/t.* repeat; say *or* tell again; *v/i.:* **avoir** (*or* **trouver** *or* **voir**) **à ~** (à) find fault (with); **~te** [~'dit] *f* repetition; **~tes** [~'dit] *2nd p. pl. pres. of* **redire**.

redondan|ce [rədɔ̃'dã:s] *f* redundancy; **~t** [~'dã] redundant.

redonner [rədɔ'ne] (1a) *v/t.* give back; give again; give more (*of s.th.*); *v/i.:* **~ dans** fall back into.

redoubler [rədu'ble] (1a) *vt/i.* redouble, intensify, increase; *v/t. school:* repeat a year; **~ de** redouble; **~ d'efforts** strive harder than ever.

redout|able [rədu'tabl] formidable; **~er** [~'te] (1a) fear, dread.

redress|ement [rədrɛs'mã] *m fig.* rectification; straightening; correction; *fig.*

recovery; **~er** [rədrɛ'se] (1a) set up again; raise; set right (*a wrong etc.*); ⚡, *a. fig.* rectify; ⊕ true; **se ~** stand up again; draw o.s. up; *fig.* recover; **~eur** [~'sœ:r] *m* righter (*of wrongs*).

redû, -due [rə'dy] **1.** *p.p. of* **redevoir**; **2.** *su./m* ✝ balance due.

réduction [redyk'sjɔ̃] *f* reduction; cut.

rédui|re [re'dɥi:r] (4h) reduce; lessen; cut down (*expenses*); put down (*a rebellion, resistance, etc.*); 🦴 set (*a fracture*); **~ en** (*qch.*) reduce to, change (in)to; **se ~ à** boil down to, come (down) to; **se ~ en** be reduced to; **~t** [~'dɥi] **1.** *su./m* retreat, nook, *pej.* hovel; **2.** *adj./m:* **à prix ~** at a reduced price.

réédifier [reedi'fje] (1o) rebuild.

rééduca|tion [reedyka'sjɔ̃] *f* rehabilitation; re-education; **~quer** 🦴 [~'ke] (1m) rehabilitate; re-educate.

réel, -elle [re'ɛl] **1.** *adj.* real; actual; **2.** *su./m* reality.

réélection [reelɛk'sjɔ̃] *f* re-election.

réélire [~'li:r] (4t) re-elect.

réévalua|tion [reevalɥa'ʒjɔ̃] *f* revaluation; **~er** [~'lɥe] (1n) revalue.

réexpédier [reɛkspe'dje] (1o) send back; send on, forward.

refaire [rə'fɛ:r] (4r) do *or* make (*s.th.*) again; redo; do up; make (some) more (*of s.th.*); ⊦ take in, have; **si c'était à ~!** if I had to do it again!; **se ~** (*sa santé*) recover (one's health); **se ~** ✝ make one's losses; *fig.* change (one's ways).

réfect|ion [refɛk'sjɔ̃] *f* remaking; rebuilding; repair; **~oire** [~'twa:r] *m* dining hall.

refend [rə'fã] *m* splitting; △ **mur m de ~** partition-wall; **~re** [~'fã:dr] (4a) split; rip (*timber*); slit.

référ|ence [refe'rã:s] *f* reference; **ouvrage m de ~** reference book; **~endum** [~rɛ̃'dɔm] *m* referendum; strike ballot; **~er** [~'re] (1f) *v/t.:* **se ~ à** refer to (*s.th.*); ask (*s.o.'s*) opinion; consult; **en ~ à q.** submit the matter to s.o.

refermer [rəfɛr'me] (1a) shut *or* close (again) (*a. se ~*); **se ~** *a.* heal up (*wound*).

refiler F [rəfi'le] (1a) pass on; give; palm off (on, *à*).

réfléchi [refle'ʃi] thoughtful; considered; *gramm.* reflexive; **~ir** [~'ʃiːr] (2a) *v/t.* reflect; reverberate; *v/i.* consider; ponder (on **à**, **sur**).

réflecteur [reflɛk'tœːr] *m* reflector; **reflet** [rə'flɛ] *m* reflection; glint; **refléter** [~fle'te] (1f) reflect (*light etc.*); **se ~** be reflected.

réflex|e [re'flɛks] *adj.*, *su./m* reflex; **~ion** [~flɛk'sjɔ̃] *f phys.*, *fig.* reflection; *fig.* thought; **~ faite** everything considered; **à la ~** on reflection.

reflu|er [rəfly'e] (1a) flow *or* surge *or* move back; **~x** [~'fly] *m* ebb(tide); flowing back.

refon|dre [rə'fɔ̃ːdr] (4a) remelt; *metall.*, *a. fig.* recast; **~te** [~'fɔ̃ːt] *f* remelting; recasting (*a. fig.*).

réform|able [refɔr'mabl] reformable; ⚖ reversible; *a. fig.* reforming; **2.** *su.* reformer; **~ation** [~ma'sjɔ̃] *f* reformation (*a. eccl.*); **~e** [re'fɔrm] *f* reform(ation); ✗ discharge; **~é** [refɔr'me] **1.** *su. eccl.* protestant; **2.** *adj. eccl.* reformed; ✗ discharged.

reformer [rəfɔr'me] (1a) (*a.* **se ~**) re-form, form (up) again.

réformer [refɔr'me] (1a) reform; ✗ discharge; reverse (*a judgment*).

refoul|ement [reful'mɑ̃] *m* driving back; *fig.*, *psych.* repression; **~er** [rəfu'le] (1a) drive back, repel; force back; *fig.*, *psych.* repress.

réfract|aire [refrak'tɛːr] **1.** *adj.* refractory; resistant, *a. fig.* impervious (to, **à**); 🐟 stubborn (*illness*); ⚙ proof (against, **à**); **2.** *su.* refractory person; **~er** [~'te] (1a) refract; **~ion** [~'sjɔ̃] *f* refraction.

refrain [rə'frɛ̃] *m* refrain; F *fig.* **le même ~** the same old story.

refréner [rəfre'ne] (1f) curb, restrain, check.

réfrigér|ant [refriʒe'rɑ̃] refrigerating; freezing; **~ateur** [~ra'tœːr] *m* refrigerator; *fig.* **mettre qch. au ~** put s.th. on ice; **~er** [~'re] (1f) refrigerate; cool; chill.

refroid|ir [rəfrwa'diːr] (2a) *v/t.* cool, chill (*a. fig.* one's enthusiasm *etc.*); *sl.* kill; **se ~** 🐟 catch a chill; get colder (*weather*); *v/i.* grow cold; cool (off *or* down); **~issement** [~dis'mɑ̃] *m* cooling (down); 🐟 chill; *temperature*: drop.

refuge [rə'fyːʒ] *m* refuge; traffic island;

réfugié *m*, **e** *f* [refy'ʒje] refugee; **réfugier** [~] (1o): **se ~** take refuge.

refus [rə'fy] *m* refusal; F *ce n'est pas de ~* I won't say no (to that); **~er** [~fy'ze] (1a) *vt/i.* refuse; decline; *v/t.* reject, turn down; turn away (customers, *du monde*); fail (*a candidate*); **~ de** (*inf.*); **se ~ à** (*inf.*) refuse to (*inf.*); **se ~ à qch.** object to s.th.

réfut|ation [refyta'sjɔ̃] *f* refutation; **~er** [~'te] (1a) refute; disprove.

regagner [rəga'ɲe] (1a) regain; win back; recover; make up for (*s.th. lost*); return to (*a place*).

regain [rə'ɡɛ̃] *m* 🌾 second growth; *fig.* renewal, revival.

régal, *pl.* **-als** [re'gal] *m* treat; **~ade** [~ga'lad] *f*: *boire à la ~* drink from the bottle held away from the lips; **~er** [~ga'le] (1a) treat (*s.o.*) to a (fine) meal; **~ q. de qch.** treat s.o. to s.th.; **se ~** have a fine meal *etc.*; *fig.* enjoy o.s.; **se ~ de** *a.* feast on.

regard [rə'ɡaːr] *m* look, glance; sewer *etc.*: manhole; ⚙ peephole; **au ~ de** from the point of view of; **en ~** opposite; **en ~ de** compared to, in comparison with; **lancer** (*or* **jeter**) **un ~ sur** cast an eye over, have a look at; **~ant** [rəɡar'dɑ̃] close-fisted; *peu ~* quite free with one's money; **~er** [~'de] (1a) *v/t.* look at; watch; face; look for; look up; *fig.* view; *fig.* consider (as, **comme**); *fig.* concern; **~ fixement** stare at; *cela me regarde* that is my business; *cela ne le regarde pas* that's none of his business; *v/i.* (have a) look; *fig.* **~ à** pay attention to (*s.th.*); think about *or* of; mind; **~ par** (**à**) **la fenêtre** look through (in at) the window; **~ voir** (*si*) have a look (and see if); *fig.* **y ~ de** (*plus*) *près* have a close(r) look (at it); *fig.* **y ~ à deux fois** think twice.

régate [re'gat] *f* regatta.

régence [re'ʒɑ̃ːs] *f* regency.

régénér|ation [reʒenera'sjɔ̃] *f* regeneration; **~er** [~'re] (1f) regenerate; *fig.* restore, fortify.

régent *m*, **e** *f* [re'ʒɑ̃, ~'ʒɑ̃ːt] regent; **~er** [~ʒɑ̃'te] (1a) lord it over.

régicide [reʒi'sid] *su.*, *su./m* regicide.

régie [re'ʒi] *f* administration; state control; state-controlled company.

regimber [rəʒɛ̃'be] (1a) balk.

régime [re'ʒim] *m pol.* régime; system, regulations *pl.*; ⚙ normal running; *mot., fig.* speed; 🍴 diet; *gramm.* object; 🍇 bunch; 🍴 **mettre au ~** put on a diet; **suivre un ~** (be on a) diet.

régiment ✗ [reʒi'mã] *m* regiment.

région [re'ʒjõ] *f* region; area; **~al** [~ʒjo'nal] regional; local.

régir [re'ʒiːr] (2a) govern; **~sseur** [~ʒi-'sœːr] *m* manager; *thea.* stage manager.

registre [rə'ʒistr] *m* register (*a.* ♪); 🍴 ledger; **~ de l'état civil** register of births, deaths and marriages.

réglable [re'glabl] adjustable; **réglage** [~'glaːʒ] *m* ⚙ regulating, adjustment; *speed:* control; *paper:* ruling; *radio:* tuning; **règle** [regl] *f* rule; ⚙ ruler, rule; 🍴 **~s** *pl.* menses; **à calcul** slide rule; **de ~** usual, customary; **en ~** in order; straight; **réglé** [re'gle] regular; steady (*pace, person*); ruled (*paper*); fixed (*hour etc.*); **règlement** [reglə'mã] *m* regulation(s *pl.*); rule; 🍴 settlement; *a. fig.* **~ de comptes** settling of scores; **réglementaire** [regləmã'tɛːr] that conforms to the regulations; regulation-...; **réglementation** [~ta'sjõ] *f* regulation; control; **~ de la circulation** traffic regulations *pl.*; **réglementer** [~'te] (1a) regulate, control; make rules for; **régler** [re'gle] (1f) ⚙, *fig.* regulate; ⚙, 🍴, *fig.* adjust; *fig.* settle (*a quarrel, a question,* 🍴 *an account*); 🍴 settle (up), pay (up); rule (*paper*); *mot.* tune (*an engine*); **~ sur** model on; adjust to.

réglisse ♣ [re'glis] *f* liquorice.

réglure [re'glyːr] *f paper:* ruling.

règne [rɛɲ] *m* 🍇, *zo.* kingdom; *pol., a. fig.* reign; **régner** [re'ɲe] (1f) reign (*a. fig.*), rule; *fig.* prevail.

regorger [rəgɔr'ʒe] (1l) overflow (with, **de**), abound (in, **de**).

régress|er [regrɛ'se] (1a) decline, decrease, fall off; **~if** [regre'sif] regressive; **~ion** [~'sjõ] *f* regression; *biol.* retrogression; *sales etc.*: drop.

regret [rə'grɛ] *m* regret (for, of **de**); **à ~** reluctantly; **~table** [rəgrɛ'tabl] regrettable; **~ter** [~'te] (1a) regret; be sorry (that *ind., que sbj.*; for *ger., de inf.*); miss; mourn (for).

regroup|ement [rəgrup'mã] *m* (regrouping; **~er** [~gru'pe] (1a) regroup; group (together); **se ~** gather (together).

régul|ariser [regylari'ze] (1a) regularize; put in order; ⚙ *etc.* regulate; **~arité** [~'te] *f* regularity; *temper:* evenness; **~ateur** [regyla'tœːr] **1.** *adj.* regulating; **2.** *su./m* regulator; **~ier** [~'lje] regular; even; steady; *fig.* in order, lawful; F *fig.* straight; on the level.

régurgiter [regyrʒi'te] (1a) regurgitate.

réhabilit|ation [reabilita'sjõ] *f* rehabilitation; **~er** [~'te] (1a) rehabilitate; bring back into favo(u)r.

réhabituer [reabi'tɥe] (1n) reaccustom (to, **à**).

rehauss|ement [rəos'mã] *m* heightening, raising; *fig.* enhancing; **~er** [~o'se] (1a) heighten, raise; increase; *fig.* enhance, bring out.

réimpr|ession [reɛ̃prɛ'sjõ] *f* reprint; **~imer** [~pri'me] (1a) reprint.

rein [rɛ̃] *m anat.* kidney; 🍴 **~ artificiel** kidney machine; **avoir mal aux ~s** have backache; **casser les ~s à q.** ruin s.o.

reine [rɛn] *f* queen; **~-claude**, *pl.* **~s-claudes** 🍇 [~'kloːd] *f* greengage.

réinsérer [reɛ̃se'rɛ] (1f) reinsert; *fig.* reintegrate (*s.o.*).

réintégrer [reɛ̃te'gre] (1f) reinstate; return to (*one's domicile*).

réitérer [reite'rɛ] (1f) reiterate.

rejaillir [rəʒa'jiːr] (2a) splash (back or up); *fig.* **~ sur** be reflected on, fall upon.

rejet [rə'ʒɛ] *m* throwing out; *food:* throwing up; ✗ dismissal, *fig. parl.,* 🍴 *etc.* rejection; 🍇 shoot; **~able** [rəʒ'tabl] rejectable; **~er** [~'te] (1c) throw back or again; fling back; throw up (*a. food*); reject (*a. parl. a bill, a* 🍴 *etc.*); 🍇 throw out (*shoots*); **~ la responsabilité sur** cast the responsibility on; **~on** [~'tõ] *m* 🍇 shoot, *fig.* offspring.

rejoindre [rə'ʒwɛ̃ːdr] (4m) rejoin; return to; get or go (back) to; meet; join; catch up (with); *fig.* touch; **se ~** meet (again).

réjou|ir [reʒwi'iːr] (2a) cheer, delight, amuse; **se ~ (de)** be delighted (at); be glad (about); **~issance** [~ʒwi'sãːs] *f* rejoicing.

relâche[1] [rə'laːʃ] *m* rest, respite, 🍴 closed; **faire ~** be closed.

relâche[2] ⚓ [~] *f:* **faire ~** put into port.

relâch|é [rəlɑ'ʃe] lax, loose; **~ement** [~lɑʃ'mã] *m* relaxing, slackening; *fig.* relaxation; *conduct:* looseness; **~er**

[~lɑ'ʃe] (1a) v/t. loosen, slacken; fig. relax; release (a prisoner etc.); se ~ loosen, slacken; fig. a. slack off or up; v/i. ♪ put into port.

relais [rə'lɛ] m ⚡ radio: relay; ~ des routiers truck stop; sp. course f de (or par) ~ relay race; prendre le ~ (de) take over (from).

relancer [rəlɑ̃'se] (1k) throw back or again; return (a ball); fig. pester (s.o.); mot. restart (the engine); fig. revive, relaunch; fig. boost, stimulate.

relater [rəla'te] (1a) relate; report.

relatif [rəla'tif] relative (to, à); ~on [~'sjɔ̃] f relation, relationshiph, connection; account; report; person: acquaintance; fig. contact, touch; obtenir un poste par ~ get a job through one's connections; ~vement relatively, comparatively; ~ à (as) compared to; concerning, about; ~vité [~tivi'te] f relativity; phys. théorie f de la ~ relativity theory.

relaxer [rəlak'se] (1a) relax; ⚖ release; se ~ relax.

relayer [rəlɛ'je] (1i) relieve, take over from; ⚡, tel., radio: relay; se ~ take turns; work in shifts.

relégation ⚖ [rəlega'sjɔ̃] f relegation; ~uer [~'ge] (1s) relegate.

relent [rə'lɑ̃] m musty smell.

relève [rə'lɛːv] f relief; relieve team; prendre la ~ take over; relevé [rəl've] **1.** adj. raised; turned up (sleeve etc.); fig. high; lofty; noble; cuis. highly seasoned; **2.** su./m summary; list; ✝ statement; admin. return; ~ du gaz gas-meter reading; relèvement [rəlɛv'mɑ̃] m raising again; picking up; bank-rate, temperature, wages: rise; raising; ♫, surv. bearing; ✝, fig. recovery; ✝ account: making out; ✗ sentry: relieving; wounded: collecting; relever [rəl've] (1d) raise (a. ✝ prices, wages, etc.); lift; stand up (again), set upright; pick up (from the ground); △ rebuild; ♪ take the bearings of; surv. survey; fig. set off, enhance; ✝ make out (an account); read (the meter); fig. call attention to, point out; notice, react to; fig. accept, take up (a challenge); relieve, take over from (s.o.); collect, take in; cuis. season; ~ q. de release s.o. from; se ~ get up; rise (a. fig.); ✝, a. fig. recover; take

turns; v/i.: ~ de be dependent on; be a matter for, pertain to; arise from; ⚖ be recovering from; have just recovered from.

relief [rə'ljɛf] m relief; ~s pl. remains; en ~ (in) relief; threedimensional; mettre en ~ bring out, set off.

relier [rə'lje] (1o) bind (a. books); link (up), connect (with, to à); ~eur [rə'ljœːr] m (book)binder.

religi|eux, -euse [rəli'ʒjø, ~'ʒjøːz] **1.** adj. religious; sacred (music), church...; **2.** su./m monk; su./f nun; ~on [~'ʒjɔ̃] f religion; (religious) faith; entrer en ~ take the vows; ~osité [~ʒjozi'te] f religiosity.

reliquaire [rəli'kɛːr] m shrine.

reliquat [rəli'ka] m remainder.

relique [rə'lik] f relic.

relire [rə'liːr] (4t) read again; read over.

reliure [rə'ljyːr] f (book)binding.

relui|re [rə'lɥiːr] (4u) gleam; shine; faire ~ polish (s.th.); ~sant [~lɥi'zɑ̃] bright, shining; fig. pas ~, peu ~ not exactly brilliant.

reluquer [rəly'ke] (1m) eye; ogle.

remâcher [rəmɑ'ʃe] (1a) chew again; F fig. ruminate or brood over.

remani|ement [rəmani'mɑ̃] m recast(ing); pol. reshuffle; ~er [~'nje] (1o) reast, reshape; pol. reshuffle.

remarier [rəma'rje] (1o) remarry; se ~ get married again.

remarqu|able [rəmar'kabl] remarkable (for, par); outstanding (for, par); ~e [~'mark] f remark; note; ~er [~mar'ke] (1m) notice; remark; faire ~ qch. à q. point s.th. out to s.o.; se faire ~ attract attention.

remballer [rɑ̃ba'le] (1a) pack up (again); F ~ ses remarques keep one's remarks to o.s.

rembarrer [rɑ̃ba're] (1a) rebuff.

rembl|ai [rɑ̃'blɛ] m embankment; ~ayer [~blɛ'je] (1i) fill (up) (a ditch etc.); bank (up).

remboîter ⚙ [rɑ̃bwa'te] (1a) set.

rembourr|age [rɑ̃bu'raːʒ] m stuffing, padding; upholstering; ~er [~'re] (1a) stuff, pad, upholster.

rembours|able [rɑ̃bur'sabl] repayable; ~ement [~sə'mɑ̃] m repayment; livraison f contre ~ cash on delivery; ~er [~'se] (1a) repay, refund.

rembrunir [rãbry'niːr] (2a): **se ~** darken; become gloomy.

rem|ède [rə'mɛd] *m* remedy, cure (for, **à**); medicine, medicament; **porter ~ à** remedy; **sans ~** beyond remedy; **~édiable** [rəme'djabl] remediable; **~édier** [~'dje] (1o): **~ à** remedy, cure.

remembrement *admin.* [rəmãbrə'mã] *m* regrouping of lands.

remémorer [rəmemɔ're] (1a): **se ~** call (*s.th.*) to mind.

remerci|ements [rəmɛrsi'mã] *m/pl.* thanks; **~er** [~'sje] (1o) thank (for, **de**); dismiss (*an employee*).

remettre [rə'mɛtr] (4v) put (*s.th.*) back (again); replace; *cost.* put (*s.th.*) on again; return; restore; put; add, put in (some) more; *&* set (*a bone*); deliver; hand over (*a. a command, an office*); remit (*a penalty, a. sins*); *fig.* postpone, put off; **~ au hasard** leave to chance; **~ en état** overhaul; F **~ ça** start all over again, do it again; F **en ~** overdo it; **se ~** recover (from, **de**); **se ~ à** (**faire**) **qch.** take up *or* start (doing) *s.th.* again; **s'en ~ à q.** rely on s.o. (for, **de**).

réminiscence [remini'sãːs] *f* reminiscence.

remis|e [rə'miːz] *su./f* putting back; postponement; *✝* discount (of, **de**; on, **sur**); restoration; *post.* delivery; *debt, penalty:* remission; *office, ticket:* handing over; coach-house; *& shed*; **~ à neuf** renovation; **~ de bagages** luggage (*Am.* baggage) reclaim; **~er** [~mi'ze] (1a) put (*a vehicle*) away; lay aside; F *fig.* snub (*s.o.*).

rémissi|ble [remi'sibl] remissible; **~on** [~'sjõ] *f *, *debt, sin:* remission; **sans ~** unremitting(ly *adv.*); without fail.

rémitten|ce *&* [remi'tãːs] *f* remission; **~t** [~'tã] remittent.

remont|age [rəmõ'taːʒ] *m ☼* (re)assembling; *clock:* winding up; **à ~ automatique** self-winding (*watch*); **~ant** [~'tã] *adj., su./m ☼* tonic; **~ée** [~mõ'te] *f* climb(ing); **~er** [rəmõ'te] (1a) *v/i.* go up (again); *v/i.* get (*into a car, on a horse, etc.*) again; rise, get higher; *fig.* date *or* go back (*to a time*); *v/t.* climb up (again); raise (up); take (*s.th.*) up; pull up (*socks, trousers*); wind up (*a watch*); *☼* reassemble; refit, reset; *✝* restock; *thea.* put (*a play*) on again; F *fig.* cheer

up; **se ~** recover one's strength *or* spirits; get in a new supply (of, **en**); **~oir** *☼* [~'twaːr] *m* watch: winder.

remontrance [rəmõ'trãːs] *f* reprimand, reproof.

remontrer [rəmõ'tre] (1a) *v/t.* show (again); point out; *v/i.:* **en ~ à q.** show one knows better than s.o.

remordre [rə'mɔrdr] (4a): **~ à** take up *or* tackle again; **remords** [~'mɔːr] *m* remorse.

remorqu|e [rə'mɔrk] *f* vessel in tow; *mot.* trailer; **prendre** (**être**) **en ~** (be on) tow; **~er** [rəmɔr'ke] (1m) tow; pull; **~eur** [~'kœːr] *m* tug(boat).

rémoulade *cuis.* [remu'lad] *f* remoulade-sauce.

rémouleur [remu'lœːr] *m* knife (and scissor) grinder

remous [rə'mu] *m* eddy; swirl; *crowd:* bustle, *ship:* wash; *fig.* stir.

rempart [rã'paːr] *m* rampart.

rempla|çant *m, e f* [rãpla'sã, ~'sãːt] substitute, deputy; **~cement** [~plas-'mã] *m* replacement; substitution; **~cer** [~pla'se] (1k) replace (by, **par**); substitute *or* deputize *or* stand in for; take the place of.

rempli [rã'pli] full (of, **de**); filled (with, **de**); *fig.* busy (*day etc.*); **~ir** [rã'piːr] (2a) fill (up) (with, **de**); *admin.* fill in *or* out *or* up (*a form*); *fig.* fulfil (*a hope, a promise*), perform (*a duty*), meet, satisfy (*conditions*), comply with (*formalities*); **se ~** fill (up); **~ssage** [~pli'saːʒ] *m* filling (up); F *fig.* padding.

rempl|oi [rã'plwa] *m* re-use; **~oyer** [~plwa'je] (1h) use again; employ again, reinvest (*money*).

remplumer F *fig.* [rãply'me] (1a): **se ~** get back on one's feet.

rempocher [rãpɔ'ʃe] (1a) put (*s.th.*) back in one's pocket.

remporter [rãpɔr'te] (1a) carry back *or* away; *fig.* win, achieve.

remu|ant [rə'mɥã] restless; bustling; **~e-ménage** [~myme'naːʒ] *m/inv.* bustle, stir, commotion; **~ement** [~my'mã] *m* movement; **~er** [~'mɥe] (1n) *v/t.* move (*a. fig. s.o.'s heart, etc.*); stir (*coffee, tea*); turn over (*the ground*); *fig.* stir up; *dog:* wag (*its tail*); **se ~** move, stir (o.s.); F bustle about; F get a move on; *v/i.* move; budge; fidget; be loose (*tooth*).

remugle [rə'my:gl] *m* stale smell.

rémunér|ateur [remynera'tœːr] remunerative, profitable; **~ation** [~ra'sjɔ̃] *f* remuneration, payment (for, **de**); **~er** [~re] (1f) remunerate, pay.

renâcler [rəna'kle] (1a) snort; *fig.* balk, jib (at, **à**).

renaissance [rənɛ'sɑ̃ːs] *f* rebirth; revival; *art etc.*: ♀ Renaissance; **renaître** [~'nɛːtr] (4x) be born again; *fig.* reappear; *fig.* revive.

rénal [re'nal] renal, kidney...; **calcul** *m* ~ renal calculus.

renard [rə'naːr] *m* fox.

renchér|i [rɑ̃ʃe'ri] fastidious (person); **~ir** [~'riːr] (2a) go up (in price), get dearer; ~ **sur** outdo; outbid; improve upon; **~issement** [~ris'mɑ̃] *m* rise in price.

rencogner F [rɑ̃kɔ'ɲe] (1a) drive *or* push (*s.o.*) into a corner.

rencontr|e [rɑ̃'kɔ̃ːtr] *f* meeting; encounter; 🚗, *mot.* collision; *fig.* occasion; **aller à la ~ de** go to meet; **de** ~ casual; chance ...; **~er** [~kɔ̃'tre] (1a) *v/t.* meet; 🚗, *mot.* collide with; *fig.* come across, find; ✗ encounter; *fig.* meet with, come up against; **se** ~ meet; collide; *fig.* happen; *fig.* appear; *fig.* agree (*persons, ideas*).

rendement [rɑ̃d'mɑ̃] *m* yield; return; output; ⚙ efficiency.

rendez-vous [rɑ̃de'vu] *m* appointment; date; rendezvous (*a.* = meeting place); **avoir (un)** ~, **avoir pris** ~ have an appointment; **donner** (*or* **fixer**) (**un**) ~ **à q.** give s.o. an appointment, make an appointment with s.o., arrange to see s.o.; **prendre** ~ make an appointment; **sur** ~ by appointment.

rendormir [rɑ̃dɔr'miːr] (2b) put to sleep again; **se** ~ go to sleep again, fall asleep again.

rend|re [rɑ̃ːdr] (4a) *v/t.* return, give back; restore (*s.o.'s liberty, s.o.'s health*); give (*an account, change, a verdict*); render (*services etc.*); pay (*homage*); *fig.* render, convey (*the meaning etc.*); ♪ pronounce (*judgment*); ♪ perform, play; ✝ deliver; ✝, ✗, ⚙ yield, produce; ✗ surrender (*a fortress*); ✗ bring up, vomit; ~ (*adj.*) make (*adj.*); *fig.* ~ **justice à** do (*s.o.*) justice; ♪♪ **la justice** dispense justice;

~ **nul** nullify; **se** ~ go (to, **à**); *fig.* yield, give way, *a.* ✗ surrender (to, **à**); *v/i.* be productive *or* profitable; give a yield; *a. fig.* pay off; **~u** [rɑ̃'dy] **1.** *adj.* arrived; exhausted; **2.** *su./m* paint. *etc.* rendering; ✝ returned article.

rêne [rɛn] *f* rein (*a. fig.*).

renégat(e *f*) *m* [rəne'ga, ~'gat] renegade.

renferm|é [rɑ̃fɛr'me] **1.** *adj.* withdrawn, uncommunicative; **2.** *su./m* fustiness; **sentir le** ~ smell stuffy; **~er** [~] (1a) contain, hold; **se** ~ (**dans, en**) withdraw (into *o.s.*, *silence*).

renfl|é [rɑ̃'fle] bulging, swelling; **~ement** [~flə'mɑ̃] *m* bulge; swelling; **~er** [~'fle] (1a): **se** ~ bulge (out), swell (out).

renflouer [rɑ̃flu'e] (1a) ♪ refloat; *fig.* put in funds.

renfonc|ement [rɑ̃fɔ̃s'mɑ̃] *m* recess; **~er** [~fɔ̃'se] (1k) knock *or* push (further) in; △ recess; pull down (*one's hat*).

renfor|cement [rɑ̃fɔrsə'mɑ̃] *m* △, ✗ strengthening (*a. fig. of opinion*); reinforcing; intensification; **~cer** [~'se] (1k) reinforce; strengthen; increase (*the sound, the expenditure*); intensify; **~t** [rɑ̃'fɔːr] *m* reinforcement(s *pl.*); **à grand** ~ **de** with a great deal of.

renfrogn|é [rɑ̃frɔ'ɲe] sullen, sulky; **~er** (1a): **se** ~ scowl; frown.

rengager [rɑ̃ga'ʒe] (1l) *v/t.* reengage; *v/i.*, **se** ~ ✗ re-enlist.

rengain|e F [rɑ̃'gɛːn] *f* old refrain, (*the same*) old story; **~er** [~gɛ'ne] (1a) withhold, hold back, save.

rengorger [rɑ̃gɔr'ʒe] (1a): **se** ~ puff o.s. up.

renier [rə'nje] (1o) deny, abjure; disown; repudiate; disavow.

renifl|ement [rəniflə'mɑ̃] *m* sniff(ing); **~er** [~'fle] (1a) *v/t.* sniff (*s.th.*) (up); *fig.* scent; *v/i.* sniff.

renne *zo.* [rɛn] *m* reindeer.

renom [rə'nɔ̃] *m* renown; **~mé, e** [rənɔ'me] **1.** *adj.* renowned (for, **pour**); **2.** *su./f* fame; reputation.

renonc|ement [rənɔ̃s'mɑ̃] *m* renouncing; renunciation; ~ **à soi-même** self-denial; **~er** [rənɔ̃'se] (1k): ~ **à** give up; renounce; abandon; **~iation** [~sja'sjɔ̃] *f* giving up; renunciation; abandonment.

renouer [rən'we] (1a) re-knot; tie up again; *fig.* ~ **avec qch.** take s.th. up again, resume s.th.; **~ avec q.** take up with s.o. again.

renouve|au [rənu'vo] *m* renewal; revival; spring(time); **~ler** [~nuv'le] (1c) renew; repeat; **se ~** be renewed; be repeated, recur, happen again; **~llement** [~nuvel'mã] *m* renewal; repetition.

rénov|ateur [renova'tœːr] *m* renovator; **~ation** [~'sjɔ̃] *f* renovation; renewal; restoration; **~er** renovate; renew; restore.

renseign|ement [rãsɛɲ'mã] *m* (piece of) information; **bureau m de ~s** inquiry office; **prendre des ~s** ask for information, make inquiries (about, **sur**); **~er** [~sɛ'ɲe] (1a) inform (*s.o.*) (about, **sur**); give (*s.o.*) information *or* directions; **se ~** ask for information, inquire, find out (about, **sur**).

renta|biliser [rãtabili'ze] (1a) make profitable, make pay; **~bilité** [~'te] *f* profitableness; **~ble** [rã'tabl] profitable.

rent|e [rãːt] *f* pension, annuity; (private) income; **~ perpétuelle** perpetuity; **~ier** *m*, **-ère** *f* [~'tje, ~'tjɛːr] stockholder; annuitant; person living on private means.

rentr|ant [rã'trã] ✔ retractable; ◎ inset; **~ée** [rã'tre] *f* return; home-coming; re-entry; *crops:* gathering; *school etc.:* reopening; *parl.* re-assembly; ✝ *taxes etc.:* collection; ✝ *money:* receipt; *actor etc.:* comeback; **~er** [~] (1a) *v/i.* re-enter (*a. thea.*); come *or* go in (again); return; come *or* go home; re-open (*school etc.*); *parl.* re-assemble; go back to school (*child*); ✝ come in (*money*); **~ dans** get back, recover (*rights etc.*); be included in, be part of; crash into (*a wall, car, etc.*); *v/t.* take *or* bring *or* get *or* pull in; retract; put away; ✔ gather in (*crops*); *fig.* suppress.

renvers|able [rãvɛr'sabl] reversible; **~ant** [~'sã] staggering; **~e** [rã'vɛrs] *f:* **à la ~** on one's back, backwards; **~ement** [rãvɛrsə'mã] *m* reversal; inversion; ◎ reversing; *wind:* shift(ing); overturning; *fig.* disorder; *fig.*, *pol.* overthrow; **~er** [~'se] (1a) *v/t.* turn upside down; knock over; upset; spill; *fig.*, *pol.* overthrow; reverse, invert; F *fig.* stun; F **~ les rôles** turn the tables; **se ~** fall over; overturn; capsize; lean back; *v/i.* F spill over (*milk etc.*).

renvoi [rã'vwa] *m* return(ing), sending back; *ball, sound:* throwing back; reflecting; dismissal; adjournment; ⚖, *pol.*, *typ.* reference; ✍ belch; **renvoyer** [~vwa'je] (1r) send back; throw back; reflect; dismiss (*s.o.*); postpone, put off, adjourn; *pol.* refer; ⚖ remand.

réoccuper [reɔky'pe] (1a) reoccupy.

réorganiser [reɔrgani'ze] (1a) reorganize.

réouverture [reuvɛr'tyːr] *f* reopening; resumption.

repaire [rə'pɛːr] *m* den; hideout.

repaître [rə'pɛːtr] (4k) feed; **se ~** eat one's fill, **se ~ de** feed on; *fig.* revel in, wallow in.

répand|re [re'pãːdr] (4a) spill; shed; spread; scatter (*flowers, money, sand, etc*); give off (*heat, a smell*); **se ~** spread; spill; *fig.* **se ~ en** let out, pour forth (*abuse etc.*); **~u** [~pã'dy] widespread, widely held (*opinion*).

réparable [repa'rabl] reparable;*cost.* repairable; remediable.

reparaître [rəpa'rɛːtr] (4k) reappear; ✍ recur.

répar|ateur [repara'tœːr] **1.** *adj.* repairing; restoring; **2.** *su.* repairman; repairer; **~ation** [~ra'sjɔ̃] *f* repair(ing); *fig.* amends *pl.*; ✕ **~s** *pl.* reparations; ⚖ **~ civile** compensation; **~er** [~'re] (1a) mend, repair, fix; *fig.* make good; *fig.* make amends for.

repart|ie [rəpar'ti] *f* repartee; retort; **avoir de la ~, avoir la ~ facile** be quick at repartee; **~ir** [~'tiːr] (2b) start off *or* set out *or* leave again; retort, reply.

réparti|r [repar'tiːr] (2a) share out; distribute; allot; divide up; **~tion** [~ti'sjɔ̃] *f* distribution; sharing out; dividing up; allotment; *statistics:* frequency.

repas [rə'pɑ] *m* meal; **petit ~** snack.

repass|age [rəpa'saːʒ] *m* ironing; ◎ sharpening; **~er** [~'se] (1a) *v/i.* come *or* go back *or* again; call again (on s.o., **chez q.**); pass again, come *or* go past again, *v/t.* go over (*s.th.*) again (*a. fig., in one's mind*), go back across; hand (over *or* round) again; hand on, pass on (*a. fig. an illness etc.*); put (back) again; take again (*an exam etc.*); *cost.* iron; ◎ sharpen (up); show again (*a film etc.*), repeat (*a show etc.*).

repayer [rəpɛ'je] (1i) pay again.

repêchage [rəpε'ʃaːʒ] *m* fishing up *or* out; *school:* second chance; **repêcher** [~'ʃe] (1a) fish up *or* out; *school:* let (*s.o.*) through.

repeindre [rə'pε̃ːdr] (4m) repaint.

repenser [rəpɑ̃'se] (1a) *v/i.* think again (about, of **à**); **y ~** think it over; *v/t.* rethink.

repent|ant [rəpɑ̃'tɑ̃] repentant; **~i** [~'ti] repentant, penitent; **~ir** [~'tiːr] **1.** (2b): **se ~** (**de qch.**) repent ([of] s.th.); be sorry (for s.th.); **2.** *su./m* repentance.

repérage [rəpe'raːʒ] *m* locating.

répercu|ssion [repεrky'sjɔ̃] *f* repercussion; consequences *pl.;* **~ter** [~'te] (1a) reverberate; reflect; **se ~** have repercussions (on, **sur**).

repère [rə'pεːr] *m* (reference *or* guide) mark; **point m de ~** landmark (*a. fig.*); **repérer** [~pe're] (1f) ✕, ⚓ *etc.* locate; spot; **se ~** get *or* take one's bearings.

répert|oire [repεr'twaːr] *m* index; list; index notebook; *thea., a. fig.* repertoire; **~orier** [~tɔ'rje] (1o) list, itemize.

répét|er [repe'te] (1f) repeat; do *or* say again; *thea.* rehearse; go over (again); learn (*a lesson etc.*); **se ~** repeat o.s.; recur, happen again; **~ition** [~ti'sjɔ̃] *f* repetition; recurrence; private lesson; *thea.* rehearsal; *picture etc.:* replica; *thea.* **~ générale** dress rehearsal.

repiquer [rəpi'ke] (1m) *v/t.* ✿ plant out; *v/i.:* F **~ au plat** have a second helping.

répit [re'pi] *m* respite; **sans ~** without (a moment's) respite, incessant(ly *adv.*).

replacer [rəpla'se] (1k) put back (in its place), replace; ✝ reinvest; find a new position for.

replet, -ète [rə'plε, ~'plεt] stoutish; **réplétion** [reple'sjɔ̃] *f* repletion.

repli [rə'pli] *m* fold; bend coil; *fig.* recess; withdrawal (*a.* ✕); **~ement** [~'mɑ̃] *m* withdrawal (into o.s.); **~er** [~'e] (1a) fold (up *or* over *or* down); tuck up; **se ~** coil up, roll up; withdraw (within o.s., **sur soi-même**).

réplique [re'plik] *f* retort, reply; *thea.* line, cue; *arts:* replica; **sans ~** irrefutable (*argument etc.*); obey without a word; **~er** [~pli'ke] (1m) retort.

répon|dant [repɔ̃'dɑ̃] *m* ⚖ surety, guarantor; F **avoir du ~** have s.th. to fall back on; **~dre** [~'pɔ̃ːdr] (4a) *v/t.* answer, reply; *v/i.* ⚙ *etc., a. fig.* re-

spond; **à** answer; comply with; correspond to, match; **~ de** answer for; guarantee; **~se** [~'pɔ̃ːs] *f* answer, reply; response; **~ payée** reply paid.

report [rə'pɔːr] *m* ✝ carrying forward; transfer; postponement; **~age** *journ.* [rəpɔr'taːʒ] *m* report(ing); story, article; (live) commentary; coverage.

reporter[1] [rəpɔr'te] (1a) carry *or* take back; transfer; postpone (to **à**); **se ~ à** refer to; *fig.* go back (in one's mind) to.

reporter[2] *journ.* [rəpɔr'tεːr] *m* reporter; **~ sportif** sports reporter.

repos [rə'po] *m* rest; peace (*of mind etc.*), ♪ pause; **au ~, en ~** at rest; **de tout ~** safe; **~ant** [rəpo'zɑ̃] restful; refreshing (*sleep*); **~é** [~'ze] rested, refreshed; **à tête ~e** at leisure; deliberately; **~er** [rəpo'ze] (1a) *v/t.* place, put, (re)lay; put down; *fig.* rest; (take a) rest; rely ([up]on, **sur**); settle (*bird, wine, etc.*); **se ~ sur ses lauriers** rest on one's laurels; *v/i.* lie, rest; be at rest; **~ sur** be built on; rest on, be based on; *ici repose* here lies.

repouss|ant [rəpu'sɑ̃] repulsive; offensive (*odour*); **~er** [~'se] (1a) *v/t.* push back *or* away; repel; reject; postpone; ✪ chase, emboss; *v/i.* grow again; **~oir** [~'swaːr] *m* foil.

répréhensible [repreɑ̃'sibl] reprehensible.

reprendre [rə'prɑ̃ːdr] (4aa) *v/t.* take again; recapture; get back; pick (s.o.) up (again); *fig.* recover; take back (*an object, a gift, a promise, a servant, etc.*); resume; repeat; *fig.* catch (cold, F *etc.*) again; *fig.* reprove (s.o.); *v/i.* start (up) *or* begin again; improve, pick up; heal again; take root (again); set again (*liquid*); come in again (*fashion*); continue, go on (*speaking*).

représailles [rəpre'zaːj] *f/pl.* reprisals; **user de ~** make reprisals.

représent|able [rəprezɑ̃'tabl] representable; **~ant** *m*; **~ante** *f* [~'tɑ̃, ~'tɑ̃t] representative; **~ de commerce** sales representative; **~atif** [~ta'tif] representative (of, **de**); **~ation** [~ta'sjɔ̃] *f* representation; *thea.* performance; ✝ sales representation; *ambassador etc.:* entertainment; **~er** [~'te] (1a) *v/t.* represent; *thea.* perform; *fig.* point (s.th.) out (to, **à**); *fig.* **se ~ qch.** imagine *or* visualize s.th.; v/i. have a good presence; keep up appearances.

répressi|f [reprɛ'sif] repressive; **~on** [~'sjɔ̃] f repression.

réprimand|e [reprimɑ̃:d] f reprimand; **~er** [~mɑ̃'de] (1a) reprimand (for, **de**).

réprimer [repri'me] (1a) repress; suppress; curb.

repris, e [rə'pri, ~'pri:z] **1.** p.p. of **reprendre; 2.** su./m. **~ de justice** old offender; su./f recapture, recovery; talks, work: resumption; thea. play, business etc.: revival; † trade-in, part exchange; box. round; ♪ repetition; fig. renewal; ✗ fresh attack; mot. engine: pick-up; cost. darn(ing); mending, repairing; **~e perdue** invisible mending; **à plusieurs ~es** repeatedly; **~er** [~pri'ze] (1a) mend; darn.

réprobat|eur [reproba'tœ:r] reproving; **~ion** [~'sjɔ̃] f reprobation.

reproch|able [rəprɔ'fabl] reproachable; **~e** [~'prɔʃ] m reproach; **sans ~** blameless; **~er** [~prɔ'ʃe] (1a): **~ qch. à q.** reproach or blame s.o. for s.th.

reprodu|cteur [rəprɔdyk'tœ:r] reproductive; **~ction** [~'sjɔ̃] f reproduction; **~ire** [rəprɔ'dɥi:r] (4h) reproduce; zo., etc. breed, reproduce.

reprographier [rəprɔgra'fje] (1a) reproduce, copy.

réprouv|é [~'ve] su. outcast; eccl. **les ~s** pl. the damned; save (up), keep; eccl. reprobate; **~er** [~'ve] (1a) reprove, disapprove of; eccl. reprobate.

rept|ation [rɛpta'sjɔ̃] f crawling; **~ile** [~'til] adj., su./m reptile.

repu [rə'py] **1.** p.p. of **repaître; 2.** adj. satiated, full.

républi|cain [repybli'kɛ̃] adj., su. republican; **~que** [~'blik] f republic.

répudier [repy'dje] (1o) repudiate.

répugn|ance [repy'ɲɑ̃:s] f repugnance; loathing (of, for **pour**); reluctance (to inf., à inf.); **~ant** [~'ɲɑ̃] repugnant, disgusting; **~er** [~'ɲe] (1a): **~ à q.** be repugnant to s.o., disgust s.o.; **~ à faire qch.** be loath to do s.th.; **il me répugne de** (inf.) I am reluctant to (inf.).

répulsi|f [repyl'sif] repulsive; **~on** [~'sjɔ̃] f repulsion (for, **pour**).

réput|ation [repyta'sjɔ̃] f reputation; **~é** [~'te] renowned.

requ|érir [rəke'ri:r] (2l) call for; request; demand; require; **~ête** [~'kɛt] f request, petition.

requin icht. [rə'kɛ̃] m shark.

requis [rə'ki] **1.** adj. required; **2.** p.p. of **requérir.**

réquisit|ion [rekizi'sjɔ̃] f requisition; **~ionner** [~sjɔ'ne] (1a) requisition; **~oire** ⚖, fig. [~'twa:r] m indictment.

rescapé [rɛska'pe] **1.** adj. rescued; **2.** su. survivor; rescued person.

rescousse [rɛs'kus] f: **aller (venir) à la ~ de** go (come) to the rescue or aid of.

réseau [re'zo] m network.

résection ✗ [resɛk'sjɔ̃] f resection; **réséquer** [rese'ke] (1s) resect.

réserv|ation [rezɛrva'sjɔ̃] f reservation, booking; **~e** [~'zɛrv] f reservation, reserve; hunt. preserve; fig. **sans ~** unreserved(ly adv); **sous ~é** subject to; **~é** [rezɛr've] reserved; cautious, guarded (attitude etc.); **~er** [~'ve] (1a) reserve; book; save (up), keep; fig. have or hold in store (for, à); **~iste** ✗ [~'vist] m reservist; **~oir** [~'vwa:r] m reservoir; (fish-)pond; ⚙, mot. tank; **~ de secours** reserve tank.

résid|ant [rezi'dɑ̃] resident; **~ence** [~'dɑ̃:s] f residence; residential flats pl.; **~ principale (secondaire)** main (second) home; **~ent** [~'dɑ̃] m résident; **~entiel** [~dɑ̃'sjɛl] residential (quarter); **~er** [~'de] (1a) reside (at, à; in, dans); fig. lie (in dans, en); **~u** [~'dy] m ✗, ⚙, ♣ residue.

résign|ation [reziɲa'sjɔ̃] f resignation; **~é** [~'ɲe] resigned (to, à); **~er** [~'ɲe] (1a): **se ~** resign o.s. (to, à).

résilier [rezi'lje] (1o) terminer.

résille [re'zij] f net(ting); hairnet.

résin|e [re'zin] f resin; **~eux** [~zi'nø] **1.** adj. resinous; coniferous (forest); **2.** su./m coniferous tree.

résist|ance [rezis'tɑ̃:s] f resistance (a. ⚡, ⚙, pol. etc.); **~ant** [~'tɑ̃] **1.** adj. resistant; tough; fast (colour); hard-wearing; **~ à la chaleur** heat-proof; **2.** su. pol. member of the **Résistance** (1939–45 war); **~er** [~'te] (1a). **~ à** resist; ⚙ take (a stress); stand up to, withstand, hold out against.

résol|u [rezɔ'ly] **1.** adj. resolute; resolved, determined (to, à; **2.** p.p. of **résoudre; ~us** [~] 1st p. sg. p.s. of **résoudre; ~ution** [rezɔly'sjɔ̃] f resolution (*a.* 🔥, 🔥 *etc.*); solution (*of a problem*); 🏛 termination; **prendre la ~ de** (*inf.*) make a resolution *or* resolve to (*inf.*), make up one's mind to (*inf.*); *admin.* **prendre une ~** pass a resolution; **~vons** [rezɔl'vɔ̃] *1st p. pl. pres. of* **résoudre**.

réson|ance [rezɔ'nɑ̃:s] *f* resonance; **~nement** [~zɔn'mɑ̃] *m* resounding; **~ner** [~zɔ'ne] (1a) resound, ring; be resonant (*room*); echo (*sound*).

résorber 🔥 [rezɔr'be] (1a) resorb; absorb; *fig.* reduce; **se ~** be resorbed; *fig.* be reduced; break up, be resolved.

résou|dre [re'zudr] (4bb) solve; resolve (to *inf.*, **de** *inf.*); **se ~ à** (*inf.*) resolve *or* decide to (*inf.*); bring o.s. to (*inf.*); **~s** 🔥 [~'zu] *p.p./m of* **résoudre**.

respect [rɛs'pɛ] *m* respect; **~ de soi** self-respect; **sauf votre ~** with all (due) respect; **tenir q. en ~** keep s.o. in check; **~able** [rɛspɛk'tabl] respectable (*a. fig.*); **~er** [~'te] (1a) respect; **se ~** have self-respect; **~if** [~'tif] respective; **~ueux** [~'tuø] respectful (of, **de**).

respir|ation [respira'sjɔ̃] *f* respiration, breathing; **~atoire** [~ra'twa:r] breathing; respiratory; **~er** [~'re] (1a) *v/i.* breathe; *fig.* breathe again; *fig.* take breath, get one's breath; *v/t.* breathe (in), inhale; *fig.* radiate, exude (health *etc.*, *la santé etc.*).

resplendi|r [rɛsplɑ̃'di:r] (2a) shine (*a. fig.* with, **de**); gleam, glisten; **~ssant** [~di'sɑ̃] resplendent.

responsab|ilité [rɛspɔ̃sabili'te] *f* (for, **de**) responsibility; liability; **~le** [~'sabl] responsible (for s.th., **de qch.**; for s.o., **pour q.**; to **devant, envers**); in charge; 🏛 *a.* liable (for, **de**); **rendre q. ~** hold s.o. responsible for.

resquiller F [rɛski'je] (1a) get in on the sly; fiddle a ride.

ressac ⚓ [rə'sak] *m* backwash, undertow; surf.

ressaisir [rəsɛ'zi:r] (2a) recapture, seize again; regain one's self-control; pull o.s. together.

ressasser [rəsa'se] (1a) repeat (*a story*) over and over.

ressaut [rə'so] *m* projection.

ressembl|ance [rəsɑ̃'blɑ̃:s] *f* likeness; resemblance (to, **avec**); **~ant** [~'blɑ̃]

lifelike, true to life; **~er** [~'ble] (1a): **~ à** be *or* look like, resemble; **se ~** be *or* look alike, resemble each other.

ressemeler [rəsəm'le] (1e) resole.

ressent|iment [rəsɑ̃ti'mɑ̃] *m* resentment; **~ir** [~'ti:r] (2b) feel; **se ~ de** feel the effects of.

resserr|e [rə'sɛr] *f* shed; **~é** [rəsɛ're] narrow, confined; **~ement** [~sɛr'mɑ̃] *m* contraction, tightening; closing up; narrowness; **~er** [~sɛ're] (1b) (*a.* **se ~**) tighten (up); close (up), contract; **se ~** *a.* narrow, grow narrow(er); **se ~ autour de** close in on.

ressort[1] [rə'sɔ:r] *m* ⚙ spring; *fig.* energy, spirit; **faire ~** spring back.

ressort[2] [~] *m* 🏛 competence, jurisdiction; *fig.* scope; **être du ~ de** fall within the competence *or* scope of; **en dernier ~** finally, eventually; 🏛 without appeal.

ressortir[1] [rəsɔr'ti:r] (2b) *v/i.* go *or* come out again; *fig.* stand out, be set off; *fig.* result, follow (from, **de**); *v/t.* bring *or* take out again.

ressorti|r[2] [rəsɔr'ti:r] (2a): **~ à** 🏛 be within the jurisdiction of; *fig.* pertain to; **~ssant, e** [~ti'sɑ̃, ~'sɑ̃t] *su.* national (*of a country*).

ressource [rə'surs] *f* possibility; **~s** *pl. a.* resources; **sans ~** hopeless.

ressouvenir [rəsuv'ni:r] (2h): **se ~** remember, recall.

ressusciter [resysi'te] (1a) *vt.* resuscitate, bring back to life; raise from the dead; *v/i.* come back to life; rise from the dead.

restant [rɛs'tɑ̃] **1.** *adj.* remaining; **2.** *su.* survivor; *su./m* remainder; left-over; *fig.* remnant.

restaur|ant [rɛstɔ'rɑ̃] *m* restaurant; **manger au ~** eat out; **~ateur** [~ra'tœ:r] *m* restorer; **~ation** [~ra'sjɔ̃] *f* restoration; **~er** [~'re] (1a) restore; refresh.

rest|e [rɛst] *m* rest, remainder, remnant(s *pl.*); **~s** *pl.* left-overs; mortal remains; **au ~, du ~** moreover; **de ~** (*time, money etc.*) to spare; **~er** [rɛs'te] (1a) remain; be left (behind); stay; *en* **~ à** go no further than; stop at; stick to; *en là* leave it at that.

restitu|er [rɛsti'tɥe] (1n) restore; return (s.th. to s.o., **qch. à q.**); **~tion** [~ty'sjɔ̃] *f* restoration; return.

restoroute (*TM*) [resto'rut] *m* roadside restaurant.

restr|eindre [rɛs'trɛ̃:dr] (4m) restrict, limit, cut down (on); **se ~** become restricted, narrow; *expenses*: cut down on things; **~ictif** [~trik'tif] restrictive; **~iction** [~trik'sjɔ̃] *f* restriction; qualification; (**~ mentale** mental) reservation.

résult|at [rezyl'ta] *m* result, issue; effect; **avoir pour ~** result in; **~er** [~'te] (1a) result, follow (from, **de**); **il en résulte que** it follows that.

résum|é [rezy'me] *m* summary; **en ~** in short; in brief; **~er** [~] (1a) summarize, sum up; **se ~** sum up; **se ~ à** boil *or* come down to, amount to; **se ~ en** be embodied in.

résurrection [rezyrɛk'sjɔ̃] *f* resurrection; *fig.* revival.

retable △ [rə'tabl] *m* altar-piece.

rétabli|r [reta'bli:r] (2a) re-establish, restore; reinstate; restore *s.o.* to health; **se ~** recover; be restored, return (*former state*); **~ssement** [~blis'mã] *m* re-establishment; reinstatement; recovery.

rétamé F [rɔta'me] worn out; stoned (= *drunk*); bust(ed).

retaper F [rɔta'pe] (1a) touch up, do up; fix up; straighten (*a bed*); buck (*s.o.*) up; **se ~** get on one's feet (again).

retard [rɔ'tair] *m* delay; lateness; *child, harvest*: backwardness; **être en ~** be late; be slow (*clock etc.*); be behind (with **dans, pour**); be backward; **être en ~ sur** be behind (*the fashion, the times*); **~ataire** [rɔtarda'tɛ:r] **1.** *adj.* late; behindhand; backward (*child, country, etc.*); **2.** *su.* late-comer; **~ateur** [~'tœ:r] retarding; **~ement** [rɔtardɔ'mã] *m* delay; retarding; **à ~** delayed action ..., time (*bomb*); **+ after** the event, afterwards; **~er** [~'de] (1a) *v/t.* delay, retard; defer (*an event, payment*); put back (*an action, a clock*); set (*s.o.*) back; *v/i.* be late; be slow, lose (*clock*); **~ sur** be behind (*the times etc.*).

retéléphoner [rɔtelefɔ'ne] (1a) **~** (**a** *q.*) phone (*s.o.*) again, call (*s.o.*) back.

retenir [rɔt'ni:r] (2h) hold back; keep (*s.o.*) back; hold (*s.o.*) up; detain (*s.o.*); hold (*s.o., s.th., s.o.'s attention*); withhold; *fig.* remember; book (*a seat, a room*); engage (*a servant etc.*); *fig.* hold

back (*a sob, tears, etc.*); restrain (from *ger.*, **de** *inf.*); **se ~** hold o.s. back; restrain o.s.; control o.s.; **se ~ à** hold on to (*s.th.*); **se ~ de** (*inf.*) stop o.s. (*ger.*), refrain from (*ger.*); **rétention** [retã'sjɔ̃] *f* retention.

retenti|r [rɔtã'ti:r] (2a) (re)sound, ring, echo; *fig.* **~ sur** affect; **~ssement** [~tis'mã] *m* resounding; *fig.* repercussion; *fig.* stir.

retenu [rɔt'ny] restrained, reserved; discreet; low-keyed; **~e** [~] *f* money: deduction; ✚ carry over; *school*: detention; holding back; *fig.* discretion; modesty; restraint.

réticence [reti'sã:s] *f* reticence; hesitation, reluctance.

réticul|e [reti'kyl] *m* opt. reticle; handbag; **~é** [~ky'le] reticulated.

rétif [re'tif] restive, stubborn.

rétine [re'tin] *f* eye: retina.

retir|é [rɔti're] retired; remote; **~er** [~] (1a) withdraw, take away; take out; remove; pull out; take off (*a garment*); derive (*profit*); obtain; *fig.* take back (*an insult, a promise, etc.*); pick up, collect (*baggage etc.*); **~ de la circulation** call in (*currency*); **se ~** retire.

retomb|ée [rɔtɔ̃'be] *f* fallout; *fig.* **~s** *pl.* repercussions, consequences; *fig.* spin-off *sg.*; *phys.* **~s** *pl.* **radio-actives** fall-out *sg.*; **~er** [~] (1a) fall (down) again; fall (back); **~ dans** lapse into; *fig.* **~ sur** blame, glory: fall upon.

retordre [rɔ'tɔrdr] (4a): *fig.* **donner du fil à ~ à** *q.* give s.o. trouble.

retorquer [rɔtɔr'ke] (1m) retort.

retors [rɔ'tɔ:r] crafty, wily.

retouch|e [rɔ'tuʃ] *f* retouch(ing); touching-up; *garment*: alteration; **~er** [~tu'ʃe] (1a) retouch, touch up; alter (*garment etc.*).

retour [rɔ'tu:r] *m* return; going back; turn; change; ♪, ♯ recurrence; *biol.* reversion; ♯ **~ d'âge** critical age; **à son ~** on his return; ✚ **billet m de ~** return ticket; **en ~** in return (for, **de**); **être de ~** be back; **être sur le ~** be past one's prime; **~ner** [~tur'ne] (1a) *v/i.* return;go back; **~ en arrière, ~ sur ses pas** turn back; **de quoi retourne-t-il?** what is it all about?; *v/t.* turn (*s.th.*) upside down *od.* over *od.* up; turn (*s.th.*) inside out; twist (*s.o.'s arm*); *fig.* upset, disturb (*s.o.*); return, send (*s.th.*) back; **se ~** turn (over); turn round; *fig.* **se ~ contre** turn against (*s.o.*); rebound on (*s.o.*); *fig.* **se ~ vers** turn to (*s.o.*, *s.th.*); **s'en ~** return, go back.

retracer [rətra'se] (1k) relate, recount.

rétracter [retrak'te] (1a) retract; draw in; **se ~** retract (*a. fig.*).

retrait [rə'trɛ] *m* withdrawal; ☉ shrinkage; recession; collection (*of baggage*); *mot.* **~ du permis (de conduire)** disqualification from driving; **en ~** set back; *a. fig.* in the background; **~e** [rə'trɛt] *f* ✗, *eccl.*, *fig.* retreat; *fig.* refuge; retirement; (retirement) pension; **en ~** retired; **mettre q. à la ~** retire s.o.; **prendre sa ~** retire; **~é** [rətrɛ'te] *adj.* retired; *su.* pensioner.

retraiter¹ [rətrɛ'te] (1a) treat or handle again; ☉ reprocess.

retraiter² [~] (1a) pension off.

retranch|ement [rətrɑ̃ʃ'mɑ̃] *m* entrenchment; **~er** [~trɑ̃'ʃe] (1a) take out; cut out *or* away *or* off; deduct (*an amount*); **se ~ derrière** (*etc.*) entrench o.s. behind *etc.*

retrans|mettre [rətrɑ̃s'mɛttre] (4v) *radio:* broadcast; *telev.* show; **~mission** [~mi'sjɔ̃] *f* broadcast; showing.

rétréci|r [retre'si:r] (2a) *v/t.* narrow; *cost.* take in (*a garment*); **se ~** (grow) narrow; *tex.*, *a. v/i.* shrink; **~ssement** [~sis'mɑ̃] *m* narrowing; contraction; *tex.* shrinking; ⚕ stricture.

retremper [rətrɑ̃'pe] (1a) soak again; *fig.* strengthen; **se ~** reimmerse o.s.

rétribu|er [retri'bɥe] (1m) pay, remunerate; **~tion** [~by'sjɔ̃] *f* payment; salary; **sans ~** honorary.

rétro [re'tro] **1.** *adj.* reminiscent of times past; **la vogue ~** nostalgia; **2.** *su./m* nostalgia; *mot.* (= *rétroviseur*) back-view mirror.

rétro... [retro] retro...; **~actif** [~ak'tif] retroactive; **~action** [~ak'sjɔ̃] *f* retroaction; ⚡, *radio:* feedback; **~fusée** *f* [~fy'ze] *f* braking rocket; **~grade** [~'grad] retrograde, backward; **~grader** [~gra'de] (1a) *v/i.* move backwards; retrograde; regress; fall back; *mot.* change (*Am.* shift) down (from ... to ..., **de ... en ...**); ✗ *etc.* demote; **~manie** [~ma'ni] *f* nostalgia; **~spectif** [~spɛk'tif] retrospective.

retrousser [rətru'se] (1a) roll up (*one's sleeves*); curl up (*one's lips*); **nez** *m* **retroussé** snub nose.

retrouv|ailles [rətru'va:j] *f/pl.* reunion, reconciliation; **~er** [~'ve] (1a) find (again); meet (*s.o.*) again; return to; recover; *aller ~* go and see (*s.o.*) again; **se ~** be found (again); meet (again); find o.s. back; *a.* **s'y ~** find one's way; F *fig.* **s'y ~** break even.

rétroviseur *mot.* [retrɔvi'zœ:r] *m* driving mirror, rear-view mirror.

réunifier [reyni'fje] (1o) reunify.

réun|ion [rey'njɔ̃] *f* meeting; bringing together, collection, gathering; reunion; **~ir** [~'ni:r] (2a) gather (together); collect; raise (*funds etc.*), get (*things*) together; bring together; join, link; reunite; *fig.* combine (*elements etc.*); **se ~** meet; unite.

réussi [rey'si] successful, good, a success; **~r** [rey'si:r] (2a) *v/i.* succeed, be successful, be a success; thrive, do well, pass (*an exam*); **~ à q.** agree with (*s.o.*), do s.o. good; **~ à** (*inf.*) succeed in (*ger.*), manage to (*inf.*); *v/t.* be successful in; carry (*s.th.*) out well; manage; **~te** [~'sit] *f* success.

revalo|ir *fig.* [rəva'lwa:r] (3l) pay back; repay; **~risation** ♱ [rəvalɔriza'sjɔ̃] *f* revalorization; **~riser** ♱ [~'ze] (1a) revalue.

revanche [rə'vɑ̃:ʃ] *f* revenge (on, *sur*); **en ~** in return; on the other hand.

rêvass|er [rɛva'se] (1a) daydream (about, **à**); **~erie** [~vas'ri] *f* daydream(ing); **~eur** *m*, **-euse** *f* [~va'sœ:r, ~'sø:z] daydreamer.

rêve [rɛ:v] *m* dream; **~ déveillé** daydream; *faire un ~* have a dream.

revêche [rə'vɛʃ] crabby, surly.

réveil [re'vɛ:j] *m* waking, awakening; revival; ✗ reveille; alarm clock; **~le-matin** [~vɛjma'tɛ̃] *m/inv.* alarm clock; **~ler** [reve'je] (1a) (a)wake; waken (*a. fig.*); **se ~** wake up, awake; **~lon** [~'jɔ̃] *m* midnight supper (*on Christmas Eve and New Year's Eve*).

révél|ateur [revela'tœ:r] **1.** *adj.* revealing; tell-tale (*sign*); **2.** *su./m phot.* developer; **~ation** [~la'sjɔ̃] *f* revelation; **~er** [~'le] (1f) reveal, disclose; make (widely) known; show; *phot.* develop; **se ~** reveal itself, be revealed; *fig.* **se ~ ...** prove (to be) ...

revenant [rəv'nɑ̃] *m* ghost.

revendeur *m*, **-euse** *f* ✝ [rəvɑ̃'dœːr, ~'døːz] retailer; secondhand dealer.

revendi|cation [rəvɑ̃dika'sjɔ̃] *f* claim; demand; **~quer** [~'ke] (1m) claim; demand.

revendre [rə'vɑ̃ːdr] (4a) resell.

revenir [rəv'niːr] (2h) return, come back *or* again (to, **à**); *fig.* **~ à** reach (*s.o.'s* ears); amount to; come to, cost; come *or* boil down to; *by right:* fall to (*s.o.*); be due to, go to (*s.o.*); ⚕ **~ à soi** come round; **~ de** get over (*s.th.*), recover from; **~** retrace (*one's steps*); go back on (*a decision, a promise*); go back over (*an affair, the past, etc.*); *cuis* **faire ~** (*meat*); ... **ne me revient pas** I don't like the look of ...; I cannot recall ...; **ne pas en ~** be unable to get over it; **cela revient à** (*inf*.) it amounts to (*ger.*); **cela revient au même** that amounts to *or* comes (down) to the same thing; **il lui revient de** (*inf*.) it's for him *or* up to him (*or* her) to (*inf*)

revente [rə'vɑ̃ːt] *f* resale.

revenu [rəv'ny] *m person:* income; *State:* revenue; ✝ yield; **impôt m sur le ~** income tax.

rêver [rɛ've] (1a) *v/i.* dream (about, of **de**); **~ à** think about; dream of; **~ de** dream of, long for; *v/t.* dream of.

réverbè|re [rever'bɛːr] *m* street lamp; reflector; **~rer** [~be're] (1f) reflect (*light*); re-echo (*a sound*).

révér|ence [reve'rɑ̃ːs] *f* reverence; bow, curtsey; **tirer sa ~** take one's leave; **~encieux** [~rɑ̃'sjø] reverential; **~end** *eccl.* [~'rɑ̃] Reverend; **~er** [~'re] (1f) revere.

rêverie [rɛv'ri] *f* reverie; daydream(ing).

revers [rə'vɛːr] *m* reverse (*a. fig.*); *hand, page etc.:* back; *tex.* wrong side; *cost. coat:* lapel; *trousers:* turn-up, *Am.* cuff; *fig.* setback; *sp.* backhand stroke.

réversible [rever'sibl] reversible.

revêt|ement [rəvɛt'mɑ̃] *m* ⚙, △ facing, coating; *road:* surface; **~ir** [~vɛ'tiːr] (2g) dress (in, **de**); *fig.* invest (with, **de**); *cost.* put on, don (*a garment*); *fig.* assume, take on (*a shape etc.*); ⚙, △ face, coat, surface.

rêveur [rɛ'vœːr] **1.** *adj.* dreamy; dreaming; **2.** *su.* (day)dreamer.

revirement [rəvir'mɑ̃] *m* sudden change *or* turn, about-face.

révis|er [revi'ze] (1a) revise; ✝ audit; ⚖ review; *mot.*, ⚙ service, overhaul; inspect; **~eur** [~'zœːr] *m* reviser; examiner; auditor; **~ion** [~'zjɔ̃] *f* revision; audit(ing); ⚖ review; ⚙, *mot.* service, servicing, overhaul(ing).

revitaliser [revitali'ze] (1a) revitalize; **crème** *f* **revitalisante** nourishing cream.

revivifier [revivi'fje] (1o) revive.

revivre [rə'viːvr] (4hh) *v/i.* revive; live again, come to life again; *v/t.* live (*s.th.*) over again.

révoca|ble [revo'kabl] revocable; removable; **~tion** [~ka'sjɔ̃] *f* ⚖ *etc.* revocation; *official:* removal, dismissal.

revoi|ci F [rəvwa'si] *prp.:* **me ~!** here I am again!; **~là** F [~'la] *prp.:* **me ~!** here I am again!; **le ~ malade!** there he is, ill again!

revoir [rə'vwaːr] **1.** (3m) see again; meet (*s.o.*) again; revise; **2.** *su./m:* **au ~** good-bye.

révolt|ant [revɔl'tɑ̃] revolting, shocking; **~e** [~'vɔlt] *f* revolt; **~é** [revɔl'te] *adj.* rebellious; outraged, shocked; *su.* rebel; **~er** [~] (1a) revolt, shock, **se ~** revolt.

révolu [revo'ly] past, bygone; full (*year*); completed (*period of time*); **~tion** [revoly'sjɔ̃] *f* revolution; **~tionnaire** [~sjɔ'nɛːr] *adj.*, *su.* revolutionary; **~tionner** [~sjɔ'ne] (1a) revolutionize; F *fig.* stir up.

revolver [revɔl'vɛːr] *m* gun, revolver.

révoquer [revo'ke] (1m) revoke; dismiss, remove (*an official*).

revue [rə'vy] *f* review; inspection (*a.* ✕); *journ.* magazine; *thea.* revue; F **nous sommes de ~** we'll meet again; **passer en ~** review, inspect (*troops*), *fig.* a. **faire la ~ de** go through, look over; revue.

révulsé [revyl'se]: **l'œil ~** with turned-up eyes.

rez-de-chaussée [retʃo'se] *m* street level; ground floor, *Am.* first floor.

rhabiller [rabi'je] (1a) dress (*s.o.*) again, ⚙ repair; △ renovate; *a. fig.* refurbish; **se ~** get dressed again.

rhénan [re'nɑ̃] Rhine ..., Rhenish.

rhésus [re'zyz] *m:* **facteur m ~** rhesus factor; **~ positif** (**négatif**) rhesus positive (negative).

rhétorique [reto'rik] *f* rhetoric.

rhodanien [rɔda'njɛ̃] of the Rhone.

rhombe ♪ [rɔ̃:b] *m* rhomb(us).

rhubarbe ♀ [ry'barb] *f* rhubarb.

rhum [rɔm] *m* rum.

rhumatis|ant ♪ [rymati'zɑ̃] rheumatic; **~mal** ♪ [~tis'mal] rheumatic; **~me** ♪ [~'tism] *m* rheumatism; **~ articulaire** rheumatoid arthritis.

rhume ♪ [rym] *m* cold; **~ de cerveau** cold in the head; **~ des foins** hayfever.

ri [ri] *p.p.* of **rire** 1; **riant** [rjɑ̃] smiling (*face, a. countryside etc.*).

ribambelle [ribɑ̃'bɛl] *f* flock, swarm, herd.

rican|er [rika'ne] (1a) snigger; giggle; **~eur** [~ka'nœːr] sniggering; giggling.

rich|ard *m, e f* F [ri'ʃaːr, ~'ʃard] wealthy person, F moneybags; **~e** [riʃ] **1.** *adj.* rich (in **en, de**); wealthy; F fig. fine; **2.** *su.* rich person; *su./m:* **les ~s** *pl.* the rich; **~esse** [ri'ʃɛs] *f* wealth; riches *pl.*; *fig.* opulence; richness.

ricin ♀ [ri'sɛ̃] *m* castor-oil plant; **huile *f* de ~** castor oil.

ricoch|er [rikɔ'ʃe] (1a) ricochet, rebound, bounce (off, **sur**); **faire ~** make (*a pebble*) jump; **~et** [~'ʃɛ] *m* rebound; ✕ ricochet; *fig.* **par ~** indirectly; **faire ~** rebound.

rictus [rik'tys] *m* grin; grimace.

rid|e [rid] *f* wrinkle; fold; *ground:* fold; *sand, water:* ripple; **~é** [ri'de] wrinkled.

rideau [ri'do] *m* curtain; shutter; **~!** that's enough!; **~ de fer** Iron Curtain; *fig.* **tirer le ~ sur** draw a veil over.

rider [ri'de] (1a) wrinkle; ripple (*water, sand*); **se ~** become wrinkled; wrinkle.

ridicul|e [ridi'kyl] **1.** *adj.* ridiculous; **2.** *su./m* absurdity; ridiculousness; ridicule; **tourner en ~** ridicule; **~iser** [~kyli'ze] (1a) ridicule; **se ~** make o.s. ridiculous, make a fool of o.s.

rien [rjɛ̃] **1.** *pron./indef.* anything; nothing; not ... anything; **~ de nouveau** nothing new; **~ du tout** nothing at all; **~ moins que** nothing less than; **cela ne fait ~** that does not matter; **de ~!** I don't mention it!; **en moins de ~** in less than no time; **il ne dit jamais ~** he never says a thing; **il n'y a ~ à faire** it can't be helped; **plus ~** nothing more; **sans ~ dire** without a word; **2.** *su./m* **un ~ a** mere nothing; **un ~ de** a hint *or* touch of; **en un ~ de temps** in no time (at all).

rieur [rjœːr] **1.** *adj.* laughing; merry; mocking; **2.** *su.* laugher.

rififi *sl.* [rifi'fi] *m* fight, brawl; trouble.

rigid|e [ri'ʒid] rigid; stiff (*a. fig.*); **~ifier** [~ʒidi'fje] (1o) make rigid; harden; **~ité** [~ʒidi'te] *f* rigidity; stiffness (*a. fig.*); tenseness.

rigolade F [rigɔ'lad] *f* fun, lark.

rigolard *sl.* [rigɔ'laːr] jolly.

rigole [ri'gɔl] *f* ditch; ⊙ channel.

rigol|er F [rigɔ'le] (1a) laugh; have fun; be joking; **~o, -ote** F [~'lo, ~'lɔt] **1.** *adj.* funny; odd; **2.** *su.* wag; phoney.

rigorisme [rigɔ'rism] *m* rigorism, strictness; **rigoriste** [~'rist] **1.** *adj.* rigorous; strict; **2.** *su.* rigid moralist; **rigoureux** [rigu'rø] rigorous; strict; severe; close (*reasoning*); **rigueur** [~'gœːr] *f* rigo(u)r, severity; *fig.* strictness; *fig.* accuracy; **à la ~** at a pinch; if (absolutely) necessary; **de ~** obligatory, compulsory.

rillettes *cuis.* [ri'jɛt] *f/pl.* potted pork mince *sg.*

rim|e [rim] *f* rhyme; **~er** [ri'me] (1a) rhyme (with, **avec**).

rinçage [rɛ̃'saːʒ] *m* rinsing; **rince-bouteilles** [rɛ̃sbu'tɛːj] *m/inv.* bottle washer; **rince-doigts** [~'dwa] *m/inv.* finger bowl; **rincée** [rɛ̃'se] *f sl.* thrashing; F downpour; **rincer** [~'se] (1k) rinse; **rinçure** [~'syːr] *f* slops *pl.*

ring *box.* [riŋ] *m* ring.

ripaill|e F [ri'paːj] *f* feast; **faire ~** = **~er** [ripa'je] (1a) feast.

ripost|e [ri'pɔst] *f* retort; reposte; **~er** [~pɔs'te] (1a) reposte.

rire [riːr] **1.** *v/i.* (4cc) laugh (at, **de**); joke; **~ au nez de q.** laugh in s.o.'s face; **~ dans sa barbe** chuckle to o.s.; **pour ~** for fun, as a joke; **~ de** take (*s.th.*) in one's stride; **2.** *su./m* laugh(ter).

ris¹ [ri]: **(~ de veau** calf) sweetbread.

ris² [~] *1st p. sg. p.s.* of **rire** 1; **risée** [ri'ze] *f* derision; *person:* laughing stock; **risette** [~'zɛt] *f:* **(faire ~** give a) smile; **risible** [~'ziːbl] ludicrous.

risqu|e [risk] *m* risk; hazard; **† à ses ~s et périls** at one's own risk; **au ~ de** (*inf.*) at the risk of (*ger.*); **~é** [ris'ke] risky; daring, risqué (*joke etc.*); **~er** [~] (1m) *v/t.* risk; venture; **~ le coup** take a chance, chance it; **se ~ dans** (*etc.*) venture into (*etc.*); **se ~ à** (*inf.*) venture or dare to (*inf.*); *v/i.:* **~ de** (*inf.*) run the risk of (ger.); be likely to (inf.); **~e-tout** [~kə'tu] m/inv. daredevil.

rissoler cuis. [risɔ'le]: (a. **faire ~**) brown.

ristourn|e ✝ [ris'turn] f rebate; **~er** [~tur'ne] (1a) repay; refund.

rite eccl. etc. [rit] m rite.

ritournelle [ritur'nɛl] f ♪ ritornello; F fig. **la même ~** the same old story.

rituel [ri'tɥɛl] adj., su./m ritual.

rivage [ri'va:ʒ] m shore, beach.

rival [ri'val] adj., su. rival; **~iser** [rivali-'ze] (1a): **~ avec** rival; compete with; vie with (in s.th., **de qch.**); hold one's own against; **~ité** [~'te] f rivalry.

rive [ri:v] f shore, river, bank.

river [ri've] (1a) rivet (a. fig.); clinch.

riverain [ri'vrɛ̃] **1.** adj. riverside ...; bordering on a road; **2.** su. riverside resident; dweller along a road.

rivet ⊙ [ri'vɛ] m rivet; **~er** [riv'te] (1a) rivet.

rivière [ri'vjɛ:r] f river.

rixe [riks] f brawl, fight; affray.

riz [ri] m rice; **~ au lait** rice pudding; **rizière** [ri'zjɛːr] f ricefield.

robe [rɔb] f dress, frock; gown; animal: coat; onion, potato: skin; **~ de chambre** dressing gown.

robinet ⊙ [rɔbi'nɛ] m tap, Am. faucet; **~ d'arrêt** stopcock; **~ mélangeur** mixer tap.

robot [rɔ'bo] m robot.

robuste [rɔ'byst] robust, sturdy; ☒ hardy; fig. firm (faith etc.); **~sse** [~bys'tɛs] f sturdiness; hardiness.

roc [rɔk] m rock (a fig.).

rocade [rɔ'kad] f road: bypass.

rocaill|e [rɔ'ka:j] f rocky ground; rock garden; rockwork; ✝ rococo; **~eux** [~ka'jø] rocky, stony; fig. rugged, rough.

roch|e [rɔʃ] f rock; **~er** [rɔ'ʃe] m rock; bolder; **~eux** [rɔ'ʃø] rocky; fig. harsh.

rocambolesque [rɔkɑ̃bɔ'lɛsk] fantastic, crazy, incredible.

rococo [rɔkɔ'ko] **1.** su./m rococo; **2.** adj./inv. rococo; fig. old-fashioned.

rodage [rɔ'da:ʒ] m mot., fig. running in, breaking in; **roder** [~'de] (1a) mot., fig. run in, break in.

rôd|er [ro'de] (1a) loiter; roam or prowl (about); **~eur** m, **-euse** f [~'dœːr, ~'dø:z] prowler.

rodomontade [rɔdɔmɔ̃'tad] f bragging; bluster.

rogatons F [rɔga'tɔ̃] m/pl. food: scraps.

rogne sl. [rɔɲ] f (bad) temper; F **se mettre en ~** blow one's top.

rogner [rɔ'ɲe] (1a) v/t. trim, pare; clip (claws, a. fig. the wings); cut down (s.o's salary); v/i. F be cross.

rognon usu. cuis. [rɔ'ɲɔ̃] m kidney.

rognures [rɔ'ɲy:r] f/pl. clippings.

rogue [rɔg] haughty, arrogant.

roi [rwa] m king (a. cards, chess); **le jour** (or **la fête**) **des ~s** Twelfth Night.

roitelet orn. [rwat'lɛ] m wren.

rôle [ro:l] m thea., fig. part, rôle, **à tour de ~** in turn.

romain [rɔ'mɛ̃] adj., su. Roman.

romaïque [rɔma'ik] adj., su./m ling. Romaic; modern Greek.

roman [rɔ'mɑ̃] **1.** adj. Romance; △ Norman (in England), Romanesque; **2.** su./m novel; ling. Romance.

romanc|e ♪ [rɔ'mɑ̃:s] f ballad; **~ier** m, **-ère** f [rɔmɑ̃'sje, ~'sjɛːr] novelist; fiction writer.

romand geog. [rɔ'mɑ̃]: **la Suisse ~e** French(-speaking) Switzerland.

roman|esque [rɔma'nɛsk] romantic; fantastic; fabulous; **~-feuilleton**, pl. **~s-feuilletons** [rɔmɑ̃fœj'tɔ̃] m serial (story).

romanichel m, **-elle** f [rɔmani'ʃɛl] gipsy; Romany.

roman|iser [rɔmani'ze] (1a) romanize; **~iste** [~'nist] su. romanist; **~tique** [rɔmɑ̃'tik] romantic; **~tisme** [~'tism] m romanticism.

romarin ☒ [rɔma'rɛ̃] m rosemary.

romp|re [rɔ̃:pr] (4a) v/t. break; break up (an alliance; the road, etc.); break off (a conversation, an engagement); burst (an artery, the river banks); **~ à** break (s.o.) in to; **~** break; snap; v/i. fig. break it off; fig. **~ avec** break with (s.o.); **~u** [rɔ̃'py] **1.** p.p. of **rompre**; **2.** adj. exhausted; **~ à** used to, experienced in; **~ de fatigue** worn out, tired out; **à bâtons ~s** desultory (conversation).

romsteck cuis. [rɔms'tɛk] m rumpsteak.

ronce [rɔ̃:s] f bramble; branch; **~ artificielle** barbed wire.

ronchon F [rɔ̃'ʃɔ̃] grumpy; **~ner** F [rɔ̃ʃɔ'ne] (1a) grumble, grouse; **~neur** F [~'nœːr] grumpy.

rond, e [rɔ̃, rɔ̃ːd] **1.** *adj.* round; plump; F tipsy; **2. rond** *adv.*: ☼, *fig.* **tourner ~** run smoothly; **3.** *su./m* circle, round, ring; *bread etc.*: slice; **en ~** in a circle; *su./f* ✗ *etc.* round; ♩ semibreve; **à la ~e** around; (*do s.th.*) in turn; **~-de-cuir**, *pl.* **~s-de-cuir** [~d'kɥiːr] *m* bureaucrat, *pej.* penpusher; **~elet** [rɔ̃d'lɛ] plumpish; nice round (*sum*); **~elle** [rɔ̃'dɛl] *f* disc; slice; ☼ washer; **~eur** [~'dœːr] *f* roundness; fullness; *figure*: curve; **~in** [~'dɛ̃] *m* log; round bar; **~point**, *pl.* **~s-points** [rɔ̃'pwɛ̃] *m* road: roundabout, *Am.* traffic circle.

ronfl|ant [rɔ̃'flɑ̃] snoring; rumbling (*noise*); *fig.* grand-sounding; **~ement** [~flə'mɑ̃] *m* snore; *noise*: roar(ing), boom(ing); hum; **~er** [~'fle] (1a) snore; roar, boom; hum; **~eur, -euse** [~'flœːr, ~'fløːz] *su.* snorer; *su./m* ♪ buzzer.

rong|er [rɔ̃'ʒe] (1l) gnaw (at); *worms etc.*: eat into; *fig.* fret (*s.o.'s heart*); **se ~ les ongles** bite one's nails; F **se ~ les sangs** fret (o.s.); *fig.* **rongé de** worn by (*care*); **~eur** [~'ʒœːr] *adj.*, *su./m zo.* rodent.

ronron(nement) [rɔ̃'rɔ̃ (~rɔn'mɑ̃)] *m* purr(ing); hum; **~ner** [~rɔ'ne] (1a) purr; hum.

roquet [rɔ'kɛ] *m* cur (*a. fig.*).

roquette ✗ [rɔ'kɛt] *f* rocket.

ros|ace △ [rɔ'zas] *f* rose window; (*ceiling*) rose; **~aire** *eccl.* [~'zɛːr] *m* rosary; **~âtre** [~'zaːtr] pinkish.

rosbif *cuis.* [rɔs'bif] *m* roast beef.

rose [roːz] **1.** *su./f* ❀ rose; *su./m* rose (colo[u]r), pink; **voir tout en ~** see things through rose-colo(u)red glasses. **2.** *adj.* pink; rosy; **rosé** [ro'ze] **1.** *adj.* pinkish; **2.** *su./m* wine: rosé.

roseau ❀ [rɔ'zo] *m* reed.

rosée [rɔ'ze] *f* dew.

ros|eraie [roz'rɛ] *f* rose garden; **~ette** [ro'zɛt] *f* ribbon: bow; rosette; **~ier** ❀ [~'zje] *m* rose bush.

rossard *sl.* [rɔ'saːr] *m* skunk, beast.

rosse [rɔs] **1.** *su./f* ✗ † *horse*: nag; *see* **rossard**; **2.** *adj.* nasty; beastly.

rossée [rɔ'se] *f* thrashing; **rosser** F [~] (1a) give (*s.o.*) a thrashing.

rossignol [rɔsi'ɲɔl] *m* nightingale; ❦ F piece of junk; ❦ skeleton key.

rossinante F [rɔsi'nãːt] *f* old horse.

rot *sl.* [ro] *m* belch.

rotatif, -ve [rɔta'tif, ~'tiːv] **1.** *adj.* rotary; **2.** *su./f typ.* rotary press; **~ion** [~'sjɔ̃] *f* rotation (*a.* ↗, ✈); *stocks etc.*: turn-over; **~oire** [~'twaːr] rota(to)ry.

roter *sl.* [rɔ'te] (1a) belch.

rôti *cuis.* [ro'ti] *m* roast (meat); **~ de bœuf** (**porc**) roast beef (pork).

rotin [rɔ'tɛ̃] *m* ❀ rattan; rattan cane.

rôtir [ro'tiːr] (2a) *vt/i.* roast; *cuis.* **faire ~**, **mettre à ~** roast; **rôtisserie** [~tis'ri] *f* grill room.

rotond|e △ [rɔ'tɔ̃ːd] *f* rotunda; 🚂 engine shed; **~ité** [~tɔdi'te] *f* rotundity; F stoutness.

rotor ↯, ✈ [rɔ'tɔːr] *m* rotor.

rotule [rɔ'tyl] *f* anat. kneecap; ☼ ball-and-socket joint; *mot.* knuckle.

roturier [rɔty'rje] **1.** *adj.* common, plebeian; **2.** *su.* commoner.

rouage ☼ [rwa'ʒ] *m* wheels pl. (*a. fig.*); work(s pl.); cog(wheel).

roublard F [ru'blaːr] wily, crafty; **~ise** [~blar'diːz] *f* craftiness.

roucouler [ruku'le] (1a) coo.

roue [ru] *f* wheel; **faire la ~** spread its tail (*peacock etc.*); *fig.* swagger; **~ avant** (**arrière**) front (back) wheel; *mot.* **~ de secours** (*or* **de rechange**) spare wheel; **rouler en ~ libre** freewheel; **mettre des bâtons dans les ~s de q.** put a spoke in s.o.'s wheel; **sur ~s** on wheels; **roué** [rwe] **1.** *su./m* rake, roué; **2.** *adj.* cunning, wily; **rouelle** [rwɛl] *f* round slice; *veal*: fillet.

roue|r [rwe] (1p) 🏛 *hist.* break on the wheel; *fig.* **~ de coups** thrash (*s.o.*) soundly; **~rie** [ru'ri] *f* cunning; trickery; **~t** [rwɛ] *m* spinning wheel; ☼ pulley wheel.

rouge [ruːʒ] **1.** *adj.* red (with, **de**); ruddy; red-hot (*metal*); **~ sang** blood-red; **2.** *adv.*: *fig.* **voir ~** see red; **3.** *su./m colour*: red; F red wine; **à ~ lèvres** lipstick; ☼ **au ~** at red heat, red-hot; *traffic*: **passer au ~** jump the lights; **se mettre du ~** put on rouge; **4.** *su. pol. person*: red; **~âtre** [ruʒ'atr] reddish; **~aud** F [~'ʒo] red-faced; **~-gorge** [ruʒ'gɔrʒ] *m* robin.

rougeole 🩺 [ru'ʒɔl] *f* measles *sg.*

roug|e-queue [ruʒ'kø] *m* redstart; **~eur** [~'ʒœːr] *f* redness; *face*: blush, flush; red spot; **~ir** [~'ʒiːr] (2a) *vt/i.* redden; turn red; *v/i.* blush; flush; *v/t.* make red-hot.

rouill|e [ruːj] f rust; ❦ mildew; **~é** [ru'je] rusty; ❦ mildewed; **~er** [~je] (1a) v/t. make rusty; **se ~** rust, get rusty; fig. get stiff; a. get out of practice; v/i. rust, get rusty; **~ure** [~jyːr] f rustiness; ❦ blight.

roul|ade [ru'lad] f roll; ♪ trill; **~age** [~'laːʒ] m ✗, mot. rolling; goods: carriage, haulage; **~ant** [~'lɑ̃] rolling; sliding (door); smooth (road); smooth-running (car); ✞ working (capital); F screamingly funny; **~eau** [~'lo] m roll; ⚙ etc. roller; coll; phot. spool; hair: curler; **~** (à pâtisserie) rolling pin; fig. **être au bout de son ~** be at one's wit's end; **~ement** [rul'mɑ̃] m rolling; ⚙ machine: running; rumble, rattle; ♪ drum: roll; ✞ capital: circulation; fig. alternation; ⚙ **~** (à billes) ball bearings pl.; mot. **bande f de ~** tread; ✗ **chemin** m **de ~** runway; par **~** in rotation; **~er** [ru'le] v/t. roll (along or about); v/t. fig. turn over (in one's mind); F cheat (s.o.); F **~ sa bosse** knock about the world; **se ~** roll (up); v/i. travel; mot. run; mot. drive; ✞ circulate (money); fig. **~ sur** turn on (conversation).

roulette [ru'lɛt] f small wheel; chair etc.: castor; tram: pastry wheel; tracing wheel; game: roulette; F **aller** (or **marcher**) **comme sur des ~s** go like clockwork; sp. **patin** m **à ~** roller-skate.

roul|is ⚓ [ru'li] m roll(ing), **~otte** f [~'lɔt] f (gipsy)van; mot. caravan, trailer.

roumain [ru'mɛ̃] adj., su. Rumanian.

roupiller F [rupi'je] (1a) snooze; sleep; **~on** F [~'jɔ̃] m snooze; nap.

rouquin F [ru'kɛ̃] m redhead.

rouspét|er F [ruspe'te] (1f) grouse; **~eur** F [~'tœːr] m grouser.

rouss|âtre [ru'saːtr] reddish; **~eur** [~'sœːr] f hair etc.: redness; **tache** f **de ~** freckle; **~i** [ru'si] m: **ça sent le ~** there's a smell of s.th. burning; fig. there's trouble ahead; **~ir** [ru'siːr] (2a) v/t. scorch; turn brown; cuis. **faire ~** scorch; turn brown; cuis. **faire ~**

route [rut] f road(way); path; route (a. ✗, ⚓, ✈); **en ~** on the way; ⚓ on her course; ✞ on the road; **en ~!** let's go!; **faire ~ sur** make for; **faire fausse ~** go the wrong way, fig. be on the wrong track; **mettre en ~** start (up).

routi|er [ru'tje] **1.** adj. road-...; **carte** f **routière** road map; **réseau** m **~** highway network; **2.** su./m mot. long-distance driver; cyclist: (road) racer; **~ne** [~'tin] f routine; par **~** as a matter of routine; **de ~** routine ...; **~nier** [~ti'nje] routine; who works to a routine.

rouvrir [ru'vriːr] (2f) reopen.

roux, rousse [ru, rus] **1.** adj. reddish(-brown); red (hair); **lune** f **rousse** April moon, **2.** su. sandy person; su./m colour: reddish-brown; cuis. brown sauce.

roy|al [rwa'jal] royal; kingly; **~aliste** [~ja'list] royalist; **~aume** [~'joːm] m kingdom; realm (a. fig.); **~auté** [~jo'te] f royalty; kingship.

ruade [rɥad] f horse: lashing out.

ruban [ry'bɑ̃] m ribbon; band; (measuring) tape; **~ adhésif** adhesive tape; ⚡ **~ isolant** insulating (Am. friction) tape; **~ magnétique** recording tape; **~ roulant** conveyor belt.

rubicond [rybi'kɔ̃] florid, ruddy.

rubigineux [rybiʒi'nø] rusty.

rubis [ry'bi] m min. ruby; watch: jewel; **payer ~ sur l'ongle** pay cash down.

rubrique [ry'brik] f journ. column; heading; rubric.

ruch|e [ryʃ] f (bee)hive; cost. a. **~é** [ry'ʃe] m ruche, trill; **~er** [~] m apiary.

rude [ryd] rough (cloth, path, sea, skin, wine); hard (blow, brush, climb, task, times, weather); harsh (voice, a. fig.); primitive (people etc.); fig. brusque; F enormous; **~ment** [~'mɑ̃] adv. roughly; hit etc.: hard; F extremely, awfully, real; **~sse** [ry'dɛs] f roughness etc.; see **rude.**

rudiment|s [rydi'mɑ̃] m/pl. rudiments; basic knowledge sg.; **~aire** [~mɑ̃'tɛːr] rudimentary.

rudoyer [rydwa'je] (1h) treat roughly; bully.

rue [ry] f street.

ruée [rɥe] f rush, stampede.

ruelle [rɥɛl] f lane, alley.

ruer [rɥe] (1n) v/i. kick (out); fig. **~ dans les brancards** become rebellious; v/t.: **se ~** fling o.s., rush, dash, pounce (on etc., **sur** etc.).

rugi|r [ry'ʒiːr] (2a) roar; **~ssement** [~ʒis'mɑ̃] m roar(ing).

rugosité [rygozi'te] f roughness, ruggedness; rough patch; **rugueux** [~'gø] rough, rugged.

ruin|e [rɥin] f ruin (a. fig.); fig. downfall; **tomber en ~s** fall in ruins; **~er** [rɥi'ne] (1a) ruin; wreck; **se ~** ruin o.s.; bankrupt o.s.; **~eux** [~'nø] ruinous; fig. extravagant; fig. disastrous.

ruisse|au [rɥi'so] m brook; stream (a. of blood); street, a. fig. pej.: gutter; **~ler** [rɥis'le] (1c) stream, run; trickle; drip; **~ de** stream with; **~let** [~'lɛ] m brooklet; **~llement** [rɥisɛl'mɑ̃] m streaming; trickling; dripping; light, jewels etc.: glitter, shimmer.

rumeur [ry'mœːr] f rumo(u)r; (distant) sound, hum(ming); hubbub; fig. rumblings pl. (of protest etc.).

rumin|ant zo. [rymi'nɑ̃] adj., su./m ruminant; **~er** [~'ne] (1a) v/t. ruminate; fig. ruminate on or over; v/i. zo., fig. chew the cud.

ruolz [ry'ɔls] m electroplate(d ware).

rupestre [ry'pɛstr] rock-...

rupin F [ry'pɛ̃] rich, wealthy.

rupteur ⚡ [ryp'tœːr] m circuit breaker; **rupture** [~'tyːr] f breaking; bursting; ✶ blood-vessel: rupture; bone: fracture; fig. break, breaking off, break-up, contract, promise: breach; fig. **en ~ (de ban) avec** at odds with; **être en ~ de stock** be out of stock.

rural [ry'ral] **1.** adj. rural, country...; **2.** su.: **les ruraux** country dwellers or people.

ruse [ryːz] f ruse, trick, wile; **~ de guerre** stratagem; **user de ~** resort to trickery; **rusé** [ry'ze] cunning, wily; **ruser** [~] (1a) use trickery.

rush [rœʃ] m sp. sprint; fig. rush.

russe [rys] adj., su. Russian.

rust|aud [rys'to] **1.** adj. boorish; **2.** su. boor; **~icité** [~tisi'te] f rusticity; boorishness; ⚘ hardiness; **~ique** [~'tik] rustic; fig. countrified, unrefined; ⚘ hardy; **~re** [rystr] = **rustaud**.

rut [ryt] m animals: rut(ting), heat.

rutilant [ryti'lɑ̃] gleaming.

rythm|e [ritm] m rhythm; fig. pace, tempo, rate; fig. **au ~ de** at the rate of; **~é** rhythmic(al); **~ique** [rit'mik] rhythmic.

S

sa [sa] see **son**[1].

sabbat [sa'ba] m eccl. Sabbath; fig. witches' sabbath; F fig. din, racket.

sable[1] [sɑːbl] m sand; **~ mouvant** quicksand; F **être sur le ~** be broke; be down and out.

sable[2] zo. [~] m sable.

sabl|é cuis. [sɑ'ble] m shortbread; **~er** [~'ble] (1a) sand; gravel; ⚘ sand-blast; F fig. swig (a drink); **~eux** [~'blø] sandy; **~ier** [~bli'e] m hourglass; cuis. egg timer; **~ière** [sɑbli'ɛːr] f sand quarry; **~onneux** [~'nø] sandy; gritty (fruit).

sabord ⚓ [sa'bɔːr] m port(hole); **~er** [~bɔr'de] ⚓ scuttle; fig. wind up, shut down.

sabot [sa'bo] m sabot, wooden shoe; zo. hoof; ⚙ (brake- etc.) shoe; F dud; toy: top; mot. **~ (de Denver)** (TM) Denver shoe; F fig. **dormir comme un ~** sleep like a log; **~age** [sabo'taːʒ] m sabotage; botching; **~er** [~'te] (1a) sabotage; botch, mess up; **~eur** m, **-euse** f [~'tœːr, ~'tøːz] ⚙ saboteur; botcher.

sabr|e [sɑːbr] m sabre; **~er** [sa'bre] (1a) sabre; slash; F botch, scamp; F fig. make drastic cuts in (a play etc.).

sac[1] [sak] m sack; bag; **~ à main** handbag; **~ de couchage** sleeping bag; **~ de voyage** travelling case; **~ en papier** paperbag; F **homme de ~ et de corde** thorough scoundrel; F **vider son ~** get it off one's chest.

sac[2] [~] m pillage, sacking.

saccad|e [sa'kad] f jerk; **par ~s** in jerks; haltingly; by fits and starts; **~é** [saka'de] jerky; irregular.

saccag|e [sa'kaːʒ] m havoc; **~er** [saka'ʒe] (1l) sack; create havock in.

sacerdo|ce [saser'dɔs] *m* priesthood; **~tal** [~dɔ'tal] priestly.

sach|ant [sa'ʃɑ̃] *p.pr.* of *savoir* 1; **~e** [sa] *1st p. sg. pres. sbj.* of *savoir* 1.

sachet [sa'ʃɛ] *m* small bag; **~ de thé** teabag.

sacoche [sa'kɔʃ] *f* (tool-, money-, saddle-, *etc.*) bag.

sacrament|al *eccl.* [sakramɑ̃'tal] *m* sacramental; **~el** [~'tɛl] *eccl.* sacramental; *fig.* ritual.

sacre [sakr] *m* king: anointing, coronation; *bishop*: consecration.

sacr|é [sa'kre] holy (*orders, scripture*); sacred (*spot, vessel, a. fig.*); *sl.* (*before su.*) damned; **un(e) ~é(e) ... a.** a hell of a ...; **~ement** *eccl.* [krɔ'mɑ̃] *m* sacrament; **derniers ~s** *pl.* last rites; **~er** [~'kre] (1a) *v/t.* anoint, crown (*a king*); consecrate (*a bishop*); *v/i.* F curse.

sacri|fice [sakri'fis] *m* sacrifice, *eccl.* **saint ~** Blessed Sacrament; **~fier** [~'fje] (1o) *v/t.* sacrifice; *v/i.*: **~ à** conform to; **~lège** [~'lɛːʒ] **1.** sacrilegious (*person*); **2.** *su./m* sacrilege.

sacripant [sakri'pɑ̃] *m* scoundrel.

sacrist|ain [sakris'tɛ̃] *m* sacristan; sexton; **~ie** *eccl.* [~'ti] *f* catholic: sacristy, *protestant:* vestry.

sacro-saint [sakrɔ'sɛ̃] sacrosanct.

sadi|que [sa'dik] **1.** *adj.* sadistic; **2.** *su.* sadist; **~sme** [~'dism] *m* sadism.

safran [sa'frɑ̃] **1.** *su./m* ♣, *culs.* saffron; ♣ crocus; **2.** *adj./inv.* saffron.

sagac|e [sa'gas] sagacious; shrewd; **~ité** [~gasi'te] *f* sagacity; shrewdness.

sage [saːʒ] **1.** *adj.* wise, sensible; well-behaved; good (*child*); **2.** *su./m* wise man; **~femme,** *pl.* **~s femmes** [saʒ'fam] *f* midwife; **~sse** [sa'ʒɛs] *f* wisdom; discretion; good behavio(u)r; *la ~* (*d'*)*après coup* hindsight.

sagittaire [saʒi'tɛːr] *su./m hist.* archer; *astr. le* ♀ Sagittarius.

saign|ant [sɛ'ɲɑ̃] bleeding; *cuis.* underdone, rare (*meat*); **~ée** [~'ɲe] *f* ♣ bleeding; *anat.* (*~ du bras*) bend of the arm; *drainage:* ditch; *fig.* resources: drain, loss(es *pl.*); ♀ (oil-)groove; **~er** [~'ɲe] (1b) *v/t.* bleed (*a. fig.*); ♀, *fig.* drain, tap.

saill|ant [sa'jɑ̃] **1.** *adj.* △ projecting; prominent; *fig.* salient; **~ie** [~'ji] *f* △ projection; *fig.* sally, witticism; *zo.* cov-

ering; *en ~* projecting; *faire ~* project, jut out, protrude.

saillir [sa'jiːr] (2a) *v/i.* project, jut out, stand out, protrude; *v/t. zo.* cover.

sain [sɛ̃] healthy (*a. climate etc.*); sound (*doctrine, fruit, view,* ♥, ♣, *etc.*); wholesome; *~ d'esprit* sane; *~ et sauf* safe and sound.

saindoux *cuis.* [sɛ̃'du] *m* lard.

saint [sɛ̃] **1.** *adj.* holy; *eccl.* saintly; consecrated; ♀ *Jean* St. John; F *toute la sainte semaine* all the blessed week; **2.** *su.* saint; **~bernard** *zo.* [sɛ̃bɛr'naːr] *m/inv.* St. Bernard; **♀-Esprit** [~tɛs'pri] *m* Holy Ghost; **~eté** [sɛ̃tə'te] *f* holiness, saintliness; *fig.* sanctity.

saint...: ~frusquin F [sɛ̃frys'kɛ̃] *m/inv.* possessions *pl.*; *tout le ~* the whole caboodle; **~glinglin** F [~glɛ̃'glɛ̃]: *à la ~* never; **♀-Père** [~'pɛːr] *m* the Holy Father, *the* pope; **♀-Siège** [~'sjɛːʒ] *m* the Holy See; **♀-Sylvestre** [~sil'vɛstrə]: *la ~* New Year's Eve.

sais [sɛ] *1st p. sg. pres.* of *savoir* 1.

sais|ie [sɛ'zi] *f* seizure (*a.* 🖥); 🖥 distraint; **~ir** [~'ziːr] (2a) take hold of; grab *or* catch (hold of); seize, grasp; *fig.* understand, grasp, F get; 🖥 seize, distrain upon (*goods*); *cuis.* fry quickly; *~ q. de* refer (*s.th.*) to s.o.; *se ~ de* seize upon (*a. fig.*); **~issable** [~zi'sabl] perceptible; **~issant** [~zi'sɑ̃] **1.** *adj.* striking; gripping (*scene, speech*); piercing (*cold*); *su./m* 🖥 distrainer; **~issement** [~zis'mɑ̃] *m* sudden chill; shock, emotion.

saison [sɛ'zɔ̃] *f* season; *tourist season;* *haute (basse) ~* high (slack) season; *(hors) de ~* (un)seasonable, (in)opportune; *hors ~* out of season; off-season (*tariff etc.*); **~nier** [~zɔ'nje] seasonal.

salad|e [sa'lad] *f* salad; lettuce; *fig.* jumble; **~ier** [~la'dje] *m* salad bowl.

salaire [sa'lɛːr] *m* wage (s *pl.*); pay; *fig.* reward; *~ de base* basic wage; *les gros ~s* the top wages.

salaison [salɛ'zɔ̃] *f* salting, curing.

salamandre [sala'mɑ̃dr] *f* zo. salamander; ♀ slow-combustion stove.

salant [sa'lɑ̃] *adj./m* salt-...

salari|at [sala'rja] *m* salaried *or* wage-earning class(es *pl.*); **~é** [~'rje] **1.** *adj.* wage-earning; paid (*work*); **2.** *su.* wage-earner.

salaud s. [sa'lo] m dirty person; fig. bastard; **sale** [sal] dirty; fig. foul.

salé [sa'le] **1.** adj. salt(ed); fig. spicy (story); biting (comment etc.); F stiff (price etc.); **2.** su./m salt pork.

saler [sa'le] (1a) salt (a. fig.); cure (bacon); fig. fleece, overcharge (s.o.).

saleté [sal'te] f dirt(iness), filth(iness); fig. indecency; dirty trick.

salière [sa'ljɛːr] f saltcellar.

salin, e [sa'lɛ̃, ~'lin] **1.** adj. saline, salty; salt (air); **2.** su./m salt marsh; su./f salt works sg; salt marsh.

salir [sa'liːr] (2a) soil; fig. sully; **~ssant** [~li'sɑ̃] dirty(ing); easily soiled.

salivaire [sali'vɛːr] salivary; **~e** [sa'liːv] f saliva; F **perdre sa ~** waste one's breath; **~er** [~li've] (1a) salivate.

salle [sal] f hall; (large) room; hospital: ward; thea. auditorium, F house; **~ à manger** dining room; **~ d'attente** waiting room; **~ de bain(s) bathroom; ~ de classe** classroom; **~ des pas perdus** waiting-hall.

salmigondis [salmigɔ̃'di] m cuis. ragout; fig. miscellany.

salmis cuis. [sal'mi] m salmi; ragout (of roasted game).

salon [sa'lɔ̃] m living or sitting room; lounge; ♀ exhibition, show; fig. **~s** pl. fashionable circles; **~ de thé** tearoom.

salope sl. [sa'lɔp] tart; bitch; **~rie** F [salɔ'pri] f filth; rubbish, trash; bungled piece of work; mess; **~s** pl. smut sg.; **faire une ~ à** play a dirty trick on; **~r** F [~'pe] mess up, sl. goof up; **~tte** [~'pɛt] f overall(s pl.); dungarees pl.

salpêtre [sal'pɛːtr] m saltpetre.

saltimbanque [saltɛ̃'bɑ̃:k] m (travelling) showman; fig. charlatan.

salubre [sa'lyːbr] salubrious, healthy; wholesome; **~ité** [~lybri'te] f salubrity; wholesomeness; **~ publique** public health.

saluer [sa'lɥe] (1n) great (a. fig.); say hello or goodbye to; salute.

salure [sa'lyːr] f saltiness; salt tang.

salut [sa'ly] m safety; eccl., a. fig. salvation; greeting; bow; ✗ salute; **~!** hello, hi!; see you!, bye!; **~aire** [saly'tɛːr] salutary, beneficial; **~ation** [~ta'sjɔ̃] f greeting; bow; **agréez mes meilleures ~s** end of letter: yours faithfully.

salve [salv] f ✗, fig. salvo.

samedi [sam'di] m Saturday.

sana(torium) [sana(tɔr'jɔm)] m sanatorium, Am. sanitarium.

sanctifier [sɑ̃kti'fje] (1o) sanctify; hallow; observe (the Sabbath).

sanction [sɑ̃k'sjɔ̃] f sanction (a. pol.); approval; penalty, punishment; **~ner** [~sjɔ'ne] (1a) sanction; approve; punish.

sanctuaire [sɑ̃k'tɥɛːr] m sanctuary.

sandale [sɑ̃'dal] f sandal.

sang [sɑ̃] m blood; biol. **à ~ chaud (froid)** warm-blooded (cold-blooded) (animal); F **avoir le ~ chaud** be quick-tempered; ⚕ **coup m de ~** (apoplectic) fit; **droit m du ~** birthright; **se faire du mauvais ~** worry; **~froid** [~'frwa] m composure, self-control; **de ~** in cold blood; **~lant** [~'glɑ̃] bloody; blood-covered; blood-red; fig. bitter (attack, tears etc.); deadly (insult).

sangle [sɑ̃'gl] f strap; (saddle-)girth; **~er** [sɑ̃'gle] (1a) strap (up); girth (a horse).

sanglier zo. [sɑ̃gli'e] m wild boar.

sanglot [sɑ̃'glo] m sob; **~er** [~glɔ'te] (1a) sob.

sangsue zo., fig. [sɑ̃'sy] f leech.

sanguin [sɑ̃'gɛ̃] blood...; sanguine (temper); **~aire** [~gi'nɛːr] bloodthirsty (person); bloody (fight); **~e** [~'gin] f blood orange; red chalk (drawing); **~olent** [~ginɔ'lɑ̃] bloody, **~** sanguinolent.

sanitaire [sani'tɛːr] **1.** adj. sanitary; **2.** su./m (bathroom) plumbing.

sans [sɑ̃] prp. without; free from or of; ...less; un...; **~ hésiter** without hesitating or hesitation; **non ~ peine** not without difficulty; **~ bretelles** strapless; **~ cesse** ceaseless; **~ exemple** unparalleled; **~ faute** without fail; faultless; **~ le sou** penniless; **~ que** (sbj.) without (ger.); **~ cela, ~ quoi** but for that; **~abri** [~za'bri] m/inv. homeless person; **~façon** [~fa'sɔ̃] m/inv. straightforwardness, bluntness; **~fil** [~'fil] f/inv. wireless message; **~filiste** [~fi'list] su. wireless enthusiast or operator; **~gêne** [~'ʒɛn] su./inv. off-handed or unceremonious person; su./m/inv. pej. off-handedness; F cheek; **~le-sou** F [~lɔ'su] su./inv. penniless person; **~parti** pol. [~par'ti] su./inv. independent.

sansonnet *orn.* [sɑ̃sɔ'nɛ] *m* starling.

sans...: **~-souci** [sɑ̃su'si] carefree; unconcerned; **~-travail** [~tra'vaj] *su./inv.* unemployed person.

santal ♀ [sɑ̃'tal] *m* sandalwood.

santé [sɑ̃'te] *f* health; **à votre ~!** cheers!; **être en bonne ~** be well; **service m de (la) ~** Health Service, ✗ medical service.

saoul [su] *see* **soûl**.

sape [sap] *f* ✗ *etc.* sap(ping); undermining (*a. fig.*); **saper** [sa'pe] (1a) sap, undermine (*a. fig.*).

sapeur ✗ [sa'pœːr] *m* sapper; pioneer; **~-pompier**, *pl.* **~s-pompiers** [~pɔ̃'pje] *m* fireman; **sapeurs-pompiers** *pl.* fire brigade.

saphir *min.* [sa'fiːr] *m* sapphire.

sapin [sa'pɛ̃] *m* fir (tree); F **toux f qui sent le ~** churchyard cough; **~ière** ♀ [~pi'njɛːr] *f* fir forest.

sapristi! [sapris'ti] *int.* hang it!

sarbacane [sarba'kan] *f* blow-pipe.

sarcasme [sar'kasm] *m* sarcasm; **sarcastique** [~kas'tik] sarcastic.

sarcl|er [sar'kle] weed (out) (*a. fig.*); **~oir** [~'klwaːr] *m* hoe.

sarcophage [sarkɔ'faːʒ] *m* sarcophagus.

sard|e [sard] *adj.*, *su.* Sardinian; **~ine** [sar'din] *f* sardine; ✗ F stripe.

sardonique [sardɔ'nik] sardonic.

sarigue *zo.* [sa'rig] *m* opossum.

sarment [sar'mɑ̃] *m* vine shoot.

sarrau, *pl. a.* **-s** [sa'ro] *m* overall.

sarriette ♀ [sa'rjɛt] *f* savory.

sas [sɑ] *m* sieve, screen; *sluse*: lock; ◎ airlock; **~ser** [su'se] (1a) ♣ pass (*a boat*) through a lock; ◎ sift (*a. fig.*), screen.

satan|é F [sata'ne] confounded; **~ique** [~'nik] satanic; diabolical.

satellite [satɛl'it] *m* satellite; **mettre en orbite** put (*a rocket*) into orbit; *fig.* make a satellite of; **~te** [~'lit] *m* satellite.

satiété [sasje'te] *f* satiety.

satin *tex.* [sa'tɛ̃] *m* satin; **~é** [sati'ne] satin(-like), satiny; **~er** [~'ne] (1a) satin, glaze; surface (*paper*); *phot.* burnish; **~ette** *tex.* [~'nɛt] *f* sateen.

satir|e [sa'tiːr] *f* satire (on, **contre**); lampoon; satirizing; **~ique** [sati'rik] **1.** *adj.* satiric(al); **2.** *su./m* satirist; **~iser** [~ri'ze] (1a) satirize.

satisfaction [satisfak'sjɔ̃] *f* satisfaction;

fig. amends *pl.* (for **pour, de**); **~faire** [~'fɛːr] (4r) *v/t.* satisfy; *v/i.*: **~ à** satisfy; *fig.* comply with, meet; *fig.* fulfil; **~faisant** [~fə'zɑ̃] satisfactory, satisfying; **~fait** [~'fɛ] satisfied, pleased (with, **de**).

saturer [saty're] (1a) saturate.

saturnisme ♣ [satyr'nism] *m* lead poisoning.

sauc|e [soːs] *f* sauce; gravy; **~ée** F [so'se] *f* downpour; **~er** [so'se] (1k) dip in the sauce (*bread*); wipe (*one's plate*); F **se faire ~** get soaked; **~ière** [~'sjɛːr] *f* sauceboat; gravy boat.

saucisse [so'sis] *f* (*fresh*) sausage.

saucisson [sosi'sɔ̃] *m* (*dry*) sausage; **~ner** F [~sɔ'ne] (1a) have a snack; picknick.

sauf¹, sauve [sof, soːv] *adj.* unharmed, unhurt, unscathed; intact; safe.

sauf² [sof] *prp.* except, but; save; **~ erreur ou omission** errors and omissions excepted; **~ imprévu** except for unforeseen circumstances; **~ que** (*sbj.*) except that (*ind.*).

sauf-conduit [sofkɔ̃'dɥi] *m* safe-conduct.

sauge ♀, *cuis.* [soːʒ] *f* sage.

saugrenu [sogrə'ny] absurd.

saule ♀ [soːl] *m* willow.

saumâtre [so'maːtr] brackish, briny; F **la trouver ~** not to be amused.

saumon [so'mɔ̃] **1.** *su./m icht.* salmon; ◎ pig, ingot; **2.** *adj./inv.* salmon-pink; **~é** [somɔ'ne] salmon.

saumure [so'myːr] *f* pickling brine.

sauna [so'na] *m* sauna.

saupoudrer [sopu'dre] (1a) sprinkle, powder, dust (with, **de**).

saur [soːr] *adj./m*: **hareng m ~** smoked red herring.

saurai [so're] *1st p. sg. fut. of* **savoir 1**.

saut [so] *m* leap, jump; (*water*)fall; **~ en hauteur (longueur)** high (long) jump; *sp.* **~ périlleux** somersault; **faire le ~** give way; take the plunge; F **faire un ~ chez X** drop in on X; **par ~s et par bonds** by leaps and bounds; *fig.* jerkily; **~-de-lit**, *pl.* **~s-de-lit** *const.* [~'d'li] *m* dressing gown; **saute** [soːt] *f* price, temperature; jump; sudden change; *wind*, *a. fig.*: shift.

saut|e-mouton *sp. etc.* [sotmu'tɔ̃] *m* leapfrog; **~er** [so'te] (1a) **1.** *v/i.* jump, leap (*a. fig.* for joy, **de joie**); ♣ shift (*wind*); blow up (*explosive etc.*); ⚡ blow (*fuse*); come off (*button*); F be fired, get the sack; **~ aux yeux** be obvious; **faire ~** blow (*s.th.*) up; spring (*a trap*); burst (*a lock*); *fig.* dismiss, F fire; *fig. pol.* bring down (*the government*); *v/t.* jump (over); *fig.* skip, omit; ⚡ blow (*a fuse*); toss; *cuis.* fry quickly; **~erelle** *zo.* [~'trɛl] *f* grasshopper; **~erie** [~'tri] *f* hopping; F dance; **~eur, ~euse** [~'tœːr, ~'tøːz] **1.** *adj.* jumping; *fig.* unreliable; **2.** *su. sp.* jumper; *fig.* unreliable individual; *su./f cuis.* shallow pan; **~iller** [~ti'je] (1a) hop, jump (about); throb (*heart*).

sautoir [so'twaːr] *m sp.* jumping pit; long neck chain; **en ~** crosswise.

sauvag|e [so'vaːʒ] **1.** *adj.* wild (*a. zo.*, ♀, *a. fig.*); savage; *fig.* shy, unsociable; *fig.* unauthorized, illegal; wildcat (*strike*); **2.** *su.* (*f a. ~esse* [~va'ʒɛs]) savage; unsociable person; **~erie** [~vaʒ'ri] *f* savagery; barbarity; *fig.* unsociability; **~ine** [~'ʒin] *f coll.* waterfowl *pl.*

sauvegard|e [sov'gard] *f* safeguard; protection; **~er** [~gar'de] (1a) safeguard.

sauv|e-qui-peut [sovki'pø] *m* stampede; headlong flight; **~er** [so've] (1a) save, rescue (from, *de*); keep up (*appearances*); ♣ salvage; **sauve qui peut!** every man for himself!; **se ~** run away; F be off; **~etage** [sov'taːʒ] *m* rescue; **bateau** *m* (*or* **canot** *m*) **de ~** lifeboat; **~eteur** [~'tœːr] *m* rescuer; **~ette** [~'vɛt]: **à la ~** hurriedly, hastily; illicit(ly); **~eur** [so'vœːr] *m* deliverer; *eccl.* ♀ Savio(u)r.

savamment [sava'mɑ̃] *adv.* learnedly; cleverly; (*speak*) knowingly.

savane ✔ [sa'van] *f* savanna(h).

savant [sa'vɑ̃] **1.** *adj.* learned (in, *en*); scholarly; performing (*dog*); *fig.* clever; skilful; studied; **2.** *su./m* scholar; scientist.

savarin *cuis.* [sava'rɛ̃] *m* rum cake.

savate [sa'vat] *f* old shoe; *sp.* French *or* foot boxing; F bungler.

saveur [sa'vœːr] *f* flavo(u)r; *fig.* savo(u)r; pungency; **sans ~** insipid.

savoir [sa'vwaːr] **1.** (3i) *v/t.* know; be aware of; know how to (*inf.*), be able to; learn, get to know; **~ l'anglais** know English; **~ vivre** know how to behave; **à ~** namely, that is; **autant (pas) que je**

sache as far as I know (not that I know of); **faire ~ qch. à q.** inform s.o. of s.th.; **je ne saurais** (*inf.*) I cannot (*inf.*), I could not (*inf.*); **ne ~ que** (*inf.*) not to know what to (*inf.*); **sans le ~** unintentionally; **se ~** be known, come out; *v/i.* know; know how; **(à) ~** namely, that is; **2.** *su./m* knowledge, learning, erudition, scholarship; **~-faire** [savwar'fɛːr] *m/inv.* ability; know-how; **~-vivre** [~'viːvr] *m/inv.* good manners *pl.*; (good) breeding.

savon [sa'vɔ̃] *m* soap; F *fig.* telling-off; **~ à barbe** shaving soap; **bulle** *f* **de ~** soap bubble; **donner un coup de ~ à** give (*s.th.*) a wash; F **passer un ~ à** tell s.o. off; **~nage** [savo'naːʒ] *m* washing, soaping; **~ner** [~'ne] (1a) soap; wash; lather; F dress (*s.o.*) down; **~nette** [savo'nɛt] *f* (cake of) toilet soap; **~neux** [~'nø] soapy.

savour|er [savu're] (1a) enjoy; *fig.* savo(u)r; **~eux** [~'rø] tasty, savo(u)ry; *fig.* enjoyable; *fig.* racy.

sbire [sbiːr] *m* henchman; cop.

scabieux [ska'bjø] scabby; scabious.

scabreux [ska'brø] risky; ticklish; delicate; risqué, improper.

scalpel ⚕ [skal'pɛl] *m* scalpel.

scandal|e [skɑ̃'dal] *m* scandal; *fig.* disgrace, shame; **faire ~** create a scandal; **~eux** [skɑ̃da'lø] scandalous; **~iser** [~li'ze] (1a) shock, scandalize; **se ~ de** be shocked at.

scander [skɑ̃'de] (1a) scan (*a verse*); stress, mark, punctuate *words etc.*

scandinave [skɑ̃di'naːv] *adj.*, *su.* Scandinavian.

scaphandr|e [ska'fɑ̃ːdr] *m* diving suit; space siut; **~ autonome** aqualung; **casque** *m* **de ~** diver's helmet; **~ier** [~fɑ̃dri'e] *m* deep-sea diver.

scarabée *zo.* [skara'be] *m* beetle.

scarifier [skari'fje] (1o) scarify.

scarlatine [skarla'tin] *f* (*a.* **fièvre** *f* **~**) scarlet fever.

sceau [so] *m* seal (*a. fig.*); *fig.* stamp, mark.

scélérat [sele'ra] **1.** *adj.* villainous; outrageous; **2.** *su.* villain, scoundrel.

scell|és ⚖ [sɛ'le] *m/pl.* seals; **~er** [~] (1a) seal; seal up.

scénario [sena'rjo] *m thea.*, *cin.* scenario; *cin.* script; *fig.* pattern; **scénariste**

[~'rist] su. scenario writer; script writer; **scène** [sɛn] f thea. stage; fig. drama; play, a. F fig.: scene; **scénique** [se'nik] theatrical; scenic; stage...

sceptique [sɛp'tik] **1.** adj. sceptical, Am. skeptical; **2.** su. sceptic, Am. skeptic.

sceptre [sɛptr] m sceptre; fig. power.

schéma [ʃe'ma] m diagram; sketch; outline; **~tique** [~ma'tik] schematic.

schisme [ʃism] m schism.

schiste geol. [ʃist] m shale, schist.

schnaps F [ʃnaps] m brandy.

schnock sl. [[nok] m blockhead.

sciatique ⚕ [sja'tik] f sciatica.

scie [si] f saw; sl. bore, nuisance; fig. catchword; fig. catch or hit tune; ~ **à chantourner** jigsaw; ~ **à ruban** bandsaw.

scie|mment [sja'mã] adv. knowingly, intentionally; **~nce** [sjã:s] f learning; science; ~**o** pl. **naturelles** natural science ⚕: **homme** m **de** ~ scientist; ~**nti fique** [sjãti'fik] **1.** adj. scientific; **2.** su. scientist.

scier [sje] (1o) saw (off); F ~ **le dos à** bore stiff; **~ie** [si'ri] f sawmill.

scinder [sɛ̃'de] (1a) (a. **se ~**) split (up).

scintill|ation [sɛ̃tilla'sjɔ̃] f, **~ement** [~tij'mã] m sparkling; star: twinkling; cin. flicker(ing); **~er** [~ti'je] (1a) sparkle, scintillate (a. fig.).

scion ✒ [sjɔ̃] m shoot, scion.

sciss|ion [si'sjɔ̃] f split, division; **faire ~** secede, split away; **~ure** [si'sy:r] f fissure, cleft.

sciure ⊙ [sjy:r] f (saw)dust.

sclér|eux ⚕ [skle'rø] sclerous; **~ose** [~'ro:z] f sclerosis; **~otique** anat. [~rɔ'tik] adj., su./f sclerotic.

scola|ire [skɔ'lɛ:r] school...; **~rité** [~lari'te] f schooling, **frais** m/pl. **de ~** school fees; **~stique** phls. [~las'tik] adj., su./m scholastic.

scolopendre [skɔlɔ'pɑ̃:dr] f zo. centipede; ♀ hart's-tongue.

scorbut [skɔr'by] m scurvy; **~ique** ⚕ [~by'tik] scorbutic.

scorie [skɔ'ri] f slag; iron: dross.

scorpion zo. [skɔr'pjɔ̃] m scorpion.

scoutisme [sku'tism] m boy-scout movement, scouting.

scribe [skrib] m hist. (Jewish) scribe; copyist; F penpusher.

script cin. [skript] m film script; **~-girl** [~'gœ:rl] f continuity girl.

scrofule ⚕ [skrɔ'fyl] f scrofula.

scrupul|e [skry'pyl] m scruple; **avoir des ~s à** (inf.) have scruples about (ger.); **sans ~** unscrupulous(ly adv.); **~eux** [~py'lø] scrupulous.

scrut|ateur [skryta'tœ:r] **1.** adj. searching; **2.** su./m scrutinizer; ballot: teller; **~er** [~'te] (1a) scrutinize; examine, lock into; search; **~in** [~'tɛ̃] m poll; ballot.

sculpt|er [skyl'te] (1a) sculpture, carve (out of, dans); **~eur** [~'tœ:r] m sculptor; **~ure** [~'ty:r] f sculpture; ~ **sur bois** wood carving.

se [sə] **1.** pron./rfl. oneself; himself, herself, itself; themselves; to express passive: ~ **vendre** be sold; ~ **roser** be(come) pink; **2.** pron./recip. each other, one another.

séan|ce [se'ã:s] f seat; sitting (a. paint.); session; cin. performance; fig. ~ **tenante** immediately, **~t** [~'ã] **1.** adj. fitting, seemly; becoming (to, **à**); **2.** su./m F posterior; **se mettre sur son ~** sit up.

seau [so] m pail, bucket.

sébile [se'bil] f wooden bowl.

sec, sèche [sɛk, sɛʃ] **1.** adj. dry (a. wine, fig. remark); dried; lean, sharp (blow, answer, tone); fig. harsh; barren; ✝ dead (loss); **2.** sec adv.: F **aussi** ~ straight away; **s'arrêter** ~ stop short; **boire** ~ drink straight; **rire** ~ laugh harshly; **3.** su./m: **à** ~ dried (up), dry; F broke; **4.** su./f F cigarette.

sécession [sese'sjɔ̃] f secession; **faire ~** secede (from, **de**); hist. **la guerre de 2** the American Civil War.

séch|age [se'ʃa:ʒ] m drying; **~er** [se'ʃe] (1f) v/i. dry (up or out); **faire ~** dry; v/t. dry (up or out), F cut (a lecture); **~eresse** [seʃ'rɛs] f dryness; drought; tone: curtness; fig. coldness; **~oir** [~'fwa:r] m drying room; ⊙ drier; towel rack.

second, e [sə'gɔ̃, ~'gɔ̃:d] **1.** adj. second (a. fig.); **2.** su. (the) second; su./m second in command; box. second; ⌂ second floor, Am. third floor; su./f time: second (a. ♪); 🚂 second (class); **~aire** [səgɔ̃'dɛ:r] secondary, subordinate; **~er** [~'de] (1a) second, support.

secouer [sə'kwe] (1p) shake; shake down or off; knock out (a pipe); F fig. shake (s.o.) up.

secour|able [səku'rabl] helpful; **~ir** [~'ri:r] (2i) aid, assist, help; **~iste** [~'rist] *su.* first-aid worker; **~s** [sə'kuːr] *m* help, assistance, aid; **au ~!** help!; **de ~** relief-...; spare (*wheel*); emergency (*exit etc.*); **~ premier ~** first aid.

secousse [sə'kus] *f* jolt, bump, jerk; ⚡, *a. fig.* shock.

secret, -ète [sə'krɛ, ~'krɛt] **1.** *adj.* secret, concealed; *fig.* reticent; **2.** *su./m* secret; secrecy; ⚏ solitary confinement; **~ postal** secrecy of correspondence; **en ~** in secret; **secrétaire** [səkre'tɛːr] *su.* secretary; *su./m* writing desk; **~ d'Etat** Secretary of State; **secrétariat** [~ta'rja] *m* secretary's office.

sécrét|er *physiol.* [sekre'te] (1f) secrete; **~ion** [~'sjɔ̃] *f* secretion.

sectaire [sɛk'tɛːr] *adj., su.* sectarian; **secte** [sɛkt] *f* sect.

secteur [sɛk'tœːr] *m* sector; district, area; ⚡ mains *pl.*; ⚓ quadrant.

section [sɛk'sjɔ̃] *f* section; ⚙ tube: bore; *bus, tram:* stage; **~ner** [~'ne] (1a) divide (up) (into sections); cut (up), sever.

sécul|aire [seky'lɛːr] secular (= *once in 100 years*); century-old; **~ariser** [~lari'ze] (1a) secularize; **~arité** [~lari'te] *f* secularity; **~ier** [~'lje] *adj. su./m* secular.

sécuri|ser [sekyri'ze] (1a) make (*s.o.*) feel (more) secure; **~té** [~'te] *f* security; *admin., mot., a.* ⚙ safety; **~ routière** road safety.

sédatif ⚕ [seda'tif] *adj., su./m* sedative.

sédentaire [sedã'tɛːr] sedentary.

sédiment [sedi'mã] *m* sediment.

séditi|eux [sedi'sjø] seditious; insurgent (*a. su.*); **~on** [~'sjɔ̃] *f* sedition, insurrection.

séduc|teur [sedyk'tœːr] **1.** *adj.* seductive; tempting; **2.** *su.* seducer; **~ion** [~'sjɔ̃] *f* seduction; *fig.* attraction, appeal, seductiveness.

sédui|re [se'dɥiːr] (4h) seduce; *fig.* appeal to, tempt, fascinate; **~sant** [~dɥi'zã] seductive; *fig.* appealing, tempting; *fig.* attractive.

segment [sɛg'mã] *m* segment; **~er** [~mã'te] (1a) segment.

ségrégation [segrega'sjɔ̃] *f* segregation (*a. pol.*), isolation.

seiche *zo.* [sɛʃ] *f* cuttlefish.

séide [se'id] *m* henchman.

seigle 🌾 [sɛgl] *m* rye.

seigneur [sɛ'nœːr] *m* lord; *eccl.* **le ⚤** the Lord; **~ie** [sɛɲœ'ri] *f* lordship; manor.

sein [sɛ̃] *m* breast; **au ~ de** within; in the midst of.

seing 🖋 [sɛ̃] *m* signature; **acte** *m* **sous ~ privé** simple contract.

séisme [se'ism] *m* earthquake.

seize [sɛːz] sixteen; *date, title:* sixteenth; **seizième** [sɛ'zjɛm] sixteenth.

séjour [se'ʒuːr] *m* stay; *place:* abode, dwelling; **permis** *m* **de ~** residence permit; **~nant** *m*, **e** *f* [~ʒur'nã, ~'nãt] visitor, guest; **~ner** [~ʒur'ne] (1a) stay, reside; stop; remain.

sel [sɛl] *m* salt; *fig.* wit, spice.

select [se'lɛkt] select, exclusive.

sélect|er F [selɛk'te] (1a) choose; **~eur** [~'tœːr] *m radio:* selector; ⚙ selective; **~if** [~'tif] *adj.* selective; **~ion** [~'sjɔ̃] *f* selection; **~ionner** [~sjɔ'ne] (1a) select.

self [sɛlf] *m* self-service restaurant.

sell|e [sɛl] *f* saddle; *physiol.* **~s** *pl.* stools; **aller à la ~** pass a motion; **~er** [se'le] (1a) saddle; **~ette** [~'lɛt] *f*: **être sur la ~** on the carpet; **~ier** [se'lje] *m* saddler.

selon [sə'lɔ̃] **1.** *prp.* according to; **~ moi** in my opinion; **c'est ~!** that depends!; **2.** *cj.:* **~ que** according as.

semailles [sə'maːj] *f/pl.* sowing *sg.*

semaine [sə'mɛn] *f* week; week's pay; **à la ~** by the week; **en ~** during the week.

sémantique [semã'tik] **1.** *adj.* semantic; **2.** *su./f* semantics *pl.*

sémaphore [sema'fɔːr] *m* semaphore; 🚩 semaphore signal.

sembl|able [sã'blabl] **1.** *adj.* similar (to, à); alike; like; such; **2.** *su.* like, equal; *su./m:* **nos ~s** *pl.* our fellow-men; **~ablement** [~blablə'mã] *adv.* in like manner; **~ant** [~'blã] *m* semblance; *fig.* show (of, **de**); **faux ~** pretence; **faire ~** be (just) pretending; **faire ~ de** (*inf.*) pretend to (*inf.*); make a show of (*ger.*); **ne faire ~ de rien** pretend to take no notice; act the innocent; **sans faire ~ de rien** as if nothing had happened; surreptitiously; **~er** [~'ble] (1a) seem, appear; **il me semble** I think.

semelle [sə'mɛl] *f shoe:* sole; *stocking:* foot; **remettre des ~s à** re-sole.

sem|ence [sə'mãːs] *f* seed (*a. fig.*); ⚙ (tin)tack; **~er** [~'me] (1d) sow (*a. fig. discord etc.*); scatter; *fig.* spread (*a rumour*); F lose; F shake off, drop (*s.o.*).

semestr|e [sə'mɛstr] *m* half-year; six

months' duty *or* pay; *univ.* term; **~iel** [~mɛstri'ɛl] half-yearly.

semeur [sə'mœːr] *su.* sower.

semi... [səmi] semi...; **~brève** ♪ [~'brɛːv] *f* semibreve, whole note; **~conducteur** ⚡ [~kɔ̃dyk'tœːr] *m* semi-conductor.

sémillant [semi'jɑ̃] vivacious.

séminaire [semi'nɛːr] *m* seminary; *fig.* training centre; *univ.* seminar.

semi-remorque [səmirə'mɔrk] *f* articulated lorry, *Am.* trailer truck.

semis ⚘ [sə'mi] *m* sowing; seedling; seed-bed.

semi-ton ♪ [səmi'tɔ̃] *m* semitone.

semoir ⚘ [sə'mwaːr] *m* seeder

semonce [sə'mɔ̃ːs] *f fig.* reprimand; ⚓ **coup** *m* **de ~** warning shot.

semoule *cuis.* [sə'mul] *f* semolina.

sempiternel [sɑ̃pitɛr'nɛl] everlasting.

sénat [se'na] *m* senate; **~eur** [sena'tœːr] *m* senator.

sénile ⚕ [se'nil] senile; **sénilité** ⚕ [~nili'te] *f* senility, senile decay.

sens [sɑ̃ːs] *m fig. smell etc.*: sense; *fig.* opinion; understanding, judg(e)ment; meaning, direction, way; **~ de la musique** musicianship; **~ de l'orientation** sense of direction; **~ dessus dessous** upside down; **~ devant derrière** back to front; **~ interdit** no entry; **~ moral** moral sense; **~ unique** one-way street; **à mon ~** in my view; **le bon ~, le ~ commun** common sense; **plaisirs** *m/pl.* **des ~** sensual pleasures; **~ation** [sɑ̃sa'sjɔ̃] *f* sensation; (*physical*) feeling; **à ~** sensational (*news*); **~ationnel** [~sjo'nɛl] sensational; F terrific; **~é** [sɑ̃'se] sensible.

sensibil|iliser [sɑ̃sibili'ze] (1a) sensitize; **~ilité** [~'te] *f* sensitiveness (*a. phot.*); *fig.* feeling, compassion; **~le** [sɑ̃'sibl] sensitive; tender (*flesh, spot*); susceptible; appreciative (of, **à**); perceptible (*progress etc.*); **~ à** *a.* aware of; **~lerie** [~sibla'ri] *f* mawkishness.

sensitif [sɑ̃si'tif] sensitive; sensory; **~vité** [~tivi'te] *f* sensitivity.

sensoriel [sɑ̃sɔ'rjɛl] sensory.

sensu|alité [sɑ̃syali'te] *f* sensuality; sensuousness; **~el** [sɑ̃'sɥɛl] sensual; sensuous.

sentenc|e [sɑ̃'tɑ̃ːs] *f* maxim; ⚖ sentence; (*a.* **~ arbitrale**) award; **~ieux** [~tɑ̃'sjø] sententious.

senteur [sɑ̃'tœːr] *f* scent, perfume.

sentier [sɑ̃'tje] *m* footpath; path.

sentiment [sɑ̃ti'mɑ̃] *m* feeling (*a. fig.*); emotion; consciousness, sense; *fig.* opinion; **avoir le ~ de** *a.* be aware of; **~al** [~mɑ̃'tal] sentimental; **~alité** [~mɑ̃tali'te] *f* sentimentality.

sentinelle ⚔ [sɑ̃ti'nɛl] *f* sentry.

sentir [sɑ̃'tiːr] (2b) *v/t.* feel; be conscious of; smell (*a. fig.*); taste of (*s.th.*); F **je ne peux pas le ~** I can't stand him; **se ~** feel, be feeling (*fine, bad etc.*); **il ne se sent pas de joie** he is beside himself with joy; *v/i.* smell (bad, **mauvais**; good, **bon**).

seoir [swaːr] (3k). **~ à q.** become s.o.

sépar|able [sepa'rabl] separable; **~ateur** [separa'tœːr] **1.** *adj.* separating, separative; **2.** *su./m* ⚙ separator; **~ation** [~'sjɔ̃] *f* separation (from, **de**); parting; *fig. meeting*: breaking up, division; ⚖ **~ de biens** separate maintenance; *pol.* **~ des pouvoirs** separation of powers; △ **~ mur** *m* **de ~** partition wall; **~atiste** [~'tist] separatist; **~ément** [sepa're'mɑ̃] *adv.* separately; **~er** [~'re] (1a) separate (from, **de**); part; drive apart; divide; *fig.* distinguish (from, **de**); **se ~** part (company); break up (*assembly*); divide; split off; **se ~ de** part with.

sept [sɛt] seven; *date, title*: seventh; **~ante** [sɛp'tɑ̃ːt] *Belgium*: seventy.

septembre [sɛp'tɑ̃ːbr] *m* September.

septentrional [sɛptɑ̃trio'nal] **1.** *adj.* north(ern); **2.** *su.* northerner.

septicémie ⚕ [sɛptise'mi] *f* septic(a)emia; blood poisoning.

septième [sɛ'tjɛm] **1.** *adj./num.*, *su.* seventh; **2.** *su./f* ♪ seventh.

septique ⚕ [sɛp'tik] septic.

sépulcr|al [sepyl'kral] sepulchral; **~e** [~'pylkr] *m* sepulchre, *Am.* sepulcher.

sépulture [sepyl'tyːr] *f* burial; burial place.

séquelles [se'kɛl] *f/pl.* after-effects; aftermath *sg*.

séquence [se'kɑ̃ːs] *f* sequence.

séquestr|ation [sekɛstra'sjɔ̃] *f* illegal confinement; **~e** ⚖ [~'kɛstr] *m* impoundment; **mettre sous ~** impound; **~er** [~kɛs'tre] (1a) confine illegally; hold captive; ⚖ impound; *fig.* **se ~** sequester o.s.

serai [sə're] *1st ps. sg. fut. of* **être** 1.

serbe [serb] *adj., su.* Serb(ian).

serein [sə'rɛ̃] serene; calm.

sérénité [sereni'te] *f* serenity; calmness.

serf, serve [serf, serv] *su.* serf.

sergent ✕ *etc.* [ser'ʒɑ̃] *m* sergeant.

série [se'ri] *f* series; sequence; *tools etc.*: set; **en** ~, **par** ~ in series; † **fait en** ~ mass-produced; † **fin** *f* **de** ~ remnants *pl.*; *fig.* **hors** ~ extraordinary; **sérier** [~'rje] (1o) classify.

sérieux [se'rjø] 1. *adj.* serious; grave; earnest; genuine (*offer, purchaser*); 2. *su./m* gravity, seriousness; **garder son** ~ keep a straight face; **prendre au** ~ take seriously.

serin [sə'rɛ̃] *m orn.* serin; canary; F fool, sap; ~**er** [səri'ne] (1a) drum (*a rule etc.*) (into s.o., **à q.**).

seringue ✗, ✿ [sə'rɛ̃:g] *f* syringe; ~**er** [~rɛ̃'ge] (1m) syringe; inject.

serment [ser'mɑ̃] *m* oath; **faux** ~ perjury; **sous** ~ on oath.

sermon [ser'mɔ̃] *m* sermon; *fig.* lecture; ~**ner** F [~mɔ'ne] (1a) lecture, reprimand.

serpe ✗ [serp] *f* billhook.

serpent [ser'pɑ̃] *m* ✗, *zo., fig.* serpent; *zo., fig.* snake; ~ **à lunettes** cobra; ~ **à sonnettes** rattlesnake; ~**er** [serpɑ̃'te] (1a) wind, curve, meander; ~**in** [~'tɛ̃] 1. *adj.* serpentine; 2. *su./m* coil; paper streamer.

serpillière [serpi'jɛ:r] *f* floorcloth.

serrage [se'ra:ʒ] *m* ⊙ tightening; gripping; *mot.* ~ **des freins** braking.

serre [se:r] *f* ✗ greenhouse; *orn.* claw; ✗ ~ **chaude** hothouse.

serré [se're] 1. *adj.* tight; compact; narrow (*defile etc.*); close (*buildings*, ✗ *order, reasoning, texture, translation, sp. finish*); tightly packed (*people etc.*); 2. *adv.*: **jouer** ~ play cautiously; **vivre** ~ live on a tight budget.

serre...: ~**freins** [ser'frɛ̃] *m/inv.* 🚂 brakesman; ~**joint** ⊙ [~'ʒwɛ̃] *m* cramp; screw clamp.

serr|ement [ser'mɑ̃] *m* squeezing; ~ **de main** handshake; *fig.* ~ **de cœur** pang; ~**er** [se're] (1b) *v/t.* press, squeeze; grasp, grip; put (away); lock up; tighten (*a knot*, ⊙ *a screw*); *fig.* condense; close (*the ranks*); skirt (*the coast, a wall*); *sp.* jostle; crowd (*s.o.'s car*); ~ **q.**

de près follow close behind s.o.; ~ **la main** **à** shake hands with; ~ **les dents** clench one's teeth; **serrez-vous!** close up!; **se** ~ crowd, stand (sit *etc.*) close together; tighten (*lips*); *fig.* contract (*heart*); *v/i.*: *mot.* ~ **sur sa droite** keep to the right; ~**e-tête** [ser'tɛːt] *m/inv.* headband; skullcap.

serrur|e [se'ry:r] *f* lock; ~**erie** [seryrə'ri] *f* locksmith's trade *or* shop; lock mechanism; metalwork; ~**ier** [~'rje] *m* locksmith.

serti|r [ser'ti:r] (2a) set (*a gem*) (in a bezel); set (*window-panes*) (in, **de**); ~**ssage** [serti'sa:ʒ] *m* setting; ~**ssure** [~'sy:r] *f* bezel; setting.

sérum 🦠 [se'rɔm] *m* serum.

servage [ser'va:ʒ] *m* bondage.

serv|ante [ser'vɑ̃:t] *f* (maid) servant; ~**eur** [~'vœːr] *m* waiter; ~**euse** [~'vø:z] *f* waitress.

servi|abilité [servjabili'te] *f* obligingness; ~**able** [~'vjabl] obliging; ~**ce** [~'vis] *m* service (*a.* ✕, ♟, *eccl., tennis*); *hotel:* service charge; 🍴, *admin.* department; *cuis.* meal: course; *tools:* set; ~ **de table** dinner service; ~ **divin** divine service; ~**s** *pl. publics* public services; ✕ **être de** ~ be on duty; † **libre** ~ self service; **rendre** (**un**) ~ **à q.** do s.o. a good turn.

serviette [ser'vjet] *f* (table)napkin, serviette; towel; briefcase.

servil|e [ser'vil] servile; slavish (*imitation*); ~**ité** [~vili'te] *f* servility.

servi|r [ser'vi:r] (2b) *v/t.* serve (*a dish, s.o. at table*, † *a customer, one's country, a. tennis a ball*); help, assist; be in the service of; wait on; *cards:* deal; † supply; pay (*a rent*); *eccl.* ~ **la messe** serve at mass; **se** ~ help o.s. to food; **se** ~ **de** use; *v/i.* serve (*a.* ✕); be used (as, **de**); be in service; be useful; **à quoi cela sert-il?** what's the good of that?; **à quoi cela sert-il** (*or* **à quoi sert**) **de** (*inf.*)**?** what's the use of (*ger.*)?; ~**teur** [~vi'tœːr] *m* servant; ~**tude** [~vi'tyd] *f* servitude; *fig.* constraint.

servo... ⊙ [servo] servo(-assisted) ..., power(-assisted) ...

ses [se] *see* **sel**.

session ⚖️, *parl.* [se'sjɔ̃] *f* session.

seuil [sœːj] *m* threshold (*a. fig.*); doorstep.

seul [sœl] *adj. before su.* one, only, single; very, mere; *after su. or verb* alone, lonely; *before art.* only; ... alone; **comme un ~ homme** like one man; **un ~ homme** only one man; **le ~ homme qui** the only man who; **un homme ~** a single or lonely man; **un des ~s hommes** one of the few men; **la ~e pensée** the very thought (of it); **tout ~** (+ *verb*) (all) by oneself; by itself; **~ement** [~'mã] *adv.* only; solely; but; **ne ... pas ~** not even; **si ~ ...** if only ...; **~et** F [sœ'lɛ] lonesome, lonely.

sève [sɛːv] *f* ♀ sap; *fig.* vigo(u)r.

sévère [se'vɛːr] severe (*a. fig.*); stern; strict; hard (*climate*); **sévérité** [~veri'te] *f* severity; sternness; *fig.* austerity; strictness.

sévices [se'vis] *m/pl.* cruelty *sg.*, ill treatment; **sévir** [~'viːr] (2a) rage (*plague, war*); **~ contre** deal severely with.

sevr|age [sə'vraːʒ] *m* weaning; **~er** [~'vre] (1d) wean (*a child, a lamb*); ♀ sever; *fig.* deprive (of, **de**).

sexagénaire [sɛksaʒe'nɛːr] *adj., su* sexagenarian.

sexe [sɛks] *m* sex; F **le beau ~, le ~ faible** the fair or weaker sex.

sextuor ♪ [sɛks'tɥɔːr] *m* sextet.

sexuel [sɛk'sɥɛl] sexual.

seyant [sɛ'jɑ̃] becoming.

shake-hand [ʃɛk'ɑ̃d] *m/inv.* hand-shake.

shampooing [ʃɑ̃'pwɛ̃] *m* shampoo.

short *cost.* [ʃɔrt] *m* shorts *pl.*

si¹ [si] *cj.* if; whether.

si² [~] *adv.* so, so much; *answer to negative question:* yes; **~ bien que** so that; **~ riche qu'il soit** however rich he may be.

si³ ♪ [~] *m/inv.* si; *note:* B; **~ bémol** B flat.

siccatif [sika'tif] *adj., su./m* siccative.

sidér|al [side'ral] sidereal; **~er** F [~'re] (1a) stagger.

sidérurgie [sideryr'ʒi] *f* metallurgy of iron; **~que** [~ryr'ʒik] ironworking; **usine** *f* ~ ironworks *usu. sg.*

siècle [sjɛkl] *m* century; *eccl.* world(ly life), *fig.* period, time, age.

sied [sje] *3rd p. sg. pres. of* **seoir**.

siège [sjɛːʒ] *m* chair etc., ⊙, disease, government, *parl.*: seat; ✝ head office; ✗ siege; ♋ bench; *eccl.* see; chair: bottom; ✝ **~ social** registered office; **siéger** [sje'ʒe] (1g) sit (♋, *a.* in Parliament, **au parlement**); ✝ have its head office; ♋ be seated.

sien, sienne [sjɛ̃, sjɛn] **1.** *pron./poss.:* **le ~, la ~e, les ~s** *pl.*, **les ~nes** *pl.* his, hers, its, one's; **2.** *su./m* his or her or its or one's own; **les ~s** *pl.* his or her or one's (own) people; *su./f:* **faire des ~nes** be up to one's tricks.

sieste [sjɛst] *f* siesta; F nap.

siffl|ant, e [si'flɑ̃, ~'flɑ̃t] **1.** *adj.* hissing; wheezing; whistling; **2.** *su./f gramm.* sibilant; **~ement** [~flə'mɑ̃] *m* whistling; hiss(ing); sizzling; wheezing; **~er** [~'fle] (1a) *v/i.* whistle, hiss, sizzle; ♀ wheeze; *v/t.* whistle (*a tune*); whistle to (*a dog*); whistle for (*a taxi*); *thea.* hiss, boo; F swig (*a drink*); **~et** [~'flɛ] *m* whistle; *thea.* hiss; **donner un coup de ~** blow a whistle; **~eur** [~slant'wise; **~eur** [~'flœːr] **1.** *adj.* whistling; hissing; **2.** *su.* whistler, *thea.* booer; **~otement** [~flɔt'mɑ̃] *m* soft whistling; **~oter** [~flɔ'te] (1a) whistle softly.

sigle [sigl] *m* initials *pl.*; abbreviation.

signal [si'nal] *m* signal; *teleph.* (dialling) tone; **~ d'alarme** alarm-signal; **~ horaire** radio: time signal; **signaux** *pl.* (**lumineux**) traffic signals; **~é** [siɲa'le] outstanding; *pej.* notorious; **~ement** [~nal'mɑ̃] *m* description; **~er** [siɲa'le] (1a) signal (*a train etc.*), *fig.* indicate; point out (s.th. to s.o., **qch. à q.**); draw attention to; give a description of (*s.o.*); report (to, **à**); **~isation** [~liza'sjɔ̃] *f* signalling; signals *pl.*, signal system; *mot.* **~ routière** road signs *pl.*; **panneau** *m* **de ~** roadsign.

sign|ataire [siɲa'tɛːr] *su.* signatory; **~ature** [~na'tyːr] *f* signature; **~e** [siɲ] *m* sign; (*bodily, punctuation*) mark; ✗ insignia; **~ de tête (des yeux)** nod (wink); **faire ~ à** beckon to; **~er** [si'ɲe] (1a) sign; **se ~et** cross o.s.; **~et** [~'ɲe] *m* bookmark; **~ificatif** [siɲifika'tif] significant; **~ification** [~'sjɔ̃] *f* meaning; sense; ♋ writ etc.: service; **~ifier** [siɲi'fje] (1o) mean, signify; notify, serve (*a writ etc.*); **~ qch. à q** make s.th. known to s.o., inform s.o. of s.th.

silenc|e [si'lɑ̃s] *m* silence; stillness; *fig.* secrecy; ♪ rest; **garder le ~** keep silent (about, **sur**); **passer qch. sous ~** pass s.th. over in silence; **~ieux** [~lɑ̃'sjø] **1.**

S

adj. silent; still (*evening etc.*); **2.** *su./m mot.* silencer.

silex *min.* [si'lɛks] *m* flint, silex.

silhouett|e [si'lwɛt] *f* silhouette; outline; profile; **~er** [~lwe'te] (1a) silhouette, outline.

sili|cate 🜛 [sili'kat] *m* silicate; **~ce** [~'lis] *f* silica; **~cium** 🜛 [~'sjɔm] *m* silicon.

sillage [si'jaːʒ] *m* ⚓ wake; ✈, *fig.* trail; *fig.* **marcher dans le ~ de** follow in (*s.o.'s*) footsteps.

sillon [si'jɔ̃] *m* furrow; *disc:* groove; **~ner** [~jɔ'ne] (1a) furrow (*a. fig.*); *fig.* criss-cross.

silo [si'lo] *m* silo; *potatoes:* clamp.

simagrée F [sima'gre] *f* pretence; **~s** *pl.* affectation *sg.*; affected airs.

simil|aire [simi'lɛːr] similar; **~arité** [~lari'te] *f* likeness; **~i** F [~'li] *m* imitation; **~icuir** [~li'kwiːr] *m* imitation leather; **~itude** [~li'tyd] *f* similitude.

simple [sɛ̃ːpl] **1.** *adj.* simple; single (*a.* 🎫 ticket); plain (*food, dress*); *fig.* simple (-minded); **2.** *su./m* the simple; *tennis:* single; ♣, ♀ medicinal herb; **~icité** [sɛ̃plisi'te] *f* simplicity; *fig.* simple-mindedness; **~ification** [~fika'sjɔ̃] *f* simplification; **~ifier** [~'fje] (1o) simplify; **~iste** [sɛ̃'plist] over-simple, simplistic.

simulacre [simy'lakr] *m* semblance, show, pretence; *un ~ de* ... *a.* a sham ...

simul|ateur *m,* **-trice** *f* [simyla'tœːr, ~'tris] pretender; ⚙ simulator; **~ation** [~'sjɔ̃] *f* simulation; ✕ malingering; **~er** [~'le] (1a) simulate; feign.

simultané [simulta'ne] simultaneous; **~ité** [~nei'te] *f* simultaneity.

sincère [sɛ̃'sɛːr] sincere; **sincérité** [~seri'te] *f* sincerity; frankness.

sing|e [sɛ̃ːʒ] *m zo.* monkey, ape; F *faire le ~* monkey about; **~er** [sɛ̃'ʒe] (11) mimic, ape; **~erie** [sɛ̃ʒ'ri] *f* grimace; **~s** *pl. a.* airs and graces.

singul|ariser [sɛ̃gylari'ze] (1a): (*se ~*) make (o.s.) conspicuous; **~arité** [~'te] *f* singularity; peculiarity; **~ier** [sɛ̃gy'lje] **1.** *adj.* singular; peculiar; strange; **2.** *su./m* singular.

sinistr|e [si'nistr] **1.** *adj.* sinister; ominous; **2.** *su./m* disaster, catastrophe; fire; loss (*from fire etc.*); **~é** [~nis'tre] **1.** *adj.* disaster-stricken; **2.** *su.* victim (*of a disaster*).

sinon [si'nɔ̃] *cj.* otherwise, if not; except (that, *que*).

sinu|eux [si'nɥø] sinuous; winding; *fig.* tortuous; **~osité** [~nɥozi'te] *f* winding; **~s** [~'nys] *m anat.* sinus; Å sine.

siphon [si'fɔ̃] *m phys. etc.* siphon; ⚙ U-bend.

sire [siːr] *m king:* Sire, Sir; *fig.* individual, fellow.

sirène [si'rɛn] *f* ⚙, *myth., zo., fig.* siren; ⚙ hooter; ⚓ fog horn.

sirop [si'ro] *m* syrup; (fruit) cordial.

siroter F [siro'te] (1a) sip.

sirupeux [siry'pø] syrupy (*a. fig.*).

sis [si] *p.p. of* **seoir**.

sismique [sis'mik] seismic.

sismo... [sismo] seismo...; **~graphe** [~'graf] *m* seismograph.

site [sit] *m* setting; site; spot; *~ propre* bus lane.

sitôt [si'to] *adv.* as *or* so soon; *~ après* immediately after; *~ dit, ~ fait* no sooner said than done; *~ que* as soon as; *ne ... pas de ~* not ... for a while.

situa|tion [sitɥa'sjɔ̃] *f* situation, position, location; *fig.* job, post; *~ économique* economic position; *~ sociale* station in life; **~é** [si'tɥe] situated (at, à); **~er** [~] (1n) set; place.

six [sis; *before consonant* si; *before vowel and h mute* siz] six; *date, title:* sixth; **~ième** [~'zjɛm] **1.** *adj./num., su.* sixth. **2.** *su./m* sixth; Am. seventh floor; **~te** ♪ [sikst] *f* sixth.

ski [ski] *m* ski; skiing; *~ nautique* water skiing; *faire du ~* = **skier** [~'e] (1a) ski; **skieur** *m,* **-euse** *f* [~'kœːr, ~'øːz] skier.

slave [slaːv] **1.** *adj.* Slavonic; **2.** *su./m ling.* Slavonic; *su.* ♀ Slav.

slip [slip] *m women:* panties *pl.;* *men:* (short) pants *pl.,* briefs.

smoking [smɔ'kiŋ] *m* dinner jacket, Am. tuxedo.

snob [snɔb] **1.** *adj.* snobbish; **2.** *su./m* snob; **~er** [snɔ'be] (1a) look down on (*s.o.*); cut, coldshoulder (*s.o.*); **~isme** [~'ism] *m* snobbery.

sobr|e [sɔbr] abstemious; sober; *fig. ~ de* sparing of; **~iété** [sɔbrie'te] *f* temperance; moderation.

sobriquet [sɔbri'kɛ] *m* nickname.

soc ✗ [sɔk] *m* ploughshare, Am. plowshare.

sociabilité [sɔsjabili'te] *f* sociability; **sociable** [~'sjabl] sociable.

social [sɔ'sjal] social; **~isation** [sɔsjaliza'sjɔ̃] *f* socialization; **~iser** [~li'ze] (1a) socialize; **~isme** [~'lism] *m* socialism; **~iste** [~'list] **1.** *adj.* socialist(ic); **2.** *su.* socialist.

sociét|aire [sɔsje'tɛːr] *su.* (full) member; ✝ shareholder; **~é** [~'te] *f* society; company (*a.* ✝); association, club; **~ à responsabilité limitée** (*sort of*) limited company; **~ d'abondance** affluent society; **~ de consommation** consumer society; **~ par actions** company limited by shares.

sociolog|ie [sɔsjɔlɔ'ʒi] *f* sociology; **~gue** [~'lɔg] *su.* sociologist.

socle [sɔkl] *m* pedestal, base.

socquettes [sɔ'kɛt] *f/pl.* (*ladies'*) ankle socks.

soda [sɔ'da] *m* fizzy drink.

sœur [sœːr] *f* sister.

sofa [sɔ'fa] *m* sofa, settee.

soi [swa] *pron.* oneself; himself, herself, itself; **amour de ~** self-love; **cela va de ~** that goes without saying; **être chez ~** be at home; **en** (*or* **de**) **~** in itself; **~-disant** [~di'zɑ̃] **1.** *adj./inv.* so-called; **2.** *adv.* ostensibly.

soie [swa] *f* silk; (*hog-*)bristle; **~rie** [~'ri] *f* silk (fabric).

soif [swaf] *f* thirst (*a. fig.* for, **de**); **avoir ~** be thirsty.

soign|é [swa'ɲe] neat, trim; well cared for; carefully done; **~er** [~'ɲe] (1a) look after; ✽ nurse (*a sick person*); attend (*a patient*); *fig.* **elle soigne sa mise** she dresses with care; ✽ **se faire ~** have treatment; **~eux** [~'ɲø] careful (of, **de**); tidy, neat; painstaking.

soi-même [swa'mɛːm] oneself.

soin [swɛ̃] *m* care, pains *pl.*; neatness, tidiness; **~s** *pl.* ✽ *etc.* attention *sg.*; **aux bons ~s de** post: care of, c/o; **par les ~s de** thanks to; **premiers ~s** *pl.* first aid *sg.*; **avoir** (*or* **prendre**) **~ de** take care of (*s.th.*); take care to (*inf.*), be *or* make sure to (*inf.*).

soir [swaːr] *m* evening; afternoon; **le ~** in the evening; **~ée** [swa're] *f* duration: evening; party; *thea.* evening performance.

sois [swa] *1st p. sg. pres. sbj. of* **être 1**; **soit 1.** *adv.* [swat] (let us) suppose...;

say...; *~!* all right!, agreed!; **ainsi ~-il** so be it!, amen!; **tant ~ peu** ever so little; **2.** *cj.* [swa]: **~ ... ~ ...**, **~ ... ou ...** either ... or ...; whether ... or ...; **~ que** (*sbj.*) whether (*ind.*).

soixant|aine [swasɑ̃'tɛn] *f* (about) sixty; **la ~** the age of sixty, the sixties *pl.*; **~e** [~'sɑ̃ːt] sixty; **~e-dix** [~sɑ̃'dis; *before consonant* ~'di; *before vowel and h mute* ~'diz] seventy; **~e-dixième** [~sɑ̃tdi'zjɛm] seventieth; **~ième** [~sɑ̃'tjɛm] sixtieth.

soja ♀ [sɔ'ja] *m* soy(a) bean.

sol¹ ♩ [sɔl] *m/inv.* sol; *note:* G.

sol² [sɔl] *m* ground; ♪ soil; floor; **~aire** ✕ [~'ɛːr] *adj./inv.* ground-to-air (*missile*).

solaire [sɔ'lɛːr] solar; sun (*dial, glasses*); ✽ sun-ray (*treatment*).

soldat [sɔl'da] *m* soldier; **~ de plomb** toy *or* tin soldier; **~ inconnu** the Unknown Warrior; **se faire ~** join the army; **simple ~** private; **~esque** *pej.* [~da'tɛsk] **1.** *adj.* barrack-room ...; **2.** *su./f* soldiery.

solde¹ ✕, ⚓ [sɔld] *f* pay.

solde² ✝ [~] *m* account: balance; remnant; **~s** *pl.* (clearance) sale *sg.*

solder [sɔl'de] (1a) balance (*accounts*); settle (*a bill etc.*); sell off; **se ~ par** (*or* **en**) end (up) in.

sole *icht.* [sɔl] *f* sole.

soleil [sɔ'lɛːj] *m* sun; sunshine; ✽ **coup de ~** sunstroke; sunburn; **il fait du ~** the sun's shining; **~leux** [~lɛ'jø] sunny.

solenn|el [sɔla'nɛl] solemn; **~iser** [~ni'ze] (1a) solemnize; **~ité** [~ni'te] *f* solemnity; ceremony.

solida|ire [sɔli'dɛːr] ⚙ *etc.* interdependent, **être ~** (**de**) show solidarity (with); **~riser** [sɔlidari'ze] (1a): **se ~** show solidarity (with, **avec**); make common cause; **~rité** [~'te] *f* solidarity; ⚖ joint responsibility.

solid|e [sɔ'lid] **1.** *adj.* solid; fast (*colour*); strong; ♪ sound (*a. reason*); *fig.* reliable; **2.** *su./m* solid; **~ifier** [~'fje] (1o) solidify; **~ité** [~'te] *f* solidity; strength; *fig.* soundness (*of judgment, a.* ✝).

soliloque [sɔli'lɔk] *m* soliloquy.

soliste ♩ [sɔ'list] *su.* soloist.

solitaire [sɔli'tɛːr] **1.** *adj.* solitary, lonely; **2.** *su./m* recluse; solitaire.

solitude [sɔli'tyd] *f* solitude; loneliness; lonely spot.

S

sollicit|ation [sɔllisita'sjɔ̃] f entreaty, earnest request; **~er** [~'te] (1a) seek, request, ask or beg for; appeal to; solicit; urge; attract; ⊚ pull; **~eur** m, **-euse** f [~'tœːr, ~'tøːz] applicant (for, de); petitioner; **~ude** [~'tyd] f concern, solicitude.

solo [sɔ'lo] **1.** su./m ♪ (pl. a. **-li** [~'li]) solo; **2.** adj./inv. solo (violin etc.).

solu|bilité [sɔlybili'te] f solubility; fig. solvability; **~ble** [~'lybl] soluble (a. fig.); **~tion** [~ly'sjɔ̃] f solution.

solva|bilité ✝ [sɔlvabili'te] f solvency; **~ble** ✝ [~'vabl] solvent; **~nt** 🧪 [~'vɑ̃] m solvent.

sombre [sɔ̃ːbr] dark, gloomy, murky (sky); dim (light); melancholy.

sombrer [sɔ̃'bre] (1a) sink.

somma|ire [sɔ'mɛːr] adj., su./m summary; **~tion** [~ma'sjɔ̃] f demand; summons sg.; warning.

somme¹ [sɔm] f sum, amount; **~ globale** lump or global sum; **~ toute** ... on the whole ...; **en ~** in short, all in all, so.

somme² [~] f burden; **bête** f **de ~** beast of burden, pack animal.

somm|e³ [sɔm] m nap; **~eil** [sɔ'mɛːj] m sleep; sleepiness; fig. **en ~ dormant**; **avoir ~** be sleepy; **~eiller** [~mɛ'je] (1a) be asleep; doze; fig. lie dormant.

sommelier [sɔmə'lje] m butler; cellarman; restaurant: wine-waiter.

sommer¹ [sɔ'me] (1a) summon; call on (s.o.) (to inf., de inf.).

sommer² [~] (1a) sum up.

sommes [sɔm] 1st a. pl. pres. of **être** 1.

sommet [sɔ'mɛ] m summit, top (a. fig.); head, arch: crown; pol. **conférence** f **au ~** summit conference.

sommier [sɔ'mje] m: **~ (à ressorts)** springing, spring mattress.

sommité [sɔmi'te] f 🌿 top; fig. person: leading light.

somn|ambule [sɔmnɑ̃'byl] **1.** adj. somnambulant; **2.** su. sleep-walker; **~ambulisme** [~nɑ̃by'lism] m sleep-walking; **~ifère** [~ni'fɛːr] su./m soporific, sleeping drug or pill.

somnolen|ce [sɔmnɔ'lɑ̃ːs] f sleepiness; **~t** [~'lɑ̃] sleepy, drowsy.

somptu|aire [sɔ̃p'tɥɛːr] sumptuary; **~eux** [~'tɥø] sumptuous; **~osité** [~tɥozi'te] f sumptuousness.

son¹ m, **sa** f, pl. **ses** [sɔ̃, sa, se] adj./poss. his, her, its, one's.

son² [sɔ̃] m sound, noise.

son³ ♪ [~] m bran; F **tache** f **de ~** freckle.

sond|age [sɔ̃'daːʒ] m ⚒ boring; ⚓ sounding; probing; fig. survey; **~ (d'opinion** opinion) poll; **~é** [~'sɔ̃ːd] f sounding rod; ⚓ lead; probe; ⚒ drill; **~er** [sɔ̃'de] (1a) sound (⚓, a. fig.); probe; investigate, explore.

song|e [sɔ̃ːʒ] m dream (a. fig.); **~er** [sɔ̃'ʒe] (1l) dream (of, de); think, muse, reflect; **~ à** a. think of or about (s.th., s.o.; ger., inf.); consider, contemplate (s.th.; ger., inf.); **~erie** [sɔ̃ʒ'ri] f reverie; **~eur** [sɔ̃'ʒœːr] pensive.

sonique [sɔ'nik] sonic; sound.

sonn|aille [sɔ'naːj] f cattle bell; **~s** pl. jingle sg. of bells; **~ant** [~'nɑ̃] hard (cash); **à trois heures ~es** on the stroke of three; **~é** [~'ne] F crazy, cracked; F groggy; **il est deux heures ~es** it is gone two (o'clock); **elle a cinquante ans ~s** she is not on the wrong side of fifty, she is well into her fifties; **vingt ans bien ~s** a full twenty years; **~er** [~'ne] (1a) v/t. sound (the alarm, a horn etc.), ring (a bell); strike (the hour); ring for (s.o., a. church service); v/i. sound; ring (bell, coin); strike (clock); fig. **~ bien (creux)** sound well (hollow); **dix heures sonnent** it is striking 10; ⊚ **~erie** [sɔn'ri] f ringing; bells pl.; ⊚ striking mechanism; teleph. etc. bell; ✕ (bugle)call.

sonnette [sɔ'nɛt] f (house-)bell; hand-bell; **coup** m **de ~** ring.

sono F [sɔ'no] f P. A. (system).

sonor|e [sɔ'nɔːr] resonant; phys. acoustic; resounding, loud; ringing (voice); gramm. voiced; **bande** f **~** sound track; **~ité** [~nɔri'te] f sonority; instrument etc.: tone; sound; room: acoustics pl.

sont [sɔ̃] 3rd a. pl. pres. of **être** 1.

sophisti|cation [sɔfistika'sjɔ̃] f sophistication; **~qué** [~'ke] sophisticated.

soporifique [sɔpɔri'fik] adj., su./m soporific.

sorbet cuis. [sɔr'bɛ] m water ice.

sorbier 🌿 [sɔr'bje] m sorb; rowan.

sorc|ellerie [sɔrsɛl'ri] f witchcraft, sorcery; **~ier** [~'sje] m sorcerer; wizard; **~ière** [~'sjɛːr] f witch.

S

sordid|e [sɔr'did] sordid; *fig.* base; **~ité** [∼didi'te] *f* sordidness.

sornettes [sɔr'nɛt] *f/pl.* nonsense *sg.*; **conter des ~** talk nonsense.

sort [sɔːr] *m* fate, destiny; lot; change; spell; **tirer au ~** draw lots; **~able** [sɔr'tabl] presentable; **~e** [sɔrt] *f* sort, kind; way, manner; **de la ~** of that sort; in that way; **de ~ que** so that; **en quelque ~** in a way; **en ~ que** so that.

sortie [sɔr'ti] *f* going out; exit; outlet (*a.* ⚙); leaving; day off; release; ⚙ outflow; ✕ sortie; trip, excursion; *fig.* outburst; **~ de bain** bathrobe; **à la ~ de** on leaving.

sortilège [sɔrti'lɛːʒ] *m* charm, spell.

sortir [sɔr'tiːr] **1.** (2b) *v/i.* go out; come out; leave; file, *etc.* come up; come through (*tooth*); stand out (from, **de**); **~ do** come from; come of (*a family*); get out of (*one's bed, a difficulty*), *fig.* deviate from (*a subject*); *fig.* be outside of (*one's competence etc.*), go or be beyond; F **~ de** (*inf.*) have just done or finished (*ger.*); **~ des rails** jump the rails; **être sorti** be out; *v/t.* bring or take or put or get or send out; publish (*a book*); F throw (*s.o.*) out; F come out with (*a remark, joke, etc.*); **se ~ de** get out of (*a difficult situation etc.*); **s'en ~** be able to cope; get through, pull through; **2.** *su./m:* **au ~ de** on leaving; *fig.* at the end of.

sosie [sɔ'zi] *m* (*person's*) double.

sot, sotte [so, sɔt] **1.** *adj.* stupid, foolish, silly; **2.** *su.* fool; **sottise** [sɔ'tiːz] *f* stupidity; silliness.

sou [su] *m* sou (*5 centimes*).

soubassement [subas'mã] *m* ⚙ base (*a.* ⚙); *fig.* substructure.

soubresaut [subrə'so] *m* jerk; (sudden) start; jolt.

souche [suʃ] *f tree:* stump; ✍, *fig.* stock; *ticket:* stub, counterfoil; *fig.* **faire ~** found a family.

souci [su'si] *m* care; worry; concern; **~er** [∼'sje] (1o): **se ~ de** trouble o.s. about; care for or about; **~eux** [∼'sjø] worried, anxious, concerned (about, **de**; to *inf.*, **de** *inf.*).

soucoupe [su'kup] *f* saucer.

soudage ⚙ [su'daːʒ] *m* soldering; welding.

soudain [su'dɛ̃] **1.** *adj.* sudden; **2.** *adv.*

suddenly, all of a sudden, instantly; **~ement** [∼dɛn'mã] suddenly; **~eté** [∼dɛn'te] *f* suddenness.

soude [sud] *f* 🌿, ⚗, ⚙ soda.

souder [su'de] (1a) solder; weld; *fig.* join; **lampe *f* à ~** blow lamp.

soudoyer [sudwa'je] (1h) hire (the services of); *fig.* buy (*s.o.*).

soudure ⚙ [su'dyːr] *f* soldering; soldered joint; weld(ing); F join; *fig.* **faire la ~** bridge the gap.

souffert [su'fɛːr] *p.p. of* **souffrir**.

souffl|age [su'flaːʒ] *m* ⚙ glass blowing; **~e** [sufl] *m* breath (*a.* ✍); breathing; blast; *fig.* inspiration; *sp.*, *fig.* wind; **à bout de ~** out of breath; **~er** [∼'fle] (1a) *v/i.* blow (*person, a. wind*); pant; get one's breath; *v/t.* blow (*a.* ⚙ *glass*); blow up (*a balloon, the fire*); *thea.* prompt; *fig.* whisper; *fig.* breathe (*a word, a sound*); blow out (*a candle*); F steal; F pinch; F flabbergast, take aback; **~erie** [∼flɑ'ri] *f* bellows *pl.*; ⚙ blower; **~et** [∼'flɛ] *m* bellows *pl.* (*a. phot.*); *carriage:* (folding) hood; *fig.* slap; *fig.* affront; **~eter** [∼flə'te] (1c) slap (*s.o.*) (in the face); *fig.* insult; **~eur** [∼'flœːr] *m* blower; *thea. etc.* prompter; **~ure** [∼'flyːr] *f* bubble; blister.

souffr|ance [su'frɑ̃ːs] *f* suffering; ⚖ sufferance; **~ant** [∼'frɑ̃] suffering; ailing; ill; **~e** [sufr] *1st p. sg. pres. of* **souffrir**; **~e-douleur** [∼frədu'lœːr] *su./inv.* drudge; scapegoat.

souffreteux [sufrə'tø] sickly, feeble.

souffrir [su'friːr] (2f) *v/t./i.* suffer (from, **de**); *v/t. a.* endure; bear; allow of.

soufr|e 🌿 [sufr] *m* sulphur; **~er** [su'fre] (1a) (treat with) sulphur.

souhait [swɛ] *m* wish; **à ~** to one's liking; **~able** [swɛ'tabl] desirable; **~er** [∼'te] (1a) wish.

souill|er [su'je] (1a) soil (with, **de**); pollute; stain (*a. fig.*); *fig.* tarnish; **~on** [∼'jɔ̃] *su.* sloven; **~ure** [∼'jyːr] *f* stain; *fig.* blemish.

soûl F [su] **1.** *adj.* drunk; **2.** *su./m* fill (*a. fig.*); **dormir tout son ~** have one's sleep out.

soulag|ement [sulaʒ'mã] *m* relief; **~er** [∼la'ʒe] (1l) relieve.

soûl|ard m, e *f* [su'laːr, ∼'lard], **~aud** m, e *f* [∼'lo, ∼'loːd] drunkard; **~er** [∼'le] (1a) satiate, glut (*s.o.*) (with, **de**); F make (*s.o.*) drunk; F get on (*s.o.'s*) nerves; F **se ~** get drunk.

soulèvement [sulɛv'mɑ̃] *m* ground, *a. fig.* people: rising; ♣ **~ de cœur** nausea;

soulever [sul've] (1d) lift (up); raise (*a. fig. a question etc.*); send up; *fig.* excite, stir up; rouse (*people*); F steal; *fig.* **~ le cœur à q.** make s.o. sick; **se ~** rise, lift o.s. up; *fig.* rise up (*people*); *fig.* turn (*stomach*).

soulier [su'lje] *m* shoe; **être dans ses petits ~s** be ill at ease.

soulign|ement [suliɲ'mɑ̃] *m* underlining; *fig.* stressing; **~er** [~li'ɲe] (1a) underline; *fig.* emphasize.

soumettre [su'mɛtr] (4v) subdue, put down (*a rebellion etc.*), subjugate (*a people*); fig. subject (s.o. to sth., **q. à qch**); *fig.* submit (*an idea, a request*) (to s.o., **à q.**); **se ~ à** submit to.

soumis [su'mi] submissive; **~sion** [~mi'sjɔ̃] *f* submission (to, **à**); ✝ tender (for, **pour**); **~sionnaire** ✝ [sumisjɔ'nɛːr] *m* tenderer; **~sionner** ✝ [~'ne] (1a) tender for.

soupape ⊙ [su'pap] *f* valve; *bath etc.*: plug; *fig.* safety valve.

soupçon [sup'sɔ̃] *m* suspicion; *fig.* inkling, *fig., a. cuis.* touch, dash; *fig.* **pas un ~ de** not the ghost of; **~ner** [~sɔ'ne] (1a) suspect; *fig.* **ne pas ~** have no idea ...; **~neux** [~sɔ'nø] suspicious.

soupe [sup] *f* soup; *fig.* **~ au lait** irritable, quick-tempered; **monter comme une ~ au lait** flare up.

souper [su'pe] **1.** (1a) have supper; **2.** *su./m* supper.

soupeser [supə'ze] (1d) feel the weight of; weigh (*s.th.*) in the hand.

soupière [su'pjɛːr] *f* soup tureen.

soupir [su'piːr] *m* sigh; ♪ crotchet (*Am.* quarter) rest; **~ail**, *pl.* **-aux** [supi'raːj, ~'ro] *m* basement window; **~ant** [~'rɑ̃] *m* suitor; **~er** [~'re] (1a) sigh; **~ après** (*or* **pour**) long *or* sigh for.

souple [supl] supple; flexible; *fig.* docile; **~sse** [su'plɛs] *f* suppleness, flexibility; *fig.* adaptability.

source [surs] *f* source (*a. fig.*); spring; **de bonne ~** on good authority; **prendre sa ~ dans** river: rise in.

sourcil [sur'si] *m* eyebrow; **~er** [~si'je] (1a) knit one's brows, frown; *fig.*

flinch, wince; **~leux** [~si'jø] finicky; supercilious.

sourd [suːr] **1.** *adj.* deaf; dull (*colour, noise, pain*); low (*cry*); hollow (*voice*); *fig.* hidden, veiled (*hostility*); *fig.* underhand; *gramm.* voiceless; **2.** *su.* deaf person.

sourdine [sur'din] *f* ♪ mute; **en ~** muted; *fig.* softly; *fig.* on the quiet; *fig.* **mettre une ~ à** tone down.

sourd-muet, sourde-muette [sur'mɥɛ, surd'mɥɛt] **1.** *adj.* deaf-and-dumb; **2.** *su.* deaf-mute.

sourdre [surdr] (4dd) spring, well up, *a. fig.* arise.

souriant [su'rjɑ̃] smiling.

souricière [suri'sjɛːr] *f* mousetrap; *fig.* trap.

sourire [su'riːr] **1.** (4cc) smile; *pej.* smirk; **~ à q.** smile at s.o.; *fig.* appeal to s.o.; **2.** *su./m* smile.

souris [su'ri] *f* mouse.

sournois [sur'nwa] underhand; deceitful; **~erie** [~nwaz'ri] *f* underhand manner *or* trick; deceitfulness.

sous [su] *prp. usu.* under; underneath; below; at (*the equator*); in (*the tropics, the rain*); within (*three months*); **~ enveloppe** under cover, in an envelope; **~ le nom de** by the name of; **~ peine de** on pain of; **~ ce pli** enclosed; **~ (le règne de) Louis XIV** under *or* in the reign of Louis XIV; **~ mes yeux** before my eyes.

sous... [su; suz] *sub...*, *under...*; **~alimenté** [~zalima'te] undernourished, underfed; **~arrondissement** [~zarɔ̃-dis'mɑ̃] *m* sub-district; **~bois** [~'bwa] *m* undergrowth.

souscri|pteur ✝ [suskrip'tœːr] *m* subscriber; **~ption** [~'sjɔ̃] *f* subscription (for shares, **à des actions**); **~re** [sus'kriːr] (4q) *v/i.*: ✝, *fig.* **à** subscribe to; **~ pour** subscribe (*a sum*).

sous...: **~cutané** [sukyta'ne] subcutaneous; **~développé** [~devlɔ'pe] underdeveloped; **~emploi** [suzã'plwa] *m* underemployment; **~entendu** [~zãtã-'dy] **1.** *adj.*: implied; understood; **2.** *su./m* implication; innuendo; **~entente** [~zã'tãt] *f* mental reservation; **~estimer** [~zɛsti'me] (1a) underestimate; **~fifre** F [su'fifr] *m* underling; sidekick; **~locataire** [~lɔka'tɛːr] *su.*

subtenant; **~location** [~loka'sjɔ̃] f sub-letting; **~louer** [~'lwe] (1p) sub-let; rent (*a house*) from a tenant; **~main** [~'mɛ̃] m/inv. writing-pad; **en ~** secretly, behind the scenes; **~marin** ⚓ [~ma'rɛ̃] adj., su./m submarine; **~officier** ✗ [suzɔfi'sje] m N. C. O.; **~produit** ⚙ [~prɔ'dɥi] m by-product; spin-off; **~signé** [~si'ne] undersigned; **~sol** [~'sɔl] m ⚡ subsoil; △ basement(-flat); **~tendre** [~'tɑ̃dr] (4a) underlie.

soustraction ⚹ [sustrak'sjɔ̃] f subtraction; **~traire** [~'trɛːr] (4ff) take away, remove; subtract (from, **de**); fig. shield (s.o. from s.th., *q. à qch*); **se ~ à** escape from; avoid (*a duty*).

sous...: ~traitance [sutrɛ'tɑ̃s] f subcontracting; **~traiter** [~trɛ'te] (1a) subcontract; **~vêtement** [~vɛt'mɑ̃] m undergarment.

soutane eccl. [su'tan] f cassock.

soute ⚓ [sut] f store, hold.

soutenable [sut'nabl] tenable (*theory etc.*); **soutenance** [~'nɑ̃ːs] f thesis: maintaining; **soutènement** [sutɛn'mɑ̃] m support(ing) (*a.* △); **souteneur** [sut'nœːr] m procurer; **soutenir** [sut'niːr] (2h) support; back (*s.o.*); keep up; maintain (*an opinion*); assert (*a fact*); fig. bear (*a comparison*), stand; **soutenu** [~'ny] sustained; unflagging; steady; fig. lofty (*style*).

souterrain [sutɛ'rɛ̃] **1.** adj. underground a. fig. subterranian; **2.** su./m underground passage.

soutien [su'tjɛ̃] m support(ing), supporter; **~-gorge**, pl. **~s-gorge** cost. [~tjɛ̃'gɔrʒ] m bra.

soutirer [suti're] (1a) draw off (*wine etc.*); fig. get (s.th. out of s.o., *qch. à q.*).

souvenir [suv'niːr] **1.** (2h) v/t.: **se ~ de** remember; v/impers.: **il me souvient de** (*inf.*) I remember (*ger.*); **2.** su./m memory, remembrance, souvenir, keepsake.

souvent [su'vɑ̃] adv. often; **assez ~** fairly often; **le plus ~** mostly, usually; **peu ~** seldom.

souverain [suv'rɛ̃] adj., su. sovereign; **~eté** [~vrɛn'te] f sovereignty.

soviet [sɔ'vjɛt] m Soviet; **soviétique** [~vje'tik] Soviet (citizen).

soyeux [swa'jø] **1.** adj. silky, silken; **2.** su./m silk manufacturer.

soyons [swa'jɔ̃] *1st p. pl. pres. sbj. of* **être 1**.

spacieux [spa'sjø] spacious, roomy.

sparadrap 💊 [spara'dra] m sticking *or* adhesive plaster.

spasme 💊 [spasm] m spasm.

spatial [spa'sjal] spatial; space ...

spatule [spa'tyl] f 💊 spatula; ⚙ spoon tool; sp. ski-tip.

speaker m, **speakerine** f [spi'kœːr, ~kə'rin] radio: announcer; newsreader, newsreader.

spécial [spe'sjal] special, particular; **~iser** [spesjali'ze] (1a): **se ~ dans** specialize in; **~iste** [~'list] su. specialist; **~ité** [~li'te] f speciality.

spécieux [spe'sjø] specious.

spécifi|cation [spesifika'sjɔ̃] f specification, **~er** [.'fje] (1o) specify; **~que** [~'fik] su./m, adj. specific.

spécimen [spesi'mɛn] specimen; *typ.* specimen *or* sample copy.

spectacle [spɛk'takl] m spectacle, sight; pej. exhibition; thea. show; **le (monde du) ~** show business.

spectateur, -trice [spɛkta'tœːr, ~'tris] su. spectator; witness (*of an event*); su./m: **~s** pl. audience sg.

spectr|al [spɛk'tral] spectral (*phys.*); **~e** [spɛktr] m ghost; *opt.* spectrum.

spécula|teur m, **-trice** f [spekyla'tœːr, ~'tris] ⚹, fig. speculator; **~atif** [~'tif] ⚹, fig. speculative; **~ation** [~'sjɔ̃] f ⚹, fig. speculation; **~er** [speky'le] (1a) ⚹, a. fig. speculate (fig. on, ⚹ in **sur**; ⚹ for, à).

sperme [spɛrm] m sperm, semen.

sphère [sfɛːr] f sphere (*a. fig.*); globe; **sphérique** [~'rik] spherical.

spiral, e [spi'ral] **1.** adj. spiral; **2.** su./f spiral; **en ~e** spiral(ly adv.).

spirit|e [spi'rit] **1.** adj. spiritualistic; **2.** su. spiritualist; **~isme** [spiri'tism] m spirit(ual)ism; **~ualiser** [~tɥali'ze] (1a) spiritualize; **~ualité** [~tɥali'te] f spirituality; **~uel** [~'tɥɛl] spiritual (*a. eccl. etc.*); fig. witty; **~ueux** ⚹ [~'tɥø] **1.** adj. spirituous; **2.** su./m spirit.

spleen [splin] m melancholy.

splend|eur [splɑ̃'dœːr] f splendo(u)r; **~ide** [~'did] splendid; magnificent.

spoli|ation [spɔlja'sjɔ̃] f despoilment; **~er** [~'lje] (1o) despoil (of, **de**).

spongieux [spɔ̃'ʒjø] spongy.

spontané [spɔ̃ta'ne] spontaneous; **~ité** [~nei'te] *f* spontaneity.

sporadique [spɔra'dik] sporadic.

spore ♀, *biol.* [spɔ:r] *f* spore.

sport [spɔ:r] *m* sport; **le ~** sports *pl.*; **sportif, -ve** [spɔr'tif, ~'tiːv] **1.** *adj.* sporting; sports...; **2.** *su./m* sportsman; *su./f* sportswoman.

spumeux [spy'mø] frothy, foamy.

squame [skwam] *f skin:* scale.

square [skwaːr] *m* (public) square (with garden).

squelett|e [skə'lɛt] *m* skeleton; **~ique** [~le'tik] skeletal; skeleton-like.

stab|ilisateur [stabiliza'tœːr] **1.** *adj.* stabilizing; **2.** *su./m* stabilizer; **~iliser** [~'ze] (1a) stabilize; **~ilité** [~'te] *f* stability; *fig.* **~le** [stabl] stable; steady; *fig.* lasting.

stade [stad] *m sp.* stadium; ♣, *a. fig.* stage; period.

stage [sta:ʒ] *m* training course *or* period; ♣♣ articles *pl.*; **stagiaire** [sta'ʒjɛːr] *adj.*, *su.* trainee.

stagna|nt [stag'nã] stagnant; **~tion** [~na'sjɔ̃] *f* stagnation.

stalle [stal] *f thea.*, *stable, etc.:* stall.

stand [stã:d] *m races, show, exhibition:* stand; **~ de tir** rifle range.

standard [stã'da:r] **1.** *su./m teleph.* switchboard; *fig.* standard (of living, **de vie**); **2.** *adj.* standard; **~isation** [stãdardiza'sjɔ̃] *f* standardization; **~iser** ⊚ [~di'ze] (1a) standardize; **~iste** *teleph.* [~'dist] *su.* switchboard operator.

standing [stã'diŋ] *m* standing, status; **(de) grand ~** luxury (*flat, apartment, etc.*).

starter *mot.* [star'tɛːr] *m* choke.

station [sta'sjɔ̃] *f* ✗, ♨, ⚡, *radio:* station; stop, halt; (*holiday*) resort; **en ~** standing; **~naire** [~sjɔ'nɛːr] stationary; **~nement** [~sjɔn'mã] *m* parking; **~ner** [~sjɔ'ne] (1a) park (*car*); **défense f de ~** no parking; **~ bilatéral** (**unilatéral**) parking on both sides (on one side only); **~ interdit** road sign: no parking; **~-service**, *pl.* **~s-service** *mot.* [~sjɔ̃ser'vis] *f* service station.

statique [sta'tik] **1.** *adj.* static; **2.** *su./f* statics *sg.*

statisticien [statisti'sjɛ̃] *m* statistician;

statistique [~'tik] **1.** *adj.* statistical; **2.** *su./f* statistics *sg.*

statu|aire [sta'tɥɛːr] **1.** *adj.* statuary; **2.** *su./m person:* sculptor; *su./f art:* statuary; **~e** [~'ty] *f* statue; image.

statuer ♣♣ [sta'tɥe] (1n): **~ sur** rule on.

stature [sta'ty:r] *f* stature; height.

statut [sta'ty] *m* statute; status; charter; **~aire** [~ty'tɛːr] statutory.

sténo... [steno] steno...; **~dactylo** [~dakti'lo] *su.* shorthand-typist; **~gramme** [~'gram] *m* shorthand report; **~graphe** [~'graf] *su.* stenographer; **~graphie** [~gra'fi] *f* shorthand.

stentor [stã'tɔːr] *npr./m: fig.* **voix f de ~** stentorian voice.

stère [stɛːr] *m* cubic metre.

stéréo... [stereo] stereo...; **~phonie** [~fɔ'ni] *f* stereo(phony); **~phonique** [~fɔ'nik] stereo(phonic); **~type** *typ.* [~'tip] *adj.*, *su./m* stereotype; **~typer** [~ti'pe] (1a) stereotype.

stéril|e [ste'ril] sterile, barren; childless (*marriage*); *fig.* fruitless, vain; **~iser** [sterili'ze] (1a) sterilize; **~ité** [~'te] *f* sterility; barrenness.

sternum *anat.* [stɛr'nɔm] *m* sternum, breastbone.

stigmat|e [stig'mat] *m* stigma; ♣ (pock-)mark; *fig.* stain; *eccl.* **~s** *pl.* stigmata; **~ique** [~ma'tik] stigmatic; **~iser** [~mati'ze] (1a) stigmatize (with, **de**); ♣ pock-mark; *fig.*

stimul|ant [stimy'lã] **1.** *adj.* stimulating; **2.** *su./m* ♣ stimulant; *fig.* incentive; **~ateur** [~la'tœːr] **1.** *adj.* stimulative; **2.** *su./m:* ♣ **cardiaque** pacemaker; **~er** [~'le] (1a) stimulate.

stipendier *pej.* [stipã'dje] (1o) hire, buy (*s.o.*).

stipul|ation ♣♣ [stipyla'sjɔ̃] *f* stipulation; **~er** [~'le] (1a) stipulate.

stock ♣ [stɔk] *m* stock; **~age** [stɔ'kaːʒ] *m* ♣ stocking; storing; **~er** [~'ke] (1a) stock, store.

stoï|cien *phls.* [stɔi'sjɛ̃] **1.** *adj.* stoic(al); **2.** *su.* stoic; **~cisme** [~i'sism] *m* stoicism; **~que** [~'ik] **1.** *adj. fig.* stoic(al); **2.** *su.* stoic.

stoma|cal [stɔma'kal] gastric; stomach (*pump, tube*); **~chique** ♣, *anat.* [~'ʃik] *adj.*, *su./m* stomachic.

stop *mot.* [stɔp] *m* stop sign; brake light, *Am.* stoplight; F hitchhiking.

subsister

stopp|age [stɔ'paːʒ] *m* invisible mending or darning; **~er** [~'pe] (1a) *vt/i.* stop; *v/t. cost.* repair by invisible mending.

store [stɔːr] *m* blind; awning.

strabi|que [stra'bik] **1.** *adj.* squinting, cross-eyed; **2.** *su.* squinter; **~sme** [~'bism] *m* squinting.

strangulation [strãgyla'sjɔ̃] *f* strangulation.

strapontin [strapɔ̃'tɛ̃] *m* bus, taxi, thea.: folding seat, jump seat.

strass [stras] *m* paste jewel(le)ry.

stratagème ✕, *fig.* [strata'ʒɛm] *m* stratagem.

stratégie [strate'ʒi] *f* strategy.

strati|fier [strati'fje] ⚘, *geol., physiol.* stratified; ⊙ laminated.

stratosphère [stratɔs'fɛːr] *f* stratosphere.

strict [strikt] strict; plain.

strident [stri'dã] *m* strident, shrill.

stridul|ant [stridy'lã] stridulant, chirring; **~ation** [~la'sjɔ̃] *f* chirring; **~eux** [~'lø] stridulous.

strie [stri] *f* groove; streak; *anat., geol.* stria; **strié** [stri'e] striated; grooved; **strlure** [~'yːr] *f see* **strie**.

strophe [strɔf] *f* verse; strophe.

structure [stryk'tyːr] *f* structure; **~s** *pl. a.* facilities; **~ gonflable** air hall; **~l** [~ty'rɛl] structural.

stuc △ [styk] *m* stucco; **stucateur** [styka'tœːr] *m* stucco worker.

studieux [sty'djø] studious; devoted to study.

studio [sty'djo] *m* radio, *a. cin.*: studio; flatlet, one-room apartment.

stup|éfaction [stypefak'sjɔ̃] *f* stupefaction; amazement; **~éfait** [~'fɛ] stupefied; **~éfiant** [~'fjã] **1.** *adj.* stupefying (⚘, *a. fig.*); **2.** *su./m* ⚘ drug, narcotic; **~éfier** [~'fje] (1o) ⚘, *a. fig.* stupefy; **~eur** [sty'pœːr] *f* stupor; *fig.* amazement.

stupide [sty'pid] stupid (person); **~ité** [~pidi'te] *f* stupidity; folly.

style [stil] *m* style; **stylé** [sti'le] (well-)trained.

stylet [sti'lɛ] *m* stiletto; ⚘ probe.

stylis|te [sti'list] *su.* stylist; **~er** [~li'ze] (1a) stylize; **~tique** [~lis'tik] *f* stylistics *sg.*

stylo [sti'lo] *m* (fountain) pen; **~ (à) bille** ball-point pen; **~(-)feutre** felt-tip pen; **~graphe** [~lɔ'graf] *m* fountain pen.

su [sy] *p.p. of* **savoir**; *see* **vu**.

suaire [sɥɛːr] *m* shroud.

suav|e [sɥaːv] sweet; bland; soft; **~ité** [sɥavi'te] *f* softness; suavity.

subalterne [sybal'tɛrn] **1.** *adj.* subordinate; junior rank (*civil servant etc.*); **2.** *su.* subordinate.

subconscient [sybkɔ̃'sjã] *adj., su./m* subconscious.

subdivis|er [sybdivi'ze] (1a) subdivide; **~ion** [~'zjɔ̃] *f* subdivision.

subir [sy'biːr] (2a) undergo; suffer; sustain; submit to; come under (*an influence*); put up with, endure; **faire ~ qch. à q.** inflict s.th. on s.o.

subit [sy'bi] sudden, unexpected.

subjectif [sybʒɛk'tif] subjective.

subjonctif *gramm.* [sybʒɔ̃k'tif] *adj., su./m* subjunctive.

subjuguer [sybʒy'ge] (1m) captivate, thrill.

sublim|ation 🜍, *psych.* [syblima'sjɔ̃] *f* sublimation; **~e** [~'blim] **1.** *adj.* sublime; lofty; **2.** *su./m* the sublime; **~** 🜍 [sybli'me] *m* sublimate; **~er** [~] (1a) sublimate; **~ité** [syblimi'te] *f* sublimity.

submer|ger [sybmɛr'ʒe] (1l) submerge; flood (*a field*); immerse (*an object*); swamp (*a boat*); *fig.* overwhelm (with, **de**); **submergé de besogne** snowed under with work; **~sible** [~'sibl] *adj., su./m* submarine; **~sion** [~'sjɔ̃] *f* submersion.

subord|ination [sybɔrdina'sjɔ̃] *f* subordination; **~onné** [~dɔ'ne] **1.** *su.* subordinate; **2.** *adj.:* **être ~** depend on, be subject to; **~onner** [~dɔ'ne] (1a) subordinate (to, **à**).

suborn|ation [sybɔrna'sjɔ̃] *f* subornation; bribing; **~er** [~'ne] (1a) suborn, bribe; † seduce.

subreptice [sybrɛp'tis] surreptitious; **~ment** surreptitiously.

subroger 🕮 [sybrɔ'ʒe] (1l) subrogate; appoint (*s.o.*) as deputy.

subséquemment [sypseka'mã] *adv.* subsequently; in due course; **subséquent** [~'kã] subsequent.

subsid|e [syp'sid] *m* grant, allowance; **~iaire** [~si'djɛːr] *f* subsidiary (to, **à**).

subsist|ance [sybzis'tãːs] *f* subsistence; keep; **~s** *pl.* provisions; **~er** [~'te] (1a) subsist; exist, continue, be extant; live (on, **de**).

substan|ce [syps'tãːs] *f* substance (*a. fig.*); ⚙ material; *anat.* ~ **grise** grey matter; **en** ~ substantially; ~**tiel** [~tã'sjɛl] substantial.

substantif *gramm.* [sypstã'tif] *adj., su./m* substantive.

substitu|er [sypsti'tɥe] (1n) substitute (for, **à**); **se** ~ **à** take the place of; substitute for; ~**t** [~'ty] *m* deputy; substitute; ~**tion** [~ty'sjɔ̃] *f* substitution; mix-up.

substrat [syps'tra] *m* substratum.

subterfuge [sypter'fyːʒ] *m* subterfuge; evasion, shift.

subtil [syp'til] subtle; fine, nice (*difference etc.*); ~**iser** [syptili'ze] (1a) *v/t.* subtilize; F steal; *v/i.* split hairs; ~**ité** [~'te] subtlety; ~**s** *pl. a.* niceties.

suburbain [sybyr'bɛ̃] suburban.

subven|ir [subvə'niːr] (2h): ~ **à** provide for, meet; ~**tion** [sybvã'sjɔ̃] *f* subsidy; grant; ~**tionner** [~sjɔ'ne] (1a) subsidize.

subversi|f [sybver'sif] subversive (of, **de**); ~**on** [~'sjɔ̃] *f* subversion.

suc [syk] *m* juice; ♣ sap; *fig.* essence.

succéd|ané [syksedaˈne] *adj., su./m* substitute (for, **de**); ~**er** [~'de] (1f): ~ **à** follow; succeed (to); inherit; **se** ~ **a.** follow one another, come one after the other.

succès [syk'sɛ] *m* success; hit; **à** ~ successful.

success|eur [syksɛ'sœːr] *m* successor (to, of **de**); ~**if** [~'sif] successive; ~**ion** [~'sjɔ̃] *f* succession; series; ☆ inheritance; ~**ivement** [~siv'mã] *adv.* in succession.

succinct [syk'sɛ̃] succinct, brief.

succion [syk'sjɔ̃] *f* suction; sucking.

succomber [sykɔ̃'be] (1a) die; succumb (to, **à**); *fig.* yield (to, **à**).

succulen|ce [syky'lãːs] *f* succulence; ~**t** [~'lã] succulent; tasty.

succursale ♥ [sykyr'sal] *f* branch; **maison** *f* **à** ~**s multiples** chainstore.

sucer [sy'se] (1k) suck; *fig.* ~ **avec le lait** imbibe (*s.th.*) from infancy; **sucette** [~'sɛt] *f* dummy, *Am.* pacifier; lollipop; **suçoir** *zo.* [~'swaːr] *m* organ; sucker; **suçon** F [~'sɔ̃] *m* kiss mark, love bite; **suçoter** [~sɔ'te] (1a) suck (at).

sucr|age ⚙ [sy'kraːʒ] *m* sugaring; ~**e** [sykr] *m* sugar; ~ **de raisin** grape sugar; ~ **en morceaux** (**poudre**) lump (castor) sugar; ~**é** sweet (*food*); sweetened; *fig.*

sugary; ~**er** [sy'kre] (1a) sugar; sweeten; ~**erie** [~krə'ri] *f* sugar refinery; ~**s** *pl.* sweets, *Am.* candies; ~**ier** [~kri'e] **1.** *adj.* sugar-...; **2.** *su./m* sugar bowl *or* basin.

sud [syd] **1.** *su./m* south; ♣ south wind; **du** ~ south(ern); **le** ♋ the south (*of a country*); **2.** *adj./inv.* southern (*latitudes*); southerly (*wind*).

sudation ✿ [syda'sjɔ̃] *f* sweating.

sud-est [sy'dɛst] **1.** *su./m* south-east; **2.** *adj./inv.* south-eastern (*region*); south-easterly (*wind*).

sud-ouest [sy'dwɛst] **1.** *su./m* south-west; **2.** *adj./inv.* south-western (*region*); south-westerly (*wind*).

suède [sɥɛd] *m:* **de** (*or* **en**) ~ suède (*gloves*); **suédois** [sɥe'dwa] **1.** *adj., su./m ling.* Swedish; **2.** *su.* ♋ Swede.

suée [sɥe] *f* F sweat(ing); *sl.* drag, pain; **suer** [~] (1n) *v/i.* sweat (*a. fig.* = *toil*); F **faire** ~ *q.* make s.o. sick; *v/t.* sweat; *fig.* reek of; *fig.* ~ **sang et eau** sweat blood; **sueur** [sɥœːr] *f* sweat.

suffi [sy'fi] *p.p.* of **suffire**; ~**re** [~'fiːr] (4i) (for, **à**) be enough; be sufficient; suffice; *fig.* ~ **à** meet (*expenses*); **il suffit de ... pour** (*inf.*) it just takes ... to (*inf.*); **il suffit que** it is enough that; ~**samment** [syfiza'mã] *adv.* sufficiently, enough; ~**sance** [~'zãːs] *f* sufficiency; *pej.* conceit; **à** (*or* **en**) ~ in plenty; ~**sant** [~'zã] sufficient; *pej.* conceited, self-important; ~**sons** [~'zɔ̃] *1st p. pl. pres. of* **suffire.**

suffixe *gramm.* [sy'fiks] *m* suffix.

suffo|cant [syfɔ'kã] suffocating, stifling; ~**cation** [~ka'sjɔ̃] *f* suffocation; ~**quer** [~'ke] (1m) *v/t.* suffocate; stifle; *v/i.* choke (with, **de**).

suffrage *pol.* [sy'fraːʒ] *m* suffrage; vote; *fig.* approval; ~**s** *pl.* **exprimés** valid votes.

sugg|érer [sygʒe're] (1f) suggest; ~**estif** [~ʒɛs'tif] suggestive; ~**estion** [~ʒɛs'tjɔ̃] *f* suggestion.

suicid|aire [sɥisi'dɛːr] suicidal; suicide-prone; ~**e** [sɥi'sid] *m* suicide; ~**é** *m*, **e** *f* [sɥisi'de] *person;* suicide; ~**er** [~] (1a): **se** ~ commit suicide.

suie [sɥi] *f* soot.

suif [sɥif] *m* tallow; *sl.* telling off; ~**fer** [sɥi'fe] (1a) tallow; grease.

suinter [sɥɛ̃'te] (1a) ooze, sweat.

suis[1] [sɥi] *1st p. sg. pres. of* **être** 1.

suis[2] [sɥi] *1st p. sg. pres. of* **suivre**.

suisse [sɥis] **1.** *adj.* Swiss; **2.** *su./m eccl.* beadle; Swiss guard; *hotel:* porter; **2** Swiss; *less* **2s** *pl.* the Swiss; *petit* ~ small cream cheese; **2sse** [sɥi'sɛs] *f* Swiss (woman).

suite [sɥit] *f* continuation; retinue, train; sequence, series; *fig.* result, consequence; *fig.* coherence; **ɸ** ~ **à** with reference to, **à la** ~ **de** following (*s.th.*); *de* ~ on end, in succession, in a row; at once, immediately; *donner* ~ **à** carry out, follow up; *et ainsi de* ~ and so on; *manquer (d'esprit) de* ~ lack method or coherence; *par la* ~ later on; *par* ~ **de** as a result of, owing to.

suiv|ant, e [sɥi'vã, ~'vã:t] **1.** *adj.* following, next; *au* ~ next!; **2.** *su.* follower; *su./f* lady's-maid; **3.** **suivant** *prp.* following, along, *fig.* according to; ~ *que* according as; **~l** [~'vi] **1.** *p.p. of* **suivre**; **2.** *adj.* consistent; steady; regular, uninterrupted; coherent (*speech, reasoning, story, etc.*); *très (peu)* ~ very popular (unpopular); (not) widely followed; well- (poorly) attended; **~re** [sɥi:vr] (4ee) *vt/i.* follow; come after; *v/t.* attend (*lectures etc.*); ~ *des yeux* look after (*s.o.*); *v/i.:* **à** ~ to be continued; *faire* ~ *post:* forward.

sujet [sy'ʒɛ] **1.** *adj.:* ~ **à** subject to, prone to, liable to; **2.** *su./m* subject (*a. gramm.*, **♪** *a. fig.* = person); theme; reason (for, *de*); **à ce** ~ about this; *au* ~ *de* about, concerning; **sujétion** [syʒe'sjɔ̃] *f* subjection; constraint.

sulf|amide **♪** [sylfa'mid] *f* sulpha drug, *Am.* sulfa drug; **~ate** **♫** [~'fat] *m* sulphate, *Am.* sulfate; **~ure** **♫** [~'fy:r] *m* sulphide, *Am.* sulfide; **~ureux** [~fy'rø] sulphurous, *Am.* sulfurous.

super... [sypɛr] super-...

superbe [sy'pɛrb] superb; fine; glorious, gorgeous.

super...: **~carburant** *mot* [sypɛrkarby'lɑ̃] *m* high octane petrol or *Am.* gasoline; **~cherie** [~ʃə'ri] *f* fraud, deceit; **~fétation** [~feta'sjɔ̃] *f* superfluity; **~ficie** [~fi'si] *f* area; surface (*a. fig.*); **~ficiel** [~fi'sjɛl] superficial (*a. fig.*); **~fin** [~'fɛ̃] superfine; **~flu** [~'fly] **1.** *adj.* superfluous; useless; **2.** *su./m* superfluity; **~fluité** [~flɥi'te] *f* superfluity.

supéri|eur [sype'rjœ:r] **1.** *adj.* superior (*a. fig.*); upper, higher; ~ **à** superior to; above; **2.** *su.* superior; **~orité** [~rjɔri'te] *f* superiority (*a. fig.*); seniority (in age, *d'âge*).

super...: **~latif** [sypɛrla'tif] *adj.*, *su./m* superlative; **~marché** **ϯ** [~mar'ʃe] *m* supermarket; **~posable** [~po'zabl] super(im)posable; **~poser** [~po'ze] (1a) super(im)pose (on, **à**); **~position** [~pozi'sjɔ̃] *f* superimposition; **~(-)puissance** *pol.* [~pɥi'sã:s] *f* superpower; **~sonique** **✈** [~sɔ'nik] supersonic; *bang* *m* ~ sonic boom; **~stitieux** [~sti'sjø] superstitious; **~stition** [~sti'sjɔ̃] *f* superstition; **~structure** [~stryk'ty:r] **♫** **♪**, **⚓** superstructure; **~viser** [~vi'ze] (1a) supervise.

supplanter [syplã'te] (1n) supplant.

supplé|ant [syple'ã] **1.** *adj.* deputy ...; **2.** *su.* deputy; supply teacher; **~s** *pl. a.* temporary staff *sg.*; **~er** [~'e] (1a) *v/t.* complete; deputize for; *v/i.:* ~ **à** make up for; remedy; **~ment** [~'mã] *m* supplement (*a. book*); addition; extra charge; *restaurant:* extra course; **~mentaire** [~mã'tɛ:r] extra, additional; supplementary; **⌚** *heures f/pl.* **~s** overtime *sg.*

suppli|ant [sypli'ã] **1.** *adj.* imploring; **2.** *su.* supplic(i)ant; **~cation** [~ka'sjɔ̃] *f* supplication, entreaty.

supplic|e [sy'plis] *m* torture; torment, agony; **⚖** *dernier* ~ capital punishment; **~ier** [~pli'sje] (1o) torture; torment.

suppli|er [sypli'e] (1a) beseech, implore; **~que** [sy'plik] *f* petition.

support [sy'pɔ:r] *m* support; stand, pedestal; *fig.* mainstay; **~able** [sypɔr'tabl] tolerable, bearable; **~er** [~'te] (1a) support; tolerate; withstand; bear, endure, put up with.

suppos|é [sypo'ze] **1.** *adj.* supposed; estimated (*number etc.*); **~er** [~'ze] (1a) suppose; *fig.* imply, presuppose; **à** ~ *que*, *en supposant que* supposing (that); **~ition** [~zi'sjɔ̃] *f* supposition.

suppositoire **♪** [sypozi'twa:r] *m* suppository.

suppôt *pej.* [sy'po] *m* hechman.

suppr|ession [sypre'sjɔ̃] *f* suppression; difficulty; removal; abolition; **~imer** [sypri'me] (1a) suppress; abolish; do away with;

stop; cut out; *fig.* omit; ⚕ conceal; F kill; cancel.

suppur|ation ⚕ [sypyra'sjɔ̃] *f* festering; **~er** [~'re] (1a) form pus.

supputer [sypy'te] (1a) calculate, reckon; work out (*expenses etc.*).

supr|ématie [syprema'si] *f* supremacy; **~ême** [~'prɛm] supreme; highest; *fig.* last (*hour etc.*).

sur¹ [syr] *prp. usu.* on (*a chair, the Thames, my word*), upon; over, above; *destination:* towards (*evening, old age*); *measurement:* by; *number:* out of; *succession:* after; **~ la droite** on or to the right; **~ place** on the spot; **~ soi** on or about one; **~ ce** thereupon, and then; **~ quoi** whereupon, and then; **être ~ un travail** be at a task; **8 ~ 10** 8 out of 10; *measurement:* 8 by 10; **coup ~ coup** blow after blow; **fermer la porte ~ soi** close the door behind one; **~ un ton sévère** in a grave voice.

sur² [sy:r] sour; tart.

sur... [syr] over-...; super...; supra...

sûr [sy:r] sure (of, *de*); safe; reliable; *fig.* certain, unfailing; **~ de soi** self-confident; **à coup ~** definitely, for certain; **bien ~!** certainly, sure(ly).

surabond|ance [syrabɔ̃'dɑ̃] *f* superabundance; **~ant** [~'dɑ̃] superabundant; **~er** [~'de] (1a) overabound; overflow (with *de, en*).

suraigu, -guë [syre'gy] high-pitched (very) shrill.

suranné [syra'ne] old-fashioned.

surcharg|e [syr'ʃarʒ] *f* overload(ing); extra *or* excess load; *manuscript etc.:* alteration, correction; **~er** [~ʃar'ʒe] (1l) overload (*a. ♪*), overburden; surcharge.

surchauffer [syrʃo'fe] (1a) overheat; superheat (*steam*); burn (*iron*).

surchoix [syr'ʃwa] *m* finest quality.

surclasser [syrkla'se] (1a) outclass.

surcoup|e [syr'kup] *f* overtrumping; **~er** [~ku'pe] (1a) overtrump.

surcroît [syr'krwa] *m:* **un ~ de ...** (an) additional *or* added...; **de** (*or par*) **~** moreover; into the bargain; what is more.

surdi|-mutité [syrdimyti'te] *f* deaf-and-dumbness; **~té** [~'te] *f* deafness.

surdoué [syr'dwe] exceptionally gifted.

sureau ♀ [sy'ro] *m* elder.

surélever [syrel've] (1d) △, ♈ heighten, raise; bank (*a road bend*).

suren|chère [syrɑ̃'ʃɛ:r] *f* higher bid; overbid; *fig.* exaggerated promises *pl.*; **~chérir** [~ʃe'ri:r] (2a) *auction:* bid higher; **~ sur q.** outbid s.o.; *fig. a.* (try and) go one better than.

surestimer [syrɛsti'me] (1a) overestimate; overrate (*s.o.*).

suret [sy'rɛ] sourish.

sûreté [syr'te] *f* safety; security (*a.* ♈); *fig.* sureness; *judgment etc.:* soundness; *memory;* reliability; **pour plus de ~** to be on the safe side; **~ de soi** self-assurance; **de ~** safety-...; **la ♀** the C.I.D., *Am.* the F.B.I.

surexcit|ation [syrɛksita'sjɔ̃] *f* overexcitement; ⚕ overstimulation; **~er** [~'te] (1a) overexcite.

surexposer *phot.* [syrɛkspo'ze] (1a) overexpose.

surface [syr'fas] *f* surface; ⊼ surface area; area.

surfaire [syr'fɛ:r] (4r) overrate (*a book etc.*); ♈ charge too much for.

surfer [sœr'fe] (1a) surf(ride).

surgelé [syrʒə'le] deep- *or* quick-frozen.

surgir [syr'ʒi:r] (2a) appear (suddenly); spoing up; *fig.* arise.

surhomme [sy'rɔm] *m* superman; **surhumain** [~ry'mɛ̃] superhuman.

surimposer [syrɛ̃po'ze] (1a) superimpose; ♈ overtax.

surimpression *phot.* [syrɛ̃prɛ'sjɔ̃] *f* double exposure.

surir [sy'ri:r] (2a) turn sour.

sur-le-champ [syrlə'ʃɑ̃] *adv.* at once, on the spot.

surlendemain [syrlɑ̃d'mɛ̃] *m* second day (after s.th., **de qch.**).

surmen|age [syrmə'na:ʒ] *m* overwork(ing); **~er** [~'ne] (1d) overwork; ❀, ♈ overrun.

surmont|able [syrmɔ̃'tabl] surmountable; **~er** [~'te] (1a) rise above (*a. fig.*), top; surmount; *fig.* overcome (*an enemy, feelings*); **se ~** control o.s.

surnager [syrna'ʒe] (1l) float (on the surface); *fig.* linger (on).

surnaturel [syrnaty'rɛl] **1.** *adj.* supernatural; *fig.* uncanny; **2.** *su./m:* **le ~** the supernatural.

surnom [syr'nɔ̃] *m* nickname; appellation, name; *hist.* agnomen.

surnombre [syr'nɔ̃:br] *m* excess number; **en ~** too many.

surnommer [syrnɔ'me] (1a) call (s.o. s.th., *q. qch.*); nickname.

surnuméraire [syrnyme'rɛ:r] *adj.*, *su./m* supernumerary.

surpasser [syrpɑ'se] (1a) surpass (*s.o.*, *o.s.*), exceed, outdo.

surpaye [syr'pɛ:j] *f* overpayment; extra pay; **~er** [~pɛ'je] (1i) overpay (*s.o.*); pay too much for (*s.th.*).

surpeupl|é [syrpœ'ple] overpopulated; **~ement** [~plə'mɑ̃] *m* overpopulation.

sur(-)place [syr'plas] *m.* **faire du ~** mark time.

surplomb [syr'plɔ̃] *m* overhang; **en ~** overhanging; **~ement** [~plɔ̃b'mɑ̃] *m* overhang(ing); **~er** [~plɔ̃'be] (1a) overhang.

surplus [syr'ply] *m* surplus, excess; **au ~** moreover; **en ~** excess ...

surpren|ant [syrprə'nɑ̃] surprising; **~dre** [~'prɑ̃:dr] (4aa) surprise; astonish; catch (*s.o.*) (unawares); pay (*s.o.*) a surprise visit; overhear; intercept (*a glance, a letter*); **~ la bonne foi de q.** abuse s.o.'s good faith.

surpris [syr'pri] surprised; **~e** [~'pri:z] *f* surprise; **par ~** by surprise.

sur(-)prix [syr'pri] *m* excessive price; overcharge.

surproduction [syrprɔdyk'sjɔ̃] *f* overproduction.

surrégénérateur *phys.* [syreʒenera'tœr] *m* fast breeder.

sursaut [syr'so] *m* start, jump; **s'éveiller en ~** wake with a start; **~er** [~so'te] (1a) (give a) start.

surseoir [syr'swa:r] (3c): **~ à** stay (*a judgment*); defer; **sursis** [~'si] **1.** *p.p. of* **surseoir**; **2.** *su./m* delay; suspension of sentence; ⚔ *call-up:* deferment; **sursitaire** ⚔ [~si'tɛ:r] *m* deferred (conscript).

surtax|e [syr'taks] *f* surcharge; **~er** [~tak'se] (1a) surcharge.

surtout [syr'tu] *adv.* above all; particularly, especially.

surveill|ance [syrvɛ'jɑ̃:s] *f* watch; supervision; ⚖, ⚕ *etc.* surveillance; **~ant** [~'jɑ̃] *su.* overseer; *prison:* warder; *school:* monitor; **~e** [syr'vɛ:j] *f:* **la ~ de** two days before ...; **~er** [~vɛ'je] (1a) watch (over); keep (a) watch on; super-

vise, oversee; ⚖ **liberté** *f* **surveillée** probation.

survenir [syrvə'ni:r] (2h) occur, happen; take place; set in (*complications etc.*); arrive unexpectedly (*person*).

survi|e [syr'vi] *f* survival; afterlife; **~vance** [~vi'vɑ̃:s] *f* survival (*a. fig.*); *estate:* reversion; **~vant** [~vi'vɑ̃] **1.** *adj.* surviving; **2.** *su.* survivor; **~vre** [~'vi:vr] (4hh): **~ à** outlive; survive.

survol [syr'vɔl] *m* flight over; *cin.* panning; **~er** [~vɔ'le] (1a) fly over.

survolté [syrvɔl'te] ⚡ boosted; *fig.* (over)excited, worked up.

sus[1] [sy] *1st p. sg. p.s. of* **savoir 1**.

sus[2] [sy(s)] **1.** *adv.:* **courir ~ à** rush at (*s.o.*); **en ~ (de)** in addition (to); **2.** *int.:* **~ à ...!** at (*s.o.*)!; up (*s.th.*)!

susceptib|ilité [sysɛptibili'te] *f* susceptibility, sensitiveness, touchiness; **~le** [~'tibl] susceptible, sensitive; **~ de** capable of; liable to.

susciter [sysi'te] (1a) cause, give rise to; provoke, arouse; stir up.

suscription [syskrip'sjɔ̃] *f letter:* address.

sus|dit [sys'di] above-mentioned; **~mentionné** [~mũsjo'ne] *see* **susdit**; **~nommé** [sysno'me] above-named.

suspect [sys'pɛ] **1.** *adj.* suspicious; suspect (*person*); **~ de** suspected of; **2.** *su.* suspect; **~er** [~pɛk'te] (1a) suspect (*s.o.*); doubt (*s.th.*).

suspen|dre [sys'pɑ̃:dr] (4a) hang up; *fig.* suspend, defer; *fig.* interrupt; **~du** [~pɑ̃'dy] hanging; **~s** [~'pɑ̃] *m:* **en ~** in suspense (*a.* ⚖); unsolved; **~se** [sys'pɑ̃s] *m* suspense; **~sion** [~'sjɔ̃] *f* suspension; hanging; (hanging) lamp; *mot.* springs *pl.*; ⚔ *armistice;* *gramm.* **points** *m/pl.* **de ~** points of suspension.

suspicion [syspi'sjɔ̃] *f* suspicion; **tenir q. en ~** suspect s.o.

sustent|ation ✈ [systɑ̃ta'sjɔ̃] *f* lift(ing force); **~er** [~'te] (1a) F **se ~** take sustenance.

susurrer [sysy're] (1a) whisper.

suture [sy'ty:r] *f* ⚕ suture; *fig.* join.

suzerain [syz'rɛ̃] *adj.*, *su.* suzerain; **~eté** [~rɛn'te] *f* suzerainty.

svelte [svɛlt] slender, slim; **~sse** [svɛl'tɛs] *f* slenderness, slimness.

sycophante [sikɔ'fɑ̃:t] *m* sycophant.

syllabe [sil'lab] f syllable.

sylph|e [silf] m, **~ide** [sil'fid] f sylph; *taille f de sylphide* sylph-like waist.

sylv|ain [sil'vɛ̃] m sylvan; **~estre ⚥** [~'vɛstr] growing in the woods; **~iculture** [silvikyl'ty:r] f forestry.

symbol|e [sɛ̃'bɔl] m symbol; *eccl.* ⚩ creed; **~ique** [sɛ̃bɔ'lik] symbolic(al); **~iser** [~li'ze] (1a) symbolize.

symétrie [sime'tri] f symmetry; **symétrique** [~'trik] symmetrical.

sympa F [sɛ̃'pa] nice, likable.

sympathi|e [sɛ̃pa'ti] f sympathy; *fig.* liking, congeniality; **~que** [~'tik] nice, likable; pleasant; *fig.* congenial; invisible (ink); *il m'est* ~ I like him; **~sant** [~ti'zɑ̃] 1. *adj.* sympathizing; 2. *su./m* fellow-traveller; sympathiser; **~ser** [~ti'ze] (1a) harmonize; have a liking (for, *avec*); sympathize (with, *avec*).

symptôme [sɛ̃p'to:m] m ⚕, *a. fig.* symptom; *fig.* sign.

syn... [*before vowel* sin...; *before consonant* sɛ̃...] syn...; **~chronique** [sɛ̃krɔ'nik] synchronological; **~chronisation** [~niza'sjɔ̃] f synchronization; **~chroniser** [~ni'ze] (1e) synchronize; **~cope** [~'kɔp] f syncope; ⚕ blackout; ♩ syncopation; **~copé** [~kɔ'pe] (1a) syncopated.

syndi|c [sɛ̃'dik] m managing agent; ⚖

receiver; **~cal** [sɛ̃di'kal] syndical; trade-union; **~caliser** [~kali'ze] (1a) unionize; **~calisme** [~ka'lism] m trade-unionism; **~caliste** [~ka'list] su. trade unionist; **~cat** [~'ka] m syndicate; association; (⚒ **ouvrier** trade) union; **~ d'initiative** tourist information bureau; **~ patronal** employers' federation; **~ professionnel** trade association; **~qué** [~'ke] 1. *adj.* associated; union-...; 2. *su.* trade unionist; **~quer** [~'ke] (1m) unionize; *se* ~ combine; form a syndicate *or* trade union; join a union.

syndrome [sɛ̃'drɔm] m syndrome.

synonyme [sinɔ'nim] 1. *adj.* synonymous (with, *de*); 2. *su./m* synonym.

synoptique [sinɔp'tik] synoptic.

syntax|e [sɛ̃'taks] f syntax; **~ique** [~tak'sik] syntactic(al).

synthèse [sɛ̃'tɛz] f synthesis; **synthétique** [sɛ̃te'tik] synthetic; **synthétiser** [~ti'ze] (1a) synthesize.

systématique [sistema'tik] systematic; *fig.* hide-bound; **systématiser** [~ti'ze] (1a) systematize; **système** [sis'tɛm] m system; F ~ **D** resourcefulness; wangling; *anat.* **~ nerveux** nervous system; *fig. esprit m de* ~ (overly) systematic mind; F *ça me tape sur le* ~ that gets on my nerves.

T

T [te] m: ⚙ *fer m en T* T-iron.

ta [ta] *see* **ton¹**.

taba|c [ta'ba] 1. *su./m* tobacco; ~ **à priser** snuff; F *passer à* ~ beat (*s.o.*) up; 2. *adj./inv.* tobacco-colo(u)red; **~gie** [taba'ʒi] f place smelling of stale tobacco smoke; **~gisme** [~'ʒism] m nicotine poisoning; **~sser** F [~'se] (1a) beat (*s.o.*) up; **~tière** [~'tjɛːr] f snuffbox.

tabl|e [tabl] f table; *stone*: slab; *teleph.* switchboard; index; ~ **à rallonges** extending table; **~ ~ de multiplication** multiplication table; ~ **d'hôte** set dinner; *à* ~*!* dinner is served!; *se mettre à* ~ sit down at table; *sl.* talk, come clean; **~eau** [ta'blo] m picture (*a. fig.*); painting; *thea.*, *a. fig.* scene; notices, *a. ⚡, sp.*: board; *hotel*: keyboard; list, table; ⚖, *a.* ⚖ *jurors*: panel; ~ **d'annonces** notice board, *Am.* bulletin board; ~ **de bord** *mot.* dashboard; ✈ instrument panel; ~ **(noir)** blackboard; **~ée** [~'ble] f (tableful of) guests *pl.*; **~er** [~'ble] (1a): ~ **sur** count on; **~ette** [~'blɛt] f shelf; *stone*: slab; sill; *sideboard etc.*: (flat) top; ⚖ plate; ⚡ lozenge; *chocolate*: bar; *rayez ça de vos* ~*s!* you can forget that!

tablier [tabli'e] *m* apron, *child*: pinafore; *bridge*: road(way); ⚙ *etc.* shutter; *fig.* **rendre son ~** give notice.

tabou [ta'bu] *adj., su./m* taboo.

tabouret [tabu're] *m* (foot)stool.

tabulaire [taby'lɛːr] tabular; **tabulateur** [~la'tœːr] *m* tabulator.

tac [tak] *m* mill: clack; click; *fig.* **riposter du ~ au ~** give tit for tat.

tache [taʃ] *f* stain; spot; blot; mark; *fig.* **faire ~** jar.

tâche [tɑːʃ] *f* task, job; **pendre à ~ de** (*inf.*) undertake to (*inf.*); **travailler à la ~** do general jobbing.

tacher [ta'ʃe] (1a) stain, spot.

tâcher [ta'ʃe] (1a) try; **~ de** (*inf.*), **~ que** (*sbj.*) try to (*inf.*); **~on** [taʃ'rɔ̃] *m* piece-worker; △ jobber.

tacheter [taʃ'te] (1c) fleck, speckle.

tachy- [taki] tachy...; **tacho...**; **~mètre** ⚙ [~'mɛtr] *m* speedometer.

tacite [ta'sit] tacit; implied; **taciturne** [~si'tyrn] taciturn; reserved.

tacot F [ta'ko] *m* jalopy.

tact [takt] *m* (sense of) touch; *fig.* tact, **manque ~ de ~** tactlessness.

tacticien [takti'sjɛ̃] *m* tactician.

tactile [tak'til] tactile.

tactique [tak'tik] **1.** *adj.* tactical; ✗, *a. fig.* tactics *pl.* **2.** *su./f* ✗, *a. fig.* tactics *pl.*

taie [tɛ] *f* (pillow)case, slip.

taillade [tɑ'jad] *f* slash, cut; **~oder** [~ja'de] (1a) slash; gash; **~ant** [~'jɑ̃] *m* (cutting) edge; **~e** [tɑːj] *f* cutting; ✁ pruning; clipping; *stone*: hewing; *hair, tool, clothes*: cut; *blade*: edge; *fig.* size, dimension *pl.*; *person*: height, stature; waist, figure; F **de ~** big; **être de ~ à** (*inf.*) be capable of (*ger.*); **~e-crayon** [tajkrɛ'jɔ̃] *m/inv.* pencil sharpener; **~er** [tɑ'je] (1a) *v/t.* cut; carve; hew; trim; ✁ prune; ⚙ mill; sharpen (*a pencil*); **bien taillé** well set-up (*person*); *cost.* well-cut; *v/i. cards*: deal; **~eur** [tɑ'jœːr] *m* ⚙ cutter; *cost.* tailor; *cost.* (*a. costume m* ~) lady's suit; **~pantalon** *m* trouser suit, pant(s) suit; **~is** [~'ji] *m* copse.

tain ⚙ [tɛ̃] *m* mirror: silvering.

taire [tɛːr] (4z) suppress, hush up, say nothing about; **faire ~** silence, hush; **se ~** stop talking; be silent, say nothing; **taisez-vous!** be quiet!; **taisons** [tɛ'zɔ̃] *1st p.pl. pres. of taire*; **tait** [tɛ] *3rd p. sg. pres. of taire*.

talent [ta'lɑ̃] *m* talent; **de ~** gifted; **~ueux** F [~lɑ̃'tɥø] talented.

talion [ta'ljɔ̃] *m* retaliation.

taloch|e [ta'lɔʃ] *f* cuff, clout; **~er** F [~lɔ'ʃe] (1a) cuff, clout.

talon [ta'lɔ̃] *m* heel; ✝ stub, counterfoil; **~ner** [talɔ'ne] (1a) follow (on the heels of); dog (*s.o.*); spur on, urge on (*s.o.*); **~nette** [~'nɛt] *f* heel.

talus [ta'ly] *m* slope; bank, embankment; **en ~** sloping.

tambouille *sl.* [tɑ̃'buːj] *f* kitchen.

tambour [tɑ̃'buːr] *m* ♪, ⚙ *etc.* drum; drummer; *coil*: cylinder; △ revolving door; ♪ **~ de basque** tambourine (*with jingles*); **sans ~ ni trompette** on the quiet; **~in** [tɑ̃bu'rɛ̃] *m* ♪ tambourine (*without jingles*); long, narrow drum; **~iner** [~ri'ne] (1a) drum (*a. fig.*).

tamis [ta'mi] *m* sieve; strainer; screen; riddle; bolter; **passer au ~** sift (*a. fig.*); **~er** [tami'ze] (1a) sift, sieve; strain; filter; *fig.* soften (*the light*); **lumière tamisée** subdued *or* soft(ened) light.

tampon [tɑ̃'pɔ̃] *m* plug; stopper; pad, wad; rubber stamp; 🚂 buffer; **coup m de ~** collision; *pol.* **État m ~** buffer State; **~nement** [~pɔn'mɑ̃] *m* plugging; collision; dabbing; F thumping; **~ner** [~pɔ'ne] (1a) dab, mop; stamp (*a letter etc.*); 🚂 *etc.* collide with (*mot.* bump into; ⚙ plug.

tam-tam [tam'tam] *m* ♪ tom-tom; ♪ (*Chinese*) gong; *fig.* fuss, to-do.

tan [tɑ̃] *m* tan, tanner's bark.

tancer [tɑ̃'se] (1k) scold, F tell off.

tandem [tɑ̃'dɛm] *m* tandem; *fig.* pair, twosome; *fig.* combination; **en ~** together.

tanche *icht.* [tɑ̃ːʃ] *f* tench.

tandis [tɑ̃'di] *cj.*: **~ que** whereas (*emphasizing difference*); while.

tangage ⚓, ✈ [tɑ̃'gaːʒ] *m* pitch.

tangent, e [tɑ̃'ʒɑ̃, ~'ʒɑ̃ːt] **1.** *adj.* ⅄ tangent(ial) (to, à); **2.** *su./f* ⅄ tangent; F **prendre la ~, s'échapper par la ~** make off; dodge the issue; **tangible** [~'ʒibl] tangible.

tanguer ⚓, ✈ [tɑ̃'ge] (1m) pitch.

tanière [ta'njɛːr] *f* den, lair (*a. fig.*).

tanne 💊 [tan] *f* face: blackhead.

tanner [ta'ne] (1a) tan; weather; F pester; F **~le cuir à q.** tan s.o.'s hide; **tannerie**

[tan'ri] *f* tannery; **tanneur** [ta'nœːr] *m* tanner; **tan(n)in** [~'nɛ̃] *m* tannin.

tan-sad [tɑ̃'sad] *m* pillion.

tant [tɑ̃] *adv.* so much; so *or* as many; so; as much, as hard (as, *que*); so *or* as long (as, *que*); ~ **de** ... so much ...; so many; ~ **de fois** so often; ~ **heureuse qu'elle paraisse** however happy she may seem; ~ **mieux!** so much the better!; ~ **pis!** too bad (for, *pour*); ~ **s'en faut** far from it; ~ **s'en faut que** (*sbj.*) far from (*ger.*); ~ **soit peu** just a bit; **en** ~ **que** in so far as (+ *adj.*); (considered) as (+ *su.*); **si** ~ **est que** if indeed.

tante [tɑ̃ːt] *f* aunt; *sl.* nancy-boy, queer; F **chez ma** ~ in pawn, in pawn.

tantième ✝ [tɑ̃'tjɛm] *m* percentage.

tantinet F [tɑ̃ti'ne] *m*: **un** ~ a bit.

tantôt [tɑ̃'to] **1.** *adv.* soon, by and by; just now; ~ ... ~ ... sometimes ... sometimes ...; **à** ~ so long!; **2.** *su./m* F afternoon.

taon *zo.* [tɑ̃] *m* gad-fly, horse-fly.

tap|age [ta'paːʒ] *m* noise; din; *fig.* row; fuss; **faire du** ~ make a stir (*news*); **~ageur** [~pa'ʒœːr] **1.** *adj.* noisy; *cost.* flashy; *fig.* blustering; **2.** *su.* rowdy; brawler; noisy person; **~e** [tap] *f* slap; **~é,** **e** [ta'pe] **1.** *adj.* dried (*fruit*); *fig.* first-class; **réponse** *f* **~e** smart answer; *sl.* crazy, nutty; **2.** *su./f* F lots *pl.*, heaps *pl.*; **~e-à-l'œil** F [tapa'lœj] **1.** *adj.* showy, flasky; **2.** *su./m* show, window-dressing; **~er** [ta'pe] (1a) *v/t.* F smack, slap; slam (*the door*); beat (*a drum*); type (*a letter etc.*); dab on (*paint*); F touch (*s.o.*) (for, *de*); *sl.* **se** ~ **qch.** eat *or* drink s.th.; do s.th.; *v/i.* knock; hit; bang; ~ **dans l'œil à** take (*s.o.'s*) fancy; ~ **du pied** stamp (one's foot); ~ **sur q.** slate s.o.; **~ette** [~'pɛt] *f* gentle tap; *sl.* queer, nancy-boy; F **avoir une (bonne)** ~ be a real chatterbox.

tapinois [tapi'nwa] *adv.*: **en** ~ quietly, on the sly.

tapir [ta'piːr] (2a): **se** ~, **être tapi** crouch; hide.

tapis [ta'pi] *m* carpet; cloth; ⊙ ~ **roulant** endless belt; ~ **vert** (gaming) table; *fig.* **mettre sur le** ~ bring (*s.th.*) up (for discussion); **~ser** [~pi'se] (1a) paper (*a room*); hang (*a wall*) with tapestry; *fig.* cover, line; **~serie** [~pis'ri] *f* tapestry; wallpaper; *fig.* **faire** ~ be a wall-

flower (*at a dance*); **~sier** [~pi'sje] *m* tapestry-maker; upholsterer; paper hanger.

tapoter F [tapo'te] (1a) tap; pat.

taquet ⊙ [ta'kɛ] *m* wedge, block.

taquin [ta'kɛ̃] **1.** *adj.* teasing; **2.** *su.* tease; **~er** [~ki'ne] (1a) tease; *fig.* worry; **~erie** [~kin'ri] *f* teasing.

tarabiscoté [tarabisko'te] ⊙ grooved; *fig.* over-elaborate (*style*).

tarabuster F [tarabys'te] (1a) worry, bother; pester.

tarauder [taro'de] (1a) ⊙ tap; ⊙ thread; *a. fig.* pierce.

tard [taːr] **1.** *adv.* late; **au plus** ~ at the latest; **il se fait** ~ it is getting late; **pas plus** ~ **que** ... not later than ...; **tôt ou** ~ sooner or later; **2.** *su./m*: **sur le** ~ late in the day; *fig.* late in life; **~er** [tar'de] (1a) take a long time (coming), be a long time coming; delay (doing s.th., **à faire qch.**) (*person*); **ça ne tardera pas à arriver** this will happpen before long; **il me tarde de** (*inf.*) I am anxious to (*inf.*); **sans (plus)** ~ without (further) delay; **~if** [~'dif] late; belated (*apology*, *regret*); *fig.* slow (to, **à**); backward (*fruit*, *a. fig. intelligence*); **~illon** [~di'jɔ̃] *m* latest born; **~ivement** late; **~iveté** [~div'te] *f* lateness; slowness; backwardness.

tare [taːr] *f* ✝ tare; *fig.* defect, flaw, taint; ✝ **faire la** ~ allow for the tare; **taré** [ta're] spoiled, damaged; with a defect; *a.* tainted; *fig.* corrupt.

tarentule *zo.* [tarɑ̃'tyl] *f* tarantula.

targette ⊙ [tar'ʒet] *f* flat bolt.

targuer [tar'ge] (1m): **se** ~ **de** pride o.s. on, boast about.

tarière [ta'rjɛːr] *f* auger; borer.

tarif [ta'rif] *m* price-list, tariff; rate(s *pl.*); scale of charges; ~ **réduit** reduced tariff; **plein** ~ full tariff *or* fare; **~aire** [tari'fɛːr] tariff-...; **~er** [~'fe] (1a) fix the rate of (*a duty*) *or* the price of (*goods*); **~ication** [~fika'sjɔ̃] *f* tariffing.

tarin *sl.* [ta'rɛ̃] *m* conk (= *nose*).

tarir [ta'riːr] (2a) *v/t.* dry up; *fig.* exhaust; *v/i.,* **se** ~ dry up, run dry; *fig.* cease; **tarissement** [~ris'mɑ̃] *m* drying up; *fig.* exhausting.

tarse [tars] *m* tarsus; F *foot:* instep.

tartarinade F [tartari'nad] *f* boast.

tart|e *cuis.* [tart] *f* (open) tart; flan;

~elette cuis. [~'lɛt] f tartlet; **~ine** [tar'tin] f slice of bread and butter or jam etc.; F rigmarole; **~iner** [~ti'ne] (1a) spread (bread; butter etc.).

tartre [tartr] m tartar (a. 🐍, a. dental); ⊚ boiler; scale, fur.

tartufe [tar'tyf] m hypocrite; **~rie** [~ty'fri] f (piece of) hypocrisy.

tas [tɑ] m heap, pile; lies, people: pack; **mettre en ~** pile up; F (**tout**) **un ~ de** (quite) a lot of; **sur le ~** at work.

tasse [tɑ:s] f cup; **~ à café** coffee-cup; **~ de café** cup of coffee.

tassée [tɑ'se] f casual.

tass|ement [tas'mɑ̃] m △ etc. settling, subsidence; 🌳 etc. fall(-off); **~er** [tɑ'se] (1a) cram together; pack (tightly); shake down; **se ~** crowd together; sqeeze up; △ settle; shrink (person); F settle down, come out in the wash.

tâter [tɑ'te] (1a) v/t. touch, feel; grope for; fig. feel out, explore; v/i.: **~ à** (or **de**) taste; try.

tatillon F [tɑti'jɔ̃] over-particular (person); **~ner** [~jɔ'ne] (1a) fuss over details; split hairs.

tâton|ner [tɑtɔ'ne] (1a) feel one's way (a. fig.); grope, fumble; **~s** [~'tɔ̃] adv.: **à ~** gropingly; **marcher à ~** grope along.

tatou|age [ta'twa:ʒ] m tattooing; tattoo; **~er** [~'twe] (1p) tattoo.

taudis [to'di] m hovel; wretched room; squalid hole; **~ pl.** slums.

taule [to:l] f see tôle.

taupe [to:p] f zo. mole; 🌳 moleskin; **tau-pinière** [topi'njɛ:r] f molehill.

taureau [tɔ'ro] m bull; **course f de ~x** bullfight; **tauromachie** [~rɔma'ʃi] f bull-fighting.

tautologie [totɔlɔ'ʒi] f tautology, redundancy.

taux [to] m rate (a. 🌳): 🌳 fixed price; 🌳 ratio; 🐍 amount; **~ de change** (rate of) exchange; **~ de la mortalité** death-rate; 🌳 **~ d'escompte** bank rate; 🌳 **~ d'intérêt** rate of interest; **au ~ de** at the rate of.

tavel|é [tav'le] marked; spotted, speckled; **~ure** [~'ly:r] f mark; spot.

taverne [ta'vɛrn] f café-restaurant.

tax|ation [taksa'sjɔ̃] f fixing of prices etc.; taxation; **~e** [taks] f tax; duty; fixed price; **~er** [tak'se] (1a) tax; put a

tax on (goods); fix (the price); fix the price or rate of; fig. accuse (of, **de**).

taxi [tak'si] m taxi(-cab); **~phone** [~si'fɔn] m telephone booth.

tchécoslovaque [tʃekɔslɔ'vak] adj., su. Czechoslovak; **tchèque** [tʃɛk] adj., su. Czech.

te [tə] **1.** pron./pers. you; to you; **2.** pron./rfl. yourself, to yourself.

té [te] m T-square; △ tee-iron.

techn|icien m, -enne f [tɛkni'sjɛ̃, ~'sjɛn] technician; **~i(ci)ser** [~(si)'ze] (1a) ⊚ mechanize; fig. technicalize; **~icité** [~si'te] f technicality; **~ique** [tɛk'nik] **1.** adj. technical; **2.** su./f technique; **~ électrique** electrical engineering; **~olo-gie** [~nɔlɔ'ʒi] f technology.

te(c)k 🐦, 🌳 [tɛk] m teak (wood).

teckel zo. [tɛ'kɛl] m dachshund

teigne [tɛɲ] f zo. moth; 🌿 ringworm; F fig. pest.

teignis [tɛ'ni] 1st p. sg. p.s. of teindre; **teignons** [~'nɔ̃] 1st p. pl. pres. of teindre; **teindre** [tɛ̃:dr] (4m) dye (blue etc.; **en bleu** etc.); stain (a. fig.); **se ~** dye one's hair; **teins** [tɛ̃] 1st p. sg. pres. of teindre; **teint, e** [tɛ̃, tɛ̃t] **1.** p.p. of teindre; **2.** su./m dye, colo(u)r; complexion; **bon** (or **grand**) **~ tex.** fast colo(u)r; fig. reliable; **petit ~** fading dye; su./f tint, hue; fig. touch, tinge; **teinture** [~'ty:r] f dye(ing); tinting; hue; fig. smattering; 🌳, 🌿 tincture; **teinturerle** [~ty'ri] f (dry) cleaners; **teinturier** [~ty'rje] m (dry) cleaner.

tel m, telle f, tels m/pl., telles f/pl. [tɛl] **1.** adj./indef. such; like; as; **~ maître, ~ valet** like master, like man; **~ que** (such) as; like; **~ quel** ordinary; just as he or it is or was; **à telle ville** in such and such a town; **de telle sorte que** in such a way that; **il n'y a rien de ~ que** there's nothing like; **un ~ repas** such a meal; **2.** pron./indef. (such a) one; some; **Monsieur un ~** Mr. So-and-so; **~ qui** he who.

télé F [te'le] f television.

télé... [tele] tele...; **~commande** [~kɔ'mɑ̃:d] f remote control; **~commu-nication** [~kɔmynika'sjɔ̃] f telecommu-nication; **~distribution** [~distriby'sjɔ̃] f cable television; **~enseignement** [~ɑ̃sɛɲ'mɑ̃] m educational broadcast or

T

television program(me)s *pl.*; **~férique** [~fe'rik] *m see* **téléphérique**; **~gramme** [~'gram] *m* telegram; **~graphie** [~gra'fi] *f* telegraphy; **~graphier** [~gra'fje] (1o) telegraph, wire; **~graphique** [~gra'fik] telegraphic; **mandat** *m* ~ telegraph(ic) money order; **~graphiste** [~gra'fist] *su.* telegraph operator; telegraph messenger; **~guidé** [~gi'de] radio-controlled; guided (*missile*); **~imprimeur** [~ɛ̃pri'mœːr] *m* teleprinter; **~objectif** *phot.* [~ɔbʒɛk'tif] *m* telephoto lens; **~phérique** [~fe'rik] *m* telpher railway; cable car; cableway; **~phone** [~'fɔn] *m* telephone; **~ intérieur** F intercom; **appeler q. au ~** phone s.o. up; **avez-vous le ~?** are you on the phone?; **~phoner** [~fɔ'ne] (1a) *vt/i.* (tele)phone; *v/i.*: **~ à q.** phone s.o. up; **~phonie** [~fɔ'ni] *f* telephony; **~ sans fil** radiotelephony; **~phonique** [~fɔ'nik] telephone...; telephonic; **cabine** *f* (*or* **cabinet** *m*) **~** telephone booth; **~phoniste** [~fɔ'nist] *su.* telephone operator.

télescop|age [telɛskɔ'paːʒ] *m* concertinaing, telescoping; **~e** [~'kɔp] *m* telescope; **~er** [~kɔ'pe] (1a) smash up; **se ~** concertina, telescope.

télé...: ~scripteur [teleskrip'tœːr] *m* teleprinter; **~spectateur** *m,* **-trice** *f* [~spɛkta'tœːr, ~'tris] TV viewer; **~travail** [~tra'vaj] *m* telecommuting; **~viser** [~vi'ze] (1a) televise; **~viseur** [~vi'zœːr] *m* television set; **~vision** [~'zjɔ̃] *f* television; **~ en couleurs** colo(u)r television; **~ par câble** cable television.

télex [telɛks] *m* telex.

tellement [tɛl'mɑ̃] *adv.* so, in such a way; to such an extent.

témér|aire [teme'rɛːr] **1.** *adj.* rash (*a. judgment etc.*); daring; **2.** *su.* rash person; dare-devil; **~ité** [~ri'te] *f* rashness; daring; bold speech.

témoi|gnage [temwa'ɲaːʒ] *m* ⛪, fig. testimony, evidence; fig. *a. proof,* token, expression; fig. **en ~ de** as a token of; **~gner** [~'ɲe] (1a) *vt/i.* testify; *v/i.* give evidence; fig. **~ de** testify to, bear witness to; *v/t.* show; **~n** [tem'wɛ̃] **1.** *su./m* witness; sample; *sp.* stick (*in relay race*); ⛪ **~ à charge** (**décharge**) prosecution (defence) witness; **2.** *adj./inv.* pilot..., test...; control...; **ap-**

partement *m* ~ show flat; **lampe** *f* ~ warning light.

tempe *anat.* [tɑ̃ːp] *f* temple.

tempérament [tɑ̃pera'mɑ̃] *m* temperament; constitution; disposition; ✝ **à ~** by instal(l)ments; on the instal(l)ment plan.

tempér|ance [tɑ̃pe'rɑ̃ːs] *f* temperance; **~ant** [~'rɑ̃] temperate; **~ature** [~ra'tyːr] *f* temperature (*a.* ✽); **~é** [~'re] temperate; *art* ♪ (1f) moderate, temper.

tempête [tɑ̃'pɛːt] *f* storm; **~êter** F [~pɛ'te] (1a) rage, rant and rave; **~étueux** [~pe'tɥø] stormy (*a. fig.*).

temple [tɑ̃ːpl] *m* temple (*a. hist.* ♀); *protestantism:* church, chapel.

temporaire [tɑ̃pɔ'rɛːr] temporary.

temporel [tɑ̃pɔ'rɛl] **1.** *adj.* secular; temporal; **2.** *su./m* temporal power.

tempori|sateur [tɑ̃pɔriza'tœːr] **1.** *adj.* temporizing; **2.** *su.* temporizer; **~er** [~'ze] (1a) temporize, play for time, stall.

temps¹ [tɑ̃] *m* time (*a.* ♪); while; *fig.* times *pl.*; ✽, ⚙ phase; *mot. etc.* stroke; ♪ *a.* beat; *gramm.* tense; **à deux ~** two-stroke (*engine*); **à ~** in time; **avec le ~** in (the course of) time; **de mon ~** in my time; **de ~ à autre** (*or* **en ~**) now and then; **en ~ de guerre** in wartime; **être de son ~** keep up with the times; **il est grand ~** it is high time (to *inf.*, *de inf.*; that *ind.*, **que** *sbj.*); **le bon vieux ~** the good old days *pl.*; (**ne pas**) **avoir le ~ de** (*inf.*) have (no) time to (*inf.*); **tout le ~** all the time; the whole time.

temps² [tɑ̃] *m* weather; **quel ~ fait-il?** what is the weather like?; **il fait beau** (**mauvais**) **~** the weather is fine (bad).

tenable [tə'nabl] tenable; habitable (*house*); *fig.* **pas ~** unbearable.

tenace [tə'nas] tenacious; clinging (*perfume,* ✽); adhesive; stiff (*soil*); tough (*metal*); *fig.* stubborn; retentive (*memory*); **ténacité** [tenasi'te] *f* tenacity *etc.*; *see* **tenace.**

tenaille ⚙ [tə'naːj] *f* pincers *pl.*; **~er** *fig.* [~nɑ'je] (1a) torture.

tenan|cier [tənɑ̃'sje] *m* manager; **~t** [~'nɑ̃] *m* supporter; *sp. title:* holder; *bet:* taker; **d'un seul ~** all in one block; **~s et aboutissants** *m/pl. estate:* adjacent parts; *fig.* the ins and outs.

tendan|ce [tɑ̃'dɑ̃ːs] *f* tendency; leanings

pl.; drift; trend (*a. fig.*); **à ~** tendentious (*book*); **avoir ~ à** tend to, be inclined to; **~cieux** [~dα'sjø] tendentious.

tendeur [tᾱ'dœːr] *m* carpet, snares: layer; *wallpaper:* hanger; ☉ tightener; trouser-stretcher; shoe-tree.

tendineux [tᾱdi'nø] stringy (*meat*).

tendon *anat.* [tᾱ'dɔ̃] *m* sinew.

tendre¹ [tᾱ'dr] (4a) *v/t.* stretch; draw tight, tighten; hold (*s.th.*) out (to, **à**); hang (*wallpaper*), paper (*a room*); lay (*a carpet, a snare*); spread (*a net, a sail*); bend (*a bow*); *fig.* strain; **~ l'oreille** prick up one's ears; *v/i.:* **~ à** tend towards *s.th.* or to *do s.th.*; aim at *s.th.* or *to do s.th.*

tendr|e² [tᾱ'dr] tender; soft; early (*childhood, years*), *fig.* affectionate, fond; **~esse** [tᾱ'drɛs] *f* tenderness; love; **~s** *pl.* caresses; **~on** [~'drɔ̃] *m* ♀ tender shoot; F *fig.* young girl.

tendu [tᾱ'dy] **1.** *p.p. of* **tendre¹**; **2.** *adj.* tight; taut; tense, strained.

ténèbres [te'nɛːbr] *f/pl.* darkness *sg.* (*a. fig.*), gloom *sg.; eccl.* tenebrae; **ténébreux** [~ne'brø] dark, gloomy; *fig.* deep, sinister; obscure (*style*).

teneur¹ [tə'nœːr] holder; ♰ **~ de livres** book-keeper.

teneur² [tə'nœːr] *f* tenor (*of book, conduct, etc.*), ♔ percentage; **~ en alcool** alcoholic content.

ténia ♀, *zo.* [te'nja] *m* tapeworm.

tenir [tə'niːr] (2h) **1.** *v/t.* hold (*a. meeting etc.*); have, possess; retain; *fig.* control; run (*a firm*); keep; contain (*a pint*), *fig.* accommodate, seat (*200 persons*); △ support; occupy, take up; consider, think; regard (as, **pour**); *thea.* play (*a rôle*); ♔ stock (*goods*); take (on) (*a bet*); **l'eau** ne water tight; **~ le lit** stay in bed; ♰ **~ les livres** do the book-keeping; **~ sa promesse** keep one's word; **~ son tempérament de son père** have got one's temper from one's father; **~ tête à** resist; **se ~** stand; keep (*quiet*), remain (*standing*); be held; take place; **s'en ~ à** keep to; be satisfied with; **2.** *v/i.* hold; hold firm; remain; *fig.* last; find room (in, **dans**); border (on, **à**) (*land*); *fig.* be attached (to, **à**); be keen (on *ger.*, **à** *inf.*); **~ à** value (*s.th.*); be due to, depend on; **~ à ce que** (*sbj.*) be anxious that (*ind.*); **~ bon** (or

ferme) stand firm; hold out; ♆ hold tight; **~ de** take after (*s.o.*); be akin to (*s.th.*); **~ pour** be in favo(u)r of; **en ~ pour** be fond of (*s.o.*), stick to (*s.th.*); **je n'y tiens pas** I don't care for it; **ne pouvoir plus y ~** be unable to stand it; **tiens!, tenez!** look (here)!; here!; **tiens!** well!; really?

tennis [te'nis] *m* tennis; tennis court; *pl.* (*a.* **chaussures f de ~**) plimsolls, *Am.* sneakers; **~ de table** table tennis.

tenon ☉ [tə'nɔ̃] *m* tenon; lug; bolt.

tension [tᾱ'sjɔ̃] *f* tension; ☉, ♔ blood, steam: pressure; ⚡ voltage; ♔ **~ sous ~** live (*wire*); ♔ **avoir de la ~** have high blood pressure.

tentacule [tᾱta'tœːr] **1.** *adj.* tempting; **2.** *su./m* tempter; **~ion** [~'sjɔ̃] *f* temptation (to *inf.*, **de** *inf.*); **~ive** [~'tiːv] *f* attempt (at, **de**).

tente [tᾱːt] *f* tent; *fair etc.:* booth.

tenter [tᾱ'te] (1a) *v/t.* tempt (*s.o.*); **être tenté de** (*inf.*) be tempted to (*inf.*); *v/i.:* **~ de** (*inf.*) try to (*inf.*).

tenture [tᾱ'tyːr] *f* hanging(s *pl.*).

tenu, e [tə'ny] **1.** *p.p. of* **tenir**; **2.** *su./f* holding (*a.* ♛); ♛ books, shop, etc.: keeping; *fig.* shape; *person:* bearing; behavio(u)r; ☉ maintenance; ♛ sitting; *cost., a.* ✗ dress; *prices:* firmness; ♪ sustained note; *mot.* **~ de route** road-holding qualities *pl.*; **~e de soirée** evening dress; **~e de ville** morning *or* street dress; **de la ~e!** behave yourself!; **en grande ~e** in full dress; **en petite ~, en ~ légère** in light clothing; F scantily dressed.

ténu [te'ny] thin, slender; *fig.* fine; **~ité** [~nɥi'te] *f* tenuousness; slenderness; thinness; fineness.

ter [tɛːr] *adv.* three times, ♪ ter; *in house numbers:* **3ter 3b.**

térébenthine ♛ [terebᾱ'tin] *f* turpentine.

tergiverser [tɛrɡiver'se] (1a) shilly-shally.

terme [tɛrm] *m* term; time limit, date; ✗, ♰ time; delay (*for payment*); ♰ instalment; end; ♰ **à ~** forward (*sale, purchase*); **avant ~** premature(ly); **à court (long) ~** ♰ short- (long-)dated; *fig.* short- (long-)term (*policy etc.*); **en d'autres ~s** in other words; **en propres ~s** in so many words; *fig.* **être en bons**

~s avec be on good terms with; *mettre un* ~ *à* put an end to, end.
termin|aison [tɛrminɛ'zɔ̃] f ending; ~al [tɛrmi'nal] adj., su./m terminal; ~er [~'ne] (1a) terminate; end, finish, complete; *se* ~ come to an end; *gramm. se* ~ *en* end in.
terminologie [tɛrminɔlɔ'ʒi] f terminology.
terminus 🚆 *etc.* [tɛrmi'nys] **1.** su./m terminus; **2.** adj.: *gare f* ~ terminus.
ternaire [🎵, A⸜] [tɛr'nɛːr] ternary.
tern|e [tɛrn] dull; ~**ir** [tɛr'niːr] (2a) tarnish (a. fig.); fig. dull; *se* ~ become tarnished or dull; ~**issure** [~ni'syːr] f tarnish; dullness; tarnished spot.
terrain [tɛ'rɛ̃] m ground; soil, land; foot. field; golf: course; ⚠ site.
terrass|e [tɛ'ras] f terrace; bank; ⚠ flat roof; café: pavement (area); *à la* ~ outside; ~**ement** [~ras'mɑ̃] m banking; earthwork; ~**er** [~ra'se] (1a) bank up; throw (s.o.) down, floor (s.o.); lay (s.o.) low; fig. crush; ~**ier** [~ra'sje] m excavation worker.
terre [tɛːr] f earth; ground; soil; clay; land; estate; fig. ~ *à* ~ prosaic; down-to-earth; ~ *cuite* terracotta; ~ *ferme* mainland; firm land; ⚡ *mettre à la* ~ earth, Am. ground; *mettre pied à* ~ alight; *toucher* ~ land; *tomber par* ~ fall (flat).
terreau [tɛ'ro] m compost.
terre-neuve zo. [tɛr'nœːv] m/inv. Newfoundland dog.
terre|r [tɛ're] (1a): *se* ~ ⚔ dig o.s. in; go to earth, burrow; fig. hide; ~**stre** [~'rɛstr] ⚙, zo. terrestrial; ⚙ ground-...; land-...; fig. worldly.
terreur [tɛ'rœːr] f terror; dread.
terreux [tɛ'rø] earthy; dirty.
terrible [tɛ'ribl] terrible, dreadful.
terrien m, **-enne** f [tɛ'rjɛ̃, ~'rjɛn] **1.** su. earthling; ⚓ landsman; **2.** adj. landed, land(owner).
terrier [tɛ'rje] m (rabbit) hole, (fox) earth; zo. terrier.
terrifier [tɛri'fje] (1o) terrify.
terri(l) [tɛ'ri] m heap, tip.
terrine [tɛ'rin] f earthenware pot.
territo|ire [tɛri'twaːr] m territory; ~**rial** [~tɔ'rjal] territorial.
terroir [tɛ'rwaːr] m soil.
terroris|er [tɛrɔri'ze] (1a) terrorize; ~**me** [~'rism] m terrorism; ~**te** [~'rist] adj., su. terrorist.
tertre [tɛrtr] m mound, hillock.
tes [te] *see* ton[1].
tesson [tɛ'sɔ̃] m potsherd; fragment, piece of broken glass.
test[1] ✂ *etc.* [tɛst] m test; ~ *mental* intelligence test.
test[2] [tɛst] m zo. shell, test; 🐚 skin.
testa|ment [tɛsta'mɑ̃] m 🏛 will; bibl. *Ancien (Nouveau)* ② Old (New) Testament; ~**mentaire** [~mɑ̃'tɛːr] testamentary; ~**teur** [~'tœːr] m testator; ~**trice** [~'tris] f testatrix.
tester[1] 🏛 [tɛs'te] (1a) make a will.
tester[2] ✂ *etc.* [~] (1a) test.
testicule anat. [tɛsti'kyl] m testicle.
testimonial [tɛstimɔ'njal] oral (evidence); *lettre f* ~*e* testimonial.
tétanos ✂ [teta'nɔs] m lockjaw.
têtard [tɛ'taːr] m zo. tadpole; sl. child, kid.
tête [tɛːt] f head (a. = leader; a. = person); face; page, class, tree, etc.: top; column, vehicle: front; chapter: heading; foot. header; ~ *carrée* sl. square-head; ~ *chercheuse* rocket etc.: homing device; fig. trail blazer; iro. ~ *d'œuf* egghead; ~ *nue* bareheaded; *agir* ~ *baissée* act blindly; *avoir la* ~ *chaude (froide)* be hot- (cool-)headed; *coup m de* ~ rash action; *de* ~ from memory; *en faire à sa* ~ go one's own way; *en* ~ *à* ~ privately; *faire la* ~ *à* frown at; *faire une* ~ look glum; *la* ~ *la première* head first; *piquer une* ~ dive; *se mettre en* ~ *de* (inf.) take it into one's head to (inf.); F *se payer la* ~ *de q.* make fun of s.o.; take s.o. for a ride; ~**-à-queue** [tɛta'kø] m/inv.: *faire un* ~ spin or slew round; ~**-à-tête** [tɛta'tɛːt] m/inv. private interview; sofa; ~**-bêche** [tɛt'bɛʃ] adv. head to tail.
tét|ée [te'te] f baby's feed; suck(ing); ~**er** [~] (1f) suck; *donner à* ~ suckle; ~**ine** [~'tin] f teat; nipple; ~**on** F [~'tɔ̃] m tit.
tétra... [tetra] tetra-...; four-...; ~**phonie** [~fɔ'ni] f quadrophony.
tétras orn. [te'trɑ] m grouse.
tette [tɛt] f animal: teat, dug.
têtu [tɛ'ty] stubborn (person).
texte [tɛkst] m text.
textile [tɛks'til] adj., su./m textile.
textu|aire [tɛks'tɥɛːr] textual; ~**el**

[~'tɥɛl] textual; word-for-word (*quotation*); **~re** [~'ty:r] f texture.

thé [te] m tea; **heure** f **du ~** tea-time.

théâtral [tea'tral] theatrical (*a. fig.*); **théâtre** [~'ɑ:tr] m theatre, Am. theater (*a. ✗ of war*); **coup** m **de ~** sensational development; **faire du ~** be on the stage; *fig.* playact.

thébaïde [teba'id] f solitary retreat.

théière [te'jɛ:r] f teapot.

thématique [tema'tik] **1.** *adj.* thematic; **2.** *su.* f subject; **thème** [tem] m theme; topic; *gramm.* stem, *school:* translation into a foreign language.

théo... [teo] théo...; **~cratie** [~kra'si] f theocracy, **~logie** [~lɔ'ʒi] f theology; *unlv. a.* divinity; **~logien** m, **-enne** f [~lɔ'ʒjɛ̃, ~'ʒjɛn] theologian.

théori|cien [teori'sjɛ̃] m theorist; **~e** [~'ri] f theory; **~que** [~'rik] theoretical; **~ser** [~ri'ze] (1a) theorize.

thérap|eute [tera'pø:t] m therapeutist; **~eutique** [~pø'tik] **1.** *adj.* therapeutic; **2.** *su.* f therapy.

therm|al [tɛr'mal] thermal; **station** f **~e** spa; **~es** [tɛrm] m/pl. thermal baths; *hist. Rome:* public baths; **~ique** [tɛr'mik] thermal; heat ...

thermo... [tɛrmo] thermo-...; **~électrique** *phys.* [~elɛk'trik] thermo-electric(al); **~mètre** [~'mɛtr] m thermometer; **~nucléaire** *phys.* [~nykle'ɛːr] thermonuclear; **~stat** [~s'ta] m thermostat.

thésauriser [tezori'ze] (1a) hoard.

thèse [tɛːz] f thesis; argument.

thon *icht.* [tɔ̃] m tunny(-fish), tuna.

thuriféraire [tyrife'rɛːr] m *eccl.* incense bearer; *fig.* flatterer.

thym ♀ [tɛ̃] m thyme.

tiare [tjaːr] f (papal) tiara; papacy.

tibia *anat.* [ti'bja] m shin(-bone).

tic [tik] m ♂ tic, twitch; *fig.* habit.

tictaquer [tikta'ke] (1m) tick (away).

ticket [ti'kɛ] m ticket; check; coupon.

tiède [tjɛd] lukewarm; warm (*wind*); **tiédeur** [tje'dœːr] f lukewarmness (*a. fig.*); **tiédir** [~'diːr] (2a) v/i. grow tepid; v/t. make tepid.

tien m, **tienne** f [tjɛ̃, tjɛn] **1.** *pron./poss.*: **le ~, la ~ne, les ~s** pl., **les ~nes** pl. yours; **2.** *su./m* your own; **les ~s** pl. your (own) people.

tiendrai [tjɛ̃'dre] *1st p. sg. fut. of* **tenir.**

tiennent [tjɛn] *3rd p. pl. pres. of* **tenir; tiens** [tjɛ̃] *1st p. sg. pres. of* **tenir.**

tier|ce [tjɛrs] f ♪, ♪ third; *cards:* tierce; **~s, ~ce** [tjɛːr, tjɛrs] **1.** *adj.* third; *hist.* **~ état** m commonalty; **le ~ monde** the Third World; **2.** *su./m* third (part); third person.

tige [tiːʒ] f ♀ stem, stalk; *column:* shaft; ⊙ rod; *boot:* upper; *key:* shank; *family:* stock.

tigre *zo.* [tigr] m tiger; **tigré** [ti'gre] striped (*fur*); spotted (*skin*).

tilleul [ti'jœl] m lime(tree).

timbale [tɛ̃'bal] f ♪ kettledrum; *cuis.* pie dish; metal drinking cup.

timbr|e [tɛ̃:br] m *date, postage, etc.:* stamp; *bicycle etc.:* bell; *voice etc.:* timbre; **~ humide** rubber stamp; **~é** [tɛ̃'bre] *sonorous* (*voice*); stamped (*paper*); F crazy; **~e-poste**, pl. **~es-poste** [~brə'pɔst] m postage stamp; **~er** [~'bre] (1a) stamp (*a paper*); post-mark (*a letter*).

timid|e [ti'mid] timid, shy; **~ité** [~midi'te] f timidity; shyness; diffidence (*in ger., à inf.*).

timon [ti'mɔ̃] m *vehicle:* pole; ♣, *fig.* helm; **~erie** ♣ [~mɔn'ri] f wheelhouse; **~ier** [~mɔ'nje] m helmsman.

timoré [timo're] timorous.

tinctorial [tɛ̃ktɔ'rjal] dye-...

tins [tɛ̃] *1st p. sg. p.s. of* **tenir.**

tint|amarre F [tɛ̃ta'maːr] m din, noise; fuss; **~ement** [tɛ̃t'mɑ̃] m ringing; tinkle; jingle; buzzing (*in the ears*); **~er** [tɛ̃'te] (1a) v/t. ring; v/i. tinkle; jingle; buzz (*ears*); **~ouin** F [~'twɛ̃] m trouble.

tique *zo.* [tik] f tick.

tiquer F [ti'ke] (1m) twitch; wince.

tir [tiːr] m shooting; gunnery; fire, firing; rifle range; shooting gallery; **à la cible** target shooting; **à ~ rapide** quick-firing (*gun*).

tirade [ti'rad] f tirade; long speech.

tir|age [ti'raːʒ] m drawing, pulling; *chimney etc.:* draught, Am. draft; ⊙ wire-drawing; *stone:* quarrying; *lottery:* draw; *typ., phot.* printing; *journ.* circulation; *book:* (print) run; F fig. friction, disagreement; *typ.* **à part** off-print; **~ au sort** drawing lots; **~aillement** [~rɑj'mɑ̃] m pulling; *fig.* friction; **~ailler** [~rɑ'je] (1a) v/t. pull about; tug at; *fig.* pester (*s.o.*); v/i.

T

shoot at random; ~ **contre** snipe at;
~ailleur [~rɑ'jœːr] m ✕, fig. skirmish-
er; **~ant** [~'rɑ̃] m drawstring; boot-
strap; ⊙ (tie-)rod; ⚓ **d'eau** draught,
Am. draft.

tiré, e [ti're] **1.** adj. haggard; **2.** su./m ✝
drawee; su./f: F **une** ~ a long haul, quite
a distance; quite a lot.

tire...: ~ **au-flanc** sl. [tiro'flɑ̃] m/inv.
shirker; **~-botte** [~'bɔt] m bootjack;
~-bouchon [~bu'ʃɔ̃] m corkscrew; curl;
en ~ corkscrew (curls); **~-clou** ⊙ [~'klu]
m nail-puller; **~d'aile** [~'dɛl] adv.: à ~
swiftly; **~-fesses** F [~'fɛs] m/inv. ski
tow; **~-larigot** F [~lari'go] adv.: à ~ to
one's heart's content.

tirelire [tir'liːr] f piggy bank.

tir|er [ti're] (1a) **1.** v/t. pull; drag; draw
(a. a wire, a line, wine; a. ✝ a bill,
money; a. ⚓ 10 feet; fig. lots); tug;
stretch; pull off (boots); raise (one's
hat) (to, **devant**); ✝ pull out (a tooth);
take out (s.th. from somewhere); fig.
derive, get (a. ⊙); fire (a gun etc.);
shoot (at); **~ en longueur** stretch (s.th.)
out; **~ la langue** put one's tongue out; **~
les cartes** tell fortunes (by the cards); **~
les conséquences** draw the consequences; **~ plaisir (vanité) de** derive
pleasure from (take pride in); **se** ~ extricate o.s. (from, **de**); **s'en** ~ get off;
pull through; make ends meet; scrape
through; **se** ~ **d'affaire** get out of
trouble; **2.** v/i. pull (at, on **sur**); draw
(chimney etc.); tend to (à, **sur**), verge
(on à, **sur**); go, make (for, **vers**); shoot,
fire (at, **sur**); ✝ **à découvert** over-
draw one's account; **~ à sa fin** draw to
a close; run low (stock); **~ en longueur**
drag on; **~ sur une cigarette** draw on a
cigarette; **~et** typ. [~'rɛ] m hyphen;
dash; **~eur, -euse** [~'rœːr, ~'røːz] su. ⊙,
✝ etc.: drawer; gunman, shooter, shot.

tiroir [ti'rwaːr] m desk etc.: drawer;
~-caisse till; **à** ~s episodic (novel etc.);
F **nom** m **à** ~s double-barrel(l)ed name.

tisane [ti'zan] f infusion; (herb-)tea.

tison [ti'zɔ̃] m smoldering log; ember;
~ner [tizo'ne] (1a) poke.

tiss|age tex. [ti'saːʒ] m weaving; weave;
~er [~'se] (1a) weave; **~erand** [~'rɑ̃] m
weaver; **~eur** m, **-euse** F [ti'sœːr, ~'søːz]
weaver; **~u** [~'sy] **1.** adj. fig. woven,

made up; **2.** su./m tex. fabric, textile,
cloth; fig. texture; tissue (a. fig.);
~-éponge terry (cloth), towelling; **~ure**
tex., a. fig. [~'syːr] f texture.

titiller [titil'le] (1a) tickle, titillate.

titr|age [ti'traːʒ] m 🔬 titration; metall.
assaying; **~e** [ti:tr] m title; book: title
page; chapter; heading; journ. headline; certificate, diploma; 🔬 titre; ⚖
deed; qualification; fig. grounds pl.,
reason, right; **à** ~ **de** by right or virtue
of; as a (friend); by way of (example
etc.); on a ... basis; **à quel** ~? on what
grounds?; **au même** ~ for the same
reason; **à** ~ **gratuit** free (of charge); **à
juste** ~ rightly, with just cause, deserv-
edly; **en** ~ titular; on the permanent
staff; **~er** [ti'tre] (1a) confer a title
on (s.o.); give a title to; cin. title (a
film); 🔬 titrate; assay; journ. run as a
headline; alcoholic beverage: ~ **12°** be
12° proof.

tituber [tity'be] (1a) stagger, reel.

titulaire [tity'lɛːr] **1.** adj. titular; full
(member); **2.** su. holder; passport:
bearer.

toast [tɔst] m toast; **porter un** ~ propose
a toast (to, **à**); **~er** [tɔs'te] (1a) toast
(s.o.), drink to (s.o.'s) health.

toc [tɔk] **1.** su./m sound: tap, rap; ⊙
catch; F sham jewel(le)ry; ✝ **en** ~
pinchbeck; **2.** adj./inv. sl. crazy.

tocante F [tɔ'kɑ̃t] f watch, F ticker.

tocsin [tɔk'sɛ̃] m alarm(-bell), warning:
alarm-bell, -signal.

toge [tɔʒ] f toga; gown; robe.

tohu-bohu [tɔybo'y] m confusion.

toi [twa] pron./pers. subject: you; object:
you; (to) you; **à** ~ to you; yours.

toil|e [twal] f linen; cloth; paint. canvas;
painting; (spider's) web; ~ **à voiles**
sailcloth; ~ **cirée** oilcloth; thea., fig. ~
de fond backdrop; **reliure** f **en** ~ cloth
binding; **~erie** [~'ri] f linen or textile
trade; linen goods pl.; **~ette** [twa'let] f
washing; dressing; dressing table;
(woman's) dress; **~s** pl. toilet, lavatory;
faire sa ~ get washed, have a wash.

toi-même [twa'mɛm] pron./rfl. yourself.

tois|e [twaːz] f measuring apparatus; fig.
standard (of comparison); † measure:
fathom; **~er** [twa'ze] (1a) measure; fig.
weigh (s.o.) up.

toison [twa'zɔ̃] f fleece; F fig. mane.

T

toit [twa] *m* roof; **~ure** [twa'ty:r] *f* roof(ing).

tôle [to:l] *f* ⊙ sheet metal, sheet-iron; plate; boiler-plate; *sl.* prison.

tolér|able [tole'rabl] tolerable; **~ance** [~'rã:s] *f* tolerance; ⊙ limits *pl.*, margin; *admin.* allowance; (*religious*) toleration; **~ant** [~'rã] tolerant; **~er** [~'re] (1f) tolerate; *fig.* overlook; F bear, endure.

tôlerie [tol'ri] *f* sheet metal goods *pl. or* works *usu. sg.*

tomate 🌶 [tɔ'mat] *f* tomato.

tombale [tõ'bal] *adj./f: inscription f ~* tombstone inscription; *pierre f ~* tombstone.

tombant [tõ'bã] falling; drooping (*moustache, shoulders*); flowing (*hair*); *à la nuit ~e* at nightfall.

tombe [tõ:b] *f* tomb, grave; tombstone; **tombeau** [tõ'bo] *m* tomb.

tomb|ée [tõ'be] *f* rain: fall; *à la ~ de la nuit* (*or du jour*) at nightfall; **~er** [~'be] (1a) 1. *v/i* fall; drop, decrease; *~ bien* (*or juste*) happen *or* come at the right moment; *~ le mardi* fall on a Tuesday (*festival*); *~ mal* be inopportune; *~ malade* (*mort, amoureux*) fall ill (dead, in love); *~ sur* run *or* come across; ⚔ fall on (*the enemy*); *faire ~* bring down; drop; *laisser ~* drop (*s.th., one's voice,* F *s.o.*); give up; 2. *v/t.* throw (*s.o.*) down; F slip off (*one's jacket*); **~ereau** [tõ'bro] *m* tip-cart; **~eur** [~'bœ:r] *m sp.* wrestler, F (*a. ~ de femmes*) ladykiller.

tombola [tõbɔ'la] *f* lottery, raffle.

tome [tɔm] *m* tome, volume.

ton¹ *m, ta f, pl. tes* [tõ, ta, te] *adj./poss.* your.

ton² [tõ] *m* tone; shade, colo(u)r; *fig.* (*good etc.*) form; ♪ pitch; ♪ key; ♪ mode; *donner le ~* ♪ give the pitch; *fig.* set the tone *or* fashion; (*ne pas*) *être dans le ~* ♪ be in (out of) tune; *fig.* match, fit in (clash, be out of place); ♪ *donner du ~* (*à q.*) brace (*s.o.*) up; **to-nal, e,** *m/pl.* **-als** ♪ [tɔ'nal] tonal.

tond|age [tõ'da:ʒ] *m* shearing; **~aille** [~'daj] *f* shearing; **~aison** [~de'zõ] *f see* **tonte**; **~eur, -euse** [~'dœr, ~'dø:z] *su.* shearer; *su./f* shears *pl.*; lawnmower; clippers *pl.*; **~re** [tõ:dr] (4a) shear; *sheep:* crop (*the grass*); clip; *fig.* fleece (*s.o.*).

toni|cité ✿ [tɔnisi'te] *f* tonicity; **~fier** [~ni'fje] (1o) tone up, brace; **~que** [~'nik] *adj., su./m, su./f* tonic.

tonitru|ant *fig.* [tɔnitry'ã] thundering; **~er** *fig.* [~'e] (1a) thunder.

tonnage ⚓ [tɔ'na:ʒ] *m* tonnage; displacement.

tonnant [tɔ'nã] thundering (*a. fig.*).

tonne [tɔn] *f* metric ton; tun; **~au** [tɔ'no] *m* cask; *mot.* **faire un ~** overturn; **~let** [~'lɛ] *m* keg; **~lier** [tɔnə'lje] *m* cooper; **~lle** [~'nɛl] *f* bower, arbo(u)r.

tonner [tɔ'ne] (1a) thunder; **~re** [~'nɛ:r] *m* thunder; *coup m de ~* thunderclap; *fig.* thunderbolt; F *du ~* (*de Dieu*) terrific.

tonte [tõ:t] *f* (sheep-)shearing(time); ♪ clipping; *lawn:* mowing.

tonton F [tõ'tõ] *m* uncle.

tonus [tɔ'nys] *m* ✿ tonus, tone; *fig.* energy.

top|e! [tɔp] *int.* agreed!; **~er** [tɔ'pe] (1a) agree; shake hands on it.

topique [tɔ'pik] 1. *adj.* local; *fig.* to the point, relevant; 2. *su./m* ✿ local remedy; *phls.* commonplace.

topograph|e [tɔpɔ'graf] *m* topographer; **~ie** [~gra'fi] *f* topography; topographical map; **~ique** [~gra'fik] topographic(al).

toquade F✿ [tɔ'kad] *f* passing craze.

toquante F [tɔ'kã:t] *f* watch.

toque *cost.* [tɔk] *f jockey*; ✿: cap.

toqué F [tɔ'ke] crazy, cracked, nuts; *~ de sl.* mad about; **toquer** [~] (1m): *se ~* lose one's head (over, *de*).

torch|e [tɔrʃ] *f* torch; straw pad; **~er** [tɔr'ʃe] (1a) wipe (*s.th.*) (clean); daub (*the wall*); F do (*s.th.*) quickly, botch; **~ère** [~'ʃɛ:r] *f* candelabra; **~on** [~'ʃõ] *m* (kitchen) cloth; dish towel; duster; *coup m de ~* wipe; clean-up; **~onner** F [~ʃɔ'ne] (1a) wipe; *sl.* botch.

tord|age [tɔr'da:ʒ] *m* twist(ing); **~ant** [~'dã] screamingly funny; **~-boyaux** [tɔrbwa'jo] *m/inv.* rot-gut; rat-poison; **~re** [tɔrdr] (4a) twist; ⊙ buckle; wring (*hands, s.o.'s neck, clothes, a. fig. s.o.'s heart*); distort (*one's features, the mouth, the meaning*); *se ~* twist, writhe; **~u** [tɔr'dy] twisted; bent; crooked; warped (*a. fig. mind*); F crazy, loony.

toréador [tɔrea'dɔ:r] *m* bull-fighter.

torgn(i)ole F [tɔr'ɲɔl] *f* slap, blow.

tornade [tɔr'nad] *f* tornado.

toron [tɔ'rɔ̃] *m* cable strand; wisp.

torpeur [tɔr'pœːr] *f* torpor; **torpide** [~'pid] torpid.

torpill|e [tɔr'piːj] *f* torpedo; **~er** [~pi'je] (1a) torpedo (*a. fig.*); **~eur** [~pi'jœːr] *m* torpedo-boat.

torré|facteur [tɔrrefak'tœːr] *m* roaster; **~fier** [~'fje] (1o) roast; scorch.

torrent [tɔ'rɑ̃] *m* torrent (*a. fig.*); **~iel** [tɔrɑ̃'sjɛl] torrential; **~ueux** [~'tɥø] torrent-like, torrential.

torride [tɔ'rid] torrid; scorching.

tors [tɔːr] twisted, △ wreathed; crooked, bandy; **~ade** [tɔr'sad] *f* hair: twist, coil; twisted cord or braid; **en ~** coiled (*hair*); **~ader** [~sa'de] (1a) twist; coil.

torse [tɔrs] *m* trunk, torso; chest.

torsion [tɔr'sjɔ̃] *f* twisting.

tort [tɔːr] *m* wrong; error, fault; harm; **à ~** wrongly; **à ~ et à travers** at random, wildly; **à ~ ou à raison** rightly or wrongly; **avoir ~** be wrong; **dans** (*or* **en**) **son ~** in the wrong, at fault; **donner ~ à** blame, lay the blame on; prove (to be) wrong; **faire** (**du**) **~ à q.** harm s.o., do s.o. harm; be detrimental to s.o.

torticolis ❦ [tɔrtiko'li] *m* stiff neck.

tortill|ement [tɔrtij'mɑ̃] *m* twist(ing); worm, *a. fig.*: wriggling; **~er** [~ti'je] (1a) *v/t.* twist, twirl; twiddle; **se ~** wriggle; writhe; *v/i.* F *fig.* wriggle (a)round; **~ des hanches** swing one's hips; **~on** [~ti'jɔ̃] *m* twist.

tortionnaire [tɔrsjɔ'nɛːr] *m* torturer.

tortue [tɔr'ty] *f zo.* tortoise; *cuis.* **soupe f à la ~** turtle-soup.

tortueux [tɔr'tɥø] tortuous (*a. fig.*), winding; twisted (*tree*); *fig.* wily.

tortur|e [tɔr'tyːr] *f* torture; **~er** [~ty're] (1a) torture (*a. fig. a text*); **se ~ l'esprit** rack one's brains.

torve [tɔrv] menacing; forbidding.

tôt [to] *adv.* soon; early; **~ ou tard** sooner or later; **au plus ~** at the earliest; **le plus ~ possible** as soon as possible; **pas de si ~** not so soon.

total [tɔ'tal] **1.** *adj.* total, complete; **2.** *su./m* (sum) total; **au ~** on the whole; **~isateur** [tɔtaliza'tœːr] **1.** *adj.* adding; **2.** *su./m* adding-machine; totalizator; **~isation** [~za'sjɔ̃] *f* totalization; adding up; **~iser** [~'ze] (1a) total (up); **~itaire** [~'tɛːr] totalitarian; **~itarisme**

[~ta'rism] *m* totalitarianism; **~ité** [~'te] *f* whole, total; **en ~** wholly.

toton [tɔ'tɔ̃] *m* teetotum; F *faire tourner q. comme un ~* twist s.o. round one's little finger.

touaille [twa:j] *f* roller-towel.

toubib F [tu'bib] *m* doctor, F doc.

touch|ant [tu'ʃɑ̃] **1.** *adj.* touching, moving; **2.** *su./m* touching thing (about s.th., *de qch.*); **~e** [tuʃ] *f* touch (*a. paint., sp.*); typewriter, ♪ key; *paint. etc., a. fig.* style, manner; *foot.* throw-in; *foot.* (*a. ligne f de ~*) touch-line; *fencing, billiards:* hit; *arbitre m de ~ foot.* linesman; *rugby:* touch-judge; *pierre f de ~* touchstone (*a. fig.*); *sl.* **avoir une drôle de ~** look funny; **~e-à-tout** [tuʃa'tu] *su./inv.* dabbler; meddler; **~er** [~'ʃe] **1.** (1a) *v/t.* touch; feel (*with one's fingers*); hit (*the mark, an opponent*); contact, reach (*s.o.*); receive, draw (*money*); *fig.* move (*s.o.*) (*to tears etc.*); deal with, allude to (*a matter, a question*); strike (*a.* ♣ *rock*); *v/i.* **~ à** tamper *or* meddle with; border on (*a place, a. fig.*); be near to (*an age, a place, a. fig.*); reach to; *fig.* affect (*interests, question, welfare*); **~ à sa fin** be drawing to a close; *défense de ~!* hands off!; **2.** *su./m* touch; feel; **~ette** ♪ [~'ʃɛt] *f* fret, stop.

touff|e [tuf] *f* tuft; cluster; *trees:* clump; **~u** [~'fy] bushy (*beard etc.*); tangled (*thicket*); *fig.* abstruse.

toujours [tu'ʒuːr] *adv.* always, ever; still; anyhow; **pour ~** forever.

toupet [tu'pɛ] *m* tuft of hair; forelock; F impudence; *faux ~* toupee.

toupie []tu'pi] *f toy:* top; **toupiller** [tupi'je] (1a) spin round.

toupillon [tupi'jɔ̃] *m* (*small*) bunch.

tour¹ [tuːr] *f* tower; high-rise *or* tower block; *chess:* castle, rook.

tour² [~] *m* turn; ⚙ revolution; ⚙ lathe; circumference; *cost.* size; turning, winding; *face:* outline; trip, walk; run, drive; tour, journey; *fig.* feat; trick; *fig.* manner, style; **~ à ~** by turns; *sp.* **~ cycliste** cycle race; *~ de force* feat; **~ de main** knack, skill, *fig.* tricks *pl.* of the trade; *sp.* **~ de piste** lap; *cost.* **~ de poitrine** woman: bust measurement; **à mon ~** in my turn; *c'est* (*à*) *son ~* it is his turn; *faire le ~ de* go *or* walk (a)round (*s.th.*); *faire* (*or* *jouer*) *un mauvais ~ à q.* play a dirty trick on s.o.; *faire un ~* take a stroll; go for a ride; *fermer à double ~* double-lock (*a door*); *par ~ de faveur* out of turn.

tourbe[1] [turb] *f* mob, rabble.

tourbe[2] [turb] *f* peat, turf; **~ière** [~'bjɛr] *f* peat-bog.

tourbillon [turbi'jɔ̃] *m* whirlwind; swirl; eddy; *fig.* vortex; *fig.* whirl; *~ de neige* snowstorm; **~ner** [~jɔ'ne] (1a) swirl; whirl round.

tourelle [tu'rɛl] *f* turret.

tourie [tu'ri] *f* carboy

tourillon ⊙ [turi'jɔ̃] *m* pivot.

touris|me [tu'rism] *m* tourism; *bureau m de ~* travel agency; **~te** [~'rist] *su.* tourist; F tripper; **~tique** [~ris'tik] travel ...; tourist ...

tourment [tur'mɑ̃] *m* torment; **~s** *pl* pangs; **~e** [~'mɑ̃:t] *f* storm; *fig.* turmoil; **~er** [turmɑ̃'te] (1a) torment; *fig.* trouble; *fig.* pester; *se* **~** worry, fret.

tourn|age [tur'na:ʒ] *m* ⊙ turning; *cin.* shooting; **~ailler** F [~nɑ'je] (1a) wander (a)round; **~ant** [~nɑ̃] **1.** *adj.* turning; revolving; winding; **2.** *su./m* road, river: turning, bend; (street) corner; *fig* turning-point; **~e-disque** [turnə-'disk] *m* record player; turntable; **~edos** [~'do] *m* fil(l)et steak; **~ée** [tur'ne] *f* admin., ⚡ round; ⚡ circuit; *thea.* tour; *fig.* round (of drinks); F *fig.* thrashing; *faire la ~ de* visit, F do; **~emain** [~o'mɛ̃] *m:* *en un ~* in no time; **~er** [~'ne] (1a) **1.** *v/t.* turn; turn over (*a page*); turn round (*a corner*); *a. fig.* get round; wind (*s.th. round s.th.*); ⊙ shape, fashion; *cuis.* stir; *cin.* shoot (*a film*), actor: star in (*a film*); *se* **~** turn (round); **2.** *v/i.* turn; revolve; ⊙ run, go; spin (*top, head*); wind (*path, road*); change (*weather, wind*); *cin.* film; turn (*sour*) (*milk etc.*); *fig.* **~ à** become, turn, tend to(wards); **~ à droite** turn to the right; **~ au beau** turn fine; *mot.* **~ au ralenti** idle; *bien (mal)* turn out well (badly); *bien tourné* handsome; *la tête me tourne* I feel giddy.

tournesol [turnə'sɔl] *m* 🌻 sunflower; 🧪 litmus.

tourn|ette [tur'nɛt] *f* reel; glass cutter; **~eur** [~'nœːr] *m* turner; lathe operator; **~evis** [~nə'vis] *m* screwdriver.

tourniquet [turni'kɛ] *m* turnstile; ✝ revolving stand; 🌿 sprinkler; *shutter:* button; ⊹ tourniquet.

tourn|oi [tur'nwa] *m* tournament; **~oiement** [turnwa'mɑ̃] *m* spinning, whirling; ⚡ dizziness; **~oyer** [~'je] (1h) spin; whirl; *fig.* quibble.

tournure [tur'nyːr] *f fig.* turn (*of events etc.*); shape; cast; phrase; *~ d'esprit* cast of mind; way of thinking; *prendre une meilleure ~* take a turn for the better.

tourterelle *orn.* [turtə'rɛl] *f* turtledove.

tous [tu; tus] *see* tout.

Toussaint *eccl.* [tu'sɛ̃] *f: la ~* All Saint's Day; *la veille de la ~* Hallowe'en.

touss|er [tu'se] (1a) cough; **~oter** [~so'te] (1a) give little coughs.

tout *m*, **toute** *f*, **tous** *m/pl.*, **toutes** *f/pl.* [tu, tut, tu, tut] **1.** *adj.* before *unparticularized noun:* all, any, every; *intensive:* very, most; *before particularized su./ sg.:* all; *before particularized su./pl.:* all, every; *with numerals:* all; *~ homme* every *or* any man; *toute la ville* the whole town; *~ Paris* all *or* the whole of Paris; *toutes les semaines* every week; *tous les cinq* all five (of them *or* us); **2.** *pron./indef.* [*m/pl.* tus] all; everything; *à ~ prendre* after all; all things considered; *c'est* (*or voilà*) *~* that's all; *c'est ~ dire* that's the long and the short of it; *et ~ et ~* and all the rest of it; *nous tous* all of us; *six fois en ~* six times in all; **3.** *su./m* the whole, all; ₣ (*pl.* **touts** [tu]) total; *du ~ au ~* entirely; *pas du ~* not at all; **4.** *adv.* (*before adj./f beginning with consonant or aspirate h, agrees as if adj.*) quite, completely; all; very; ready (*-made etc.*); right; straight (*ahead*); *~ à fait* completely; *~ à l'heure* a few minutes ago, in a few minutes; *~ au plus* at the very most; *~ autant* quite as much *or* many; *~ d'abord* at first; *~ de suite* at once; *~ en* (*ger.*) while (*ger.*); although (*ind.*); *~ en étant riche* for all his riches, though he is rich; *~ sobre qu'il paraît* however sober he may seem; *c'est ~ un* it's all the same; *elle est toute contente* she is quite happy; *elle est tout étonnée* she is quite astonished; *c'est ~ autre chose* that's quite another matter.

tout-à-l'égout [tutale'gu] *m/inv.* mains drainage; sewage system.

toute [tut] *see* **tout; ~fois** [~'fwa] *cj.* however, still; yet; **~puissance** [~pqi'sã:s] *f* omnipotence.

toux [tu] *f* cough; coughing.

tout(-)va F [tu'va]: **à ~** enormous(ly).

toxi|cité [tɔksisi'te] *f* toxicity; **~comane** ✻ [~kɔ'man] **1.** *adj.* drug-addicted; **2.** *su.* drug-addict; **~comanie** [~kɔma'ni] *f* drug-habit; **~ne** [tɔk'sin] *f* toxin; **~que** [~'sik] **1.** *adj.* poisonous; **2.** *su./m* poison.

trac F [trak] *m* stage fright.

tracas [tra'kɑ] *m* bother, worry, trouble; **~ser** [~ka'se] (1a) bother, worry; **se ~** worry, fret; **~serie** [~kas'ri] *f* harassment; **~sier** [~ka'sje] irksome.

trace [tras] *f* trace; *vehicle:* track; *animal:* footprints *pl.;* *fig.* footsteps *pl.;* *fig.* sign, mark; **~é** [tra'se] *m* layout; line; course; **~er** [~] (1k) *v/t.* trace; draw (*a line, a plan*); *fig.* open up (*a route etc.*); *fig.* show (*the way*); *v/i. sl.* get a move on.

trachée *anat.* [tra'ʃe] *f* windpipe.

tract [trakt] *m* tract; leaflet.

tractations *pej.* [trakta'sjɔ̃] *f/pl.* dealings.

tract|eur [trak'tœ:r] *m* tractor; **~ion** [~'sjɔ̃] *f* traction; pulling; draught, *Am* draft; *sp.* pull-up; *mot.* (*a.* **~ avant**) car with front-wheel drive.

tradition [tradi'sjɔ̃] *f* tradition; **~aliste** [~sjɔna'list] *su.* traditionalist; **~nel** [~sjɔ'nɛl] traditional; habitual.

traduc|teur *m,* **-trice** *f* [tradyk'tœ:r, ~'tris] translator; **~ction** [~'sjɔ̃] *f* translation; **~ire** [tra'dɥi:r] (4h) translate (into, *en*); *fig.* render, convey, express; 🏛 **en justice** sue; **se ~ par** be translated by; *fig.* find it's expression in, be expressed by; **~isible** [~dɥi'zibl] translatable.

trafi|c [tra'fik] *m* traffic (*a. fig. pej.*); trading; **faire le ~ de** traffic in; **~quant** [trafi'kɑ̃] *m* trader; trafficker (in *de, en*); **~quer** [~'ke] (1m) *v/i.* trade, deal (in, *en*); *pej.* traffic; *v/t.* doctor (*s.th.*) (up).

trag|édie [traʒe'di] *f* tragedy; **~édien** [~'djɛ̃] *m* tragic actor; **~édienne** [~'djan] *f* tragic actress; **~ique** [tra'ʒik] **1.** *adj.* tragic; **2.** *su./m* tragic side; trage-

dy; tragic poet; **prendre au ~** make a tragedy of.

trahi|r [tra'i:r] (2a) betray; deceive (*s.o.*); *fig.* give away (*a secret*); reveal; *fig.* strength: fail (*s.o.*); be false to (*one's oath*); fall short of (*hopes etc.*); **~son** [~i'zɔ̃] *f* treachery; betrayal (of, *de*); 🏛 treason; **haute ~** high treason.

train [trɛ̃] *m* 🚂 train; *vehicles etc.:* string; wheels, admin. laws, etc.: set; ⚙ gear; *zo.* horse: quarters *pl.;* pace (*a. sp.*), speed; F noise, row; *fig.* mood; 🚂 **~auto** car sleeper train; **~correspondant** connection; 🚂 **~ de marchandises** (*plaisir, voyageurs*) goods, *Am* freight (excursion, passenger) train; ⚙ **~ d'engrenages** gear train; 🚂 **~ express** express train; 🚂 **~ rapide** fast express (train); **aller son petit ~** jog along; **en bon ~** doing *or* going well; **être en ~ de** (*inf.*) be (engaged in) (*ger.*); be in a mood for (*ger. or su.*); **mal en ~** out of sorts; *fig.* **manquer le ~** miss the bus; **mener grand ~** live in great style; **mettre en ~** set (*s.th.*) going; *fig.* **monter dans le ~ (en marche)** jump on the bandwagon.

train|age [trɛ'na:ʒ] *m* hauling; sleighing; **~ant** [~'nɑ̃] dragging; trailing (*robe*); *fig.* sluggish; **~ard** [~'na:r] *su.* dawdler, *Am* F slowpoke; **~asser** [~na'se] (1a) hang about; dawdle; **~e** [trɛn] *f* dress: train; *fishing:* dragnet; **à la ~** in tow (*a. fig.*); lagging behind; **~eau** [trɛ'no] *m* sleigh, sledge; **~ée** [~'ne] *f* blood, light, smoke, snail: trail; *gunpowder:* train; *sl.* prostitute; **~er** [~'ne] (1b) *v/t.* draw, pull; drag out; **~ la jambe** limp; **se ~** crawl; drag o.s. along; *fig.* linger; drag (*time*); *v/i.* trail; lie about; *fig.* linger on; hang about; dawdle; lag behind; flag; lay around *or* about (*things*); (*a.* **~ en longueur**) drag on; **~eur** [~'nœ:r] *su.* dawdler; loafer.

train-train F ['trɛ̃'trɛ̃] *m* (*daily*) round; (humdrum) routine.

traire [trɛ:r] (4ff) milk (*a cow*); **trait, e** [trɛ, trɛt] **1.** *p.p. of* **traire; 2.** *su./m* pulling; shooting; throwing; arrow, dart; *pen:* stroke; mark, line; gulp; *light:* shaft, beam; *fig.* act; stroke (*of genius*); trait; feature; *fig.* reference, relation; *paint.* outline; **~ d'esprit** witticism; **~ d'union** hyphen; **avoir ~ à** have reference to; **cheval** m **de ~** cart-horse; su./f road: stretch; journey: stage; ✝ bank: draft; trade; milking; **~e des blanches** white-slave traffic; **~e des Noirs** slave-trade; **d'une (seule) ~e** at a stretch; in one go.

traitable [trɛ'tabl] treatable; manageable; fig. tractable.

traité [trɛ'te] m treatise (on **de, sur**); pol. etc. treaty, agreement.

trait|ement [trɛt'mɑ̃] m treatment (a. ✲); salary; material, data: processing; **~er** [trɛ'te] (1a) v/t. treat (✲, ⊙, s.o., a. fig.); call (s.o. s.th., **q. de qch.**); entertain (s.o.); discuss (a subject); negotiate (a deal etc.); v/i. negotiate (for **de, pour**); with, **avec**); **~** **de** deal with (a subject); **~eur** [~'tœːr] m caterer.

traîtr|e, -esse [trɛːtr, trɛ'trɛs] **1.** adj. treacherous (a. fig.); fig. dangerous; **ne pas dire un ~ mot** not to say a (single) word; **2.** su./m traitor; su./f traitress; **~eusement** [trɛtrøz'mɑ̃] adv. of **traître 1**; **~ise** [~'triːz] f treachery.

trajectoire phys. ✗, etc. [traʒɛk'twaːr] su./f, adj. trajectory.

trajet [tra'ʒɛ] m ⛴, journey, passage, crossing; mot. etc. ride; ✈ flight, ✲, projectile, etc.: course.

tralala F [trala'la] m fuss, ceremony; **en grand ~** dressed up to the nines.

tram F [tram] m tram, Am. streetcar.

tram|e [tram] f tex. woof; fig. framework; fig. texture; telev. frame; **~er** [tra'me] (1a) hatch; plot; fig se **~** be brewing.

tramontane [tramɔ̃'tan] f north wind; north; astr. North Star.

tramway [tram'wɛ] m tramway; tram(car), Am. streetcar.

tranch|ant [trɑ̃'ʃɑ̃] **1.** adj. cutting; sharp (a. fig.); fig. trenchant; glaring (colour, a. fig. contradiction); **2.** su./m (cutting) edge; fig. **argument** m **à deux ~s** argument that cuts both ways; **~e** [trɑ̃:ʃ] f bread, meat, etc., a. fig.: slice; book, coin, plank: edge; ✗ ridge; ✝ shares: block; ✗ section; **couper en ~s** slice, **~é, e** [trɑ̃'ʃe] **1.** adj. distinct, sharp; **2.** su./f trench; forest etc.: cutting; **~er** [trɑ̃'ʃe] v/t. slice, cut (off); fig. cut short; settle (a question); **~ le mot** speak plainly; v/i. cut; contrast sharply (with, **sur**); **~oir** [~'ʃwaːr] m cutting board.

tranquill|e [trɑ̃'kil] tranquil; still; quiet; fig. untroubled; **laissez-moi ~** leave me alone; **~isant** ✲ [trɑ̃kili'zɑ̃] m tranquil(l)izer; **~iser** [~'ze] (1a) reassure; **~ité** [~'te] f tranquil(l)ity, quiet; peace.

trans... [trɑ̃s, trɑ̃z] trans...; **~action** [trɑ̃zak'sjɔ̃] f transaction; ✝ deal; ♣ settlement, composition; **~atlantique** [~zatlɑ̃'tik] **1.** adj. transatlantic; **2.** su./m Atlantic liner; deck-chair; **~border** [~'de] (1a) ⚓ tranship; ferry across (a river); **~cendant** phls [trɑ̃sɑ̃'dɑ̃] transcendent(al).

transcription [trɑ̃skrip'sjɔ̃] f transcription; copy; **transcrire** [~'kriːr] (4q) transcribe; copy (out).

transe [trɑ̃s] f (hypnotic) trance; **~s** pl. fear sg., fright sg.

trans...: ~férer [trɑ̃sfe're] (1f) transfer; (re)move from one place to another; **~fert** [~'fɛːr] m transfer (a. phot., ✝); **~figuration** [~figyra'sjɔ̃] f transfiguration; **~figurer** [~'figy're] (1a) transfigure, **~formable** [trɑ̃sfɔr'mabl] transformable; mot. convertible; **~formateur** [~ma'tœːr] **1.** adj. transforming; **2.** su./m ⚡ transformer; **~formation** [~ma'sjɔ̃] f transformation (into, **en**); ⊙ processing; **~former** [~'me] (1a) transform, convert (a. foot., a. phls.), change (into, **en**); **~fuge** [trɑ̃s'fyːʒ] m renegade; defector; **~fuser** usu. ✲ [~fy'ze] (1a) transfuse; **~fusion** [~fy'zjɔ̃] f (**~ sanguine** or **de sang** blood) transfusion; **~gresser** [~grɛ'se] (1a) transgress, break (a law etc.).

transi [trɑ̃'zi] (**~ de froid**) chilled to the bone; **~ de peur** paralyzed with fear.

transiger [trɑ̃zi'ʒe] (1l) compromise, come to terms (with, **avec**).

transistor [trɑ̃zis'tɔr] m radio: transistor.

transit ✝ [trɑ̃'zit] m transit; **~aire** ✝ [trɑ̃zi'tɛːr] **1.** adj. transit...; **2.** su./m forwarding agent; **~er** ✝ [~'te] (1a) pass in transit; **~if** [~'tif] transitive; **~ion** [~'sjɔ̃] f transition; **~oire** [~'twaːr] m transient; provisional, interim...

trans...: ~lation [trɑ̃sla'sjɔ̃] f transfer; ⊙, eccl. translation; **~lucidité** [~lysidi'te] f semi-transparency; **~metteur** [~me'tœːr] m transmitter; **~mettre** [~'mɛtr] (4v) transmit; pass on (a disease, a message); hand down (to other genera-

tions); **~migrer** [~mi'gre] (1a) transmigrate; **~missibilité** [~misibili'te] *f* transmissibility; **~missible** [~mi'sibl] transmissible; **~mission** [~mi'sjɔ̃] *f* transmission; *disease, order:* passing on; ⊙ drive, (transmission) gear; 🚗 transfer; *foot. passing;* **~muable** [~'mɥabl] transmutable (into, **en**); **~muer** [~'mɥe] (1n) transmute (into, **en**); **~mutation** [~myta'sjɔ̃] *f* transmutation (into, **en**); **~paraître** [trɑ̃spa'rɛːtr] (4k) show through; **~parence** [~pa'rɑ̃ːs] *f* transparency; **~parent** [~pa'rɑ̃] **1.** *adj.* transparent; **2.** *su./m* transparent screen; **~percer** [~pɛr'se] (1k) pierce (through); run (*s.o.*) through; *fig. rain:* soak.

transpir|ation [trɑ̃spira'sjɔ̃] *f* 🌿 perspiring, perspiration, sweat; transpiration (*a. fig.*); **en ~** in a sweat; **~er** [~'re] (1a) perspire, sweat; transpire; *fig.* leak (out).

trans...: ~plantable 🌿, 🌿 [trɑ̃splɑ̃'tabl] transplantable; **~plantation** [~plɑ̃ta'sjɔ̃] *f* transplantation; **~planter** [~plɑ̃'te] (1a) transplant; **~port** [~'pɔːr] *m* 🚢 transport, carriage; 🚗, 🚗 conveyance; 🚢 transfer; *fig. anger:* (out)burst; *delight, joy:* rapture; 🌿 **~ au cerveau** stroke; **~ d'aviation** aircraft transport; 🚗 **~ sur les lieux** visit to the scene (of the occurrence); 🚢 **compagnie** *f* **de ~** forwarding company; ⊙ **de ~** conveyor-...; **~portation** [~pɔrta'sjɔ̃] *f* conveyance; 🚢, 🚗 transportation; **~porter** [~pɔr'te] (1a) transport; carry; bring; *fig.* carry (*s.o.*) away; **transporté de joie** beside o.s. with joy; **se ~** betake o.s.; ⊙ conveyor; **~porteur** [~pɔr'tœːr] *m* 🚢 carrier; ⊙ conveyor; **~poser** [~po'ze] (1a) transpose; **~position** [~pozi'sjɔ̃] *f* transposition; **~suder** [~sy'de] (1a) transude; **~vasement** [~vaz'mɑ̃] *m* liquid: decanting; **~vaser** [~vɑ'ze] (1a) decant; **~versal** [~vɛr'sal] cross..., transversal; **~versalement** [~versal'mɑ̃] *adv.* crosswise.

trapèze [tra'pɛːz] *m* Ⓐ trapezium; *sp.* trapeze; *anat.* trapezius.

trappe [trap] *f* trap door; hatch.

trappeur [tra'pœːr] *m* trapper.

trapu [tra'py] thick-set, squat.

traqu|enard [trak'naːr] *m* trap (*a. fig.*); **~er** [~'ke] (1m) beat up (*game*); track

down (*a criminal*); hound (*s.o.*); **~eur** *hunt.* [~'kœːr] *m* beater.

trauma [tro'ma] *psych.*, 🌿 trauma; **~tique** [troma'tik] traumatic; **~tiser** [~ti'ze] (1a) traumatize; **~tisme** [~'tism] *m* traumatic experience.

travail, *pl.* **-aux** [tra'vaːj, ~'vo] *m* work; 🌿, 🚗 *pol.* labo(u)r; ⊙, *physiol.*, *a. wine:* working; employment; piece of work, F job; workmanship; business; ⊙ power; **~ intellectuel** (**manuel**) brain-work (manual work); **être sans ~** be out of work; 🚗 **~aux** *pl.* **forcés** hard labo(u)r *sg.*; **~ler** [tra'va'je] (1a) *v/i.* work; be at work; strive; ferment (*wine*); warp (*wood*); fade (*colour*); be active (*mind, volcano*); strain (*cable, ship, etc.*); 🌿 produce interest; **~ à** [work on *or* for *or* towards; *v/t.* work (*a.* 🌿, ⊙); shape, fashion; knead (*dough*); work on, work at; ♪ *etc.* practise; *fig.* worry, torment, distract; **~leur, -euse** [~'jœːr, ~'jøːz] **1.** *adj.* hard-working; **2.** *su.* worker; **~ intellectuel** intellectual worker; *su./f* (*lady's*) work-table; *zo.* worker (bee).

travée [tra've] *f* row; Ⓐ bay; span.

travers [tra'vɛːr] **1.** *su./m* fault, failing; **~ de doigt** finger's breadth; **2.** *adv.*: **de ~** askew, awry; (*look*) askance; *fig.* the wrong way, wrong; **en ~** (**de**) across (*s.th.*); **3.** *prp.*: **à ~**, **au ~ de** through (*s.th.*); **~able** [~vɛr'sabl] traversable; **~e** [~'vɛrs] *f* Ⓐ traverse beam *or* girder; *ladder:* rung; 🚂 sleeper, *Am.* tie; (*a. chemin m de ~*) short cut; **~er** [traver'se] *f* crossing, passage; **~er** [~'se] (1a) cross (*a. fig.*); pass *or* go through; **~in** [~'sɛ̃] *m* crossbar; *bed:* bolster.

travest|i [traves'ti] **1.** *adj.* disguised; fancy-dress (*ball*); **2.** *su./m* fancy dress; *thea.* man's part (played by a woman) (*or vice versa*); **~ir** [~'tiːr] (2a) misrepresent; **se ~** put on fancy dress; dress up (as, **en**); **~issement** [~tis'mɑ̃] *m* dressing up; *fig.* misrepresentation; travesty.

tray|eur [trɛ'jœːr] *m* milker; **~euse** [~'jøːz] *f* milkmaid; milking-machine; **~on** [~'jɔ̃] *m* teat, dug.

trébuch|ant [treby'jɑ̃] stumbling; of full weight (*coin*); **~er** [~'ʃe] (1a) *v/i.* stumble; trip; *v/t.* weigh; **~et** [~'ʃɛ] *m* assay balance; trap.

tréfiler [trefi'le] (1a) wiredraw.

trèfle [trɛfl] m ♣ clover(leaf); ∆, ♣ trefoil; *cards*: club(s *pl.*); *mot.* **croisement** m **en ~** cloverleaf (crossing).

tréfonds [tre'fɔ̃] m *fig.* (inmost) depths *pl.*

treillag|e [trɛja'ʒ] m trellis (work); **~er** [~ja'ʒe] (1l) trellis.

treille [trɛij] f vine arbo(u)r; ♣ climbing vine, grape vine; F **le jus de la ~** the wine.

treillis [trɛ'ji] m trellis (work), lattice; grid (*for maps etc.*); *tex.* canvas, sackcloth; ⚔ fatigues *pl.*

treize [trɛz] thirteen; *date, title*: thirteenth; **treizième** [trɛ'zjɛm] thirteenth.

trembl|ant [trã'blã] trembling *etc.*; *see* **trembler; ~e** ♣ [trã'bl] m aspen; **~ement** [trãblə'mã] m trembling, shaking; *voice*: quaver(ing); *fig.* shudder(ing); ♣ tremolo; 🎣, *fig.* tremor; **~ de terre** earthquake; F **tout le ~** the whole caboodle; **~er** [~'ble] (1a) tremble, shake, quiver (with, **de**); quaver (🎣, *voice*); flicker (*light*); *fig.* be afraid, fear; **~eur** [~'blœːr] m anxious person; *tel., teleph.* buzzer; **~oter** F [~blɔ'te] (1a) quiver; shiver (with, **de**).

trémolo [tremo'lo] m 🎣 tremolo; *fig.* quaver.

trémousser [tremu'se] (1a): **se ~** fidget; wiggle; jig about.

tremp|age [trã'pa:ʒ] m ⚙ soaking, steeping; **~e** [trã:p] f ⚙ quenching; *metall.* temper(ing); *fig.* calibre, stamp; F thrashing; **~é** [trã'pe] soaked, wet (through); *metall.* tempered; *fig.* sturdy; **~er** [~'pe] (1a) v/t. soak; drench; dip; dunk; ⚙ quench; dilute (*wine*) with water; v/i. soak; *fig.* be a party (to, **dans**); **~ette** [~'pɛt] f: **faire ~** dunk a biscuit *etc.*; F have a dip.

tremplin [trã'plɛ̃] m *sp. etc.* springboard; diving board; *ski*: platform; *fig.* stepping stone (to, **pour**).

trémulation [tremyla'sjɔ̃] f vibration, trepidation; 🎣 tremor.

trentaine [trã'tɛn] f (about) thirty; **la ~** the age of thirty, the thirties *pl.*; **trente** [trã:t] thirty; *date, title*: thirtieth; **~-trois tours** m long-playing record, album; **trentième** [trã'tjɛm] thirtieth.

trépan [tre'pã] m ⚚ trepan; ⚙ drill; **~ation** [~pana'sjɔ̃] f trepanning; **~er** [~pa'ne] (1a) trepan.

trépas *poet.* [tre'pɑ] m death, decease; **~sé** [trepa'se] *su.* deceased; **~ser** [~] (1a) die, pass away.

trépidation [trepida'sjɔ̃] f trepidation, vibration.

trépied [tre'pje] m tripod; trivet.

trépigner [trepi'ɲe] (1a) v/i. stamp one's feet; jump (for joy, **de joie**); dance (with, **de**); v/t. trample.

très [trɛ] *adv.* very (much), most.

Très-Haut [trɛ'o]: **le ~** God.

trésor [tre'zɔːr] m treasure (*a. fig.*); *pol.* ⚚ Treasury; **~s** *pl.* wealth *sg.*; **~erie** [~zɔr'ri] f treasury; **~ier** [~zo'rje] m treasurer.

tressaill|ement [trɛsaj'mã] m surprise: start; *fear*: shudder; *joy*: thrill; *pain*: wince; **~ir** [~sa'jiːr] (2s) give a start, flutter (*heart*); **~ de** shudder with (*fear*); thrill with (*joy*); wince with (*pain*).

tressauter [trɛso'te] (1a) jump, start (with fear *etc.*); jolt (*things*).

tress|e [trɛs] f tress, plait, braid; **~er** [trɛ'se] (1a) plait, braid, weave.

tréteau [tre'to] m trestle, support; *thea.* **~x** *pl.* stage *sg.*

treuil ⚙ [trœːj] m winch, windlass.

trêve [trɛːv] f truce; *fig.* respite; **sans ~** unremitting, relentlessly; **~ de ...** enough of ...; **~ de plaisanteries!** no more joking!

tri(age) [tri('a:ʒ)] m sorting (out).

triang|le [tri'ã:gl] m triangle; **~ulaire** [triãgy'lɛːr] triangular.

tribord ⚓ [tri'bɔːr] m starboard; **à** (*or* **par**) **~** to starboard.

tribu [tri'by] f tribe.

tribulation [tribyla'sjɔ̃] f tribulation; *fig.* trial; F worry, trouble.

tribun|al ⚖ [triby'nal] m (law)court; **~ arbitral** arbitration court; **~ de police** police court; **~ pour enfants** juvenile court; **~e** [~'byn] f platform, rostrum; gallery; *fig.* forum.

tribut [tri'by] m tribute (*a. fig.*); *fig.* reward; **~aire** [~by'tɛːr] tributary (*a. geog.*); dependent (on, **de**).

trich|er [tri'ʃe] (1a) cheat, **~erie** [triʃ'ri] f cheating; **~eur** m, **-euse** f [tri'ʃœːr, ~'ʃøːz] cheat.

trichromie *phot., typ.* [trikrɔ'mi] f three-colo(u)r process.

tricolore [trikɔ'lɔːr] tricolo(u)r(ed); **drapeau** m **~** French flag.

tricot [tri'ko] *m* knitting; ✝ knitwear; (*a. ~ de corps*) vest, *Am.* undershirt; jersey; **~er** [~'te] (1a) *v/t.* knit; F **se ~** make off; *v/i.* F *fig.* move or walk fast.

tridimensionnel [tridimɑ̃sjɔ'nɛl] three-dimensional.

trièdre ⚥ [tri'ɛdr] three-sided.

triennal [triɛn'nal, ~'no] triennal.

trier [tri'e] (1a) sort (out); **trieur** *m* **-euse** *f* [~'œːr, ~'øːz] sorter.

trifolié ⚘ [trifɔ'lje] three-leaved.

trigone ⚥ [tri'gɔn] trigonal, three-cornered; **trigonométrie** ⚥ [~gɔnɔme'tri] *f* trigonometry.

trilatéral [trilate'ral] three-sided.

trilingue [tri'lɛ̃ːg] trilingual.

trille ♪ [tri:j] *m* trill.

trillion [tri'ljɔ̃] *m* a million of billions, *Am.* a billion of billions.

trilogie [trilɔ'ʒi] *f* trilogy.

trimard|er *sl.* [trimar'de] be on the tramp; **~eur** [~'mar'dœːr] *m* tramp, hobo.

trimbaler F [trɛ̃ba'le] (1a) carry about; trail along; lug about.

trimer F [tri'me] (1a) drudge, toil.

trimestr|e [tri'mɛstr] *m* quarter, three month; quarter's rent or salary; *univ.* term; **~iel** [~mɛstri'ɛl] quarterly; trimestrial.

tringle [trɛ̃ːgl] *f* rod; bar; tingle.

trinité trini'te] *f* trinity (*a.* ♀ *eccl.*).

trinquer [trɛ̃'ke] (1m) clink glasses (with, **avec**); (have) a drink (with, **avec**); *sl.* get the worst of it.

triolet [triɔ'le] *m* ♪ triplet; triolet.

triomph|al [triɔ̃'fal] triumphal; **~ale-ment** [~fal'mɑ̃] *adv.* triumphantly; **~ant** [~'fɑ̃] triumphant; **~ateur** [~fa'tœːr] triumphing; **~e** [tri'ɔ̃ːf] *m* triumph; *arc m de ~* triumphal arch; **~er** [~ɔ̃'fe] (1a) triumph (over, **de**); *fig.* rejoice (over, **de**); **~ de** *a.* overcome, get over (*s.th.*).

tripaille F [tri'pɑ:j] *f* guts; offal.

triparti [tripar'ti], **~te** [~'tit] tripartite; *pol.* three-power.

tripe [trip] *f cuis.* (*usu. ~s pl.*) tripe; F **~s** *pl.* guts; **~rie** [tri'pri] *f* tripe shop; **~tte** F [~'pɛt] *f*: *ça ne vaut pas ~* it's not worth tuppence (*Am. a* cent).

triphasé ⚡ [trifa'ze] three-phase.

tripl|e [tripl] **1.** *adj.* threefold; triple; F *fig.* out-and-out; **2.** *su./m* treble; **~é** *m*,

~ée *f* [tri'ple] children: triplet; **~er** [~] (1a) treble.

triporteur [tripɔr'tœːr] *m* carrier-tricycle; (*commercial*) tri-car.

tripot [tri'po] *m* gambling house; dive; **~age** [tripɔ'ta:ʒ] *m* messing about; F *fig.* dealings *pl.*; tampering; **~ée** *f* [~'te] *f* thrashing, hiding; lots *pl.*; **~er** [~'te] (1a) *v/i.* mess about; rummage about; tamper; *v/t.* finger, fiddle with, play with; paw (*s.o.*); meddle with (*s.th.*); **~eur** [~'tœːr] *m* shady dealer.

trique F [trik] *f* cudgel, big stick.

trisaïeul [triza'jœl] *m* great-great grandfather.

trisannuel [triza'nɥɛl] triennial.

triste [trist] sad; *fig.* sorry; **~sse** [tris'tɛs] *f* sadness.

triton *zo.* [tri'tɔ̃] *m* newt.

triturer [trity're] (1a) grind (up); knead; manipulate; F *se ~ la cervelle* rack one's brains.

trivalen|ce 🜍 [triva'lɑ̃:s] *f* trivalence; **~t** [~'lɑ̃] trivalent.

trivial [tri'vjal] trite; vulgar; **~ité** [~vjali'te] *f* triteness; vulgarism.

troc [trɔk] *m* barter, exchange.

troglodyte [trɔglɔ'dit] *m zo., orn.* troglodyte; *person:* cave-dweller.

trogne [trɔɲ] *f* bloated face.

trognon [trɔ'ɲɔ̃] *m fruit:* core; *cabbage:* stump, stalk; *sl.* darling.

trois [trwa] three; *date, title:* third; ⚥ *règle f de ~* rule of three; **~-étoiles** [trwaze'twal] *adj.* (*su./inv.*) three-star (hotel *or* restaurant *etc.*); **~ième** [~'zjɛm] **1.** *adj./num.*, *su.* third; **2.** *su./m* third, *Am.* fourth floor; **~-mâts** ⚓ [trwa'ma] *m/inv.* three-master; **~-pièces** *cost.* [~'pjɛs] *m/inv.* three-piece suit; **~-quarts** [~'ka:r] *m/inv.* three-quarter length coat.

trombe [trɔ̃:b] *f* waterspout; *fig. entrer en ~* burst in; *passer en ~* dash by.

trombone [trɔ̃'bɔn] *m* ♪ trombone; paper-clip.

trompe [trɔ̃:p] *f* ♪ horn; *zo.* proboscis, *elephant:* trunk; *anat.* tube; **~s utérines** Fallopion tubes.

trompe-l'œil [trɔ̃'plœ:j] *m/inv. art:* trompe-l'œil; *fig.* eyewash, window dressing; **~er** [~'pe] (1a) deceive; cheat; mislead; delude (about, **sur**); be unfaithful to (*one's wife*); outwit, elude; *fig.* disappoint (*hopes etc.*); **se ~** be wrong; make a mistake; **se ~ de chemin** take the wrong road; **~erie** [~'pri] *f* deception; illusion; (piece of) deceit.

trompett|e [trɔ̃'pɛt] *su./f* trumpet; **en ~** turned-up (*nose*); *su./m* = **~iste** [~pɛ'tist] *m* trumpeter.

trompeur [trɔ̃'pœːr] **1.** *adj.* deceitful; lying; *fig.* deceptive; **2.** *su.* deceiver; cheat; betrayer.

tron|c [trɔ̃] *m* ♃, △, ♅, *anat.* trunk; collection box; **△ ~ de cône** truncated cone; **~che** *sl.* [trɔ̃ʃ] *f* head; **~çon** [~'sɔ̃] *m* stump; piece; offcut; **🎗**, *tel., etc.* section; **~conner** [~sɔ'ne] (1a) cut up; cut into lengths or sections.

trône [troːn] *m* throne; **trôner** [tro'ne] (1a) sit enthroned; lord it.

tronquer [trɔ̃'ke] (1m) △, ♅ truncate; *fig.* shorten; *fig.* cut down.

trop [tro] **1.** *adv.* too; to much or many; **~ de ...** too much ...; too many ...; **c'en est ~!** enough is enough!; **de ~, en ~** too many; **être de ~** be in the way, not to be welcome; be out of place; **... ne serait pas de ~** one could do with ...; **... would be welcome**; **je ne sais pas ~** I am not quite sure; **2.** *su./m* excess, too much; **ne ... que ~** far too ...; **par ~** altogether too ...

trophée [tro'fe] *m* trophy.

tropi|cal [tropi'kal] tropical; **~que** *astr., geog.* [~'pik] *m* tropic.

trop-plein [tro'plɛ̃] *m* overflow; excess; **⚙** overflow (pipe).

troquer [trɔ'ke] (1m) barter.

troquet F [trɔ'kɛt] *m* (*small*) café.

trot [tro] *m* trot; **aller au ~** trot; F **au ~** quickly; **~te** F [trɔt] *f* (*a good*) distance; **~ter** [trɔ'te] (1a) *v/i.* trot; scamper about; F *fig.* be on the go; *v/t.*: F **se ~** be off; **~teur, -euse** [~'tœːr, ~'tøːz] **1.** *adj.* walking(-*costume etc.*); **2.** *su.* horse: trotter; *fig.* quick walker; *su./f clock, watch*: second hand; **~tiner** [~ti'ne] (1a) trot short (*horse*); *fig.* toddle; *fig.* trot about; **~tinette** [~ti'nɛt] *f* scooter; **~toir** [~'twaːr] *m* pavement, *Am.* sidewalk; F *pej.* **faire le ~** walk the streets.

trou [tru] *m* hole; *needle*: eye; gap; ✈ **~ d'air** air pocket.

troubl|ant [tru'blɑ̃] disturbing; disquieting; **~e** [trubl] **1.** *adj.* blurred; cloudy

(*liquid etc.*); confused; murky, dim; **2.** *su./m* confusion; agitation, distress; discord, dissension; *fig.* uneasiness, turmoil; **~s** *pl. pol.* unrest *sg.*, disturbances; **☭** trouble *sg.*, disorders; **~e-fête** [trubləˈfɛt] *su./inv.* spoil-sport, wet blanket; **~er** [~'ble] (1a) disturb; cloud (*a liquid*); *fig.* interrupt; *fig.* disconcert; make (*s.o.*) uneasy; **se ~** become cloudy; become confused; show concern.

trouée [tru'e] *f* gap; ✗ breach; **trouer** [~] (1a) make a hole or holes in; *fig.* make gaps in; **être troué** have a hole or holes (in it).

trouille *sl.* [truːj] *f* funk, scare.

troup|e [trup] *f* troop (*a.* ✗), band; *pej.* gang; *thea.* company; herd; flock; swarm; *birds*: flight; **~eau** [tru'po] *m* herd; flock; *fig.* set, pack; **~ier** F [~'pje] *m* soldier.

trouss|e [trus] *f* case, kit; *doctor's* instrument case; **~ de toilette** toilet or sponge bag; **aux ~s de** on (*s.o.'s*) heels; **~eau** [tru'so] *m* keys *etc.*: bunch; outfit; *bride*: trousseau; **~er** [tru'se] (1a) tuck up; turn up; *cuis.* truss (*fowl*); F *fig.*, dash (*s.th.*) off.

trouv|able [tru'vabl] findable; **~aille** [~'vaj] *f* (lucky) find, godsend; **~er** [~'ve] (1a) find; discover; hit or come upon; meet (with); *fig.* consider, think; **~ bon (mauvais)** *a.* (not to) like; **~ bon de** (*inf.*) think fit to (*inf.*), **~ la mort** meet one's death; **aller (venir) ~ q.** go (come) and see s.o.; **comment trouvez-vous ...?** what do you think of ...?; **vous trouvez?** do you think so?; **se ~** be (present, situated); feel (*better etc.*); happen; **il se trouve que ...** it happens that; **se ~ mal** pass out, faint; **se ~ bien (mal) de qch.** feel all the better (worse) for s.th.

truand [try'ɑ̃] *m* crook, villain; **~er** F [~ɑ̃'de] (1a) swindle, do.

truc F [tryk] *m* knack, hang; trick; thingumajig, thing, gadget.

trucage [try'kaːʒ] *m* faking; cheating; fake; *cin.* trick picture.

truchement [tryʃ'mɑ̃] *m*: **par le ~ de** through (the intervention of).

trucider F [trysi'de] (1a) kill.

truculent [tryky'lɑ̃] colo(u)rful.

truelle [try'ɛl] *f* trowel; fish-slice.

truff|e [tryf] *f* ♅, *cuis.* truffle; F idiot; **~er**

[try'fe] (1a) *cuis.* stuff with truffles; *fig.* **truffé de** bristling with.

truie [trɥi] *f* sow.

truisme [trɥ'ism] *m* truism.

truite *icht.* [trɥit] *f* trout; **truité** [trɥi'te] spotted; speckled.

truqu|age [try'ka:ʒ] *m see* **trucage;** **~er** [~'ke] (1m) fiddle with, fix; fake; **~eur** *m*, **-euse** *f* [~'kœːr, ~'køːz] faker.

trust ✝ [trœst] *m* trust; **~er** [trœs'te] (1a) monopolize.

tsar [tsa:r] *m* czar.

tu[1] [ty] *pron./pers.* you.

tu[2] [~] *p.p. of* **taire.**

tuant F [tɥɑ̃] killing; annoying.

tuba [ty'ba] *m* ♪ tuba; *sp.* snorkel.

tube [tyb] *m* tube; ⚙ pipe; *radio:* valve; *anat.* duct; hit (song); *sl.* (tele)phone.

tubercul|e [tybɛr'kyl] *m* ⚘ tuber; ⚕ tubercle; **~eux** [~ky'lø] **1.** *adj.* ⚘ tubercular; ⚕ tuberculous; **2.** *su.* ⚕ tubercular patient; **~ose** ⚕ [~ky'lo:z] *f* tuberculosis.

tubulaire [tyby'lɛ:r] tubular.

tubulure [tyby'ly:r] *f* pipe; nozzle; *mot.* manifold.

tudesque [ty'dɛsk] Teutonic.

tue-chien ⚘ [ty'ʃjɛ̃] *m/inv.* meadow saffron; **tue-mouches** [~'muʃ] *m/inv.* ⚘ fly agaric; (*a.* **papier** *m* **~**) fly paper; **tuer** [tɥe] (1n) kill; *fig.* wear (*s.o., o.s.*) out; **tuerie** *fig.* [ty'ri] *f* slaughter; **tue-tête** [~'tɛt] *adv.:* **à ~** at the top of one's voice; **tueur** [tɥœːr] *m* killer.

tuf [tyf] *m geol.* tuff; *fig.* foundation.

tuile [tɥil] *f* tile; F *fig.* (spot of) bad luck, blow; **~rie** [tɥil'ri] *f* tile works *sg.*

tulipe [ty'lip] *f* ⚘ tulip.

tuméfac|tion [tymefak'sjɔ̃] *f* swelling; **~ié** [~'fje] swollen.

tumeur ⚕ [ty'mœːr] *f* tumo(u)r.

tumulaire [tymy'lɛːr] tomb...

tumult|e [ty'mylt] *m* commotion; tumult, uproar; turmoil; rush, bustle; riot; **~ueux** [~myl'tɥø] tumultuous.

tunique [ty'nik] *f* ⚕ ⚘, ✗, *cost.* tunic.

tunnel [ty'nɛl] *m* tunnel.

turbin F [tyr'bɛ̃] *m* work, F grind.

turbine ⚙ [tyr'bin] *f* turbine.

turbiner F [tyrbi'ne] (1a) work, toil.

turboréacteur ✈ [tyrbɔreak'tœːr] *m* turbojet.

turbulen|ce [tyrby'lɑ̃:s] *f* turbulence;

boisterousness; unruliness; **~t** [~'lɑ̃] turbulent; boisterous; stormy (*life, sea*): *fig.* unruly.

turc, turque [tyrk] **1.** *adj., su./m ling.* Turkish; **2.** *su.* ♀ Turk; **tête** *f* **de** ♀ scapegoat.

turf [tyrf] *m* racecourse; racing; **turfiste** [tyr'fist] *su.* race-goer.

turgide [tyr'ʒid] turgid, swollen.

turpitude [tyrpi'tyd] *f* turpitude, depravity; low trick; base act.

turquoise [tyr'kwa:z] **1.** *su./f* turquoise; **2.** *adj./inv.* turquoise.

tus [ty] *1st p. sg. p.s. of* **taire.**

tutélaire [tyte'lɛːr] tutelary; guardian ...; **tutelle** [~'tɛl] *f* guardianship; trusteeship; *fig.* protection.

tuteur, -trice [ty'tœːr, ~'tris] *su.* ⚖ guardian; *su./m* ⚘ prop, stake.

tutoiement [tytwa'mɑ̃] *m* use of *tu* and *toi* (*as a sign of familiarity*); **tutoyer** [~'je] (1h) address as **tu;** be on familiar terms with (*s.o.*).

tuyau [tɥi'jo] *m* pipe; tube; *cost.* fluting; pipe: stem; *chimney:* flue; F *fig.* tip, hint; **~ d'arrosage** garden hose; **~ de poêle** stovepipe; **~ d'incendie** fire hose; *mot.* **~ d'échappement** exhaust (pipe); **~ d'écoulement** drain pipe; **~ter** [~'te] (1a) flute (*linen*); F give (*s.o.*) a tip; **~terie** [~'tri] *f* pipe system.

tuyère ⚙ [tɥi'jɛ:r] *f* nozzle.

tympan [tɛ̃'pɑ̃] *m* △, *anat.* tympanum; *anat.* eardrum; **crever le ~ à q.** split s.o.'s ears.

type [tip] **1.** *su./m* type (*a. typ., fig.*); standard model *or* pattern; ✝ sample; F fellow, guy; **2.** *adj.* typical; standard...; **~sse** *sl.* [ti'pɛs] *f* female.

typhique [ti'fik] typhous; **typhoïde** ⚕ [~fɔ'id] **1.** *adj.* typhoid; **2.** *su./f* typhoid (fever).

typhon *meteor.* [ti'fɔ̃] *m* typhoon.

typhus ⚕ [ti'fys] *m* typhus.

typique [ti'pik] typical (of, **de**).

typograph|e [tipɔ'graf] *m* printer; **~ie** [~gra'fi] *f* typography.

tyran [ti'rɑ̃] *m* tyrant; **~nicide** [tirani'sid] *su., su./m* tyrannicide; **~nie** [~'ni] *f* tyranny; **~nique** [~'nik] tyrannical; **~niser** [~ni'ze] (1a) tyrannize; *fig.* bully.

tyrolien [tirɔ'ljɛ̃] *adj., su.* Tyrolese.

tzigane [tsi'gan] *su.* gipsy, Tzigane.

U

ubiquité [ybikɥi'te] f ubiquity; *avoir le don d'~* be everywhere at the same time.

ulcère 🦮 [yl'sɛːr] m ulcer; sore; *~ à l'estomac* stomach ulcer.

ulcér|er [ylse're] (1f) ulcerate; *fig.* embitter; *~eux* [~'rø] ulcerous.

ultérieur [ylte'rjœːr] ulterior; subsequent (to, à), later.

ultim|atum [yltima'tɔm] m ultimatum; *~e* [~'tim] ultimate, final; *~o* [~ti'mo] *adv.* lastly, finally.

ultra *pol.* [yl'tra] m extremist, ultra.

ultra... [yltra] ultra...; *~court* [~'kuːr] ultra-short (*wave*); *~sensible* [~sɑ̃'sibl] high-speed (*film*); *~son* [~'sɔ̃] m ultra-sound; *~sonore* [~sɔ'nɔːr] supersonic.

un, une [œ̃, yn] **1.** *art./indef.* a, an; *fig.* someone like; *not translated before abstract nouns qualified by an adj.*: *avec une grande joie* with great joy; *~ jour ou l'autre* some day or other; **2.** *adj./num./inv.* one; *une fois* once; *une heure* one o'clock; *~ jour sur deux* every other day; **3.** *su.* one; *~ à ~* one by one; *su./f: journ.* **la une** page one; *su./m:* **le un** (number) one; **4.** *pron./indef.* one; *les ~s ..., les autres ...* some ..., others ...; *l'~ l'autre* each other.

unanim|e [yna'nim] unanimous (in s.th., *dans qch.*; in *ger.* **à**, *pour inf.*); *~ité* [~nimi'te] f unanimity; *à l'~* unanimously, with one voice.

uni [y'ni] **1.** *p.p. of* **unir**; **2.** *adj.* level, even; plain (*colour, tex.*); *fig.* united; *fig.* close-(knit) (*family etc.*); **3.** *su./m* plain material.

unicité [ynisi'te] f uniqueness.

unicolore [yniko'lɔːr] unicolo(u)red.

unième [y'njɛm] *in compounds:* first; *vingt et ~* twenty-first.

unification [ynifika'sjɔ̃] f unification; † standardization; **unifier** [~'fje] (1o) unify; † standardize.

uniform|e [yni'fɔrm] **1.** *adj.* uniform, unvarying; **2.** *su./m* ✕ uniform; *~ément* [yniforme'mɑ̃] *adv. of* **uniforme 1**; *~iser* [~mi'ze] (1a) make (*s.th.*) uniform; *~ité* [~mi'te] f uniformity; *fig.* evenness.

unilatéral [ynilate'ral] unilateral.

union [y'njɔ̃] f union; association.

unipolaire ⚡ [ynipɔ'lɛːr] unipolar.

unique [y'nik] unique; single, alone; only; united; *fig.* unrival(l)ed; *seul et ~* one and only; *~ment* [ynik'mɑ̃] *adv.* solely; simply, merely.

unir [y'niːr] (2a) unite *or* combine (with, **à**); join in marriage; *s'~* unite *or* combine (with **à**, **avec**); be joined in marriage.

unisson [yni'sɔ̃] m ♩ unison; *à l'~* in unison (with, *de*); in harmony.

unitaire [yni'tɛːr] unitary; unitarian; ♣, ✝ unit-...; **unité** [~'te] f ✕, ♣ unit; ♣, *phls.*, *fig.*, *thea.* unity.

univers [yni'vɛːr] m universe, *~aliser* [yniversali'ze] (1a) universalize; *~alité* [~sali'te] f universality; *~el* [~'sel] universal; ⊙ *etc.* all-purpose, general-purpose; world(-wide); *homme m ~* all-rounder; 🦮 *remède m ~* panacea.

universitaire [yniversi'tɛːr] **1.** *adj.* university..., academic; **2.** *su.* academic; **université** [~'te] f university.

univoque [yni'vɔk] univocal; *fig.* unequivocal; *fig.* uniform.

Untel [œ̃'tɛl] m: *Monsieur (Madame) ~* Mr (Mrs) so-and-so.

urane 🜍 [y'ran] m uranium oxide; **uranium** [yra'njɔm] m uranium.

urbain [yr'bɛ̃] urban, town..., city...; urbane.

urbani|ser [yrbani'ze] (1a) urbanize; *~sme* [~'nism] m town planning, *Am.* city planning, *~ste* [~'nist] m town planner, *Am.* city planner; *~té* [~ni'te] f urbanity.

urin|aire *anat.* [yri'nɛːr] urinary; *~e physiol.* [y'rin] f urine; *~er* [yri'ne] (1a) urinate; *~oir* [~'nwaːr] m (public) urinal.

urne [yrn] f urn; (*a. ~ électorale*) ballot box; *~ funéraire* cinerary urn; *aller* (*or se rendre*) *aux ~s* go to the polls.

us [y] *m/pl.*: ~ **et coutumes** *f/pl.* ways and customs.

usage [y'za:ʒ] *m* use, employment; *cost. etc.*: service, wear; *fig.* custom; usage; ~ **du monde** good breeding; **à ~s multiples** multi-purpose; **à l'~ de** intended for; **faire** ~ **de** use; **faire bon** ~ **de** put to good use; **hors d'~** disused; **il est d'~ de** (*inf.*) it is usual to (*inf.*); **usagé** [yza'ʒe] worn; used; **usager** [~'ʒe] **1.** *su.* user; **2.** *adj.* in everyday use; ✍ for personal use; **usant** [y'zɑ̃] wearing; tiresome; **usé** [y'ze] worn (out); *cost.* threadbare; *fig.* hjackneyed; **user** [~] **1.** (1a) *v/t.* use up; consume (*fuel*); wear out; spoil, waste; **s'~** wear away *or* out; *fig.* be spent; *v/i.*: ~ **de** use; make use of; resort to.

usin|age ⊚ [yzi'na:ʒ] *m* machining, tooling; **~e** [y'zin] *f* works *usu. sg.*, factory, mill, plant; ~ **atomique** atomic plant; ~ **électrique** powerhouse; *cost.* **maremotrice** tidal power station; **~er** [yzi'ne] (1a) ⊚ machine, tool; process.

usité [yzi'te] in use, current.

ustensile [ystɑ̃'sil] *m* utensil; tool, implement.

usuel [y'zɥɛl] usual; common.

usufruit ✍ [yzy'frɥi] *m* usufruct; **~ier** [~frɥi'tje] *su.* usufructuary.

usuraire [yzy'rɛːr] usurious.

usure¹ [y'zyːr] *f* ⊚, *cost., etc.*: wear (and terar); F **avoir q. à l'~** wear s.o. down (in the end).

usure² [y'zyːr] *f* usury; *fig.* **rendre avec** ~ repay (*s.th.*) with interest; **usurier** [yzy'rje] *m* usurer.

usurp|ateur [yzyrpa'tœːr] **1.** *adj.* usurping; **2.** *su.* usurper; **~ation** [~'sjɔ̃] *f* usurpation (of, **de**); *fig.* encroachment (upon, **de**); *fig.* invade usurpatory; **~er** [yzyr'pe] (1a) *v/t.* usurp (from, **sur**); *v/i. fig.* encroach (upon, **sur**).

ut ♪ [yt] *m/inv.* ut; *note*: C.

utérin [yte'rɛ̃] uterine.

util|e [y'til] useful; *fig.* convenient; **~isable** [ytili'zabl] usable; **~isateur** [~za'tœːr] *m* user; **~isation** [~za'sjɔ̃] *f* use; **~iser** [~'ze] (1a) use; utilize; **~itaire** [~'tɛːr] utilitarian; **~itarisme** [~ta'rism] *m* utilitarianism; **~ité** [~'te] *f* usefulness; use; *thea.* minor part.

utopi|e [yto'pi] *f* utopia; utopian idea; **~que** [~'pik] utopian; **~ste** [~'pist] *su.* utopian, utopist.

uval [y'val] grape-...

V

V, v [ve] *m* V, v; **double v** W, w.

va! [va] *int.* believe me!; ~ **pour cette somme!** agreed (at that figure!).

vacan|ce [va'kɑ̃:s] *f* vacancy; vacant post; **~s** *pl.* holidays, *Am.* vacation *sg.*; **~cier** *m*, **-ière** *f* [~kɑ̃'sje, ~'sjɛːr] holidaymaker, *Am.* vacationist; **~t** [~'kɑ̃] vacant, unoccupied.

vacarme [va'karm] *m* uproar, row.

vacation ✍ [vaka'sjɔ̃] *f* sitting; **~s** *pl.* fees; *law-courts:* vacation *sg.*

vaccin ✍ [vak'sɛ] *m* vaccine; **~ation** [~sina'sjɔ̃] *f* vaccination; **~e** [vak'sin] *f* cowpox; **~er** [~si'ne] (1a) vaccinate.

vach|e [vaʃ] **1.** *su./f* cow; ✝ cowhide; F *fig.* **manger de la** ~ **enragée** have a hard time of it; **2.** *adj. sl.* harsh; mean;

~ement *sl.* [vaʃ'mɑ̃] damned, terribly, real; **~er** *m*, **-ère** *f* [va'ʃe, ~'ʃɛːr] cowherd; **~erie** [vaʃ'ri] *f* cowshed; *sl.* dirty trick; nasty remark.

vacill|ant [vasi'jɑ̃] unsteady; flickering; shaky; *fig.* undecided; uncertain (*health*); **~ation** [~ja'sjɔ̃] *f* unsteadiness; flickering; shakiness; wavering; **~er** [~'je] (1a) be unsteady; sway (to and fro); be shaky; flicker (*light*); *fig.* waver.

vacu|ité [vakɥi'te] *f* emptiness, vacuity; **~um** [~'kɥɔm] *m* vacuum.

vadrouill|e F [va'druːj] *f* stroll; **~er** F [vadru'je] (1a) stroll, roam.

va-et-vient [vae'vjɛ̃] *m/inv.* comings and goings *pl.*; movement to and fro; ⚡

two-way switch; *faire le ~ entre* 🚋, ⚓, *etc.* ply between.

vagabond [vaga'bɔ̃] **1.** *adj.* wandering; roving (*a. fig.*); **2.** *su.* vagabond; tramp; **~age** [~bɔ̃'daːʒ] *m* wandering; vagrancy; **~er** [~bɔ̃'de] (1a) be a vagabond; wander, roam (*a. fig.*).

vagin *anat.* [va'ʒɛ̃] *m* vagina.

vagi|r [va'ʒiːr] (2a) wail (*newborn infant*); squeak (*hare*); **~ssement** [~ʒis'mɑ̃] *m* wail; squeak.

vague¹ [vag] *f* ⚓ wave; *fig.* surge.

vague² [vag] **1.** *adj.* vague; hazy; dim; loose(-fitting) (*garment*); **2.** *su./m* vagueness.

vague³ [vag] **1.** *adj.* vacant, empty (*look, stare*); **2.** *su./m* empty space; *regarder dans le ~* look *or* gaze into space.

vaguer [va'ge] (1m) roam, wander.

vailla|mment [vaja'mɑ̃] valiantly; **~nce** [~'jɑ̃ːs] *f* courage; **~nt** [~'jɑ̃] valiant, brave; vigorous, in good health.

vaille [vaj] *1st p. sg. pres. sbj. of valoir.*

vain [vɛ̃] **1.** *adj.* vain; empty (*words etc.*); useless (*effort*); conceited; **2.** *adv.*: *en ~* vainly, in vain.

vain|c [vɛ̃] *3rd p. sg. pres. of vaincre,* **~cre** [vɛ̃ːkr] (4gg) defeat, beat (*s.o.*); overcome (*s.th.*); *fig.* outdo; **~cu** [vɛ̃'ky] **1.** *p.p. of vaincre;* **2.** *su.* defeated person *or* party; loser; **~queur** [~'kœːr] **1.** *su./m* victor, conqueror; *sp. etc.* winner; **2.** *adj.* victorious; **~quis** [~'ki] *1st p. sg. p.s. of vaincre;* **~quons** [~'kɔ̃] *1st p. pl. pres. of vaincre.*

vais [vɛ] *1st p. sg. pres. of aller 1.*

vaisseau [vɛ'so] *m* 🚢, ⚓, 🌊, *anat., cuis.* vessel; ⚓ ship; 🌊, *anat.* duct; *church:* nave; **~ spatial** spacecraft.

vaissel|ier [vɛsə'lje] *m* china cupboard; **~le** [~'sɛl] *f* crockery; dishes *pl.;* tableware; *eau f de ~* dishwater; *faire la ~* wash up, *Am.* wash the dishes.

val, *pl.* **vals,** *a.* **vaux** [val, vo] *m* vale, dale; *par monts et par vaux* up hill and down dale.

valable [va'labl] valid (*a. fig.*).

valence '⚛ [va'lɑ̃ːs] *f* valency.

valet [va'lɛ] *m* (man-)servant; *cards:* jack; ⚙ clamp; ⚙ stand; *fig.* toady.

valétudinaire [valetydi'nɛːr] sickly.

valeur [va'lœːr] *f* value, worth; asset (*a. fig.*); ♪ *note:* length; ✕ valo(u)r; ✝ **~s** *pl.* securities; *de ~* valuable; *fig.* of

value; able (*person*); *mettre en ~* enhance the value of; develop, reclaim (*land*); *fig.* emphasize, bring out; *objets m/pl. de ~* valuables; **~eux** [~'lœrø] brave.

valid|ation [valida'sjɔ̃] *f* validation; ratifying; **~e** [~'lid] valid; healthy; (*fig.* sound; ✕ fit (*for service*); **~er** [vali'de] (1a) validate; ratify; **~ité** [~di'te] *f* validity.

valise [va'liːz] *f* suitcase; (*diplomatic*) bag; *faire sa ~* (*or* *ses ~s*) *a. fig.* pack one's bags.

vall|ée [va'le] *f* valley; **~on** [~'lɔ̃] *m* small valley; dale, vale; **~onné** [~lɔ'ne] undulating; **~onnement** [~lɔn'mɑ̃] *m* undulation.

valoir [va'lwaːr] (3l) *v/i.* be worth; be profitable; be as good as; be equal to; apply, hold, be valid; ✝ *à ~* on account (of, *sur*); *ça vaut la peine (de inf.)* it's worth while (*to inf.*); *faire ~* make the most of (*s.th.*); turn to account; insist on (*a claim*); *fig.* emphasize, bring out; *v/t.*: *qch à q.* earn *or* win s.o. s.th.; *se faire ~* make the most of o.s.; show off; *v/impers.*: *il vaut mieux (inf.)* it's better to (*inf.*); *mieux vaut tard que jamais* better late than never.

valoriser [valɔri'ze] (1a) increase the value or importance of; upgrade.

vals|e [vals] *f* waltz; **~er** [val'se] (1a) waltz; F *aller (envoyer) ~* go (send) flying.

valu, e [va'ly] **1.** *p.p. of valoir;* **2.** *su./f* see *moins-value; plus-value;* **valus** [~] *1st p. sg. p.s. of valoir.*

valve [valv] *f* valve; **valvule** [~'vyl] *f* valvule; *anat.* valve.

vampire [vɑ̃'piːr] *m* vampire.

vanill|e, *cuis.* [va'niːj] *f* vanilla; **~é** [~ni'je] vanilla(-flavo[u]red)

vanit|é [vani'te] *f* vanity; *fig.* futility; **~eux** [~'tø] conceited.

vanne [van] ⚙ (sluice *or* flood) gate; sluice; F jibe.

vanneau *orn.* [va'no] *m* lapwing, plover.

vanner [va'ne] (1a) 🌾 winnow, sift, *fig.* exhaust, wear out.

vann|erie [van'ri] *f* basket work; **~ier** [va'nje] *m* basket maker.

vannure [va'nyːr] *f* chaff, husks *pl.*

vantail, *pl.* **-aux** [vɑ̃'taːj, ~'to] *m* door, shutter, *etc.*: leaf.

vant|ard [vã'ta:r] **1.** *adj.* boastful; **2.** *su.* braggart; **~ardise** [~tar'di:z] *f* boasting; **~er** [~'te] (1a) praise, extol; F boost; **se ~** (*de*) boast (of); **~erie** [vã'tri] *f* boast(ing).

va-nu-pieds [vany'pje] *m/inv.* tramp, hobo; beggar.

vapeur [va'pœ:r] *su./f* steam; vapo(u)r; fumes *pl.*; **machine f à ~** steam engine; *su./m* ♣ steamer; **vaporeux** [vapɔ'rø] misty; steamy; *fig.* hazy; **vaporisateur** [~riza'tœ:r] *m* vaporizer; atomizer; ⚙ evaporator; **vaporiser** [~ri'ze] (1a) vaporize; atomize, spray.

vaquer [va'ke] (1m): **~ à** attend to, see to; **~ à ses affaires** *a.* go about one's business.

varappe *mount.* [va'rap] *f* rock climbing *or* climb.

varech ♀ [va'rɛk] *m* seaweed, wrack.

vareuse [va'rø:z] *f* (pea) jacket.

varia|bilité [varjabili'te] *f* variability; changeableness; **~ble** [~'rjabl] **1.** *adj.* variable; changeable; *fig.* fickle; **2.** *su./f* A variable; **~nte** [~'rjã:t] *f* variant; **~tion** [~rja'sjɔ̃] *f* variation.

varice ♂ [va'ris] *f* varicose vein.

varicelle [vari'sɛl] *f* chicken-pox.

vari|é [va'rje] varied; various; variegated; miscellaneous; **~er** [~'rje] (1o) *v/t.* vary; variegate; *v/i.* vary; change; change one's opinion; **~été** [~rje'te] *f* variety; wide range.

vario|le ♂ [va'rjɔl] *f* smallpox; **~é** [varjɔ'le] pock-marked; **~eux** [~'lø] **1.** *adj.* variolous; **2.** *su.* smallpox patient; **~ique** [~'lik] variolous.

vascul|aire ♀, *anat.* [vasky'lɛ:r], **~eux** ♂, *anat.* [~'lø] vascular.

vase¹ [va:z] *m* vase; vessel; *fig.* **en ~ clos** in seclusion.

vase² [~] *f* mud, silt.

vaseux [va'zø] muddy, silty; F *fig.* woolly (*ideas*); *sl. fig.* seedy, ill.

vasistas [vazis'tas] *m* fanlight, *Am.* transom.

vasque [vask] *f* fountain: basin.

vassal [va'sal] *su.* vassal.

vaste [vast] vast, immense; wide.

vaticin|ation [vatisina'sjɔ̃] *f* (pompous) prediction *or* prophecy; **~er** [~'ne] (1a) prophesy; make pompous predictions.

va-tout [va'tu] *m/inv.*: **jouer son ~** stake one's all.

vaudeville [vod'vil] *m* light comedy.

vaudrai [vo'dre] *1st p. sg. fut. of* **valoir.**

vau-l'eau [vo'lo] *adv.*: **† à ~** downstream; *fig.* **aller à ~** go to ruin.

vaurien [vo'rjɛ̃] *m* good-for-nothing.

vautour *orn.* [vo'tu:r] *m* vulture.

vautrer [vo'tre] (1a): **se ~** wallow (in, *dans*) (*a. fig.*); F *fig.* sprawl (*on a sofa, etc.*); revel (in, *dans*).

vaux [vo] *1st p. sg. pres. of* **valoir.**

va-vite [va'vit]: **à la ~** hurriedly; carelessly.

veau [vo] *m* calf; *meat.*: veal; † calfskin; **~ marin** seal; F clod (*person*); F tank (*car*).

vécu [ve'ky] *p.p. of* **vivre 1.**

vécus [~] *1st p. sg. p. s. of* **vivre 1.**

vedette [və'dɛt] *f person*: star; ♣ patrol boat; motor boat; **en ~** *fig.* in the limelight.

végéta|l [veʒe'tal] **1.** *adj.* plant(-*life*); vegetable; **2.** *su./m* plant; **~rien** [~ta'rjɛ̃] *su.* vegetarian.

végét|atif [veʒeta'tif] vegetative; **~ation** [~ta'sjɔ̃] *f* vegetation; growth; **~er** [~'te] (1d) vegetate.

véhémen|ce [vee'mã:s] *f* vehemence; **~t** [~'mã] vehement.

véhicul|e [vei'kyl] *m* vehicle (*a. fig.*); *fig. a.* medium; **~er** [~ky'le] (1a) convey, carry; cart.

veill|e [vɛ:j] *f* staying up (*at night*); wakefullness, waking; *eccl.* vigil; eve (of, *de*); day before; *fig.* verge, brink; (night) watch; *fig.* **à la ~ de** on the brink *or* eve *or* point of; **la ~ de Noël** Christmas Eve; **~ée** [vɛ'je] *f* evening (spent in company); watch; *fig.* **~ d'armes** night before combat; **~er** [~'je] (1a) stay *or* sit up (late); remain *or* lie awake; *eccl.* keep vigil; ✕, ♣ watch; stand by; **~ à** see to; attend to; **~ à ce que** (*sbj.*) see to it *or* make sure that (*ind.*); **~ sur** look after; watch over; *v/t.* attend to (*a patient etc.*); sit up with (*a patient, a dead body*); **~eur** [~'jœ:r] *m*: **~ de nuit** (night) watchman; **~euse** [~'jø:z] *f* night lamp; *mot.* sidelight; *gaz*: pilot lamp; **mettre en~** turn down; dim (*a lamp*); *fig.* put (*a project etc.*) on ice.

vein|ard [vɛ'na:r] lucky (person); **~e** [vɛn] *f* vein; ✕ lode; seam; *fig.* inspiration; F (good) luck; **avoir de la ~** be lucky; **être en ~ de ...** be in a ... mood; **~é** [~'ne] veined; grained (*wood*); **~eux** [~'nø] veiny; *anat.* venous; **&** venose; **~ule** [~'nyl] *f* small vein.

vêler [vɛ'le] (1b) calve (*cow*).

velléité [vɛlei'te] *f* stray impulse; slight fancy; **F** half a mind (to, **de**).

vélo F [ve'lo] *m* (push-)bike, cycle.

vélocité [velɔsi'te] *f* speed, velocity; **vélodrome** [~'droːm] *m* cycle racing track; **vélomoteur** [~mɔ'tœːr] *m* light motorcycle.

velou|rs [vəˈluːr] *m* velvet; **~ côtelé, ~ à côtes** corduroy; **~té** [vəluˈte] **1.** *adj.* velvety; mellow (*wine*), downy, **2.** *su./m* softness, velvetiness; *cuis.* creamed soup; **~ter** [~'te] (1a) (*a.* **se ~**) soften, mellow; **~teux** [~'tø] soft, velvety.

velu [vəˈly] hairy; △ uncut.

vélum [veˈlɔm] *m* awning.

venaison *cus.* [vənɛˈzɔ̃] *f* venison.

vénal [veˈnal] venal (*a. pej.*); **†** **valeur *f* ~e** market value; **~ité** [~naliˈte] *f* venality; *pej.* corruptibility.

venant [vəˈnɑ̃]: **à tout ~** to all and sundry, to anyone.

vendable [vɑ̃ˈdabl] saleable.

vendang|e [vɑ̃ˈdɑ̃ːʒ] *f* wine-harvest; (*a.* **~s** *pl.*) vintage; **~er** [vɑ̃dɑ̃ˈʒe] (1l) *v/t.* gather the grapes of; *v/i.* harvest grapes; **~eur** *m*, **-euse** *f* [~ˈʒœːr, ~ˈʒøːz] wine-harvester.

vendeur [vɑ̃ˈdœːr] *m* vendor; seller; shop assistant, *Am.* sales clerk; salesman; **vendeuse** [~ˈdøːz] *f* seller, shop assistant, *Am.* sales clerk; saleswoman; **vendre** [vɑ̃ːdr] (4a) sell (for, **à**); **à ~** for sale; **se ~** sell, be sold (at, for **à**).

vendredi [vɑ̃drəˈdi] *m* Friday; **le ~ saint** Good Friday.

vendu [vɑ̃ˈdy] **1.** *su./m* traitor; **2.** *p.p.* of **vendre**.

vénéneux **🎏, &** [veneˈnø] poisonous.

vénér|able [veneˈrabl] venerable; **~ation** [~raˈsjɔ̃] veneration; **~er** [~ˈre] (1f) venerate; revere.

vénerie *f* hunting, venery.

vénérien **&** [veneˈrjɛ̃] venereal.

veng|eance [vɑ̃ˈʒɑ̃ːs] *f* revenge; vengeance; **tirer ~ de** be revenged for (*s.th.*); take vengeance on (*s.o.*); **~er** [~ˈʒe] (1l) avenge (for, **de**); **se ~** take one's revenge (for, **de**); be revenged (on s.o.,

de q.); **~eur, -eresse** [vɑ̃ˈʒœːr, vɑ̃ʒˈrɛs] **1.** *su.* avenger; **2.** *adj.* avenging.

véniel *eccl.* [veˈnjɛl] venial (*sin*).

veni|meux [vəniˈmø] *zo. a. fig.* venomous; *zo.* poisonous; **~mosité** [~moziˈte] *f* sting, *a. fig.*: venomousness; **~n** [vəˈnɛ̃] *m* venom.

venir [vəˈniːr] (2h) come; be coming; grow (*a.* **&**, *child, tooth*); **~ à** come or reach up or down to; **~ à bien** be successful; **~ au monde** be born; **~ de ce que** (*ind.*) come or result from (*ger.*); **~ de faire (qch.)** have just done (s.th.); **~ prendre** come and fetch (s.o.); **à ~** future (*event*), (*years*) to come; **bien ~** thrive; **d'où cela vient-il?** what's the reason for that?; **en ~ aux coups** come to blows; **en ~ aux faits** get down to business; **faire ~** send for; call (*a doctor etc.*); **où voulez-vous en ~?** what are you getting or driving at?; **s'il venait à** (*inf.*) if he (*or* it) should (happen to) (*inf.*); *v/impers.* come; happen; occur; **d'où vient(-il) que** (*ind.*)? how is it that (*ind.*)?; **est-il venu q.?** has anyone called?; **il est venu quatre hommes** four men have come; *see a.* **venu**.

vénitien [veniˈsjɛ̃] Venetian.

vent [vɑ̃] *m* wind; **~ arrière** tailwind; **~ debout** headwind; **~ de travers** crosswind; *fig.* **avoir ~ de** get wind of; **coup** *m* **de ~** gust of wind; *fig.* **en coup de ~** very fast; **F** *fig.* **dans le ~** with(-)it; **♩** **instrument** *m* **à ~** wind instrument.

vente [vɑ̃ːt] *f* **~** sale; timber; *timber*: felling; **~ forcée** compulsory sale; **de ~ difficile** hard to sell; **en ~** on sale; **être de bonne ~** sell well; **mettre en ~** put up for sale.

vent|er [vɑ̃ˈte] (1a) *v/impers.*: **il vente** it is windy; **qu'il pleuve ou qu'il vente** (come) rain or shine, in all weathers; **~eux** [~ˈtø] windy.

ventil|ateur [vɑ̃tilaˈtœːr] *m* ventilator; **⚡** fan; **~ation** [~laˈsjɔ̃] *f* ventilation; **†** apportionment; **~er** [~ˈle] (1a) ventilate, air (*a. fig.*); **†** apportion; value separately.

ventosité [vɑ̃tɔziˈte] *f* flatulence.

ventous|e [vɑ̃ˈtuːz] *f* **&** cupping glass; suction pad; *zo.* leech: sucker.

ventre [vɑ̃ːtr] *m* belly; stomach; **~ à terre** at full speed; **à plat ~** flat on one's stomach; *avoir* (*prendre*) *du* ~ be (grow) stout.

ventricule [vãtri'kyl] *m* ventricle.

ventriloqu|e [vãtri'lɔk] *su.* ventriloquist; **~ie** [~lɔ'ki] *f* ventriloquy.

ventr|ipotent F [vãtripɔ'tã], **~u** [vã'try] corpulent; big-bellied.

venu, e [və'ny] **1.** *p.p. of* **venir**; **2.** *adj.*: *bien* (*mal*) ~ well- (poorly) developped; (un)timely (*remark etc.*); *être mal* ~ *de* (*or à*) (*inf.*) be in no position to (*inf.*) (*person*); **3.** *su.* (*first, last, new-*)comer; *le premier* ~ *a.* anybody; *su./f* arrival; coming; *✶* growth; **~e** *au monde* birth; *d'une belle* ~ well-grown.

vêpres *eccl.* [vɛːpr] *f/pl.* vespers.

ver [vɛːr] *m* worm; maggot, grub; ~ *à soie* silk-worm; ~ *de terre* earthworm; ~ *luisant* glow-worm; ~ *solitaire* tapeworm; *tirer les* ~*s du nez à q.* worm secrets out of s.o.

vérace [ve'ras] veracious; **véracité** [~rasi'te] *f* veracity, truth(fulness).

véranda △ [verã'da] *f* veranda(h), *Am.* porch.

verb|al [vɛr'bal] verbal; *ⱴⱴ* oral (*contract*), **~aliser** [~'ze] (1a) draw up an official report; verbalize; ~ *contre police*: take (*s.o.'s.*) name and address; **~e** [vɛrb] *m gramm.* verb; *eccl.* ♀ *the* Word; F *avoir le* ~ *haut* be overbearing; **~eux** [vɛr'bø] verbose; **~iage** [~'bjaːʒ] *m*, **~osité** [~bozi'te] *f* wordiness.

verd|âtre [vɛr'daːtr] greenish; **~elet** [~dɔ'lɛ] slightly acid (*wine*); **~eur** [~'dœːr] *f* greenness; *fig.* acidity; *fig.* vigo(u)r.

verdict *ⱴⱴ* [vɛr'dikt] *m* verdict (against, *contre*; for, *en faveur de*).

verd|ier *orn.* [vɛr'dje] *m* greenfinch; **~ir** [~'diːr] (2a) turn green; **~oyant** [vɛrdwa'jã] green, verdant; **~oyer** [~'je] (1h) become green.

verdunisation [vɛrdyniza'sjɔ̃] *f water*: chlorination.

verdur|e [vɛr'dyːr] *f* greenness; ♀ greenery; *cuis.* greenstuff.

véreux [ve'rø] wormy (*fruit*); *fig.* shady (*firm, person*); shaky (*case*).

verge [vɛrʒ] *f* rod; *anat.* penis.

verger [vɛr'ʒe] *m* orchard.

vergeté [vɛrʒə'te] streaked.

vergla|cé [vɛrgla'se] icy (*road*); **~s** [~'gla] *m* black ice; frozen rain.

vergogne [vɛr'gɔɲ] *f* shame; *sans* ~ shameless(ly *adv.*).

vergue ⚓ [vɛrg] *f* yard.

véri|dique [veri'dik] veracious, truthful; **~fication** [~'sjɔ̃] *f* check(ing), verification; confirmation; **~fier** [veri'fje] (1o) check; verify; confirm, bear out.

vérin ⚙, *mot.* [ve'rɛ̃] *m* jack.

véritable [veri'tabl] true; real, genuine (*a. fig.*); *fig.* downright.

vérité [veri'te] *f* truth; sincerity; *à la* ~ as a matter of fact; *dire la* ~ tell the truth; *en* ~ really, truly.

verjus [vɛr'ʒy] *m* verjuice.

vermeil [vɛr'mɛːj] **1.** *adj.* ruby, bright red; rosy; **2.** *su./m* silver-gilt.

vermillon [vɛrmi'jɔ̃] **1.** *su./m* vermilion; **2.** *adj./inv.* bright red.

verm|ine [vɛr'min] (*a. fig.*); **~oulu** [~'ly] worm-eaten; *fig.* decrepit; **~oulure** [~'lyːr] *f* worm holes *pl.*; worm-eaten state.

vernaculaire [vɛrnaky'lɛːr] *adj.*, *su./m* vernacular.

vernal ♀, *astr.* [vɛr'nal] vernal.

verni [vɛr'ni] varnished; patent (*leather*); F lucky.

verni|r [vɛr'niːr] (2a) varnish; glaze; *fig.* gloss over; **~s** [~'ni] *m* varnish; polish; gloss (*a. fig.*); glaze; ~ *à ongles* nail varnish; **~ssage** [vɛrni'saːʒ] *m* varnish(ing); glaze; glazing; *exhibition*: varnishing-day; **~sser** ⚙ [~'e] (1a) glaze.

vérole *⚕* [ve'rɔl] *f* F syphilis; *petite* ~ smallpox.

verrai [vɛ're] *1st p. sg. fut. of* **voir**.

verrat *zo.* [vɛ'ra] *m* boar.

verr|e [vɛːr] *m* glass; *opt.* lens; ~ *à vin* wine glass; *⚕* ~ *de contact* contact lens; *mot.* ~ *de sûreté* safety glass; ~ *de vin* glass of wine; *prendre* (*or boire*) *un* ~ have a drink; *se noyer dans un* ~ *d'eau* make a mountain out of a molehill; **~é** [vɛ're] *adj.*: *papier* *m* ~ glass-paper; **~erie** [vɛr'ri] *f* ⚙ glassworks *usu. sg.*; *♰* glassware; **~ier** [vɛ'rje] *m* glassmaker; glassblower; **~ière** [~'rjɛːr] *f* glass (*casing*); stained glass window; glass roof; **~oterie** [~rɔ'tri] *f* small glassware; glass beads *pl.*

verrou [vɛ'ru] *m* bolt; *ⱴⱴ sous les* ~*s* under lock and key; **~iller** [~ru'je] (1a) bolt; lock (up).

verru|e 🐝 [vɛˈry] f wart; **~queux** [~ryˈkø] 🐝 warty; 🌱 warted.

vers[1] [vɛːr] m poetry: line, verse.

vers[2] [~] prp. direction: to, towards; time: towards; about (3 o'clock), around (noon); ~ **l'est** eastwards.

versant [vɛrˈsɑ̃] m slope; hillside.

versatile fig. [vɛrsaˈtil] changeable.

verse [vɛrs] adv.: **à** ~ in torrents; **il pleut à** ~ a. it's raining cats and dogs.

versé [vɛrˈse] (well-)versed (in, **dans**).

Verseau astr. [vɛrˈso] m: **le** ~ Aquarius.

vers|ement [vɛrsəˈmɑ̃] m pouring (out); 🌱 payment; 🌱 instalment; **~er** [~ˈse] (1a) v/t. pour (out); overturn, tip (a truck); shed (blood, light, tears); 🌱 pay (in); ✕ assign (men); v/i. turn over; fig. ~ **dans** lapse into.

verset [vɛrˈsɛ] m bibl. etc. verse.

verseur, -euse [vɛrˈsœːr, ~ˈsøːz] su. pourer; su./f coffeepot.

versicolore [vɛrsikɔˈlɔːr] variegated.

versi|ficateur [vɛrsifikaˈtœːr] m versifier; **~fier** [~ˈfje] (1o) versify.

version [vɛrˈsjɔ̃] f version; school: translation into one's own language.

verso [vɛrˈso] m back (of the page), **au** ~ overleaf, on the back.

vert [vɛːr] 1. adj. green; unripe (fruit); young (wine); raw (hide); callow (youth); hale and hearty (old man); fig. severe (reprimand, punishment); sharp (reply); smutty, spicy (story); **langue** f ~**e** slang; 2. su./m colour, 🐎, a. min.: green; (green) grass; wine: sharpness; **~-de-gris** [vɛrdəˈgri] m verdigris.

vert|ébral anat. [vɛrteˈbral] vertebral; **colonne** f ~**e** backbone; **~èbre** [~ˈtɛːbr] f vertebra; **~ébré** zo. [~teˈbre] adj., su./m vertebrate.

vertement [vɛrtəˈmɑ̃] adv. sharply.

vertical, e [vɛrtiˈkal] 1. adj. vertical; upright; 2. su./f ⚗ vertical; **~ité** [~kaliˈte] f uprightness.

vertig|e [vɛrˈtiːʒ] m giddiness; fear of heights; **avoir le** ~ feel dizzy; **cela me donne le** ~ it makes me dizzy; **~ineux** [~tiʒiˈnø] breathtaking, dizzy, giddy; **~o** vet. [~tiˈgo] m staggers pl.

vertu [vɛrˈty] f virtue; chastity; substance: property; **en** ~ **de** by virtue of; in accordance with; **~eux** [~ˈtɥø] virtuous.

verve [vɛrv] f (witty) eloquence; **être en** ~ be in the best of form.

vésanie [vezaˈni] f madness.

vesce 🌱 [vɛs] f vetch, tare.

vésic|atoire 🐝 [vezikaˈtwaːr] adj., su./m vesicatory; **~ule** [~ˈkyl] f vesicle, bladder (a. icht.); **~ bilaire** gall bladder.

vespasienne [vɛspaˈzjɛn] f street urinal.

vespéral [vɛspeˈral] evening-...

vesse sl. [vɛs] f silent fart.

vessie [vɛˈsi] f bladder; zo. ~ **natatoire** swim bladder.

vest|e cost. [vɛst] f jacket; fig. **ramasser une** ~ come a cropper; fig., pol. etc. **retourner sa** ~ turn one's coat; **~iaire** [vɛsˈtjɛːr] cloakroom, Am. checkroom; hat-and-coat rack; sp. etc. changing room.

vestibule [vɛstiˈbyl] m (entrance) hall; vestibule (a. anat.).

vestige [vɛsˈtiːʒ] m relic, remnant, vestige.

veston [vɛsˈtɔ̃] m (man's) jacket.

vêtement [vɛtˈmɑ̃] m garment; **~s** pl. clothes; dress sg.; eccl. vestments; **~s** pl. **de dehors** outdoor things; **~s** pl. **de dessous** underwear.

vétéran [veteˈrɑ̃] m veteran.

vétérinaire [veteriˈnɛːr] 1. adj. veterinary; 2. su./m veterinary surgeon, F vet, Am. veterinarian.

vétille [veˈtiːj] f trifle; **~eux** [~ˈjø] punctilious.

vêtir [vɛˈtiːr] (2g) clothe, dress (in, **de**); **se** ~ dress o.s.; get dressed.

veto [veˈto] m/inv. veto; **droit** m **de** ~ power of veto.

vêts [vɛ] 1st p. sg. pres. of **vêtir**; **~u** [vɛˈty] p.p. of **vêtir**; ~ **de** dressed in; **chaudement** ~ warmly dressed.

vétuste [veˈtyst] timeworn; decrepit; **~é** [~tysˈte] f decrepitude.

veuf, veuve [vœf, vœːv] 1. adj. widowed; **être** (or **rester**) ~ **de q.** be left s.o.'s widow(er); 2. su./m widower; su./f widow.

veuille [vœj] 1st p. sg. pres. sbj. of **vouloir 1.**

veule [vøːl] flabby, spineless.

veulent [vœl] 3rd p. pl. pres. of **vouloir 1.**

veulerie [vølˈri] f flabbiness, spinelessness.

veuvage [vœˈvaːʒ] m woman: widowhood; man: widowerhood.

veux [vø] 1st p. sg. pres. of **vouloir 1.**

vexation [vɛksa'sjɔ̃] f humiliation; **ve-xatoire** [~'twaːr] humiliating; harassing; **vexer** [vɛk'se] (1a) upset; annoy; **se ~** get upset or annoyed.

via [vi'a] prp. via, by way of.

viabilité [vjabili'te] f viability; road: practicability; **~le** [vjabl] viable.

viaduc [vja'dyk] m viaduct.

viager [vja'ʒe] **1.** adj. for life; life ...; **2.** su./m life income.

viande [vjãːd] f meat; F substance; **~s** pl. froides cold buffet.

viander [vjã'de] (1a) graze (deer).

viatique [vja'tik] m eccl. viaticum; fig. provisions pl. for a journey; fig. resource.

vibrant [vi'brã] vibrating; fig. ringing (voice, tone); fig. rousing (speech); **~aphone** ♪ [vibra'fɔn] m vibraphone, vibes pl.; **~ation** [~'sjɔ̃] f vibration; voice: resonance; **~er** [vi'bre] (1a) vibrate; fig. **faire ~** stir, thrill; **~eur** ⚡ [~'brœːr] m buzzer.

vicaire [vi'kɛːr] m curate, vicar.

vice [vis] m vice; defect, fault; **~ de conformation** malformation; **~ propre** inherent defect.

vice-... [vis] vice-...

vichy [vi'ʃi] m vichy water.

vicier [vi'sje] (1o) vitiate (a. ♐); corrupt, taint, spoil; pollute; **~eux** [~'sjø] vicious (a. fig. circle); faulty.

vicinal [visi'nal] local, by(road).

vicissitude [visisi'tyd] f vicissitude.

victime [vik'tim] f victim (a. fig.); disaster: casualty; **être ~ de** be a or the victim of.

victoire [vik'twaːr] f victory; **remporter la ~** gain a or the victory (over, **sur**); **~rieux** [~tɔ'rjø] victorious (over, **de**); triumphant.

victuailles F [vik'tɥaːj] f/pl. eatables, victuals.

vidange [vi'dãːʒ] f emptying; draining; mot. oil change; **~s** pl. sewage sg.; mot. **faire la ~** change the oil; **vidanger** [vidã'ʒe] (1l) empty; drain; clean out; **vide** [vid] **1.** adj. empty; blank (space); fig. vain; **~ de sens** (de)void of meaning; **2.** su./m (empty) space; blank (in document); gap; phys. vacuum; fig. emptiness; **à ~** empty; ⚡ no-load; **frapper à ~** miss (the mark etc.); ✈ emballé **sous ~** vacuum packed; ⚙ **marcher à ~** run light.

vide-ordures [vidɔr'dyːr] m/inv. rubbish-shoot; **vide-poches** [~'pɔʃ] m/inv. compartment, container: tidy; mot. glove compartment.

vider [vi'de] (1a) empty; drain; clear (out); fig. exhaust; F chuck (s.o.) out; F give (s.o.) the sack; cuis. gut, draw; core, stone (fruit); fig. settle (accounts, a question); **videur** [~'dœːr] m F bouncer.

vidimer [vidi'me] (1a) attest.

viduité [vidɥi'te] f widowhood.

vidure [vi'dyːr] f poultry: entrails pl.; fish: guts pl.; **~s** pl. rubbish sg.

vie [vi] f life; lifetime; way of life; livelihood, living; fig. animation; **~ utile** machine: life; **à ~** for life; **de ma ~** in all my life; **donner la ~ à** give birth to; **être en ~** be alive; F **jamais de la ~!** never!

vieil [vjɛj] see vieux 1; **~lard** [vjɛ'jaːr] m old man; **~s** pl. old people; **~le** [vjɛ:j] see vieux; **~lerie** [vjɛj'ri] f old stuff; **~lesse** [vjɛ'jɛs] f old age; coll. old people pl.; fig. custom, wine, etc.: age; **~lir** [~'jiːr] (2a) vt/i. age; v/i. grow old; fig. go out of fashion, become dated; **~lissement** [~jis'mã] m growing old; ageing; **~lot** F [~'jo] antiquated; oldish.

viendrai [vjɛ̃'dre] 1st p. sg. fut. of venir; **viennent** [vjɛn] 3rd p. pl. pres. of venir; **viens** [vjɛ̃] 1st p. sg. pres. of venir.

vierge [vjɛrʒ] **1.** su./f virgin; **2.** adj. virgin (forest, soil); fig. blank, clean; unexposed (film); **~ de** clear of.

vieux [vjø] (adj. before vowel or h mute **vieil**) m, **vieille** f, m/pl. **vieux** [vjø, vjɛːj, vjø] **1.** adj. old; aged; **~ jeu** old-fashioned; **2.** su./m old man; old things pl.; **mon ~!** old boy!; **prendre un coup de ~** grow old overnight; su./f old woman.

vif, vive [vif, viːv] **1.** adj. alive, living; fig. lively, brisk; sharp (wind, edge); bright (colour); quick (temper, wit); **vives eaux** pl. spring tide sg.; **2.** su./m ♐ living person; flesh; paint. life; fig. heart; **blesser au ~** wound to the quick; **entrer dans le ~ du sujet** go to the heart of the matter; **pris sur le ~** lifelike; **vif-argent** [vifar'ʒã] m quicksilver.

vigie [vi'ʒi] f look-out (post).

vigilamment [viʒila'mã] adv. of vigilant; **~ance** [~'lãːs] f vigilance; caution; **~ant** [~'lã] vigilant, alert.

vign|e [viɲ] f ℅ vine; ⟋ vineyard; ℅ ~ **blanche** clematis; ℅ ~ **vierge** virginia creeper; *fig. dans les ~s du Seigneur* drunk; **~eron** [viɲə'rɔ̃] *m* wine grower; **~ette** [~'nɛt] f vignette; manufacturer's label; *admin.* revenue seal; *mot. approx.* road tax disc; **~oble** [vi'nɔbl] *m* vineyard(s *pl.*).

vigoureux [vigu'rø] vigorous, strong; powerful; **vigueur** [~'gœːr] f vigo(u)r, strength; *fig.* force; *entrer en ~* come into force.

vil [vil] base (*a. metal*), vile; ✝ *à ~ prix* (very) cheaply, at a (very) low price.

vilain [vi'lɛ̃] **1.** *adj.* ugly; nasty, unpleasant; *fig.* mean; dirty (*trick*); *su./m* F *fig.* trouble.

vilebrequin [vilbrə'kɛ̃] *m* ⊚ brace (and bit); ⊚, *mot.* crankshaft.

vilenie [vil'ni] f vileness, meanness, dirty trick.

vilipender [vilipã'de] (1a) vilify.

villa [vi'la] f villa; country house; cottage; **~ge** [~'laːʒ] *m* village; **~geois, e** [~la'ʒwa, ~'ʒwaːz] **1.** *adj.* country-...; **2.** *su.* villager.

ville [vil] f town, city; ~ *natale* hometown; *à la ~* in town; *aller en ~* go downtown; *dîner en ~* dine out; *en ~ post:* Local.

villégiature [vileʒja'tyːr] f holiday, *Am.* vacation, holiday resort.

vin [vɛ̃] *m* wine; ~ *de pays* local wine; *grand ~* vintage wine; *gros (petit) ~* full-bodied (light) wine; **~aigre** [vi'nɛːgr] *m* vinegar; *tourner au ~* turn sour; **~aigrer** [vinɛ'gre] (1a) season with vinegar; **~aigrette** *cuis.* [~'grɛt] f vinegar sauce; French dressing; **~aigrier** [~gri'e] *m* vinegar cruet; **~asse** [~'nas] f poor wine.

vindicatif [vɛ̃dika'tif] vindictive; **vindicte** ⚖ [~'dikt] f prosecution; ~ *publique* public condamnation.

vinée [vi'ne] f vintage; **vineux** [~'nø] vinous, wine-colo(u)red; full-bodied (*wine*); vintage (*year*).

vingt [vɛ̃; *before vowel and h mute, and when followed by another numeral* vɛt] twenty; *date, title:* twentieth; ~ *et un* twenty-one; **~-deux** twenty-two; **vingtaine** [vɛ̃'tɛn] f (about) twenty; score; **vingtième** [~'tjɛm] twentieth.

vinicole [vini'kɔl] wine growing; **viniculture** [~kyl'tyːr] f wine-growing.

vins [vɛ̃] *1st p. sg. p.s. of* **venir**.

viol ⚖ [vjɔl] *m* rape; violation.

violacé [vjɔla'se] purplish-blue.

violat|eur [vjɔla'tœːr] *m* violator; **~ion** [~'sjɔ̃] f violation; *fig.* breach (*of secrecy etc.*).

violâtre [vjo'laːtr] purplish.

viol|emment [vjɔla'mã] *adv.* of **violent**; **~ence** [~'lãːs] f violence, force; *faire ~ à* do violence to; violate; **~ent** [~'lã] violent; fierce; *fig.* intense; excessive; **~enter** [~lã'te] (1a) do violence to; ⚖ rape; **~er** [~'le] (1a) violate; ⚖ rape.

violet, -ette [vjɔ'lɛ, ~'lɛt] **1.** *ad.* violet, purple, **2.** *su./m colour:* violet; *su./f* ℅ violet.

violon [vjɔ'lɔ̃] *m* ♪ violin; F jail; *fig.* ~ *d'ingres* (*artistic*) hobby; **~celle** [~lɔ̃'sɛl] *m* cello; **~celliste** [~lɔ̃se'list] *su.* cellist; **~iste** [~lɔ̃'nist] *su.* violinist.

viorne ♀ [vjɔrn] f viburnum.

vipère *zo.* [vi'pɛːr] f viper.

virage [vi'raːʒ] *m* turning; *road etc.:* turn, bend; ✈ bank(ing); *phot.* toning; ~ *à droite* right turn; right-hand bend; ~ *à visibilité réduite* blind corner; *prendre un ~* take a corner.

viral ⚕ [vi'ral] viral; virus (*disease*); infectious.

vir|ée [vi'te] f trip, tour; joyride; **virement** [vir'mã] *m* turn; ✝ transfer; **virer** [vi're] (1a) *v/i.* turn; ✈ bank; ⚓ heave; change colo(u)r; ~ *au bleu* turn blue; *v/t.* ✝ transfer (*money*); *phot.* tone; *sl.* chuck (*s.o.*) (out).

virevolte [vir'vɔlt] f spinning round; half turn; *fig.* sudden change.

virgin|al [virʒi'nal] virginal, maidenly; **~ité** [~ni'te] f virginity.

virgule [vir'gyl] f *gramm.* comma; ⅄ (decimal) point.

viril [vi'ril] male; *fig.* manly, virile; *âge m ~* manhood; *anat. membre m ~* penis; **~iser** [virili'ze] (1a) make (*s.o.*) look like a man; **~ité** [~'te] f virility; manliness, manhood.

virole [vi'rɔl] f ferrule.

virtu|alité [virtuali'te] f potentiality; virtuality; **~el** [~'tuɛl] potential; virtual; **~ellement** [~tuɛl'mã] *adv.* potentially; virtually, practically.

V

virtuose [vir'tɥo:z] su. virtuoso; **virtuo-sité** [~tɥozi'te] f virtuosity.

virulence [viry'lɑ̃:s] f virulence; **virulent** [~'lɑ̃] virulent; **virus** ✽ [vi'rys] m virus; **maladie f à ~** virus disease.

vis[1] [vis] f screw.

vis[2] [vi] 1st p. sg. pres. of **vire** 1.

vis[3] [~] 1st p. sg. p.s. of **voir**.

visa [vi'za] m visa; signature; certification; authentification.

visag|**e** [vi'za:ʒ] m face; countenance; **faire bon (mauvais)** ~ **à** be friendly (unfriendly) towards; **à ~ découvert** openly; **~iste** [viza'ʒist] su. beautician.

vis-à-vis [viza'vi] 1. adv. opposite; 2. prp.: ~ **de** opposite, facing; fig. in relation to, with respect to; 3. su./m person etc. opposite.

viscères anat. [vi'sɛːr] m/pl. viscera.

viscos|**e** [vis'ko:z] f viscose; **~ité** [~kozi'te] f viscosity; stickiness.

visée [vi'ze] f aim (a. fig.); aim(ing); sight(ing); **~s** pl. designs.

viser[1] [vi'ze] (1a) v/i. aim (at, **à**) (a. fig.); v/t. aim at; sight; fig. have (s.th.) in view; fig. allude to; sl. (take a) look at; **~ q. à la tête** aim at s.o.'s head.

viser[2] [~] (1a) visa (a passport); sign; stamp (a ticket); certify.

viseur [vi'zœːr] m gun: sights pl.; phot. view-finder.

visib|**ilité** [vizibili'te] f visibility; **~le** [~'zibl] visible; fig. obvious; fig. ready to receive (visitors) (person).

visière [vi'zjɛːr] f helmet: visor; cap: peak; eyeshade; fig. **rompre en ~ avec q.** quarrel openly with s.o.

vision [vi'zjɔ̃] f vision; (eye)sight; sight.

visit|**e** [vi'zit] f visit (a. ✽); (social or ceremonial) call; admin. inspection; customs: examination; **heures f/pl. de ~** calling hours; hospital: visiting hours; **rendre ~ à** pay (s.o.) a visit; **~er** [vizi'te] (1a) visit; inspect; search; **~eur** [~'tœːr] 1. adj. visiting; 2. su. visitor, caller; inspector; customs: searcher.

vison zo. [vi'zɔ̃] m mink.

visqueux [vis'kø] viscous; sticky; gooey; slimy (a. fig.).

visser (1a) screw (on or down); F clamp down on.

visuel [vi'zɥɛl] visual; **champ m ~** field of vision.

vital [vi'tal] vital (a. fig. question); **~ité** [~'te] f vitality.

vitamine [vita'min] f vitamin.

vite [vit] 1. adj. quickly, fast; soon; 2. adj. fast; **~sse** [vi'tes] f speed; quickness; mot. gear; mot. ~ **limitée** speed limit; mot. **première (quatrième) ~** first (fourth) gear; **à toute ~** at top speed; **en ~** quickly; in a hurry; **prendre q. de ~** outrun s.o.

viti|**cole** [viti'kɔl] vine-...; **~culteur** [~kyl'tœːr] m vine grower; **~culture** [~kyl'ty:r] f vine growing.

vitr|**age** [vi'tra:ʒ] m windows pl.; glass door or roof or partition; net curtain; glazing; **~ail**, pl. **-aux** [~'tra:j, ~'tro] m stained glass window; **~e** [vitr] f pane (of glass); window-pane; **~er** [~'tre] (1a) ⊙ glaze (a window etc.); **~erie** [~tra'ri] f glaziery; **~eux** [~'trø] vitreous (a. ✽); glassy; **~ier** [vitri'e] m glassmaker; ⊙ glazier; **~ifier** [~'fje] (1o) vitrify; **~ine** [vi'trin] f shop window; ☞ showcase.

vitupér|**ation** [vitypera'sjɔ̃] f vituperation; **~er** [~'re] (1f): ~ **contre** rail against.

vivac|**e** [vi'vas] long-lived; ✿ hardy; fig. enduring; fig. inveterate; **~ité** [~vasi'te] f promptness; alertness; vividness; liveliness; intensity; sharpness.

vivant [vi'vɑ̃] 1. adj. living (a. fig.), alive; modern (language); fig. lively, vivid; 2. su./m: **les ~** the living; **bon ~** man who enjoys life; **de son ~** in his lifetime.

vivat(s) [vi'vat] m (pl.) cheer(s).

vivier [vi'vje] m fish pond; fish tank.

vivi|**fier** [vivi'fje] (1o) vitalize; give life to; invigorate; **~pare** [~'pa:r] viviparous (animal); **~section** [~sɛk'sjɔ̃] f vivisection.

vivoter F [vivo'te] (1a) live from hand to mouth; struggle or rub along; **vivre** [vi:vr] 1. (4hh) v/i. live (on, **de**; at, in **à**); be alive; fig. survive (memory etc.); **difficile à ~** difficult to get along with; **se laisser ~** take life as it comes; ✗ **qui vive?** who goes there?; **qui vivra verra** time will show; **vive ...!** long live ...!; v/t. live (one's life); live through (experiences); 2. su./m food; **~s** pl. provisions; **le ~ et le logement (or couvert)** board and lodging.

vocab|**le** [vɔ'kabl] m word, term; **~ulaire** [~kaby'lɛːr] m vocabulary; word list.

voca|l [vɔ'kal] vocal; **~lique** *gramm.* [vɔka'lik] vocalic, vowel-...; **~tion** [~'sjɔ̃] *f* vocation.

vociférer|ations [vɔsifera'sjɔ̃] *f/pl.* screams, outcries; **~er** [~'re] (1f) shout (out), scream (out).

vœu [vø] *m* wish; vow.

vogue [vɔg] *f* fashion, vogue.

voguer [vɔ'ge] (1m) sail; float.

voici [vwa'si] *prp.* here is, here are; **~ un an que je suis ici** I have been here for a year; **me ~!** here I am!

voie [vwa] *f* way; road; path; route; *anat.* duct, tract; *road:* lane; **#** track, line; **~ aérienne** air route, airway; **~s** *pl.* **de communication** routes; **~s** *pl.* **de droit** legal channels; **⚖** **~s de fait** assault *sg.* and battery *sg.*; *fig.* **~s et moyens** ways and means, **♣ ~ d'eau** leak; **➤ à deux ~s** double-track (*line*); **en ~ de** in process of; under (*repair*); **par ~ de** *fig.* by (means of); **par ~ ferrée** by rail; **par la ~ aérienne (maritime)** by air (by sea).

voilà [vwa'la] *prp.* there is, there are; that is, those are; **~!** here they are!; **~ ce que je dis** that's what I say; **~ qui est drôle** that's funny; **~ un an que je suis ici** I have been here for a year; **en ~ assez!** that's enough!; **me ~!** here I am!

voile [vwal] *su./m* veil (a. *fig., a. eccl.*); *phot.* fog; **♣** shadow (*on the lungs*); **⚙** buckle, warping; *anat.* **~ du palais** soft palate; *su./f* **♣** sail; flap, ship; **bateau m à ~s** sailing-boat; **faire ~** set sail (for, **pour**); F **mettre les ~s** clear out; **~er** [vwa'le] (1a) veil; shade, dim; *fig.* cloak, hide; *phot.* fog; **⚙** buckle, warp; **♣** rig with sails; *fig.* **voix f voilée** husky voice; **se ~** wear a veil; *fig.* mist over, cloud over; become husky (*voice*); **⚙** buckle, warp; **~ette** [vwa'let] *f* (hat) veil; **~ier** [~'lje] *m* sailing ship; **~ure** [~'ly:r] *f* **♣** sails *pl.*; **⚙** buckling, warping.

voir [vwa:r] (3m) see; inspect; **⚚** attend (*a patient*); **⚚** see, consult (*a doctor*); *fig.* imagine, figure; *fig.* understand; *fig.* experience, go through; **~ à** (*inf.*) see to it that (*ind.*); **~ le jour** be born; **~ venir q.** see s.o. coming; *fig.* see what s.o. is up to; **~ venir** wait and see; **à ce que je vois** from what I see; **aller ~** (go and) see (*s.o.*), look (*s.o.*) up, visit;

se **~** be obvious, show; happen, occur; *se* **~ préférer** (*disqualifier etc.*) be preferred (disqualified *etc.*); **il s'est vu décerner un prix** he was awarded a prize, a prize was awarded to him; **c'est à ~** that remains to be seen; F **écoutez ~** just listen; **être bien** (**mal**) **vu** be highly (poorly) thought of; be good (bad) form; **faire ~** show; **laisser ~** show, reveal; **n'avoir rien à ~ avec** (*or* **à**) have nothing to do with; **venir ~** call on (*s.o.*); **voyons!** look here!; come (on) now!

voire [vwa:r] *adv.* even, indeed.

voirie [vwa'ri] *f* system of roads, rubbish (*Am.* garbage) dump; refuse (*Am.* garbage) collection.

voisin [vwa'zɛ̃] **1.** *adj.* neighbo(u)ring; adjacent; next; **~ de** in the vicinity of; *fig.* similar to; **2.** *su.* neighbo(u)r; **~age** [~zi'na:ʒ] *m* neighbo(u)rhood; vicinity; **~er** [~zi'ne] (1a): **~** (**avec**) be side by side (with).

voiture [vwa'ty:r] *f* car (a. *mot.*); carriage; cart; **#** coach, *Am.* car; **~ d'enfant** perambulator, *Am.* baby carriage; F **~-pie** radio patrol car; **en ~!** all aboard!

voix [vwa] *f* voice (a. *gramm.*); *pol.* vote; **à haute ~** aloud; **à ~ basse** softly, in a low voice; *pol.* **aller aux ~** vote; **♪ chanter à deux ~** sing in two parts; **de vive ~** by word of mouth.

vol¹ [vɔl] *m* theft, larceny, robbery; **~** **⚖ à l'étalage** shop lifting.

vol² [vɔl] *m* flying; flight (a. *of birds*); **~ à voile** gliding; **~ habité** manned space flight; **prendre son ~** take off; *orn.* take wing; **~age** [vɔ'la:ʒ] flighty, fickle.

volaille [vɔ'la:j] *f* poultry; *cuis.* fowl; **~r** [~la'je] *m* poultry yard.

volant [vɔ'lɑ̃] **1.** *adj.* flying; *fig.* loose (*sheet*); **~ personnel m** flight staff; **2.** *su./m mot.* steering wheel; shuttlecock; badminton; **⚙** flywheel; flounce; *mot.* **prendre le ~** drive.

volatil [vɔla'til] *adj.* volatile.

volatile [~] *m* fowl; winged creature.

volatiliser [vɔlatili'ze] (1a) volatilize; *se* **~** volatilize; *fig.* vanish (into thin air).

vol-au-vent *cuis.* [vɔlo'vɑ̃] *m/inv.* vol-au-vent (*small filled puff-pie*).

volcan [vɔl'kɑ̃] *m* volcano.

volée [vɔ'le] *f bird, bullet, stairs:* flight;

V

birds etc.: flock, flight; *bullets etc.*: volley; *bells*: peal; *fig. blows etc.*: shower; thrashing, hiding; **à la ~** in the air; *catch etc.*: in mid air; *a.* **à toute ~** with full force; *fig.* **de haute ~** top-flight (*people*).

voler[1] 🐦 [vɔ'le] (1a) *vt./i.* steal; *v/t.* rob (*s.o.*); swindle, cheat (*s.o.*).

voler[2] [~] (1a) fly; **~ à voile** glide.

volet [vɔ'le] *m* shutter; flap; *fig.* section, portion, part; *fig.* **trier sur le ~** select carefully.

voleter [vɔl'te] (1c) flit; flutter.

voleur [vɔ'lœːr] **1.** *adj.* thieving; pilfering; **2.** *su.* thief; **au ~!** stop thief!

volière [vɔ'ljɛːr] *f* aviary.

volontaire [vɔlɔ̃'tɛːr] **1.** *adj.* voluntary; intentional; spontaneous; *fig.* headstrong; determined; **2.** *su./m* ✗ volunteer; **~é** [~'te] *f* will; willpower; will. wish; **à ~** at will; as (much as) you like; **montrer de la bonne ~** show willingness; **~iers** [~'tje] *adv.* willingly, gladly; *fig.* readily.

volt ⚡ [vɔlt] *m* volt; **~age** [vɔl'taːʒ] *m* voltage; **~aïque** [~ta'ik] voltaic.

volte-face [vɔltə'fas] *f* about-turn.

voltiger [vɔlti'ʒe] (1l) *orn.* flit (*a. fig.*); fly about; flutter; **~eur** [~ti'ʒœːr] *m* acrobat.

volubile [vɔly'bil] voluble.

volume [vɔ'lym] *m* volume; tome; **~ineux** [~lymi'nø] voluminous.

volupté [vɔlyp'te] *f* (sensual) pleasure; **voluptueux** [~'tɥø] **1.** *adj.* voluptuous; **2.** *su.* sensualist.

volute [vɔ'lyt] *f* volute; scroll; curl.

vomir [vɔ'miːr] (2a) 🗡 vomit, bring up; *fig.* belch (forth); *fig.* hate, abhor; **~ssement** 🗡 [~mis'mɑ̃] *m* action: vomiting; vomit; **~tif** 🗡 [~mi'tif] *adj., su./m* emetic.

vont [vɔ̃] *3rd p. pl. pres. of* **aller 1.**

vorace [vɔ'ras] voracious; **voracité** [~rasi'te] *f* voracity.

vortex [vɔr'teks] *m* whorl; vortex.

vos [vo] *pl. of* **votre.**

vosgien [vo'ʒjɛ̃] of the Vosges.

votant [vo'tɑ̃] *su.* voter; **vote** [vɔt] *m* vote; voting; passing (of a bill, **d'une loi**); **~ par correspondance** postal vote; **voter** [vɔ'te] (1a) *vt./i.* vote; *v/t.* vote for; pass (*a bill*).

votif *eccl. etc.* [vɔ'tif] votive.

votre, *pl.* **vos** [vɔtr, vo] *adj./poss.* your.

vôtre, *pl.* **vos** [voːtr] **1.** *pron./poss.*: **le (la)** **~, les ~s** yours; F **à la ~** cheerio!; your health!; **je suis des ~s** I am on your side; **2.** *su./m* yours, your own; **les ~s** *pl.* your (own) people.

voudrai [vu'dre] *1st p. sg. fut. of* **vouloir 1.**

vuer [vɥe] (1p) dedicate; pledge.

vouloir [vu'lwaːr] **1.** (3n) *v/t.* want; need; require; claim; **~ bien** be willing; **~ dire** mean; **se ~ ...** want or claim to be ...; **je voudrais ...** I would like ...; **je veux que ce soit fait** I want this to be done; **le moteur ne voulut pas marcher** the engine refused to work; **sans le ~** unintentionally; **veuillez me dire** please tell me; *v/i.*: **en ~ à** bear (*s.o.*) a grudge; **2.** *su./m* **bon ~** goodwill; *s.o.'s* pleasure; **mauvais ~** ill will; **~u** [~'ly] *p.p. of* **vouloir 1**; **~us** [~'ly] *1st p. sg. p.s. of* **vouloir 1.**

vous [vu] **1.** *pron./pers.* subject: you; object: you; (to) you; **à ~** to you; yours; **2.** *pron./rfl.* yourself, yourselves; **3.** *pron./recip.* one another; **~même** [~'mɛːm] *pron./rfl.* yourself; **~s** *pl.* yourselves.

voussure △ [vu'syːr] *f* arching.

voûte [vut] △ vault (*a. fig.*); *anat.* **~ du palais** roof of the mouth; *anat.* **~ plantaire** arch of the foot; **~é** [vu'te] △ vaulted; round-shouldered, bent (*person*); **~er** [~] (1a) vault; arch; *fig.* bend.

vouvoyer [vuvwa'je] (1h) address (*s.o.*) as **vous.**

voyage [vwa'aːʒ] *m* journey; tour; trip; *coll.* **le ~, les ~s** travel(l)ing; **~ d'affaires** business trip; **... de ~** travel(l)ing...; **il est en ~** he is travel(l)ing; **partir en ~** go on a journey; **~er** [~ja'ʒe] (1l) travel (*a.* ✈); (make a) journey; *fig.* get about; **~eur, ~euse** [~ja'ʒœːr, ~'ʒøːz] **1.** *su.* travel(l)er; passenger; fare (*in a taxi*); ✈ (*a.* **~ de commerce**) commercial travel(l)er; **2.** *adj.* travel(l)ing.

voyant, e [vwa'jɑ̃, ~'jɑ̃t] **1.** *adj.* loud, gaudy; conspicuous; **2.** *su.* sighted person; seer; *su./f* clairvoyant; *su./m* ⚙ warning or signal light.

voyelle *gramm.* [vwa'jɛl] *f* vowel.

voyons [vwa'jɔ̃] *1st p. pl. pres. of* **voir.**

voyou [vwa'ju] *m* street urchin; hooligan, hoodlum.

V

vrac [vrak] *m*: ✝ **en ~** in bulk; loose; *fig.* higgledy-piggledy.

vrai [vre] **1.** *adj.* true; real; F *pour de ~* really; **2.** *adv.* truly; really; *dire ~* tell the truth; **3.** *su./m* truth; *à ~ dire* to tell the truth; *être dans le ~* be right; **~ment** [~mɑ̃] *adv.* really, truly; indeed; **~semblable** [~sã'blabl] likely, probable; **~ment** in all likelihood, probably; **~semblance** [~sã'blɑ̃:s] *f* probability, likelihood; verisimilitude; *selon toute ~* in all probability *or* likelihood.

vrill|e [vri:j] *f* ⚙ gimlet; ♀ tendril; spiral; ✈ spin; **~er** [vri'je] (1a) *v/t.* ⚙ bore (into); *v/i.* spiral, spin; become twisted (*thread*).

vrombi|r [vrɔ̃'bi:r] (2a) buzz; ⚙, ✈ hum; throb; **~ssement** [~bis'mɑ̃] *m* buzz(ing); hum(ming).

vu [vy] **1.** *p.p. of voir*; **2.** *prp.* seeing (that, *que*); **~ que** *a.* since; **3.** *su./m*: *au ~ et au su de tout le monde* openly (and publicly).

vue [~] *f* sight; eyesight; view; *à ~ ♪*, ✝ at sight; *à ~ de* within sight of; *à ~ d'œil* visibly; *fig.* at a rough estimate; *à la ~ de* in the *or* at the sight of; *à première ~* at first sight; *fig. avoir des ~s sur* have one's eye(s) on; *avoir en ~* have in mind; have it in mind (*to do*); *avoir la ~ courte* be shortsighted; *en ~* in sight; *fig.* conspicuous; *fig.* prominent (*person*); *en ~ de* with a view to; in order to; *garder q. à ~* keep a close watch on s.o.; *perdre de ~* lose sight of.

vulga|ire [vyl'gɛ:r] vulgar (*a. pej.*); common, ordinary, simple; **~riser** [~gari'ze] (1a) popularize, *pej.* coarsen; **~rité** [~'te] *f* vulgarity

vulnérab|ilité [vylnerabili'te] *f* vulnerability; **~le** [~'rabl] vulnerable.

vulve *anat.* [vylv] *f* vulva.

W

wagon 🚃 [va'gɔ̃] *m* carriage, *Am.* car; *goods*: wagon, truck, *Am* freight car; *monter en ~* board the train; **~-citerne**, *pl.* **~s-citernes** [~si'tɛrn] *m* tank car; **~-lit**, *pl.* **~s-lits** [~'li] *m* sleeping car; **~-poste**, *pl.* **~s-poste** [vagɔ̃'pɔst] *m* mail van, *Am.* mail car; **~-restaurant**, *pl.* **~s-restaurants** [~rɛstɔ'rɑ̃] *m* dining car, diner.

wallon [va'lɔ̃] *adj.*, *su.* Walloon.

watt ⚡ [wat] *m* watt; **~-heure**, *pl.* **~s-heures** ⚡ [wa'tœ:r] *m* watt hour.

week-end [wi'kɛnd] *m* weekend.

X

xénophob|e [ksenɔ'fɔb] **1.** *adj.* xenophobic; **2.** *su.* xenophobe; **~ie** [~fɔ'bi] *f* xenophobia.

xérès [ke'rɛs] *m* sherry.

xylo|graphie [ksilɔgra'fi] *f* xylography, xylograph; **~phone** ♪ [~'fɔn] *m* xylophone.

Y

y [i] **1.** *adv.* there; here; in; *il y a* there is *or* are; *il y a deux ans* two years ago; *je l'y ai rencontré* I met him there; **2.** *pron.* to *or* by *or* at *or* in *or* about *or* on it (him, her, them); *il n'y peut rien* there's nothing he can do about it; *il y va de* it is a matter of; *je n'y suis pour rien* I had nothing to do with it; *vous y êtes?* F do you get it?

yacht ⚓ [jak] *m* yacht.
yaourt *cuis.* [ja'urt] *m* yog(h)urt.
yeux [jø] *pl. of* œil.
yoga [jɔ'ga] *m* yoga.
yole ⚓ [jɔl] *f* yawl; skiff.
yougoslave [jugɔ'slav] *adj.*, *su.* Yugoslav(ian).
youpin F *pej.* [ju'pɛ̃] *su.* Jew.
youyou ⚓ [ju'ju] *m* dinghy.

Z

zèbre [zɛbr] *m zo.* zebra; F chap, guy; **zébrer** [ze'bre] (1f) streak.
zélateur *m*, **-trice** *f* [zela'tœːr, ‿'tris] zealot, zealous worker (for, *de*); **zèle** [zɛl] *m* zeal (for, *pour*); F *faire du ~* make a show of zeal; **zélé** [ze'le] zealous.
zénith [ze'nit] *m* zenith (*a. fig.*).
zéro [ze'ro] **1.** *su./m* zero; nought, cipher; *tennis:* love; F nobody; **2.** *adj./inv.:* zero, no (at all).
zeste [zɛst] *m:* *un ~ de citron* a piece of lemon peel.
zézaiement [zezɛ'mɑ̃] *m* lisp(ing); **zézayer** [‿zɛ'je] (1i) lisp.
zibeline *zo.*, ✝ [zi'blin] *f* sable.
zigouiller *sl.* [zigu'je] (1a) kill.
zig(ue) *sl.* [zig] *m* chap, *Am.* guy.

zigzag [zig'zag] *m* zigzag; *en ~* zigzag...; **~uer** [‿za'ge] (1m) zigzag.
zinc [zɛ̃ːg] *m* zinc; F counter, bar.
zinguer [zɛ̃'ge] (1m) coat *or* cover with zinc.
zizanie [ziza'ni] *f:* *semer* (*or mettre*) *la ~* stir up ill-feeling.
zodia|cal *astr.* [zɔdja'kal] zodiacal; **~que** [‿'djak] *m* zodiac.
zona ✝ [zɔ'na] *m* shingles *pl.*
zonard F [zɔ'naːr] *m* hobo; dropout.
zone [zoːn] *f* zone; *geog.* belt; area; *fig.* *~ sombre* grey zone.
zoo F [zɔ'ɔ] *m* zoo.
zoo... [zɔɔ] zoo...; **~logie** [‿lɔ'ʒi] *f* zoology; **~logique** [‿lɔ'ʒik] zoological.
zozoter F [zɔzɔ'te] (1a) lisp.
zut! *sl.* [zyt] *int.* darn it!

English-French Dictionary

A

a *gramm. article*: un(e *f*); *20 miles a day* 20 milles par jour.

A 1 F de première qualité.

aback: F *taken* ~ déconcerté, étonné.

abac|us, *pl.* **-ci** boulier *m*.

abandon 1. abandonner; renoncer à (*a plan, a right, etc.*); **2.** abandon *m*, laisser-aller *m*; ~**ed** *adj.* abandonné; dévergondé; ~**ment** abandon *m*.

abase abaisser, humilier.

abash confondre, déconcerter, ~**ed** confus, embarrassé.

abate *v/i.* diminuer, s'affaiblir, baisser; s'apaiser; *v/t.* supprimer (*a nuisance etc.*); ~**ment** diminution *f*; suppression *f*.

abb|ess abbesse *f*; ~**ey** abbaye *f*; ~**ot** abbé *m*, supérieur *m*.

abbreviat|e abréger (*a*, *A*); ~**ion** abréviation *f*.

ABC ABC *m*; ~ *warfare* guerre *f* atomique, bactériologique et chimique.

abdicat|e abdiquer; renoncer à; se démettre de (*a function*); ~**ion** abdication *f*; démission *f*.

abdom|en *anat.* abdomen *m*; ventre *m*; ~**inal** abdominal.

abduct enlever.

abet encourager; prêter assistance à; (*usu. aid and* ~) être complice de; ~**tor** complice *mf*; fauteur (-trice *f*) *m* (de, *in*).

abeyance: *fall into* ~ tomber en désuétude; ♣ *in* ~ en suspens (*matter*).

abhor abhorrer; ~**rence** horreur *f*; aversion *f* (pour, *of*); *hold in* ~ avoir en horreur; ~**rent** répugnant (à, *to*); incompatible (avec, *to*).

abide *v/i.* † demeurer; ~ *by* respecter (*rules etc.*); accepter (*consequences etc.*); rester fidèle à (*a promise*); *v/t.* supporter.

ability capacité *f*; **abilities** *pl.* intelligence *f*; *to the best of one's* ~ de son mieux.

abject misérable; servile.

abjure abjurer; renoncer à.

ablaze en flammes; *fig.* ~ *with* enflammé de (*anger etc.*); resplendissant de.

able capable; compétent; *be* ~ *to* (*inf.*) pouvoir (*inf.*); savoir (*inf.*); être à même *or* en mesure de (*inf.*); ~**-bodied** robuste.

abnegat|e renoncer à; ~**ion** renoncement *m*; désaveu *m*.

abnormal anormal; ~**ity** caractère *m* anormal; difformité *f*.

aboard ♣ à bord (de); *Am* 🚋 🚊 *bus, tram: all* ~! en voiture!; ♣ embarquez!

abode demeure *f*; séjour *m*.

aboli|sh abolir, supprimer; ~**tion** abolissement *m*, suppression *f*.

A-bomb *see atomic bomb.*

abomina|ble abominable; ~**te** abominer; ~**tion** abomination *f*.

aborigin|al aborigène, indigène; ~**es** *pl.* aborigènes *m/pl.*

abort *v/i.* 🌡, *fig.* avorter; *fig. a.* échouer; *v/t.* 🌡, *fig.* faire avorter; *fig.* ~ *a mission* interrompre *or* abandonner une mission; ~**ion** avortement *m* (*a. fig.*); ~**ive** manqué, raté (*plan etc.*); infructueux (*attempt, measure, etc.*).

abound abonder (en **with**, **in**); foisonner (de **with**, **in**).

about 1. *prp.* autour de; environ, presque; au sujet de; ~ *the streets* dans les rues; *I had no money* ~ *me* je n'avais pas d'argent sur moi; ~ *ten o'clock* vers 10 heures; *he is* ~ *my height* il a à peu près la même taille que moi; **2.** *adv.* tout autour, à l'entour, çà et là; de ci, de là; *be* ~ *to* (*inf.*) être sur le point de (*inf.*).

above 1. *prp.* au-dessus de; *fig.* supérieur à; ~ *all* surtout; *fig. it is* ~ *me* cela me dépasse; **2.** *adv.* en haut; là-haut; au-dessus; **3.** *adj.* précédent; ~**board** loyal; ~**-mentioned** susmentionné, (cité) ci-dessus.

abreast de front; côte à côte; ~ *of* (*or with*) à la hauteur de; *fig. be* (*keep*) ~ *of* être (se tenir) au courant de.

abridg|e abréger; raccourcir; ~**(e)ment**

raccourcissement *m*; diminution; abrégé *m*, résumé *m*.

abroad à l'étranger; *fig. there is a report* ~ le bruit court que.

abrogat|e abroger; **~ion** abrogation *f*.

abrupt brusque, précipité; abrupt (*style*); à pic, escarpé (*mountain*).

abscond s'évader (de, *from*); se soustraire à la justice; F décamper.

absence absence *f*, éloignement *m*; ~ *of mind* distraction *f*.

absent 1. absent, manquant; *fig.* distrait; **2.:** ~ *o.s.* s'absenter (de, *from*); **~-minded** distrait; **~tee** absent(e *f*) *m*; *pol.* ~ *ballot* vote *m* par correspondance; ~ *voter* électeur (-trice *f*) *m* par correspondance.

absolut|e absolu; autoritaire; illimité (*power*); réel (*truth*); ⚖ irrévocable; **~ion** absolution *f*.

absolve absoudre (de, *from*); relever (de, *from*).

absorb absorber; amortir (*a shock*); *become ~ed in* s'absorber dans.

absorption absorption *f* (*a. fig.*).

abstain s'abstenir (de, *from*); *parl.* ~ (*from voting*) s'abstenir (de voter).

abstemious sobre, tempérant.

abstention abstinence *f* (de, *from*); *parl.* abstention *f*.

abstinent abstinent, sobre.

abstract 1. abstrait; 2. abstrait *m*; résumé *m*; 3. *v/t.* soustraire, dérober (à, *from*); détourner (*s.o.'s attention*); résumer (*a book*); **~ed** *fig.* distrait, rêveur; **~ion** soustraction *f*; *phls.* abstraction *f*; *fig.* distraction *f*.

abstruse *fig.* abstrus, obscur; caché.

absurd absurde, déraisonnable; F idiot; **~ity** absurdité *f*.

abundan|ce abondance *f* (*a. fig.*), affluence *fig*; **~t** abondant, copieux.

abus|e 1. abus *m*; insultes *f/pl.*; 2. abuser de; insulter, injurier (*q.*); **~ive** injurieux, insultant.

abut aboutir, confiner (à, *upon*).

abyss abîme *m*, gouffre *m*.

academ|ic 1. universitaire (*studies, year, etc.*); (purement) théorique, abstrait; ~ *freedom* liberté *f* de l'enseignement; 2. universitaire *mf*; **~y** académie *f*.

accede: ~ *to* accéder à; entrer en possession de (*a position*); monter sur (*the throne*).

accelerat|e (s')accélérer (*a. mot.*); *v/t. fig.* activer; **~ion** accélération *f*; *mot.* ~ *lane* rampe *f* d'accès; **~or** *mot.* accélérateur *m*.

accent 1. accent *m*; ton *m*; 2. accentuer; appuyer sur, souligner; **~uate** accentuer; faire ressortir.

accept accepter; **~able** acceptable; **~ance** acceptation *f*; ✝ *article:* réception *f*.

access accès *m* (à, *to*); ⚖ droit *m* de visite (*de*, of *children*); *easy of* ~ d'accès facile; *have* ~ *to* avoir accès à (*qch.*) or auprès de (*q.*); **~ible** accessible; **~ion** admission *f* (auprès, *to*); entrée *f* en fonctions; accroissement *m*; ~ *to the throne* avènement *m* au trône; **~ory** 1. accessoire, 2. accessoire *m*.

accident accident *m*; hasard *m*; *motor* ~ accident *m* de voiture; *road* ~ accident *m* de la route; ~ *insurance* assurance *f* contre les accidents; *by* ~ accidentellement; par hasard; *be killed in an* ~ perdre la vie dans un accident; *meet with an* ~ avoir un accident; **~al** accidentel; fortuit; accessoire; ~ *death* mort *f* accidentelle; **~ally** par hasard; **~-prone** sujet aux accidents.

acclaim acclamer.

acclamation acclamation *f*.

acclimatiz|ation acclimatation *f*; **~e** acclimater; habituer.

acclivity montée *f*; côte *f*; rampe *f*.

accommodat|e accommoder; adapter; fournir (de, *with*); recevoir, loger; **~ing** obligeant; **~ion** adaptation *f*, ajustement *m*; arrangement *m*; logement *m*; place *f* (*for people etc.*); *Am.* ~ *s pl. a.* hébergement *m*, hôtels *m/pl.*; *Am.* ~ *train* train *m* omnibus.

accompany accompagner.

accomplice complice *mf* (de, *to* or *in a crime*).

accomplish accomplir; **~ed** accompli; **~ment** accomplissement *m*; *usu.* ~ *s pl.* talents *m/pl.*

accord 1. accord *m*: *of one's own* ~ de son plein gré; *with one* ~ d'un commun accord; 2. *v/i.* concorder (avec, *with*); *v/t.* accorder; **~ance:** *in* ~ *with* conformément à, suivant; **~ant** conforme (à *with, to*); **~ing:** ~ *as* selon que; ~ *to* selon, suivant, d'après; **~ingly** en conséquence; donc.

accost aborder, accoster.

account 1. ✝ compte; compte rendu; *fig.* profit; *fig.* importance; **current ~** compte en courant; **have** (*or* **hold**) **an ~ with** avoir un compte chez; **have a bank ~** avoir un compte en banque; **of no ~** de peu d'importance; **on no ~** en aucun cas; **on ~ of** à cause de; **take into ~, take ~ of** tenir compte de; **keep ~s** tenir les livres; **call s.o. to ~** demander compte à q.; F **give a good ~ of o.s.** s'acquitter bien; **2.** *v/i.*: **~ for** expliquer (*qch.*); rendre compte de; justifier (de); *sp.* avoir à son actif; *v/t.* estimer, tenir pour; **~able** responsable; **~ant** comptable *m*; **chartered ~,** *Am.* **certified public ~** expert *m* comptable diplômé.

accredit accréditer (*q.*) (auprès de, **to**); **~ s.th. to** mettre qch. sur le compte de, attribuer qch. à (*q., qch.*); **~ed** accrédité (*ambassador etc.*); admis, reçu (*belief etc.*).

accretion accroissement *m*; addition *f*.

accrue provenir, dériver (de, **from**); ✝ s'accumuler (*interest*).

accumulat|e (s')accumuler; (s')amasser; **~ion** accumulation *f*.

accura|cy exactitude *f*, précision *f*; **~te** exact; précis; juste.

accurs|ed, ~t maudit; exécrable.

accus|ation accusation *f*; ✝✝ *a.* plainte *f*; **~ative** *gramm.* (*a.* **~ case**) accusatif *m*; **~e** accuser; **~er** accusateur *m*.

accustom accoutumer, habituer (à, **to**); **~ed** accoutumé, habitué (à, **to**); habituel, coutumier; **be ~ to do**(**ing**) **a.** avoir l'habitude *or* avoir coutume de faire; **get** *or* **become ~ to** (**doing**) **s.th.** s'habituer *or* s'accoutumer à (faire) qch.

ace as *m*; **within an ~ of** à deux doigts de.

acerbity âpreté *f*, aigreur *f*.

acet|ic acétique; **~one** acétone *f*.

ache 1. faire mal (à); **be aching all over** avoir mal partout; **2.** mal *m*, douleur *f*.

achieve atteindre, parvenir à; obtenir; accomplir, exécuter; **~ment** accomplissement *m*; *project:* exécution *f*; exploit *m*.

acid acide (*a. su./m*); **~ rain** pluies *f/pl.* acides; **~ity** acidité *f*.

acknowledg|e reconnaître (pour, **as**); accuser réception de (*a letter*); **~(e)ment** reconnaissance *f*; aveu *m*; ✝ accusé *m* de réception.

acne 🌟 ['æknɪ] acné *f*.

acorn 🌿 gland *m*.

acoustics *sg. and pl.* acoustique *f*.

acquaint informer; renseigner (sur, **with**); **be ~ed with** connaître; **become ~ed with** faire la connaissance de (*q.*); prendre connaissance de (*qch.*); **~ance** connaissance *f*.

acquiesce: **~ in** acquiescer à.

acquire acquérir; *fig.* prendre (*a habit, taste, etc.*); **~ment** acquisition *f*; *usu.* **~s** *pl. a.* connaissances *f/pl.*

acquisit|ion acquisition *f*; **~ive** avide.

acquit acquitter (de, **of**); *fig.* **~ o.s. well** bien s'en tirer; **~tal** acquittement *m*.

acre acre *f*; (*approx.*) arpent *m*.

acrid âcre; mordant (*style*).

across 1. *adv.* à travers; de l'autre côté; **2.** *prp.* à travers, sur; en travers de; **come ~** rencontrer; tomber sur.

act 1. *v/i.* agir (en, **as**; sur, **on**); *thea.* jouer; *v/t. thea.* jouer (*a part*); **2.** acte *m*; action *f*; *thea.* acte *m*; ✝✝ loi *f*, décret *m*; **~ing 1.** action *f*; *thea.* jeu *m*; *play:* exécution *f*; **2.** suppléant, provisoire; gérant.

action action *f*, acte *m*; ✝✝ procès *m*; ✗ combat *m*; **take ~** prendre les mesures.

activ|ate activer; *phys.* rendre radioactif; **~e** actif, vif; en activité (*volcano*); **~ity** activité *f*.

act|or acteur *m*; **~ress** actrice *f*.

actual réel, véritable; **~ity** réalité *f*; **~ize** réaliser; **~ly** en fait; réellement, en réalité; à vrai dire.

actuate *fig.* pousser, animer.

acupuncture acupuncture *f*.

acute aigu (*a.* 🌟, *a.* angle, accent, sound); pénétrant (*sense, mind, etc.*); vif (*pain*); fin (*ear*).

ad F *see* **advertisement.**

adamant *fig.* inflexible.

adapt (s')adapter (à, **to**); **~ation** adaptation *f* (à, **to**); **~er** *radio, telev.:* adaptateur *m*.

add *v/t.* ajouter; joindre; (*a.* **~ up**) additionner; *v/i.* **~ to** augmenter.

adder vipère *f*.

addict 1. ~ o.s. s'adonner (à, **to**); **2.**: **drug ~** toxicomane *mf*; **~ed** adonné (à, **to**); **become ~ to** s'adonner à (*drink etc.*), s'abandonner à (*a vice*).

addition addition *f* (*a.* ᴿ); *Am. land:* agrandissement *m*; **in ~** (**to**) en plus (de); **~al** additionnel, supplémentaire; nouveau.

address 1. adresser; (*a.* **~ o.s. to**) s'adresser à (*q.*), adresser la parole à (*q.*); **2.** adresse *f*; discours *m*; **~ee** destinataire *mf*.

adenoids ❀ *pl.* végétations *f/pl.* adénoïdes.

adept: ~ in, ~ at expert en *or* à.

adequate adéquat, suffisant; qui convient.

adhere (to) adhérer (à); s'en tenir (à); **~nce** adhésion *f*; **~nt** adhérent *m*.

adhesion ❀, *phys.* adhérence *f*; *fig.* adhésion *f*.

adhesive adhésif (*a. su./m*).

adjacent adjacent (à, **to**).

adjective adjectif *m*.

adjoin *v/t.* avoisiner (*qch.*), être adjacent à; *v/i.* se toucher; **~ing** voisin, adjacent.

adjourn *v/t.* ajourner; remettre; lever (*a session*) (jusque, **to**); *v/i.* suspendre *or* lever la session; **~ment** ajournement *m*; remise *f*.

adjudge juger.

adjust *v/t.* (r)ajuster; régler; *v/i.* **or ~ o.s. to** s'adapter à; **~ing screw** vis *f* de serrage; **~ment** (r)ajustement *m*; réglage *m*.

ad lib 1. improviser; **2.** à discrétion, à volonté, F à gogo; **3.** impromptu, improvisé; **4.** improvisation(s) *f/(pl.)*.

administ|er administrer (*a country, affairs, a remedy*); **~ justice** rendre la justice; **~ration** administration *f*; gestion *f*; *esp. Am.* gouvernement *m*; **~rative** administratif; **~rator** administrateur (-trice *f*) *m*.

admirable admirable.

admiral amiral *m*.

admir|ation admiration *f*; **~e** admirer; **~er** admirateur (-trice *f*) *m*.

admiss|ible admissible; **~ion** admission *f*, accès *m* (à, **to**); *fee:* entrée *f*; aveu *m*.

admit *v/t.* admettre (à, dans **to, into**); laisser entrer; reconnaître, avouer; *v/i.:* **~ of** permettre; comporter; **~tance** entrée *f*; accès *m*; **~ed** avoué; **~ly** il faut reconnaître (que) ...

admixture mélange *m*; mixture *f*.

admoni|sh admonester; avertir, prévenir; **~tion** admonestation *f*; avertissement *m*.

ado affairement *m*, bruit *m*; **without**

more (*or* **further**) **~** sans plus de cérémonies.

adolescen|ce adolescence *f*; **~t** adj., *su./mf* adolescent(e *f*).

adopt adopter (*a. fig.*); *fig. a.* choisir; **~ed country** patrie *f or* pays *m* d'adoption; **~ion** adoption *f*; choix *m*; **~ive** adoptif; **~ country** patrie *f or* pays *m* d'adoption.

ador|able adorable; **~ation** adoration *f*; **~e** adorer; **~ingly** avec adoration.

adorn orner, parer; **~ment** parure *f*; ornementation *f*.

adroit adroit; exercé.

adulat|e aduler; **~ion** adulation *f*.

adult *adj., a. su./mf* adulte *mf*.

adulter|ate falsifier, frelater; **~er** adultère *m*; **~ess** adultère *f*; **~ous** adultère; **~y** adultère *m* (*act*).

advance 1. *v/i.* s'avancer; avancer (*in age*); monter (*in rank*); hausser (*prices*); *v/t.* avancer; augmenter, hausser (*the prices*); élever (*in rank*); faire avancer; **2.** avance *f*; marche *f* en avant; avancement *m*; *prices:* hausse *f*; **in ~** d'avance, en avance; en avant; **3.** avant-; **~d** avancé; **~ment** avancement *m*; progrès *m*.

advantage avantage *m* (*a. in tennis*); **gain an ~ over** se procurer un avantage sur; **gain the ~ over** l'emporter sur; **take ~ of** profiter de (*qch.*); abuser de (la crédulité de) (*q.*); **~ous** avantageux (pour, **to**); utile.

adventur|e aventure *f*; **~er** aventurier *m*; **~ous** aventureux.

adverb adverbe *m*.

advers|ary adversaire *m*; **~e** adverse; contraire; défavorable; **~ to** hostile à; **~ity** adversité *f*.

advertis|e faire de la réclame (pour); *v/t.* annoncer, faire connaître; *v/i.* insérer une annonce; **~ement** publicité *f*, réclame *f*; *journ.* annonce *f*; affiche *f* (*on a wall*); **~ing: ~ agency** agence *f* de publicité; **~ campaign** campagne *f* publicitaire; **~ film** film *m* publicitaire; **~ manager** chef *m* de la publicité; **~ medium** organe *m* de publicité, support *m* publicitaire.

advice conseil *m*, -s *m/pl.*; avis *m*; **on the ~ of** sur le conseil de; **take medical ~** consulter un médecin.

advis|able recommandable; **~e** recommander (*qch.*); conseiller (*q.*; à q. de *inf.*, **s.o. to** *inf.*); ♣ aviser (*de*, **of**); **~er** conseiller (-ère *f*) *m*; **~ory** consultatif.

advocate 1. avocat *m*; *fig. a.* défenseur *m*, partisan *m*; **2.** plaider en faveur de (*qch.*), préconiser.

aerial 1. aérien; **2.** *radio, telev.*: antenne *f*; **~ high ~** antenne *f* haute.

aero... aéro-; **~drome** aérodrome *m*; **~nautic(al)** aéronautique; **~nautics** *sg.* aéronautique *f*; **~plane** avion *m*; **~sol (can)** aérosol *m*, atomiseur *m*.

aesthetic‖(al) esthétique; **~s** *sg.* esthétique *f*.

afar au loin; **from ~** de loin.

affable affable.

affair affaire *f*; (*love* **~**) affaire *f* de cœur *or* amoureuse.

affect affecter, toucher, agir sur, avoir un effet sur, *stronger*: attaquer (*s.o.'s health etc.*); *feign*: affecter, feindre; *prefer*: affectionner; **~ation** affectation *f*; *speech, style*: affèterie *f*; **~ed** affecté, maniéré (*style, manners*); **~ion** affection *f*; **~ionate** affectueux.

affidavit ♣♣ déclaration *f* sous serment.

affiliat‖e 1. affilier (à **to**, **with**); **~d company = 2.** filiale *f*; **~ion** affiliation *f*.

affinity affinité *f*.

affirm affirmer, soutenir; **~ation** affirmation *f*; assertion *f*; **~ative 1.** affirmatif; **2.** affirmative *f*; **in the ~** affirmativement.

affix apposer (sur, à, **to**).

afflict affliger; **~ion** affliction *f*.

affluen‖ce abondance *f*, **~t 1.** abondant (en, **in**); **2.** affluent *m*.

afford se permettre, avoir les moyens de; *give*: donner, offrir, fournir; *I can't ~ it* je ne peux pas me l'offrir *or* payer.

affront 1. offenser; **2.** affront *m*.

afield: (*far ~* très) loin; *too far ~* trop loin.

afire en feu; *fig.* enflammé (de, **with**); *set ~* mettre le feu à.

afloat ♣, *a. fig.* à flot; en circulation (*ideas, rumours*): *set ~* lancer (*a ship, a business*).

afraid: *be ~* (*of*, *that*) avoir peur (de, que *sbj.*); craindre (*q. or qch.*, que *sbj.*).

afresh de *or* à nouveau.

African 1. africain; **2.** Africain(e *f*) *m*.

after 1. *adv.* après; plus tard; ensuite; **2.** *prp. time*: après; *place*: après; à la suite de; *manner*: suivant, selon, d'après; **~ all** après tout, enfin; **~ having seen him** après l'avoir vu; **3.** *cj.* après que; **4.** *adj.* subséquent; futur; **5.** *su.*: **~s** *pl.* dessert; **~effect** répercussion *f*; **~glow** dernières lueurs *f/pl.* du couchant; **~math** ✍ regain *m*; *fig.* suites *f/pl.*; **~noon** après-midi *m/inv.*; **~sales service** service *m* après-vente; **~shave (lotion)** lotion *f* après rasage, after-shave *m*; **~taste** arrière-goût *m*; **~wards** après, par la suite.

again encore; encore une fois, de nouveau; d'autre part; **~ and ~**, *time and ~* maintes et maintes fois; *as much ~* deux fois autant; *now and ~* de temps en temps.

against contre; **~ the wall** contre le mur; **~ a background** sur un fond; **over ~** vis-à-vis de.

age 1. âge *m*; époque *f*; (*old*) **~** vieillesse *f*; **~ bracket**, **~ group** tranche *f* d'âge; *act or be your ~!* tu n'es pas un enfant!; *at the ~* à l'âge de; *of ~* majeur; *under ~* mineur; *what is your ~?* quel âge avez-vous?; F *wait for ~s* attendre des éternités; *when I was your ~* à ton âge, quand j'avais ton âge; **2.** vieillir; **~d** âgé, vieux; âgé de (*twenty years etc.*); **~less** sans âge; éternel; toujours jeune (*beauty*); **~-old** séculaire.

agency agence *f*; *by* (*or through*) *the ~ of* par l'action de (*qch.*), par l'entremise de (*q.*).

agenda ordre *m* du jour.

agent agent *m* (*a.* 🐾).

agglomerate (s')agglomérer.

agglutinate (s')agglutiner.

aggravat‖e aggraver; F agacer (*q.*); **~ion** aggravation *f*; F agacement *m*.

aggregate 1. (s')agréger (à, **to**); *v/t.* s'élever à *or* au total de; **2.** global; total; **3.** ensemble *m*, total *m*.

aggress‖ion agression *f*; **~ive** agressif; **~war** guerre *f* offensive; **~iveness** agressivité *f*; **~or** agresseur *m*.

aggrieve chagriner, affliger.

aggro *sl.* aggressivité *f*; violences *f/pl.*

aghast consterné; stupéfait (de, **at**).

agil‖e agile, leste; **~ity** agilité *f*.

agitat‖e *v/t.* agiter, remuer; *fig.* rendre (*q.*) inquiet, troubler; *v/i.* faire de l'agitation; **~ion** agitation *f*; **~or** agitateur *m*.

ago: *a year* ~ il y a un an.

agon|ize *v/t.* torturer, mettre au supplice; *v/i.* être au supplice; **~ized** angoissé, d'angoisse (*cry*, *look*, *etc.*); **~y** angoisse *f.*

agree (*tally*) concorder (avec, **with**); (*admit*) *v/t.* admettre, avouer; (*be of the same opinion*) être d'accord (avec **with**); (*come to terms*) se mettre d'accord (sur, **on**), s'accorder; ~ **on** convenir de; ~ **to s.th.** consentir à qch., accepter qch.; ~ **to do s.th.** être d'accord pour *or* accepter de *or* consentir à faire qch.; s'accorder pour faire qch.; **s.th. does not ~ with s.o.** (*food etc.*) qch. ne réussit pas à q.; **~able** agréable; d'accord; consentant (à, **to**); **be ~ to** (*doing*) qch. consentir à (faire) qch., accepter de (faire) qch.; **~d** d'accord; **~ment** accord *m*; **come to an ~** arriver à une entente, tomber d'accord.

agricultur|al agricole; **~e** agriculture *f*; **~ist** agriculteur *m.*

aground: **run ~** s')échouer.

ague fièvre *f* (intermittente).

ahead en avant, sur l'avant; **straight ~** droit devant; **go ~** avancer.

aid 1. aider; **2.** aide *f*; **by** (*or* **with**) **the ~ of** avec l'aide de (*q.*); à l'aide de (*qch.*).

ail *v/i.* être souffrant; *v/t.* faire souffrir (*q.*); **what ~s him?** qu'est-ce qu'il a?; **~ing** souffrant, indisposé; **~ment** mal *m*, maladie *f.*

aim 1. *v/i.* viser, pointer (à, **at**); *fig.* ~ **at** (*ger.*) viser à (*inf.*); *esp.* Am. ~ **to** (*inf.*) aspirer à (*inf.*); *v/t.*.. ~ **a gun at** viser (*q.*); **2.** but *m* (*a. fig.*); **take ~** viser; **~less** sans but.

air¹ 1. air *m*; **by ~** en avion; **in the open ~** en plein air; **castles in the ~** châteaux *m/pl.* en Espagne; **on the ~** radiodiffusé; à la radio; **take the ~** prendre l'air; **2.** aérer, ventiler (*a room*, *a tunnel*); faire connaître, faire parade de (*one's opinions*, *one's knowledge*); (*radio*)diffuser, téléviser (*a program*).

air² air *m*, mine *f*, apparence *f*; **give o.s. ~s** se donner des airs.

air³ ♪ air *m*, mélodie *f.*

air...: **~-base** base *f* d'aviation; **~bed** matelas *m* pneumatique; **~borne** ✈ en vol; ✕ aéroporté; **~brake** frein *m* à air comprimé; **~bus** aerobus *m*, airbus *m*; **~-conditioned** climatisé; **~-conditioner** climatiseur *m*; **~-conditioning** cli-

matisation *f*; **~-cooled** (*engine*) à refroidissement par l'air; **~s** *m/pl.*; ~ **carrier** porte-avions *m/inv.*; **~-cushion** coussin *m* à air; **~drop 1.** parachuter; **2.** parachutage *m*; **~force** armée *f* de l'air; **~freight** fret *m* aérien; transport *m* par air; **by ~** par voie aérienne, par avion; **~gun** fusil *m* à air comprimé; ~ **hostess** hôtesse *f* de l'air; ~ **letter** aérogramme, lettre *f* par avion; **~lift** pont *m* aérien; **~line** ligne *f* aérienne; **~mail** poste *f* aérienne; **by ~** par avion; **~man** aviateur *m*; **~mechanic** mécanicien *m* d'avion; **~passenger** passager (-ère *f*) *m*; **~plane** *esp.* Am. avion *m*; **~-pocket** ✈ trou *m* d'air; **~port** aéroport *m*; **~pump** pompe *f* à air; **~raid** ✕ raid *m* aérien; ~ **precautions** défense *f* anti-aérienne; ~ **shelter** abri *m*; **~sick: be ~** avoir la nausée; **~strip** piste *f* d'atterrissage; ~ **terminal** ✈ aérogare *f*; **~tight** étanche à l'air; **~-to-~** ✕ avion-avion; **~-to-ground** ✕ avion-terre; ~ **traffic controller** contrôleur de la navigation aérienne, F aiguilleur du ciel; **~way** voie *f* aérienne; **~worthy** navigable.

airy bien aéré; léger; désinvolte; peu sérieux.

aisle △ nef *f* latérale; passage *m.*

ajar entrouvert, entrebâillé.

akin apparenté (à, avec **to**).

alarm 1. alarme *f*, alerte *f*; **2.** alarmer (*a. fig.*); **~-clock** réveille-matin *m/inv.*, réveil *m.*

Albanian 1. albanais; **2.** Albanais(e *f*) *m.*

album album *m*; *disk: a.* 33 tours *m/inv.*

alcohol alcool *m*; **~ic** alcoolique (*a. su.*); **~ism** alcoolisme *m.*

alcove alcôve *f*; niche *f.*

alderman magistrat *m* municipal.

ale ale *f*, bière *f* anglaise.

alert 1. alerte, éveillé; **2.** alerte *f*; **on the ~** sur le qui-vive; éveillé.

alibi alibi *m*; F excuse *f.*

alien 1. étranger; *fig.* ~ **to** étranger à; **2.** étranger (-ère *f*) *m*; **~able** aliénable, mutable; **~ate** aliéner (*property*); *fig.* (s')aliéner (*q.*); **~ation** aliénation *f*; **~ist** aliéniste *m.*

alight¹ allumé; en feu.

alight² descendre; mettre pied à terre; se poser (*bird*); ✈ atterrir.

align (s')aligner; **~ment** alignement *m.*

amateurish **A**

alike 1. *adj.* semblable, pareil; **2.** *adv.* de la même manière; de même; pareillement.

aliment|ary alimentaire; **~ation** alimentation *f*.

alimony pension *f* alimentaire.

alive vivant, en vie; sensible (à, *to*), conscient (de, *to*); *fig.* éveillé; *ǃ* sous tension; **~ with** grouillant de.

all 1. *adj.* tout; entier; **for ~ that** toutefois, cependant; **2.** *su.* tout *m*; totalité *f*; **~ of them** eux tous; (*nothing*) **at ~** quoi que ce soit; **not at ~** (pas) du tout; **for ~ (that) I care** pour ce que cela me fait; **for ~ I know** autant que je sache; **~ told** somme toute; **3.** *adv.* tout; entièrement; **~at once** tout à coup; tout d'un coup; **~ the better** tant mieux; **~ but** à peu près, presque; **~ right** en règle; entendu!; bon!

allay apaiser; calmer.

alleg|ation allégation *f*; **~e** alléguer; prétendre; **~ed** allégué, prétendu; présumé; **~ly** à ce qu'on dit.

allegiance fidélité *f*, obéissance *f*.

allerg|ic *ǃ*, *fig.* allergique (à, *de*); **~y** allergie *f* (à, *to*).

alleviat|e alléger, soulager; **~ion** allègement *m*, soulagement *m*.

alley ruelle *f*, *town.* passage *m*; *Am.* ruelle *f* latérale; *garden:* allée *f*.

alliance alliance *f*.

all...: ~important capital, extrêmement important; **~In** tout compris; inclusif; **~night** de nuit; ouvert toute la nuit.

allocat|e allouer, assigner; distribuer; **~ion** allocation *f*; répartition *f* (*of shares*); distribution *f*.

allot assigner, attribuer; affecter (*qch.*) (à, *to*); répartir; **~ment** attribution *f*; *sum:* affectation *f*; distribution *f*; portion *f*.

all-out total, maximum; *adv. a.* à fond.

allow permettre; admettre; tolérer; laisser; prévoir; accorder; allouer; **~ for** tenir compte de; **~able** admissible; **~ance** tolérance *f* (*a,* ⊙); pension *f* alimentaire, rente *f*; argent *m* de poche; rabais *m*; **make ~(s) for** tenir compte de.

alloy 1. alliage *m*; *fig.* mélange *m*; **2.** (s')allier; *v/t. fig.* altérer.

all...: ~purpose universel, à tout faire; **~round** général; complet; **⚬ Saint's**

Day la Toussaint *f*; **~star** composé de joueurs de premier ordre.

allude faire allusion (à, *to*).

allur|e attirer; séduire; **~ing** séduisant; **~ement** attrait *m*; séduction *f*.

allusion allusion *f* (à, *to*).

ally 1. (s')allier, (à, avec *to*, *with*); **2.** allié *m*.

almighty 1. tout-puissant; **2.** ⚬ le Tout-Puissant.

almond amande *f*.

almost presque, à peu près.

alms *usu. sg.* aumône *f*.

aloft en haut; en l'air.

alone seul; **let** (*or* **leave**) **~** laisser (*q.*) tranquille; **let ~** sans compter; sans parler de.

along 1. *adv.:* **come ~!** venez donc!; **all ~** depuis longtemps; tout le temps; **~ with** avec; **2.** *prp.* le long de; **~side** le long de; *a. fig.* à côté de.

aloof à l'écart (de, *from*); **2.** distant; réservé; **~ness** réserve *f* (à l'égard de, *from*).

aloud à haute voix; tout haut.

alp alpe *f*; **2. the ~s** *pl.* les Alpes *f/pl.*

already déjà; dès à présent.

Alsatian 1. alsacien; **2.** Alsacien(ne *f*) *m*.

also aussi; encore; également.

altar autel *m*.

alter changer; modifier; **~ation** changement *m*, modification *f*.

altercation dispute *f*, querelle *f*.

alternat|e 1. (faire) alterner; *ǃ alternating current* courant *m* alternatif; **2.** alternatif, alterné; **2.** *Am.* suppléant(e *f*) *m*; remplaçant(e *f*) *m*; **~ion** alternation *f*; alternance *f*; **~ive 1.** second, autre, de remplacement; alternatif; **~ly** ou bien, sinon; **2.** solution *f* de rechange; alternative *f*; **I have no ~** je n'ai pas le choix.

although quoique, bien que (*sbj.*).

altitude altitude *f*.

altogether 1. tout à fait, entièrement; somme toute; en tout, au total; **2.** **F in the ~** tout nu, F à poil.

alumin|ium, *Am.* **~um** aluminium *m*.

always toujours; **as ~** comme toujours, comme d'habitude.

amalgamat|e (s')amalgamer; **~ion** amalgamation *f*.

amass amasser, accumuler.

amateur amateur *m* (*a. adj.*); **~ish**

d'amateur, de dilettante; **~ism** amateurisme *m*.

amaz|e stupéfier; **~ement** stupéfaction *f*; stupeur *f*; **~ing** stupéfiant, étonnant.

ambassador ambassadeur *m*.

amber ambre *m*; *traffic*: ~ **light** feu *m* orange; **at** ~ à l'orange.

ambigu|ity ambiguïté *f*; **~ous** ambigu; équivoque; obscur.

ambit|ion ambition *f* (*de, to*); **~ious** ambitieux (*de of, to*); prétentieux (*style*).

amble 1. *horse*: amble *m*; pas *m* tranquille; **2.** aller (à) l'amble (*horse*); déambuler; marcher d'un pas tranquille.

ambula|nce ambulance *f*; **~nt** ambulant; **~tory** ambulatoire.

ambush 1. guet-apens (*pl.* guets-apens) *m*; embuscade *f*; **lay an** ~ tendre une embuscade (à q., *for s.o.*); **lie in** ~ se tenir en embuscade; **2.** tendre une embuscade à.

ameliorat|e (s')améliorer; **~ion** amélioration *f*.

amend 1. *v/t.* amender (*a. parl.*); réformer; corriger; *v/i.* s'amender; **2.** *make* **~s** faire amende honorable; *make* **~s** *for* q. réparer; **~ment** modification *f*; rectification *f*; *parl.* amendement *m*.

amenity *place*: aménité *f*, charme *m*; amabilité *f*; *amenities pl.* commodités *f/pl.* (*of life*).

American 1. américain; ~ *cloth* toile *f* cirée; *tourism*: ~ *plan* pension *f* complète; **2.** Américain(e *f*) *m*.

amiable aimable.

amicable amical.

amid(st) *prp.* au milieu de; entre.

amiss mal; de travers; mal à propos; *be* ~ ne pas tourner rond, loucher; *take* ~ prendre de travers.

amity amitié *f*; concorde *f*.

ammonia ammoniaque *f*.

amoral amoral.

ammunition munitions *f/pl.*

amnesty 1. amnistie *f*; **2.** amnistier.

among(st) *prp.* parmi, entre.

amorous amoureux (*de, of*).

amortiz|ation amortissement *m*; **~e** amortir.

amount 1.: ~ *to* s'élever à, monter à; revenir à; *fig.* équivaloir à; **2.** somme *f*, montant *m*, total *m*; quantité *f*; *to the* ~ *of* jusqu'à concurrence de.

ampere ⚡ ampère *m*.

ample ample, large; vaste; gros; *have* ~ ... avoir (bien) assez de ...

ampli|fication amplification *f* (*a. phys., a. rhetoric*); **~fier** *radio*: amplificateur *m*; **~fy** amplifier (*a. radio*); *fig.* développer; **~tude** *phys. etc.* amplitude; *fig.* abondance *f*.

amputat|e amputer; **~ion** amputation *f*.

amus|e amuser; distraire; **~ement** amusement *m*; distraction *f*; ~ *arcade* luna-park *m*; ~ *park* parc *m* d'attractions; *for* ~ pour se distraire; pour (faire) rire; **~ing** amusant, divertissant (pour, *to*).

an *gramm. article*: un(e *f*).

an(a)estheti|c anesthésique (*a. su./m*); **~st** anesthésiste *mf*; **~ze** anesthésier, insensibiliser.

analog|ous analogue (à *with, to*); **~y** analogie *f*.

analys|e analyser; faire l'analyse de (*a. gramm.*); **~is**, *pl.* -ses analyse *f*; **~t** (*psych*)analiste *mf*.

anarch|ist anarchiste (*mf, adj.*); **~y** anarchie *f*.

anatomy anatomie *f*.

ancest|or ancêtre *m*; aïeul (*pl.* -eux) *m*; **~ry** ancêtres *m/pl.*; lignage *m*.

anchor 1. ancre *f*; *at* ~ à l'ancre; mouillé; **2.** *v/t.* ancrer, mettre à l'ancre; *v/i.* jeter l'ancre, mouiller; **~age** ancrage *m*, mouillage *m*.

anchovy anchois *m*.

ancient 1. ancien; antique; **2.** *the* **~s** *pl.* les anciens *m/pl.* (*Greeks and Romans*).

and et.

anecdote anecdote *f*.

anew de nouveau; à nouveau.

angel ange *m*; **~ic(al)** angélique.

anger 1. colère *f*; **2.** irriter, mettre (*q.*) en colère.

angina 🏥 angine *f*.

angle¹ angle *m*; *fig.* point *m* de vue.

angle² pêcher à la ligne; *fig.* chercher, quêter; **~r** pêcheur *m* à la ligne.

Anglican anglican (*a. su.*).

Anglo-Saxon 1. Anglo-Saxon(ne *f*) *m*; **2.** anglo-saxon.

angora (laine *f*) angora *m*; (*a.* ~ *cat* chat *m*) angora *m*.

angry fâché, furieux (contre q., *with*

s.o.; de qch., *about or at s.th.*); en colère; **make ~** mettre (*q.*) en colère.

anguish angoisse *f*; *fig.* supplice *m*.

angular anguleux.

animal animal; **~ home** asile *m* pour animaux; *zo.* **~ kingdom** règne *m* animal; **~ lover** ami(e *f*) *m* des animaux; **~ shelter** asile *m* pour animaux.

animat|e 1. animer; stimuler; **~d cartoon** dessins *m/pl.* animés; **~ion** animation *f*; vivacité *f*; entrain *m*; stimulation *f*.

animosity animosité *f*.

ankle cheville *f*; **~ bone** astragale *m*.

annals *pl.* annales *f/pl.*

annex 1. annexer (à, *to*); **2.** annexe *f*; **~aton** annexion *f*.

annihilate anéantir, annihiler.

anniversary anniversaire *m*.

annotat|e annoter; **~ion** annotation *f*.

announce annoncer; faire connaître; faire part de (*marriage, birth, etc.*); **~ment** annonce *f*; avis *m*; faire-part *m/inv.*; **~r** radio: speaker(ine *f*) *m*.

annoy agacer, fâcher, contrarier; ennuyer; **~ance** ennui *m*; contrariété *f*; **~ing** ennuyeux, fâcheux; agaçant.

annual 1. annuel (*a.* ♀); **2.** ♀ plante *f* annuelle; *book*: annuaire *m*.

annuity rente *f*; **life ~** rente *f* viagère.

annul annuler; résilier (*a contract*); abroger (*a law*); **~ment** annulation *f*; résiliation *f*; abrogation *f*.

anoint oindre.

anomalous anomal.

anonym|ity anonymat *m*, anonyme *m*; **~ous** anonyme.

another encore un, un(e) de plus; un autre; F **tell me (or us) ~!** à d'autres!, tu ne le crois pas toi-même!

answer 1. *v/t.* répondre (*qch.*) (à q., *s.o.*); faire réponse à; remplir (*a purpose*); répondre à (*a charge*); **~ the bell** (*or door*) aller *or* venir ouvrir; *v/i.* répondre (à, *to*); **~ for** être responsable de; répondre de (*q.*), se porter garant de; **don't ~ back!** ne réponds pas!; **2.** réponse *f* (à, *to*), *A, fig.* solution *f*; **~able** responsable.

ant *zo.* fourmi *f*.

antagonis|m antagonisme *m* (entre, de *between*); opposition *f* (à, *to*; avec, *with*); **~t** antagoniste *m*; **~tic** opposé, hostile (à, *to*).

antarctic antarctique; **♀ Circle** cercle *m* polaire antarctique.

antenna, *pl.* **-nae** antenne *f*.

anterior antérieur (à, *to*).

anthem *eccl.* antienne *f*; **national ~** hymne *m* national.

anthill fourmilière *f*.

anthropolog|ist anthropologue *mf*; **~y** anthropologie *f*.

anti... *pref.* anti-; anté-; contre-; **~aircraft: ~ alarm** alerte *f* (aux avions); **~ defense** défense *f* contre avions, D.C.A.; **~biotic** ♉ antibiotique (*a. su./m*).

anticipat|e aller au-devant de, devancer (*s.o.'s wishes etc.*); reckon with: s'attendre à, prévoir, escompter; devancer (*competitors*); anticiper sur (*the end of a story etc.*); **~ion** attente *f*, expectative *f*; **in ~** d'avance.

anti...: ~climax déception *f*; **~clockwise** dans le sens inverse des aiguilles de la montre.

antics *pl.* singeries *f/pl.*

anti...: ~cyclone anticyclone *m*; **~ dote** antidote *m*, contrepoison *m*; **~freeze** antigel *m*; **~pathy** antipathie *f*; **~pollution device** équipement *m* anti-pollution.

antiqua|rian 1. d'antiquaire, d'antiquités; **2.** (*a.* **~ry**) amateur *m* d'antiquités; antiquaire *m*; **~ted** vieilli; désuet; démodé.

antiqu|e 1. antique; ancien; **2.** antiquité *f*; objet *m* (d'art) antique; **~ity** (*Roman etc.*) antiquité *f*; ancienneté *f*.

anti...: ~septic antiseptique (*adj. su./m*); **~social** insociable (*behaviour, person*); antisocial (*measures*); **~thesis** opposé; antithèse *f*; **~thetical** opposé; antithétique.

antlers *pl.* bois *m* (*pl.*).

anvil enclume *f*.

anxiety anxiété *f*, angoisse *f*; *fig.* désir *m* (de *inf.*, *to inf.*); *fig.* sollicitude *f* (pour, *for*).

anxious anxieux, inquiet; *fig.*: désireux (de *inf.*, *to inf.*); impatient (de *inf.*, *to inf.*); **be ~ to** (*inf.*) *a.* tenir à (*inf.*).

any *adj., a. pron.* un; tout; n'importe quel; n'importe lequel; **not ~** aucun, nul; **~body** quelqu'un; n'importe qui; tout le monde; quiconque; *after negative*: personne; **not ~** personne; **~how 1.**

cj. en tout cas; **2.** *adv.* n'importe comment; ~**one** *see* **anybody**; ~**thing** quelque chose; *after negative:* rien; ~ **but** rien moins que; ~**way** *see* **anyhow**; ~**where** n'importe où.

apart séparé, éloigné (l'un de l'autre), écarté; (*to one side*) à part, de côté; (*to pieces*) en morceaux; **come** *or* **fall** ~ tomber en morceaux; se désagréger; **joking** ~ plaisanterie à part; ~ **from** à part, en dehors de, excepté.

apartment appartement *m*; *Br. a.* pièce *f*, *Am. a.* logement *m.*

apath|etic apathique; indifférent; ~**y** apathie *f*; indifférence *f.*

ape 1. (grand) singe *m*; **2.** singer.

aperture ouverture *f.*

apiary rucher *m.*

apiece chacun; la pièce.

aplomb assurance *f.*

apogee *astr.* apogée *m* (*a. fig.*).

apolitical apolitique.

apolog|ize s'excuser (de, *for*; auprès de, *to*); ~**y** excuses *f/pl.*; apologie *f*; F (mauvais) substitut *m* (de, *for*).

apoplexy ♂ apoplexie *f.*

apostate apostat *m*; relaps(e *f*) *m.*

apostle apôtre *m.*

apostroph|e *gramm., a. rhetoric:* apostrophe *f*; ~**ize** apostropher.

appal épouvanter; consterner; ~**ling** épouvantable, effroyable.

apparatus appareil *m*; dispositif *m.*

appar|ent apparent, évident; ~**ition** apparition *f.*

appeal 1. faire appel (à, *to*); demander (qch., *for s.th.*; à, *to*); interjeter appel; ~ **to** plaire à, attirer; ♂♯ invoquer l'aide de (*the law*); *see* **country; 2.** ♂♯ appel *m*; recours *m*; *fig.* prière *f*, supplication *f*; attrait *m*; ~ **for mercy** demande *f* de grâce; ♂♯ **lodge** (*or* **file**) **an** ~ interjeter appel; ~**ing** suppliant; émouvant; attirant, sympathique.

appear paraître (*a.* books); se montrer; *telev.* passer (à la télé, **on television**); ♂♯ comparaître; *seem:* sembler, paraître: ~**ance** apparition *f*; *book:* parution *f*; apparence *f*, aspect *m*; **to all** ~**s** selon toute apparence.

appease apaiser, calmer (*passions, pain*); assouvir (*one's hunger*); ~**ment** apaisement *m*; assouvissement *m*; ~ **policy** politique *f* d'apaisement.

append apposer (*one's signature*); annexer (*a document*); ~**age** appendice *m*; ~**icitis** appendicite *f*; ~**ix**, *pl.* **-dixes, -dices** appendice *m.*

appertain: ~ **to** appartenir à; incomber à.

appeti|te appétit *m*; ~ **suppressant** coupe-faim *m/inv.*, anorexigène *m*; ~**zing** appétissant.

applaud applaudir.

applause applaudissements *m/pl.*

apple pomme *f*; ~ **cart:** F **upset s.o.'s** ~ bouleverser les plans de q.; ~ **pie** tourte *f* aux pommes; ~**pie:** F **in** ~ **order** rangé en ordre parfait; ~**sauce** compote *f* de pommes; *Am. sl.* salades *f/pl.*; ~**tree** pommier *m.*

appliance appareil *m.*

applica|ble (à, **to**) applicable; ~**nt** candidat(e *f*) *m* (à, **for**); ~**tion** application *f* (à, sur **to**); utilisation *f*; assiduité *f*; demande *f* (de, **for**); (**letter of**) ~ (lettre *f* de) demande *f* d'emploi.

apply *v/t.* appliquer (sur, **to**; *fig.* à, **to**); ~ **o.s. to** s'appliquer à; ~ **the brakes** actionner les freins; *v/i.* (**to**) s'appliquer (à); s'adresser (à); avoir recours (à); ~ (**for**) poser sa candidature (pour); ~ (**for a** *or* **the job**) faire une demande d'emploi.

appoint nommer (q. gouverneur, **s.o. governor**); désigner (pour *inf.*, **to** *inf.*); fixer (*a date, a place*); prescrire (que, **that**); ~**ment** rendez-vous *m*; entrevue *f*; nomination *f*; désignation *f*; ~ **book** agenda *m*, calepin *m.*

apportion répartir; distribuer; ~**ment** répartition *f.*

apprais|al évaluation *f*; ~**e** priser.

apprecia|ble appréciable, sensible; ~**te** *v/t.* apprécier; faire (grand cas de), être reconnaissant de; ✝ évaluer; *v/i.* augmenter de valeur; ~**tion** appréciation *f* (de, **of**); reconnaissance *f*; évaluation *f*; amélioration *f*, hausse *f*; ~**tive** sensible, compréhensif; reconnaissant.

apprehen|d appréhender; saisir, arrêter; comprendre; ~**sion** appréhension *f*; arrestation *f*; ~**sive** inquiet, craintif.

apprentice 1. apprenti(e *f*) *m*; **2.** placer en apprentissage (chez, **to**); ~**ship** apprentissage *m.*

approach 1. *v/i.* (s')approcher; *fig.* se rapprocher (de, **to**); *v/t.* (s')approcher de; s'adresser à (q.); *fig.* s'attaquer à, aborder (*a question*); **2.** approche *f*; voie *f* d'accès; abord *m*; *fig.* rapprochement *m*; *fig.* démarche *f*; *fig.* méthode *f*.

approbation approbation *f*.

appropriat|e 1. (s')approprier; s'attribuer; *parl. etc.* affecter (*funds*, **for**); **2.** (*to*) approprié (à); convenable, propre (à); **~ion** appropriation *f*; budget *m*.

approv|al approbation *f*; **on ~** à l'essai; **~e** approuver; ratifier (*a. ~ of*); **~ing** approbateur; **~ly** d'un air approbateur.

approximate 1. se rapprocher (de, **to**); **2.** proche (de, **to**); approximatif; **~ly** environ, à peu près.

apricot ♀ abricot *m*.

April avril *m*; **~ fool** poisson *m* d'avril.

apron tablier *m*; *fig.* **be tied to s.o.'s ~ strings** être pendu aux jupes de q.

apt enclin (à, **to**); susceptible (de, **to**); apte (à, **to**); **~itude** disposition *f*, penchant *m* (à, **to**); talent *m* (pour, **for**).

aqualung scaphandre *m* autonome.

aquaplan|e 1. aquaplane *f*; **2.** *sp.* faire de l'aquaplane; *mot.* faire de l'aquaplaning; **~ing** *mot.* aquaplaning *m*.

aquarium aquarium *m*.

Aquarius *astr.* le Verseau.

aquatic aquatique.

aqueduct aqueduc *m*.

aquiline nose nez *m* aquilin.

Arab Arabe *mf*; *sl.* **street ~** gavroche *m*; **~ian 1.** arabe; **2.** Arabe *mf*; **~ic 1.** arabe; **2.** *ling.* arabe *m*.

arable labourable.

arbit|er arbitre *m*; **~rariness** arbitraire *m*; **~rary** arbitraire; **~rate** arbitrer; juger; **~ration** arbitrage *m*; **~rator** ⚖ arbitre *m*.

arbo(u)r tonnelle *f*.

arc ♀, *astr.* arc *m* (⚡ électrique); **~ade** arcade *f*, galerie *f*, passage *m* couvert.

arch¹ 1. *esp.* △ voûte *f*; cintre *m*; *bridge*: arche *f*; **2.** (se) voûter; *v/t.* bomber (*a. v/i.*); cintrer; cambrer.

arch² espiègle; malin; malicieux.

arch³ insigne, grand; archi-.

arch(a)eolog|ist archéologue *mf*; **~y** archéologie *f*.

archaic archaïque.

archangel archange *m*.

archbishop archevêque *m*.

archduke archiduc *m*.

archenemy ennemi *m* par excellence.

archetype archétype *m*.

archipelago *geog.* archipel *m*.

architect architecte *m*; **~ural** architectural; **~ure** architecture *f*.

archives *pl.* archives *f/pl.*

archway passage *m* voûté; porte *f* cintrée; portail *m*.

arctic 1. arctique; ♀ **Circle** cercle *m* polaire; ♀ **Ocean** Arctique *m*; **2. the ♀** l'Arctique *m*.

ardent fervent, ardent.

ardo(u)r ardeur *f*; chaleur *f*.

arduous ardu.

area aire *f*, superficie (*a.* ♒); secteur *m*; région *f*; zone *f*; *fig.* domaine *m*; *Am. teleph.* **~ code** numéro *m* de présélection; *danger* **~** zone *f* dangereuse; *foot.* **goal ~** surface *f* de but; *prohibited* **~** zone *f* interdite.

arena arène *f*.

Argentine 1. argentin, **2.** Argentin(e *f*) *m*.

argue *v/t.* discuter; raisonner sur; prouver; **~ s.o. into doing s.th.** persuader q. de faire qch.; *v/i.* argumenter (sur, **about**); discuter; raisonner.

argument argument *m*; raisonnement *m*; débat *m*, dispute *f*; **~ative** ergoteur.

arid aride; **~ity** aridité *f*.

Aries *astr.* le Bélier *m*.

arise survenir; se produire; **~ from** résulter de.

aristocra|cy aristocratie *f*; **~t** aristocrate *mf*; **~tic(al)** aristocratique.

arithmetic arithmétique *f*, calcul *m*; **~al** arithmétique.

arm¹ bras *m*; **keep s.o. at ~'s length** tenir q. à distance.

arm² 1. arme *f*; **~s race** course *f* aux armements; **~s reduction** désarmement *m*; **be (all) up in ~s** être en révolte; se gendarmer, s'élever (contre, *against*); **2.** armer; **~ o.s. with s.th.** s'armer de qch. (*a. fig.*).

Armada *hist.* l'Armada *f*.

armament armement *m*.

armature armure *f* (*a.* ♀, *zo.*); △, *phys.* armature *f*.

armchair fauteuil *m*.

armistice armistice *m* (*a. fig.*).

armo(u)r 1. ✗ armure *f*, blindage *m*; blindés *m/pl.*; cuirasse *f* (*a. fig.*, *zo.*); **2.** cuirasser; blinder; **~ed car** char *m* blindé; **~-clad**, **~-plated** blindé, cuirassé; **~y** arsenal *m*; *Am.* fabrique *f* d'armes.

army armée f.

around 1. *adv.* autour; dans les parages, là; **2.** *prp.* autour de; environ, vers.

arouse *usu. fig.* éveiller; susciter (*suspicions etc.*).

arraign accuser, inculper.

arrange arranger (*a.* ♪); ranger; convenir de, fixer (*a date etc.*); **~ment** arrangement *m* (*a.* ♪); disposition *f*.

array 1. rang *m*, ordre *m*; collection *f* (de, **of**); **2.** déployer (*troops etc.*); revêtir (de, **in**).

arrears arriéré *m*; **in ~** en retard; **get in(to) ~** se mettre en retard.

arrest 1. arrestation *f*; **under ~** en état d'arrestation; **put under ~** arrêter; **2.** arrêter (*a criminal etc.*); retenir, attirer (*s.o.'s attention, etc.*).

arriv|al arrivée *f*; ✝ arrivage; ⚓ entrée *f*; **~s** *pl.* nouveaux venus *m/pl. or* arrivés *m/pl.*; **on ~** à l'arrivée; **~e** arriver; **~ at** arriver à, parvenir à, atteindre (*a. an age*).

arroga|nce arrogance *f*; **~nt** arrogant; **~te** s'attribuer (*qch.*) (à tort), s'arroger (*qch.*).

arrow flèche *f*; **~head** pointe *f* de flèche.

arsenic arsenic *m*.

arson crime *m* d'incendie.

art art *m*; métier *m*; *fig.* artifice *m*; **~ critic** critique *mf* d'art; **~ dealer** marchand(e *f*) *m* d'art; **~ gallery** musée *m* d'art; galerie *f* (d'art); **~s and crafts** métiers *m/pl.* d'art; **applied ~s** arts *m/ pl.* appliqués *or* industriels; **fine ~s** les beaux-arts *m/pl.*; **Faculty of ₂s** Faculté *f* des Lettres.

arter|ial artériel; **~ road** artère *f*; **~y** artère *f* (*a. fig.*); **traffic ~** artère *f* de circulation.

artful ingénieux; rusé.

article 1. article *m*; **2.** placer comme apprenti (chez, **to**); mettre en stage (chez, auprès de **to**).

articulat|e 1. *v/t.* articuler (*anat., a. words*); énoncer; **2.** *a.* **~ed** net, distinct; articulé (*a. speech*); mot. **~ lorry** semi-remorque *m*; **~ion** articulation *f*; netteté *f* d'énonciation.

artific|e artifice *m*, ruse *f*; **~ial** artificiel.

artillery artillerie *f*.

artisan artisan *m*.

artist artiste *mf*; **~e** artiste *mf*; **~ic** artistique; **~ry** art *m*.

artless naturel, sans artifice; ingénu.

as 1. *adv.*, *a. cj.* aussi, si; comme, puisque; au moment où; (au)tant que; **~ good ~** aussi bon que; **~ if, ~ though** comme si; **~ if** (*ger.*) comme pour (*inf.*); **~ it were** pour ainsi dire; **~ well** aussi, également; **~ well ~** de même que; **~ yet** jusqu'à présent; **so kind ~ to** (*inf.*) assez aimable pour (*inf.*); **such ~ to** (*inf.*) de sorte à (*inf.*); de façon que; **2.** *prp.*: **~ for, ~ to** quant à; **~ from** à partir de, depuis; ✝ **~ per** suivant.

ascend *v/i.* monter; s'élever; comme, (*a ladder*); gravir (*a hill etc.*); monter sur (*the throne*); **~ancy, ~ency** ascendant *m*, influence *f*.

ascension ascension *f*; ₂ (*Day*) jour *m* de l'Ascension.

ascent ascension *f*; montée *f*.

ascertain constater; vérifier.

ascetic 1. ascétique; **2.** ascète *mf*.

ascribe imputer, attribuer (a, **to**).

ash[1] ♀ frêne *m*.

ash[2] *usu.* **~es** *pl.* cendre *f*; **Ash Wednesday** mercredi *m* des Cendres.

ashamed: be (*or feel*) **~** (**of**) avoir honte (de); **be ~ of o.s.** avoir honte.

ashcan boîte *f* à ordures; poubelle *f*.

ashen cendré; gris; blême (*face*).

ashore à terre; échoué; **go ~** débarquer; **run ~, be driven ~** s'échouer.

ashtray cendrier *m*.

Asiatic 1. asiatique, d'Asie; **2.** Asiatique *mf*.

aside 1. de côté; à part; à l'écart; **~ from** à part, en plus de; **2.** à-côté *m*; *thea.* aparté *m*.

ask *v/t.* demander (qch. à q., *s.o. s.th.*; que, *that*); inviter (à, **to**); prier (q. de *inf.*, *s.o. to inf.*); **~ (s.o.) a question** poser une question (à q.); *v/i.* **~ about** se renseigner sur; **~ after** s'informer de; **~ for** demander (*qch.*); chercher à voir (*q.*); ✝ **~ing price** prix *m* de départ.

askance, askew de côté, de travers.

asleep endormi; engourdi (*foot etc.*); **be ~** dormir; **fall ~** s'endormir.

asparagus ♀ asperge *f*, *cuis.* **~s** *f/pl.*

aspect exposition *f*, vue *f*, aspect *m*, air *m*; point *m* de vue.

asperity âpreté *f*; rudesse *f*.

asphalt 1. asphalte *m*; bitume *m*; **2.** asphalter; bitumer.

aspir|ate 1. *gramm.* aspiré; **2.** aspirer;

~ation aspiration *f*; **~e** aspirer, viser (à **to**, **after**, **at**); ambitionner (*qch.*); **~ing** ambitieux.

ass¹ âne(sse *f*) *m*.

ass² *Am. sl.* derrière *m*, *sl.* cul *m*.

assail assaillir (*a. fig.* de, *with questions etc.*); **~ant** assaillant(e *f*) *m*; agresseur *m*.

assassin assassin *m*; **~ate** assassiner; **~ation** assassinat *m*.

assault 1. assaut *m*; ⚖ agression *f*; *see* **battery**; 2. attaquer, assaillir.

assembl|age assemblage *m*; ⚙ *a.* montage *m*; **~e** (s')assembler; (se) rassembler; (se) réunir; *v/t.* ⚙ *a.* monter, **~y** assemblée *f*, réunion *f*; ⚙ montage *m*; ⚙ **~ line** chaîne *f* de montage.

assent 1. assentiment *m*, consentement *m*; 2. consentir (à, **to**).

assert affirmer, soutenir (*one's rights*); protester (*one's innocence*); **~ o.s.** s'affirmer, s'imposer; **~ion** assertion *f*, affirmation *f*; revendication *f* (*of rights*).

assess estimer, établir (*taxes*); fixer (*a sum*); **~able** évaluable (*damage*); imposable (*property*); **~ment** évaluation *f*.

asset *fig.* avantage *m*, atout *m*, valeur *f*; † **~s** biens *m/pl.*, avoir *m*, actif *m*; † **~s and liabilities** actif et passif *m*.

assiduous assidu.

assign 1. assigner; attribuer; **~ation** assignation; affectation; *co.* rendez-vous *m*; **~ment** mission *f*, tâche *f*; allocation *f*, attribution *f*.

assimilat|e (s')assimiler (à, **to**); **~ion** assimilation *f*.

assist assister (*q.*), aider (*q.*); **~ance** assistance *f*, aide *f*, secours *m*; **~ant** 1. sous-; 2. adjoint(e *f*) *m*, auxiliaire *m/f*; **shop:** vendeur (-euse *f*)*m*.

assize ⚖ assises *f/pl.*

associat|e 1. *v/t.* associate (à, **with**); *v/t.* **~ with** fréquenter (*q.*), entretenir des relations avec; 2. associé *m* (*a.* †), **~ion** association *f* (*a. of ideas*); fréquentation *f*; société *f*, amicale *f*.

assort *v/t.* assortir (*a.* †), classer, *v/t.* **~ with** aller bien avec (*a colour*); cadrer avec (*a statement*); s'associer avec; **~ed** assorti, **~ment** assortiment *m* (*a.* †).

assuage apaiser; soulager.

assume assumer, prendre; adopter (*an attitude, a name, etc.*); supposer, ad-

mettre; **~ed name** nom *m* d'emprunt; **~ption** supposition *f*, hypothèse *f*; adoption *f*; **on the ~ that** en supposant que.

assur|ance assurance *f*; *Brit.* **life ~** assurance-vie (*pl.* assurances-vie) *f*; **~e** assurer; **~ s.o. of s.th.** assurer q. de qch.; **~ed** 1. assuré (*a.* = *certain*); 2. assuré(e *f*) *m*; **~edly** assurément, sans aucun doute; avec assurance.

asthma ♣ asthme *m*.

astir debout; agité, en émoi.

astonish étonner; **be ~ed** s'étonner (de **at**, **to**); **~ment** étonnement *m*.

astound stupéfier.

astray: **go ~** s'égarer; *fig.* se dévoyer.

astride à califourchon (sur, **of**).

astro|logy astrologie *f*; **~naut** astronaute *m/f*; **~nautics** astronautique *f*; **~nomer** astronome *m*; **~nomy** astronomie *f*.

astute astucieux, habile.

asunder en morceaux.

asylum asile *m*, refuge *m*.

at *prp.* à; en (*war, peace, sea*); (au)près de; sur (*request*); **~ my aunt's** chez ma tante; **~ night** la nuit; **~ school** à l'école; **~ the age of** à l'âge de; **~ one blow** d'un seul coup; **~ five o'clock** à cinq heures.

athei|sm athéisme *m*; **~st** athée *m/f*; **~ic(al)** athée.

athlet|e athlète *m*; **~ic** athlétique; **~ics** *pl.* athlétisme *m*.

Atlantic 1. atlantique; 2. (*a.* **~ Ocean**) Atlantique *m*.

atmospher|e atmosphère *f*; **~ic(al)** atmosphérique.

atom atome *m*; **~ic** atomique; **~ bomb** (**energy**, **weight**) bombe *f* (énergie *f*, poids *m*) atomique; **~ pile** (*or* **reactor**) pile *f* atomique, réacteur *m* nucléaire; **~ waste** déchets *m/pl.* nucléaires; **~ize** atomiser; pulvériser (*a liquid*); **~izer** atomiseur *m*.

atone: **~ for** expier (*qch.*), racheter (*qch.*); **~ment** expiation *f*.

atop en haut, au sommet.

atroc|ious atroce; affreux; **~ity** atrocité *f*.

attach *v/t.* (**to**) attacher (*a. value, importance, etc.*) (à); lier, fixer (à); joindre (à); ajouter (*credence*) (à); ⚖ arrêter (*q.*), saisir (*qch.*); **~ o.s. to** s'attacher à; **~ment** attachement *m*, affection *f* (pour, *for*); ⚙, *machine*: accessoire *m*; 🚉 *person*: arrestation *f*, *goods*: saisie *f* (de, *on*).

attack 1. attaquer (*a. fig.*); s'attaquer à (*a problem, a task, etc.*); **2.** attaque *f*; ⚕ accès *m*, crise *f*, attaque *f*; ~ *on s.o.'s life* attentat *m* contre q.; ⚕ *heart* ~ crise *f* cardiaque; ~er agresseur *m*.

attain *v/t.* atteindre, parvenir à; acquérir (*knowledge*); *v/i.*: ~ *to* atteindre (à); ~ment arrivée *f*; *fig.* réalisation *f*; ~s *pl.* connaissances *f/pl.*

attempt 1. essayer, tenter (de, *to*); **2.** tentative *f*; attentat *m* (contre q., [*up*-] *on s.o.'s life*).

attend *v/t.* assister à; aller à (l'école, *school*); suivre (*a course etc.*); soigner (*a sick person*); accompagner; *v/i.*: ~ *to* s'occuper de; ~ *on* soigner (*a sick person*); ~ance présence *f*; assistance *f* (à, *at*); ⚕ soins *m/pl.* (pour, *on*); *be in* ~ être de service (auprès de, *on*); ~ant **1.** qui accompagne; concomitant; **2.** employé(e *f*) *m*; surveillant(e *f*) *m*.

atten|tion attention *f*; ✗ ~! garde à vous!; ~ive attentif (à, *to*); prévenant.

attest attester; ~ *to* témoigner de.

attic grenier *m*.

attire 1. vêtir; **2.** tenue *f*, vêtements *m/pl.*

attitude attitude *f*; pose *f*; position *f*.

attorney mandataire *m/f*; *Am.* avoué *m*; *power of* ~ pouvoirs *m/pl.*; ⚖ *General* avocat *m* du Gouvernement; procureur *m* général; *Am.* chef *m* du Ministère de Justice.

attract attirer; ~ion attraction *f* (*a. thea. etc.*); *fig.* attrait *m*; ~ive attrayant, attirant; ✝ *etc.* intéressant; ~iveness attrait *m*, charme *m*.

attribute 1. imputer, attribuer (à, *to*); **2.** attribut *m* (*a. gramm.*).

attune harmoniser (avec, *to*).

auburn châtain roux.

auction 1. (*a. sale by* or *Am. at* ~) vente *f* aux enchères; *sell by* (or *at*) ~, *put up for* ~ vendre aux enchères; **2.** (*usu.* ~ *off*) vendre aux enchères; ~eer commissaire-priseur (*pl.* commissaires-priseurs) *m*.

audaci|ous audacieux, hardi; *pej.* effronté; ~ty audace *f*; hardiesse *f*.

audible audible.

audience *people*: assistance *f*; *thea.* spectateurs *m/pl.*; *concert*: auditeurs *m/pl.*; *interview*: audience *f*.

audio-visual audio(-)visuel; ~ *aids* support *m* audiovisuel; ~ *apparatus* matériel *m* audiovisuel.

audit 1. *accounts*: vérification *f*; **2.** vérifier; ~ion *thea. etc.* **1.** audition *f*; **2.** *vt/i.* auditionner; ~or expert *m* comptable; ~orium salle *f* (de concert, de conférence, *etc.*).

auger ⚙ perçoir *m*; tarière *f*.

aught: *for* ~ *I care* pour ce qui m'importe; *for* ~ *I know* autant que je sache.

augment augmenter; ~ation augmentation *f*.

augur 1. augure *m*; **2.** présager; *v/i.*: ~ *well* (*ill*) être de bon (mauvais) augure; ~y augure *m*.

August 1. août *m*; **2.** ♌ auguste.

aunt tante *f*.

au pair 1. (*a.* ~ *girl*) jeune fille *f* au pair; **2.** au pair; **3.** travailler au pair.

auspic|es: *under the* ~ *of* sous les auspices de; ~ious propice, heureux.

auster|e austère; ~ity austérité *f*.

Australian 1. australien; **2.** Australien(ne *f*) *m*.

Austrian 1. autrichien; **2.** Autrichien(ne *f*) *m*.

authentic authentique; ~ate établir l'authenticité *f*.

author auteur *m*; ~itarian autoritaire; ~itative autoritaire; qui fait autorité (*document*); ~ity autorité *f*; autorisation *f*; *the authorities pl.* les autorités *f/pl.*; l'administration *f*; ~ize autoriser; ~ship qualité *f* d'auteur; *book*: paternité *f*.

autis|m autisme *m*; ~tic autistique.

autocra|cy autocratie *f*; ~tic(al) autocratique; autocrate (*person*).

automat restaurant *m* à distributeurs automatiques; ~ic automatique (*a. su./m = gun*); ~ion ⚙ automatisation *f*; ~on automate *m* (*a. fig.*).

automobile automobile *f*.

autonomy autonomie *f*.

autumn automne *m*; ~al automnal.

auxiliary auxiliaire (*a. su.*).

avail 1. servir (à); ~ *o.s. of* profiter de (*qch.*); user de (*qch.*); **2.** *of no* ~ inutile, en vain; ~ability disponibilité *f*; ~able disponible; libre.

avalanche avalanche *f*.

avaric|e avarice *f*; ~ious avare.

avenge venger; ~ *o.s.* (or *be* ~d) (*up*)on

se venger de *or* sur; **~r** vengeur (-eresse *f*) *m*.

avenue avenue *f*; *fig.* **explore every ~** tout essayer.

aver déclarer, affirmer.

average 1. moyenne *f*; ⚓ avarie *f*; **on ~** en moyenne; **above** (**below**) **~** au-dessus (au-dessous) de la moyenne; **2.** moyen; **3.** atteindre *or* faire une moyenne de; faire *etc.* en moyenne.

avers|e opposé (à, *to*); **not to be ~ to** ne pas refuser, ne pas dire non à; **~ion** aversion *f*, répugnance *f* (**pour, contre** to).

avert détourner (*a. fig*); écarter.

aviat|ion aviation *f*; **~or** aviateur *m*.

aviary volière *f*.

avid avide (de *of, for*); **~ity** avidité *f* (de, pour *for*).

avocado (*a.* **~ pear**) avocat *m*.

avoid éviter; se soustraire à; **~able** évitable; **~ance** action *f* d'éviter.

avow avouer; **~al** aveu *m*; **~edly** franchement, ouvertement.

await attendre.

awake 1. éveillé; *fig. a.* en éveil; **be ~ to** avoir conscience de; **wide ~** tout éveillé; **2.** *v/t.* (*a.* **~n**) éveiller; réveiller; *v/i.* se réveiller, s'éveiller; **~ to** se rendre compte de, prendre conscience de.

award 1. adjudication *f*, sentence *f* arbitrale; récompense *f*; *univ. etc.*: bourse *f*; **2.** adjuger; accorder; conférer.

aware au courant, avisé; sensible; **be ~** avoir connaissance (de, *of*); avoir conscience (de, *of*); ne pas ignorer (qch., *of s.th.*); que, *that*); **become ~ of** prendre conscience de; se rendre compte de; **~ness** conscience *f*.

awash inondé (de, *with*).

away (au) loin; absent; parti; à (une distance de ...); **work** *etc.* **~** travailler *etc.* sans arrêt *or* tant qu'on peut; **do ~ with** supprimer.

awe crainte *f*; respect *m*.

awful affreux; **~ly** F énormément, F vachement.

awhile un moment, (pendant) quelque temps.

awkward gauche, maladroit (*person*); fâcheux, gênant; délicat (*problem*); peu pratique; malaisé, difficile; **~ness** gaucherie *f*, maladresse *f*; difficulté *f*.

awl alêne *f*.

awning *shop*: store *m*, banne *f*; *hotel etc.*: marquise *f*; *tent*: auvent *m*.

awry de travers, de guingois; **go ~** tourner *or* finir mal.

ax(e) hache *f*.

axis, *pl.* **axes** axe *m*.

axle (*a.* **~ tree**) essieu *m*; arbre *m*.

ay(e) 1. oui; **2.** *parl.* voix *f* pour; **the ~s have it** le vote est pour.

azure 1. d'azur, azuré; **2.** azur *m*.

B

babble 1. babiller; **2.** babillage *m m*.

baboon *zo.* babouin *m*.

baby 1. bébé *m*; **~ carriage** voiture *f* d'enfant; **~ tooth** dent *f* de lait; F **be left holding the ~** rester avec l'affaire sur les bras; F **it's your ~** c'est votre affaire; **2.** d'enfant, de bébé; petit; **~hood** première enfance *f*; **~sit** faire du baby-sitting.

bachelor célibataire *m*; *univ.* licencié(e *f*) *m*.

back 1. *su.* dos *m*; reins *m/pl.*; revers *m*; *chair*: dossier *m*; *room*: fond *m*; *house*,

car: derrière *m*; arrière *m*, (**at the**) **~ of** au fond de; **2.** *adj.* arrière, de derrière; sur la cour (*hotel room*); **3.** *adv.* en arrière, de retour; **4.** *v/t.* renforcer (*a wall*); endosser (*a book, a.* † *a cheque*); miser sur (*a horse*), (*a.* **~ up**) appuyer, soutenir; servir de fond à; mettre en arrière (*an engine*); financer (*q.*); *v/i.* aller en arrière; marcher à reculons; 🚗, *mot.* faire marche arrière; F se dégager (de, *out of*); **~ alley** rue *f* misérable (*in the slums*); **~ache** mal *m* aux reins; **~bite** médire de (*q.*); **~bone** échine *f*;

colonne *f* vertébrale; *fig.* caractère *m*, fermeté *f*; ~**chat** répliques *f/pl.* impertinentes; ~**cloth**, ~**drop** *thea.*, *fig.* toile *f* de fond; ~**date** antidater; ~**d** (**to**) avec effet rétroactif (à); ~**er** parieur (-euse *f*) *m*; partisan *m*; ♣ donneur *m* d'aval; commanditaire *m*; ♣ **fire** mot. pétarder; *fig.* échouer; ~**ground** fond *m*, arrière-plan *m*; *fig.* milieu *m*, cadre *m*; *fig.* formation (professionnelle) *f*; ~**lash** contre-coup *m*, répercussion(s *pl.*) *f*; ~**log** arriéré *m* (de travail); ~**pay** rappel *m* de salaire; ~**pedal** *fig.* faire marche arrière; ~**side** derrière *m*; ~**slide** retomber dans l'erreur; rechuter; ~**stage** derrière la scène, dans les coulisses; ~**street** *see* **back alley**; ~**stairs** *pl.* escalier *m* de service; ~**stroke** (*or* ~**swimming**) nage *f* sur le dos; ~**talk** répliques *f/pl.* impertinentes; ~**ward 1.** *adj.* attardé, arriéré (*a. child*); en arrière; en retard; timide, hésitant; **2.** *adv.* (*a.* ~**wards**) en arrière; ~**wash** remous *m*; ~**water** eau stagnante; *fig.* bled *m* perdu; *fig.* (petit) coin *m* tranquille; ~ **wheel** roue *f* arrière; ~**yard** arrière-cour *m*.

bacon lard *m*; F **save one's** ~ sauver sa peau; se tirer d'affaire.

bacteriological bactériologique.

bad mauvais (*action, person, habit*); grave (*accident*); faux (*coin*); vilain (*child*); **not** (**so** *or* **too**) ~ pas mal; **it's** (*or* **that's**) **too** ~ (c'est) dommage; **be** ~**ly off** être mal loti; ~**ly wounded** gravement blessé; F **want** ~**ly** avoir grand besoin de.

badge insigne *m*; plaque *f*.

badger 1. *zo.* blaireau *m*; **2.** tracasser, harceler, importuner.

bad...: ~**lands** *pl.* terres *f/pl.* incultivables; ~**ness** mauvaise qualité *f*; mauvais état *m*; person: méchanceté; ~**tempered** grincheux.

baffle déconcerter, dérouter; frustrer; faire échouer (*a plan*); défier (*description*).

bag 1. sac *m*; *anat.* poche *f*; ~**s and baggage** avec armes et bagages; **2.** (se) gonfler; *v/t.* empocher; mettre en sacs.

bagatelle bagatelle *f*; billard *m* anglais.

baggage *Am.* bagages *m/pl.*; ✗ équipement *m*; ~ **car** fourgon *m*; ~ **check** bulletin *m* de consigne; ~ **rack** mot.

galerie *f*, 🚆 porte-bagages *m/inv.*; ~ **reclaim** (guichet *m* de) remise *f* des bagages; ~ **room** consigne *f*.

baggy qui fait des poches (*pants*), flottant; avachi.

bagpipe ♪ cornemuse *f*.

bail¹ 1. caution *f*; ⚖ **admit to** ~ accorder la liberté provisoire sous caution à (*q.*); **2.** cautionner; ~ **out** se porter caution pour (*q.*).

bail² ⚓ écoper; ✈ ~ **out** sauter en parachute.

bailiff ⚖ intendant *m*; huissier *m*.

bait 1. amorce *f*; appât *m* (*a. fig.*); *a. fig.* **rise to** (*or* **swallow** *or* **take**) **the** ~ mordre à l'hameçon; **2.** amorcer (*a fish hook, a trap, etc.*); *fig.* harceler, tourmenter.

bak|e [beik] *v/t.* (faire) cuire au four; *v/i.* cuire au four; *a. fig.* cuire; ~**d potatoes** pommes *f/pl.* au four; ~**er** boulanger *m*; ~**ery** boulangerie *f*; ~**ing** cuisson *f*; ~ **powder** levure *f* (chimique); ~ **soda** bicarbonate *f* de soude.

balance 1. balance *f*; *fig.* équilibre *m*; watch: balancier *m*; ♣ solde *m*; bilan *m*; ~ **of power** balance *f* politique; ~ **of trade** balance *f* commerciale; **2.** *v/t.* balancer; équilibrer; compenser; faire contrepoids à; ♣ balancer, solder; dresser le bilan de; *fig.* peser; *v/i.* faire équilibre; se balancer.

balcony balcon *m*.

bald chauve; ~**ness** calvitie *f*.

baldachin baldaquin *m*.

bale¹ ♣ balle *f*, ballot *m*.

bale² *see* **bail²**.

baleful sinistre; funeste.

balk *v/t.* contrarier; arrêter; frustrer; *v/i.*: ~ **at** regimber (contre), reculer (devant).

ball¹ 1. *tennis, rifle, etc.:* balle *f*; *croquet, snow:* boule *f*; *foot.* ballon *m*; *billard:* bille *f*; *thread, wool:* pelote *f*, peloton *m*; *cannon:* boulet *m*; *Am. baseball:* coup *m* manqué; F *fig.* **be on the** ~ être à la hauteur (de la situation); connaître son affaire; **keep the** ~ **rolling** soutenir la conversation; *Am.* F **play** ~ coopérer (avec, **with**); **2.** (s')agglomérer.

ball² bal (*pl.* -s) *m*; F *fig.* **have a** ~ s'amuser bien, prendre du bon temps.

ballad ballade *f*.

ballast 1. ⚓ lest *m*; **2.** lester.

ball-bearing(s *pl.*) ⊙ roulement *m* à billes.

ballet ballet *m*.

balloon ballon *m*; *comics*: bulle *f*.

ballot 1. (tour *m* de) scrutin *m*; **2.** voter au scrutin; tirer au sort; **~ box** urne *f*.

ball-point-pen stylo *m* à bille.

ballroom salle *f* de bal.

balm baume *m*; **~y** balsamique; *fig.* embaumé, doux.

baloney *sl.* sottises *f/pl.*

balsam baume *m*.

balustrade balustrade *f*.

bamboo bambou *m*.

bamboozle F embob(el)iner; déboussoler.

ban 1. interdiction *f*; **2.** interdire.

banana banane *f*.

band¹ bande *f* (*a. radio*); ruban *m* (*a. saw, rubber, etc.*); cercle (*barrel etc.*).

band² 1. bande *f*, troupe *f*; ♩ orchestre *m*; **2.** **~ together, ~ up** former une bande, se liguer.

bandage 1. bandage *m*; bandeau *m*; pansement *m*; **2.** mettre un pansement à.

Band-Aid (*TM*) *Am.* sparadrap *m*.

bandit bandit *m*, brigand *m*.

band...: **~master** chef *m* d'orchestre *or* de musique *etc.*; **~stand** kiosque *m* à musique; **~wagon:** *jump* (*or climb or get*) *on the* **~** se ranger du bon côté.

bandy 1. (se) renvoyer (*balls, words, etc.*); échanger (*blows, jokes*); **~ about** faire circuler; **2.** **~-legged** bancal.

bane *fig.* tourment *m*, malheur *m*; **~ful** *fig.* funeste; pernicieux.

bang 1. boum! pan!; *go* **~** éclater; **2.** exactement, F pile; directement, en plein; **3.** coup *m*; détonation *f*; claquement *m*; **4.** frapper; (faire) claquer *or* heurter à (*the door*); **~er** F (*old* **~** vieux) tacot *m*; saucisse *f*; **~on** F exactement, tout juste; **~ time** à l'heure pile; **~-up** F vachement bien, chic.

bangle bracelet *m*.

banish bannir; **~ment** exil *m*.

banisters *pl.* rampe *f* (d'escalier).

bank 1. ✝ banque *f*, *river, lake etc.*: rive *f*, bord *m*; *oysters, sand etc.*: banc *m*; *clouds*: couche *f*; *earth*: remblai *m*, talus *m*; *in a road*: bord *m* relevé; *row*: rang *m*, rangée *f*; *clavier m*; **2.** *v/t.* (*a. ~ up*) relever (*a road in a bend*); amonceler, entasser; couvrir (*a fire*); endiguer;

entreposer; ✝ déposer en banque; *v/i.* s'amonceler; avoir un compte de banque (*chez*, *with*); ✈ virer; **~ on** compter sur; **~ account** compte *m* en banque; **~ bill**, **~ note** billet *m* de banque; **~ holiday** jour *m* férié; **~ rate** taux *m* de l'escompte; **~er** banquier *m* (*a. gambling*). **~ing 1.** affaires *f/pl.* de banque *f*; la banque; **2.** de *or* en banque; **~hours** heures *f/pl.* d'ouverture des banques; **~rupt 1.** failli(e *f*) *m*; *fraudulent* **~** banqueroutier (-ère *f*) *m*; **2.** failli; *be* **~** être en faillite; *go* **~** faire faillite; **3.** *v/t.* mettre (*q.*) en faillite; **~ruptcy** faillite *f*, *fraudulent* **~** banqueroute *f*.

banner bannière *f*; étendard *m*.

banns *pl.* bans *m/pl.* (*of marriage*); *call the* **~ of** annoncer le mariage de (*q.*).

banquet 1. banquet *m*; **2.** *v/t.* offrir un banquet à (*q.*); *v/i.* festoyer.

banter plaisanteries *f/pl.*

bapti|sm baptême *m*; **~st** (*ana*)baptiste *mf*; **~ze** baptiser.

bar 1. barre *f* (*a. metal, sand, harbour, a.* ⚖, ♩); ⚖ barreau *m*, traverse *f*; bar *m*; *soap*: brique *f*; *gold*: lingot *m*; *thea. etc.*: buvette *f*; *fig.* obstacle *m*; ♩ the ♩ le barreau; **2.** barrer; griller (*a window*); barricader (*a door*); exclure (de, *from*); empêcher (q. de *inf.*, *s.o. from ger.*); **3.** excepté, sauf; **~ none** sans exception.

barb *arrow*: barbelure *f*; *fishhook*, *feather*: barbe *f*.

barbar|ian barbare (*a. su./mf*); **~ous** barbare; cruel, inhumain.

barbecue 1. barbecue *m*; **2.** griller au charbon de bois; rôtir tout entier.

barbed barbelé; *fig.* tranchant (*remark etc.*); **~ wire** (fil *m* de fer) barbelé *m*.

barber coiffeur *m*.

bare 1. nu; dégarni; *the* **~** *idea* la seule pensée; **2.** mettre à nu; **~faced** F éhonté, cynique; **~footed** aux pieds nus; nu-pieds; **~headed** nu-tête, (1a) tête nue; **~ly** à peine, tout juste.

bargain 1. marché *m*, affaire *f*, occasion *f*; **~ basement** coin *or* sous-sol des bonnes affaires; *a good* (*bad*) **~** une bonne (mauvaise) affaire; F *it's a* **~!** entendu!; *into the* **~** par-dessus le marché; *make* (*or strike*) *a* **~** conclure un marché; **2.** négocier; traiter (de, *for*); marchander (*qch.*, *about s.th.*); **~ for** F s'attendre à.

B

barge 1. péniche *m*; **2.** ~ **in** faire irruption.

bark¹ 1. écorce *f*; **2.** écorcer; écorcher (*one's skin*).

bark² 1. aboyer; F *fig.* **be ~ing up the wrong tree** faire fausse route; **2.** aboiement *m*.

barley orge *f*.

barn grange *f*; *Am.* étable *f*; **~storm** *pol. Am.* faire une tournée de discours électoraux.

baromet|er baromètre *m*; **~ric(al)** barométrique.

baron baron *m*; **~ess** baronne *f*.

barracks *pl.* caserne *f*.

barrage barrage *m*.

barrel 1. tonneau *m*; *wine etc.*: fût *m*; *rifle etc.*: canon *m*; *lock*: cylindre *m*; **2.** mettre (*qch.*) en fût; **~organ** ♪ orgue *m* de Barbarie.

barren stérile; aride; *fig.* improductif.

barricade 1. barricade *f*; **2.** barricader.

barrier barrière *f*.

barrister (*a.* **~at-law**) avocat *m*.

barrow brouette *f*; voiture *f* des quatre saisons.

bartender barman *m*.

barter 1. échange *m*; troc *m*; **2.** échanger, troquer (contre, **for**); *pej.* ~ **away** vendre, faire trafic de.

base¹ bas, vil; ignoble; faux (*money*).

base² 1. base *f* (*a.* 🐾, A, ✈); ⚡ *bulb*: culot *m*; **2.** *fig.* baser, fonder (sur, [up]on); **~less** sans base; **~ment** soubassement *m*; sous-sol *m*.

baseness bassesse *f*.

bash F **1.** frapper *or* cogner (dur *or* fort); **2.** coup *m* (violent); **have a ~ at** essayer; s'essayer à.

bashful timide; modeste.

basic 1. fondamental; de base; 🐾 basique; **2.** the **~s** les éléments *m/pl.*, l'essentiel *m*; **~ally** fondamentalement; *fig.* au fond.

basin bassin *m* (*a.* ⚓, *geog.*); *soup*: bol *m*; *milk*: cuvette *f*; lavabo *m*.

basis, *pl.* **~ses** base *f*.

bask: ~ **in the sun** se chauffer au soleil; *fig.* ~ **in** jouir de.

basket corbeille *f*; panier *m*; **~ball** basket-ball *m*.

bass ♪ basse *f*; ~ **clef** clé *f* de fa.

bastard 1. bâtard; corrompu; **2.**

bâtard(e *f*) *m*; enfant *mf* naturel(le *f*); *sl.* salaud(e *f*) *m*.

baste¹ *cuis.* arroser (de graisse).

baste² *cost.* bâtir, baguer.

bat¹ chauve-souris (*pl.* chauves-souris) *f*; **be blind as a ~** ne pas y voir plus clair qu'une taupe; F **have ~s in the belfry** être cinglé.

bat² 1. *cricket*: batte *f*; *ping-pong*: raquette *f*; *fig.* **off one's own ~** de sa propre initiative; **2. not ~ an eyelid** ne pas sourciller.

batch *bread, a. fig.*: fournée *f*; *paper*: paquet *m*; lot *m*.

bated: with ~ breath en retenant son souffle.

bath 1. bain *m*; *Br.* baignoire *f*; ♿ **chair** fauteuil *m* roulant; **2.** baigner; *a.* **have a ~** prendre un bain.

bathe 1. (se) baigner; **2.** bain *m* (*in the sea etc.*); baignade *f*.

bathing bains *m/pl.* (*in the sea etc.*); baignades *f/pl.*; *attr.* de bain(s); ~ **cap** bonnet *m* de bain; ~ **costume,** ~ **suit** maillot *m* (de bain); ~ **trunks** slip *m* de bain.

bath...: ~ **mat** tapis *m* de bain; **~robe** peignoir *m* de bain; **~room** salle *f* de bains; *Am. a.* toilettes *f/pl.*; ~ **towel** serviette *f* de bain; **~tub** baignoire *f*.

baton *marshal*: bâton *m*; ♪ baguette *f*.

battalion bataillon *m*.

batten 1. latte *f*; **2.** *v/t.* latter.

batter 1. *cricket*: batteur *m*; *cuis.* pâte *f* lisse; **2.** battre; (*a.* ~ **at**) frapper avec violence; **~ed** cabossé (*thing*); meurtri (*person*); ~ **baby** (*wife*) enfant (épouse) martyr(e).

battery batterie *f* (*a.* ✂, ☉); ⚡ pile *f*; ⚖ **assault and ~** voies *f/pl.* de fait; **~operated** ⚡ à piles.

battle 1. bataille *f*, combat *m*; **2.** se battre, lutter; **~axe** hache *f* d'armes; F *fig.* mégère *f*; **~field** champ *m* de bataille; **~ments** *pl.* créneaux *m/pl.*; parapet *m*; **~ship** cuirassé *m*.

bawdy obscène; impudique.

bawl brailler; hurler; beugler.

bay¹ baie *f*.

bay² △ travée *f*; claire-voie (*pl.* claires-voies) *f*; ~ **window** fenêtre *f* en saillie.

bay³ laurier *m*.

bay⁴ 1. aboyer; hurler (*dog*); **2.: hold** (*or*

B

keep) *at* ~ tenir (*q.*) à distance *or* en respect; *stand at* ~ être aux abois; *bring to* ~ acculer.

bay⁵ (cheval *m*) bai.

bayonet baïonnette *f*.

bazaar bazar *m*; vente *f* de charité.

be 1. être; se trouver; *there is, there are* il y a; *here you are again!* vous revoilà!; ~ *about* (*ger.*) être occupé à (*inf.*) *or* de (*qch.*); ~ *after* venir après (*q.*); F être en quête de (*q.*); ~ *off* s'en aller; partir; ~ *on at* harceler; ~ *on to* être en contact avec; être sur la piste de; être aux trousses de (*q.*); **2.** *v/aux. and p.pr., used to express the progressive form;* ~ *reading* (être en train de) lire; **3.** *v/aux. and inf., used to express permission, a duty, intention or possibility:* **I am to inform you** je suis chargé de vous faire savoir; *it is* (*not*) *to* ~ *seen* on (ne) peut (pas) le voir; *if he were to die* s'il mourait; **4.** *v/aux and p.p. used to express the passive voice: usually translated by* on *and the active voice, or by the passive voice, or by a reflexive verb;* **I am asked** on me demande.

beach 1. plage *f*; ~ *ball* ballon *m* de plage; **2.** ⚓ échouer; ~ *comber* rôdeur *m* de grève; propre *m* à rien; ~ *wear* tenue(s *pl.*) *f* de plage.

beacon 1. fanal *m*; phare *m*; balise *f*; **2.** baliser; éclairer.

bead perle *f*, goutte *f* (*of sweat etc.*); *rifle:* guidon *m*; ~*s pl.* a. chapelet *m*.

beak bec *m*; F nez *m* crochu.

beam [biːm] **1.** poutre *f*; *lights:* rayon *m*; F *fig.* *be off* (*the*) ~ faire fausse route; F *fig.* *be on* (*the*) ~ être sur la bonne voie; **2.** rayonner; ~*ing* radieux.

bean fève *f*; *coffee:* grain *m*; *sl.* tête *f*, caboche *f*; *full of* ~*s* plein d'entrain; F *spill the* ~*s* vendre la mèche.

bear¹ ours(e *f*) *m*; ♱ baissier *m*.

bear² 1. *v/t.* porter (*qch., sword, name, title, date, etc.*); supporter; (rap)porter; donner naissance à (*a child*); ~ *down* vaincre; accabler; ~ *out* corroborer, confirmer; ~ *up* soutenir; résister à; **2.** *v/i.* endurer; se rapporter, avoir rapport (à, *upon*); porter; ~ *to the right* prendre à droite; ~ *up* tenir bon; ~ (*up*)*on* porter sur; peser sur; ~ *with* supporter; *bring to* ~ mettre (*qch.*) en action; ~*able* supportable.

beard 1. barbe *f*; **2.** narguer (*q.*).

bearer porteur (-euse *f*) *m*; *passport:* titulaire *mf*; ♱ *cheque:* porteur *m*.

bearing port *m*, maintien *m*, allure *f*; rapport *m*, relation *f*; ⚙ position *f*; *beyond* (*or past*) (*all*) ~ (absolument) insupportable; *find one's* ~*s* s'orienter; *lose one's* ~*s* perdre le nord, être désorienté; *take one's* ~*s* s'orienter, se repérer.

beast bête *f*; ~*ly* F **1.** sale, infect; **2.** terriblement.

beat 1. *v/t.* battre; dépasser (*q.*); F devancer (*q.*); *Am.* ♱ rouler, escroquer; *sl.* ~ *it!* filez!; ~ *down* (①abattre; ~ *up* fouetter (*eggs, cream, etc.*); ♱ rosser, cogner (*q.*); recruter; *v/i.* battre; ~ *about the bush* tourner autour du pot; **2.** battement *m*; pulsation *f*; ♪ mesure *f*; *police:* ronde *f*; *fig.* domaine *m*; **3.** ♱ battu, confondu; ~ *out* épuisé, F à plat; ~*en* battu (*path, metal*).

beatitude béatitude *f*.

beautician esthéticien(ne *f*) *m*, visagiste *mf*.

beautiful beau; ~*ly* admirablement; parfaitement.

beautify embellir.

beauty beauté *f* (*a.* belle femme); ~ *parlo(u)r*, ~ *shop* institut *m* de beauté; ~ *spot place:* coin *m* pittoresque.

beaver *zo.* castor *m*; *eager* ~ travailleur (-euse *f*) *m* acharné(e).

becalm ⚓ déventer, immobiliser.

because parce que; ~ *of* à cause de.

beckon faire signe (à *q.*).

becloud ennuager, voiler.

become *v/i.* devenir; se faire; *v/t.* convenir à, aller (bien) à; ~*ing* convenable, bienséant; seyant (*dress etc.*).

bed lit *m* (*a.* of a river); banc *m* (*of oysters*); *flowers:* parterre *m*; ~ *and breakfast* chambre et petit déjeuner; *go to* ~ (aller) se coucher; ~*clothes pl.* draps *m/pl.* de lit; ~*ding* literie *f*.

bedevil embrouiller; tourmenter.

bedew humecter, mouiller.

bed...: ~*linen* draps *m/pl.* de lit; ~*rid*(*den*) cloué au lit; ~*room* chambre *f* (à coucher); ~*side* chevet *m*; ~*spread* couvre-lit *m*, dessus-de-lit *m*; ~*stead* châlit *m*; ~*time* heure *f* du coucher.

bee abeille *f*; F réunion *f* (*pour travaux*

en commun); F **have a ~ in one's bonnet** avoir une manie.

beech ♀ hêtre *m*; **~nut** faine *f*.

beef 1. bœuf *m*; F muscle *m*; énergie *f*; F plainte *f*; F grommeler, se plaindre; **~steak** bifteck *m*; **~ tea** cuis. consommé *m*; **~y** F musculeux.

bee...: **~hive** ruche *f*; **~keeper** apiculteur *m*; **~line**: **make a ~ for** aller droit vers (*qch.*).

beer bière *f*; F **small ~** peu important.

beet ♀ betterave *f*; **white ~** bette *f*; **red ~** betterave *f* rouge.

beetle 1. coléoptère *m*; cafard *m*; **2.** F **~ off** ficher le camp.

beetroot betterave *f*.

befall arriver *or* survenir à (*q.*).

befit convenir à, seoir à.

before 1. *adv. place*: en avant; devant; *time*: auparavant; avant; **2.** *cj.* avant que; **3.** *prp. place*: devant; *time*: avant; **~hand** préalablement; à l'avance.

befriend venir en aide à; secourir.

beg *v/t.* mendier; solliciter; prier (*q.* de *inf.*, **s.o.** *to inf.*); **I ~ your pardon** je vous demande pardon; plaît-il?; **~ the question** supposer la question résolue; éluder la question; *v/i.* mendier (*qch.* à *q.*, **for s.th.** *of s.o.*); demander, prier; faire le beau (*dog*); **~ off** se faire excuser.

beget engendrer.

beggar 1. mendiant(e *f*) *m*; **2.** **it ~s all description** cela défie toute description; **~y** mendicité *f*.

begin commencer (à, de **to**; par, à **at**); se mettre (à *inf.*, **to** *inf.*); **~ner** commençant(e *f*) *m*; **~ning** commencement *m*; début *m*.

begone! partez!; hors d'ici!

begrudge donner à contre-cœur, mesurer; envier (*qch.* à *q.*, **s.o. s.th.**).

beguile (*a.* **~ away**) faire passer (*time*); **~ing** séduisant.

behalf: **on** (*or* **in**) **~ of** au nom de; de la part de; en faveur de.

behave se conduire, se comporter; **~io(u)r** comportement *m*, conduite *f*; ☉ fonctionnement *m*; **~io(u)ral** *psych.* de comportement; **~ pattern** type *m* de comportement; **~ psychology** psychologie *f* du comportement.

behead décapiter.

behind 1. *adv.* (par) derrière; en arrière; en retard; **2.** *prp.* derrière; en arrière de;

en retard sur; *see* **time 1**; **3.** F derrière *m* postérieur *m*; **~hand** en retard.

behold voir, apercevoir.

beho(o)ve incomber à (*q.*).

being être *m*; existence *f*; **in ~** vivant; **come into ~** prendre naissance.

belabo(u)r F rouer (*q.*) de coups.

belated attardé; tardif.

belch éructer; *sl.* roter; **~ forth** (*or* **out**) vomir (*flames etc.*).

beleaguer assiéger.

Belisha beacon globe *m* orange.

belfry beffroi *m*, clocher *m*.

Belgian 1. belge; **2.** Belge *mf*.

belie démentir.

belief croyance *f* (à, **in**; en Dieu, **in God**); *fig.* conviction *f*, foi *f*.

believ|able croyable; **~e** croire (à, en **in**); **~er** croyant(e *f*) *m*.

belittle déprécier, rapetisser.

bell cloche *f*; sonnette *f*; timbre *m*; *electric*: sonnerie *f*.

belle beauté *f*.

bellhop *sl.* chasseur *m*.

bellied ventru.

belligerent belligérant (*a. su./m.*).

bellow beugler.

bellows *pl.*: (**a pair of** un) soufflet *m*.

belly ventre *m*; **~ button** F nombril *m*; **~ flop** plat-ventre *m/inv.*; ✈ **~ landing** atterrissage *m* sur le ventre; **~ laugh** gros rire *m*; **~ache 1.** mal *m* au ventre; **2.** *sl.* rouspéter.

belong avoir sa place *or* aller (*somewhere*); **~ to** appartenir à; faire partie de; être à; **~ with** aller avec; **~ings** *pl.* affaires *f/pl.*; effets *m/pl.*

beloved 1. aimé; **2.** chéri(e *f*) *m*.

below 1. *adv.* en bas, en dessous, (au-)dessous; **2.** *prp.* au-dessous de.

belt 1. ceinture *f*; *fig.* zone *f*; ☉ courroie *f*; **2.** *v/t.* boucler (*a. sl.*); F battre, rosser; F **~ out** faire retentir; *v/i.* F filer (à toute allure).

bemoan pleurer, déplorer (*qch.*).

bemused confus, embrouillé; rêveur.

bench banc *m*; ☉ établi *m*; ⚖ siège *m*; magistrature *f*; *see* **treasury**.

bend 1. tournant *m*; ☉ *pipe*: coude *m*; **2.** (se) courber; *v/i.* tourner (*road*); *v/t.* plier; fléchir; baisser (*one's head*); tendre (*a spring*); appliquer (*one's mind*).

beneath *see* **below.**

benediction bénédiction *f*.

bide

benefact|ion bienfait *m*; don *m*, donation *f*; **~or** bienfaiteur *m*; **~ress** bienfaitrice *f*.

benefic|ence bienfaisance *f*; **~ent** bienfaisant; salutaire; **~ial** avantageux, salutaire.

benefit 1. avantage *m*, profit *m*; *thea.* représentation *f* au bénéfice (de *q.*); *unemployment, sickness, etc.*: indemnité *f*; **for the ~ of** au bénéfice de; **2.** *v/t.* faire du bien à, profiter à; être avantageux à; *v/i.* profiter (de *by*, *from*).

benevolen|ce bienveillance *f*, bonté *f*; **~t** (envers, *to*) bienveillant; charitable; **~ society** association *f* de bienfaisance.

benign bénin (*a.* 🏥); doux.

bent 1. penchant *m*, disposition *f*; **2.** *sl.* malhonnête, véreux; **be ~ on** (*ger.*) vouloir absolument (*inf.*).

bequeath léguer.

bequest 🏛 legs *m*.

berate réprimander.

bereave priver; **~d** afflige; **the ~** la famille du disparu.

berry 🌿 baie *f*.

berth 1. ⚓ mouillage *m*; couchette *f*; *fig.* emploi *m*; **give s.o. a wide ~** éviter q.; **2.** *v/t* accoster (*a ship*) le long du quai; *v/i.* ⚓ mouiller.

beseech supplier, implorer.

beset assaillir; **~ with** *a.* entouré de, pressé de; **~ting sin** grand défaut.

beside 1. *adv. see* **besides 1**; **2.** *prp.* à côté de; **~ o.s.** hors de soi; **~ the question** en dehors du sujet; **~s 1.** *adv.* en plus, d'ailleurs; **2.** *prp.* sans compter; excepté.

besiege assiéger; *fig. a.* assaillir, harceler.

besmear barbouiller.

bespatter éclabousser; salir.

bespeak témoigner de; **bespoke: ~ tailor** tailleur *m* à façon.

best 1. *adj.* meilleur; **~ man** garçon *m* d'honneur; **at ~** au mieux; **2.** *adv.* le mieux; **3.** *su.* meilleur *m*; mieux *m*; **all the ~!** bonne chance!; **do one's ~** faire de son mieux, faire tout son possible (pour *inf.*, **to** *inf.*); **for the ~** pour le mieux; **make the ~ of** s'accommoder de.

bestial bestial; **~ity** bestialité *f*.

bestow accorder, conférer (à, **on**).

bet 1. pari *m*; **2.** parier; F **you ~** tu parles, vous parlez!

betake: ~ o.s. to se rendre à.

bethink: ~ o.s. of se rappeler.

betimes de bonne heure.

betoken présager.

betray trahir; **~al** trahison *f*; **~er** traître(sse *f*) *m*.

betroth fiancer; **~al** fiançailles *f/pl.*

better 1. *adj.* meilleur; mieux; **he is ~** il va mieux; **get ~** s'améliorer; **2.** *su.* meilleur *m*; mieux *m*; **~s** *pl.* supérieurs *m/pl.*; **get the ~ of** l'emporter sur (*q.*); rouler (*q.*); surmonter (*un obstacle*), **3.** *adv.* mieux; **so much the ~** tant mieux; **you had ~** vous feriez mieux de vous en aller; **4.** (s')améliorer.

between 1. *prp.* entre; **2.** *adv. a.* **in ~** au milieu; dans l'intervalle; *time:* a. entre-temps.

betwixt *see* **between**; **something ~ and between** quelque chose entre les deux.

bevel oblique.

beverage boisson *f*.

bevy bande *f*, troupe *f*.

bewail pleurer (*qch.*).

beware se méfier (de q., **of s.o.**); **~ of the dog!** chien méchant!

bewilder confondre, ahurir; **~ment** confusion *f*, ahurissement *m*.

bewitch ensorceler, enchanter.

beyond 1. *adv.* au-delà; **2.** *prp.* au-delà de; *fig.* au-dessus de; en dehors de; *fig.* **be ~ s.o.** dépasser q.

bi... bi(s)-; di(s)-; semi ; **~annual** *twice a year*: semestriel; *lasting two years, occurring every two years*: biennal.

bias 1. parti *m* pris; préjugé *m*; penchant *m*; **2.** rendre partial; prévenir (contre, **against**; en faveur de, **towards**).

Bible Bible *f*.

biblical biblique.

bicarbonate 🧪 bicarbonate *m*.

biceps *anat.* biceps *m*.

bicker se chamailler.

bicycle 1. bicyclette *f*; **2.** faire de la bicyclette; aller à bicyclette.

bid 1. commander; dire; *at auction etc.*: faire une offre *or* enchère de; *fig.* **~ fair** promettre (de *inf.*, **to** *inf.*); s'annoncer; **~ farewell** faire ses adieux à; **~ welcome** souhaiter la bienvenue à; **2.** offre *f*, mise *f*, enchère *f*; **a ~ to** (*inf.*) un effort pour (*inf.*).

bide: ~ one's time attendre le bon moment.

B

biennial biennal.

bier civière (*for a coffin*).

big grand; gros; ~ **business** grosses affaires *f/pl.*; F *fig.* ~ **shot** personnage *m* important, F grosse légume *f*; *sl.* **hit** (*or* **make**) **the** ~ **time** réussir, arriver; **talk** ~ faire l'important; fanfaronner.

bigamy bigamie *f*.

bigmouth F gueulard(e *f*) *m*.

bigness grandeur *f*; grosseur *f*.

bigot fanatique *mf*; sectaire *mf*; **~ed** fanatique, sectaire; **~ry** fanatisme *m*.

big-time *sl.* de première ordre; important, gros.

bigwig F grosse légume *f*.

bike F vélo *m*.

bilateral bilatéral.

bile bile *f* (*fig. anger*).

bilious bilieux; *fig.* irritable.

bill¹ *bird, anchor, geog.*: bec *m*.

bill² **1.** note *f*, facture *f*; *restaurant*: addition *f*; **†** effet *m*; ~ **of exchange** traite *f*; *Am.* billet *m* (de banque); *parl.* projet *m* de loi; ~ **of fare** carte *f* du jour; ~ **of lading** connaissement *m*; **2.** facturer (*goods*); afficher; **~board** panneau *m* d'affichage; **~fold** porte-billets *m/inv.*

billiards *sg. or pl.* billard *m*.

billion *Am.* milliard *m*; *Br.* billion *m*.

billow 1. lame *f*, vague *f*; *fig.* flot *m*; **2.** se soulever (en vagues); ondoyer; se gonfler; **~y** houleux.

billy *Am. police:* bâton *m*; ~ **goat** bouc *m*.

bin boîte *f*; coffre *m*; (*dust* ~) poubelle *f*.

binary binaire.

bind *v/i.* lier, attacher; (res)serrer; relier (*books*); fixer (*a ski*); obliger, engager; *v/i.* se lier; durcir; **~er** lieur (-euse *f*) *m*; *machine:* lieuse *f*; *agent:* liant *m*; **~ing 1.** obligatoire (pour, **on**); **2.** *livres:* reliure *f*; *ski:* fixation *f*.

binocular jumelles *f/pl.*

bio... bio...; **~chemistry** biochemie *f*; **~graphic(al)** biographique; **~graphy** biographie; **~logic(al)** biologique; **~logist** biologue *mf*; **~logy** biologie *f*.

birch ❦ (*or* **~tree**) bouleau *m*.

bird oiseau *m*; *sl.* nana *f* (= *girl*); F *that's* (*strictly*) *for the* ~s ça ne vaut rien; *kill two* ~s *with one stone* faire d'une pierre deux coups; ~**'s-eye view** vue *f* à vol d'oiseau; *fig.* vue d'ensemble.

birth naissance *f*; ~ **certificate** acte *m* de

naissance; ~ **control** limitation *f* des naissances; **bring to** ~ faire naître; **come to** ~ naître, prendre naissance; **~day** anniversaire *m*; **~place** lieu *m* de naissance; **~rate** natalité *f*.

biscuit biscuit *m* (*a. porcelaine*).

bishop évêque *m*; *chess:* fou *m*; **~ric** évêché *m*.

bissextile: ~ **year** = année *f* bissextile.

bit morceau *m*; bout *m*; *money:* pièce *f*; *horse:* mors *m*; ⚙ mèche *f*; *computer:* bit *m*; *a* ~ (+ *adj.*) un peu; *a* ~ *of* un peu de (*qch.*).

bitch chienne *f*; *sl.* garce *f*.

bite 1. mordre (*a. acid, tool, anchor, fish, etc.*); piquer (*insect, pepper*); ronger (*corrosion*); **2.** coup *m* de dent; morsure *f*; *insect:* piqûre *f*; *fish:* touche *f*; *food:* bouchée *f*.

biting mordant; perçant (*cold*).

bitter 1. amer; aigre; glacial (*wind*); **to the** ~ **end** jusqu'au bout; **2.** bière *f* (amère); **~ness** amertume *f*; goût *m* amer; **~sweet** aigre-doux.

biz F affaire *f*, -s *f/pl*.

blab F *v/i.* jaser, bavarder; *v/t.* (*a.* ~ **out**) aller raconter, laisser échapper (*a secret*).

black 1. noir; *fig.* sombre; ~ **eye** œil *m* poché; ~ **ice** verglas *m*; ~ **market** marché *m* noir; **2.** noircir; cirer (*shoes*); F pocher (*s.o.'s eye*); ~ **out** *v/t.* obscurcir; *v/i.* s'évanouir; **3.** noir *m*; noir(e *f*) *m* (*negro*); **~berry** ❦ mûre *f* (sauvage); **~bird** merle *m*; **~board** tableau *m* noir; **~en** *v/t.* noircir (*a. fig.*); *fig.* calomnier; *v/i.* (se) noircir; s'assombrir; **~guard 1.** vaurien *m*; ignoble personnage *m*; **2.** ignoble, canaille; **~head** ⚕ comédon *m*; **~ing** cirage *m*; **~ish** noirâtre; **~jack 1.** *surt. Am.* assommoir *m*; **2.** donner un coup d'assommoir à (*q.*); **~leg** briseur *m* de grève, jaune *m*; **~list 1.** liste noire; **2.** mettre sur la liste noire; **~letter** *typ.* caractères *m/pl.* gothiques; **~mail 1.** chantage *m*; **2.** faire chanter (*q.*); **~ness** noirceur *f*; obscurité *f*; **~out** ⚡ panne *f* d'électricité; ⚕ trou *m* de mémoire; ⚕ évanouissement *m*; **~smith** forgeron *m*.

bladder *anat., a. foot.* vessie *f*.

blade *grass:* brin *m*; *knife, saw, sword:* lame *f*; *oar:* plat *m*; *f propeller:* ailette *f*; *blower:* vanne *f*.

blame 1. reproches *m/pl.*; blâme *m*; faute *f*; **2.** blâmer; **~ s.o. for s.th.** reprocher qch. à q.; **~ s.o. for** (*ger.*) reprocher à q. de (*inf.*); **he is to ~ for** il est responsable de; **~ful** blâmable; **~less** innocent; irréprochable.

blanch blanchir; pâlir.

blank 1. blanc; vierge (*page*); sans expression, étonné (*look*); ✝ en blanc (*credit, cheque*); *fig.* **give s.o. a ~ cheque** (*Am.* **check**) donner carte blanche à q. (pour faire, **to do**); **2.** blanc *m*; vide *m*; lacune *f* (*memory*): trou *m*; *lottery*: billet *m* blanc; ✗ (*a.* **~ cartridge**) cartouche *f* à blanc; F *fig.* **draw a ~** n'arriver à rien.

blanket 1. couverture *f*; F *snow, smoke*: manteau *m*; *fig.* **wet ~** trouble-fête *m/ inv*; rabat-joie *m/inv.*; **2.** couvrir; envelopper; F supprimer; **3.** général, d'une portée générale.

blare beugler.

blarney F baratin *m*.

blasphem|e: ~ (*against*) blasphémer contre; **~er** blasphémateur (-trice *f*) *m*; **~ous** blasphématoire (*words etc.*); blasphémateur (*person*); **~y** blasphème *m*.

blast 1. *wind*: rafale *f*; *wind, explosion*: souffle *m*; *trumpet*: sonnerie *f*; explosion *f*; (**at**) **full ~** à plein volume; **2.** faire sauter; *fig.* ruiner; **~ furnace** ⚙ haut fourneau *m*; **~-off** *rocket*: lancement *m*.

blatant flagrant; criant (*injustice*)

blather F déconner.

blaze 1. flamme *f*; feu *m*, incendie *f*; **~s** *pl.* F enfer *m*; **2.** *v/i.* flamber; flamboyer (*sun, colours*); étinceler; *v/t.* **~ a trail** montrer la voie, faire œuvre de pionnier.

blazon blason *m*; armoiries *f/pl.*

bleach 1. blanchir; oxygéner (*hair*); **2.** eau *f* de Javel; **~er** blanchisseur (-euse *f*) *m*; **~ers** *Am. pl.* places *f/pl.* découvertes d'un terrain de base-ball.

bleak morne; désolé.

bleary trouble, chassieux (*eyes*); **~eyed** aux yeux troubles.

bleat 1. bêlement *m*; **2.** bêler.

bleed saigner; **~ing** 🩸 saignée *f*.

blemish 1. défaut *m*; *fig.* tache *f*; tacher; gâter.

blench sourciller; pâlir.

blend 1. (se) mélanger; *v/t.* couper (*wine etc.*); **2.** mélange *m*.

bless bénir; **~ s.o. with** accorder à q. le bonheur de; F **~ me!**, **my soul!** tiens!; **~ed** bien-heureux; saint; heureux (*event*); *sl.* fichu; **~ing** bénédiction *f*; *fig.* bienfait *m*.

blether *see* **blather**.

blind 1. aveugle (*a. fig. anger, passion, etc.*); faux (*door*); sans visibilité (*corner, flying, etc.*); **be ~ to** ne pas voir (*qch.*); **~ alley** impasse *f* (*a. fig.*); **~ spot** *anat.* point *m* aveugle; *mot. etc.* angle *m* mort; **2.** store *m*, jalousie *f*, F masque *m*, prétexte *m*; **the ~** *pl.* les aveugles *m/pl.*; **3.** aveugler (*sun, to*); *fig.* éblouir; **~fold 1.** aveuglément; **2.** bander les yeux (à *or* se q., *s.o.*); **~ness** cécité *f*; *fig.* aveuglement *m*.

blink 1. clignotement *m*; lueur *f*; F *fig.* **on the ~** detraqué; **2.** clignoter (*light, eyes*); (*a.* **~ one's eyes**) cligner des yeux; **~ers** *pl.* *horse*: œillères *f/pl.* (*a. fig.*).

bliss félicité *f*, béatitude *f*.

blister 1. ampoule *f*; *peint., skin*: cloque *f*; **2.** (se) couvrir d'ampoules; (se) cloquer (*painting*)

blitz bombardement *m* aérien.

blizzard tempête *f* de neige.

bloat gonfler; boursoufler; bouffir; saurer (*herrings*).

block 1. *marble, metal, paper, etc.*: bloc *m*; *houses*: pâté *m*; obstruction *f*; embouteillage *m*; **2.** (*a.* **~ up**) bloquer.

blockade 1. blocus *m*; **2.** bloquer; faire le blocus de.

block...: ~head imbécile *m/f*, sot(te *f*) *m*; **~ letter** *typ.* caractère *m* gras.

blond(e 1. blond; **2.** blond(e *f*) *m*.

blood sang *m* (*a. fig.; a. descent*): race *f*; **in cold ~** de sang-froid; **~ donor** donneur (-euse *f*) *m* de sang; **~ group** groupe *m* sanguin; **~ poisoning** empoisonnement *m* du sang; **~ pressure** tension *f* (artérielle); **~ sample** prélèvement *m* de sang; **~ transfusion** transfusion *f* de sang; **~curdling** à faire frémir; **~shed** carnage *m*; **~shot** éraillé (*eye*); **~thirsty** avide de sang; **~vessel** vaisseau *m* sanguin; **~y 1.** ensanglanté; sanguinaire; *sl.* sacré; **2.** *sl.* vachement; **~yminded** *sl.* mauvais coucheur, obstiné.

bloom 1. fleur *f* (*a. fig.*); épanouissement

B

m; duvet (of peaches etc.); **2.** fleurir (a. fig.), être en fleur; **~ing** fleurissant; F sacré, fichu; **~er** F gaffe f.

blossom 1. fleur f (esp. on trees); **2.** fleurir.

blot 1. tache f; **2.** v/t. tacher; sécher; (usu. **~ out**) effacer (a. fig.); fig. cacher, masquer.

blotch tache f (a. on the skin); **~y** couvert de taches.

blott|er buvard m; Am. registre m d'arrestations etc.; **~ing-paper** papier m buvard.

blouse blouse f; ✕ Am. vareuse f.

blow¹ coup m (de poing, de bâton, etc.).

blow² v/i. souffler; **~ over** s'apaiser, passer; **~ up** éclater; se mettre en colère; v/t. souffler (a. glass); wind: pousser; sonner (a wind-instrument); ⚡ faire sauter (a fuse); sl. manger (one's money); **~ one's nose** se moucher; F **~ one's top** sortir de ses gonds; **~ up** faire sauter; gonfler (a tyre); agrandir (a photo etc.); fig. exagérer, faire toute une affaire de; F (scold) engueuler (q.); **2.** coup m de vent, bourrasque f; **~er** souffleur (-euse f) m; ◎ ventilateur m; sl. téléphone m; **~lamp** ◎ chalumeau m; **~out** mot. éclatement m (of tyres); sl. gueuleton m; **~torch** ◎ chalumeau m; **~up** explosion f; phot. agrandissement m; F accès m de colère; sl. engueulade f.

bludgeon matraque f.

blue bleu (a. su.); triste, cafardeux; obscène, porno; **out of the ~** à l'improviste, sans crier gare; **~berry** myrtille f, airelle f; **~print** dessin m négatif; fig. projet m; **~s** pl. a. sg. humeur f noire, cafard m; ♪ blues m.

bluff bluff m; geog. cap m à pic; falaise f; **2.** bluffer; **3.** brusque.

bluish bleuâtre; bleuté.

blunder 1. bévue f, gaffe f, faux pas m; **2.** faire une bévue etc.

blunt 1. émoussé (knife, edge, etc.); épointé (pencil); obtus (angle); fig. brusque; **2.** émousser; épointer; **~ly** brusquement, carrément.

blur 1. masse f or tache f or apparence f confuse; **2.** v/t. barbouiller; brouiller.

blush 1. rougeur f; **2.** rougir (de for, with, at); **~ to** (inf.) avoir honte de (inf.).

bluster 1. storm: hurlement m; talk: fan-

faronnades f/pl.; **2.** souffler en rafales (wind); fig. faire le fanfaron.

boar sanglier m.

board 1. planche f; panneau m, tableau m (for posting notices etc.); carton m; ⚓ bord m; pension f; commission f, comité m, conseil m; ✝ (a. **~ of directors**) conseil m d'administration; **~ and lodging** chambre f avec pension; Br. ♔ **of Trade** ministère m du Commerce; Am. **~ of trade** chambre f de commerce; fig. **above ~** dans les règles, régulier; **on a ~ a ship** (a train etc.) à bord d'un navire (dans un train etc.); **2.** v/t. planchéir; cartonner (a book); (a. **~ out**) mettre en pension; aller à bord de; monter (en, dans); v/i. être en pension (chez, **with**); **~er** pensionnaire mf; school: interne mf.

boarding...: ~house pension f de famille; **~ school** internat m.

boast 1. se vanter (de, **of**); être fier de posséder; **2.** fanfaronnade; (sujet m de) fierté f (or d')orgueil m; **~er** vantard(e f) m; **~ful** vantard.

boat 1. bateau m; canot m; **2.** aller en bateau; faire du canotage; **~ing** canotage m; **~ race** régate f.

bob 1. fishing line: bouchon m; queue f écourtée; petite révérence f; **2.** v/t. couper (one's hair); s'agiter, se balancer; faire une petite révérence; **~ up** surgir (tout d'un coup).

bobbin bobine f (a. ⚡).

bobble cost. pompon m.

bobby Brit. sl. agent m de police.

bob|sled, ~sleigh bobsleigh m.

bode: ~ well (ill) être de bon (mauvais) augure.

bodice corsage m; child: brassière f.

bodily corporel (a. ⚖ harm).

body corps m (a. ◎, △); people: masse f; (a. **dead ~**) cadavre m; ✈ fuselage m; mot. (a. **~work**) carrosserie f; **~guard** garde f du corps.

bog 1. marécage m; **2.** (s')embourber; **get ~ged** (down) s'enliser.

boggle rechigner (devant **at**, **over**; à inf. **at**, **about** ger.).

bogus faux, bidon.

boil 1. v/i bouillir (a. fig.); **~ down** se réduire; fig. **~ down to** revenir à; v/t. faire bouillir; cuire à l'eau; **~ed egg** œuf m à la coque; **2.** ébullition f; furoncle *m*; ~er chaudière *f*; ~ suit bleu *m* (de travail).

boisterous tapageur.

bold hardi, courageux; assuré; escarpé; *pej.* effronté; *typ.* gras; ~face *typ.* charactères *m/pl.* gras; ~ness hardiesse *f etc.; pej.* effronterie *f*.

bolster 1. traversin *m*; ⚙ matrice *f*; coussinet *m*; **2.** (*usu.* ~ up) soutenir.

bolt 1. *door:* verrou *m*; *lock:* pêne *m*; ⚙ boulon *m*; *fig., a. poet.* coup *m* de foudre; **2.** *v/t.* verrouiller; F gober; *Am. pol.* abandonner (*one's party, q.*); *v/i.* F filer (à toute vitesse).

bomb 1. bombe *f*; **2.** bombarder, ~ard rbombarder (*a. fig.*).

bombastic enflé, ampoulé (*style*).

bomber ✈ bombardier *m*.

bomb-proof à l'épreuve des bombes; blindé (*shelter*).

bona fide de bonne foi (*a. adv.*); sérieux (*offer etc.*).

bond lien *m* (*a. fig.*); engagement *m*, *a.* ✝ obligation *f*; ✝ bon *m*; titre *m*; ⚙ joint *m*; ✝ in ~ entrepôse; ~age esclavage *m*; ~(s)man *hist.* serf *m*.

bone 1. os *m*; *fish:* arête *f*; ~ of contention pomme *f* de discorde; *frozen to the* ~ glacé jusqu'à la moelle; F make no ~s about (*ger.*) ne pas se gêner pour (*inf.*), **2.** désosser (*les arêtes de*); F (*a.* ~ up) potasser; ~idle, ~lazy paresseux comme une couleuvre.

bonfire feu *m* de joie; feu *m* (de jardin), F conflagration *f*.

bonnet bonnet *m*; *Br mot.* capot *m*.

bonus ✝ prime *f*.

bony osseux; anguleux.

boob nigaud(e *f*) *m*.

book 1. livre *m*; registre *m*; *tickets etc.:* carnet *m*; cahier *m*; **2.** *v/t.* inscrire; prendre (*a ticket*), retenir, réserver (*a room etc.*), louer (*a seat*); enregistrer; ~ed up complet (*hotel etc.*); *fig.* (complètement) pris (*person*); *v/i.* prendre un billet; *hotel etc.:* ~ in prendre une chambre; arriver; ~binder relieur (-euse *f*) *m*; ~case bibliothèque *f*; ~ing clerk employé (-e *f*) *m* du guichet; ~ing office 🎦, *thea.* guichet *m*; guichets *m/pl.*; ~ish studieux; livresque (*style*); ~keeper comptable *m*, teneur *m* de livres; ~keeping tenue *f* des livres; comptabilité *f*; ~let livret *m*; ~seller libraire *m*.

boom[1] ✝ hausse *f* rapide, boom *m*; vogue *f*; **2.** être en hausse; prospérer, aller très fort (*trade*).

boom[2] **1.** gronder, bourdonner; **2.** grondement *m*, bourdonnement *m*.

boon avantage *m*, bienfait *m*.

boor *fig.* rustre *m*; ~ish rustre, grossier; ~ishness grossièreté *f*.

boost stimuler; faire de la réclame pour; ⚡ survolter; ~er ⚙ *etc.* booster *m*; ⚕ (*a.* ~ shot*) rappel *m*.

boot[1]: *to* ~ par-dessus le marché, de plus.

boot[2] botte *f*; chaussure *f*; *Br. mot.* coffre *m*; F get the ~ se faire flanquer à la porte; Γ give s.o. the ~ flanquer q. à la porte.

booth baraque *f*; stand *m* de foire.

boot...: ~lace lacet *m*; ~legger contrebandier *m* de boissons alcooliques.

booty butin *m*.

border 1. bordure *f*, bord *m*; *wood:* lisière *f*; *country:* frontière *f*; **2.** *v/t.* border; encadrer; avoisiner; *v/i.: fig.* ~(up)on frôler, être voisin de.

bore[1] *gun etc.:* calibre *m*; (~hole) perçage *m*, trou *m*; **2.** percer; creuser.

bore[2] **1.** ennuyer, Γ raser, assommer; **2.** raseur (-euse *f*) *m*; casse-pieds *mf/inv.* (*person*), ennui *m* (*thing*); ~dom ennui *m*.

borough bourg *m*; municipalité *f*; *Am. a.* quartier *m* de New York City.

borrow emprunter (à, *from*).

bosom sein *m*, giron *m*; poitrine *f*; ~ friend ami(e *f*) *m* intime, intime *mf*.

boss 1. patron *m*; **2.** commander; mener, régenter.

botany botanique *f*.

botch 1. F travail *m* mal fait; travail *m* bousillé; **2.** bousiller, saboter.

both tous (les) deux; l'un et l'autre; ~ ... and ... et ...; ~ of them tous (les) deux.

bother F **1.** ennui *m*; tracas *m*; **2.** *v/t.* gêner; importuner; tracasser; *v/i.* s'inquiéter (de, *about*).

bottle 1. bouteille *f*; **2.** mettre en bouteille(s); *fig.* ~ up embouteiller; refouler (*emotions*); ~neck *road etc.:* rétrécissement *m*, étranglement *m*; *fig.* goulet *m* d'étranglement; ~opener ouvre-bouteilles *m/inv.*

bottom 1. *mountain, staircase, page:* bas *m*; *box, barrel, ship, sea, etc. a. fig.* fond

B

m; chair: siège *m; glass, plate*: dessous *m; geogr.* creux *m;* F derrière *m;* **at the ~** (**of**) au fond (de); au bas bout (de); **2.** inférieur; (d')en bas; du bas; dernier; fondamental; **~less** sans fond; *fig.* insondable.

bough branche *f,* rameau *m.*

boulder bloc *m* de pierre, rocher.

bounc|e 1. bond *m;* rebondissement *m;* **2.** rebondir; F **~** être refusé (*cheque*); **~er** *sl. nightclub:* videur *m;* **~ing** F plein de vie.

bound¹ 1. limite *f,* borne *f;* **out of ~s** accès interdit (à, **to**); **2.** borner, limiter.

bound² 1. bond *m,* saut *m;* **2.** bondir, sauter; *fig.* sursauter.

bound³: **~ for ...,** **~..~** à destination de ..., en route *or* partance pour; **be ~ to** (*inf.*) être obligé de (*inf.*), devoir (*inf.*); **be ~ to happen** arriver inévitablement; **~ up** pris; **~ up with** lié à.

boundary limite *f,* frontière *f.*

boundless sans bornes; illimité.

bount|eous, ~iful généreux; libéral; **~y** générosité *f;* prime *f.*

bouquet *flowers, wine:* bouquet *m.*

bout *✝, fig.* accès; *fig.* (courte) période *f; boxing:* match *m.*

bow¹ 1. révérence *f,* inclination *f* de tête; **2.** *v/i.* s'incliner (devant, **to**); faire une révérence; *v/t.* plier; courber.

bow² ⚓ avant *m.*

bow³ *sp.* arc *m; ribbon:* nœud *m; ♪* archet *m; cost.* **~ tie** (neud *m*) papillon *m.*

bowdlerize expurger (*a text*).

bowels *pl.* intestins *m/pl.;* entrailles *f/pl.* (*a. fig.*).

bower tonnelle *f.*

bowl ¹ bol *m,* jatte *f;* cuvette *f;* coupe *f; pipe:* fourneau *m.*

bowl² 1. boule *f;* **~s** *pl.* (jeu *m* de) boules *f/pl.; Am.* (jeu *m* de) quilles *f/pl.;* **2.** faire rouler; **~ along** rouler (bon train) **~ over** renverser.

bow-legged aux jambes arquées, bancal.

bowl|er (*a.* **~ hat** chapeau *m*) melon *m.*

bowling *sp.* bowling *m; Br. a.* jeu *m* de boules; **~ alley** bowling *m.*

box¹ 1. boîte *f; hats:* carton *m; mot.* carter *m; thea.* loge *f;* ⚖ barre *f (for the witnesses); stable:* stalle *f; thea.* **~ office** bureau *m* de location; *window:* guichet *m;* **2.** emboîter; mettre en boîte.

box² boxer; **~ s.o.'s ear** gifler q.; **~er** *sp.* boxeur *m;* **~ing** *sp.* boxe *f;* **~ gloves** gants *m/pl.* de boxe; **~ match** match *m* de boxe; **~ ring** ring *m.*

Boxing-day jour *m* des étrennes.

boy garçon *m.*

boycott 1. boycotter; **2.** boycottage *m.*

boy ...: **~friend** (petit) ami *n;* **~hood** enfance *f,* adolescence *f;* **~ish** puéril, de garçon.

brace 1. ⚙ attache *f;* △ support *m,* étrésillon *m; ⚕* appareil (dentaire) *m; ♪ typ.* accolade *f; hunt.* couple *f;* ⚙ **~ (and bit)** vilebrequin *m; Br.* **~s** *pl.* pantalon: bretelles *f/pl.;* **2.** attacher; fortifier, soutenir.

bracelet bracelet *m.*

bracket 1. console *f;* support *m; typ.* [] crochet *m;* ( ) parenthèse *f;* ≈ accolade *f; ⚡, gas:* applique *f;* **2.** mettre entre crochets *etc.*

brackish saumâtre.

brag 1. vanterie *f;* **2.** se vanter (de **of,** **about**); **~gart** fanfaron *m.*

braid 1. *hair:* tresse *f;* galon *m* (*a.* ✖); **2.** tresser; galonner.

brain *anat.* cerveau *m;* F cervelle *f* (*a. cuis*); *usu.* **~s** *pl.* intelligence; **~less** stupide; *fig.* irréfléchi; **~child** F idée *f,* invention *f;* **~wash** faire (subir) un lavage de cerveau à (*q.*); **~washing** lavage *m* de cerveau; *media etc.:* bourrage *m* de crâne; **~wave** F idée *f* lumineuse; **~work** travail *m* cérébral.

brake 1. frein *m;* **~ fluid** liquide *m* pour freins; **~ pedal** pédale *f* de frein; **2.** freiner; **braking distance** (**power**) distance *f* (puissance *f*) de freinage.

bramble ⚘ ronce *f* sauvage.

bran son *m.*

branch 1. branche *f;* ✝ (*a.* **local ~**) succursale *f;* **2.** (*a.* **~ out**) se ramifier; (*a.* **~ off**) (se) bifurquer (sur, **from**).

brand 1. ✝, *fig.* marque *f;* ✝ **~ name** marque *f* (de fabrique); **2.** marquer; *fig.* stigmatiser.

brandish brandir.

bran(d)-new tout (battant) neuf.

brandy cognac *m,* eau-de-vie *f.*

brash effronté.

brass cuivre *m* jaune; laiton *m;* F (*impertinence*) culot *m;* F argent *m;* **~ band** fanfare *f; Am.* **~ knuckles** *pl.* coup-de--poing (*pl.* coups-de-poing) *m* américain.

bring

brassière soutien-gorge (*pl.* soutiens-gorge) *m.*

brav|ado bravade *f*; **~e 1.** courageux, brave; **2.** braver; défier (*q.*); **~ery** bravoure *f*.

brawl 1. rixe *f*, bagarre *f*, querelle *f*; **2.** se bagarrer.

brawn muscle(s *pl.*) *m*; *cuis.* fromage *m* de tête; **~y** musculeux; musclé (*person*).

bray 1. braiment *m*; **2.** braire.

brazen 1. d'airain; *fig.* effronté; **2. ~ it out** crâner.

breach 1. rupture *f*; *fig.* infraction *f* (à, **of**); ✕ brèche *f*; **2.** *v/t.* ouvrir une brèche dans; *v/i.* se rompre.

bread pain *m* (*a. subsistence*) *m*; (= *money*); **~ and butter** tartines *f/pl.* (beurrées); *fig.* gagne pain *m*, subsistance *f*.

breadth largeur *f* (*a. fig. of mind*); *style:* ampleur *f*; *cloth:* lé *m*.

break 1. rupture *f*; fracture *f*; brèche *f*; lacune *f*; arrêt *m*, pause *f*, *school:* récréation *f*; chance *f*; **2.** *v/t.* briser, casser; rompre; enfoncer; résilier (*a contract*); faire sauter (*a bank*); s'évader de (*prison*); violer (*a law, the truce*); **~ down** démolir; *fig.* dresser (*a horse*); rompre (à, **to**); **~ up** mettre (*qch.*) en morceaux; disperser (*a crowd*); démolir; **3.** *v/i.* (*se*) casser, se briser, se rompre; déferler (*waves*); se dissiper (*clouds*); tourner (*weather*); s'altérer (*voice*); **~ away** se détacher (de, **from**); **~ down** s'effondrer; *mot.* ⊕ tomber en panne; ✚ faire une dépression nerveuse; **~ up** se briser; prendre fin; se séparer; **~able** fragile; **~age** rupture *f*; *glass:* casse *f*; **~down** rupture *f*; arrêt *m* complet; ✚ dépression *f* nerveuse; *mot.* panne *f*; **~ lorry**, **~ truck** dépanneuse *f*; **~fast 1.** petit déjeuner *m*; **2.** déjeuner; **~through** percée *f*; **~up** dissolution *f*, rupture *f*; **~water** brise-lames *m/inv.*

breast sein *m*; poitrine *f*; *make a clean ~ of it* dire ce qu'on a sur la conscience; **~feed** élever au sein; **~stroke** brasse *f*.

breath haleine *f*, souffle *m*; **~alyser** *mot.* alcootest *m*; **~e** *vt/i.* respirer; *v/t. a.* pousser (*a sigh*); murmurer (*words*); **~less** essoufflé; **~taking** stupéfiant, ahurissant.

breeches *pl.* culotte *f*.

breed 1. race *f*; espèce *f*; **2.** *v/t.* engendrer; *zo.* élever; *v/i.* se reproduire; se multiplier; **~er** éleveur *m*; **~ing** reproduction *f*; *zo.* élevage *m*; bonnes manières *f/pl.*

breez|e 1. brise *f*; **2.** F **~ in** (**out**) entrer (sortir) d'un air désinvolte; **~y** venteux; léger; désinvolte; jovial (*person*).

brethren *pl.* frères *m/pl.*

brevity brièveté *f*.

brew 1. brasser; *fig.* (se) tramer; *v/i.* infuser (*tea*); couver (*thunderstorm*); **2.** brassage *m*; **~ery** brasserie *f*.

bribe 1. pot-de-vin *m*; **2.** acheter (*q.*); soudoyer; **~ry** corruption *f*.

brick 1. brique *f*; *sl.* **drop a ~** faire une gaffe; **2.** briqueter; **~ up** murer; **~layer** maçon *m*; **~works** *usu. sg.* briqueterie *f*.

bridal nuptial, de noce(s).

bride (nouvelle) mariée *f*; **~groom** (nouveau) marié *m*; **~smaid** demoiselle *f* d'honneur; **~to-be** future fiancée *f* or épouse *f*.

bridge 1. pont *m*; ♟ passerelle *f*; **2.** jeter un pont sur; *fig.* relier; *fig.* **~ the gap** faire la soudure.

bridle 1. bride *f*; *fig.* frein *m*; **2.** *v/t.* brider (*a. fig.*); *fig.* refréner; *v/i.* (*a.* **~ up**) redresser la tête; **~path** piste *f* cavalière.

brief 1. bref; court; passager; **2.** ⚖ dossier *m*; **hold a ~ for** défendre; *cost.* **~s** *pl.* slip *m*; **3.** donner des instructions à (*q.*); mettre (*q.*) au courant; **~case** serviette *f*, porte-documents *m/inv.*; **~ing** instructions *f/pl.*; séance *f* d'information.

brier ⚘ bruyère *f* arborescente.

brigade ✕ brigade *f*.

bright brillant; éclatant; vif; clair; animé; F intelligent; **~en** *v/t.* faire briller; éclairer; *fig.* égayer; *v/i.* s'éclaircir; *eyes:* s'animer; *fig.* s'animer; **~ness** éclat *m*; clarté *f*; vivacité *f*; intelligence *f*.

brillian|cy brillant *m*; éclat *m*; **~t** brillant, éclatant; lumineux (*idea*).

brim 1. bord *m*; **2.** **~ over** déborder (de, **with**); **~ful(l)** débordant (de, **of**).

brimstone soufre *m*.

brine saumure *f*; eau *f* salée.

bring amener; apporter; intenter (*a legal action*); avancer (*arguments*); **~ about** provoquer, causer; amener; **~ down** abattre; faire tomber; faire baisser

B

(*prices*); **~ forth** produire; enfanter; mettre bas (*young*); **~ s.th. home to s.o.** faire sentir qch. à q.; **~ off** réussir; **~ out** faire ressortir; **~ round** ramener à la vie; **~ under** assujettir; **~ up** approcher; élever (*a child*).

brink bord *m*.

brisk vif, alerte, animé.

bristl|e 1. soie *f*; *beard:* poil *m*; **2.** (*oft.* **~ up**) se hérisser; *fig.* **~ with** être hérissé de; **~ed**, **~y** hérissé; poilu.

British 1. britannique; **2. the ~** *pl.* les Britanniques *m/pl.*; **~er** natif (-ive *f*) *m* de la Grande-Bretagne.

Briton Britannique *mf*.

brittle fragile, cassant.

broach percer, entamer (*a cask*); *fig.* aborder (*a subject*).

broad large; plein, grand (*day*); peu voilé (*view, allusion*); épanoui (*smile*); **~ly speaking** généralement parlant; **~cast** *v/t.* radiodiffuser; téléviser; transmettre; répandre; *v/i.* émettre; parler *etc.* à la radio; **~(ing) station** station *f* de radiodiffusion; **2.** émission *f*; **~minded** tolérant; à l'esprit large; **~ness** largeur *f*; grossièreté *f*.

brocade ♉ brocart *m*.

broil *v/t. cuis.* (faire) cuire sur le gril; *vt/i.* griller (*a. fig.*); **~er** poulet *m* à rôtir.

broke F fauché, à sec; **dead ~** fauché comme les blés.

broken: **~ health** santé *f* délabrée *or* ruinée; **speak ~ English** écorcher l'anglais; **~hearted** qui a le cœur brisé.

broker ♉ courtier *m*; agent *m* de change; **~age** ♉ courtage *m*.

bronchial *anat.* bronchial.

bronze 1. bronze *m*; **2.** de *or* en bronze; **3.** (se) bronzer; (se) hâler.

brooch broche *f*, épingle *f*.

brood 1. couvée *f*; **2.** couver; F broyer du noir, ruminer; **~er** couveuse *f*; **~y** mélancholique.

brook ruisseau *m*.

broom balai *m*; ♉ genêt *m*; **~stick** manche *m* à balai.

broth bouillon *m*.

brothel bordel *m*.

brother frère *m*; **~hood** fraternité *f*; **~-in-law** beau-frère (*pl.* beaux-frères) *m*; **~ly** fraternel.

brow front *m*; *slope:* sommet *m*; (*eye* **~**) sourcil; **knit** (*or* **pucker**) **one's ~s** fron-

cer les sourcils; **~beat** intimider; rudoyer.

brown 1. brun; châtain (*hair*); **2.** brun *m*, marron *m*; **3.** (se) brunir; *cuis.* (faire) dorer.

browse brouter, paître; *fig.* bouquiner; feuilleter.

bruise 1. bleu *m*, meurtrissure *f*; **2.** (se) meurtrir; *v/t.* se faire un bleu à.

brunt choc *m*; attaque *f*; violence *f*; **the ~ of** le plus fort de.

brush 1. brosse *f*; pinceau *m*; *fox:* queue *f*; accrochage *m* (*with an enemy*); broussaille *f/pl.*; **2.** *v/t.* brosser; balayer (*a carpet*); frôler; **~ up** donner un coup de brosse à (*qch.*); *fig.* se remettre à, dérouiller; *v/i.* **~ against** frôler *or* froisser (*q.*) en passant; **~ by** (*or* **past**) passer rapidement auprès de; frôler en passant; **~off** *sl.:* **give s.o. the ~** envoyer promener q.; **~up** coup *m* de brosse; **~wood** broussailles *f/pl.*; menu bois *m*, brindilles *f/pl*.

brusque brusque.

Brussels: ♉ **~ sprouts** *pl.* choux *m/pl.* de Bruxelles.

brut|al brutal; **~ality** brutalité *f*; **~e 1.** bête *f* brute; brute *f* (*a. fig. homme brutal*); **2.** = **~ish** de brute; bestial; brutal.

bubble 1. bulle *f*; **2.** pétiller; faire des bulles, bouillonner.

buccaneer pirate *m*.

buck 1. *zo.* mâle *m*; *Am.* F dollar *m*; ◎ chevalet *m*; **2.** *v/i.* ruer; F **~ up** se remuer; prendre courage; *v/t.* F résister à, opposer; (*a.* **~ off**) jeter, désarçonner; F **~ up** remonter (*q.*).

bucket seau *m*; *sl.* **kick the ~** casser sa pipe.

buckle 1. boucle *f*; **2.** *v/t.* boucler; attacher; ceindre; *vt/i.* ◎ gauchir; (se) voiler (*sheet metal*); **~ to** s'appliquer à (*a task*); *mot.* **~ up** mettre la ceinture.

buck...: **~shot** chevrotine *f*; **~skin** (peau *f* de) daim *m*.

bud 1. ♉ bourgeon *m*; *flower:* bouton *m*; *fig.* germe *m*; *fig.* **in the ~** en germe, en herbe; **2.** bourgeonner; boutonner (*flower*).

buddy *Am.* F ami *m*; copain *m*.

budge *v/i.* bouger; *v/t.* faire bouger.

budgerigar perruche *f*.

budget 1. budget *m*; **2.** budgétaire; bon

marché, économique; **3.** (*a.* ~ *for*) budgétiser.

buff 1. (peau *f* de) buffle *m*; (couleur *f*) chamois *m*; F fana *fm* (de), mordu(e *f*) *m* (de); **2.** (couleur) chamois.

buffalo, *pl.* -**loes** *zo.* buffle *m*; *Am.* bison *m*.

buffer 🏛 tampon *m*; (*a.* ~ *stop*) butoir *m*; ~ *state* état *m* tampon.

buffet¹ 1. frapper; secouer, ballotter; **2.** coup *m*.

buffet² buffet *m*.

buffoon bouffon *m*.

bug 1. punaise *f*; insecte *m*; bacille *m*; F appareil *m* d'écoute, microphone clandestin; **2.** installer des appareils d'écoute dans.

bugger *sl.* pédéraste *m*; con *m*, salaud; bougre *m*, bonhomme *m*.

bugle (*a.* ~ *horn*) clairon *m*.

build 1. construire; bâtir (sur, **on**); ~ *up* (s')accumuler; (se) faire; **2.** *person:* carrure *f*; construction *f*; ~**er** entrepreneur *m* en bâtiments; constructeur *m*; ~**ing** construction *f*; bâtiment *m*; immeuble *m*; édifice *m*; *attr.* de construction; ~ **(p)lot** terrain *m* à bâtir; ~ *site* chantier *m*; ~**up** accumulation *f*, intensification *f*.

built|-in encastré (*cupboard*); *fig.* immanent, intrinsèque; ~**up:** ~ *area* agglomération *f*.

bulb ♀ bulbe *m*, oignon *m*; ⚡ ampoule *f*.

bulge 1. gonflement *m*, bombement *m*; saillie *f*; (*a.* ~ *out*) bomber; faire saillie; être gonflé (de, **with**).

bulk masse *f*, volume *m*; *fig.* gros *m* (*a.* ✝); *la* plus grande partie (de, **of**); *in* ~ en bloc; ~**y** gros; volumineux, encombrant.

bull¹ taureau *m*.

bull² *sl.* connerie(s) *f*/(*pl.*).

bulldog bouledogue *m*.

bulldoze passer au bulldozer; *fig.* forcer; ~**r** ⚙ bulldozer *m*.

bullet *gun, revolver:* balle *f*; ~**proof** blindé, pare-balles.

bulletin bulletin *m*, communiqué *m*; *radio:* informations *f*/*pl.*; *Am.* ~ *board* tableau *m* d'affichage.

bullfight course *f* de taureaux; ~**er** torero *m*; ~**ing** tauromachie *f*.

bullion *or m* en barres; *or m or* agent *m* en lingot.

bully 1. brute *f*, tyran *m*; **2.** brutaliser, rudoyer; intimider.

bulwark *usu. fig.* rempart *m*.

bum F **1.** derrière *m*; vagabond *m*; *be* (*or go*) *on the* ~ = **2.** vagabonder.

bumble bee bourdon *m*.

bump 1. choc *m*; coup *m*; cahot *m*, heurt *m*; bosse *f*; **2.** (se) cogner; (se) heurter; ~ *along* avancer en cahotant; ~ *into* tamponner, rentrer dans; F *fig.* (*meet*) rencontrer (par hasard); *v*/*t.* cogner, heurter; *sl.* ~ *off* descendre (*q.*); ┌ ~ *up* faire monter; ~**er** pare-chocs *m*/*inv.*; *Am.* 🏛 *a.* tampon *m*; ~ *crop* récolte *f* exceptionnelle, ~ *house* *thea.* salle *f* comble.

bun petit pain *m* au lait; *hair:* chignon *m*.

bunch 1. *flowers:* bouquet *m*; *people:* groupe *m*; *keys:* trousseau *m*; *grapes:* grappe *f*; **2.** (se) grouper.

bundle 1. paquet *m*; ballot *m*; *wood:* fagot *m*; **2.** *v*/*t.* fourrer, flanquer (dans, *into*); ~ *off* expédier; ~ *out* flanquer dehors; ~ *up* faire un paquet de, empaqueter; *fig.* emmitoufler (*q.*).

bung 1. bouchon *m*; **2.** F flanquer; *usu.* ~ *up* bouchonner.

bungalow bungalow *m*.

bungle 1. gâchis *m*; maladresse *f*; **2.** bousiller, rater.

bunk¹ couchette *f*; ~ *beds* lits *m*/*pl.* superposés.

bunk² F bêtises *f*/*pl.*

bunny F Jeannot lapin *m*.

buoy ⚓ **1.** bouée *f*; **2.** baliser (*a canal*); (*usu.* ~ *up*) faire flotter; *fig.* appuyer, soutenir; ~**ancy** flottabilité *f*; *fig.* élasticité *f* de caractère, ressort *m*; *fig.* entrain *m*; ~**ant** flottable; *fig.* allègre; *fig.* élastique.

bunting pavoisement *m*.

burden 1. fardeau *m*, charge *f*; **2.** charger; *fig.* accabler; *some* onéreux; fâcheux.

bureau *office:* bureau *m*, *Am.* *a.* service *m* (*of government*); *furniture:* *Br.* secrétaire *m*, *Am.* commode *f*; ~**cracy** bureaucratie *f*; ~**crat** bureaucrate *m*/*f*; ~**cratic** bureaucratique.

burglar cambrioleur *m*; ~ *alarm* sonnerie *f* d'alarme *or* antivol; ~**ize** cambrioler; ~**proof** incrochetable (*lock*); ~**y** cambriolage *m*.

burgle cambrioler.

burial enterrement *m*.

B

burlesque 1. burlesque; **2.** burlesque *m*; parodie *f*; **3.** parodier.

burly costaud, de forte carrure.

burn 1. brûler; **~ down** détruire par le feu; **2.** brûlure *f*; **~er** brûleur *m*; bec *m* de gaz.

burnish polir.

burnt: ~ sugar caramel *m*.

burrow 1. terrier *m*; **2.** *v/t.* creuser; *v/i.* se terrer; *fig.* fouiller.

burst 1. éclat(ement) *m*; explosion *f* (*a. fig.*); *flames:* jaillissement *m*; *fig.* poussée *f* (*of activity*); **2.** *v/i.* éclater, exploser; crever (*abscess, tyre, bubble, etc.*); *fig.* déborder (de, **with**); **~ forth** (*or* **out**) jaillir; s'exclamer; apparaître (*sun*); **~ into tears** fondre en larmes; **~ out laughing** éclater de rire; *v/t.* faire éclater; crever; enfoncer (*a door*).

bury enterrer, ensevelir; inhumer; *fig.* cacher.

bus autobus *m*; **~ stop** arrêt *m* d'autobus.

bush buisson *m*; arbrisseau *m*.

bushel boisseau *m* (*a. measure*).

bushy touffu; broussailleux.

business affaire *f*; besogne *f*; occupation *f*; devoir *m*; affaire *f/pl.* (*a. ✝*); **~ address** adresse *f* du bureau (*de q.*); **~ end** côte *m* opérant (*of a tool*), tranchant *m* (*of a knife*), canon *m* (*of a gun*); **~ hours** *pl.* heures *f/pl.* d'ouverture; **~ quarter** quartier *m* commerçant; **~ research** analyse *f* du marché; **~ tour, ~ trip** voyage *m* d'affaires; **on ~** pour affaires; **get down to ~** en venir au fait; **have no ~ to** (*inf.*) ne pas avoir le droit de (*inf.*); **mind one's own ~** s'occuper de ses affaires; **that's none of your ~** cela ne vous regarde pas; **~like** pratique; sérieux (*manner*); capable; **~man** homme *m* d'affaires.

busman conducteur *m* or receveur *m* d'autobus.

bust¹ buste *m*, gorge *f*, poitrine *f*.

bust² *sl.* **1.** fiasco *m*, four *m* (noir); faillite *f*; coup *m* (violent); bringue *f*, bombe *f*; **2.** casser; (faire) crever; abîmer; arrêter, choper (*a criminal*); **3.** foutu, fichu; abîmé; fauché, à sec; **go ~** faire faillite; s'abîmer.

bustle affairement *m*; remue-ménage *m/inv.*; va-et-vient *m/inv.*; **2.** *v/i.* s'affairer; s'activer; faire l'empressé; *v/t.* faire dépêcher (*q.*); bousculer.

bust-up *sl.* grabuge *f*; engueulade *f*; rupture *f*.

busy 1. occupé (à, de **at, with**); affairé; fréquenté (*quarter, street*); **~ packing** occupé à faire ses malles; **2.** (*usu. ~ o.s.*) s'occuper (à **with, in, about**; à, de *inf.* **with** *ger.*).

but 1. *cj.* mais; or; toutefois; **2.** *prp.* sans; **the last ~ one** l'avant-dernier; **the next ~ one** le (la) deuxième; **~ for** sans; ne fût-ce pour; **3.** *adv.* ne ... que; seulement; **all ~** presque; **nothing ~** rien que; **I cannot ~** (*inf.*) je ne peux m'empêcher de (*inf.*).

butcher 1. boucher *m*; **~('s) shop** boucherie *f*; **2.** tuer; *fig.* massacrer.

butler maître *m* d'hôtel.

butt 1. gros bout *m*; *tree:* souche *f*; *gun:* crosse *f*; *fig.* souffre-douleur *m*; *~:* cible *f* (*of mockery etc.*); F mégot *m*; **2.** *v/t.* donner un coup de corne *or* de tête à.

butter 1. beurre *m*; **2.** beurrer; (*a. ~ up*) F flatter; **~cup** bouton-d'or (*pl.* boutons-d'or) *m*; **~-fingered** maladroit, empoté; **~fly** papillon *m* (*a. fig.*); F **have butterflies in one's stomach** avoir le trac.

buttocks *pl.* fesses *f/pl.*, derrière *m*.

button 1. bouton *m* (*a.* ✿); **2.** (*a. ~ up*) (se) boutonner; *fig.* refermer; **~hole 1.** boutonnière *f*; **2.** retenir, accrocher (*q.*).

buttress contrefort *m*.

buxom dodu, rondelet.

buy *v/t.* acheter (à, **from**); prendre (*a. ticket*); *fig.* payer; offrir (qch à q., **s.o. s.th.**); **~ up** acheter en bloc; **~er** acheteur (-euse *f*) *m*; acquéreur *m*.

buzz 1. bourdonnement *m*; *Am.* **~ saw** scie *f* circulaire; F **give s.o. a ~** donner un coup de fil à q.; **2.** bourdonner.

buzzard *orn.* busard *m*.

by 1. *prp. place:* (au)près de, à côté de; au bord de; *direction:* par; *time:* avant, pour; *means:* par, de; à (*hand, machine, horse, etc.*); en (*car, tram*); *origin:* de; *oath:* au nom de; par (*qch.*); *measure:* sur; selon; **~ side ~ side** côte à côte; **~ day** de jour, le jour; **a play ~ Shaw** une pièce de Shaw; **~ lamplight** à la lumière de la lampe; **~ the dozen** à la douzaine; **~ far** de beaucoup; **5 feet ~ 2** cinq pieds sur deux; **~ land** par terre; **~ rail** par le chemin de fer; **day ~ day** de jour en jour; **2.** *adv.* près; de côté; **~ and ~** tout à l'heure, bientôt, par la suite; **close ~** tout près; **go ~** passer; **~ and large** à tout prendre; **3.** *adj.* latéral.

bye-bye F au revoir!; adieu!

by...: ~election élection *f* partielle; **~gone** passé, d'autrefois; **let ~s be ~s**

passons l'éponge; **~law** arrêté *m* municipal; **~name** sobriquet *m*; **~pass 1.** déviation *f*; détour *m*; **2.** éviter; dévier (*the traffic*); **~product** sous-produit *m*; **~stander** spectateur (-trice *f*) *m*; **~word** synonyme *m*; **be a ~ for** être synonyme de.

C

cab taxi *m*; fiacre *m*; *train, truck, crane, etc.*: cabine *f*.

cabbage chou *m*.

cabin cabane *f*; ♣ cabine *f*.

cabinet meuble *m* à tiroirs; vitrine *f*, *radio*: coffret *m*; *pol.* cabinet *m*, ministère *m*; **~ council** conseil *m* des ministres; **~-maker** ébéniste *m*.

cable 1. câble *m*; **~ car** téléphérique *m*; *on rails*: funiculaire *m*; **~ television** télédistribution *f*, télévision *f* par câble(s); **2.** *tel.* câbler; **~gram** câblogramme *m*.

caboose ♣ cuisine *f*; 🚂 *Am.* fourgon *m*.

cab ...: ~ rank, ~stand station *f* de voitures.

cacao cacao *m*; *tree*: cacaotier *m*.

cackle 1. caquet(ement) *m*; **2.** caqueter.

cactus, *pl.* **-ti** cactus *m*.

cad F goujat *m*; canaille *f*.

cadence ♪ cadence *f*; intonation *f*.

cadet élève *m* officier.

c(a)esarian 🔆 (*a.* **~ section**) césarienne *f*.

café café(-restaurant) *m*.

cafeteria cafétéria *f*.

cage 1. cage *f*; **2.** mettre en cage.

cagey méfiant; prudent.

cajole cajoler; persuader (à q. de *inf.*, *s.o. into ger.*).

cake 1. gâteau *m*; *chocolate*: tablette *f*; *soup*: pain *m*; **2.** faire croûte.

calamit|ous calamiteux, désastreux, **~y** calamité *f*; désastre *m*.

calcify (se) calcifier.

calculat|e *v/t.* calculer; estimer; *Am. a.* supposer; *v/i.* compter (sur, **on**); **~ion** calcul *m*; **~or** machine *f* à calculer, calculatrice *f*.

caldron *see* **cauldron.**

calendar calendrier *m*; **~ year** année *f* civile.

calf, *pl.* **calves** veau *m*; *other animals*: petit(e *f*) *m*; *anat.* mollet *m*; **~skin** (cuir *m* de) veau *m*.

calib|er, ~re calibre *m*; **~rate** étalonner, calibrer.

Californian 1. californien; de Californie; **2.** Californien(ne *f*) *m*.

call 1. appel *m* (*a. teleph.*); cri *m* (*a bird*); visite *f*; demande *f* (de, **for**); vocation *f*; nomination *f* (*to a post, etc.*); (*a telephone ~*) coup *m* de téléphone; ☏ **on ~** sur demande; **2.** *v/t.* appeler (*a.* 🕮), crier; convoquer (*a meeting*); héler (*a taxi*); faire venir (*a doctor*); attirer (*s.o.'s attention*) (sur, **to**); décréter (*a strike*); *fig.* nommer (à, **to**); **be ~ed** s'appeler; *Am.* F **~ down** injurier; **~ in** retirer (*a coin*) de la circulation; faire (r)entrer (*q.*); **~ up** évoquer; ✕ mobiliser; *Am. a.* téléphoner à (*q.*); **3.** *v/i.* téléphoner; faire une visite, passer (chez **at**, **on**); **~ at a port** faire escale; **~ for** faire venir (*q.*) *or* apporter (*qch.*); commander; venir chercher (*q.*, *qch.*); **to be** (**left till**) **~ed for** poste restante; **~ on** invoquer; réclamer (qch. à q., *s.o. for s.th.*); requérir, demander; **~box** cabine *f* téléphonique; **~er** personne *f* qui appelle; visiteur (-euse *f*) *m*; *teleph.* demandeur (-euse *f*) *m*; **~ing** appel *m*; convocation *f*; métier *m*; visite *f* (à, **on**); *Am.* **~ card** carte *f* de visite.

callous calleux; *fig.* insensible, dur; **~ness** insensibilité *f*, dureté *f*.

callow sans plumes; *fig.* imberbe, sans expérience.

callus callosité *f.*

calm 1. calme (*a. su./m*); **2.** (*a. ~ down se*) calmer, (s') apaiser.

calorie *phys.* calorie *f.*

column|iate calomnier; **~iation** calomnie *f.*; **~y** calomnie *f.*

calve vêler (*a. geol.*); **~s** *pl. of* **calf.**

camber 1. bombement; cambrure *f*; **2.** bomber.

camel *zo.* chameau *m.*

camera *phot.* appareil(-photo) *m*; *for moving pictures:* caméra *f*; **in ~** à huis clos.

camomile camomille *f.*

camouflage 1. camouflage *m*; **2.** camoufler.

camp 1. camp *m*; campement *m*; **~ bed,** **~ cot** lit *m* de camp; **~ chair** chaise *f* pliante; **~(ing) stool** pliant *m*; **2.** camper; **~ out** faire du camping.

campaign 1. campagne *f* (*a. pol., a. fig.*); **election ~** campagne *f* électorale; **2.** faire une (*or des*) campagne(s).

camp|er campeur (-euse *f*) *m*; *Am.* mot. *a.* caravane *f*; **~ing** camping *m*; **~ site** = **~site** (terrain *m* de) camping *m.*

campus *univ. Am.* terrains *m/pl.*

can¹ *v/aux.* (*defective*) je peux *etc.*, je suis *etc.* capable de (*inf.*).

can² 1. bidon *m*; *Am.* boîte *f* (de conserve); **~ opener** ouvre-boîtes *m/invr.*; **2.** *Am.* mettre en conserve *or* boîte(s).

Canadian 1. canadien; **2.** Canadien(ne *f*) *m.*

canal canal *m* (*a. *); **~ization** canalisation *f*; **~ize** canaliser.

canard canard *m*; fausse nouvelle *f.*

canary (*a. ~ bird*) serin *m.*

cancel *give up, revoke:* annuler; révoquer; (*call off:* decommander; biffer, rayer (*s.th. written*); oblitérer (*a stamp, ticket*); supprimer (*a flight, train, etc.*); **~ out** éliminer; *fig.* neutraliser; **~lation** annulation; révocation *f*; oblitération *f*; suppression *f*; élimination *f.*

cancer cancer *m*; *attr.* cancéreux; **~ous** cancéreux.

candid franc; sincère; impartial.

candidate candidat *m*, aspirant *m.*

candied candi; confit.

candle bougie *f*; chandelle *f*; cierge *m*; **~stick** chandelier *m*; bougeoir *m.*

cando(u)r franchise *f*, sincérité *f.*

candy 1. sucre *m* candi; *Am.* bonbons *m/pl.*, confiseries *f/pl.*; **~ floss** barbe *f* à papa; **2.** *v/t.* glacer (*fruit*).

cane 1. jonc *m*; canne *f*; rotin *m*; **2.** battre à coups de canne.

canine de chien, canin.

canister boîte *f* (*en fer blanc*).

canker , , *fig.* chancre *m.*

cannabis *drug:* cannabis *m*; chanvre *m* (indien).

canned *Am.* (conservé) en boîte; **~ music** musique *f* enregistrée *or* en boîte.

cannery *Am.* conserverie *f.*

cannibal cannibale (*a. su./mf*).

cannon 1. canon *m*; **2.** caramboler; se heurter (contre *against, into*); **~ade** canonnade *f.*

cannot *je ne peux pas etc.*

canoe canoë *m*; périssoire *f.*

canon canon *m*; **~ize** canoniser.

canopy dais *m*; baldaquin *m.*

cant¹ 1. inclinaison *f*; **2.** (s')incliner; pencher.

cant² jargon *m*, argot *m*; langage *m* hypocrite; boniments *m/pl.*

cantankerous F revêche, acariâtre.

canteen cantine *f*; bidon *m.*

cantilever console *f*; cantilever *m.*

canvas toile *f* (*a. paint.*); *ship:* voiles *f/pl.*

canvass 1. prospecter (*an area etc.*); solliciter (*votes, orders*); *v/i. pol.* faire une tournée électorale; **2.** (*a. ~ing*) prospection *f*; démarchage *m.*

caoutchouc caoutchouc *m.*

cap 1. casquette *f*; *bottle:* capsule *f*; *pen:* capuchon *m*; **2.** *v/t.* coiffer; couvrir; capsuler (*a bottle*); *fig.* couronner; F surpasser; **to ~ it all** pour comble.

capab|ility capacité *f*, aptitude *f*, faculté *f*; **~le** capable (de, *of*); susceptible (de, *of*).

capaci|ous vaste; ample; **~ty** capacité *f* (pour *inf.*, *for ger.*); volume *m*; aptitude *f*, faculté *f*; qualité *f* (professionnelle); **legal ~** capacité *f* juridique; **in my ~ as** en ma qualité de.

cape¹ cap *m*, promontoire *m.*

cape² pèlerine *f*, cape *f.*

caper¹ cabriole *f*; **cut ~s = 2.** gambader.

caper² *cuis.* câpre *f.*

capital 1. capital (*letter, crime, town*); **2.** (*~ city*) capitale *f*; capital *m*, fonds *m/pl.*; *typ.* (*a. ~ letter*) majuscule *f*;

chapiteau *m*; ♦ **~ gains** plus-values *f/pl.* (en capital); **~intensive** d'un contenu fort en travail; **~ism** capitalisme *m*; **~ist** capitaliste *mf*; **~ize** capitaliser; écrire avec une majuscule.

capitul|ate capituler; **~ion** capitulation *f*, reddition *f*.

capric|e caprice *m* (*a. ♪*), lubie *f*; **~ious** capricieux.

capsize *v/i.* chavirer; se renverser; *v/t.* faire chavirer.

capsule capsule *f*.

captain 1. capitaine *m*; *sp.* chef *m* d'équipe; **2.** être le capitaine de; commander.

caption légende *f*.

captious pointilleux.

captiv|ate *fig.* captiver, fasciner, charmer; **~e** captif (*adj., su.*); **~ity** captivité *f*.

capture 1. capitaine ⚔, ♣ *etc.* capturer; *fig.* capter (*attention etc.*); **2.** capture *f*.

car voiture *f*, auto *f*; **~ park** parking *m*, parc *m* de stationnement; **~ wash** lave-auto *m/inv.*

caramel (bonbon *m* au) caramel *m*.

caravan caravane *f* (*a. Br. mot.*); *gipsies:* roulotte *f*; **~ site** camping *m* pour caravanes.

caraway ♀ carvi *m*.

carbine carabine *f*.

carbohydrate hydrate *m* de carbone; F **~s** *pl.* nourriture *f* riche en hydrate de carbone.

carbolic acid 🜍 phénol *m*.

carbon 🜍 carbone *m*; (*a. ~ copy*) carbone *f*; (*a. ~ paper*) papier *m* carbone.

carbure(t)tor *mot.* carburateur *m*.

car|case, ~cass carcasse *f*.

carcino|ma 🜍 carcinome *m*; **~genic** cancérigène.

card carte *f*, F *house of ~s* château *m* de cartes; **~board** carton *m*; cartonnage *m*; **~ box** carton *m*.

cardiac cardiaque; **~ arrest** arrêt *m* du cœur.

cardigan cardigan *m*.

cardinal 1. cardinal; **~ number** nombre *m* cardinal; **2.** *eccl., orn.* cardinal *m*.

card...: **~ index** fichier *m*, classeur *m*; **~-sharp(er)** tricheur *m*.

care 1. souci *m*; soin *m*; attention *f*; *medical* **~** soins *m/pl.* médicaux; **~ of** (*abbr. c/o.*) aux bons soins de; chez;

take ~ faire attention; **take ~ of** s'occuper de; garder; **take ~ (of yourself)!** fais bien attention (à toi)!; **take ~ to do** faire attention à *or* prendre soin de faire; **with ~!** fragile!; **2.** se soucier; s'inquiéter; **~ for** soigner; se soucier de; tenir à; F **I don't ~** (*if I do*)! ça m'est égal.

career 1. carrière *f*; **2.** (*a. ~ along*) aller à toute vitesse.

care...: **~free** insouciant; exempt de soucis; **~ful** soigneux (de *of, for*); attentif (à, *of*); prudent; *be* **~I** fais attention!; *be* **~ to** (*inf.*) avoir soin de (*inf.*); **~fulness** soin *m*, attention *f*; prudence *f*; **~less** sans soin; négligent; inconsidéré; nonchalant; insouciant (de *of, about*); **~lessness** inattention *f*; insouciance *f*.

caress 1. caresse *f*; **2.** caresser.

care...: **~taker** concierge *mf*; gardien(ne *f*) *m*, **~worn** usé par le chagrin.

carfare *Am.* prix *m* du voyage.

cargo ♣ cargaison *f*.

caricature 1. caricature *f*; **2.** caricaturer.

carmine 1. carmin *m*; **2.** carmin.

carna|ge carnage *m*; **charnel**; de la chair; sensuel.

carnation 🜍 œillet *m*.

carnival carnaval (*pl. -s*) *m*.

carnivor|e carnivore *m*, carnassier *m*; **~ous** carnivore, carnassier.

carol: (*Christmas ~*) chanson *f* (de Noël).

carous|e 1. (*a. ~al*) buverie *f*, F bombe *f*; **2.** faire la fête.

carousel manège *m*.

carp carpe *f*.

carpen|ter charpentier *m*; menuisier *m*, **~ry** charpente(rie) *f*.

carpet 1. tapis *m* (*a. fig.*); *bring on the ~* soulever (*a question*); **2.** recouvrir d'un tapis; **~ sweeper** balai *m* mécanique.

carriage port *m*; transport *m*; voiture *f*; *person:* allure *f*; *typewriter:* chariot *m*; frais *m/pl.* de port; **~-free, ~-paid** franco de port; **~ road, ~way** chaussée *f*; route *f* carrossable.

carrier porteur (-euse *f*) *m* (*a. ✈*); ♦ entrepreneur *m or* entreprise *f* de transport, transporteur *m*; *bicycle:* porte-bagages *m/inv.*; **~ bag** sac *m* (en plastique); **~ pigeon** pigeon *m* voyageur.

carrion 1. charogne *f*; **2.** pourri.

carrot carotte *f*.

carry 1. *v/t.* porter; transporter; remporter (a price); fig. comporter, avoir pour conséquence; faire adopter (a proposal); ⚔ retenir (a number); ✗ enlever (a fortress); **be carried** être voté; ✝ ~ **forward** reporter (a sum); ~ **on** continuer; entretenir; exercer (a trade); poursuivre (a process); ~ **out**, ~ **through** exécuter; fig. **get carried away** se laisser entraîner; s'emballer; **2.** gun: portée f; trajet m.

cart 1. charrette f, fig. **put the ~ before the horse** mettre la charrue devant les bœufs; **2.** charrier, transporter; **~er** charretier m.

cartilage cartilage m.

carton carton m; cigarettes: cartouche f.

cartoon cin. dessin m animé.

cartridge cartouche f.

cartwheel gym. roue f.

carv|e v/t. découper (meat); tailler; se frayer (a way); vt/i. sculpter (dans, in); graver (sur, in); **~er** couteau m à découper; person: découpeur m; **~ing** sculpture f.

cascade chute f d'eau; cascade f.

case¹ case m (a. ♣, ⚖ gramm.); fait m; ⚖ a. cause f, affaire f; réclamation f; **in ~** au cas où; à tout hasard; **in any ~** en tout cas.

case² 1. caisse f; étui m; violin: boîte f; watch: boîtier m; shop: vitrine f; typ. casse f; **2.** encaisser; envelopper (de, with); **~-harden** ⚙ aciérer; **~-hardened** fig. endurci; **~ment** fenêtre f à deux battants; croisée f.

cash 1. espèces f/pl.; argent m comptant; ~ **desk** caisse f; ~ **dispenser** changeur m de monnaie; ~ **down**, **for ~** argent comptant; **be in (out of) ~** (ne pas) être en fonds; ~ **payment** paiement m (au) comptant; ~ **on delivery** livraison f contre remboursement; ~ **price** prix m au comptant; ~ **register** caisse f enregistreuse; **2.** encaisser (a coupon); toucher (a cheque); **~book** livre m de caisse; sommier m; **~ier** caissier (-ère f) m; **~less** sans argent, F à sec.

casing revêtement m; encaissement m; enveloppe f; book: cartonnage m.

cask fût m, tonneau m.

casket boîte f; Am. cercueil m.

casserole cocotte f.

cassette cassette f; ~ **player** lecteur m de

cassettes; ~ **recorder** magnétophone m à cassettes.

cast 1. jet m; coup m; ⚙ metall. coulée f; moulage m; thea. distribution f des rôles; fig. tournure f (of fancy); 🎣 (a. **plaster ~**) plâtre m; **2.** v/t. jeter (a. a glance); ⚓ anchor; zo. its slough); lancer; donner (one's vote); perdre (👁 its leaves, one's teeth); (pro)jeter (light, a shadow); metall. couler; thea. distribuer les rôles de; (a. ~ **up**) faire le total de; ~ **iron** fonte f (de fer); ~ **steel** fonte f d'acier; ~ **lots** tirer au sort (pour, for); ~ **away** or **off** rejeter; ~ **down** jeter bas; baisser (one's eyes); **be ~ down** être découragé; **3.** v/i. ~ **about** or **around for** chercher.

castanet castagnette f.

castaway ⚓ naufragé; fig. reprouvé(e f) m.

caste caste f; classe f.

castigate châtier; fig. critiquer.

casting 1. ⚙ moulage m; thea. distribution f; **2.** ~ **vote** voix f prépondérante.

cast-iron en fonte; fig. de fer, rigide.

castle château m (fort); chess: tour f.

castor¹: ~ **oil** huile f de ricin; ~ **sugar** sucre m semoule.

castor² furniture: roulette f.

castrate châtrer.

casual (unconcerned) désinvolte, insouciant; chance: de hasard; fait (etc.) en passant or au hasard (remark etc.); temporaire (work, worker, etc.); (de) sport (clothes); ~ **wear** vêtements m/pl. (de) sport; **~ty** victime f, accidenté(e f) m; ✗ **casualties** pl. pertes f/pl.

cat chat(te f) m; **~'s eye** cataphote m.

cata|logue, Am. a. **~log 1.** catalogue m, répertoire m; univ. Am. annuaire m; prospectus m; **2.** cataloguer.

catalyst catalyseur m.

catapult 1. lance-pierres m/inv.; ✈ catapulte f; **2.** catapulter.

cataract cataracte f (a. fig., a. 🎣).

catarrh catarrhe m; rhume m de cerveau.

catastrophe catastrophe f.

catch 1. prise f, capture f; ⚙ cliquet m; door: loquet m, window: loqueteau m; fig. attrape f; fig. aubaine f; **2.** v/t. attraper (a. an illness), prendre; saisir; F obtenir; rencontrer (a glance); sound: frapper (one's ear); ne pas manquer (*the train*); attirer *s.o.'s attention*); *thunderstorm etc.*: surprendre; *fig.* comprendre; **~ cold** prendre froid; s'enrhumer; **~ s.o.'s eye** attirer l'attention de q.; *parl.* **~ the Speaker's eye** obtenir la parole; **~ up** ramasser vivement; **3.** *v/i.* prendre, s'engager (*lock etc.*); F **~on** avoir du succès, prendre; F comprendre; **~ up** se rattraper; **~ up with** rattraper; **~all** fourre-tout *m/inv.*; **~er** *baseball:* rattrapeur *m*; **~ing** contagieux; **~phrase**, **~word** slogan *m*, **~y** facile à retenir; entraînant.

categor|ical catégorique; **~ize** catégoriser; **~y** catégorie *f*.

cater s'occuper de *or* fournir la nourriture (de, **for**); **~ for** (*Am. a.* **~ to**) s'adresser à; satisfaire (les besoins de); **~ to** satisfaire, aller au-devant de; **~er** traiteur *m*; **~ing** (**trade**) restauration *f*.

caterpillar (*TM*) chenille *f*.

cathedral cathédrale *f*.

cathode ⚡ cathode *f*.

catholic 1. universel; catholique; **2.** catholique *mf*.

catkin ♣ chaton *m*.

catnap 1. (petit) somme *m*; **2.** faire un petit somme.

cattle bétail *m*, bestiaux *m/pl.*

catwalk passerelle *f*.

catty F méchant.

cauldron chaudron *m*; chaudière *f*.

cauliflower ♣ chou-fleur (*pl.* choux-fleurs) *m*.

caulk ⚓ calfater.

caus|al causal; causatif; **~e 1.** cause *f*; **2.** causer; faire (faire qch. à q., **s.o. to do s.th.**); **~eless** sans cause.

causeway chaussée *f* (surélevée).

caustic caustique; *fig. a.* mordant.

caution 1. précaution *f*; prudence *f*; avertissement *m*; **2.** avertir.

cautious prudent, circonspect; **~ness** prudence *f*; circonspection *f*.

cavalry ✗ cavalerie *f*.

cave 1. caverne *f*; grotte *f*; **2.:** **~ in** s'effondrer; céder; **~man** homme *m* des cavernes; F malotru *m*.

cavern caverne *f*.

caviar(e) caviar *m*.

cavil ergoter.

cavity cavité *f*; creux *m*.

cavort F cabrioler; faire des galopades.

cavy *zo.* cobaye *m*, cochon *m* d'Inde.

caw 1. croasser; **2.** croassement *m*.

cease cesser; **~fire** ✗ cessez-le-feu *m/inv.*; **~less** incessant; sans arrêt.

cedar ♣ cèdre *m*.

cede céder.

ceiling plafond *m* (*a. fig.*); **~ price** prix *m* plafond.

celebrat|e célébrer; **~ed** célèbre; **~ion** célébration *f*.

celebrity célébrité *f*.

celerity célérité *f*.

celery ♣ céleri *m*.

celestial céleste.

celibacy célibat *m*.

cell cellule *f*; ⚡ élément *m* de pile.

cellar cave *f*.

cell|ist violoncelliste *mf*; **~o** violoncelle *m*.

cellul|ar cellulaire; **~ose** cellulose *f*.

Celt Celte *mf*; **~ic** celte; celtique.

cement 1. ciment *m*; **~ mixer** betonnière *f*; **2.** cimenter.

cemetery cimetière *m*.

censor 1. censeur *m*; censurer; **2.** censurer; **~ious** porté à censurer; sévère; **~ship** censure *f*; censorat *m*.

censur|able censurable, blâmable; **~e 1.** critique *f*, réprimande *f*; **2.** critiquer, blâmer (publiquement).

census recensement *m*.

cent *Am.* cent *m* (= $^1/_{100}$ *dollar*); F sou *m*; **per ~** pour cent.

centenary centenaire *m*.

centennial centennal.

centigrade centigrade.

central central; **~ heating** chauffage *m* central; **~ office**, ⚡ **~ station** centrale *f*; **~ize** (*sc*) centraliser.

cent|re, *Am.* **~er 1.** centre *m*; milieu *m*; *foot.* **~ forward** avant-centre *m*; **2.** central; **3.** *v/t.* centrer; concentrer; *v/i.:* **(a)round**, **~ (up)on** tourner autour de; **~rifugal** centrifuge.

century siècle *m*.

cereal 1. céréale; **2.** céréale *f*; *usu.* **~s** *pl.* céréales *f/pl.* en flocons.

cerebral *anat.* cérébral.

ceremon|ial 1 (*a* **~ious**) cérémonieux, de cérémonie; **2.** cérémonial (*pl.* -s) *m*; **~y** cérémonie *f*; **stand on ~** faire des façons *or* cérémonies.

certain certain, sûr; **for ~** certainement, à coup sûr; **make ~ (of)** s'assurer (de); **~ty** certitude *f*; chose *f* certaine.

certi|ficate 1. certificat *m*; attestation *f*; ~ **of birth** (**death, marriage**) acte *m* de naissance (décès, mariage); **medical ~** certificat *m* médical; **2.** délivrer un certificat à (*q.*); **~fiable** qu'on peut certifier; *Br.* F à bon à enfermer, fou; **~fication** certification *f*; **~fy** certifier; diplômer; authentiquer; **~tude** certitude *f*.

cessation cessation *f*, arrêt *m*.

cession cession *f*.

cesspool fosse *f* d'aisance; *fig.* cloaque *f*.

chafe *v/t.* frictionner; frotter; *fig.* irriter; *v/i.* s'user par le frottement; s'irriter.

chaff **1.** balle *f* (*of wheat*); F raillerie *f*; **2.** railler (*q.*).

chaffinch *zo.* pinson *m*.

chagrin 1. déception *f*; dépit *m*; **2.** contrarier.

chain 1. chaîne *f* (*a. fig.*); suite *f* (*of events*); chaînette *f*; *phys., fig.* ~ **reaction** réaction *f* en chaîne; ~ **store** maison *f* à succursales multiples; **2.** (*a. ~ up*) attacher par des chaînes; enchaîner; **~-smoke** fumer une cigarette après l'autre; **~-smoker** fumeur (-euse *f*) *m* invétéré(e) (qui fume sans arrêt).

chair 1. chaise *f*; (*arm ~*) fauteuil *m*; (*a. professorial ~*) chaire *f*; **be in the ~** présider; **2.** présider; **~man** président *m*.

chalk 1. craie *f*; **2.** écrire à la craie; ~ **out** esquisser; ~ **up** remporter (*a victory etc.*), établir (*a record etc.*); **~y** crayeux.

challenge 1. défi *m*; provocation *f* (en duel, **to a duel**); ⚖ récusation *f*; **2.** défier; mettre en doute; **~r** provocateur (-trice *f*) *m*.

chamber chambre *f*; **~maid** *hotel*: femme *f* de chambre.

chamois *zo.* chamois *m*; ✝ (*or ~ leather*) (peau *f* de) chamois *m*.

champagne champagne *m*.

champion 1. champion *m* (*a. sp.*); **2.** soutenir, défendre; **~ship** *sp.* championnat *m*.

chance 1. chance *f*, hasard *m*; occasion *f* (de, **of**); risque *m*; **by ~** par hasard; **take a** (*or* **one's**) ~ prendre un risque; **2.** fortuit, accidentel; de rencontre; **3.** *v/i.* ~ **to see** voir par hasard; avoir l'occasion de voir; ~ (**up**)**on** rencontrer par

hasard; *v/t.* risquer; essayer; ~ **it** risquer le coup.

chancellor chancelier *m*; **~ship** dignité *f* de chancelier.

chandelier lustre *m*.

chandler marchand *m* (de couleurs), droguiste *m*.

change 1. *v/t.* (*alter*) changer de; (*transform*) changer; transformer (en, **into**); (*exchange*) échanger (contre, **for**); ~ **one's mind** changer d'avis; *v/i.* changer; se transformer; (*~ clothes*) se changer; 🚃 (*~ trains*) changer (de train); ~ **into** se changer *or* transformer en; **2.** changement *m*; *money* (*a. small ~*) monnaie *f*; **give ~ for** faire la monnaie à q. (de); **~able** changeant; variable; **~less** immuable; fixe; **~over** changement *m*.

channel *geog.* canal *m*; conduit *m*; *river*: lit *m*; *irrigation*: rigole *f*; *telev.* chaîne *f*; *fig.* voie *f*; **go through the usual ~s** suivre la filière habituelle.

chant 1. chant *m*; psalmodie *f*; **2.** psalmodier; *fig.* chanter.

chaos chaos *m*.

chap¹ 1. gerçure *f*, crevasse *f*; **2.** (se) gercer, (se) crevasser.

chap² F garçon *m*, type *m*.

chapel chapelle *f* oratoire *m*.

chaplain aumônier *m*.

chapter chapitre *m* (*a. eccl.*); *Am.* filiale *f* (*of a society*); ~ **of accidents** série *f* noire; **give** (*or* **quote**) ~ **and verse** citer ses autorités; fournir des preuves.

char (se) carboniser.

character caractère *m* (*a. typ.*); *thea., novel*: personnage *m*; F personnalité *f*; F original *m*, numéro *m*; ~ **assassination** assassinat *m* moral; **that's in** (**out of**) ~ **for him** cela (ne) lui ressemble (pas); **~istic** characteristique (*a. su./f*); **~ize** caractériser.

charcoal charbon *m* (de bois).

charge 1. ✗, ⚡, ⚔, ⚡, *foot.* charge *f* (*a. fig.*) (de, **of**); soin *m*, garde *f*; ✗ *a.* attaque *f*; prix *m*; *admin.* droits *m/pl.*; ✝ ~**s** *pl.* frais *m/pl.*; ~ **account** compte *m* crédit d'achat; **be in** ~ être responsable (de, **of**); **free of** ~ exempt de frais; franco; **take** ~ **of** s'occuper de; se charger de; prendre en charge; **2.** *v/t.* charger (*a.* ✗); passer (*expenditure*) (à, **to**); débiter (*postage*); accuser, inculper (q.

de qch., *s.o. with s.th.*); ~ (up)on foncer sur (q.); ~ *s.o. a price* demander un prix à q. (pour, *for*).

chariot *poet.*, *hist.* char m.

charit|able charitable; **~y** charité f; bienfaisance f; aumônes f/pl.; œuvre f de bienfaisance.

charlatan charlatan m.

charm 1. charme m; **2.** charmer; **~ing** charmant, ravissant.

chart 1. ♫ carte f marine; diagramme m, graphique m; **2.** porter sur une carte.

charter 1. charte f; ~ *flight* (vol m en) charter m; ~ *member* membre m fondateur; ~ *plane* charter m; **2.** ♫, ✈ affréter.

charwoman femme f de ménage.

chary prudent; *be ~ of* être avare de (qch.), hésiter à (inf.)

chase 1. chasse f; poursuite f; **2.** chasser; poursuivre.

chasm gouffre m, abîme m.

chaste chaste; **~n** châtier.

chastise punir, châtier.

chastily chasteté f; fig. pureté f.

chat 1. causerie f; **2.** causer, bavarder.

chattels pl. (usu. *goods and ~*) biens m/pl. et effets m/pl.

chatter 1. bavarder; jaser; claquer (teeth); **2.** bavardage m; **~box** F babillard(e f) m; **~er** bavard(e f) m.

chatty qui aime bavarder; fig. familier, de conversation (style).

chauffeur chauffeur m.

cheap 1. bon marché, pas cher; à prix réduit; fig. trivial; **2.** adv.(à) bon marché; **~en** v/t. baisser le prix de; v/i. diminuer de prix, baisser; **~ly** (à) bon marché.

cheat 1. v/t. tromper; frauder; frustrer (q. de qch., *s.o.* [out] *of s.th.*); fig. échapper à; v/i. tricher; **2.** (person) tricheur (-euse f) m; escroc m; (action) tricherie f.

check 1. contrôle f, vérification f; fig. frein m; chess, fig.: échec m; tex. carreaux m/pl.; Am. see **cheque**; Am. restaurant: addition f; Am. bulletin m (de bagages, de consigne, etc.); *keep (or hold) in ~* tenir en échec; **2.** v/t. contrôler, vérifier; fig. freiner, arrêter; ~ *in* (faire) enregistrer (one's luggage); ~ *off* cocher; ~ *out* retirer (one's luggage); ~ *over* vérifier, examiner; ~ *up(on)*

examiner, se renseigner sur; v/i.: ~ *in* arriver; *hotel*: s'inscrire; *airport*: se présenter à l'enregistrement; ~ *out* partir; *hotel*: régler sa note; **~erboard** échiquier m; damier m; ◉ **~ered** see **chequered**; **~ers** jeu m de dames; **~list** liste f (de contrôle); **~mate 1.** échec et mat m; **2.** faire échec et mat à (a. fig.); **~point** contrôle m; **~room** vestiaire m; **~up** vérification f, contrôle m; ✚ examen m (médical).

cheek joue f; F toupet m; **~bone** pommette f; **~y** F insolent, effronté.

cheer 1. encouragement m; joie f; **~s** pl. applaudissements m/pl.; *~s!* (à votre) santé!; *three ~s for ...!* une ban pour ...!; **2.** v/t. applaudir (q.); (a. ~ *up*) égayer, remonter; (a. ~ *on*) encourager; v/i. applaudir; pousser des vivats, (a. ~ *up*) (re)prendre courage; s'égayer; **~ful** gai, joyeux; **~fulness** gaieté f; **~io** F à bientôt!; à la vôtre!; **~less** triste; **~y** gai, joyeux.

cheese fromage m.

chef chef m de cuisine.

chemical 1. chimique, **2.** **~s** pl. produits m/pl. chimiques

chemist chimiste mf; ✚ pharmacien(ne f) m; **~ry** chimie f.

cheque ✚ chèque m; ~ *account* compte m courant; *not negotiable*, *crossed ~* chèque m barré; **~book** carnet m de chèques.

chequered à carreaux; fig. varié, accidenté (life).

cherish chérir; fig. entretenir, nourrir (hopes etc.).

cherry cerise f; *tree*: cerisier m.

chess (jeu m d'échecs m/pl.; **~board** échiquier m; **~man** chess: pièce f.

chest caisse f, coffre m; anat. poitrine f; ~ *of drawers* commode f.

chestnut 1. châtaigne f; *edible*: marron m; (~ *tree*) châtaignier m; marronnier m; fig. vieille histoire f; **2.** châtain.

chew v/t. mâcher; sl. ~ *the fat* (or *rag*) bavarder; v/i. fig. méditer (sur [up]on, over); **~ing gum** chewing-gum m.

chick poussin m; sl. nana f.

chicken 1. poulet m; ✚ ~ *pox* varicelle f; **2.** sl.: ~ *out* dégonfler; **~feed** sl. bagatelle f; **~hearted**, **~livered** froussard.

chief 1. principal; premier; en chef; ~ *clerk* chef m de bureau; premier clerc *m*; **2.** chef *m*; **...-in-~ ...** en chef; **~tain** chef *m* de clan.

chilblain engelure *f.*

child, *pl.* **-ren** enfant *mf*; **~'s play** jeu *m* d'enfant; *from a* **~** dès l'enfance; *with* **~** enceinte; **~bed** couches *f/pl.*; **~birth** accouchement *m*; **~hood** enfance *f.*; **~ish** enfantin; *pej.* puéril; **~ishness** *pej.* enfantillage *m*; puérilité *f.*; **~like** enfantin; *fig.* naïf.

chill 1. froid, glacé; **2.** froideur *f*; froid *m*; ⚕ coup *m* de froid, refroidissement *m*; **3.** *v/t.* refroidir, glacer; *fig.* donner le frisson à (*q.*); *v/i.* se refroidir, se glacer; **~y** froid; frais.

chime 1. carillon *m*; **2.** carillonner; *fig.* s'accorder; **~ in** interrompre, se mêler (à la conversation).

chimney cheminée *f*; **~sweep(er)** ramoneur *m.*

chimpanzee *zo.* chimpanzé *m.*

chin menton *m.*

china porcelaine *f*; *attr.* de *or* en porcelaine; **⚹man** Chinois *m.*

Chinese 1. chinois; **2.** *ling.* chinois *m*; Chinois(e *f*) *m*; *the* **~** *pl.* les Chinois *m/pl.*

chink fente *f*, fissure *f*, lézarde *f*; *door:* entrebâillement *m*; *sound:* tintement *m.*

chinwag *sl.* causerie *f.*

chip 1. éclat *m*; *wood, metal:* copeau *m*; *gambling:* jeton *m*; *computer:* chip *m*; *cuis.* (**potato**) **~s** *pl. Br.* frites *f/pl., Am.* chips *m/pl.*; **2.** (s')ébrécher (*plate etc.*); **~ings** *pl.* gravillons *m/pl.*

chirp 1. gazouiller, pépier; grésiller (*cricket*); **2.** gazouillement *m*, pépiement *m*; *cricket:* grésillement *m.*

chisel 1. ciseau *m*; burin *m*; **2.** ciseler; buriner (*metal*); *sl.* carotter.

chit-chat bavardages *m/pl.*

chivalr|ous chevaleresque; courtois; **~y** chevalerie *f*; courtoisie *f.*

chive ⚘ ciboulette *f.*

chlor|ide chlorure *f*; **~ine** chlore *m*; **~oform 1.** chloroforme *m*; **2.** chloroformer.

chock 1. cale *f*; **2.** caler; (*a.* **~ up**) mettre sur cales; **~-full** plein à craquer.

chocolate chocolat *m.*

choice 1. choix *m*; **2.** de choix; ⚹ **~ quality** première qualité *f.*

choir △, ♪ chœur *m.*

choke 1. étouffer; *v/t. a.* étrangler; (*usu.* **~ up**) obstruer; (*usu.* **~ down**) ravaler; *mot.* fermer (*the gas*); **~ back** réprimer; contenir; **2.** étranglement *m*; *mot.* starter *m.*

choose choisir; juger bon (de *inf.*, *to inf.*).

chop 1. coup *m* de hache; *cuis.* côtelette *f*; **~s** *pl.* mâchoires *f/pl.* (*a.* ⚙); babines *f/pl.*; **2.** couper, fendre, hacher; (*oft.* **~ up**) couper en morceaux; **~per** couperet *m*; hachoir *m*; **~py** variable; clapoteux (*sea*).

choral choral; chanté en chœur; **~ (e)** ♪ choral *m.*

chord ♪, *fig.* corde *f*; ♪ accord *m.*

chore *usu.* **~s** *pl.* travaux *m/pl.* domestiques.

chorus 1. chœur *m*; refrain *m*; **2.** répéter en chœur.

chow *Am. sl.* mangeaille *f.*

Christ le Christ; F **~!, for ~'s sake** Bon Dieu (de Bon Dieu)!

christen baptiser; **⚹dom** chrétienté *f*; **~ing** baptême *m.*

Christian 1. chrétien; **~ name** prénom *m*; **2.** chrétien(ne *f*) *m*; **~ity** christianisme *m.*

Christmas 1. Noël *m*; **2.** de Noël; **~ box** étrennes *f/pl.*; **~ Day** le jour de Noël; **~ Eve** la veille de Noël; **~ tree** arbre *m* de Noël.

chromium chrome *m*; **~-plated** chromé.

chronic chronique; **~le 1.** chronique *f*; **2.** faire la chronique de.

chronolog|ical chronologique; **~y** chronologie *f.*

chubby F potelé; joufflu (*face*).

chuck¹ 1. gloussement *m*; **2.** glousser.

chuck² ** F lancer; *a.* **~ in, **~ up** laisser tomber, plaquer; **~ out** flanquer dehors.

chuckle rire tout bas.

chum F copain *m*, copine *f.*

chump F idiot(e *f*) *m*; tête *f.*

chunk F gros morceau *m*; *bread: a.* quignon *m.*

church église *f*; *attr.* d'église; de l'Église; **~ service** office *m*; **~-goer** pratiquant(e *f*) *m*; **~yard** cimetière *m.*

churlish mal élevé; grincheux.

churn 1. baratte *f*; bidon *m* à lait; **2.** *v/t.* baratter; *fig.* agiter (*qch.*); *v/i* faire du beurre.

chute chute *f* d'eau; *river:* rapide *m*; *sp.*

glissière f; toboggan m; (*rubbish* ~) vide-ordures m/inv.; F parachute m.

cider cidre m.

cigar cigar m.

cigarette cigarette f; ~ *case* étui m à cigarettes; ~ *end* mégot m; ~ *holder* fume-cigarette m/inv.; ~ *paper* papier m à cigarettes.

cinch chose f certaine *or* facile.

cincture ceinture f.

cinder cendre f; ℒ**ella** Cendrillon f; ~*track* sp. piste f cendrée.

cine...: ~ *camera* caméra f; ~ *film* film m (de format réduit).

cinema cinéma m.

cinnamon cannelle f.

cipher 1. zéro m (*a. fig.*); *fig.* nullité f; *code*: chiffre m; **2.** chiffrer.

circle 1. cercle m (*a. fig.*); *fig.* milieu m; *Br. thea.* balcon m; **2.** *v/t.* (en)cercler; tourner autour de; *v/i.* (~ [*a*]round, ~ *about*) tournoyer, circuler; tourner (autour de).

circuit circuit m; ⚡ *short* ~ court-circuit (*pl.* courts circuits) m; ⚡ ~ *breaker* coupe-circuit m/inv.; ~*ous* détourné, sinueux.

circular 1. circulaire; ~ *saw* scie f circulaire; (*a.* ~ *letter*) = **2.** (lettre f) circulaire f.

circulat|e (faire) circuler; circuler; ~*ing*: ~ *library* bibliothèque f circulante; ~*ion* circulation f; *newspaper*: tirage m; ~*ory* circulatoire; ⚕ ~ *system* appareil m circulatoire; ~ *troubles* troubles m/pl. de la circulation.

circum... circon..., circum...; ~*cise* circoncire; ~*ference* circonférence f; ~*locution* circonlocution f; ~*navigate* faire le tour de; ~*scribe* ⚕ circonscrire; *fig.* limiter; ~*scription* ⚕ circonscription f; ~*spect* circonspect; ~*spection* circonspection f; ~*stance* circonstance f; ~*s pl. fig.* situation financière; *under no* ~ en aucun cas; ~*vent* contrevenir.

circus cirque m; *place*: rond-point (*pl.* ronds-points) m.

cirrhosis cirrhose f.

cistern réservoir m d'eau.

citadel citadelle f.

cit|ation citation f; ~*e* citer.

citizen citoyen(ne f) m; habitant(e f) m; *attr.* civique; ~*ship* citoyenneté f.

citrus fruits agrumes m/pl.

city 1. ville f; *London*: *the* ℒ la Cité de Londres; **2.** urbain, municipal; ~ *editor* rédacteur m chargé des nouvelles locales; ~ *father* conseiller m municipal; ~ *hall* hôtel m de ville.

civic 1. civique; municipal; ~ *rights pl.* droits m/pl. civiques; **2.** ~*s pl.* instruction f civique.

civil civil (*a.* ⚖; *a. engineer*); poli; civique (*rights*); ~ *engineering* travaux m/pl. publics; ℒ *servant* fonctionnaire m/f; ℒ *service* Administration f; ~*ian* ✕ civil m; ~*ity* politesse f; ~*ization* civilisation f; ~*ize* civiliser.

claim 1. demande f, réclamation f, revendication f; droit m, titre m (à, *to*); *esp. Am.* terrain m revendiqué par un chercheur d'or *etc.*; *lay* ~ *to* prétendre à; **2.** *v/t.* revendiquer, réclamer, demander; prétendre; *v/i.* faire une réclamation; ~*ant* prétendant(e f) m; réclamant(e f) m; ⚖ réquérant(e f) m.

clairvoyant voyant(e f) m.

clamber grimper.

clammy moite; froid et humide.

clamo(u)r 1. clameur f; cris m/pl.; **2.** vociférer.

clamp 1. agrafe f, crampon m; étau m (à main); **2.** *v/t.* agrafer; cramponner; fixer; serrer; *v/i.* ~ *down on* sévir contre.

clan clan m; tribu f; *fig.* coterie f.

clandestine clandestin.

clang 1. bruit m métallique *or* retentissant; **2.** (faire) retentir.

clank 1. bruit m métallique, cliquetis m; **2.** *v/i.* faire un bruit métallique; *v/t.* faire sonner.

clap 1. battement m de mains; applaudissements m/pl.; tape f (légère); ~ *of thunder* coup m de tonnère; **2.** applaudir; *v/t.* donner à (*q.*) une tape (dans le dos, *on the back*); ~ *one's hands* battre des mains; ~*board* *Am.* bardeau m; ~*trap* F baratin m.

claret bordeaux m (rouge).

clari|fication clarification f; ~*fy* (se) clarifier; *fig. a.* (s')éclaircir; ~*ty* clarté f.

clash 1. choc m; *fig.* conflit m; **2.** (se) heurter; (s')entrechoquer; (faire) résonner; *v/i.* s'opposer (*opinions*).

clasp 1. *medal*: agrafe f; *book*: fermoir m; *necklace*: fermeture f; *fig.* prise f, étreinte f; **2.** agrafer; *fig.* étreindre; serrer; ~*knife* couteau m pliant.

class 1. classe *f*; *univ. Am.* année; ~ **struggle, ~ war(fare)** lutte *f* des classes; **2.** classer; ranger par classes.

classic 1. classique *m*; ~**s** *pl.* études *f*/*pl.* classiques; **2.** = ~**al** classique.

classif|ication classification *f*; ~**ied** classifié; secret; ~ **ads** petites annonces *f*/*pl.*; ~**y** classifier; classer.

class...: ~mate camarade *mf* de classe; ~**room** salle *f* de classe; ~**y** chic.

clatter 1. vacarme *m*; bruit *m* (*of cups etc.*); *fig.* bavardage *m*; **2.** *v/i.* faire du bruit; retentir; *fig.* bavarder; *v/t.* faire retentir.

clause clause *f*; *gramm.* proposition *f*.

claw 1. griffe *f*; *eagle etc.*: serre *f*; *crayfish*: pince *f*; **2.** griffer; déchirer; s'accrocher à (*qch.*).

clay argile *f*; glaise *f*; *sp.* ~ **pigeon** pigeon *m* d'argile.

clean 1. *adj.* propre; net (*a. fig.*); **2.** *adv.* tout à fait, absolument; **3.** nettoyer; balayer; faire (*a room*); ~ **out** nettoyer à fond; ~ **up** nettoyer; ~**cut** net, bien défini; ~**er** nettoyeur (-euse *f*) *m*; femme *f* de ménage; (*a. dry* ~) teinturier *m*; ~'**s** teinturerie *f*; ~**ing** nettoyage *m*; ~ **woman** femme *f* de ménage; ~**liness** propreté *f*; netteté *f*; ~**ly 1.** proprement, nettement; **2.** propre; ~**ness** propreté *f*; netteté *f*.

cleanse nettoyer; purifier; ~**r** détergent; *make-up*: démaquillant *m*.

clean-shaven rasé de près.

clean-up nettoyage *m*; *fig.* épuration *f*.

clear 1. *adj.* clair; net (*idea, voice, etc.; a.* ✝); *fig.* libre, dégagé; débarrassé; **2.** *adv.* nettement, distinctement; complètement; **3.** *v/t.* éclaircir (*a. fig.*); nettoyer; déblayer (*the ground; a. fig.*); écarter (*an obstacle*); dégager (*a road*); acquitter (*a debt*); ⚖ innocenter (de *of*, *from*); sortir (*a prison*), quitter, s'éloigner de; (faire) évacuer; franchir, sauter (*an obstacle etc.*); ~ **out** vider, débarrasser (*a drawer, room etc.*); jeter, se débarrasser de (*objects*); ✝ ~ **off** solder, liquider (*goods*); ~ **up** mettre en ordre; fig. mettre bon ordre à; *fig.* éclairci, résoudre (*a secret*); *v/i.* (*a.* ~ **up**) s'éclaircir; (*a.* ~ **off**) se dissiper (*clouds, fog*); ~ **up** remettre de l'ordre; **4. in the** ~ hors de danger; **in** ~ en clair; ~**ance** dégagement *m*; déblaiement *m*; *letter box*:

levée *f*; ✝ compensation *f*; ⚓, ✝ dédouanement *m*; ✝ (*a.* ~ **sale**) solde *m*; ⚙ jeu *m*; ~**cut** précis; bien défini; ~**ing** éclaircissement *m* etc. (*see clear* **3**); *forest*: clairière *f*; ♀ **House** chambre *f* de compensation.

cleav|age clivage *f*; *woman*: naissance des seins; ~**e** (se) fendre; ~**er** couperet *m*.

clef ♪ clef *f*, clé *f*.

cleft fente *f*, fissure *f*, crevasse *f*.

clemen|cy clémence *f*; ~**t** clément.

clench (se) serrer (*teeth, fists*).

clergy (membres *m*/*pl.* du) clergé *m*; ~**man** ecclésiastique *m*; *protestantism*: pasteur *m*.

clerical *eccl.* clérical; de bureau.

clerk employé(e *f*) *m* de bureau; *Am.* vendeur (-euse *f*) *m*.

clever habile, adroit; intelligent; ingénieux (*device, invention*; etc.); *sl.* ~ **dick** gros malin; ~**ness** habileté *f*; adresse *f*; intelligence *f*.

click 1. cliquetis *m*, bruit *m* sec; ⚙ cliquet *m*; déclic *m*; **2.** *v/i.* cliqueter; faire un déclic; F *fig.* become clear; ~ **with** plaire à; *v/t.* faire claquer *or* cliqueter.

client client(e *f*) *m*; ~**èle** clientèle *f*.

cliff falaise *f*; escarpement *m*.

climate climat *m*.

climacteric ⚕ ménopause *f*, retour *m* d'âge; *fig.* tournant *m*.

climax gradation *f*; *fig.* apogée *m*.

climb monter (sur), grimper (sur *or* à); ~ **down** descendre; *fig.* en rabattre; ~**er** ascensionniste *mf*; arriviste *mf*; ⚘ plante *f* grimpante; ~**ing** montée *f*, escalade *f*; ~ **iron** crampon *m*.

clinch 1. ⚙ rivetage *m*; *fig.* étreinte *f*; **2.** *v/t.* river; confirmer (*an argument etc.*); accrocher.

cling (à, **to**) s'accrocher, se cramponner à; adhérer.

clinic clinique *f*; ~**al** clinique.

clink 1. tintement *m*, choc *m*; **2.** (faire) tinter *or* cliqueter; ~ **glasses with** trinquer avec; ~**er** escarbilles *f*/*pl.*

clip¹ 1. attache *f*; pince *f*; *hair*: barrette *f*; (*a. paper* ~) trombone *f*; **2.** (s')attacher, (s')agrafer.

clip² 1. couper, tailler; tondre (*sheep, a hedge*, etc.); rogner (*wings*); (*cut out*) dépouper; (*shorten*) écourter, (*abbreviate*) abréviate) abréger; F (*hit*) taper, gifler, F talocher; F *fig.* (*fleece*) tondre, fusiller, vider (*q.*); **2.** coupe *f*; tonte *f*; F (*speed*) vitesse *f*, allure *f*; **~er** clipper *m*; (***a pair of***) **~s** *pl.* (une) tondeuse *f*; **~pings** *pl.* coupures *f/pl.* de presse; **~-on** qui s'attache.

clique coterie *f*; F clan *m*.

cloak 1. manteau *m*; *fig.* voile *m*; **2.** revêtir d'un manteau; *fig.* masquer, voiler; **~room** vestiaire *m*; 🚂 consigne *f*.

clobber *sl.* **1.** battre, F rosser; **2.** *Br. a.* frusques *f/pl.*, barda *m*.

clock 1. horloge *f*; pendule *f*; ***~ radio*** radio-réveil *m* (*pl.* radios-réveils); **2.** *v/i.*: ***~ in*** (***out***) pointer à l'arrivée (au départ) (*workers*); **~face** cadran *m*; **~wise** à droite; **~work** *clock*: mouvement *m*; ⚙ mécanisme *m*.

clod motte *f* (de terre); *fig.* terre *f*; (*a.* ***~hopper***) lourdaud *m*.

clog 1. entrave *f*; sabot *m*; **2.** (se) boucher, (s')obstruer.

cloister cloître *m*.

close 1. *v/t.* fermer; barrer; terminer; arrêter (*an account*); ***~ down*** fermer (*a factory*); *v/i.* (se) fermer; finir; se prendre corps à corps (avec, ***with***); ***~ in*** tomber (*night*); ***~ on*** (*prp.*) se (re)fermer sur; ***closing time*** heure *f* de fermeture; ***closing time!*** on ferme!; **2.** proche, (tout) près; bien fermé; clos; avare; étroit (*garments etc.*); exclusif (*society*); serré; soutenu (*attention*); minutieux; impénétrable (*secret*); intime (*friend*); fidèle (*translation*); ***~ by*** (*or* ***to***) tout près (de); ***~ fight*** combat *m* corps à corps; *hunt.* ***~(d) season*** (*or* ***time***) chasse *f* fermée; ***have a ~ call*** (*or* ***shave***) l'échapper belle, y échapper de justesse; **3.** conclusion *f*, fin *f*; ***bring to a ~*** terminer; ***come to a ~*** prendre fin; finir; ***draw to a ~*** approcher de sa fin.

closet 1. armoire *f*, placard *m*; **2.** secret; **3.** enfermer; ***be ~ed with*** être enfermé *or* en tête à tête avec (*q.*).

close-up *cin.* gros plan *m*.

closure fermeture *f*; clôture *f*.

clot 1. *blood*: caillot *m*; *ink*: bourbillon *m*; **2.** se coaguler (*blood etc.*); former des caillots.

cloth étoffe *f*, tissu *m*; drap *m*; toile *f*; linge *m*; torchon *m*; lavette *f*; (*a.* ***table-~***) nappe *f*; *fig.* ***the ~*** le clergé.

clothe habiller, vêtir (de ***in, with***); revêtir (de, ***with***) (*a. fig.*).

clothes *pl.* vêtements *m/pl.*, habits *m/pl.*; **~basket** panier *m* à linge; **~ hanger** cintre *m*; **~horse** séchoir *m*; **~-line** corde *f* à linge; **~peg, ~pin** pince *f*.

clothier drapier *m*; marchand *m* de confections.

clothing vêtements *m/pl*.

cloud 1. nuage *m* (*a. fig.*); **2.** (se) couvrir; *fig.* (s')assombrir; **~burst** rafale *f* de pluie; trombe *f*; **~-cuckooland:** ***live in ~*** planer dans les nuages; **~less** sans nuages; **~y** nuageux (*sky*); trouble (*liquid*).

clout F **1.** taloche *f*; **2.** gifler.

clove clou *m* de girofle.

cloven *adj.* fendu, fourchu.

clover ⚘ trèfle *m*; **~leaf** ⚘ feuille *f* de trèfle; *mot.* (*a.* ***~ crossing*** *or* ***junction***) croisement *m* en) trèfle.

clown 1. clown *m*; **2.** ***~ about, ~ around*** faire le clown.

cloy *v/t.* rassasier (de, ***with***); *v/i.* devenir fade; **~ing** écœurant, douceâtre.

club 1. massue *f*; *sp.* crosse *f*; cercle *m*, club *m*; **~s** *pl. cards*: trèfle *m*; **2.** *v/t.* frapper avec une massue; *v/i.* (*usu.* ***~ together***) s'associer (*pour faire qch.*); **~foot** pied-bot (*pl.* pieds-bots) *m*.

clue indice *m*; *fig.* idée *f*.

clump 1. bloc *m*; *trees*: groupe *m*; *flowers*: massif *m*; **2.** marcher lourdement; se grouper en massif.

clums|iness gaucherie *f*, maladresse *f*; **~y** gauche, maladroit, lourd; informe.

cluster 1. ⚘ *flowers*: bouquet *m*; *trees*: groupe *m*; *grapes*: grappe *f*; *people etc.*: essaim *m*, groupe *m*; **2.** (se) grouper; (se) rassembler; former un groupe (*etc.*) (autour de, ***[a]round***).

clutch 1. ⚙ embrayage *m*; *fig. usu.* **~es** *pl.* griffes *f/pl.*; *mot.* ***~ pedal*** pédale *f* d'embrayage; **2.** *v/t.* saisir; étreindre; *v/i.*: ***~ at*** s'agripper à, agripper.

clutter 1. méli-mélo (*pl.* mélis-mélos) *m*; encombrement *m*; désordre *m*; **2.** encombrer (de, ***with***).

coach 1. carrosse *m*; 🚂 voiture *f*; *Am.* autocar *m*; *univ.* répétiteur *m*; *sp.* entraîneur *m*; **2.** donner des leçons particulières à; *sp.* entraîner; **~work** carrosserie *f*.

coagulate (se) coaguler.

coal charbon *m*; houille *f*; **carry ~s to Newcastle** porter de l'eau à la mer; **~field** bassin *m* houiller.

coalesce se fondre; s'unir.

coalition coalition *f*; *pol.* cartel *m*.

coal-pit houillère *f*.

coarse grossier; **~ness** grossièreté *f*; rudesse *f*.

coast 1. côte *f*, rivage *m*; plage *f*; *esp. Am.* piste *f* (*for toboggans*); **2.** suivre la côte; descendre (en toboggan, en roue libre); **~er** *Am.* bobsleigh *m*; ♻ caboteur *m*; **~er brake** *cycl. Am.* frein *m* à contre-pédalage; **~ing** cabotage *m*.

coat 1. manteau *m*; *Am. a.* veston *m*; *animal:* peau *f*, fourrure *f*; *paint:* couche *f*; **~ of arms** armoiries *f/pl.*; **2.** enduire (de, **with**); revêtir, couvrir (de, **with**); **~hanger** cintre *m*; **~ing** enduit *m*, revêtement *m*; couche *f*; *tex.* étoffe *f* pour vêtements.

coax cajoler; encourager (*q.*) à force de cajoleries (à *inf.*, **into** *ger.*).

cob *zo.* cygne *m* mâle; ♺ épi *m* de maïs.

cobbler cordonnier *m*.

cobweb toile *f* d'araignée.

cock 1. coq *m*; *rifle:* chien *m*; *hay:* meulon *m*; robinet *m*; **2.** dresser (*the ears*); armer (*a gun*); **~chafer** *zo.* hanneton *m*; **~erel** jeune coq *m*; **~eyed** *sl.* qui louche; de travers; absurde; gris (*drunken*).

cockney Londonien(ne *f*) *m*.

cockpit poste *m* du pilote, cockpit *m*.

cockroach *zo.* cafard *m*.

cock|sure F outrecuidant; **~tail** cocktail *m*; **~y** outrecuidant, suffisant, effronté.

cocoa cacao *m*.

coconut noix *f* de coco.

cocoon *zo.* cocon *m*.

cod *icht.* morue *f*.

coddle gâter, câliner; dorloter.

code 1. code *m*; *secret:* chiffre *m*; **2.** coder; chiffrer.

codger F vieux bonhomme *m*.

cod-liver oil huile *f* de foie de morue.

co-ed *Am.* élève *f* d'une école coéducationelle.

co-education coéducation *f*.

coerc|e contraindre; forcer; **~ion** contrainte *f*.

coeval (**with**) du même âge (que).

coexist coexister (avec, **with**).

coffee café *m*; **~ bar, ~ shop** café *m*,

cafétéria *f*; **~ bean** grain *m* de café; **~ grounds** *pl.* marc *m* de café; **~ pot** cafetière *f*.

coffer coffre *m*.

coffin cercueil *m*.

cogent valable, incontestable.

cogitate *v/i.* réfléchir, méditer (sur, [*up*]on); *v/t.* méditer (*qch.*).

cognate (**with**) parent (de); analogue (à).

cognition connaissance *f*.

cognizan|ce connaissance *f* (*a.* ♃); **~t: be ~ of** avoir connaissance de; être conscient de.

cog-wheel ⚙ roue *f* dentée.

coheir cohéritier *m*.

coherent cohérent.

cohes|ion cohésion *f*; **~ive** cohésif.

coil 1. *cord, wire, hair:* rouleau *m*; *cable:* glène *f*; ⚡ bobine *f*; *snake:* repli *m*; **~ spring** ressort *m* en spirale; **2.** (*oft.* **~ up**) (s')enrouler.

coin 1. (pièce *f* de) monnaie *f*; **2.** frapper (*money*); *fig.* inventer; **~age** monnayage *m*; monnaie *f*; *fig.* invention *f*.

coincide (**with**) coïncider (avec); *fig.* s'accorder (avec); **~nce** coïncidence *f*; *fig.* rencontre *f*, concours *m*; **~nt** coïncident; *fig.* d'accord.

coke (*TM*) coke *m* (*a. sl.* cocaine); F Coca-Cola *f*.

cold 1. froid; *person:* **be ~** avoir froid; *it is ~* il fait froid; **2.** froid *m*; ♬ rhume *m*; **~-blooded** *zo.* à sang froid; *fig.* insensible, sans pitié (*person*); accompli de sang-froid (*action*); **~-hearted** au cœur froid; **~ness** froideur *f*; **~-shoulder** battre froid à (*q.*).

coleslaw salade *f* de choux.

colic ♬ colique *f*.

collaborat|e collaborer; **~ion** collaboration *f*; **~or** collaborateur (-trice *f*) *m*.

collaps|e 1. s'affaisser; s'écrouler; s'effondrer; **2.** affaissement *m* *etc.*; **~ible** pliant, démontable.

collar 1. col *m*; *coat:* collet *m*; *shirt:* (faux) col *m*; ⚙ anneau *m*, collet *m*; **2.** saisir au collet; *cuis.* rouler (*meat*) pour la ficeler; **~bone** *anat.* clavicule *f*.

collate collationner (*texts*).

collateral collatéral; parallèle (*street*); accessoire; concomitant.

colleague collègue *mf*.

collect *v/t.* (r)assembler; amasser

(*wealth*); collectionner (*stamps*); (*pick up*) ramasser; aller chercher (*q., qch.*); lever (*letters*); percevoir (*taxes*); encaisser (*money owed*); ~ **one's thoughts** se recueillir; *teleph.* ~ **call** PCV (= Per-ce-voir); *v/i.* s'assembler; ~**ed** *fig.* plein de sang-froid; ~**ion** rassemblement *m*; collection *f*; perception *f*; encaissement *m*; *eccl.* quête *f*; ~**ive** collectif; ~ **bargaining** convention *f* collective; ~**or** collectionneur (-euse *f*) *m*; percepteur *m*; encaisseur *m*; ~**'s item** pièce *f* de collection.

colleg|e collège *m*; *oft.* université *f*; école *f* secondaire, lycée *m*; école *f* (*militaire or navale*); ~**ian** étudiant(e *f*) *m*; lycéen(ne *f*) *m*.

collide se heurter; ~ **with** heurter.

collie colley *m*.

collier houilleur *m*, mineur *m*; ~**y** houillère *f*; mine *f* de charbon.

collision collision *f* (*a. fig.*); heurt *m*; *fig.* conflit *m*.

colloqu|ial familier; ~**y** colloque *m*.

colon *typ.* deux-points *m/inv.*

colonel ✕ colonel *m*.

colon|ial colonial (*a. su./m*); ~**ist** colon *m*; ~**ize** *v/t.* coloniser; *v/i.* former une colonie; ~**y** colonie *f*.

colossal colossal.

colo(u)r 1. couleur *f*; ~**s** *pl. a.* drapeau *m*; ~ **bar**, ~ **line** discrimination *f* raciale; ~ **film** film *m* en couleur, *camera:* pellicule *f* (en) couleur; ~ **television** télévision *f* (en) couleur; ~ **television set** téléviseur *m* couleur; **2.** colorer, colorier, peindre; *fig.* fausser, présenter sous un faux jour (*news etc.*); ~**blind** daltonien; ~**blindness** daltonisme *m*; ~**ed** coloré; encouleur; de couleur (*person*); ~**s** *pl.* personnes *f/pl.* de couleur; ~**fast** bon teint; ~**ful** coloré; *fig. a.* pittoresque; ~**ing 1.** colorant; **2.** coloration *f*; *face:* teint *m*; *shade:* teinte *f*; *fig.* dénaturation *f*.

colt poulain *m*, pouliche *f*; *fig.* débutant(e *f*) *m*.

column colonne *f* (*a. typ., a.* ✕); ~**ist** *Am. journ.* collaborateur *m* régulier d'un journal.

comb 1. peigne *m*; *cock, mountain, wave:* crête *f*; ☼ *a.* carde *f*; **2.** *v/t.* peigner; *a.* carder (*wool*); ~ **out** démêler; *fig.* éliminer.

combat 1. combat *m*; **2.** combattre (contre, **with**; pour, **for**) ~**ant** combattant *m*; ~**ive** combattif; agressif.

combin|ation combinaison *f*; ~**e 1.** (se) réunir; (s')allier; **2.** association *f*; ✝ trust *m*, cartel *m*.

combust|ible combustible (*adj., su.*); ~**ion** combustion *f*.

come venir, arriver; **to** ~ futur, à venir, qui vient; ~ **about** arriver, se passer; ~ **across s.o.** tomber sur q.; ~ **along** se dépêcher; arriver; ~ **at** se jeter sur; *fig.* parvenir à; ~ **by** passer par; obtenir; ~ **down** descendre; *fig.* s'abaisser; déchoir; .. **down with** être frappé par (*an illness*); ~ **for** venir chercher; ~ **in!** entrez!; ~ **off** se détacher (*button*); avoir lieu; tomber (*hair*); ~ **on** s'avancer; survenir; ~ **round** *fig.* reprendre connaissance; ~ **to** (*u.s.*) revenir à soi; reprendre ses sens; ~ **up to** s'élever jusqu'à; s'approcher de (*q.*); égaler; ~ **upon** tomber sur; rencontrer par hasard; ~**back** rentrée *f*, retour *m* en vogue *or* au pouvoir; réplique *f*.

comed|ian comédien(ne *f*) *m*; comique *m*; ~**y** comédie *f*.

comeliness mine *f* avenante.

comet comète *f*.

comfort 1. confort *m*, bien-être; consolation *f*, réconfort *m*; **2.** consoler; réconforter; ~**able** confortable; à son aise; ~**er** consolateur (-trice *f*) *m*; *fig.* cache-nez *m/inv.*; *Am.* couvre pied *m* piqué; *Brit.* sucette *f*; ~**less** incommode; ~ **station** toilette *f*.

comic 1. comique; *fig.* (*usu.* ~**al**) pour rire; ~ **strips** = **2.** ~**s** *pl. journ.* bandes *f/pl.* dessinées (*often humorous*).

coming 1. futur, qui vient; **2.** venue *f*; approche *f*.

comma virgule *f*; **inverted** ~**s** *pl.* guillements *m/pl.*

command 1. ordre *m*; maîtrise *f* (*of a language*); ✕ commandement *m*; **have at one's** ~ avoir à sa disposition; **2.** ordonner; commander; *fig.* être maître de, maîtriser; disposer de; ~**er** chef *m*; ✕ commandant *m*; ~**ment** commandement *m*.

commemorat|e commémorer; célébrer le souvenir de; ~**ion** commémoration *f*.

commence commencer; ~**ment** commencement *m*.

commend recommander; confier; louer; F **~ me to ...** saluez ... de ma part; **~ation** éloge m, louange f; **~atory** élogieux.

commensurable commensurable (avec **with, to**).

comment 1. commentaire m; **2.** faire des commentaires or des remarques (sur, **on**); **~ on** a. commenter; **~ary** commentaire m; radioreportage m; **~ator** commentateur (-trice f) m; radioreporter m.

commerc|e commerce m; affaires f/pl.; **~ial 1.** commercial; mercantile; marchand; de (du) commerce; **~ traveller** voyageur m de commerce, représentant(e f) m; **2.** telev., radio: réclame f.

commiserat|e **~ with** compatir à; **~ion** commisération.

commissary commissaire m.

commission 1. commission f (a. ✝); ordre m; délégation f (of authority); crime: perpétration f; ✗ brevet m, grade m d'officier; **in (out of) ~** en (hors de) service; **2.** commander (work of art etc.); passer commande à (q.); charger (q.) (de inf., **to** inf.); **~er** commissaire m; délégué m d'une commission.

commit (a. a crime, an error); confier (à, **to**); **~ (o.s.** s')engager (à, **to**); (se) compromettre; **~ to prison** envoyer en prison; **~ to writing** coucher (qch.) par écrit; **~ed** engagé; **~ment** engagement m; responsabilité(s) f/ (pl.); obligation(s) f/ (pl); **~tal** internement m; **~ to** remise f à; **~tee** comité m, commission f.

commodity (usu. **commodities** pl.) marchandise f; produit m; denrée f.

common 1. commun; courant; ordinaire; vulgaire; **~ law** droit m commun or coutumier; ✝ ♀ **Market** Marché m commun; **~ sense** bon sens m; **in ~** en commun (avec, **with**); **2.** terrain m communal; **~er** bourgeois m, roturier m; **~place 1.** lieu m commun; **2.** banal; médiocre; **~s** pl. (usu. **House of**) ♀ Chambre f des Communes; **~wealth: the British** ♀ l'Empire m Britannique.

commotion agitation f; troubles m/pl.

communal communal.

communicat|e v/t. communiquer (à, **to**); v/i. communiquer (avec, **with**; par, **by**); eccl. recevoir la communion; **~ion** communication f (a. ✗, teleph.); voie f

d'accès; **be in ~ with** être en relation avec; **~ive** communicatif; expansif.

communion eccl., fig. communion f.

communis|m communisme m; **~t 1.** communiste mf; **2.** (or **~tic**) communiste.

community communauté f.

communize collectiviser; rendre communiste.

commut|ation commutation f (en **into**, **for**); Am. **~ ticket** carte f d'abonnement; **~ator** ⚡ commutateur m; **~e 1.** v/t. échanger (pour, contre **for**, **into**); ⚖ etc. commuer (en, **into**); v/i. faire le trajet journalier (entre domicile et lieu de travail); faire la navette; **~er** personne f qui fait le trajet journalier (entre domicile et lieu de travail).

compact 1. (agreement) convention f; (a. **~car** voiture f) compact f; (a. **powder ~**) poudrier m; **2.** compact; serré; **3.** v/t. rendre compact.

companion compagnon m, compagne f; **~able** sociable; **~ship** camaraderie f; compagnie f.

company compagnie f (a. ✝, thea., ✗); **have ~** avoir du monde or de la visite; **keep s.o. ~** tenir compagnie à q.; **part ~ with** se séparer de.

compar|able comparable (avec, à **with**, **to**); **~ative 1.** comparatif; comparé; relatif; **~ degree = 2.** gramm. comparatif m; **~e 1. beyond** (or **without** or **past**) **~** sans pareil; **2.** v/t. comparer (avec, à **with**, **to**); **(as) ~d with** en comparaison de; v/i. être comparable (à, **with**); **~ison** comparaison f (a. gramm.).

compartment compartiment m (a. △, a. 🚂); luggage: soute f.

compass boussole f; fig. limite(s) f/ (pl.); **(a pair of) ~es** pl. (un) compas m.

compassion compassion f (de, **on**); **~ate** compatissant.

compatible compatible (avec, **with**).

compatriot compatriote mf.

compel contraindre, forcer, obliger (q. à inf., **s.o. to** inf.).

compensat|e v/t. dédommager (de, **for**); compenser (a. ⊜) (avec **with, by**); v/i. **~ for** compenser (qch.); **~ion** compensation f (a. ⊜); dédommagement m; réparation f.

compère 1. animateur (-trice f) m,

présentateur (-trice *f*) *m*; **2.** animer (*a show*), présenter.

compete concourir (pour qch., **for s.th.**); rivaliser (avec q. de qch., **with s.o. in s.th.**); **~nce**, **~ncy** compétence *f*; **~nt** capable; compétent (*a.* 🏛).

competit|ion concurrence *f* (*a.* ♥); *sp.* concours *m*, compétition *f*; **~ive** de concurrence; de concours; compétitif (*price etc.*); **~or** concurrent(e *f*) *m*.

compile compiler; dresser (*a list, an inventory etc.*).

complacen|ce, **~cy** contentement *m* de soi-même; **~t** content de soi-même.

complain se plaindre (de **of**, **about**; à **to**; que, **that**); porter plainte (contre **against**, **about**); **~ant** plaignant(e *f*) *m*; **~t** grief *m*; plainte *f*; doléances *f/pl.*; maladie *f*.

complaisan|ce complaisance *f*, obligeance *f*; **~t** complaisant, obligeant.

complement 1. complément *m*; ♣ effectif *m* (complet); **2.** compléter; **~ary** complémentaire.

complete 1. complet; entier; total; **2.** compléter; achever; remplir (*a form*); **~ion** achèvement *m*.

complex 1. complexe; **2.** ensemble *m*; *psych.* complexe *m*; **~ion** teint *m*; aspect *m*, caractère *m*; **~ity** complexité *f*.

complian|ce acquiescement *m* (à, **with**); obéissance *f*; **in ~ with** en conformité avec, conformément à; **~t** accommodant.

complicat|e compliquer; **~ed** compliqué; **~ion** complication *f* (*a.* 🏥).

complicity complicité *f* (à, **in**).

compliment 1. compliment *m*; **2.** *v/t.* complimenter (de, **on**); **~ary** flatteur; (*free*) (à titre) gracieux; **~ ticket** billet *m* de faveur.

comply *v/i.:* **~ with** se conformer à; se soumettre à; accomplir (*a condition*); observer (*a rule*).

component 1. partie *f* constituante; composant *m*; **2.** constituant; composant.

compos|e composer; calmer (*s.o.'s mind*); **~ed** calme, tranquille, posé; **be ~ of** se composer de; **~er** ♪ compositeur (-trice *f*) *m*; **~ition** composition *f*; **~t** compost *m*; **~ure** sang-froid *m*, calme *m*.

compound 1. composé; **~ interest** intérêts *m/pl.* composés; **2.** composé *m* (*a.* 🐍); enclos *m*; **3.** *v/t.* arranger (*a difference*); *v/i.* s'arranger.

comprehen|d comprendre; **~sible** compréhensible; **~sion** compréhension *f*; **~sive** compréhensif; ♥ **~ insurance** assurance *f* tous risques.

compress 1. comprimer; **2.** 🩹 compresse *f*; **~ion** compression *f*.

comprise comprendre, contenir.

compromise 1. compromis *m*; **2.** *v/t.* compromettre; *v/i.* aboutir à *or* accepter un compromis.

compuls|ion contrainte *f*; **~ive** compulsif; **~ory** obligatoire.

compunction remords *m*; componction *f*.

comput|ation calcul *m*, estimation *f*; compte *m*; **~e** calculer, estimer (à, **at**).

computer ordinateur *m*; **~ language** langage *m* machine; **~ science** informatique; **~ scientist** informaticien(ne *f*) *m*; **~-controlled** commandé par ordinateur; **~ization** informatisation *f*; **~ize** informatiser.

comrade camarade *mf*.

con[1] *abbr.* of **contra**; **pro and ~** pour et contre; **the pros and ~s** le pour et le contre.

con[2] *sl.* **1.** (*a.* **~ game**) escroquerie *f*; **~ man** escroc *m*; **2.** duper; escroquer.

conceal cacher; masquer; voiler.

concede concéder; admettre.

conceit vanité *f*; prétention *f*; **~ed** vaniteux, prétentieux.

conceiv|able imaginable, concevable; **~e** *v/i.* devenir enceinte; **~ of s.th.** (s')imaginer qch.; *v/t.* concevoir (*a child, a project, etc.*).

concentrat|e (se) concentrer; **~ion** concentration *f* (*a.* 🏛).

concept concept *m*; **~ion** conception *f*.

concern 1. affaire *f*; intérêt *m* (dans, **in**); inquiétude *f*, souci *m* (à l'égard de, **about**); ♥ entreprise *f*; maison *f* de commerce; **2.** concerner; **~ o.s. with** s'occuper de, **~ o.s. about** (*or* **for**) s'intéresser à; s'inquiéter de; **~ed** inquiet (de **at**, **about**, **for**; au sujet de, **about**); soucieux; impliqué (dans, **in**); **be ~ with** s'occuper de; s'intéresser à; **~ing** *prp.* au sujet de, concernant, en ce qui concerne.

C

concert concert *m*; **in ~ ♪** en concert; *fig. act* de concert; **~ hall** salle *f* de concert; **~ pitch** diapason *m* (de concert); *fig.* **at ~ pitch** au maximum de la forme; en pleine forme.

concess|ion concession *f*; **~ive** concessif.

concilia|te (ré)concilier; **~ion** conciliation *f*; **~or** conciliateur (-trice *f*) *m*; **~ory** conciliant, conciliatoire.

concise concis; bref; serré (*style*).

conclude *v/t.* conclure; terminer, achever; arranger, régler (*one's affairs*); **to be ~d in our next** la fin au prochain numéro; *v/i.* conclure.

conclus|ion conclusion *f*; **~ive** concluant, décisif.

concoct confectionner; *fig.* imaginer; tramer; **~ion** confection *f*, mixtion *f*; *fig. plan etc.*: élaboration *f*.

concord concorde *f*, harmonie *f* (*a.* ♪); *gramm.* concordance *f*; **~ance** accord *m* (avec, **with**); concordance *f* (*a. eccl.*); **~ant** concordant.

concourse foule *f*; rassemblement *m*; hall *m*.

concrete 1. concret; △ de *or* en béton; **2.** △ *béton-m; phls., gramm.* concret *m*; **3.** (se) concréter *v/t.* solidifier; *v/t.* bétonner.

concur (r)enfermer coïncider; être d'accord (avec, **with**); concourir (à, **in**); contribuer (à, **to**); **~rence** coïncidence *f*; accord *m*; **~rent** concordant; simultané; **~rently** simultanément.

concussion secousse *f*; commotion *f* (cérébrale).

condemn condamner; **~ation** condamnation *f*.

condens|ation condensation *f*; **~e** (se) condenser.

condescen|d condescendre (à, **to**); **~ing** condescendant; **~sion** condescendance *f*.

condiment condiment *m*.

condition 1. condition *f*; **on ~ that** à condition que; **2.** déterminer; conditionner (*a.* the air, *a. psych.*); **~al 1.** conditionnel; dépendant (de, [*up*]on); **~ mood** = **2.** *gramm.* conditionnel *m*.

condol|e (**with s.o.**) partager la douleur (de q.); exprimer ses condoléances (à q.); **~ence** condoléance *f*.

conduc|e: **~ to** conduire à; **~ive** (**to**) favorable (à); qui contribue (à).

conduct 1. conduite *f*; **2.** conduire; mener; diriger (*a.* ♪); **~ o.s.** se comporter; **~ed tour** voyage *m* organisé; **~ion** conduction *f*; **~or** conducteur *m* (*a. phys., a.* ⚡); *tram etc.*: receveur *m*; 🚋 *Am.* chef *m* de train; ♪ chef *m* d'orchestre.

conduit conduit *m*; tuyau *m*.

cone cône *m*; *icecream*: cornet *m*; ♣ pomme *f* (de pin).

confection *cuis.* sucrerie(s) *f*/ (*pl.*); **~er** confiseur *m*; **~ery** confiserie *f*; pâtisserie *f*.

confedera|te 1. confédéré (*a. su.*); **2.** (se) confédérer; **~tion** confédération *f*.

confer *v/t.* (à, **on**) conférer; accorder (*a favour*); décerner (*an honour*); *v/i.* conférer; **~ence** conférence *f*.

confess *v/t.* confesser; avouer (*qch.*; que, **that**; *inf.*, **to** *ger.*); *v/i. eccl.* se confesser; **~ion** confession *f* (*a. eccl.*); **~ional** confessionnal *m*; **~or** confesseur *m*.

confide *v/t.* confier; avouer (*qch.*) en confidence (à q., **to s.o.**); *v/i.* se (con)fier (à q., **in s.o.**); **~nce** confiance *f* (en, **in**); (*self-confidence*) confiance *f* en soi, assurance *f*; confidence *f*; **~ man** escroc *m*; truc escroquerie *f*; **~nt** assuré, sûr (de, **of**); **~ntial** confidentiel.

confine (r)enfermer (dans, **to**); limiter (à, **to**); **be ~d to bed** être alité, garder le lit; **be ~d** faire ses couches; accoucher; **~ment** emprisonnement *m*; alitement *m*; restriction *f*; *woman*: couches *f*/*pl.*

confirm confirmer (*a. eccl.*); affermir (*one's power*); ratifier (*a treaty etc.*); 🏛 entériner; **~ation** confirmation *f*; affermissement *m*.

confiscat|e confisquer; F voler; **~ion** confiscation *f*; F *fig.* vol *m*.

conflagration incendie *m*.

conflict 1. conflit *m*. lutte *f*; **2.** (**with**) être en conflit (avec); se heurter (à).

conflu|ence *rivers etc.*: confluent *m*; concours *m* (*of people etc.*).

conform: **~ to** se conformer à; obéir à; **~ with** se soumettre à; **~able** conforme (à, **to**); **~ity** conformité *f* (à **with**, **to**); **in ~ with** conformément à.

confound confondre: **~ed** F maudit, sacré.

confront être en face de; faire face à; confronter (avec, **with**).

confus|e confondre (*a. fig.*); mêler; em-

consistent

brouiller; troubler; **~ion** confusion f; désordre m.

confute réfuter.

congeal (se) congeler; (se) cailler; (se) figer; geler.

congenial sympathique; agréable; convenable (à, **to**); **~ with** du même caractère que.

congenital congénital, de naissance.

congest|ed congestionné (#, a road etc.), fig. encombré; **~ion** congestion f; encombrement m (a. traffic).

conglomeration conglomérat m.

congratulat|e féliciter (q. de qch., s.o. [**up**]**on s.th.**); **~ion** félicitation f.

congregat|e (se) rassembler; **~ion** eccl. assistance f, paroissiens m/pl.

congress congrès m; **~man**, **~woman** membre m du Congrès.

congruous conforme (à **to**, **with**).

conical conique.

conifer conifère m.

conjecture 1. conjecture f; **2.** conjecturer.

conjoin (s') unir; **~t** joint, associé.

conjuga|l conjugal; **~te** conjuguer; **~tion** conjugaison f.

conjunction conjonction f.

conjur|e conjurer, supplier (q. de inf., s.o. to inf.); by magic etc.: conjurer (a demon); (a. **~ up**) faire apparaître; **~ up** évoquer (a. fig.); **~er** m prestidigitateur m, illusionniste m f; **~ing trick** tour m de prestidigitation.

conk sl. **1.** pif m (= nose); **2. ~ out** tomber en panne; sl. crever.

connect (se) (re)lier, (se) joindre; v/t. ≠ (inter)connecter; brancher (a lamp); **~ed** connexe; apparenté; fig. cohérent; **be ~ with** être allié à or avec; se rattacher à; avoir des rapports avec; **~ion** rapport m, lien m; ideas: suite f, cohérence f; ≠ connexion f; tel. communication f; ⊕ raccord m; correspondance f; family: parenté f; person: relations f/pl. (a. ♥); fig. liaison f.

conning tower submarine: kiosque m; cruiser: tourelle f de commandement.

connive: ~ at fermer les yeux sur.

connoisseur connaisseur (-euse f) m (en **of**, **in**).

connotation connotation f.

connubial conjugal.

conquer conquérir; vaincre; **~or** conquérant(e f) m; vainqueur m.

conquest conquête f.

conscience conscience f.

conscientious consciencieux; de conscience; **~objector** objecteur m de conscience; **~ness** conscience f.

conscious conscient; (de, **of**); **be ~ of** a. avoir conscience de; **be ~ that** a. savoir que; **~ness** conscience f; ♥ connaissance f.

conscript ✗ conscrit m; **~ion** ✗ conscription f.

consecrat|e consacrer; **~ion** consécration f.

consecutive consécutif.

consensus consensus m.

consent 1. consentement m; **by common** (or **general**) **~** de l'aveu de tout le monde; **by mutual ~** par consentement mutuel; **age of ~** âge m nubile; **2.** consentir (a, **to**).

consequen|ce conséquence f; suites f/pl.; importance f (pour q., à qch.); **in ~ of** par suite de; en conséquence de; **~t** résultant (de, **on**); **be ~ on** a. résulter de; **~tial** conséquent (à **to**, [**up**]**on**); consécutif (à, **to**); person: suffisant; **~tly** par conséquent; donc.

conserva|tion préservation f, protection f; défense f de l'environnement; **~tionist** écologiste m f; **~tive 1.** conservateur (a. pol.); prudent; **2.** conservateur (-trice f) m; **~tory** ♪ serre f; ♪ etc. conservatoire m; **~e** conserver; préserver.

consider considérer; estimer; prendre en considération; réfléchir à; **~able** considérable, important; **~ate** plein d'égards (pour, envers **to**[**wards**]); **~ation** considération f; égard m, -s m/pl.; compensation f, rémunération f; fig. importance f; **be under ~** être en délibération or à l'examen; **take into ~** prendre en considération; tenir compte de; **on no ~** sous aucun prétexte; **~ing 1.** prp. eu égard à; **2.** F adv. malgré tout.

consign expédier, envoyer; remettre, confier; **~ment** ♥ expédition f; envoi m.

consist: ~ in consister en (qch.), consister à (faire qch.); **~ of** se composer de; **~ence**, **~ency** liquid: consistance f (a. fig.); soil: compacité f; behaviour: uniformité f, logique f; **~ent** conséquent; logique; compatible (avec, **with**).

consol|ation consolation *f*; **~atory** consolant, consolateur; **~e 1.** console *f* (*a.* ♫); **2.** consoler.

consolidate (se) consolider (*a. fig.*); (se) tasser (*road*); *v/t.* solidifier.

consonan|ce consonance *f*; **~t 1.** ♪ harmonieux; consonant; conforme (à *with, to*); **2.** consonne *f*.

consort époux *m*, épouse *f*.

conspicuous apparent, manifeste; *fig.* frappant; insigne; *make o.s. ~ by* se faire remarquer par.

conspir|acy conspiration *f*; **~ator** conspirateur (-trice *f*) *m*; **~e** conspirer (contre, *against*).

constab|le agent *m* de police; gendarme *m*; **~ulary** police *f*; *county ~* gendarmerie *f*.

constan|cy constance *f*; **~t** continuel; constant; invariable; loyal, fidèle; **~tly** continuellement, constamment.

constellation *astr.* constellation *f*.

consternation consternation *f*.

constipation ⚕ constipation *f*.

constituen|cy circonscription *f* électorale; électeurs *m/pl.*; **~t 1.** constituant, constitutif; **2.** élément *m* (constitutif), composant *m*; *pol.* électeur (-trice *f*) *m*.

constitut|e constituer; **~ion** constitution *f*; **~ional** constitutionnel (*a.* ⚕).

constrain contraindre (à, *de inf. to inf.*); **~t** contrainte *f*.

constrict (res)serrer; rétrécir; gêner; **~ion** resserrement *m*.

construct construire; bâtir; **~ion** construction *f*; interprétation *f*, explication *f*; *~ site* chantier *m*; *under ~* en construction; **~ive** constructif; créateur (*mind*); **~or** constructeur *m*; ingénieur *m*.

construe *gramm.* analyser; *fig.* interpréter, expliquer.

consul consul *m*; *~ general* consul *m* général; **~ate** consulat *m* (*a. building*).

consult *v/t.* consulter; *v/i.* conférer (avec, *with*); (*a. ~ together*) délibérer; **~ant** consultant (*adj., su.*); (*expert*-) conseil *m*; ⚕ médecin *m* consultant; *legal ~* conseiller *m* juridique; **~ation** ⚕, ⚖, *book*: consultation *f*, délibération *f*; **~ative** consultatif; **~ing** consultant; *~ hours* heures *f/pl.* de consultation; *~ room* cabinet *m* de consultation.

consume *v/t.* consommer (*food, sup-*plies, *fuel, etc.*); *fig.* consumer; **~r** consommateur (-trice *f*) *m*; *~ durables pl.* biens *m/pl.* de consommation durables; *~ goods pl.* biens *m/pl.* de consommation; *~ society* société *f* de consommation.

consummate 1. achevé; **2.** consommer (*a crime, marriage*).

consumpt|ion consommation *f*; ⚕ tuberculose *f*; **~ive** tuberculeux.

contact 1. contact *m* (*a.* ⚡); *opt.* **~ lenses** *pl.* lentilles *f/pl.* cornéennes; ⚡ *make* (*break*) établir (rompre) le contact; **2.** contacter (*q.*).

contagi|on ⚕ contagion *f*; maladie *f* contagieuse; **~ous** contagieux.

contain contenir; *fig. a.* maîtriser; **~er** récipient *m*; ⚓ conteneur *m*; **~erize** conteneuriser.

contaminat|e contaminer; *fig.* corrompre; **~ion** contamination *f*.

contemplat|e considérer, envisager, songer à; contempler; **~ion** contemplation *f*; **~ive** contemplatif.

contempora|neous contemporain; **~ry 1.** contemporain (de, *with*); moderne; **2.** contemporain(e *f*) *m*.

contempt mépris *m*, dédain *m*; **~ible** méprisable; indigne; **~uous** dédaigneux (de, *of*); méprisant.

contend *v/i.* lutter, rivaliser (avec, *with*); *v/t.* soutenir (que, *that*).

content¹ contenu *m*; *document, mineral etc.*: teneur *f*; **~s** *pl.* contenu *m*; *table of ~s* table *f* des matières.

content² 1. satisfait (de, *with*); **2.** contenter, satisfaire; *~ o.s. with* se contenter de; **3.** contentement *m*; *to one's heart's ~* à souhait; **~ed** content, satisfait (de, *with*).

content|ion dispute *f*, contestation *f*; assertion *f*, affirmation *f*; **~ious** contentieux; disputeur; **~ment** contentement *m*.

contest 1. lutte *f*; concours *m*; *sp.* match *m*; **2.** (se) disputer; contester.

context contexte *m*.

contiguous contigu, (à, *to*).

continent 1. continent *m*; *Br. the ~* l'Europe *f* (continentale); **2.** chaste; **~al 1.** continental; *Br. a.* de l'Europe; *~ breakfast* petit déjeuner *m* à la française; *~ quilt* duvet *m*; **2.** *Br.* Européen(ne *f*) *m* continental(e).

contingen|cy éventualité f; cas m imprévu; **~ plan** plan m d'urgence; **~t 1.** contingent; **be ~ on** dépendre de; **2.** ✕ contingent m.

continua|l continuel, incessant; **~nce** continuation f; durée f; **~tion** continuation f; suite f; reprise f.

continue continuer; reprendre; **to be ~d** à suivre; **~ity** continuité f (a. cin.); **~ girl** script(-girl) f; **~ous** continu; suivi.

contort tordre, crisper; **~ion** contorsion f; torsion f, crispation f.

contour contour m, profil m.

contra contre.

contraband contrebande f.

contract 1. v/t. contracter (habits, an illness, debts, a marriage, etc.); v/i. se contracter, se resserrer; s'engager (de, to); **~ing party** contractant(e f) m; **2.** contrat m, **by ~** par contrat; **~ work** travail m à forfait; **~ion** contraction f; **~or** building: entrepreneur m.

contradict contredire (q., qch.); **~ion** contradiction f; **~ory** contradictoire; opposé (à, to).

contrar|iety contrariété f; **~y 1.** contraire, opposé (à, to); F indocile; **2.** contraire m; **on** ou **the ~** au contraire; **to the ~** a. à l'encontre.

contrast 1. contraste m (avec to, with); **in ~ to** par contraste avec; v/t. faire contraster (avec, with); opposer; mettre en contraste (avec, with); v/i. contraster (avec, with).

contraven|e enfreindre; **~tion** infraction f (à, of); **in ~ of** en violation de.

contribut|e v/i. .. **~ to** contribuer (à); donner, offrir (a sum) (pour, to[wards]); journ. etc. écrire (an article); **~ion** contribution f; journ. article m; **~or** contributeur(-trice f) m; collaborateur (-trice f) m (d'un journal, **to a newspaper**); **~ory** contribuant.

contrit|e contrit, pénitent; **~ion** contrition f, pénitence f.

contriv|ance invention f; combinaison f; artifice m, appareil m, dispositif m; F truc m; **~e** v/t. inventer, combiner; arranger; v/i.: **~ to** (inf.) s'arranger ou trouver (le) moyen ou se débrouiller pour (inf.); **~ed** forcé.

control 1. autorité f; maîtrise f; contrôle m; train, ship: manœuvre f; mot. (a. **~ lever**) manette f de commande; ⊙ **~s**

pl. commandes f/pl.; ⊙ **~ desk** pupitre m de commande; **remote ~** télécommande f; **~ knob** bouton m de réglage; ✈ **~ tower** tour f de contrôle; **2.** diriger; régler; maîtriser; gouverner; réglementer (the traffic); ⊙ commander (a. ✈); ✝ **~ling interest** participation majoritaire.

controver|sial controversé, discuté; **~sy** controverse f; polémique f.

contumacious rebelle, récalcitrant.

contumely insolence f; mépris m.

contuse ✗ contusionner.

convalesce être en convalescence; se remettre (de sa maladie), relever de maladie; **~nce** convalescence f, **~nt** convalescent (a. su.).

convene (s')assembler, (se) réunir; v/t. convoquer (an assembly).

convenien|ce commodité f, confort m; (a. **public ~**) cabinets m/pl. d'aisance; **at your earliest ~** dans les meilleurs délais; **~t** commode.

convent couvent m; **~ion** convention f; **~ional** conventionnel.

converge converger.

convers|ant: be ~ with être au courant de, connaître; **~ation** conversation f, entretien m; **~ational** de (la) conversation; **~e 1.** contraire, inverse (adj., su.); **2.** causer, s'entretenir; causer (avec, with); **~ion** conversion f.

convert 1. converti(e f) m; **2.** transformer (a. ✍); changer; convertir (a. ⊙, eccl., pol., phls.); **~er** ⊙, ⚡ convertisseur m; **~ible** convertible (en, into) (thing); mot. décapotable.

convex convexe.

convey (trans)porter; communiquer (a thought, news, etc.); transmettre (a. phys.); **~ance** transport m; moyen(s) m(pl.) de transport; transmission f (a. ⚖, a. phys.); communication f (a. ✍); voiture f, véhicule m; **~or** ⊙ (a. **~ belt**) bande f transporteuse.

convict 1. forçat m; **2.** reconnaître ou déclarer (q.) coupable; **~ion** conviction f; ⚖ condamnation f

convince convaincre, persuader (q. de qch., s.o. of s.th.).

convivial joyeux, jovial.

convoke convoquer.

convoy 1. convoi m; **2.** convoyer.

convuls|e ébranler, bouleverser; **be ~d**

with laughter se tordre de rire; **~ion** convulsion *f*; *fig.* bouleversement *m*; **~ive** convulsif.

cook 1. cuisinier (-ière *f*) *m*; (*a. head ~*) chef *m*; **2.** *v/t.* (faire) cuire; F cuisiner (*an account*); *v/i.* faire la cuisine; **~book** livre *m* de cuisine; **~ery** cuisine *f*; **~ie** *Am.* galette *f*.

cool 1. frais; froid, tiède (*sentiments*); *fig.* calme, de sang-froid; *pej.* sans gêne; **2.** frais *m*; **3.** (se) rafraîchir; **~ing** ☉ refroidissement *m*; *attr.* de réfrigération; **~ness** fraîcheur *f*; *fig.* person: froideur *f*; sang-froid *m*.

coon *Am.* F *zo. abbr. of* rac(c)oon: raton-laveur *m*; *sl. pej.* nègre *m*.

coop 1. cage *f* à poules; poulailler *m*; **2. ~ up** (*or* **in**) enfermer.

co-op F *see* **co(-)operative store.**

cooper tonnelier *m*.

co(-)operat|e coopérer, collaborer; **~ion** coopération, *f* collaboration *f*; **~ive 1.** coopératif; **~ society** société *f* coopérative; **~ store** société *f* coopérative de consommation; F coopérative *f*; **2.** coopérative *f*; **~or** coopérateur (-trice *f*) *m*.

co-ordinat|e 1. coordonné; **2.** coordonner (à, with); **~ion** coordination *f*.

cop *sl.* flic *m*.

copartner coassocié(e *f*) *m*.

cope se débrouiller, s'en tirer, F se défendre; **~ with** tenir tête à, faire face à; s'occuper de; venir à bout de.

co-pilot copilote *m*.

copier machine *f* à photocopier.

copious copieux, abondant; **~ness** profusion *f*, abondance *f*.

copper[1] **1.** cuivre *m* (rouge); petite pièce *f* (d'argent); **2.** de *or* en cuivre.

copper[2] *Brit. sl.* (*cop*) flic *m*.

coppice, copse taillis *m*, hallier *m*.

copy 1. copie *f*; reproduction *f*; *book*: exemplaire *m*; *newspaper*: numéro *m*; *printing*: manuscrit *m*; *journ.* matière *f* à reportage; (*a. carbon ~*) double *m*; *fair* (*or* *clean*) **~** copie *f* au net; *rough* **~** brouillon *m*; **2.** copier; reproduire; **~ fair** mettre au net; **~book** cahier *m*; **~cat** F copieur (-euse *f*) *m*; imitateur (-trice *f*) *m*; **~ist** copiste *mf*; scribe *m*; **~right** propriété *f* littéraire; droit *m* d'auteur.

coral corail *m*.

cord 1. corde *f*; cordon *m*; *tex.* velours *m* côtelé; **2.** corder.

cordial 1. cordial; chaleureux; **2.** sirop *m*; cordial *m*; **~ity** cordialité *f*.

corduroy *tex.* velours *m* côtelé.

core 1. *fruit*: trognon *m*, *a. wood*: cœur *m* (*a. fig.*); ☉ noyau *m*; *fig.* **to the ~** complètement, jusqu'à la moelle; **2.** enlever le trognon *or* cœur de.

cork 1. liège *m*; *bottle*: bouchon *m*; **2.** boucher; *fig.* (*a. ~ up*) étouffer, réprimer (*emotions etc.*); **~ing** F épatant, fameux; **~ jacket** gilet *m* de sauvetage; **~screw** tire-bouchon *m*; **~tree** ♠ chêne-liège (*pl.* chênes-lièges) *m*.

corn[1] **1.** grain *m*; *Br.* blé *m*; *Am.* (*a. Indian ~*) maïs *m*; *Am.* **~ bread** pain *m* de maïs; **~ flakes** paillettes *f*/*pl.* de maïs; **2.** saler; **~ed beef** corned-beef *m*.

corn[2] ♠ *toe*: cor *m*.

corner 1. coin *m*; tournant *m*; *mot.* virage *m*; *fig.* dilemme *m*; *foot.* (*a. ~ kick*) corner *m*; **2.** acculer, coincer; ♣ accaparer (*the market*); **~ed** à angles; **~stone** pierre *f* angulaire (*a. fig.*).

cornflower bl(e)uet *m*; **~ blue** bleu barbeau.

cornice △, *mount.* corniche *f*; chapiteau *m* d'armoire.

coronary ♠[1] **1.** coronaire; **~ thrombosis** = **2.** F infarctus *m* (du myocarde).

coron|ation couronnement *m*, sacre *m*; **~er** ☉ coroner *m*; **~et** cercle *m*, couronne *f*; diadème *m*.

corpora|l 1. ~ punishment châtiment *m* corporel; **2.** ✗ caporal *m*; brigadier *m*; **~te** (en) commun; **~ body, body ~** corps *m* constitué; **~ image** image *f* de la firme; **~ name** raison *f* sociale; **~tion** corporation *f*; personne *f* civile; municipalité *f*; conseil *m* municipal; *Am.* société *f* par actions.

corpse cadavre *m*.

corpulen|ce, **~cy** corpulence *f*; **~t** corpulent.

corral *esp. Am.* **1.** corral *m*; **2.** renfermer dans un corral.

correct 1. *adj.* correct; juste; exact; **2.** *v/t.* corriger; rectifier (*an error*); reprendre (*a child*); **~ion** correction *f*; rectification *f*.

correlat|e *v/t.* mettre en corrélation (avec, with); *v/i.* être en corrélation (avec **with**), correspondre (à **with, to**); **~ion** corrélation *f.*

correspond correspondre (à **with, to**); **~ence** correspondance *f.*; **~ course** cours *m* par correspondance; **~ent** correspondant(e *f*) *m.*

corridor couloir *m*, corridor *m.*

corroborat|e *v/t.* corroborer; **~ion** corroboration *f.*

corro|de *v/t.* corroder, ronger (*metal*, *a.* *fig.*); *v/i.* se corroder; **~sion** corrosion *f.*; **~sive** corrosif (*adj., su./m*).

corrugated plissé; ondulé; **~ cardboard** carton *m* ondulé; **~ iron** tôle *f* ondulée.

corrupt 1. corrompu; **2.** corrompre; **~ible** corruptible; **~ion** corruption *f.*

corset corset *m.*

coruscate scintiller; briller.

co-signatory cosignataire (*a. su.*).

cosine ⅄ cosinus *m.*

cosiness atmosphère *f* chaleureuse, confortable *m.*

cosmetic cosmétique (*adj., su./m*).

cosmonaut cosmonaute *m.*

cosmopolit|an, ~e cosmopolite (*a. su.*).

cost 1. coût *m*; frais *m/pl.*; dépens *m/pl.*; *fig.* **at all ~s** à tout prix, coûte que coûte; **first** (*or* **prime**) **~** prix *m* coûtant; **~ of revient**; **~ of living** coût *m* de la vie; **2.** coûter.

co-star 1. partenaire *mf*; **2.** partager la vedette.

costly coûteux; de grande valeur, précieux.

costume costume *m.*

cosy douillet, confortable.

cot lit *m* d'enfants; lit *m* de camp.

cottage chaumière *f*; petite maison *f* de campagne; *Am.* résidence *f* d'été; **~ cheese** fromage *m* blanc; **~ industry** industrie *f* à domicile; **~r** paysan(ne *f*) *m*; habitant(e *f*) *m* d'une chaumière; *Am.* estivant(e *f*) *m.*

cotton 1. coton *m*; **2.** de coton; **~ candy** barbe *f* à papa; **~ wool** ouate *f*; **3.** ⊢ **~ on** (**to s.th.**) piger (qch.).

couch 1. canapé *m* divan *m*; **2.** formuler, rédiger.

cough 1. toux *f*; **~ drop** (**mixture**) pastille *f* (sirop *m*) pour la toux; **2.** *v/i.* tousser.

council conseil *m*; **city ~, town ~** conseil *m* municipal; *eccl.* concile *m*; **~(l)or,** **~man, ~woman** conseiller *m*; membre *m* du conseil.

counsel 1. conseil *m*; ⚖ avocat *m*; **~ for the defence** défenseur *m*; avocat *m* du défendeur; **~ for the prosecution** avocat *m* de la partie publique; **2.** conseiller (à q. de *inf.*, **s.o. to** *inf.*); **~(l)or** conseiller *m.*

count¹ 1. compte *m*; calcul *m*; *votes*: dépouillement *m*; **2.** *v/t.* compter; dénombrer; *fig.* tenir (*q.*) pour, estimer; **~ o.s. lucky** s'estimer heureux; *v/i.* compter (sur, **on**; pour **as, for**; au nombre de, **among**); **~ for little** ne compter guère.

count² *foreign title*: comte *m.*

countable comptable

countdown *rocket launching*: compte *m* à rebours.

countenance 1. expression *f* (du visage), mine *f*; appui *m*, encouragement *m*; **2.** appuyer, encourager.

counter¹ comptoir (-euse *f*) *m*; ⚙ compteur *m*; *gambling*: jeton *m*; *shop*: comptoir *m*; *bank etc.*: guichets *m/pl.*; caisse *f*; *phys.* **Geiger ~** compteur *m* Geiger; **under the ~** clandestinement.

counter² 1. *adj., adv.*: **~ to** à l'encontre de, *adv. a.* contrairement à; **2.** *box.* coup *m* d'arrêt; **3.** *v/t.* aller à l'encontre de; *box.* parer.

counteract neutraliser, contrebalancer; parer à.

counter-attack 1. contre-attaque *f*; **2.** contre-attaquer.

counterbalance 1. contrepoids *m*; **2.** contrebalancer; compenser.

counter-clockwise en sens inverse des aiguilles d'une montre.

counter-espionage contre-espionnage *m.*

counterfeit 1. contrefait, faux; **2.** contrefaçon *f*; *document*: faux *m*; ⊢ fausse monnaie *f*; **3.** contrefaire; **~er** contrefacteur *m.*

counterfoil souche *f*, talon *m.*

countermand annuler, contremander; **unless ~ed** sauf contrordre.

countermeasure contre-mesure *f.*

counterpart *person*: homologue *mf*; *thing*: double *m.*

counterpoint ♪ contrepoint *m.*

counterpoise 1. contrepoids *m*; équilibre *m*; **2.** contrebalancer.

counter-productive improductif; inutile; absurde.

countersign 1. mot *m* d'ordre; **2.** contresigner.

countersink ⊚ fraiser.

counterweight contrepoids *m*.

countess comtesse *f*.

counting-house (bureau *m* de la) comptabilité *f*.

countless innombrable.

countrified rustique, rustaud.

country 1. pays *m*; région *f*; patrie *f*; campagne *f*; **2.** campagnard *m* de *or* à la campagne; **~man** campagnard *m* paysan *m*; compatriote *m*; **~side** campagne(s) *f*/ (*pl.*); **~woman** campagnarde *f*, paysanne *f*; compatriote *f*.

county comté *m*; **~town,** *Am.* **~seat** chef-lieu *m* (*pl.* chefs-lieux) de comté.

coup coup *m* (audacieux).

coupl|e 1. couple *m*, deux...; couple *f*; **F a ~ of** quelques; **2.** *v/t.* coupler; *fig.* associer; ⊚ engrener; 🚂 atteler; ⚡ interconnecter; *v/i.* s'accoupler; **~ing** couplage *m*, accouplement *m*; 🚂 attelage *m*.

coupon coupon *m* (*a.* 🛡).

courage courage *m*; **~ous** courageux.

courier courrier *m*, messager *m*.

course 1. *events, river, time, univ.:* cours *m*; route *f* (*a.* ⚓); *affairs:* courant *m*; *bullet:* trajet *m*; *meal:* plat *m*; *fig.* chemin *m*; *sp.* piste *f*; *terrain m: sp.* champ *m* de course(s); *golf:* parcours *m*; ⚓ cap *m*; ⚕ (*a. ~ of treatment*) traitement *m*; △ assise *f* (*of bricks etc.*); **~ of action** ligne *f* de conduite; *in due* **~** en temps utile; *of* **~** (bien) entendu, naturellement; **2.** *v/t.* (faire) courir; *v/i.* courir, couler (*liquid, esp. blood*).

court 1. cour *f* (*a. royal,* ⚖); ⚖ tribunal *m*; *sp.* court *m* (de tennis); *terrain m:* ⚖ **settle s.th. out of ~** arranger qch. à l'amiable; **2.** courtiser, faire la cour à (*a woman*); solliciter (*qch.*); **~eous** courtois, poli (envers, *to*); **~esy** courtoisie *f*, politesse *f*; **~ call** visite *f* de politesse; *mot.* **~ light** plafonnier *m*; **~house** palais *m* de justice; **~ier** courtisan *m*; **~ly** courtois; élégant; **~-martial,** *pl.* **~s- -martial** ⚔ **1.** conseil *m* de guerre; **2.** faire passer en conseil de guerre; **~ship** cour *f* (*paid to a woman*); **~yard** *house:* cour *f*.

cousin cousin(e *f*) *m*.

cove anse *f*; petite baie *f*.

covenant 1. convention *f*, contrat *m*; **2.** s'engager (de, *to inf.*).

cover 1. couverture *f*; *table:* tapis *m*; couvercle *m*; abri *m*; *letter:* enveloppe *f*; *fig.* voile *m* (*at table*); **~ story** *journ.* article *m* principal; *spy:* couverture *f*; **2.** couvrir (de, *with*) (*a.* ⚡ *risk,* ✕ *retreat, expenses*); revêtir, recouvrir; parcourir (*a distance*); **~ing** recouvrement *m*; couverture *f* (*a. of bed*); enveloppe *f*; *furniture:* housse *f*.

covert 1. voilé, caché; secret; **2.** *hunt.* abri *m*, couvert *m*; retraite *f*.

cover-up camouflage *m*.

covet convoiter; aspirer à; **~ous** avide (de, *of*); avare; cupide.

cow¹ vache *f*.

cow² intimider, dompter.

coward lâche *mf*; **~ice** lâcheté *f*; **~ly** lâche.

cow|boy cow-boy *m*; **~catcher** 🚂 chasse-pierres *m*/*inv.*

cower se recroqueviller, se tapir; *fig.* trembler (devant, *before*).

cow|herd vacher *m*; bouvier *m*; **~hide** peau *f* de vache *f*.

cowl *monk, chimney:* capuchon *m*; ⊚ capot *m*.

cowshed étable *f*.

coxcomb fat *m*.

coxswain barreur *m*; ⚓ patron *m*.

coy modeste, farouche, réservé.

crab¹ crabe *m*; *astr.* le Cancer *m*.

crab² 1. (*a. ~ apple*) pomme *f* sauvage; **2.** F rouspéter; **~by** F grincheux.

crack 1. craquement *m*; fente *f*, fissure *f*; lézarde *f*; *glass, chinaware, etc.:* fêlure *f*; F coup *m* sec; *sp. sl.* crack *m*, as *m*; *esp. Am. sl.* remarque *f* mordante; **2.** de premier ordre; **3.** *v/t.* faire claquer (*a whip*); fêler; crevasser; fendre; casser (*a nut*); **~ a joke** faire une plaisanterie; F **~ up** vanter (*q., qch.*); *v/i.* craquer (*a.*); claquer; se fêler; se crevasser; se lézarder; se gercer (*skin*); se casser (*voice etc.*); F **~ up** s'effondrer; flancher (*a. person*); s'écraser (*vehicle etc.*); **~down** razzia (*f*); **~ed** fêlé, fendu *etc.*; F timbré, toqué; **~er** pétard *m*; biscuit *m* dur; **~le** craqueter; crépiter; pétiller (*fire*); **~pot** (*type m*) cinglé; **~up** F effondrement *m*; crise *f* nerveuse; *mot. etc.* collision *f*; ✈ crash *m*.

cradle berceau *m*.

craft habileté f; ruse f; artifice m; métier m manuel; profession f; coll. pl. embarcations f/pl., petits navires m/pl.; avion, appareil; **~sman** artisan m, ouvrier m; **~y** astucieux, rusé.

crag rocher m à pic; **~gy** escarpé.

cram 1. fourrer (dans, *into*); bourrer (de, *with*); empâter (*fowl*); F bûcher.

cramp 1. ✻ crampe f; ☉ crampon m; *fig.* contrainte f; **2.** ☉ cramponner; *fig.* gêner; **~ed** resserré; (a. **~ for space**) à l'étroit.

crank manivelle f; F excentrique m/f; **~shaft** ☉ vilebrequin m; **~y** excentrique; *Am. a.* grincheux.

cranny fente f, crevasse f; niche f.

crape crêpe m noir.

crash 1. fracas m; catastrophe f; accident m, collision f; ✈ crash m; *mot.* **~ barrier** glissière f de sécurité; **~ course** cours m intensif; **~ diet** régime m radical; **~ landing** atterrissage m en catastrophe; **2.** s'écraser (*plane etc.*); **~ down** tomber (par terre) avec fracas; **~ into** emboutir, rentrer dans; **~ through** passer à travers (qch.) avec fracas.

crate caisse f à claire-voie.

crater cratère m; ✗ entonnoir m.

crave **~ for** désirer avidement (qch.).

craven poltron, lâche.

crawfish *fresh water*: écrevisse f; *sea*: langouste f.

crawl 1. rampement m; *swimming*: crawl m; **2.** ramper (a. *fig.* devant, to); *slowly*: avancer au pas (*vehicle, traffic, etc.*).

crayfish *see* **crawfish**.

crayon craie f à dessiner; *esp.* (crayon m de) pastel m.

craz|e manie f (de, for); **be the (latest) ~** faire fureur; **~y** fou (de **with, about,** for).

creak grincer, crier.

cream 1. crème f (a. *fig.*); **2.** crème *inv.*; **~ery** *factory*: laiterie f; *shop*: crémerie f; **~y** crémeux; *fig.* velouté.

crease 1. (faux) pli m, *tex.* ancrure f; **2.** (se) plisser; (se) froisser.

creat|e v/t. créer; faire; **~ion** création f (a. *fashion*); **~ive** créateur, créatif; **~or** créateur (-trice f) m; **~ure** créature f.

crèche crèche f, garderie f.

creden|ce foi f, croyance f; **~tials** pl. références f/pl.; lettres f/pl. de créance; papiers m/pl. d'identité.

credib|ility crédibilité f; **~le** croyable; digne de foi.

credit 1. crédit m (a. ✝); honneur m; ✝ *school*: unité f de valeur, U. V. f; **~ card** carte f de crédit; **2.** ajouter foi à; attribuer, prêter (une qualité à q.); **~ s.o. with a quality**); ✝ créditer (q. d'une somme **s.o. with a sum, a sum to s.o.**); porter (a sum) au crédit; *fig.* **~ s.o. with s.th.** prêter qch. à q.; **~able** honorable, estimable; **~or** créancier (-ère f) m.

credulous crédule.

creed crédo m (a. pol.); croyance f.

creek crique f; *Am.* ruisseau m.

creel panier m de pêcher

creep 1. ramper; se faufiler; se glisser; glissement m; F flagorneur (-euse f) m; **~s** pl. chair f de poule; **~er** ♀ plante f rampante.

cremat|e incinérer; **~ion** incinération f, **~orium** (pl. a. **-ria**), **~ory** four m crématoire.

crescent croissant (adj., su./m); ⨀ *City* la Nouvelle-Orléans f.

cress ♀ cresson m.

crest ⛰, *cock, mountain, wave*: crête f; arête f, *hill*: sommet m; *peacock*: aigrette f; *helmet*: cimier m; **~fallen** abattu, découragé.

crevasse crevasse f (glaciaire).

crevice fente f; lézarde f; fissure f.

crew équipage m; *workers*: équipe f; *pej.* bande f; **~cut** cheveux m/pl. en brosse.

crib 1. mangeoire f; lit m d'enfant; *eccl.* crèche f; **2.** F copier.

crick crampe f; **~ in the neck** torticolis m.

cricket[1] *zo.* grillon m.

cricket[2] *sp.* cricket m; F **not ~** déloyal.

crime crime m.

criminal criminel (adj., su.); ⨀ *Investigation Department* (*CID*) police f judiciaire (P.J.); **~ity** criminalité f.

crimp crêper (*hair*); gêner, enraver.

crimson cramoisi (a. su./m).

cringe reculer, se faire tout petit; *fig.* ramper (devant to, before)

crinkle 1. pli m, ride f; **2.** (se) froisser; onduler.

cripple 1. boiteux (-euse f) m, estropié(e f) m; **2.** estropier; *fig.* paralyser.

crisis, pl. **-ses** crise f.

crisp 1. croquant; vif, (air, wind); brusque; **2.** donner du croustillant à; **3.** (*a. potato*) **~s** *pl.* (pommes) chips *f/pl.*

criss-cross 1. entrecroisement *m*; **2.** (s')entrecroiser; **3.** entrecroisé.

criterion, *pl.* **-ria** critère *m.*

critic (*literary etc.*) critique *m*; censeur *m*; **~al** critique; **in ~ condition** dans un état critique; **~ism** critique *f*; **~ize** critiquer.

croak *v/t.* coasser (*frog*); croasser (*crow*).

crochet 1. (*a. ~ work*) travail *m* au crochet; **~ hook** crochet *m*; **2.** *v/t.* faire (*qch.*) au crochet; *v/i.* faire du crochet.

crock pot *m* de terre; **~ery** vaisselle *f*; faïence *f*, poterie *f.*

crocodile *zo.* crocodile *m.*

crocus ♣ crocus *m.*

crone F commère *f*, vieille *f.*

crony F copain (copine *f*) *m.*

crook 1. courbe *f*; *shepherd*: houlette *f*; F escroc *m*; **2.** (se) recourber; **~ed** (re-) courbé; tordu; *fig.* malhonnête.

croon fredonner; **~er** chanteur (-euse *f*) *m* de charme.

crop 1. récolte *f*, moisson *f*; *fruit*: cueillette *f*; *hair*: coupe *f*; *bird*: jabot; (*a. riding ~*) cravache *f*; **2.** tondre, couper; brouter, paître; **~ up** surgir.

cropper: F **come a ~** faire une (*fig.* faire la) culbute.

cross 1. croix *f* (*a. decoration, a. fig.*); croisement *m* (*of races*); **2.** (entre-) croisé; mis en travers; oblique; contraire; maussade (*person*); **3.** *v/t.* croiser (*two things, races, s.o. in the street*); traverser; passer (*the sea*); franchir (*the threshold*); barrer (*a cheque*); *fig.* contrarier (*q., a project*); **~ o.s.** se signer; **~ out** rayer, biffer; **~ over** traverser; **~bar** foot. barre *f* (transversale); **~breed** hybride *m*, métis(se *f*) *m*; **~check** (verifier par) contre-épreuve *f*; **~country** à travers champs; **~examination** interrogatoire *m* contradictoire; **~eyed** qui louche; **~ing** passage *m* (pour piétons); intersection *f* (*of roads*); 🚂 passage *m* à niveau; traversée *f*; **~reference** renvoi *m*, référence *f*; **~road** chemin *m* de traverse; **~s** *pl. or sg.* carrefour *m* (*a. fig.*); croisement *m* de routes; **~section** coupe *f* en travers; **~walk** passage *m* clouté; **~wind** vent *m* de travers; **~wise** en croix; **~word puzzle** mots *m/pl.* croisés.

crotch entre-jambes *m/inv.* (*in a garment*); fourche *f.*

crotchet ♩ noire *f*; **~y** grincheux.

crouch se blottir, s'accroupir (*devant, to*).

crow 1. corneille *f*; chant *m* du coq; *Am.* F **eat ~** avaler des couleuvres; **2.** chanter (*cock*); *fig.* chanter victoire (*sur, over*).

crowd 1. foule *f*; **2.** *v/t.* remplir (*de, with*); entasser dans (*into*); *v/i.* se presser (en foule); s'attrouper; **~ed** bondé, plein.

crown 1. *king, tooth, flower, etc.*: couronne *f*; *head*: sommet *m*; *tree*: cime *f*; **2.** couronner; F mettre le comble à.

crucial crucial (*a. fig.*); **~fix** crucifix *m*; **~fixion** crucifixion *f*; **~fy** crucifier (*a. fig.*).

crude (à l'état) brut (*metal, material, oil, etc.*); cru (*a. light, colour*); brutal; grossier (*style*).

cruel cruel; **~ty** cruauté *f.*

cruet huilier *m* et vinaigrier *m*; (*a. ~set*) salière *f* et poivrier *m.*

cruise ⚓ **1.** croisière *f*; voyage *m* d'agrément; **2.** ⚓ croiser; **cruising speed** vitesse *f* de croisière; **~r** ⚓ croiseur *m.*

crumb *bread*: miette *f*; *fig.* brin *m.*

crumble *v/t.* émietter (*bread*); *v/i.* s'émietter; s'effriter; s'écrouler (*a. fig. hopes etc.*).

crummy *sl.* minable, moche.

crumple *v/t.* froisser (*bread*); *v/i.* se froisser; s'effondrer.

crunch 1. *v/t.* croquer (*with one's teeth*); faire craquer or crisser; *crush*; *v/i.* craquer; s'écraser; **2.** craquement *m*, crissement *m*; *fig.* instant *m* décisif or critique.

crusade 1. croisade *f*; **2.** mener une campagne; **~r** croisé *m.*

crush 1. écrasement *m*; F presse *f*; F **have a ~ on** avoir un béguin pour; **2.** *v/t.* écraser; froisser; *fig.* anéantir; *v/i.* se presser en foule.

crust 1. croûte *f*; **2.** (se) couvrir d'une croûte; **~y** qui a une forte croûte; *fig.* bourru.

crutch béquille *f.*

cry 1. cri *m*; plainte *f*; **2.** crier; *v/i.* s'écrier; pleurer; **~ down** décrier; **~ for** demander (en pleurant); crier à (*help*); réclamer; **~ off** (se) décommander.

crystal 1. cristal *m*; *esp. Am.* verre *m* de montre; **2.** de cristal; **~clear** clair comme de l'eau de roche; absolument clair; **~line** cristallin; **~lize** (se) cristalliser.

cub petit *m* (*of an animal*); *bear*: ourson *m*; *lion*: lionceau *m*.

cub|e *&* cube *m*; **~ root** racine *f* cubique; **~ic(al)** cubique.

cuckoo coucou *m*.

cucumber concombre *m*.

cud: chew the ~ ruminer.

cuddle 1. *v/t.* serrer (doucement) dans ses bras, caresser; *v/i.* se pelotonner, se blottir; **2.** caresse *f*, étreinte *f*.

cudgel 1. gourdin *m*; **2.** bâtonner; **~ one's brains** se creuser la cervelle.

cue 1. *esp. thea.* réplique *f*; *billiards*: queue *f*, **2.** (*u.* **~ in**) donner la réplique *or* le signal à.

cuff *shirt*: poignet *m*; manchette *f*, *Am. trousers*: bord *m* relevé; **off the ~** à l'improviste.

cull sélectionner.

culminat|e culminer; **~ion** culmination *f*.

culottes *pl.* (**a pair of** une) jupe-culotte *f* (*pl.* jupes-culottes).

culpable coupable.

culprit coupable *mf*; prévenu(e *f*) *m*.

cultivat|e *usu.* cultiver; *biol.* faire une culture de; **~ion** culture *f*, **~or** *person*: cultivateur (-trice *f*) *m*; *implement*: cultivateur *m*, motoculteur *m*.

cultur|al culturel; *&* cultural; **~e** culture *f*, **~ed** cultivé, lettré.

cumb|ersome, ~rous encombrant, gênant; difficile à remuer; lourd.

cumulative cumulatif.

cunning 1. rusé; astucieux; malin; *Am. a.* mignon; **2.** ruse *f*, *pej.* astuce *f*.

cup tasse *f*, calice *m* (*a. &*); *sp.* coupe *f*, **~board** armoire *f*.

cupidity cupidité *f*.

cupola coupole *f*.

cur roquet *m*.

curable guérissable.

curate vicaire *m*.

curb 1. *fig.* frein *m*; *horse*: gourmette *f*, *Am. a.* bordure *f* du trottoir; (*a.* **~ stone**) bordure *f* (*of pavement*); **2.** mettre un frein à, refréner; gourmer (*a horse*).

curd (*a.* **~s** *pl.*) (lait *m*) caillé *m*.

curdle *v/t.* (faire) cailler; figer; *v/i* se cailler; se figer.

cure 1. cure *f*; remède *m*; **2.** *&* guérir (de, *of*); *fig.* remédier à; *cuis.* saler; fumer; sécher; **~all** panacée *f*.

curfew couvre-feu *m*.

curi|o curiosité *f*; bibelot *m*; **~osity** curiosité *f*; **~ous** curieux.

curl 1. *hair*: boucle *f*; *smoke, wave*: spirale *f*; **2.** boucler; *v/t.* friser; *v/i.* s'élever en spirales (*smoke*); **~ up** s'enrouler; **~er** bigoudi *m*, rouleau *m*.

curling *sp.* curling *m*.

curly frisé, bouclé.

currant groseille *f*; (*a.* **dried ~**) raisin *m* de Corinthe.

currency monnaie *f*; circulation *f*; **foreign ~** devises *f/pl. or* monnaie *f* étrangère; *fig.* **have ~** avoir cours; **gain ~** s'accréditer.

current 1. courant (*money, report, month, price, opinion, etc.*); qui court (*rumour*); **~ events** *pl.* actualités *f/pl.*; **~ issue** dernier numéro *m* (*of a publication*); **2.** courant *m* (*a. &, a. of air*); *fig.* cours *m*.

curriculum, *pl.* **-la** programme *m* d'études.

curry¹ cari *m*, curry *m*.

curry² corroyer (*leather*); étriller (*a horse*); **~ favo(u)r with** chercher à gagner la faveur de.

curse 1. malédiction *f*; juron *m*; **2.** *v/i.* jurer, blasphémer; *v/t.* maudire; **~d** maudit; *F* sacré.

curt brusque; sec; cassant.

curtail réduire, couper (*expenses etc.*); raccourcir, écourter; tronquer; **~ment** réduction *f*, raccourcissement *m*.

curtain 1. rideau *m*; *thea.* **~ call** rappel *m*; **2.** garnir de rideaux.

curts(e)y 1. révérence *f*; **drop a ~ = 2.** faire une révérence (à, **to**).

curvature courbure *f*.

curve 1. courbe *f*; *road*: tournant *m*; *mot.* virage *m*; **2.** (se) courber; *v/i. a.* faire une courbe (*road etc.*).

cushion 1. coussin *m*; bourrelet *m*; **2.** garnir de coussins; rembourrer; *fig.* amortir (*a shock, blow, etc.*).

cuss *sl.* **1.** juron *m*; type *m*; **2.** jurer.

custod|ian gardien(ne *f*) *m*; *museum*: conservateur *m*; **~y** garde *f*; détention *f* préventive.

custom coutume *f*, usage *m*; ⚖ droit *m* coutumier; ✝ clientèle *f*; **~ary** habituel; d'usage; coutumier (*right*); **~er** client(e *f*) *m*; F type *m*; **~house** (bureau *m* de la) douane *f*; **~made** fait sur commande; *cost.* fait sur mesure; **~s** *pl.* douane *f*; **~ clearance** dédouanement *m*; **~** droits *m*/*pl.* de douane; **~ inspection** visite *f* douanière; **~ officer** douanier *m*.

cut 1. *v*/*t.* couper (*a. cards*), tailler; trancher; hacher; réduire; *mot.* prendre (*a curve*); F manquer exprès à; **~ one's finger** se couper le *or* au doigt; **he is ~ting his teeth** ses dents percent; F **~ a figure** faire figure; **~ across** prendre un raccourci par; **~ away** *see cut off*; **~ back** rabattre (*a tree*); *fig.* réduire, couper; **~ down** abattre (*a tree*); couper (*a distance, the price*), restreindre (*the production*); **~ off** couper; enlever; *fig.* isoler, couper (*be, from*); **~ out** couper; découper (*pictures*); *fig.* supplanter; *fig.* cesser; **be ~ out for** être taillé pour (*qch.*); *v*/*i.* **~ in** intervenir; **~ up** découper, couper en morceaux (*or* tranches *etc.*); F affliger, déprimer; **2.** *usu.* coupure *f*; *clothes, hair, etc.*: coupe *f*; *fig.* réduction *f*, réstriction *f*; *piece*: morceau *m*, tranche *f*; *blow*: coup *m*; *art*: gravure *f*; *cuis.* **cold ~s** *pl.* viandes *f*/*pl.* froides; **3.** coupé *etc.*; *sl.* ivre; **~ glass** cristal *m* taillé; **~-and-dried** arrêté, tout fait (*ideas etc.*); décidé d'avance; **~back** restriction(s) *f*/ (*pl.*).

cute mignon, coquet, chouet; malin.

cuticle *anat.* épiderme *m*; **~ scissors** *pl.* ciseaux *m*/*pl.* de manucure.

cutlery couverts *m*/*pl.*; ✝ coutellerie *f*.

cutlet *mutton*: côtelette *f*; *veal*: escalope *f*.

cut|off ⚙ arrêt *m*; *road*: raccourci *m*; **~out** *figure*: découpage *m*; ⚡ coupe-circuit *m*/*inv.*; **~-price**, **~-rate** à prix réduit; bon marché; **~ter** coupeur *m* (*a. of clothing*); *stone etc.*: tailleur *m*; *cin.* monteur *m*; *tool*: coupoir *m*; ⚓ cutter *m*; *Am.* traîneau *m*; **~throat 1.** assassin *m*, tueur *m*; *Br.* rasoir *m* à manche; **2.** acharné (*competition*); meurtrier; **~ting 1.** tranchant; cinglant (*wind*); ⚙ *a.* de coupe, à couper; **~ edge** coupant *m*; *tool*: fil *m*; **2.** coupe *f*; *clothing*: taille *f*; tranchée *f*; ⚘ bouture *f*; *newspaper*: coupure *f*; **~s** *pl.* bouts *m*/*pl.*; ⚙ copeaux *m*/*pl.*; rognures *f*/*pl.*

cycl|e 1. cycle *m*; bicyclette *f*; **2.** faire de la *or* aller à bicyclette; **~ist** cycliste *mf*.

cyclone cyclone *m*.

cylinder cylindre *m*; **~ block** bloc-cylindres *m*; **~ capacity** cylindrée *f*; **~ head** culasse *f*.

cynic cynique *mf*; **~al** cynique; **~ism** cynisme *m*.

Czech 1. tchèque; **2.** *ling.* tchèque *m*; Tchèque *mf*.

Czecho-Slovak 1. tchécoslovaque; **2.** Tchécoslovaque *mf*.

D

dab 1. coup *m* léger; tache *f*; petit morceau *m* (*of butter*), petit coup *m* de (*paint, oil etc.*); *sl.* **~s** *pl.* empreintes *f*/*pl.* digitales; **2.** tamponner (*wound, etc.*); tapoter; appliquer légèrement (*colours*); *typ.* clicher.

dabble: ~ in barboter dans; *fig.* s'occuper *or* se mêler un peu de; **~r** dilettante *mf*.

dad(dy) F papa *m*.

daddy-longlegs *zo.* F tipule *f*.

daffodil ⚘ narcisse *m* des bois.

dagger poignard *m*; **be at ~s drawn** être à couteaux tirés; **look ~s at s.o.** foudroyer q. du regard.

dago *Am. sl. pej.* Espagnol *m*, Portugais *m*, *esp.* Italien *m*.

daily 1. quotidien, journalier; F **~ dozen** gymnastique *f* quotidienne; **2.** tous les jours, quotidiennement; **3.** *journ.* quotidien *m*.

dainty 1. délicat (*person, a. thing*); mi-

daze

gnon; **2.** friandise *f*; morceau *m* de choix.

dairy laiterie *f* (*a. shop*); crémerie *f*; *attr.* laitier.

daisy ♀ pâquerette *f*; (*as*) *fresh as a ~* frais comme une rose; *push up the daisies* être mort.

dall|iance badinage *m*; **~y** s'attarder; lambiner; *fig.* **~ with** caresser (*an idea etc.*).

dam 1. barrage *m* de retenue; digue *f*; lac *m* de retenue; **2.** (*a. ~ up*) endiguer.

damage 1. dégâts *m/pl.*; ⚖ **~s** *pl.* dommages-intérêts *m/pl.*; **2.** endommager; *fig.* nuire à (*q.*).

damask damas *m*.

dame dame *f* (*a. title*); *sl.* femme *f*.

damn 1. condamner; maudire; **2.** *sl.* (*a. ~ed*) sacré, fichu; **3.** *sl.* **~(it)** *I* merde! **4.** *sl.* *I don't care* (*or give*) *a* **~** je m'en fous; **5.** *sl.* vachement (= *very*); **~ation** damnation *f*.

damp 1. humide; moite; **2.** humidité *f*; **3.** (*a. ~en*) mouiller; humecter; assourdir, étouffer (*a sound*); *fig.* refroidir; *fig.* décourager; **~er** rabat-joie *m/inv.*; ⚙ amortisseur *m*.

danc|e 1. danse *f*; bal *m*; **2.** danser; **~er** danseur (-euse *f*) *m*; **~ing** danse *f*; *attr.* de danse.

dandelion ♀ pissenlit *m*.

dandle faire sauter (*a child*) (sur ses genoux).

dandruff pellicules *f/pl.*

dandy 1. dandy *m*, **2.** F chic.

Dane Danois(e *f*) *m*; *dog*: danois *m*

danger danger *m*; **~ous** dangereux.

dangle (faire) pendiller, pendre; (se) balancer; *fig.* faire miroiter (*hopes etc.*).

Danish 1. danois; **2.** *ling.* danois *m*.

dank humide.

dapper F pimpant; vif.

dapple|d tacheté; pommelé; **~-grey** (*cheval m*) gris pommelé.

dare *v/i.* oser; *v/t.* oser faire; risquer; défier (*q.*); **~devil** casse-cou *m/inv.*

daring 1. audacieux; **2.** audace *f*.

dark 1. *usu.* sombre; obscur; foncé (*colour*); **2.** obscurité *f*; nuit *f*; noir; *before* (*after*) **~** avant (après) la tombée de la nuit; *fig.* *in the ~ about* dans l'ignorance sur; **~en** (s')obscurcir; (s')assombrir; **~ness** obscurité *f*; ténèbres *f/pl.*

darling 1. bien-aimé(e *f*) *m*; chéri(e *f*) *m*; **2.** bien-aimé; favori.

darn¹ repriser, raccommoder.

darn² *sl.* see **damn 2, 3**.

dart 1. flèchette *f*; trait *m* (*a. fig.*); élan *m*, mouvement *m* soudain en avant; s'élancer, se précipiter, foncer (sur *at*, [*up*]*on*).

dash 1. mouvement *m* soudain en avant, élan *m*; *typ.* tiret *m*; *fig.* entrain *m*; tiret *m* (vers *for, to*); *fig.* *salt etc.*: soupçon *m*; *liquid*: goutte *f*; **2.** *v/t.* lancer violemment; éclabousser (de boue, *with mud*); (*usu.* *~ to pieces*) fracasser; anéantir (*s.o.'s hopes*); flanquer, jeter; déconcerter, confondre; abattre (*s.o.'s courage*); *v/i.* se précipiter, s'élancer (sur, *at*); courir; se jeter (contre, *against*); **~board** ✓, *mot.* tableau *m* de bord; **~ing** plein d'élan; *fig.* brillant.

dastardly lâche, ignoble.

data *pl., sg.* donnée *f*, **-s** *f/pl.*; **~ bank** (*file*) banque *f* (fichier *m*) de données; **~ processing** traitement *m* de données, informatique *f*.

date¹ ♀ datte *f*, *tree*: dattier *m*.

date² 1. date *f*; rendez-vous *m*; *out of* **~** démodé; *up to* **~** au courant, à jour; Fà la page; **2.** *v/t.* dater; assigner une date à; F être un rendez-vous avec *or* à (*q.*); **~ back** antidater; *v/i.* dater, être démodé; **~d** démodé; **~ back to, ~ from** remonter à.

daub barbouiller (de, *with*) (*a. paint*).

daughter fille *f*; ♀ **~ company** société *f* filiale; **~-in-law** belle-fille (*pl.* belles-filles) *f*.

daunt intimider, décourager; **~less** intrépide.

dawdle F lambiner, traînasser, traîner; **~r** traînard(e *f*) *m*, lambin(e *f*) *m*

dawn 1. aube *f* (*a. fig.*), aurore *f*; point *m* du jour; **2.** poindre; se lever (*day*); *fig.* venir à l'esprit (de, *upon*).

day jour *m* (*a. dawn*); journée *f*; *oft.* **~s** *pl.* temps *m*; vivant *m*; âge *m*; **~ off** jour *m* de congé; *carry* (*or win*) *the* **~** remporter la victoire; *this* **~** aujourd'hui; *the other* **~** l'autre jour; *this* **~ week** (d')aujourd'hui en huit; *the next* **~** le lendemain; *the* **~ before** la veille (de qch., *s.th.*); **~break** point *m* du jour; aube *f*; **~-care centre** crèche *f*; **~light** (lumière *f* du) jour *m*; **~-nursery** garderie *f*, crèche *f*; **~time** journée *f*.

daze étourdir; stupéfier.

dazzle éblouir, aveugler.

dead 1. *adj. usu.* mort; de mort (*silence, sleep*); engourdi (*limb*); terne (*colour*); aveugle (*window*); *fig.* sourd (à, **to**); ✝ sans courant; épuisé (*battery etc.*); ✝ **bargain** véritable occasion *f*; **~ calm** *fig.* silence *m* de mort; **~ letter** lettre *f* de rebut; *fig.* lettre morte; **~ loss** perte *f* sèche; *sl.* bon à rien; **~ man** mort *m*; *sl.* bouteille *f* vide; **~ march** marche *f* funèbre; F **~ ringer** sosie *f* (de, **for**,); **~ shot** tireur *m* sûr de son coup, tireur *m* qui ne rate jamais son coup; **2.** *adv.* absolument; complètement; **~ against** absolument opposé à; **~ asleep** profondément endormi; **~ tired** mort de fatigue; **3.** *su.* **the ~** *pl.* les morts *m/pl.*; **in the ~ of winter** au cœur de l'hiver; **in the ~ of night** au plus profond de la nuit; **~en** amortir (*a blow*); assourdir (*a sound*); **~end: ~ (street)** cul-de-sac *m*; *Am.* **~ kids** *pl.* gavroches *m/pl.*; **~line** limites *f/pl.*; date *f* limite; **~lock** impasse *f*; situation *f* insoluble; **~ly** mortel.

deaf sourd (à, **to**); **~ aid** appareil *m* auditif, audio-prothèse *f*; **~en** rendre sourd; assourdir; **~-mute** sourd(e)-muet(te *f*) *m*; **~ness** surdité *f*.

deal 1. *cards:* main *f*; *fig.* marché *m*; **a good ~** quantité *f*, beaucoup; **a great ~** beaucoup; **2.** *v/t.* donner (*a. a blow*), (*a. ~ out*) distribuer; *v/i.* faire le commerce (de, **in**); **~ with** ✝ commercer avec, faire du commerce avec; faire ses achats chez; *fig.* s'occuper de; se charger de; faire avec; *fig.* s'y prendre avec; *fig.* traiter de (*a subject*); **~er** *cards:* donneur *m*; ✝ négociant(e *f*) *m* (en, **in**); marchand(e *f*) *m*; **~ing** *usu.* **~s** *pl.* commerce *m*; *fig.* relations *f/pl.*

dean doyen *m*.

dear cher; coûteux; **~ me!** mon Dieu!; **my ~** mon cher!, ma chère!

death mort *f*; décès *m*; **tired to ~** mort de fatigue; épuisé; **~bed** lit *m* de mort; **~ blow** coup *m* fatal; **~ duty** droit *m* de succession; **~less** immortel; **~rate** (taux *m* de la) mortalité *f*; **~'s-head** tête *f* de mort.

debar exclure (q. de qch., **s.o. from s.th.**); défendre (à q. de *inf.*, **s.o. from ger.**).

debase avilir; ✝ déprécier (*currency*); **~ment** avilissement *m*; *money:* dépréciation *f*.

debat|able discutable; contestable; **~e 1.** débat *m*, discussion *f*; **2.** discuter, disputer (sur qch., [**on**] **s.th.**); se demander, réfléchir.

debauch|ery débauche *f*; **~ed** débauché.

debilitate débiliter.

debit ✝ **1.** débit *m*, doit *m*; **2.** débiter; porter (*a sum*) au débit.

debris débris *m/pl.*

debt dette *f*; **be in ~** avoir des dettes; **~or** débiteur (-trice *f*) *m*.

debug F réparer; (re)mettre en ordre.

debunk F déboulonner (*q.*).

decade décade *f*.

decaden|ce décadence *f*; **~t** décadent; en décadence.

decaffeinated décaféiné.

decamp lever le camp; F décamper.

decant décanter; **~er** carafe *f*.

decapitat|e décapiter; **~ion** décapitation *f*.

decay 1. décomposition *f*, pourriture *f*; délabrement *m*; déclin *m*; *teeth:* carie *f*; **2.** se décomposer, pourrir; ✝ *etc.* se carier; *fig.* décliner; se délabrer, se détériorer; tomber en décadence.

decease *esp.* ✝✝ **1.** décès *m*; **2.** décéder; **the ~d** le défunt *m*, la défunte *f*; *pl.* les défunts *m/pl.*

deceit tromperie *f*; fourberie *f*; **~ful** trompeur.

deceive tromper; **be ~d** se tromper; **~r** trompeur *m*.

decelerat|e ralentir; **~ion** ralentissement *m*.

December décembre *m*.

decen|cy bienséance *f*; pudeur *f*; **decencies** *pl.* les convenances *f/pl.*; **~t** convenable; honnête; assez bon.

deception tromperie *f*; fraude *f*.

decide *v/i.* décider (de, **to**); se décider (pour **in favour of, for**); à *inf.*, **on** *ger.*); prendre son parti; **~d** décidé; résolu; **~ly** *a.* incontestablement.

decimal 1. décimal; **2.** décimale *f*.

decipher déchiffrer.

decis|ion décision *f*; **take a ~** prendre une décision *or* un parti; **~ive** décisif.

deck 1. ♿ pont *m*; jeu *m* (de cartes, **of cards**); (*a. ~ out*) parer, orner (de,

defray

with); **~chair** chaise *f* longue, trans-at(lantique) *m*.

declaim déclamer (contre, *against*).

declar|able déclarable; à déclarer; **~ation** déclaration *f* (en douane); *make a ~* déclarer; émettre une déclaration; **~e** déclarer (*qch. à q.*, *war*, *s.th. at the customs*, *s.o. guilty*, *etc.*).

declension *gramm.* déclinaison *f*.

declin|ation *astr.*, *phys.* déclinaison *f*; **~e 1.** déclin *m*; baisse *f*; **2.** *v/t.* refuser (courtoisement); *gramm.* décliner; *v/i.* décliner; baisser; s'incliner.

declivity pente *f*, déclivité *f*.

declutch *mot.* débrayer.

decode déchiffrer.

decompose (se) décomposer.

decontrol libérer (*qch.*) des contrôles du gouvernement.

decorat|e décorer (*a. with a medal*); orner; peindre (et tapisser) (*a room*); **~ion** décoration *f*; **~ive** décoratif; **~or** décorateur (-trice *f*) *m*; (*a. house ~*) peintre *m* (en bâtiments *or* décorateur).

decor|ous bienséant; **~um** bienséance *f*.

decoy 1. leurre *m*; (*a. ~-duck*) oiseau *m* de leurre; F compère *m* (*of a swindler*); **2.** leurrer; attirer.

decrease 1. diminution *f*; **2.** diminuer; (s')amoindrir.

decree 1. décret *m*; arrêté *m*; ⚖ jugement *m*; **2.** décréter.

decrepit décrépit (*person*); qui tombe en ruine, délabré (*thing*).

decry dénigrer, décrier.

dedicat|e dédier; *fig.* consacrer (*time*, *life*, *etc.*) (à, *to*); **~ion** dédicace *f*; *fig.* dévouement *m*.

deduce déduire, conclure (de, *from*).

deduct déduire; retenir, retrancher (de, *from*); **~ion** déduction *f*; *salary*: retenue *f*.

deed 1. action *f*, acte *m*; ⚖ acte *m* (notarié); **2.** transférer par un acte.

deem juger, estimer.

deep 1. profond; grave (*voice*, *tone*); foncé (*colour*); F malin (*person*); **~en** (s')approfondir; **~-freeze 1.** surgeler; **2.** congélateur *m*; **~ness** profondeur *f*; **~-rooted** profondément enraciné; **~-seated** enraciné.

deer (*red ~*) cerf *m*; *coll.* cervidés *m/pl.*; **~skin** peau *f* de daim; *fallow ~* daim *m*; *roe ~* chevreuil *m*.

de-escalat|e réduire; limiter; **~ion** réduction *f*; limitation *f*.

deface défigurer; mutiler;

defam|ation diffamation *f*; **~e** diffamer.

default 1. manquement *m*; ✝, ⚖ défaut *m*; *criminal law*: contumace *f*; *sp. by ~* par forfait; *in ~ of which* faute de quoi; **2.** *v/i.* manquer à ses engagements.

defeat 1. défaite *f*; *suffer a ~* essuyer une défaite; **2.** battre, vaincre; faire échouer; *parl.* mettre en minorité.

defect 1. défaut *m*; **2.** *~ to* passer à; **~ive** défectueux; **~or** transfuge *mf*.

defence, *Am.* **defense** défense *f*; ⚖ *witness for the ~* témoin *m* à décharge; **~less**, *Am.* **defenseless** sans défense; désarmé.

defend défendre; **~ant** ⚖ défendeur (-eresse *f*) *m*; accusé(e *f*) *m*; **~er** défenseur *m*.

defense(less) *Am. see* **defence(less)**.

defens|ible défendable, soutenable (*opinion*); **~ive 1.** défensif; de défense; **2.** défensive *f*.

defer différer, remettre; ajourner (*a meeting etc.*).

defer² (to) déférer (à); se soumettre (à); s'incliner (devant); **~ence** déférence *f*; **~ential** respectueux, (plein) de déférence.

defian|ce défi *m*; *bid ~ to* porter un défi à; *in ~ of* au mépris de; **~t** provocant; intraitable.

deficien|cy manque *m*, insuffisance *f*; défaut *m*; ✱ *etc.* carence *f*; *~ disease* maladie *f* de carence; **~t** défectueux; insuffisant; *be ~ in* manquer de.

deficit déficit *m*.

defile¹ défilé *m*; *geog.* gorge *f*; **2.** défiler (*troops etc.*).

defile² salir; polluer; **~ment** souillure *f*; pollution *f*.

defin|e définir; délimiter (*a territory*); **~ite** défini; bien déterminé; **~ition** définition *f*; **~itive** définitif.

defle|ct *v/t.* faire dévier; détourner; *v/i.* dévier, défléchir; **~ction**, *oft.* **~xion** déflexion *f*; *compar.* déviation *f*.

deform déformer; **~ed** *a.* difforme; **~ation** déformation *f*; **~ity** difformité *f*.

defraud frustrer (q. de qch., *s.o. of s.th.*); ⚖, ✝ frauder.

defray rembourser, couvrir (*the cost*); **~ s.o.'s expenses** rembourser ses frais à q.

defrost dégivrer; décongeler (*food*).

deft adroit, habile.

defunct 1. défunt; décédé; *fig.* désuet; **2.** défunt(e *f*) *m*.

defuse désamorcer.

defy défier; *fig.* résister à (*efforts etc.*).

degenerat|e 1. dégénérer (en, *into*); **2.** dégénéré; **~ion** dégénération *f*.

degrad|ation dégradation *f*; **~e** (se) dégrader; **~ing** dégradant.

degree degré *m* (*a.* A, *geog.*, *gramm.*, *phys.*); *univ.* grade *m*; *fig. a.* rang *m*; **by ~s** par degrés; **in no ~** pas le moins du monde; **to a ~** au plus haut dégré, énormément, *a.* **in some ~, to a (certain)** à un certain degré; **take one's ~** prendre ses grades.

dehydrated déshydraté.

de-ice dégivrer.

deign daigner (faire, **to do**).

deity divinité *f*.

deject décourager; **~ed** abattu, deprimé; **~edness, ~ion** découragement *m*, tristesse *f*.

delay 1. délai *m*; **2.** *v/t.* retarder; différer; *v/i.* tarder (à *inf.*, **in** *ger.*); s'attarder; **~ed-action ...** ...à retardement.

delegat|e 1. déléguer; **2.** délégué(e *f*) *m*; **~ion** délégation *f*; députation *f*.

delete rayer, supprimer.

deliberat|e 1. *v/i.* délibérer (de, sur **on**); *v/t.* délibérer au sujet de; **2.** délibéré, prémédité; réfléchi (*person*); mesuré; (*step etc.*); **~ely** exprès, à dessein, délibérément; **~ion** délibération *f*; lenteur *f* réfléchie.

delica|cy délicatesse *f* (*a. fig.*); sensibilité *f*; *health*: faiblesse *f*; *cuis.* friandise *f*; **~te** délicat (*a. fig.*); *fig.* raffiné; fin; faible, fragile; **~tessen** charcuterie *f*.

delicious délicieux.

delight 1. délices *f/pl.*, délice *m*, plaisir *m*; **take ~ in** prendre plaisir à; **2.** *v/t.* enchanter, ravir; *v/i.* se délecter (à, **in**); se complaire (à *inf.*, **in** *ger.*); adorer (*inf.*, **in** *ger.*); **~ful** ravissant; charmant; délicieux.

delineate tracer; dessiner; délinéer.

delinquen|cy délinquance *f*; *act*: délit *m*; **~t** délinquant (*a. su*).

deliri|ous en délire; délirant; F fou; **~um** délire *m*; fièvre *f* délirante.

deliver livrer (*goods*); distribuer (*the mail*); remettre (*a parcel, a message etc.*); délivrer (de, **from**); (*a.* **~ up**) rendre, faire (*a conference*); prononcer (*a speech*); ✠ (faire) accoucher (de, **of**); donner (*a blow*); lancer (*an attack, a ball*); **~ance** délivrance *f*; **~er** libérateur (-trice *f*) *m*; ✝ livreur (-euse *f*) *m*.

delivery ✝ livraison *f*; *letters etc.*: distribution *f*; ✠ accouchement *m*; *speech*: débit *m*; **~ man** livreur *m*; ✠ **~ room** salle *f* d'accouchement; **~ truck, ~ van** voiture *f* de livraison; **(by) special ~** par exprès; **special ~ letter** lettre *f* exprès.

dell vallon *m*, combe *f*.

delouse épouiller.

delta delta *m*.

delude leurrer.

deluge 1. déluge *m*; 2 le Déluge *m*; **2.** inonder (de, **with**).

delus|ion illusion *f*; fantasme *m*; **~ive** illusoire; trompeur.

demagog|ic démagogique; **~ue** démagogue *m*.

demand 1. exigence *f*; revendication *f*, réclamation *f*; ⚖ requête *f* (à **on, to**); ✝ demande *f*; **on ~** sur demande; **make ~s** faire des demandes (à q., **on s.o.**); **2.** exiger (de, **from**), réclamer (à, **from**).

demarcat|e délimiter; **~ion** démarcation *f*; (*usu.* **~ line of ~**) ligne *f* de démarcation.

demean (*usu.* **~ o.s.** s')abaisser.

demeano(u)r attitude *f*, comportement *m*; maintien *m*.

demented fou.

demerit démérite *m*.

demi... demi-...

demijohn dame-jeanne (*pl.* dames-jeannes) *f*.

demilitarize démilitariser.

demise décès *m*; ⚖ cession *f*.

demobilize démobiliser.

democra|cy démocratie *f*; **~t** démocrate *mf*; **~tic(al)** démocratique.

demoli|sh démolir; F dévorer, avaler; **~tion** démolition *f*.

demon démon *m*; F **a ~ for work** un bourreau de travail.

demonstrat|e démontrer; manifester; **~ion** démonstration *f*; *pol.* manifestation *f*; **~ive** démonstratif.

demote rétrograder.

demur 1. hésitation *f*; objection *f*; **without ~** sans hésiter. **2.** hésiter; soulever des objections.

demure sage, réservé.

den tanière *f*; antre *m* (*a*. F *fig.*).

denial dénégation *f*, démenti *m*.

denominat|e dénommer; **~ion** dénomination *f*; catégorie *f*; *money:* valeur *f*; *eccl.* confession *f*, culte *m*; **~or** dénominateur *m*.

denote dénoter; signifier; indiquer.

denounce dénoncer.

dens|e dense; épais; (*stupid*) obtus, bouché; **~ly populated** à forte densité de population; **~ness** densité, stupidité *f*.

dent 1. bosse(lure) *f*; *fig.* **make a ~ in** faire un trou dans; **2.** cabosser.

dent|al dentaire, **~ surgeon** chirurgien(ne *f*)*m* dentiste; **~ifrice** dentifrice *m*; **~ist** dentiste *mf*; **~ure** dentier *m*; *zo.* denture *f*.

denude dénuder; dépouiller.

denunciat|ion dénonciation *f*; condamnation *f*; accusation *f* publique; **~or** dénonciateur (-trice *f*) *m*.

deny nier; renier (*one's faith*); refuser (qch. à q. *s.o. s.th., s.th. to s.o.*).

depart *v/i.* partir; **~ from** partir de; *fig.* s'écarter de; **~ this life** mourir; **the ~ed** le défunt *m*, la défunte *f*, *pl.* les morts *m/pl.*; **~ment** département *m* (*a. geog.*); service *m*; **~** rayon *m*; *Am.* ministère *m*, **State ~** Ministère *m* des Affaires étrangères; **~ store** grand magasin *m*; **~ure** départ *m* (*a.* 🚂, ⚓); *fig.* écart *m*, déviation (de, *from*).

depend: **~ (up)on** dépendre de; se trouver à la charge de; compter sur; se fier à; F **it ~s** cela dépend; **~able** bien fondé; digne de confiance (*person*); **~ant** personne *f* à charge; **~ence** dépendance *f* (de, [up]on); confiance *f* (en, *on*), **~ency**, *oft.* **dependencies** *pl.* dépendance *f*; **~ent 1.** (**on**) dépendant (de); à la charge (de); **2.** *see* **dependant**.

depict (dé)peindre.

deplane descendre d'avion.

deplete épuiser; réduire.

deplor|able déplorable; lamentable; **~e** déplorer; regretter vivement.

deploy (se) déployer.

depopulate (se) dépeupler.

deport expulser (*a foreigner*); **~ o.s.** se conduire; **~ation** expulsion *f*; **~ment** tenue *f*; conduite *f*.

depose déposer (*a.* 🏛).

deposit 1. *usu.* dépôt *m*; *geol.* gisement

m, couche *f*; 🪨 sédiment *m*; ⚓ acompte *m*, arrhes *f/pl.*; *for bottle etc.:* consigne *f*; (*surety*) cautionnement *m*, garantie *f*; **2.** déposer; mettre en dépôt; donner en acompte; **~ion** déposition *f*; 🏛 témoignage *m*; 🪨 dépôt *m*; **~or** déposant *m*; **~ory** dépôt *m*.

depot ⚔, ⚓ dépôt *m*; *Am.* gare *f*.

deprav|e dépraver; **~ity** dépravation *f*.

deprecat|e désapprouver; **~ory** désapprobateur; humble.

depreciate *v/t.* déprécier, dénigrer; *v/i.* se déprécier.

depredation déprédation *f*.

depress déprimer; appuyer sur (*a button*); faire baisser (*prices*); **~ed** déprimé; ⚓ en crise, languissant; **~ing** déprimant; **~ion** dépression *f*.

deprive priver (q. de qch., *s.o. of s.th.*); **~d** *a.* déshérité.

depth profondeur *f*; *forest, water:* fond *m*; *layer:* épaisseur *f*; *colour:* intensité *f*; *sound:* gravité *f*; **in the ~s of** au plus profond de.

deput|ation délégation *f*, députation *f*; **~e** déléguer; **~ize: ~ for s.o.** remplacer q.; **~y 1.** remplaçant(e *f*) *m*; 🏛 fondé *m* de pouvoir; délégué(e *f*) *m*; **2.** adjoint; vice-...

derail 🚂 (faire) dérailler.

derange dérégler; déranger; **~d** dérangé (*mind, stomach*).

derelict 1. abandonné; délaissé; négligé; négligent; **2.** épave *f* (humaine); **~ion** abandon *m*, délaissement *m*; négligeance *f*.

deride tourner en dérision.

deris|ion dérision *f*; ridicule *m*; **~ive** moqueur; *fig.* dérisoire (*offer*).

deriv|ation dérivation *f*; **~ative** dérivé (*adj., su./m*); **~e** *v/t.* tirer (de); prendre (*du plaisir etc.*) (à); devoir (*qch.*) (à); **be ~ed from** = *v/i.* **~ from** dériver de, provenir de.

derogat|e: ~ from diminuer; **~ory** péjoratif, dépréciateur.

derrick *oil:* derrick *m*; ⚓ mât *m* de charge.

descend descendre; **~ (a. be ~ed) from** descendre de; **~ant** descendant(e *f*) *m*.

descent descente *f*; origine *f*.

descri|be décrire; **~ption** description *f*; espèce *f*, sorte *f*, genre *m*.

descry apercevoir, distinguer.

desecrate profaner.

desegregate abolir les distinctions légales or sociales entre les blancs et les races de couleur dans.

desensitize désensibiliser.

desert 1. désert *m*; **2.** désert; désertique; **~ island** île *f* déserte; **3.** *v/t.* déserter; abandonner (*q.*); *v/i.* ✗ déserter; **~er** déserteur *m*; **~ion** désertion *f*.

deserv|e mériter; **~ing** méritant (qch., *of s.th.*); méritoire (*action*).

design 1. dessein *m* (*pej. a.* **~s** *pl.*); projet *m*; dessin *m* (décoratif); conception *f*, plan *m*; modèle *m* (*a. mot.*, ☉); ✝, ☉ design *m*, esthétique *f* industrielle; **2.** projeter; concevoir; créer; dessiner.

designat|e désigner; **~ion** désignation *f*.

designer dessinateur (-trice *f*) *m*; ✝, ☉ designer *m*.

desir|able désirable; **~e 1.** désir *m* (de, *for*; de *inf.*, **to** *inf.*); envie *f* (de *inf.*, **to** *inf.*); **2.** désirer (*qch., q.*; faire qch., **to do s.th.**); vouloir (que q. *sbj.*, *s.o.* **to** *inf.*); **~ous** désireux (de *inf. of ger.*, **to** *inf.*).

desist cesser (de *inf.*, *from ger.*).

desk *office:* bureau *m*; *hotel, airport:* réception *f*; *shop:* caisse *f*, ♪, *school:* pupitre *m*; **~ pad** sous-main *m* (*pl.* sous-mains); bloc-notes *m* (*pl.* blocs-notes).

desolat|e désolé; désert, morne; **~ion** désolation *f*.

despair 1. désespoir *m*; **2.** désespérer (de, *of*); **~ing** désespéré.

desperat|e *adj.* désespéré; *fig.* acharné; **~ion** désespoir *m*.

despicable méprisable.

despise mépriser, dédaigner.

despite en dépit de.

despoil dépouiller (de, *of*).

desponden|cy découragement *m*, abattement *m*; **~t** découragé, abattu.

despot despote *m*, tyran *m*.

dessert dessert *m*; **~ spoon** cuiller *f* à dessert.

destin|ation destination *f*; **~e** destiner (à *for, to*); **be ~d to** (*inf.*) être destiné à (*inf.*); **~y** destin *m*, destinée *f*; sort *m*.

destitute dépourvu, dénué (de, *of*); sans ressources.

destroy détruire; **~er** destructeur (-trice *f*) *m*; ♣ contre-torpilleur *m*.

destruct|ible destructible; **~ion** destruc-

tion *f*; **~ive** destructeur; destructif (*criticism, intentions, etc.*); **~or** incinérateur *m*.

desultory décousu, sans suite.

detach détacher; **~able** détachable; **~ed** détaché (*a. fig. attitude etc.*); **~ house** maison *f* individuelle; **~ment** ✗ *u. fig.* détachement *m*.

detail 1. détail *m*; **in ~** en détail; **2.** énumérer; raconter en détail; ✗ affecter (à, *for*).

detain retenir; ✝✝ détenir.

detect découvrir; apercevoir, distinguer; détecter; **~ion** découverte *f*, détection *f*; **~ive** agent *m* de la sûreté; policier *m*; (*a. private* **~**) détective *m* privé; **~ story** (roman *m*) policier *m*; **~or** découvreur (-euse *f*) *m*.

détente *pol.* détente *f*.

detention détention *f*; retenue *f* (*of a pupil*).

deter détourner (de, *from*).

detergent détersif, détergent (*adj., su./m*).

deteriorat|e (se) détériorer; **~ion** détérioration *f*.

determin|ation détermination *f*; **~e** *v/t.* déterminer; décider (de, *to*); résoudre (*a contract*); *v/i.* décider (de *inf. on ger.*, **to** *inf.*); se décider (à *inf. on ger.*, **to** *inf.*); **~ed** déterminé; résolu; **be ~ to** (*inf.*) être décidé à (*inf.*).

deterrent 1. préventif, de dissuasion; ✗ **~ weapon** arme *f* de dissuasion; **2.** préventif *m*, force *f* de dissuasion.

detest détester; **~able** détestable.

dethrone détrôner.

detonat|e (faire) détoner; **~ion** détonation *f*, explosion *f*.

detour, détour détour *m*.

detract: **~ from** diminuer, amoindrir; **~ion** détraction *f*.

detriment préjudice *m* (de, *to*); **to the ~ of** au détriment *or* pejudice de; **~al** nuisible, préjudiciable (à, *to*).

deuce *games:* deux *m*; *tennis:* égalité *f*; F diable *m*.

devalu|ation dévaluation *f*; **~e** dévaluer.

devastat|e dévaster; *a. fig.* anéantir; **~ing** dévastateur; écrasant (*criticism etc.*); irrésistible (*charm etc.*); **~ion** dévastation *f*.

develop *v/t.* développer; manifester; ex-

dilapidate

ploiter (*a region*); contracter (*a habit, an illness*); *Am.* mettre à jour; *v/i.* se développer; se révéler; **~ing country** pays *m* en voie de développement; **~ment** développement *m*; exploitation *f*; événement *m*; déroulement *m* (*of events*).

deviat|e (*from*) s'écarter (de); dévier (de); **~ion** déviation *f*; écart *m*.

device appareil *m*, dispositif *m*; expédient *m*; **leave s.o. to his own ~s** livrer q. à lui-même.

devil devil *m*; **poor ~** pauvre diable *m*; **~ish** diabolique; **~(l)ed** *cuis.* fortement relevé; **~(t)ry** diablerie *f*.

devious détourné (*road, fig. means, fig.*); pas franc (*person*).

devise inventer, imaginer; combiner; *⁂* disposer par testament de.

devoid: ~ of dépourvu de.

devot|e consacrer (à, *to*); **~ed** dévoué; **~ion** dévouement *m* (à, pour q., *to s.o.*); dévotion *f* (*to God*).

devour dévorer.

devout dévot, pieux, fervent.

dew rosée *f*; **~drop** goutte *f* de rosée; **~y** couvert de rosée.

dexter|ity dextérité *f*; **~ous** adroit, habile (à *inf.*, *in ger.*).

diabet|es *⚕* diabète *m*; **~ic** diabétique (*a. mf.*).

diabolic(al) diabolique.

diagnos|e *⚕* diagnostiquer; **~is**, *pl.* **-ses** diagnostic *m*.

diagram diagramme *m*, tracé *m*, schéma *m*; graphique *m*.

dial 1. cadran *m* (*a. teleph.*); **2.** composer, faire (*a number*); **~(l)ing tone** tonalité *f*.

dialect dialecte *m*.

dialog(ue) dialogue *m*.

diameter diamètre *m*.

diamond diamant *m*; (*shape*) losange *m*; *Am. baseball*: terrain *m* (de baseball); *cards*: **~s** *pl.* carreau *m*.

diaper 1. couche *f* (*for babies*); **2.** changer (*a baby*).

diaphragm diaphragme *m*.

diarrhoea *⚕* diarrhée *f*.

diary journal *m*; agenda *m*.

dice 1. *pl. die* dé*²*! **F** *no ~!* rien à faire!; **2.** *cuis.* couper en cubes; **~y** risqué.

dicker F marchander.

dicky F **1.** peu solide, fragile; **2.** (*a. ~*

bird) (petit) oiseau; (*a. ~ seat*) strapontin *m*.

dictat|e 1. ordre *m* injonction *f*; **2.** dicter; dictée *f*; ordres *m/pl.*; **~or** *pol.* dictateur *m*; **~orship** dictature *f*.

diction diction *f*; **~ary** dictionnaire *m*.

die¹ mourir (de *of, from*); F *fig.* brûler (de *inf.*, *to inf.*); **~ away** s'éteindre (*voice*); s'affaiblir (*sound*); s'effacer (*colour*); disparaître (*light*); **~ down** s'éteindre; se calmer; diminuer, tomber, baisser; **~ out** s'éteindre; disparaître.

die² (*pl. dice*) dé *m*.

die³, *pl* **dies** matrice *f*; étampe *f*; *money:* coin *m*.

die...: ~-casting ⚙ moulage *m* sous pression; **~hard 1.** conservateur *m* à outrance; **2.** intransigeant; pur et dur.

diet 1. nourriture *f*; *restricted food:* régime *m*; diète *f* (*a. pol.*); **2.** *v/t.* mettre (q.) au régime; *v/i.* être au *or* suivre un régime.

differ différer (de *in, from*); être différent (de); ne pas s'accorder *or* être d'accord (sur, *about*); **~ence** différence *f*; différend *m*; être différent (de *from, to*); autre (que, *from*); **~entiate** (se) différencier; *⚕* différentier; faire une différence (entre, *between*); **~ently** différemment, autrement.

difficult difficile; **~y** difficulté *f*.

diffiden|ce manque *m* d'assurance; **~nt** qui manque d'assurance.

diffus|e 1. (se) diffuser; **2.** diffus; **~ion** diffusion *f*.

dig 1. *v/t/i.* creuser; **~ up** déterrer; *v/t.* bêcher; enfoncer; **2.** coup *m* (*de coude etc.*).

digest 1. (se) digérer; **2.** abrégé *m*, résumé *m*; **~ible** digestible; **~ion** digestion *f*; **~ive** digestif *m*.

digit *⚕* chiffre *m*; *anat.* doigt *m*; **~al** digital; numérique (*computer etc.*); à affichage numérique (*watch etc.*).

digni|fied digne; plein de dignité; **~fy** donner de la dignité à; *fig.* décorer (de, *with*); **~tary** dignitaire *m*; **~ty** dignité *f*.

digress s'écarter, faire une digression (de, *from*); **~ion** digression *f*.

digs F piaule *f*.

dike 1. digue *f*; chaussée *f* surélevée; **2.** protéger par des digues.

dilapidate (se) délabrer.

dilate (se) dilater.

dilatory dilatoire.

dilemma dilemme *m*.

diligen|ce assiduité *f*; **~t** assidu.

dilute 1. diluer, délayer (*a. fig.*); 2. dilué, délayé.

dim 1. faible; effacé (*colour*); vague (*memory*); 2. *v/t.* obscurcir; réduire, baisser (*the light*); ternir (*a. fig.*); *mot.* **~ the headlights** se mettre en code; *v/i.* s'obscurcir; *fig.* s'estomper.

dimension dimension *f*.

dimin|ish diminuer; **~ution** diminution *f*; **~utive** 1. minuscule; 2. *gramm.* diminutif *m*.

dimmer ⚡ rheostat *m*; **~s** *pl. mot.* **phares** *m/pl.* code; feux *m/pl.* de position.

dimple fossette *f*.

din fracas *m*, vacarme *m*.

dine dîner *v/i.*; **~ out** dîner en ville; **~r** dîneur (-euse *f*) *m*; wagon-restaurant (*pl.* wagons-restaurants) *m*.

dingy sale, minable.

dining...: **~car** 🚃 wagon-restaurant (*pl.* wagons-restaurants) *m*; **~ room** salle *f* à manger.

dinner dîner *m*; banquet *m*; F déjeuner *m*; **~ jacket** smoking *m*; **~ party** dîner *m* (par invitations); **~ service**, **~ set** service *m* de table.

dint: **by ~ of** à force de; *see a.* **dent.**

dip 1. *v/t.* plonger; tremper; immerger; *mot.* **dip the headlights** se mettre en code; *v/i.* plonger; baisser (*sun*); *geol.* s'incliner; 2. plongement *m*; pente *f*, déclivité *f*; F baignade *f*; F **have** *or* **take a ~** faire trempette.

diploma diplôme *m*; **~cy** diplomatie *f*; **~t** diplomate *m*; **~tic(al)** diplomatique; **~tist** diplomate *m*.

dipper plongeur (-euse *f*) *m*; *orn.* merle *m* d'eau; *mot.* basculeur *m*; cuiller *f* à pot, louche *f*; *Am.* **Great** (*or* **Big**) ⚹ *astr.* la Grande Ourse.

diprod, dipstick *mot.* jauge *f* (de niveau de huile).

dire désespéré, extrême.

direct 1. direct; ⚡ **~ current** courant *m* continu; *teleph.* **~ dial(l)ing** (numéro *m* interurbain) automatique *m*; *gramm.* **~ speech** discours *m* direct; **~ train** train *m* direct; 2. tout droit; *see* **~ly 1**; 3. diriger; adresser (*a letter* à q., **to s.o.**);

ordonner (à q. de *inf.*, **s.o. to** *inf.*); indiquer.

direction direction *f*; **~s** *pl.* indications *f/pl.*, instructions *pl.*; **~s** *pl.* **for use** mode *m* d'emploi.

direct|ive directif; **~ly** 1. *adv.* directement, tout droit; tout de suite; absolument; 2. *cj.* aussitôt que.

director directeur *m*; administrateur *m*; *thea.*, *cin.* metteur en scène; **~ate** (conseil *m* d')administration *f*; (*a.* **~ship**) directorat *m*; **~y** répertoire *m* d'adresses; *teleph.* annuaire *m* (des téléphones); *teleph.* **~ assistance**, **~ enquiry** renseignements *m/pl.*

dirigible dirigeable (*a. m.*).

dirt saleté *f*, crasse *f*; boue *f*; terre *f*; **~ road** route *f* non macadamisée; *sp.* **~ track** piste *f*; **~cheap** F (à) très bon marché; **~y** 1. sale; 2. (se) salir.

disability incapacité *f*; invalidité *f*, infirmité *f*.

disable mettre hors de service *or* de combat; mettre (q.) hors d'état (de *inf.* **from**, **for** *ger.*); **~d** invalide; mutilé; impotent.

disabuse désabuser (de, **of**).

disadvantage désavantage *m*, inconvénient *m*; **~ous** défavorable.

disagree (**with**) ne pas être d'accord (avec); donner tort (à); ne pas convenir (à q.); ne pas concorder (avec) (*things*); **~able** désagréable (*a. fig.*); **~ment** différend *f*; désaccord *m*.

disappear disparaître; **~ance** disparition *f*.

disappoint décevoir; **~ment** déception *f*.

disappro|bation, **~val** désapprobation *f*; **~ve** (*a.* **~ of**) désapprouver.

disarm désarmer (*a. fig.*); **~ament** désarmement *m*.

disarrange mettre en désordre; déranger; **~ment** désordre *m*; dérangement *m*.

disarray désordre *m*.

disast|er désastre *m*; catastrophe *f*; **~rous** désastreux.

disbelie|f incrédulité *f*; **~ve** ne pas croire (q.) *or* à (qch.); **~ver** incrédule *mf*.

disburse débourser; **~ment** déboursement *m*; **~s** *pl.* débours *m/pl.*

disc disque *m*; *see a.* **disk.**

discard 1. se défaire de, se débarrasser de; abandonner (*a theory etc.*); *cards:*

se défausser (de qch., **s.th.**); **2.** *cards*: défausse *f*; *fig.* (pièce *f* de) rebut *m*.

discern discerner; **~ing** judicieux; **~ment** discernement *m*; jugement *m*.

discharge 1. *v/t.* décharger (a. ⚡, ⚡); lancer (*a projectile*); congédier, renvoyer (*an employee*), débaucher (*a worker*); s'acquitter de (*a duty*); aquitter (*a prisoner, a debt*); payer (*a bill*); *v/i.* suppurer; se déverser; partir (*gun*); **2.** décharge *f* (a. ⚡); ⚓ déchargement *m*; *employee*: renvoi *m*; ⚔ libération *f*; *prisoner*: élargissement *m*; *debt*: paiement *m*; *duty*: accomplissement *m*.

disciple disciple *mf*; **~inary** disciplinaire; **~ine 1.** discipline *f*; **2.** discipliner; punir.

disclaim désavouer; (re)nier; ⚖ renoncer à.

disclose révéler, divulguer; **~ure** révélation *f*, divulgation *f*.

discolo(u)r se décolorer; (se) ternir (*mirror*); jaunir (*teeth*).

discomfit confondre, embarrasser; **~ure** confusion *f*, embarras *m*.

discomfort 1. manque *m* de confort, gêne *m*, malaise *m*; **2.** incommoder.

discompose troubler.

disconcert déconcerter; troubler.

disconnect ⚡etc. débrancher; détacher, déconnecter; couper (*the phone, power* etc.); ⊙ débrayer; **~ed** détaché; *fig.* décousu.

disconsolate désolé.

discontent mécontentement *m*; **~ed** mécontent (de, **with**); peu satisfait.

discontinue cesser, arrêter; se désabonner à.

discord discorde *f*; ♪ dissonance *f*; **~ant** discordant.

disco(theque) disco(thèque) *f*.

discount 1. ✝ remise *f*, rabais *m*; *bank* etc.: escompte *m*; **~ store** magasin *m* à demi-gros; **2.** ✝ escompter; *fig.* ne pas tenir compte de.

discountenance désapprouver.

discourage décourager (de, **from**); **~ing** décourageant, **~ement** découragement *m*.

discourse 1. discours *m*; dissertation *f*; **2.** discourir.

discourteous impoli; **~sy** impolitesse *f*.

discover découvrir; **~er** découvreur (-euse *f*) *m*; **~y** découverte *f*.

discredit 1. discrédit *m*; doute *m*; **2.** mettre en doute; discréditer.

discreet discret; avisé.

discrepancy divergence *f*; désaccord *m*; écart *m*.

discretion discrétion *f*; **age** (or **years** *pl.*) **of ~** âge *m* de raison; **at ~** à discrétion.

discriminate faire une différence; **~ from** faire la différence *or* la distinction *or* la discrimination entre; **~ against** (*in favour of*) constituer (*thing*) *or* pratiquer (*person*) une discrimination contre (en faveur de); **~ing** avisé; plein de discernement; différentiel (*tariff*); **~ion** racial, social etc.: discrimination *f*, discernement *m*; jugement *m*; distinction *f*.

discuss discuter (de); **~ion** discussion *f*.

disdain 1. dédain *m* (de, **of**), mépris *m*; **2.** dédaigner.

disease maladie *f*; **~d** malade.

disembark débarquer; **~ation** débarquement *m*.

disembodied désincarné.

disembowel étriper.

disenchant désenchanter; désillusionner.

disengage (se) dégager; ⊙ (se) déclencher; *mot.* **~ the clutch** débrayer; **~d** libre.

disentangle (se) démêler.

disfavo(u)r 1. défaveur *f*; disgrâce *f*; désapprobation *f*; **2.** désapprouver; défavoriser.

disfigure défigurer; gâter.

disgorge rendre, dégorger; déverser (*water*).

disgrace 1. disgrâce *f*; honte *f*; déshonneur *m*; **2.** déshonorer; disgracier; **~ful** honteux; scandaleux.

disgruntled mécontent (de **at, about, with**).

disguise 1. déguiser (en, **as**); masquer; camoufler; **2.** déguisement *m*; **in ~** déguisé.

disgust 1. dégoût *m*; répugnance *f*; **2.** dégoûter; **~ing** dégoûtant.

dish 1. plat *m*; **do** or **wash the ~es** faire la vaisselle; **2.** (*usu.* **~ up** or **out**) servir; *fig.* débiter.

disharmony dissonance *f*; désaccord *m*.

dishcloth torchon *m*; lavette *f*.

dishearten décourager.

dishevel(l)ed échevelé; ébouriffé.

dishonest malhonnête; déloyal; **~y** malhonnêteté f.

dishono(u)r 1. déshonneur m; honte f; **2.** déshonorer; ✝ ne pas honorer; **~able** déshonorant; sans honneur (*person*).

dish...: ~washer laveur (-euse f) m de vaisselle; ⊙ lave-vaisselle m/inv.; **~water** eau f de vaisselle; sl. lavasse f; **~y** F appétissante.

disillusion 1. désillusion f, désabusement m; **2.** a. **~ize** désillusionner, désabuser; **~ment** see disillusion 1.

disinclined peu disposé (à for, to).

disinfect désinfecter; **~ant** désinfectant (a. su./m).

disinherit déshériter; **~ance** déshéritement m; ♇ exhérédation f.

disintegrat|e (se) désintégrer; (se) désagréger; **~ion** désintégration f.

disinterested désintéressé.

disjointed incohérent.

disk disque m; plaque f (of identity); mot. **~ brakes** freins m/pl. à disque; **~ jockey** présentateur m (de disques), disc-jockey m; **~ette** disquette f.

dislike 1. aversion f, antipathie f (pour for, of, to); **2.** ne pas aimer; détester; trouver mauvais.

dislocat|e disloquer; déboîter (a limb); fig. désorganiser; **~ion** dislocation f; fig. désorganisation f.

dislodge pousser, déplacer; faire bouger; déloger (the enemy).

disloyal déloyal; **~ty** déloyauté f.

dismal sombre; morne; lugubre.

dismantle démanteler; ⊙ démonter (a machine); **~ment** démantèlement m; ⊙ démontage m.

dismay 1. consternation f; in **~** d'un air consterné; **2.** consterner.

dismember démembrer; écarteler.

dismiss congédier; renvoyer; abandonner, écarter, laisser tomber (an idea etc.); ♇ rejeter (a request); **~al** congédiement m; renvoi m; rejet m; abandon m.

dismount descendre (de cheval, de voiture).

disobedien|ce désobéissance f (à to, of); **~t** désobéissant.

disobey désobéir à.

disoblige désobliger (q.).

disorder 1. désordre m; confusion f; tumulte m; ♣ troubles m/pl.; **mental ~** dérangement m d'esprit; **2.** déranger; mettre le désordre dans; **~ly** en désordre; désordonné.

disorganize désorganiser.

disown désavouer; renier.

disparag|e déprécier, décrier; **~ing** désobligeant.

disparity disparité f.

dispassionate impartial; calme; sans passion, froid.

dispatch 1. expédition f, envoi m; dépêche f; **~ note** bulletin m d'expédition; **2.** expédier (a. kill); envoyer.

dispel dissiper, chasser.

dispens|able dont on peut se passer; **~ary** pharmacie f; officine f; policlinique f; **~ation** distribution f; décret m; eccl. dispense f; **~e** distribuer; administrer (justice, sacrament, etc.); eccl. dispenser; **~ with** se passer de; rendre superflu; **~er** distributeur m.

dispers|al dispersion f; fig. déconcentration f; (se) disperser; v/t. disséminer, répandre.

dispirit décourager.

displace déplacer; supplanter; **~ment** déplacement m.

display 1. étalage m (a. ✝); manifestation f; exposition f; parade f; **~ case** vitrine f (d'exposition); **~ stand** présentoir m; **2.** étaler; afficher; montrer; faire preuve de; révéler.

displeas|e déplaire (à q., s.o.); fig. contrarier; **~ed** mécontent (de at, with); **~ure** mécontentement m (de at, over); déplaisir m.

dispos|al disposition f; destruction f; rubbish etc.: enlèvement m; goods: vente f; résolution f (of a question); at s.o.'s **~** à la disposition de q.; **~e** v/t. disposer (a. q. à, s.o. to); v/i. **~ of** se débarrasser de, se défaire de; se passer de; ✝ vendre; résoudre (a problem); **~ed** enclin (à to, for); disposé (à, to); **~ition** disposition f; naturel m, caractère m.

dispossess déposséder; exproprier.

disproof réfutation f.

disproportionate disproportionné.

disprove réfuter.

dispute 1. discussion f; conflit m; **industrial ~** conflit m social; **wages ~** conflit m salarial; **beyond ~** incontesta-

dive

ble(ment); *in or under* ~ en discussion; *open to* ~ contestable; **2.** contester; débattre; disputer (qch. à q., *s.th. with s.o.*).

disqualif|ication disqualification *f*; ~**y** rendre incapable (de *inf.*, *from ger.*); *sp.* disqualifier; ~ *s.o. for s.th.* (*from doing s.th.*) rendre q. inapte à (faire) qch.; ~ *s.o. from driving* retirer son permis (de conduire) à q.

disquiet inquiéter, alarmer; troubler.

disregard 1. indifférence *f* (à l'égard de *of, for*); inobservation *f* (*of law*); **2.** ne tenir aucun compte de.

disreput|able de mauvaise réputation, peu recommandable; louche; ~**e** discrédit *m*.

disrespect manque *m* de respect *or* d'égards; ~**ful** irrespectueux.

disrupt perturber, déranger; (inter)rompre; ~**ion** perturbation *f*, dérangement *m*; interruption *f*, rupture *f*; ~**ive** perturbateur.

dissatis|faction mécontentement *m* (de *with, at*); dissatisfaction *f*; ~**factory** peu satisfaisant; ~**fied** mécontent, insatisfait (de, *with*); ~**fy** mécontenter; ne pas satisfaire (*q.*).

dissect disséquer.

dissemble *v/t.* dissimuler; feindre; *v/i.* déguiser sa pensée.

dissension dissension.

dissent 1. dissentiment *m*; *eccl.* dissidence *f*; différer (de, *from*); *eccl.* être dissident; ~**er** dissident(e *f*) *m*.

dissimilar (*to*) différent (de); dissemblable (à).

dissimulation dissimulation *f*.

dissipat|e (se) dissiper; *v/t. a.* disperser (*one's fortune etc.*); ~**ed** dissolu (*life etc.*); ~**ion** dissipation *f*.

dissociate dissocier.

dissolute dissolu, débauché; ~**ion** dissolution *f*.

dissolve *v/t.* (faire) dissoudre; *v/i.* se dissoudre; fondre; *fig.* s'évanouir, disparaître.

dissonan|ce dissonance *f*; ~**t** *♪* dissonant; *fig. a.* en désaccord (avec, *from, to*).

dissuade dissuader (de, *from*).

distan|ce 1. *place, time:* distance *f*; éloignement *m*; lointain *m*; intervalle *m*; *fig.* réserve *f*; *at a* ~ de loin; à une

distance (de, *of*); **2.** éloigner; *fig.* reculer; ~**t** éloigné; lointain; distant, réservé (*person*); *two miles* ~ à deux milles de distance; ~ *control* commande *f* à distance; ~ *relative* cousin(e *f*) *m* éloigné(e).

distaste dégoût *m* (de, *for*); ~**ful** désagréable, dégoûtant.

distemper *vet.* maladie *f* des chiens; (*paint*) détrempe *f*; ~**ed** dérangé (*mind*).

distend (se) dilater; (se) distendre.

distil (se) distiller; ~**late** distillat *m*; ~**lery** distillerie *f*.

distinct distinct (de, *from*); net; (*unmistakable*) marqué; ~**ion** distinction *f*; *draw a* ~ *between* faire une distinction entre; *have the* ~ *of* (*ger.*) avoir l'honneur de (*inf.*); ~**ive** distinctif.

distinguish distinguer; différencier (de, *from*); ~**ed** distingué; remarquable (par, *for*); ~**ing** distinctif (*feature etc.*).

distort tordre; déformer; *fig.* fausser; ~**ion** distorsion *f*; déformation *f* (*a. opt., a. tel.*).

distract distraire, détourner; affoler (*q.*); brouiller (*s.o.'s mind*); ~**ed** éperdu, affolé; ~**ion** distraction *f*; affolement *m*, folie *f*; *drive s.o. to* ~ rendre q. fou.

distress 1. détresse *f*; douleur *f*; affliction *f*; embarras *m*, gêne *f*; ~ *signal* signal *m* de détresse; **2.** affliger; ~**ed** *area* zone *f* sinistrée.

distribut|e distribuer; répartir; ~**ion** distribution *f*; répartition *f*.

district région *f*; district *m* (*a. admin.*); quartier *m* (*of a town*); *election:* circonscription *f*; *Br. admin.* ~ **council** conseil *m* départemental; *Am.* ⚖ **court** cour *f* fédérale.

distrust 1. méfiance *f*; **2.** se méfier *or* défier de; ~**ful** méfiant.

disturb déranger; troubler; inquiéter; ~**ance** troubles *m/pl.*, émeute *f*; tapage *m*, bruit *m*; ~**ed** *psych.* inadapté.

disun|ite (se) désunir; ~**ity** désunion *f*.

disuse: *fall into* ~ tomber en désuétude; ~**d** désaffecté.

ditch 1. fossé *m*, **2.** ⨍ planter là, plaquer; **ditto** de même.

divagate s'éloigner du sujet.

divan divan *m*.

dive 1. plonger (dans, *into*); ✈, *a. fig.* piquer (du nez); ⨍ *into* s'enfoncer dans, entrer précipitamment dans; **2.**

plongeon m; *submarine*: plongée f; ✓ (vol m) piqué m; (*club etc.*) bouge m; ~r plongeur m.

diverge diverger; ~nce, ~ncy divergence f; ~nt divergent.

divers|e divers; ~ion détournement m; (*distraction*) diversion f (a. ✗, a. of *mind*); ~ity diversité f.

divert détourner; dévier (*traffic etc.*); *fig.* divertir.

divest dépouiller (de, *of*).

divide 1. *v/t.* diviser (a. ♉); partager, répartir (entre, *among*); séparer (de, *from*); *v/i.* se diviser; se séparer; ♉ être divisible (par, *by*); 2. *Am.* ligne f de partage des eaux; ~nd ♱, a. ♉ dividende m; ~r *mot.* bande f médiane.

divine[1] 1. divin (a. *fig.*); ~ *service* office m divin; 2. théologien m, ecclésiastique m.

divine[2] deviner, prédire; (~ *for* chercher à) découvrir (*underground water etc.*); *divining rod* baguette f divinatoire.

diving action f de plonger; *sp.* plongeon m; *attr.* de plongeurs; ~ *bell* cloche f à or de plongeur.

divinity divinité f; théologie f.

divis|ible divisible; ~ion division f (a. *disunion*, a. ✗, ♉); partage m; classe f; ~or ♉ diviseur m.

divorce 1. divorce m ([d']avec, *from*); 2. divorcer (d')avec *or* de; ~e divorcé(e f) m.

divulge divulguer, révéler.

dizz|iness vertige m; ~y pris de vertige (*person*); vertigineux (*chose*); ~ *spell* étourdissement m; *feel* ~ avoir le vertige; avoir la tête qui tourne; *make s.o.* ~ donner le vertige à q.

do (*see a.* **done**) 1. *v/t. usu.* faire; (faire) cuire; finir; jouer (*a part*); F duper, rouler, avoir (q.); F ~ *London* visiter Londres; *what is to be done?* que faire?; *have done reading* avoir fini de lire; ~ (*over*) *again* refaire; F ~ *in* éreinter, épuiser; tuer; ~ *into* traduire en; ~ *over* couvrir de (*peinture etc.*); ~ *up* envelopper, emballer; attacher; fermer, boutonner (*one's coat etc.*); refaire, remettre à neuf (*redecorate*) a. repeindre; F éreinter (q.); ~ *o.s. up* se faire beau (belle), se maquiller; 2. *v/i.* faire l'affaire; aller; suffire; convenir; *that*

will ~ c'est bien; cela va; cela suffira; cela faira l'affaire; *that won't* ~ cela ne va *or* n'ira pas; *how* ~ *you* ~? comment allez-vous?; comment vous portez-vous?, F ça va?; ~ *well* aller bien; réussir; ~ *away with* abolir; supprimer (a. F = *kill*); *I could* ~ *with some coffee* je prendrais volontiers du café; ~ *without* se passer de; ~ *up* s'attacher, se fermer (*garment*); 3. *v/aux. interr.*: ~ *you know him?* le connaissez-vous?; *with not*: *I don't know him* je ne le connais pas; *emphasis*: *I* ~ *feel better* je me sens vraiment mieux; ~ *come and see me* venez me voir, je vous en prie; ~ *be quick* dépêchez-vous donc; *you write better than I* ~ vous écrivez mieux que moi; *I take a bath every day.* — *So* ~ *I* je le prends un bain tous les jours. — Moi aussi.

docile docile; ~ity docilité f.

dock[1] couper, écourter; *fig.* réduire.

dock[2] 1. ♻ bassin m; *esp. Am.* quai m; ⚖ banc m des prévenus; *dry* ~ cale f sèche; 2. ♻ (faire) entrer au bassin; ~*yard* chantier m de construction de navires.

doctor 1. docteur m; médecin m; 2. F droguer; F falsifier; *vet.* châtrer, couper (*an animal*); soigner (q.).

doctrine doctrine f.

document 1. document m; 2. documenter; ~ary documentaire.

doddering gâteux.

dodg|e 1. esquive f; ruse f, F truc m; 2. *v/t.* esquiver; éviter; ~er malin m, finaud m; *Am. a.* prospectus m; ~y F risqué (*thing*); louche (*person*).

doe biche f; lapine f; hase f.

dog 1. chien(ne f) m; ~ *collar* collier m de chien; ~ *days* canicule f; ~*eared* écorné (*book*); 2. filer (q.); suivre (q.); ~*ged* tenace.

dogma dogme m; ~tic(al) dogmatique.

dog('s)-ear F corne f (*in a book*).

dog-tired éreinté.

doing action f de faire; travail m (dur); *this is his* ~ c'est lui qui a fait cela; ~s *pl.* activités f/pl., faits et gestes m/pl.; *Br.* F truc m, machin m.

do-it-yourself bricolage m.

doldrums zone f des calmes; *fig. be in the* ~ avoir le cafard (*person*); être dans le marasme (*business etc.*).

dole allocation f de chômage; *be on the*

~ être en chômage, chômer; (*usu.* ~ *out*) distribuer (avec parcimonie).

doleful lugubre; douloureux; triste.

doll 1. poupée *f*; *sl.* jeune fille *f*, *sl.* nana *f*. **2.** F ~ *up* bichonner.

dollar dollar *m*.

dolly poupée *f*.

dolorous douloureux.

dolphin *icht.* dauphin *m*.

dolt F cruche *f*.

domain domaine *m* (*a. fig.*).

dome dôme *m*.

domestic 1. domestique; de ménage; de famille; intérieur (*commerce, flight, etc.*); ~ **appliance** appareil *m* ménager; **2.** domestique *mf*; ~**ate** apprivoiser, domestiquer (*an animal*); ♀, *zo.* acclimater.

domicile *esp.* 🏠 domicile *m*; ~**d** domicilié, demeurant (à, *at*).

domin|ant dominant; ~**ate** dominer; ~**ation** domination *f*; ~**eer** se montrer autoritaire; ~ **over** tyranniser; ~**eering** autoritaire.

dominion domination *f*, maîtrise *f*; territoire *m*, dominion *m*.

domino domino *m*; ~ **effect** effet *m* (de) domino.

don[1] professeur *m* d'université.

don[2] revêtir.

donat|e donner; faire un don de; ~**ion** don *m*, donation *f*.

done *adj.* fait; cuit; (*or* ~ *up*) épuisé, F claqué, à plat; *the* ~ *thing* ce qui se fait; *well* ~ bien cuit.

donkey âne(sse *f*) *m*.

donor donateur (-trice *f*) *m*; ♥ donneur (-euse *f*) *m* de sang.

doodle 1. griffonnage *m*; **2.** griffonner.

doom 1. *esp. pej.* sort *m*, destin *m*; mort *f*; ruine *f*; **2.** condamner; ~**ed** (*to failure*) voué à l'échec; ~**sday** jour *m* du Jugement dernier.

door porte *f*; *car, carriage, etc.*: portière *f*; *next* ~ (*to*) à côté (de); *fig.* approchant (de); *within* ~**s** chez soi; *out of* ~**s** dehors; en plein air; ~**bell** sonnette *f*; ~**handle** poignée *f* de port(ièr)e; ~**man** concierge *m*; portier *m*; ~**step** pas *m* de porte; ~**way** porte *f*; portail *m*.

dope 1. drogue *f*; dopant *m*; *sl.* idiot(e *f*) *m*; *sl.* tuyau *m* (= *information*); ~ *fiend* toxico(mane). **2.** doper.

dop(e)y F abasourdi, abruti.

dormant *usu. fig.* en sommeil; inappliqué (*rule, etc.*); ♀ *etc.* dormant.

dormer (*a.* ~ *window*) lucarne *f*; (*fenêtre f* en) mansarde *f*.

dormitory dortoir *m*; *esp. Am.* maison *f* d'étudiants.

dose 1. dose *f*; **2.** médicamenter.

doss *sl.* somme *m*, roupillon *m* (= *sleep*); ~ *house* asyle *m* de nuit.

dossier dossier *m*, documents *m/pl.*

dot 1. point *m*; *on the* ~ F à l'heure tapante; **2.** mettre un point sur; pointiller; *fig.* (par)semer (de, *with*).

dote radoter; ~ [*up*]*on* aimer (*q.*) à la folie.

double 1. double à deux personnes *or* lits (*room*); deux (*letters*), ~ *bed* grand lit *m*; ~ *bend* virage *m* en S; ~ *parking* stationnement *m* en double file; **2.** double *m* (*a.* tennis); deux fois autant, *river, hare*: détour *m*; **3.** *v/t.* doubler (*a.* ♪); serrer (*one's fist*); plier en deux (*a paper*); *thea.* jouer deux (*parts*); ~ *up* replier; faire plier (*q.*) en deux; *v/i.* (se) doubler; ~ *back* revenir sur ses pas; ~**breasted** croisé (*jacket etc.*); ~**cross** F tromper, duper; ~ *dealing* duplicité *f*, fourberie *f*; ~**decker** autobus *m* à impériale; *cuis.* sandwich *m* double; ~**park** stationner en double file; ~**talk** paroles *f/pl.* ambiguës.

doubt 1. douter de (*q., qch.*); ~ *that*, ~ *whether* douter que; **2.** doute *m*; incertitude *f*; *no* ~ sans (aucun) doute; ~**ful** douteux; incertain; ~**fulness** incertitude *f*; irrésolution *f*; caractère *m* douteux; ~**less** sans aucun doute.

dough pâte *f*; *sl.* argent *m*; ~**nut** *cuis.* beignet *m*.

dove colombe *f*.

dowel ⚙ goujon *m*; cheville *f* (en bois).

down[1] *see* dune; ⚙s *pl.* hautes plaines *f/pl.* (du Sussex *etc.*).

down[2] duvet *m*.

down[3] **1.** *adv.* vers le bas; en bas; d'en haut; par terre; *be* ~ être en baisse (*prices*); F *be* ~ *upon* en vouloir à (*q.*); être toujours sur le dos de (*q.*); **2.** *prp.* vers le bas de; en bas de; au fond de; en descendant; le long de; ~ *the river* en aval; ~ *the wind* à vau-vent; **3.** *int.* à bas!; **4.** *adj.* F déprimé, en pleine déprime; ♥ ~ *payment* acompte *m*; **5.** *v/t.* abattre (*a. a plane*), terrasser; ~ *tools* se

mettre en grève; **6.** *su. see* **up** 5;
~-and-out sans-le-sou *m/inv.*;
~-at-heel écule (*shoe*); miteux (*person*);
~beat 1. ♪ (*temps m*) frappé *m*; **2.** F
pessimiste; **~cast** abattu; baissé (*look*);
~fall chute *f* (*a. fig.*); *fig.* ruine *f*; écrou-
lement *m*; **~grade** déprécier; dégrader;
~hearted déprimé, découragé; **~hill 1.**
en descendant; **2.** incliné; en pente;
~pour grosse averse *f*; déluge *m*; **~right
1.** *adv.* tout à fait; carrément; nette-
ment; **2.** *adj.* franc; direct; carré; éclatant (*lie*); **~stairs 1.** d'en bas, du
rez-de-chaussée (*room*); **2.** en bas de
l'escalier; **~stream** en aval; **~to-earth**
terre-à-terre; **~town** *esp. Am.* centre *m*
(*of a town*); **~ward 1.** de haut en bas;
fig. fatal; dirigé en bas; **2.** (*a.* **~wards**)
de haut en bas.

downy duveteux; velouté.
dowry dot *f*.
doze 1. sommeiller; **2.** petit somme *m*.
dozen douzaine *f*.
dozy somnolant; F *Br.* gourde.
drab terne.
draft 1. *see* **draught**; ✝ traite *f*; ✗ détachement *m*; *Am.* conscription *f*; ✗ ~
dodger insoumis *m*; **2.** rédiger; faire
le brouillon de; *Am.* appeler sous les
armes; **~ee** ✗ *Am.* conscrit *m*; **~sman**
see **draughtsman**.
drag 1. *v/t.* (en)traîner, tirer; draguer; ~
along (en)traîner; *v/i.* traîner; draguer
(à la recherche de, **for**); ~ **on, ~ out**
s'éterniser; **2.** entrave *f*, résistance *f*;
F corvée *f*; F casse-pieds *mf*; *sl.* (**in ~** en)
travesti *m*.
dragon dragon *m*; **~fly** libellule *f*.
drain 1. égout *m*; tuyau *m* d'écoulement;
fig. saignée *f*; F **down the ~** perdu, F
fichu; **2.** *v/t.* assécher, dessécher; vider
(*a pond, a glass, etc.*); *fig.* épuiser; (*a.* **~
off**) faire écouler; évacuer (*the water*); *v/i.*
s'écouler; **~age** écoulement *m*; ✎ drainage *m*; ~ **pipe** tuyau *m* d'écoulement;
gouttière *f*.
drake canard *m* (mâle).
dram goutte *f*; petit verre *m*.
drama drame *m*; **~tic** dramatique; **~tist**
auteur *m* dramatique; **~tize** dramati-
ser; *thea.* adapter à la scène.
drape 1. (se) draper (de **with, in**); **2.** **~s**
pl. Br. tentures *f/pl.*; *Am* rideaux *m/pl.*
drastic énergique; radical.

draught tirage *m* (*of chimney etc.*); courant *m* d'air; *drink*: coup *m*; ✦ potion *f*;
⚓ tirant *m* d'eau; **~s** *pl.* dames *f/pl.*; *see*
draft 1; ~ **beer** bière *f* à la pression;
~board damier *m*; **~sman** dessinateur
(-trice *f*) *m*; **~y** plein de courants d'air.
draw 1. *v/t. oft.* attirer (*a crowd*);
tracer, dessiner; retirer, toucher
(*money*); aspirer (*air*); arracher (*tears*)
(à, **from**); ~ **in** retirer, rentrer, tirer (*to*)
dedans; ~ **out** étirer; allonger, prolonger; ~ **up** tirer en haut; faire monter;
dresser (*a list*), rédiger (*a contract etc.*);
~ (**up**)**on** fournir (*a draft*) sur (*q.*); tirer
(*a cheque*) sur (*a bank*); *fig.* tirer sur
(*savings etc.*); *fig.* faire appel à (*one's
memory etc.*); *v/i.* infuser (*tea*); ~
in raccourcir (*days*); ~ **near** approcher;
s'approcher de; ~ **on** approcher; ~ **up**
s'arrêter; **2.** tirage *m*; loterie *f*; *sp.* partie *f* nulle; F attraction *f*; **~back** désavantage *m*, inconvénient *m*; *Am. a.*
remboursement *m*; **~bridge** pont-levis
m; **~ee** ✝ tiré *m*; payeur *m*; **~er** dessinateur *m*; tireur *m* (*a.* ✝); tiroir *m*; (*usu.*
chest of ~s *pl.*) commode *f*.
drawing dessin *m*; ~ **board** planche *f* à
dessin; **~pin** punaise *f*; **~room** salon *m*.
drawl (parler *ou* dire d'un) accent *m*
traînant.
drawn tiré; ◎ étiré; *sp.* égal.
dread 1. épouvante *f*; **2.** redouter; **~ful
1.** épouvantable, redoutable; **2.:** **penny
~** roman *m* à sensation.
dream 1. rêve *m*; songe *m*; **2.** rêver (de,
of); **~er** rêveur (-euse *f*) *m*; **~y** rêveur;
langoureux.
drear|iness tristesse *f*; aspect *m* morne;
~y triste; morne.
dredge¹ draguer; *fig.* ~ **up** déterrer (*s.th.
forgotten*).
dredge² *cuis.* saupoudrer.
dregs *pl.* lie *f*.
drench tremper, mouiller (de, **with**); **~er**
F pluie *f* battante.
dress 1. robe *f*, costume *m*; *fig.* habillement *m*, habits *m/pl.*; *thea.* ~ **circle**
premier balcon *m*; **2.** (s')habiller; ~ **up**
déguiser (en, **as**); F s'endimancher; *v/t.*
panser (*a wound*); tailler (*a fruit-tree*);
◎ dresser; *cuis.* apprêter; **~er** buffet *m*
de cuisine; *Am.* dressoir *m*.
dressing habillement *m*, toilette *f*; pansement *m* (*of a wound*); *cuis.* sauce *f*,

assaisonnement *m; cuis.* farce *f;* ☉ apprêt *m; ✚* pansements *m/pl.;* ~ *gown* robe *f* de chambre; ~ *room* vestiaire *m; thea.* loge *f;* ~ *table* coiffeuse *f;* ~-*down* semence *f,* F savon *m;* **get a (good)** ~ recevoir un savon; **give s.o. a (good)** ~ passer un savon à q.

dressmak|er couturier (-ère *f*) *m;* ~**ing** couture *f.*

dribble dégoutter; baver (*child etc.*); *foot.* dribbler.

dribs and drabs F: *in* ~ petit à petit, peu à peu.

dried (des)séché; ~ *milk* lait *m* en poudre; ~ *vegetables pl.* légumes *m/pl.* déshydratés.

drift 1. mouvement *m;* direction *f,* sens *m;* ⚓ dérive *f,* cours *m, fig.* tendance *f; snow:* amoncellement *m; rain:* rafale *f;* ~ *from the land* dépeuplement *m* des campagnes; **2.** *v/t.* entasser; *v/i.* flotter; aller à la dérive, être entraîné; ⚓ dériver; se laisser aller (*a. fig.*); ~*ice* glaces *f/pl.* flottantes; ~*wood* bois *m* flotté.

drill¹ ☉ perceuse *f,* foret *m; dentist:* roulette *f,* fraise *f;* **2.** forer; percer; fraiser (*a tooth*).

drill² **1.** exercice(s) *m/pl.;* **2.** faire faire l'exercice à (*q.*).

drink 1. boisson *f; have a* ~ boire un verre; **2.** boire; ~ *s.o.'s health* boire à la santé de q.; ~*able* buvable; potable (*water*).

drinking...: ~ *fountain* fontaine *f* publique; ~ *water* eau *f* potable.

drip 1. (d)égouttement *m;* goutte *f;* F nouille *f* (*person*); ✚ (*be on the* ~ avoir le) goutte-à-goutte *m/inv.;* **2.** (laisser) tomber goutte à goutte; *v/i.* dégoutter; ~*ping cuis.* graisse *f* (de rôti).

drive 1. *v/i. mot.* aller (en voiture), conduire (une voiture); (*a.* ~ *along*) rouler (à, *at a certain speed*); *fig.* **be driving at s.th.** en vouloir venir à qch., vouloir dire qch.; ~ *away,* ~ *off* partir; ~ *in* entrer; ~ *on* continuer (sa route), *v/t. mot.* conduire (*a car, a person*); emmener (*a person*) (en voiture); (*chase*) chasser, pousser (devant soi); enfoncer (*a nail etc.*); *fig.* (*force*) pousser (à, *to*); ☉ faire marcher, actionner (*a machine*); ☉ percer, creuser (*a tunnel etc.*); ~ *away,* ~ *off,* ~ *out* chasser; ~ *back* repousser; ~ *in*

enfoncer (*a nail etc.*); ~ *on* pousser; **2.** promenade *or* voyage *or* trajet (en voiture); (*a.* ~*way*) allée *f; fig.* énergie *f,* entrain *m,* dynamisme *m; psych.* besoin, pulsion(s) *f/pl.);* ✚ *etc.* campagne *f,* efforts *m/pl.;* ☉ traction *f;* transmission *f; mot.* **left-(right-)hand** ~ conduite *f* à gauche (à droite); *mot.* **front-wheel** ~ traction *f* avant; *mot.* **back-wheel** ~ propulsion *f* arrière; ~*in* (restaurant *m or* cinéma *m*) où l'on accède en voiture.

drivel 1. radoter; **2.** radotage *m.*

driver conducteur (-trice *f*) *m; bus, taxi:* chauffeur (-euse *f*) *m;* ~*'s license* permis *m* de conduire.

driving 1. conduite *f;* **2.** de transmission; conducteur; ~ *force* force *f* motrice (*a. fig.*); ~ *instructor* moniteur *m* de conduite; ~ *licence* permis *m* de conduire; ~ *school* auto-école *f;* ~ *test* examen *m* du permis de conduire.

drizzle 1. bruine *f;* **2.** bruiner.

drone 1. *zo.* faux bourdon *m;* fainéant *m;* **2.** bourdonner.

drool baver.

droop *v/t.* baisser; laisser pendre; *v/i.* pendre; languir; s'affaisser; pencher; ~*ing* (re)tombant; (a)baissé; languissant.

drop 1. goutte *f;* baisse *f,* chute *f;* descente *f* brusque *or* à pic; *in ground:* dénivellation *f; cuis.* bonbon *m; earring etc.:* pendeloque *m; fig.* **at the** ~ *of a hat* sans hésiter; **2.** *v/t.* lâcher; laisser tomber (*qch., a question, one's voice*); mouiller (*anchor*); lancer (*a bomb*); jeter à la poste (*a letter*); verser (*tears*); laisser (*a subject*); laisser échapper (*a remark*); baisser (*one's voice, one's eyes, the curtain*); supprimer (*a letter, a syllable*); perdre (*money*); F ~ *it!* assez!; *v/i.* tomber; dégoutter; s'abaisser (*terrain*); se laisser tomber (*into an armchair*); baisser (*price, temperature*); ~ *away* diminuer, baisser; ~ *in* entrer en passant (à, chez *at,* [*up*]*on*); ~ *in on s.o. a.* passer voir q.; ~ *off* diminuer; s'endormir; ~ *out* se retirer, abandonner; ~*let* gouttelette *f;* ~*pings pl.* crottes *f/pl.*

drought sécheresse *f.*

drove troupeau *m;* foule *f.*

drown *v/t.* noyer; étouffer (*a sound*); *v/i.* (*or* **be** ~*ed*) se noyer; être noyé.

drows|e v/i. somnoler, s'assoupir; v/t. assoupir; **~y** somnolent; assoupi.

drudge 1. fig. bête f de somme; **2.** peiner, F trimer; **~ry** corvée f.

drug 1. drogue f; stupéfiant m; **be a ~ in the market** être invendable; **~ addict** toxicomane mf; **~ pusher** (or **peddler**) revendeur (-euse f) m de stupéfiants; **~ traffic(king)** trafic m des stupéfiants; **2.** droguer; **~gist** Am. pharmacien m; **~store** drugstore m.

drum 1. tambour m (a. ⚙); tonneau m; **2.** battre du tambour; tambouriner; **~mer** tambour m; **~stick** ♪ baguette f de tambour; cuis. pilon m.

drunk ivre, soûl (a. fig.); **get ~** s'enivrer, se soûler; **~ard** ivrogne(sse f) m; **~en** ivre; d'ivrogne(s) (party, quarrel, etc.); **~ driving** conduite f en état d'ivresse; **~enness** ivresse f; ivrognerie f; **~ometer** alcootest m.

dry 1. usu. sec (F a. = prohibitionist); aride (subject, terrain); fig. caustique; ⚡ **~ cell** pile f sèche; **~ goods** pl. F Am. tissus m/pl.; articles m/pl. de nouveauté; **2.** sécher; v/t. faire sécher; essuyer (one's eyes); v/i. (a. **~ up**) tarir; F **~ up!** taisez-vous!; **~-clean** nettoyer à sec; **~-cleaning** nettoyage m à sec; **~-nurse** nourrice f sèche.

dual double.

dubious douteux; hésitant; incertain.

duchess duchesse f.

duck 1. canard m; cane f; **2.** v/i. se baisser (subitement); v/t. plonger (q.) (dans l'eau); baisser subitement (one's head); fig. éviter; **~ling** caneton m.

dud F **1.** nullard(e f) m, raté(e f) m (person); thing: **... is a ~** ... ne marche pas, ... ne vaut rien; **2.** raté; qui ne vaut rien; faux (cheque etc.).

dude Am sl. gommeux m; type m, mec m.

dudgeon: in (high) ~ (extrêmement) furieux.

due 1. dû (f due); qui convient (respect etc.); ✝ échu; **in ~ course** en temps utile; **be ~ to** être dû à, être causé par; **be ~ to** (inf.) devoir (inf.); **... is due to** (inf.) **... is due (to arrive) at ...** ... doit arriver à ...; ✝ **fall ~** échoir; **2.** adv. ⚓ droit; **3.** dû m; fees: usu. **~s** pl. droits m/pl.; frais m/pl.; cotisation f.

duel 1. duel m; **2.** se battre en duel.

duke duc m; **~dom** duché m.

dull 1. terne (a. style), mat (colour); sans éclat (eye); dur (ear); sourd (noise, pain); lourd (mind); sombre (weather); émoussé; ✝ inactif (market); ennuyeux; **2.** v/t. émousser; assourdir; ternir; amortir (a pain); engourdir (s.o's mind); hébéter (q.); v/i. se ternir; s'engourdir; **~ness** manque m d'éclat or de tranchant; lenteur f de l'esprit; ennui m; ✝ marasme m.

duly dûment; comme il se doit; convenablement; en temps voulu.

dumb muet; F bête; **deaf and ~** sourd-muet; **~found** ahurir; abasourdir; **~ness** mutisme m; silence m; **~waiter** desserte f; Am. monte-plats m/inv.

dummy 1. chose f factice; mannequin m; Br. tétine f; Am. imbécile m/f, sot(te f) m; **2.** faux; factice.

dump 1. décharge f (publique), dépotoir m; dépôt m; F dirty place: trou m; F **be (down) in the ~s** avoir le cafard; **2.** déposer; jeter; se débarrasser de; déverser; ✝ vendre à vil prix; **~ing** ✝ dumping m; **,no ~!'** ,décharge interdite!'

dumpling cuis. boulette f.

dun harceler (a debtor); **~ning letter** demande f pressante.

dunce F crétin(e f) m.

dune dune f.

dung 1. ⚜ engrais m, fumier m; **2.** fumer (a field).

dungarees pl. salopette f.

dungeon cachot m.

dunghill fumier m.

dunk tremper (dans son café etc.).

dupe 1. dupe f; **2.** duper, tromper.

duplex 1. ⚙ double; **2.** Am. maison f comprenant deux appartements indépendants.

duplic|ate 1. double; en double; **2.** double m, copie f (exacte); **in ~** en double; **3.** reproduire; copier; **~ity** duplicité f; mauvaise foi f.

dura|ble durable; résistant; solide; **~tion** durée f.

duress(e) ⚖ contrainte f.

during prp. pendant.

dusk demi-jour m/inv.; crépuscule m; obscurité f; **~y** sombre.

dust 1. poussière f; **2.** épousseter; saupoudrer (de, with); **~bin** boîte f à ordures; poubelle f; **~bowl** région f désertique; **~er** *Br.* chiffon *m* (à poussière); *Am.* cache-poussière *m/inv.*; **~ cover, ~ jacket** *book*: jaquette *f*; **~man** éboueur *m*, boueux *m*; **~y** poussiéreux; poudreux.

Dutch 1. hollandais, de Hollande; **~ treat** repas *m* où chacun paie sa part; **go ~** partager les frais; **2.** *ling.* hollandais *m*; **the ~** *pl.* les Hollandais *m/pl.*; **~man** Hollandais *m*.

duti|able soumis à des droits de duane *etc.*; taxable; **~ful** respectueux, soumis.

duty devoir *m* (envers, **to**); respect *m*; obéissance *f*; fonction(s) *f/(pl.)*; service *m*; *customs etc.*: droit(s) *m/(pl.)*; **on ~** de service; **off ~** libre; **~-free** exempt de douane; **~ shop** magasin *m* hors-taxe.

dwarf 1. nain(e *f*) *m*; **2.** rabougrir; *fig.* rapetisser, éclipser, faire paraître petit.

dwell habiter; demeurer (dans, *à*); *fig.* **~ (up)on** s'étendre sur; **~ing** demeure *f*.

dwindle diminuer; se réduire (à, [*in*]to).

dye 1. teint(ure *f*) *m*; **2.** teindre.

dying (*see* **die¹**) **1.** mourant, agonisant, moribond; **2.** mort *f*.

dynam|ic 1. dynamique; **2. ~s** *usu. sg.* dynamique *f*; **~ite 1.** dynamite *f*; **2.** faire sauter à la dynamite; **~o** dynamo *f*.

dynasty dynastie *f*.

dysentery ⚕ dysenterie *f*.

dyspepsia ⚕ dyspepsie *f*.

E

each 1. *adj.* chaque; **2.** *pron.* chacun (-e *f*); **~ other** l'un(e) l'autre, les un(e)s les autres.

eager passionné; impatient (de *inf.*, **to** *inf.*); désireux; avide (de *after*, **for**); *fig.* vif; acharné; **be ~ to do s.th.** *a.* désirer vivement faire qch., brûler de faire qch.; **~ness** ardeur *f*; vif désir *m*; empressement *m*.

eagle aigle *mf*; pièce *f* de 10 dollars.

ear¹ *♦* épi *m*.

ear² oreille *f*; **turn a deaf ~ to** faire la sourde oreille à; **~-deafening** assourdissant; **~drum** *anat.* tympan *m*.

earl comte *m* (*of England*).

early 1. *adj.* matinal; premier; précoce; **be an ~ bird** être matinal; **in the ~ afternoon** au début de l'après-midi, en début d'après-midi; **2.** *adv.* de bonne heure; tôt; **as ~ as** dès; pas plus tard que.

earmark: ~ for destiner *or* réserver (*funds etc.*) à.

earn gagner; ✝ rapporter (*interest etc.*); *fig. a.* mériter (*a reward etc.*); *fig.* **~ s.o. s.th.** valoir qch. à q.; **~ed income** revenu *m* du travail.

earnest 1. sérieux; **2.** sérieux *m*; **in ~** sérieusement; **be in ~** être sérieux.

earnings *pl.* salaire *m*; gains *m/pl.*; profits *m/pl.*

ear...: ~phones *pl. radio*: casques *m/pl.* (d'écoute); **~piece** *teleph.* écouteur *m*; **~plugs** *pl.* boules *f/pl.* Quiès (*TM*); **~ring** boucle *f* d'oreille; **~shot** portée *f* de la voix.

earth 1. terre *f*; *radio*: (*a.* **~connection**) contact *m* à la terre; **2.** *v/t.* ⚡ relier à la terre *or* à la masse; **~en** de *or* en terre; **~enware** poterie *f*; **~ly** terrestre; **F not an ~ ...** pas le *or* la moindre ...; **~quake** tremblement *m* de terre; **~worm** lombric *m*; **~y** terreux, de terre; *fig.* grossier, terre à terre.

ease 1. repos *m*, bien-être *m*, aise *f*; tranquillité *f* (*of mind*); *manners*: aisance *f*; **at ~** tranquille; à son *etc.* aise; **with ~** facilement; **live at ~** vivre à l'aise; **2.** *v/t.* adoucir, soulager (*pain*); calmer; (re)lâcher (*one's grip etc.*); diminuer; **~ in (out)** faire entrer (sortir) doucement; *v/i.* **~ off, ~ up** diminuer; se détendre.

easel chevalet *m*.

easi|ly facilement; sans aucun doute, bien; **~ness** facilité *f*, aisance *f*.

east 1. *su.* est *m*; **the** ⚙ l'Orient *m*; *Am.* les États *m/pl.* de l'Est; **2.** *adj.* d'est, de l'est; **3.** *adv.* à *or* vers l'est.

Easter Pâques *m/pl.*; *attr.* de Pâques; ~ **egg** œuf *m* de Pâques.

easter|ly de *or* à l'est; ~**n** de l'est; oriental.

eastward 1. *adj.* à *or* de l'est; 2. *adv. a.* ~**s** vers l'est.

easy facile; à l'aise; aisé (*air, style, task*); ~ **does it!** doucement!; *in* ~ *circumstances* dans l'aisance; *on* ~ *street* très à l'aise; *take it* (*or things*) ~ ne pas s'en faire; ne pas se le fouler; se la couler douce; ~ **chair** fauteuil *m*; bergère *f*; ~**going** accommodant; insouciant.

eat manger; ~ *out* manger au restaurant; ~ *up* manger jusqu'à la dernière miette; consumer; dévorer (*a. fig.*); *v/t.* manger; déjeuner *etc.*; ~**able** mangeable; 2. ~**s** *pl.* comestibles *m/pl.*

eaves *pl.* avant-toit *m*; ~**drop** écouter de façon indiscrète; être aux écoutes; ~ *on* écouter (de façon indiscrète).

ebb 1. (*a.* ~**tide**) reflux *m*; *be on the* ~ descendre; *fig.* **be at a low** ~ être en baisse; 2. descendre (*tide*); *fig.* baisser, (*a.* ~ *away*) diminuer.

ebony (bois *m* d')ébène *f*.

ebullien|ce exubérance *f*; ~**t** exubérant.

eccentric 1. excentrique (*a. fig.*); 2. ◎ excentrique *m*; original(e *f*) *m*.

ecclesiastic 1. ecclésiastique; 2. *a.* ~**al** ecclésiastique.

echo 1. écho *m*; 2. *v/t.* répéter; *fig.* se faire l'écho de; *v/i.* faire écho; retentir.

eclipse 1. éclipse *f*; 2. *v/t.* éclipser; *v/i.* être éclipse.

ecolog|ical écologique; ~**ist** écologiste *mf.*; ~**y** écologie *f*.

econom|ic économique; ~**ical** économique; économe (*person*); ~**ics** *sg.* économie *f* politique; ~**ist** économiste *m*; personne *f* économe (de, *of*); ~**ize** économiser (qch. *on* or *with s.th.*); ~**y** économie *f*; *economies pl.* économies *f/pl.*; épargnes *f/pl.*; ~ *class* classe *f* touriste; *political* ~ économie *f* politique.

ecsta|sy extase *f*; *fig.* **go into** (*or be in*) *ecstasies* (*over*) s'extasier (sur); ~**tic** extatique.

eddy 1. remous *m*; tourbillon *m*; 2. faire des remous; tourbillonner.

edge 1. bord *m*; *knife etc.*: tranchant *m*; *forest*: lisière *f*; *be* ~ *up* être nerveux; *have the* ~ *on* être avantage par rapport à; 2. *v/t.* border; *v/i.* (se) faufiler; (se) glisser; ~**d** tranchant; ...-~**d** à ...

tranchant(s), à tranchant(s) ...; ~**ing** bordure *f*; *dress*: liséré *m*; ~**y** F énervé.

edible 1. comestible, bon à manger; mangeable (*meal*); 2. ~**s** *pl.* comestibles *m/pl.*

edi|fication édification *f*; ~**fice** édifice *m*; ~**fying** édifiant.

edit éditer (*a book*); diriger (*a newspaper*); ~**ion** édition *f*; ~**or** éditeur *m*; *journ.* rédacteur *m* en chef; *letters pl. to the* ~ courrier *m* des lecteurs; ~**orial** 1. de la rédaction; ~ *office* (bureau *m* de) rédaction; ~ *staff* la rédaction; 2. *article*: éditorial *m*.

educat|e instruire; (*train*) former; éduquer; ~**ion** instruction *f*; enseignement *m*; formation *f*; éducation *f*; *elementary* ~ enseignement *m* primaire; *Ministry of* ~ Ministère *m* de l'Éducation nationale; ~**ional** d'enseignement; pédagogique; ~**or** éducateur (-trice *f*) *m*.

eel *ichth.* anguille *f*.

efface effacer (*a. fig.*), oblitérer.

effect 1. effet *m*; action *f* (*a.* ◎); vigueur *f* (於 *of a law*); sens *m*; ~**s** *pl.* effets *m/pl.*; *bring* (*or put*) *into* ~ effectuer, réaliser, appliquer; *take* ~ produire un effet; *a.* *come into* ~ prendre effet, entrer en vigueur; *of no* ~ sans effet, inefficace; *in* ~ en fait, en réalité; 2. effectuer; opérer; réaliser; ~**ive** efficace; effectif (*a.* ◎); 於 en vigueur; *fig.* frappant; ~ *date* date *f* d'entrée en vigueur; ~**ual** efficace; valide, en vigueur.

effeminate efféminé.

effervesce entrer en effervescence; pétiller; mousser; ~**nce** effervescence *f*; ~**nt** effervescent; gazeux (*drink*).

effete veule; décadent.

effica|cious efficace; ~**y** efficacité *f*.

efficien|cy efficacité *f*; capacité *f*; ◎ rendement *m*; bon fonctionnement *m*; ~ *expert* expert *m* de l'organisation rationnelle (*in industry*); ~**t** efficace; capable, compétent (*person*); à bon rendement.

effigy (*in* ~ en) effigie *f*.

efflorescence efflorescence *f* (*a.* 🌱); ♀ fleuraison *f*.

effluent effluent *m*.

effort effort *m*; ~**less** aisé; facile (*achievement etc.*).

effrontery effronterie *f*; toupet *m*.

effulgent resplendissant, brillant.

effus|ion effusion f, épanchement m (a. fig.); **~ive** expansif; **~iveness** effusion f; volubilité f.

egg¹ (usu. ~ **on**) pousser, inciter.

egg² œuf m; **scrambled ~s** pl. œufs m/pl. brouillés; **boiled ~s** pl. œufs m/pl. à la coque; **fried ~s** pl. œufs m/pl. sur le plat; **~cup** coquetier m; **~head** intellectuel m; **~plant** aubergine f; **~shell** coquille f (d'œuf); **~whisk** fouet m (à œufs).

ego le moi; **~centric(al)** égocentrique; **~ism** égoïsme m; **~ist** égoïste mf; **~istical** égoïste.

egregious iro. insigne; fameux.

egress sortie f, issue f.

Egyptian 1. égyptien; **2.** Égyptien(ne f) m.

eight 1. huit; **2.** huit m; **~een** dix-huit; **~eenth** dix-huitième; **~fold** octuple; adv. huit fois autant; **~h** huitième (a. su./m); **~hly** en huitième lieu; **~ieth** quatre-vingtième; **~y** quatrevingt(s); **~first** quatre-vingt-unième.

either 1. adj. chaque; l'un et l'autre de; l'un ou l'autre de; **2.** pron. chacun; l'un et or ou l'autre; **3.** cj. **~ ... or ...** ou ... ou ...; soit ... soit ...; **not ... ~** ne ... non plus.

ejaculat|e éjaculer; s'écrier; **~ion** éjaculation f; exclamation f.

eject éjecter; expulser (q.); **~or seat** siège m éjectable.

eke: ~ out suppléer à l'insuffisance de; allonger (a liquid); **~ out a miserable existence** (or a living) gagner une maigre pitance.

elaborat|e 1. compliqué; travaillé (style); recherché; soigné; **2.** élaborer; donner des détails (sur, on); **~ion** élaboration f.

elapse (se) passer; s'écouler.

elastic élastique (a. su./m); **~ity** élasticité f.

elat|ed transporté (de joie); **~ion** exultation f.

elbow 1. coude m; **at one's ~** tout à côté; **out at ~s** troué aux coudes, fig. déguenillé; **2.** pousser du coude; **~ one's way through** se frayer un passage à travers (en jouant des coudes); **~ out** évincer (de, of); **~grease** F huile f de coude; **~room: have ~** avoir de la place (pour se retourner); avoir les coudes franches.

elder¹ 1. plus âgé, aîné; **2.** plus âgé(e f) m; aîné(e f) m; eccl. ancien m; **my ~s** pl. mes aînés m/pl.

elder² ♀ sureau m.

elderly assez âgé.

eldest aîné.

elect 1. élu (a. eccl.); futur; **the president ~** le président désigné, le futur président; **2.** élire; choisir (de inf., to inf.); **~ion** élection f; attr. électoral (campaign, speech, etc.); **~ioneer** faire de la propagande électorale; **~or** électeur (-trice f) m; **~oral** électoral; **~orate** électorat m.

electr|ic électrique; fig. électrisant; **~cal** électrique; **~ engineering** ingénieur m électricien; **~ engineering** technique f électrique; **~cian** (monteur-)électricien m; **~city** électricité f; **~fy, ~ze** électriser (a. fig.). ⚡ électrifier.

electro|cute électrocuter; **~magnet** électro-aimant m; **~motor** électromoteur m.

electron électron m; **~ ray tube** oscillographe m cathodique; **~ic** électronique; **~ics** sg. électronique f.

electroplate plaquer (par galvanoplastie).

elegan|ce élégance f, **~t** élégant.

element élément m; **~s** pl. rudiments m/pl., éléments m/pl.; **~al** élémentaire; des éléments; fig. premier; **~ary** élémentaire; primaire (school).

elephant éléphant m.

elevat|e élever; **~ed** (a. **~ railroad** or **train**) chemin m de fer aérien; **~ion** élévation f (a. ⊙, △, astr., eccl., hill); altitude f, hauteur f; **~or** ⊙ élévateur m; Am. ascenseur m.

eleven onze (a. su./m); **~ses** F pause-café f; **~th** onzième.

elfin féerique; d'elfe.

elicit tirer (au jour); obtenir; fig. arracher (à, from) (an avowal etc.).

eligible admissible; éligible; acceptable; **be ~ for** avoir droit à (qch.).

eliminat|e éliminer; **~ion** élimination f.

élite élite f.

elk zo. élan m.

ellipse Å ellipse f.

elm ♀ orme m.

elocution élocution f, diction f.

elongat|e (s')allonger; (s')étirer; **~ion** allongement m; prolongement m.

elope s'enfuir (avec un amant); ~**ment** fugue f (amoureuse).

eloquen|ce éloquence f; ~**t** éloquent.

else 1. *adv.* autrement; ou bien; **2.** *adj.* autre; encore; *anyone* ~ quelqu'un d'autre; *what* ~? quoi encore?; ~**where** ailleurs.

elucidat|e élucider, éclaircir; ~**ion** élucidation f, éclaircissement m.

elude échapper à; éluder, éviter, esquiver.

elus|ive insaisissable; évasif (*answer*); ~**ory** évasif.

emaciated émacié, décharné.

emanat|e émaner (de, *from*); ~**ion** émanation f; effluve m.

emancipat|e émanciper; affranchir; ~**ion** émancipation f.

embalm embaumer.

embank endiguer; remblayer (*a road*); ~**ment** digue f; talus m, remblai m; quai m.

embargo 1. embargo m; *put an* ~ *on* = **2.** mettre l'embargo sur, frapper (*qch.*) d'embargo.

embark (s')embarquer (*a. fig.* dans, [*up*]*on*); *v/t.* prendre (*qch.*) à bord; *v/i.*: ~ (*up*)*on s.th.* s'embarquer dans qch.; ~**ation** embarquement m.

embarrass embarrasser; gêner; ~**ed** embarrassé; gêné; dans l'embarras; ~**ment** embarras m; gêne f.

embassy ambassade f.

embellish embellir; enjoliver.

embers braise f.

embezzle détourner (*funds*); ~**ment** détournement m de fonds.

embitter aigrir (*q.*); envenimer (*a quarrel etc.*).

emblem emblème m; *sp.* insigne m.

embod|iment incarnation f; ~**y** incarner, personnifier; comporter, renfermer; réunir (*qualities*, *features*, *etc.*).

embolden enhardir.

embolism ✝ embolie f.

emboss graver en relief; repousser (*metal*).

embrace 1. *v/t.* prendre *or* serres dans ses bras, étreindre; *fig.* embrasser; *v/i.* se prendre dans les bras (l'un l'autre), s'étreindre; **2.** étreinte f.

embroider broder (*a. fig.*); ~**y** broderie f (*a. fig.*).

embroil entraîner (dans, *in*).

emend corriger; ~**ation** correction f.

emerald émeraude f.

emerge émerger, surgir; *fig. a.* apparaître; ~**ncy** urgence f; cas m imprévu; circonstance f critique; ~ *brake* frein m de secours; *teleph.* ~ *call* appel m urgent; ~ *exit* sortie f de secours; ✈ ~ *landing* atterrissage m forcé; ~ *measure* mesure f extraordinaire; ~**nt** émergent; surgissant.

emery ~ *paper* papier m émeri.

emigra|nt émigrant(e f) m; ~**te** émigrer; ~**tion** émigration f.

eminen|ce éminence f; élévation f; monticule m; ~**t** éminent; ~**ly** éminemment; admirablement, parfaitement.

emissary émissaire m.

emit émettre (*a.* ✝); dégager.

emoluments *pl.* émoluments m/pl.

emotion émotion f; ~**al** *psych. etc.* émotionnel; émotif (*person*); qui fait appel aux émotions, touchant, émouvant; *be* ~**ly** *disturbed* souffrir de troubles de l'affectivité.

emotive émotif.

emperor empereur m.

empha|sis accent m; *gramm. a.* accentuation f; *place* (*or* *put*) ~ *on* mettre l'accent sur; ~**size** accentuer; appuyer sur; souligner; faire ressortir; ~**tic** énergique; catégorique.

empire empire m.

empirical empirique.

employ 1. employer; *be* ~**ed in** (*ger.*) être occupé à (*inf.*); **2.** emploi m; *in the* ~ *of* au service de; ~**ee** employé(e f) m; ~**er** patron(ne f) m; maître(sse f) m; employeur m; ~**ment** emploi m; occupation f; situation f; travail m; ~ *agency* bureau m de placement; *full* ~ plein emploi m.

empower autoriser (à, *to*); ✝✝ habiliter, donner (plein) pouvoir à (*q.*).

empress impératrice f.

empt|iness vide m; *fig.* vanité f; ~**y 1.** vide; *fig.* vain; **2.** (se) vider; *on an* ~ *stomach* à jeun; ~**y-handed** les mains vides; *return* ~ *a.* revenir bredouille.

emulat|e imiter; rivaliser avec; ~**ion** émulation f.

emulsion émulsion f; ~ *paint* peinture f mate.

enable permettre, mettre à même (de *inf.*, *to inf.*); ✝✝ donner pouvoir à (*q.* de *inf.*, *to inf.*).

enact décréter, ordonner; *thea.* représenter.

enamel 1. émail *m*; **2.** émailler.

enamo(u)red amoureux (de, *of*); *fig. a.* enchanté (par, *of*).

encase enfermer; revêtir (de, *with*).

enchain enchaîner.

enchant ensorceler; *fig.* enchanter; **~ing** ravissant; **~ment** enchantement *m*.

encircle encercler, entourer.

enclos|e clôturer, enclore; entourer; renfermer; joindre (à une lettre, **in a letter**); **please find ~d** veuillez trouver ci-joint; **~ure** ‡ *etc.* annexe *m*.

encode chiffrer.

encompass entourer; renfermer.

encore 1. bis!, **2.** bisser; **3.** bis *m*.

encounter 1. rencontre *f*; combat *m*; **2.** rencontrer; éprouver (*difficulties*); affronter.

encourage encourager; inciter; favoriser; **~ment** encouragement *m*.

encroach: **~ (up)on** empiéter sur; **~ment** empiétement *m* (sur, **upon**).

encumb|er encombrer (de, **with**); grever (*a property*); **~rance** embarras *m*; charge *f*.

encyclop(a)edia encyclopédie *f*.

end 1. *time:* fin *f* (*a.* = *purpose*); *farthest part:* bout *m*; ۞ **~ product** produit *m* fini; **bring to an ~, put an ~ to** mettre fin à, terminer; **come to an ~** prendre fin, finir; **no ~ of** infiniment de, ... sans nombre; **in the ~** enfin; à la longue, **on ~** de suite; debout; **stand on ~** se dresser (sur la tête) (*hair*); **make both ~s meet** joindre les deux bouts; **2.** *v/t.* terminer; finir; *v/i.* finir, se terminer; **~ up in** terminer par; aboutir à (*road*); échouer à (*person*).

endanger mettre en danger.

endear rendre cher, **~ing** sympathique; **~ment** (*or term of* **~**) mot *m* tendre.

endeavo(u)r 1. effort *m*, tentative *f*; **2.** (**to** *inf.*) essayer (de *inf.*); chercher (à *inf.*); s'efforcer (de *inf.*).

end|ing fin *f*; conclusion *f*; *gramm.* terminaison *f*; **~less** sans fin (*a.* ۞); infini, interminable.

endorse ‡ endosser (*a document*); avaliser (*a money order*); *fig.* appuyer, approuver; **~ment** ‡ endos(sement) *m*; approbation *f*.

endow doter, *fig. a.* douer (de, **with**);

~ment dotation *f*; fondation *f*; *fig.* don *m* (*quality*).

endue douer (de, **with**).

endur|able supportable; **~ance** endurance *f*, résistance *f*; patience *f*; **~e** *v/t.* supporter, souffrir (*qch.*); *v/i.* durer.

enema ☞ lavement *m*.

enemy ennemi(e *f*) *m* (*a. adj.*).

energ|etic énergique; **~y** énergie *f* (*a. phys.*); **~-saving** à faible consommation d'énergie.

enervate énerver; affaiblir.

enfeeble affaiblir.

enfold envelopper.

enforce appliquer (*a law etc.*), mettre en vigueur; faire observer; imposer (à *qch.*, **upon s.o.**); **~d** forcé; **~ment** application *f*.

enfranchise donner le droit de vote à (*q.*); affranchir.

engage *v/t.* engager (*an assistant etc.*); embaucher (*a worker*); retenir (*a place*); ۞ mettre en prise (*a gear*); fixer (*s.o.'s attention*); attaquer (*the enemy*); **be ~d** être fiancé; être pris; être occupé (*a. teleph.*); **be ~d in** être occupé à; prendre part à; *v/i.* s'engager; s'obliger (à, **to**); s'embarquer (dans, **in**); **~ment** engagement *m*; obligation *f*; promesse *f*; rendez-vous *m*; fiançailles *f/pl.*; ۞ mise *f* en prise; ✗ action *f*.

engaging attrayant, séduisant.

engender faire naître, produire.

engine machine *f*, *car etc.:* moteur *m*; 🚂 locomotive *f*; 🚂 *Br.* **~ driver** mécanicien *m*.

engineer 1. ingénieur *m*; 🚂 *Am.* mécanicien *m*; **2.** construire; F machiner; **~ing** ingénierie *f*, engineering *m*; technique *f*; construction *f* mécanique.

English 1. anglais; **the ~ Channel** la Manche; ♪ *ling* anglais *m*; **the ~** *pl.* les Anglais *m/pl.*; **~man** Anglais *m*; **~-speaking** anglophone; **~woman** Anglaise *f*.

engrav|e graver; **~er** *person:* graveur *m*; **~ing** gravure *f*.

engross absorber (*q.*, *attention etc.*)

engulf engloutir, engouffrer.

enhance rehausser, mettre en valeur; augmenter; relever.

enigma énigme *f*; **~tic(al)** énigmatique.

enjoin imposer (à, **on**).

enjoy aimer, prendre plaisir à; goûter;

jouir de; ~ **o.s.** s'amuser; se divertir; **I ~ my dinner** je trouve le dîner bon; **~able** agréable; **~ment** plaisir *m*; ⚖ jouissance *f*.

enlarge *v/t.* agrandir (*a. phot.*); étendre, élargir; *v/i.* s'agrandir *etc.*; *fig.* ~ (**up**)**on** s'étendre sur (*a topic*); **~ment** agrandissement *m* (*a. phot.*).

enlighten éclairer (q. sur qch., **s.o. on s.th.**); **~ing** révélateur; **~ment** éclaircissements *m/pl.*; *hist.* **the Age of ♀** le Siècle *m* des lumières.

enlist *v/t.* enrôler (*a soldier*); engager; ✗ **~ed man** (simple) soldat *m*; *v/i.* s'enrôler; s'engager (dans, **in**).

enliven animer; *fig.* égayer.

enmity inimitié *f*.

ennoble anoblir; *fig.* ennoblir.

enorm|ity énormité *f*; **~ous** énorme.

enough assez (de *qch.*); suffisamment (de *qch.*); **strangely** ~ chose curieuse, curieusement; **sure** ~! assurément!

enquire *see* **inquire.**

enrage faire enrager, rendre furieux; **~d** furieux (contre, **at**).

enrapture ravir.

enrich enrichir.

enrol(l) *v/t.* inscrire (*members etc.*); immatriculer (*a student*); engager (*workers*); ✗ enrôler; *v/i.* (*or* ~ **o.s.**) s'inscrire *etc.*; **~ment** enrôlement *m*; engagement *m*.

ensign ⚓ pavillon *m*.

enslave asservir.

ensnare prendre au piège.

ensue s'ensuivre (de **from, on**).

ensure assurer, garantir; ~ **that** s'assurer que; *see a.* **insure.**

entail entraîner, comporter, avoir pour conséquence.

entangle emmêler, embrouiller; empêtrer; **~ment** emmêlement *m*, embrouillement *m*; ✗ barbelé(s) *m(/pl.).*

enter *v/t.* entrer dans, pénétrer dans; monter dans (*a taxi etc.*); inscrire (*qch.*) (dans une liste); entrer à (*the army, a school*); s'inscrire à (*a university etc.*); prendre part à (*a discussion*); ⚖ interjeter (*appeal etc.*); *v/i.* entrer; s'inscrire; *sp.* s'engager (pour, **for**); entrer (à, **at** *school etc.*); ~ **into** entrer dans (*details*); entrer en (*a conversation*); prendre part à; ~ (**up**)**on** entrer en (*a function*); entreprendre; embrasser (*a career*); s'engager dans (*qch.*).

enterpris|e entreprise *f*; *fig.* (esprit *m* d')initiative *f*; **~ing** entreprenant.

entertain *v/t.* amuser, divertir; recevoir (*guests*); *fig.* envisager, considérer (*plans etc.*); avoir (*doubts, a thought*); *v/i.* recevoir; **~er** hôte(sse *f*) *m*; artiste *mf* de variété; **~ing** amusant, divertissant; **~ment** spectacle *m*; divertissement *m*, amusement *m*.

enthral(l) captiver, ensorceler.

enthrone introniser.

enthusias|m enthousiasme *m*; **~t** enthousiaste *mf*; **~tic** enthousiaste.

entice séduire, attirer; **~ment** séduction *f*; attrait *m*.

entire entier; **~ly** entièrement, tout entier; **~ty** intégr(al)ité *f*.

entitle intituler; donner à (*q.*) le droit (à, **to**; de *inf.*, **to** *inf.*); **be ~d** s'intituler, s'appeler; **be ~d to** avoir droit à (*qch.*); avoir le droit de (*inf.*).

entity entité *f*.

entomb ensevelir.

entrails *pl.* entrailles *f/pl.*

entrance[1] entrée *f* (dans, **into**; *a.* en fonctions, **into** [*or* **upon**] **office**); accès *m*; (*a.* ~ **fee**) prix *m* d'entrée.

entrance[2] ravir, enchanter.

entrap prendre au piège; amener (*q.*) par ruse (à *inf.*, **into** *ger.*).

entreat supplier, prier; **~y** prière *f*, supplication *f*.

entrench retrancher.

entrust confier (qch. à q., **s.th. to s.o.**); charger (**de, with**).

entry entrée *f*; inscription *f*; ⚖ prise *f* de possession (de, [**up**]**on**); ♰ *book-keeping:* partie *f*; *sp.* liste *f* des inscrits; *fig.* commencement *m*; **no ~** entrée interdite; *street:* sens interdit; ~ **permit** permis *m* d'entrée; *book-keeping by* **double** (**single**) ~ tenue *f* des livres *or* comptabilité *f* en partie double (simple).

enumerate énumérer.

enunciate prononcer, articuler; exposer, énoncier (*a theory etc.*).

entwine (s')entrelacer; (s')enlacer.

envelop envelopper; **~e** enveloppe *f*; **in an** ~ sous enveloppe; **~ment** enveloppement *m*.

envi|able enviable, digne d'envie; **~ous** envieux (de, **of**).

environ entourer, environner (de, **with**);

estimate

~ment environnement *m*; milieu *m*; ambiance *f*; **~mental** du milieu; de l'environnement, écologiste; **~s** *pl.* environs *m/pl.*, alentours *m/pl.*

envisage, envision prévoir.

envoy envoyé *m*.

envy 1. envie *f*; **2.** envier (qch. à q., *s.o. s.th.*).

enzyme enzyme *m*.

epic 1. (*a.* **~al**) épique; **2.** épopée *f*.

epidemic ✶ 1. épidémique; **~ disease** = **2.** épidémie *f*.

epidermis *anat.* épiderme *m*.

epigram épigramme *f*.

epilep|sy ✶ épilepsie *f*, **~tic ✶** épilop tique (*a. su./mf*).

epilogue épilogue *m*.

episcopa|cy épiscopat *m*; **~l** épiscopal; **~te** épiscopat *m*.

episode épisode *m*.

epitaph épitaphe *f*.

epoch époque *f*; **~making** qui fait époque.

equable égal (*character, climate, etc.*).

equal 1. égal; **~ to** à la hauteur de; égal à; **2.** égal *m*; **my ~s** *pl.* mes pareils; **3.** égaler; **not to be ~led** sans égal; **~ity** égalité *f*; **~ization** égalisation *f*; compensation *f*; **~ize** égaliser; **~izer** *sp.* but *m or* point *m* égalisateur.

equanimity égalité d'humeur *or* d'esprit.

equate mettre sur le même pied; comparer; **~ion** équation *f*.

équator équateur *m*; **at the ~** sous l'équateur.

equestrian cavalier (-ère *f*) *m*.

equilibrium équilibre *m*.

equip équiper; munir; **~ment** équipement *m*; outillage *m*.

equity équité *f*.

equivalen|ce équivalence *f*; **~t** équivalent (à, *to*) (*a. su./m*).

equivoca|l équivoque; ambigu; **~lity, ~lness** équivoque *f*; **~te** s'exprimer de manière équivoque, équivoquer; **~tion** équivocation *f*.

era ère *f*; époque *f*; âge *m*.

eradicate supprimer.

eras|e effacer; **~er** gomme *f*; **~ure** rature *f*.

ere (à) avant (que).

erect 1. droit; debout; **2.** ériger, élever; édifier (*a theory etc.*); **~ion** construction *f*; érection *f* (*a. physiol.*).

eremite ermite *m*.

erogenous érogène.

ero|de éroder; ronger (*metal*); **~sion** érosion *f*.

erotic érotique.

err se tromper; s'égarer (de, *from*).

errand commission *f*; message *m*; **go (on) ~s** faire des commissions; **~ boy** garçon *m* de courses; *hotel:* chasseur *m*.

errant errant.

errat|ic irrégulier; *geol.*, **✶** erratique; **~um**, *pl.* **-ta** erratum (*pl.* -ta) *m*.

erroneous erroné.

error erreur *f*, faute *f*; **~ rate** pourcentage *m* de fautes.

erudit|e érudit, savant; **~ion** érudition *f*.

erupt entrer en éruption (*volcano etc.*); percer (*tooth*); *fig.* éclater; **✶ ~ in pimples** se couvrir de pustules, **~ion** *volcano, u. fig., a.* **✶**: éruption *f*; *fig.* éclat *m*.

escalat|e *v/i.* s'intensifier; monter (en flèche) (*prices etc.*); *v/t.* intensifier; **~ion** intensification *f*; montée *f* (en flèche); **~or** escalier *m* roulant, escalator *m*.

escap|ade escapade *f*; **~e 1.** *v/t.* échapper à; *v/i.* s'échapper, s'évader (de, *from*); se dégager (*gas etc.*); **2.** évasion *f*, fuite *f*; *vapour:* échappement *m*; **~ hatch** trappe *f* de secours; **have a narrow ~** l'échapper belle; **~ism** évasion *f*.

eschew éviter.

escort 1. escorte *f*; *companion:* cavalier *m*; **2.** escorter; accompagner.

escutcheon écusson *m* (*a.* ⊙).

especial spécial; particulier; **~ly** particulièrement, surtout; exprès

espionage espionnage *m*.

essay essai *m*; *school:* composition *f*; tentative *f* (de, *at*); **~ist** essayiste *mf*.

essen|ce essence *f*; **~tial 1.** essentiel; fondamental; **2.** essentiel *m*.

establish établir; fonder, créer; affermir, asseoir; **~ o.s.** s'établir; **~ment** établissement *m* (*a.* ✝); création *f*, fondation *f*; ✝ maison *f*.

estate propriété *f*; ⚑ immeuble *m*, bien *m*; ⚖ succession *f*; **real ~** biens-fonds *m/pl.*, propriété *f* immobilière; **~ agent** agent *m* immobilier.

esteem 1. estime *f*; **2.** estimer.

estima|ble estimable; **~te 1.** estimer; évaluer (à, *at*); **2.** estimation *f*; évaluation *f*; ✝ devis *m* (estimataire); **~tion** opinion *f*; estime *f*.

estrange aliéner l'estime (de, *from*).

estuary estuaire *m*.

etch graver (à l'eau-forte); **~ing** (gravure *f* à l')eau-forte *f*; art *m* de graver à l'eau-forte.

etern|al éternel; **~ity** éternité *f*.

ether éther *m* (*a*. 🐦); **~eal** éthéré.

ethic|al éthique; moral; **~s** *usu*. *sg*. morale *f*, éthique *f*.

etiquette étiquette *f*; cérémonial *m* (*oft*. de cour).

etymology étymologie *f*.

euphemism euphémisme *m*.

European 1. européen; **2.** Européen(ne *f*) *m*.

evacuat|e évacuer; **~ion** évacuation *f*.

evade éviter; échapper à; éluder.

evaluat|e évaluer; **~ion** évaluation *f*.

evanescent évanescent.

evangelic(al) évangélique.

evaporat|e *v/t.* faire évaporer; *v/i.* s'évaporer; **~ion** évaporation *f*.

evas|ion évasion *f*, dérobade *f*, évitement *m*; **~ive** évasif.

eve veille *f*; *on the ~ of* à la veille de.

even 1. *adj.* uni, plat, uniforme; régulier; égal; pair (*number*); *get ~ with s.o.* prendre sa revanche sur q.; **~ with the ground** au ras du sol; **2.** *adv.* même; *before comp.*: encore; *with negative particle*: seulement, même; *not ~* pas même; **~ though, ~ if** quand même; **3.** (s')égaliser; **~ up** compenser; **~-handed** impartial.

evening soir *m*; soirée *f*; **~ dress** tenue *f* or toilette *f* de soirée; **~ star** étoile *f* du berger.

evenness régularité *f*; égalité *f*.

evensong office *m* du soir.

event événement *m*; cas *m*; *sp.* épreuve *f*; **athletic ~s** *pl.* concours *m* athlétique; *after the ~* après coup; *at all ~s* en tout cas; *quoi qu'il arrive*; *in any ~* en tout cas; *in the ~* en fait; *in the ~ of* en cas de; dans le cas où (*cond*.); **~ful** mémorable.

eventual qui en résulte; final, définitif; **~ly** à la fin; en fin de compte, en définitive.

ever jamais; toujours; *~ so* très, infiniment; *... au possible*; *as soon as I can* aussitôt que je pourrai; *le plus vite possible*; *~ after, ~ since* depuis lors; depuis le jour où ...; *~ and anon* de temps en temps; *for ~ a. for ~ and ~, for ~ and a day* à tout jamais; F *~ so much* infiniment; **~glade** *Am.* région *f* marécageuse; **~green** (arbre *m*) toujours vert; **~lasting** éternel; inusable; **~more** toujours; éternellement.

every chaque; tous *m/pl.* les; *~ now and then* de temps à autre; par moments; *~ other day* tous les deux jours; un jour sur deux; *~ twenty years* tous les vingt ans; **~body, ~one** chacun; tout le monde; **~day** de tous les jours; **~thing** tout; **~where** partout.

evict évincer; expulser.

eviden|ce 1. évidence *f*; preuve *f*; témoignage *m*; *fig.* signe *m*; *in ~* en vue; en évidence; *give ~* témoigner (de, *of*; en faveur de, *for*; contre, *against*); **2.** manifester; prouver; **~t** évident; **~tly** de toute évidence; à ce qu'il paraît.

evil 1. mauvais; méchant; **2.** mal *m*; malheur *m*.

evince manifester.

evoke évoquer.

evol|ution évolution *f*; développement *m*; **~ve** *v/i.* évoluer; se développer (à partir de, *from*); *v/t.* élaborer, développer.

ewe brebis *f*.

ex 1. *prefix*: ex-; *before su.*: *a.* ancien; **~minister** ex-ministre *m*; **2.** F ex *mf*.

exact 1. exact; précis; juste; **2.** exiger (*a fee*); extorquer; réclamer; **~ing** exigeant; astreignant (*work*); **~itude**, **~ness** exactitude *f*.

exaggerat|e exagérer; **~ion** exagération *f*; **~ive** exagératif; exagéré.

exalt exalter; élever; **~ation** exaltation *f*; **~ed** élevé; exalté.

exam F *school*: examen *m*.

examin|ation examen *m*; *customs*: visite *f*; inspection *f*; **~e** examiner; *customs*: visiter; contrôler.

example exemple *m*; *for ~* par exemple.

exasperat|e exaspérer; **~ion** exaspération *f*.

excavat|e excaver; mettre à jour (*an object*); **~ion** excavation *f*; *archeol.* fouille *f*; **~or** excavateur *m*.

exceed dépasser; **~ingly** extrêmement.

excel *v/t.* surpasser; *v/i.* exceller (à *in*, *at*); **~lence** excellence *f*; **⌂lency** Excellence *f*; **~lent** excellent.

except 1. v/t. excepter; **2.** prp. excepté, à l'exception de, sauf; **~ for** à part; **~ if (when)** sauf si (quand); **~ that** excepté or sauf que, si ce n'est que; **3.** cj. à moins que (sbj.); **~ing** prp. à l'exception de; **~ion** exception f; objection f (à, **to**); **take ~ to** s'offenser de; **~ional** exceptionnel; **~ly** par exception.

excerpt 1. extraire (a passage) (de, **from**); **2.** extrait m (de, **from**).

excess excès m; excédent m; **in ~ of** au-dessus de; **carry to ~** pousser (qch.) trop loin; **~ charge, ~ fare** supplément m; **~ baggage, ~ luggage** excédent m de bagages, **~ postage** surtaxe f postale; **~ive** excessif; **~ly** à l'excès.

exchange 1. échanger (contre, **for**); **2.** échange m; ✝ change m; (a. 2) Bourse f; teleph. central m; ✝ **bill of ~** traite f; **foreign ~(s** pl.) devises f/pl. étrangères; **(foreign) ~ office** bureau m de change; **(rate of) ~** cours m du change; **~able** échangeable (contre, pour **for**).

exchequer Ministère m des Finances; **Chancellor of the** 2 Ministre m des Finances.

excise¹ taxe f, contributions f/pl. indirectes.

excise² exciser.

excit|able excitable; **~ation** excitation f; **~e** exciter; **get ~d** s'exciter; **~ement** excitation f; **~ing** passionnant.

exclaim s'exclamer; s'écrier.

exclamation exclamation f; **~ mark** point m d'exclamation.

exclude exclure.

exclus|ion exclusion f; **~ive** exclusif; sélect, très fermé (circle); **~ of** non compris; **be mutually ~** s'exclure mutuellement.

excommunicat|e excommunier; **~ion** excommunication f.

excrement excrément m.

excrete excréter; ⚕ etc. sécréter.

excruciating atroce, affreux.

exculpate disculper.

excursion excursion f; randonnée f.

excus|able excusable; **~e 1.** excuser; pardonner (qch. à q., **s.o. s.th.**); **2.** excuse f; prétexte m.

execra|ble exécrable; épouvantable; **~te** exécrer, détester.

execut|e exécuter; **~ion** exécution f; **~ioner** bourreau m; **~ive 1.** exécutif; ✝

de cadre, de directeur; **~ committee** bureau m (of a company); **~ suite** bureaux m/pl. de la direction; **2.** ✝ cadre m, directeur m; pol. exécutif m; **~or** exécuteur (-trice f) m testamentaire.

exempl|ary exemplaire; **~ify** illustrer, exemplifier.

exempt 1. exempt, dispensé (de, **from**); **2.** exempter, dispenser (de, **from**); **~ion** exemption f.

exercise 1. exercice m (a. of a faculty, a. school, ♪, etc.); ~s pl. Am. a. cérémonies f/pl.; **2.** v/t. exercer (one's body, one's mind, influence, a profession, etc.); user de; faire preuve de (patience etc.); tracasser; v/i. faire l'exercice.

exert exercer (influence etc.); employer (force); **~ o.s. physically:** se dépenser; fig. s'efforcer (de inf., **to** inf.), se donner du mal (à inf., **to** inf.); **~ion** effort m.

exhale exhaler (smell, breath, smoke, fig. one's anger); respirer.

exhaust 1. épuiser; **2.** ⊙ échappement m; (a. **~ fumes** pl.) gas m d'échappement; (a. **~ pipe**) tuyau m d'échappement; **~ed** épuisé; **~ion** épuisement m; **~ive** approfondi.

exhibit 1. exhiber; faire preuve de; **2.** object m exposé; **~ion** exposition f; fig. manifestation f; **~ionist** exhibitionniste mf.

exhilarat|e égayer; ranimer; **~ion** gaieté f, joie f, allégresse f.

exhort exhorter.

exigen|ce, ~cy exigence f; nécessité f; situation f critique; **~t** urgent.

exiguous exigu; modique (income etc.).

exile 1. exil m; person: exilé(e f) m; **2.** exiler.

exist exister; **~ence** existence f; **be in ~** exister; **call into ~** créer; **come into ~** être créé; naître; **~ent** existant; actuel.

exit 1. sortie f; **2.** thea. ... sort.

exodus bibl., a. fig. exode m.

exonerate (de, **from**) disculper; exonérer, dispenser.

exorbitant exorbitant.

exorcize exorciser.

exotic exotique.

expan|d phys. (se) dilater; fig. (s')étendre, (s')accroître, augmenter, (se) développer; *fig.* (*start to talk*) devenir expansif (*person*); **~ing** *a.* en (pleine) expansion (*market, industry, etc.*); *fig.* **~ on** (*explain*) s'étendre sur, expliquer; **~se** étendue *f*; **~sion** expansion *f* (*a. pol.,* ✝ *etc.*); dilatation *f*; développement *m*; **~sive** expansif (*a. fig.*); dilatable; étendu.

expatiate s'étendre (sur, **on**).

expatriate expatrier.

expect s'attendre à; escompter; exiger; attendre (de **of, from**); *think:* penser, croire, songer à; **~ant** qui attend; **be ~ of** attendre (*qch.*); **be ~** attendre un bébé; **~ mother** future maman *f*; **~ation** attente *f*; espérance *f*; probabilité *f*.

expectorate expectorer.

expedi|ent 1. opportun; pratique; **2.** expédient *m*; **~te** expédier; accélérer, hâter; **~tion** expédition *f*; **~tious** prompt.

expel expulser, chasser; renvoyer (q. de l'école, **s.o. from** [**the**] **school**).

expen|d dépenser (*money, energy, etc.*); épuiser (*resources etc.*), consommer; **~diture** dépense *f*; dépenses *f/pl.*; **~se** dépense *f*; frais *m/pl.*; dépens *m/pl.*; **~s** *pl.* dépenses *f/pl.*, frais *m/pl.*; **at my ~** à mes frais; à mes dépens; **at my ~ of** aux dépens de; **~sive** cher, coûteux.

experience 1. expérience *f*; **2.** connaître, éprouver; **~d** éprouvé; expérimenté.

experiment 1. expérience *f*; **2.** faire des expériences; **~al** expérimental.

expert 1. expert (en **at, in**); (de) connaisseur; **~ opinion** avis *m* d'expert; **~'s report** expertise *f*; **2.** expert *m*; **~ise** compétence *f*.

expiate expier.

expir|ation expiration *f*; **~e** expirer; **~y** expiration *f*.

explain expliquer (a, **to**); **~able** explicable; justifiable (*conduct*).

explanat|ion explication *f*; **~ory** explicatif.

explicable explicable.

explicit explicite; formel.

explode (faire) exploser.

exploit 1. exploiter; **2.** exploit *m*; **~ation** exploitation *f*.

explor|ation exploration *f*; **~atory** d'exploration; préliminaire (*talks*); **~er** explorateur (-trice *f*) *m*.

explos|ion explosion *f*; **~ive** explosif *adj.*; *su./m.*

exponent interprète *mf*, représentant(e *f*) *m*; ✝ exposant *m*.

export 1. exporter; exportation *f*; **~ation** exportation *f*.

expos|e exposer (*a. phot.*); démasquer; dévoiler; **~ition** exposition *f*; exposé *m*.

expostulate faire des remontrances (à, **with**).

exposure exposition *f*; ❄ *etc.* effets *m/pl.* du froid; *phot.* pose *f*; **~ meter** photomètre *m*; **~ time** temps *m* de pose.

expound expliquer; exposer (*a doctrine*).

express 1. exprès; formel; 🖪 rapide; *Br. post:* exprès; **~ company** compagnie *f* de messageries; **2.** (*a.* **~ train**) rapide *m*, express *m*; **by ~** par messagerie; **3. send s.th. ~** envoyer qch. exprès; **4.** exprimer (*feelings, a. juice, etc.*); énoncer (*a principle*); émettre (*an opinion*); **~ion** ♪, ✝, *gramm., paint., face:* expression *f*; **~ive** expressif; **~ly** expressément; **~way** voie *f* exprès.

expropriate exproprier.

expulsion expulsion *f*.

expunge effacer, supprimer.

expurgate expurger (*a book*); épurer (*a text*); supprimer (*a passage*).

exquisite exquis; **~ly** exquisément; *fig.* extrêmement.

extant existant, qui existe.

extempor|aneous, ~ary, ~e impromptu; **~ize** improviser.

extend *v/t.* étendre (*a. fig.*); prolonger; tendre (*one's hand*); agrandir (*a territory*); offrir (*an invitation etc.*); *v/i.* s'étendre; se prolonger, continuer.

extens|ion extension *f*; prolongation *f*; *table:* (r)allonge *f*; *teleph. office:* poste *m*, *private:* appareil *m* supplémentaire; ⚡ **~ cord** allonge *f* de câble; *University* Ⓤ cours *m* populaire organisé par une université; **~ive** étendu, vaste (*area etc.*); *fig.* considérable, important.

extent étendue *f*; importance *f*, ampleur *f*; degré *m*, mesure *f*; **to the ~ of** au point de; **to a certain ~** jusqu'à un certain point; **to some ~** dans une certaine mesure.

extenuate atténuer.

exterior 1. extérieur (à, **to**); **2.** extérieur *m*.

exterminate exterminer.

external externe; **~ly** extérieurement; **~s** pl. l'extérieur m.

extinct éteint; **~ion** extinction f.

extinguish éteindre.

extirpate extirper.

extol chanter les louanges de, exalter.

extort extorquer (à, *from*); **~ion** extorsion f.

extra 1. adj. en plus, en supplément; supplémentaire (*pay, work, etc.*); **~-time** prolongation f; **2.** adv. extra-; plus que d'ordinaire; **3.** su. supplément m; *thea.* figurant(e f) m; *journ.* édition f spéciale; **~s** pl. frais m/pl. or dépenses f/pl. supplémentaires; **~ special** deuxième édition f spéciale (*of an evening paper*).

extract 1. extrait m; concentré m (a. 🐟); **2.** extraire (a 🐟 ⚒, *a tooth, a passage*); soutirer (*money*) (de, *from*); arracher (*money, a tooth*) (à, *from*); **~ion** extraction f (a. = origin).

extracurricular hors programme.

extradit|e extrader; **~ion** extradition f.

extramarital extra-conjugal.

extraneous étranger (à, *to*).

extraordinary extraordinaire.

extravagan|ce extravagance f; prodigalité f; **~t** extravagant; prodigue (*person*); exorbitant (*price*); dispendieux (*tastes etc.*).

extrem|e 1. extrême; *eccl.* **~ unction** extrême-onction f; **2.** extrême m; **in the ~** au plus haut degré; **go to ~s** pousser les choses à l'extrême; **~ity** extrémité f; **extremities** pl. extrémités f/pl. (*of the body*).

extricate dégager, libérer.

extrovert extroverti, extraverti (a. su.).

exuberan|ce exubérance f; **~t** exubérant; surabondant.

exude exsuder; *fig.* répandre, respirer.

exult exulter, se réjouir (de qch. *at, in s.th.*).

eye 1. œil m; *needle:* trou m; **keep an ~ on** surveiller; **mind your ~!** gare à vous!; **with an ~ to** en vue de; **2.** regarder; examiner; mesurer (q.) des yeux; *pej.* lorgner; **~ball** globe m oculaire; **~brow** sourcil m; **~catcher** F attraction f; **~d** aux yeux ...; **~drops** pl. gouttes f/pl. pour les yeux; **~lash** cil m; **~lid** paupière f; **~-opener** *fig.* révélation f; **~shadow** ombre f à paupières; **~shot** portée f de (la) vue; **~sight** vue f; portée f de la vue; **~sore** *fig.* chose f qui offense les regards; horreur f; **~wash** F *fig.* de la frime; **~-witness** témoin m oculaire.

fable fable f, conte m.

fabric *tex.* tissu m; *fig.* édifice m, bâtiment m; **~ate** fabriquer, inventer; **~ation** invention f, fabulation f.

fabulous légendaire.

facade △ façade f.

face 1. visage m, figure f, (a. = side, front) face f; air m, mine f; *clock:* cadran m; *cloth:* endroit m; **in (the) ~ of** devant, face à, en présence de; **~ to ~ with** vis-à-vis de; **save one's ~** sauver la face; **on the ~ of it** à première vue; **set one's ~ against** s'opposer à, s'élever contre; **✝ ~ value** valeur f nominale; *fig.* **take s.th. at ~ value** prendre qch. au pied de la lettre; **2.** v/t. affronter, braver; donner sur (*the yard, etc.*); envisager (*the facts*); revêtir (*a wall*); faire face à (q.); **be ~d with** se trouver devant (*a difficulty etc.*); être menacé de; v/i. **~ about** faire demi-tour; **~ up to** affronter (*a danger etc.*); **~cloth** gant m de toilette; **~-lift(ing)** lifting m; *fig.* retapage m, retouche f.

facetious facétieux, plaisant.

faci|le facile; complaisant (*person*); **~tate** faciliter; **~ity** facilité f; **facilities** pl. installations f/pl.

facing ⊚ revêtement m.

fact fait m; **~s** pl. (**of the case**) faits m/pl. (de la cause), vérité f; **in ~** en fait, en vérité; **the facts of life** les choses de la vie.

faction faction f; dissension f.
factitious factice, contrefait; faux.
factor A, fig. facteur m.
factory usine f, fabrique f.
faculty pouvoir m; faculté f (a. univ.); fig. talent m; Am. corps m enseignant.
fad F lubie f, marotte f, dada m.
fad|e v/i. se faner (flower, colour, fig. person); se décolorer, passer (material); (a. ~ away) s'affaiblir, diminuer, disparaître, (a. ~ out) s'évanouir, s'éteindre; v/t. faner, flétrir; décolorer; ~ing radio: fading m.
fag 1. corvée f, travail m pénible; Br. sl. sèche f (cigarette); Am. sl. pédé m (= homosexual); ~ end bout m, restes m/pl.; Br. sl. mégot m; **2.** travailler dur; ~ged (out) F éreinté, crevé.
fail v/i. faire défaut; manquer (heart, strength, voice, etc.); diminuer, échouer; ✝ faire faillite; baisser (day, light, health); v/t. échouer à (qch.); faire défaut à (q.); manquer à (q., qch.); recaler, refuser (a candidate etc.); ~ to (inf.) négliger de (inf.); **2.** without ~ sans faute; à coup sûr; ~ing défaut m; faiblesse f; ~ure échec m; ☢ panne f; person: raté(e f) m; défaut m, manque(ment) m.
faint 1. faible; léger; **2.** s'évanouir; **3.** évanouissement m; ~hearted timide; lâche.
fair¹ 1. adj. beau (person, weather, etc.); juste; blond; assez bon; ~ copy copie f au net; corrigé m; ~ play jeu m loyal; traitement m juste; the ~ sex le beau sexe; **2.** adv. loyalement; play etc. franc jeu.
fair² foire f.
fair|ly adv. de fair¹; honnêtement; avec impartialité, équitablement; assez; ~ness justice f, impartialité f; équité f; sp. franc jeu m; ~sized assez grand; ~way ⚓ passage m, chenal m.
fairy fée f; ~tale conte m de fées.
faith foi f (en, in God); confiance f (en, in); croyance f; culte m, religion f; ~ful fidèle; the ~pl. les fidèles m/pl.; Yours ~ly Agréez l'expression de mes sentiments distingués; ~fulness fidélité f; ~less infidèle; perfide.
fake sl. **1.** chose f truquée; article m faux; (Am. a. ~r) person: simulateur (-trice f) m; **2.** truquer.

falcon faucon m.
fall 1. chute f (a. of water); barometer, water, curtain, temperature: baisse f; night, rain: tombée f; Am. automne m; **2.** tomber; baisser (prices etc.); with adj.: devenir; s'effondrer (building); descendre; se projeter (shadow); ~ asleep s'endormir; ~ back tomber en arrière; reculer; ~ behind rester en arrière; ~ for se laisser prendre à (tricks etc.); être dupe de; F tomber amoureux de; ~ ill (or ~ sick) tomber malade; ~ in love with tomber amoureux de; ~ out se brouiller (avec, with); ~ short tomber en deçà (de, of); ~ short of ne pas atteindre; ~ through tomber à l'eau (project etc.).
fallac|ious trompeur; ~y erreur f; faux raisonnement m.
fall guy dupe f; bouc m émissaire.
fallible faillible.
falling baisse f; chute f etc.; ~ star étoile f filante.
fallout retombées f/pl. (radioactives).
fallow zo. fauve; ✎ en friche.
false adj. faux; ~ teeth pl. fausses dents f/pl., dentier m; ~hood mensonge m; fausseté f; ~ness fausseté f.
falsi|fication falsification f; ~fy falsifier; ~ty fausseté f.
falter v/i. chanceler, vaciller; fig. hésiter; trembler (voice); v/t. balbutier.
fame renom m, renommée f; ~d célèbre, renommé (pour, for).
familiar 1. familier (à, to); au courant (de, with); **2.** ami(e f) m intime; ~ity familiarité f, fig. a. connaissance f (de, with); ~ize familiariser.
family 1. famille f; **2.** de famille, familial; in the ~ way F enceinte (f); ~ tree arbre m généalogique.
famine famine f; disette f.
famous célèbre; adv. F à merveille.
fan¹ 1. éventail m (a. ⚓); ventilateur m; **2.** éventer; souffler (the fire); fig. attiser.
fan² F fervent(e f) m, fan mf.
fanatic 1. (a. ~al) fanatique; **2.** fanatique mf.
fanci|ed imaginaire; ~ful fantasque; fantaisiste.
fancy 1. fantaisie f, imagination f; idée f; caprice m, goût m, lubie f; take a ~ to prendre goût à (qch.); s'éprendre de

(*q.*); **2.** de fantaisie; de luxe; de pure imagination; **~dress** travesti *m*, déguisement *m*; **~dress ball** bal *m* masqué; **3.** s'imaginer, se figurer; croire, penser; avoir envie de (*qch.*); aimer, se sentir attiré vers (*q.*); *just* **~***!* figurez-vous (ça)!; **~free** libre comme l'air; **~work** broderie *f*.

fang *dog*: croc *m*; *snake*: crochet *m*.

fantas|tic fantastique; bizarre; **~y** fantaisie *f*.

far 1. *adv.* loin; **~ away**, **~ off** loin; au loin, dans le lointain; beaucoup, bien; **~ the best** de beaucoup le meilleur; **as ~ as** jusqu'à; **by ~** de beaucoup; **~ from** loin de; **in so ~ as** dans la mesure où; **2.** *adj.* lointain, éloigné; *fig.* absent, distrait (*look*).

fare prix *m* (du ticket, du voyage, du trajet, *etc.*); *taxi*: client(e *f*) *m*; voyageur (-euse *f*) *m*; chère *f*; **2.** se débrouiller, s'en tirer; aller (*well or ill*); **~ well!** adieu!; **~well 1.** adieu *m*, -x *m*/*pl*.

far...: **~-fetched** *fig.* tiré par les cheveux, recherché, forcé; **~-gone** F (dans un état) avancé.

farm 1. ferme *f*; **2.** cultiver; (*a.* **~ out**) donner à ferme; exploiter (*the soil*), *v*/*i.* cultiver la terre; **~er** fermier *m*; **~hand** ouvrier (-ère *f*) *m* agricole; **~house** (maison *f* de) ferme *f*; **~ing** agriculture *f*; exploitation *f*; culture *f*; **~yard** cour *f* de ferme.

far...: **~-off** lointain, éloigné; **~-out** F insolite; extravagant; super; **~-sighted** presbyte; *fig.* prévoyant.

fart V **1.** pet *m*; **2.** péter.

fascinat|e fasciner, charmer; **~ion** fascination *f*; charme *m*, attrait *m*.

Fascis|m *pol.* fascisme *m*; **~t** fasciste (*a. su.*/*mf*).

fashion 1. mode *f*; vogue *f*; façon *f*, manière *f*; forme *f*; **in ~** à la mode; **out of ~** démodé; **set the ~** mener la mode; donner le ton; **after a ~** tant bien que mal; **2.** façonner, former; confectionner (*a dress*); **~able** à la mode, élégant, **~ parade**, **~ show** présentation *f* de collections.

fast¹ 1. *adj.* rapide; bon teint (*colour*); ferme; **be ~** avancer (*watch*, *clock*); **make ~** attacher; **2.** *adv.* ferme; vite; **be ~ asleep** dormir profondément.

fast² 1. jeûne *m*; **2.** jeûner.

fasten *v*/*t.* attacher (à, *to*); fixer (*a.* les yeux sur, *one's eyes* [*up*]*on*); *v*/*i.* s'attacher; se fixer; **~ upon** *fig.* saisir (*qch.*); **~er** attache *f*; *dress*: agrafe *f*; *window*: *etc.* fermeture *f*.

fastidious difficile, exigeant, délicat.

fastness fermeté *f*; *colours*: solidité *f*; vitesse *f*; légèreté *f* de conduite.

fat 1. gras; gros; **2.** graisse *f*; *meat*: gras *m*; *fig.* **live on** (*or* **off**) **the ~ of the land** vivre grassement; F **the ~ is in the fire** le feu est aux poudres; **3.** (s')engraisser.

fatal fatal; mortel; **~ly** mortellement; **~ity** fatalité *f*; *accident*: victime *f*, mort(e *f*) *m*; *accident* *m* mortel, sinistre *m*.

fate destin *m*; sort *m* (*of a person*); **~ful** fatidique.

fathead *sl.* idiot(e *f*) *m*.

father 1. père *m*; **2.** engendrer, créer; **~hood** paternité *f*; **~-in-law** beau-père (*pl.* beaux-pères) *m*; **~less** sans père; **~ly** paternel.

fathom 1. *measure*: toise *f*; ♣ brasse *f*; **2.** ♣ (*a. fig.*) sonder; **~less** sans fond.

fatigue fatigue *f*; ✗ corvée *f*.

fat|ness graisse *f*; *person*: grosseur *f*, corpulence *f*; **~ten** engraisser.

fatuous sot, imbécile.

faucet ☉ *esp. Am.* robinet *m*.

fault 1. faute *f*; défaut *m* (*a.* ♂, ☉); **find ~ with** trouver à redire à; **be at ~** être en tort *or* en défaut, **to a ~** à l'excès; **2.** prendre en défaut; **~finder** censeur (-euse *f*) *m*; **~less** sans défaut; parfait; **~y** défectueux.

favo(u)r 1. faveur *f*; service *m*; bonté *f*; **in ~ of** en faveur de; **I am** (**not**) **in ~ of it** moi, je suis pour (contre); **do s.o. a ~** rendre (un) service à q.; **2.** être en faveur de; favoriser; honorer (de, *with*); **~able** (**to**) favorable (à); propice (à); bon; **~ite 1.** favori, préféré; **2.** favori(te *f*) *m*; *sp.* favori *m*.

fawn¹ *zo.* faon *m*; (couleur *f*) fauve *m*; **2.** (*a.* **~-colo**[**u**]**red**) fauve.

fawn²: **~** (**up**)**on** aduler, flatter (*q.*) (servilement).

fax 1. télécopie *f*; *machine*: télécopieur *m*; **2.** envoyer par télécopie.

faze *Am.* F bouleverser.

fear 1. peur *f*, crainte *f*; **through** (*or* **from**) **~ of** de peur de; **for ~ of** (*ger.*) de crainte de (*inf.*); **2.** craindre; avoir peur (de); redouter; **~ful** craintif (*person*); épouvantable, affreux; **~fulness** crainte *f*; caractère *m* épouvantable; **~less** intrépide; sans peur.

feasib|lity possibilité *f* (de réalisation); **~le** possible, faisable.

feast 1. fête *f* (*a. eccl.*); festin *m*; *fig.* régal *m*; **2.** *v/t.* fêter; **~ one's eyes on** assouvir ses yeux de; *v/i.* faire bonne chère; se régaler (*de*, [*up*]**on**).

feat exploit *m*, haut fait *m*.

feather 1. plume *f*; *wing, tail*: penne *f*; **2.** *v/t.* empenner (*an arrow*); **~brained**, **~headed** étourdi, écervelé; **~weight** *box.* poids *m* plume; **~y** plumeux; léger.

feature 1. trait *m* (*a. of the face*); caractéristique *f*, particularité *f*, spécialité *f*; *journ.* article *m*; **2.** *v/t.* mettre (*q.*) en vedette; avoir (*q.*) pour vedette; *v/t.* figurer; être représenté; **~ film** grand film *m* du programme.

February février *m*.

fecund fécond.

fed: *be ~ up with* en avoir marre de.

federa|l fédéral; **~lism** fédéralisme *m*; **~lize** (se) fédérer; **~tion** fédération *f*; **~tive** fédératif.

fee droits *m/pl.*; *lawyer, doctor, etc.*: honoraires *m/pl.*; *school*: frais *m/pl.*

feeble faible.

feed 1. alimentation *f* (*a.* ⚙); nourriture *f*; *baby*: tétée *f*; **2.** *v/t.* nourrir (*q.*); alimenter (⚙, *sp., an engine, a stove, a fire, a family*); donner à manger à (*an animal*); **~ s.th. into** mettre qch. dans; **~ on** se nourrir de; **~back** feedback *m*; **~er** mangeur (-euse*f*) *m*; ⚙ *etc.* artère *f* or conducteur *m* alimentaire; **~er line** 🚆 embranchement *m*; **~ing bottle** biberon *m*.

feel 1. *v/t.* sentir; tâter; ressentir (*pain, pity, etc.*); éprouver; penser; *v/i.* être ... au toucher (*thing*); sembler; se sentir (*person*); **~ cold** avoir froid (*person*), être froid (au toucher) (*thing*); **I ~ like** (*ger.*) j'ai envie de (*inf.*); **2.** toucher (*q.*); sensation *f*; **~er** *zo.* antenne *f*; *snail*: corne *f*; *octopus etc.*: tentacule *m*; **~ing 1.** sensible; **2.** toucher *m*; émotion *f*; sentiment *m*; sensibilité *f*.

feign feindre, simuler.

feint 1. feinte *f*; **2.** feinter.

felicit|ate féliciter (de, sur **on**); **~ous**

heureux; à propos (*remark etc.*); **~y** félicité *f*; à-propos *m*.

fell abattre; assommer.

felloe jante *f*.

fellow garçon *m*, bonhomme *m*, F type *m*; camarade *m*; compagnon *m*; collègue *m*; semblable *m*; *univ.* agrégé(e *f*) *m*; *society*: membre *m*; *attr.* camarade ..., compagnon de, co(n)-; **~** *old* ~ mon vieux *m*; *the ~ of a glove* l'autre gant *m*; **~ citizen** concitoyen(ne *f*) *m*; **~ countryman** compatriote *mf*; **~ creature** semblable *m*; **~ feeling** sympathie *f*; **~ travel(l)er** *pol.* sympathisant(e *f*) *m*; **~ship** association *f*; camaraderie *f*; *univ.* bourse *f*.

felon criminel(le *f*) *m*; **~y** crime *m*.

felt feutre *m*; **~-tip pen** stylo *m* feutre.

female 1. féminin (*person*); femelle (*animal*); de(s) femme(s); **2.** femme *f*; *animal*: femelle *f*; *sl. pej.* bonne femme *f*.

femini|ne féminin; *gramm.* du féminin; *oft. pej.* de femme; **~ism** féminisme *m*; **~ist** féministe (*adj.*), *mf*).

fen marais *m*, marécage *m*.

fence 1. clôture *f*; palissade *f*; barrière *f*; *sp.* haie *f*; *sl.* receleur (-euse *f*) *m*; *sit on the ~* attendre d'où vient le vent; **2.** *v/t.* (*a. ~ in*) enclore, clôturer; enfermer; *sl.* receler; *v/i. sp.* faire de l'escrime.

fencing clôture *f*, palissade *f*; escrime *f*.

fend: ~ off détourner; éviter, éluder; **~ for o.s.** se débrouiller.

fender garde-feu *m/inv.*; *mot. Am.* aile *f*; *mot.* pare-chocs *m/inv.*

fennel ❧ fenouil *m*.

ferment 1. ferment *m*; *fig.* effervescence *f*, agitation *f*; **2.** (faire) fermenter; *fig.* (s')échauffer; **~ation** fermentation *f*; *fig.* effervescence *f*.

fern ❧ fougère *f*.

feroci|ous féroce; **~ty** férocité *f*.

ferret *zo.* furet *m*; **2.** *v/t.* **~ out** découvrir; *v/i.* chasser au furet.

Ferris wheel *fun fair*: grande roue *f*.

ferry 1. passage *m*; bac *m*; **2.** passer en bac; transporter; **~boat** bac *m*; **~man** passeur *m*.

fertil|e fertile; fécond; **~ity** fertilité *f*; **~ize** fertiliser; **~izer** engrais *m*.

ferv|ent fervent, ardent; **~o(u)r** ferveur *f*.

fester suppurer.

festiv|al fête *f*; ♪, *thea.* festival *m*; **~e** de fête; **~ity** fête *f*, réjouissance *f*.

filthy

festoon feston *m.*

fetch *v/t.* apporter; aller chercher; amener (*q.*); atteindre, sell for (*a price*); F flanquer (*a blow*); F ~ up finir par arriver (à, dans *at, in*); ~ing attrayant.

fetid fétide, puant.

fetter 1. chaîne *f;* **2.** enchaîner.

feud 1. querelle *f;* **2.** se quereller; ~al féodal; ~alism féodalité *f.*

fever fièvre *f;* ~ish fiévreux.

few 1. *adj.* peu de; quelques; **2.** *pron.:* a ~ quelques-uns; a good ~ pas mal (de).

fiancé(e) fiancé(e *f*) *m.*

fib 1. petit mensonge *m;* F bobard *m;* **2.** raconter des bobards.

fib|**re,** *Am.* ~er fibre *f;* ~rous fibreux.

fickle inconstant, volage; ~ness inconstance *f;* humeur *f* volage.

fiction fiction *f;* (*a works of* ~) romans *m/pl.,* littérature *f* romanesque; ~al fictif, d'imagination.

ficti|**tious** fictif, imaginaire, inventé; ~ve fictif, imaginaire.

fiddle violon *m;* **2.** *v/t.* jouer du violon; ~ (*about or around*) *with* tripoter; *v/t. sl.* maquiller, truquer (*accounts*); ~ *away* perdre (*one's time*), ~stick archet *m.*

fidelity fidélité *f.*

fidget F **1.** *usu.* ~s *pl.* agitation *f,* énervement *m; person:* énervé(e *f*) *m;* **2.** se trémousser, remuer; gigoter; (s')énerver; s'agiter; ~y agité, nerveux.

field champ *m; sp.* terrain *m; fig.* domaine *m;* ✝ marché *m;* ~ **glasses** *pl.* jumelles *f/pl.;* ~**work** travaux *m/pl. or* recherches *f/pl.* sur les lieux.

fiend démon *m;* F *fig.* ... ~ mordu(e *f*) *m* de ...; ~ish diabolique; infernal.

fierce féroce; violent; furieux; ~ness férocité *f;* violence *f;* fureur *f.*

fiery de feu; enflammé; ardent; fougueux.

fif|**teen** quinze; ~**teenth** quinzième (*a. su./m*); ~**th** cinquième (*a. su./m*); ~**tieth** cinquantième (*a. su./m*); ~**ty** cinquante.

fig figue *f; tree:* figuier *m.*

fight 1. combat *m;* lutte *f;* bagarre *f;* **show** ~ offrir de la résistance; **2.** *v/t.* se battre avec *or* contre; combattre; lutter contre; se défendre contre (*a. fig. emotions etc.*); ~ *off* résister à; *v/i.* se battre; combattre; lutter; se bagarrer; ~ *against* combattre (*q., qch.*); ~ *shy of*

(faire tout pour) éviter, fuir devant; ~er combattant *m,* guerroyeur *m;* ✈ ~ **plane** chasseur *m;* ~**ing** combat *m; attr.* de combat.

figurative figuratif; figuré.

figure 1. figure *f* (*a.* ♪, *dance, geometry, book*); forme *f;* silhouette *f;* ✝ chiffre *m;* **2.** *v/t.* se figurer; figurer (*qch.*); supposer, penser; ~ *out,* ~ *up* (arriver à) comprendre, trouver (*a solution*); résoudre (*a problem*); calculer; *v/i.* figurer; être plausible, cadrer; ~ *on* compter sur; ~**head** ⚓ figure *f* de proue; *fig.* prête-nom *m;* ~**skating** patinage *m* artistique.

filament filament *m* (*a.* ⚡); ⚛, *zo., phys.* filet *m.*

filch chiper (à, *from*).

file¹ 1. dossier *m;* classeur *m,* fichier *m; people etc.:* file *f; In single* ~ en file indienne; **2.** *v/t.* classer; ⚖ déposer (*a petition*); *v/i.* marcher en file, passer.

file² 1. lime *f;* **2.** limer.

filial filial.

filibuster 1. (*or* ~er) obstructionniste *m;* **2.** faire de l'obstruction.

fill 1. (se) remplir (de, *with*); (se) combler; *v/t.* plomber (*a tooth*); occuper (*an office*); satisfaire (*a desire*); *Am.* ✝, *pharm.* exécuter; ~ *in* (*or out, up*) boucher, combler (*a hole etc.*); remplir (*a form*); ~ *in for* remplacer; **2.** suffisance *f;* soûl *m,* plumée *f.*

fillet filet *m; veal:* rouelle *f;* ~**ed** ... filet(s) *m/(pl.)* de ... (*fish*).

fill-in remplaçant(e *f*) *m;* bouche-trou *m/inv.*

filling remplissage *m; cuis.* farce *f,* garniture *f; tooth:* plombage *m; mot.* ~ **station** poste *m* d'essence.

fillip *finger:* chiquenaude *f;* encouragement *m,* stimulant *m.*

filly *zo.* pouliche *f.*

film 1. *cin.* film *m;* pellicule *f* (*a. phot.*); voile *m* (*of mist, smoke*); taie *f* (*over the eyes*); ~ **cartoon** dessin *m* animé; ~ **cartridge** *phot.* (pellicule *f* en) bobine *f; take a* ~ tourner un film; **2.** *v/t. phot., cin.* filmer; *v/i.* (*a.* ~ *over*) se couvrir (d'une pellicule); se voiler.

filter 1. filtre *m;* ~ **tip** (cigarette *f* à) bout *m* filtre; **2.** filtrer.

filth saleté *f;* ~**y** sale; dégoûtant; crapuleux.

filtrate (s'in)filtrer.

fin nageoire f; sl. main f.

final 1. final (a. gramm.); dernier; définitif; sp. ~ **whistle** coup m de sifflet final; **2.** a. ~**s** pl. examen m final; sp. finale f; ~**ist** sp. finaliste mf; ~**ize** terminer; rendre définitif; ~**ly** enfin; définitif.

finance 1. finance f; **2.** v/t. financer; v/i. être dans la finance; ~**ial** financier; ~ **year** année f budgétaire; ~**ier** financier m.

finch orn. pinson m.

find 1. trouver; retrouver; découvrir; ⚖ déclarer (guilty etc.); fournir; ~ **out** découvrir; ~ **out about** apprendre; se renseigner sur; **2.** trouvaille f, découverte f; ~**ing** découverte f; a. ~**ings** trouvaille f; constatations f/pl.; ⚖ conclusion f; verdict m.

fine¹ 1. bon; beau; joli (a. iro.); fin; petit; ~ **arts** pl. beaux arts m/pl.; **2.** adv. finement; F bien, admirablement.

fine² 1. amende f; contravention f; **2.** mettre (q.) à l'amende; donner une contravention à (q.); frapper (q.) d'une amende (de).

fineness finesse f; subtilité f.

finery parure f.

finesse finesse f; ruse f.

finger 1. doigt m; **2.** manier, toucher; tripoter; ~**nail** ongle m; ~**print** empreinte f digitale; ~**tip** bout m du doigt.

finish 1. v/t. finir; terminer; ~ **off, up** achever; ⚙ usiner; v/i. finir; cesser; se terminer; **2.** fin f; ⚙ etc. finition f; sp. arrivée f.

finite fini (a. &, gramm.), limité.

fink sl. jaune m; salaud m.

Finn Finlandais(e f) m, Finnois(e f) m; ~**ish 1.** finlandais; **2.** ling. finnois m.

fir sapin m; Scotch ~ pin m rouge; ~**cone** pomme f de sapin.

fire 1. feu m; incendie m; ✕ tir m; fig. ardeur f; ~! au feu!; on ~ en flammes; **2.** v/t. mettre le feu à; (a. ~ **off**) ✕ tirer; cuire (bricks etc.); fig. enflammer; F renvoyer, vider (q.); ⚙ (a. ~ **up**) chauffer (a stove etc.); v/i. prendre feu; s'enflammer (a. fig.); ~**alarm** signal m d'incendie; ~**arms** pl. armes f/pl. à feu; ~**brigade** sapeurs-pompiers m/pl.; ~**bug** F incendiaire m; ~**department** Am. sapeurs-pompiers m/pl.; ~**engine** ⚙ pompe f à incendie; ~**escape**

échelle f or escalier m de sauvetage; ~**extinguisher** extincteur m (d'incendie); ~**insurance** assurance f contre l'incendie; ~**man** (sapeur-)pompier m; ⚙ chauffeur m; ~**place** cheminée f; foyer m; ~**proof** ignifuge; ~**screen** devant m de cheminée; ~**side** foyer m (a. fig.); coin m du feu; ~**station** poste m de pompiers; ~**wood** bois m à brûler; ~**work** pièce f d'artifice; ~**works** pl. feu m d'artifice.

firing chauffage m; ✕ feu m, tir m; ✕ ~ **squad** peloton m d'exécution.

firm 1. ferme; **2.** maison f (de commerce), firme f; raison f sociale; ~**ness** fermeté f.

first 1. adj. premier; ~ **aid** premiers secours or soins m/pl.; ~ **name** prénom m; **2.** adv. d'abord; pour la première fois; at ~, ~ **of all** pour commencer; tout d'abord; **3.** su. premier (-ère f) m; ✝ ~ **of exchange** première f de change; **from the** ~ dès le premier jour; ~**aid box** or **kit** trousse f de premiers secours; ~**born** premier-né; ~**class** de première classe; de première qualité; ~**ly** premièrement; d'abord; ~**rate** de premier ordre.

firth estuaire m, golfe m.

fiscal fiscal; financier.

fish 1. poisson m; coll. poissons m/pl.; F type m; cuis. ~ **fingers**, ~ **sticks** pl. bâtonnets m/pl. de poisson; **2.** v/i. pêcher (qch., **for s.th.**); aller à la pêche (de, **for**); v/t. pêcher; ~**bone** arête f; ~**erman** pêcheur m; ~**ery** pêche f; pêcherie f; ~**hook** hameçon m.

fishing pêche f; ~ **line** ligne f de pêche; ~ **pole**, ~ **rod** canne f à pêche; ~ **tackle** attirail m de pêche.

fishmonger marchand(e f) m de poisson.

fission fission f; ~**ionable** phys. fissile; ~**ure** fissure f, fente f.

fist poing m.

fit¹ 1. bon, propre, convenable (à, **for**); en (bonne) forme; en bonne santé; capable; F prêt (à, **for**); **2.** v/t. adapter, accommoder (à **to, for**); installer, poser, s'accorder avec; aller à (q.); (a. ~ **together**) assembler (pieces); ⚙ (a. ~ **in**) emboîter; pourvoir (de, **with**); ~ **out** équiper (de, **with**); ~ **up** monter; appareiller; v/i. s'ajuster; aller (dress etc.); convenir; **3.** coupe f; ajustement m.

fit² ⚹, *fig.* crise *f*, attaque *f*, accès *m*; *by or in* ~*s and starts* par à-coups; *have a* ~ piquer une crise.

fit|ful intermittent (*showers etc.*); troublé (*sleep etc.*); irrégulier; capricieux; ~**ness** convenance *f*; aptitude *f*; (bonne) forme *f*; santé *f*; ~**ter** monteur *m*; *cost.* essayeur (-euse *f*) *m*; ~**ting 1.** convenable, propre; **2.** montage *m*; *cost. etc.* essayage *m*; ~**tings** *pl.* garniture *f* (*in a room*); installations *f*/*pl.*; ⚡ appareillage *m*.

five 1. cinq (*a, su.*/*m*); **2.** ~*s sg.* (jeu *m* de) balle *f* au mur; ~**fold** quintuple.

fix 1. fixer (*a, phot., a. one's eyes upon s.o.*); attacher; nommer (*u day*); décider; *esp. Am.* F arranger, faire (*the bed etc.*); ~ *v.s.* s'établir; ~ *up* arranger; installer; *Am.* réparer; **2.** F embarras *m*, difficulté *f*; ~**ed** fixe; arrêté, permanent; invariable; ~ **star** étoile *f* fixe; ⚡ ~**interest** à intérêt fixe; ~**ing** fixage *m*; *tex.* bousage *m*; ~**ings** *pl.* équipement *m*; garniture *f*; ~**ture** meuble *m* fixe; appareil *m* fixe; ~**tures** *pl.* meubles *m*/*pl.* fixes; appareil *m*.

fizz 1. pétiller; **2.** pétillement *m*; F champagne *m*; ~**le** pétiller (légèrement); ~ *out* rater; ~**y** pétillant.

flabbergast F abasourdir, ahurir.

flabby, flaccid flasque, mou.

flag 1. drapeau *m*; ⚓ pavillon *m*; (*a.* ~**stone**) dalle *f*; ~ **day** *Br.* jour *m* de quête; *Am.* **Flag Day** le quatorze juin; **2.** *v/t.* pavoiser; (*usu.* ~ **down**) héler, arrêter (*a taxi, car etc.*); *v/i.* languir; fléchir; s'affaiblir; ~**pole** mât *m* (de drapeau).

flagon bonbonne *f*.

flagrant flagrant.

flag...: ~**staff** mât *m* or hampe *f* de drapeau; ~**stone** pierre *f* à paver; dalle *f*.

flail 1. *v/t.* battre; *v/i.* (*a.* ~ *about*) battre l'air; **2.** ⚡ fléau *m*.

flair flair *m*; F aptitude *f* (à, *for*).

flake 1. flocon *m*; *soap*: paillette *f*; *metal*: écaille *f*; **2.** (s')écailler.

flamboyant flamboyant; éclatant; voyant.

flame 1. flamme *f*; **2.** flamber; ~ *up* s'enflammer; *fig. a.* s'emporter (*person*).

flammable inflammable.

flan *cuis.* tarte *f*.

flange ⊚ boudin *m*.

flank 1. flanc *m*; **2.** flanquer (de, **by**, **with**).

flannel *tex.* flanelle *f*; *attr.* de flanelle; ~*s* *pl.* pantalon *m* de flanelle.

flap 1. patte *f*; pan *m*; *shoe*: oreille *f*; léger coup *m*; clapotement *m*; **2.** *v/t.* frapper légèrement; battre de (*its wings*); *v/i.* battre; claquer.

flare 1. flamboyer; brûler avec une lumière inégale; ~ *up* s'enflammer; s'emporter (*person*); **2.** flamme *f* vacillante; ⚡ feu *m*.

flash 1. éclair *m*; éclat *m*; *phot.* flash *m*; (*a. news* ~) flash *m* (d'information); *in a* ~ en un clin d'œil; ~ *of wit* boutade *f*; **3.** *v/i.* lancer des étincelles; briller; étinceler; clignoter (*light*); *v/t.* faire étinceler; projeter (*a beam of light*); darder (*a look*); câbler, télégraphier; *it* ~*ed on me* l'idée me vint tout d'un coup; ~ **back** retour *m* en arrière; ~ **bulb** *phot.* ampoule *f* (de) flash; ~**light** *Am.* lampe *f* de poche; *phot.* flash *m*; ~**y** voyant, tapageur.

flask flacon *m*; fiole *f*; bouteille *f*; *vacuum* ~ thermos *m*.

flat 1. plat, à plat (*tyre*); *fall*: à plat ventre; fade, éventé (*beer*); *fig.* monotone; *fig.* net, catégorique (*denial etc.*); ♩ B *etc.* ~ si *etc.* bémol; *fall* ~ rater; F ~ *out* à toute allure; à plat, épuisé; **2.** pays *m* plat; plaine *f*; appartement *m*; ♩ bémol *m*; *mot.* pneu *m* crevé; ~**foot** pied *m* plat; *Am. sl.* agent *m*, flic *m*; ~**footed** à pieds plats; F catégorique; ~**iron** fer *m* à repasser; ~**let** studio *m*; ~**ly** catégoriquement; ~**ness** nature *f* plate; égalité *f*; *fig.* monotonie *f*; ~**ten** (s')aplatir.

flatter flatter; ~**er** flatteur (-euse *f*) *m*; ~**y** flatterie *f*.

flavo(u)r 1. saveur *f*; goût *m*; arome *m*; *wine*: bouquet *m*; **2.** assaisonner (de, **with**); parfumer.

flaw 1. défaut *m*; imperfection *f*; *fig.* inconvénient *m*; **2.** gâter; endommager; ~**less** sans défaut; parfait.

flax ⚷ lin *m*.

flay écorcher; *fig.* rosser; *fig.* éreinter.

flea puce *f*.

fledg(e)ling oisillon *m*; *fig.* novice *mf*.

flee *v/i.* s'enfuir; *v/t.* fuir.

fleece 1. toison *f*; **2.** tondre; F *fig.* estamper (*q.*); ~**y** floconneux; moutonné (*clouds, waves*).

fleet 1. flotte *f*; *fig.* série *f*; **2.** rapide; **~-footed** au pied léger.

flesh 1. chair *f*; **2.** *fig.* **~ out** étoffer; **~ly** charnel; sensuel; **~y** charnu; gras.

flex 1. fléchir; tendre (*muscles*); **2.** *⚡* fil *m* (souple); *teleph.* cordon; **~ibility** flexibilité *f*; **~ible** flexible; souple; **~ working hours** *pl.* horaire *m* souple.

flick 1. légère tape *f*; chiquenaude *f*; **~s** *pl.* F ciné *f*; **2.** donner une légère tape *or* une chiquenaude à; **~ away, ~ off** enlever *or* chasser d'une chiquenaude; **~ over, ~ through** feuilleter.

flicker 1. trembler, vaciller; clignoter; **2.** vacillement *m*; clignement *m*, clignotement (*of lights*); *fig.* lueur (d'espoir *etc.*, **of hope** *etc.*).

flight vol *m* (*a. ✈*); *ball etc.*: trajectoire *f*; *bees*: essaim *m*; *birds*: volée *f*; fuite *f*; (**~ of steps** *or* **stairs**) escalier *m*; **put to ~** mettre (*q.*) en fuite; **take (to) ~** prendre la fuite; **~ deck** *✈* pont *m* de pilotage; *⚓* pont *m* d'envol; **✈ ~ recorder** enregistreur *m* de vol; **~y** frivole; volage; inconstant.

flimsy mince; fragile; léger; frivole.

flinch broncher; reculer (devant, **from**); tressaillir.

fling 1. coup *m*, jet *m*; *horse*: ruade *f*; **have one's ~** jeter sa gourme; **2.** *v/t.* s'élancer; *v/t.* lancer; **~ o.s.** se précipiter; **~ open** ouvrir tout grand.

flint silex *m*; pierre *f* à briquet.

flip 1. chiquenaude *f*; **2.** *v/t.* donner une chiquenaude à; *v/i. sl.* devenir fou; s'affoler.

flippan|cy irrévérence *f*; **~t** irrévérencieux.

flipper *zo.* nageoire *f*; *sl.* main *f*.

flirt 1. flirter; **2.** flirteur (-euse *f*)*m*; **~ation** flirt *m*; coquetterie *f*.

flit voltiger, voler.

flivver *Am.* F tacot *m* (= *cheap car*).

float 1. *⊙, fishing*: flotteur *m*; radeau *m*; wagon *m* en plate-forme; **2.** *v/t.* faire flotter; (re)mettre à flot; *⚓* lancer; *v/i.* flotter; *⚓* être à flot; **~ing** flottant.

flock 1. troupeau *m*; *birds*: volée *f*; *fig.* foule *f*; **2.** s'attrouper; **~ in (out** *etc.*) aller (entrer *etc.*) en foule; **~ together** s'assembler, se rassembler.

floe glaçon *m* (flottant).

flog fouetter; fustiger.

flood 1. déluge *m*; inondation *f*; *river*: débordement *m*; **the ♌** le Déluge; **~ tide** marée montante; **2.** *v/t.* inonder (de, **with**); noyer (*a. mot.*); *v/i.* déborder; **~gate** écluse *f*; vanne *f*; **~light 1.** illumination *f* par projecteurs; **2.** illuminer (aux projecteurs).

floor 1. sol *m*; plancher *m* (*a. fig.*); *house*: étage *m*; *Br.* **ground ~,** *Am.* **first ~** rez-de-chaussée *m*; *Br.* **first ~,** *Am.* **second ~** premier étage *m*; **~ lamp** lampadaire *m*; *♰* **~ manager** chef *m* de rayon; *night club, etc.*: **~ show** attractions *f/pl.*; **hold the ~** avoir la parole; **take the ~** prendre la parole; **2.** planchéier; terrasser (*q.*); *fig.* consterner, atterrer (*q.*); **~walker** *♰* chef *m* de rayon.

flop 1. bruit *m* sec; F échec *m*, F four, fiasco *m*, flop *m*; **2.** se laisser tomber, s'affaler (dans, **into**); F faire fiasco, F être un four.

florid fleuri; flamboyant; rubicond (*complexion*).

flora flore *f*; **~l** floral.

florist fleuriste *mf*.

floss (*a.* **~ silk**) bourre *f* de soie.

flounce¹ *cost. etc.* volant *m*.

flounce² s'élancer; **~ out** sortir en trombe.

flounder¹ *icht.* flet *m*.

flounder² patauger.

flour farine *f*.

flourish 1. fioriture *f*; *♪* fanfare *f*; **2.** *v/i.* fleurir; prospérer; *v/t.* brandir; **~ing** fleurissant, prospère.

flout se moquer de.

flow 1. courant *m*, cours *m*; passage *m*; écoulement *m*; *tide*: flux *m*; **~ chart** organigramme *m*; **2.** couler; circuler; flotter (*hair*); s'écouler; monter (*tide*).

flower 1. fleur *f*; **~ girl** marchande *f* de fleurs; **2.** fleurir; **~pot** pot *m* à fleurs; **~y** fleuri.

flu F *see* **influenza**.

fluctuat|e varier; **~ion** fluctuation *f*.

flue conduit *m* de cheminée.

fluen|cy facilité *f* (*in speaking etc.*); **~t** coulant, facile (*speech etc.*); **be ~ in German, speak ~ German** parler l'allemand couramment; **be a ~ speaker** avoir la parole facile; **~tly** *speak etc.* couramment, avec aisance.

fluff peluche *f*; duvet *m*; **~y** pelucheux; duveteux.

fluid fluide (*a. su./m*).

flunk *Am.* F *v/i.* (*a. ~ out*) échouer (*in an examination*); *v/t.* recaler (*q.*).

flunk(e)y laquais *m*.

flurry *snow, wind, etc.*: rafale *f*; *fig. activity etc.*: accès *m*, poussée *f*; **~ of excitement** excitation *f* soudaine.

flush[1] ◎ de niveau, affleuré; très plein; abondant; F en fonds.

flush[2] flux *m*, flot; rouge(oiement) *m*; *W. C.*: chasse *f* d'eau, *fig.* élan *m*, accès *m* (*of emotion etc.*); *fig.* fraîcheur *f*; **3.** *v/t.* inonder; laver à grande eau; *v/i.* rougir; jaillir.

fluster 1. confusion *f*; **2.** (s')agiter; **~ed** énervé.

flute 1. ♪ flûte *f*; **2.** jouer (*qch.*) sur la flûte, **~d** cannelé.

flutter 1. *wings*: battement *m*, palpitation *f*; agitation *f*; **2.** (s')agiter; palpiter; battre des ailes.

flux *fig.* flux *m* (*a.* ♣); *fig.* changement *m* continuel.

fly[1] *v/t.* voler (*bird etc.*); voyager en avion; flotter (*flag, hair, etc.*); passer rapidement (*time*), **~ at** s'élancer sur; **~ into a passion** se mettre en colère; *v/t.* transporter (par avion); piloter (*a plane*); faire voler (*a kite etc.*); arborer, battre (*a flag*); **2.** *zo.* mouche *f*; *cost.* (*a.* flies *pl.*) braguette *f*; **~ing 1.** l'aviation *f*; **2.** volant; d'aviation; rapide; **~ ~ buttress** arc-boutant *m*; **~ saucer** soucoupe *f* volante; *sp.* **~ start** départ *m* lancé; *fig.* **get off to a ~ start** faire un départ brillant; **~ visit** visite *f* éclair; (**come off** *etc.*) **with ~ colo(u)rs** (s'en tirer *etc.*) brillamment.

fly...: ~over *Br. mot.* autopont *m*; **~sheet** *tent.* double toit *m*; **~weight** *box.* poids *m* mouche; **~wheel** volant *m* (de commande).

foal 1. poulain *m*, pouliche *f*; **2.** mettre bas (a filly), pouliner.

foam 1. écume *f*; mousse *f*; **2.** écumer; mousser; **~y** écumeux; mousseux.

focus 1. foyer *m*; *fig. a.* centre *m*, siège *m*; **in** (**out of**) **~** (pas) au point; **2.** (faire) converger; *v/t.* concentrer (*rays, fig. one's attention*); *opt.* mettre au point.

fodder fourrage *m*.

foe ennemi(e *f*) *m*.

fog 1. brouillard *m*; ♣ brume *f*; *phot.*

voile *m*; **2.** *v/t.* embrumer; *phot.* voiler; *v/i.* (*a.* **~ up**) se voiler.

fog(e)y F: **old ~** vieille baderne *f*.

foggy brumeux; *fig.* confus.

foible faible *m*, marotte *f*.

foil[1] feuille *f* (de métal *etc.*); (*kitchen ~*) papier *m* d'aluminium; *mirror*: tain *m*; *fig.* repoussoir *m*.

foil[2] **1.** faire échouer; déjouer, contrecarrer, contrarier; **2.** *fencing*: fleuret *m*.

fold[1] **1.** enclos *m*; parc *m* à moutons; *fig.* sein *m*; **2.** (em)parquer.

fold[2] **1.** pli *m*; **2.** **-fold** *plus number*: ... fois, par ..., -uple; **3.** *v/t.* plier; plisser; croiser (*one's arms*); serrer (dans, **in**); **~ back** rabattre; **~ up** plier; *v/t.* se (re)plier; **~ up** fermer boutique; **~er** classeur *m*, dossier *m*; brochure *f*, dépliant *m*; chemise *f* (*for papers*); **~ bed, table** *etc.*: pliant; **~ door** porte *f* accordéon; **~ screen** paravent *m*; **~ seat** pliant *m*; *thea. etc.* strapontin *m*.

foliage feuillage *m*.

folk gens *mf/pl.*; F **~s** *pl.* famille *f*; **~lore** folklore *m*; **~song** chanson *f* populaire.

follow *v/t.* suivre (*up* (pour)suivre; tirer parti de, exploiter (*a success etc.*); donner suite à (*a suggestion etc.*); **~ up with** faire suivre de; *v/i.* (s')en suivre; **to ~** à suivre; **~er** partisan(e *f*) *m*, disciple *m/f*; **~ing 1.** suivant; **2.** partisans *m/pl.*; **~-up** poursuite *f*; rappel *m*; contrôle *m*; ♣ soins *m/pl.* post-hospitaliers.

folly folie *f*.

foment fomenter.

fond affectueux, tendre; **be ~ of** (*ger.*) aimer (*inf.*); **~le** caresser; **~ness** (pour, **for**) tendresse *f*, affection *f*; penchant *m*.

font *eccl.* fonts *m/pl.* baptismaux.

food nourriture *f*; aliment(s) *m*(*pl.*); **~stuffs** *pl.* produits *m/pl.* alimentaires.

fool 1. idiot(e *f*) *m*, imbécile *mf*; *hist.* bouffon, fou; **make a ~ of s.o.** se moquer de q.; duper q.; **make a ~ of o.s.** se rendre ridicule; **2.** *v/t.* duper (*q.*); F **~ away** gaspiller; *v/i.* faire la bête; **~ about, ~ around**, (**a)round** faire le clown; **3.** F imbécile; **~ery** bêtise *f*, **~hardy** téméraire; **~ish** idiot, bête; imprudent; **~ishness** bêtise *f*; imprudence *f*; **~proof** ◎ indétraquable; à toute épreuve.

foot 1. (*pl.* **feet**) pied *m* (*a. measure*); *animal, bird*: patte *f*; *page*: bas *m*; **on ~**

à pied; **set on ~** mettre en train; **2.** *v/t.*: **~ the bill** payer la note; **~ it** marcher; **~ball** football *m*; ballon *m* (de football); **~brake** frein *m* à pied; **~bridge** passerelle *f*; **~fall** (bruit *m* de) pas *m*; **~hills** *pl.* contreforts *m/pl.*; **~hold** prise *f* (de pied); **~ing** prise *f* (de pied); *fig.* situation *f*, position *f*; **get a ~** prendre pied; **lose one's ~** perdre pied.

foot...: ~lights *pl. thea.* rampe *f*; **~loose** (*and fancy-free*) libre comme l'air; **~man** laquais *m*; **~note** note *f* (en bas de la page); commentaire *m*, explication *f*; **~path** sentier *m*; *town:* trottoir *m*; **~print** empreinte *f* de pas; pas *m*; **~sore** aux pieds endoloris; **~step** pas *m*; trace *f*; **~wear** chaussures *f/pl.*

fop fat *m*, dandy *m*.

for 1. *prp. usu.* pour (*a. destination*); de (*fear, joy, etc.*); par (*example etc.*); pendant (*a week*); depuis, il y a (*a year*); *distance:* jusqu'(à); malgré; *destination:* à (*London*); vers; **I walked ~ a mile** j'ai fait un mille; **~ 3 days** pour *or* pendant 3 jours; **~ all that** en dépit de *or* malgré tout; **come ~ dinner** venir dîner; **I ~ one** moi entre autres; **~ us** aller chercher (*q.*); **it is good ~ us to** (*inf.*) il est bon que nous (*sbj.*); **it is ~ you to decide** c'est à vous à décider (*q.*); **2.** *cj.* car.

forage 1. fourrage *m*; **2.** fourrager; **~ cap** calot *m*.

foray incursion *f*; raid *m*.

forbear¹ ancêtre *m*.

forbear² s'abstenir (de, *from*).

forbid défendre (qch. à q., *s.o. s.th.*); interdire (qch. à q., *s.o. s.th.*); **~ding** menaçant; rebarbatif.

force 1. force *f*; ✕ **armed ~s** *pl.* forces *f/pl.* armées; **come** (*put*) **in ~** entrer (mettre) en vigueur; **2.** forcer; contraindre, obliger; imposer (qch. à q., *s.th.* [*up*]*on s.o.*); **~ one's way** se frayer un chemin; **~ open** ouvrir de force; **~d** *landing, march etc.*: forcé; **~feed** alimenter (*q.*) de force; **~ful** énergique; plein de force; vigoureux; violent.

forceps ✄ forceps *m*.

forcib|le forcé; vigoureux, énergique; **~ly** de force, par la force; énergiquement.

fore 1. *adv.*: **bring** (**come**) **to the ~** (se)

mettre en évidence; **2.** *adj.* de devant; antérieur; pré-; **~arm** avant-bras *m*; **~bode** présager; *person:* pressentir; **~boding** présage *m*, pressentiment *m*; **~cast 1.** prévision *f*; pronostic *m*; **weather ~** bulletin *m* météorologique, F météo *f*; **2.** prédire; prévoir; **~father** aïeul (*pl.* -eux) *m*; **~finger** index *m*; **~foot** pied *m* antérieur; **~go** *see* forgo; **~going** précédent; **~gone: ~ conclusion** chose *f* prévue; **~ground** premier plan *m*; **~hand** avant-main *f*; **~head** front *m*.

foreign étranger (*a. fig.*); **~ body** corps *m* étranger; **✝ ~ exchange** devises *f/pl.* étrangères; **~ minister** ministre *m* des Affaires étrangères; ♀ **Office** ministère *m* des Affaires étrangères; **~ policy** politique *f* extérieure; **~ trade** commerce *m* extérieur; **~er** étranger (-ère *f*) *m*.

fore...: ~leg patte *f or* jambe *f* de devant; **~lock** mèche *f* sur le front; **take time by the ~** saisir l'occasion aux cheveux; **~man** ⚖ chef *m* du jury; ☉ chef *m* d'équipe; contremaître *m*; **~most 1.** *adj.* premier, le plus en avant; **2.** *adv.* tout d'abord; **~noon** matinée *f*.

forensic: ~ medicine médecine *f* légale; **~ expert** médecin *m* légiste.

fore...: ~runner avant-courrier *m*, précurseur *m*; **~see** prévoir; **~shadow** présager, laisser prévoir; **~sight** prévoyance *f*; prévision *f*.

forest 1. forêt *f*; **2.** boiser.

forest|er (garde-)forestier *m*; **~ry** sylviculture *f*.

fore...: ~taste avant-goût *m*; **~tell** prédire, présager; **~thought** prévoyance *f*; préméditation *f*; sagesse *f*; **~warn** avertir, prévenir; **~woman** contremaîtresse *f*; **~word** avant-propos *m/inv.*; préface *f*.

forfeit 1. *fig.* prix *m*; *game:* gage *m*; **pay the ~ of ones life** payer de sa vie; **2.** perdre (*a right etc.*); payer de (*one's life etc.*); **~ure** perte *f*.

forge¹ foncer (de l'avant, *ahead*).

forge² **1.** forge *f*; **2.** forger; contrefaire (*a signature etc.*); inventer; **~ry** falsification *f*; contrefaçon *f*; faux *m*.

forget oublier; F **I ~** j'ai oublié; **~ful** oublieux; **~me-not** ♣ myosotis *m*, F ne-m'oubliez-pas *m*.

forgiv|able pardonnable; **~e** pardonner

(à q., *s.o.*; qc. [*for*] *s.th.*); ~**eness** pardon *m*; ~**ing** peu rancunier.

forgo se priver de, renoncer à; s'abstenir de.

fork 1. fourchette *f*; ⚓, *roads*: fourche *f*; **2.** fourcher (*tree*); bifurquer (*road*); F ~ **out** *v/t.* allonger (*money*); *v/i.* casquer; ~**lift** (**truck**) chariot *m* élévateur (à fourches).

forlorn abandonné; malheureux, triste; désespéré.

form 1. forme *f*; taille *f*; formule *f*, bulletin *m*; *school*: classe *f*; banc *m*; *sp.* **in** ~ en forme; **2.** *v/t.* former, faire; contracter (*an alliance, a habit*); *v/i.* se former.

formal formel, en due forme; officiel (*reception, wear, style etc.*); cérémonieux; ~**ty** formalité *f*; cérémonie *f*.

format format *m*.

format|ion formation *f*; ~**ve** formateur.

former précédent; ancien; antérieur; premier; ~**ly** autrefois, jadis.

formidable formidable; redoutable.

formula, *pl.* -**lae**, -**las** formule *f*.

formulate formuler.

forsake abandonner; renoncer à.

fort ✕ fort *m*; forteresse *f*.

forte (point *m*) fort *m*.

forth en avant; *and so* ~ et ainsi de suite; ~**coming** qui arrive; futur; prochain; aimable, gentil (*person*); *fig.* **be** ~ paraître; ne pas se faire attendre; ~**with** tout de suite.

fortieth quarantième (*a. su./m*).

forti|fication fortification *f*; ~**fy** fortifier; ~**tude** courage *m*; force *f* d'âme.

fortnight quinze jours *m/pl.*; quinzaine *f*; ~**ly 1.** tous les quinze jours; **2.** bimensuel.

fortress forteresse *f*.

fortuitous fortuit.

fortunate heureux; *it is ~ that* heureusement, c'est une chance que; ~**ly** par bonheur, heureusement.

fortune fortune *f*; chance *f*; ~ **hunter** coureur *m* de dot; ~**teller** diseur (-euse *f*) *m* de bonne aventure.

forty quarante (*a. su./m*); F ~ **winks** *pl.* petit somme *m*.

forward 1. *adj.* en avant (*movement etc.*); de devant, d'avant; avancé (*development etc.*); *fig.* direct, pej. effronté (*person*); **2.** *adv.* en avant; *from this time* ~ désormais; **3.** *su. foot.* avant *m*; **4.** *v/t.*

avancer; expédier; faire suivre (*mail*); ~**ing agent** expéditeur *m*; entrepreneur *m* de transports; ~**s** *see* **forward 2.**

foster 1. prendre en nourrice (*a child*); (*a.* ~ **up**) élever; *fig.* nourrir (*thoughts etc.*); *fig.* stimuler, encourager; **2.** *fig.* adoptif.

foul 1. infect (*a. odour*); sale (*a. weather*); *fig.* dégoûtant; *box.* bas; déloyal (*play*); infâme (*action*); impur (*thought*); **fall** (*or* **run**) ~ **of** entrer en collision avec; *fig.* se brouiller avec; **2.** *sp.* faute *f*; *box.* coup *m* bas; *foot.* passe *f* irrégulière; **3.** salir; souiller; *sp.* commettre une faute contre; F ~ **up** bousiller.

found[1] fonder; établir.

found[2] ⚙ fondre.

foundation fondation *f*; △, *a. fig.* fondement *m*; base *f*.

founder[1] fondateur (-trice *f*) *m*.

founder[2] *v/i.* ⚓ couler (à fond); *fig.* échouer.

foundling enfant *mf* trouvé(e).

foundry ⚙ fonderie *f*.

fount *fig.* source *f*; ~**ain** fontaine *f*; jet *m* d'eau; *fig.* source *f*; ~ **pen** stylo *m* à encre.

four quatre (*a. su./m*); ~**flusher** *Am. sl.* bluffeur (-euse *f*) *m*; ~**fold** quadruple; ~**letter word** mot *m* obscène, obscénité *f*; ~**square** carré(ment *adv.*); *fig.* inébranlable; *fig.* franc; ~**stroke** mot. à quatre temps; ~**teen** quatorze (*a. su./m*); ~**teenth** quatorzième (*a. su./m*); ~**th** quatrième (*a. su./m*); & quart *m*; ~**thly** en quatrième lieu.

fowl volaille *f*; ~**ing** chasse *f* aux oiseaux.

fox 1. renard *m*; **2.** F mystifier; tromper; ~**glove** ♣ digitale *f*; ~**y** rusé; malin.

fraction fraction *f*.

fracture 1. fracture *f* (*oft.* 🦴); **2.** fracturer.

fragile fragile.

fragment fragment *m*; morceau *m*.

fragran|ce parfum *m*; bonne odeur *f*; ~**t** parfumé, odorant.

frail peu solide; fragile; frêle (*person*); délicat; ~**ty** fragilité *f*; *fig.* faiblesse *f*; défaut *m*.

frame 1. cadre *m*; construction *f*, ⚙ charpente *f*; ✈ fuselage *m*; ♣ carcasse *f* (*ship*); *window*: chambranle *m*; ~ **aerial** antenne *f* en cadre; ~ **of mind** état *m* d'esprit; **2.** former, construire; encadrer; *fig.* imaginer, fabriquer; **~-up** F coup *m* monté; **~work** ☉ squelette *m*; charpente *f*; *fig.* cadre *m*.

franchise droit *m* de vote; autorisation *f*, permis *m*.

frank 1. franc; sincère; ouvert; 2. affranchir (*mail*).

frankfurter saucisse *f* de Francfort.

frankness franchise *f*, sincérité *f*.

frantic frénétique; fou (de, **with**).

fratern|al fraternel; **~ity** fraternité *f*; confrérie *f*; *Am. univ.* association *f* estudiantine.

fraud *crime*: imposture *f*, fraude *f*; *person*: imposteur *m*, fraudeur *m*; **~ulent** frauduleux.

fray 1. (s')érailler; (s')effiler; (s')user; *fig.* s'énerver; 2. bagarre *f*.

frazzle *worn to a* ~ à plat, éreinté.

freak 1. phénomène *m*, anomalie *f*; F excentrique *mf*; F mordu(e *f*) *m*, fana *mf*; 2. F ~ *out* se défoncer; **~ish** excentrique; bizarre.

freckle tache *f* de rousseur, **~d** taché de son.

free 1. libre; en liberté; franc; gratuit; débarrassé; dégagé; généreux; *he is* ~ *to* (*inf.*) il lui est permis de (*inf.*); ~ *and easy* sans gêne; *make* ~ prendre des libertés (avec q., **with s.o.**); *make* ~ *to* (*inf.*) se permettre de (*inf.*); *set* ~ libérer; 2. (*from, of*) libérer (de); dégager (de); débarrasser (de); exempter (de); **~booter** F maraudeur *m*; **~dom** liberté *f*; ~ *of speech* franc-parler *m*.

free...: **~-for-all** mêlée *f* générale; **~lance** indépendant(e *f*) *m*; **~ly** librement; *speak*: franchement; *spend*: libéralement; **~mason** franc-maçon (*pl.* francs-maçons) *m*; **~masonry** franc-maçonnerie *f*; **~way** autoroute *f*.

freez|e 1. *v/i.* geler; se figer; ~ *to death* mourir de froid; *v/t.* (con)geler; glacer; bloquer (*prices, accounts*); 2. gel *m*; ✝ *etc.* blocage *m*; **~e-dry** lyophiliser; **~er** congélateur *m*; **~ing** glacial; 2. (~ *point* point *m* de) congélation *f*; (...)*below* ~ (...) au-dessous de zéro.

freight 1. fret *m* (*a. price*); cargaison *f*; ~ *car* wagon *m* de marchandises; 2. affréter; **~er** ⚓ cargo *m*; ✈ avion *m* de fret.

French 1. français; *cuis.: take* ~ *leave* filer à l'anglaise; *cuis.* ~ *dressing* vinaigrette *f*; *cuis.* ~ *fried potatoes*, ~ *fries pl.*

(pommes *f/pl.* [de terre]) frites *f/pl.*; ~ *window* porte-fenêtre (*pl.* portes-fenêtres) *f*; 2. *ling.* français *m*, langue *f* française; *the* ~ *pl.* les Français *m/pl.*; **~man** Français *m*.

frenz|ied forcené; **~y** frénésie *f*.

frequen|cy fréquence *f* (*a. ⚡*); **~t** 1. fréquent; 2. fréquenter; hanter.

fresh frais; récent; nouveau; effronté; ~ *water* eau *f* douce; **~en** *vt/i.* rafraîchir; **~ness** fraîcheur *f*; nouveauté *f*; **~water** d'eau douce.

fret 1. se tracasser; 2. inquiétude *f*; **~ful** énervé.

fret|saw scie *f* à découper; **~work** ouvrage *m* à claire-voie.

friar moine *m*, frère *m*.

friction friction *f*; frottement *m*; ⚡ ~ *tape* ruban *m* isolant.

fridge F frigo *m*.

Friday vendredi *m*.

friend ami(e *f*) *m*; connaissance *f*; *make* ~*s with* se lier d'amitié avec; **~liness** attitude *f* amicale; **~ly** amical; bienveillant; gentil; *be* ~ *with* être ami(e) avec; **~ship** amitié *f*.

frigate ⚓ frégate *f*.

fright peur *f*, épouvante *f*; F épouvantail *m*; **~en** effrayer, faire peur à; *be* **~ened at** (*or* **of**) avoir peur de; **~ful** affreux.

frigid frigide; *fig. a.* froid.

frill *cost.* volant *m*, ruche *f*; jabot *m*; F ~*s pl.* chichis *m/pl.*

fringe 1. frange *f*; bord(ure *f*) *m*; *on the* ~ *of* en bord(ure) de; *fig.* en marge de (*society etc.*); ~ *benefits* avantages *m/pl.* sociaux *or* supplémentaires *m/pl.*; ~ *group* groupe *m* marginal; 2. border.

frippery fanfreluche *f*.

frisk gambader, folâtrer; *for drugs, weapons etc.*: fouiller; **~y** vif; animé.

fritter 1. beignet *m*; 2. ~ *away* gaspiller.

frivol|ity frivolité *f*; **~ous** frivole; futile.

frizzle (*a.* ~ *up*) *cuis.* (laisser) brûler.

frizzy crépu (*hair*).

fro: *to and* ~ de long en large; *go to and* ~ aller et venir.

frock *woman*: robe *f*; *monk*: froc *m*.

frog grenouille *f*; **~man** homme-grenouille (*pl.* hommes-grenouilles) *m*.

frolic 1. gambades *f/pl.*; ébats *m/pl.*; 2. folâtrer, gambader.

from *prp.* de; depuis; à partir de; par

suite de; de la part de; par; **defend ~**
protéger contre; **drink ~** boire dans.

front 1. devant *m*; avant *m*; premier rang
m; façade *f* (*a. fig.*); X *pol.*, *meteor.*,
etc.: front; F prête-nom *m*; (*a. sea ~*)
bord *m or* front *m* de mer; **in ~** en avant,
devant; **in ~ of** devant; **2.** antérieur, de
devant; X, *fig.* **~ line** front *m*, première
ligne *f*; *journ.* **~ page** première page *f*;
mot. **~ wheel drive** traction *f* avant; **3.**
(*a. ~ on, towards*) faire face à; donner
sur; **~age** façade *f*; devanture *f*; **~al**
frontal; de front; **~ier** frontière *f*.

frost 1. (*a. hoar ~, white ~*) gelée *f* blanche, givre *m*; F déception *f*; **2.** geler;
givrer; **~ed glass** verre *m* dépoli; **~bite**
gelure *f*; **~y** gelé; glacial (*a. fig.*); couvert de givre.

froth 1. écume *f*; mousse *f*, **2.** écumer,
mousser; **~y** écumeux; *fig.* léger, amusant.

frown 1. froncement *m* de sourcils; air *m*
désapprobateur, **2.** froncer les sourcils;
se renfrogner; *fig.* **~ at, ~ (up)on** désapprouver.

frow|sty, ~zy qui sent le renfermé; mal
tenu, sale.

frozen gelé; frigorifié.

frugal frugal; **~ity** frugalité *f*.

fruit 1. fruit *m* (*a. fig. result*); *coll.* fruits
m/pl.; **2.** porter des fruits; **~erer** frui-
tier (-ère *f*) *m*; **~ful** fécond, fertile; *fig.*
fructueux; **~ition: bring (come) to ~**
(se) réaliser; **~less** stérile; *fig.* vain.

frustrat|e frustrer; faire échouer (*a plan
etc.*); **~ion** frustration *f*; anéantisse-
ment *m*.

fry 1. *cuis.* friture *f*; **2.** (faire) frire; **~ing
pan** poêle *f*.

fuchsia ♀ fuchsia *m*.

fudge *cuis.* fondant *m*.

fuel 1. *heating:* combustible *m*; ⊕ carburant *m*; **2.** *mot.* s'approvisionner en
combustible *or* carburant.

fugitive fugitif.

fulfil remplir; accomplir; réaliser, satisfaire; **~ment** accomplissement *m*; réalisation *f*.

full 1. *adj.* plein; rempli; entier; complet;
comble; à part entière (*member etc.*); **at
~ length** tout au long; **~ dress** grande
tenue *f*; **~ employment** plein emploi *m*;
of ~age majeur; **~ stop** *gramm.* point
m; **2.** *adv.* tout à fait; en plein;

précisément; parfaitement; bien; **3.** *su.*
plein *m*; **in ~** intégralement; en toutes
lettres; **to the ~** complètement, tout à
fait.

full...: ~bodied corsé (*wine*); **~dress**
de cérémonie; solennel; **~fledged**
qualifié, achevé; *zo.* qui a toutes ses
plumes (*bird*); **~grown** grand, adulte;
~length: ~ film film *m* principal.

ful(l)ness plénitude *f*.

full-time à plein temps.

fully entièrement; **~ 3 hours** bien 3 heures; *for compounds see* **full-**.

fulminate fulminer.

fumble fouiller, tâtonner.

fume fumée *f*, vapeur *f*; **2.** (en)rager,
être furieux.

fumigate fumiger; désinfecter.

fun amusement *m*; plaisanterie *f*; rigolade *f*; **for ~** pour s'amuser; **have ~**
s'amuser; **in ~** par plaisanterie; **it's no ~**
ce n'est pas drôle; **make ~ of** se moquer
de.

function 1. fonction *f* (*a. physiol.*, *a. Å*);
cérémonie *f*; **2.** fonctionner; **~al** fonc-
tionnel; **~ary** fonctionnaire *m*.

fund 1. fonds *m* (*a. fig.*); **~s** *pl.* fonds
m(pl.); ressources *f/pl.* pécuniaires;
bank: provision *f*; **2.** consolider (*a
debt*); financer.

fundament fondement *m*; **~al 1.** fondamental; essentiel; **2. ~s** *pl.* premiers
principes *m/pl.*

funer|al funérailles *f/pl.*; obsèques
f/pl.; **~ director** entrepreneur *m* de
pompes funèbres; **2.** funèbre; des
morts; **~eal** funèbre.

fun fair foire *f*, fête *f* foraine.

funicular 1. funiculaire; **~ railway = 1.**
funiculaire *m*.

funnel entonnoir *m*; 🚂 cheminée *f*.

funny drôle, comique, F rigolo, marrant;
curieux, bizarre; **~ or funnily enough**
chose curieuse, curieusement.

fur 1. fourrure *f*; *animal:* pelage *m*; *boiler:* dépôt *m* de tartre; **~s** *pl.* peaux *f/pl.*;
~ coat manteau *m* de fourrure; **2.** *v/t.*
fourrer, garnir de fourrure; 🪥 **~red
tongue** langue *f* chargée.

furbish fourbir.

furious furieux.

furl rouler (*an umbrella, a flag, etc.*); ⚓
ferler (*a sail*).

furlough 1. permission *f*, congé *m*; **2.** X

envoyer (*q.*) en permission; accorder un congé à.

furnace four(neau) *m.*

furnish meubler (*a house, a room*); fournir; ~ **with** munir de; **~ed rooms** meublé *m.*; **~er** fournisseur *m.*; **~ing** fourniture *f.*; **~ings** *pl.* ameublement *m.*

furniture meubles *m/pl.*; ameublement *m.*; mobilier *m.*; **a piece of ~** un meuble *m.*

furrier pelletier *m.*

furrow 1. sillon *m.*; **2.** sillonner.

further 1. *adv.* plus loin; (*more*) davantage, plus; (*moreover*) de plus; **2.** *adj.* autre; supplémentaire, additionnel; **3.** *v/t.* faire avancer; **~ance** avancement *m.*; **~more** en outre, de plus; **~most** le plus lointain, le plus éloigné.

furthest le plus loin.

furtive furtif.

fury fureur *f.*; acharnement *m.*

fuse 1. (se) fondre; (se) fusionner, (s') amalgamer; *⚡* faire sauter; **2.** *⚡* plomb *m.*, fusible *m.*; *bomb:* amorce *f.*

fuselage *✈* fuselage *m.*

fusion fusion *f.*; fonte *f.*

fuss 1. façons *f/pl.*, chichi(s) *m/(pl.*); histoire(s) *f/(pl.*); tapage *m.*, agitation *f.*; **2.** faire des façons *etc.*; **~y** chichiteux.

fusty qui sent le renfermé; démodé.

futile futile; vain.

future 1. futur; à venir; **2.** avenir *m.*; *in the* ~ à l'avenir; *gramm.* futur *m.*

fuzz duvet *m.*; **a ~ of hair** des cheveux bouffants; *sl.* **the** ~ les flics *m/pl.*, la flicaille (= *police*); **~y** duveteux; crépu (*hair*); flou (*outline*).

G

gab F **1.** jacasser; **2.** *the gift of the* ~ la langue bien pendue.

gabble 1. bredouillement *m.*; caquet *m.*; **2.** bredouiller; caqueter.

gable pignon *m.*

gad: ~ *about* vadrouiller (dans *or* en, à).

gadfly *zo.* taon *m.*; œstre *m.*

gadget dispositif *m.*; machin *m.*, truc *m.*; gadget *m.*

gag 1. bâillon *m.*; gag *m.*; plaisanterie *f.*; **2.** *v/t.* bâillonner (*a. fig.*); *v/i.* blaguer, plaisanter.

gage garantie *f.*; défi *m.*; *Am. see* **gauge.**

gaiety gaieté *f.*; réjouissances *f/pl.*

gain 1. gain *m.*, profit *m.*; **2.** *v/t.* gagner; prendre (*speed, weight, etc.*); *v/i.* avancer (*watch*); **~ful** profitable; ~ *employment* travail *m.* rémunéré.

gainsay contredire.

gait allure *f.*, démarche *f.*

gal *Am. sl.* jeune fille *f.*

gala 1. gala *m.*; **2.** de gala.

galaxy galaxie *f.*

gale coup *m.* de vent; tempête *f.*

gall¹ bile *f.*; *a. fig.* fiel *m.*; F effronterie *f.*; ~ *bladder* vésicule *f.* biliaire.

gall² *⚘* galle *f.*

gall³ 1. écorchure *f.*; *fig.* blessure *f.*; **2.** écorcher; *fig.* froisser, ulcérer.

gallant 1. vaillant, brave; *to women:* galant; **2.** galant *m.*; **~ry** vaillance *f.*; galanterie *f.* (auprès des femmes).

gallery galerie *f.*

galley *⚓* galère *f.*; (*kitchen*) cambuse *f.*; (*a. ~ proof*) placard *m.*

gallon *measure:* gallon *m.*

gallop 1. galop *m.*; **2.** (faire) aller au galop.

gallows *usu. sg.* potence *f.*

gallstone calcul *m* bilaire.

galore à gogo.

gamble 1. *v/i.* jouer (de l'argent); *v/t.* ~ *away* perdre (*qch.*) au jeu; **2.** jeu *m* de hasard; *fig.* affaire *f* de chance; **~r** joueur (-euse *f*) *m.*

gambol 1. cabriole *f.*; **2.** cabrioler.

game 1. jeu *m*; *cards:* partie *f*; *cuis. etc.* gibier *m*; *play the* ~ *fig.* agir loyalement; **2.** brave; *be* ~ *for* être prêt à; *be* ~ *to* (*inf.*) avoir le courage de (*inf.*); **~keeper** garde *m* de chasse.

gammy F estropié; boiteux.

gander jars m; *Am. sl.* coup m d'œil.

gang 1. groupe m; bande f; équipe f; *pej.* clique f; **2.** ~ **up** se liguer (contre **against, on**); ~**plank** ⚓ planche f à débarquer.

gangster bandit m, gangster m.

gangway ⚓ passerelle f; *bus:* couloir m (central); *cinema, theater:* allée f.

gap lacune f; trou m; intervalle m.

gape rester bouche bée (devant, **at**); ~**ing** bouche bé (*person*); *fig.* béant (*opening*).

garage 1 garage m; **2.** *mot.* mettre au garage.

garb costume m, vêtement m.

garbage ordures f/pl.; détritus m; ~**can** poubelle f; ~**collector** boueux m, éboueur m.

garden 1. jardin m; **2.** jardiner; ~**er** jardinier m; ~**ing** jardinage m, horticulture f.

gargle 1. se gargariser; **2.** gargarisme m.

gargoyle gargouille f.

garish criard; cru (*light*).

garland guirlande f; couronne f.

garlic ♣ ail (*pl.* aulx, ails) m.

garment vêtement m.

garnish garnir (de, **with**).

garret mansarde f.

garrison ⚔ **1.** garnison f, **2.** mettre en garnison.

garrulous loquace; verbeux.

garter *Br.* jarretière f, *Am.* jarretelles f/pl.

gas 1. gaz m; *F* bavardage m; *Am. F mot.* essence f; ~ **cooker**, ~ **range**, ~ **stove** cuisinière f à gaz; ~ **meter** compteur m à gaz; *mot.* ~ **pedal** accélérateur m; *mot.* ~ **station** poste m d'essence, station-service f; *mot.* **step on the** ~ mettre les gaz; **2.** asphyxier; ⚔ gazer; *F* jaser; ~**eous** gazeux.

gash 1. entaille f (*in the flesh*), taillade f; **2.** entailler, taillader.

gasket ⊙ joint m en étoupe etc.

gas...; ~**light** lumière f du gaz; ~**mask** masque m à gaz; ~**oline** *Am. mot.* essence f; ~**ometer** réservoir m à gaz.

gasp 1. souffle m; halètement m; **2.** haleter; avoir le souffle coupé.

gasworks *usu sg.* usine f à gaz.

gate porte f (*a. fig.*); barrière f; grille f; *sp. public* m; *lock:* vanne f; ~**crash** s'introduire sans invitation (dans); ~**keeper** portier (-ère f) m; ~**man** 🚂 gar-

de-barrière (*pl.* gardes-barrière[s]) m; ~**way** entrée f.

gather 1. *v/t.* recueillir; cueillir (*fruit, flowers, etc.*); (*a.* ~ **together**) rassembler, réunir, amasser; (*a.* ~ **up**) ramasser; (*a.* ~ **in**) rentrer (*the harvest*), récolter (*corn etc., a. fig.*); *cost.* froncer; *fig.* ~ **from** inférer de, déduire de; ~ **dust** s'empoussiérer; ~ **rust** s'enrouiller; ~ **speed** prendre de la vitesse; ~ **strength** reprendre des forces; ~ **weight** prendre du poids; ~ **s.o. in one's arms** serrer q. dans ses bras; *v/i.* se rassembler; se réunir; s'accumuler; se préparer (*thunderstorm*); grossir (*river etc.*); 🐛 mûrir (*abscess*); **2.** *cost.* fronce f; ~**ing** rassemblement m; accumulation f; assemblée f.

gaudy voyant, criard, tapageur.

gauge 1. calibre m, *instrument*; jauge f, indicateur m; 🚂 écartement m; **2.** calibrer; mesurer, jauger; standardiser.

gaunt décharné; désolé.

gauntlet *fig.* gant m; *fig.* **run the** ~ soutenir un feu roulant.

gauze gaze f.

gawk ⌐ **1.** godiche mf, personne f gauche; **2.** regarder bouche bée, ~**y** gauche, godiche.

gay gai; joyeux; *F* homosexuel.

gaze 1. regard m (fixe); **2.** ~ **at** regarder fixement.

gazette journal m (officiel).

gear ⊙ équipement m, appareil m; attirail m; ⊙ engrenage m; *mot.* (low première, **top** grande) vitesse f; **in** ~ *mot.* embrayé, en prise; en action; **out of** ~ hors d'action; *mot.* débrayé; ~ **lever**, ~ **shift**, ~ **stick** levier m de changement de vitesse; **2.** (s')engrener; ~ **to** adapter à.

gee eh bien!

geezer *F* bonhomme m.

gem pierre f précieuse; bijou m (*a. fig.*).

Gemini *astr. pl.* les Gémaux m/pl.

gender *gramm.* genre m.

general 1. général; ~ **election** élections f/pl. générales; ♙ **Post Office** poste f centrale; 🏥 ~ **practitioner** (*G. P.*) généraliste mf; médecin m traitant; **in** ~ en général; **2.** ⚔ général m; ~**ity** généralité f; *la* plupart m; ~**ize** généraliser; populariser; ~**ly** généralement; universellement; *F* pour la plupart; ~**-purpose** universel.

generat|e engendrer; produire; **~ion** génération f; **~ive** générateur; producteur; **~or** ⚙ générateur m; esp. mot. Am. dynamo f d'éclairage.

gener|osity générosité f; **~ous** généreux; abondant.

genial jovial; doux (climate).

genitive gramm. génitif m.

genius génie m.

gent F homme m, monsieur m.

genteel distinguée; excessivement poli; **~ poverty** décente misère.

gentile gentil m.

gentle doux; modéré, léger; co. noble; **~man** monsieur (pl. messieurs m); **~manlike**, **~manly** comme il faut; bien élevé, **~ness** douceur f.

gentry petite noblesse f.

genuine authentique; véritable; vrai, sincère.

geograph|ical géographique; **~y** géographie f.

geolog|ical géologique; **~ist** géologue m; **~y** géologie f.

geometr|ic(al) géométrique; **~y** géométrie f.

germ biol. germe m; microbe m.

German 1. allemand; **~ Ocean** mer f du Nord; **2.** ling. allemand m; Allemand(e f) m.

germinate (faire) germer.

gesticulat|e v/i. gesticuler; v/t. exprimer par des gestes; **~ion** gesticulation f.

gesture 1. geste m; **2.** faire signe (à, to).

get 1. v/t. obtenir; gagner; prendre; se faire (a reputation etc.); recevoir; aller chercher; attraper (a blow, an illness); faire (inf., p.p.); **have got** avoir; **~ one's hair cut** se faire couper les cheveux; **~ away** arracher; éloigner; **~ in** rentrer (a. v/i.); **~ off** enlever, ôter (one's clothes); **~ out** tirer; (faire) sortir; **~ through** parl. faire adopter; **~ s.th. over** (with) en finir avec qch.; **~ together** se réunir; se rencontrer (avec, with); **~ up** faire monter; **2.** v/i. devenir; se faire; aller; se rendre (à, to); en arriver (à inf., to inf.); se mettre; **~ ready** se préparer; **~ ahead** prendre de l'avance; **~ along** se débrouiller; **~ along with** s'entendre or s'accorder (bien) avec; **~ at** atteindre; parvenir à; **~ away** partir; s'échapper; **~ into** entrer or monter dans; mettre (one's clothes etc.); **~ off** descendre; **~ on** monter sur or dans; avancer; fig. se débrouiller; **~ out** (of, from) sortir (de); s'échapper (de); **~ through** passer; teleph. obtenir la communication; **~ to hear** (or know or learn) apprendre; **~ over** traverser; passer; se remettre de (illness, loss, etc.); **~ up** se lever; monter; s'élever; **~away** fuite f; **~together** réunion f; rencontre f; **~up** mise f, tenue f; présentation f.

ghastly horrible, affreux; blême.

gherkin cornichon m.

ghost fantôme m, spectre m, revenant m; **~like**, **~ly** spectral.

giant géant (adj., su./m).

gibber baragouiner; bafouiller (de, with); **~ish** baragouin m, charabia m.

gibbet 1. gibet m; **2.** pendre.

gibe 1.: **~ at** railler; se moquer de; **2.** raillerie f; moquerie f.

giblets pl. abatis m.

gidd|iness vertige m; **~y** pris de vertige (person); étourdi; vertigineux (height); **be ~** avoir le vertige.

gift cadeau m, don m; **~ed** (bien) doué; de talent.

gigantic géant, gigantesque.

giggle 1. rire sottement; **2.** petit rire m sot.

gild dorer.

gill icht. ouïe f; fig. usu. **~s** pl. bajoue(s) f/(pl.); mushroom: lame f.

gilt 1. dorure f; **2.** doré; **~-edged** ♦ qui n'implique aucun risque, de tout repos (shares etc.); doré sur tranche (book).

gimlet vrille f.

gimmick F truc m; **~ry** trucs m/pl.

gin¹ gin m.

gin² piège m; ⚙ cotton: égreneuse.

ginger 1. gingembre m; F énergie f; **~ group** groupe m de pression; **2.** F (oft. **~ up**) secouer, animer; **3.** roux (hair); **~bread** pain m d'épice; **~ly** avec précaution.

gipsy bohémien(ne f) m.

gird ceindre (de, with).

girder poutre f.

girdle 1. ceinture f; cost. gaine f; **2.** ceindre.

girl (jeune) fille f; **~friend** of girl: amie f, of boy: petite amie f; **~hood** jeunesse f; adolescence f; **~ish** de jeune fille.

girth sangle f (de selle); circonférence f; tour m (de taille).

gist essence *f*; point *m* essentiel.

give 1. *v/t. usu.* donner; remettre; causer; pousser (*a sigh etc.*); présenter (*compliments*); porter (*a blow*); céder; **~ birth to** donner naissance à (*a. fig.*); **~ credit to** ajouter foi à; **~ ear to** prêter l'oreille à; **~ away** trahir; F trahir; **~ back** rendre; **~ forth** émettre; dégager; **~ in** donner; remettre; **~ out** distribuer; annoncer; **~ up** renoncer à; abandonner, lâcher, laisser tomber; arrêter (de faire, *doing*); vouer, consacrer (*one's life, time, etc.*) (à, **to**); **~ o.s. up to** s'abandonner à, se livrer à (*dispair etc.*); *v/i. tex.* prêter (*fabric etc.*); (*a. ~ way*) céder; s'affaisser (*sous*, **under**); **~ in** céder; se rendre; **~ out** manquer, s'épuiser (*supplies, patience, etc.*); être à bout; **~ up** renoncer, capituler, lâcher, abandonner (la partie); **~and-take** concessions *f/pl.* mutuelles; **~away 1.** révélation *f* (involontaire); ✝ *article*: prime *f*; **2. ~ price** prix *m* dérisoire; **~ show** audition *f* où on décerne des prix à des concurrents; **given: ~ to** adonné à; **~ name** prénom *m*.

glaci|al *anat.* glacial; *geol.* glaciaire; **~er** glacier *m*.

glad content, ravi, heureux (de **of**, **at**, **to**); joyeux; heureux (*news etc.*); **~ly** volontiers, avec plaisir; **~den** réjouir.

glade clairière *f*.

gladness joie *f*.

glamo|rous séduisant, fascinant; magnifique; **~(u)r 1.** éclat *m*, fascination *f*; **2.** fasciner.

glance 1. coup *m* d'œil; regard *m*; **2.** jeter un coup d'œil (sur, **at**); lancer un coup d'œil (à, **at**); **~ off** dévier; ricocher (sur); **~ over** examiner rapidement.

gland *anat.* glande *f*.

glare 1. éclat *m* (éblouissant); éblouissement *m*; regard *m* fixe et furieux; **2.** briller d'un éclat éblouissant; lancer un regard furieux (à, **at**)

glass 1. verre *m*; (*a. looking ~*) miroir *m*; *coll.* verrerie *f*; (**a pair of ~**) *es pl.* (des) lunettes *f/pl.*; **2.** de ou en verre; **3.** vitrer; **~y** vitreux.

glaze 1. vernis *m*; *cuis.* glace *f*; **2.** (se) glacer; *v/t.* vitrer; vernir; *v/i.* devenir vitreux (*eye*); **~d** vitreux (*eye*); **~ier** vitrier *m*.

gleam 1. lueur *f*; reflet *m*; **2.** (re)luire; miroiter (*water*).

glean *v/t.* glaner; *v/i.* faire la glane.

glee joie *f*, allégresse *f*; **~ club** chorale *f*; **~ful** joyeux.

glen vallon *m*.

glib qui a du bagou (*person*); désinvolte (*excuse etc.*); **a ~ tongue** la langue bien pendu; **~ talker** beau parleur.

glid|e 1. glissement *m*; ✈ vol *m* plané; **2.** (faire) glisser; *v/i. in the air*: planer; **~er** ✈ planeur *m*; **~ing** vol *m* à voile.

glimmer 1. faible lueur *f*; *water*: miroitement *m*; *min.* mica *m*; **2.** jeter une faible lueur; miroiter.

glimpse 1. vision *f* momentanée; **catch a ~ of** entrevoir; **2.** entrevoir; **~ at** jeter un rapide coup d'œil sur.

glint 1. luire, briller; **2.** lueur *m*, éclair *m*, reflet *m*.

glisten luire; briller.

glitter 1. étinceler; scintiller; briller; **2.** scintillement *m*.

gloat jubiler; **~ over** savourer.

glob|al global; mondial; universel; **~e** globe *m*; *for fish*: bocal *m*.

gloom, ~iness obscurité *f*, ténèbres *f/pl.*; mélancolie *f*, tristesse *f*; **~y** sombre; morne.

glori|fy glorifier; **~ous** glorieux; magnifique; éclatant.

glory 1. gloire *f*; splendeur *f*; **2.** (**in**) se glorifier (de); être fier (de); F se réjouir (de).

gloss[1] 1. glose *f*; commentaire *m*; **2.** gloser; **~ over** minimiser, passer sur; cacher, dissimuler.

gloss[2] 1. brillant *m*, éclat *m*, vernis *m*, lustre *m*; **~ paint** peinture *f* brillante; **2.** lustrer.

glossary glossaire *m*, lexique *m*.

glossy lustré, brillant, glacé.

glove gant *m*; *mot.* **~ comparment** boîte *f* à gants.

glow 1. lueur *f*; chaleur *f*; **2.** rayonner; rougir; **~worm** ver *m* luisant.

glue 1. colle *f*; **2.** coller.

glum morose.

glut 1. ✝ *etc.* inonder, encombrer; (**~ o.s.** se) rassasier; **2.** surabondance *f*.

glutton gourmand(e *f*) *m*; glouton(ne *f*) *m*; **~y** gourmandise *f*.

G-man agent *m* armé du F.B.I.

gnarled noueux.

gnash grincer (des dents, *one's teeth*).

gnat moustique *m*, moucheron *m*.

gnaw ronger; **~er** rongeur *m*.

gnome gnome *m*; gobelin *m*.

go 1. aller; passer; marcher (*machine, heart*); sonner (*bell*); partir (de, *from*); s'en aller; *with adj.*: devenir; s'étendre (jusqu'a, *to*); **~ bad** se gâter; *see* **mad, sick**; *sl.* **here ~es!** allons-y!; *sl.* **~ it!** vas-y!; allez-y!; **let ~** lâcher; laisser aller; **~ shares** partager; **~ to** (or **and**) *see* aller voir; **~ about** circuler; se mettre à (*a task*); **~ ahead** avancer; persister; **~ at** s'attaquer à; **~ by** (*adv.*) passer; (*prp.*) se régler sur; **~ by the name of** être connu sous le nom de; **~ for** aller chercher; (aller) faire (*a walk, a journey, etc.*); attaquer; *Am. a.* aimer, prendre plaisir à; **~ in for an examination** passer un examen; **~ into** entrer dans; *fig.* examiner, se pencher sur (*a question*); se lancer dans; **~ off** partir (*a. gun etc.*), s'en aller; **~ on** continuer (de, à *inf.*, *ger.*); passer (à, *to*); **~ on!** avancez!; *iro.* allons donc!; **~ out** sortir; s'éteindre (*fire*); **~ over** passer (à, *to*); **~ through** passer par; traverser; subir (*a trial*); **~ with** accompagner; s'accorder avec, aller avec (*qch*); **~ without** se passer de; **2.** F aller *m*; coup *m*, essai *m*; F énergie *f*, entrain *m*; F dernier cri *m*; *on the* **~** à courir, remuant; *in one* **~** d'un seul coup; *have a* **~** essayer (de *inf.*, *at ger.*).

goad 1. aiguillon *m*; **2.** aiguillonner.

go-ahead F **1.** entreprenant, dynamique; **2.** *le* feu vert.

goal but *m* (*a. sp., a. foot.*); **~ie** F, **keeper** *foot.* gardien *m* de but, F goal *m*.

goat *zo.* chèvre *f*; F **get s.o.'s** **~** faire enrager q.

gob *sl.* crachat *m*; gueule *f*.

gobble dévorer; glouglouter (*turkey*); **~dygook** F style *m* ampoulé; jargon *m* (*of civil servants*); **~r** dindon *m*.

go-between intermédiaire *mf*.

goblin gobelin *m*, lutin *m*.

god dieu *m*; *eccl.* ♀ dieu *m*; **~child** filleul(e *f*) *m*; **~dess** déesse *f*; **~father** parrain *m*; **~forsaken** perdu (*place*); **~head** divinité *f*; **~less** impie; athée; **~like** de dieu; divin; **~ly** saint; pieux, dévot; **~mother** marraine *f*; **~speed** bon voyage *m*, adieu *m*.

go-getter personne *f* énergique.

goggle 1. (*a.* **~ one's eyes**) rouler de gros yeux; **2.** (*a pair of*) **~s** *pl.* (des) lunettes *f/pl.*; **~box** *sl.* télé *f*.

going 1. qui marche; *fig.* prospère, qui va bon train; *fig.* actuel; **be ~ to** (*inf.*) être sur le point de (*inf.*); **2.** marche *f*; départ *m*; état *m* du sol; **~s-on** *pl.* F conduite *f*.

gold or *m*; **2.** d'or; **~en** d'or (*a. fig.*); en or; **~finch** chardonneret *m*; **~fish** poisson *m* rouge; **~mine** mine *f* d'or; **~-plated** plaqué or; **~smith** orfèvre *m*.

golf *sp.* golf *m*; **~ball** balle *f* de golf; **~club** club *m* de golf; *stick:* crosse *f* de golf; **~course**, **~links** *pl.* terrain *m* de golf; **~er** golfeur (-euse *f*) *m*.

gondola gondole *f*.

gone *adj.* parti; disparu; mort; F fou, dingue (de, **on**); **be ... months ~** être enceinte de ... mois; **be far ~** (*ill*) être très mal; *on drink, drugs, etc.*: être complètement parti.

good 1. *usu.* bon; sage (*child*); **~ morning!** bonjour!; **~ afternoon!** bon jour, *later:* bonsoir!; **~ evening!** bonsoir!; **~ night!** bonne nuit!; ♀ **Friday** (le) Vendredi *m* saint; **~ at** bon or fort en; **2.** bien *m*; **~s** *pl.* articles *m/pl.*; marchandises *f/pl.*; **that's no ~** cela ne vaut rien; **it is no ~ talking** inutile de parler; **for ~** pour de bon; **~bye 1.** adieu *m*; **2.** au revoir!, adieu!; **~for-nothing** vaurien(ne *f*) *m*; **~humo(u)red** jovial; **~looking** beau, joli; **~natured** bon; au bon naturel; **~ness** bonté *f*; bonne qualité *f*; *int.* dieu *m*!; **~ will** bonne volonté *f*; bienveillance *f*; ✝ clientèle *f*.

goody bonbon *m*; *fig.* bonne chose *f*; *fig.* **the goodies and the badies** les bons et les méchants *m/pl.*; **~goody** F enfant *mf* (*etc.*) modèle.

gooey gluant; F *fig.* sentimental.

goof *sl.* **1.** idiot(e *f*) *m*; gaffe *f*; **2.** (*a.* **~ up**) saloper, bousiller; **~y** *sl.* idiot.

goon F idiot(e *f*) *m*; *Am.* voyou *m*.

goose oie *f*; **~berry** groseille *f* (à maquereau); **~flesh**, *esp. Am.* **~pimples** *pl. fig.* chair *f* de poule; **~step** pas *m* de l'oie.

gopher saccophore *m*; chien *m* de prairie.

gore 1. sang *m* coagulé; **2.** blesser avec les cornes.

gratify

gorge 1. gorge *f* (*a. geog.*); gosier *m*; *my ~ rises at it* j'en ai des nausées; **2.** ~ *o.s.* se gorger (de **on, with**).

gorgeous magnifique; superbe.

gory sanglant.

go-slow grève *f* perlée.

gospel évangile *m*.

gossip 1. causerie *f*; cancans *m/pl.*; bavard(e *f*) *m*; *journ.* ~ *column* échos *m/pl.*; **2.** bavarder.

Gothic gothique.

gouge 1. ✪ gouge *f*; **2.** (~ *out*) creuser à la gouge; *fig.* crever.

gourd ♀ courge *f*.

gout ✗ goutte *f*; podagre *f*.

govern gouverner; **~ess** gouvernante *f*; **~ment** gouvernement *m*; *Am. a.* conseil *m* municipal, *attr.* d'État, gouvernemental; **~mental** gouvernemental; **~or** gouverneur *m* (*Am. of a U.S. state*); F vieux *m*.

gown robe *f*; *univ.*, ✗✗ toge *f*.

grab (*a. ~ at, make a ~ at*) saisir, *fig.* se saisir de; ~ *bag* sac *m* à surprise.

grace 1. grâce *f*; bénédicité *m*, ✠ délai *m*; *style:* aménité *f*; **2.** honorer (de, **with**); **~ful** gracieux; **~fulness** élégance *f*, grâce *f*; **~less** gauche, inélégant.

gracious bienveillant; miséricordieux.

gradation gradation *f*.

grade 1. grade *m*; rang *m*; degré *m*; catégorie *f*; qualité *f*; calibre *m*; *esp. Am. level m; Am. school:* classe *f*; *Am.* **make the ~** arriver; surmonter les difficultés; *esp. Am.,* ~ *crossing* passage *m* à niveau; *esp. Am.* ~ *school* école *f* primaire; **2.** classer; graduer; calibrer.

gradient pente *f*, inclinaison *f*; ⚡ gradient *m*.

gradua|l graduel; progressif; **~lly** *a.* peu à peu; **~te 1.** *v/t.* graduer; *v/i. Am.* recevoir son diplôme; *univ.* passer sa licence; prendre ses grades; **2.** *univ.* gradué(e *f*) *m*; **~tion** graduation *f*; *on scale:* graduation *f*; *Am.* remise *f* d'un diplôme, *univ.* réception *f* d'un grade.

graft 1. ✗ greffe *f*; *Am.* corruption *f*; *Br. sl.* corvée *f*; **2.** ✗ greffer (*a.* ✗) (sur, **on**[**to**]).

grain grain *m*; **go against s.o.'s** (*or* the) ~ aller à l'encontre de la nature de q.

gramma|r grammaire *f*; **~tical** grammatical.

gram(me) gramme *m*.

granary grenier *m*.

grand 1. magnifique; *fig.* grand, noble; *Am.* ♀ *Old Party* parti *m* républicain; *sp.* ~ *stand* grande *f* tribune; **2.** ♪ (*a.* ~ *piano*) piano *m* à queue; *Am.* F mille dollars *m/pl.*; **~child** petit-fils (*pl.* petits-fils) *m*; petite-fille (*pl.* petites-filles) *f*; **~children** *pl.* petits-enfants *m/pl.*; **~eur** grandeur; splendeur *f*; ✗ *delusions of* ~ folie *f* des grandeurs; **~father** grand-père (*pl.* grands-pères) *m*.

grandiose grandiose; pompeux.

grand...: **~mother** grand-mère (*pl.* grand[s]-mères *f*; **~parents** *pl.* grands--parents *m/pl.*; ~ *stand* tribune *f*.

grange manoir *m*, château *m*.

granny F grand-maman (*pl.* grand[s]-mamans) *f*.

grant 1. concession *f*; (*monetary*) subvention *f*, *univ.* bourse *f*; **2.** accorder; céder; admettre; *take for* ~*ed* considérer comme allant de soi.

granul|ated granulé; grainé; grenu (*surface*); ~ *sugar* sucre *m* semoule; **~e** granule *m*.

grape (grain *m* de) raisin *m*; **~fruit** pamplemousse *m* or *f*; **~vine** vigne *f*; *fig.* rumeur *f*, *on* (*or through*) *the* ~ par le téléphone arabe.

graph graphique *m*, courbe *f*; **~ic(al)** graphique; *fig.* pittoresque, vivant (*description*), **graphic arts** *pl.* graphique *f*; **~ite** *min.* graphite *m*.

grapple en venir *or* être aux prises (avec, **with**), s'attaquer (à, **with**).

grasp 1. prise *f*; étreinte *f*; *fig.* emprise *f*; *fig.* compréhension *f*; **2.** *v/t.* saisir; empoigner, *fig.* comprendre.

grass herbe *f*; pâture *f*; gazon *m*; *at* ~ au vert (*a. fig. off duty*); ~ *roots* *pl.* pol. etc. base *f*; *fig. les faits m/pl.* fondamentaux; ~ *widow* veuve *f* (veuf *m*) temporaire; divorcée *f* (divorcé *m*); **~hopper** sauterelle *f*; **~land** prairie *f*; **~y** herbeux, herbu.

grate *fireplace, a.* ✪: grille *f*; *v/t.* râper; grincer de (*one's teeth*); *fig.* agacer (*the nerves*).

grateful reconnaissant; **~ly** avec reconnaissance.

grater râpe *f*.

grati|fication satisfaction *f*; plaisir *m*; **~fy** satisfaire; faire plaisir à.

grating 1. grinçant; **2.** grillage *m*; grincement *m*.

gratis gratis.

gratitude gratitude *f*.

gratuit|ous gratuit; **~y** gratification *f*; F pourboire *m*.

grave 1. grave; sérieux; **2.** tombe(au *m*) *f*; **~digger** fossoyeur *m*.

gravel 1. gravier *m*; ⚕ gravelle *f*; **2.** graveler; sabler.

grave...: ~stone pierre *f* tombale; **~yard** cimetière *m*.

gravitate: ~ to(wards) être attiré par; se déplacer vers; **~ion** gravitation *f*.

gravity gravité *f*; *fig.* a. sérieux *m*.

gravy jus *m*; sauce *f* au jus.

gray *esp. Am. see* **grey.**

graze¹ *v/i.* paître; *v/t.* pâturer (*a meadow*).

graze² écorcher; *fig.* raser, frôler, effleurer.

greas|e 1. graisse *f*; ☉ lubrifiant *m*; ☉ **~ gun** graisseur *m*; **2.** graisser; ☉ lubrifier; **~y** graisseux; gras.

great *usu.* grand; important; F magnifique; **~grandchild** arrière-petit-fils *m*, arrière-petite-fille *f* (*pl.* **~ grandchildren** arrière-petits-enfants *m/pl.*); **~grandfather** arrière-grand-père (*pl.* arrière-grands-pères) *m*; **~coat** pardessus *m*; **~ly** beaucoup, fortement; **~ness** grandeur *f*; importance *f*.

Grecian grec.

greed, ~iness avidité *f*; gourmandise *f*; **~y** avide (de *of*, *for*); gourmand.

Greek 1. grec; **2.** *ling.* grec *m*; Grec(que *f*) *m*.

green 1. vert (*a.* ☉); inexpérimenté, jeune; naïf; frais; **2.** vert *m*; gazon *m*, pelouse *f*; **~s** *pl.* légumes *m/pl.* verts.

green...: ~back *Am.* billet *m* d'un dollar; **~grocer** marchand(e *f*) *m* de légumes; **~grocery** commerce *m* de légumes; légumes *m/pl.* et fruits *m/pl.*; **~horn** F blanc-bec (*pl.* blancs-becs) *m*, bleu *m*; **~house** serre *f* (chaude); **~ish** verdâtre; 2**lander** Groenlandais(e *f*) *m*.

greet saluer; accueillir; **~ing** salut(ation *f*) *m*; accueil *m*; **~s card** carte *f* de vœux; *birthday* (*Christmas*) **~s** *pl.* souhaits *m/pl.* de bon anniversaire (de Noël).

grenade ⚔ grenade *f*.

grey 1. gris (*a. su./m*); *fig.* sombre; **~ area** zone *f* sombre; **~ matter** *anat.* substance *f* grise; *fig.* intelligence *f*; **2.** grisonner (*hair*); **~haired** aux cheveux gris; **~hound** lévrier *m*, levrette *f*; *Am.* (*TM*) a. autocar *m* (à longue distance); **~ish** grisâtre.

grid grille *f*; ⚡ etc. réseau *m*; **~iron** *cuis.* gril *m*; *sp.* terrain *m* de rugby.

grief douleur *f*, chagrin *m*.

griev|ance grief *m*; ⚡ *v/t.* faire de la peine, désoler, chagriner; *v/i.* se désoler; **~ for** pleurer (*q.*, *qch.*); **~ous** pénible; cruel; grave.

grill 1. griller; *v/t. sl.* cuisiner (*a suspect etc.*); **2.** gril *m*; *cuis.* grillade *f*; **~room** grill-room *m*.

grim sinistre; sévère; farouche.

grimace 1. grimace *f*; **2.** grimacer.

grim|e saleté *f*, crasse *f*; **~y** crasseux, sale.

grin 1. large sourire *m*; **2.** sourire d'une oreille à l'autre.

grind 1. *v/t.* broyer, moudre, écraser; aiguiser (*a knife, scissors, etc.*); dépolir (*glass*); tourner (*a handle*); F faire (*q.*) travailler dur; **~ one's teeth** grincer des dents; *fig.* **~ down** écraser, opprimer; *fig.* **~ out** produire (machinalement); *v/i.* grincer; F (*swot*) bûcher (*student etc.*); **2.** grincement *m*; F corvée *f* (*swot*) bûcheur(-euse*f*) *m*; **~stone** meule *f* à aiguiser.

grip 1. empoigner; saisir (*a. fig.*); *mot.* adhérer à (la route, *the road*); **2.** prise *f*; serrement *m*; poignée *f*; sac *m* (de voyage); *come* (*or* get) *to* **~s with** s'attaquer à.

gripe 1. F rouspéter; **2.** plainte *f*; ennui *m*; **~s** *pl.* colique *f*.

gripping prenant, passionnant.

grisly macabre; effrayant.

gristle cartilage *m*.

grit 1. gravillon *m*; grès *m*; F cran *m*, courage *m*; **2.** couvrir de gravillon (*a road etc.*); *fig.* **~ one's teeth** serrer les dents.

grizzle F pleurnicher.

grizzly 1. grisonnant (*hair etc.*); **~ bear** = **2.** ours *m* grizzlé.

groan 1. gémissement *m*; **2.** gémir.

grocer épicier (-ère *f*) *m*; **~y** épicerie *f*; *groceries pl.* (articles *m/pl.* d')épicerie *f*; provisions *f/pl.*

groggy chancelant; groggy.

groin *anat.* aine *f*; △ nervure *f*.

groom 1. palefrenier m; (*bridegroom*) marié m; **2.** panser (*a horse*); soigner (*o.s.*); *fig.* former, façonner (*q.*).

groove 1. rainure f; cannelure f; *disc:* sillon m; *fig.* routine f; **2.** rainer, canneler.

grope tâtonner; ~ **for** chercher (à tâtons).

gross 1. gros; gras; grossier; global; ✝ brut; **2.** grosse f (*12 dozen*); **in** (**the**) ~ à tout prendre.

grotto grotte f.

grouch F **1.** rouspéter, ronchonner; **2.** ronchonnement m; *person:* grogneur (-euse f) m; ~y grognon.

ground[1]: ~ **glass** verre m dépoli.

ground[2] **1.** sol m; terre f; terrain m; raison f, motif m; fond m; **on the** ~(**s**) **of** en raison de; **fall to the** ~ tomber par or à terre; **stand one's** ~ tenir bon; **2.** *v/t.* fonder; enseigner à fond; ✈ retenir au sol, empêcher de décoller; F empêcher de sortir *or* partir; ♣ *etc.* échouer; ⚡ mettre à la terre; *v/i.* ♣ *etc.* s'échouer; ~ **crew** ✈ *see* **ground staff;** ~**floor** rez-de-chaussée m/*inv.*; ~**hog** *esp. Am.* marmotte f d'Amérique; ~**less** sans fondement; ~**staff** ✈ personnel m rampant; ~**work** fond(ement) m.

group 1. groupe m; **2.** (se) grouper.

grove bosquet m, bocage m.

grovel *usu. fig.* ramper.

grow *v/i.* pousser; croître; grandir, augmenter; ~ **up** grandir; *v/t.* cultiver; laisser pousser; ~**er** cultivateur (-trice f) m; planteur m.

growl 1. grondement m, grognement m; **2.** gronder, grogner; ~**er** grognon(ne f) m.

grown-up adulte (*adj., mf*).

growth croissance f; accroissement m; augmentation f; poussée f; 🎗 tumeur f.

grub 1. larve f; ver m; F (*food*) bouffe f, mangeaille f; **2.** *v/i.* fouiller (pour trouver qch., **for s.th.**); *sl.* bouffer (*eat*); ~**by** malpropre.

grudge 1. rancune f, *bear u.o. a* ~ garder rancune à q.; en vouloir à q. (de, **for**); **2.** accorder à contrecœur; voir d'un mauvais œil; ~ **doing s.th.** rechigner à faire qch; ~**ing** accordé à contrecœur; réticent; ~**ingly** à contrecœur; en rechignant.

gruel gruau m (d'avoine).

gruel(l)ing éreintant, épuisant.

gruesome épouvantable.

gruff bourru, revêche, rude.

grumble 1. grommeler; grogner; **2.** grommellement m; grognement m; ~**r** grognon(ne f) m.

grunt 1. grogner; **2.** grognement m.

guarant|ee 1. garanti(e f) m; **2.** garantir; ~**or** garant(e f) m; ~**y** garantie f; caution f.

guard 1. garde f (a. ✕); ⚙ protecteur m (*in machinery*); 🚂 chef m de train; ✕ ~**s** pl. Garde f; **be on one's** ~ être sur ses gardes; **2.** *v/t.* protéger; garder; surveiller; *v/i.* ~ **against** se méfier de (qch.); se garder de (*inf.*); ~**ed** prudent; ~**ian** gardien(ne f) m; 🏛 tuteur (-trice f) m; ~ **angel** ange m guardien; ~**ship** garde f; tutelle f; ~**rail** barrière f de sécurité.

gue(r)rilla guérillero m; (~ *warfare*) guérilla f.

guess 1. conjecture f; **2.** *v/t.* deviner; *esp. Am.* supposer, penser, croire; *v/i.* deviner; estimer (qch., at s.th.).

guest invité(e f) m; pensionnaire mf; ~**house** pension f de famille; ~**room** chambre f d'amis.

guffaw 1. gros rire m; **2.** rire grossièrement.

guid|able dirigeable; ~**ance** gouverne f; conseils m/pl.; ⚙ guidage m.

guide 1. guide m; ~ **dog** chien m d'aveugle; **2.** guider; conduire; diriger; ~**book** guide m; ~**lines** pl. directives f/pl.; ~**post** poteau m indicateur.

guild association f; *hist.* corporation f; ~**hall** hôtel m de ville.

guile ruse f, astuce f; ~**ful** rusé; ~**less** candide; franc.

guilt, a. ~**iness** culpabilité f; ~**less** innocent (de, **of**); ~**y** coupable.

guinea guinée f; ~ **pig** cobaye m (a. *fig.*).

guise aspect m, forme f, apparence f.

guitar ♪ guitare f.

gulch *Am.* ravin m étroit.

gulf *geog.* golfe m; *usu. fig.* gouffre m, abîme m.

gull[1] *orn.* mouette f, goéland m.

gull[2] duper, tromper.

gullet gosier m.

gulp 1. avaler (a. ~ **down**); *fig.* ~ **back** refouler; **2.** bouchée f; coup m (de gosier).

gum[1] *usu.* ~s *pl.* gencive *f.*

gum[2] **1.** gomme *f.*; colle *f.*; **2.** gommer; coller; F ~ **up** bousiller.

gun 1. arme *f* à feu; revolver *m*, pistolet; fusil *m*; canon *m*; F **big** (*or* **great**) ~ grand personnage *m*; **2.** ~ **down** abattre; F ~ **for** chercher; ~**boat** (chaloupe *f*) canonnière *f*; ~ **licence** permis *m* de port d'armes; ~**man** *Am.* bandit *m*, gangster *m*; ~**powder** poudre *f*; ~**smith** armurier *m.*

gurgle 1. glouglouter, gargouiller; **2.** glouglou *m*, gargouillement *m.*

gush 1. jaillissement *m*; jet *m*; débordement *m* (sentimental); **2.** jaillir (de, *from*); sortir à flots; ~**er** *fig.* personne *f* expansive; ~**ing** *fig.*, ~**y** exubérant, expansif.

gust rafale *f*, coup *m* de vent; bouffée *f* (*of rage*).

gut 1. boyau *m*, intestin *m*; ~s *pl.* F cran *m* (*courage*); **2.** vider (*a fish*); ~**less** F mou, qui manque de cran; ~**sy** F qui a du cran; qui a du punch.

gutter 1. *roof:* gouttière *f.*; *street:* ruisseau *m*; *road:* caniveau *m*; **2.** couler (*candle*); vaciller (*flame*).

guy *esp. Am.* F type *m*; (*a.* ~ **rope**) corde *f.*

guzzle manger *or* boire (avidement); F bouffer; siffler; ~**r** glouton(ne *f*) *m.*

gym F gymnase *f*; gym(nastique) *f*; *attr.* de gymnastique, ~ **shoes** tennis *m/pl.*, baskets/*pl.*

gymnas|ium gymnase *m*; ~**tics** gymnastique *f*; éducation *f* physique.

gyrate tourn(oy)er.

H

haberdasher mercier (-ère *f*) *m*; *esp. Am.* chemisier *m*; ~**y** mercerie *f*; *esp. Am.* chemiserie *f.*

habit habitude *f*; *monk:* habit *m*; **be in the** ~ **of** (*ger.*) avoir pour habitude de (*inf.*); **get into** (**out of**) **the** ~ **of** (*ger.*) prendre (perdre) l'habitude de (*inf.*); ~**able** habitable; ~**ation** habitation *f*; demeure *f.*

habitual habituel; invétéré (*liar etc.*); ~**ly** habituellement; d'habitude.

hack[1] **1.** ⊙ pic *m*; taillade *f*, entaille *f*; **2.** hacher, tailler.

hack[2] (*oft.* ~ **writer**) nègre *m*; (*horse*) haridelle *f*; F *Br.* (*ride*) promenade *f* à cheval; F *Am.* taxi *m.*

hackneyed rebattu.

hacksaw scie *f* à métaux.

haddock *icht.* aiglefin *m*; **smoked** ~ haddock *m.*

hag sorcière *f*; *fig. sl.* vieille taupe *f.*

haggard hagard; égaré (*look*).

haggle marchander; chicaner (sur, *over*).

hail[1] **1.** grêle *f*; **2.** *v/impers.* grêler; *v/t. fig.* faire pleuvoir.

hail[2] héler; *fig.* acclamer, saluer; ~ **from** venir de; être originaire de; **within** ~**ing distance** à portée de (la) voix.

hail...: ~**stone** grêlon *m*; ~**storm** abat *m* de grêle.

hair *head:* cheveu *m*, -x *m/pl.*; *body:* poil *m*; ~ **remover** dépilateur *m*; ~'s **breadth** = ~**breadth: by a** ~ de justesse; **within a** ~ **of** à deux doigts de; ~**cut** taille *f* (de cheveux); **have a** ~ se faire couper les cheveux; ~**do** coiffure *f*; ~**dresser** coiffeur (-euse *f*) *m*; ~**dryer** sèche-cheveux *m/inv.*; séchoir *m*; ~**less** sans cheveux, chauve; ~**piece** postiche *m*; ~**pin** épingle *f* à cheveux; ~**raising** horrifique; ~**splitting** ergotage *m*; ~**spray** laque *f* (pour les cheveux); ~**style** coiffure *f*; ~**y** chevelu; poilu.

hale vigoureux; robuste.

half 1. demi; **2.** à moitié, à demi; **it isn't** ~ **bad** ce n'est pas mauvais du tout; **3.** moitié *f*; **by halves** à demi; **go halves** se mettre de moitié (avec *q.*, **with s.o.**), partager; ~**bred** demi-sang *m/inv.*; ~**brother** demi-frère *m*; ~**caste** métis(se *f*) *m*; ~**hearted** tiède, hésitant; ~**length** (*a.* ~ **portrait**) portrait *m* en buste; ~**mast:** (**at**) ~ à mi-mât; en berne (*colours*); **~moon** demi-lune *f*; **~penny** demi-penny *m*; F sou *m*; **~-price: at ~** à moitié prix; **~time** *sp.* mitemps *f*; **~way** à mi-chemin; à moitié; *fig.* **meet s.o. ~** faire un compromis avec q; **~way house** centre *m* de réadaptation; *fig.* chose *f* qui tient le milieu (entre, *between*); **~-witted** niais.

halibut *icht.* flétan *m*.

hall salle *f*; vestibule *m*; *hotel*: hall *m*; *univ.* (*a.* **~ of residence**) maison *f* estudiantine.

hallmark 1. poinçon *m*; *fig.* marque *f*; **2.** poinçonner; *fig.* marquer.

hallow sanctifier, consacrer; **~ed** *a.* saint, béni (*ground*).

hallucinat|e avoir des hallucinations; **~ion** hallucination *f*; **~ory** hallucinatoire.

hallway vestibule *m*.

halo *astr.*, *anat.* halo *m*; auréole *f*.

halt 1. halte *f* (*a.* ♠), arrêt *m*; **2.** faire halte; s'arrêter; *fig.* hésiter, balancer; **3.** boiteux, **~ing** hésitant; *fig.* entrecoupé.

halter *horse*: licou *m*; corde *f*.

halve diviser en deux; réduire de moitié; **~s** *pl.* **of half.**

ham jambon *m*; F (*a.* **~ actor**) cabotin *m*; (*oft.* radio) amateur *m*.

hamburger hamburger *m*; *Am. a.* viande *f* de bœuf hachée.

hamlet hameau *m*.

hammer 1. marteau *m*; **2.** marteler, battre au marteau; enfoncer (*a nail etc.*) (à coups de marteau); F *fig.* battre à plates coutures; démolir; *fig.* **~ out** élaborer.

hammock hamac *m*.

hamper 1. panier *m*, banne *f*; **2.** gêner; entraver.

hand 1. main *f* (*a. zo.*, *a. fig.* aid, *protection*); *watch*: aiguille *f*; ouvrier (-ère *f*) *m*; *cards*: jeu *m*; *measure*: paume *f*; écriture *f*; *barometer etc.*: indicateur *m*; **at ~** tout près; **at first ~** de première main; **a good** (*poor*), **~** à fort à (faible en); **by ~** à la main; **change ~s** changer de propriétaire or de mains; **give** (*or lend*) **s.o. a** (*helping*) **~** aider q; **~ on ~** en main; ♠ **en** magasin; *esp. Am.* tout près; prêt; **on one's ~s** à sa charge; **on the one ~** d'une part; **on the other ~** d'autre part; par contre; **~ over fist** main sur main;

rapidement; **~ to ~** corps à corps; **come to ~** parvenir, arriver (*letters*); **put one's ~ to** entreprendre; **~s up!** haut les mains! **2.** passer; **~ about** faire circuler; **~ down** descendre (*qch.*); transmettre; **~ in** remettre; présenter (*a request*); **~ out** distribuer; tendre; **~ over** remettre; céder; **~bag** sac *m* à main; **~bill** affiche *f* à la main; ♠ prospectus *m*; **~brake** ⊙ frein *m* à main; **~cuff 1.:** **~s** *pl.* menottes *f*/*pl.*; **2.** mettre les menottes à (*q.*), **~ful** poignée.

handicap 1. *sp. u. fig.* handicap *m*; **2.** handicaper, **~ped 1.** handicapé; **2.** *pl.* the (*mentally or physically*) **~** les handicapés (mentaux or physiques).

handi|craft travail *m* d'artisan; artisanat *m*; **~ness** *person*: adresse *f*, *thing*: commodité *f*; **~work** travail *m* manuel; ouvrage *m*.

handkerchief mouchoir *m*.

handle 1. *door*, *sword*: poignée *f*; *tool*: manche *m*; *pail*, *jar*: anse *f*; *pump*: balancier *m*; F **fly off the ~** s'emporter, *sl.* sortir de ses gonds; **2.** manier, manipuler; manœuvrer; traiter; s'occuper de; ♠ faire, avoir (*commodities*); **~bar** *cycl.* guidon *m*.

hand...: **~-me-down** *Am.* F *pl.* costume *m* de confection; décrochez-moi-ça *m*/*inv.*; **~rail** main *f* courante; garde-fou *m*; **~saw** scie *f* à main; égoïne *f*; **~shake** poignée *f* de main; **~some** beau; généreux (*gift*); joli (*sum*); **~work** travail *m* à la main; **~writing** écriture *f*; **~y** adroit, habile; commode, pratique; sous la main, à portée de la main; (bien) accessible.

hang 1. *v/t.* (sus)pendre (à *from*, *on*); tapisser (de, *with*); accrocher (à *from*, *on*); coller (*a wallpaper*); **~ up** accrocher; *v/i.* être suspendu (à, *on*); *fig.* planer (*over*); **~ about** traîner; rôder; **~ back** rester en arrière; *fig.* hésiter; **~ on** s'accrocher (à, *to*); F attendre; *teleph.* **~ up** raccrocher; **2.** F **get the ~ of** comprendre.

hangar hangar *m*.

hangdog: ~ look air *m* de chien battu.

hanger cintre *m*; porte-vêtements *m*/*inv.*; **~-on**, *pl.* **~s-on** parasite *m*.

hang-gliding *m* vol libre.

hanging 1. suspendu; tombant; **2.:** **~s** *pl.* tapisserie *f*; rideaux *m*/*pl.*

hangman bourreau *m*.

hangout *sl.* repaire *m*, boîte *f*.

hangover *sl.* gueule *f* de bois.

hangup *sl.* problème *m*; complexe *m*.

hanker: ~ *after* désirer vivement.

hap|hazard au hazard, au petit bonheur, fortuit; ~**less** malheureux; infortuné.

happen arriver (à, *to*); se passer, se produire; **he** ~**ed to be at home** il se trouvait chez lui; ~ (**up)on** trouver *or* rencontrer par hasard; ~**ing** événement *m*.

happiness bonheur *m*.

happy heureux; content; satisfait (de, *with*); ~**-go-lucky** F insouciant.

harangue 1. harangue *f*; **2.** haranguer.

harass harceler; tourmenter; tracasser; ~**ment** tracasseries *f/pl.*

harbo(u)r 1. port *m*; *fig.* asile *m*; **2.** héberger; *fig.* entretenir, nourrir (*hopes etc.*).

hard 1. *adv. usu.* dur; sévère; fort (*frost*); rigoureux (*weather*); pénible; cruel; difficile; incorrigible; ~ **currency** devises *f/pl.* fortes; ~ **drink** (*or liquor*) alcool *m* fort; **no ~ feelings!** sans rancune!; ~ **luck!** pas de chance!; **have a** ~ **time** (*of it*) avoir des moments difficiles; avoir du mal (à faire qch., **doing s.th.**); ~ *of hearing* dur d'oreille; **2.** *adv.* fort; dur; durement; de toutes ses forces; ~ *by* tout près; ~ *up* sans moyens; dans la gêne; **rain** ~ pleuvoir à verse; ~**-boiled** dur (*eggs*); tenace; *esp. Am.* expérimenté; ~**en** (se) durcir; (s')endurcir; rendre *or* devenir dur; ~**ening** durcissement *m*; ~**-headed** pratique; positif; ~**-hearted** au cœur dur; ~**ihood** hardiesse *f*; ~**iness** vigueur *f*, robustesse *f*; ~**ly** sévèrement; avec difficulté; à peine; ne ... guère; ~**ness** dureté *f*, difficulté *f* (*a. fig.*); rudesse *f*; ~**pan** *Am.* sol *m* résistant; ~**ship** privation *f*; gêne *f*; épreuve *f*; ~**ware** quincaillerie *f*; *data processing*: hardware *m*, matériel *m*.

hare lièvre *m*; ~**bell** jacinthe *f* des bois; clochette *f*; ~**-brained** écervelé; *fig.* anat. bec-de-lièvre (*pl.* becs-de-lièvre) *m*.

hark: ~! écoutez!

harm 1. mal *m*; tort *m*; **come to** ~ se faire mal; **mean no** ~ ne pas avoir de mauvaises intentions; **out of** ~**'s way** à l'abri du danger; en lieu sur; **2.** faire du mal *or* tort à; nuire à (*a person*); endommager, abîmer (*a thing*); ~**ful** nuisible; ~**less** inoffensif; anodin; innocent.

harmon|ic harmonique; ~**ious** harmonieux; ~**ize** (s')harmoniser; ~**y** harmonie *f*.

harness 1. harnais *m*; **die in** ~ mourir à la besogne; **2.** harnacher; atteler; *fig.* exploiter (*resources*).

harp ♪ 1. harpe *f*; **2.** ~ **on** rabâcher (*qch.*).

harpoon 1. harpon *m*; **2.** harponner.

harrow herse *f*; ~**ed** torturé; ~**ing** déchirant; navrant.

harry ravager, piller (*a country*); harceler (*a person*).

harsh rude; dur; âpre (*taste*); discordant (*sound*); rugueux (*surface etc.*).

hart *zo.* cerf *m*.

harvest 1. *grain*: moisson *f*; *fruit*: récolte *f*; *vine*: vendange *f*; **2.** moissonner; récolter; vendanger; ~**er** moissonneuse *f*.

hash 1. *cul.* hachis *m*; *fig.* pagaille *f*, gâchis *m*; *fig.* réchauffé *m*; *see a.* **hash(ish)**; **2.** hacher (*meat*).

hash(ish) ha(s)chisch *m*, hash *m*.

hassle F chamaillerie *f*; affaire *f*, histoire *f*.

haste hâte *f*; précipitation *f*; **make** ~ se dépêcher; ~**n** (se) hâter, se presser; ~**iness** précipitation *f*, hâte *f*; ~**ily** précipitamment; à la hâte; ~**y** précipité; hâtif.

hat chapeau *m*.

hatch 1. *chickens*: couvée *f*; *mot.* hayon *m* arrière; (*a. service* ~) guichet *m*; ⚓ (*a.* ~**way**) écoutille *f*; **2.** (faire) éclore; ~**back** *mot.* (voiture *f* à) hayon *m* arrière.

hatchet hachette *f*.

hat|e 1. haine *f* (de, contre *to*[*wards*]); **2.** détester, haïr; ~**eful** odieux, détestable; ~**red** haine *f*.

haught|iness arrogance *f*, morgue *f*; ~**y** arrogant, hautain.

haul 1. *fishing*: coup *m* de filet; prise *f*, butin *m*; trajet *m*, voyage *m*; **2.** tirer, traîner; transporter par camion(s); ~**age** transport *m* (routier); ~**ier** transporteur *m*, camionneur *m*.

haunch hanche *f*; *cuis.* cuissot *m*.

haunt 1. lieu *m* fréquenté; repaire *m*; **2.** hanter.

have 1. v/t. avoir; prendre (a bath, a meal); faire (a walk, s.th. done); ~ **to** (inf.) être obligé de (inf.); **I would ~ you know that ...** sachez que ...; **I had as well** (inf.) j'aurais pu aussi bien (inf.); **I had better** (**best**) (inf.) je ferai(s) mieux de (inf.); **I had rather** (inf.) j'aime(rais) mieux (inf.); ~ **on** porter; ~ **it out with** s'expliquer avec. **2.** v/aux. avoir; sometimes être; ~ **come** être venu.

haven port m; fig. havre m, asile m.

have-not pauvre m; see haves.

haversack sac m à dos.

haves: the ~ and the have-nots les riches et les pauvres.

havings pl. biens m/pl.

havoc ravages m/pl.; **wreak ~ on, make ~ of** ravager; **play ~ with** mettre sens dessus dessous.

haw ♀ cenelle f.

hawk¹ orn. faucon m.

hawk² colporter; **~er** colporteur m.

hawthorn ♀ aubépine f.

hay 1. foin m; **2.** faire les foins; **~fever** rhume m des foins; **~loft** grenier m à foin; **~maker** machine: faneuse f; **~rick, ~rick** meule f de foin.

hazard 1. danger m, risque m; hasard m; **2.** hasarder; risquer; **~ous** dangereux, risqué; hasardeux.

haze 1. brume f légère; **2.** v/i.: ~ **over** se couvrir de brume; v/t. harasser (q.) de corvées; Am. brimer.

hazel 1. ♀ noisetier m; **2.** couleur noisette; **~nut** noisette f.

hazy brumeux; estompé (outline etc.); fig. vague.

H-bomb bombe f H.

he 1. il, (accentuated) lui; ~ (**who**) celui qui; **2.** attr. mâle.

head 1. usu. tête f (a. fig.); ship: nez m, proue f; mot. capote f; bed: chevet m; table: haut bout m; river: source f; geog. cap m; person: chef m; ✝, school: directeur -trice f m; patron(ne f) m; coin: (le côté m) face f; **~s or tails?** pile ou face?; **come to a ~** aboutir; mûrir; **get it into one's ~ that** se mettre dans la or en tête que; ~ **over heels** éperdument (amoureux, **in love**); **go ~ over heels** faire la culbute; **2.** premier; principal; ... en chef; **~ office** bureau m or siège m central; **3.** v/t. mener, être en tête de; être à la tête de; conduire; foot.

jouer de la tête; ~ **off** intercepter; Am. prendre sa source (à, **at**); v/i. ~ **for** diriger vers; **~ache** mal m or maux m/pl. de tête; **~dress** coiffure f, garniture f de tête; **~gear** garniture f de tête; coiffure f; chapeau m; **~ing** en-tête m; rubrique f; manchette f; titre m; sp. (jeu m de) tête f; **~land** cap m, promontoire m; **~less** sans tête; fig. sans chef; **~light** mot. phare m; **~line** titre m; manchette f; typ. titre m courant; **~long 1.** adj. précipité; impétueux; **2.** adv. la tête la première; **~man** chef m; **~master** directeur m; school: proviseur m; **~mistress** directrice f; **~phones** pl. casque m (à écouteurs); **~quarters** pl. ✕ quartier m général; ✝ etc. siège m (social); **~rest** appui-tête m (pl. appuis-tête); **~strong** entêté; obstiné; **~waters** pl. cours m supérieur d'une rivière; **~way** progrès m; **make ~** faire des progrès; **~wind** vent m contraire; **~word** mot-souche (pl. mots-souches) m; **~work** travail m intellectuel; foot. jeu m de tête; **~y** capiteux (wine etc.), emporté (person).

heal guérir (de, **of**); ~ **up** (se) guérir; **~ing** guérison f.

health santé f; ~ **food(s** pl.) aliments m/pl. naturels; **~ful** salubre; salutaire; **~ resort** station f estivale or thermale; **~y** en bonne santé; sain.

heap 1. tas m; monceau m; F **~s** pl. of des tas de; **2.** empiler; fig. accabler (de, **with**); ~ **up** (s') empiler; (s')entasser.

hear entendre; écouter; avoir des nouvelles (de, **from**); apprendre; **~er** auditeur (-trice f) m; **~ing** sense: ouïe f, audition f (a. ✝, a. ♪); ✝✝ audience f; **~aid** appareil m acoustique, audiophone m; **~say** (**by** ~ par) ouï-dire m/inv.

hearse corbillard m.

heart cœur m; ~ **attack** crise f cardiaque; ~ **failure** arrêt m du cœur; ~ **transplant** greffe f du cœur; ~ **and soul** corps et âme; **by** ~ par cœur; **in his** ~ (**of** ~**s**) au plus profond de son cœur; **with all my** ~ de tout mon cœur; **lose** ~ perdre courage; **take** ~ prendre courage; **take** (or **lay**) **to** ~ prendre (qch.) à cœur; **~ache** chagrin m; **~beat** battement m de cœur; **~break** déchirement m de cœur; **~breaking** navrant; **~broken** le cœur brisé, navré; **~burn** brûlures f/pl.

d'estomach; **~en** encourager; **~felt** sincère; profond.

hearth foyer *m*, âtre *m*.

heart|less insensible; cruel; **~rending** navrant; **~sick** *fig.* découragé; désolé; **~y** cordial; sincère; vigoureux, robuste.

heat 1. chaleur *f*; *fig.* ardeur *f*; *animal*: rut *m*; *sp.* épreuve; **2.** (*a.* **~ up**) (s')échauffer; *v/t.* chauffer; **~ up** *a.* (se) rechauffer; **~ed** chauffé; *fig.* échauffé (*person*), passionné (*a. debate etc.*); **~er** ⚙ radiateur *m*; *Am. sl.* revolver *m*.

heath lande *f*; ♀ bruyère *f*, brande *f*.

heathen païen (*a. su.*).

heather ♀ bruyère *f*, brande *f*.

heating chauffage *m*; *attr.* de chaleur; **~ battery** batterie *f* de four *etc.*; **~ cushion, ~pad** coussin *m* chauffant *or* électrique.

heat ...: ~resistant résistant à la chaleur; **~stroke** 💊 coup *m* de chaleur; **~ wave** vague *f* de chaleur.

heave 1. soulèvement *m*; effort *m*, poussée *f*; **2.** *v/t.* (sou)lever; lancer; pousser (*a sigh*); **~ the anchor** déraper; *v/i.* se soulever.

heaven ciel *m*; *cieux m/pl.*; **~s** *pl.* ciel *m*; **~ly** céleste; divin.

heaviness pesanteur *f*, lourdeur *f*.

heavy *usu.* lourd; pesant; gros (*heart, rain, etc.*); violent (*blow*); grand (*smoker etc.*); dense (*traffic*); **be ~ going** être difficile; **~duty** très résistant; à haute tenue (*oil*); **~weight** *box.* poids *m* lourd.

heckle interpeller; chahuter.

hectic agité, bousculé, fiévreux; *a.* 💊 hectique.

hedge 1. haie *f*; *fig.* protection *f*; **2.** *v/t.* (*a.* **~ in, ~ up**) entourer d'une haie; enfermer; *fig.* **~d about** (*or around*) **with** entouré de (*problems etc.*); **~one's bet** se couvrir; *v/i.* éviter de répondre franchement; se défier; **~hog** *zo.* hérisson *m*; *Am. a.* porc-épic *m*; **~row** bordure *f* de haies; haie *f*.

heed 1. attention *f* (à, *to*); **pay ~ to, take ~ of = 2.** faire attention à; tenir compte de; **~ful** attentif (à, *of*); **~less** insouciant.

heel 1. talon *m*; *sl.* salaud *m*; **be at** (*or* **on**) **s.o.'s ~s** être aux trousses de q.; **bring s.o. to ~** faire obéir (*q.*); **down at**

~ éculé; *fig.* de pauvre apparence, miteux; **2.** retalonner.

hefty costaud (*person*); gros.

heifer génisse *f*.

height hauteur *f*; *person*: taille *f*; altitude *f*; *fig.* sommet *m*, apogée *m*; comble *m*; **~en** *v/t.* rehausser; *vt/i. fig.* augmenter.

heinous atroce; odieux.

heir héritier *m* (de, *to*); **~ apparent** héritier *m* présomptif; **~at-law** héritier *m* légitime; **~ess** héritière *f*; **~loom** meuble *m or* bijou *m* de famille; *fig.* apanage *m*.

helicopter hélicoptère *m*.

hell enfer *m*; *attr.* de l'enfer; **like ~** comme fou; F **a ~ of a ...** un(e) sacré(e) ...; F **what the ~ ...?** que diable ...?; **raise ~** faire un bruit infernal; **~bent** F résolu; acharné; **~ish** infernal; diabolique.

hello holà!; *teleph.* allô!

helm ♣, *fig.* barre *f*.

helmet casque *m*.

helmsman timonier *m*.

help 1. aide *f*; secours *m*; *fig.* remède *m*; *person*: aide *mf*, *household*: femme *f* de ménage; **by the ~ of** à l'aide de; **2.** *v/t.* aider; secourir; faciliter; *at table*: servir (q., *s.o.*); qch., *s.th.*; qch. à q., *s.o. to s.th.*); **~ o.s.** se servir; **~ out** dépanner, tirer (*q.*) d'embarras; **I could not ~ laughing** je ne pouvais m'empêcher de rire; **I can't ~ it** je n'y peux rien; *v/i.* aider, servir; **~er** aide *mf*; assistant(e f) *m*; **~ful** utile; salutaire; serviable (*person*); **~ing** portion *f*; **~less** sans ressource; désarmé; impuissant; **~lessness** impuissance *f*; **~mate** aide *mf*; compagnon *m*, compagne *f*.

helter-skelter à la débandade.

helve manche *m*.

Helvetian helvétien, suisse.

hem 1. *cost.* ourlet *m*; bord *m*; **2.** *cost.* ourler; border; *fig.* **~ in** cerner, entourer; *hinder*: entraver.

hemisphere hémisphère *m*.

hemp chanvre *m*.

hen poule *f*; *bird*: femelle *f*.

hence (*oft. from ~*) d'ici; désormais; de là; **a year ~** dans un an; **~forth, ~forward** désormais, à l'avenir.

hen...: ~ party F assemblée *f* de jupes; **~pecked** dominé par sa femme.

her 1. *accusative*: 1a; *dative*: lui; à elle; se, soi; celle; **2.** son, sa; ses.

herald 1. héraut *m*; *fig. a.* messager (-ère *f*) *m*; **2.** annoncer; **~ry** blason *m*.

herb herbe *f*; *cuis.* **~s** *pl.* fines herbes *f/pl.*; **~ivorous** herbivore.

herd 1. troupeau *m*; **2.** *v/t.* assembler; *v/i.* (*a.* **~ together**) s'assembler en troupeau; s'attrouper; **~sman** bouvier *m*.

here ici; **~ is** voici; **~'s to ...!** à la santé de ...!

here|after 1. dorénavant; **2.** avenir *m*; *la* vie *f* à venir; **~by** par là.

hered|itary héréditaire; **~ity** héréditié *f*.

herein ici; en ceci; **~of** of ceci.

here|sy hérésie *f*; **~tic** hérétique *m/f*; **~tical** hérétique.

here|tofore jusqu'ici; **~upon** là-dessus; **~with** avec ceci; ci-joint.

heritage héritage *m*.

hermetic hermétique.

hermit ermite *m*.

hero, *pl.* **-roes** héros *m*; **~ic** héroïque; épique; **~in** *drug*: héroïne *f*; **~ine** héroïne *f*; **~ism** héroïsme *m*.

heron *orn.* héron *m*.

herring *icht.* hareng *m*.

hers le sien, la sienne, les siens, les siennes; à elle.

herself elle-même; *rfl.* se, *stressed*: soi.

hesitat|e hésiter (à, **to**; sur **about**, **over**); **~ion** hésitation *f*.

hessian (toile *f* de) jute *m*.

hetorodox hétérodoxe.

het up F excité, agité, nerveux.

hew tailler.

hey hé!; holà!; hein?

heyday âge *m* d'or, apogée *m*, beaux jours *m/pl.*

hi salut!

hiccup, *a.* **hiccough 1.** hoquet *m*; **2.** avoir le hoquet; hoqueter.

hide¹ 1. peau *f*; **†** cuir *m*; **2.** F tanner le cuir à (*q.*).

hide² 1. cacher (qch. à q., **s.th. from s.o.**); *v/t.* se cacher (de q., **from s.o.**); **~-and-seek** cache-cache *m*; **~away** F cachette *f*.

hidebound *fig.* aux vues étroites.

hideous affreux; horrible.

hiding¹ F rossée *f*.

hiding²: go into ~ se cacher; **in ~** caché; **~ place** cachette *f*.

hi-fi (*abbr. of* **high fidelity**) sound: de haute fidélité.

high 1. *adj.* (*see a.* **~ly**) *usu.* haut; élevé; fort (*wind*); grand (*speed*); avancé (*meat*); *sl. on drink*: parti, *on drugs*: drogué; *sl.* **get ~** se défoncer; **it is ~ time** il est grand temps; **leave ~ and dry** planter là, laisser en plan; **with a ~ hand** arbitrairement; **~ spirits** *pl.* gaieté *f*; ♀ **Church** haute Église *f* (anglicane); *esp. Am. sl.* **~ life** la vie *f* mondaine; **⚡ tension** haute tension *f*; **~ water** marée *f* haute; **~ wind** gros vent *m*; **2.** *su. meteor.* zone *f* de haute pression; **✝**, *fig.* pointe *f*, plafond *m*; *esp. Am.* ♀ *see* **High School; on ~** en haut; **3.** *adv.* haut; en haut; fort(ement); **~-and-mighty** F arrogant; **~boy** commode *f*; **~brow F 1.** intellectuel(le *f*) *m*; **2.** iro. prétendu intellectuel; **~-class** de première classe *or* qualité; **~-flown** ampoulé (*style etc.*); **~-flying** ambitieux; **~-handed** arbitraire; **~lander** montagnard *m* écossais; **~lands** hautes terres *f/pl.*; **~light 1.** point *m* marquant *or* culminant; **2.** mettre en lumière, souligner; **~ly** fort(ement); très; bien; extrêmement; **speak ~ of** vanter; **~-minded** à l'esprit élevé; **~ness** élévation *f*; *fig.* grandeur *f*; **~-pitched** *sound*: aigu; **~-rise block** (*or* **flats** *pl.*) tour *f* (d'habitation). **~road** grand-route *f*; *fig.* bonne voie *f*; **~ school** collège *m*, lycée *m*; **~ street** grand-rue *f*; **~-strung** (au tempérament) nerveux; **~ water** marée *f* haute; **~way** grande route *f*; *fig.* bonne voie *f*.

hijack détourner (*a plane*); **~er** pirate *m* de l'air.

hike 1. marcher à pied, faire une randonnée à pied; *increase:* (sou)lever; **2.** randonnée *f* à pied; **✝** hausse *f* (*of prices*); **~r** excursionniste *mf* (à pied).

hilari|ous hilarant; désopilant; joyeux; **~ousness, ~ty** hilarité *f*.

hill colline *f*; côte *f*; *mot.* **~ start** démarrage *m* en côte; **~ock** petite colline *f*; **~slde** (flanc *m* de) coteau *m*; **~y** montueux; montagneux.

hilt *sword:* poignée *f*.

him *accusative:* le; *dative:* lui; se, soi; celui.

himself lui-même; *rfl.* se, *stressed:* soi; **of ~** de lui-même; de son propre choix; **by ~** tout seul.

hind¹ *zo.* biche *f.*

hind² de derrière; postérieur.

hinder gêner, entraver; retarder; empêcher (*q.*) (de, *from*).

hindmost dernier.

hindrance empêchement *m*; obstacle *m*.

hindsight sagesse *f* (d') après coup.

hinge 1. gond *m* charnière *f*; 2. ~ (*up*)*on fig.* dépendre de.

hint 1. allusion *f*; signe *m*; 2. suggérer; faire allusion (à, *at*).

hip¹ hanche *f*; ~ *flask* flacon *m* plat.

hip² ⚓ F gratte-cul *m*/*inv.*

hip³ *sl.* dans le vent.

hippo F = **hippopotamus** hippopotame *m.*

hire 1. louage *m*; *house*: location *f*; gages *m*/*pl.*; ⚓ ~ *purchase* achat *m* à crédit *or* à tempérament; *on* ~ à louer; 2. louer; engager, embaucher (*a person*); ~ *out* louer; ~ *o.s. out* accepter un emploi.

his 1. son, sa, ses; 2. le sien, la sienne, les siens, les siennes; à lui.

hiss 1. siffler; 2. sifflement.

histor|ian historien *m*; ~**ic(al)** historique; ~**y** histoire *f.*

hit 1. coup *m*; touche *f*; succès *m*, coup *m* réussi; *thea.*, ♪ succès *m*; 2. *v/t.* frapper; heurter; atteindre (*an aim*); porter (*a blow*); trouver; F arriver à; ~ *it off with* s'entendre (bien) avec; ~ *v/i.* ~ (*up*)*on* découvrir; trouver; tomber sur.

hitch 1. saccade *f*; nœud *m*; *fig.* empêchement *m* soudain, anicroche *m*, accroc *m*; 2. attacher; ~ *up* remonter (d'une saccade); ~**hike** faire de l'auto-stop; ~**hiking** auto-stop *m.*

hither *poet.* ici; ~**to** jusqu'ici.

hive 1. ruche *f*; *fig.* fourmilière *f*; 2. ~ *off* (se) séparer.

hoard 1. amas *m*; provision(s) *f*/ (*pl.*); réserve(s) *f*/ (*pl.*); *fig.* trésor *m*, *money*: magot *m*; 2. amasser; thésauriser.

hoarfrost gelée *f* blanche; givre *m.*

hoarse rauque, enroué.

hoary blanchi (*hair*); chenu (*person*); *fig.* séculaire.

hoax 1. canular *m*, mystification *f*; faire un canular à, jouer un tour à.

hob *range*: plaque *f* chauffante.

hobble 1. boitillement *f*; F embarras *m*; 2. *v/i.* boitiller *v/t.* entraver.

hobby passe-temps *m* (favori), hobby *m*; ~ *horse* cheval *m* à bascule; *fig.* dada *m.*

hobgoblin lutin *m.*

hobo vagabond *m.*

hock vin *m* du Rhin.

hoe ✐ 1. houe *f*; 2. houer.

hog 1. *Br.* porc *m* châtré, *Am.* cochon *m*; F *go* (*the*) *whole* ~ aller jusqu'au bout; 2. accaparer, monopoliser; *mot.* ~ *the road* tenir toute la route; ~**gish** de cochon; grossier; ~**skin** peau *f* de porc.

hoist 1. palan *m*; 2. hisser.

hokum *Am. sl.* balivernes *f*/*pl.*

hold 1. *v/t. usu.* tenir; retenir (*s.o.'s attention, one's breath, in memory*); maintenir; détenir; avoir, posséder; juger, estimer; professer (*an opinion*); arrêter; célébrer (*a holiday*); tenir (*a meeting*); ~ *one's own* défendre sa position; ~ *back* retenir; ~ *down* maintenir à terre; *fig.* maintenir bas (*prices etc.*); *fig.* réprimer, opprimer; ~ *down a job* occuper *or* garder une situation; ~ *off* tenir à distance, tenir à l'écart; ~ *out* offrir, promettre; présenter; ~ *over* remettre à plus tard; ~ *together* maintenir (ensemble); ~ *up* soutenir; (re)lever; arrêter; exposer; 3. *v/i.* tenir (bon); se maintenir; persister; valoir, être vrai; ~ *good* être valable; ne pas se démentir; ~ *forth* pérorer; ~ *off* se tenir à distance; ~ *on* s'accrocher, se cramponner (à, *to*); ne pas lâcher; F ~ *on! teleph.* ne quittez pas!; ~ *out* tenir (bon); durer (*supplies etc.*); ~ *to* s'en tenir à; ~ *together* tenir (bon *or* ensemble); ~ *up* se maintenir; 2. prise *f*; *fig.* influence *f*, empire *m*; ♺ cale *f*; *catch* (*or get, lay, seize, take*) ~ *of* saisir; *get* ~ *of* à trouver, se procurer, F dégot(t)er, dénicher; *get* ~ *of o.s.* se contrôler; *on* ~ en attente; *put s.o. on* ~ faire attendre q.; ~**er** titulaire *mf*; *sp.*, ⚓ détenteur (-trice *f*) *m*; ~ *of shares* actionnaire *mf*; ~**ing** tenue *f*; possession *f*; ~ *company* holding *m*; ~**over** *Am.* survivance *f*; ~**up** hold-up *m*; *mot.* embouteillage *m.*

hole 1. trou *m*; *pick* ~*s in* critiquer; 2. trouer, faire un trou dans.

holiday jour *m* de fête; congé *m*; ~*s pl.* vacances *f*/*pl.*; ~**maker** vacancier (-ère *f*) *m.*

holler F 1. brailler; 2. braillement *m*, (grand) cri *m.*

hollow 1. *adj.* creux; sourd (*sound*); *fig. a.* faux; 2. *adv. sound* ~ sonner creux;

3. *su.* creux *m*, cavité *f*; *ground*: dépression *f*, cuvette *f*; **4.** (*a.* ~ *out*) creuser.
holly ♣ houx *m*.
holster étui *m* de revolver.
holy saint; bénit (*water*); sacré (*ground*); ♀ *Thursday* le jeudi *m* saint; ♀ *Ghost* (*or Spirit*) le Saint-Esprit *m*; ~ *orders* ordres *m/pl.* (majeurs); ♀ *Week* la semaine *f* sainte.
homage hommage *m*; *do* (*or pay, render*) ~ rendre hommage (à, *to*).
home 1. *su.* foyer *m*; maison *f*, chez-soi *m*; patrie *f*; *at* ~ chez moi (lui, elle *etc.*); **2.** *adj.* domestique; intérieur (*trade, affairs, etc.*); qui porte (*blow*); ♀ *Office* Ministère *m* de l'Intérieur; ~ *rule* autonomie *f*, ♀ *Secretary* Ministre *m* de l'Intérieur; ~ *straight*, ~ *stretch* sp. dernière ligne *f* droite; *fig.* phase *f* finale; *F tell s.o. a few* ~ *truths* dire ses quatre vérités à q.; **3.** *adv.* à la maison, chez moi *etc.*; à son pays; ~ *delivery* livraison *f* à domicile; *come* ~, *go* ~ rentrer; *hit* (*or strike*) ~ frapper juste; ~*bred* indigène; *fig.* naturel; ~ *economics* sg. Am. économie *f* domestique; ~*grown* indigène; du cru (*wine*); ~*help* aide *f* ménagère; ~*less* sans asile; ~*like* intime; ~*liness* simplicité *f*; Am. manque *m* de beauté; ~*ly fig.* simple, modeste; Am. sans beauté; ~*made* fait à la maison; du pays; ~*sick*: *be* ~ avoir le mal du pays; s'ennuyer de sa famille; ~*sickness* mal *m* du pays; nostalgie *f*; ~*spun* **1.** *fig.* simple, rude; **2.** tissu *m* fait à la maison; ~*town* ville *f* natale; ~*ward* **1.** *adv.* (*or* ~*wards*) vers la maison; vers son pays; **2.** *adj.* de retour; ~*work* school: devoirs *m/pl.*
homicide homicide *m*; meurtre *m*; *person*: homicide *mf*.
homing qui retourne au point de départ; ✕ à tête chercheuse (*missile etc.*); ~ *pigeon* pigeon *m* voyageur.
homogeneous homogène.
hone aiguiser.
honest honnête; sincère, franc, ~ *truth* pure vérité *f*; ~*y* honnêteté *f*.
honey miel *m*; F chéri(e) *f*; ~*comb* rayon *m* de miel; nid d'abeilles (*pattern*); ~*combed* alvéolé; ~*ed fig.* mielleux; ~*moon* **1.** lune *f* de miel; voyage *m* de noces; **2.** passer sa lune de miel; faire son voyage de noces.

honk *mot.* klaxonner.
honky-tonk *sl.* bouge *m*.
honorary honoraire (*member, president etc.*); honorifique (*title etc.*).
hono(u)r 1. honneur *m*; *your* ♀ Monsieur le juge; **2.** honorer; ~*able* honorable.
hood capuchon *m*; ⊙ *a.* hotte *f*; *mot.* Br. capote *f*, Am. capot *m* (*of the engine*).
hoodlum *sl.* voyou *m*.
hoodoo porteur (-euse *f*) *m* de malheur.
hoodwink tromper.
hooey Am. *sl.* bêtises *f/pl.*
hoof sabot *m*; F pied *m*.
hook 1. crochet *m*; *dress*: agrafe *f*; *fishing*: hameçon *m*; *by* ~ *or by crook* d'une manière ou d'une autre; F ~, *line and sinker* totalement; sans réserve; **2.** *v/t.* accrocher; agrafer (*a dress*); prendre (*a fish*); attraper; ~ *up* agrafer; suspendre; relier, ℰ brancher; *radio, TV*: faire un duplex entre; *v/i.* (*a.* ~ *on*) s'accrocher; ~*ed* crochu, recourbé; *sl.* toxicomane; ~*up* alliance *f*; *radio, TV*: duplex *m*; ~*y*: Am. *play* ~ faire l'école buissonnière.
hoop 1. cerceau *m*, *cask*: cercle *m*; **2.** cercler.
hooping-cough coqueluche *f*.
hoot 1. *su. person*: huée *f*; *mot.* coup *m* de klaxon; **2.** huer; *mot.* klaxonner, *thea.* siffler; ~*er* sirène *f*; *mot.* klaxon *m*.
hop¹ ♣ houblon *m*; ~*s pl.* houblon *m*.
hop² **1.** saut *m*; F sauterie *f*; **2.** sauter; sautiller.
hope 1. espoir *m* (de, *of*); espérance *f*; **2.** espérer (qch., *for s.th.*); *I* ~ *so* je l'espère, j'espère que oui; *I* ~ *not* j'espère que non; ~*ful* plein d'espoir; qui promet; ~*fully* on espère (que); ~*less* désespéré; sans espoir; incorrigible.
horde horde *f*.
horizon horizon *m*; ~*tal* horizontal.
horn *usu.* corne *f*; *zo.* antenne *f*; ♪ cor *m*; ♪ F instrument *m* à vent; *mot.* klaxon *m*; (*stag's*) ~*s pl.* bois *m/pl.*; ~ *of plenty* corne *f* d'abondance.
hornet *zo.* frelon *m*.
horr|endous horrible, terrible; ~*ible* horrible, affreux; ~*id* horrible, affreux; ~*ific* horrifique; ~*ify* horrifier; ~*or* horreur *f* (de, *of*); ~ *film* film *m* d'horreur *m*.

horse 1. su. cheval m; **~back: on ~** à cheval; sur un cheval; **~hair** crin m (de cheval); **~laugh** F gros rire m bruyant; **~man** cavalier m; **~manship** manège m, équitation f; **~ opera** Western m; **~power** measure: cheval-vapeur (pl. chevaux-vapeur) m; **~race** course f de chevaux; **~radish** ⚘ raifort m; **~ sense** bon sens m; **~shoe** fer m à cheval.

horticulture horticulture f.

hose 1. ⚓ bas m/pl.; ⊙; (a. **~pipe**) tuyau m; **garden ~** tuyau m d'arrosage; **2.** laver (a car etc.) or arroser (the garden) au jet.

hosiery ⚓ bonneterie f; bas m/pl.; in a store: rayon m des bas.

hospitable hospitalier.

hospital hôpital m; **~ity** hospitalité f.

host¹ hôte m radio, telev. présentateur (-trice f) m.

host² fig. foule f, multitude f.

host³ eccl. hostie f.

hostage otage m; **take s.o. ~** prendre q. en otage.

hostel foyer m.

hostess hôtesse f.

hostile hostile; **~ity** hostilité f.

hostler valet m d'écurie.

hot chaud; brûlant; violent (temper); piquant, fort, relevé (sauce, food); pol. **~ line** téléphone m rouge; **~ spot** point m névralgique; **go** (or **sell**) **like ~ cakes** se vendre comme des petits pains; **~bed** fig. foyer m.

hotchpotch salmigondis m; fig. méli-mélo (pl. mélis-mélos) m.

hotel hôtel m.

hot...: ~head tête f chaude, impétueux m; **~house** serre f chaude; **~ness** chaleur f; **~plate** chauffe-assiettes m/inv.; **~ly** fig. passionnément; **~ rod** mot. Am. sl. bolide m; **~spur** tête m brûlé; **~water bottle** bouillotte f.

hound 1. chien m (usu. de chasse); **2.** chasser; fig. s'acharner après.

hour heure f; **~ hand** petite aiguille f; **~ly** toutes les heures; pay: à l'heure.

house 1. su. maison f (a. ⚓ de commerce); parl. Chambre f; thea. salle f; **keep ~** faire le ménage; **2.** v/t. loger; héberger; v/i. habiter; **~agent** agent m de location; **~breaker** voleur m avec effraction; **~broken** propre (animal); docile (person); **~hold** ménage m; famille

f; **~holder** propriétaire m, locataire m; chef m de famille; **~hunting** recherche d'un appartement or d'une maison; **~keeper** ménagère f; gouvernante f; **~keeping 1.** ménage m; **2.** du ménage; **~trained** see housebroken; **~warming (party)** pendaison f de la crémaillère; **~wife** ménagère f, maîtresse f de maison; trousse f de couture; **~wifery** économie f domestique; **~work** travaux m/pl. domestiques.

housing logement m; **~ estate** (or **project** or **scheme**) cité f, grand ensemble m; **~ shortage** crise f du logement.

hovel taudis m, masure f.

hover planer; **~(a)round** rôder (autour de); **~ between** hésiter entre; être entre; **~craft** aéroglisseur m.

how comment; **~ much** (or **many**) combien (de); **~ about ...?** et ...?; si on ...?; **~ever 1.** adv. de quelque manière que (sbj.); before adj. or adv.: quelque ... que (sbj.), tout ... que (ind.); F comment diable?; **2.** conj. cependant, pourtant.

howl 1. hurler; **2.** hurlement m; **~er** F gaffe f; **~ing** F énorme.

hub moyeu m; fig. centre m; mot. **~ cap** enjoliveur m.

hubbub brouhaha m, vacarme m.

hub(by) F mari m.

huckleberry ⚘ airelle f, myrtille f.

huckster colporteur m.

huddle 1. v/t. entasser (pêle-mêle); v/i. (a. **~ together**, **~ up**) s'entasser; se blottir (l'un contre l'autre); **2.** su. tas m (confus); méli-mélo (pl. mélis-mélos) m; F **go into a ~** faire un petit comité.

hue¹ teinte f, nuance f.

hue²: (**raise a**) **~ and cry** (soulever un) tollé m (général).

huff 1. su.: in a **~** froissé, fâché, blessé; **take** (**the**) **~** se froisser; **2.** (se) froisser; **~ed** froissé, blessé, fâché; **~y** irascible; susceptible; fâché.

hug 1. étreinte f; **2.** étreindre, embrasser; serrer dans ses bras; fig. serrer (the shore, the kerb etc.).

huge immense, énorme; **~ness** immensité, énormité f.

hulk of car, ship etc.: carcasse f; F fig. mastodonte m; **~ing** gros; lourdaud (person).

hull 1. ⚘ cosse f; fig. enveloppe f; ⚓, ✈ coque f; **2.** écosser (peas).

hullabaloo vacarme *m*, brouhaha *m*.

hullo ohé!; tiens!; *teleph.* allô!

hum 1. bourdonnement *m*; ronflement *m*; fredonnement *m*; **2.** *v/i.* bourdonner; ronfler; fredonner; vrombir (*aircraft*); *v/t.* fredonner (*a song*).

human 1. humain; ~ **rights** *pl.* droits *m/pl.* de l'homme; **~ly** en être humain; **~e** humain; humanitaire; **~itarian** humanitaire; **~ity** humanité *f*, **~kind** le genre *m* humain.

humble 1. humble, modeste, **eat ~ ple** en rabattre; avouer qu'on a tort; **2.** humilier.

humble-bee bourdon *m*.

humbleness humilité *f*.

humbug 1. blagues *f/pl.*; *person:* blagueur (-euse *f*) *m*; **2.** mystifier.

humdrum 1. monotone; banal; **2.** monotonie *f*; banalité *f*.

humid humide; moite (*skin*); **~ity** humidité *f*; moiteur *f*.

humili|ate humilier; **~ating** humiliant; **~ation** humiliation *f*; **~ty** humilité *f*.

hummingbird *orn.* colibri *m*.

humorous comique, drôle; humoristique (*representation etc.*); plein d'humour (*person*).

humo(u)r 1. humour *m*; humeur *f*; **sense of ~** (sens *m* de l') humeur *f*; **out of ~** de mauvaise humeur; **2.** se prêter aux caprices de (*q.*); faire plaisir à.

hump 1. bosse *f*; *sl.* cafard *m*; **2.** voûter; arrondir (*one's back*); F carry (*on one's back*); **~back** bossu(e *f*) *m*.

humpty-dumpty F petite personne *f* boulotte.

hunch 1. bosse *f*; intuition *f*, pressentiment *m*; **2.** (*a. ~ out, ~ up*) voûter; **~back** bossu(e *f*) *m*.

hundred 1. cent; **2.** cent *m*; centaine *f* (de); **~fold** centuple; **~th** centième (*a. su./m*); **~weight** quintal *m*.

Hungarian 1. hongrois; **2.** Hongrois(e *f*) *m*; *ling.* hongrois *m*.

hunger 1. *su.* faim *f.a. fig.* de, **for**); (**go on a**) ~ **strike** (faire la) grève de la faim; **2.** *fig.* ~ **for** (*or* **after**) avoir faim de.

hungry affamé (*de* **for**, **after**) (*a. fig.*); **be ~** avoir faim.

hunk F gros morceau *m*.

hunt 1. *su.* chasse *f*, recherche *f* (de, **for**); **2.** *v/t.* chasser; chercher; ~ **out, ~ up** découvrir; *v/i.* chasser (au chien courant *or* à courre); ~ **for** chercher; **~er** chasseur *m*; **~ing 1.** chasse *f*; **2.** de chasse.

hurdle claie *f*; *sp.* haie *f*; **~r** *sp.* sauteur *m* de haies; ~ **race** *sp.* course *f* de haies.

hurl lancer, jeter.

hurricane ouragan *m*.

hurried pressé; précipité (*fait etc.*) à la hâte; **~ly** précipitamment; à la hâte.

hurry 1. hâte *f*; précipitation *f*; **in a** ~ à la hâte, en vitesse; **be in a** ~ être pressé; F **not ... in a** ~ ne ... pas de sitôt; **2.** *v/t.* hâter, presser; ~ **on, ~ up** faire hâter le pas à; *v/i.* (*a. ~ up*) se presser, se hâter, se dépêcher; presser le pas.

hurt 1. *v/t.* faire mal à; blesser (*a. s.o.'s feelings*), faire de la peine à; **get** ~ se faire mal; *v/i.* faire mal; **3.** mal *m*, blessure *f*; **4.** blessé; **~ful (to)** nuisible (à).

hurtle *v/i.* dévaler, passer en trombe; *v/t.* lancer.

husband 1. mari *m*; **2.** ménager; **~ry** agronomie *f*; industrie *f* agricole.

hush 1. *int.* silence!; chut!; **2.** *su.* silence *m*; **3.** *v/t.* calmer; faire taire; ~ **up** étouffer (*a scandal*); faire taire; se taire; ~ **money** prix *m* du silence (de *q.*).

husk 1. *sp. grain:* balle *f*, *rice etc.:* enveloppe *f*, *peas, cosse f*, *fig.* carcasse *f*; **2.** écosser (*peas*); décortiquer; **~y** rauque (*voice*); F fort, costaud.

hustle 1. *v/t.* bousculer, pousser; *v/i.* se dépêcher; **2.** *su.* bousculade *f*; activité *f* énergique; ~ **and bustle** tourbillon *m*; remue-ménage *m/inv.*

hut cabane *f*, hutte *f*.

hutch cage *f*, *rabbits:* clapier *m*.

hyacinth ♀ jacinthe *f*.

hya(e)na *zo.* hyène *f*.

hybrid hybride (*adj.*, *su./m*).

hydrant prise *f* d'eau; (*a. fire* ~) bouche *f* d'incendie.

hydro... hydr(o)-; **~electric:** ~ **generating station** centrale *f* hydroélectrique; **~gen** ♀ hydrogène *m*; ~ **bomb** bombe *f* à hydrogène; **~plane** hydravion *m*.

hyena hyène *f*.

hygien|e hygiène *f*; **~ic** hygiénique.

hymn 1. *eccl.* hymne *f*, cantique *m*; (*national etc.*) hymne *m*; **2.** glorifier.

hyphen trait *m* d'union; **~ate** écrire avec un trait d'union.

hypno|sis hypnose *f*; **~tist** hypnotiseur (-euse *f*) *m*; **~tize** hypnotiser.

hypo|chondria hypocondrie *f*; F spleen *m*; **~chondriac 1.** hypocondriaque; **2.** hypocondre *mf*; **~crisy** hypocrisie *f*; **~crite** hypocrite *mf*; F *man: a.* tartufe *m*;

~critical hypocrite; **~thesis**, *pl.* **-ses** hypothèse *f*; **~thetic(al)** hypothétique.

hyster|ia 𝒳 hystérie *f*; F crise *f* de nerfs; **~ical** hystérique; **~ics** *pl.* crise *f* or attaque *f* de nerfs; *go into* **~** avoir une crise de nerfs.

I

I je; *stressed:* moi.

ice 1. glace *f* (*a. cuis.*); F *cut no* **~** ne faire aucune impression (sur, *with*); **2.** *v/t. cuis.* (faire) rafraîchir (*a drink*); *cuis.* glacer (*a cake*); *vt/i.* (*a.* **~** *up,* **~** *over*) geler (*water etc.*); (se) givrer (*window etc.*); **~axe** piolet *m*; **~berg** iceberg *m*; **~bound** fermé or retenu par les glaces; **~box** glacière *f*; *Br. a.* compartiment *m* à glace; *Am. a.* frigidaire *m*; **~cold** glacé; **~cream** glace *f*; **~ cube** glaçon *m*; **~ hockey** hockey *m* sur glace.

Icelander Islandais(e *f*) *m*.

ice ...: **~ rink** patinoire *f*; **~skate** patiner, faire du patinage (sur glace); **~skating** patinage *m* (sur glace).

icicle glaçon *m*.

icing *cuis.* glaçage *m*; ✈ givrage *m*.

icy glacial.

idea idée *f*; **~l** idéal (*adj., su./m*).

identi|cal identique (à, *with*); **~fication** identification *f*; **~fy** identifier; **~kit** portrait-robot *m* (*pl.* portraits-robots); **~ty** identité *f*; **~ card** carte *f* d'identité.

ideolog|ical idéologique; **~y** idéologie *f*.

idiom idiome *m*; locution *f*, expression *f* idiomatique.

idiot 𝒳 idiot(e *f*) *m*; imbécile *mf* (*a.* F); **~ic** idiot; stupide, bête.

idle 1. paresseux; inoccupé; en chômage (*factory*); *fig.* inutile; dormant (*capital*); **~ hours** *pl.* heures *f*|*pl.* perdues; *lie* **~** ne pas marcher (*machinery etc.*); ⊙ *run* **~** marcher à vide; **2.** *v/t.* (*usu.* **~** *away*) perdre; *v/i.* fainéanter; muser;

~ness paresse *f*; oisiveté *f*; chômage *m*; *fig.* inutilité *f*; **~r** fainéant(e *f*) *m*, oisif (-ive *f*) *m*, désœuvré(e *f*) *m*.

idol idole *f*; **~atrous** idolâtre; **~ater** idolâtre *f*; **~ize** idolâtrer; adorer (à l'excès).

idyl|l(l) idylle *f*; **~llic** idyllique.

if 1. si; **~ not** sinon; *as* **~** comme si; **2.** si *m*|*inv.*; **~fy** F douteux.

ignit|e *v/t.* mettre le feu à, enflammer; *v/i.* prendre feu; **~ion** ignition *f*; ⚡, *mot.* allumage *m*; *mot.* **~ key** clef *f* de contact; *mot.* **switch on (off) the** **~** mettre (couper) le contact.

ignoble ignoble; vil, infâme.

ignominious ignominieux.

ignor|ance ignorance *f*; **~ant** ignorant (de, *of*); **~e** ne tenir aucun compte de; faire semblant or feindre de ne pas voir; méconnaître (*a fact etc.*).

ill 1. *adj.* mauvais; malade (de, *with*); *fall* (or *be taken*) **~** tomber malade; **2.** *adv.* mal; **~ at ease** mal à l'aise; **3.** *su.* mal *m*; **~advised** impolitique; malavisé (*person*); **~bred** mal élevé.

illegal illégal.

illegible illisible.

illegitimate illégitime.

ill ...: **~fated** néfaste; **~favo(u)red** laid; **~humo(u)red** de mauvaise humeur; maussade.

illiberal peu libéral.

illicit illicite; clandestin.

illiterate illettré (*person*); plein de fautes.

ill ...: **~mannered** malappris, mal élevé; **~natured** méchant; désagréable; **~ness** maladie *f*.

illogical illogique.

ill...: ~-starred malheureux; **~-tempered** de mauvaise humeur; de méchant caractère; **~-timed** mal à propos; **~-treat** maltraiter.

illuminat|e éclairer (a. fig. a question etc.); from outside: illuminate; **~d advertising** enseigne f lumineuse; **~ing** éclairant; **~ion** éclairage m; illumination f.

illus|ion illusion; **be under an ~** se faire or avoir une illusion; **~ive, ~ory** illusoire.

illustrat|e illustrer; **~ion** illustration f; **~ive** explicatif; **be ~ of** illustrer, expliquer.

illustrious illustre; célèbre.

ill will rancune f, malveillance f.

image image f; **~ry** images f/pl.

imagin|able imaginable; **~ary** imaginaire; **~ation** imagination f; **~ative** d'imagination; imaginatif (person); **~e** imaginer; s'imaginer, supposer, se figurer.

imbecile imbécile (adj., su./mf).

imbibe boire; absorber (a. fig.).

imbued: ~ with imbu de, pénétré de.

imitat|e imiter; **~ion** imitation f.

immaculate immaculé (a. rel.); impeccable.

immaterial immatériel; peu important; indifférent; négligeable.

immature pas mûr(i).

immeasurable immesurable.

immediate immédiat; **~ly 1.** adv. tout de suite, immédiatement; directement; **2.** cj. dès que.

immemorial immémorial.

immense immense; énorme.

immerse immerger, plonger; fig. **~ o.s. in** se plonger dans.

immigra|nt immigrant(e f) m, immigré(e f) m; **~te** immigrer; **~tion** immigration f.

imminent imminent, proche.

immobil|e immobile; fixe; **~ize** immobiliser.

immoderate immodéré.

immodest immodeste.

immoral immoral; **~ity** immoralité f.

immortal immortel; **~ity** immortalité f.

immovable 1. immobile, fixe; fig. immuable, inébranlable; **2. ~s** pl. biens m/pl. immeubles.

immun|e immunisé (contre **from, against**); **~ity** immunité f; **diplomatic ~** immunité f diplomatique; **~ize** immuniser (contre **from, against**).

immutable immuable; inaltérable.

imp lutin m; petit démon m.

impact choc m; impact m (a. fig.).

impair détériorer; dégrader; abimer.

impale empaler.

impalpable impalpable.

impart communiquer, transmettre.

impartial impartial; **~ity** impartialité f.

impassable infranchissable; impraticable (road).

impasse impasse f.

impassioned passionné.

impassive impassible; insensible (aux émotions).

impatien|ce impatience f; **~t** impatient.

impeach accuser (de, **of, with**); attaquer; mettre en accusation (a public official); mettre (qch.) en doute.

impeccable impeccable, irréprochable.

imped|e gêner; empêcher (de inf., **from** ger.); **~iment** obstacle m; (a. **speech ~**) défaut m d'élocution.

impending imminent.

impenetrable impénétrable.

impenitent impénitent.

imperative 1. (absolument) nécessaire, urgent; impérieux; ~ **mood = 2.** gramm. (mode m) impératif m.

imperceptible imperceptible.

imperfect 1. imparfait; défectueux; ~ **tense = 2.** gramm. (temps m) imparfait m; **~ion** imperfection f; défectuosité f.

imperial impérial; fig. majestueux; Br. légal (weights and measures); **~ism** impérialisme.

imperil mettre en péril.

imperious impérieux.

imperishable impérissable.

impermeable imperméable.

impersonal impersonnel.

impersonate imiter (q.), se faire passer pour.

impertinen|ce impertinence f; insolence f; **~t** impertinent (a. ⚡); insolent.

imperturbable imperturbable.

impervious imperméable (à, **to**); fig. insensible (à, **to**).

impetu|ous impétueux; **~s** force f, élan m, poussée f; impulsion f.

impiety impiété f.

impinge: ~ *on* affecter; empiéter sur (*rights etc.*).

impious impie.

implacable implacable.

implant implanter (dans, *in*); inculquer (à, *in*).

implement 1. instrument *m*, outil *m*; **2.** exécuter (*a contract, a promise*); accomplir.

implicat|e impliquer (dans, *in*); **~ion** implication *f*; insinuation.

implicit implicite; absolu, sans réserve (*trust fig.*).

implore implorer; supplier.

imply laisser entendre *or* supposer; suggérer.

impolite impoli.

import 1. † importation *f*; signification *f*; portée *f*; importance *f*; † ~s *pl.* importations *f*/*pl.*; **2.** † importer (*goods*); signifier; **~ance** importance *f*; **~ant** important; **~ation** importation *f*; **~er** importateur (-trice *f*) *m*.

importun|ate importun; ennuyeux; **~e** importuner; presser.

impos|e *v*/*t.* imposer (à, [*up*]*on*); *v*/*i.* ~ (*up*)*on s.o.* abuser de la bonté de q.; **~ing** imposant; grandiose; **~ition** *eccl.*, *typ.* imposition *f*; impôt *m*; *school*: pensum *m*.

impossib|ility impossibilité *f*; **~le** impossible.

impost|or, **~er** imposteur *m*; **~ure** imposture *f*.

impoten|ce impuissance *f* (*a. physiol.*); **~t** impuissant.

impoverish appauvrir.

impracticable impraticable.

impractical peu pratique.

imprecation imprécation *f*.

imprecis|e imprécis; **~ion** imprécision *f*.

impregn|able imprenable (*fortress*); *fig.* inattaquable; **~ate** ♀, ♣, *biol.* imprégner; saturer; pénétrer (*a. fig.*).

impresario impérsario *m*.

impress 1. *seal etc.*: empreinte *f*; *fig.* marque *f*; **2.** imprimer (à, *on*); inculquer (*an idea*) (à, *on*); ◎ empreindre (qch. sur qch. *s.th. on s.th.*, *s.th. with s.th.*); *fig.* impressionner; **~ion** impression *f* (*a. fig.*); ◎, *seal etc.*: empreinte *f*; *be under the ~ that* avoir l'impression que; **~ive** impressionnant.

imprint 1. imprimer (sur, *on*); **2.** empreinte *f* (*a. fig.*); *typ.* nom *m* (*of the printer*); rubrique *f* (*of the editor*).

imprison emprisonner; mettre en prison **~ment** emprisonnement *m*.

improbable improbable; invraisemblable; peu plausible.

improp|er incorrect; indécent; malséant, inconvenant; déplacé; malhonnête; **~riety** impropriété *f*; indécence *f*; inconvenance *f*.

improve *v*/*t.* améliorer; perfectionner; bonifier (*the soil*); *v*/*i.* s'améliorer; faire des progrès; ~ (*up*)*on* surpasser; **~ment** amélioration *f*; perfectionnement *m*.

improvis|ation improvisation *f*; **~e** improviser.

impruden|ce imprudence *f*; **~t** imprudent.

impuden|ce impudence *f*, insolence *f*; **~t** impudent, insolent.

impuls|e, **~ion** impulsion *f*; **~ive** impulsif.

impunity impunité *f*; *with ~* impunément.

impure impur (*a. fig.*).

imput|ation imputation *f*; **~e** imputer, attribuer.

in 1. *prp.* dans (*these circumstances, the house, the street*); en (*a word, silk, English, June*); à (*the house, the country, bed, despair, spring*); de (*this way*); par (*groups, writing*); sous (*the reign of*); chez (*Shaw*); pendant (*the daytime*); comme; ~ *England* en Angleterre; ~ *Canada* au Canada; ~ *a few words* en peu de mots; ~ *all probability* selon toute probabilité; ~ *crossing the road* en traversant la rue; *engaged ~* (*ger.*) occupé à (*inf.*); ~ *a ... voice* d'une voix ...; ~ *our time* de nos jours; *at ten* (*o'clock*) ~ *the morning* à deux heures du matin; ~ *the rain* à *or* sous la pluie; *one ~ ten* un sur dix; ~ *excuse of* comme excuse de; ~ *1970* en 1970; ~ *so far as* dans la mesure où; tant que; **2.** *adv.* dedans; au dedans; rentré; au pouvoir; *be ~* être chez soi; être élu; être au pouvoir; *be ~ for* avoir à attendre; être inscrit pour (*an examination etc.*); F *be ~ with* être en bons termes avec; **3.** *adj.* intérieur; F à la mode, dans le vent, in; **4.** *su. parl. the ~s pl.* le parti au pouvoir.

inability incapacité *f* (de, *to*).

inaccurate inexact; incorrect.

inaction inaction f.

inactive inactif; inerte (a. 🐾); **~ity** inactivité f; inertie f.

inadequate insuffisant; inadéquat (means etc.).

inadmissible inadmissible.

inadvertent inattentif; fait par mégarde; **~ly** par mégarde.

inalienable inaliénable.

inalterable immuable; inaltérable.

inane stupide, inepte; insensé.

inanimate inanimé, sans vie.

inappropriate peu approprié; déplacé, mal à propos.

inapt inapte, incapable (person); peu approprié.

inarticulate inarticulé (a. zo.); qui s'exprime mal.

inasmuch adv.: **~ as** vu que, puisque.

inattention inattention f, **~ive** inattentif; négligent.

inaudible inaudible.

inaugural inaugural; **~te** inaugurer; investir (q.) de ses fonctions; **~tion** inauguration f; investiture f; **2 Day** Am. entrée f en fonction du nouveau président des É.-U.

inborn inné.

incandescent incandescent; **~ light** lumière f à incandescence.

incapable incapable (de, of); **~citate** rendre incapable (de for, from); **~city** incapacité f (de for, to).

incarnate 1. incarner; 2. incarné.

incautious imprudent; inconsidéré.

incendiary incendiaire (adj., mf).

incense[1] encens m.

incense[2] exaspérer, irriter.

incentive encouragement m, stimulant m.

incessant incessant, continuel.

incest inceste m.

inch 1. measure: pouce m; fig. pas m; by **~es** peu à peu, petit à petit; fig. **within an ~ of** à deux doigts de; 2. (a. ~ one's way) aller (or avancer etc.) petit à petit.

incidence fréquence f.

incident incident m; épisode m; **~al** accessoire; **~ music** musique f de fond; **be ~ to** accompagner, comporter; 2. chose f fortuite.

incinerate incinérer; **~or** incinérateur m.

incise inciser; **~ion** incision f; **~ive** incisif; mordant; pénétrant; **~or** (dent f) incisive f.

incite inciter; pousser (à, to); **~ment** incitation f.

inclination inclination f (a. fig.); inclinaison f, pente f; fig. a. penchant m, tendance f.

incline 1. v/t. incliner (a. fig. à inf., to inf.); pencher; v/i. s'incliner; se pencher; fig. **~ to** (a. **be ~d to**) (inf.) être enclin à, incliner à, pencher à (inf.); **~ to(wards)** (a. **be ~d to[wards]**) (inf.) être enclin à, incliner à; pencher pour (qch.); 2. pente f, déclivité f; plan m incliné; **~d** incliné; see incline v/i.; **be well ~d towards** être bien disposé à l'égard de.

include inclure, comprendre; comporter; **~ing** (y) compris.

inclusion inclusion f; **~ve** inclus, compris; **be ~ of** comprendre, inclure; **~ terms** prix m tout compris.

incognito incognito.

incoheren[ce **~cy** incohérence f; **~t** incohérent.

income revenu m, **~ tax** impôt m sur le revenu.

incommode incommoder, gêner.

incommunica[do sans contact avec l'extérieur; **~tive** taciturne; peu communicatif.

incomparable incomparable (à to, with); sans pareil.

incompatible incompatible.

incompetent incompétent (a. ⚖️); incapable.

incomplete incomplet.

incongruous incongru; sans rapport (avec to, with).

inconsequential sans importance.

inconsidera[ble insignifiant; **~te** irréfléchi, inconsidéré; sans égards (pour, towards).

inconsisten[cy inconsistance f; incompatibilité f; **~t** inconsistant; incompatible (avec, with).

inconstant inconstant, variable.

inconvenien[ce 1 inconvénient m; 2. gêner, déranger; **~t** incommode, inopportun; gênant.

incorporate v/t. incorporer (à in[to], with; avec, with); contenir, comprendre; ⚖️ constituer en société commerciale; v/i. s'incorporer (en, in; à, avec with); 2. incorporé; faisant corps; **~ed:** **~ company** société *f* constituée, *Am.* société *f* anonyme (*abbr.* S. A.); **~ion** incorporation *f* (à, avec, dans *in*[*to*], with); ⚖ constitution *f* en société commerciale.

incorrect incorrect; inexact.

increas|e 1. augmenter; 2. augmentation *f*; croissance; **~ing** croissant; **~ingly** de plus en plus.

incredible incroyable.

incredulous incrédule.

increment augmentation *f*.

incriminate incriminer.

incrustation incrustation *f*; ⚙ entartrage *m*.

incub|ate couver (*a. fig.*, *a.* 🐛); **~ation** incubation *f* (*a. biol.*, *a.* 🐛).

inculcate inculquer (à q.; **upon s.o.**; dans l'esprit, **in the mind**).

incumbent: **be ~ on s.o.** incomber à q.

incur encourir, s'attirer; contracter (*a debt*); courir (*a risk*); faire (*expenses*).

incurable incurable.

incurious sans curiosité, indifférent.

incursion incursion *f*.

indebted endetté; redevable (de, **for**).

indecen|cy indécence *f*; **~t** indécent.

indecisi|on indécision *f*; **~ve** peu concluant (*argument etc.*); indécis (*person, a. battle*), irrésolu.

indecorous malséant; inconvenant.

indeed 1. *adv.* en effet; en vérité; à vrai dire; 2. *int.* vraiment?; (*a.* **yes, ~!**) certainement!

indefatigable infatigable, inlassable.

indefensible indéfendable.

indefinable indéfinissable.

indefinite indéfini; imprécis; **~ly in time:** indéfiniment; **postponed ~** remis à une date interminée.

indelible ineffaçable, indélébile.

indelicate grossier; indélicat; indiscret, sans tact.

indemni|fy indemniser, dédommager (de, **for**); **~ty** assurance *f*; indemnité *f*.

indent 1. denteler; *typ.* renfoncer; ♦ passer une commande pour; 2. dentelure *f*; ♦ ordre *m* d'achat; **~ation** découpage *m*; dentelure *f*; découpure *f*; empreinte *f*; bosse *f*; *typ* alinéa *m*; **~ure** 1. contrat *m* bilatéral; **~s** *pl.* contrat *m* d'apprentissage; 2. lier par contrat.

independen|ce indépendance *f* (à

l'égard de, **from**); *Am.* ♀ **Day** le 4 juillet; **~t** indépendant; **~ means** fortune *f* personnelle; **~tly** de façon indépendante; **~ of** indépendamment de.

in-depth en profondeur.

indescribable indescriptible.

indeterminate indéterminé.

index (*pl. a.* **indices**) *eccl., book:* index *m*; ⚙ **balance** *etc.*: aiguille *f*; *library etc.*: catalogue *m*; **ratio, indication:** indice *m*; A exposant *m*; **~ card** fiche *f*; **~ figure** indice *m*; **~ finger** index *m*.

Indian 1. indien; **~ corn** maïs *m*; **~ ink** encre *f* de Chine; **in ~ file** en file indienne; **~ summer** été *m* de la Saint-Martin; 2. Indien(ne) *m (f)*.

Indiarubber gomme *f* (à effacer).

indicat|e indiquer; **~ion** indication *f*; indice *m*, signe *m*; **~ive** 1. indicatif (de, **of**); **be ~ of** (dé)montrer; **~ mood** = 2. *gramm.* indicatif *m*; **~or** indicateur *m* (*a.* ⚙); *mot.* clignotant *m*.

indict accuser (de **for, on a charge of**); **~able** punissable; **~ment** accusation *f*.

indifferen|ce indifférence *f* (pour, à l'égard de **to, towards**); **~t** indifférent (à, **to**); médiocre; ⚛ neutre.

indigenous indigène; du pays.

indigent indigent; nécessiteux.

indigest|ible indigeste; **~ion** dyspepsie *f*; indigestion *f*.

indign|ant indigné (de, **at**; contre, **with**); d'indignation; **~ation** indignation *f*; **~ity** indignité *f*; affront *m*.

indirect indirect.

indis|creet indiscret; imprudent, inconsidéré; **~cretion** indiscrétion *f*; imprudence *f*; F faux pas *m*.

indiscriminate sans discernement; qui ne fait pas de distinction; aveugle; **~ly** au hasard, à tort et à travers.

indispensable indispensable.

indispos|ed indisposé; *fig.* peu disposé (à *inf.*, **to** *inf.*); **~ition** indisposition *f*, malaise *m*.

indisputable incontestable, indiscutable; hors de controverse.

indistinct indistinct, vague.

indistinguishable indistinguible; imperceptible, insaisissable (*difference etc.*).

individual 1. individuel; particulier; 2. individu *m*; **~ist** individualiste *mf*; **~ity** individualité *f*.

indivisible indivisible; ⊕ insécable.

indoctrinat|e endoctriner; ~ion endoctrination f.

indolen|ce indolence f; paresse f; ~t indolent; paresseux.

indomitable indomptable.

indoor de maison; d'intérieur; intérieur; sp. (pratiqué) en salle; ~ **aerial** antenne f d'appartement; ~ **plant** plante f d'appartement; ~ **swimming pool** piscine f couverte; ~s à la maison.

indorse etc. see **endorse**.

induce persuader, décider (à faire, **to do**), provoquer (an effect etc.), amener; phls., ⨍ induire; ~ment encouragement m; motif m.

induct établir (q.) dans ses fonctions, installer; ~ance ⨍ inductance f; ~ion installation f; ⊕, phls., phys. induction f.

indulge v/t. céder à; céder aux désirs de (q.), gâter (q.); v/i.: ~ **in** se permettre; s'adonner à; ~nce indulgence f; satisfaction; gâterie f, faiblesse f, abandon m (à, **in**); ~nt indulgent (envers, à, pour **to**); faible.

industri|al industriel; professionnel; de l'industrie; ~ **action** action f revendicative; ~ **art** art m mécanique; ~ **court** tribunal m industriel; ~ **disease** maladie f professionnelle; ~ **espionage** espionnage m industriel; ~ **estate**, ~ **park** zone f industrielle; ~ **tribunal** conseil m de prud'hommes; ~ **school** école f des arts et métiers; ~alist industriel m, industrialiste m; ~alize industrialiser; ~ous travailleur, assidu.

industry industrie f; assiduité f au travail.

inebriate enivrer; ~d ivre.

ineffable ineffable, indicible.

ineffective, ~ual inefficace.

inefficien|cy inefficacité f; ~t inefficace.

inelegant sans élégance; inélégant.

ineligible inéligible; fig. peu acceptable; **be** ~ **for** ne pas avoir droit à.

inept inepte; déplacé; mal à propos.

inequality inégalité f.

inequitable inéquitable.

inert inerte; ~ia, ~ness inertie f.

inescapable inévitable, inéluctable.

inevitable inévitable.

inexcusable inexcusable.

inexhaustible inépuisable.

inexorable inexorable.

inexpedient inopportun, malavisé.

inexpensive bon marché; peu coûteux; pas cher.

inexperience inexpérience f; ~d inexpérimenté, sans expérience.

inexpert inexpert; maladroit.

inexpressible inexprimable.

inexpressive sans expression.

inextinguishable inextinguible.

inextricable inextricable.

infallible infaillible; sûr.

infam|ous infâme; abominable; mal famé; ~y infamie f.

infan|cy petite or première enfance f, bas âge m; ⚖ minorité f; fig. (still) **in it's** ~ (encore) dans l'enfance; ~t **1.** enfant mf; ⚖ mineur(e f) m; ~ **school** école f maternelle; **2.** d'enfance; enfantin.

infantile infantile.

infantry ✕ infanterie f.

infatuat|ed entiché, engoué (de, **with**); ~ion toquade f, engouement m.

infect infecter; ⚕ contaminer; fig. corrompre; ~ion ⚕ f, fig. infection f; contamination f; ~ious ⚕ infectieux; fig. contagieux.

infer inférer, conclure; ~ence inférence f, conclusion f.

inferior 1. inférieur (à, **to**); **2.** inférieur m; subordonné(e f) m; ~ity infériorité f (par rapport à, **to**); ~ **complex** complexe m d'infériorité.

infernal infernal; Γ ~ly terriblement.

infertile stérile.

infest infester (de, **with**) (fig.).

infidel infidèle; ~ity infidélité f.

infighting guerre f intestine.

infiltrat|e v/i. s'infiltrer; v/t. s'infiltrer dans; faire (persons) s'infiltrer (dans, **into**); ~ion infiltration f.

infinite infini; ~ive (a. ~ **mood**) gramm. infinitif m.

infirm infirme; ~ary infirmerie f; hôpital m; ~ity infirmité f.

inflame (s')enflammer.

inflamma|ble inflammable; ~tion inflammation f; ~tory incendiaire (a. fig.); ⚕ inflammatoire.

inflat|e gonfler (a. fig.); ✝ faire monter, hausser (prices); ~ed gonflé (a. fig.); fig. a. enflé, exagéré; ~ion gonflement m; ⚕, ✝ inflation f; ~ionary ✝ inflationniste.

inflect fléchir; moduler (*one's voice*); *gramm.* conjuguer (*a verb*), décliner (*a noun*).

inflexi|ble inflexible (*a. fig.*); **~on** inflexion *f*; *voice*: modulation *f*; *gramm.* flexion *f*.

inflict infliger (à, *on*); **~ion** infliction *f*; affliction *f*.

influen|ce 1. influence *f*; **under the ~ of** sous l'effet de; **under the ~ of drink** en état d'ébriété; F **under the ~** paf, ivre; **2.** influencer; influer sur; **~tial** influent.

influenza ✻ grippe *f*.

influx affluence *f*, entrée *f*; *fig.* invasion *f*, inondation *f*.

inform *v/t.* informer (de, *of*); renseigner (sur, *about*); avertir; mettre au courant; **keep s.o. ~ed** tenir q. au courant (de, *of*); *v/i.* dénoncer (q., **against** *or* **on s.o.**); **~al** simple; sans cérémonie; non-officiel; **~ality** simplicité *f*; absence *f* de cérémonie; **~ation** renseignements *m/pl.*, informations *f/pl.*; instruction *f*; ⚖ dénonciation *f* (contre, **against**, **on**); **~ film** documentaire *m*; **~ science** informatique *f*; **~ative** instructif; **~er** dénonciateur (-trice *f*) *m*, F mouchard *m*.

infra dig F au-dessous de la dignité (de q.), deshonorant.

infrared infrarouge.

infrastructure infrastructure *f*.

infringe enfreindre (*a law etc.*); contrefaire (*a patent*); **~ upon** empiéter sur.

infuriate rendre furieux; **~ing** exaspérant.

infuse infuser.

ingen|ious ingénieux; **~uity** ingéniosité *f*; **~uous** ingénu, naïf.

ingot lingot *m*.

ingratiate: **~ o.s.** s'insinuer (dans les bonnes grâces de, **with**).

ingratitude ingratitude *f*.

ingredient ingrédient *m*.

ingress entrée *f*; droit *m* d'accès.

inhabit habiter; **~able** habitable; **~ant** habitant(e *f*) *m*.

inhal|ation inhalation *f*; **~e** *v/t.* inhaler; aspirer; respirer; *v/i.* avaler la fumée (*smoker*).

inherent inhérent, propre (à, *in*).

inherit hériter (de) (*qch.*); *fig. a.* tenir (de, *from*); **~ance** succession *f*; héritage *m*; *biol.* hérédité *f*.

inhibit empêcher (q. de, *s.o. from*); *psych.* inhiber; **~ing** gênant; **~ion** défense *f* expresse; *psych.* inhibition *f*.

inhospitable inhospitalier.

inhuman inhumain; barbare; **~e** inhumain, cruel.

inimical (à, *to*) hostile; défavorable.

inimitable inimitable.

initia|l 1. initial; premier; de début; **2.** *letter*: initiale *f*; **~s** *pl. signature*: parafe *m*; **3.** parafer (*a document etc.*); **~lly** au début; **~te 1.** initié(e *f*) (*a. su.*); **2.** lancer (*a plan etc.*), entreprendre; inaugurer; initier (à, *into*); **~tion** initiation *f*; **~tive** initiative *f*; **on one's own ~** de sa propre initiative; **~tor** initiateur (-trice *f*) *m*.

inject injecter; ✻ faire une piqûre à; **~ion** injection *f*; ✻ *a.* piqûre *f*.

injudicious malavisé, peu judicieux.

injunction injonction *f*, ordre *m*.

injur|e blesser; faire du mal à, faire du tort à; endommager; **~ious** nuisible; **~y** blessure *f*, lésion *f*; tort *m*; mal *m*; dommage *m*.

injustice injustice *f*.

ink encre *f*.

inkling soupçon *m*, (vague) idée *f*.

ink ...: **~pot** encrier *m*; **~y** taché d'encre.

inlaid (de, **with**) *metal, mother-of-pearl etc.*: incrusté, *wood, ivory*: marqueté; **~ work** incrustation *f*; marqueterie *f*.

inland 1. du pays, intérieur (*commerce etc.*); ♀ **Revenue** le fisc *m*; **2.** intérieur *m*; **3.** à l'intérieur.

in-laws *pl.* beaux-parents *m/pl.*; parents *m/pl.* par alliance.

inlet *geog.* bras *m* de mer, crique *f*; ⊙ arrivée *f*, admission *f*.

inmate habitant(e *f*) *m*, occupant(e *f*) *m*; *asylum*: interné(e *f*) *m*; *prison*: détenu(e *f*) *m*.

inmost le plus profond.

inn auberge *f*; *town*: hôtellerie *f*.

innate inné.

inner intérieur; interne; intime (*emotions etc.*); ⊙ **~ tube** chambre *f* à air; **~most** le plus profond *or* intime.

innervate *physiol.* innerver.

innings *pl. or sg. sp.* tour *m* de batte.

innkeeper aubergiste *mf*; hôtelier *m*.

innocen|ce innocence *f*; **~t** innocent (de, *of*).

innocuous inoffensif.

innovation innovation *f.*

innuendo insinuation *f.;* allusion *f.*

innunmerable innombrable.

inoperative inopérant.

inopportune inopportun.

inordinate démesuré.

in-patient malade *fm* hospitalisé(e).

input 1. ⚙ *etc.* énergie *f etc.* (fournie); *computer:* données *f/pl.; fig.* apport *m;* **2.** introduire, mettre.

inquest 🏛 enquête *f* (sur, **on**); *coroner's* ~ enquête *f* judiciaire après mort d'homme.

inquir|e demander (qch., *for s.th.*); se renseigner (*sur about, after*); ~ *into* faire des recherches *or* une enquête sur; ~*ing* curieux; interrogateur; ~*y* enquête *f;* demande *f* de renseignements; *make inquiries* prendre des renseignements (sur *about,* on); ~ *desk,* ~ *office* bureau *m* de renseignements.

inquisit|ion investigation *f;* ~*ive* questionneur; curieux.

inroad ✗ incursion *f; fig.* empiétement *m; fig. make* ~*s on* (*or into*) empiéter sur (*privileges etc.*); entamer (*savings, health etc.*); porter atteinte à (*s.o.'s renown etc.*).

insane fou; ⚕ aliéné.

insanitary insalubre.

insanity folie *f;* ⚕ aliénation *f* mentale.

insatiable insatiable (de, **of**).

inscribe inscrire; dédicacer (à, **to**) (*a book*).

inscription inscription *f* (✝ au grand livre); dédicace *f.*

inscrutable impénétrable.

insect insecte *m;* ~*icide* insecticide *m.*

insecure peu sûr; incertain.

insens|ate insensé; insensible (*matter*); ~*ible* insensible (à **of, to**); sans connaissance, évanoui; ~*itive* insensible (à, **to**).

insert 1. *usu.* insérer (dans, *in*[**to**]); introduire; **2.** insertion *f;* encart *m* (*in book*); ~*ion* insertion *f;* introduction *f.*

inshore 1. *adj.* côtier; **2.** *adv.* vers *or* près de la côte.

inside 1. *su.* intérieur *m;* F ~*s pl.* ventre *m;* **2.** *adj.* (d')intérieur; interne; **3.** *adv.* à l'intérieur, (en) dedans; **4.** *prp.* à l'intérieur de.

insidious insidieux.

insight perspicacité *f; glimpse:* aperçu *m.*

insignificant insignifiant.

insignia *pl.* insignes *m/pl.*

insincere peu sincère; faux.

insinuat|e insinuer; ~*ion* insinuation *f.*

insipid insipide, fade.

insist: ~ (*up*)*on* insister sur; ~ **on** (*ger.*) insister pour (*inf.*); ~ *that* insister pour que (*sbj.*); maintenir que; ~*ence* insistance *f;* ~*ent* instant.

insolent insolent.

insolvent insolvable; en faillite.

insomnia insomnie *f.*

insomuch: ~ *that* au point que; tellement que; ~ *as* d'autant que.

inspect inspecter; contrôler; ~*ion* inspection *f;* contrôle *m;* ~*or* inspecteur *m;* contrôleur *m.*

inspir|ation inspiration *f;* ~*e* inspirer; ~ *inspirant.*

install installer, ~*ation* installation *f*

instal(l)ment ✝ versement *m* partiel, acompte *m;* *fig.* épisode *f* (*of a story etc.*); *buy s.th. on the* ~ *plan* acheter qch. à tempérament.

instance cas *m,* circonstance *f;* exemple *m, for* ~ par exemple.

instant 1. instant *m,* moment *m; in an* ~ tout de suite; **2.** instantané; urgent; ~*aneous* instantané; ~*ly* immédiatement, aussitôt.

instead au lieu de cela; ~ *of* (*ger.*) au lieu de (*inf.*); ~ *of s.o.* (*or s.th.*) à la place de q. (*or* qch.).

instep cou-de-pied (*pl.* cous-de-pied) *m; shoe:* cambrure *f.*

instigat|e inciter (à, **to**); provoquer; entreprendre, commencer; entamer (*proceedings*); ~*ion* instigation *f;* ~*or* instigateur (-trice *f*) *m;* auteur *m* (*of a revolt*).

instil(l) inculquer (à, *into*), inspirer (à, *into*).

instinct instinct *m;* ~*ive* instinctif.

institut|e 1. institut *m;* **2.** instituer; 🏛 intenter (*an action*); ~*ion* institution *f;* établissement *m;* ⚕ hôpital *m* psychiatrique; ~*ionalize* institutionnaliser; mettre (*q.*) dans un établissement *or* hôpital.

instruct instruire; donner des ordres à (*q.*), charger (de, **to**); ~*ion* instruction *f;* ordre *m;* ~*s pl. a.* directives *f/pl.,* ⚙ *etc.* indications; ~*s pl. for use* mode *m* d'emploi; ~*ive* instructif; ~*or* moniteur

J

m, professeur *m*; *Am.* chargé *m* de cours.

instrument instrument *m*; ⚙ ~ *panel* tableau *m* de bord; ~al instrumental; *be* ~ *in* contribuer à (*qch. or inf.*).

insubordinate insubordonné.

insufferable insupportable.

insula|r insulaire; *fig.* borné; ~te ⚡, *a. fig.* isoler; *insulating tape* ruban *m* isolant; ~tion isolement *m*; ~tor *phys.* isolant *m*.

insulin insuline *f*.

insuperable insurmontable.

insult 1. insulte *f*, affront *m*; **2.** insulter.

insur|ance assurance *f*; *attr.* d'assurance; ~ *fraud* escroquerie *f* à l'assurance; ~e (faire) assurer; *fig. a.* garantir.

insurgent insurgé *m*. (*a. su.*).

insurmountable insurmontable.

insurrection insurrection *f*, soulèvement *m*.

intact intact.

intake ⚙ adduction *f*, admission *f*, *water etc.*: prise *f*; *food*: consommation *f*.

intangible intangible; ✝ immatériel (*assets*).

integr|al intégrant; intégral, entier; ~rate (s') intégrer; ~rity intégrité *f*; probité *f*; totalité *f*.

intellect intellect *m*; intelligence *f*; ~ual intellectuel (*adj., mf*).

intellig|ence intelligence *f*; informations *f/pl.*; ~ *department* service *m* des renseignements; ~ent intelligent; ~ible intelligible.

intempera|nce intempérance *f*; alcoolisme *m*; ~te immodéré, intempérant; adonné à la boisson.

intend: ~ *for* destiner à; ~ *to* (*inf.*) avoir l'intention de (*inf.*), compter (*inf.*); ~ed **1.** projeté (*enterprise*); voulu (*effect*); intentionnel; **2.** prétendu(e *f*) *m*, futur(e *f*) *m*.

intense intense; vif (*a. colour*); fort.

intensi|fy (s')intensifier; ~ty intensité *f*; ~ve intensif; ⚕ ~ *care unit* service *m* de réanimation *or* de soins intensifs.

intent 1. intention *f*; dessein *m*; *to all* ~s (*and purposes*) pratiquement, à peu près; **2.** attentif; absorbé (par, *on one's work etc.*); fixe (*look*); *be* ~ *on* (*ger.*) être (bien) décidé à (*inf.*); ~ion intention *f*; dessein *m*; but *m*; ~ional voulu,

intentionnel; ~ness application *f*; attention *f* soutenue.

inter enterrer, ensevelir.

inter... entre-; inter-.

interact agir l'un sur l'autre; ~ion interaction *f*.

intercede intercéder.

intercept intercepter (*a letter, a ship, a message*); prendre *or* arrêter au passage; ~ion interception *f*.

intercession intercession *f*.

interchange 1. échanger; mettre à la place l'un de l'autre; changer de place; **2.** échange *m*; alternance *f*; *mot.* échangeur *m*.

intercom interphone *m*.

intercourse rapports *m/pl.*

interest 1. intérêt *m*; ✝ intérêt(s) *m* (*pl.*); *take an* ~ *in* s'intéresser à; **2.** intéresser; *be* ~ed *in* s'intéresser à; ~-free sans intérêts; ~ing intéressant.

interfere se mêler (de *in, between*); ~ *with* gêner; déranger; toucher à, tripoter (*qch., q.*); contrecarrer (*projects etc.*); ~nce intrusion *f*, ingérence *f*; *radio:* interférence *f*.

interim 1. *su.* intérim *m*; *in the* ~ en attendant, entretemps; **2.** *adj.* intérimaire, provisoire.

interior 1. (de l')intérieur; *fig.* intime; **2.** intérieur *m*; ~ *decorator* artiste *mf* décorateur.

interject interrompre; faire (*a remark*); ~ion interjection *f*.

interlace (s')entrelacer.

interlock (s')enclencher.

interlocutor interlocuteur *m*.

interloper intrus(e *f*) *m*.

interlude intermède *m*.

intermarriage intermariage *m*.

intermediary intermédiaire *mf*.

intermediate intermédiaire; moyen (*course, school etc.*); ✈ ~ *landing* escale *f*; ~range ballistic missile fusée *f* de portée moyenne; *Am.* ~ *school* école *f* secondaire.

interment enterrement *m*.

interminable interminable.

intermingle (s')entremêler.

intermission pause, interruption *f*; *thea.* entracte *m*.

intermittent intermittent; ~ly par intervalles.

intern interner.

intern(e) *hospital*: interne *m*.

internal interne; intérieur; intestin (*war, quarrel etc.*); **~ combustion engine** moteur *m* à combustion interne; **2 Revenue** le fisc *m*.

international international.

interplay effet *m* réciproque; interaction *f*.

interpolate interpoler; intercaler.

interpose *v/t.* interposer; faire (*an observation*); *v/i.* intervenir.

interpret interpréter; **~ation** interprétation *f*; **~er** interprète *mf*.

interrelat|ed en rapport (l'un de l'autre), en corrélation, **~ion** rapport *m*, corrélation *f*.

interrogat|e interroger; **~ion** interrogation *f*; *police*: interrogatoire *m*; **note** (*or* **mark** *or* **point**) **of ~** point *m* d'interrogation; **~ive 1.** interrogateur; *gramm.* interrogatif; **2.** *gramm.* pronom *m* interrogatif.

interrupt interrompre; **~ion** interruption *f*.

intersect (s')(entre)couper, (s')(entre)croiser; **~ion** intersection *f*; *roads*: carrefour *m*.

intersperse parsemer (de, **with**).

interstate *Am.* entre États.

intertwine (s')entrelacer.

interval intervalle *m* (*a. of time, a.* ♪); *sp.* mi-temps *m*; *thea.* entracte *m*; *school*: récréation *f*; *weather*: **bright ~s** *pl.* éclaircies *f/pl.*

interven|e intervenir; s'écouler (*years*); survenir; **~tion** intervention *f*.

interview 1. entrevue *f*; *journ.* interview *f*; **2.** avoir une entrevue avec; *journ.* interviewer; **~ee** personne *f* interviewée, interviewé(e *f*) *m*; **~er** interviewe(u)r *m*.

interweave (s')entrelacer; *fig. a.* (s')entremêler.

intestine intestin (*a. su./m.*).

intima|cy intimité *f*; **~te 1.** faire savoir, laisser entendre; suggérer; **2.** intime; *fig.* approfondi; **3.** intime *mf*; **~tion** avis *m*, annonce *f*, suggestion *f*.

intimidat|e intimider; **~ion** intimidation *f*.

into *prp.* dans, en; à; entre (*s.o.'s hands*).

intolera|ble intolérable, insupportable; **~nt** intolérant.

intonation intonation *f*.

intoxica|nt 1. enivrant; **2.** boisson *f* alcoolique; **~te** enivrer; *fig.* enivrement *m*; **♣ poison**: intoxication *f*.

intractable intraitable; obstiné; difficile (*task*); insoluble (*problem*).

intramuscular **♣** intramusculaire.

intransitive intransitif.

intravenous **♣** intraveineux.

intrepid intrépide.

intrica|cy complication *f*, complexité *f*; **~te** compliqué, complexe, embrouillé.

intrigu|e 1. intrigue *f*; **2.** intriguer; **~er** intrigant(e *f*) *m*; **~ing** fascinant.

intrinsic(al) intrinsèque.

introduc|e introduire, faire entrer; présenter (q. à q., **s.o. to s.o.**; *a. parl. a bill*); initier (q. à qch., **s.o. to s.th.**); **~tion** introduction *f*; *person*: présentation *f*; **~tory** préliminaire; de recommandation (*letter*); **♣ ~ price** prix *m* de lancement.

introspect|ion introspection *f*; **~ive** introspectif.

introvert 1. **♣** retourner, introvertir; **2.** introverti(e *f*) *m*.

intru|de *v/t.* introduire de force (dans, **into**); imposer (à, [*up*]**on**); *v/i.* faire intrusion (auprès de, [*up*]**on**); être importun; s'imposer; **~ into** (*or* [*up*]**on**) *a.* s'immiscer dans; déranger; **am I intruding?** est-ce que je dérange?; **~der** intrus(e *f*) *m*; importun(e *f*) *m*; **~sion** intrusion *f*, empiétement *m*; **~sive** importun.

intrust see **entrust**.

intuit savoir intuitivement; **~ion** intuition *f*; **~ive** intuitif.

inundate inonder (de, **with**).

inure habituer (à, **to**).

invade envahir; **~r** envahisseur *m*.

invalid¹ invalide; nul.

invalid² 1. malade (*adj.*, *mf*); infirme (*adj.*, *mf*); **2.** invalide *m*.

invalidate rendre nul, invalider; **♣** casser (*a sentence*).

invaluable inestimable.

invasion invasion *f*.

invective invective *f*.

inveigh: ~ against fulminer contre, maudire (*qch.*).

inveigle séduire; attirer (dans, **into**).

invent inventer; **~ion** invention *f*; **~ive** inventif; **~iveness** esprit *m* inventif;

esprit *m* d'invention; imagination *f*; ~or inventeur (-trice *f*) *m*; ~ory inventaire *m*.

invers|e inverse (*adj.*, *su./m*); ~ion renversement *m*; *gramm. etc.* inversion *f*.

invert renverser; invertir; ~ed commas *pl.* guillemets *m/pl.*

invest *v/t.* ✝ investir *or* placer (*money*) (dans, **in**); *fig.* ~ with investir *or* revêtir de; *v/i.* ✝ placer de l'argent (dans, **in**).

investigat|e examiner, étudier, rechercher; enquêter sur (*a crime etc.*); investigating committee commission *f* d'enquête; ~ion investigation *f*, recherches *f/pl.*; *crime etc.*: enquête *f*; ~or investigateur (-trice *f*) *m*.

invest|ment ✝ investissement *m*, placement *m*; ~or investisseur (-euse *f*) *m*.

inveterate invétéré.

invidious désobligeant (*person*); désagréable.

invigorate fortifier, donner de la vigueur à.

invincible invincible.

inviola|ble inviolable; ~te inviolé.

invit|ation invitation *f*; ~e inviter (q. à *inf.*, **s.o. to** *inf.*); *fig.* demander, appeler, solliciter (*qch.*).

invoice ✝ facture *f*.

invoke invoquer.

involve entraîner, nécessiter (*qch.*); impliquer (*q.*) (dans, **in**); ~ **s.o. in s.th.** *a.* mêler q. à qch.; ~d impliqué; concerné, engagé(*person*); en jeu (*factor etc.*); *fig.* compliqué, contourné; *be* ~ *with* **s.o.** avoir des rapports avec q.; ~ment implication *f*, participation *f*.

invulnerable invulnérable.

inward 1. *adj.* (dirigé vers l') intérieur; interne; 2. *adv.* (*usu.* ~s) vers l'intérieur; ~ly *fig.* en son for intérieur.

I O U (*abbr. of* **I owe you**) reconnaissance *f* de dette.

irascible irascible; colérique.

irate en colère, furieux.

iridescent irisé, chatoyant.

iris ♀, *anat.*, *cin.*, *opt.* iris *m*.

Irish 1. irlandais; d'Irlande; 2. *ling.* irlandais *m*; *the* ~ les Irlandais *m/pl.*; ~man Irlandais *m*; ~woman Irlandaise *f*.

irk ennuyer; ~some ennuyeux.

iron 1. fer *m*; **cast** ~ fonte *f*; ~s *pl.* fers *m/pl.*; 2. de fer (*a. fig.*); en fer; *pol.* ☾ **Curtain** le rideau *m* de fer; 3. repasser;

~ **out** faire disparaître (*wrinkles, fig. difficulties etc.*); ~clad cuirassé; *fig.* inflexible.

ironic(al) ironique.

ironing repassage *m*; ~ **board** planche *f* à repasser.

iron...: ~monger quincaillier (-ère *f*) *m*; ~mongery quincaillerie *f*; ~work construction *f* en fer; serrurerie *f*; ~s *usu. sg.* usine *f* de sidérurgie.

irony ironie *f*.

irradiant rayonnant (de, **with**).

irradiate irradier; *v/t. a.* éclairer; illuminer.

irrational irrationnel, déraisonnable, absurde.

irreconcilable irréconciliable; *fig.* inconciliable, incompatible (avec, **with**).

irredeemable irréparable, irrémédiable.

irrefutable irréfutable.

irregular irrégulier.

irrelevant hors de propos; sans rapport avec le problème.

irreligious irréligieux.

irremediable irrémédiable.

irremovable immuable.

irreparable irréparable.

irrepressible irrésistible; irrépressible.

irreproachable irréprochable.

irresistible irrésistible.

irresolute irrésolu, indécis.

irrespective (**of**) indépendant (de); *adv.* sans tenir compte (de).

irresponsible étourdi, irréfléchi; ⚖ irresponsable.

irretrievable irréparable, irrémédiable.

irreverent irrévérencieux.

irrevocable irrévocable.

irrig|ate irriguer; ~ion irrigation *f*.

irrita|ble irritable; ~nt irritant *m*; ~te irriter; ~ting irritant; ~tion irritation *f*.

irruption irruption *f*.

island île *f*; (*a. traffic* ~) refuge *m*; ~er insulaire *mf*.

isle île *f*; ~t îlot *m*.

isola|te isoler; *fig.* ~d case cas *m* isolé; ~tion isolement *m*; ~ hospital hôpital *m* de contagieux.

issue 1. sortie *f*; problème *m*, question *f*, enjeu *m*; résultat *m*; distribution *f* (*of goods etc.*); ✝ émission *f* (*of banknotes etc.*); publication *f* (*of a book*; *a.* ✗, ♫ *of orders*); *newspaper:* édition *f*; *be at* ~

être en débat (sur, **on**); être en question; **2.** *v/i.* provenir (de, *from*); *v/t.* publier (*a. books*); distribuer (qch. à q., **s.o. with s.th.**); donner (*an order*); ⚓ émettre (*banknotes*).

isthmus isthme *m.*

it 1. *pron.* il, *stressed:* lui; elle (*a. stressed*); ce, *stressed:* cela; *direct object:* le, la; *indirect object:* lui; **of** (*or from*) ~ en; **to** (*or at*) ~ y; *sl.* **go** ~! vas-y!; allez-y!; **2.** *su.* F quelque chose.

Italien 1. italien; **2.** *ling.* italien *m*; Italien(ne *f*) *m.*

italics *typ.* italiques *m/pl.*

itch 1. démangeaison *f* (*a. fig.*, de *inf.*, to *inf.*); **2.** démanger; *person:* éprouver des démangeaisons; *fig.* avoir une démangeaison (de *inf.*, **to** *inf.*); **I am**

~ing to (*inf.*) *a.* ça me démange de (*inf.*); **~ing** démangeaison *f* (*a. fig.*); **~y** qui démange.

item article *m*, objet *m*; *on agenda:* point *m*, détail *m*, question *f*; **news** ~ nouvelle *f*; **~ize** spécifier, détailler.

iterate réitérer.

itiner|ant itinérant, ambulant; **~ary** itinéraire *m.*

its son, sa; ses.

itself lui-même, elle-même; *rfl.* se, *stressed:* soi; **of** ~ tout seul; de lui-même, d'elle-même; **in** ~ en lui-même *etc.*; en soi, de soi; **by** ~ à part; tout seul.

ivory 1. ivoire *m*; F **tickle the ivories** jouer du piano; **2.** en ivoire; d'ivoire; ~ **tower** tour *f* d'ivoire.

ivy ♣ lierre *m.*

J

jab F **1.** enfoncer (dans, **in**[**to**]); donner un coup de (qch.) (à, **at**); *box.* lancer un coup sec à; **2.** coup *m* (de pointe); *box.* coup *m* sec; F 🪡 piqûre *f.*

jabber baragouiner.

jack 1. *cards:* valet *m*; *mot.* cric *m*; *bowling:* cochonnet *m*; F **every man** ~ chacun, tout le monde; **2.** ~ **up** soulever (au cric).

jackal *zo.* chacal (*pl.* -als) *m.*

jack...: ~**ass** baudet *m*; imbécile *m*; ~**boot** bottes *f/pl.* à l'écuyère; *fig.* régime *m* autoritaire; ~**daw** *orn.* choucas *m.*

jacket *man:* veston *m*; *woman:* jaquette *f*; veste *f*, ⊗ chemise *f*; *book:* couverture *f.*

jack...: ~**knife** couteau *m* de poche; 2 **of all trades** factotum *m*; ~**pot** gros lot *m*; *poker:* pot *m.*

jade¹ *precious stone:* jade *m.*

jade² rosse *f*, haridelle *f*, *pej.* drôlesse *f*; ~**d** épuisé; fatigué (de, **with**).

jag F bombe *f*, noce *f*; ~**ged** ébréché; *sl.* soûl.

jail 1. prison *f*; **2.** mettre en prison; ~**bird** F gibier *m* de potence; ~ **break** évasion *f* de prison; ~**er** gardien *m* de prison.

jalop(p)y *mot.* F (vieux) tacot *m.*

jam¹ confiture *f.*

jam² 1. presse *f*, foule *f*; encombrement *m*, ⊗ arrêt *m* (de fonctionnement); *radio:* brouillage *m*; **traffic** ~ embouteillage *m*; *sl.* **be in a** ~ être dans le pétrin; **2.** *v/t.* serrer, presser; fourrer *or* enfoncer *or* (en)tasser (de force) (dans, **into**); bloquer; ⊗ coincer; *radio:* brouiller; ~ **in** serrer; *mot.:* ~ **on the brakes**, ~ **the brakes on** freiner à bloc; *v/i.* se bloquer, se coincer.

jamboree rassemblement *m*; F bombance *f*; *boy scouts:* jamboree *m.*

jam-|full, ~**packed** plein à craquer.

jangle 1. (faire) rendre un son discordant; (faire) cliqueter; ~**d nerves** nerfs *m/pl.* en pelote; **2.** son *m* discordant; cliquetis *m.*

janitor portier *m*; *Am.* concierge *m.*

January janvier *m.*

Japanese 1. japonais; **2.** *ling.* japonais *m*; Japonais(e *f*) *m.*

jar¹ pot *m* (*for mustard etc.*); bocal *m*; récipient *m.*

jar² 1. son *m* grinçant *or* discordant; choc *m*, secousse *f*; *v/i.* grincer; *fig.* se heurter, détonner; jurer (*colours*); ~ **on** irriter, agacer; *v/t.* ébranler, secouer.

jargon jargon *m*; *pej.* charabia *m*.

jaundice jaunisse *f*; ~**d** ictérique.

jaunt balade *f*, randonnée *f*, sortie *f*; ~**y** enjoué; vif; insouciant.

javelin javeline *f*; javelot *m* (*a.* sp.).

jaw mâchoire *f*; ~**bone** os *m* maxillaire.

jay orn. geai *m*; ~**walk** traverser (la rue) sans regarder; ~**walker** piéton *m* imprudent.

jazz 1. *J* jazz *m*; F *and all that* ~ et tout le bataclan; **2.** ~ **up** animer; égayer; ~**y** voyant, tapageur.

jealous jaloux (de, *of*); ~**y** jalousie *f*.

jeer 1. huée *f*; raillerie *f*; **2.** se moquer (de, *at*), se railler (de qch., *at s.th.*); railler (q., *at s.o.*); huer.

jejune stérile, aride; *a.* maigre (*soil*).

jell *cuis.* épaissir, prendre; F *fig.* prendre forme, se réaliser.

jelly 1. gelée *f*; **2.** se prendre en gelée; ~**fish** *zo.* méduse *f*.

jeopardize mettre en péril.

jerk 1. *su.* secousse *f*, saccade *f*; **2.** *v/t.* donner une secousse à; tirer d'un coup sec; *v/i.* se mouvoir par saccades; cahoter; ~**water** F petit, de province, sans importance; ~**y** saccadé; ~**ily** par saccades.

jersey tricot *m*.

jest 1. plaisanterie *f*, *in* ~ en plaisantant; **2.** plaisanter; ~**er** *hist.* bouffon *m*.

jet 1. jet *m* (*of water etc.*); *gas:* bec *m*; gicleur *m*; avion *m* à réaction, jet *m*; ✕ ~ *fighter* chasseur *m* à réaction; ~ *lag* troubles *m/pl.* dus au décalage horaire; **2.** (faire) jaillir; ✈ voyager en jet.

jet-black (noir comme) jais *m*.

jetty ⚓ digue *f*; estacade *f*.

Jew juif *m*; *attr.* juif, des juifs.

jewel bijou *m*, joyau *m*; *watch:* rubis *m*; ~(**l**)**er** bijoutier *m*; ~(**le**)**ry** bijouterie *f*.

Jewess juive *f*; **Jewish** juif.

jibe 1. *see gibe*; **2.** *Am.* F cadrer, F coller.

jiffy F (*in a* ~ en un) clin d'œil.

jiggle *v/t.* secouer légèrement; *v/i.* sautiller.

jigsaw scie *f* à chantourner.

jilt laisser tomber (*a lover*).

Jim Crow *Am. sl.* nègre *m* (*a. attr.*); discrimination *f* (entre blancs et noirs).

jingle 1. cliquetis *m*; *bell:* tintement *m*; **2.** (faire) tinter *or* cliqueter.

jitter F **1.** frétiller (de nervosité); **2.** F *the* ~*s pl.* la frousse, le trac.

Job': ~'*s news* nouvelle *f* fatale.

job² **1.** tâche *f*, travail *m*, F boulot *m*; place *f*, emploi *m*; ~ *creation* création *f* d'emplois (nouveaux); ~ *hunting* chasse *f* à l'emploi; *a bad* ~ une mauvaise affaire; *odd* ~*s pl.* petits travaux *m/pl.*; *do a good* ~ faire du bon travail; bien faire; *on the* ~ *training* formation *f* sur le tas; **2.** *v/i.* faire des petits travaux; travailler à la tâche; ~*less* sans travail.

jockey 1. *su.* jockey *m*; **2.** *v/t.* manœuvrer; *v/i.* intriguer.

jocose facétieux; jovial; ~*ness* jocosité *f*; humeur *f* joviale.

jocular facétieux; gai.

jog 1. *su.* coup *m* léger; petit trot *m*; **2.** *v/t.* donner un coup léger à; ~ *s.o.'s memory* rafraîchir la mémoire de q.; *v/i.* (*usu.* ~ *along*, ~ *on*) trotter.

John: ~ *Bull* l'Anglais; *Am.* ~ *Hancock* (*s.o.'s*) signature *f*.

join 1. *v/t.* joindre (*a.* ⊙), (ré)unir; rejoindre, retrouver (*q.*); se joindre à; s'inscrire à, devenir membre de, adhérer à; *v/i.* s'unir, se (re)joindre (à, *with*); (*a.* ~ *together*) se réunir; ~ *battle* livrer bataille (à, *with*); ~ *hands* se donner la main; *fig.* se joindre (à, *with*); ~ *in* prendre part (à); se mettre de la partie; s'associer (à); ~ *up* s'engager dans l'armée; **2.** *su.* joint *m*.

joiner menuisier *m*; ~**y** menuiserie *f*.

joint 1. joint *m*; jointure *f*; articulation *f*; *Br. cuis.* rôti *m*; *sl.* (*place, pub etc.*) boîte *f*; *sl.* (*hash*) joint *m*; *out of* ~ disloqué (*a. fig.*); *put out of* ~ disloquer; **2.** (en) commun; combiné; collectif; co-; ~ *ownership* copropriété *f*; ~*ly* en commun; ~*-stock:* ~ *company* société *f* par actions.

jok|**e 1.** *su.* plaisanterie *f*; (*a.* *practical* ~) tour *m*, farce *f*; *play a* ~ *on* jouer un tour à; **2.** plaisanter; ~*er* farceur (-euse *f*) *m*; *cards:* joker *m*; F type *m*; ~*y* facétieux.

jolly 1. gai, joyeux; **2.** drôlement.

jolt 1. cahoter; **2.** cahot *m*, secousse *f*.

josh *Am.* F **1.** blague *f*; **2.** blaguer.

joss stick bâton *m* d'encens.

jostle 1. *v/t.* coudoyer; *v/i.* jouer des coudes; **2.** *su.* bousculade *f*.

jot 1.: *not a* ~ *of* pas un grain *or* brin de;

2. ~ **down** prendre note de; ~**ter** bloc-notes m (*pl.* blocs-notes).

journal journal m; ~**ism** journalisme m; ~**ist** journaliste mf.

journey 1. voyage m; trajet m; parcours m; **2.** voyager; ~**man** compagnon m, ouvrier m.

jovial jovial.

joy joie f; ~**ful** joyeux; ~**less** triste, sans joie; ~**ous** joyeux.

jubila|nt débordant de joie; exultant; ~**tion** jubilation, exultation f.

judge 1. su. juge m; **2.** v/i. juger.

judg(e)ment jugement m; décision f judiciaire; *fig.* avis m; *fig.* discernement m; **sit in** ~ **on** juger; *eccl.* ~**day** jugement m dernier.

judicature judicature f; (cour f de) justice f; *coll.* magistrature f.

judicial judiciaire; *fig.* impartial.

judicious judicieux, sensé.

jug cruche f; pot m; *sl.* prison f.

juggernaut monstre m; *truck etc.*: mastodonte m.

juggle 1. jonglerie f; **2.** jongler (avec) (*a. fig.*); ~**r** jongleur (-euse f) m.

Jugoslav 1. Yougoslave mf; **2.** yougoslave.

juice jus m (*a. mot. sl., a. ⚡ F*).

jukebox juke-box m.

July juillet m.

jumble 1. méli-mélo (*pl.* mélis-mélos) m; fatras m; **2.** ~ brouiller.

jumbo (*a.* ~**sized**) géant, énorme; ~**jet** jumbo-jet m, gros-porteur m.

jump 1. su. saut m (*a. sp.*); bond m; sursaut m; F **get** (**have**) **the** ~ **on** devancer; **2.** v/i. sauter, bondir; sursauter; ~ **at** *fig.* sauter sur; ~ **off** sauter (de); ~**ing-off point** (*or* **place**) (point m de) départ m; ~ **on** (**to**) sauter sur; sauter dans (*a bus etc.*); *fig.* ~ **on** attaquer; prendre à partie; disputer (q.); ~ **to conclusions** conclure à la légère, juger trop vite; v/t. franchir; faire sauter (*a horse*); sauter dans (*a train etc.*); sauter de, quitter; ~ **the gun** *sp.* partir avant le départ; *fig.* (*r.*)agir prématurément; *mot.* ~ **the lights** brûler le feu (rouge), passer au rouge; ~ **the queue** (*Am.* **the line**) passer avant son tour; 🚂 ~ **the**

rails dérailler; ~**er** sauteur m; chandail m, pull(-over) m, *Am.* robe f à bretelles; ~**seat** strapontin m; ~**y** nerveux, agité.

junct|ion jonction f; bifurcation f; *rivers*: confluent m; 🚂 gare f d'embranchement; ⚡ ~ **box** boîte f de dérivation; ~**ure** jointure f; conjoncture f.

June juin m.

jungle jungle f.

junior 1. cadet; plus jeune (que, **to**); *univ. Am.* de troisième année (*student*); *Am.* ~ **high school** moyennes classes f/pl. d'une école secondaire; ~ **partner** second associé m; *Br.* ~ **school** école f primaire; **2.** cadet(te f) m; second associé m; *Am.* élève mf de troisième année (*at a college*); F le jeune m; **he is my** ~ (**by**) il est mon cadet (de ...*ans*).

junk vieilleries f/pl.; *pej.* pacotille f; *sl.* drogue f, *sl.* came f; ⚓ jonque f; ~ **heap**, ~ **yard** dépotoir m; ~ **shop** (boutique f de) brocanteur m.

junket lait m caillé; *Am.* voyage m d'agrément aux frais du gouvernement.

junkie *sl.* drogué(e f) m, camé(e f) m.

junta junte f.

juris|diction juridiction f, ~**prudence** jurisprudence f.

juror 🏛 membre m du jury.

jury 🏛 jury m; jurés m/pl.; ~**man** membre m du jury.

just 1. *adj.* juste; **2.** *adv.* juste; précisément; absolument, tout à fait; seulement; ~ **as** au moment où; ~ **now** actuellement; tout à l'heure.

justice justice f; *person*: juge m, magistrat m; **court of** ~ tribunal m; **do** ~ **to** rendre justice à (q.).

justi|fiable justifiable; légitime; ~**fication** justification f; ~**fy** justifier.

justly avec raison; légitimement.

justness justesse f.

jut 1. (*a.* ~ **out**) être en *or* faire saillie, dépasser; **2.** saillie f.

juvenile 1. juvénile; de (la) jeunesse; pour enfants; ~ **delinquency** délinquance f juvénile; ~ **delinquent** mineur(e) délinquant(e f) m; **2.** jeune mf, adolescent(e f) m.

juxtapose juxtaposer.

K

kale chou *m* (frisé); *Am. sl.* argent *m*.

kangaroo *zo.* kangourou *m*.

kaput *sl.* fichu.

keel ⚓ quille *f*.

keen perçant (*cold, eye, wind etc.*); vif (*cold, competition etc.*); mordant (*satire*); ardent; vorace (*appetite*); **be ~ on** aimer (beaucoup) (*qch., q*); **be ~ on** (*ger.*) *or* **to** (*inf.*) avoir envie de, aimer (beaucoup), tenir à (*inf.*); **~ness** âpreté *f*; *fig.* ardeur *f*.

keep 1. *v/t. usu.* tenir (*a shop, accounts, a newspaper, a promise etc.*); *a. before adj.*); garder (*one's bed*; *qch.* pour, **for**); avoir (*a car*); (*a. ~ up*) maintenir; contenir; préserver (de, **from**); retenir (*in prison, s.o.'s attention*); suivre (*a rule*); célébrer (*a holiday*); cacher (qch. à q., **s.th. from s.o.**); **~ s.o. company** tenir compagnie à q.; **~ company with** sortir avec; **~ silence** garder le silence; **~ one's temper** se contenir; **~ time** être exact (*watch*); ♪ suivre la mesure; **~ waiting** faire attendre q.; **~ away** tenir à distance; **~ down** empêcher de monter; maintenir bas (*prices*); *fig.* retenir, réprimer (*emotions etc.*); opprimer (*people etc.*); **~ s.o. from** (*ger.*) empêcher q. de (*inf.*); **~ in** retenir; contenir (*one's anger*); mettre en retenue (*a pupil*); **~ in view** ne pas perdre de vue; **~ off** tenir à distance (de); **~ on** garder; **~ out** empêcher d'entrer; **~ up** soutenir; tenir haut; maintenir (*a price etc.*); entretenir (*a correspondence*); sauver (*appearances*); **2.** *v/i.* rester; se conserver (*food etc.*); continuer; **~ doing** ne pas cesser de faire, continuer de faire; **~ away** se tenir *or* rester à l'écart; **~ from** s'abstenir de; **~ off** se tenir à l'écart; **~ on** (*ger.*) continuer de (*inf.*); **~ out** ne pas entrer; **'~ out'** 'défense d'entrer!'; **~ to** s'en tenir à; suivre; **~ up** se maintenir; **~ up with** se maintenir au niveau de; **3.** *su.* (moyens *m/pl.* de) subsistance *f*; F **for ~s** pour de bon.

keep|er gardien(ne *f*) *m*; **~ing** garde *f*; **be in** (**out of**) **~ with** (ne pas) être en accord avec; **~sake** souvenir *m*.

keg tonnelet *m*, barillet *m*.

kennel *dog*: niche *f*; **~s** *pl.* chenil *m*.

kerb(stone) *see* **curb(stone)**.

kerchief fanchon *f*, fichu *m*.

kernel *hazel-nut etc.*: amande *f*; noyau *m* (*a. fig.*).

kettle bouilloire *f*; **~drum** ♪ timbale *f*.

key 1. clé *f*, clef *f* (*a. ♪, a. fig.*); *typewriter, piano*: touche *f*; ♪ ton *m* (*a. fig.*); **2.** *in compounds* (*most important*): ... clé, clef; **~ industry** (**position** *etc.*) industrie *f* (position *f or* poste *m*) clé; **~ money** pas *m* de porte; **~ punch** poinçonneuse *f*; **~ ring** porte-clefs *m/inv.*; ♪ **~ signature** armature *f*; **3.** ♪ accorder; **~ to** adapter à; **~ up** (sur)exciter; **~board** clavier *m*; porte-clefs *m/inv.*; **~hole** trou *m* de serrure; **~man** pivot *m*; **~note** tonique *f*; *fig.* note *f* dominante; **~stone** clef *f* de voûte.

kick 1. coup *m* de pied; *gun*: recul *m*; F énergie *f*, allant *m*; F **for ~s** pour s'amuser, pour le plaisir; F **get a ~ out of** éprouver du plaisir à; **2.** *v/t.* donner des coups *or* un coup de pied à; F congédier (*q.*); F **~ out** ficher à la porte; F **~ s.o. around** maltraiter q.; *sl.* **~ up a row** faire du chahut; *fig.* faire un scandale; *v/i.* donner un coup de pied, reculer (*gun*); ruer (*animal*); rechigner (à **against, at**); **~ around, ~ about** traîner (*quelque part*); *Am. sl.* **~ in with** contribuer (*qc.*); **~back** *esp. Am.* F réaction *f* violente; **~er** cheval *m* qui rue; *sp.* joueur *m*; *Am. sl.* rouspéteur (-euse *f*) *m*; **~off** *foot.* coup *m* d'envoi.

kid 1. chevreau *m*; F gamin(e *f*) *m*, gosse *mf*; **~ glove** gant *m* de chevreau; gant *m* glacé; **2.** *v/i. sl.* plaisanter; taquiner.

kidnap kidnapper, enlever (*esp. a. child*); **~(p)er** kidnappeur (-euse *f*) *m*.

kidney *anat.* rein *m*; *cuis.* rognon *m*; **~ bean** ♀ haricot *m* nain; ⚕ **~ machine** rein *m* artificiel.

kill tuer; *fig.* supprimer, faire échouer; **~ off** exterminer; **~er** tueur (-euse *f*) *m*; meurtrier (-ère *f*) *m*; **~ing** meurtrier, mortel; écrasant (*work etc.*); F tordant; **~joy** rabat-joie *m/inv.*

kiln four *m*; séchoir *m*, meule *f*.

kilo|gram(me) kilogramme *m*; F kilo *m*; **~metre**, *Am.* **~meter** kilomètre *m*.

kilt kilt *m*.

kin parents *m/pl.*

kind 1. bon (pour *to*); aimable (à, *of*); **2.** espèce *f*; sorte *f*; genre *m*; nature *f*; *... of a kind* du même genre, de la même sorte; F *of ...* plus ou moins, un peu; *pay in ~* payer en nature; *fig. repay s.o. in ~* rendre la pareille à qu.

kindergarten jardin *m* d'enfants; **~ teacher** jardinière *f* d'enfants.

kind-hearted bienveillant, bon.

kindle (s')allumer; (s')enflammer.

kind|ly *adj.* bienveillant, bon; avec bonté; *not take ~ to ger.* ne pas aimer que *sbj.*; *will you ~ ...* voulez-vous bien ...; **~ness** bonté *f*; bienveillance *f*; amabilité *f* (envers, *to*).

kindred 1. apparenté; **2.** parenté *f*.

king roi *m*; *draughts*: dame *f*; **~dom** royaume *m*; *esp.* ♀, *zo.* règne *m*; **~like**, **~ly** royal, de roi; **~pin** ⊙, *fig.* cheville *f* ouvrière; **~size(d)** long (*cigarettes*); très grand, géant; F à tout casser (*hangover etc.*).

kink 1. *rope etc.*: entortillement *m*, nœud *m*; *wire*: faux pli *m*; défaut *m*; *fig.* anomalie *f*; **2.** s'entortiller; **~y** crépu (*hair*); F *fig.* bizarre, excentrique.

kinship parenté *f*.

kip *sl.* **1.** roupillon *m*; **2.** roupiller.

kipper hareng *m* fumé or doux.

kiss 1. baiser *m*; **2.** (s')embrasser.

kit équipement *m*; trousse *f* (*of tools etc.*); *set*: kit *m*; **~bag** sac *m* (de voyage); ⊙ trousse *f* d'outils.

kitchen cuisine *f*, **~ garden** (jardin *m*) potager *m*; **~ sink** évier *m*; **~ette** kitchenette *f*.

kite cerf-volant (*pl.* cerfs-volants) *m*; *orn.* milan *m*; *fig.* ballon *m* d'essai.

kitten chaton *m*, petit(e *f*) chat(te *f*) *m*.

knack F *have* (*get*) *the ~ of* (*ger.*) avoir (attraper) le chic pour (*inf.*).

knapsack (havre)sac *m*.

knave fripon *m*; *cards*: valet *m*; **~ry** friponnerie *f*, fourberie *f*.

knead pétrir; travailler.

knee genou *m* (*a.* ⊙); **~cap** *anat.* rotule *f*; **~joint** articulation *f* du genou; rotule *f*; **~l** s'agenouiller.

knell glas *m*.

knickers *pl.* culotte *f* (*for women*).

knickknack babiole *f*, bibelot *m*.

knife 1. (*pl.* **~es**) couteau *m*; **2.** poignarder.

knight 1. chevalier *m*; *chess*: cavalier *m*; **2.** créer chevalier; **~hood** chevalerie *f*; titre *m* de chevalier; **~ly** chevaleresque.

knit tricoter; **~ together** (se) lier, (s') unir; se souder (*bone*); **~ the brows** froncer les sourcils; **~ting 1.** tricot *m*; *action*: tricotage *m*; **2.** à tricoter; **~needle** aiguille *f* à tricoter; **~wear** tricot *m*.

knob *drawer, door*: bouton *m*; *coal, sugar etc.*: morceau *m*; *butter*: noix *f*.

knock 1. coup *m*, choc *m*; **2.** *v/i.* frapper; taper (sur, *at*); *mot.* cogner; F se heurter (à, *against*); F **~ about**, **~ around** vagabonder, F se balader (*quelque part*) (*person*); traîner (*quelque part*) (*thing*); **~ off** (s')arrêter (de travailler); *v/t.* frapper, heurter; F dire du mal de, critiquer; **~ about** maltraiter; **~ down** abattre; renverser; *auction*: adjuger; ⊙ démonter; **~ off** faire tomber de; rabattre (*a sum from a price*); s'arrêter (de travailler), finir; **~ out** assommer; *box.* knockouter; **~over** renverser; **~er** heurtoir *m*, marteau *m* (de porte); **~kneed** cagneux; **~out** *box.* (*a. ~ blow*) knock-out *m*; *sl.* chose *f* or personne *f* épatante.

knoll tertre *m*, butte *f*.

knot 1. nœud *m*; **2.** (se) nouer; **~ty** noueux; *fig.* difficile, épineux.

know 1. savoir (*a fact*); connaître (*q., a place*); reconnaître; *come to ~* apprendre; **2.** F *be in the ~* être au courant (de l'affaire); **~how** savoir-faire *m/inv.*; connaissances *f/pl.* techniques; **~ing** entendu (*look, smile*); **~ingly** *smile* d'un air entendu; *do s.th.* sciemment.

knowledge connaissance *f*; savoir *m*, connaissances *f/pl.*; *to my ~* autant que je sache.

known connu; *come to be ~* se répandre (*rumour*); se faire connaître; *make ~* faire connaître; signaler.

knuckle 1. (*a. ~bone*) articulation *f* du doigt; *veal*: jarret *m*; **2.** **~ down** (or *under*) se soumettre; céder.

L

lab labo(ratoire) *m.*

label 1. étiquette *f*; *fig.* désignation *f*; ✝ marque *f*; **2.** étiqueter.

laboratory laboratoire *m.*

laborious laborieux.

labo(u)r 1. travail *m*, peine *f*; main--d'œuvre *f*, travailleurs *m/pl.*; *pol.* les travaillistes *m/pl.*; ⚒ travail *m*; **Ministry of** ⚒ Ministère *m* du Travail; *hard* ~ travail *m* forcé; travaux *m/pl.* forcés; **2.** travailliste (*party*); du travail; ⚒ **Day** fête *f* du travail; ~ **dispute** conflit *m* social; ~ **force** personnel *m*, main--d'œuvre *f*; *Am.* ~ **union** syndicat *m* ouvrier; **3.** *v/i.* travailler; peiner (*a. fig.*); *v/t.* insister sur; ~ **under** être victime de (*an illusion etc.*); ~**ed** lourd (*style*); pénible (*respiration*); ~**er** travailleur *m*; manœuvre *m*; ~**ing** ouvrier; ~**intensive** d'un contenu fort en travail.

lace 1. lacet *m*; *tex.* dentelle *f*; **2.** lacer (*a shoe*); arroser (*a beverage*) (à, *with*); garnir de dentelle(s); *fig.* (*a. into*) rosser (*q.*), éreinter (*qch.*).

lacerate lacérer; déchirer.

lack 1. *su.* manque *m*, défaut *m*; *for* (*or through*) ~ **of** par manque de; **2.** *v/t.* manquer de; ne pas avoir; *v/i.* **be** ~**ing** manquer (*in*, de), faire défaut; ~ **for nothing** manquer de rien; ~**lustre,** *Am.* ~**luster** terne.

laconic laconique.

lacquer 1. laque *m*; **2.** laquer.

lad garçon *m*; jeune homme *m.*

ladder 1. échelle *f* (*a. fig., a.* ♣); *stocking:* maille *f* qui file; **2.** filer (*stocking etc.*); ~**proof** indémaillable (*stocking etc.*)

laden chargé (de, *with*).

ladle 1. louche *f*; **2.** (~ **out**) servir (avec une louche); F *fig.* ~ **out** débiter.

lady dame *f*; Lady *f*; *my* ~ madame *f*; *ladies!* mesdames!; ⚒ **Day** (fête *f* de) l'Annonciation *f*; ~ **doctor** femme *f* docteur; *ladies (room)* les toilettes *f/pl.* (des dames); ~**bird,** ~**bug** coccinelle *f*; ~**killer** don Juan *m*; ~**like** distingué.

lag¹ 1. traîner (*a.* ~ **behind**) rester en arrière; **2.** retard *m.*

lag² ⚙ isoler, calorifuger.

lager (beer) bière *f* blonde.

laggard traînard(e *f*) *m.*

lagoon lagune *f*; *atoll:* lagon *m.*

laid: ~ **up** alité, au lit.

lair tanière *f*, repaire *m.*

laity les laïques *m/pl.*

lake lac *m*; *paint.* laque *f.*

lamb agneau *m*; ~ **chop** côtelette *f* d'agneau; ~**skin** peau *f* d'agneau; *fur:* agnelin *m*; ~**swool** laine *f* d'agneau.

lame 1. boiteux; estropié; *fig.* faible, piètre (*excuse etc.*); **be** ~ (**in one leg**) boiter (d'une jambe); ~ **duck** canard *m* boiteux; *Am.* député *m* non réélu; **2.** rendre boiteux; estropier.

lament 1. lamentation *f*; **2.** se lamenter (sur, *for*); pleurer (*q., for s.o.*); ~**able** lamentable, déplorable; ~**ation** lamentation *f.*

lamp lampe *f*; *mot.* feu *m.*

lampoon pamphlet *m.*

lamp ...: ~**post** (poteau *m* de) réverbère *m*; ~**shade** abat-jour *m/inv.*

lance 1. lance *f*; **2.** percer, ouvrir (*a.* ⚕); ~**corporal** ✗ caporal *m.*

land 1. pays *m*; terre *f*, sol *m*; terrain *m*; propriété *f* foncière; ♣ débarquer; ✈ atterrir; *fig. fall:* (re)tomber; F ~ **up** finir par se retrouver (dans, à **in, at**); *v/t.* débarquer; amener à terre (*a fish etc.*); F décrocher (*a prize*); F ~ **s.o. in** mettre *q.* dans; ~**agent** courtier *m* en immeubles; ~**ed** foncier; terrien; F **be** ~ **with s.th.** avoir qch. sur les bras; ~**holder** propriétaire *m* foncier.

landing débarquement *m*; ✈ atterrissage *m*; *staircase:* palier *m*; ✈ ~ **gear** train *m* d'atterrissage; ~ **ground** terrain *m* d'atterrissage; ~ **stage** débarcadère *m*, embarcadère *m.*

land...: ~**lady** propriétaire *f*; *boarding house etc.:* logeuse *f*; aubergiste *f*, F patronne *f*; ~**lord** propriétaire *m*; *boarding house etc.:* logeur *m*; aubergiste *m*, F patron *m*; ~**lubber** ♣ terrien *m*; ~**mark** point *m* de repère; *fig.* événement *m* marquant; ~**owner** propriétaire *mf* foncier; ~**scape** paysage *m*; ~ **architecture** (*or* **design**) architecture *f* de paysage; ~ **gardener** jardinier *m* paysagiste; **~ gardening** jardinage *m* paysagiste; **~slide** éboulement *m* (de terrain) (*a.* **landslip**); *pol.* victoire *f* écrasante.

lane chemin *m* (vicinal); *town:* ruelle *f*; *mot.* voie *f*; *sp.* couloir *m*.

language langue *f*; langage *m*; **bad ~** gros mots; **strong ~** langage *m* violent; injures *f*/*pl.*

languid languissant.

languish languir (après, pour **for**).

languor langueur *f*.

lank plat (*hair*); **~y** grand et maigre.

lantern lanterne *f*; ⚓ fanal *m*.

lap 1. *su. cost.* pan *m*; *sp.* tour *m* (de piste); *sp.* **~ of hono(u)r** tour *m* d'honneur; **in** (or **on**) **s.o.'s ~** sur les genoux de q.; **2.** *v*/*t.* (*a.* **~ up**) laper; envelopper (de, **in**); *v*/*i.* clapoter (*waves*).

lapel *cost.* revers *m*.

lapse 1. erreur *f*; faux pas *m*; intervalle *m*, laps *m* (de temps); défaillance *f* (*of memory*); **2.** déchoir; ✝ cesser d'être en vigueur; **~ into** (re)tomber dans.

larceny larcin *m*, vol *m*.

larch ♀ mélèze *m*

lard 1. saindoux *m*, graisse *f* de porc; **2.** larder (de, **with**) (*a. fig.*); **~er** garde-manger *m*/*inv.*

large grand; gros; nombreux; large; **at ~** en liberté; en général; pour la plupart; en détail; **~ly** en grande partie; **~ness** grandeur *f*; grosseur *f*; *fig.* largeur *f*; **~minded** à l'esprit large; tolérant; **~scale** à grande échelle; *fig. a.* important.

lark 1. *orn.* alouette *f*; farce *f* blague *f*; **2. ~ about**, **~ around** faire le fou (la folle); **~spur** ♀ pied *m* d'alouette.

larva *zo.*, *pl.* **-vae** larve *f*.

lascivious lascif.

laser laser *m*; **~ beam** rayon *m* laser.

lash 1. coup *m* de fouet; lanière *f*; *eye:* cil *m*; **2.** cingler, fouetter; lier (à, **to**); **~ out** ⌐ dépenser, F allonger (*money*); **~ out at** (or **against**) attaquer.

lass jeune fille *f*; **~ie** fillette *f*.

lassitude lassitude *f*.

last¹ *adj.* dernier; **~ but one** avant-dernier; **~ night** hier soir; la nuit dernière; **2.** *su.* dernier (-ère *f*) *m*; **at ~** enfin, à la fin; **at long ~** enfin; **3.** *adv.* la dernière fois; le dernier; **~, but not least** enfin et surtout.

last² durer; **~ out** tenir; passer, faire (*time*).

last³ forme *f* (*for shoes*).

last-ditch ultime, désespéré (*efforts etc.*).

lasting durable; résistant.

lastly en dernier lieu; pour finir.

last-minute de dernière minute *or* heure.

latch loquet *m*; **~key** clef *f* de maison.

late en retard; retardé; tardif (*fruit etc.*); avancé (*hour*); ex-; feu (*dead person*); récent; **at** (**the**) **~st** au plus tard; **as ~ as** pas plus tard que; **of ~** récemment; **of ~ years** depuis quelques années; **~r on** plus tard; **be ~** être en retard (de 5 minutes, **5 minutes**); avoir du retard; avoir un retard de ...; **~comer** retardataire *mf*; tard-venu(e *f*) *m*; **~ly** récemment; **~ness** retard *m*; *time:* heure *f* tardive.

latent latent.

lateral latéral.

lath latte *f*; *roof:* volige *f*.

lathe ⊙ tour *m*.

lather 1. *su.* mousse *f* de savon; **2.** *v*/*t.* savonner; *v*/*i.* mousser.

Latin latin (*adj.*, *su.*/*m*); **~ America** Amérique *f* latine; **~ American** d'Amérique latine.

latitude latitude *f*.

latter: **the ~** celui-ci *m* (celle-ci *f*, ceux-ci *m*/*pl.*, celles-ci *f*/*pl.*); **~ly** récemment, dernièrement.

lattice treillage *m*, treillis *m*.

laudable louable.

laugh 1. rire *m*; **2.** (**at**) rire (de); se moquer (de); **~able** risible, ridicule; **~ing** ricur; **~ingstock** risée *f*; **~ter** rire(s) *m*/(*pl.*).

launch 1. lancement *m*; chaloupe *f*; **2.** *v*/*t.* lancer (*a. a ship, a rocket, a. fig.*); *v*/*i.* ~ (**out**) **into** se lancer dans; **~ing 1.** lancement *m*, **2.** **~ pad** (*site etc.*) rampe *f* (aire *f* etc.) de lancement.

laund|er blanchir; **~(e)rette** *Br.*, **~romat** *Am.* (TM) laverie *f* automatique; **~ress** blanchisseuse *f*; **~ry** blanchisserie *f*; linge *f*; lessive *f*.

laurel ♀ laurier *m* (*a. fig.*).

lava lave *f*.

lavatory toilettes *f*/*pl.*

lavender ♀ lavande *f*.

lavish 1. prodigue (de **in**, **of**); abondant; **2.** prodiguer (à, **on**).

law loi *f*; *science*: droit *m*; **go to ~** avoir recours à la justice; **lay down the ~** faire la loi, donner le ton; **~-abiding** ami de l'ordre; **~court** cour *f* de justice; tribunal *m*; **~ful** légal; permis; légitime; **~less** sans loi.

lawn pelouse *f*; gazon *m*; **~mower** tondeuse *f*.

law...: ~suit procès *m*; **~yer** avocat *m*; homme *m* de loi; juriste *m*.

lax flasque; relâché (*morals*); **~ative** laxatif (*a. su./m*).

lay¹ laïque, lai.

lay² 1. *v/t.* coucher; abattre; mettre (*the table*, *s.th. on s.th.*, *taxes etc.*); parier (*money*; *a. fig.* que, **that**); pondre (*eggs*); poser (*the foundations*, *a carpet*, *s.th. on s.th.*); **~ before** exposer, présenter à (*q.*); **~ down** déposer; ✗ rendre (*one's arms*); résigner (*one's office*); poser; imposer (*a condition*); formuler (*a principle*); **~ in** s'approvisionner de; **~ low** étendre, abattre; **~ off** licencier (*workers etc.*); **~ open** exposer; **~ out** arranger, étaler (*before s.o.'s eyes*); concevoir, faire le plan de; dessiner; dépenser (*a. fig.*); **~ up** amasser, emmagasiner (*provisions*), mettre (*qch.*) en réserve; ⚓ mettre en rade (*a ship*), remiser (*a car*); forcer (*q.*) à garder le lit (*illness*); 2. *v/i.* pondre (*des œufs*); 3. *su.*: **find out the ~ of the land** tâter le terrain; **~about** fainéant(e *f*) *m*; **~-by** *mot.* parking *m* (à côté d'une autoroute).

layer couche *f*; *geol.* strate *f*.

layman profane *m*; *eccl.* laïque *m*.

lay...: ~-off licenciement *m*; **~out** disposition *f*, plan *m*; *typ.* layout *m*.

lazy paresseux, fainéant.

lead¹ plomb *m*; *pencil*: mine *f*.

lead² 1. *su.* (*position*) tête *f*; *sp.*, *fig.* avance *f*; (*clue*) piste *f*; *thea.* premier rôle *m*; *cards*: main *f*; ⚡ câble *m*; *dog*: laisse *f*; *journ.* (*a.* **~ story**) article *m* de tête; **take the ~** prendre la tête; *fig.* prendre les devants (sur *of*, *over*); 2. *v/t.* mener, conduire (à, **to**); amener, induire (en, **into**); guider; être en *or* à la tête de; **~ on** entraîner; F *fig.* faire marcher; *fig.* encourager (à parler); *v/i.* mener, conduire (à, **to**); **~ off** commencer (par, **with**); **~ up to** conduire à.

leaden de plomb (*a. fig.*).

leader chef *m*, dirigeant(e *f*) *m*; *journ.*

article *m* de fond, éditorial *m*; *pol.* leader *m*; **~ship** direction *f*.

leading premier, principal; de tête; **~ article** article *m* de fond, éditorial *m*; *thea.* **~ lady** (**man**) vedette *f*; **~ light** sommité *f*.

leaf feuille *f*; *book*: feuillet *m*; *door*, *table*: battant *m*; **~age** feuillage *m*; **~less** sans feuilles; **~let** prospectus *m*; **~y** feuillu.

league 1. ligue *f*; *measure*: lieue *f*; *sp.* ⚽ **match** match *m* de championnat; 2. se liguer.

leak 1. fuite *f*, ⚓ voie *f* d'eau; 2. fuir (*liquid*, *recipient*); prendre l'eau, faire eau; **~ out** fuir, couler; *fig.* s'ébruiter, transpirer; **~age** fuite *f* (*a. fig. secrets*); perte *f*; **~y** qui coule; qui prend l'eau; *fig.* peu discret.

lean¹ maigre (*a. su./m*).

lean² (s')appuyer (contre, **against**); *v/i.* s'adosser (à, contre **against**); s'accouder; se pencher (sur, **over**; vers, **towards**); en arrière, **back**); pencher (*a. fig.* pour, **towards**); *fig.* **~ on** s'appuyer sur; faire pression sur; **~ over** se pencher; **~ing** 1. penché; 2. penchant *m* (pour, **towards**).

leanness maigreur *f*.

leap 1. *v/i.* saut *m*, bond *m*; *fig.* **in ~s and bounds** à pas de géant; 2. sauter; **~frog** 1. saute-mouton *m*; 2. sauter (par-dessus, **over**); **~year** année *f* bissextile.

learn apprendre; **~ed** instruit, savant; **~er** débutant(e *f*) *m*; **~ing** savoir *m*, érudition *f*.

lease 1. bail *m*; 2. louer à bail.

leash laisse *f*; **keep on a ~** tenir en laisse.

least 1. *adj.* le moindre; le plus petit; 2. *adv.* (le) moins; 3. *su.*: **at (the) ~** au moins; du moins; **not in the ~** pas le moins du monde; **to say the ~** pour ne pas dire plus.

leather 1. cuir *m*; F *foot.* ballon *m*; 2. de *or* en cuir.

leave 1. *v/t.* laisser; abandonner; léguer (*a fortune etc.*); quitter (*a place*); sortir de; F **~ it at that** en demeurer là; **~ behind** laisser (*a. traces*); distancer; **~ off** cesser; renoncer à; **be left** rester; *v/i.* partir; 2. permission *f*; (*a.* **~ of absence**) congé *m*.

leaven levain *m*.

lecture 1. conférence *f* (sur, **on**); cours

m; *fig.* sermon *m*; **2.** *v/i.* faire une conférence (sur, **on**); faire un cours (de, **on**); *vt/i.* sermonner; **~r** conférencier (-ère *f*) *m*; *univ.* maître *m* de conférences; professeur *m*.

ledge rebord *m*; saillie *f*, corniche *f*.

ledger ✝ grand livre *m*, registre *m*.

lee (côté *m*) sous le vent; *in the ~ of* à l'abri de.

leech *zo.* sangsue *f* (*a. fig.*).

leek ♣ poireau *m*.

leer 1. regard *m* en dessous; **2.** ~ *at* lorgner d'un air méchant.

lees *pl.* lie *f* (*a. fig.*).

lee|ward ⚓ sous le vent; **~way** ⚓ dérive *f*; *fig.* **make up ~** rattraper le temps perdu; se rattraper.

left 1. *adj.* gauche; **2.** *adv.* à gauche; **3.** *su.* gauche *f*; **~-hand** le *or* à gauche; *mot.* ~ **drive** conduite *f* à gauche; **~-handed** gaucher (*person*); *fig.* gauche; *fig.* ambigu.

leftist gauchiste (*adj.*, *su.*/*mf*).

left...: ~ **luggage** bagages *m/pl.* en consigne; **~-luggage locker** casier *m* à consigne automatique; ~ **luggage office** consigne *f*; **~-overs** *pl.* restes *m/pl.*

leg jambe *f*; *animal:* patte *f*; *table:* pied *m*; ♣ branche *f*; *trip:* étape *f*; *cuis.* cuisse *f*, *mutton:* gigot *m*; F **give s.o. a ~ up** faire la courte échelle à q.; **be on one's last ~s** être à bout de ses ressources; **pull s.o.'s ~** se payer la tête de q.

legacy legs *m*, héritage *m*.

legal légal; juridique; judiciaire; légitime; ~ **adviser** conseiller *m* juridique; ~ **aid** assistance *f* judiciaire; ~ **costs** *pl.* frais *m/pl.* judiciaires; dépens *m/pl.* (à la charge du succombé); ✝ ~ **department** (service *m* du) contentieux *m*; ~ **dispute** litige *m*; ~ **entity** personne *f* morale; ~ **tender** monnaie *f* légale; **take ~ action** (*against*) intenter un procès (à), engager un procès (contre); **~ize** légaliser.

legend légende *f*; **~ary** légendaire.

leggings *pl.* guêtres *f/pl.*

legible lisible.

legion légion *f*.

legislat|ion législation *f*; **~ive** législatif; **~or** législateur *m*.

legitim|acy légitimité *f*; **~ate** légitime; **~ize** legitimer.

legroom place *f* pour les jambes.

leisure loisir(s) *m*(*/pl.*); ~ **activities** *pl.* loisirs *m/pl.*; ~ **centre** centre *m* de loisirs; ~ **time** temps *m* libre, loisir; ~ **wear** tenue *f* de détente; **at ~** (tout) à loisir; libre; **at your ~** quand vous en aurez le loisir; **~ly 1.** posé, tranquille; **2.** sans se presser.

lemon citron *m*; ~ **soda** lemonade *f*; ~ **squash** citron *m* pressé; citronnade *f*; ~ **squeezer** presse-citron *m/inv.*; **~ade** *Br.* lemonade *f*, *Am.* citronnade *f*.

lend prêter; *fig.* donner; **~ing library** bibliothèque *f* de prêt.

length longueur *f*; morceau *m*; pièce *f*; *time:* durée *f*; **at ~** enfin, à la fin; **~en** (s')allonger; (se) prolonger; **~ways**, **~wise** dans le sens de la longueur, en long; **~y** assez long; plein de longueurs (*book*, *speech etc.*).

lenient clément, indulgent.

lens lentille *f*; *phot.* objectif *m.*

Lent carême *m.*

lentil ♣ lentille *f.*

Leo *astr.* le Lion *m.*

leopard léopard *m.*

lep|rosy ✞ lèpre *f*; **~ous** lépreux.

less 1. *adj.* moins de; **2.** *adv.* moins; ~ **and** ~ de moins en moins; **the ~ ...** moins ...; **3.** *prp.* ♣ moins; ✝ sans; **~en** diminuer; (s')amoindrir; **~er** (plus) petit; moindre.

lesson leçon; **~s** *pl.* cours *m.*

lest de peur *or* de crainte que ... ne (*sbj.*) *or* de (*inf.*).

let *v/t.* laisser; faire (*inf.*); louer (*a house etc.*); ~ **alone** laisser tranquille *or* en paix; laisser (*q.*) faire; *adv.* sans parler de ...; ~ **down** baisser; descendre; F décevoir, laisser (*q.*) en panne; ~ **go** *v/t.* lâcher; *v/i.* lâcher prise; ~ **into a secret** mettre (*q.*) dans un secret; ~ **loose** lâcher; ~ **off** laisser descendre (*a passenger etc.*); faire partir (*a shot etc.*); dégager (*a smell etc.*); *fig.* faire grâce à (*q.*); *fig.* dispenser (de *inf.*, **from** *gen.*); F ~ **on** dire, raconter, avouer; ~ **out** laisser sortir; laisser échapper; *cost.* élargir (*a dress*); ~ **up** diminuer; cesser; **~down** F déception *f.*

lethal mortel.

lethargy léthargie *f*; *fig.* inaction *f.*

letter lettre *f*; caractère *m*; **~s** *pl.* (belles-)lettres *f/pl.*; ~ **paper** papier *m* à lettres; **to the ~** au pied de la lettre; **~box**

boîte *f* aux lettres; **~head** en-tête *m*; **~ing** lettrage *m*; inscription *f*.
lettuce ♣ laitue *f*.
letup arrêt *m*; diminution *f*; **without (a) ~** *a.* sans s'arrêter.
levee *Am.* river: digue *f*, levée *f*.
level 1. *adj.* plat, plan, ras; **~ with** au niveau de; à la hauteur de; à égalité avec; **my ~ best** tout mon possible; 🚋 **~ crossing** passage *m* à niveau; **2.** *su.* niveau *m* (*a.* ☉, *a.* fig.); terrain *m* or surface *f* plat(e); **sea ~** niveau *m* de la mer; **on a ~ with** à la hauteur de; fig. au niveau de; F **on the ~** loyal; tout à fait sincère; **3.** *v/t.* niveler, égaliser; pointer (*a gun*); fig. raser (*a town*); **~ a blow at** allonger un coup à; **~ off, ~ out** égaliser; fig. se stabiliser; **~ up** élever (*qch.*) au niveau (de *qch.*, **to s.th.**); *v/i.* **~ at** (or **against**) viser; **~-headed** à la tête bien équilibrée.
lever 1. levier *m*; **2.** déplacer (à l'aide d'un levier); **~ out** déloger; **~ up** soulever; **~age** force *f* de levier; fig. prise *f*.
levity légèreté *f*.
levy 1. taxation *f*; taxe *f*; ✗ levée *f*; **2.** imposer (*a tax, fine etc.*) (sur, **on**); ✗ lever.
lewd obscène; impudique.
liability responsabilité *f*; fig. disposition *f* (à, **to**); **liabilities** *pl.* engagements *m/pl.*, obligations *f/pl.*, ✝ passif *m*.
liable responsable (de, **for**); passible (de, **for**) (*a fine*); sujet, disposé (à, **to**); **be ~ to** avoir une disposition à; être sujet à; être susceptible de (*faire*).
liais|e entrer or rester en liaison; **~on** liaison *f*.
liar menteur (-euse *f*) *m*.
libel 1. diffamation *f* (par écrit); **2.** diffamer (par écrit).
liberal 1. libéral (*a. pol.*); généreux, prodigue (de, **with**); abondant; **2.** *pol.* libéral (-aux *pl.*) *m*; **~ity** libéralité *f*; générosité *f*.
liberat|e libérer; **~ion** libération *f*; **~or** libérateur (-trice *f*) *m*.
libertarian libertaire *mf*.
libertine libertin (*adj.*, *mf*).
liberty liberté *f*; **be at ~** être libre (de, à faire, **to**).
Libra *ast.* la Balance *f*.
librar|ian bibliothécaire *mf*; **~y** bibliothèque *f*.
licen|ce *Am.* **~se 1.** *admin.* permis *m*,

autorisation *f*; ✝, fig. licence *f*; *radio, TV*: redevance *f*; *mot.* **~ number** numéro *m* d'immatriculation; *mot.* **~ plate** plaque *f* minéralogique or d'immatriculation; *mot.* **driving (*Am.* driver's) ~** permis *m* (de conduire); **2.** donner un permis or une licence à; autoriser; *Brit.* **(fully) ~d** autorisé à vendre des boissons alcoolisées; **~see** détenteur (-euse *f*) m d'une licence or d'un permis; *pub*: propriétaire *mf*.
licentious licencieux.
lichen ♣, ♣ lichen *m*.
lick 1. coup *m* de langue; F vitesse *f*; F **a ~ of** un peu de, un coup de; **2.** lécher; F battre; **~ the dust** mordre la poussière; **~ into shape** façonner.
licorice ♣ *Am.* réglisse *f*.
lid couvercle *m*; paupière *f*.
lie¹ 1. mensonge *m*; **give the ~ to** démentir; **tell a ~** mentir; **2.** mentir.
lie² 1. être étendu or allongé or couché (*person*); être, se trouver (*thing*); *rest*: reposer; (*a.* **~ down**) s'étendre, s'allonger, se coucher; **~ about** or **around** traîner; **~ back** se renverser; **~ in** rester au lit; **~ over** être ajourné; **~ up** garder le lit; se cacher; **2.** *see* **lay² 3**.
lieu: in ~ of au lieu de.
lieutenant lieutenant *m*.
life, *pl.* **-ves** vie *f*; **~ assurance, ~ insurance** assurance-vie *f*; **~ expectancy** espérance *f* de vie; **~ jacket**, *Am. a.* **~ preserver** gilet *m* de sauvetage; 🛥 **~ sentence** condamnation *f* à vie; **~belt** ceinture *f* de sauvetage; **~boat** canot *m* de sauvetage; **~guard** garde *f* du corps; *Am.* sauveteur *m* (*on the beach*); **~less** sans vie; *mot.* fig. sans vigueur; **~like** vivant; **~long** de toute sa vie; **~-size** de grandeur naturelle; **~span** (durée *f* de) vie *f*; **~time** vie *f*; **in s.o.'s ~** du vivant de q.
lift 1. *su.* haussement *m*; levée *f* (*a.* ☉); ✈ poussée *f*; fig. élévation *f*; *Br.* ascenseur *m*; **give s.o. a ~** donner un coup de main à q.; *Br.* emmener q. en voiture; **2.** *v/t.* (*oft.* **~ up**) (sous)lever; F voler, F chiper; *v/i.* se lever; **~ off** space: décollage *m*.
liga|ment ligament *m*; **~ture** ligature *f*; ♪ liaison *f*.
light¹ 1. *su.* lumière *f*; jour *m* (*a.* fig.); lampe *f* mot. (**head~**) phare *m*; *mot.*

(*rear* ~, *traffic* ~) feu *m*; *cigarette*: feu *m*; *phot.* ~ **meter** photometre *m*; ~ **wave** onde *f* lumineuse; ~ **year** année--lumière *f* (*pl.* années-lumière); **will you give me a** ~ voudriez-vous bien me donner du feu?; **2.** *adj.* clair; éclairé; blond; **3.** *v/t.* (*oft.* ~ **up**) éclairer; illuminer (*the street, s.o.'s face etc.*); *v/i.* (*usu.* ~ **up**) s'allumer; s'éclairer (*face*); *Am. sl.* ~ **out** détaler, ficher le camp.

light² **1.** *usu.* léger; facile; ~ **current** ⚡ courant *m* faible; ~ **reading** lecture distrayante; **make** ~ **of** faire peu de cas de; prendre à la légère; **2.** ~ **on** tomber sur, trouver par hasard.

lighten¹ (s')éclairer.

lighten² *v/t.* alléger (*a. fig.*); réduire le poids de; *v/i.* être soulagé.

lighter¹ (*a.* **cigarette** ~) briquet *m*.

lighter² ⚓ péniche *f*, chaland *m*.

light...: ~**headed** étourdi; ~**hearted** gai; ~**house** phare *m*.

lighting éclairage *m*.

lightness légèreté *f*.

lightning éclairs (*s pl.*) *m*; foudre *f*; ~ **conductor**, ~ **rod** paratonnerre *m*; ⚡ ~ **strike** grève *f* surprise.

light weight *sp.* poids *m* léger.

like 1. *adj., adv.* pareil, semblable, tel; F **feel** ~ (*ger.*) avoir envie de (*inf.*); ~ **that** de la sorte; **what is he** ~? comment est-il?; **2.** *su.* semblable *mf*, pareil(le *f*) *m*; ~'*s* goûts *m/pl.*, préférences *f/pl.*; F **the** ~(**s**) **of** des personnes *or* choses comme; **3.** *v/t.* aimer; avoir de la sympathie pour; vouloir; *I should* ~ **to know** je voudrais bien savoir.

like|lihood probabilité *f*; ~**ly** probable; vraisemblable; plausible; susceptible (**de, to**); **be** ~ **to** (*inf.*) *a.* risquer de (*inf.*); ~**minded** de (la) même opinion; ~**n** comparer (**à, with to**); ~**ness** ressemblance *f*; apparence *f*; aspect *m*; portrait *m*; ~**wise** de même; de plus, aussi.

liking affection *f*, sympathie *f*; goût *m*, penchant *m*; **take a** ~ **to** se mettre à aimer; prendre goût à (*qch*).

lilac 1. lilas; **2.** ⚘ lilas *m*.

lily ⚘ lis *m*; ~ **of the valley** muguet *m*.

limb *body*: membre *m*; *tree*: (grosse) branche *f*.

limber 1. ~ **up** se dégourdir; ~**ing up exercises** exercices *f/pl.* d'assouplissement; **2.** souple.

phot. ~ **meter** photometre *m*;

lime chaux *f*; ⚘ lime *f*; ⚘ (*a.* ~**tree**) tilleul *m*; ⚘ limon *m*; ~**juice** jus *m* de limon; ~**light** *thea.* rampe *f*; *fig.* **in the** ~ très en vue; ~**stone** *geol.* calcaire *m*.

limit 1. limite *f*; **in** (**off**) ~**s** accès *m* permis (interdit); F **that is the** ~! ça, c'est le comble!; ça c'est trop fort! F **go the** ~ aller jusqu'au bout; **2.** limiter (**à, to**); ~**ation** restriction *f*, limitation *f*; ~**ed** limité, restreint (**à, to**); ~ (**liability**) **company** (*abbr. Co. Ltd.*) société *f* à responsabilité limitée; société *f* anonyme; ~ **in time** à terme; de durée restreinte; ~**less** illimité.

limp 1. have a ~ = **2.** boiter.

limp² flasque; mou.

limpid limpide, clair.

line 1. ligne *f*; voie *f*; corde *f*, fil *m*; rangée *f*; file *f*, queue *f*; colonne *f* (*of vehicles etc.*); *territory*: limite *f* ✝ articles *m/pl* genre *m*; F renseignement *m*, ✝ tuyau *m*; *thea.* ~**s** *pl.* texte *m*; *hard* ~**s** *pl.* mauvaise chance *f*; **all down the** ~ sur toute la ligne; **in** ~ **with** d'accord avec; **that is not in my** ~ ce n'est pas dans mon rayon *or* ma partie; **stand in** ~ faire la queue; ~**s** s'aligner; *fig.* se conformer (**à, with**), **2.** *v/t.* aligner; ligner, régler; rayer; border; *cost. etc.* doubler; ~ **out** tracer; *v/i.* ~ **up** s'aligner; faire la queue.

linea|ge lignée *f*; famille *f*; ~**ment** trait *m*; ~**r** linéaire.

linen linge *m* (*de corps*); (*cloth*) lin *m*; ~ **basket** panier *m* à linge.

liner paquebot *m* (*de ligne*).

linger tarder; s'attarder (sur, **over on**); traîner; *fig.* persister, subsister.

lingerie ✝ lingerie *f* (*de dame*).

lining *garment*: doublure *f*; *hat*: coiffe *f*; △ revêtement *m*.

link 1. chaînon *m*; *chain*: anneau *m*; *fig.* lien *m*; **cuff** ~ bouton *m* de manchette; **2.** (se) joindre; *v/t. a.* relier, enchaîner.

links *pl.* (*a.* **golf**~) terrain *m* de golf.

linkup connexion *f*; lien *m*, rapport *m*; jonction *f*.

linseed graine *f* de lin, ~ **oil** huile *f* de lin.

lint tissu *m* ouaté.

lintel linteau *m*.

lion lion *m*; ~**ess** lionne *f*.

lip lèvre *f* (*a.* ⚘); *animal*: babine *f*; *cup*: (re)bord *m*; F insolence *f*; ~**read** lire sur les lèvres; **~stick** rouge *m* à lèvres; bâton *m* de rouge.

liquefy (se) liquéfier.

liqueur liqueur *f*.

liquid liquide (*adj.*, *su./m*).

liquidat|e ✝ liquider (*a debt*); **~ion** liquidation *f*.

liquidize *cuis.* passer au mixeur; **~r** mixeur *m*, centrifugeuse *f*.

liquor boisson *f* alcoolique.

liquorice ♣ réglisse *f*.

lisp 1. zézayement *m*; **2.** zézayer.

list¹ 1. liste *f*; **✝ ~ price** prix *m* de catalogue; **2.** mettre sur la *or* une liste; faire la *or* une liste de; énumérer; *Br.* **~ed** classé, historique (*building*).

list² ♺ 1. inclinaison *f*; **2.** donner de la bande.

listen écouter; **~ to** écouter; **~ in radio:** se mettre à l'écoute; écouter (qch., **to s.th.**); **~er** auditeur (-trice *f*) *m*.

listless apathique, sans énergie; indifférent.

literal littéral.

litera|ry littéraire; de lettres; **~ture** littérature *f*; **✝** prospectus *m/pl.*

lithe(some) souple, agile, leste.

lithography lithographie *f*.

litiga|nt ⚖ plaideur (-euse *f*) *m*; **~te** *v/i.* plaider; être en procès; *v/t.* mettre (*qch.*) en litige, contester (*qch.*); **~tion** litige *m*.

litter 1. ordures *f/pl.*, détritus *m/pl.*; *zo.* portée *f*; **2.** *v/t.* éparpiller; laisser (traîner) des détritus dans (*a room etc.*); joncher *ou* couvrir de; *v/i.* laisser traîner des détritus; *zo.* mettre bas; **~bag, ~bin** boîte *f* à ordures.

little 1. *adj.* petit; peu de ...; *fig.* mesquin (*mind*); **a ~ one** un petit (*child*); **2.** *adv.* peu; **3.** *su.* peu *m* (de chose); **~ by ~, by ~ and ~** peu à peu; petit à petit; **a ~** un peu (de); **not a ~** beaucoup.

live 1. vivre (de, **on**); se nourrir (de, **on**); habiter; *v/t.* mener (*a life*); **~ to see** vivre assez longtemps pour voir (*qch.*); **~ out** passer; **~ up to one's promise** remplir sa promesse; **~ up to a standard** atteindre un niveau; **2.** vivant, ardent (*coal*); **⚡** sous tension; *telev.*, *radio:* (transmis) en direct; **~lihood** vie *f*; gagne-pain *m/inv.*); **~ly** vif; animé; mouvementé.

liven (*a.* **~ up**) *v/t.* animer, égayer; *v/i.* s'animer; s'activer.

liver foie *m*.

livery *cost.* livrée *f*.

livestock bétail *m*, bestiaux *m/pl.*

livid furious; blême, livide.

living 1. vivant, en vie; **2.** vie *f*, gagne-pain *m/inv.*; **make** (*or* **earn**) **a ~** gagner sa vie (en, **by** *ger.*); **~ room** living *m*, (salle *f* de) séjour *m*; **~ space** espace *m* vital; **~ standard** niveau *m* de vie.

lizard lézard *m*.

load 1. *su.* fardeau *m*, poids *m*; **⚙** *etc.* charge *f*; *F* **~s of** des tas de, pas mal de; **2.** *v/t.* (**~ with**) charger (de) (*a vehicle etc.*), charger (avec) (*a camera, gun etc.*); **~ed** plombé (*cane*); pipé (*dice*); *fig.* insidieux (*question*); *sl.* soûl (= *drunk*); *sl.* bourré de fric (= *rich*).

loaf 1. (*pl.* **-ves**) pain *m* (*a.* of sugar), bread: miche *f*; **2.** traîner, flâner; **~er** flâneur *m*.

loam ✿ terre *f* grasse.

loan 1. prêt *m*; avance *f*; emprunt *m*; **2.** *esp. Am.* prêter.

loath: be ~ to (*inf.*) répugner à (*inf.*); **~e** détester; abhorrer; **~ing** aversion *f*, répugnance *f* (pour **for**, **of**); **~some** dégoûtant.

lobby 1. vestibule *m* (*a. parl.*); *thea.* foyer *m*; *parl.* lobby *m*; **2.** faire pression (sur).

lobe *anat.*, **♣** lobe *m*.

lobster homard *m*.

local 1. local; regional; du pays; *admin.* municipal; *teleph.:* **~ call** communication *f* interurbaine; *pol.* **~ elections** (élections *f/pl.*) municipales *f/pl.*; **2.** personne *f* (*pl. les gens m/pl.*) du pays; *Br. F* café *m* du coin; *Am.* train *m* omnibus; **~ity** localité *f*; région *f*; **~ize** localiser.

locat|e *v/t.* repérer, trouver; situer; **be ~d** être situé; *v/i. Am.* s'établir; **~ion** repérage *m*; emplacement *m*; *cin.* extérieurs *m/pl.*

loch *Sc.* lac *m*; bras *m* de mer.

lock¹ 1. *su. door etc.:* serrure *f*; *gun:* platine *f*; écluse *f*; verrou *m* (*a. fig.*); **2.** *v/t.* fermer à clef; (*a.* **~ up**) enfermer; **⚙** enrayer (*a wheel*); verrouiller *fig.* serrer; **~ in** enfermer à clef; **~ out** fermer la porte à; lockouter (*workers*); **~ up** bloquer; immobiliser (*capital*); *v/i.* se fermer à clef; s'enclencher, se bloquer.

lock² hair: boucle *f*.

locker casier *m*.

lop-sided

locket médaillon *m.*

lock...: ~out lockout *m*; **~smith** serrurier *m.*

loco *sl.* toqué, fou.

locomotive locomotive *f.*

locust *zo.* grande sauterelle *f.*

lodestar *fig.* point *m* de mire.

lodg|e 1. *su.* pavillon (*de chasse*); *porter*, *Freemasons*: loge *f*; **2.** *v/t.* loger (*q.*); déposer; *admin.* présenter; **~ a complaint** porter plainte; **~ itself** se loger; *v/i.* demeurer (chez, **with**); être en pension (chez, **with**); **~er** locataire *mf*; **~ing** hébergement *m*; **~ings** *pl.* meublé *m.*

loft grenier *m*; *church etc.*: galerie *f*; **~y** haut, élevé; *fig.* hautain (*person*).

log (grosse) bûche *f*; (*book*) registre *m*, ♪ journal *m* de bord; *r* carnet *m* de vol; *truck*: carnet *m* de route; **~ cabin** cabane *f* de bois; **sleep like a ~** dormir comme une souche.

loggerheads: at ~ (**with**) à couteaux tirés (avec).

logic logique *f*; **~al** logique.

logistics logistique *f.*

logrolling échange *m* de faveurs.

loin *cuis.* filet *m* (*of mutton or veal*), aloyau *m* (*of beef*), longe *f* (*of veal*); **~s** *pl.* reins *m/pl.*

loiter traîner, flâner.

loll pendre; être étendu, être prélassé (*person*); **~ about** flâner.

lollipop suzette *f.*

London de Londres; **Londoner** Londonien(ne *f*) *m.*

lone|liness solitude *f*, isolement *m*; **~ly**, **~some** solitaire, isolé; **~r** solitaire *mf.*

long¹ *adj.* long; *adv.* a) longtemps, b) depuis longtemps; **before ~** sous peu; avant peu; **for ~** pendant longtemps; **take ~** prendre du temps (*things*); tarder (à *inf.* **to** *inf.*, [**in**] *ger.*) (*person*); **take a ~ time** mettre longtemps (à *or* pour *inf.*, *ger. or* to *inf.*); *sp.* **~jump** saut *m* en longueur; *radio:* **~ waves** grandes ondes *f/pl.*; **in the ~ run** à la longue; **all night ~** toute la nuit; **no ~er** ne ... plus.

long² désirer ardemment (qch., **for s.th.**); brûler (de *inf.*, **to** *inf.*).

long...: ~distance à longue distance; **~evity** longévité *f.*

longing 1. impatient, avide; **2.** désir *m* ardent, grande envie *f* (de, **for**).

longitude *geog.* longitude *f.*

long...: ~playing record (disque *m*) 33 tours *m/inv.*; **~range** à longue *or* grande portée; **~shoreman** débardeur *m*, docker *m*; **~sighted** presbyte; *fig.* prévoyant; **~suffering** patient; longanime; **~term** à long terme (*a. memory*); **~winded** interminable; diffus.

loo F *les* cabinets *m/pl.*, F *le* petit coin.

look 1. *su.* regard *m*; air, aspect *m*; (*usu.* **~s** *pl.*) mine *f*; **have a ~ at s.th.** jeter un coup d'œil sur qch.; **2.** *v/i.* regarder (qch., **at s.th.**; pour, **out of**); avoir l'air (*sick etc.*); sembler (que, **as if**); paraître; **it ~s like rain** on dirait qu'il va pleuvoir; **~ about** chercher (q.); **~ after** s'occuper de; soigner; garder; **~ at** regarder; **~ for** chercher; **~ forward to** attendre avec plaisir; **~ in** faire une petite visite (à, **on**); *telev.* regarder; **~ into** examiner, étudier; **~ out** regarder dehors; faire attention, prendre garde (à, **for**); **~ out for** a. (re)chercher; **~ over** jeter un coup d'œil sur (qch.); **~ up** regarder en haut, lever les yeux; s'améliorer; *fig.* **~ up to** respecter; *fig.* **~ (up)on** regarder (comme, **as**); **3.** *v/t.*: **~ disdain** lancer un regard dédaigneux; **~ up** chercher, consulter; passer voir (*q.*); **~alike** double *m.*

looker-on spectateur (-trice *f*) *m* (de, **at**).

look ...: ~out guetteur *m*; poste *m* de guet; *fig. esp. Br.* perspective *f*, **be on the ~ for** (re)chercher; **that is my ~** ça c'est mon affaire; **~over** examen *m* superficiel; coup *m* d'œil; **give s.th. a ~** examiner qch. rapidement; jeter un coup d'œil à *or* sur.

loom 1. métier *m* (à tisser); **2.** se dessiner; surgir; *fig.* menacer.

loony *sl.* dingue (*= fou*).

loop 1. *su.* cord, river: boucle *f*; ♀ stérilet *m*; **2.** faire une boucle; **~hole** échappatoire *f.*

loose 1. branlant; détaché; défait; échappé, en liberté; libre; mobile; lâche; vague; débauché (*life*); **2.** *v/t.* dénouer; détacher; **~n** (*se*) défaire (ou) relâcher; (se) desserrer.

loot 1. piller, pillage *m*; butin *m.*

lop tailler (*a tree etc.*); **~ off** couper; **~eared** aux oreilles pendantes; **~sided** de guingois; déjeté.

loquacious loquace.

lord seigneur *m*, maître *m*; *title*: lord *m*; **the** 2 le Seigneur (*God*); *parl.* **the (House of)** 2s la Chambre des Lords; 2 **Mayor** maire *m*; **my ~** monsieur le baron *etc.*; **the** 2**'s Prayer** l'oraison *f* dominicale; **the** 2**'s Supper** la Cène *f*; **~ly** de grand seigneur; magnifique; noble; hautain; **~ship** seigneurie *f*; **your** 2! Monsieur le Juge (*or* Compte)!

lore science *f*, savoir *m*.

lorry camion *m*.

lose *v/t.* perdre; égarer; manquer (*the train*); **~ o.s.** s'égarer; fig. s'absorber; ~ **sight of s.th.** perdre qch. de vue; **get lost** se perdre, s'égarer; *v/i.* perdre; retarder (*watch*); **~r** perdant(e *f*) *m*.

loss perte *f*; 🕈 **~ leader** article-réclame *m* (*pl.* articles-réclame); **at a ~** désorienté; embarrassé (*pour inf.*, **to** *inf.*).

lost perdu; *fig. a.* désorienté; égaré; **get ~** être perdu; s'égarer; *sl.* **get ~!** fiche le camp!; *Br.* ~ **property** (*office*), *Am.* **~-and-found** (**department**) (service *m* des) objets *m/pl.* trouvés.

lot 1. sort *m* destinée *f*; *a.* 🕈 lot *m*; F **a ~**, **~s** *pl.* beaucoup (de, **of**); **the ~** tous (toutes) *pl.*; (le) tout; **draw ~s for s.th.** tirer qch. au sort; **~tery** loterie *f*.

loud bruyant; retentissant; criard (*colour*); *adv.* fort; **~hailer** porte-voix *m/inv.*; **~mouth** gueulard(e *f*) *m*; **~speaker** haut-parleur *m* (*pl.* haut-parleurs).

lounge 1. flâner; s'étendre à son aise; s'étaler; **2.** salon *m*; ~ **suit** complet *m* veston.

lous|e, *pl.* **lice** pou *m*; **~e up** F bousiller; **~y** pouilleux; F mauvais (= *bad*), F moche (= *ugly*), F sale (= *dirty*); F ~ **with** bourré de.

lout rustre *m*, lourdaud *m*.

louvre, *Am.* **louver** persienne *f*.

lovable adorable; aimable.

love 1. amour *m*; ~ **at first sight** le coup *m* de foudre; **give** (*or* **send**) **her my ~** dis-lui bien des choses (de ma part); **in ~ with** amoureux de; **make ~** (**to**) faire l'amour (avec); faire la cour (à); **2.** aimer (d'amour), affectionner; ~ **to do** aimer à faire; **3.** d'amour; ~ **affair** liaison *f* amoureuse; **~child** enfant *m* naturel; **~liness** beauté *f*; **~ly** beau; ravis-

sant; F charmant; **~r** amoureux *m*; amateur *m*; **~song** chanson *f* d'amour.

loving affectueux.

low¹ 1. bas; faible (*speed, standard etc.*); grave (*sound*); (*a.* **in ~ spirits**) déprimé, abattu; *adv.* bas; **in a ~ voice** à voix basse, doucement; **bring ~** abattre; humilier; **lie ~** se tapir; se cacher; *fig. a.* se tenir coi; **2.** *meteor.* dépression *f*; *fig.* niveau *m* le plus bas.

low² 1. meugler; **2.** meuglement *m*.

low...: ~-brow 1. peu intellectuel; **2.** homme *m etc.* terre à terre; philistin(e *f*) *m*; **~cost** (à) bon marché; **~down** bas; ignoble.

lower 1. *adj.* plus bas; inférieur; **2.** *v/t.* baisser; abaisser; descendre; *v/i.* baisser.

lowering menaçant; sombre.

low...: ~income à revenus modérés; **~key(ed)** discret, retenu; **~land** plaine *f* basse; pays *m* plat; **~liness** humilité *f*; **~ly** *adj.* humble, modeste; **~necked** décolleté (*dress*); **~spirited** abattu, découragé.

loyal (**to**) loyal (envers); fidèle (à); **~ty** fidélité *f*; loyauté *f*.

lozenge *pharm.* pastille *f*, tablette *f*.

lubric|ant lubrifiant *m*; **~ate** lubrifier, graisser; **~ation** lubrification *f*, ⚙ graissage *m*.

lucid lucide; **~ity** lucidité *f*.

luck chance *f*, fortune *f*; **good ~** bonne chance *f*, bonheur *m*; **bad** (*or* **hard** *or* **ill**) ~ malchance *f*, malheur *m*; **~ily** par bonheur; heureusement; **~less** malchanceux; **~y** heureux; qui porte bonheur.

lucrative lucratif.

ludicrous grotesque, risible.

ludo jeu *m* des petits chevaux.

lug traîner, tirer.

luge 1. luge *f*; **2.** faire de la luge.

luggage bagages *m/pl.*; ~ **rack** filet *m* (à bagages); ~ **van** 🚂 fourgon *m* aux bagages.

lugubrious lugubre.

lukewarm tiède (*a. fig.*).

lull 1. endormir (en berçant); **2.** *su.* moment *m* de calme; accalmie *f*; **~aby** berceuse *f*.

lumber 1. *su.* bric-à-brac *m*; fatras *m*; bois *m* de charpente; **2.** *v/t.* (*usu.* ~ **up**) encombrer; *v/i.* aller lourdement *or* à pas pesants; ~**jack**, ~**man** bûcheron *m*; ~**room** débarras *m*.

lumin|ary sommité *f*, lumière *f*; ~**ous** lumineux.

lump 1. *su. stone, sugar etc.*: morceau *m*; bloc *m*; masse *f*; *fig. person*: lourdaud *m*; *in the ~* en bloc; en gros; ~ **sugar** sucre *m* en morceaux; ~ **sum** somme *f* globale; **2.** *v/t.* (*usu.* ~ **together**) mettre en bloc; réunir; *v/i.* former des mottes; ~**ish** (ba)lourd; ~**y** grumeleux (*sauce*); défoncé (*mattress etc.*).

lunacy folie *f*; ✚ démence *f*.

lunar de (la) lune; lunaire.

lunatic 1. fou; ~ **asylum** maison *f* d'aliénés; **2.** fou (folle *f*) *m*; aliéné(e *f*) *m*.

lunch 1. (*abbr. of* ~**eon**) *su.* déjeuner *m*; **2.** *v/i.* déjeuner; *v/t.* offrir un déjeuner à (*q.*); ~**time** *l'* heure *f* du déjeuner.

lung *anat.* poumon *m*.

lunge 1. *su. fencing*: botte *f*; *fig.* mouvement brusque *m* en avant; **2.** *fencing*, *fig.*: porter une botte (à, **at**); *fig.* se précipiter.

lupin(e) ♀ lupin *m*.

lurch 1. embardée *f*; *leave in the ~* laisser (*q.*) dans l'embarras, planter (*q.*) là; **2.** tituber.

lure 1. attrait *m*; leurre *m*; **2.** attirer, séduire; persuader.

lurid effrayant.

lurk se cacher; rester tapi.

luscious succulent.

lust 1. desir *m*; soif *f* (de, **for**); **2.** ~ **for**, ~ **after** désirer (ardemment); convoiter; ~**ful** avide.

lust|re *Am.* ~**er** lustre *m*; éclat *m*; ~**rous** brillant.

lusty vigoureux.

lute ♪ luth *m*.

luxur|iant luxuriant, exubérant; ~**ious** luxueux; ~**y 1.** luxe *m*; **2.** de luxe.

lying menteur.

lymph ✚ lymphe *f*.

lynch lyncher; ~ **law** loi *f* de Lynch.

lynx *zo.* lynx *m*.

lyric 1. lyrique; **2.** ~**s** *pl.* paroles *f/pl.* (*of a song*); ~**al** lyrique.

M

M

ma'am *see* **madam**.

macaroni macaroni(s) *m*/(*pl.*).

macaroon macaron *m*.

mace[1] *spice*: macis *m*.

mace[2] massue *f*, masse *f*.

macerate macérer.

machin|ation machination *f*; ~**e 1.** machine *f*; *attr.* des machines; à la machine; **2.** façonner (*cost. a.* coudre) à la machine; ~**gun** mitrailleuse *f*; ~**e-made** fait à la machine; ~**ery** machinerie *f*; (*parts, a. fig.*) rouages *m/pl.*; ~**e-tool** machine-outil (*pl.* machines-outils) *f*; ~**e-washable** lavable en machine; ~**ist** machiniste *m*.

machismo machisme *m*.

mackerel *icht.* maquereau *m*.

mackinaw *Am.* couverture *f* épaisse.

mackintosh imperméable *m*.

macro|biotic macrobiotique; ~**biotics** *sg.* macrobiotisme *m*; ~**cosm** macrocosme *m*.

mad fou (de *about, with, on*); *Am.* fâché (contre, *with*); F furieux; *go ~* devenir fou; *drive ~* rendre fou.

madam madame *f*; mademoiselle *f*.

mad|cap écervelé (*a. su.*); ~**den** rendre fou, exaspérer.

made|-to-measure fait sur mesure; ~**-to-order** fait sur commande; ~**-up** assemblé; inventé; faux (*story*); artificiel; tout fait (*clothes*); maquillé (*woman*).

mad|house maison *f* de fous; asile *m* d'aliénés; ~**man** fou *m*, aliéné *m*; ~**ness** folie *f*; *Am. a.* colère *f*; ~**woman** folle *f*, aliénée *f*.

magazine (*illustrated*) magazine *m*; *gun*: magasin *m*; ✗ dépôt *m*.

maggot asticot *m*, ver *m*.

Magi *pl.* les Rosis *m/pl.* Mages.

magic 1. (*a.* ~**al**) magique; **2.** magie *f*; ~**ian** magicien (-ne *f*) *m*.

magistrate magistrat *m*; juge *m* de paix.
magnanimous magnanime.
magnet aimant *m*; **~ic** magnétique; aimanté; **~ field (pole)** champ *m* (pôle *m*) magnétique; **~ize** aimanter, *a. fig.* magnétiser.
magni|fication grossissement *m*; **~ficence** magnificence *f*; **~ficent** magnifique; somptueux; **~fy** grossir; **~fying glass** loupe *f*; **~tude** grandeur *f*.
magpie *orn.* pie *f*; *fig.* bavard(e *f*) *m*.
mahogany acajou *m*; *attr.* en acajou.
maid bonne *f*; **old ~** vieille fille *f*; **~ of all work** bonne *f* à tout faire; **~ of hono(u)r** fille *f* d'honneur; *Am.* première demoiselle *f* d'honneur.
maiden 1. jeune fille *f*; **2.** de jeune fille; non mariée; *fig.* premier, inaugural, de début; **~ name** nome *m* de jeune fille; **~ speech** discours *m* de début; **~ voyage** ♣ premier voyage *m*, ✈ premier vol *m*; **~head, ~hood** virginité *f*; célibat *m*; **~ly** virginal; modeste.
mail 1. *post:* courrier *m*; poste *f*; **2.** envoyer par la poste; expédier; **~ing list** liste *f* d'adresses; **~bag** sac *m* de dépêches *or* de poste; **~box** boîte *f* aux lettres; **~man** facteur *m*; **~-order firm**, *Am. oft.* **~-order house** maison *f* qui vend par correspondance.
maim mutiler.
main 1. principal, premier, essentiel; grand (*road*); **the ~ chance** son propre intérêt; **by ~ force** de vive force; **2.** ⊕ canalisation *f* maîtresse; ⚡ conducteur *m* principal; **~s** *pl.* ⚡ secteur *m*; **in the ~** en général; dans l'ensemble; **~land** terre *f* ferme; continent *m*; **~ly** surtout; **~spring** ressort *m* moteur; *fig.* mobile *m* essentiel; **~stay** ♣ étai *m* de grand mât; *fig.* soutien *m* principal; **~stream** tendence *f* principale; ♀ **Street** *Am.* grand-rue *f*; habitants *m/pl.* d'une petite ville.
maintain entretenir; maintenir; soutenir (*an opinion, one's family etc.*); conserver, garder; **~ that** affirmer *or* maintenir que.
maintenance entretien *m*; maintenance *f* (*a.* ⊛); **~ costs** *pl.* frais *m/pl.* d'entretien.
maize ❀ maïs *m*.
majest|ic majestueux; **~y** majesté *f*.
major 1. majeur; le plus grand; *mot.* de

priorité (*road*); principal; ♪ **A ~** la *m* majeur; ♪ **~ key** ton *m* majeur; **2.** ✕ commandant *m*; *Am. univ.* sujet *m* principal; **~ity** majorité *f* (*a. age*); le plus grand nombre; **~ rule** gouvernement *m* majoritaire; **~ decision** décision *f* prise à la majorité.
make 1. *v/t. usu.* faire; construire; fabriquer; confectionner (*clothes*); fixer (*conditions*); établir (*a rule*); conclure (*peace, a treaty*); ⚡ fermer (*a circuit*); nommer (*s.o. a judge*); **~ the best of it** en prendre son parti; **~ good** réparer (*an error*); tenir (*one's word*); **~ it** arriver à temps; (*ed*) réussir; **do you ~ one of us?** êtes-vous des nôtres?; **~ a place** arriver à un endroit; **~ shift** s'accommoder (de, *with*); **~ into** transformer en; **~ out** dresser (*an account, a list*); faire (*a cheque*); prouver; discerner; déchiffrer (*a handwriting*); **~ over** céder; transférer; **~ up** faire; assembler; façonner (*a dress etc.*); dresser (*a list, an account*); inventer (*a story*); compenser; compléter; **made up of** composé de; *see* **~ up for** (*v/i.*); **~ up one's mind** se décider (à, *to*; pour **for, in favo[u]r of**); **~ it up** se réconcilier, faire la paix; **2.** *v/i.* **~ as if** faire semblant de; faire comme si; **~ after** s'élancer sur *or* après; **~ away with** enlever; détruire; dérober (*money*); **~ for** se diriger vers; **~ off** se sauver; décamper; **~ sure** s'assurer (de, *of*); s'arranger (pour *inf.*, *that*); **~ up** compenser; se réconcilier; se maquiller; **~ up for** compenser; réparer; se rattraper de (*a loss*); suppléer à; **3.** fabrication *f*; façon *f*; *person:* taille *f*; marque *f*; ⚡ *circuit:* fermeture *f*; **~-believe 1.** illusion *f*, fantaisie *f*, chimères *f/pl.*; (faux) semblant; **2.** imaginaire, de fantaisie; **~r** faiseur (-euse *f*) *m*; ✝ fabricant *m*; **the ♀** le Créateur *m* (*God*); **~shift 1.** pis-aller *m/inv.*; **2.** de fortune; **~-up** composition *f*; maquillage *m*; invention *f*.
making: **in the ~** en train de se faire.
maladjust|ed *psych.* inadapté; **~ment** inadaptation *f*.
maladministration mauvaise administration *f*.
maladroit maladroit.
malady maladie *f*.
malaise malaise *m*.

malark(e)y F baratin *m*.

malcontent mécontent (*a. su.*).

male 1. mâle; masculin; ~ **screw** vis *f* mâle; **2.** mâle *m*.

malediction malédiction *f*.

malevolen|ce malveillance *f*; ~**t** malveillant.

malfunction 1. fonctionnement *m* défectueux, dérèglement *m*; **2.** fonctionner mal.

malice malveillance *f*; méchanceté *f*; *bear s.o.* ~ en vouloir à q., vouloir du mal à q.; ★ **with** ~ **aforethought** avec intention criminelle.

malicious méchant; malveillant; ~**ness** méchanceté *f*, malice *f*.

malign calomnier; diffamer; ~**ancy** malignité *f* (*a.* ★); ~**ant** malin (*a.* ★); méchant *m/pl.*; ~**ity** malignité *f* (*a.* ★); méchanceté *f*.

mall centre *m* commercial.

malleable malléable.

mallet maillet *m*.

malnutrition malnutrition *f*.

malodorous malodorant.

malpractice faute *f* or négligence *f* professionnelle.

malt malt *m*.

maltreat maltraiter, malmener.

mam(m)a maman *f*.

mammal mammifère *m*.

mammoth 1. *zo.* mammouth *m*; **2.** géant, monstre.

mammy F maman *f*; *Am. a.* nourrice *f* noire.

man 1. *pl.* **men** homme *m*; F mari *m*; *chess*: pièce *f*; *draughts*: pion *m*; *attr.* d'homme(s); **2.** garnir d'hommes.

manage *v/t.* gérer, diriger (*a firm etc.*), (*handle*) manier; venir à bout de; *v/i.* s'arranger, se débrouiller (*pour inf.*, **to** *inf.*); ~ **to** (*inf.*) *a.* arriver à, réussir à (*inf.*); ~**able** maniable; traitable (*person*); ~**ment** direction *f*, administration *f*, gestion *f*; administrateurs *m/pl.*; ~**r** directeur *m*; *hotel, restaurant etc.*: gérant *m*; *departmental* ~ chef *m* de rayon; chef *m* de service; *sales* ~ directeur *m* commercial; ~**ress** directrice *f*, gérante *f*.

managing directeur; gérant; ~ *director* directeur *m* général, P.D.G.

mandarin *person*: mandarin *m*; (*a.* ~ *orange*) mandarine *f*.

mandat|e *pol.* mandat *m*; ~**ory** obligatoire; *pol.* mandataire.

mane crinière *f*.

maneuver *Am. see* **manœuvre**.

manful courageux.

mange *vet.* gale *f*; F rogne *f*.

manger crèche *f*.

mangle déchirer; mutiler.

mangy galeux; *fig.* minable.

manhood âge *m* viril; virilité *f*.

mania manie *f*; ~**c** fou.

manicure 1. soin *m* des mains; **2.** soigner les mains de; manucurer (*a. fig.*).

manifest 1. manifeste, évident; **2.** manifester; ~**ation** manifestation *f*; ~**o** *pol. etc.* manifeste *m*.

manifold 1. divers, varié; nombreux; **2.** *mot.* **intake** (**exhaust**) ~ collecteur *m* d'admission (d'échappement); **3.** polycopier.

manipulat|e manipuler (*a. fig. pej.*); ◎ manœuvrer; ~**ion** manipulation *f*; ◎ manœuvre *f*; *pej.* tripotage *m*.

man|kind le genre *m* humain, l'humanité *f*; ~**ly** viril, d'homme; ~**made** artificiel; ~ **fibre** fibre *f* synthétique.

manner manière *f* (*a. art. a. literature*); façon *f*; ~**s** *pl.* mœurs *f/pl.*; manières *f/pl.*; *in a* ~ d'une façon; *in such a* ~ *that* de manière que, de sorte que; ~**ed** aux manières ...; *art:* maniéré; ~**ly** courtois, poli.

manœuvre, *Am. a.* **maneuver 1.** manœuvre *f*; **2.** manœuvrer.

man-of-war vaisseau *m* de guerre.

manor (*a.* ~ *house*) manoir *m*; *lord of the* ~ seigneur *m*.

manpower main-d'œuvre (*pl.* mains d'œuvre) *f*.

man-servant domestique *m*.

mansion château *m*; hôtel *m* particulier (*in town*).

man-size(d) F gros; de grande personne.

manslaughter homicide *m* involontaire.

mantelpiece cheminée *f*.

mantle 1. *fig.*, △, *anat.*, *zo.* manteau *m*; **2.** (*sc*) (re)couvrir.

manual 1. manuel; **2.** manuel *m*; ♪ clavier *m*.

manufactur|e 1. fabrication *f*; **2.** fabriquer; ~**er** fabricant *m*.

manure 1. fumier *m*; engrais *m*; **2.** fumer; engraisser.

manuscript manuscrit m.

many 1. beaucoup de; bien des; ~ *a* maint; bien des; *one too* ~ un de trop; **2.** un grand nombre; *a good* ~ un assez grand nombre (de); *a great* ~ un grand nombre (de).

map 1. *geog.* carte f; *town*: plan m; **2.** dresser une carte *or* un plan (de qch., *s.th.*); *fig.* ~ *out* tracer; organiser, arranger.

maple ♀ érable m.

mar gâter, gâcher, troubler.

marathon marathon m.

maraud marauder; ~**er** maraudeur m.

marble 1. marbre m; *game*: bille f; **2.** de marbre; ~**d** marbré.

March mars m.

march 1. marche f; **2.** marcher (au pas); ~ *off* se mettre en marche; ~ *past* défiler.

marchioness marquise f.

mare jument f.

margarine margarine f.

margin marge f; *wood*: lisière f; *river etc.*: bord m; ~ *of profit* marge f (bénéficiaire); *safety* ~ marge f de sécurité; *by a wide* (*narrow*) ~ de loin (de peu); ~**al** marginal (*note*); en marge.

marihuana, marijuana marihuana f.

marine 1. marin; de mer; de (la) marine; **2.** ✕ fusilier m marin; ~**r** marin m.

marital matrimonial; conjugal.

maritime maritime.

mark¹ *coin*: mark m.

mark² 1. marque f (a. ♆, *of a product*); *but* m, cible f; signe m; *school*: note f; point m (*a. punctuation*); *sp.* ligne f de départ; ♆ cote f; *fig. up to the* ~ à la hauteur; dans son assiette (*health*); *hit the* ~ frapper juste; *miss the* ~ manquer le but; **2.** marquer; tâcher; *scol.* noter; ~ *time* marquer le pas; *fig. a.* faire du sur place; ~ *down* inscrire; désigner; ♆ baisser (le prix de); ~ *off* séparer; délimiter; ~ *out* tracer; délimiter, borner; distinguer; désigner; ~ *up* hausser (le prix de); ~**ed** marqué, prononcé, net; ~**edly** sensiblement; ~**er** marqueur m (*a. pen*); *tool*: marquoir m.

market 1. marché m; ~ *garden* jardin m maraîcher; ~ *place* place f du marché; ~ *price* prix m courant; ~ *research* étude f de marché; *be in the* ~ *for* être acheteur de; **2.** *v/t.* lancer sur le marché; trouver des débouchés pour; ven-

dre; *v/i.*: *go* ~*ing* faire son marché; ~**able** vendable; ~**ing** marketing m.

marksman bon tireur m.

marmalade confiture f d'oranges.

maroon 1. abandonner (*q.*) sur une île déserte; *fig.* bloquer; **2.** *colour*: bordeaux; **3.** *firework*: fusée f à pétard.

marquee chapiteau m.

marquis marquis m.

marriage mariage m; ~**able** mariable.

married marié (*person*); conjugal (*life*); ~ *couple* ménage m.

marrow moelle f; *fruit*: courge f; ~**y** plein de moelle (*a. fig.*).

marry *v/t.* marier (q. à q., *s.o. to s.o.*); se marier avec; épouser (*q.*); *v/i.* (*a. get married*) se marier.

marsh marais m, marécage m.

marshal 1. maréchal m; *Am.* commissaire m de (la) police; **2.** (ar)ranger; ressembler; réunir; conduire; 🚂 trier (*carriages*).

marshy marécageux.

mart salle f de vente; marché m.

marten *zo.* mart(r)e f.

martial martial; ~ *law* loi f martiale.

martyr 1. martyr(e f) m; **2.** martyriser; ~**dom** martyre m.

marvel 1. merveille f; **2.** (de, *at*) s'émerveiller; s'étonner; ~**(l)ous** merveilleux.

Marxis|m marxisme m; ~**t** marxiste (*adj., mf*).

mascot mascotte f.

masculine masculin; mâle.

mash 1. pâte f; *Br. cuis.* purée f; **2.** écraser; ~**ed potatoes** *pl.* purée f (de pommes de terre).

mask 1. masque m; **2.** masquer.

mason maçon m; (*a. free-*~) franc-maçon (*pl.* francs-maçons) m; ~**ry** maçonnerie f.

masquerade 1. mascarade f; bal m masqué; **2.** *fig.* ~ *as* se déguiser en; se faire passer pour.

mass¹ *eccl.* messe f; *High* ♀ grand-messe f.

mass² 1. masse; ~ *media* pl. media m/ pl.; ~ *meeting* réunion f en masse; ~ *production* fabrication f en série; ~ *psychology* psychologie f des foules; ~ *society* société f de masse; **2.** se masser.

massacre 1. massacre m; **2.** massacrer.

massage 1. massage m; **2.** masser.

massive massif; énorme; solide.

mast ⚓ mât m; *radio*: pylône m.
master 1. maître m (a. fig.); *employer*: patron m, chef m; *school*: instituteur m; professeur m; *univ.* (di)recteur m; *title*: monsieur m; ♀ *of Arts* licencié m ès lettres; **~ of ceremonies** maître des cérémonies; *show etc.*: animateur m; **2.** maître; de maître; *fig.* supérieur; **~card** carte f maîtresse; **3.** maîtriser; apprendre (*a subject*); *show etc.*: **~builder** entrepreneur m de bâtiments; **~ful** impérieux; autoritaire; **~key** passe-partout m/inf.; **~ly** magistral, de maître; **~mind 1.** fig. cerveau m; **2.** diriger, être le cerveau de; **~piece** chef-d'œuvre m; **~ stroke** coup m de maître; **~y** maîtrise f (de **over, of**); connaissance f approfondie.
masticate mastiquer; mâcher.
mastiff mâtin m; dogue m anglais.
mat¹ 1. *straw*: natte f; *wool etc.*: tapis m, (*door* **~**) paillasson m; (*table* **~**) napperon m; **2.** (s')emmêler.
mat² mat; mati.
match¹ allumette f.
match² 1. égal m, pareil(le f) m; *colours*: assortiment m; mariage m; *sp.* match (*pl.* match, matches) m; **bo or make a good ~** être bien assorti(e)s; **2.** v/t. aller (bien) avec, s'assortir à, être assorti à; (*a.* **~ up to**) égaler, valoir; (*a.* **~ up**) assortir; unir (*q.*) (à, **with**); **well ~ed** bien assorti; v/i. aller (bien) ensemble, être bien assorti; **with shoes to ~** avec (des) chaussures assorties; **~box** boîte f à *or* d'allumettes; **~ing** assorti; **~less** incomparable, sans pareil, sans égal.
mate¹ *chess*: faire échec et mat.
mate² 1. camarade mf; compagnon m; *animal*: mâle m, femelle f; *school*: camarade mf; ⚓ second m; **2.** (s')accoupler; (s')unir.
material 1. matériel; essentiel (pour, **to**); **2.** matière f; tissu f; **~s** pl. matériaux m/pl.; fournitures f/pl.; **~ism** matérialisme m; **~istic** matérialiste; **~ize** se matérialiser, se réaliser.
maternal maternel; de mère; d'une mère; **~ity** maternité f, **~ benefit** allocation f de maternité; **~ dress** robe f de grossesse *or* de future maman; **~ hospital** maternité f; **~ ward** salle f des accouchées.
mathematician mathématicien(ne f) m; **~s** *usu. sg.* mathématiques f/pl.

mating accouplement; **~ season** saison f des amours.
matriculate s'inscrire.
matrimonial matrimonial; conjugal; **~y** mariage m.
matrix ◎ matrice f.
matron matrone f; *hospital*: infirmière f en chef; **~ of hono(u)r** dame f d'honneur.
matter 1. matière f; substance f; sujet m; chose f; affaire f; ♣ matière f purulente; **printed ~** imprimés m/pl.; **what's the ~?** qu'est-ce qu'il y a?; **what's the ~ with you?** qu'est-ce que vous avez?; **no ~** n'importe; **no ~ who** qui que ce soit; **as a ~ of course** tout automatiquement; **as a ~ of fact** en fait; **~ of fact** question f de(s) fait(s); **2.** avoir de l'importance; importer (à, **to**); **it does not ~** n'importe; cela ne fait rien; **~-of-fact** pratique; prosaïque.
mattres matelas m.
mature 1. mûr; *cuis.* fait (*cheese*); **2.** mûrir; **~ity** maturité f; ♦ échéance f.
maudlin larmoyant; pleurard.
maul meurtrir, malmener.
Maundy Thursday jeudi m saint.
mauve mauve (m, adj.).
maw zo. caillette f; fig. gueule f.
mawkish exagérément sentimental.
maxim maxime f; **~al** maximal; **~ize** maxim(al)iser; **~um 1.** pl. usu. **-ma** maximum (pl. a. **-ma**) m; **2.** maximum.
May¹ mai m; **~ Day** le Premier mai m.
may² defective verb: je peux etc.; il se peut que.
maybe peut-être.
mayday, ♀ S.O.S.
mayhem Am. 🕮 mutilation f; F chaos m, F tohu-bohu m.
mayor maire m.
maze labyrinthe m, dédale m.
me accusative: me, dative: moi.
mead hydromel m; *poet.* pré m.
meadow pré m, prairie f.
meag|re, Am. ~er maigre.
meal repas m; farine f; **~s** pl. **on wheels** repas m/pl. livrés à domicile; **~time** heure f du repas.
mean¹ mesquin, radin; misérable, minable; small F **no ~** assez bon.
mean² 1. moyen; **2.** milieu m; moyen terme m; Å moyenne f; **~s** pl. moyens m/pl.; voies f/pl.; **a ~s of** (ger.) *or* **to**

(*inf.*) un moyen (de *inf.*); *by all* ~s mais certainement!; *by no* ~s en aucune façon; *by this* ~s par ce moyen; *by* ~s *of* au moyen de.

mean³ avoir l'intention (de *inf.*, *to inf.*); se proposer (de *inf.*, *to inf.*); vouloir; vouloir dire; entendre (par, *by*); destiner (pour, *for*); ~ *well* (*ill*) vouloir du bien (mal) (à, *by*).

meaning sens *m*, signification *f*; **2.** significatif, éloquent; qui en dit long; ~**ful** constructif; *see a. meaning* 2; ~**less** dénué de sens; insensé (*effort etc.*).

mean|time, ~while (*a. in the* ~) en attendant, dans l'intervalle.

measles *sg.* 🐟 rougeole *f*.

measure 1. mesure *f* (*a.* ♩, *a. fig.*); ☉ règle *f*, mètre *m*; *made to* ~ fait sur mesure; **2.** mesurer (pour, *for*); métrer (*a wall*); ~ *up to s.th.* se montrer à la hauteur de qch.; ~**d** mesuré; ~**less** illimité; ~**ment** mesurage *m*; mesure *f*.

meat viande *f*; ~ *pie* pâté *m* en croûte; ~**ball** boulette *f* de viande; ~**y** *fig.* substantiel.

mechan|ic 1. mécanicien *m*; **2.** ~**s** *pl.* mécanique *f*; mécanisme *m*; ~**ical** mécanique; ~**ism** mécanisme *m*; ~**istic** mécaniste; ~**ization** mécanisation *f*; ~**ize** mécaniser.

medal médaille *f*; ~**lion** médaillon *m*; ~**(l)ist** médaillé(e *f*) *m*.

meddle (*with, in*) se mêler (de); toucher (à); ~**some** officieux; qui touche à tout.

media *pl.* les media *m/pl.*

mediaeval *see medieval.*

medial médian; moyen.

median 1. médian; **2.** ⚕ médiane *f*; *Am. mot.* (*a.* ~ *strip*) bande *f* médiane.

mediat|e s'interposer; agir en médiateur; ~**ion** médiation *f*; ~**or** médiateur (-trice *f*) *m*.

medic F *doctor:* toubib *m*; *student:* carabin *m*.

Medicaid assistance médicale aux économiquement faibles.

medical médical; de médecine; ~ *certificate* attestation *f* de médecin; ~ *man* médecin *m*; ~ *student* étudiant *m* en médecine.

Medicare assistance *f* médicale aux personnes âgées.

medicate médicamenter; ~**d** médical.

medicin|al médicinal; ~**e** médecine *f*; médicament *m*.

medieval médiéval.

mediocre médiocre.

meditat|e *v/i.* méditer (sur, [*up*]*on*); *v/t.* méditer (*qch.*; de faire qch., *doing s.th.*); projeter; ~**ion** méditation *f*; ~**ive** méditatif.

medium 1. *pl.* **-dia, -diums** milieu *m*; intermédiaire *m*; moyen *m*; *psych.* médium *m*; **2.** moyen; *radio:* ~ *wave* onde *f* moyenne; ~**-sized** de grandeur *or* de taille moyenne.

medlar 🌰 nèfle *f*; *tree:* néflier *m*.

medley mélange *m*; ♩ pot-pourri (*pl.* pots-pourris) *m*.

meek doux; humble; soumis; ~**ness** humilité *f*; soumission *f*.

meerschaum (*pipe f en*) écume *f* de mer.

meet *v/t.* rencontrer, tomber sur; faire la connaissance de; rejoindre, retrouver; croiser (*in the street*); aller chercher (*s.o. at the station*); satisfaire à (*s.o.'s wishes*); faire face à (*commitments, misfortune etc.*); trouver (*death*); faire honneur à (*a bill*); *come* (*go, run*) *to* ~ *s.o.* venir (aller, courir) à la rencontre de q.; *v/i.* se rencontrer; se voir; se réunir; confluer (*rivers*); ~ *with* rencontrer, se heurter à (*difficulties*); essuyer (*a loss etc.*); ~ *up* se rencontrer; se retrouver; ~ *up with* rencontrer.

meeting rencontre *f*; réunion *f*; assemblée *f*; *pol., sp.* meeting *m*.

megaton mégatonne *f*.

melancholy 1. mélancolie *f*; **2.** mélancolique.

mellow 1. mûr (*a. fig.*); moelleux; doux (*sound, light, wine*); *fig.* tendre (*colour*); **2.** (faire) mûrir; (se) velouter; (s')adoucir (*person*).

melod|ious mélodieux; ~**y** mélodie *f*.

melon 🌰 melon *m*.

melt fondre; *fig.* (se) dissoudre; *v/t.* attendrir (*s.o.'s heart*); *v/i.:* ~ *away fig.* fondre, se dissiper; ~ *down* fondre; ~**ing point** point *m* de fusion; ~**ing pot** creuset *m*.

member membre *m*; ~ *of Parliament* député *m*; ~**ship** adhésion *f* (à, *of*); qualité *f* de membre; (nombre *m* des) membres *m/pl.*; ~ *card* carte *f* de membre.

membrane membrane *f*.

memento souvenir *m*, mémento *m*.

memoir mémoire *m*; notice *f* biographique; **~s** *pl.* mémoires *m/pl.*

memorable mémorable.

memorandum mémorandum *m* (*a. pol.*); *pol.* note *f* (diplomatique).

memorial 1. commémoratif (*monument*); **2.** mémorial *m*.

memorize apprendre par cœur.

memory mémoire *f* (*a. data processing*); souvenir *m*; **in ~ of** en mémoire de; en souvenir de.

men (*pl. of* **man**) hommes *m/pl.*; le genre *m* humain, l'humanité *f*.

menace 1. menacer; **2.** menace *f*.

mend 1. *v/t.* raccommoder (*clothes*); réparer; **~ one's ways** s'amender; **2.** reprise *f*, raccommodage *m*; **on the ~** en voie de guérison.

mendacious menteur, mensonger.

mendicant mendiant (*a. su./m*)

menial 1. de domestique, inférieur; **2.** domestique *mf*.

menopause ménopause *f*.

menstruat|e avoir ses règles; **~ion** menstruation *f*, règles *f/pl.*

mental mental; de l'esprit; **~ arithmetic** calcul *m* de tête; **~ hospital** (*or* **home**) hôpital *m* psychiatrique; **~ block** blocage *m* mental; **make a ~ note** prendre note mentalement; **~ity** mentalité *f*; esprit *m*.

mention 1. mention *f*; **2.** mentionner; **don't ~ it!** il n'y a pas de quoi!; **not to ~** sans parler de.

menu menu *m*; carte *f*.

mercantile mercantile; commercial, de commerce; commerçant.

mercenary mercenaire (*a. su./m*).

merchandise marchandise(s) *f*(*pl.*).

merchant 1. négociant *m*; marchand(e *f*) *m*; **2.** marchand; de *or* du commerce; **~ bank** banque *f* de commerce; **~ navy** (*Am.* **marine**) marine *f* marchande; **law ~** droit *m* commercial; **~man** navire *m* marchand *or* de commerce.

merci|ful miséricordieux, clément; **~less** impitoyable.

mercury ♀ mercure *m*.

mercy pitié *f*, miséricorde *f*; **at s.o.'s ~** à la merci de q.

mere simple, seul, pur; **~ words** rien que des mots; **~ly** simplement.

meretricious factice (*style*).

merge *v/t.* fusionner; amalgamer (avec **with, into**); *v/i.* se fondre (dans **with, into**); s'amalgamer; **~r** fusion *f*.

meridian 1. méridien; **2.** *geog.* méridien *m*; *fig.* apogée *m*.

merit 1. mérite *m*; valeur *f*; *usu.* **~s** *pl.* bien-fondé *m*; le pour et le contre; **2.** mériter; **~orious** méritoire; méritant (*person*).

mermaid sirène *f*.

merriment gaieté *f*, réjouissance *f*.

merry joyeux, gai; F éméché; **make ~** se divertir; **~-go-round** manège *m*; **~-making** réjouissances *f/pl.*

mesh 1. maille *f*; *fig. usu.* **~es** *pl.* réseau *m*; filet *m*; ⊙ **In ~** en prise (avec, **with**); **2.** *fig.* (s')engrener.

mess[1] 1. désordre *m*; gâchis *m*; F embrouillamini *m*, pagaille *f*; **make a ~ of** gâcher; F **look a ~** être dans un état épouvantable; **2.** *v/t. a.* **~ up** gâcher, chambarder, bousiller; salir; *v/i.* F **~ about** gaspiller son temps; **~ about with** tripoter.

mess[2] ✕, ♣ mess *m* (*for officers*).

message message *m*; commission *f*; F **get the ~** comprendre, F piger; **give s.o. the ~** faire la commission à q.; **take a ~** faire la commission.

messenger messager (-ère *f*) *m*.

Messiah Messie *m*.

Messieurs, *usu.* **Messrs.** ✝ Messieurs *m/pl.*; maison *f*.

mess-up *see* **mess[1]**.

messy F en désordre; embrouillé; sale.

metal 1. métal *m*; **2.** empierrer; **~lic** métallique; **~lurgy** métallurgie *f*.

metamorphos|e (se) métamorphoser (en, **into**); **~is** métamorphose *f*.

metaphor métaphore *f*, image *f*.

mete out infliger.

meteor météore *m*; **~ology** météorologie *f*.

meter (*a.* **gas ~**) compteur *m*; *Am. see a.* **metre**; **~ maid** contractuelle *f*.

method méthode *f*; **~ic(al)** méthodique.

meticulous méticuleux.

met|re, *Am.* **~er** mesure *f*; mètre *m*.

metric métrique.

metropoli|s métropole *f*; **~tan** métropolitain.

mettle *person*: courage *m*, ardeur *f*; *horse*: fougue *f*; **~some** courageux, ardent, fougueux.

M

mews *sg.,* † *pl.* écuries *f/pl.*; *London*: impasse *f*, ruelle *f*.

Mexican 1. mexicain; **2.** Mexicain(e *f*) *m*.

miaow 1. miaulement *m*, miaou *m*; **2.** miauler.

mickey F: *take the ~ out of s.o.* se payer la tête de q.

microbe microbe *m*.

micro|cosm microcosme *m*; **~phone** microphone *m*; **~processor** microprocesseur *m*; **~scope** microscope *m*; **~wave** micro-onde *f*.

mid mi-; **~air:** (*in ~*) en plein ciel; **~day** midi *m*.

middle 1. milieu *m*; *fig.* taille *f*; **2.** du milieu; moyen; intermédiaire; 2 *Ages pl.* Moyen Âge *m*; **~class(es** *pl.*) classe *f* moyenne; bourgeoisie *f*; **~-aged** F entre deux âges; **~class** bourgeois; **~man** intermédiaire *m*; **~-of-the-road** modéré, qui évite les extrêmes; **~sized** de grandeur *or* taille moyenne; **~weight** *box.* poids *m* moyen.

middling passable; moyen.

midge moucheron *m*.

midget[1] nain(e *f*) *m*; **2.** nain; minuscule.

mid|land intérieur (*sea*); **2. the** 2*s pl.* les Midlands *m/pl.*; **~most** le plus près du milieu; **~night** minuit *m*; **~riff** diaphragme *m*; **~st** *su.* milieu *m*; *in the ~ of* au milieu de; parmi; **~summer** milieu *m* de l'été; **~way** mi-chemin; **~wife** sage-femme *f*; **~wives** *pl.* sages-femmes) *f*; **~winter** milieu *m* de l'hiver.

might puissance *f*, force *f*; **~y** puissant; F rude; **2.** rudement, sacrément.

migrat|e émigrer; passer; **~ion** migration *f*; **~ory** migrateur.

mike F micro(phone) *m*.

mild doux; léger; *fig.* peu strict (*rule*).

mildew *plants*: rouille *f*; *vine etc.*: mildiou *m*; moisissure *f*; **~ed** piqué (*books etc.*).

mildness douceur *f*.

mile mille *m*.

mil(e)age distance *f or* vitesse *f* en milles; *fig.* parcours *m*

milestone borne *f*; *fig.* événement *m* marquant.

milit|ant militant; **~ary 1.** militaire; **2.** les militaires *m/pl.*; l'armée *f*; **~ate:** ~ *contre* militer contre.

milk 1. lait *m*; **2.** traire; *fig.* dépouiller; ~

tooth dent *f* de lait; **~maid** laitière *f*; trayeuse *f*; **~man** laitier *m*; **~sop** F poule *f* mouillée; **~y** laiteux; lacté; *astr.* 2 *Way* Voie *f* lactée.

mill 1. moulin *m*; usine *f*; fabrique *f*; filature *f*; **2.** *v/t.* moudre (*coffee, grain etc.*); ⚙ fraiser; creneler (*coin etc.*); broyer (*ore*); *v/i.* ~ *about*, ~ *around* grouiller (*people*); tourner en rond.

millenium millenaire *m*.

miller meunier *m*.

millet 𝕐 millet *m*.

millimetre millimètre *m*.

milliner modiste *f*; **~y** (articles *m/pl.* de) modes *f/pl*.

million million *m*; **~aire** millionnaire *mf*; **~th** millionième (*a. su./m*).

millipede *zo.* mille-pattes *m/inv.*

millstone meule *f*.

milt laitance *f* (*of fish*).

mime 1. mime *m*; **2.** mimer.

mimeograph 1. polycopieur *m*; **2.** polycopier.

mimic 1. imitateur; **2.** mime *m*; imitateur (-trice *f*) *m*; **3.** imiter; contrefaire; F *singer* (*q.*); **~ry**; imitation *f*; *zo.* mimétisme *m*.

mince 1. *v/t.* hacher; *he doesn't ~ matters* (*or his words*) il ne mâche pas ses mots; *v/i.* marcher d'un air affecté; **2.** (*a. ~d meat*) hachis *m*; **~meat** compôte *f* de raisins secs, de pommes, d'amandes *etc.*; F *fig. make ~ of* pulvériser; ~ *pie* petite tarte *f* au *mincemeat*; **~r** hachoir *m*.

mind 1. esprit *m*; idée *f*, avis *m*; *to my ~* à mon avis; *out of one's ~* hors de son bon sens; *change one's ~* changer d'avis; *bear s.th. in ~* ne pas oublier qch.; tenir compte de qch.; F *blow s.o.'s ~* renverser q.; *have* (*half*) *a ~ to* avoir (bonne) envie de; *have in ~* penser à; songer à; compter (*faire qch.*); *have s.th. on one's ~* avoir l'esprit préoccupé de qch.; *keep in ~* ne pas oublier; *make up one's ~* se décider; **2.** faire attention à; s'occuper de; ne pas manquer de (*inf.*); *never ~!* ça ne fait rien!; ~ *the step!* attention à la marche!; *I don't ~* (*it*) cela m'est égal; peu (m')importe; *do you ~ if* ... est-ce que cela vous gêne si ...; *do you ~ smoking?* la fumée ne vous gêne pas?; *would you ~ doing* (*s.th.*) cela vous ennuierait *or* dérangerait de faire (qch.); ~ *your own business!* mêlez-vous de ce qui vous regarde!; ~**bending** F hallucinant; ~**blowing** F renversant, bouleversant; ~**boggling** F inconcevable; ~**ful** (*of*) attentif (à); soigneux (de); ~**less** (*of*) insouciant (de); indifférent (à); oublieux (de).

mine¹ 1. le mien, la mienne, les miens, les miennes; à moi; **2.** les miens *m*/*pl.*

mine² 1. ✕, ✕, *fig.* mine *f*; **2.** miner (*a.* ✕); ✕ exploiter (*coal*); creuser; ~*r* mineur *m.*

mineral 1. minerai *m*; ~**s** *pl.* boissons *f*/*pl.* gazeuses; **2.** minéral.

mingle (se) mêler (à, *with*); (se) mélanger (avec, *with*).

miniature 1. miniature *f*; **2.** (en) miniature; de petit format.

mini|bus minibus *m*, ~**cab** minitaxi *m.*

minim|ize réduire au minimum; *fig.* minimiser; ~**um 1.** *pl.* **-ma** minimum (*pl.* -s, -ma) *m*; **2.** minimum.

mining 1. minier; de mine(s); **2.** exploitation *f* minière.

minion serviteur *m.*

miniskirt mini-jupe *f.*

minister 1. *pol.* ministre *m*; *eccl.* pasteur *m* (*protestant*); **2.** *v*/*i.* ~ **to** soigner (*q.*); ~**ial** *pol.* ministériel.

ministry ministère *m.*

mink *zo.* vison *m.*

minor petit, mineur, peu important; ♪ mineur; *A* ~ la *m* mineur; **2.** mineur(e *f*) *m*; *Am. univ.* sujet *m* (d'étude) secondaire; ~**ity** minorité *f* (*a.* ✝✝), ~ *government* gouvernement *m* minoritaire.

minster cathédrale.

minstrel ménestrel *m.*

mint¹ ♀ menthe *f.*

mint² 1. Hôtel *m* de la Monnaie; F *a* ~ (*of money*) une somme *f* fabuleuse; *in* ~ *condition* à l'état de neuf; **2.** battre (*coins*); *fig.* forger.

minuet ♪ menuet *m.*

minus 1. *prp.* moins; F sans; **2.** *adj.* négatif; **3.** (*a.* ~ *sign*) signe *m* moins.

minute¹ minute *f*, ~**s** *pl.* procès-verbal (*pl.* procès-verbaux) *m*; ~ *hand* grande aiguille *f*; *just a* ~! minute!

minute² 1. tout petit; minuscule; détaillé; ~**ly** dans ses moindres détails.

mirac|le miracle *m*; *by a* ~ par miracle; ~**ulous** miraculeux.

mirage mirage *m.*

mire boue *f*, fange *f*; *fig.* **drag through** *the* ~ traîner dans la boue.

mirror 1. miroir *m*, glace *f*; **2.** refléter (*a. fig.*).

mirth gaieté *f*; ~**ful** gai, joyeux.

miry bourbeux, fangeux; vaseux.

mis... mé-, més-, mal-, mauvais ...

misadventure mésaventure *f*; ✝✝ accident *m.*

misapply mal appliquer.

misapprehend mal comprendre.

misappropriate détourner (*funds*).

misbehav|e se conduire mal; ~**io(u)r** mauvaise conduite *f.*

misbelief fausse croyance *f.*

miscalculat|e *v*/*t.* mal calculer; *v*/*i.* se tromper; ~**ion** erreur *f* (de calcul).

miscarriage ✝ fausse couche *f*; ~ *of justice* erreur *f* judiciaire.

miscellan|eous varié; divers; ~**y** mélange *m*; recueil *m.*

mischance malchance *f*; accident *m.*

mischief bêtises *f*/*pl.*, sottises *f*/*pl.*; malice *f*, espièglerie *f*; mal *m*, dommage *m*; méchanceté *f.*

mischievous *child:* espiègle; méchant, nuisible.

miscon|ceive mal concevoir; mal comprendre; ~**ception** fausse idée *f*, malentendu *m.*

misconduct 1. mauvaise conduite *f*; mauvaise gestion *f*; *professional* ~ faute *f* professionnelle; **2.** mal diriger *or* gérer.

misconstru|ction fausse interprétation *f*; ~**e** mal interpréter.

miscount mal compter.

misdeed méfait *m.*

misdemeano(u)r écart *m* de conduite; ✝✝ infraction *f.*

misdirect mal diriger; mal adresser.

misdoing méfait *m.*

miser avare *mf.*

miserable malheureux; triste; misérable; déplorable.

miserly avare.

misery souffrances *f*/*pl.*; misère *f*, détresse *f*; tristesse *f.*

misfire 1. *mot.* avoir des ratés *fig.* rater; **2.** *mot.* raté *m* d'allumage.

misfit inadapté(e *f*) *m.*

misfortune malheur *m*; infortune *f.*

misgiving pressentiment *m*, crainte *f*, soupçon *m.*

misguide mal guider *or* conseiller.

mishap mésaventure *f*; accident *m*.

misinform mal renseigner.

misinterpret mal interpréter.

mislay égarer.

mislead tromper; fourvoyer; **~ing** trompeur.

mismanage mal administrer.

misnomer nom *m or* terme *m* mal approprié.

misplace déplacer; mal placer; égarer.

misprint 1. imprimer incorrectement; **2.** faute *f* d'impression.

mispronounce mal prononcer.

misquote citer inexactement.

misread mal lire *or* interpréter.

misrepresent présenter (*q.*) sous un faux jour; dénaturer (*facts*).

miss¹ mademoiselle.

miss² 1. coup *m* manqué *or* perdu *or* raté; F **give s.th. (s.o.) a ~** ne pas aller à qch. (chez q.); sauter, omettre qch.; **2.** *v/t.* manquer; F rater (*the mark, an opportunity, the train*); ne pas trouver; ne pas saisir; se tromper de (*one's way*); ne pas avoir; remarquer *or* regretter l'absence de; ~ (*ger.*) faillir (*inf.*); ~ **out** sauter, oublier; ~ **out on** rater, perdre; *v/i.* manquer le coup; frapper à vide.

misshapen difforme.

missile projectile *m*; ✕ missile *m*; ~ **site** base *f* de lancement.

missing manquant; absent; *esp.* ✕ disparu; **be ~** manquer; être égaré *or* perdu.

mission mission *f*; **~ary** missionnaire.

missive missive *f*.

mis-spell mal épeler *or* écrire.

mis-spend mal employer.

mist 1. brume *f*; brouillard *m*; buée *f* (*on glass*); **2.** (*usu.* ~ **over**, ~ **up**) (s') embruer; (s')embuer (*glass*).

mistake 1. se tromper de; se méprendre sur; mal comprendre; ~ **for** prendre pour, confondre avec; **2.** erreur *f*; faute *f*; **by ~** par méprise; **~n** erroné; mal compris; **be ~** se tromper.

mister (*abbr.* **Mr**) monsieur (*pl.* messieurs) *m*.

mistletoe ♣ gui *m*.

mistress maîtresse *f*; *primary school*: institutrice *f*; (*abbr.* **Mrs**) madame (*pl.* mesdames) *f*.

mistrust 1. se méfier de; **2.** méfiance *f*,

défiance *f* (de **in**, **of**); **~ful** méfiant, soupçonneux.

misty brumeux; *fig.* vague, confus.

misunderstand mal comprendre; **~ing** malentendu *m*; mésentente *f*; erreur; ✝ méprise *f*.

misuse 1. mal employer; abuser de; **2.** abus *m*; mauvais emploi.

mite *zo.* mite *f*, *fig.* brin *m*, grain *m*, atome *m*.

mitigate adoucir, atténuer (*a. fig.*).

mitten mitaine *f*.

mix (se) mélanger; (se) mêler (à, avec **with**); **~ed** mélangé; mixte; *esp. cuis.* assorti; ~ **up** mélanger; *fig.* confondre; embrouiller; **~ed up with** engagé dans (*an affair*); **~er** *cuis.* mixe(u)r *m*; *fig.* **be a good ~** être très sociable; **~ture** mélange *m*, assortiment *m*; *pharm.* mixture *f*; **~-up** confusion *f*.

moan 1. gémissement *m*; **2.** gémir; se lamenter, se plaindre.

moat fossé *m*; douve *f*.

mob foule *f*; populace *f*; **2.** *v/t.* assiéger; *v/i.* s'attrouper.

mobil|e mobile; **~ize** mobiliser.

mock 1. faux; contrefait; d'imitation; **2.** *v/t.* imiter, singer; *a. v/i.*: ~ **at** ridiculiser, se moquer de; **~ery** raillerie *f*; (sujet *m* de) moquerie *f*; **~ing** moqueur; **~-up** moquette *f*.

mode mode *m* (*a.* ♪, *gramm.*).

model 1. modèle *m* (*a. fig.*); *person:* mannequin *mf*; **2.** modèle, exemplaire; *toy etc.*: modèle réduit; **3.** *v/t.* modeler (*a. fig.* sur, [**up**]**on**); *fashion show:* présenter (*clothes*); *v/i.* être mannequin.

moderat|e 1. modéré; **2.** (se) modérer; **~ion** modération *f*; **in ~** avec modération.

modern moderne; **~ize** moderniser.

modest modeste; **~y** modestie *f*.

modi|fication modification *f*; **~fy** modifier.

modulate moduler.

module: lunar ~ module *m* lunaire.

moist humide; **~en** humecter, mouiller; **~ure** humidité *f*; **~urize** humidifier (*the air*); hydrater (*the skin*); **moisturizing cream** crème *f* hydratante.

molar (*a.* ~ **tooth**) molaire *f*.

molasses mélasse *f*.

M

mortgage

mole¹ *zo.* taupe *f.*

mole² grain *m* de beauté.

molecule *phys.* molécule *f.*

molehill taupinière *f.*

molest attaquer; molester.

mollify adoucir; apaiser.

mollycoddle chouchouter.

molten en fusion; fondu.

mom F maman *f*; ~-and-pop store épicerie *f* du coin.

moment moment *m*, instant *m*; importance *f*; at (or for) the ~ pour le moment; ~ary momentané, passager; ~ous important; grave; ~um force *f*, élan *m*; vitesse *f* (acquise); gather ~ prendre de la vitesse.

monarch monarque *m*; ~y monarchie *f.*

monastery monastère *m*

Monday lundi *m.*

monetary monétaire.

money argent *m*; ready ~ argent *m* comptant; get (or have) one's ~'s worth en avoir pour son argent; make ~ gagner de l'argent; out of ~ à sec; ~lender prêteur *m*; ~maker mine *f* d'or; ~order mandat-poste (*pl.* mandats-poste) *m.*

mongrel bâtard(e *f*) *m.*

monitor 1. ⊙, *telev. etc.* moniteur *m*; 2. contrôler; surveiller.

monk moine *m*, religieux *m.*

monkey 1. singe *m*; F ~ business, ~ tricks *pl.* qch. de louche; ⊙ ~ wrench clé *f* anglaise; F make a ~ out of s.o. ridiculiser q.; 2. ~ about, ~ around s'amuser; faire l'imbécile; ~ (about or around) with tripoter.

monkish de moine, monacal.

mono 1. mono(phonique); 2. (in ~ en) monophonie *f*; F disque *m* mono.

mono|gamy monogamie *f*; ~logue monologue *m*; ~polist accapareur (-euse *f*) *m*; ~polize monopoliser; *fig.* s'emparer de; ~poly monopole *m* (de, of); ~rail monorail *m*; ~tonous monotone; ~tony monotonie *f.*

monsoon mousson *f.*

monster monstre *m.*

monstrosity monstruosité *f*; ~trous monstrueux; atroce; scandaleux; énorme, colossal.

month mois *m*; ~ly 1. mensuel; 2. revue *f* mensuelle.

monument monument *m*; ~al monumental.

mood humeur *f*, disposition *f*; be in the ~ for avoir envie de; ~y lunatique; maussade, mal luné.

moon 1. lune *f*; F be over the ~ être aux anges; F cry for the ~ demander la lune; F promise the ~ promettre la lune; F once in a blue ~ tous les trente-six du mois; 2. (*usu.* ~ about): F muser; ~light 1. clair *m* de lune; F do a ~ flit décamper à la cloche de bois; 2. F faire du travail noir; F ~lighting travail *m* noir; ~lit éclairé par la lune; ~shine clair *m* de lune; F balivernes *f/pl.*; alcool *m* de contrebande; ~struck halluciné, F hébété.

Moor¹ Maure *m*, Mauresque *f.*

moor² lande *f*, bruyère *f.*

moor³ ⚓ *v/t.* amarrer, *v/i.* mouiller.

moorings ⚓ *pl.* amarres *f/pl.*

moose *zo.* (*a.* ~ deer) élan *m.*

moot: ~ point point *m* litigieux.

mop 1. balai *m* à franges; F hair: tignasse *f*; 2. essuyer, (*a.* ~ up) éponger (*water*).

mope avoir le cafard.

moped cyclomoteur *m*, mobylette *f* (*TM*).

moral 1. moral; 2. morale *f*; moralité *f* (*of a story*); ~s *pl.* moralité *f*; ~e moral *m*; ~ity moralité *f*; ~ize moraliser.

morass marais *m*, marécage *m.*

morbid morbide; malsain.

more 1. *adj.* plus de, davantage de; 2. *adv.* plus, davantage; once ~ encore (une fois); de nouveau; so much (or all) the ~ d'autant plus; à plus forte raison; no ~ ne ... plus; ~ and ~ de plus en plus; ~ or less plus ou moins.

moreover d'ailleurs, du reste.

morgue morgue *f.*

moribund moribond.

morning 1. matin *m*; matinée *f*; in the ~ le matin; ... o'clock in the ~ ... heures du matin; tomorrow ~ demain matin; 2. du matin; matinal.

moron idiot(e *f*) *m.*

morose morose, maussade.

morph|ia, ~ine morphine *f.*

morsel (petit) morceau *m.*

mortal 1. *adj.* mortel; 2. *su.* mortel(le *f*) *m*; ~ity mortalité *f.*

mortar mortier *m.*

mortgag|e 1. hypothèque *f*; 2. hypo-

M

théquer; **~ee** créancier *m* hypothécaire; **~or** débiteur *m* hypothécaire.

mortician *Am.* entrepreneur *m* de pompes funèbres.

morti|fication mortification *f*; humiliation *f*; **~fy** *v/t.* mortifier; humilier.

mortise ⚙ mortaise *f*.

mortuary morgue *f*.

mosaic mosaïque *f*.

Moslem musulman (*a. su.*).

mosque mosquée *f*.

mosquito *zo.* moustique *m*.

moss ♣ mousse *f*; **~y** moussu.

most 1. *adj.* le plus de; la plupart de; **2.** *adv.* le plus; très, fort, bien; **3.** *su.* le plus; la plupart; **~** tout au plus; *make the* **~** *of* tirer le meilleur parti possible de; **~ly** pour la plupart; le plus souvent.

moth mite *f*; papillon *m* de nuit; **~eaten** rongé des mites.

mother 1. mère *f*; ♀**'s Day** fête *f* des Mères; **2.** chouchouter, dorloter; **~hood** maternité *f*; **~-in-law** belle-mère (*pl.* belles-mères) *f*; **~ly** maternel; **~-of-pearl** en or de nacre; **~tongue** langue *f* maternelle.

motif motif *m*.

motion 1. mouvement *m*, marche *f* (*a.* ⚙); geste *m* (*of hand*); *parl.* motion *f*; *set in* **~** mettre en mouvement *or* en marche; **2.** *v/t.* faire signe à (*q.*) (*de inf.*, *to inf.*); *v/i.* faire un signe *or* geste; **~less** immobile; **~ picture** *Am.* film *m*.

motivat|e motiver; **~ion** motivation *f*.

motive 1. moteur; **2.** motif *m*, mobile *m*; **3.** motiver; **~less** immotivé.

motley bariolé; bigarré.

motor 1. moteur *m*; **2.** moteur; à moteur; d'automobile; **3.** voyager *or* aller en auto; *v/t.* conduire (*q.*) en auto; **~bike** F moto *f*; **~boat** canot *m* automobile; **~cade** file *f* d'automobiles; **~car** auto(mobile) *f*, voiture *f*; **~cycle** motocyclette *f*; **~cyclist** motocycliste *m*; **~ing** automobilisme *m*; tourisme *m* en auto; **~ist** automobiliste *mf*; **~ize** motoriser; **~man** conducteur *m*; **~ scooter** scooter *m*; **~way** autoroute *f*.

mottled moucheté, tacheté.

motto devise *f*.

mo(u)ld¹ humus *m*; moisissure *f*.

mo(u)ld² 1. moule *m*; **2.** mouler; façonner (sur, [*up*]on).

mo(u)lder s'effriter; (*a.* **~ away**) tomber en poussière; moisir.

mo(u)ldy moisi; chanci (*bread*).

mo(u)lt *v/i.* muer; *v/t.* perdre (*hair*, *feathers*).

mound tertre *m*; monceau *m*, tas *m*.

mount 1. montagne *f*, *poet.*, *a. geog.* mont *m*; *horse*, *jewel*: monture *f*; **2.** *v/i.* monter (à cheval); **~ up** s'élever; *v/t.* monter sur (*a horse*, *a bicycle etc.*); ⚙ monter (*diamonds*).

mountain 1. montagne *f*; **~ range** chaîne *f* de montagnes; *make a* **~** *out of a* **molehill** (se) faire d'une mouche un éléphant; **2.** des montagnes; montagneux; **~eer** montagnard(e *f*) *m*; alpiniste *mf*; **~eering** alpinisme *m*; **~ous** montagneux.

mountebank charlatan *m*.

mourn *v/i.* porter le deuil; *v/t.* (*or* **~ for**, **over**) pleurer (*q.*), déplorer (*qch.*); **~er** affligé(e *f*) *m*; **~ful** lugubre; mélancolique; **~ing** deuil *m*; *attr.* de deuil; *be in* **~ for** proter le deuil de (*q.*).

mouse, *pl.* **mice** souris *f*.

moustache moustache(s) *f*(*pl.*).

mousy effacé (*person*); terne; gris.

mouth bouche *f*; *dog*, *cat etc.*: gueule *f*; *river*: embouchure *f*; *bottle*: goulot *m*; *tunnel*, *hole*: entrée *f*; (*opening*) arifice *f*; *by word of* **~** de vive voix; *down in the* **~** déprimé; *shut your* **~!** *keep your* **~!** ferme-la!; *stop s.o.'s* **~** former la bouche à q.; **~ful** bouchée *f*; **~organ** harmonica *m*; **~piece** ♩ bec *m*, embouchure *f*; *megaphone*: embout *m*; *fig.* porte-parole *m*/*inv.*; **~watering** qui fait venir l'eau à la bouche, appétissant.

move 1. *v/t.* déplacer (*qch.*); bouger (*qch.*); remuer; émouvoir (*q.*); proposer (*a motion*); mouvoir; *v/i.* se déplacer; circuler; bouger; s'avancer; déménager; *chess*: marcher; **~ for s.th.** demander qch.; **~ in** entrer; emménager; **~ on** se remettre en marche; **~ out** déménager; **2.** mouvement *m*, déménagement *m*; *chess*: coup *m*; *fig.* démarche *f*; *on the* **~** en marche; **~ables** biens *m*/*pl.* mobiliers; **~ment** mouvement *m*.

movie *cin.* film *m*; **~s** *pl.* cinéma *m*; **~ house** cinéma *m*; **~goer** amateur *m* de cinéma, cinéphile *mf*.

moving en mouvement; en marche; mobile; *fig.* émouvant; *cin.* **~ picture** film *m*; **~ staircase** escalier *m* roulant.

mow faucher; tondre (*lawn*); **~er** faucheur (-euse *f*) *m*; tondeuse *f* (*of lawn*).

much 1. *adj.* beaucoup de; **2.** *adv.* beaucoup, bien, fort; **as ~ as** autant que; **not so ~ as** ne ... pas (au)tant que; **as I would like** pour autant que je désire; **I thought as ~** je m'y attendais, je m'en doutais; **make ~ of** faire grand cas de.

muck F **1.** boue *f*; crasse *f*; **2.** *v/t.* **~ up** bousiller, esquinter; *v/i.* **~ about** faire le fou.

mud boue *f*; *river:* vase *f*.

muddle 1. *v/t.* (*a.* **~ up**, **together**) embrouiller; *v/i.* s'embrouiller; **~ through** se débrouiller; **2.** embrouillement *m*; désordre *m*, F pagaille *f*; **get into a ~** s'embrouiller.

mud|dy boueux; fangeux; vaseux; trouble (*liquid*); **~guard** garde-boue *m/inv.*; **~slinger** calomniateur (-trice *f*) *m*.

muff (*a.* **~ up**) rater; F bousiller.

muffle 1. ⊙ moufle *m*; **2.** (*oft.* **~ up**) (s')emmitoufler; amortir (*a sound*); étouffer; **~r** cache-nez *m/inv.*; *mot.* pot *m* d'échappement.

mug 1. tasse *f*; bol *m*; pot *m*; *sl.* gueule *f*, bille *f* (= *face*); *sl.* idiot(e *f*) *m*; **2.** attaquer, agresser (et voler); **~ger** agresseur; **~ging** (vol *m* avec) agression *f*.

muggy chaud et humide, lourd.

mugwump *pol.* indépendant *m*

mulatto mulâtre(sse *f*) *m*.

mulberry mûre *f*; *tree:* mûrier *m*.

mule mulet *m*, mule *f*.

mulled chaud (et) épicé (*wine*).

multi|farious varié; multiple; **~form** multiforme; **~lateral** multilatéral; complexe; **~millionaire** milliardaire *mf*; **~national** multinational.

multi|ple multiple (*adj.*, *su.*); *Br.* (*a.* **~ store**) magasin *m* à succursales multiples); ⚕ **~ sclerosis** sclérose *f* en plaques); **~plication** multiplication *f*; **compound (simple)** ~ multiplication *f* de nombres complexes (de chiffres); **~table** table *f* de multiplication, **~plicity** multiplicité *f*; **~plier** multiplicateur *m*; **~ply** (se) multiplier; **~purpose** universel; polyvalent.

multitude multitude *f*; foule *f*.

mum¹: **keep ~** ne pas souffler mot; **~'s the word!** motus!, chut!

mum² F maman *m*.

mumble marmotter.

mummy¹ momie *f*.

mummy² F maman *f*.

mumps *sg.* ⚕ oreillons *m/pl.*

munch mâcher, mâchonner.

mundane banal; terrestre.

municipal municipal; **~ity** municipalité *f*.

munificent munificent.

munitions *pl.* munitions *f/pl.*

murder 1. assassinat *m*, meutre *m*; *fig.* **get away with** (**blue**) ~ pouvoir faire n'importe quoi impunément; **2.** assassiner; *fig.* massacrer; **~er** assassin *m*, meurtrier *m*; **~ess** assassine *f*, meurtrière *f*; **~ous** meurtrier.

murk obscurité *f*; **~y** obscur, sombre; *fig. a.* trouble (*past*).

murmur 1. murmure *m*; **2.** murmurer.

musc|le 1. muscle *m*; **2.** **~ in** s'immiscer dans; **~ular** musculaire; musculeux, musclé (*person*).

muse méditer (sur, [up]on).

museum musée *m*.

mush bouillie *f*; *fig.* sentimentalités *f/pl.*

mushroom 1. champignon *m*; **2.** s'élever; (*a.* **~ up**) pousser comme des champignons.

music musique *f*; **set to ~** mettre en musique; **~al 1.** musical; musicien (*person*); **~ instrument** instrument *m* de musique; **~ paper** papier *m* à musique; **~ stand** pupitre *m* (à musique); **~al 1.** musical; de musique; musicien (*person*); **2.** comédie *f* musicale; **~ian** musicien(ne *f*) *m*; **~ianship** sens *m* de la musique.

musk musc *m*.

musket mousquet *m*.

musquash *zo.* rat *m* musqué.

muss F (*a.* **~ up**) froisser; bousiller.

mussel moule *f*.

must¹ 1. *defective verb:* **I ~** (*inf.*) je dois (*inf.*), il faut que je (*sbj.*); **I ~ not** (*inf.*) il ne faut pas que je (*sbj.*); **2.** nécessité *f* absolue.

must² moût *m*, vin *m* doux.

must³ moisi *m*, moisissure *f*.

mustache moustache *f*.

mustard moutarde *f*.

muster 1. rassemblement *m*; **pass ~** être passable, (pouvoir) passer; **2.** (*usu.* **~ up**) rassembler.

M

musty de moisi (*smell*); qui sent le renfermé (*room, air etc.*, *a. fig.*).
mutation mutation *f*.
mute 1. muet; 2. muet(te *f*) *m*; ♪ sourdine *f*; 3. assourdir; ♪ mettre la sourdine à; **~d** sourd; *fig.* voilé (*enthusiasm etc.*); ♪ en sourdine.
mutilate mutiler.
mutin|eer mutin *m*; **~ous** mutin; **~y** 1. mutinerie *f*; 2. se mutiner.
mutter 1. marmotter; 2. marmottement *m*.
mutton mouton *m*; **leg of ~** gigot *m*; **~chop** côtelette *f* de mouton.
mutual mutuel; réciproque; **~ insurance company** (compagnie *f* d'assurance)

mutuelle *f*; **~ fund** société *f* d'investissement; **by ~ consent** par consentement mutuel.
muzzle 1. museau *m*; *dog*: muselière *f*; *gun*: bouche *f*; 2. museler.
my mon, ma, mes.
myrrh ♀ myrrhe *f*.
myrtle ♀ myrte *m*.
myself moi-même; *rfl.* me, *stressed*: moi.
mysterious mystérieux.
mystery mystère *m*; (*a. ~ story*) roman *m* à suspens.
mysti|c 1. *a.* **~cal** mystique; esotérique (*rite*); 2. *eccl.* mystique *mf*; **~cism** mysticisme *m*, mystique *f*; **~fy** désorienter.
myth mythe *m*; **~ology** mythologie *f*.

N

nab *sl.* saisir, arrêter.
nadir *astr.* nadir *m*; *fig.* stade *m* le plus bas.
nag[1] F canasson *m* (= *horse*).
nag[2] (*a. ~ at*) être après (*q.*); harceler (*q.*); **~ging** criailleries *f/pl.*; harcèlement *m*.
nail 1. *finger, toe*: ongle *m*; ◎ clou *m*; **~ clippers** *pl.* pince *f* à ongles; **~ file** lime *f* à ongles; **~ polish**, **~ varnish** vernis *m* à ongles; *fig.* **hit the ~ on the head** frapper juste; 2. clouer; *fig.* **~ s.o. down** obliger (*q.*) à prendre position *or* à se décider.
naïve, naive naïf; ingénu.
naked nu; dénudé (*country etc.*); dépouillé (*tree*); **~ facts** *pl.* faits *m/pl.* bruts; **with the ~ eye** à l'œil nu; **~ness** nudité *f*.
name 1. nom *m*; *fig.* réputation *f*; **of** (*or* **by**) **the ~ of** du nom de, nommé; **Christian ~, given ~** prénom *m*; **in the ~ of** au nom de; **call s.o. ~s** injurier q.; **know s.o. by ~** connaître q. de nom; 2. nommer; dénommer; citer; fixer (*a date, price etc.*); **~less** sans nom; inconnu; anonyme; *fig.* indicible; **~ly** à savoir, c'est-à-dire; **~plate** plaque *f*; écusson *m*; **~sake** homonyme *m*.

nanny nounou *f*, bonne *f* (d'enfants); **~goat** chèvre *f*, bique *f*.
nap[1] *velvet etc.*: poil *m*.
nap[2] 1. petit somme *m*; 2. sommeiller; **catch s.o. ~ping** prendre q. au dépourvu *or* en défaut.
nape (*usu. ~ of the neck*) nuque f.
napkin (*oft. table ~*) serviette *f*; (*a. baby's ~*) couche *f*.
narcosis ♂ narcose *f*.
narcotic narcotique (*a. su./m*).
nark *sl.* mettre en rogne; **~ed** en rogne; **~y** F de mauvais poil.
narra|te raconter; **~ion** narration *f*; récit *m*; **~ive** 1. narratif; 2. récit *m*; **~or** narrateur (-trice *f*) *m*.
narrow 1. étroit; *fig. a.* borné, limité, restreint; faible (*majority*); *see* escape 2; 2. **~s** *pl.* passe *f* étroite; *port*: goulet *m*; 3. (se) rétrécir; (se) restreindre; (se) resserrer; **~ down** (se) réduire; (se) limiter; **~-minded** borné; **~ness** étroitesse *f*.
nasal nasal; nasillard (*accent*).
nasty méchant; mauvais; désagréable; dégoûtant; sale.
nation nation *f*.
national 1. national; 2. national (e *f*) *m*; *abroad*: ressortissant(e *f*) *m*; **~ism** na-

tionalisme *m*; **~ist** nationaliste *mf*; **~ity** nationalité *f*; **~ize** nationaliser.

nationwide national.

native 1. du pays; indigène (de, **to**) (*person*, *plant*); inné (*quality*); de naissance (*place*); **~ language** langue *f* maternelle; **2.** habitant(e *f*) *m* de pays; indigène *mf*.

nativity nativité *f*.

natural naturel; de la nature; **~ disaster** catastrophe *f* naturelle; **~ gas** gaz *m* naturel; **2.** ♪ (*a.* **~ sign**) bécarre *m*; ♪ (*note*) note *f* naturelle; F talent *m* naturel; **~ist** naturaliste *mf*; **~ize** naturaliser; ♀, *zo* acclimater.

nature nature *f*; **by ~** de nature.

naught zéro *m*; *fig.* rien *m*, néant *m*; **come** (**bring**) **to ~** (faire) échouer; **~y** pas sage; vilain; méchant.

nause|a nausée *f*, **~ate** *v/t.* avoir la nausée (de, **at**); *v/t.* dégoûter; donner des nausées à.

nautical nautique, marin.

naval naval; de marine; **~ architect** ingénieur *m* des constructions navales; **~ base** port *m* de guerre, base *f* navale.

nave¹ △ nef.

nave² *wheel:* moyeu *m*.

navel nombril *m*; **~ orange** (orange *f*) navel *f*.

naviga|ble navigable; **~te** *v/i.* naviguer; *v/t.* naviguer sur; gouverner (*a ship*); **~tion** navigation *f*; *ship:* conduite *f*; **~tor** navigateur *m*.

navy marine *f* de guerre.

near 1. *adj.* proche; voisin; (le plus) court (*way*); **~ at hand** tout près; *it was* **a ~ miss** (*or thing*) il s'en est fallu de peu, le coup est passé très près; **2.** *adv.* près, proche; **3.** *prp.* (*a.* **~ to**) près de; **4.** *v/t.* (s')approcher de; **~by** tout près, tout proche; **~ly** (de) près; presque; à peu près; près de; manquer; **~ness** proximité *f*; **~side** *mot. in Britain:* de gauche; *other countries:* de droite; **~sighted** myope.

neat bien rangé *or* tenu; soigné; net; pur, sec (*drink*); bon; habile; **~ness** netteté *f*; ordre *m*.

nebulous nébuleux.

necess|arily 1. nécessaire (à, **for**); **2.** *usu.* **necessaries** *pl.* nécessités *f/pl*; **~itate** nécessiter (*qch.*); **~ity** nécessité *f*; chose *f* essentielle.

neck 1. cou *m*; *cuis.* collet *m*; *bottle:*

goulot *m*; *dress:* encolure *f*; **~ and ~** à égalité; *stick one's* **~ out** prendre un risque *or* des risques, se compromettre; *up to one's* **~** complètement, totalement, jusqu'au cou; **2.** F se peloter; **~band** col *m*; encolure *f*; **~erchief** foulard *m*; **~lace** collier *m*; **~line** encolure *f*.

née: *Mrs X,* **~ Y** Mme X, née Y.

need 1. besoin *m* (de, **for**); indigence *f*; **be** (*or* **stand**) **in ~ of** avoir besoin de; **2.** avoir besoin de; demander (*qch.*); être obligé de; **~ful 1.** nécessaire; **2.** F le fric *m* (*money*).

needle 1. aiguille *f*; **2.** agacer.

needless inutile.

needle...: ~woman couturière *f*; **~work** travail *m* à l'aiguille.

needy nécessiteux.

ne'er-do-well propre-à-rien (*pl.* propres-à-rien) *mf*, vaurien(ne *f*) *m*.

nefarious abominable.

negat|e nier; **~ion** négation *f*; **~ive 1.** négatif; **2.** négative *f*; *gramm.* négation *f*; *phot.* négatif *m*; *answer in the ~* répondre par la négative.

neglect 1. manque *m* de soin; négligence *f*; abandon *m*; **2.** négliger; **~ful** négligent; insoucieux (de, **of**).

negligent négligent.

negligible négligeable.

negotia|te *v/t.* négocier; prendre, franchir (*an obstacle*), négocier (*a bend*), *a.* *fig.* surmonter; *v/i.* négocier; **~ting ta-ble** table *f* de conférence; *at the ~* par des négociations, par voie de négociation; **~tion** négociation *f*; pourparlers *m/pl.*; *under ~* en négociation.

negr|ess négresse *f*; **~o,** *pl.* **-oes** nègre *m*.

neigh 1. hennissement *m*; **2.** hennir.

neighbo(u)r voisin(e *f*) *m*; **~hood** voisinage *m*; quartier *m*; **~ing** avoisinant, voisin; **~ly** de bon voisinage; obligeant.

neither 1. *adj.* *or pron.* ni l'un ni l'autre; aucun; **2.** *adv.* **~ ... nor** ni ... ni ...; *not ... ~* (ne ... pas) ... ne ... pas non plus.

neon néon *m*; **~ light(ing)** éclairage *m* au néon; **~ sign** enseigne *m* au néon.

nephew neveu *m*.

nerve nerf *m*; ♀, △ nervure *f*; *fig.* courage *m*; *fig.* vigueur *f*; F audace *f*; *F be all* **~s** être un paquet de nerfs; F *get on* **s.o.'s ~s** taper sur les nerfs à q.; F *have* *the* ~ *to* (*inf.*) avoir le toupet de (*inf.*); *lose one's* ~*s* perdre son sang-froid; ~**racking** énervant.

nervous nerveux; ~ *breakdown* dépression *f* nerveuse; ~ *system* système *m* nerveux; ~**ness** nervosité *f*.

nest 1. nid *m*; **2.** (se) nicher; ~**le** se nicher; se blottir.

net¹ 1. filet *m*; ~ *curtains pl.* voilage *m*; **2.** prendre (*qch.*) au filet.

net² 1. net; **2.** rapporter net.

nether inférieur.

nettle 1. ⚘ ortie *f*; **2.** *fig.* piquer, irriter.

network réseau *m*.

neuron neurone *m*.

neuro|sis ⚕ névrose *f*; ~**tic** névrosé (*a. su.*).

neuter 1. neutre; **2.** châtrer.

neutral 1. neutre; **2.** neutre *m*; ⊕ point *m* mort; ~**ity** neutralité *f*; ~**ize** neutraliser.

neutron *phys.* neutron *m*; ~ *bomb* bombe *f* à neutrons.

never ne ... jamais; jamais (de la vie); ~**more** (ne ...) plus jamais; (ne ...) jamais plus; ~**theless** néanmoins, pourtant.

new nouveau; neuf; frais; ~**comer** nouveau venu *m*; nouvel arrivé *m*; ~**ly** récemment, nouvellement.

news *pl. or sg.* nouvelle(s) *f*(*pl.*); *radio, telev.*: informations *f*/*pl.*; *what's the* ~? quoi de neuf?; *break the* ~ *to s.o.* annoncer les nouvelles à q. (avec ménagement); ~ *agency* agence *f* de presse; ~ *agent*, ~ *dealer* marchand(e *f*) *m* de journaux; ~*boy* vendeur *m* de journaux; ~ *bulletin*, ~**cast** bulletin *m* d'informations; ~**monger** débiteur (-euse *f*) *m* de nouvelles; ~**paper** journal *m*; *attr.* de journaux; ~**print** papier *m* de journal; ~**reel** film *m* d'actualité; actualités *f*/*pl.*; ~**stall**, *Am.* ~**stand** étalage *m* de marchand de journaux; *France*: kiosque *m* (à journaux); ~ *vendor* vendeur *m* de journaux.

New Year nouvel an *m*; nouvelle année *f*; ~'*s Day* le jour de l'an; ~'*s Eve* la Saint-Sylvestre *f*.

next 1. *adj.* prochain; voisin; *le* plus proche; suivant; ~ *but one* le deuxième; ~ *door* à côté; *d'à côté*; ~ *time* la prochaine fois; ~ *to* à côté de; près de; ~ *to nothing* ne ... presque rien; **2.** *adv.* ensuite, après; ~**door** voisin.

nexus connexion *f*, lien *m*.

nibble (*a.* ~ *at*) grignoter.

nice aimable, gentil (*person*); agréable; joli; fin, subtil (*distinction*); ~**ty** exactitude *f*; subtilité *f*; *to a* ~ exactement.

niche niche *f*.

nick 1. entaille *f*, encoche *f*; *in the* ~ *of time* juste à temps; **2.** entailler; *sl.* piquer (= *arrest; steal*).

nickel 1. *min.* nickel *m*; *Am. a. piece of 5 cents*; **2.** nickeler.

nickname 1. surnom *m*; sobriquet *m*; **2.** surnommer.

nicotine nicotine *f*.

niece nièce *f*.

nifty chic.

niggard grippe-sou *m*; ~**ly** *adj.* chiche, mesquin.

nigger *pej.* nègre *m*, négresse *f*.

night nuit *f*, soir *m*; obscurité *f*; *by* ~ de nuit; *in the* ~ (pendant) la nuit; *at* ~ la nuit; ~**cap** bonnet *m* de nuit; *fig.* grog *m* (qui se prend avant de se coucher); ~**club** boîte *f* de nuit; ~**dress** chemise *f* de nuit (*for ladies*); ~**fall** tombée *f* de la nuit; ~**gown** *see* nightdress; ~**ingale** *orn.* rossignol *m*; ~**ly** nocturne; (de) tous les soirs; ~**mare** cauchemar *m*; ~ *shift* *time*: poste *m* de nuit; *people*: équipe *f* de nuit; *be on* or *work* (*on*) *the* ~ être (au poste) de nuit; ~**shirt** chemise *f* de nuit (*for men*); ~**spot** F boîte *f* de nuit; ~**time** nuit *f*; ~ *watchman* gardien *m* de nuit.

nil rien *m*; *sp.* zéro *m*.

nimble agile, leste; délié (*mind*); ~**ness** agilité *f*; *fig.* vivacité *f*.

nimbus nimbe *m*, auréole *f*.

nine 1. neuf; **2.** neuf *m*; neuf fois; ~**pins** *pl.* quilles *f*/*pl.*; ~**teen** dix-neuf (*a. su./m*); ~**ty** quatre-vingt-dix.

ninny F niais(e *f*) *m*.

ninth 1. neuvième; **2.** ♪ neuvième *f*.

nip¹ 1. pincement *m*; **2.** pincer; ~ *in the bud* tuer dans l'œuf.

nip² goutte *f* (*of spirits*).

nipper *lobster etc.*: pince *f*; (*a pair of*) ~*s* *pl.* pince *f*, tenailles *f*/*pl.*

nipple mamelon *m*.

nippy leste, vif; âpre; piquant (*taste*).

nit|re, *Am.* ~**er** nitre *m*, salpêtre *m*.

nitrogen ⚗ azote *m*.

nitty-gritty *sl.*: *come* (or *get down*) *to the* ~ en venir au fait or au fond.

nitwit F imbécile *mf*.

nix F **1.** non; rien à faire!; **2.** dire non à (*qch.*).

no 1. *adj.* aucun, pas de; *in ~ time* en un clin d'œil; *~ one* personne (... ne); **2.** *adv.* peu; non; pas (plus); **3.** non *m/inv.*

Nobel: *~ prize* Prix *m* Nobel; *~ peace prize* Prix *m* Nobel de la paix; *~ prize-winner* (lauréat *m* du) Prix Nobel *m*.

nobility noblesse *f* (*a. fig.*).

noble noble; **~man** noble *m*; **~ness** noblesse *f*.

nobody personne, aucun (... ne).

no-claims bonus bonification *f* pour non-sinistre.

nocturnal nocturne.

nod 1. *v/i.* faire signe que oui; incliner la tête; (*a. ~ off*) somnoler; *have a ~ding acquaintance* se connaître vaguement; *v/t.* incliner (*one's head*); **2.** signe *m* de (la) tête.

node nœud *m*; ⚕ nodosité *f*.

noise 1. bruit *m*; *~ abatement* lutte *f* anti-bruit or contre le bruit; *~ level* niveau *m* des bruits; F *big ~* gros bonnet *m*; **2.** *~ abroad*, *~ about* ébruiter; *~less* sans bruit; silencieux.

noisome fétide; *fig.* désagréable.

noisy bruyant; tapageur; turbulent.

nomad nomade *mf*.

nomin|al nominal; fictif, symbolique (*price, value*); *~ate* nommer; proposer; *~ation* nomination *f*.

non ... non-; in-; sans ...

non-aggression: (*~ pact* pacte *m* de) non-agression *f*.

non-alcoholic non-alcoolisé.

non-align|ed non-aligné; *~ment* non--alignement *m*.

non-breakable incassable.

nonce: *for the ~* pour l'occasion; *~ word* mot *m* de circonstance.

nonchalant nonchalant.

non-commissioned sans brevet; ✗ *~ officer* sous-officier *m* gradé.

non-committal évasif.

non-conductor non-conducteur *m*.

nonconformist non-conformiste *mf*; dissident(e *f*) *m*.

nondescript 1. indéfinissable; **2.** *fig.* personne *f* or chose *f* indéfinissable.

none 1. aucun; pas de; **2.** aucunement; *~ the less* pourtant.

nonentity nullité *f*.

non-existent non-existant.

non-fiction ouvrages *m/pl.* autres que les romans.

non-(in)flammable ininflammable.

non-interference, non-intervention non-intervention *f*.

non-iron ne pas repasser!

nonpareil personne *f* or chose *f* sans pareille.

non-partisan impartial.

non-payment non-paiement *m*; défaut *m* de paiement.

nonplussed perplexe.

non-proliferation: (*~ treaty* traité *m* de) non-prolifération *f*.

non-resident non-résident (*a. su.*).

nonsense absurdités *f/pl.*

non-skid antidérapant.

non-smoker non-fumeur *m*.

non-stop sans arrêt; *~* sans escale direct (*train*).

non-union non-syndiqué (*worker*).

nook (re)coin *m*.

noon (*a. ~day*) midi *m*.

noose nœud *m* coulant; corde *f*.

nope *Am.* F non!

nor *preceded by* **neither:** ni; *at the beginning of a sentence:* ne ... pas non plus; *~ do I* (ni) moi non plus.

norm norme *f*; règle *f*; *~al* normal; *~alize* normaliser.

north 1. *su.* nord *m*; **2.** *adj.* du nord; septentrional; *~-east 1.* nord-est *m*; **2.** (*a. ~eastern*) du nord-est; *~erly* du or au nord; *~ern* du nord; septentrional; *~erner* habitant(e *f*) *m* du nord; *Am.* 2 nordiste *mf*; *~ward 1.* *adj.* au or du nord; **2.** *adv.* (*a. ~wards*) vers le nord; *~-west 1.* nord-ouest *m*; **2.** (*a. ~western*) du nord-ouest.

Norwegian 1. norvégien; **2.** Norvégien(ne *f*) *m*.

nose 1. nez *m*; *fig.* flair *m*; **2.** *v/t.* (*a. ~ out*) sentir, flairer; *~ out* à découvrir; *~ one's way* s'avancer avec précautions; *v/i.* *~ about*, *~ around* fouiner; *~dive* ✈ (vol *m*) piqué *m*; *~gay* bouquet *m* de fleurs.

nostalgi|a nostalgie *f*; goût *m* du passé; *~c* nostalgique *f*.

nostril narine *f*, *horse:* naseau *m*.

nostrum panacée *f*.

nosy F curieux; indiscret.

not (ne) pas, (ne) point.
notabl|e notable (*a. su./m*); **~y** notamment, en particulier.
notary (*a. ~ public*) notaire *m*.
notation notation *f*.
notch 1. encoche *f*; *scale etc.*: cran *m*; *geog.* défilé *m*; **2.** encocher.
note 1. note *f* (*a. ♱, ♪, pol.*); *bank*: billet *m*; *information*: mot *m*; **take ~s of** prendre des notes de; **2.** noter; constater; faire attention à; (*a. ~ down*) prendre note de; **~book** carnet *m*; **~d** réputé (pour, *for*); **~paper** papier *m* à lettres; **~worthy** remarquable, notable; digne d'attention.
nothing 1. rien *m*; **2.** rien *m*; *for ~* gratis, gratuitement; *good for ~* bon à rien; *bring to ~* faire échouer; *come to ~* échouer.
notice 1. avis *m*; affiche *f*; écriteau *m*; annonce *f*, *journ.* notice *f*; *fig.* attention *f*; *employer*: congé *m*, *employee*: démission *f*; *at short ~* à bref délai; *give ~ that* prévenir que; *give s.o. a week's ~* donner ses huit jours à q.; *take ~ of* faire attention à; *until further ~* jusqu'à nouvel ordre; *without ~* sans avis préalable; **2.** remarquer, observer; s'apercevoir de or que; **~able** perceptible; **~board** porte-affiches *m/inv.*
noti|fication avis *m*, annonce *f*; notification *f*; **~fy** signaler; annoncer; **~ s.o. of** avertir q. de.
notion notion *f*, idée *f*; *Am.* **~s** *pl.* mercerie *f*.
notorious notoire, (re)connu.
notwithstanding 1. *prp.* malgré, en dépit de; **2.** *adv.* néanmoins.
nought zéro *m*; *fig. see* **naught**.
noun *gramm.* nom *m*, substantif *m*.
nourish nourrir; **~ing** nourrissant, nutritif; **~ment** nourriture *f*.
novel 1. nouveau; original; **2.** roman *m*; **~ist** romancier (-ère *f*) *m*; **~ty** nouveauté *f* (*a. ♱*).
November novembre *m*.
novice novice *mf*.
now 1. *adv.* maintenant; *with past tense*: alors; *just ~* tout à l'heure (*every*) *~ and then*, *~ and again* de temps à autre; *from ~ on* désormais; **2.** *cj.* (*a. ~ that*) maintenant que; or; **~adays** de nos jours.
nowhere nulle part.

noxious nuisible.
nozzle ⊕ jet *m*.
nub essentiel *m* (*of a matter*).
nucle|ar nucléaire; **~ deterrent force** force *f* de dissuasion nucléaire; **~ power** énergie *f* nucléaire; **~ power plant** centrale *f* (électro-)nucléaire; **~ reactor** réacteur *m* atomique; **~ research** recherches *f/pl.* nucléaires; **~ submarine** sous-marin *m* atomique; **~ warfare** guerre *f* nucléaire or atomique; **~us**, *pl.*-**i** noyau *m*.
nude 1. nu; **2.** *paint.* nu *m*; *in the ~* (tout) nu.
nudge 1. pousser (*q.*) du coude; **2.** coup *m* de coude.
nugget pépite *f* (*of gold*).
nuisance *person*: peste *f*; *thing*: ennui *m*; *what a ~!* quel ennui!; *make o.s.* (*or be*) *a ~* être assommant.
nuke F attaquer avec des armes nucléaires.
null ♱♱, *a. fig.* nul; *fig.* inefficace; *~ and void* nul et sans effet; **~ity** nullité *f*.
numb 1. engourdi; **2.** engourdir.
number 1. ♱♱, *gramm.*; *person*: nombre *m*; chiffre *m*; *house, car etc.*: numéro *m*; **2.** numéroter; compter; **~less** sans nombre; innombrable; **~plate** *mot.* plaque *f* minéralogique.
numera|l 1. numéral *m*; **2.** chiffre *m*; **~tion** numération *f*.
numerical numérique.
numerous nombreux.
nun religieuse *f*; **~nery** couvent *m*.
nurse 1. infirmière *f*; (*male ~*) infirmier *m*; *for children*: nurse *f*, bonne *f* d'enfants; (*wet-~*) nourrice *f*; **2.** allaiter (*a baby*); soigner (*sick people, a plant*); bercer (*dans ses bras*); *fig.* traiter avec ménagement; *fig.* cultiver; *fig.* entretenir (*a hope, feelings*); **~ling** nourrisson *m*; **~maid** bonne *f* d'enfants.
nursery nursery *f*, chambre *f* des enfants; ✗ pépinière *f* (*a. fig.*); **~ rhyme** comptine *f*; **~ school** (école *f*) maternelle *f*.
nursing allaitement *m*; soins *m/pl.*; profession *f* de garde-malade; **~ bottle** biberon *m*; **~ home** clinique *f*; maison *f* de retraite.
nurture nourrir (*a. fig.*); élever.
nut noix *f*; noisette *f*; ⊕ écrou *m*; *sl.*

personne *f* difficile; F *the* **~s and bolts** les connaissances rudimentaires; *sl.* **be ~s** être dingue; **~cracker(s)** casse-noisettes *m/inv.*; **~meg** (noix *f* de) muscade *f*.

nutriment nourriture *f*.

nutri|tion nutrition *f*; **~tional** alimentaire; nutritif (*value*); **~tious**, **~tive** nourrissant, nutritif.

nut|shell coquille *f* de noix; *in a ~* en peu de mots; **~ty** *sl.* un peu fou.

nylon *tex.* nylon *m*; **~s** *pl.* bas *m* | *pl.* nylon.

nymph nymphe *f*.

O

o 1. ♀ *teleph.* zéro *m*; **2.** *int.* O, ô, oh.

oaf idiot(e *f*) *m*; lourdaud(e *f*) *m*.

oak ♀ chêne *m*.

oar aviron *m*, rame *f*; F *stick one's ~ in* s'immiscer.

oasis, *pl.* **-ses** oasis *f* (*a. fig.*).

oat *usu.* **~s** *pl.* avoine *f*; F *fig.* **feel one's ~s** se sentir gaillard; *sow one's wild ~s* faire des fredaines.

oath serment *m*; *pej.* juron *m*; *swear or take an ~* prêter serment (sur, *on*); *on ~* sous serment.

oatmeal farine *f* d'avoine.

obdurate obstiné; inflexible.

obedien|ce obéissance *f*; *eccl.* obédience *f*; **~t** obéissant.

obeisance révérence *f*.

obey *v/t.* obéir à; *v/i.* obéir.

obituary nécrologie *f*.

object 1. objet *m*; *fig. a.* but *m*; *gramm.* complément *m*; **2.** *v/t.* objecter (que, *that*); *v/i.* **~** protester contre; désapprouver; *if you don't ~* si cela ne vous (*or* te) fait rien; **~ion** objection *f*; *if you have no ~* si vous n'y voyez pas d'objection; **~ionable** choquant; répugnant; **~ive 1.** objectif; **2.** objectif *m* (*a. opt.*).

obligat|ion obligation *f* (*a.* ✝); devoir *m*; dette *f* de reconnaissance; *be under* (*an*) *~ to s.o.* avoir des obligations envers q.; *be under a ~ to* (*inf.*) être dans l'obligation de (*inf.*); *without ~* sans engagement; **~ory** obligatoire (à q., *on s.o.*); de rigueur.

oblig|e *v/t.* obliger (à, *to*); rendre service à (*q.*); **~ed** reconnaissant; *much ~!* merci bien!; *v/i.* **~ing** obligeant, complaisant.

oblique oblique (*a.* ♈, *gramm.*); indirect (*a. fig.*); de biais (*look*).

obliterate effacer; oblitérer.

oblivi|on oubli *m*; *fall* (*or sink*) *into ~* tomber dans l'oubli; **~ous** oublieux (de, *of*).

oblong 1. oblong; **2.** rectangle *m*.

obnoxious odieux; répugnant.

obscen|e obscène; **~ity** obscénité *f*.

obscur|e obscur (*a. fig.*); sombre; **2.** *v/t.* obscurcir (*a. fig.*); voiler; éclipser; **~ity** obscurité *f*.

obsequies *pl.* obsèques *f/pl.*

obsequious obséquieux.

observ|able observable, visible; *observance* observance *f*; **~ant** observateur (de, *of*); attentif (à, *of*); **~ation** observation *f*; surveillance *f*; **~atory** observatoire *m*; **~e** observer; *say:* faire observer.

obsess obséder; **~ion** obsession *f*.

obsolete désuet; démodé.

obstacle obstacle *m*.

obstina|cy obstination *f*; persistance *f*; **~te** obstiné.

obstruct *v/t.* obstruer (*a.* ✿), boucher; encombrer; gêner; **~ion** obstruction *f*; obstacle *m*; **~ive** obstructif.

obtain *v/t.* obtenir; *v/i.* exister, avoir cours; **~able** procurable.

obtru|de (s')imposer (*on*, à); **~sive** importun, indiscret (*person*); voyant, tapageur; trop en évidence.

obtuse obtus.

obviate éviter.

obvious évident, manifeste, clair.

occasion 1. occasion *f*; événement *m*; *on the ~ of* à l'occasion de; *rise to the ~* être *or* se montrer à la hauteur de la situation; **2.** occasionner, causer, donner lieu à; ~**al** ... de temps en temps; occasionnel.

occident occident *m*, ouest *m*; ~**al** occidental; de l'ouest.

occult occulte.

occup|ant *country:* occupant(e *f*) *m*; *house:* locataire *mf*; ~**ation** occupation *f* (*a.* ✗); emploi *m*, métier *m*, profession *f*; ~**ational:** ~ **disease** maladie *f* professionnelle; ~ **hazard** risque *m* du métier; ~ **therapy** thérapie *f* or thérapeutique *f* occupationnelle, ergothérapie *f*; ~**y** occuper (*q.*, *qch.*, *a.* ✗ *a town*); ~ **o.s.** (*or* **be occupied**) **with** (*or* **in**) s'occuper à.

occur se produire; se trouver; ~ **to s.o.** venir à l'esprit à q.; ~**rence** événement *m*; occurrence *f*.

ocean océan *m*; ~ **liner** paquebot *m*; ~**going** de haute mer (*ship*); ~**ic** océanique; de l'océan.

o'clock: **five** ~ cinq heures.

October octobre *m*.

ocul|ar oculaire; ~**ist** oculiste *m*.

odd impair (*number*); dépareillé; déparié (*glove etc.*); *fig.* quelconque; étrange, curieux; **40** ~ une quarantaine; quelque quarante ...; **12 pounds** ~ 12 livres et quelques shillings; ~**ly enough** curieusement; ~**ball** F drôle de type *m*; ~**ity** singularité *f*; F original(e *f*) *m*; ~**s** *pl.*, *a. sg.* chances *f/pl.*; avantage *m*; différence *f*; *sp.* cote *f*; **at** ~ brouillé, en désaccord; ~ **and ends** bribes *f/pl.* et morceaux *m/pl.*; **it makes no** ~ ça ne fait rien; **the** ~ **are for** (**against**) **him** les chances sont pour (contre) lui.

odious odieux; détestable.

odo(u)r odeur *f* (*a. fig.*); parfum *m*.

of *prp. usu.* de; *material:* de, en (*silk*, *wood etc.*); parmi, (d')entre; **doctor** ~ **science** (~ **philosophy**) docteur *m* ès sciences (en philosophie); **north** ~ au nord de; **the 2nd** ~ **May** le 2 mai; **the remedy** ~ **remedies** le remède par excellence; **he** ~ **all men** lui entre tous; ~ **an evening** le soir.

off 1. *adv.* détaché; *distance:* à ... (de distance); **5 months** ~ à 5 mois d'ici ou de là; ~ **and on** par intervalles; **be** ~ s'en aller; *fig.* être fermé (*gas etc.*); être coupé; être avancé (*food*), avoir tourné (*milk*); **day** ~ jour *m* de congé; **have**

one's shoes ~ avoir ôté ses souliers; **be well** (**badly**) ~ être dans l'aisance (dans la gêne); **2.** *prp. usu.* de; *after certain verbs such as:* ôter, emprunter *etc.*: de; *distance:* éloigné de; *fig.* dégoûté de; ⚓ au large de; **a street** ~ **the Strand** une rue aboutissant au Strand; **be** (**or feel**) ~ **colo(u)r** ne pas être en forme *or* dans son assiette; **3.** *adj.* de dehors; extérieur; droit, *Am.* gauche (*side*); latéral (*street*); ~ **chance** chance *f* douteuse; ~ **day** jour où l'on n'est pas en forme; **on the** ~ **chance** à tout hasard; dans le vague espoir (**de** *that*, **of** *ger.*); **4.** *su. cricket:* **to the** ~ en avant à droite; **5.** *int.* filez!

offal déchets *m/pl.*; *cuis.* abats *m/pl.*

off...: ~**beat** F excentrique; ~**cast 1.** rebut; **2.** de rebut; ~**centre** décentré; ~**colo(u)r** scabreux (*joke etc.*).

offence offense *f*; 🏛 délit *m*; **give** ~ offenser, froisser, blesser (q., **to s.o.**); **take** ~ s'offenser; être fâché.

offend *v/t.* offenser, blesser; *v/i.* pécher (**contre**, **against**); violer (la loi, **against the law**); ~**er** 🏛 délinquant(e *f*) *m*; offenseur *m*; **first** ~ délinquant(e *f*) *m* primaire.

offens|e *Am. see* **offence**; ~**ive 1.** offensif; choquant, offensant; ~ désagréable. **2.** offensive *f*.

offer 1. offre *f*; 🌱 **on** ~ en promotion; **2.** *v/t.* offrir; présenter (*problems*); faire (*resistance*); proposer; *v/i.* s'offrir; ~**ing** offrande *f*.

off-hand 1. brusque; **2.** sans y réfléchir, F comme ça.

office bureau *m*; *admin.* ♙ ministère *m*; fonction(s) *f/*(*pl.*), charge *f*; **good** ~**s** bons offices *m/pl.*; ~**block** immeuble *m* de bureaux; ~**boy** garçon *m* de bureau; ~ **hours** *pl.* heures *f/pl.* de bureau; **in** ~ au pouvoir (*government*, *party*); **take** ~ entrer en fonctions; ~**holder** employé(e *f*) *m* de l'État; ~**r** fonctionnaire *m*; officier *m* (*a.* ✗).

official 1. officiel; **2.** fonctionnaire *m*; employé *m*; ~**dom** fonctionnarisme *m*; ~**ese** jargon *m* administratif.

officiate officier; ~ **as** exercer les fonctions de.

officious trop empressé.

offing: **in the** ~ en perspective.

off...: ~**key** ♪, *fig.* faux; ~**peak:** ~

charges pl. tarif *m* réduit (aux heures creuses); **~hours** *pl.* heures *f/pl.* creuses; **~putting** peu engageant, rebutant, répugnant; **~season 1.** morte-saison *f;* **2.** hors-saison (*tariff etc.*); **~set** compenser; **~shoot** rejeton *m;* ramification *f; fig.* conséquence *f;* **~shore** côtier, littoral; **~side** *sp.* hors jeu; **~spring** descendants *m/pl.; fig.* produit *m;* **~stage** *thea.* dans la coulisse *fig.;* dans la vie privée; en privé; **~the-cuff** impromptu, au pied levé; **~the-peg** *cost.* de confection, prêt à porter; **~the-record** confidentiel; **~the-white** blanc cassé.

often souvent, fréquemment.

ogre ogre *m.*

oh O!, ô!

oil 1. huile *f;* pétrole *m; heating:* mazout *m;* **2.** huiler; graisser; **~ change** vidange *m;* **~ cloth** toile *f* cirée; **~ field** gisement *m* de pétrole; **~ paint** peinture *f* à l'huile, *art:* couleur *f* à l'huile; **~ painting** peinture *f* à l'huile; **~-producing:** **~ countries** *pl.* pays *m/pl.* producteurs de pétrole; **~ rig** plate-forme *f* pétrolière; **~skin** toile *f* cirée ou huilée; **~s** *pl.* ciré *m;* **~ slick** nappe *f* de pétrole; **~y** huileux; gras (*a. voice*); *fig.* onctueux.

ointment onguent *m.*

O.K., okay, oken 1. d'accord!; **2.** bon, en bon état; **3.** approuver; contresigner (*an order*).

old vieux; âgé; ancien; de jadis; *how ~ is he* quel âge a-t-il?; *he is ... years* il a ... ans; **~ age** vieillesse *f;* **~ age pension** retraite *f,* pension *f* vieillesse; **~ age pensioner** retraité(e) *f) m;* **an ~ boy** un ancien élève; *esp. Am.* ≥ *Glory* la bannière étoilée; **~ wives' tale** conte *m* de bonne femme; **~-fashioned** démodé; vieux jeu; **~ish** vieillot.

olive ♀ olive *f; tree:* olivier *m.*

Olympic games *pl.* jeux *m/pl.* Olympiques.

ombudsman médiateur *m,* protecteur du citoyen.

ominous de mauvais augure.

omission omission *f.*

omit omettre.

omnipoten|ce toute-puissance *f;* **~t** tout-puissant.

on 1. *prp. usu.* à (*horseback, foot etc.*); en (*holiday, the road, sale*); après; de (*this side*); dans (*the train*); **~ exami-**

nation après considération; **~ both sides** des deux côtés; **~ all sides** de tous côtés; **~ business** pour affaires; *be ~ a committee* faire partie d'un comité; **~ Friday** vendredi; **~ the 5th of April** le 5 avril; **~ the left** à gauche; **~ these conditions** dans ces conditions; **~ hearing it** lorsque je (*etc.*) l'entendis; **2.** *adv.* (en) avant; *oft. not translated: put ~* mettre; *thea. be ~* être en scène; *have one's shoes ~* être chaussé; *write ~* continuer à écrire; *and so ~* et ainsi de suite; **~ and ~** sans fin; **~ to** sur, à; *from that day ~* à partir de ce jour; *what's ~?* thea. qu'est-ce qui se joue?

once 1. *adv.* une (seule) fois; autrefois; jadis; *at ~* tout de suite; à l'instant; *all at ~* soudain; **~ for all** une fois pour toutes; (*just*) *for ~* pour le coup, pour un coup; *in a while* (une fois) de temps en temps; *this ~* cette fois-ci; **~ more** une fois de plus, encore une fois; **2.** *cj.* (*a. ~ that*) dès que; une fois (que); **~-over:** F *give* (*s.th., s.o.*) *the* (*or a*) ~ jeter un coup d'oeil sur *ou* à.

oncoming 1. imminent; qui approche; **~ traffic** circulation *f* en sens inverse; **2.** arrivée; approche *f.*

one 1. un; unique; seul; celui; *impersonal pronoun.* on; **~ Mr. Miller** un certain M. Miller; *give ~'s view* donner son avis; *a large dog and a little ~* un grand chien et un petit; *for ~ thing* entre autres raisons; **2.** (*a. ~ f) m; the little ~s* les petit(e)s; **~ another** l'un(e) l'autre, les un(e)s les autres; *at ~* d'accord; **~ by ~,** *~ after another* un(e) à un(e), l'un(e) après l'autre; *it is all ~* (*to me*) cela m'est égal; *I for ~ ...* quant à moi, je ...; **~-night stand** *thea.* soirée *f* unique.

onerous onéreux; pénible.

one...: **~self** soi-même; *rfl.* se, *stressed:* soi; *by ~* tout seul; **~sided** inégal; asymétrique (*form*); **~upmanship** art *m* de faire mieux que les autres; **~way:** **~ street** (rue *f* à) sens *m* unique.

ongoing en cours.

onion oignon *m.*

onlooker spectateur(-trice *f) m.*

only 1. *adj.* seul, unique; **2.** *adv.* seulement, ne ... que; rien que; **~ yesterday** pas plus tard qu'hier; **3.** *cj.* seulement, mais; **~ that** si ce n'est *or* n'était que.

onrush ruée *f.*

N
O

onset (première) attaque *f*; commencement *m*.

onshore à terre; du large (*wind*).

onslaught assaut *m*; attaque *f*.

onward 1. *adj.* en avant, progressif; **2.** *adv.* (*a.* ~s) en avant; plus loin.

ooz|e 1. vase *f*; boue *f*; **2.** suinter; ~ *out*, ~ *away* s'écouler; ~y vaseux; suintant.

opaque opaque; *fig.* obscur, difficile à comprendre; *fig.* peu intelligent.

open 1. *adj. usu.* ouvert; plein (*air*, *country*, *sea*); grand (*air*); dégagé (*road etc.*); nu (*fire*); public (*trial*); haut (*sea*); non résolu, discutable (*question*); manifeste; déclaré (*enemy*); franc; doux (*weather*); découvert (*car*); ~ *to* accessible à; exposé à; *in the* ~ *air* en plein air; *the* ~ *sea* le large; ♀ *University* (Centre *m* de) Téléenseignement *m* universitaire; **2.** *su.* *bring into the* ~ exposer au grand jour; **3.** *v/t. usu.* ouvrir; *v/i.* s'ouvrir; s'étendre (*view*); commencer; ~ *into* donner dans; ~ *on to* donner sur (*window*); ~-*air* en or de plein air; ~-*ended* sans limite de durée; illimité; flexible (*offer*); ~*er* person: ouvreur (-euse *f*) *m*; ~-*handed* libéral; ~*ing* **1.** ouverture *f*; *fence*, *wall*: percée *f*; clairière *f* (*in a wood*); *fig.* occasion *f*; poste *m* vacant; **2.** d'ouverture, inaugural; *thea.* ~ *night* première *f*; ~ *time* heure *f* d'ouverture; ~-*minded* qui a l'esprit large; ~*ness* situation *f* exposée; *fig.* franchise *f*.

opera opéra *m*.

operable praticable; ✚ opérable.

opera...: ~ *glasses* *pl.* jumelles *f/pl.* d'opéra; ~ *house* opéra *m*.

operat|e *v/t.* ⊕ *etc.* faire marcher or fonctionner; ✚ diriger, gérer (*a company etc.*); ⚒ *etc.* exploiter (*a mine*); *v/i.* ⊕ marcher, fonctionner; faire effet (*drug etc.*); ~*ing*: ~ *expenses* *pl.* dépenses *f/pl.* courantes; ~ *system* système *m* d'exploitation; ~ *table* (*theatre*) ✚ table *f* (salle *f*) d'opération; ~*ion* fonctionnement *m*; ✦, ⚒, ✚ opération *f*; *be in* ~ fonctionner; être en vigueur; *come into* ~ entrer en vigueur; ~*ional* opérationnel; ~*ive* **1.** en vigueur **2.** ouvrier (-ère *f*) *m*; ~*or* opérateur (-trice *f*) *m*; téléphoniste *f*.

opinion opinion *f*, avis *m*; ~*poll* sondage *m* (d'opinion); *in my* ~ à mon avis;

~*ated* opiniâtre.

opium opium *m*; ~ *addict* opiomane *mf*; ~ *den* fumerie *f* d'opium.

opponent 1. adversaire *mf*.

opportun|e opportun; ~*ity* occasion *f*.

oppos|e s'opposer à; opposer (*two things*, *persons*); ~*ed* opposé (à, *to*); *as* ~ *to* à l'opposé de, par opposition à; ~*ite* **1.** *su.* opposé *m*, contraire *m*; **2.** *adj.* (d')en face; **3.** *adv.* en face, vis-à-vis; **4.** *prp.* (*a.* ~ *to*) en face de, vis-à-vis de; ~*ition* opposition *f* (*a. parl.*).

oppress opprimer; ~*ion* oppression *f*; ~*ive** oppressif.

opt: ~ *for* (*against*) opter pour (contre); ~ *to* (*inf.*) choisir de (*inf.*); ~ *out* (*of it*) se retirer.

optic optique; ~*al* optique; ~ *illusion* illusion *f* d'optique; ~*ian* opticien *m*.

optimis|m optimisme *m*; ~*tic* optimiste.

optimize optimiser.

option choix *m*; option *f*; ~*al* facultatif; ✚ en supplément.

opulence opulence *f*, richesse *f*.

opus opus *m*; *magnum* ~ œuvre *f* maîtresse.

or ou; *either ...* ~ ou ... ou; soit ... soit; ~ *else* ou bien; sinon.

orac|le oracle *m*; ~*ular* d'oracle; *fig.* sibyllin.

oral oral.

orange 1. orange *f*; **2.** orangé; orange; ~*ade* orangeade *f*.

orat|ion discours *m*; ~*or* orateur (-trice *f*) *m*; ~*ory* éloquence *f*; *art m* oratoire.

orb orbe *m*; ~*it* **1.** orbite *f*; **2.** tourner autour de.

orchard verger *m*.

orchestra ♪ orchestre *m*; ~ *pit* *thea.* fosse *f* d'orchestre.

orchid ⚘ orchidée *f*.

ordain *eccl.* ordonner; *fig.* décréter.

ordeal épreuve *f*; *hist.* ordalie *f*.

order 1. *usu.* ordre *m* (*a. eccl.*, *of knights*, *a. fig.*); ✚ commande *f*; ordonnance *f* (*for payment*); *post-office*: mandat *m*; instruction *f*; ~ *book* carnet *m* de commande; ~ *blank* (or *form*) bulletin *m* de commande; *in* ~ en ordre; *admin. etc.* en règle; *fig.* normal, permis, dans les règles; *put in* ~ mettre en ordre; *in* ~ *to* (*inf.*) pour (*inf.*); *in* ~ *that* pour que (*sbj.*), afin que (*sbj.*); *make to* ~ faire sur commande; faire sur mesure (*a suit*); *parl.* **standing** ~**s** *pl.* ordres *m/pl.* permanents; **2.** *v/t.* mettre en ordre; régler; ordonner; ✝ prescrire; ✝ commander; *v/i. restaurant etc.*: passer sa commande; ~**ly 1.** ordonné (*room, person etc.*); réglé, rangé (*life etc.*); discipliné; **2.** ✕ planton *m*; (**medical**) ~ infirmier *m*.

ordinal ordinal (*a. su./m*).

ordinance ordonnance *f*, règlement *m*.

ordinary 1. ordinaire; normal; courant; **2.** *out of the* ~ exceptionnel.

ordnance ✕ artillerie *f*.

ordure ordure *f*; immondice *f*.

ore minéral *m*.

organ organe *m*; ♪ orgue(s) *m* (*f/pl.*); ~**ic** organique; ~**ism** organisme *m*; ~**ist** ♪ organiste *mf*; ~**ization** organisation *f*; .... organisateur (trice *f*) *m*.

orgy orgie *f* (*a. fig.*); *fig.* profusion *f*.

orient 1. orient *m*; **2.** orienter; ~**al** oriental (*adj., mf*); ~**ate** orienter.

orifice orifice *m*, ouverture *f*.

origin origine *f*; provenance *f*.

original 1. original (*book, style, idea etc.*); originel, premier; **2.** original *m*; *person:* original(e *f*) *m*; ~**ity** originalité *f*.

originate *v/t.* faire naître, être l'auteur de; *v/i.* (**from, in**) provenir (de), avoir son origine (dans); ~**or** auteur *m*; initiateur (-trice *f*) *m*.

ornament 1. ornement *m*; **2.** orner; agrémenter (*a dress*); ~**al** ornemental; d'agrément.

ornate orné.

orphan orphelin(e *f*) *m*; **2.** (*a.* ~**ed**) orphelin; ~**age** orphelinat *m*.

orthodox orthodoxe.

oscillate osciller; ~**ion** oscillation *f*.

ostensible prétendu; feint; ~**ly** en apparence, soi-disant.

ostentation ostentation *f*; ~**us** fastueux, plein d'ostentation; ostentatoire.

ostracism ostracisme *m*; ~**ze** frapper (*q.*) d'ostracisme.

ostrich *orn.* autruche *f*.

other autre (**than, from** que); *the* ~ *day* l'autre jour, récemment; *every* ~ *day* tous les deux jours; ~**wise** autrement; sinon.

otter *zo.* loutre *f* (*a. skin*).

ought *defective verb*: **I** ~ **to** (*inf.*) je dois *or*

devrais (*inf.*); *you* ~ *to have done it* vous auriez dû le faire.

ounce once *f* (*a. fig.*).

our notre; nos; ~**s** le (la) nôtre, les nôtres; à nous; *a ... of* ~ un(e) de nos ...; ~**selves** nous-mêmes; *rfl.* nous (*a. stressed*).

oust évincer; supplanter; déloger.

out 1. *adv.* (au, en) dehors; au clair; sorti; éteint (*light, switch, fire etc.*); *be* ~ être sorti; sortir; être bas (*tide*); être en grève (*workers*); être en fleur; être paru (*book*); être épuisé, manquer (*provisions etc.*); être éventé (*secret*); être luxé (*arm etc.*); être à bout (*patience, month etc.*); *pol.* n'être plus au pouvoir; *sp.* être hors jeu; F *be* ~ *for s.th.* être à la recherche de qch.; *be* ~ *to* (*inf.*) avoir pour but de (*inf.*); *hear s.th.* ~ entendre qch. jusqu'au bout; ~ *and* ~ complètement; *have it* ~ *with* s'expliquer avec (*q.*); *way* ~ sortie *f*; ~ *with him!* à la porte!; **2.** *su.* F excuse *f*; *parl. the* ~**s** *pl.* l'opposition *f*; **3.** *adj.* exceptionnel (*size*); hors série; **4.** *prp.* ~ *of* hors de, au en dehors de; par (*the window*); parmi; *drink* ~ *of* boire dans (*a glass*), à (*the bottle*); *3* ~ *of 10* 3 sur 10; ~ *of respect* par respect; (*made*) ~ *of metal etc.* en or de metal *etc.*; *be* (*or have run*) ~ *of* n'avoir plus de, être à court de; **5.** F flanquer dehors *or* à la porte; ~**and-out** achevé; total; ~**bid** renchérir sur; ~**board** hors bord; extérieur; ~**break** éruption *f*; début *m*; ~**building** bâtiment *m* extérieur; ~**burst** explosion *f*, éruption *f*; ~**cast** expulsé(e *f*) (*a. su.*); *fig.* réprouvé(e *f*) (*a. su.*); ~**class** surclasser; ~**come** issue *f*, conséquence *f*; ~**cry** cri *m*; clameur *f*; tollé *m*; ~**dated** vieilli, démodé; ~**distance** dépasser, distancer; ~**do** surpasser; dépasser; ~**door** *adj.*, ~**doors** *adv.* au dehors; en plein air.

outer extérieur; externe; ~**most** le plus en dehors; extrême.

out...: ~**fit 1.** équipement *m*; matériel *m*; *clothes:* tenue *f*, (*group*) équipe *f*; **2.** équiper; ~**going 1.** sortant; **2.** sortie *f*; ✝ ~**s** *pl.* dépenses *f/pl.*; ~**grow** devenir plus grand que (*q.*); devenir trop grand pour (*qch.*); *fig.* ~**growth** conséquence *f* naturelle.

outing sortie *f*, excursion *f*.

out...: ~**last** survivre à; ~**law 1.** hors-la-loi *m/inv.*; **2.** mettre hors la loi (*a person*); proscrire; ~**lay** dépenses *f/ pl.*; frais *m/pl.*; ~**let** sortie *f*, issue *f*; tube, *a.* ✝: débouché *m*; *psych. etc.* exutoire *m*; ~**line 1.** silhouette *f*, contour *m*; *fig.* esquisse *f*, résumé *m*; aperçu *m*, grandes lignes *f/pl.*; **2.** tracer (les contours de), silhouetter; *fig.* esquisser (à grands traits), donner un aperçu de; ~**live** survivre à; ~**look** perspective *f* (*a. fig.*); *fig.* façon de voir (qch., *on s.th.*); ~**lying** éloigné, écarté; ~**moded** démodé; ~**most** le plus en dehors; extrême; ~**number** surpasser en nombre; ~**of-the-way** écarté (*place*); *fig.* insolite; ~**post** poste *m* avancé; ~**put** rendement *m*; débit *m*; production *f*; *computer:* sortie *f*.

outrage *m*; scandale *m*; outrage *m* (à *on*, *against*); **2.** outrager; ~**ous** scandaleux; atroce.

out...: ~**reach** tendre la main plus loin que; *fig.* prendre de l'avance sur; ~**right 1.** *adj.* catégorique, net; **2.** *adv.* complètement; catégoriquement; franchement; sur le coup; ~**rival** surpasser; l'emporter sur (*q.*); ~**run** dépasser; ~**set** commencement *m*, début *m*; **2.** tracer au plus; **2.** *adj.* extérieur; du dehors; maximum (*price*); *foot:* ~ **right** (**left**) ailier *m* droit (gauche); **3.** *adv.* (en) dehors; à l'extérieur; ~ **of** = **4.** *prp.* en dehors de; à l'extérieur de; hors de; ~**sider** étranger (-ère *f*) *m*; *in competition:* outsider *m*; ~**size 1.** ✝ grande taille *f*; **2.** énorme; ~**skirts** *pl.* *town:* faubourgs *m/pl.*, banlieue *f*; *forest:* lisière *f*; *fig.* marge *f*; ~**smart** être plus malin que; déjouer; ~**spoken** franc; ~**standing** éminent; en suspens (*matter*); ✝ dû; ~**stretched** tendu (*arm*); étendu, allongé (*body etc.*); ~**strip** dépasser; surpasser; ~**vote** obtenir une majorité sur.

outward 1. *adj.* en dehors; extérieur; (d')aller (*journey*); **2.** *adv.* (*usu.* ~**s**) au dehors; vers l'extérieur.

out...: ~**weigh** dépasser en poids; *fig.* l'emporter sur; ~**wit** déjouer, être plus malin que.

oval 1. (en) ovale; **2.** ovale *m*.

oven four *m*; ~**proof** allant au four; ~**ready** prêt à rôtir.

over 1. *adv.* par-dessus (*qch.*); en plus; fini; *with adj. or adv.:* trop; *with verb:* sur-, trop; *with su.:* excès *m*; ~ **and above** en outre; (*all*) ~ **again** de nouveau; ~ **against** vis-à-vis de; *all* ~ partout; ~ **and** ~ (*again*) à plusieurs reprises; **get s.th.** ~ (**and done**) **with** en finir avec qch.; venir à bout de qch.; **read** ~ lire (*qch.*) en entier; parcourir; **2.** *prp.* sur, (par)dessus; au-dessus de; au-delà de; *all* ~ **the town** dans toute la ville; ~ **night** pendant la nuit.

over...: ~**act** exagérer; ~**all 1.** tablier *m*; blouse; sarrau *m*; ~**s** *pl.* salopette *f*; F bleus *m/pl.*; **2.** total, d'ensemble; **3.** dans l'ensemble, au total; ~**awe** intimider; ~**balance** (se) renverser; ~**bearing** arrogant; ~**board** ✝ par-dessus bord; *man:* à la mer; ~**burden** surcharger (de, *with*); ~**cast** couvert; ~**charge** surcharger; demander un prix (*or* des prix) excessif(s) (à q., *s.o.*); ~ **s.o. for s.th.** faire payer qch. trop cher à q.; ~ **s.o. 10 francs** faire payer 10 francs de trop à q.; ~**clouded** couvert (de nuages); *fig.* assombri (de, *with*); ~**coat** pardessus *m*; ~**come** vaincre (*an enemy etc.*); surmonter (*difficulties etc.*); maîtriser (*emotions etc.*); **be** ~ **by** (*or* **with**) succomber à; *fig.:* être saisi de; ~**crowded** bondé, trop plein; ~**do** exagérer; prendre trop de (*qch.*); excéder (ses forces *etc.*, *one's strength etc.*); *cuis.* trop cuire; ~**done** exagéré; trop cuit; ~**dose** dose *f* trop forte *or* excessive; ~**draw** exagérer; ✝ mettre (*an account*) à découvert; ~**due** en retard (*a.* 🚃); ✝ échu; ~**eat:** ~ **o.s.** trop manger; ~**expose** *phot.* surexposer; ~**flow 1.** déborder; **2.** trop plein *m*; ~**grow** (re-)couvrir; envahir; ~**hang 1.** surplomber; **2.** saillie *f*; ~**haul** examiner en détail; réparer; ~**head 1.** *adv.* en haut; **2.** *adj.* ✝ général (*expenses etc.*); ⊕ ~ **wire** câble *m* aérien; **3.** *su.* ✝ ~**s** *pl.* frais *m/pl.* généraux; ~**hear** surprendre (*q.*, *a conversation*); ~**heat** ⊕ surchauffer; ~ **o.s.** s'échauffer; ~**indulge** avoir trop d'indulgence pour (*q.*); gâter (*q.*); céder trop facilement à (*qch.*); ~ **in** faire abus de; manger *or* boire *etc.* trop de (*qch.*); ~**joyed: be** ~ être aux anges; ~**kill** ✗

capacité *f* de surextermination; *fig.* excès *m*; ~**lap** (par) trop; ~**night 1.** *adv.* (pendant) la nuit; jusqu'au lendemain; *fig.* du jour au lendemain; **2.** *adj.* d'une nuit; de nuit; *fig.* soudain; ~**bag** sac *m* de voyage; ~**stay** séjour *m* d'une nuit; ~**stop** arrêt *m* pour la nuit; ~**pay** surpayer; ~**play** exagérer; *fig.* ~ **one's hand** aller trop loin; présumer de ses forces; ~**plus** surplus *m*; ~**populated** surpeuplé; ~**power** maîtriser, vaincre; *fig.* accabler, écraser; ~**ing** *a.* irrésistible; ~**pressure** surpression *f*; surmenage *m* (*of the mind*); ~**rate** surestimer; ~**reach** dépasser; *fig.* tromper, duper, escroquer; *fig.* ~ **o.s.** présumer de ses forces; ~**react** réagir excessivement; ~**ride** outrepasser (*an order*); fouler aux pieds (*rights*); ~**rule** décider contre; *t²* annuler; rejeter; envahir; *fig.* dépasser; ~**seas** d'outre-mer; étranger; ~ **trade** commerce *m* extérieur; ~**see** surveiller; surveillant(e *f*) *m*; ⊕ contremaître *m*; ~**shadow** ombrager; éclipser (*q.*); ~**shoot** dépasser; *fig.* ~ **the mark** aller trop loin, exagérer; ~**sight** oubli *m*; surveillance *f*; ~**sleep** (*a.* ~ **o.s.**) dormir trop longtemps; ~**spill** excédent *m* de

population; ~**staffed** avec trop de personnel; ~**state** exagérer; ~**strain 1.** surtendre; *fig.* surmener; **2.** tension *f* excessive; *fig.* surmenage *m*.

overt mal caché, manifeste.

over...: ~**take** dépasser (*qch.*); doubler (*a car*); rattraper (*q.*); ~**tax** surtaxer; *fig.* trop exiger de (*q.*); ~**throw 1.** renverser (*a. fig.*); vaincre; **2.** renversement *m*; défaite *f* (*a. fig.*, *a.* ✗); ~**time** heures *f/pl.* supplémentaires; ~**tone** ♪ harmonique *m*; *fig.* (*a.* ~**s** *pl.*) sousentendu *m*, note *f*, accent *m*.

overture ouverture *f* (*a.* ♪); offre *f*.

over...: ~**turn** (se) renverser; ~**value** surestimer; ~**weight** excédent *m*; ~**whelm** accabler; submerger; ~**work 1.** surmenage *m*; **2.** (se) surmener; ~**wrought** excédé, surexcité.

owe devoir.

owing dû; ~ **to** par suite de, à cause de.

owl *orn.* hibou *m*; chouette *f*.

own 1. propre; à moi (toi *etc.*); **2.** *my* ~ le mien (la mienne *etc.*); *a house of one's* ~ une maison à soi; *hold one's* ~ tenir ferme; maintenir sa position; *on one's* ~ (tout) seul. **3.** posséder; ~ *up* avouer.

owner propriétaire *mf*; ~**less** sans propriétaire; ~**ship** (droit *m* de) propriété *f*; possession *f*.

ox, *pl.* **oxen** bœuf *m*.

oxid|ation 🜍 oxydation *f*; ~**e** oxyde *m*; ~**ize** (s')oxyder.

oxtail: ~ *soup* soupe *f* à la queue de bœuf.

oxygen 🜍 oxygène *m*.

oyster huître *f*.

ozone 🜍 ozone *m*.

P

pace 1. pas *m*; allure *f*, vitesse *f*; *keep* ~ *with* aller aussi vite que, *fig.* suivre; *fig.* se (main)tenir au courant de; *put s.o. through his* (*her*) ~*s* mettre q. à l'épreuve; *set the* ~ donner l'allure, *fig.* donner le ton; **2.** *v/i.* marcher (à pas mesurés); ~ *up and down* faire les cent pas; *v/t.* (*a.* ~ *up and down a room etc.*) arpenter (*une pièce etc.*); (*a.* ~ *out*, ~ *off*) mesurer (*qch.*) au pas; ~**maker** *sp.* (*a.* ~**setter**) meneur *m* de train; *♥* stimulateur *m* cardiaque, pacemaker *m*.

pacific pacifique; paisible; *the* 2 *Ocean* l'océan *m* Pacifique, le Pacifique *m*.

pacif|y pacifier; calmer, apaiser; **~ist** pacifiste *mf*.

pack 1. paquet *m*; ballot *m*; *wolves*: meute *f*, *thieves etc.*: bande *f*; *cards*: jeu *m*; *fig.* tas *m*; **2.** *vt/i.* tasser; remplir, bourrer; (*oft.* **~ up**) emballer, empaqueter; envelopper (*a.* 🐾); (*a.* **~ off**) envoyer promener; faire (*a suitcase*); conserver en boîtes (*meat etc.*); (*a.* **~ up, ~ one's bags**) faire ses bagages *or* sa valise; *v/i.* F **~ up** arrêter (de travailler), finir; *sl.* tomber en panne; *sl.* fermer sa gueule (= *shut up*).

package 1. paquet *m*; **~ deal** marché *m or* accord *m* global; **~ holiday** vacances *f/pl.* organisées; **~ tour** voyage *m* organisé à prix forfaitaire; **2.** emballer.

packet paquet *m*.

pack ice banquise *f*.

packing emballage *m*; *meat etc.*: conservation *f*; matière *f* pour emballage; ⊕ garniture *f*; **~ case** caisse *f* (d'emballage); **~ house, ~ plant** fabrique *f* de conserves.

packthread ficelle *f*.

pact pacte *m*, contrat *m*.

pad 1. coussinet *m*; tampon *m* (*for inking, a.* ⊕); bloc-notes (*pl.* blocs-notes) *m* (*for writing*); *launching* **~** rampe *f* de lancement; **2.** rembourrer; ouater; *a. fig.* remplir, *fig. a.* étoffer; **~ding** rembourrage *m*; *a. fig.* remplissage *m*, *fig. a.* étoffement *m*.

paddle 1. pagaie *f*; palette *f*; **2.** pagayer; barboter.

paddy waggon *sl.* panier *m* à salade (= *prison van*).

paddock enclos *m*; *sp.* paddock *m*.

padlock cadenas *m*.

pagan païen(ne *f*) (*a. su.*).

page¹ *book*: page *f*; **2.** paginer.

page² **1.** page *m*; (*a.* **~ boy**) chasseur *m*; **2.** appeler.

pageant spectacle *m* historique; cérémonie *f*.

pail seau *m*.

pain 1. douleur *f*; peine *f* (*a. fig.*); **~s** *pl.* douleurs *f/pl.*; *sl.* (*a.* **~ in the neck**) casse-pieds *mf*; (*up*)**on ~ of** sous peine de; **be in ~** souffrir; **take ~s** prendre *or* se donner de la peine (pour *inf.*, **to** *inf.*); **2.** faire souffrir (*q.*); faire de la peine à (*q.*); **~ful** douloureux; *fig.* pénible; **~less** sans douleur; **~killer** anal-

gésique *m*; **~staking** assidu; appliqué (*pupil*); soigné (*work*).

paint 1. peinture *f*; **~s** *pl.* couleurs *f/pl.*; *wet* **~!** attention à la peinture!; **2.** peindre; *v/i. a.* faire de la peinture; **~brush** pinceau *m*; **~er** peindre *m*; **~ing** *art*: peinture *f*; *picture*: tableau *m*, toile *f*.

pair 1. paire *f*; *people*: couple *m*; **2.** (s')apparier; *v/i.* faire la paire (avec, **with**).

pal F copain *m*, copine *f*.

palace palais *m*.

palat|able agréable (au goût), bon; **~e** *anat.* palais *m*.

pale¹ 1. pâle (*a. colour*), blême; **~ ale** bière *f* blonde; **2.** pâlir.

pale² pieu *m*; *fig.* limites *f/pl.*

paleness pâleur *f*.

palette palette *f* (*a. fig.*).

palisade palissade *f*.

pall¹ *fig.* manteau *m*; voile *f*.

pall² devenir ennuyeux (pour, **on**); **~ on** *a.* lasser.

pallet paillasse *f*; ✝ palette *f*.

palliat|e pallier; atténuer; **~ive** palliatif *m*; anodin *m*.

pall|id blafard; blême; **~idness, ~or** pâleur *f*.

pally F: **be ~** être copains (copines *f*); **be ~ with** être copain (copine *f*) avec.

palm 1. *hand*: paume *f*; ♀ *tree*: palmier *m*; *branch*: palme *f*, *eccl.* rameau *m*; **2. Sunday** (dimanche *m* des) Rameaux *m/pl.*; **~ tree** palmier *m*; **2.** cacher dans la main; **~ off on s.o.** refiler (*qch.*) à q.

palpable palpable; *fig.* évident.

palpitat|e palpiter; **~ion** palpitation *f*.

paltry mesquin, misérable.

pamper choyer, dorloter.

pamphlet brochure *f*.

pan casserole *f*; (*frying* **~**) poêle *f*; cuvette *f*.

panacea panacée *f*.

pancake crêpe *f*.

panda *zo.* panda *m*; **~ car** voiture *f* pie (de la police); **~ crossing** passage *m* clouté.

pandemonium tohubohu *m*.

pander: ~ to satisfaire (à).

pane vitre *f*, carreau *m*.

panel 1. △ panneau *m*; *ceiling*: caisson *m*; ⊙ (*a.* **instrument ~**) tableau *m* de bord; *people*: jury *m*, invités *m/pl.*; **~ discussion** réunion-débat *f* (*pl.* réunions-débats), panel *m*; **~ doctor**

médecin *m* conventionné; **2.** recouvrir de panneaux.

pang tiraillement *m*, pincement *m*; serrement *m* de cœur.

panhandle 1. *Am. geog.* enclave *f*; **2.** *Am.* F mendigoter.

panic 1. panique *f*; **2.** paniquer.

pansy ♀ pensée *f*; *sl.* homme *m* efféminé.

pant haleter; *fig.* ~ **for** (*or* **after**) soupirer après.

panther *zo.* panthère *f*.

panties slip *m* (*for women*).

pantry garde-manger *m/inv.*; *hotel etc.*: office *f*.

panto *esp. Am.* F *pl.*: (**a pair of**) ~ (un) pantalon *m*; (un) caleçon *m*; ~ **suit** tailleur-pantalon *m* (*pl.* tailleurs-pantalons).

panty hose collant *m*.

pap bouillie *f*.

papa papa *m*.

papa|cy papauté *f*; ~**l** papal; du Pape.

paper 1. papier *m*; (*news~*) journal *m*; (*wall~*) papier *m* peint; (*examination ~*) épreuve *f* écrite; article *m*, exposé *m*, papier *m*; (*identity*) ~**s** *pl.* papiers *m/pl.* (d'identité); *fig.* **on** ~ sur le papier; **2.** de *or* en papier; en carton; ~ **money** papier-monnaie *m*; **~back** livre *m* broché, livre *m* de poche; **~bag** sac *m* de *or* en papier; **~clip** agrafe *f*, pince *f*; **~hanger** colleur *m* de papiers peints; **~mill** papeterie *f*, **~weight** presse-papiers *m/inv.*; **~work** écriture(s) *f/ (pl.)*; *pej.* paperasserie *f*.

par égalité *f*; pair *m*; **on a ~ with** au même niveau que.

parable parabole *f*.

parachut|e 1. parachute *m*; ~ **jump** saut *m* en parachute; **2.** *v/t* parachuter; *v/i* sauter en parachute; **~ist** parachutiste *mf*.

parade 1. parade *f*; défilé *m*; *fig.* étalage *m*; **make a ~ of** faire parade de; **2.** *v/t.* faire parade de; *v/i.* défiler.

paradise paradis *m*.

paradox paradoxe *m*; **~ical** paradoxal.

paragon parangon *m*; modèle *m*.

paragraph paragraphe *m*; alinéa *m*.

parallel 1. parallèle (à **to**, **with**); *fig. a.* analogue; **2.** *lines:* parallèle *f*; *geog.* parallèle *m* (*a. fig.*); **3.** égaler (*qch.*); être égal à (*qch.*).

paraly|se paralyser; **~sis** paralysie *f*.

paramount souverain; suprême.

paranoi|a paranoïa *f*; **~ac** paranoïque (*adj.*, *mf*).

parapet garde-corps *m/inv.*

paraphernalia *pl.* F affaires *f/pl.*; attirail *m*, appareil *m*.

parapleg|ia paraplégie *f*; **~ic** paraplégique (*adj.*, *mf*).

parasite parasite *m*.

parasol ombrelle *f*.

paratrooper para(chutiste) *m*.

parboil faire bouillir à demi.

parcel 1. paquet *m*, colis *m*; parcelle *f* (*of land*); **2.** (*usu.* ~ **up**) empaqueter; (*usu.* ~ **out**) morceler.

parch (se) dessécher.

parchment parchemin *m*.

pardon 1. pardon *m*; ₤ grâce *f*; **2.** pardonner (*qch.* à q., **s.o.** à **s.th.**); ₤ faire grâce à; **~able** pardonnable.

pare rogner (*one's nails etc.*); peler, éplucher; *fig.* ~ **down** réduire.

parent père *m*, mère *f*; ~**s** *pl.* parents *m/pl.*; **~al** parental.

parenthesis, *pl.* **-ses** parenthèse *f*.

parings *pl.* rognures *f/pl.*; pelures *f/pl.*

parish 1. paroisse *f*; (*a. civil* ~) commune *f*; **2.** paroissial; municipal; **~ioner** paroissien(ne *f*) *m*.

Parisian Parisien(ne *f*) *m*.

parity égalité *f*; parité *f* (*a.* ✝).

park 1. parc *m*, jardin (public) *m*; **2.** *mot.* garer, parquer; *v/i. mot.* stationner, se garer.

parking stationnement *m*; ~ **light** feu *m* de position; ~ **lot** parc *m* de stationnement, parking *m*; ~ **meter** parc(o)mètre *m*; ~ **place**, ~ **space** créneau *m*; ~ **ticket** contravention *f*.

parlance langage *m*, parler *m*.

parley 1. conférence *f*; pourparlers *m/pl.*; **2.** *v/i.* parlementer.

parliament parlement *m*; **~arian** parlementaire (*a. su.*); **~ary** parlementaire.

parlo(u)r salon *m*.

parochial paroissial; communal; *fig.* de clocher, borné.

parody 1. parodie *f*; **2.** parodier.

parole parole *f* (d'honneur); ₤ **on** ~ en liberté conditionnelle; *release on* ~ = **2.** mettre (*q.*) en liberté conditionnelle.

parquet 1. parquet(age) *m*; *Am. thea.* parterre *m*; **2.** parqueter.

P

parrot 1. *orn.* perroquet *m*; **2.** répéter *or* parler comme un perroquet.

parry 1. *sp. etc.* parade *f*; **2.** parer.

parsimonious parcimonieux.

parsley ♣ persil *m*.

parson (*catholic*) curé *m*; (*protestant*) pasteur *m*; **~age** presbytère *m*.

part 1. *su.* partie *f* (*a. gramm., a.* ♪) (de, **of**); part *f* (à, **in**); *thea.*, *fig.* rôle *m*; ⊕ pièce *f*; parages *m/pl.*; **take ~ in** prendre part à (*qch.*); **take in good (bad) ~** prendre en bonne (mauvaise) part; **for my (own) ~** pour ma part, quant à moi; **for the most ~** pour la plupart; **in ~** en partie; partiellement; **on my ~** de ma part; **2.** *adv.* en partie, mi-, moitié ...; **3.** *v/t.* séparer; **~ one's hair** se faire une raie; *v/i.* se diviser; se quitter; se séparer (de, **with**).

partake participer (à **in, of**); **~ of** prendre (*a meal*); *fig.* tenir de.

partial partiel, en partie, partial (*person*); **be ~ to** avoir un faible pour; **~ly** en partie; **~ity** partialité *f* (pour, envers **for, to**); prédilection *f* (pour, **for**).

particip|ant participant(*e f*) *m* (à, **in**); **~ate** participer, prendre part (à, **in**); **~ation** participation *f* (à, **in**); **~le** *gramm.* participe *m*.

particle particule *f* (*a. gramm.*).

particular 1. particulier; spécial; détaillé; méticuleux; exigeant (sur **about, as to**); délicat (sur **on, about**); **~ly** en particulier; **2.** détail, point *m*; **in ~** en particulier; **in every ~, in all ~s** en tout point; **~s** *pl.* détails *m/pl.*; renseignement(s) *m(/pl.)*; **~ity** particularité *f*; méticulosité *f*; minutie *f*; **~ize** spécifier; détailler.

parting 1. séparation *f*; départ *m*; *hair*: raie *f*; **~ of the ways** *esp. fig.* carrefour *m*; **2.** d'adieu (*kiss etc.*).

partisan 1. partisan *m* (*a.* ✗); **2.** partisan, partial; **~ship** esprit *m* partisan; appartenance *f* à un parti.

partition 1. *pol. etc.* partition *f*; (*a. ~ wall*) cloison *m*; **2.** morceler, démembrer; cloisonner (*a room*).

partitive *gramm.* partitif (*a. su./m.*).

partly en partie, partiellement.

partner 1. associé(*e f*) *m* (*a.* ✝); *sp.* partenaire *mf*; danseur (-euse *f*) *m*; ✝ **sleeping** (*or* **silent**) ~ commanditaire *m*; **2.** s'associer à; *sp.* être le partenaire de; **be**

~ed by s.o. avoir q. pour associé *etc.*; **~ship** association *f* (*a.* ✝); ✝ société *f*.

part-owner copropriétaire *mf*.

partridge *orn.* perdrix *f*.

part-time à temps partiel; à mi-temps; **have a ~ job, work ~** travailler à temps partiel; **be on ~** être en chômage partiel.

party *pol.* parti *m*; soirée *f*, fête *f*, parti *m*; groupe *m*, équipe *f*, ✗ détachement *m*; *fig.* complice *mf*; F individu *m*; **~ line** *parl.* directive *f* du parti.

pass 1. *su. geog.* col *m*, défilé *m*; ⚓, *sp.* passe *f*; *univ.* mention *f* passable; *permit.*: coupe-file *m/inv.*; **2.** *v/i.* passer (de ... à *or* en, **from ... to**); s'écouler (*time*); disparaître; arriver; être voté (*law etc.*), être reçu (*in examination*); **bring to ~** faire arriver; **come to ~** avoir lieu, arriver; **~ away** disparaître; trépasser, mourir; **~ by** passer, défiler (devant); **for** passer pour; **~ off** disparaître; **~ on** continuer; F trépasser; **~ out** F s'évanouir; **3.** *v/t.* passer devant *or* près de; dépasser; croiser; *sp.* devancer; passer (*one's time, things in review*); laisser passer (*q.*); (faire) passer, faire circuler; subir (*a test*) avec succès; réussir à (*an examination*); voter (*a bill*); prononcer (*a judgement*); **~ by** (*or* **over**) négliger (*q.*); ne pas faire attention à; **~ down** transmettre; **~ off** faire passer pour; **~ up** laisser passer, perdre (*a chance etc.*); ne pas faire attention à; **~able** praticable (*way*); passable, acceptable.

passage passage *m* (*a. of a text*); traversé *f* (*of sea etc.*); ruelle *f*; corridor *m*; ⊕ conduit *m*; adoption *f* (*of a bill*); ♪ trait *m*; **bird of ~** oiseau *m* de passage; **~way** couloir *m*; ruelle *f*.

passenger ⚓, ✈ passager (-ère *f*) *m*; voyageur (-euse *f*) *m*; **~ train** train *m* de voyageurs.

passer-by passant(*e f*) *m*.

passion passion *f* (de, **for**); colère *f*; **2 Week** *eccl.* semaine *f* sainte; **~ate** passionné; véhément.

passive passif.

passport passeport *m*.

password ✗ mot *m* de passe.

past 1. *adj.* passé (*a. gramm.*); ancien; **~ master** maître *m* passé; **for some time ~** depuis quelque temps; *gramm.*: **~ tense** passé *m*; **2.** *prp.* au-delà de; plus de; *half* ~ *two* deux heures et demie; **5** (***minutes***) ~ *eight* huit heures cinq *or* passé de cinq (minutes); *be* ~ *fifty* avoir dépassé la cinquantaine; *be* ~ *comprehension* être hors de toute compréhension; ~ *endurance* insupportable; *I would not put it* ~ *her* je ne l'en crois pas incapable; **3.** *su.* passé *m*; *... is a thing of the* ~ ... n'existe plus; ... n'a plus cours; ..., c'est du passé.

paste 1. pâte *f* (*a. cuis.*); colle *f*; *jewellery*: strass *m*; **2.** coller; **~board** carton *m.*

pastel 1. (crayon *m*) pastel *m*; **2.** pastel.

pasteurize pasteuriser; stériliser

pastime passe-temps *m/inv.*; distraction *f.*

pastor pasteur *m*; *Am.* prêtre *m.*

pastry pâtisserie *f*; pâte *f*; **~cook** pâtissier (-ère *f*) *m.*

pasture 1. pâturage *m*; **2.** paître.

pat 1. coup *m* léger; petite tape *f*; caresse *f*; *butter*: noisette *f*, rondelle *f*; **2.** tap(ot)er; caresser; **3.** ~ *answer* réponse *f* toute prête; *answer* ~ répondre sur-le-champ; *have* (*or know*) *s.th.* (*off*) ~ savoir qch. sur le bout du doigt.

patch 1. manifeste, patent; *colour*: tache *f*; *land*: parcelle *f*; *fig. bad* ~ moment *m* *or* période *f* difficile; **2.** rapiécer, raccommoder, mettre une pièce à; ~ *up* réparer; *roughly*: rafistoler; **~work** patchwork *m.*

pate *sl.* tête *f*, caboche *f.*

patent 1. manifeste, patent; ✝ breveté; ~ *leather* cuir *m* verni; **2.** brevet *m* (d'invention); ~ *office* bureau *m* des brevets; **3.** faire breveter.

patern|al paternel; **~ity** paternité *f.*

path chemin *m*, sentier *m*; *phys.* trajectoire *f*; *sp.* piste *f.*

pathetic pathétique; attendrissant.

patholog|ical pathologique; **~ist** pathologiste *mf*; **~y** pathologie *f.*

pathos pathétique *m.*

pathway sentier *m*, chemin *m.*

patien|ce patience *f*; *cards*: réussite *f*; **~t 1.** patient; **2.** malade *mf*; *dentist*: patient(e *f*) *m*; *doctor*: client(e *f*) *m*

patio patio *m.*

patrimony patrimoine *m.*

patriot patriote *mf.*

patrol 1. patrouille *f*; **2.** *v/t.* faire la patrouille dans; *v/i.* patrouiller; **~man** patrouilleur *m*; *Am. a.* agent *m* de police.

patron protecteur *m*; *eccl.* patron(ne *f*) *m*; ✝ client(e *f*) *m*; *charity*: patron *m*; ~ *saint* saint(e) patron(ne *f*) *m*; **~age** protection *f*, appui *m*; patronage *m*; clientèle *f*; **~ize** ✝ accorder sa clientèle à; *fig.* traiter avec condescence.

patter 1. tapoter; **2.** tapotement; *talk*: boniment *m.*

pattern 1. modèle *m*; dessin *m*, motif *m*; *sewing*: patron *m*; échantillon *m*; **2.** modeler (sur *after, on*).

paunch panse *f*, ventre *m.*

pauper indigent(e *f*) *m.*

pause 1. pause *f*, arrêt *m*; **2.** faire une pause; s'arrêter.

pave paver; *fig.* préparer; **~ment** pavé *m*, pavage *m*; dallage *m*; *Br.* trottoir *m*, *Am.* chaussée *f.*

paw 1. patte *f* (*sl. a. hand*); **2.** donner des coups de patte à, piaffer (*horse*); F tripoter.

pawn 1. gage *m*; *chess*: pion *m*; *in* (*or at*) ~ en gage; **2.** mettre en gage; **~broker** prêteur (-euse *f*) *m* sur gage(s); **~shop** maison *f* de prêt.

pay 1. salaire *m*; paie *f*, *servant*: gages *m/pl.*; ✗ solde *f*; ✝ ~ *freeze* blocage *m* des salaires; ~ *packet* (*Am.* ~ *envelope*) paie *f*; (*Am.* ~ *check*) salaire *m*; ~ *phone*, ~ *station* téléphone *m* public; **2.** *v/t.* payer; régler (*a bill*); présenter (*one's respect to s.o.*); faire (*honour, a visit to s.o.*); ~ *attention* (*or heed*) *to* faire attention à, tenir compte de; ~ *down* payer comptant; ~ *in* verser; ~ *off* régler; rembourser (*a creditor*); congédier (*an employee*); payer (*qch.*); rémunérer (*q., qch.*); *fig.* expier; ~ *up* régler; **~able** payable (*a.* ✝); acquittable; **~day** jour *m* de paye; **~ee** ✝ preneur (-euse *f*) *m*; **~ing** payant; profitable; **~load** charge *f* payante; ✗ poids *m* utile; **~ment** paiement *m*; rémunération *f*; **~off** règlement *m*; remboursement *m*; F résultat *m*; F comble *m*; **~roll** feuille *f* de paie; **~slip** bulletin *m* de paie.

pea ❀ (petit) pois *m.*

peace paix *f*; tranquillité *f*; ~ *movement* mouvement *m* pacifiste; ~ *talks* pourparlers *m/pl.* de paix; *break the* ~ troubler l'ordre public; **~able** pacifique; en paix; paisible; **~ful** paisible; pacifique; **~maker** conciliateur (-trice *f*) *m.*

P

peach ♀ pêche f; *tree:* pêcher m.

pea|cock paon m; **~hen** paonne f.

peak 1. pic m, cime f, sommet m; *cap:* visière f; *fig.* maximum m; *fig.* sommet m, apogée m, faîte m; *attr.* maximum, record, de pointe; **~ hours** heures f/pl. d'affluence *or* de pointe (*traffic*); **~ season** pleine saison; **2.** atteindre son maximum; **~ed** en pointe.

peal 1. *bells:* carillon m; *thunder:* grondement m; **~ of laughter** éclat m de rire; **2.** carillonner; retentir; gronder (*thunder*).

peanut ♀ arachide f.

pear ♀ poire f; *tree:* poirier m.

pearl perle f; **~y** perlé, nacré.

peasant paysan(ne f) m.

peat tourbe f.

pebble caillou m; *beach:* galet m.

peck¹ 1. (*a.* **~ at**) donner un coup (*or* des coups) de bec (à); picoter, picorer (*food*); F donner une bise à (= *kiss*); **~(ing) order** ordre m des préséances; **2.** coup m de bec; F bise f (= *kiss*).

peck² *measure:* picotin m.

peculate détourner des fonds.

peculiar bizarre, singulier; particulier (à, to); **~ity** particularité f; bizarrerie f.

pecuniary pécuniaire; d'argent.

pedal 1. pédale f; **2.** pédaler.

pedantic pédant(esque).

peddle v/t. colporter; v/i. faire le colportage; **~r** colporteur m.

pedestal piédestal m.

pedestrian 1. piéton m; **~ crossing** passage m clouté; **~ precinct** zone f piétonnière; **~ traffic** piétons m/pl.; **2.** *fig.* terre-à-terre.

pedicur|e soins m/pl. des pieds; **~ist** pedicure mf.

pedigree *animal:* pedigree m; *person:* lignée f; *attr.* de (pure) race.

pedlar colporteur m.

pee F faire pipi.

peek 1. jeter un coup d'œil furtif (sur, at); **2.** coup d'œil furtif.

peel 1. pelure f; peau f; *lemon:* écorce f. **2.** (*a.* **~ off**) v/t. peler; éplucher; v/i. peler; s'écailler; F se déshabiller.

peep¹ 1. coup m d'œil rapide *or* furtif; **2.** jeter un coup d'œil rapide *or* furtif (sur, at); se montrer; **~ing Tom** voyeur m.

peep² 1. pépiement m; **2.** pépier.

peephole judas m.

peer 1.: **~ at** scruter du regard; **2.** pair m; **~less** sans pareil.

peevish irritable; maussade.

peg 1. cheville f (*a.* ♪); fiche f; *whisky:* doigt m; (*a. clothes* **~**) pince f à linge; *fig.* **take s.o. down a ~** *or* **two** remettre q. à sa place; **2.** cheviller; *fig.* maintenir (*prices, wages etc.*); F **~ away** (*a.* **~ along**) travailler ferme (à, at).

pekin(g)ese pékinois m.

pelican *orn.* pélican m.

pellet boulette f; *pharm.* pilule f; grain m de plomb.

pelt 1. fourrure f, peau f; **2.** v/t. *fig.* bombarder (de, with); v/i. tomber à verse (*rain*).

pelvis *anat.* bassin m.

pen¹ 1. plume f; **~ friend**, **~ pal** correspondant(e f) m; **~ pusher** gratte-papier mf/inv.; **2.** écrire.

pen² 1. enclos m; **2.** (*usu.* **~ up**, **~ in**) parquer (*animals*), enfermer.

penal pénal (*law, code*); **~ servitude** travaux m/pl. forcés; **~ize** sp. pénaliser; *fig.* désavantager, punir; **~ty** peine f; pénalité f (*a. sp.*); *foot.* **~ area** surface f de réparation; **~ kick** penalty m.

penance pénitence f.

pence pl. of **penny**.

pencil 1. crayon m; **2.** marquer (*or* dessiner) au crayon; noter; **~ sharpener** taille-crayon m/inv.

pendant *necklace:* pendentif m.

pending 1. *adj.* en suspens; **2.** *prp.* pendant; en attendant.

pendulum pendule m; balancier m.

penetrat|e pénétrer (dans); **~ing** pénétrant; **~ion** pénétration; **~ive** pénétrant, perçant.

penfriend correspondant(e f) m.

penguin *orn.* pingouin m.

peninsula presqu'île f; péninsule f.

peniten|ce pénitence f; **~t** pénitent; **~tiary** prison f.

pen...: **~knife** canif m; **~ name** nom m de plume.

pennant banderole f, flamme f.

penniless sans le sou.

penny, *pl. value:* **pence,** *coins:* **pennies** penny m; **~ dreadful** roman m à deux sous; **~-in-the-slot machine** distributeur m automatique.

pension 1. pension f (*a.* ✗); (*old age* **~**) pension f vieillesse, retraite f; **~ scheme**

caisse *f* de retraite; **2.** *usu.* **~ off** mettre
(*q.*) à la retraite; pensionner; **~able** qui
a droit à une retraite; **~er** retraité *m*;
pensionnaire *mf*.

pensive pensif; songeur.

pent-up enfermé; *fig.* refoulé (*emotions
etc.*), réprimé.

Pentecost la Pentecôte *f*.

penthouse appartement *m* (*built on the
roof of a tall building*).

penury pénurie *f*.

people 1. *persons:* gens *m/pl.*, *crowd: a.*
monde *m*; *other persons:* les gens *m/pl.*,
on; *nation, population:* peuple *m*; **~ pl.
say** on dit; **English ~** *pl.* des *or* les
Anglais *m/pl.*; **many ~** *pl.* beaucoup de
monde; F **my ~** *pl.* mes parents *m/pl.*;
ma famille *f*; *pol.* **~'s republic** république *f* populaire; **2.** peupler (de, with).

pep F **1.** vigueur *f*, dynamisme *m*, pep *m*; **~
pill** excitant *m*, remontant *m*; **~ talk**
mots *m/pl.* d'encouragement; **2. ~ up**
remonter (le moral à) (*q.*); animer, mettre de l'entrain dans (*qch.*).

pepper 1. poivre *m*; **2.** poivrer;
~and-salt poivre et sel (*hair*); **~box,
~pot** poivrière *f*; **~mint** ♀ menthe *f*
poivrée; (*a. ~ lozenge*) pastille *f* de
menthe; **~y** poivré; *fig.* irascible.

per par; **~ cent** pour cent (%).

perambulat|e se promener dans; par-
courir; **~or** voiture *f* d'enfant.

perceive (a)percevoir; s'apercevoir de;
voir, comprendre.

percentage pourcentage *m*.

percept|ible perceptible, sensible; **~ion**
perception *f*; sensibilité *f*.

perch¹ *icht.* perche *f*.

perch² **1.** perchoir *m*; **2.** (se) percher;
~ed perché.

percipient percepteur.

percolat|e passer; **~or** percolateur *m*.

percussion percussion *f*; ♪ (*a. ~ instruments pl.*) instruments *m/pl.* de *or* à
percussion.

perdition perte *f*, ruine *f*.

peremptory péremptoire.

perennial éternel; ♀ persistant.

perfect 1. parfait; *complete, absolute:*
complet, absolu; ♪ **~ pitch** l'oreille *f*
absolue; **~ly** parfaitement; **2.** *gramm.*
(*or ~ tense*) parfait *m*; **3.** parfaire,
(par)achever; rendre parfait; **~ion** perfection *f*; **~ionist** perfectionniste *mf*.

perfid|ious perfide; **~y** perfidie *f*.

perforate perforer.

perform *v/t.* exécuter, faire; s'acquitter
de (*a duty*); ♪, *thea.* jouer; *v/i. thea. etc.:*
donner *or* des représentations; *fig.*
fonctionner, marcher; se comporter;
~ance exécution *f*; exploit *m*, presta-
tion *f*; *thea.* représentation *f*; *sp.*, *mot.*
performance *f*; F affaire *f*, histoire *f*;
~er artiste *mf*.

perfume 1. parfum *m*; odeur *f*; **2.** parfumer; **~ry** parfumerie *f*.

perfunctory superficiel; négligent.

perhaps peut-être.

peril péril *m*; **~ous** périlleux.

period période *f*; *history:* époque *f*;
school: leçon *f*; *gramm.* point *m*; ♂
règles *f/pl.*; **~ic** périodique; *attr.*
d'époque (*furniture etc.*); **~ical 1.**
périodique; **2.** (*publication f*) périodique *m*.

peripher|al périphérique; **~y** périphérie
f.

perish (faire) périr *or* mourir; (se)
détériorer; **~able** périssable; **~ing** glacial (*cold*).

periwig perruque *f*.

perjur|e: **~ o.s.** se parjurer; **~y** parjure
m; ♣ faux témoignage *m*.

perk F (*usu. ~ up*) (se) ragaillardir; (se)
retaper.

perk(s *pl.*) F à-côté(s) *m(/pl.*).

perky guilleret.

perm F *hair:* **1.** permanente *f*; **2.** faire
une permanente à; **have one's hair
~ed** se faire faire une permanente.

permanen|ce permanence *f*; **~t** perma-
nent, **~tly** en permanence; constam-
ment.

permea|ble perméable; **~te** *v/t.* filtrer à
travers; *v/i.* pénétrer; s'infiltrer (dans
into, among).

permissi|ble permis, tolérable; **~on** per-
mission *f*; autorisation *f*; **~ve** tolérant.

permit 1. permettre (à *inf.*, *to inf.*); **~ of
s.th.** permettre qch.; **2.** autorisation *f*,
permis *m*.

pernicious pernicieux.

perpendicular perpendiculaire.

perpetrate perpétrer; commettre.

perpetu|al perpétuel; **~ate** perpétuer;
~ity: (*in ~ en*) perpétuité *f*.

perplex rendre perplexe; **~ed** perplexe;
~ity perplexité *f*.

perquisites *pl.* (petits) avantages *m/pl.*

persecut|e persécuter; *fig. a.* harceler; **~ion** persécution *f;* **~or** persécuteur (-trice *f*) *m.*

persever|ance persévérance *f;* **~e** persévérer (à *inf.*, **in** *ger.*).

persist persister; s'obstiner (dans, **in**; à *inf.*, **in** *ger.*); **~ence, ~ency** persistance *f;* obstination *f;* **~ent** persistant; continu.

person personne *f; thea.* personnage *m;* **~able** agréable (de sa personne); **~age** personnage *m* (*a. thea.*); personnalité *f;* **~al** personnel; individuel; particulier; **~ assistant** secrétaire *m/f* privé(e); **~ality** personnalité *f;* **~ify** personnifier; **~nel** personnel *m;* **~to-~ call** *teleph.* communication (téléphonique) avec préavis.

perspic|acious perspicace; **~ity** perspicacité *f.*

perspir|ation transpiration *f;* sueur *f;* **~e** transpirer; suer.

persua|de persuader (de, *of;* que, *that;* à q. de *inf. s.o. into ger., s.o. to inf.*); convaincre; **~sion** persuasion *f;* conviction *f;* religion *f,* confession *f, a. fig.* croyance *f;* F *fig.* genre *m;* **~sive** persuasif.

pert effronté; coquin; gaillard.

pertain to avoir rapport à.

pertinacious obstiné, entêté.

pertinent pertinent, à propos; **~ to** ayant rapport à.

perturb perturber; inquiéter.

perus|al lecture *f;* examen *m;* **~e** lire attentivement; *fig.* examiner.

pervade pénétrer; se faire *f* sentir un peu partout dans.

pervers|e pervers; contrariant; **~ion** perversion *f;* **~ity** perversité *f.*

pervert 1. pervertir; **2.** perverti(e *f*) *m.*

pessimis|m pessimisme *m;* **~tic** pessimiste.

pest animal *m or* insecte nuisible; F *fig.* casse-pieds *mf/inv.*

pester importuner, harceler.

pesti|cide pesticide *m;* insecticide *m;* **~lent(ial)** *co.* embêtant, ennuyeux.

pestle pilon *m;* **2.** broyer au pilon.

pet 1. animal *m* favori; *fig.* enfant *mf* gâté(e); **2.** favori; **~ dog** chien *m* favori *or* de salon; **~ name** diminutif *m;* **3.** choyer, chouchouter; câliner; F (se) peloter.

petal ❧ pétale *m.*

petition 1. pétition *f;* **2.** adresser une pétition à.

petrify (se) pétrifier.

petrol *mot. Brit.* essence *f;* **~ station** poste *m* d'essence.

petticoat jupon *m.*

pettifogging chicanier; insignifiant.

petting F pelotage *m; heavy ~* pelotage *m* poussé.

pettish irritable, grognon.

petty insignifiant, petit; mesquin.

petulant irritable.

pew banc *m* d'église; siège *m.*

pewter étain *m,* potin *m.*

phantasm fantasme *m.*

phantom fantôme *m;* vision *f.*

Pharisee pharisien *m* (*a. fig.*).

pharmac|eutical pharmaceutique; **~ist** pharmacien(ne *f*) *m;* **~y** pharmacie *f.*

phase 1. phase *f;* **2.** **~ in (out)** introduire (supprimer) graduellement.

pheasant *orn.* faisan(e *f*) *m.*

phenomenon, *pl.* **-na** phénomène *m.*

philanderer coureur *m* (de jupons).

philanthropist philanthrope *mf.*

philolog|ist philologue *mf;* **~y** philologie *f.*

philosoph|er philosophe *mf;* **~ical** philosophique; **~ize** philosopher; **~y** philosophie *f.*

phlegm flegme *m* (*a.* ✿), calme *m.*

phobia phobie *f.*

phone 1. téléphone *m;* **2.** téléphoner; **~ back** rappler; **~ book** annuaire *m* (téléphonique); *see* **telephone;** **~-in** programme *m* à ligne ouverte.

phonetics *pl.* phonétique *f.*

phon(e)y F **1.** faux; factice; (du *or* en) toc; **2.** charlatan *m* (*person*); faux *m* (*thing*).

phosphorus ☸ phosphore *m.*

photo photo *f;* **~copier** photocopieur *m;* **~copy 1.** photocopie *f;* **2.** photocopier; **~electric:** (**~ cell** cellule *f*) photo-électrique; **~flash** flash *m;* **~genic** photogénique; **~graph 1.** photographie *f,* photo *f; take a ~ of* prendre *or* faire une photo(graphie) de; **2.** photographier; **~grapher** photographe *m/f;* **~graphic** photographique; **~graphy** photographie *f;* **~sensitive** photosensible; **~stat** *TM see* **photocopy.**

phrase 1. locution *f;* expression *f;* **2.** exprimer, rédiger; ♩ phraser.

physic|al physique; **~ian** médecin *m*; **~ist** physicien(ne *f*) *m*; **~s** *sg.* physique *f*.

physiotherap|ist kinésithérapeute *m/f*; **~y** kinésithérapie *f*.

pian|ist pianiste *m/f*; **~o** piano *m*.

pick 1. choix *m*; le meilleur *m*; pic *m*, pioche *f*; *the ~ of the bunch* le dessus du panier; *take one's ~* faire son choix, choisir; **2.** *vt/i.* cueillir (*flowers, fruits*); choisir; enlever; *♪* pincer (*a string*); se curer (*one's teeth*); ronger (*a bone*); crocheter (*a lock*); *~ pockets* voler à la tire; *~ a quarrel with* chercher querelle à *q.*; *~ at* chipoter à (*food*); *~ on* harceler, être (toujours) après *q.*; *~ out* choisir, trouver; distinguer, reconnaître; *~ up v/t.* ramasser, (passer) prendre, aller *or* venir chercher, (passer) prendre, aller *or* venir chercher, remonter (*q.*) (*tonic etc.*); apprendre (en passant); attraper, chiper (*an illness*); trouver; décrocher (*the receiver*); *~ up speed* prendre de la vitesse; *~ o.s. up* se relever; *v/i.* s'améliorer; se rétablir; *~a-back* sur le dos; *~axe* pioche *f*.

picket 1. piquet *m* (de grève); membre *m* d'un piquet; **2.** installer un piquet (de grève) à *or* devant.

pickings *pl.* restes *m/pl.*; *F fig.* gratte *f*.

pickle 1. marinade *f*; saumure *f*; conserve *f* au vinaigre; **~s** *pl.* pickles *m/pl.*; **2.** mariner.

pick...: ~lock crochet *m*; **~pocket** voleur (-euse *f*) *m* à la tire; **~-up 1.** personne *f or* chose *f* ramassée; *record-player*: pick-up *m/inv.*; *mot.* (*a. ~ truck, ~ van*) pick-up *m/inv.*; *mot.* accélération *f*, reprise(s) *f/(pl.)*; *✝* (*a. ~ in prices*) hausse *f*; **2.** improvisé.

picky difficile (à satisfaire).

picnic 1. pique-nique *m*; **2.** pique-niquer.

pictorial illustré.

picture 1. image *f*; tableau *m*, peinture *f*; **~s** *pl.* cinéma *m*; *attr.* d'images; du cinéma; *~ (post)card* carte *f* postale illustrée; **2.** dépeindre; (se) représenter; se figurer.

picturesque pittoresque.

pie *meat etc.*: pâté *m*; *fruit*: tourte *f*.

piece 1. pièce *f* (*a. thea., coin, ✝*); morceau *m* (*a. ♪*); *~ of advice* conseil *m*; *~ of news* nouvelle *f*; *take to ~s* mettre en morceaux, démonter; **2.** (*a. ~ up*) rac-

commoder; *~ together* rassembler; **~meal** peu à peu; **~work** travail *m* à la tâche.

pier jetée *f*; *bridge*: pilier *m*.

pierce (trans)percer.

piety piété *f*.

pig porc *m*, cochon *m*.

pigeon *zo.* pigeon *m*; **~hole 1.** casier *m*; **2.** classer; *fig.* enterrer (temporairement) (*a project etc.*).

pigg|ery porcherie *f*; *fig.* cochonnerie *f*; **~ish** sale; goinfre; **~y 1.** petit cochon; **2.** de cochon; *fig.* goinfre, glouton; **~yback** sur le dos; **~ybank** tirelire *m*.

pigheaded obstiné, têtu.

piglet petit cochon *m*, porcelet *m*.

pigment pigment *m*.

pig...: ~skin peau *f* de porc; **~sty** porcherie *f*; **~tail** tresse *f*, natte *f*.

pike ✕ pique *f*; *geog.* pic *m*; *icht.* brochet *m*; *Am.* barrière *f* de péage.

pile¹ 1. pile *f*, tas *m*; *fig.* fortune *f*, *atomic ~* pile *f* atomique; **2.** (*usu. ~ up*) (s')empiler; (s')entasser.

pile² pieu *m*.

pile³ *tex.* poil *m*.

piles F hémorroïdes *f/pl.*

pileup *F* carambolage *m or* télescopage *m* (en série).

pilfer chiper, chaparder.

pilgrim pèlerin(e *f*) *m*; **~age** pèlerinage *m*.

pill pilule *f*.

pillage 1. pillage *m*; **2.** piller.

pillar pilier *m*; *~ box* boîte *f* aux lettres.

pillion *mot.* siège *m* arrière.

pillory 1. pilori *m*; **2.** mettre au pilori.

pillow oreiller *m*; coussin *m*; *~ case, ~ slip* taie *f* d'oreiller.

pilot 1. pilote *m*; **2.** piloter; conduire; **3.** ...(-)pilote, ... d'essai; ⊕ *~ light* veilleuse *f*.

pimp souteneur *m*, maquereau *m*.

pimp|le *♂* bouton *m*; **~y** boutonneux.

pin 1. épingle *f*; ⊕ cheville *f*; clou *m*; *game*: quille *f*; *~ money* argent *m* de poche; **2.** épingler; attacher avec des épingles; *fig.* clouer; *~ down* définir (*qch.*); coincer (*q.*), obliger (*q.*) à prendre position.

pinafore tablier *m*.

pinball machine flipper *m*.

pincers *pl.* tenailles *f/pl.*

pinch 1. pincement *m*; *salt etc.*: pincée *f*;

P

at (*or* in) *a* ~ au besoin; à la rigueur; **2.** *v/t.* pincer (*a. sl.* = *arrest*); serrer (*shoe etc.*); *sl.* chiper (= *steal*); *v/i.* serrer (*shoe etc.*); (*a.* ~ *and scrape*) rogner sur tout.

pinchhit remplacer (q., *for s.o.*).

pincushion pelote *f* (à épingles).

pine¹ ⚓ pin *m*; bois *m* de pin.

pine² languir (après, *for*); (*a.* ~ *away*) dépérir.

pineapple ananas *m*.

pinion 1. aileron *m*; ⊕ pignon *m*; **2.** lier les bras à (*q.*).

pink 1. œillet *m*; *colour*: rose *m*; F *in the* ~ en parfaite santé; **2.** rose; **3.** *mot.* cliqueter.

pinnacle pinacle *m*.

pin...: ~**point 1.** localiser (précisément); (bien) définir; mettre le doigt sur (*a problem etc.*); **2.** (absolument) précis; ~**prick** piqûre *f* d'épingle; *fig.* coup *m* d'épingle; ~**stripe** rayure *f* (très fine).

pint *measure*: pinte *f*.

pioneer ✗, *fig.* pionnier *m*.

pious pieux.

pip *fruit*: pépin *m*; *signal*: top *m*; *cards*, *dice*: point *m*; ✗ *ranks*: étoile *f*.

pipe 1. tuyau *m*, conduite *f*, tube *m*; *tobacco*: pipe *f* (*a. measure of wine*); ♩ pipeau *m*; ♩ ~**s** *pl.* cornemuse *f*; ~ *dream* château *m* en Espagne; **2.** canaliser; amener par tuyaux; siffler; F ~ *down* se taire; ~**d music** musique *f* de fond enregistrée; ~**line** pipe-line *m*.

piping 1.: ~ *hot* tout chaud; **2.** tuyauterie *f*.

pipsqueak rien-du-tout *mf/inv.*

pique 1. ressentiment *m*, dépit *m*; **2.** blesser, froisser.

pira|cy piraterie *f*; ~**te 1.** pirate *m*; **2.** pirater; contrefaire; plagier; ... pirate (*radio, station etc.*).

pistol pistolet *m*.

piston ⊕ piston *m*; ~ *displacement* cylindrée *f*; ~ *rod* tige *f* de piston.

Pisces *ast.* les Poissons *m/pl.*

piss V ~ pisse *f*; **2.** pisser; ~ *off* fous le camp!; ~**ed** soûl, plein (= *drunk*); (*a.* ~ *off*) fâché.

pistachio pistache *f*.

pit¹ 1. fosse *f*; trou *m*; creux *m* (*a. anat.*); dépression *f*; marque *f*, *on face*: *a.* cicatrice *f*; *Br. thea.* parterre *f*; (*a. coal* ~ puits *m* de) mine; ♩ *the* (*orchestra*) ~ la

fosse *f* (d'orchestre); ~ *worker* mineur *m* de fond; **2.** opposer (à, *against*); ~**ted** grêlé (*face*); marqué, troué.

pit² 1. *fruit*: noyau *m*; **2.** dénoyauter (*fruit*).

pitch¹ poix *f*, brai *m*.

pitch² 1. lancement *m*; ♩ ton *m*; *voice*: hauteur *f*; ♩ tangage *m*; *hawker*: place *f* habituelle; *sp.* terrain *m*; *fig.* degré *m*; **2.** *v/t* lancer; dresser (*a tent*); ♩ ~ *higher* (*lower*) hausser (baisser) (*a tune*); ~ *one's hope too high* viser trop haut; *v/i.* tomber; ♩ tanguer; F ~ *into* s'attaquer à.

pitcher cruche *f*; broc *m*.

pitchfork 1. fourche *f* à foin; **2.** lancer; *fig.* parachuter, bombarder (dans, *into a post etc.*).

piteous pitoyable, piteux.

pitfall trappe *f*; piège *m*.

pith moelle *f*; *orange*: peau *f* blanche; *fig.* essence *f*; *fig.* vigueur *m*; ~**y** vigoureux; nerveux.

piti|able pitoyable; ~**ful** pitoyable; lamentable; ~**less** impitoyable.

pittance maigre salaire *m*.

pity 1. pitié *f*; *it is a* ~ c'est dommage; **2.** plaindre; avoir pitié de.

pivot 1. pivot *m*; **2.** (faire) pivoter.

pixie lutin *m*; fée *f*.

placard 1. affiche *f*; **2.** afficher.

placate apaiser.

place 1. lieu *m*, endroit *m*; place *f*; rang *m*; emploi *m*; ~ *name* nom *m* de lieu; *at my* ~ chez moi; *in* ~ *of* au lieu de; *in the first* ~ d'abord; premièrement; *in the second* ~ (et) puis; deuxièmement; *out of* ~ déplacé; *put s.o. in his* ~ remettre q. à sa place; *take* ~ avoir lieu; *take first* ~ être (le) premier; *fig.* être le plus important; **2.** placer (*a. money*); (re)mettre; ✝ passer (*an order*); ~**name** nom *m* de lieu.

placid placide; ~**ity** placidité *f*.

plagiar|ism plagiat *m*; ~**ize** plagier.

plague 1. peste *f*; fléau *m*; **2.** tourmenter, harceler.

plaice *icht.* plie *f*.

plain 1. *adj.* évident, clair; simple; ordinaire; pur; *cuis.* nature; laid, sans beauté; carré, franc; *in* ~ *English* pour parler clairement; ~ *chocolate* chocolat *m* à craquer; ~ *paper* papier *m* non réglé; **2.** *adv.* clairement; carrément; complètement; **3.** *su.* plaine *f*; **~clothes man** agent *m* en civil; agent *m* de la sûreté; **~ness** simplicité *f*.

plaint|iff ⚖ demandeur (-eresse *f*) *m*; **~ive** plaintif.

plait 1. *hair:* tresse *f*; **2.** tresser.

plan plan *m*; projet *m*; **2.** tracer le plan de; organiser; *fig.* projeter; **~ned economy** économie *f* planifiée.

plane[1] **1.** avion *m*; **2.** planer.

plane[2] **1.** uni; plat; égal; **2.** ♈ plan *m*; *fig.* niveau *m*; ⊕ rabot *m*; **3.** aplanir; ⊕ raboter.

plane ♃ (*a.* **~ tree**) platane *f*.

planet *astr.* planète.

plank planche *f*; *parl.* point *m* d'un programme électoral.

planning planification *f*; **family~** planning *m* familial.

plant 1. plante *f*; ⊕ usine *f*; ⊕ matériel *m*, installation *f*; *sl.* coup *m* monté; **2.** planter; *fig.* installer; (dé)poser; **~ation** plantation *f*; **~er** planteur *m*.

plaque plaque *f*; ✴ (*a.* **dental ~**) plaque *f*.

plaster 1. plâtre *m*; (*usu.* **~ of Paris**) plâtre *m* de moulage; ✴ (*a.* **sticking ~**) sparadrap *m*; **2.** plâtrer; recouvrir (de, **with**).

plastic 1. plastique; **2.** *usu.* **~s** *pl.* (matière *f*) plastique *m*.

plate 1. *dish:* assiette *f*; ⊕ plaque *f* (*a. mot., photo*); *book:* gravure *f*; **2.** plaquer.

platform terrasse *f*; estrade *f*; *geog.* 🚋 quai *m*; *pol.* programme *m*.

platinum *min.* platine *m*.

platitude platitude *f*.

platoon peloton *m*.

platter plat *m*; écuelle *f*.

plausible plausible; convainquant.

play 1. jeu *m*; *thea.* pièce *f*; **~ on words** jeu *m* de mots; **2.** *v/t.* jouer à (*a game cards etc.*); jouer (*a part, a song, a play etc.*); jouer de (*an instrument etc.*); *sp.* jouer contre (*a team*); **~ the flute** jouer de la flûte; **~ back** (faire) repasser; **~ down** minimiser; **~ off** opposer (à, **against**); **~ up** souligner, insister sur (*qch.*); *v/i.* jouer (avec, **with**); **~ at** jouer à; **~ for time** temporiser; **~ on** jouer sur; **~ up** faire des siennes; **~ up to** flatter, faire de la lèche à (*q.*); **~act** faire du théâtre, jouer la comédie; **~acting** (pure) comédie *f*; **~back** play-back *m*;

~ed-out épuisé; **~er** joueur (-euse *f*) *m* (*a. sp.*); acteur (-trice *f*) *m*; ♪ musicien(ne *f*) *m*; **~fellow** camarade *mf* de jeu; **~ful** badin, enjoué; **~goer** amateur (-trice *f*) *m* du théâtre; **~ground** (*a.* **~ing-field**) terrain *m* de jeu(x); cour *f* de récréation; **~house** théâtre *m*; *Am.* maison *f* de poupée; **~-off** *sp.* belle *f*; **~pen** parc *m* (pour bébés); **~thing** jouet *m*; **~wright** auteur *m* dramatique.

plea ⚖ argument *m*; prière *f*, appel *m*; excuse *f*, prétexte *m*.

plead *v/i.* plaider (pour, en faveur de **for**); **~ for mercy** demander grâce; *v/t.* plaider; alléguer (*an excuse*); **~ with** implorer, supplier.

pleasant agréable, aimable; affable; **~ries** *pl.* civilités *f/pl.*

please *v/i.* plaire; être agréable; **if you ~** s'il vous plaît; je vous en prie; **~ come in!** veuillez entrer; *v/t.* plaire à; **~ o.s.** agir à sa guise, **be ~d to do s.th.** faire qch. avec plaisir; **be ~d with** être (très) content de; **~d** content, satisfait.

pleasing agréable; doux.

pleasur|able agréable; **~e** plaisir *m*; *attr.* d'agrément; **at ~** à volonté; **give s.o. ~** faire plaisir à q.; **take ~** prendre (du) plaisir (à qch., **in s.th.**).

pleat 1. pli *m*; **2.** plisser.

plebiscite plébiscite *m*.

pledge 1. gage *m*; promesse *f*; **2.** engager; promettre.

plenary plénier.

plenipotentiary plénipotentiaire (*a. su./m*).

plent|eous abondant; **~iful** abondant; **~y** abondance *f*; **~ of** beaucoup de; assez de.

pliable flexible; souple.

pliers *pl.* pinces *f/pl.*

plimsoll (chaussure *f* de) tennis *m*.

plight état *m* (*or* situation *f*) difficile.

plod (*a.* **~ along, on**) marcher lourdement *or* péniblement.

plonk F **1.** pinard *m* (= *cheap wine*); **2.** laisser tomber *or* poser lourdement.

plot[1] (lot *m* de) terrain *m*.

plot[2] **1.** complot *m*, intrigue *f*, *novel etc.:* plan *m*; **2.** *vt/i.* comploter; *v/t.* (*a.* **~ down**) tracer; relever.

plough, *Am.* **plow 1.** charrue *f*; **2.** labourer; creuser (*a furrow*); *fig.* avancer péniblement; **~share** soc *m* de charrue.

ploy stratagème *m*, truc *m*.

pluck 1. arracher; plumer (*a chicken etc.*, *a. fig.*); cueillir (*a flower etc.*); ♪ pincer (*a string*); **~ at** tirer; **~ up courage** s'armer de courage; **2.** courage *m*, F cran *m*; **~y** courageux.

plug 1. bouchon *m*, bonde *f*; tampon *m*; ⚡ fiche *f*; ⚡ prise *f* (de courant); *mot.* (*spark~*) bougie *f*; ✝ matraquage *m*; *v/t.* boucher; tamponner F ✝ faire de la publicité pour, matraquer; ⚡ **~ in** brancher.

plum 1. prune *f*; **2.** F chouet.

plumage plumage *m*.

plumb 1. vertical, droit; **2.** plomb *m*; ⚓ sonde *f*; **3.** sonder; **~er** plombier *m*; **~ing** plomberie *f*, tuyauterie *f*.

plume plume *f*, panache *m*.

plummet tomber (à pic).

plump 1. *adj.* rebondi, grassouillet; **2.** tomber lourdement; F **~ for** se décider pour.

plunder 1. pillage *m*; **2.** piller.

plunge 1. plongeon *m*; *fig.* **take the ~** sauter le pas; **2.** *v/t.* plonger (dans, **in**[**to**]); *v/i.* plonger, s'enfoncer; ⚓ tanguer.

pluperfect *gramm.* plus-que-parfait *m*.

plural *gramm.* (*a.* **~ number**) pluriel *m*; **~ity** pluralité *f*; cumul *m*.

plus 1. *prp.* plus; **2.** *adj.* positif; **3.** *su.* plus *m*; *fig.* atout *m*, avantage *m*.

plush peluche *f*; *attr.* en or de peluche.

ply 1. *wood:* feuille *f*, épaisseur *f*; *wool:* fil *m*; **2.** *v/t.* manier; exercer (*a trade*); presser (*s.o. with questions*); *v/i.* faire le service; faire la navette; **~wood** contre-plaqué *m*.

pneumatic pneumatique.

pneumonia ✚ pneumonie *f*.

poach braconner; **~ed eggs** œufs *m/pl.* pochés; **~er** braconnier *m*.

pock ✚ pustule *f*.

pocket 1. poche *f*; **be 10 pounds out of ~** avoir perdu 10 livres; **2.** empocher; **3.** de poche; **~ knife** canif *m*; **~ money** argent *m* de poche; **~book** carnet *m* (de poche); portefeuille *m*; livre *m* de poche.

pod 1. ♀ cosse *f*; **2.** écosser.

poem poème *m*.

poet poète *m*; **~ess** poétesse *f*; **~ic(al)** poétique; **~ics** *sg.* art *m* poétique; **~ry** poésie *f*; vers *m/pl.*

poignan|cy piquant *m*; âpreté *f*; **~t** poignant.

point 1. point *m* (*a.* ⚡, *sp.*, *typ.*, *cards*, *dice*); ⊕, *knife*, *needle*, *geog.* pointe *f*; *fig.* point *m*, question *m*, sujet; *in time:* moment *m*; ⚡ (*a.* **decimal ~**) virgule *f*; ⚡ contact *m*; 🚉 **~s** *pl.* aiguillage *m*; **~ of view** point *m* de vue; **the ~ is** ce dont il s'agit c'est; **come to the ~** en venir au fait; **make a ~ of** (*ger.*) ne pas manquer de (*inf.*); tenir à (*inf.*); **in ~ of fact** en réalité; **off** (*or* **beyond**) **the ~** hors de propos; **be on the ~ of** (*ger.*) être sur le point de (*inf.*); **win on ~s** gagner aux points; **to the ~** à propos; **there is no ~ in** (*ger.*) cela ne sert à rien de (*inf.*), ce n'est pas la peine de (*inf.*); **2.** *v/t.* marquer de points; (*oft.* **~ out**) indiquer; **~ at** braquer (*a weapon*) sur; *v/i.* **~ at** montrer du doigt; **~ out** faire remarquer, signaler; indiquer; **~ to** indiquer; signaler; **~blank** à bout portant; *fig.* catégoriquement, carrément; **~ed** pointu; *fig.* mordant; significatif; **~edly** d'une manière significative; **~er** aiguille *f*, index *m*; *school:* baguette *f*; *hunt.* chien *m* d'arrêt; F tuyau *m*; **~less** inutile.

poise 1. équilibre *m*; port *m*, maintien *m*; *fig.* calme *m*, assurance; **2.** mettre or tenir (en équilibre); **be ~d for** être prêt à.

poison 1. poison *m*; **2.** empoisonner; **~ous** toxique; vénimeux (*animal*); vénéneux (*plant*).

poke 1. poussée *f*, coup *m*; **2.** *v/t.* pousser, donner un coup à; enfoncer, fourrer; (*a.* **~ up**) tisonner (*the fire*); **~ fun at** se moquer de; *v/i.* (*a.* **~ about**) fouiller.

poker tisonnier *m*; *cards:* poker *m*.

poky F étriqué, exigu.

polar polaire; **~ bear** ours *m* blanc.

Pole¹ Polonais(e *f*) *m*.

pole² *geog.*, *astr.*, *fig.* pôle *m*; ⚡ électrode *f*; **~ star** étoile *f* polaire.

pole³ poteau *m* (*a.* télégraphique); perche *f* (*a. sp.*); mât *m*; *sp.* **~ vault** saut *m* à la perche.

poleax(e) 1. hache *f*; **2.** assommer; terrasser.

polemic, *a.* **~al** polémique.

police 1. police *f*; **~ car** voiture *f* de police; **~ force** la police *f*; **~man**, **~officer** agent *m* (de police); **~ record** casier *m* judiciaire; **~ state** état *m* policier; **~ station** commissariat *m* de police; **2.** surveiller par la police; contrôler.

policy politique *f*; (*a.* **insurance ~**) police *f* (d'assurance).

polio F, **~myelitis** *🗲* poliomyélite *f*.

Polish¹ polonais.

polish² 1. *cream*: cire *f*, *a.* action: cirage *m*, (*nail~*) vernis *m*; *shine*: poli *m*, éclat *m*; *fig.* raffinement *m*; **2.** *put cream on*: cirer, *make shiny*: faire briller, astiquer; F *fig.* **~ off** expédier (*work etc.*), finir, s'envoyer (*food etc.*); *flg.* **~ up** perfectionner.

polite poli; **~ness** politesse *f*.

politic diplomatique, indiqué; **~al** politique; **~ian** homme *m* politique; **~s** *pl.*, *oft. sg.* politique *f*.

poll 1. vote (*par bulletins*); scrutin *m*; (*a.* **opinion ~**) sondage *m* (d'opinion); **2.** *v/t.* sonder l'opinion de (*people*); réunir (*votes*).

polling elections *f/pl.*; participation *f* électorale; **~ booth** isoloir *m*; **~ station** bureau *m* de vote.

pollster sondeur (-euse *f*) *m*

pollut|e polluer; **~ion** pollution *f*.

polo polo *m*; **~ neck** (chandail *m* à) col *m* roulé.

polyester polyester *m*.

polygamy polygamie *f*.

polyglot polyglotte (*adj.*, *su./mf*).

polyp polype *m*.

polytechnic Institut *m* universitaire de technologie, I.U.T. *m*.

polythene, polyethylene polyéthylène *m*, **~ bag** sac *m* en plastique.

pommel pommeau *m*.

pomp pompe *f*, apparat *m*; **~ous** pompeux; suffisant (*person*).

pond étang *m*; mare *f*; réservoir *m*.

ponder *v/i.* réfléchir (sur, **on, over**); *v/t.* réfléchir à, peser; **~ous** lourd.

pone pain *m* de maïs.

pong F **1.** puanteur *f*; **2.** puer.

pontiff pontife *m*; prélat *m*.

pontoon ponton *m*.

pony poney *m*; **~tail** queue *f* de cheval.

poodle caniche *m/f*.

pool¹ flaque *f* d'eau; mare *f*.

pool² 1. cagnotte *f*; poule *f* (*a. billard*); *football* **~s** *pl.* concours *m* de pronostics; *✝* syndicat *m*; fonds *m/pl.* communs; *Am.* **~ room** salle *f* de billard;

swimming ~ piscine *f*; **2.** mettre en commun; *✝* mettre en syndicat.

poop *♻* poupe *f*; dunette *f*.

poor *usu.* pauvre; médiocre, mauvais; faible; **~ health** santé *f* débile; **~ly 1.** *adj.* souffrant; **2.** *adv.* pauvrement; **~ness** pauvreté *f*; infériorité *f*.

pop¹ 1. bruit *m* sec; **2.** *v/t.* faire éclater *or* sauter; mettre, fourrer; porter; *v/i.* éclater; sauter; **~ in** entrer; **~ off** partir; F crever (= *die*); **~ out** sortir; **~ up** apparaître.

pop² pop (*su./m, adj*).

pop³ *Am.* F papa *m*; pépère *m*, pépé *m*.

pope pape *m*.

poplar *♣* peuplier *m*.

poppy *♣* pavot *m*; **~cock** F fadaises *f/pl.*

populace peuple *m*; *pej:* populace *f*.

popular populaire; vogue, à la mode; **~ity** popularité *f*; **~ize** populariser.

populat|e peupler; **~ion** population *f*; **~ explosion** explosion *f* démographique.

populous très peuplé.

porcelain porcelaine *f*.

porch porche *m*; *Am.* véranda *f*.

porcupine *zo.* porc-épic (*pl.* porcs-épics) *m*.

pore¹ pore *m*.

pore²: **~ over** s'absorber dans.

pork porc *m*, **~ butcher** charcutier *m*; **~ chop** côtelette *f* de porc; **~y** F gras (*person*).

porous poreux.

porpoise *zo.* marsouin *m*.

porridge bouillie *f* d'avoine.

port port *m*; *♻* sabord *m*; *♻* (*left side*) bâbord *m*; (*wine*) porto *m*.

portable portatif.

portal portail *m*; *fig.* entrée *f*.

porten|d présager; **~t** présage *m*; **~tious** sinistre; pompeux.

porter concierge *m*, gardien *m*; *hotel, railway:* porteur *m*.

portion 1. part *f*, partie *f*; portion *f*; **2.** (*a.* **~ out**) répartir.

portly corpulent.

portrait portrait *m*.

portray faire le portrait de (*q*); *fig.* (dé)peindre, décrire; **~al** portrait *m*, représentation *f*.

Portuguese 1. portugais; **2.** *ling.* portugais *m*; Portugais(e *f*) *m*.

pose 1. pose *f*; **2.** *v/i.* se poser; se faire

passer (pour, *as*); *v/t.* poser (*a question*); créer; présenter (*difficulties etc.*).

posh F chic, chouette.

position 1. position *f* (*a. fig.*, ✗, *posture*); situation *f*; place *f*; emploi *m*; *fig.* attitude *f*; **2.** placer; mettre en place.

positive 1. positif (*a.* ⚡, *phot.*); formel, indéniable; sûr, certain; **2.** positif *m* (*a. phot.*).

possess posséder; ⁓**ion** possession *f*; ⁓**ive** possessif; ⁓**or** possesseur *m*.

possib|**ility** possibilité *f*; ⁓**le** possible; ⁓**ly** peut-être; **he cannot ⁓ ...** il lui est impossible de ...

post¹ poteau *m*; **2.** afficher.

post² ✗ *etc.*: poste *m*; *job*: poste *m*, situation *f*; *mail*: courrier *m*; *institution*: poste *f*; **by** (**the**) ⁓ par la poste; **2.** ✗ poster, mettre en faction (*a sentinel*); poster, mettre à la poste; envoyer par la poste; F (*oft.* ⁓ **up** *or* **keep** *s.o.* ⁓**ed**) mettre au courant.

postage port *m*, affranchissement *m*; ⁓ **stamp** timbre-poste (*pl.* timbres-poste) *m*.

postal postal; *Am.* ⁓ (**card**) carte *f* postale; ⁓ **order** mandat-poste (*pl.* mandats-poste) *m*.

post...: ⁓**box** boîte *f* aux lettres; ⁓**card** carte *f* postale; ⁓**code** code *m* postal.

poster affiche *f*; poster *m*.

posterior 1. postérieur (à, **to**); **2.** F derrière *m*, postérieur *m*.

posterity postérité *f*.

post-free franco *inv.*

post-graduate 1. postscolaire; **2.** candidat *m* à un diplôme supérieur.

post-haste en toute hâte.

posthumous posthume.

post...: ⁓**man** facteur *m*; ⁓**mark 1.** cachet *m* de la poste; **2.** timbrer; ⁓**master** receveur *m* des postes.

post-mortem autopsie *f*.

post...: ⁓(-)**office** bureau *m* de poste; ⁓ **box** boîte *f* postale; ⁓**paid** franco, affranchi.

postpone ajourner, remettre *or* renvoyer (à plus tard); ⁓**ment** ajournement *m*; remise *f* à plus tard.

postscript post-scriptum *m/inv.*

postulate 1. postulat *m*; **2.** postuler.

posture 1. posture *f*, *body*: attitude *f*; position *f*; **2.** poser.

post-war d'après guerre.

posy bouquet *m* (de fleurs).

pot 1. pot *m*; marmite *f*; casserole *f*; *sl.* marijuana *f*; F **go to ⁓** aller à vau-l'eau; **2.** mettre en pot.

potato, *pl.* ⁓**es** pomme *f* de terre; ⁓ **chips**, ⁓**crisps** *pl.* (pommes *f/pl.*) chips *m/pl.*; *fig.* **hot ⁓** affaire *f* épineuse; **mashed** ⁓**es** *pl.* purée *f* de pommes de terre, pommes *f/pl.* mousseline.

pot-belly panse *f.*

potted en pot; en terrine; en conserve.

poten|**cy** puissance *f*; force *f*; ⁓**t** puissant; fort; ⁓**tial** potentiel (*adj.*, *su./m*).

pot...: ⁓**herb** herbe *f* potagère; ⁓**hole** *mot.* nid-de-poule (*pl.* nids-de-poule) *m*; caverne *f.*

potion potion *f.*

potluck: take ⁓ manger à la fortune du pot; *fig.* tenter sa chance.

potshot F coup *m* (de fusil *etc.*) tiré au hasard; **take a ⁓ at** tirer sur (*q.*, *qch.*) au hasard.

potter¹ (*usu.* ⁓ **about**, ⁓ **around**) bricoler; (*usu.* ⁓ **along**) aller doucement.

potter² potier *m*; ⁓**y** poterie *f.*

pouch *anat.* poche *f*; *tobacco*: blague *f.*

poultice ⚕ cataplasme *m.*

poultry volaille *f.*

pounce 1. ⁓ **on** sauter *or* fondre *or* se précipiter sur; **2.** bond *m*; attaque *f.*

pound 1. *weight*: livre *f*; ⁓ (**sterling**) livre *f* (sterling); fourrière *f*; **2.** broyer; battre (*a. v/i.*).

pour *v/t.* verser; ⁓ **out** verser, servir (*a drink*); répandre (*a smell etc.*); *fig.* épancher; ⁓ **away** vider, jeter; *v/i.* couler, ruisseler; tomber à verse (*rain*); *fig.* ⁓ **in** (**out**) entrer (sortir) en foule (*people etc.*).

pout 1. moue *f*; **2.** faire la moue.

poverty pauvreté *f*; ⁓**-stricken** pauvre; indigent; misérable.

powder 1. poudre *f*; **2.** pulvériser; poudrer (*one's face*); saupoudrer (de, **with**); ⁓**ed** *a.* en poudre (*milk etc.*); ⁓ **keg** *fig.* poudrière *f*; ⁓ **room** toilettes *f/pl.* (pour dames).

power 1. pouvoir *m* (*a.* ⚖, *pol. executive etc.*); puissance *f* (*a.* ⊕, ⚛, *pol. country*, *influence*); force *f*; ⚡ courant *m*; **be in ⁓** être au pouvoir; *Western* ⁓**s** *pl.* pol. puissances *f/pl.* occidentales; ⁓ **struggle** lutte *f* pour le pouvoir; **2.** ⚡ de courant; ⚡ à haute tension; ⊕ à moteur; ⊕ servo...; **~ cut** coupure *f* de courant; **~ point** prise *f* de courant; **~ plant, ~ station** centrale *f* électrique; **~ steering** servodirection *f*; **~ed:** ⊕ **~ by ...** qui marche à ...; actionné par ...; **~ful** puissant, fort; **~less** impuissant; inefficace.

powpow F conférence *f*.

practica|ble praticable; faisable; **~l** pratique; **~lly** pratiquement.

practice 1. pratique *f*; *profession:* exercice *m*; entraînement *m*; *doctor, lawyer:* clientèle *f*; *put into* **~** mettre en pratique *or* en action; **2.** *Am. see* **practise**.

practioo *v/t.* pratiquer; exercer (*a profession*); s'exercer à, s'entraîner à; *v/i.* s'exercer, s'entraîner; **~d** expérimenté; versé; expert.

practitioner praticien *m*; *general* **~** médecin *m* ordinaire.

prairie prairie *f*; savane *f*.

praise 1. éloge(s) *m*/(*pl.*), louange(s) *f*/(*pl.*); **2.** louer, faire l'éloge de; F vanter; **~worthy** digne d'éloges; louable.

pram voiture *f* d'enfant; landau *m*.

prance caracoler (*horse etc.*); *fig.* **~** se pavaner, aller en se pavanant.

prank farce *f*, tour *m*.

pray prier (q., *to s.o.*); **~er** prière *f*; *Lord's* ♀ oraison *f* dominicale; pater *m*; **~ book** livre *m* de prières.

pre... pré-; avant; antérieur à.

preach prêcher; Γ **~ at** sermonner (q.); **~er** prédicateur *m*.

preamble préambule *m*.

precarious précaire; incertain.

precaution précaution *f*; **~ary** de précaution; d'avertissement.

precede (faire) précéder; **~nce, ~ncy** priorité *f*; préséance *f*; **~nt** précédent *m* (*a.* ⚖).

precept précepte *m*; règle *f*.

precinct enceinte *f*; zone *f*.

precious 1. *adj.* précieux; F *a. iro.* fameux; **2.** F *adv.* très, bien.

precipi|ce précipice *m*; **~tate 1.** *v/t.* précipiter (*a.* 🜊); hâter; **2.** précipité; irréfléchi; **~tation** précipitation *f*; **~tous** à pic; escarpé; abrupt.

précis résumé *m*, abrégé *m*.

precis|e précis; méticuleux; **~ion** précision *f*.

preclude exclure; empêcher (de *inf.*, *from ger.*).

precocious précoce.

preconceived préconçu (*idea*).

preconception préconception *f*.

precondition condition *f* requise *or* nécessaire.

precursor précurseur *m*.

predator prédateur *m*; **~y** rapace; *zo.* de proie.

predecessor prédécesseur *m*.

predestin|ation prédestination *f*; **~ed** prédestiné.

predetermine déterminer d'avance.

predicament situation *f* difficile.

predicate *phls.* prédicat *m*.

predict prédire; **~ion** prédiction *f*.

predilection prédilection *f*.

predispos|e prédisposer (à, *to*); **~ition** prédisposition *f* (à, *to*).

predomina|nce prédominance *f*; **~nt** prédominant; **~ntly** surtout; en majeure partie; **~te** prédominer.

pre-eminent prééminent.

pre-empti|on (droit *m* de) préemption *f*; **~ve** ✝ de préemption; *fig.* préventif.

preen lisser; **~ o.s.** se lisser les plumes (*bird*); s'arranger (*person*), se pomponner.

prefab F maison(ette) *f* préfabriquée; **~ricate** préfabriquer.

preface préface *f*.

prefect préfet *m*; *school:* élève *mf* surveillant(e *f*).

prefer préférer (à, *to*; faire, *doing*); **~able** préférable; **~ably** de préférence; préférablement; **~ence** préférence *f*; **~ential** préférentiel; de préférence; **~ment** avancement *m*.

prefix préfixe *m*.

pregnan|cy grossesse *f*; **~t** enceinte (*woman*); *fig.* **~ with** gros de.

prejudice 1. préjugé *m*; préjudice *m*, dommage *m*; **2.** prévenir, prédisposer; porter préjudice à; **~d** plein de préjugés; préconçu (*view etc.*).

prejudicial préjudiciable, nuisible.

prelate prélat *m*.

preliminary préliminaire (*adj., su./m*).

prelude 1. prélude *m* (*a.* ♪); **2.** *v/i.* ♪ préluder; *v/t. fig.* préluder à

premarital prématrimonial, avant le mariage.

premature prématuré.

premeditat|ed prémédité; **~ion** préméditation *f*.

premier 1. premier, primordial; **2.** *pol.* premier ministre *m*.

première 1. première *f*; **2.** donner la première de.

premise prémisse *f*; **~s** *pl.* locaux *m/pl.*; **on** (**off**) **the ~s** sur les (hors des) lieux.

premium prime *f*; *put a ~ on* faire cas de.

premonition prémonition *f*.

preoccup|ation préoccupation *f*; **~y** préoccuper.

prep F *see* **preparation**; **preparatory school.**

prepaid payé d'avance.

prepar|ation préparation *f*; **~s** *pl.* préparatifs *m/pl.*; **~ory** préparatoire; **~ school** école *f* préparatoire.

prepare *v/t.* préparer; *v/i.* se préparer (à, *for*; à *inf.*, *to inf.*); **~d** préparé; prêt (à, *for*; pour *inf.*, *for ger.*).

prepay payer d'avance.

preponderan|ce prépondérance *f*; **~nt** prépondérant; **~te** l'emporter (sur, *over*).

preposition *gramm.* préposition *f*.

prepossess prévenir (favorablement); **~ing** avenant.

preposterous absurde.

prerequisite condition *f* préalable.

prerogative prérogative *f*.

presage 1. présage *m*; **2.** présager.

preschool préscolaire.

prescribe prescrire.

prescription prescription *f*; **⚕** ordonnance *f*; **~ charge** somme *f* fixe à payer pour l'exécution d'une ordonnance.

presence présence *f*; **~ of mind** présence *f* d'esprit.

present¹ 1. présent; actuel (*year etc.*); **2.** présent *m*; *at ~* à présent, actuellement, en ce moment; *for the ~* pour le moment.

present² présenter; remettre; **~ s.o. with s.th.** *give:* offrir qch. à q.; *fig.* mettre q. devant qch.; *be ~ed with s.th.* se trouver devant qch.

present³ cadeau *m*; *make s.o. a ~ of s.th.* faire cadeau de qch. à q.

presentable présentable.

presentation présentation *f*; remise *f*; introduction *f*; **~ copy** exemplaire *m* gratuit.

present-day actuel, d'aujourd'hui.

presentiment pressentiment *m*.

presently bientôt; tout à l'heure; F actuellement.

preservati|on conservation *f*; préservation *f*; **~ve** agent *m* de conservation.

preserve 1. préserver, garantir (de, *from*); maintenir; garder; conserver (*a. food*); **2.** *game:* réserve *f*; *cuis.* confiture *f*.

preside présider (qch., à qch. *over s.th.*).

presiden|cy présidence *f*; **~t** président(e *f*) *m*; **~tial** présidentiel.

press 1. ⊕, *newspaper:* presse *f*; *for wine, oil etc.:* pressoir *m*; *typ.* imprimerie *f*; **2.** *v/t.* presser; (*a. ~ down*) appuyer sur (*a button etc.*), faire pression sur (*a lid etc.*); *cost.* repasser, donner un coup de fer à (*a dress etc.*); *fig.* forcer, presser (q.), insister sur (qch.); *fig.* poursuivre, talonner, serrer (q.) de près; **~ s.th. on s.o.** presser q. d'accepter qch.; *be ~ed for time* être pressé, manquer de temps; *v/i.* presser (*a. fig. time*); *fig.* presser; *fig.* **~ for s.th.** réclamer qch. instamment; **3.** de presse; **~ agency** (*conference, cutting*) agence *f* (conférence *f*, coupure *f*) de presse; **~gang: ~ s.o. into doing s.th.** faire pression sur q. pour qu'il fasse qch., forcer q. à faire qch.; **~ing** 1. pressant; urgent, pressé; **2.** *dress etc.:* repassage *m*; **~man** F journaliste *m*; **~stud** pression *f*, bouton-pression *m* (*pl.* boutons-pression); **~up: do ~s** faire des tractions *or* des pompes; **~ure 1.** pression *f* (*a. fig.*); *fig. a.* tension *f*, contrainte *f*; **~ cabin** cabine *f* surpressurisée; **~ cooker** cocotte-minute *f*; **~ gauge** manomètre *m*; **~ group** groupe *m* de pression; *put ~ on = 2.* faire pression sur (*a. fig.*); **~urize** faire pression sur (q.), forcer (q.) à faire qch., *into doing s.th.*); ⊕ **~d** pressurisé.

prestig|e 1. prestige *m*; **2.** de prestige; **~ious** prestigieux.

presum|ably vraisemblablement; **~e** présumer; prendre des libertés; se permettre (de, *to*); **~ (up)on** abuser de; **~ing** impertinent.

presumpt|ion présomption *f*; **~uous** présomptueux.

presuppos|e présupposer; **~ition** présupposition *f*.

preten|ce, *Am.* **~se** (faux) semblant *m*;

prétexte *m*; prétention *f* (à, **to**); **make a
~ of** (*ger.*) faire semblant de (*inf.*).

pretend *v/t.* feindre, simuler; prétendre
(que, **that**; être, **to be**); **~ to do** faire
semblant de faire; *v/i.* faire semblant; **~
to s.th.** prétendre à qch.; **~ed** feint,
faux; soi-disant (*person*); prétendu.

pretense *Am. see* **pretence**.

pretension prétention *f* (à, **to**).

preterit(e) *gramm.* prétérit *m*.

pretext prétexte *m*.

pretty 1. *adj.* joli; **2.** *adv.* assez.

prevail prédominer, avoir cours, régner;
prévaloir (sur, **over**); contre, **against**);
l'emporter (sur **over**, **against**); **~
(up)on s.o. to** (*inf.*) décider *or* persuader q. à (*inf.*); **~ing** courant; en vogue;
dominant.

prevalent (pré)dominant; répandu.

prevaricate équivoquer, **~ion** faux-
fuyants *m/pl.*

prevent empêcher (de, **from**); empêcher
de se produire; prévenir (*an accident,
illness, abuse etc.*); **~ion** prevention *f*;
~ive préventif; **~ custody** détention *f*
préventive.

preview *thea., cin.* avant-première *f*; *fig.*
aperçu *m*.

previous antérieur; précédent; préalable; F trop pressé; **~ to** *a.* avant; **~ly** *a.*
auparavant.

pre-war d'avant-guerre.

prey 1. proie *f*; **beast** (**bird**) **of ~** bête *f*
(oiseau *m*) de proie; **2.: ~ (up)on** faire
sa proie de (*animal*); *fig.* ronger.

price 1. prix *m*; *Stock Exchange*: cours
m; **2.** fixer le prix de; évaluer; demander le prix de; **~ down** réduire le prix de;
3. (des) prix; **~ bracket**, **~ range** éventail *m* or gamme *f* des) prix *m/pl.*;
within my ~ range dans mes prix; **~ list**
prix *m* courants; **~ ticket** étiquette
f (de prix); **~less** inestimable.

pric(e)y F coûteux, F cherot.

prick 1. piqûre *f*; **2.** piquer; **~ up one's
ears** dresser l'oreille; **~le** ♀ épine *f*,
piquant *m*; picotement *m*; **2.** picoter;
~ly épineux.

pride 1. orgueil *m*; fierté *f*; **take ~ in** être
fier de; **2.: ~ o.s. (up)on** se piquer de.

priest prêtre *m*.

prig poseur (-euse *f*) *m*.

prim guindé, collet monté.

prima|cy primauté *f*; **~rily** principale-

ment; **~ry** primaire; premier, primordial; *colour:* fondamental.

prime 1. premier, de premier ordre;
principal; **♰ ~ cost** prix *m* coûtant; **2
Minister** président *m* du Conseil; premier ministre *m*; **~ number** nombre *m*
premier; *radio, telev.:* **~ time** heures *f*
(*pl.*) d'écoute maximum; **2.** (*a. ~ of life*)
fleur *f* de l'âge; **3.** *v/t.* amorcer (*a
pump*); *paint.* apprêter; *fig.* renseigner,
mettre (*q.*) au courant.

primer premier cours *m* or livre *m* de
lecture; *colour:* apprêt *m*

primeval primitif, primordial.

primitive primitif.

primrose ♀ primevère *f*.

prince prince *m*; **~ss** princesse *f*.

principal 1. principal; **2.** principal(e *f*)
m; (di)recteur *m*; **~ity** principauté *f*.

principle principe *m* (*a.* ♘); **in ~** en
principe; **on ~** par principe.

print 1. *mark:* empreinte *f*; *typ.* caractères *m/pl.*; *typ.* matière *f* imprimée;
phot. épreuve *f*; *art:* gravure *f*, estampe
f; *tex.* imprimé *m*; **out of ~** épuisé; *v/t.*
imprimer; *in newspaper etc.* publier;
écrire (*a word*) en majuscules; *phot.* tirer une épreuve de; **~ed matter** imprimés *m/pl.*; **~er** imprimeur *m*; **~ing** impression *f*; *art:* imprimerie *f*; **~ press**
presse *f* typographique; **~-out** listage
m.

prior 1. *adj.* préalable; précédent;
antérieur (à, **to**); **2.** *adv.:* **~ to** antérieu-
rement à; **3.** *su. eccl.* prieur *m*; **~ity**
priorité *f* (sur, **over**); **give s.th. first** (*or*
top) **~** donner la priorité absolue à qch.;
get one's priorities right décider de ce
qui est le plus important pour q.

prism prisme *m*.

prison prison *f*; **~er** prisonnier (-ère *f*)
m; détenu(e *f*) *m*; **take s.o. ~** faire q.
prisonnier.

privacy intimité *f*; secret *m*.

private 1. privé; particulier; personnel;
~ company société *f* en nom collectif; **~
lessons** *pl.* leçons *f/pl.* particulières; **2.**
✗ (*or* **~ soldier**) simple soldat *m*; **in ~
—** **~ly** en privé.

privation privation *f*.

privilege privilège *m*; prérogative *f*;
~d privilégié.

privy: ~ to instruit de; **2 Council** Conseil
m privé.

P

prize 1. prix *m*; *lottery:* lot *m*; ⚓ prise *f*;
2. primé (*bull etc.*); F de premier ordre;
3. estimer, faire (grand) cas de; → *a.*
pry²; **~winner** gagnant|(e *f*) *m*; **~winning** gagnant; primé.

pro F pro *m/f* (= *professional*).

probab|ility probabilité *f*; **~le** probable.

probation *job:* essai *m*; ⚖ liberté *f* surveillée; **on ~** à l'essai; ⚖ en liberté surveillée; **~ary** d'essai.

probe ⚕ **1.** sonde *f*, poinçon *m*; *esp. Am.
parl., pol.* enquête *f*; **2.** (*a.* **~ into**) sonder.

probity probité *f*.

problem problème *m*; **~ child** enfant *mf*
difficile *or* caractériel; **no ~!** de rien!; ça
fait rien!; **~atic(al)** problématique.

procedure procédure *f*, procédé *m*.

proceed procéder; avancer; aller; continuer (qch., *with s.th.*); se mettre (à *inf.,
to *inf.*); **~ from** (pro)venir de; **~ing** procédé *m*; façon d'agir; **~s** *pl.* ⚖ procès
m; ⚖ **take ~s against** intenter un procès à; **~s** *pl.* produit *m*, recette *f*.

process 1. processus *m* (*a. anat.*); procédé *m*, méthode *f*; ⚖ procès *m*; **in the
~** (*ger.*) en train de (*inf.*); **in ~ of
construction** en cours de construction;
2. ⊕ traiter; **~ed cheese** fromage *m*
fondu; **~ing** ⊕ traitement *m*.

procession cortège *m*; défilé *m*; procession *f*.

proclaim proclamer; déclarer.

proclamation proclamation *f*.

proclivity penchant *m*, tendance *f*.

procrastinat|e remettre les affaires à
plus tard; **~ion** procrastination *f*.

procreate engendrer.

procure *v/t.* se procurer, obtenir; procurer (qch. à q. *s.o. s.th., s.th. for s.o.*);
v/i. faire le métier de proxénète.

prod 1. coup *m* (leger), poussée *f*; **2.**
pousser; donner un (petit) coup à.

prodigal prodigue (*a. su.*).

prodig|ious prodigieux; **~y** prodige *m*;
~ child ~ enfant *m* prodige.

produce 1. produits *m/pl.*; **2.** produire
(*a. cin.*); causer; présenter, montrer;
thea. mettre en scène; **~r** producteur
(-trice *f*) *m* (*a. cin.*); *thea.* metteur *m* en
scène; *cin.* directeur *m* de productions.

product produit *m*; **~ion** production *f* (*a.
of a film*); *thea.* mise *f* en scène; **~ive**
productif; **~ivity** productivité *f*.

prof F prof(esseur) *m*.

profan|ation profanation *f*; **~e 1.** profane; impie, blasphématoire; non initié;
2. profaner.

profess professer; **~ed** déclaré; soi-disant, pretendu; **~ion** profession *f*; **~ional 1.** professionnel; de *or* d'un professionnel (*work etc.*); **2.** professionnel(le
f) *m*; **~or** professeur *m*.

proffer 1. offrir; **2.** offre *f*.

proficien|cy compétence *f*, capacité *f*
(en, **in**); **~t** compétent.

profile 1. profil *m*; *fig.* **keep a low ~**
rester dans l'ombre; **2.** profiler.

profit 1. profit *m*; ✝ *a.* bénéfice *m*; ✝ **~
margin** marge *f* bénéficiaire; **2. ~ by** (*or
from*) tirer profit de; **~able** ✝ rentable,
lucratif; *fig.* profitable; **~eer 1.** faire
des bénéfices excessifs; **2.** profiteur
(-euse *f*) *m*; **~sharing** participation *f*
aux bénéfices.

profligate débauché; prodigue.

profound profond (*a. fig.*).

profundity profondeur *f* (*a. fig.*).

profus|e prodigue (de **in, of**); profus;
~ion profusion *f*.

progen|itor ancêtre *m*; **~y** progéniture *f*.

prognosis ⚕, *pl.* **-ses** pronostic *m*.

program|(me) 1. programme *m* (*a. data
processing*); *radio, telev.:* emission *f*; **2.**
programmer; **~mer** *radio:* programmateur (-trice *f*) *m*; *data processing:*
programmeur (-euse *f*) *m* (*person*), programmateur *m* (*machine*), programming *radio, data processing:* programmation
f.

progress 1. progrès *m*; **in ~** en cours;
make ~ faire des progrès; avancer;
~ion progression *f*; **~ive** progressif.

prohibit défendre, interdire (qch., *s.th.*;
à q. de *inf., s.o. from ger.*); empêcher
(q. de *inf., s.o. from ger.*); **~ion** prohibition *f*, défense *f*; *Am.* la prohibition *f*;
~ive prohibitif.

project 1. projet *m*; **2.** *v/t.* projeter; *v/i.*
faire saillie; **~ile** projectile *m*; **~ion** projection *f*; saillie *f*; **~or** projecteur *m*.

proletaria|n prolétaire (*a. su.*); prolétarien; **~t** prolétariat *m*.

prolif|erate proliférer; **~eration** prolifération *f*; prolifique.

prolix prolixe, diffus.

prolog(ue) prologue *m*.

prolong prolonger; ✝ proroger.

promenade 1. promenade *f*; esplanade *f*; **2.** (se) promener.

prominen|ce proéminence *f*; *fig.* importance *f*; **~t** proéminent, saillant; *fig.* important.

promiscu|ity promiscuité (sexuelle) *f*; **~ous** confus; de mœurs légers.

promis|e 1. promesse *f*; **2.** promettre; **~ing** prometteur.

promontory *geog.* promontoire *m*.

promot|e promouvoir; organiser, mettre (*qch.*) sur pied; ✝ lancer *or* promouvoir (*an article*); *esp. Am. school:* faire passer; **~ion** promotion *f*; avancement *m*; ✝ lancement *m* (*of an article*): ✝ (*u. sales* ~) promotion *f* de la vente; **~ prospects** *pl.* possibilités *f/pl.* d'avancement.

prompt 1. prompt; rapide; **~ly** *a.* ponctuellement; **2.** inciter, pousser (à, *to*); suggérer (*qch.* à *q.*, *s.o. to s.th.*); donner (*an idea*); *thea.* souffler, souffler ses répliques à (*q.*); **3.** ponctuellement; **4.** *thea.* réplique *f*; *a.* = **~er** *thea.* souffleur (-euse *f*) *m*; **~ness** promptitude *f*; rapidité *f*; ponctualité *f*.

promulgate promulguer.

prone couché sur le ventre; **~ to** enclin à, sujet à.

prong *fork:* dent *f*; pointe *f*.

pronoun *gramm.* pronom *m*.

pronounce *v/t.* prononcer; *v/i.* se prononcer (sur, *on*; pour, *in favour of*); **~d** prononcé; marqué.

pronto F tout de suite.

pronunciation prononciation *f*.

proof 1. preuve *f*; *test, typ., phot.* épreuve *f*; *alcohol:* degré *m*; *put to the* **~** mettre à l'épreuve; *in* **~** *of* pour *or* en preuve de; **2.** **~ against**, **...~** à l'épreuve de, résistant à; **3.** *tex. etc.* imperméabiliser (*a fabric*).

prop 1. support *m*, étai *m*; appui *m*; *thea. sl.* accessoire *m*; **2.** (*or* **~ up**) appuyer; étayer, soutenir.

propaganda propagande *f*.

propaga|te (se) propager; **~tion** propagation *f*.

propel propulser; **~ler** hélice *f*.

propensity propension *f*.

proper adéquat, bon, vrai; comme il faut, approprié; convenable (*behavior etc.*); vrai, véritable; **~ name** nom *m* propre; **~ly** comme il faut; **~ty** pro-

priété *f*; biens *m/pl.*; immeuble(s) *m| (pl.)*; *fig.* qualité *f*; *thea.* accessoire *m*.

prophe|cy prophétie *f*; **~sy** *vt/i.* prophétiser; *v/t. a.* prédire.

prophet prophète *m*; **~ic** prophétique.

propi|tiate apaiser; rendre favorable; **~tious** propice, favorable.

proponent partisan(e *f*) *m*, défenseur (-euse *f*) *m*.

proportion 1. proportion *f*; partie *f*, part *f*; **2.** proportionner; **~al** proportionnel; en proportion (de, *to*); **~ate** proportionnel.

propos|al proposition *f*, offre *f*; demande *f* en mariage; projet *m*; **~e** *v/t.* proposer; suggérer; **~ to do** (*s.th.*) compter faire (*qch.*); *v/i.* faire la demande en mariage; **~ition** proposition *f*.

propound soumettre.

proprlet|ary de propriété; ✝ de marque déposée; **~or** propriétaire *m|f*; **~y** bienséance(s) *f|pl.*

propulsion ⊕ propulsion *f*.

prorata au prorata.

pros *see* **con¹**.

prosaic *fig.* prosaïque, banal.

proscri|be proscrire.

prose 1. prose *f*; **2.** en prose.

prosecut|e poursuivre (*a.* ⚖); **~ion** ⚖ poursuites *f|pl.* (judiciaires); *witness for the* **~** témoin *m* à charge; **~or** ⚖ procureur *m*; *public* **~** ministère *m* public.

prospect 1. perspective *f* (*a. fig.*); *fig. a.* espoir *m*, chance *f*; ✝ client *m* possible; **~s** *pl. a.* possibilités *f|pl.*; **2.** ⚒ prospecter; **~ for** chercher; **~ive** futur; éventuel (*buyer etc.*); **~us** prospectus *m*.

prosper prospérer; **~ity** prospérité *f*; **~ous** prospère.

prostitut|e 1. prostituée *f*; **2.** prostituer; **~ion** prostitution *f*.

prostrat|e 1. prosterné; *fig.* prostré; **2.** abattre; **~ o.s.** se prosterner (*devant, before*); **~ion** prosternation *f*; prostration *f*.

prosy ennuyeux, verbeux.

protagonist protagoniste *m*.

protect protéger (*contre, from*); **~ion** protection *f*; **~ive** protecteur; **~ custody** détention *f* préventive; **~ duty** droit *m* protecteur; **~or** protecteur (-trice *f*) *m*; **~orate** protectorat *m*.

protest 1. protestation *f*; *in* **~ against**

pour protester contre; *under* ~ en protestant; **2.** *v/i.* protester (contre, *against*); *v/t.* protester de (*one's innocence etc.*); *Am.* protester contre.

Protestant protestant (*a. su.*).

protestation protestation *f.*

protocol protocole *m.*

prototype prototype *m.*

protract prolonger.

protru|de dépasser; avancer; faire saillie; ~**sion** saillie *f.*

protuberance protubérance *f.*

proud fier (de *of, to*); orgueilleux.

prove *v/t.* prouver; *v/i.* se révéler, s'avérer, se montrer; ~ *true* (*false*) se révéler *etc.* vrai (faux).

provenance origine *f,* provenance *f.*

provender fourrage *m,* provende *f; F, a. co.* nourriture *f.*

proverb proverbe *m;* ~**ial** proverbial.

provide *v/t.* pourvoir, munir (de, *with*); fournir (qch. à q., *s.o. with s.th.*); ⅛⅛ stipuler (que, *that*); *v/i.:* ~ *for* pourvoir aux besoins de; ~ *against* se prémunir contre; ~*d that* pourvu que (*sbj.*); à condition que (*sbj.*).

providen|ce providence *f* (divine); ~*t* prévoyant; ~*tial* heureux.

provider pourvoyeur (-euse *f*) *m.*

providing (*that*) à condition que (*sbj.*).

provinc|e province *f;* ~*ial* provincial (*a. su.*).

provision 1. fourniture *f;* ✝ provision *f;* ⅛⅛ disposition *f; make* ~ *for* prendre des dispositions pour; **2.** approvisionner; ~*al* provisoire.

proviso condition *f.*

provocat|ion provocation *f;* ~*ive* provocateur; provocant.

provoke provoquer; inciter (à, *to*).

prow ⚓ proue *f.*

prowess prouesse *f;* exploit *m.*

prowl 1. *v/i.* (*a.* ~ *about,* ~ *around*) rôder; *v/t.* rôder dans (*the streets etc.*). **2.** *be on the* ~ rôder; *fig. on the* ~ *for* à la recherche de, en quête de; ~ *car police:* voiture *f* de patrouille; ~*er* rôdeur (-euse *f*) *m.*

proximity proximité *f.*

proxy (*by* ~ par) procuration *f.*

prude prude *f.*

pruden|ce prudence *f;* ~*t* prudent.

prud|ery pruderie *f,* pudibonderie *f;* ~*ish* prude, pudibond.

prune¹ pruneau *m.*

prune² (*a.* ~ *away, off*) élaguer.

pry¹ fureter; fouiller; ~ *into* fourrer le nez dans.

pry²: ~ *open* forcer (avec un levier).

psalm psaume *m.*

pseudo... pseud(o)-; faux; ~*nym* pseudonyme *m.*

psyche psyché, psychè *f;* psychisme *m.*

psychiatr|ic psychiatrique; ~*ist* psychiatre *m;* ~*y* psychiatrie *f.*

psychic psychique; métapsychique.

psychoanaly|sis (*pl. -es*) psychanalyse *f;* ~*st* psychanalyste *mf;* ~*ze* psychanalyzer.

psycholog|ical psychologique; ~*ist* psychologue *m;* ~*y* psychologie *f.*

psychopath psychopathe *mf.*

psychosis psychose *f.*

pub bistrot *m.*

puberty puberté *f.*

public 1. public; ~ *address system* sonorisation *f,* haut-parleurs *m/pl.;* ~ *company* société *f* anonyme; ~ *convenience* toilettes *f/pl.;* ~ *holiday* jour *m* férié; ~ *library* bibliothèque *f* municipale; ~ *relations pl.* relations *f/pl.* publiques; ~ *school* école *f* privée; ~ *spirit* civisme *m;* **2.** public; *the general* ~ le grand public; *in* ~ en publique; ~*an* patron(ne *f*) *m* d'un bistrot; ~*ation* publication *f;* ~*ist* publiciste *m;* ~*ity* publicité *f;* ~*ly* publiquement.

publish publier; ~*er* éditeur *m;* ~*ing* publication *f; trade:* édition *f.*

pucker (*a.* ~ *up*) (se) plisser.

pudding pudding *m,* pouding *m;* dessert *m; black* ~ boudin *m.*

puddle flaque *f* (d'eau).

pudent pudique.

puerile puéril, *pej. a.* enfantin.

puff 1. *smoke:* bouffée *f;* houppe(tte) *f* (*for powder*); *cake:* feuilleté *m;* réclame *f* tapageuse; F souffle *m,* haleine *f; cuis.* ~ *pastry* pâte *f* feuilletée; **2.** *v/t.* lancer, émettre (*puffs of smoke*); (*a.* ~ *out, up*) gonfler; (*a.* ~ *at*) tirer sur (*one's pipe etc.*); (*a.* ~ *up*) vanter; ~ *up* augmenter (*prices*); *v/i.* souffler; lancer des bouffées (*of smoke*); sortir en bouffées; ~*ed* essoufflé; à l'haleine courte; ~*y* bouffi, gonflé; boursouflé; bouffant (*sleeve*).

pug (*or* ~ *dog*) carlin *m;* petit dogue *m;* ~ *nose* nez *m* camus.

pugnacious batailleur; querelleur.

puke *sl.* vomir, *sl.* dégobiller.

pull 1. traction *f*; *phys.*, *fig.* attraction *f*; *give* (*s.th.*) *a* ~ tirer (sur qch.); **2.** *v/t.* tirer; arracher (*weeds, a tooth etc.*); ✥ ramer; ~ *the trigger* presser la détente; ~ *down* faire descendre; démolir; ~ *in* tirer (en) dedans; rentrer; ~ *off* arracher; ôter; F réussir; ~ *out* arracher; sortir; retirer; ~ *through* tirer d'affaire; ~ *up* (re)monter; arrêter; *v/i.* tirer; ~ *in* entrer, arriver; ~ *out* sortir; se retirer (de, *of*); ~ *through* s'en sortir; ~ *up* s'arrêter.

pulley ⊕ poulie *f*.

pull...: ~*-in* parking *m* (avec restaurant); ~*-out* **1.** supplément *m* détachable; **2.** détachable; rétractable; ~*over* pull-over *m*, F pull *m*; ~*-up* arrêt *m*; restaurant *m* (de routiers).

pulp 1. pulpe *f*; **2.** à sensation (*magazine etc.*); **3.** réduire en pulpe.

pulpit chaire *f*.

puls|ate palpiter; vibrer; battre (*heart*); ~*ation* pulsation *f*; battement *m*; ~*e* **1.** pouls *m*; battement *m*; **2.** palpiter; vibrer; battre.

pulverize pulvériser.

pumice (pierre *f*) ponce *f*.

pump 1. pompe *f*; **2.** *v/t.* pomper; F faire parler; ~ *up* gonfler.

pumpkin ♀ citrouille *f*; potiron *m*.

pun jeu *m* de mots.

Punch[1] polichinelle *m*; guignol *m*; *as pleased as* ~ heureux comme un roi.

punch[2] F **1.** coup *m* de poing; F force *f*, punch *m*; *drink:* punch *m*; ⊕ poinçon *m*; ~ *line* pointe *f* (d'une plaisanterie); **2.** donner un coup de poing à; ⊕ poinçonner, perforer; ~ *a hole* faire un trou; ~*ed card* = ~*card* carte *f* perforée; ~*-drunk* abruti (par les coups); ~*-up* F bagarre *f*.

punctilious méticuleux.

punctual ponctuel; ~*ity* ponctualité *f*.

punctuat|e ponctuer; ~*ion* ponctuation *f*.

puncture 1. crevaison *f*; **2.** crever.

pungen|cy goût *m* piquant; âcreté *f*; *fig.* mordant *m*; ~*t* piquant (*taste etc.*) âcre; *fig.* mordant.

punish punir; ~*able* punissable; ~*ment* punition *f*; châtiment *m*.

puny chétif; malingre.

pupil[1] élève *mf*.

pupil[2] *anat.* pupille *f*.

puppet marionnette *f*, pantin *m*.

puppy chiot *m*.

purchase 1. achat *m*; **2.** acheter; ~*r* acheteur (-euse *f*) *m*.

pure pur; ~*bred* de race pure.

purgatory purgatoire *m*.

purge 1. purge *f*; **2.** purger.

purify purifier; épurer.

Puritan puritain(e *f*) (*a. su.*).

purity pureté *f*.

purl 1. (*a.* ~ *stitch*) maille *f* à l'envers; **2.** tricoter à l'envers.

purlieus *pl.* alentours *m/pl.*

purloin dérober.

purple pourpre; cramoisi.

purport 1. signification *f*, teneur *mf*; **2.** ~ *to be* (se) prétendre.

purpose but *m*, intention *f*, fin *f*; *for the* ~ *of* pour; dans le but de; *on* ~ exprès; *to no* ~ en vain; ~*-built* construit spécialement; fonctionnalisé; ~*ful* résolu; ~*less* inutile; irrésolu; sans but; ~*ly* *adv.* à dessein, exprès.

purr ronronner.

purse 1. bourse *f*, portemonnaie *m/inv.*; **2.** pincer, serrer.

pursu|ance: *in* (*the*) ~ *of* dans l'exécution de; ~*e* poursuivre; *fig.* rechercher (*pleasure*); ~*er* poursuivant(e *f*) *m*; ~*it* poursuite *f*; recherche *f* (de, *of*); occupation *f*; *usu.* ~*its* *pl.* travaux *m/pl.*

purvey fournir; ~*or* fournisseur *m*.

pus ⚕ pus *m*; sanie *f*.

push 1. poussée *f*, impulsion *f*; coup *m*; effort *m*; F énergie *f*, allant *m*; **2.** *v/t.* pousser; bousculer; appuyer sur (*a button*); enfoncer (dans, *in*[*to*]); (*a.* ~ *through*) faire passer (à travers, *through*); (*a.* ~ *ahead* *or* *forward* *or* on) (faire) avancer, pousser (en avant); ~ *aside* écarter; ~ *over* renverser; ~ *s.th.* (*up*)*on* *s.o.* imposer qch. à q.; ~ *one's way* se frayer un chemin (à travers, *through*); ~ *up* faire monter (*prices etc.*); *v/i.* avancer; pousser; F ~ *off* filer; ~ *on* se presser, se hâter; se remettre en route; ~*-button* **1.** pressoir *m*, bouton *m*; **2.** presse-bouton; ~*cart* charrette *f* à bras; ~*chair* poussette *f*; ~*over* F chose *f* facile à faire, *la* facilité même; *be a* ~ *for* ne pas pouvoir résister à; ~*-up:* *do* ~*s* faire des tractions *or* des pompes; ~*y* dynamique; *pej.* qui se met trop en avant, arriviste.

pusillanimous pusillanime.

puss(y), pussy-cat minet(te *f*) *m*, minou *m*.

put 1. *v/t.* mettre, poser; placer; exprimer, dire; ~ *about* faire circuler (*a rumour*); ~ *across* boucler (*an affair*); ~ *back* remettre; retarder (*a watch etc.*); ~ *by* mettre de côté (*money*); ~ *down* (dé)poser; noter; supprimer; mettre fin à; attribuer (à, *to*); inscrire (q. pour, *s.o. for*); ~ *forth* émettre; publier (*a book etc.*); pousser (*leaves etc.*); ~ *forward* avancer (*a watch, an opinion etc.*); émettre; ~ *o.s. forward* se mettre en avant; ~ *in* introduire, insérer; placer (*a word*); présenter (*a document*); F passer (*one's time*); ~ *off* enlever, retirer, ôter (*one's hat, one's coat etc.*); remettre (à plus tard) (*an appointment*) ajourner; déconcerter (*q.*); décourager (*q.*) (de, *from*); ~ *on* mettre (*a garment etc.*); prendre (*weight, speed*); ✝ augmenter (*prices*); ajouter à; allumer (*the light etc.*); *mot.* serrer (*the brake*); **he is ~ting it on** il fait l'important; *fig.* ~ *it on thick* exagérer; ~ *on airs* se donner des airs; F ~ *s.o. on* faire q. marcher, rouler q.; ~ *out* mettre dehors; tendre (*one's hand*); étendre (*one's arms*); tirer (*one's tongue*); sortir (*one's head*); placer (*money*) (à intérêt, *to interest*); émettre (*a document etc.*); publier, éteindre (*the light, the gas etc.*); *fig.* déconcerter;

fig. gêner; ~ *s.o. out* expulser q. (de, *of*); ~ *through teleph.* mettre en communication (avec, *to*); ~ *to* attacher; accrocher (*an engine etc.*); ~ *up* monter, dresser; (re)lever; construire, ériger; organiser (*qch.*) sur pied; faire monter, hausser (*prices*); mettre (*for sale*); afficher, accrocher (*a notice*); loger (*guests*); ~ *s.o. up to* inciter q. à; **2.** *v/i.* ⚓ ~ *in* entrer dans; faire escale dans (*a port*); ⚓ ~ *off* (*or* out *or* to sea) démarrer, pousser au large; ~ *up at* loger à *or* chez; descendre à *or* chez; ~ *up for* poser sa candidature à; ~ *up with* s'arranger de; supporter, tolérer; se résigner à; ~*on* **1.** faux, affecté, feint; **2.** manières *f/pl.* affectées; mystification *f*, farce *f*.

putre|faction putréfaction *f*; ~**fy** (se) putréfier.

putrid putride; infect; *sl.* moche.

putter see **potter**[1].

putty 1. mastic *m*; **2.** mastiquer.

puzzl|e 1. énigme *f*; problème *m*; (*jig-saw* ~) puzzle *m*; **2.** rendre perplexe; ~ *out* découvrir, trouver; résoudre (*a problem*); *v/i.* (*oft.* ~ *one's brains*) se creuser la tête (pour comprendre qch., *over s.th.*); ~**ement** perplexité *f*; ~**ing** déconcertant.

pygmy pygmée *fm*.

pyjamas *pl.* pyjama *m*.

pylon pylône *m*.

pyramid pyramide *f*.

Pyrrhic victory victoire *f* à la Pyrrhus.

Q

quack[1] (faire) coin-coin *m*.

quack[2] charlatan *m*; ~**ery** charlatanisme *m*.

quadrangle ⅋ quadrilatère *m*; *school etc.*: cour *f*.

quadru|ped quadrupède *m*; ~**ple 1.** quadruple; **2.** (se) quadrupler; ~**plet** quadruplé(e *f*) *m*.

quagmire bourbier *m* (*a. fig.*).

quail[1] *orn.* caille *f*.

quail[2] trembler, fléchir, faiblir.

quaint bizarre; singulier; au charme vieillot, pittoresque.

quake 1. trembler; **2.** tremblement *m* (de terre).

quali|fication titre *m* (à un emploi, *for a post*); aptitude *f*; réserve *f*; ~**fied** qui a les qualités requises; diplômé; qualifié, compétent; restreint; ~**fy** *v/t.* qualifier (de, *as*); apporter des réserves à, nuancer (*a statement etc.*); *v/i.* se qualifier (pour, **for**); remplir les conditions requises (pour, **for**); ~ **as** obtenir son diplôme de; **~tative** qualitatif; **~ty 1.** qualité *f*; **2.** de qualité (*goods etc.*).

qualm scrupule *m*; hésitation *f*.

quandary embarras *m*; impasse *f*.

quantity quantité *f*.

quantum, *pl.* **-ta** quantum (*pl.* -ta) *m*; ~ **theory** théorie *f* des quanta.

quarantine quarantaine *f*.

quarrel 1. querelle *f*; dispute *f*; **2.** se quereller; se disputer; **~some** querelleur.

quarry 1. carrière *f*; *hunt.* proie *f*; *fig.* mine *f*; **2.** extraire (*stones*).

quart quart *m* (*of a gallon*).

quarter 1. quart *m*; *year;* trimestre *m*; *Am.* quart *m* de dollar (*25 cents*); *town:* quartier *m*; **~s** *pl.* logement *m*; ✕ quartiers *m/pl.*; **2.** couper *or* diviser en quatre; équarrir; *hist.* écarteler; ✕ cantonner; **~day** jour *m* du terme; **~deck** ♣ plage *f* arrière; **~ly 1.** trimestriel; **2.** tous les trois mois; **3.** publication *f* trimestrielle.

quartet(te) ♩ quatuor *m*.

quartz quartz *m*.

quash ⚖ annuler; *fig.* étouffer.

quasi quasi-, presque.

quaver 1. ♩ croche *f*; **2.** trembloter, (*a ~ out*) chevroter (*voice*).

quay quai *m*.

queasy: feel ~ avoir envie de vomir.

queen reine *f*; *cards etc.:* dame *f*; ~ **bee** reine *f*, abeille *f* mère.

queer bizarre, étrange; suspect, louche; ⚥ homosexuel; **feel ~** ne pas se sentir bien.

quell réprimer, étouffer.

quench éteindre; ~ **one's thirst** se désaltérer.

querulous plaintif; grognon.

query 1. question *f*, doute *f*; **2.** mettre en question, mettre en doute.

quest recherche *f*; **in ~ of** à la recherche de, en quête de.

question 1. question *f*, (*mise f en*) doute *m*; ~ **mark** point *m* d'interrogation; **beyond** (*all*) ~ sans aucun doute; **in ~** en question, en doute; **call in ~** mettre en doute; **the ~ is whether** il s'agit de savoir si; **that is out of the ~** c'est impossible; **2.** interroger; mettre en

doute; **~able** discutable; *pej.* douteux; **~ing 1.** interrogateur (*look etc.*); **2.** interrogatoire *m*; **~naire** questionnaire *m*.

queue 1. queue *f*, file *f*; **2.** (*usu.* ~ **up**) faire la queue.

quibble chicaner.

quick 1. rapide; prompt (*reply*); vif (*a. fig., mind*); **be ~** (*about it*)! fais vite!, dépêche-toi!; **2.** vif *m*, chair *f* vivante; *fig.* **cut s.o. to the ~** piquer *or* blesser *or* atteindre q. au vif; **~en** *v/t.* accélérer, presser; stimuler; *v/i.* s'accélérer, devenir plus rapide; **~frozen** surgelé; **~ie** F chose *f* faite à la va-vite; **~ly** vite, rapidement, **~ness** vitesse *f*, rapidité *f*; promptitude *f* (*of mind*).

quick...: ~sand sable *m* mouvant; fig.; **~set** (*a.* ~ **hedge**) haie *f* vive; **~silver** *min.* mercure *m*; **~tempered** irascible, F soupe au lait, **~witted** à l'esprit prompt; adroit.

quid F livre *f* (sterling).

quiet 1. tranquille, calme; silencieux; discret; **2.** tranquillité *f*; calme *m*; F **on the ~** en douce, en cachette; **3.** = **~en** (*oft.* ~ **down**) (sc) calmer, (s')apaiser; **~ness**, **~ude** tranquillité *f*, calme *m*.

quill penne *f*; plume *f* (d'oie); tuyau *m* de plume, *hedgehog:* piquant *m*.

quilt 1. édredon *m*; (*a.* **continental ~**) couverture *f* édredon; ouater (*a dress*).

quince ♦ coing *m*.

quinine *pharm.* quinine *f*.

quintessence quintessence *f*.

quintuple quintuple (*a. su./m*).

quip mot *m* piquant; sarcasme *m*.

quirk bizarrerie *f*; caprice *f*.

quisling *pol.* F collaborateur *m*.

quit 1. *v/t.* quitter; lâcher; cesser, arrêter (de faire, *doing*); *v/i.* déménager; démissionner; *fig.* abandonner la partie; **2.** libéré, débarrassé (de, *of*).

quite tout à fait, entièrement; parfaitement, très bien; assez, plutôt; ~ **a hero** un véritable *or* vrai héros; F ~ **a** pas mal de; ~ (**so** *or* **that**)! exactement!

quittance quittance *f*.

quitter F lâcheur (-euse *f*) *m*.

quiver[1] tremblement *f*; frémissement *m*; **2.** trembl(ot)er; tressaillir, frémir.

quiver[2] carquois *m*.

quiz 1. (série *f* de) questions *f/pl.*; (*a.* ~

show, ~ *program*[*me*]) jeu-concours *m*, quiz *m*; **2.** interroger; **~zical** interrogateur; narquois.

quoit (*a. game*: ~*s sg.*) palet *m*.

quorum *parl.* quorum *m*.

quota quote-part *f*, quota *m*.

quotation citation *f*; ✝ cours *m*; ~ **marks** *pl.* guillemets *m/pl.*

quote citer; *typ.* guillemeter; *Stock Exchange*: coter (à, **at**); ✝ indiquer, faire (*a price*).

quotient ⋏ quotient *m*.

R

rabbi rabbin *m*; *title*: rabbi *m*.

rabbit lapin *m*.

rabble populace *f*; **~-rousing** qui incite à la violence.

rab|id enragé; **~ies** *vet.* rage *f*.

ra(c)coon *zo.* raton *m* laveur.

race¹ race *f*; ~ *riot* bagarre *f* raciale.

race² **1.** course *f*; **2.** *v/i.* faire la course (contre, *against*); courir (à toute vitesse), filer; emballer (*engine etc.*); *v/t.* faire la course avec (*q.*); faire courir (*a horse*); emballer (*the engine etc.*); **~course** champ *m* de courses; piste *f*; ~ **horse** cheval *m* de course; **~r** coureur (-euse *f*) *m* (*a. mot.*); cheval *m* de course.

racial de (la) race.

racing courses *f/pl.*; *attr.* de course (*car, driver etc.*).

racis|m racisme *m*; **~t** raciste (*adj., su./mf*).

rack **1.** casier *m*; classeur *m*; râtelier; étagère *f*; *draining* ~, *plate* ~ égouttoir *m*; *luggage* ~ porte-bagages *m/inv.*; filet *m* (à bagages); *fig.* **on the** ~ au supplice; *in* ~ *and ruin* en ruine(s); *go to* ~ *and ruin* aller à vau-l'eau; **2.** *fig.* tourmenter; torturer; ~ *one's brains* se creuser la cervelle.

racket¹ *tennis etc.*; raquette *f*.

racket² vacarme *m*, tapage *m*; escroquerie *f*; *organized*: racket *m*.

racy plein de verve; savoureux (*story*).

radar radar *m*.

radial **1.** radial; **2.** (*a.* ~ *tyre*, ~ *tire*) pneu *m* à carcasse radiale.

radian|ce rayonnement *m*; **~t** rayonnant; *phys.* radiant.

radiat|e *v/i.* rayonner; émettre des rayons; *v/t.* émettre; répandre; **~ion** rayonnement *m*; *radium etc.*: radiation *f*; **~or** radiateur *m*.

radical radical.

radio **1.** radio *f*; ~ *set* poste *m* de radio; *on the* ~ à la radio; **2.** envoyer (*a message etc.*) par radio, appeler (*q.*) par radio; **~active** radioactif; **~activity** radioactivité *f*; **~graphy** radiographie *f*; **~logist** radiologue *mf*, radiologiste *mf*; **~therapy** radiothérapie *f*.

radish ♀ radis *m*.

radius, *pl.* -**dii** ⋏, *a. fig.* rayon *m*.

raffle tombola *f*, loterie *f*.

raft **1.** radeau *m*; **2.** transporter *etc.* sur un radeau; **~er** △ chevron *m*.

rag¹ chiffon *m*; lambeau *m*; *in* ~*s* en haillons (*person*); en lambeaux (*garment*); F *in one's glad* ~*s* en grand tralala.

rag² F chahuter; railler.

ragamuffin gamin *m* des rues.

rag...: **~and-bone man** chiffonnier *m*; **~bag** F ramassis *m*.

rage **1.** rage *f*, fureur *f* (*a. of the wind*), emportement *m*; manie *f*; F *be all the* ~ être le dernier cri, faire fureur. **2.** être furieux (*person*); faire rage (*wind*); *fig.* tempêter (contre, *against*); sévir (*epidemic*).

ragged déguenillé (*person*); ébréché; (*rock*); en lambeaux (*clothes*).

ragman chiffonnier *m*.

raid **1.** ✕ raid *m*; *police*: rafle *f*; *bandits*: razzia *f*; *see* **air-raid**; **2.** *v/i.* faire une rafle *etc.*; *v/t. a.* marauder.

rail¹ **1.** barre(au *m*) *f*; *bridge*: parapet *m*; (*a.* ~*s pl.*) palissade *f* (*of wood*), grille *f* (*of iron*); 🚆 rail *m*; (*by* ~) chemin *m* de fer; ✥ lisse f; **go off the ~s** dérailler (a. fig.); **2.** (a. **~ in** or **off**) entourer d'une grille.

rail² crier, se répandre en invectives (contre **at, against**).

railing(s pl.) grille f.

railroad esp. Am. chemin m de fer.

railway chemin m de fer; **~man** cheminot m; **~station** gare f.

rain 1. pluie f; **in the ~** sous la pluie; **2.** pleuvoir (a. fig.); v/t. fig. faire pleuvoir (qch.) (sur, on); **~bow** arc-en-ciel (pl. arcs-en-ciel) m; **~check** F: **take a ~ on s.th.** profiter de or se souvenir de qch. plus tard; **give s.o. a ~ on s.th.** offrir qch. à q. une autre fois; **~coat** imperméable m; **~fall** averse f; chute f de pluie; **~proof** imperméable; **~y** pluvieux; de pluie.

raise 1. lever; relever; soulever (a. fig. an objection etc.); hausser; augmenter; ériger (a building etc.); élever (children, cattle etc.), cultiver, faire pousser (plants); fig. causer, provoquer; fig. réunir, rassembler (funds etc.); fig. obtenir (a loan etc.); **2.** (a. **pay ~**) augmentation f (de salaire).

raisin raisin m sec.

rake 1. râteau m; roué m; **2.** ratisser; fig. fouiller (dans); hausser (a. balayer) F ~ **in** amasser (money etc.); F ~ **out** découvrir, dénicher; ~ **up** tisonner (a fire etc.); fig. remuer sur, fouiller dans, remuer (past events etc.); **~off** profit m (illicite), ristourne f.

rakish désinvolte; libertin.

rally 1. ralliement m; réunion f; mot. rallye m; **2.** (se) rallier, (se) rassembler; v/i. a. se remettre (person); reprendre; ~ **round** entourer; fig. venir en aide (à).

ram 1. bélier m; ⊕ piston m (plongeur); **2.** battre; heurter; mot. tamponner (a car); ✥ éperonner.

ramble 1. randonnée f; **2.** marcher or se promener (à l'aventure); faire une randonnée; fig. discourir; **~er** promeneur (-euse f)m, randonneur (-euse f)m, ✿ rosier m grimpant, **~ing** décousu (speech etc.); ✿ grimpant.

ramification ramification f; **~y** (se) ramifier.

ramp rampe f; mot. pont m (élévateur); road: dénivellation f.

rampage 1. be or **go on the ~ = 2.** se comporter comme des fous; se livrer à des actes de violence.

rampant: be ~ sévir.

rampart rempart m.

ramshackle délabré; déglingué (car etc.).

ranch ferme f d'élevage; ranch m.

rancid rance, ranci.

ranco(u)r rancune f, rancœur f.

random 1.: at ~ au hasard, au jugé; à l'aveuglette; **2.** fait au hasard; **~ sample** échantillon m prélevé au hasard.

range 1. rangée f; chaîne f (of mountains); ✠ assortiment m, a. fig. choix m, échelle f, gamme f; série f; portée f (of voice etc., a. of a gun); rayon m d'action; fig. champ m, sphère f; fig. étendue f, rayon m; Am. prairie f; (a. **shooting-~**) champ m de tir; (a. **kitchen ~**) fourneau m de cuisine; **2.** v/t. aligner, ranger; placer; disposer; parcourir (a region); v/i. s'étendre (de ... à, **from ... to**); **~r** Br. garde m forestier; Am. gendarme m à cheval.

rank¹ 1. rang m (social, ✗, a. fig.); ✗, ✥ grade m; **the ~s** pl., **the ~ and file** les hommes m/pl. de troupe f, fig. la masse, la base; **2.** v/t. ranger; compter, classer (avec, **with**; parmi, **among**); Am. a. être supérieur à; v/i. compter (parmi, **among**; pour, **as**), se classer.

rank² luxuriant, exubérant (plant); riche, gras (soil); rance; fétide.

rankle rester sur le cœur (de, **with**).

ransack fouiller (dans); saccager.

ransom 1. rançon f; **2.** racheter.

rant 1. rodomontades f/pl.; **2.** déclamer avec extravagance; (a. **~ and rave**) fulminer, tempêter.

rap¹ 1. petit coup m (sec); F bavardage m; **2.** frapper (à or sur); taper (sur); fig. critiquer (sévèrement); F bavarder.

rap²: I don't care a ~ je m'en fiche.

rapacious rapace; **~ty** rapacité f.

rape¹ 1. viol m; **2.** violer (a woman).

rape² ♀ colza m.

rapid 1. rapide; **2.** **~s** pl. rapides m/pl.; **~ity** rapidité f.

rapier violeur m.

rapt fig. ravi, extasié; absorbé (dans, **in**); **~ure** ravissement m; **in ~s** ravi, go into **~s** s'extasier.

rare rare; cuis. saignant (steak).

rarebit: Welsh ~ toast m au fromage fondu.

rarefy (se) raréfier; *fig.* affiner.

rarity rareté *f*.

rascal fripouille *f*; fripon(-ne *f*)*m*.

rash[1] irréfléchi, inconsidéré.

rash[2] 🐝 éruption *f*.

rasher tranche *f* de lard.

rasp 1. râpe *f*; grincement *m*; **2.** *v/t.* râper; racler; *v/i.* grincer.

raspberry 🌿 framboise *f*.

rat 1. *zo.* rat *m*; *pol.* renégat *m*; *sl.* salaud *m*; ~ **poison** mort-aux-rats; *fig.* ~ **race** foire *f* d'empoigne; **smell a** ~ soupçonner anguille sous roche; **2.** F ~ **on s.o.** lâcher q.; moucharder q.

ratchet ⊕ (*a.* ~ **wheel**) roue *f* à rochet.

rate 1. taux *m*, raison *f*, pourcentage *m*; vitesse *f*, cadence *f*; tarif *m*, cours *m*; *Br.* impôts *m/pl.* locaux; **at the** ~ **of** au taux de; à la vitesse de; **at any** ~ en tout cas; ~ **of exchange** cours *m* du change; ~ **of interest** taux *m* d'intérêt; **2.** *v/t.* estimer; évaluer; considérer; classer; *v/i.* être classé; être estimé; ~**payer** contribuable *mf*.

rather plutôt; quelque peu, un peu; assez; **I had** (*or* **would**) ~ (*inf.*) j'aime mieux (*inf.*).

ratify ratifier.

rating[1] évaluation *f*; classement *m*; ⚓ matelot *m*; (*a.* **popularity** ~) **person**: (indice *m* de) popularité *f*, cote *f*, *radio*, *telev.*: *a.* taux *m* d'écoute.

ratio proportion *f*, raison *f*.

ration 1. ration *f*; **2.** rationner.

rational rationel; raisonnable; sensé; raisonné; ~**ist** rationaliste (*a. su.*); ~**ize** rationaliser.

rattle 1. bruit *m*; fracas *m*; crépitement *m*; *chain*: cliquetis *m*; *toy*: hochet *m*; 🐝 râle *m*; **2.** *v/i.* crépiter; cliqueter; 🐝 râler; *v/t.* faire sonner; faire cliqueter; agiter, secouer; faire entre-choquer; ~ **off** (*or* **out**) réciter rapidement; ~**snake** serpent *m* à sonnettes; ~**trap** F tacot *m*.

raucous rauque.

ravage 1. ravage *m*; **2.** *v/t.* ravager.

rave être en délire; *fig.* pester (contre, **at**); s'extasier (sur, **about**).

ravel (s')embrouiller; *usu.* ~ **out** (s')effilocher.

raven corbeau *m*; ~**ous** affamé.

ravine ravin *m*.

ravings *pl.* délires *m/pl.*

ravish ravir; ~**ing** ravissant.

raw cru; brut (*metal*); âpre (*weather*); vif (*wound*); inexpérimenté (*person*); ~ **material** matières *f/pl.* premières *or* brutes; ~**boned** décharné; efflanqué (*horse*); ~**hide** cuir *m* vert.

ray rayon *m*; *fig.* lueur *f* (*of hope*); 🐝 ~ **treatment** radiothérapie *f*.

rayon rayonne *f*, soie *f* artificielle.

raze (*a.* ~ **to the ground**) raser.

razor rasoir *m*; ~ **blade** lame *f* de rasoir.

razzia *police*: razzia *f*.

re ✝, *admin.* concernant.

reach 1. portée *f*, atteinte *f*; étendue *f* (*a. fig.*); partie *f* droite (*of a river*) entre deux coudes; **beyond** ~, **out of** ~ hors de (la) portée, hors d'atteinte; **within s.o.'s** ~ à (la) portée de q.; **within easy** ~ tout près; **2.** *v/i.* (*a.* ~ **out**) tendre la main (pour, **for**); s'étendre ([jusqu']là, **to**); (*a.* ~ **to**) atteindre; *v/t.* arriver à, atteindre; (*oft.* ~ **out**) (é)tendre.

react réagir; ~**ion** réaction *f*; ~**ionary** réactionnaire (*adj., mf*); ~**or** *phys.* réacteur *m*.

read 1. *v/t.* lire; étudier; *fig.* interpréter; ~ **out** lire à haute voix; ~ **to s.o.** faire la lecture à q.; ~ **up** (**on**) étudier; s'informer *or* se renseigner (sur); *v/i.* lire; ⊕ indiquer, marquer (*thermometer*); **2.** lecture *f*; ~**able** lisible; ~**er** lecteur (-trice *f*) *m*; *univ.* maître *m* de conférences; livre *m* de lecture; ~**ership** lecteurs *m/pl.*

readi|ly *adv.* volontiers, avec empressement; facilement; ~**ness** empressement; facilité *f*; **in** ~ prêt.

reading lecture *f*; *gas-meter*: relevé *m*; *on instrument, scale etc.* indication(s) *f(pl.)*; interprétation *f*; variante *f*; ~ **lamp** lampe *f* de bureau; ~ **matter** lecture(s) *f(pl.)*; de quoi lire; ~ **room** salle *f* de lecture.

readjust *v/t.* rajuster; remettre à point (*an instrument*); ~ **o.s. to** = *v/t.* ~ **to** s'adapter à; ~**ment** rajustement *m*.

ready prêt (à *inf.*, **to** *inf.*); sous la main, disponible; *fig.* facile; prompt (à, **with**); ✝ comptant (*money*); ~ **for use** prêt à l'usage; **make** (*or* **get**) ~ (se) préparer; (s')apprêter; ~**made** tout fait; de confection (*clothes*); ~**to-wear** prêt à porter.

real 1. *adj.* vrai; véritable; réel ~ **property** (*or* **estate**) propriété *f* immobilière; F

for ~ pour de bon, sérieusement; sérieux; **2.** *adv.* F vraiment; très, F rudement, vachement; **~ism** réalisme *m*; **~istic** réaliste; **~istically** avec réalisme; **~ity** réalité *f*; réel *m*; *fig.* vérité *f*; **~izable** réalisable; imaginable; **~ization** réalisation *f* (*a.* ✝); *fig.* perception *f*; **~ize** réaliser (*a project*); bien comprendre, se rendre compte de; rappporter (*a price*); **~ly** vraiment; à vrai dire; réellement.

realm royaume *m*; *fig.* domaine *m*.

realt|or *Am.* agent *m* immobilier; **~y ☆** biens *m/pl.* immobiliers.

reap moissonner (*grain*); *a. fig.* récolter; **~er** ⊕ moissonneuse *f*.

reappear reparaître.

rear¹ *v/t.* élever; dresser; ✿ cultiver; *v/i.* (*a.* ~ **up**) se cabrer (*horse*).

rear² 1. arrière *m*, derrière *m*; queue *f*; dernier rang *m*; **at the** ~ **of, in (the)** ~ **of** derrière, en queue de; **2.** (d')arrière; de derrière; dernier; ~ **exit** sortie *f* de derrière; *mot.* ~ **light** feu *m* arrière; ~ **wheel** roue *f* arrière; *mot.* **~-wheel drive** traction *f* arrière; *mot.* ~ **window** glace *f* arrière; ~ **guard** arrière-garde *f*.

re-arm réarmer; **~ament** réarmement *m*.

rearmost dernier, de queue.

rearview: ~ **mirror** rétroviseur *m*.

rearward(s) à *or* vers l'arrière.

reason 1. raison *f*; **by** ~ **of** à cause de; **listen to** ~ entendre raison; **have** ~ **to** (*inf.*) avoir lieu de (*inf.*); **it stands to** ~ **that** il est de toute évidence que; **2.** *v/i.* raisonner (*a. q.*, **with s.o.**); *v/t.*: ~ **s.o. into** (*out of*) (*ger.*) amener q. à (dissuader q. de) (*inf.*); **~able** raisonnable (*a. fig.*); bien fondé; **~ed** raisonné; **~ing** raisonnement *m*.

reassemble (se) rassembler (*people etc.*); ⊕ remonter.

reassur|e rassurer; **~ing** rassurant.

rebate ✝ rabais *m*, escompte *m*; remboursement *m*.

rebel rebelle *mf*; **2.** se rebeller; **~lion** rébellion *f*; **~lious** rebelle.

rebirth renaissance *f*.

rebound 1. rebondir; ricocher (*bullet etc.*); **2.** rebondissement *m*; ricochet *m*.

rebuff 1. rebuffade *f*; **2.** repousser.

rebuild rebâtir, reconstruire.

rebuke 1. réprimande *f*; **2.** réprimander; faire des reproches à.

rebut réfuter.

recall 1. rappel *m*; rappel *m* (d'un souvenir), évocation *f*; **have total** ~ être capable de se souvenir de tout détail; **beyond** (*or* **past**) ~ irrémédiable; irrévocable; **2.** rappeler (*an ambassador etc.*); se rappeler, se souvenir de.

recant (se) rétracter; abjurer.

recap F **1.** récapituler; résumer; **2.** récapitulation *f*; résumé *m*.

recapitulate récapituler; résumer.

recapture reprendre.

recast ⊕, *fig.* refondre; *fig. a.* réorganiser.

reced|e s'éloigner, reculer; **~ing** fuyant (*chin etc.*).

receipt 1. réception *f*; reçu *m*; accusé *m* de réception; ✝ recette *f* (*a. cuis.*); **2.** acquitter.

receiv|e recevoir; **~ed** admis; **~er** *letter:* destinataire *mf*; *teleph.* récepteur *m*; (*a.* ~ **of stolen goods**) receleur (*-euse f*) *m*; ☆ **official** ~ administrateur *m* judiciaire; *teleph.* **lift the** ~ décrocher.

recent récent; **~ly** récemment.

receptacle récipient *m*.

reception réception *f* (*a. radio*); accueil *m*; (*a.* ~ **desk**) réception *f*; **~ist** réceptionniste *m*.

receptive réceptif.

recess vacances *f/pl.*; △ renfoncement *m*, recoin *m*; niche *f*.

recession récession *f*.

recipe *cuis., pharm.* recette *f* (*a. fig.*).

recipient destinataire *mf*, *grant etc.*: bénéficiaire *mf*.

reciproc|al réciproque; **~ate** *v/t.* retourner, donner en retour; *v/i.* rendre la pareille.

recit|al récit *m*; ♪ récital (*pl.* -s) *m*; **~ation** récitation *f*; **~e** réciter (*a poem etc.*); énumérer.

reckless insouciant; imprudent.

reckon *v/t.* calculer; estimer; compter (*a. fig.* parmi **among, as**); considérer comme; F penser, croire, juger; ~ **in** compter (*qch.*), tenir compte de; ~ **up** additionner; *v/i.* calculer; ~ **(up)on** compter sur; ~ **with** compter avec, tenir compte de; s'attendre à; prévoir; ~ **without** compter sans; ne pas tenir compte de, négliger, oublier; **~ing** compte *m*; calcul *m*; estimation *f*; **be out in one's** ~ se tromper (dans son calcul), mal calculer.

reclaim réformer (*q.*); récupérer (*waste materials etc.*); défricher (*land*); réclamer (la restitution de qch., le remboursement de *money*).

recline (s')appuyer; reposer; être allongé.

recluse reclus(e *f*) *m*; solitaire *mf*.

recogni|tion reconnaissance *f*; ~zable reconnaissable; ~ze reconnaître (à, **by**).

recoil 1. se détendre; reculer (devant, **from**) (*person, gun*); **2.** *spring*: détente *f*; *gun, fig.*: recul *m*.

recollect se souvenir de, se rappeler; ~ion souvenir *m*.

recommend recommander; ~ation recommandation *f*.

recompense 1. récompense *f*; dédommagement *m* (de, **for**); **2.** récompenser *or* dédommager (q. de qch., **s.o. for s.th.**).

reconcil|able conciliable; ~e réconcilier (avec *m*, **to**); concilier, faire accorder (*facts etc.*); ~ **o.s. to, become ~d to** se résigner à; ~iation (ré)conciliation *f*.

recondition remettre à neuf.

reconnaissance ✕ reconnaissance *f*.

reconnoit|re, *Am.* ~**er** ✕ *v/t.* reconnaître; *v/i.* faire une reconnaissance.

reconsider reconsidérer.

reconstitute reconstituer.

reconstruct reconstruire; reconstituer (*a crime*); ~ion reconstruction *f*; *crime*: reconstitution *f*.

record 1. rapport *m*; ⚖ procés-verbal *m*; récit *m*; dossier *m*, registre *m*; ♩ disque *m*; *sp. etc.*: record *m*; (*a.* **police ~**) casier *m* (judiciaire); *sp.* ~ **holder** détenteur (-trice *f*)*m* du record; ~ **library** discothèque *f*; ~ **player** électrophone *m*; **beat** (*or* **break**) **the** ~ battre le record; **set up a** ~ établir un record; **off the** ~ non officiel; confidentiel; **2.** enregistrer; consigner par écrit; rapporter; (**by**) ~**ed delivery** en recommandé; **3.** ... record (*time, speed, crop etc.*); **in** ~ **time** en un temps record; ~**er** ⚖ *approx.* juge *m* municipal; (*tape* ~) magnétophone *m*; ♩ flûte *f* à bec; ~**ing** enregistrement *m*.

recount raconter; recompter.

recoup récupérer; ~ **o.s.** se dédommager (de, **for**); se rattraper.

recourse recours *m*; expédient *m*; **have** ~ **to** avoir recours à.

recover¹ *v/t.* retrouver, recouvrer (*a. one's health*); regagner; rentrer en possession de; reprendre (*one's breath*); récupérer (*money, materials etc.*); **be** ~**ed** être remis; *v/i.* guérir; se remettre.

re-cover² recouvrir.

recovery recouvrement *m* (*a. from debts*); rétablissement *m* (*a. fig.*), guérison *f*; ⚖ redressement *m*.

re-create recréer.

recreation récréation *f*, detente *f*; ~ **centre** centre *m* de loisirs; ~ **ground** terrain *m* de jeux; ~ **room** salle *f* de récréation.

recrimination récrimination *f*.

recruit 1. recrue *f*; **2.** recruter.

rectang|le rectangle *m*; ~**ular** rectangulaire.

rectify rectifier; réparer.

rector *rel.* pasteur *m*; *univ.* recteur *m*; ~**y** presbytère *m*; cure *f*.

recumbent couché, étendu.

recuperate *v/i.* se remettre; *v/t.* récupérer (*one's health*); recouvrer.

recur revenir; se reproduire; ~**rence** réapparition *f*; répétition *f*; ~**rent** périodique.

recycl|e retraiter; recycler; ~**ing** retraitement *m*; recyclage *m*.

red 1. rouge (*a. pol.*); roux (*hair*); ♀ **Cross** Croix-Rouge *f*; *zo.* ~ **deer** cerf *m* commun; ⊕ ~ **heat** chaude *f* rouge; ~ **herring** hareng *m* saur; *fig.* manœuvre *f* de diversion; ~ **tape** bureaucratie *f*; **2.** rouge *m* (*a. pol. mf*); **in** ~ en déficit, à découvert; ~**-carpet:** (*give s.o.*) ~ **treatment** (recevoir q. en) grande de pompe *f*; ~**den** rougir; ~**dish** rougeâtre.

redecorate repeindre (et retapisser) (*a room etc.*).

redeem racheter (*eccl., a slave etc.*); amortir, rembourser (*a debt*); purger (*a mortgage*); dégager, retirer (*from pawn*); tenir (*a promise*); F réparer; *fig.* arracher (à, **from**); ~**ing feature** qualité *f* qui rachète les défauts (*de q. or qch.*), le seul bon côté (*de q. or qch.*); ♀**er** Rédempteur *m*, Sauveur *m*.

redemption *eccl.* rédemption *f*; *crime, slave etc., a.* ✝: rachat *m*; ✝ amortissement *m*; purge *f*.

redeploy réorganiser; redéployer.

redevelop réaménager (*an area*); rénover (*housing*).

red...: ~-faced rougeaud; **~-haired** roux, rouquin; **~-handed: catch s.o. ~** prendre q. en flagrant délit; **~head** F rouquin(e f)m; **~hot** ⊕ (chauffé au) rouge; fig. ardent; fig. tout chaud, (de) dernière heure.

redirect faire suivre (mail).

redistribute redistribuer.

red-letter day jour m de fête; fig. jour m mémorable.

red-light district quartier m réservé or malfamé.

redness rougeur f; hair, foliage: rousseur f.

redo refaire.

redolent: be ~ of sentir.

redouble redoubler.

redoubtable redoutable.

redound: ~ to contribuer à; **~ (up)on** rejaillir sur.

redress 1. réparation f (a. ⚖); **2.** réparer; rétablir (the balance).

reduc|e réduire; diminuer; baisser; affaiblir; ralentir (speed); atténuer (a contrast); **~tion** réduction f; diminution f; ✝ rabais m; baisse f (of temperature, in prices); phot. atténuation f.

redundan|cy superfluité f; ✝ licenciement m; **~t** superflu; ✝ mis au chômage, licencié; ✝ **make ~** licencier.

reed roseau m; ♩ anche f.

reef récif m, écueil m.

reek 1. relent m; **2.** puer (qch., **of s.th.**).

reel 1. bobine f; fishing rod: moulinet m; cin. bande f; **2.** v/t. bobiner; **~ off** dévider; fig. débiter; v/i. chanceler.

re-elect réélire; **~ion** réélection f.

re-ent|er rentrer (dans); **~ry** rentrée f.

re-establish rétablir.

refer v/i. **~ to** parler de, mentionner; se reporter à (a document, notes etc.) s'appliquer à; **~ to** (s.o., s.th.) **as** appeler, traiter de; **~ring to** en réponse à (votre lettre, **your letter**); v/t. **s.th. to** soumettre qch. à; **~ s.o. to** renvoyer q. à.

referee 1. arbitre m; **2.** v/t. arbitrer; v/i. être arbitre, faire fonction d'arbitre.

reference renvoi m, référence f (to an authority); rapport m; mention f, allusion f; **~s** (pl.) référence(s f/pl.); (a. **foot-note ~**) appel m de note; **in** (or **with**) **~ to** comme suite à, quant à; **~ book** ouvrage m de référence; **~ num-**

ber cote f; **~ point** point m de repère; **make ~ to** signaler, faire mention de.

referendum référendum m.

refill 1. remplir (de nouveau), recharger (a lighter etc.); **2.** recharge f.

refine ⊕, fig. (se) raffiner; fig. a. (s')affiner; **~ upon** raffiner sur; **~d** raffiné; **~ment** ⊕ raffinage m; fig. raffinement m; **~ry** raffinerie f.

reflect v/t. réfléchir, refléter; fig. être le reflet de; v/i. réfléchir (sur, à **on**); fig. **~ (up)on** porter atteinte à; **~ion** réflexion f (a. fig.); reflet m (a. fig.), image f; critique (de, **on**); **on ~** à la réflexion; **~ive** réfléchi (mind, person).

reflex 1. réflexe m; **~ action** (mouvement m) réflexe m; **~ive** réfléchi.

reform¹ 1. réforme f; **2.** (se) réformer; (se) corriger.

reform² (se) reformer.

reform|ation réforme f (a. eccl. 2); **~ed** amendé; **~er** réformateur (-trice f) m.

refract|ion réfraction f; **~ory** réfractaire (a. ♈, ⊕); rebelle.

refrain 1. v/i. se retenir, s'abstenir (de, **from**); **2.** refrain m.

refresh (se) rafraîchir; revigorer; **~er** cours m de recyclage; **~ment** rafraîchissement m (a. cuis.); **~ room** buffet m.

refrigerat|e (se) réfrigérer; v/t. a. frigorifier; **~or** réfrigérateur m.

refuel (se) ravitailler (en carburant).

refuge refuge m; **take ~ in** se réfugier dans; **~e** réfugié(e f) m.

refulgent resplendissant.

refund 1. remboursement m; **2.** rembourser.

refurbish remettre à neuf.

refurnish meubler de neuf.

refus|al refus m; **~e¹** refuser.

refuse² ordures f/pl.

refute réfuter.

regain regagner; retrouver.

regal royal.

regale régaler (de, **with**).

regard 1. estime f, respect m; considération f, attention f; **in this ~** à cet égard; **with ~ to** quant à, en ce qui concerne; **with kind ~s** avec les sincères amitiés (de, **from**); **2.** regarder (comme, **as**); considérer; **as ~s** en ce qui concerne; **~ing** en ce qui concerne; **~less: ~ of** sans se soucier de.

regatta régate f.

regenerate (se) régénérer.

regen|cy régence f; **~t** régent(e f) m.

regime régime m; **~nt** régiment m.

region région f; fig. **in the ~ of** environ, dans les (amount); **~al** régional.

register 1. registre m (a. ♥, ♪, ⊕ furnace); matricule f; election: liste f; ⊕ chimney: rideau m; ⊕ compteur m; **2.** v/t. enregistrer (a. luggage, a. fig.); inscrire; immatriculer (a car, a student); ⊕ indiquer, marquer (degrees etc.); ♥ déposer (a trade mark); recommander (a letter); fig. exprimer; v/i. s'inscrire (person); fig. pénétrer, rentrer; **~ed** ♥ déposé; (en) recommandé (letter).

registr|ar officier m de l'état civil; secrétaire m; **~ation** enregistrement m; inscription f; car etc.: immatriculation f; trade mark: dépôt m; **~y** enregistrement m; (a. **~ office**) bureau m d'enregistrement or de l'état civil.

regress régresser; **~ion** régression f; retour m en arrière.

regret 1. regret m; **2.** regretter (de inf., ger. or to inf.); **~ful** plein de regrets; **~ly** avec or à regret; **~table** regrettable.

regroup (se) regrouper; **~ment** regroupement m.

regular régulier; usual: habituel; ordinaire (size, petrol, gas etc.); F pej. vrai, véritable (idiot etc.); F **a ~ guy** un chic type; **~ity** régularité f.

regulat|e régler; **~ion 1.** règlement m; ⊕ réglage m. **2.** réglementaire.

rehash 1. F resucée f; **2.** réchauffer.

rehears|al ♪, thea. répétition f; récit m détaillé; **~e** ♪, thea. répéter; énumérer; raconter (tout au long).

reign 1. règne m; **2.** régner; **~ing** actuel (champion etc.).

reimburse rembourser.

rein 1. rêne f; bride f; fig. **give ~ to** lâcher la bride à; **2.:** **~ in** (or up or back) brider, retenir.

reindeer zo. renne m.

reinforce renforcer; ⊕ **~d concrete** béton m armé; **~ment** ✗ pl. renfort(s) m/(pl.).

reinstate réintégrer; rétablir.

reinsure réassurer.

reissue 1. rééditer (a book, record); ressortir (a film); **2.** réédition f.

reiterate réitérer, répéter.

reject 1. rejeter (a. ✗); refuser; repousser; ♥ mettre au rebut (an article etc.); **2.** ♥ marchardise f or objet m de rebut; **~ion** rejet m; refus m; repoussement m.

rejoice se réjouir (de **at, in**).

rejoin[1] (se) rejoindre.

rejoin[2] répliquer.

rejuvenat|e vt/i. rajeunir; **~ion** rajeunissement m.

rekindle (se) rallumer.

relapse 1. ✗, a. fig. rechute f; **2.** retomber; ✗ rechuter.

relate v/t. raconter; établir un rapport; v/i. se rapporter, avoir rapport (à, **to**); **relating to** concernant; **~d** ayant rapport; apparenté; allié.

relation rapport m (à **to, with**); parent(e f) m; **in ~ to** par rapport à; **~ship** rapport m; parenté f.

relative 1. relatif (a. gramm.); respectif; **~ to** relatif à; **2.** parent(e f) m.

relax v/i. se relaxer (person), se détendre; se relâcher; v/t. relâcher; détendre; modérer (restrictions etc.); **~ation** relâchement m; détente f.

relay[1] 1. relais m (a. ♪); relève f (of workers); sp. (a. **~ race**) course f de relais; **2.** transmettre.

re-lay[2] poser de nouveau.

release 1. libération f, prisoners: a. élargissement m; dégagement m; cin. sortie f; ♪ disque m; ⊕ déclencheur m; **2.** relâcher; libérer (de **from**), dégager; cin. sortir; ⊕ déclencher.

relegate reléguer (a. a team etc.).

relent s'adoucir; se laisser attendrir; **~less** implacable; impitoyable.

relevant (à, **to**) pertinent; applicable; qui se rapporte.

reliab|ility sûreté f; sérieux m, solidité f; ⊕ fiabilité f; **~le** sûr; digne de foi (source) or de confiance (person); ⊕ etc. fiable (car etc.).

reliance confiance f; dépendance f (de, **on**); **place ~ on** se fier à.

relic relique f (a. eccl.); fig. vestige m; **~s** pl. restes m/pl.

relief soulagement m; ✗ town: délivrance f; guard: relève f; secours m (a. aux pauvres); △ relief m.

relieve soulager; venir en aide à, secourir; relayer; ✗ relever (the guard); ✗ délivrer (a fortress etc.); fig. débarrasser.

religi|on religion *f;* **~ous** religieux.

relinquish renoncer à (*an idea, a project etc.*); abandonner; lâcher.

relish 1. goût *m; cuis.* condiment *m,* assaisonnement *m; fig.* attrait *m;* **2.** *v/t.* savourer; *fig.* trouver du plaisir à, aimer.

relocat|e transférer, déplacer; **~ion** transfert *m,* déplacement *m.*

reluctan|ce répugnance *f;* **~t** qui résiste; fait *or* donné à contrecœur; **be ~ to** (*inf.*) être peu disposé à (*inf.*); **~tly** à contrecœur.

rely: ~ (up)on compter sur; dépendre de.

remain 1. rester. **2. ~s** *pl.* restes *m/pl.;* **~der** reste *m.*

remake nouvelle version *f or* réalisation *f,* remake *m.*

remand 🏛 (*a ~ in custody*) renvoyer en détention provisoire.

remark 1. remarque *f,* observation *f;* attention *f;* **2.** *v/t.* remarquer; *v/i.* ~ (*up*)*on* faire des remarques sur; **~able** remarquable.

remedy 1. remède *m;* **2.** remédier à.

rememb|er se souvenir de, se rappeler; **~ me to him!** dites-lui bien des choses de ma part!; **~rance** souvenir *m,* mémoire *f.*

remind rappeler (qch. à q., **s.o. of s.th.**); **~ s.o. of** *a.* faire q. penser à; **~er** (✝ lettre *m* de) rappel *m;* pense-bête *m.*

reminisce parler de *or* évoquer ses souvenirs (de, *about*); **~nces** souvenirs *m/ pl.;* **~nt** qui se souvient (de, *of*); **be ~ of** rappeler, faire penser à.

remiss négligent.

remission *debts, punishment:* remise *f;* ✝, *eccl.* rémission *f.*

remit *v/t.* envoyer; remettre (*a debt, a punishment; a.* ✝, *a. eccl.*); *v/i.* diminuer d'intensité; **~tance** paiement *m;* versement *m.*

remnant reste *m;* restant *m;* coupon *m* (*of cloth*).

remodel remodeler; remanier.

remonstra|nce remontrance *f.*

remorse remords *m;* **~ful** plein de remords; **~less** sans remords; impitoyable.

remote écarté; éloigné; reculé; lointain; *fig.* vague; **~ control** télécommande *f,* téléguidage *m;* **~-control** téléguidé, télécommandé; **~ness** éloignement *m.*

remov|al enlèvement *m; employee:* renvoi *m; nuisance:* suppression *f;* 🏥 ablation *f; to another place:* déménagement *m;* **~ man** déménageur *m;* **~ van** camion *m* de déménagement; **~e 1.** *v/t.* enlever; éloigner; écarter; retirer; faire partir (*stains etc.*); renvoyer (*an employee*); supprimer (*a nuisance etc.*); déménager (*furniture etc.*); *v/i.* déménager; **2.** distance *f;* recul *m;* degré *m;* **be only (at) one ~ from** être tout proche de, confiner à, friser; **many ~s from** loin de; **~er** *for stains etc.:* détachant *m; for paint etc.:* décapant *m;* **~s** *pl.* entreprise *f* de déménagement.

remunerat|e rémunérer; **~ion** rémunération *f;* **~ive** rémunérateur.

renaissance Renaissance *f.*

rename rebaptiser.

rend déchirer; *fig. a.* fendre.

rend|er rendre; *cuis.* clarifier, **~ering,** **~ition** ♪ interprétation *f;* traduction *f.*

renegade renégat(e *f*) *m.*

renew renouveler; reprendre; **~al** renouvellement *m;* reprise *f.*

renounce *v/t.* renoncer à; répudier.

renovate renouveler; remettre à neuf, restaurer.

renown renom(mée *f*) *m;* **~ed** renommé.

rent[1] déchirure *f; land:* fissure *f.*

rent[2] 1. *room, house etc.:* loyer *m; car etc.:* location *f;* **2.** louer (*a. = ~ out*); **~-a-car (service)** location *f* de voitures; **~al** (montant *m* du) loyer *m* (prix *m* de) location *f.*

renunciation (of) renoncement *m* (à); reniement *m* (de).

reopen (se) rouvrir; **~ing** réouverture *f.*

reorganize réorganiser.

repair[1] 1. réparation *f;* **~ kit** trousse *f* de réparation; **~ man** réparateur *m;* **~ shop** atelier *m* de réparations; **in (good) ~** en bon état; **2.** réparer (*a. fig.*); refaire.

repair[2] se rendre (à, *to*).

repar|able réparable; **~tion** réparation *f* (*a. pol., a. fig.*); **make ~s** réparer.

repartee repartie *f,* **be good at ~** avoir de la repartie.

repay rembourser (q., *money*); *fig.* récompenser; **~able** remboursable; **~ment** remboursement *m; fig.* récompense *f.*

repeal 1. abrogation *f*; ⚖ annulation *f*;
2. abroger; annuler.

repeat 1. *v/t.* répéter; réitérer; renouveler (*an order etc.*); *v/i.* (*a. ~ o.s.*) se
répéter; revenir (*food*); **2.** reprise *f* (*a.
♪*); ♪ (*oft. ~ order*) commande *f* renouvelée; **~edly** plusieurs fois.

repel repousser; **~lent** repoussant.

repent (*a. ~ of*) se repentir de; **~ance**
repentir *m*; **~ant** repenti.

repercussion répercussion *f*.

repertory répertoire *m*.

repetition répétition *f*; ♪ *etc.* renouvellement *m*; ♪ reprise *f*.

replace replacer; remplacer (par, **by**);
teleph. raccrocher (*the receiver*); **~ment**
remplacement *m*.

replenish remplir (de nouveau); (se)
réapprovisionner (de, en **with**).

replete rempli, plein (de, **with**); *after
meal*: rassasié.

replica réplique *f*.

reply 1. répondre; **2.** réponse *f*.

report 1. rapport *m* (sur, **on**); *journ.* reportage *m*; *meteor. etc.* bulletin *m*; *fig.*
rumeur *f*; réputation *f*; *gun*: détonation
f; (*a. ~ card, school ~*) bulletin *m* (scolaire); **2.** *v/t.* rapporter; faire un rapport sur; *journ.* faire un reportage sur;
annoncer, signaler; dire, mentionner;
dénoncer (*a suspect etc.*), signaler (*an
abuse etc.*) (à, **to**); **he is ~ed ...** on dit
qu'il ..., on nous apprend qu'il ...; *v/i.*
faire un rapport *or* un reportage (sur,
on); se présenter (*person*) (chez, **to**); **~
sick** se (faire) porter malade; **~ed:**
gramm.: **~ speech** discours *m* indirect;
~edly à ce qu'on dit; on dit que ...; **~er**
reporter *m*.

repos|e 1. repos *m*; **2.** reposer; **~itory**
dépôt *m*; entrepôt *m*; *fig.* répertoire *m*.

reprehensible répréhensible.

represent représenter; signaler (qch. à
q., **s.th. to s.o.**); **~ation** représentation
f; **~s** *pl.* démarche *f*; **~ative 1.** représentatif; **2.** représentant(e *f*) *m*; *pol.* député
m.

repress réprimer; *psych. a.* refouler;
~ion (*a. psych.* **conscious ~**) répression
f; *psych.* (*a.* **unconscious ~**) refoulement *m*.

reprieve 1. ⚖ grâce *f*; délai *m*, sursis *m*;
2. grâcier; accorder un délai *or* un sursis à.

reprimand 1. réprimande *f*; **2.** réprimander.

reprisals *pl.* représailles *f/pl.*

reproach 1. reproche *m*; **2.** reprocher
(qch. à q., **s.o. with s.th.**); faire des
reproches à; **~ful** de reproche.

reprint 1. réimprimer; **2.** réimpression *f*.

reprobate dépravé.

reprocess retraiter; recycler; **~ plant**
usine *f* de retraitement *or* de recyclage.

reproduc|e (se) reproduire; (se) multiplier; **~tion** reproduction *f*.

reproof reproche *m*; réprimande *f*.

reprove réprimander.

reptile reptile *m*.

republic république *f*; **~an** républicain
(*a. su.*).

repudiate répudier.

repugnan|ce répugnance *f*; **~t** répugnant.

repuls|e repousser; **~ive** répulsif.

reput|able honorable (*person, a. employment*); estimé; **~ation** réputation *f*;
~e réputation *f*, renom *m*; **~ed** supposé; **be ~ to be** (*or* **as**) passer pour; **~edly**
d'après ce qu'on dit.

request 1. demande *f*; requête *f*; **at
s.o.'s ~** à *or* sur la demande de q.; **by ~**
sur demande; **~ stop** arrêt *m* facultatif;
(*musical*) **~ programme** disques *m/pl.*
etc. or programme *m* des auditeurs; **2.**
demander (qch. à q., **s.th. of s.o.**; à q.
de *inf.*, **s.o. to** *inf.*); prier (q. de *inf.*, **s.o.
to** *inf.*).

require demander, avoir besoin de,
nécessiter; exiger (qch. de q., **s.th. of
s.o.**); **~** (*of*) **s.o. to** (*inf.*) *a.* vouloir que
q. (*sbj.*); **~d** requis, voulu; **~ment** besoin *m*, exigence *f*; condition *f* (requise).

requisit|e 1. requis, nécessaire; **2.** chose
f nécessaire; **toilet ~s** *pl.* accessoires
m/pl. de toilette; **~ion 1.** demande *f*; ✗
réquisition *f*; **2.** ✗ réquisitionner.

requit|al récompense *f*; revanche *f*; **~e**
récompenser; venger.

rerun 1. repasser, passer (*a film etc.*) de
nouveau; **2.** reprise.

resale revente *f*; **~ price** prix *m* de revente; **~ value** valeur *f* à la revente.

rescind abroger (*a law*); annuler.

rescue 1. sauvetage *m*; secours *m*; délivrance *f*; **~ party** équipe *f* de sauvetage
or de secours; **come** (*or* **go**) **to s.o.'s ~**

aller (*or* venir) à la rescousse de q.; **2.** sauver; secourir, porter secours à; délivrer; **~ s.o. from danger** arracher q. à un *or* au danger; **~r** sauveteur (-euse *f*) *m*; secoureur (-euse *f*) *m*; libérateur (-euse *f*) *m*.

research recherche *f* (de *for, after*); recherches *f/pl.*; **marketing ~** étude *f* du marché; **~ work** recherches *f/pl.*; **~worker = ~er** chercheur (-euse *f*) *m*.

resembl|ance ressemblance *f* (à, avec **to**); **~e** ressembler à.

resent ne pas aimer (du tout), être indigné de; **~ful** rancunier; **~ment** mécontentement *m*; rancune *f*.

reserv|ation room, seat etc.: réservation *f*; doubt, restriction; a. territory: réserve *f*; **~e 1.** réserve *f* (a. fig. attitude); **2.** réserver, retenir (a room, a place etc.); **~ed** réservé (a. fig.).

reservoir réservoir *m* (a. fig.).

reside résider; **~nce** résidence *f*; **~ permit** permis *m* de séjour; **~nt 1.** résidant; **2.** habitant(e *f*) *m*, résident(e *f*) *m*.

residue 🔬, ⚕ résidu *m*; reste *m*.

resign *v/t.* se démettre de; **~ o.s. to** se résigner à; *v/i.* démissionner; **~ation** démission *f*; résignation *f* (à, to); **~ed** résigné.

resilien|ce élasticité *f*; a. fig. ressort *m*; **~t** élastique; qui a du ressort.

resin résine *f*; colophane *f*.

resist *v/t.* résister à; s'opposer à; *v/i.* résister; **~ance** résistance *f*.

resolut|e résolu; ferme; **~eness** fermeté *f*; **~ion** résolution *f*.

resolve *v/t.* 🔬, ♩, fig. résoudre; se résoudre à, résoudre de (*inf.*); *v/i.* (a. **~ o.s.**) se résoudre; **~ (up)on** se résoudre à; ♩ 🔬 résolution *f*; **~d** résolu.

resonanc|e résonance *f*; **~t** résonnant; sonore (*voice*).

resort 1. recours *m*; lieu *m* de séjour; **health ~** station *f* thermale; **seaside ~** station *f* balnéaire; **summer ~** station *f* d'été; **in the last ~** en dernier ressort; **2. ~ to** avoir recours à.

resound résonner, retentir (de, *with*).

resource ressource *f*; **~ful** ingénieux; débrouillard.

respect 1. respect *m*; **in this ~** à cet égard; **in some ~s** à certains égards; **in all ~s** à tous égards; **in many ~s** à bien des égards; **in no ~** à aucun égard; **with**

~ to quant à, en ce qui concerne; **without ~ of** sans acception de (*race, sex etc.*); **pay one's ~s to** présenter ses respects à; **2.** *v/t.* respecter; **as ~s** quant à; **~ability** respectabilité *f*; **~able** respectable; **~ful** respectueux (envers, pour **to[wards]**); **~ing** en ce qui concerne, quant à; **~ive** respectif.

respirat|ion respiration *f*; **~or** respirateur *m*; **~ive** respiratif.

respite répit *m*; ⚖ sursis *m*.

resplend|ent resplendissant.

respon|d répondre; réagir; **~se** réponse *f*; réaction *f*.

responsi|bility responsabilité *f* (de *for, of*); **~ble** responsable (de, *for*); qui comporte des responsabilités (*job*); sérieux, digne de confiance.

rest[1] 1. repos *m*; arrêt *m*, pause *f*; ♩ silence *f*, support *m*, appui *m*; **~ home** maison *f* de repos; **~ room** toilettes *f/pl.*; *v/i.* reposer; (a. **~ up**) se reposer; **~ (up)on** reposer sur, appuyer sur (a support); **~ against** appuyer contre; *v/t.* (faire) reposer; **~ s.th. against s.th.** appuyer qch. contre qch.; **~ s.th. on s.th.** appuyer *or* reposer qch. sur qch.

rest[2] 1. reste *m*, restant *m*; les autres *m/pl.*; **for the ~** quant au reste; **2.** rester; demeurer; (**you can**) **~ assured** soyez certain, **~ with s.o.** dépendre de q. (decision etc.); **it ~s with you to ...** (inf.) a. c'est à vous de ... (inf.).

restaurant restaurant *m*.

restful reposant; paisible.

restitution restitution *f*; **make ~ of** restituer (qch.).

restive nerveux; rétif.

restless sans repos; agité; inquiet; **~ness** agitation *f*; nervosité *f*.

restock (se) réapprovisionner.

restor|ation rétablissement *m*; restauration *f*; restitution *f*; **~e** rétablir; restaurer; restituer.

restrain retenir (de, *from*); refréner; contenir; **~ed** sobre; mesuré; **~t** contrainte *f*; restriction *f*; sobriété *f*.

restrict restreindre; limiter; **~ion** restriction *f*; limitation *f*; **~ive** restrictif.

result 1. résultat *m*; **2.** résulter, provenir (de, *from*); **~ in** aboutir à.

resume reprendre.

resurgen|ce réapparition *f*, reprise *f*; **~t** renaissant.

resurrect ressusciter; **~ion** résurrection f.

resuscitate réanimer.

retail 1. su. (vente f au) détail m; **by ~** au détail; **2.** adj. de détail; au détail (sale); **~ trader** détaillant m; **~ bookseller** libraire m; **3.** adv. au détail; **4.** (se) vendre au détail; **~er** détaillant m.

retain garder, conserver; retenir; engager (a lawyer); **~er** acompte m.

retaliat|e se venger, user de représailles; rendre la pareille (à, **on**); **~ion** vengeance f, représailles f/pl.

retard retarder; **~ed** retardé; (a. **mentally ~**) arriéré.

rethink repenser.

reticen|ce réticence f, **~t** réticent.

retina rétine f.

retinue suite f (of a nobleman).

retir|e v/t. mettre à la retraite; v/i. se retirer (de, **from**); prendre sa retraite; **~ed** retraité; **~ pay** pension f de retraite; **~ement** retraite f; **early ~** préretraite f; **~ing** sortant; de retraite; fig. réservé, timide.

retort 1. réplique f; riposte f; 🜊 cornue f; **2.** répliquer, riposter.

retouch retoucher (a. phot.).

retrace reconstituer; **~ one's steps** revenir sur ses pas.

retract (se) rétracter; rentrer; ⚙ escamoter; **~able** ⚙ escamotable.

retrain (se) recycler; **~ing** recyclage m.

retreat 1. retraite f; **2.** reculer; se retirer; ✗ battre en retraite.

retrench faire des économies.

retribution châtiment m.

retriev|al récupération f; réparation f; (re)cherche f; **~ system** système m de recherche documentaire; **beyond** (or **past**) **~** irréparable; (definitivement) perdu; **~e** récupérer; (re)trouver; réparer (a mistake etc.), sauver (the situation etc.).

retro- rétro...; **~active** rétroactif; **~grade 1.** rétrograde; **2.** rétrograder; **~gression** rétrogression f; **~spect: in ~** rétrospectivement; **~spection** examen m or coup m d'œil rétrospectif; **~spective 1.** rétrospectif; **2.** rétrospective f.

return 1. retour m; renvoi m; parl. élection f; ✝ (oft. **~s** pl.) recettes f/pl., rendement m; remboursement m (of a sum); déclaration f (of income); admin.

relevé m; restitution f; fig. récompense f; fig. échange m; attr. de retour; **many happy ~s of the day** mes meilleurs vœux pour votre anniversaire; **in ~** en retour; en échange (de, **for**); **by ~** (of **post**) par retour du courrier; **~ ticket** billet m d'aller et retour; **2.** v/i. revenir; rentrer; retourner; fig. **~ to** revenir à (a subject etc.); retomber dans (a habit); v/t. rendre; renvoyer; adresser (thanks); fig. répliquer; ✝ rapporter (a benefit, a. admin.); parl. élire.

reun|ion réunion f; **~ite** (se) réunir.

rev F mot. **1.** tour; **2.** (a. **~ up**) (s')emballer.

revaluat|e réévaluer; **~ion** réévaluation f.

reveal révéler; faire connaître or voir; **~ing** révélateur.

revel se delecter (à, de **in**).

revelation révélation f.

revel|(l)er noceur (-euse f) m; **~ry** orgie(s) f/pl.

revenge 1. vengeance f; games: revanche f; **take ~** se venger (de, **for**; on, **on**); **2.** v/i. se venger (de qch., sur q. **on**); v/t. venger; **~ o.s.** (or **be ~d**) **on** se venger de (qch.) or sur (q.); **~ful** vindicatif; **~r** vengeur (-eresse f) m.

revenue (a. **~s** pl.) revenu m.

reverberat|e résonner (sound); se réverbérer (light); **~ion** réverbération f.

revere révérer, vénérer; **~nce** vénération f; révérence f; **~nd** vénérable; eccl. révérend; **~nt(ial)** respectueux; révérentiel.

reverie rêverie f.

revers|al renversement m; revirement m (of opinion); fig. revers m, échec m; **~e 1.** contraire m, inverse m; ✗, a. fig. revers m; mot. (a. **~ gear**) marche f arrière; **2.** contraire, opposé, inverse; **~ side cloth:** envers m; **3.** retourner, renverser, invertir (an order); révoquer (a decree); mot. v/i. faire marche arrière; **~ible** réversible; **~ion** réversion f; retour m.

revert **~ to** revenir à; retourner à (a. biol. etc.).

review 1. révision f; ✗, ⚓, periodical, fig.: revue f; critique f, compte rendu m; **2.** réviser; ✗, ⚓, mot. passer en revue; faire le compte rendu de; **~er** critique m (littéraire).

revis|e 1. réviser; revoir (*a manuscript etc.*); **~ion** révision *f*.

reviv|al reprise *f*; renouveau *m*, renaissance *f*; **~e** *v/t.* ressusciter; ranimer; renouveler; *v/i.* reprendre; se ranimer.

revo|cation révocation *f*; **~ke** révoquer; revenir sur (*a decision etc.*).

revolt 1. révolte *f*; **2.** se révolter.

revolution ⊕, *pol.* révolution *f*; ⊕ *a.* tour *m*; **~ary** révolutionnaire (*adj., mf*); **~ize** révolutionner.

revolv|e tourner; **~er** revolver *m*; **~ing** tournant; ⊕ *a.* rotatif; pivotant (*chair*); **~ door** tambour *m*.

revulsion répugnance *f*.

reward 1. récompense *f*; **2.** récompenser (de, **for**); **~ing** qui (en) vaut la peine *or* le coup.

rewind remonter (*a watch*).

rhapsody rhapsodie *f*.

rhetoric rhétorique *f*; éloquence *f*.

rheumatism ❦ rhumatisme *m*.

rhubarb ♣ rhubarbe *f*.

rhyme 1. rime *f* (à, **to**); vers *m/pl.*; *without* **~** *or* *reason* sans rime ni raison; **2.** (faire) rimer (avec, **with**).

rhythm rythme *m*; **~ic(al)** rythmique.

rib 1. côte *f*; ♣ nervure *f*; *umbrella*: balcine *f*; **2.** F taquiner (*a p.*).

ribald paillard; **~ry** paillardises *f/pl.*; propos *m/pl.* grossiers.

ribbon ruban; **~s** *pl.* lambeaux *m/pl.*

rice riz *m*; **~ field** rizière *f*; **~ pudding** riz *m* au lait.

rich riche (en, **in**); généreux (*wine*); *the newly* **~** les nouveaux riches *m/pl.*; **~es** *pl.* richesses *f/pl.*; **~ness** richesse *f*.

rick meule *f* (*of hay*).

ricket|s ❦ *sg. or pl.* rachitisme *m*; **~y** rachitique; F branlant, bancal.

ricochet 1. ricochet *m*; **2.** (faire) ricocheter.

rid débarrasser (de, **of**); *get* **~** *of* se débarrasser de; **~dance: good** **~!** bon débarras!

riddle¹ énigme *f* (*a. fig.*), devinette *f*.

riddle² 1. crible *m*; **2.** cribler (de, **with**).

ride 1. promenade *f*; voyage *m*; course *f*; *bus etc.*: trajet *m*; **2.** *v/i.* se promener, aller (*on horseback, in a bus, on a bicycle*); voyager; *fig.* voguer; ♣ **~ at anchor** être à l'ancre; *v/t.* monter (*a horse*); aller à (*a bicycle etc.*); diriger (*a horse*); voguer sur (*the waves*); **~r** cava-

lier (-ère *f*) *m*; *race*: jockey *m*; *circus*: écuyer (-ère *f*) *m*.

ridge 1. *mountain*: arête *f*, crête *f*; faîte *m* (*a.* △); *rocks*: banc *m*; *hills*: chaîne *f*; ⏞ billon *m*; **2.** sillonner.

ridicul|e 1. ridicule *m*; **2.** ridiculiser; **~ous** ridicule.

riding 1. équitation *f*; **2.** d'équitation; **~ breeches** *pl.* culotte *f* de cheval.

rife abondant (en, **with**); répandu.

riff-raff canaille *f*.

rifle 1. fusil *m* (à canon rayé); **~ range** *outdoors*: champ *m* (*or indoors*: stand *m*) de tir; **2.** piller ❦ vider.

rift fente *f*, fissure *f*.

rig 1. ♣ gréement *m*; ⊕ derrick; F *clothes*: accoutrement *f*; **2.** ♣ gréer; F truquer; F **~ out** accoutrer; **~ up** monter, installer; arranger; **~ging** ♣ gréement *m*.

right 1. droit; bon; correct, juste; convenable, approprié; bien placé; *be* **~** avoir raison (*person*); être correct (*answer, guess etc.*); être à l'heure (*clock*); *be* **~ to** (*inf.*) avoir raison de (*inf.*); bien faire de (*inf.*); *pol.* **~ wing** (aile *f*) droite *f*; *all* **~!** entendu!; très bien!; c'est bon!; *put* (*or set*) **~** réparer; corriger; **2.** *adv.* droit; tout ...; bien; correctement; à droite; **~ away** tout de suite; sur-le-champ; **~ in the middle** au beau milieu; **~ on** tout droit; **3.** *su.* droit *m*; bien *m*; droite *f* (*a. pol.*); **~ of way** *road*: priorité *f*; (droit *m* de) passage *m*; *by* **~** de droit; *by* **~s** en toute justesse; *by* **~ of** par droit de; à titre de; *have a* **~ to** avoir droit à (*qch.*); avoir le droit de (*inf.*), être en droit de (*inf.*); *on* (*or to*) *the* **~** à droite; *put* (*or set*) *to* **~s** (re)mettre en ordre; **4.** *v/t.* redresser; *fig.* corriger; **~-angled** à angle droit; rectangle (*triangle*); **~eous** juste, vertueux; justifié (*indignation etc.*); **~ful** légitime; **~-hand** à *or* de droite; *mot.* **~ drive** conduite *f* à droite; **~ man** le bras *m* droit (*de q.*); **~-hander** droitier (-ère *f*) *m*; *sl.* *pol.* droitiste (*adj., su./mf*); **~ly** correctement, bien; à juste titre, avec raison; **~ or wrongly** à tort ou à raison; **~-minded** sensé; **~-wing** *pol.* de droite.

rigid rigide; **~ity** rigidité *f*.

rigo|rous rigoureux; **~(u)r** rigueur *f*.

rim bord *m*; *spectacles*: monture *f*; *wheel*: jante *f*.

rime rime *f*; givre *m*.

rind écorce *f*, peau *f* (*a. of a fruit*); *cheese*: croûte *f*; *bacon*: couenne *f*.

ring¹ 1. anneau *m*; bague *f*; rond *m*; *persons*: cercle *m*; ✝ cartel *m*; *circus*: arène *f*; *box.* ring *m*; **~ binder** classeur *m* à anneaux; **~ road** rocade *f*, (boulevard *m*) périphérique *m*; **2.** baguer (*a finger, bird etc.*); (*usu.* **~ in** or **round** or **about**) entourer.

ring² 1. tintement *m*; coup *m* de sonnette; F coup *m* de téléphone; son *m* (*a. fig.*), *fig. a.* accent *m*; **2.** *v/i.* sonner; tinter (*a. ears*); (*oft.* **~ out**) résonner (**the, with**); *teleph.* **~ off** raccrocher; **the bell is ~ing** on sonne; *v/t.* (faire) sonner; **~ the bell** sonner; *v/t.* F *teleph.* donner un coup de téléphone à.

ring...: **~leader** meneur *m*; chef *m* de bande; **~let** *hair*: boucle *f*.

rink patinoire *f*; skating *m*.

rinse 1. rinçage *m*; **2.** rincer.

riot 1. émeute *f*, bagarres *f/pl.*; *fig.* orgie *f*, profusion *f* (*of colours etc.*); **~ squad** police *f* secoure; F *fig.* **read s.o. the ~ act** semoncer q.; **~ = 2.** faire une or des émeute(s); se livrer à des bagarres; **~er** émeutier *m*; **~ous** tumultueux; tapageur (*person*); dissolu (*life*).

rip 1. déchirure *f*; **~ cord** tirette *f* (*of a parachute*); **2.** *v/t.* déchirer; **~ off** arracher; F voler, F chiper; *v/i.* se déchirer; *mot.* F filer.

ripe mûr; fait (*cheese*); **~n** *vt/i.* mûrir; **~ness** maturité *f*.

rip-off F estampage *m*; vol *m*.

riposte 1. riposte *f*; **2.** riposter.

ripple 1. ride *f*; ondulation *f*; gazouillement *m*; murmure *m*; **2.** (se) rider; *v/i.* onduler; murmurer.

rise 1. *water, road*: montée *f*; *hill*: élévation *f*, hausse *f* (*a.* ✝, ♩); *sun, thea., curtain*: lever *m*; *water*: crue *f*; *prices etc.*: augmentation *f*; *rank*: avancement *m*; *river, a. fig.*: source *f*; **give ~ to** engendrer, faire naître, mener à; **take** (**one's**) **~** prendre sa source (**dans, in**); **2.** monter; se lever (*person, sun etc.*); s'élever (*building site*); se soulever (contre, **against**); prendre sa source (dans, **in**; à, **at**); **~ to the occasion** se montrer à la hauteur de la situation; **~r: be an early** (**a late**) **~** se lever tôt (tard).

rising montant; en hausse; *fig.* nouveau, jeun (*generation etc.*).

risk 1. risque *m*; **at ~** en danger; **at the ~ of** (*ger.*) au risque de (*inf.*); **run a** (or **the**) **~** courir un or le risque; **2.** risquer; **~y** risqué (*a. fig.*), hasardeux.

rit|e rite *m*; **~ual** rituel (*adj., su./m*).

rival 1. rival(e) *f*) *m*; concurrent(e) *f*) *m*; **2.** rival; ✝ concurrent; **3.** rivaliser (avec); **~ry** rivalité *f*; concurrence *f*.

riven fendu, déchiré.

river rivière *f*; *big one, a. fig.* fleuve *m*; **~ basin** bassin *m* fluvial; **~bank, ~side** rive *f*, berge *f*; *bord m* de la rivière *or* du fleuve; **~bed** lit *m* de rivière *or* de fleuve.

rivet 1. ⊕ rivet *m*; **2.** rive(te)r; *fig.* fixer (à, **to**; sur, [**up**]**on**).

rivulet ruisseau *m*.

road route *f* (de, **to**); *in town, village*: rue *f*; chemin *m* (*a. fig.*); voie *f* (*a. fig.*); F **hit the ~** se mettre en route; **on the ~** en route; *fig.* **on the ~ to** sur le chemin du (*success etc.*); **'~ up'** 'attention travaux'; **~block** barrage *m* (*a. fig.*); **~hog** *mot.* chauffard *m*; **~house** relais *m*; **~man** cantonnier *m*; **~ map** carte *f* routière; **~side** bord *m* de la route; **~way** chaussée *f*; **~worthy** en état de marche.

roam *v/i.* errer, rôder; *v/t.* parcourir.

roar 1. *v/i.* hurler; *v/i.* rugir; tonner; ronfler (*car, fire*); *v/t.* beugler (*a song*); **2.** hurlement *m*; rugissement *m*; éclat *m* (*of laughter*).

roast 1. (faire) rôtir; **2.** rôti; **~ beef** rôti *m* de bœuf; rosbif *m*.

rob voler (*q.*); dévaliser (*a bank*); **~ber** voleur (-euse *f*) *m*; **~bery** vol *m*.

robe robe *f* (*ceremony etc.*).

robin *orn.* rouge-gorge (*pl.* rouges-gorges) *m*.

robot robot *m*; automate *m*.

robust robuste; solide.

rock¹ rocher *m*; roc *m*, roche *f*; *Am. a.* pierre *f*.

rock² *v/t.* bercer; basculer; *v/i.* osciller; *vt/i.* balancer.

rocker bascule *f*; *Am. a.* rocking-chair *m*; F **off one's ~** cinglé.

rocket 1. fusée *f*; **2.** passer en trombe; (*a.* **~ up**) monter en flèche.

rock...: **~face** paroi *f* rocheuse; **~fall** chute *f* de pierres.

rocking...: ~ **chair** rocking-chair m; ~ **horse** cheval m à bascule.

rocky¹ rocailleux; rocheux.

rocky² branlant; chancelant.

rod baguette f; *curtain*: tringle f; ⊕ tige f; *sp.* canne f à pêche; *sl.* revolver m.

rodent rongeur m.

rodeo rodéo m.

roe¹ (*a.* **hard** ~) œufs m/pl. (*of fish*); **soft** ~ laite f, laitance f.

roe² chevreuil m; ~**buck** chevreuil m (mâle).

rogue coquin(e f) m; ~**ish** coquin.

role, rôle *thea.* rôle m (*a. fig.*).

roll 1. ⊕, *tex.*, *cloth*, *paper*: rouleau m; *banknotes*: liasse f; *typ.*, *phot.* bobine f; *cuis.* petit pain m; *drum*, *thunder*: roulement m; ♪ roulis m; *adm. etc.* liste f; ~ **call** appel m; ♪ 2. v/t. rouler; ♪ *laminer*; ~ **out** étendre (au rouleau); ~ **up** (en)rouler; ⊕ ~**ed gold** doublé m; v/i. rouler; couler (*tears*); gronder (*thunder*); ♪ rouler; ~ **up** s'enrouler; ~**er** rouleau m; roulette f; *tex.*, *paper*: calandre f; ♪ lame f de houle; *Am.* ~ **coaster** montagnes f/pl. russes; ~ **skate** patin m à roulettes.

rollicking joyeux; rigoleur.

rolling roulant; onduleux (*landscape*); houleux (*sea*); ⊕ ~ **mill** usine f de laminage; ~ **pin** rouau m à pâtisserie; ~ **stock** matériel m roulant.

roll...: ~**neck** col m roulé; ~**top desk** bureau m à cylindre.

roly-poly 1. *cuis.* rouleau m à la confiture; **2.** F grassouillet.

Roman 1. romain; ~ **Catholic** catholique (*adj.*, *su./mf*); **2.** Romain(e f) m.

romance 1. roman m (d'amour), idylle f; charme m, attrait m; ♪ romance f; **2.** 2 *ling.* roman (*language*).

Romanesque roman (*a. su./m*).

romantic romantique; romantique *mf*; ~**ism** romantisme m.

romp 1. gambades f/pl.; **2.** s'ébattre.

rood crucifix m.

roof 1. toit m; *tunnel etc.*: plafond m; *anat.* ~ **of the mouth** voûte f du palais; *mot.* ~ **rack** galerie f; **2.** (*oft.* ~ **over**) (re)couvrir d'un toit; ~**ing** toiture f; ~ **felt** carton-pierre m (*pl.* cartons-pierres) m.

rook 1. *chess*: tour f; *orn.* freux m; *fig.* escroc m; **2.** escroquer.

room *in building*: pièce f; salle f; (*a.* **bed**~) chambre f; *space*: place f, espace m; ~**s** *pl.* appartement m; **in my** ~ à ma place; ~ **and board** pension f (complète); ~**er** sous-locataire m; ~**ing house** hôtel m garni, maison f meublée; ~**mate** compagnon m (compagne f) de chambre; ~**y** spacieux; ample.

roost 1. juchoir m, perchoir m; **2.** se jucher, se percher; ~**er** coq m.

root¹ 1. racine f; **take** ~, **strike** ~ prendre racine; **2.** (s')enraciner; ~ **out** *fig.* extirper.

root² (*a.* ~ **about**) fouiller; ~ **for** encourager par des cris; F ~ **out** trouver, F dénicher.

rope 1. corde f; ♪ cordage m; *bell*: cordon m; ~ **ladder** échelle f de corde; *mount.* ~ **team** cordée f; **know the** ~**s** connaître son affaire; être au courant; **show s.o. the** ~**s** mettre q. au courant; ~**dancer** funambule *mf*; ~**way** funiculaire m.

rosary *eccl.* rosaire m; chapelet m.

rose ♀ rose f; *colour*: rose m (*a. adj.*); *watering-can*: pomme f; ~**bud** bouton m de rose; ~**bush** rosier m; ~ **colo(u)red** (couleur de) rose; *fig.* **look at** (*or* **see**) **the world through** ~ **glasses** (*or* **spectacles**) voir tout *or* la vie en rose; ~**hip** gratte-cul m/*inv.*; ~**mary** romarin m.

rosin colophane f.

rostrum tribune f.

rosy (de) rose; vermeil (*complexion*).

rot 1. pourriture f; ♪ carie f; F bêtises f/pl.; **2.** pourrir.

rota liste f; **on a** ~ **basis** par roulement, à tour de rôle; ~**ry** rotatif; ~**te** v/t. faire tourner *or* pivoter; faire (*qch.*) par roulement, alterner; v/i. tourner, pivoter; ~**tion** rotation f; **in** ~ à tour de rôle; ~**tory** rotatoire.

rotor ⊕, ⚡, ✈ *helicopter*: rotor m.

rotten pourri (*a. fig.*); gâté.

rotund rondelet (*person*); rond.

rouge rouge m, fard m.

rough 1. rêche, rugueux (*surface*, *skin*), rude (*surface*, *road*, *skin*, *voice*, *climate*, *treatment*, *work etc.*); brutal; *fig.* approximatif (*guess etc.*); ébauché (*plan etc.*); sommaire; ⊕ brut; *fig.* grossier, fruste (*manners*); **be** ~ **on s.o.** être un coup dur pour q. (*event etc.*); *be ~ with s.o.*, *give s.o. a ~ time* (*of it*) être dur avec q.; *~ and ready* primitif; grossier; sans façon (*person*); *~ draft* brouillon *m*; *at a ~ guess* approximativement; **2.** état *m* brut; terrain *m* accidenté; *person*: voyou *m*; **3.** *~ it* vivre à la dure; *~ out* esquisser, ébaucher; *usu. ~ up* malmener; **4.** brutalement, dur; F *cut up ~* se mettre en rogne; *sleep ~* coucher à la dure; **~age** matières *f/pl.* non digestibles; **~-and-tumble** lutte *f*, bagarre *f*; **~cast 1.** △ crépi; **2.** crépir (*a wall*); **~en** rendre *or* devenir rude.

rough...: **~hewn** taillé à coups de hache; dégrossi; *fig.* ébauché; **~ly** rudement; grossièrement; *fig.* approximativement, à peu près, environ; **~neck** F dur *m* (à cuire); **~ness** rudesse *f*; rugosité *f*; grossièreté *f*; **~shod: ride ~ over** fouler (*q.*) aux pieds.

round 1. rond; circulaire; *~ trip* aller *m* et retour *m*; **2.** *adv.* (tout) autour; (*oft. ~ about*) à l'entour; *all ~* tour autour; *fig.* sans exception; *all the year ~* (*pendant*) toute l'année; **3.** *prp.* (*oft. ~ about*) autour de; vers (*three o'clock*); environ; **4.** *su.* cercle *m*, rond *m* (*a.* △); *tennis, journey etc.*: tour *m*; *postman, doctor*: tournée *f*; *sp.* circuit *m*; *box.* round *m*; *applause etc.*: salve *f*; **5.** (s')arrondir; *v/t.* contourner; ⚓ doubler (*a cape*); *~ down* arrondir (au chiffre inférieur); *~ off* arrondir (*a figure, price etc.*); *fig.* achever; *~ up* rassembler; faire une rafle de (*criminals etc.*); arrondir (au chiffre supérieur); **~about 1.** indirect, détourné; **2.** détour *m*; *Br. mot.* rond--point, sens *m* giratoire; *Br.* manège *m*; **~ish** presque rond; **~trip** aller et retour (*ticket*); **~up** rassemblement *m*; rafle *f* (*of criminals etc.*).

rous|e (r)éveiller; susciter; activer; **~ing** enthousiaste.

rout 1. déroute *f*; *put to ~* = **2.** mettre en déroute; F *~ out* déloger, chasser.

route route *f*; itinéraire *m*.

routine 1. routine *f*; *fig.* train-train *m* (journalier); **2.** courant; ordinaire.

rov|e errer (dans); **~ing** vagabond.

row¹ rang *m*; rangée *f*; file *f* (*of cars, people etc.*); ligne *f* (*of houses etc.*); *~ house* maison *f* attenante aux maisons voisines.

row² **1.** ramer; faire du canotage; **2.** promenade *f* en canot.

row³ F **1.** vacarme *m*; chahut *m*; dispute *f*; F réprimande *f*; **2.** se quereller (avec, *with*).

rowan ⚘ sorbier *m*; *a.* **~berry** sorbe *f*.

row-boat bateau *m* à rames, canot *m*.

rowdy chahuteur *m*; voyou *m*.

rower rameur (-euse *f*) *m*.

rowing-boat = **row-boat**.

royal royal; **~ty** royauté *f*; *royalties pl.* droits *m/pl.* d'auteur.

rub 1. frottement *m*; friction *f*; coup *m* de torchon; F *there is the ~* c'est là le diable; **2.** *v/t.* frotter; frictionner; F *don't ~ it in!* n'insiste(z) pas!; *~ off* enlever *or* faire partir en frottant; *fig. ~ off on* déteindre sur; *~ out* effacer; *~ up the wrong way* prendre (*q.*) à rebrousse-poil; *v/i.: fig. ~ along* (*or on or through*) se débrouiller.

rubber caoutchouc *m*; *Br. a.* gomme *f* à effacer; *~ band* élastique *m*; *~ stamp* tampon *m*; **~neck** F **1.** badaud(e *f*) *m*; **2.** faire le badaud; **~-stamp** tamponner; *fig.* approuver sans discuter.

rubbish *Br. household*: ordures *f/pl.*; déchets *m/pl.*; *fig.* fatras *m*, camelote *f*; *fig.* bêtises *f/pl.*; *~ bin* boîte *f* à ordures; poubelle *f*; *~ dump* dépotoir *m*.

rubble décombres *m/pl.*

ruby *min.* rubis *m*.

rucksack sac *m* à dos.

ructions *pl.* F grabuge *m*.

rudder ⚓, ✈ gouvernail *m*.

ruddy rouge; rougeâtre; F sacré; *adv.* F vachement.

rude grossier; impoli, malélevé; brutal, brusque.

rudiment rudiment *m*; **~ary** rudimentaire.

rueful triste; plein de regret.

ruffian voyou *m*.

ruffle *v/t.* ébouriffer (*hair etc.*); froisser (*cloth, a. fig. a person*); irriter; troubler, agiter; *v/i.* s'ébouriffer; s'agiter.

rug couverture *f*; (*a. floor ~*) carpette *f*; descente *f* de lit.

rugged accidenté, déchiqueté; rude; solide, robuste.

ruin 1. ruine *f*; **2.** ruiner; abîmer; **~ous** ruineux.

rul|e 1. règle *f*; règlement *m*; (*a. standing ~*) règle *f* fixe; *pol.* gouvernement *m*, autorité *f*; **as a ~** en règle générale; *mot.* **~ of the road** code *m* de la route; **2.** *v/t.* gouverner; (*a.* **~ over**) régner sur; commander à; régler (*paper*); **~ out** éliminer; *v/i.* régner; **~er** souverain(e *f*) *m*; règle *f*.

rum 1. rhum *m*; **2.** étrange.

Rumanian 1. roumain *m*; **2.** *ling.* roumain *m*; Roumain(e *f*) *m*.

rumble 1. *thunder*: grondement *m*; *stomach*: grouillement *m*; *sl.* bagarre *f*; **2.** gronder; gargouiller.

rumbustious F exubérant.

rumina|nt ruminant (*a. su./m*); **~te** ruminer (*a. fig.*); *fig.* **a.** méditer.

rummage 1. fouille *f*; (*usu.* **~ goods** *pl.*) choses *f/pl.* de rebut; **~ sale** vente *f* de charité; **have a ~** (far)fouiller; **2.** *v/t.* (far)fouiller; *v/i.* fouiller (pour trouver, **for**).

rumo(u)r 1. rumeur *f*; **2. it is ~ed that** bruit court que.

rump *anat.* croupe *f*.

rumple froisser, chiffonner; ébouriffer (*hair*).

rumpus F tapage *m*; querelle *f*, prise *f* de bec; **kick up a ~** *a.* faire un scandale; **~ room** salle *f* de jeux.

rumpsteak *cuis.* rumsteck *m*.

run 1. *v/i. usu.* courir; passer; couler (*liquid*); glisser (*slide etc.*); *mot.* aller, rouler, marcher (*a.* ⊕); faire le service (*bus, train*); ⊕ fonctionner; s'écouler (*time*); couler (*river, ⊕ a. colour*); se démailler (*stocking*); *thea.* se donner (*play, film etc.*); **~ across s.o.** rencontrer *q.* par hasard; **~ away** se sauver, s'échapper; **~ down** descendre en courant; s'arrêter (*watch etc.*); *fig.* décliner; **~ dry** se dessécher; **~ for** *parl.* se porter candidat à *or* pour; **~ high** s'échauffer (*sentiments*); **~ into** rentrer dans (= *hit*); rencontrer (*q.*) par hasard; s'élever à (*a figure*); **~ low** baisser; s'épuiser; **~ off** se sauver; **~ on** continuer; *print.* **~ out** s'épuiser; **~ out of** manquer de; **I have ~ out of tobacco** *a.* je n'ai plus de tabac; **~ short of** être à court de; **~ through** parcourir du regard; aboutir (*a fortune*); **~ to** se monter à, s'élever à (*a sum*); **~ up** s'accumuler; **~ up against** se heurter à; **2.** *v/t.* courir (*a distance*); (faire) passer (qch. sur, à travers *etc.* **s.th. over, through etc.**); faire couler

(*water*); faire courir (*q., an animal etc.*); diriger (*a ship, a train*) (sur, **to**); assurer le service de (*a ship, a bus*); ⊕ faire marcher *or* fonctionner (*a machine etc.*); avoir (*a car*); diriger (*a hotel, a shop etc.*); tenir (*a shop, a household*); éditer (*a newspaper etc.*); passer en contrebande (= *smuggle*); **~ down** renverser; *fig.* dénigrer; F attraper; **be ~ down** être à plat; être épuisé; **~ errands** faire des courses *or* commissions; **~ in** *mot. etc.* roder; F arrêter (*a criminal*); **~ on** faire suivre; **~ over** écraser (*q.*); parcourir (*a text*); **~ s.o. through** transpercer *q.*; **~ up** faire monter; *fig.* faire accumuler; bâtir à la va-vite (*a new building*); **3.** course *f*; *mot.* tour *m*; ⚓ traversée *f*; ☃ *etc.* trajet *m*; ⊕ marche *f*; *fig.* cours *m*; suite *f*; ✝ ruée *f* (sur, [up]on); petit ruisseau *m*; *stockings*: échelle *f*; *cards*: séquence *f*; **be on the ~** être à courir, être en fuite; **the common ~** le commun, l'ordinaire; **in the long ~** à la longue; **in the short ~** ne songeant qu'au présent; **have the ~ of** avoir libre accès à.

run...: **~about** *mot.* voiturette *f*; (*a.* **~ car**) petite auto *f*; **~away 1.** fugitif (-ive *f*) *m*; **2.** fugitif; qui c'est échappé *or* enfui *or* sauvé *fig.* galopant (*inflation etc.*); **~down** épuisé; ruiné; délabré; **~down** F compte *m* rendu (minutieux).

rung échelon *m*; *ladder*: traverse *f*.

run-in F querelle *f*, prise *f* de bec.

runner coureur (-euse *f*) *m*; *sledge*: patin *m*; *drawer*: coulisseau *m*; **~up** *sp.* second(e *f*) *m*.

running 1. courant; **two days ~** deux jours de suite; **~ commentary** commentaire *m* suivi; **in ~ order** en état de marche; **~ hand** écriture *f* cursive; **2.** course *f*; fonctionnement *m*, marche *f*; *company etc.*: direction *f*, gestion *f*; **make the ~** mener la course.

run-of-the-mill ordinaire; banal; médiocre.

runt avorton *m*.

run-up période *f* préparatoire.

runway ✈ piste *f*.

rupture 1. rupture *f*; 🩺 hernie *f*; **2.** (se) rompre.

rural rural; de (la) campagne.

ruse ruse *f*.

rush¹ 🌿 jonc *m*.

rush² 1. course *f* précipitée; ruée *f*; hâte *f*; ~ *hours* pl. heures *f*/pl. d'affluence; ~ *job* travail *m* d'urgence *or* fait à la va-vite; 2. *v*/*i*. se précipiter, s'élancer (sur, *at*); se jeter; F ~ *to conclusions* conclure trop hâtivement; *v*/*t*. transporter *or* expédier d'urgence; faire à la hâte; presser (*q.*, *qch.*), bousculer (*q.*); ✕ *etc.* prendre d'assaut; *sl.* faire payer (*q.*), estamper.

russet roussâtre.

Russian 1. russe; 2. *ling.* russe *m*; Russe *mf.*

rust 1. rouille *f*; 2. (se) rouiller.

rustic 1. rustique; 2. rustre *m*.

rustle 1. (faire) bruire; *v*/*t.* a. froisser; *Am.* F voler; F ~ *up* trouver *or* faire à la hâte; 2. frou-frou *m*; froissement *m*.

rust...: ~*proof* inoxydable; ~*y* rouillé.

rut ornière *f* (*a. fig.*); *zo.* rut *m*.

ruthless impitoyable.

rye ♀ seigle *m*.

S

sabotage 1. sabotage *m*; 2. saboter.

sack¹ 1. pillage *m*; 2. piller, mettre à sac.

sack² 1. sac *m*; F *get the* ~ se faire renvoyer *or* F vider; F *give s.o. the* ~ = 2. renvoyer, F vider (*q.*); F *hit the* ~ (aller) se coucher *or* F se pieuter; ~*cloth*, ~*ing* toile *f* à sac.

sacrament *eccl.* sacrement *m*.

sacred sacré; saint.

sacrifice 1. sacrifice *m*; ✝ *at a* ~ à perte; 2. sacrifier.

sacrileg|e sacrilège *m*; ~*ious* sacrilège.

sacrosanct sacrosaint.

sad triste; ~*den** attrister.

saddle 1. selle *f*; 2. (*a.* ~ *up*) seller; *fig.* encombrer (de, *with*).

sadis|m sadisme *m*; ~*t** sadique *mf*; ~*tic** sadique; ~*ally** avec sadisme.

sadness tristesse *f.*

safe 1. en sécurité (contre, *from*), à l'abri (de, *from*), hors de danger; sûr (*method etc.*); sans danger; sans risque; ~ *and sound* sain et sauf; *to be on the* ~ *side* par précaution; 2. coffre-fort (pl. coffres-forts) *m*; *cuis.* garde-manger *m*/*inv.*; ~*breaker*, ~*cracker* crocheteur *m* de coffres-forts; ~*conduct* sauf-conduit *m*; ~*guard* 1. sauvegarde *f*; 2. sauvegarder, protéger; ~ *keeping* garde *f*; ~*ly* sans risque; sans accident; *arrive* ~ arriver sain et sauf; ~*ness* sûreté *f*; sécurité *f.*

safety sûreté *f*; sécurité *f*; ~ *belt* ceinture *f* de sécurité; ~ *curtain thea.* rideau *m*

de fer; ~ *glass* verre *m* Sécurit (*TM*); ~ *island* refuge; ~ *pin* épingle *f* de nourrice; ~ *net* filet *m* de protection; ~ *razor* rasoir *m* de sûreté; ~ *valve* soupape *f* de sûreté.

saffron safran *m* (*a. colour*).

sag fléchir; s'affaisser; pendre.

sagacious sagace, avisé.

sage¹ 1. sage, prudent; 2. sage *m*.

sage² ♀ sauge *f.*

sagittarius *astr.* le Sagittaire *m*.

sail 1. voile *f*; tour *m* en bateau; *windmill:* aile *f*; *set* ~ prendre la mer; *set* ~ *for* partir pour; 2. *v*/*i.* naviguer; aller (en bateau); *under* ~ à la voile; planer (*in the air*); *fig.* ~ *into* attaquer; ~ *through* réussir haut la main; *v*/*t.* piloter; manœuvrer (*a boat*); parcourir *or* traverser (en bateau) (*the sea etc.*); ~*boat* bateau *m* à voiles; ~*cloth* toile *f* à voile, canevas *m*; ~*er ship:* voilier *m*; ~*ing sp.* la voile *f*; départ *m*; ~ *boat* bateau *m* à voiles; ~*ing sp.* voilier *m*; *fig.* *be plain* ~ aller sans anicroches *or* accrocs; ~*or* marin *m*; matelot *m*; *be a good* (*bad*) ~ (ne pas) avoir le pied marin; ~*plane* ✈ planeur *m*.

saint saint(e *f*) *m*; ~*ly adj.* (de) saint; plein de bonté (*smile*).

sake: *for the* ~ *of* pour; dans l'intérêt de; *for my* ~ pour moi; *for God's* ~ pour l'amour de Dieu.

salad salade *f.*

salary traitement *m*; salaire *m*.

sale vente f; (a. public ~) vente f aux enchères; for ~ à vendre; on ~ en vente; **~able** vendable; de vente facile.

sales...: ~clerk vendeur (-euse f) m; **~girl** vendeuse f; **~man** vendeur m; représentant m (de commerce); **~manship** l'art de vendre; **~woman** vendeuse f.

salient saillant.

saliva salive f.

sallow[1] ♀ saule m.

sallow[2] jaunâtre, cireux.

sally 1. ✕ sortie f; fig. saillie f (of wit); 2. (a. ~ out) faire une sortie.

salmon saumon m (a. colour).

saloon salon m, Am. bar m; mot. berline f.

salt 1. sel m; ~ cellar, ~ shaker salière f; 2. salé, de sel; 3. saler; **~free** sans sel; **~petre**, Am. **~peter** ♣ salpêtre m, nitre m; **~y** salé; de sel.

salubrious salubre, sain.

salutary salutaire (à, to).

salut|ation salutation f; **~e** 1. salut m; 2. saluer (a. ✕, ♣).

salvage 1. sauvetage m; objets m/pl. sauvés; 2. récupérer.

salvation salut m (a. fig.); ♀ Army Armée f du Salut.

salve 1. usu. fig. baume m; 2. usu. fig. adoucir; calmer.

salvo ✕ salve f (a. fig.).

same: the ~ le (la) même; les mêmes pl.; all the ~ tout de même; it is all the ~ to me ça m'est égal; cela ne me fait rien; F (the) ~ again! la même chose!

sample 1. esp. ♦ échantillon m; blood, ore etc.: prélèvement m; 2. échantillonner; fig. goûter.

sanatorium sanatorium m.

sanct|ify sanctifier; **~imonious** moralisateur; **~ion** 1. sanction f; 2. sanctionner; **~ity** sainteté f; caractère m sacré; **~uary** sanctuaire m; asile m.

sand 1. sable m; sl. cran m (= courage); **~s** pl. (étendue f de) sable; 2. de sable; sablé; 3. sabler.

sandal sandale f.

sand...: ~box tas m de sable; **~hill** dune f; **~man** marchand m de sable; **~paper** papier m de verre; **~piper** zo. bécasseau m; **~pit** tas m de sable; **~stone** grès m.

sandwich 1. sandwich m; ham etc. ~ sandwich m au jambon etc.; 2. (a. ~ in) serrer, coincer; insérer, intercaler.

sandy sabl(onn)eux; sablé; blond roux (hair).

sane sain d'esprit; sensé; sain (judgement).

sanguin|ary sanglant; **~e** confiant, optimiste.

sanitary hygiénique; sanitaire; ~ towel, ~ napkin serviette f hygiénique.

sanit|ation installations f/pl. sanitaires; système m sanitaire; salubrité f publique; **~y** santé f d'esprit; bon sens m.

Santa Claus Père m or bonhomme m Noël.

sap 1. ♀ sève f (a. fig.); sl. idiot(e f) m; 2. saper; **~less** sans sève; sans vigueur; **~ling** jeune arbre m, fig. jeune homme m.

sapphire min. saphir m.

sappy plein de sève; sl. nigaud.

sarcas|m sarcasme m; **~tic** sarcastique.

sardine icht. sardine f.

sash châssis m (of a window); ceinture f; écharpe f; ~ window fenêtre f à guillotine.

satchel cartable m.

sateen satinette f.

satellite satellite m (a. fig.); ~ country (town) pays m (cité f) satellite.

satiate rassasier (de, with).

satin tex. satin m.

satir|e satire f; **~ical** satirique; **~ist** satirique m; **~ize** satiriser.

satisfact|ion satisfaction f (de at, with); acquittement m; promise: exécution f; réparation f (of an insult); **~ory** satisfaisant.

satisfy satisfaire, contenter; satisfaire à (conditions etc.); convaincre, assurer.

saturat|e saturer (de, with); **~ion:** (~ point point m de) saturation f.

Saturday samedi m.

sauce sauce f; **~pan** casserole f; **~r** soucoupe f.

saucy F effronté, impertinent.

sauna sauna m or f.

saunter flâner; se balader.

sausage saucisse f; saucisson m.

savage 1. féroce; brutal; sauvage; 2. attaquer (férocement); **~ry** sauvagerie f; férocité f.

save 1. v/t. sauver; économiser, épargner, mettre de côté (money); (faire) gagner (time); garder; éviter, épargner (qch. à q., s.o. s.th.; à q. de faire, s.o. [from] doing); 2. v/i. (a. ~ up) faire des économies, épargner; **~ up for** mettre de l'argent de côté pour; **~ on** économiser; 3. *prp.* excepté, sauf; 4. *cj.* **~ that** excepté que; **~r † F** épargnant(e *f*) *m*; *fig.* économiseur *m* (*of time etc.*).

saving 1. économique; économe (*person*); *fig.* **~ grace** qualité qui rachète les défauts (*de q. or qch.*); 2. épargne *f*; **~s** *pl.* économies *f/pl.*

savings...: **~ account** compte *m* d'épargne; **~ bank** caisse *f* d'épargne; **~ deposit** dépôt *m* à la caisse d'épargne.

savio(u)r sauveur *m*.

savo(u)r 1. saveur *f*; goût *m*; 2. *v/i. fig.* **~ of** sentir (*qch.*); *v/t.* savourer; **~y** savoureux; salé, piquant.

savvy *sl.* jugeote *f*.

saw¹ adage *m*; dicton *m*.

saw² 1. scie *f*; 2. scier; **~dust** sciure *f*; **~mill** scierie *f*.

say 1. dire; *that is to* ~ c'est-à-dire; *you don't* ~ *so!* pas possible!, vraiment!; *I* ~! dites donc!; *he is said to be rich* on dit qu'il est riche; on le dit riche; *no sooner said than done* sitôt dit, sitôt fait; 2. mot *m*, parole *f*; *it is my* ~ *now* maintenant à moi la parole; *have one's* ~ dire son mot; *have a* (*no*) ~ *in the matter* (ne pas) avoir voix au chapitre; **~ing** dicton *m*, proverbe *m*; *it goes without* ~ cela va sans dire.

scab *wound:* croûte *f*; *vet. etc.* gale *f*; *sl.* jaune *m*; **~by** croûteux; galeux; *sl.* moche; **~ies** **⚕** gale *f*.

scabrous scabreux.

scads *pl.* F **~ of** beaucoup de, F un *or* des tas de.

scaffold **⚖** échafaud *m*; **△** échafaudage *m*; **~ing** échafaudage *m*.

scald 1. ébouillanter, échauder; faire chauffer (*milk*); 2. brûlure *f*.

scale¹ *fish, reptile:* écaille *f*; **⊕** tartre *m*; 2. (s')écailler.

scale² 1. balance *f*; 2. peser.

scale³ 1. échelle *f*; **♩, ♪** gamme *f*; *etc.* barème *m*; *on a large* (*small*) ~ sur une grande (petite) échelle, en grand (petit); 2. escalader (*a wall etc.*); **~ down** réduire; **~ up** augmenter.

scallop 1. coquille *f* (Saint-Jaques); 2. *cost.* festonner.

scalp 1. cuir *m* chevelu; scalper; **~el** scalpel *m*.

scamp 1. coquin(e *f*) *m*; 2. bâcler; **~er** galoper; **~ away**, **~ off** détaler.

scan scruter; promener son regard sur; *read quickly:* parcourir; **⊕** balayer (*beams etc.*); *poetry:* scander (*verses*).

scandal scandale *m*; ragots *m/pl.*, cancans *m/pl.*; **~ize** scandaliser; **~ous** scandaleux.

Scandinavian 1. scandinave; 2. Scandinave *mf*.

scant, ~y insuffisant.

scapegoat bouc *m* émissaire.

scar 1. cicatrice *f*; balafre *f*; 2. *v/t.* laisser une cicatrice sur; marquer d'une cicatrice; balafrer; *v/i.* **~ over** (se) cicatriser.

scarce rare; peu abondant; F *make o.s.* ~ s'éclipser; **~ely** à peine; (ne) guère; **~ity** rareté *f*; manque *m*.

scare 1. effrayer; faire peur à (*q.*); epouvanter; *be* **~d** avoir peur (de, *of*); 2. peur *f*, frousse *f*; panique *f*; **~crow** épouvantail *m*; **~monger** alarmiste *mf*.

scarf écharpe *f*; foulard *m*.

scarlet écarlate (*a. su./f*); **⚕** ~ *fever* (fièvre *f*) scarlatine *f*; **♀** ~ *runner* haricot *m* d'Espagne.

scary Feffroyable, qui donne la frousse (*thing*); peureux, timide (*person*).

scathing *fig.* mordant, caustique.

scatter (se) disperser; (s')éparpiller; (se) répandre; (se) dissiper; **~brained** écervelé; **~ed** épars; isolé (*rainshowers etc.*).

scavenger éboueur *m*, balayeur *m*.

scenario *cin., thea.* scénario *m*.

scene scène *f*; *fig. a.* lieu(x) *m/pl.* (*of an event*); paysage *m*; spectacle *m*; *fig.* **be-hind the** **~s** dans les coulisses; **~ry** décors *m/pl.*, scène *f*; paysage *m*, vue *f*.

scenic scénique; *fig.* pittoresque (*road etc.*); ~ *car* voiture *f* panoramique.

scent 1. parfum *m*; odeur *f*; odorat *m*; *hunt.* vent *m*; piste *f* (*a. fig.*); 2. parfumer; (*oft.* ~ *out*) flairer; **~less** inodore.

sceptic sceptique *mf*; **~al** sceptique; *be* ~ *about* douter de.

scept|re, *Am.* **~er** sceptre *m*.

schedule 1. programme *f*; plan *m*; liste *f*; horaire *m*; *according to* ~ comme prévu; *ahead of* ~ avant le moment *or* l'heure prévu(e); *be ahead of* ~ être en avance; *behind* ~ avec du retard; *be behind* ~ être en retard; *on* ~ être à l'heure; au moment prévu; 2. prévoir;

⤳ ~d flight vol *m* de ligne, vol *m* régulier.

schem|e 1. plan *m*; projet *m*; système *m*; arrangement *m*; **2.** comploter; combiner (de, **to**); **~ing** *pej.* **1.** intrigant; **2.** machinations *f/pl.*

schism schisme *m*; *fig.* division *f.*

scholar savant *m*; érudit(e *f*) *m*; *univ.* boursier (-ère *f*) *m*; **~ly** *adj.* savant; **~ship** érudition *f*, science *f*; *univ.* bourse *f* (d'études).

scholastic scolaire; *fig.* pédant; *phls.* scolastique (*a. su./m*).

school 1. école *f*; académie *f*; **at** ~ à l'école; **put to** ~ envoyer à l'école; **2.** instruire; habituer; discipliner; **~boy** écolier *m*, élève *m*; **~fellow**, **~mate** camarade *mf* de classe; **~girl** élève *f*, écolière *f*; **~ing** instruction *f*, éducation *f.*

school...: ~leaver jeune *mf* qui a terminé ses études scolaires; **~master** *primary school*: maître *m*; *secondary school*: professeur *m*; **~mistress** *primary school*: institutrice *f*; *secondary school*: professeur *m*; **~room** (salle *f* de) classe *f.*

schooner goélette *f*; verre *f* (à boire).

sciatica sciatique *f.*

science science *f.*

scientific scientifique.

scientist homme *m* de science; savant *m.*

scintillate scintiller, étinceler.

scissors *pl.*: (**a pair of** des) ciseaux *m/pl.*

scoff 1. sarcasme *m*; **2.** se moquer (de, **at**); *Br. sl. a.* bouffer (= *eat*).

scold 1. mégère *f*; **2.** gronder.

scon(e) *cuis.* galette *f* au lait.

scoop 1. pelle *f* à main; *Ⓣ* rafle *f*, coup *m*; *journ.* nouvelle *f* sensationnelle; **2.** ramasser (*a.* ~ **up**); *fig.* devancer (*q.*), *fig.* s'emparer de; (*a.* ~ **out**) écoper (*water*); vider; creuser.

scooter trottinette *f*; scooter *m.*

scope envergure *f*; portée *f*; cadre *m*, limites *f/pl.*; place, possibilité(s) *f/(pl.)*.

scorch *v/t.* roussir, brûler; *v/i.* F mot. brûler le pavé.

score¹ 1. *sp. etc.* score *m*, nombre *m* de points; *Ⓣ* partition *f*; (*a.* ~ **mark**) éraflure *f*, entaille *f*; **on the** ~ **of** en raison de; **on that** ~ à cet égard; **what's the** ~? *sp.* où en est le jeu?, *fig.* qu'est-ce qu'il y a?; **know the** ~? être au courant; *fig.* **settle a(n old)** ~ régler un compte; **2.** *v/t. sp.* marquer (*a goal, hit etc.*), *fig.* remporter (*a success*); F obtenir; *Ⓣ* composer, écrire, inciser, érafler; ~ **out** rayer; *v/i. sp.* marquer (un but *or* des buts), marquer un point *or* des points; mettre dans le mille (*a. fig.*); *fig.* avoir du succès.

score² 2 vingtaine *f*; **three** ~ soixante.

scorn 1. mépris *m*, dédain *m*; **2.** mépriser, dédaigner; **~ful** méprisant.

Scorpio *astr.* le Scorpion *m.*

scorpion *zo.* scorpion *m.*

Scot Écossais(e *f*) *m*; *hist.* Scot *m.*

Scotch 1. écossais *f*; ~ **tape** (*TM*) scotch *m* (*TM*), **2.** *ling.* écossais *m*; *Ⓣ* whisky *m*; écossais, scotch *m*; **the** ~ *pl.* les Écossais *m/pl.*; **~man** Écossais *m.*

scot-free indemne.

Scots, ~man *see* **Scotch(man).**

scoundrel scélérat *m*; vaurien *m.*

scour¹ nettoyer; frotter; récurer (*a pan*); décaper (*a metallic surface*).

scour² parcourir; battre (*a region*) (à la recherche de, **for**).

scourge fléau *m*; **2.** affliger.

scout 1. *✕ etc.* éclaireur *m*; reconnaissance *f*, **Boy ⓈS** *pl.* (boys-)scouts *m/pl.*; **2.** aller en reconnaissance; ~ **for** chercher.

scowl 1. air *m* renfrogné; **2.** se renfrogner.

scrabble chercher à tâtons.

scraggy décharné; famélique.

scram F filer le camp, filer.

scramble 1. monter *etc.* à quatre pattes; se bousculer (pour avoir qch., **for s.th.**); **~d eggs** *pl.* œufs *m/pl.* brouillés; **2.** marche *f etc.* difficile; *fig.* ruée *f*, lutte *f.*

scrap¹ 1. bagarre *f*; **get into** *or* **have a** ~ = se bagarrer.

scrap² 1. (petit) morceau *m*, bout *m*; fragment *m*; (*a.* ~ **iron**) ~**s** *pl.* restes *m/pl.*; déchets *m/pl.*; ~ **merchant** marchand *m* de ferraille; *fig.* (**throw**) **on the** ~ (mettre) au rancart, (jeter) au rebut; **2.** mettre à la casse *or* la ferraille; *a. fig.* mettre au rancart; **~book** album *m.*

scrap|e 1. grattement *m*; éraflure *f*; **2.** gratter; érafler; (*a.* ~ **along**, ~ **past**) frôler; **~er** grattoir *m*, racloir *m.*

scrappy mal fait; incomplet; F querelleur, batailleur.

scrapyard chantier *m* de ferraille; *for cars*: cimetière *m* de voitures.

scratch 1. coup *m* d'ongle *or* de griffe; égratignure *f*; *polished surface*: rayure *f*; *fig.* **start from** ~ partir à zéro; *fig.* **up to** ~ à la hauteur, au niveau voulu; **2.** improvisé; **3.** *v/t.* gratter; égratigner; donner un coup de griffe à; ~ **out** rayer; *v/i.* gratter; grincer.

scrawl 1. griffonner; **2.** griffonnage *m*.

scrawny *Am.* F décharné.

scream 1. cri *m* perçant; F **he is a** ~ il est tordant; **2.** crier.

scree éboulis *m*.

screech 1. cri *m* strident; crissement *m*; **2.** crier, hurler; crisser, grincer.

screen 1. ✕, *cin.*, *radar*, *a. furniture*: écran *m*; (*a.* **draught** ~) paravent *m*; scrible *m*; *fig.* rideau *m*; **on the** ~ à l'écran; ~ **advertising** publicité *f* à l'écran; *mot.*: ~ **wiper** essuie-glace *m*; **2.** abriter, protéger; voiler; dérober (a, **from**); *cin.* mettre à l'écran; tamiser; *a. fig.* filtrer; ~**play** *cin.* scénario *m*.

screw 1. vis *f*; **2.** ⚓ hélice *f*; visser; V baiser; ~ **up** visser; plisser (*one's eyes*); pincer (*one's lips*); ~**ball** dingue *mf*; ~**driver** tournevis *m*.

scribble 1. griffonnage *m*, gribouillage *m*; **2.** griffonner, gribouiller.

script écriture *f*; *cin.* scénario *m*; *univ.* copie *f*.

Scripture Écriture *f* sainte.

scroll *paper*: rouleau *m*; △, *violin*: volute *f*.

scrounge F *v/t.* se faire payer (*qch.*) (par **off**, **s.o.**); chiper; *v/i.* ~ **on** vivre aux crochets de (*q.*); ~**r** parasite *mf*.

scrub 1. broussailles *f/pl.*; nettoyage *m* à la brosse; F personne *f* rabougrie; **2.** nettoyer à la brosse; frotter; récurer (*pans etc.*); F abandonner, laisser tomber; ~**by** rabougri; couvert de broussailles; ~**woman** femme *f* de ménage.

scrup|le scrupule *m*; ~**ulous** scrupuleux.

scrutin|ize scruter; examiner à fond; ~**y** examen *m* minutieux.

scuba scaphandre *m* autonome; ~ **diving** plongée *f* sous-marine autonome.

scud courir, fuir.

scuff 1. éraflure *f*; **2.** (s')érafler.

scuffle rixe *f*, mêlée *f*; bagarre *f*.

scull ⚓ aviron *m*; godille *f*.

scullery arrière-cuisine *f*.

sculptor sculpteur *m*.

sculpture 1. sculpture *f*; **2.** sculpter.

scum écume *f*, *pej.* rebut *m*, lie; *single person*: salaud(e *f*) *m*.

scurf pellicules *f/pl.* (*on the scalp*).

scurrilous heineux; grossier.

scurry aller à pas précipités.

scurvy 🟥 scorbut *m*.

scuttle 1. seau *m* à charbon; ⚓ écoutille *f*; **2.** *v/t.* ⚓ saborder; *v/i.* filer; ~ **away**, ~ **off** détaler.

scythe 🗡 **1.** faux *f*; **2.** faucher.

sea 1. mer *f*; *fig.* océan *m*; lame *f*; **at** ~ en mer; F *fig.* **be all at** ~ être perdu *or* déboussolé, nager; **by** ~ par mer; **put to** ~ prendre la mer; **2.** de mer; maritime; naval; ~**board** littoral *m*; rivage *m*; ~ **faring** de mer; ~ **man** marin *m*; ~**food(s** *pl.*) fruits *m/pl.* de mer; ~**front** (quartier *m* au) bord *m* de la mer; ~**going** de haute mer.

seal¹ *zo.* phoque *m*.

seal² 1. *bottle*, *letter*: cachet *m*; *document*: sceau *m*; plomb *m*; ⊕ joint *m* étanche; **2.** sceller; cacheter; ~ **up** fermer hermétiquement.

sea level niveau *m* de la mer.

seam 1. couture *f*; *min.* filon *m*, veine *f*; *geol.* couche *f*; **2.** faire une couture à.

seaman marin *m*, matelot *m*.

seam...: ~**less** sans couture; ~**y** désagréable.

sea...: ~**plane** hydravion *m*; ~**port** port *m* de mer; ~**power** puissance *f* navale.

sear dessécher; brûler; cautériser.

search 1. recherche *f* (de, **for**); *admin.* visite *f*; *police*: perquisition *f*; fouille *f*; **in** ~ **of** à la recherche de; **2.** *v/t.* chercher dans; fouiller dans; ~ **out** découvrir, trouver; *fig.* scruter; *v/i.* faire des recherches; ~ **after**, ~ **for** rechercher; ~ **through** fouiller; ~**ing** minutieux; pénétrant (*look*, *wind*); ~**light** projecteur *m*.

sea...: ~**shore** rivage *m*; côte *f*; ~**sick**: **be** ~ avoir le mal de mer; ~**sickness** mal *m* de mer; ~**side** bord *m* de la mer; ~ **resort** plage *f*; bains *m/pl.* de mer.

season 1. saison *f*; **height of the** ~ (pleine) saison *f*; *cherries are in* ~ c'est la saison des cerises; **out of** ~ hors de saison; *2's Greetings!* meilleurs souhaits de nouvel *etc.*; **2.** *v/t.* dessécher (*tim-*

ber); *cuis.*, *fig.* assaisonner, relever; *v/i.* se sécher (*timber*); mûrir; **~able** de (la) saison; opportun; **~al** saisonnier; **~ing** *cuis.* assaisonnement *m*; **~ ticket** carte *f* d'abonnement.

seat 1. siège *m*; *thea.*, *bus*: place *f*; *pants*: fond *m*; **take a ~** s'asseoir; **2.** (faire) asseoir; placer; avoir des places assises pour (*public etc.*); **~ed** assis; **~ belt** ceinture *f* de sécurité.

sea...: **~water** eau *f* de mer; **~weed** ♂ algue *f*; varech *m*; **~worthy** en état de naviguer.

secede se séparer (de, *from*).

seclu|ded retiré; isolé, à l'écart; **~sion** solitude *f*, isolement *m*.

second 1. second; deuxième; **on ~ thoughts** toute réflexion faite; **2.** *arrive etc.*: en deuxième (position); **3.** *unit of time*: seconde *f*; le (la) second(e *f*) *m* or deuxième *mf*; *box.* second *m*; **♀** article *m* de deuxième choix; **4.** seconder; appuyer (*a proposition*); **~ary** secondaire; **~hand** d'occasion; **~ bookseller** bouquiniste *mf*; **~ly** en second lieu; deuxièmement; **~rate** inférieur; de qualité inférieure.

secre|cy discrétion *f*; secret *m*; **in ~** en (or dans le) secret; **~t 1.** secret; **2.** secret *m*; **in ~** en secret; **be in the ~** être au courant.

secretary secrétaire *mf*; **♀ of State** ministre *m*; *Am.* ministre *m* des Affaires étrangères.

secre|te *physiol.* sécréter; cacher; **~ion** *physiol.* sécrétion *f*, **~ive** dissimulé, cachottier.

sect secte *f*; **~arian** sectaire.

section 1. section *f*; coupe *f*; *typ.* paragraphe *m*; *town:* quartier *m*; sectionner.

secular séculier; laïque.

secure 1. sûr; assuré; en sûreté; à l'abri (de *against*, *from*); ferme; **2.** mettre en sûreté *or* à l'abri (de *from*, *against*); fixer, attacher, obtenir, se procurer.

security sûreté *f*; **♀** *for loan etc.*: garantie *f*, caution *f*, **securities** *pl.* valeurs *f/pl.*, titres *f/pl.*; **2.** conseil, forces *etc.* de sécurité.

sedan limousine *f*; (*a.* **~ chair**) chaise *f* à porteurs.

seda|te 1. calme, posé; **2. ♂** mettre sous sédation; **~ion** sédation *f*; **~ive** sédatif; calmant (*a. su./m*).

sedentary sédentaire.

sediment sédiment *m*, dépôt *m*.

sediti|on sédition *f*; **~ous** séditieux.

seduc|e séduire; **~tion** séduction *f*; **~tive** séduisant, séducteur.

sedulous assidu.

see¹ *v/i.* voir; *fig.* comprendre; *I ~* je comprends; **~ about** s'occuper de; **~ through s.o.** pénétrer les intentions de q.; **~ to** s'occuper de; *v/t.* voir; visiter; accompagner; consulter (*a doctor*); comprendre; **go to ~ s.o.** aller voir q.; rendre visite à q.; **~ s.o. home** accompagner q. chez lui; **~ off** reconduire (*a guest to the station*); **~ out** accompagner (q.) jusqu'à la porte; **~ through** mener (*qch.*) à bonne fin; **~ that** veiller à ce que, s'assurer que, prendre soin que (*sbj.*).

see² évêché *m*; archevêché *m*.

seed 1. grain(e *f*) *m*; *apple etc.*: pépin *m*; *fig.* germe; **go** (*or run*) **to ~** monter en graine (*plant*); **2.** se décatir; **2.** *v/t.* ensemencer; enlever la graine de (*a fruit*); **~ed players** têtes *f/pl.* de série; *v/i.* monter en graine; **~ling** ♂ (jeune) plant *m*; **~y** F minable; indisposé.

seeing: **~ that** étant donné, puisque.

seek (*a.* **~ after, for**) (re)chercher.

seem sembler; paraître; **~ingly** apparemment; **~ly** convenable.

seep (s'in)filtrer; suinter.

seer voyant(e *f*) *m*, prophète *m*.

seesaw 1. bascule *f*; **2.** *fig.* balancer, osciller.

seethe bouillonner; bouillir.

segment 1. segment *m*; **2.** (se) segmenter.

segregat|e (se) séparer; **~ion** ségrégation *f*.

seiz|e *v/t.* saisir; attraper; s'emparer de; *th, admin.* confisquer; **~** (*up*)**on** saisir, profiter de; **⊕ ~ up so** gripper; s'immobiliser; **~ure** saisie *f*.

seldom *adv.* peu souvent, rarement.

select 1. choisir; sélectionner; trier; **2.** sélect; choisi; d'élite; **~ion** choix *m*; sélection *f* (*a. biol.*); **~ive** sélectif; **~or** ⊕ sélecteur *m*.

self (*pl.* **selves**) **1.** *the* **~** le moi; **2. ~...** *oft.* de soi; auto-; ⊕ *etc. a.* automatique(ment); **~adhesive** auto-collant; **~assertive** impérieux; autoritaire; **~assurance** assurance; **~assured**

plein d'assurance, sûr de soi; **~cen-
tered** égocentrique; **~command**
maîtrise f de soi; sang-froid m; **~con-
ceit** suffisance f, vanité f; **~conceited**
vaniteux; **~confidence; ~confident**
plein de confiance en soi, sûr de soi;
confiance f en soi; **~conscious** gêné;
contraint; **~contained** indépendant;
~control maîtrise f de soi; possession f
de soi-même; **~defence** auto-défense
f, self-défense f; ⚖ (**in ~**) en légitime
défense f; **~denial** abnégation f (de
soi); **~educated** autodidacte;
~esteem respect m de soi; **~evident**
évident, qui va de soi; **~explanatory**
qui se passe d'explication, qui s'expli-
que de soi-même; **~governing** autonome; **~government** autonomie f;
~help efforts m/pl. personnels; **~im-
portance** suffisance f, présomption f;
~important suffisant, présomptueux;
~indulgent qui ne se refuse rien; **~in-
terest** intérêt m personnel; **~ish**
égoïste; **~ishness** égoïsme m; **~less**
désintéressé; altruiste; **~lessly** sans
penser à soi; **~lessness** altruisme m;
désintéressement m; **~locking** à fermeture automatique; **~love** amour m de
soi; **~opinionated** entêté, opiniâtre;
~pity apitoiement m sur soi-même;
~portrait autoportrait m; **~pos-
sessed** maître de soi, plein de
sang-froid; **~possession** maîtrise f de
soi, sang-froid; **~praise** auto-louange
m, éloge(s) m/(pl.) de soi-même;
~preservation conservation f de soi;
~reliant indépendant; **~respect** respect m de soi-même; dignité f; **~re-
specting** qui se respecte; **~righteous**
pharisaïque; **~righteousness** phari-
saïsme m; **~rule** autonomie f; **~sacri-
fice** abnégation f, **~same** même;
~satisfied suffisant, content de soi;
~seeking égoïste; **~service** libre-ser-
vice m, self-service m; **~ restaurant** restaurant m self-service, self m; **~styled**
soi-disant *inv.*, prétendu; **~sufficient**
(économiquement *etc.*) indépendant;
~supporting (financièrement) indé-
pendent; **~taught** autodidacte; **~-
willed** obstiné, entêté; **~winding** (à
remontage) automatique.

sell *v/t.* vendre; F *fig.* ~ **s.o. s.th.,** ~ **s.th.
to** (*or* **on**) **s.o.** faire accepter qch. à q.,

convaincre q. de qch.; F **sold on** convaincu de; enthousiasmé par; ✝ **~ by ...**
(*date*) à consommer avant le ...; **~ out**
vendre tout son (stock de); **sold out**
épuisé (*article*); **we are sold out of ...**
on n'a plus de ...; **this show is sold out**
il n'y a plus de billets pour cette séance;
~ off liquider; *v/i.* se vendre; **~ out** vendre son affaire; **~er** vendeur (-euse f) m;
✝ **good** *etc.* ~ article m de bonne *etc.*
vente; **best ~** livre m à (gros) succès,
best-seller m.

sellotape (*TM*) scotch m (*TM*).

sell-out trahison f; capitulation f; F succès m énorme, pièce f *etc.* pour laquelle
tous les billets sont vendus.

semblance semblant m.

semi... semi-; (à) demi; à moitié; mi-;
~breve ♪ ronde f; **~circle** demi-cercle
m; **~colon** point-virgule m (*pl.* points-vir-
gules) m; **~conductor** ⚡ semi-conduc-
teur m; **~detached**: **~ house** maison f
jumelle; **~final** *sp.* demi-finale f.

seminar *univ.* séminaire m.

semi...: ~official semi-officiel, officieux;
~precious: **~ stone** pièrre f fine *or*
semi-précieuse; **~quaver** ♪ double croche f; **~skilled**: **~ worker** ouvrier (-ère
f) m spécialisé(e); **~tone** ♪ demi-ton m.

semolina semoule f.

senate sénat m; **~or** sénateur m.

send *v/t.* envoyer; remettre (*money*); **~
back** renvoyer; **~ forth** envoyer (dehors); répandre; lancer; **~ in** faire
(r)entrer; envoyer; **~ off** expédier; envoyer; **~ up** faire monter (*a. fig.*); *v/i.*: **~
for** faire venir, envoyer chercher; **~er**
letter etc.: expéditeur (-trice f) m.

senile sénile; **~ity** sénilité f.

senior 1. aîné; plus âgé (que, **to**);
supérieur (à, **to**); premier (*clerk etc.*); **~
citicens** *pl.* personnes f/pl. âgées; ✝ **~
partner** associé m principal; 2. aîné(e f)
m; le (la) plus ancien(ne f) m;
supérieur(e f) m; **~ity** priorité f d'âge;
ancienneté f.

sensation sensation f; **~al** sensationnel;
à sensation (*novel etc.*).

sense 1. sens m; sentiment m; sensation
f; bon sens m, intelligence f; signification f; **~ of direction** sens m de l'orientation; **~ of duty** sentiment m du devoir;
~ of humo(u)r (sens m de l')humour m;
~ of time notion f de l'heure; **in one's**

~s sensé, sain d'esprit; *be out of one's ~s* avoir perdu le sens *or* la tête; *bring s.o. to his ~s* ramener q. à la raison; *make ~* être logique *or* compréhensible; *make ~ of* arriver à comprendre; *talk ~* parler raison; **2.** sentir; deviner, pressentir; **~less** absurde, insensé, stupide; sans connaissance; **~lessness** absurdité *f*.

sensibility sensibilité *f* (à, *to*).

sensible raisonnable, sensé; pratique; appréciable, sensible (*difference, change etc.*); *be ~ of* avoir conscience de.

sensitiv|e sensible (à, *to*); **~eness, ~ity** sensibilité *f* (à, *to*).

sensual sensuel.

sensuous sensuel; voluptueux.

sentence 1. 🏛 jugement *m*; condamnation *f*; peine *f*; *gramm.* phrase *f*; *serve one's ~* subir sa peine; *see life*; **2.** condamner (à, *to*).

sententious sentencieux.

sentient doué de sensation.

sentiment sentiment *m*; opinion *f*, avis *m*; **~al** sentimental; **~ality** sentimentalité *f*.

sentinel, ~ry ✕ sentinelle *f*.

separa|ble séparable; **~te 1.** séparé, détaché; indépendant; particulier; **~ly** séparément; **2.** (se) séparer; **3.** *cost.* **~s** *pl.* coordonnés *m/pl.*; **~tion** séparation *f*.

sepsis 🩺 septicémie *f*.

September septembre *m*.

septic septique; infecté.

sepul|chral sépulcral; **~chre, ~cher** *poet.* sépulcre *m*.

sequel suite *f* (*a. of a story etc.*), conséquence *f*; *as or in a ~ to* à la suite de.

sequence ordre *m*; succession *f*; ♪, *cards, cin.* séquence *f*; *gramm. ~ of tenses* concordance *f* des temps.

sequestrate 🏛 séquestrer (*property*); confisquer.

sequin paillette *f*.

serenade 1. ♪ sérénade *f*; **2.** donner une sérénade à.

seren|e serein; **~ity** sérénité *f*.

sergeant ✕ sergent *m*; (*a. police ~*) brigadier *m*.

serial 1. de série; en série; **2.** *journ.* feuilleton.

series *sg.*, *a. pl.* série *f*; *books etc.*: collection *f*.

serious sérieux; grave; sincère; *take s.th. ~* prendre qch. au sérieux; **~ness** gravité *f*; sérieux *m*.

sermon sermon *m*.

serrated denté|e.

serum sérum *m*.

servant serviteur *m*, servante *f*; domestique *mf*.

serve 1. *v/t.* servir; être utile à; 🏛 faire (*a sentence*); (*it*) *~s him right* cela lui apprendra; *~ out* distribuer, servir; *v/i.* servir (à, *for*; de, *as*); ✕ servir dans l'armée; être utile; *~ at table* servir à table; **2.** *tennis*: service *m*.

service 1. service *m* (*a.* ✕, 🛥, *rel.*, *crockery, servant, meals, tennis, a. fig.*); ⊕, *mot.* révision *f*; *the ~s pl.* l'armée *f* la marine *f etc.*; *mot.* **~ area** aire *f* de service, **~ charge** service; *mot.* **~ station** station-service (*pl.* stations-service) *f*; *be of ~ to* rendre service à, être utile à; *do s.o. a ~* rendre un service à; *mot. put one's car in for (a) ~* donner sa voiture à réviser; **~able** utile, pratique; solide; **~man** militaire *m*.

servil|e servile; **~ity** servilité *f*.

session session *f* (*a.* 🏛); séance *f*; *univ.* année *f* universitaire; *be in ~ parl,* siéger; 🏛 être en session.

set 1. *v/t.* mettre (*a. the table, an alarm-clock*), poser (*a problem, a question*); placer; imposer (*a task*); régler (*a clock, a.* ⊕); dresser (*a trap*); donner (*an example*); fixer (*a day*); ♪ planter; lancer (*a dog*) (contre *at, on*); ajuster; affiler (*a tool*); monter (*a gem*); mettre en plis (*one's hair*); 🩺 remettre; *~ s.o. laughing* faire rire q.; *~ the fashion* lancer la mode; *~ sail* faire voile; *~ one's teeth* serrer les dents; *~ aside* mettre de côté; *fig.* rejeter; écarter; *~ at ease* mettre à son aise; *~ at rest* calmer; *~ at declarer (a question)*; *~ back* in time: retarder (de, *by*); reculer; *~ store by* attacher grand prix à; *~ off* compenser (par, *against*); faire ressortir; faire partir (*a rocket*); *~ up* monter, dresser; faire; relever; organiser; fonder; mettre en avant; rétablir (*s.o.'s health*); **2.** *v/i.* se coucher (*sun etc.*); prendre (*jelly, concrete etc.*); *fig.* se figer (*face, expression etc.*); 🩺 se ressouder (*fracture etc.*); prendre racine (*plant*); *~ to work etc.* se mettre au travail *etc.*; *~ about* se mettre à ([faire] qch., [*doing*] *s.th.*); ~ **in** commencer; survenir (*difficulties etc.*); ~ **off** se mettre en route; partir; ~ **out** se mettre en route; partir; *fig.* entreprendre (de faire, **to do**); ~ **up** se poser (en, **as**); s'établir (qch., **as s.th.**); ~ (**up**)**on** attaquer; **3.** fixe; résolu; pris; assigné; prescrit; ~ (**up**)**on** déterminé à; résolu à; ~ **with** orné de; ~ **fair** au beau fixe (*barometer*); **hard** ~ fort embarrassé; ~ **speech** discours *m* étudié; **4.** *tools etc.*: jeu *m*; serie *f*; ensemble *m*; garniture *f* (*of buttons etc.*); *china etc.*: service *m*; *people*: groupe *m*, cercle *m*; *radio*: poste *m*; ♪ plaçon *m*; *tennis*: set *m*; *poet.* sun: coucher *m*; *hairdressing*: mise *f* (en plis); *thea.* décor *m* (monté).

set...: ~**back** revers *m* (de fortune); ~**down** humiliation *f*; ~**off** contraste *m*; ♱ compensation *f*; ~**journey**: départ *m*; ~**square** ⚹ équerre *f* à dessin.

settee canapé *m*.

setting cadre *m*, encadrement *m*; *gem*: monture; ⊕ *etc.* mise; *astr.* couchant *m*.

settle *v/t.* fixer; établir; calmer (*a child*); régler (*a bill*); arranger (*a dispute*); résoudre (*a question*); décider; coloniser (*a country*); *v/i.* (*oft.* ~ **down**) s'établir; se calmer (*excitement*); (*a.* ~ **o.s.**) s'installer; s'adapter; ~ **up** régler (la note); ~**d** sûr (*a. weather*); fixe (*idea*); ♱ réglé (*bill*); ~**ment** établissement *m*; arrangement *m*; *problem*: solution *f*; colonie *f*; ♱ règlement *m* (*of a bill*); ~**r** colon *m*.

set...: ~**to** dispute *f*; prise *f* de bec; ~**up** organisation *f*; situation *f*; affaire *f*, F truc *m*.

seven sept; ~**teen**(**th**) dix-sept(ième) (*a. su./m*); ~**th 1.** septième; **2.** septième *m*, ♪ *f*; ~**tieth** soixante-dixième; ~**ty** soixante-dix.

sever (se) séparer, rompre; *v/t.* couper, trancher; *fig.* désunir.

several plusieurs.

severance séparation *f*; rupture *f*.

sever|e sévère (*person, look, style etc.*); grave (*wound, illness*); rigoureux (*person, sentence, climate, weather etc.*); dur; ~**ity** sévérité *f*; gravité *f*; rigueur *f*.

sew coudre; brocher (*a book*).

sewage vidanges *m/pl.*

sewer égout *m*; ~**age** système *m* d'égouts.

sewing couture *f*; *attr. machine etc.* à coudre.

sex sexe *m*; *attr.* sexuel; **have** ~ (**with**) avoir des rapports sexuels (avec).

sexton sacristain *m*; F fossoyeur *m*.

sexual sexuel; ~ **intercourse** rapports *m/pl.* sexuels; ~ **urge** pulsion *f* sexuelle.

sexy sexy *inv.*

shabby râpé, usé; miteux; *fig.* mesquin.

shack cabane *f*.

shackles *pl.* entraves *f/pl.*

shade 1. ombre *f*; *fig.* obscurité *f*; *lamp*: abat-jour *m/inv.*; *colour, opinion*: nuance *f*; teinte *f*, soupçon *m*; *Am.* store *m*; ... **degrees in the** ~ à l'ombre; ~**s** *pl.* lunettes *f/pl.* de soleil; **2.** *v/t.* ombrager; abriter de la lumière *or* du soleil; voiler, masquer (*the light*); abriter (de, **from**); *paint.* nuancer.

shadow 1. ombre *f*; *pol.* ~ **cabinet** cabinet *m* fantôme; **2.** ombrager; *police*: filer (*q.*); ~**box** *sp.* boxer à vide; ~**y** ombragé; *fig.* vague, flou.

shady ombragé; F louche.

shaft *spear etc.*: hampe *f*; *lumière*: trait *m*; ⊕ arbre *m*; *wagon*: brancard *m*; ⚒ puits *m*.

shaggy hirsute; à longs pails.

shake 1. *v/t.* secouer; agiter; ébranler; *fig.* bouleverser; ~ **down** faire tomber (*qch.*) en secouant; tasser (*qch.*) en le secouant; ~ **off** secouer; *fig.* se defaire *or* débarrasser de; semer (*q.*); ~ **hands** serrer la main (à, **with**); ~ **up** secouer (*a.* F *fig.*); agiter; *v/i.* trembler (de, **with**; devant, **at**); chanceler; branler (*head*); **2.** secousse *f*; tremblement *m*; ♪ trille *m*; F instant *m* moment *m*; ~**down** lit *m* improvisé; F fouille *f*; F chantage *m*, extorsion *f*; ~ **cruise** voyage *m* d'essai; ~**hands** serrement *m or* poignée *f* de main; ~**up** remaniement *m*.

shaky peu solide; chancelant; tremblant.

shall *defective verb used for expressig the future or an obligation.*

shallow 1. peu profond; *fig.* superficiel; **2.** ~**s** *pl.* bas-fond *m*.

sham 1. faux, simulé; feint; **2.** *thing*: imitation *f*; *fig.* comédie, frime *f*; *per-*

son: imposteur *m*; **3.** *v/t.* feindre, simuler; *v/i.* faire semblant.

shamble aller à pas traînants.

shambles F *pl.* pagaïe *f.*

shame 1. honte *f*; **it is a ~** (*that*) c'est dommage que (*sbj.*); **put to ~** = **2.** faire honte à; **~faced** honteux; embarrassé; **~ful** honteux; **~less** sans honte.

shampoo 1. shampooing *m*; (**have a**) **~ and set** (se faire un) shampooing (et) mise en plis, **2.** faire un shampooing à, shampooiner.

shamrock ♣ trèfle *m* d'Irlande.

shandy panaché *m.*

shank ⊕ tige *f*; manche *m*; *cuis.* jarret *m* (*of beef*); jambe *f.*

shanty cabane *f*, hutte *f.*

shape 1. forme *f*; **take ~** prendre forme, **2.** façonner, former; *v/i.* (*a.* **~ up**) se développer; promettre; **~d** façonné; en forme de; **~less** informe; difforme; **~ly** bien fait; beau.

share 1. part *f*, portion *f*; contribution *f*; ♥ action *f*; **have a ~ in** avoir part à; **go ~s** partager (*qch.* avec q., **in s.th. with s.o.**); **2.** *v/t* partager; avoir en commun; avoir part à (*qch.*); *v/i.* prendre part (à, *in*), participer (à, *in*); **~cropper** *Am.* métayer (-ère *f*) *m*; **~holder** ♥ actionnaire *mf.*

shark *icht.* requin *m*; *fig.* escroc *m.*

sharp 1. *adj.* tranchant, aiguisé (*edge, knife etc.*); aigu (*point, a. voice*); piquant, fort (*taste, flavour*) vif (*wind, frost, a. intelligence*); fin (*ear*); net, marqué (*outline, features*); perçant (*look*); vert (*wine, a. rebuke*); saillant (*angle*); prononcé (*curve*); sévère (*discipline*); peu honnête; F élégant, chic *inv.* (*dress, car, person etc.*); ♪ **C ~** do *m* dièse; **2.** *adv.* ♪ trop haut; *stop, turn etc.* brusquement; **at 3 o'clock ~** à 3 heures précises *or* F pile; **3.** *su.* ♪ dièse *m*; F escroc *m*; *Am. sl.* as *m*; **~en** aiguiser (*a. fig, s.o.'s appetite*); tailler (*a pencil*); accentuer (*a contrast*); **~ener** (*a.* **pencil ~**) taille-crayon *m/inv.*; (*a.* **knife ~**) aiguisoir *m*; **~er** escroc *m*; **~ness** tranchant *m*; pointe *f*; acuité *f*; violence *f*; acidité *f*; *fig.* rigueur *f.*

sharp...: ~-eyed à la vue perçante; à qui n'échappe rien; **~-set** en grand appétit, affamé; **~shooter** tirailleur *m*; **~sight-**
ed à la vue perçante; *fig.* perspicace; **~-witted** à l'esprit vif.

shatter (se) fracasser; (se) briser (en éclats); *v/t. fig.* ruiner; briser (*hopes*), bouleverser; **~proof**: **~ glass** verre *m* Sécurit (*TM*).

shave 1. *v/t.* raser; planer (*wood*); friser; *fig.* rogner; *v/i.* se raser; **~ through** se faufiler entre (*cars etc.*); **2. have a ~** se (faire) raser; **have a close** (*or* **narrow**) **~** l'échapper belle; **~n** rasé; **~r** rasoir *m* électrique.

shaving 1. *beard*: rasage *m*, **~s** *pl. wood*: copeaux *m/pl.*; *metal*: rognures *f/pl.*; **2.** à raser; à barbe; **~ brush** blaireau *m*; **~ cream** crème *f* à raser; **~ foam** mousse *f* à raser; **~ soap** savon *m* à barbe.

shawl châle *m*; fichu *m.*

she 1. elle, **2.** femelle *f*; **she-** femelle *f* (*of an animal*).

sheaf *corn*: gerbe *f*; *paper*: liasse *f.*

shear 1. tondre; **2.** (**a pair of**) **~s** *pl.* (des) cisailles *f/pl.*

sheath gaine *f* (*a.* ♀, *a. anat.*); *sword*: fourreau *m*; **~e** rengainer; ⊕, *a. fig.* revêtir, recouvrir.

shebang ⊢ affaire *f*; truc *m.*

shed¹ perdre (*its leaves, one's teeth*); verser, répandre.

shed² hangar *m*, remise *f.*

sheen lustre *m*, éclat *m*, luisant *m.*

sheep mouton *m*; **~dog** chien *m* de berger; **~fold** parc *m* à moutons; **~ish** timide; penaud; **~skin** peau *f* de mouton.

sheer *adj.* pur, vrai; absolu; à pic (*a. adv.*), escarpé, abrupt.

sheet *metal, paper, glass etc.*: feuille *f*; *water etc.*: nappe *f*; *snow*: couche *f*; *bed*: drap *m*; ♪ écoute *f*; **~ lightning** éclairs *m/pl.* en nappe; **~ metal** tôle *f.*

shelf rayon *m*, étagère *f*, planche *f*, *underwater*: écueil *m*; ♥ **~ life** durée *f* de conservation avant vente; *fig.* **on the ~** vieille fille (*woman*); au rancart (*person, project etc.*).

shell 1. coquille *f*; *oysters*: *a.* écaille *f*; *lobster etc.*: carapace *f*; *pea*: cosse *f*; *on beach*: coquillage *m*; ✕ obus *m*; *house*: carcasse *f*; **2.** décortiquer, écaler; écosser (*peas*); ✕ bombarder; **~fish** coquillage *m*; crustacé *m.*

shelter 1. abri *m*; asile *m*; *fig.* protection *f*; **2.** *v/t.* abriter; donner asile à; *v/i.* (*a.* **~ o.s.**) s'abriter; **~ed** protégé.

shelve v/t. mettre sur un rayon; fig. ajourner, mettre en suspens; v/i. aller en pente douce.

shenanigan(s pl.) F mystification f.

shepherd 1. berger m; **2.** escorter; guider, conduire; garder.

sherbet sorbet m.

sheriff shérif m.

shield 1. bouclier m; **2.** protéger.

shift 1. changement m; workers, time: poste m, workers: a. équipe f; mot. ~ **stick** levier m de vitesse; ~ **work** travail m par relais or roulement; fig. **make ~ (with)** se contenter (de), se débrouiller (avec); **2.** v/t. changer (de place etc.); déplacer; v/i. changer de place; bouger; changer (scene); tourner (wind); mot. changer de vitesse; ~ **for o.s.** se débrouiller; **~less** peu débrouillard; indifférent; **~y** sournois; fuyant (eyes).

shilly-shally F tergiverser.

shimmer 1. scintiller, miroiter, chatoyer; **2.** scintillement m, miroitement m, chatoyement m.

shin 1. (or ~**bone**) tibia m; **2.:** ~ **up** grimper à.

shine 1. éclat m; brillant m; F **take a ~ to** s'enticher de; **2.** v/i. briller (a. fig.); (re)luire; v/t. (a. ~ **up**) polir; cirer.

shingle △ bardeau m; galets m/pl.; Am. petite enseigne f; ✎ ~**s** pl. zona m.

shiny brillant, luisant.

ship 1. bateau m, navire m; **2.** ⚓, a. F expédier; transporter; embarquer; **~board:** ⚓ **on ~** à bord; **~building** construction f navale; **~-canal** canal m maritime; **~ment** cargaison f; **~owner** armateur m; **~ping** navigation f; navires m/pl.; **~shape** en ordre impeccable; **~wreck** naufrage m; **~wrecked** naufragé; **~yard** chantier m de constructions navales.

shire esp. in compounds: comté m.

shirk se dérober à, esquiver.

shirt chemise f (for men); F **keep one's ~ on** ne pas se fâcher or s'emballer; **~sleeve** manche f de chemise; **in (one's) ~s** en bras de chemise; **~y** F irritable; **get ~** se mettre en rogne.

shit V **1.** merde f; **2.** chier.

shiver¹ 1. frisson; **it gives me the ~s** ça me donne le frisson, ça me fait trembler; **2.** frissonner; grelotter; **~y** tremblant; fiévreux.

shiver² 1. fragment m, éclat m; **2.** (se) fracasser.

shoal fish: banc m; fig. foule f, masse f; geog. haut-fond (pl. hauts-fonds) m.

shock 1. choc m (a. ✿, ⊕, ✗); secousse f (a. ⚡); heurt m, coup m; **2.** fig. choquer; bouleverser; offenser; **~ed at** choqué de; scandalisé par; mot. ~ **absorber** amortisseur m; ~ **therapy** (or **treatment**) thérapeutique f (or traitement m) (de) choc; **~ing** choquant; affreux; scandaleux; **~proof** anti-choc inv.

shoddy mal fait; fig. mesquin.

shoe 1. chaussure f, soulier m; horse: fer m; ⊕ sabot m; sledge: patin m; **2.** ferrer (a horse); **~black** cireur m (de chaussures); **~cream** crème f pour chaussures; **~horn** chausse-pied m; **~lace** lacet m; **~maker** cordonnier m; **~shine** cirage m de chaussures; (a. ~ **boy**) cireur m de chaussures; **~shop** magasin m de chaussures; **~string** lacet m; F fig. **on a ~** avec très peu d'argent.

shoot 1. ♀ pousse f; rejeton m; partie f or terrain m de chasse; river: rapide m; **2.** v/t. tirer (a gun); tuer d'un coup de feu, abattre; fusiller; chasser (game); darder (rays); lancer; décharger; phot. prendre un instantané de; tourner (a film); sp. marquer (a goal); ~ **down** abattre; v/i. tirer (sur, **at**); fig. se précipiter, filer; (a. ~ **forth**) pousser; ~ **ahead** aller rapidement en avant; ~ **up** jaillir; pousser rapidement; monter en flèche (prices etc.); **~er** tireur (-euse f) m.

shooting 1. tir m; chasse f; fusillade f; film: tournage m; **go ~** aller à la chasse; **2.** lancinant (pain); ~ **gallery** stand m de tir; ~ **licence** permis m de chasse; ~ **range** champ m de tir; ~ **star** étoile f filante.

shoot-out F échange m de coups de feu.

shop 1. magasin m; small one: boutique f; ⊕ atelier m; ~ **assistant** vendeur (-euse f) m; ⊕ ~ **floor** les ouvriers m/pl.; **talk ~** parler métier; **2.** (usu. F **go ~ping**) faire ses courses; **~keeper** boutiquier (-ère f) m; marchand(e f) m; **~lifter** voleur (-euse f) m à l'étalage; **~man** commis m de magasin; **~per** acheteur (-euse f) m; **~ping** achats m/pl.; emplettes f/pl.; **~centre** quartier m commerçant; **~steward** délégué m (syndical) d'atelier; **~walker** chef m de rayon; inspec-

teur (-trice f) m; ~**window** vitrine f;
devanture f.

shore 1. rivage m, bord m; côte f; **on ~** à
terre; **2.:** ~ **up** étayer.

short 1. adj. court; petit (person); in
time: court, bref; insuffisant (weight
etc.); fig. brusque; cuis. croquant; **be ~
of** manquer de; **fall** (or **run**) ~ manquer;
s'épuiser (provisions); ~ **list** liste f des
candidats sélectionnés; ~ **time**
chômage m partiel; **2.** adv. court; brusquement, ~ **of** sauf; à moins de; **come**
(or **fall**) ~ **of** manquer à; ne pas atteindre; **cut** ~ couper la parole à; **stop** ~
of s'arrêter au seuil de; ne pas aller
jusqu'à; **3.** su. cin. court métrage m;
≸ court-circuit (pl. courts-circuits)
m; **F ~s** pl. culotte f de sport; short m;
in ~ bref, en un mot; ~**age** manque
m, insuffisance f; admin. crise f; **†** déficit m; ~**change** F estamper, rouler; ~**coming** défaut m; ~**cut** raccourci
m; ~**dated †** à courte échéance;
~**en** v/t. raccourcir; abréger; v/i. (se)
raccourcir; diminuer; ~**ening** raccourcissement m; cuis. matière f grasse;
~**hand** sténographie f; ~ **typist** sténo-
dactylo f; ~**handed** à court de personnel; ~**haul** (à) courte distance;
~**list** mettre (q.) sur la liste des candidats sélectionnés; ~**livod** de courte
durée; ~**ly** adv. brièvement; bientôt;
~**ness** brièveté f; brusquerie f; manque
m; ~**range** à courte portée (weapon
etc.); à court rayon d'action (plane
etc.); in time à court terme; ~**sighted**
myope; fig. imprévoyant; ~**term †** à
court terme; ~**winded** à l'haleine
courte.

shot gun: coup m de feu; tireur (-euse f)
m; sp. shot m; phot. prise f de vue; **≸**
piqûre f; sl. alcool: goutte f; fig. essai m,
coup m; **have a ~ at** essayer (qch.); **not
by a long ~** tant s'en faut; pas à beaucoup près; **within** (**out of**) ~ à (hors de)
portée; F fig. **big ~** grosse légume f
(important person); ~**gun** fusil m de
chasse; F ~ **marriage** mariage m forcé;
~**put** sp. lancer m du poids.

shoulder 1. épaule f; ~ **bag** sac m à
bandoulière; ~ **blade** omoplate f; ~
strap garment: bretelle f; bag: bandoulière; uniform: patte f d'épaule; **give
s.o. the cold ~** battre froid à q.; mettre

sur l'épaule; fig. endosser; ~ **ones way**
se frayer le chemin à coups d'épaule; ~
aside écarter d'un coup d'épaule.

shout 1. cri m; laughter: éclat m; **2.** crier;
~ **down** faire (q.) taire par des huées.

shove 1. poussée f; coup m d'épaule; **2.**
pousser; bousculer.

shovel 1. pelle f; **2.** pelleter.

show 1. v/t. montrer, faire voir; manifester; faire preuve de; laisser paraître;
indiquer; représenter; cin. présenter;
exposer (paintings etc.); ~ **in** introduire;
faire entrer; ~ **off** faire valoir or ressortir; faire parade de; ~ **out** reconduire; ~
up faire monter; révéler; v/i. se voir,
être visible (emotion, sign etc.); (a. ~ **up**)
se montrer, se laisser voir; ~ **off** faire
l'important; épater la galerie; **2.** spectacle m, show m; cin. séance f; thea.
représentation f; exposition f, salon m,
concours m; parade f (a. fig.); fig. a.
étalage m, a. of feelings etc.: manifestation f, démonstration f; **make-believe**:
semblant m, apparence f; F affaire f; ~
business le monde m or l'industrie f du
spectacle, le show-business m; ~ **dumb**
pantomime f; **on ~** exposé, F **give the ~
away** vendre la mèche; **make a ~ of**
(ger.) faire semblant de (inf.); **put up a
good** (**poor**) ~ faire bonne (piètre) figure; **3.** d'exposition; de démonstration;
... témoin (flat etc.); ~**case** vitrine f;
~**down** épreuve f de force, confronta-
tion f.

shower 1. averse f; hail, snow: giboulée
f; fig. pluie f; **2.** v/t. verser; fig. combler
(de, **with**); v/i. se doucher; ~**bath**
bain-douche (pl. bains-douches) m;
douche f; ~**y** pluvieux.

show...: ~**man** forain m; fig. showman
m; ~**off** crâneur (-euse f) m;
m'as-tu-vu(e f) m; ~**piece** objet m
exemplaire, modèle m (du genre);
joyau m (of a collection etc.); ~**room**
salle f d'exposition; ~**window** étalage
m; ~**y** voyant; prétentieux.

shred 1. lambeau f; petit morceau m;
fig. grain m, brin m; **2.** déchirer (en
morceaux).

shrew zo. (a. ~**mouse**) musaraigne f;
person: mégère f.

shrewd perspicace; sagace; fin.

shriek 1. cri m (perçant or aigu); **2.** crier;
hurler.

S

shrift: *give short ~ to* expedier vite; *get short ~* être expédié vite.

shrill aigu, perçant.

shrimp *zo.* crevette *f*.

shrine châsse *f*; lieu *m* saint.

shrink 1. *v/i.* rétrécir (*cloth*), rapetisser; se contracter; se réduire; (*a. ~ back*) reculer (devant qch., *from s.th.*; à *inf.*, *from ger.*); *v/t.* (faire) rétrécir (*cloth*); **2.** F psychanalyste *m*, F psy *m*; **~age** rétrécissement *m*; contraction *f*.

shrivel (*a. ~ up*) (se) ratatiner.

shroud 1. linceul *m*; **2.** envelopper.

Shrove Tuesday mardi *m* gras.

shrub arbrisseau *m*; arbuste *m*; **~bery** bosquet *m* d'arbustes.

shrug 1. (*a. ~ one's shoulders*) hausser les épaules; *~ off* faire fi de; **2.** haussement *m* d'épaules.

shrunken contracté; ratatiné.

shudder 1. frissonner, frémir (de, *with*); **2.** frisson *m*, frémissement *m*.

shuffle 1. *v/t.* traîner (*one's feet*); remuer; mêler, brouiller; battre (*cards*); *~ off* se débarrasser de; *v/i.* marcher en traînant les pieds; **2.** pas *m/pl.* traînants; marche *f* traînante; *cards:* battement *m*.

shun fuir, éviter.

shunt 1. 🚂 changement *m* de voie; **2.** 🚂 *u. fig.* aiguiller; manœuvrer; *fig.* expédier, envoyer.

shut *v/t.* fermer; *~ down* fermer (*a factory*); *~ in* enfermer; *~ out* exclure; *~ up* enfermer; *v/i.* (se) fermer; F *~ up!* taisez-vous!, *sl.* la ferme!; **~down** fermeture *f*; *~ter* volet *m*; *phot.* obturateur *m*.

shuttle 1. navette *f*; *~ service* (service *m* de) navette; **2.** *v/t.* transporter; (r)envoyer, expédier; *v/i.* faire la navette.

shy 1. timide (avec, *of*); farouche (*animal*); *be ~ of* ne pas oser de (*faire*); **2.** faire un écart (*horse*); *~ away from* reculer devant, craindre (de faire, *from doing*); **~ness** timidité *f*.

shyster *sl.*, *esp. Am.* homme *m* d'affaires véreux; avocassier *m*.

Siberian sibérien, de Sibérie.

sibling frère *m*; sœur *f*.

Sicilian sicilien.

sick malade (de **of**, *with*); *fig.* dégoûté (de, *of*); *fig.* malsain (*mind*), macabre (*joke etc.*); *~ pay* indemnité *f* de maladie; *be ~* vomir; *fig.* *be ~* (*and tired*) *of*

(en) avoir assez de, F en avoir marre de; *feel ~* avoir mal au cœur; *go ~* se faire porter malade; *~bed* lit *m* de malade; *~en* *v/i.* tomber malade; *fig.* se lasser (de qch., *of s.th.*); *~ at* être écœuré par; être dégoûté de; *v/t.* rendre malade; dégoûter; *~fund* caisse *f* de maladie.

sickle faucille *f*.

sick...: *~ leave* congé *m* de maladie; *~ly* maladif; écœurant (*odour etc.*); malsain (*climate*); *~ness* maladie *f*; nausée(s) *f*(*pl.*).

side 1. *usu.* côté *m*; *road, river etc.:* bord *m*; *pol. etc.* parti *m*; *~ by* côte à côte; *~ by ~* à côté de; *at* (*or by*) *s.o.'s ~* à côté de q.; **2.** latéral, de côté; secondaire (*effect, issue etc.*); **3.** prendre parti (pour, *with*); se ranger du côté (de, *with*); *~board* buffet *m*; *Am. ~s pl.* = *~burns pl.* pattes *f/pl.*; *~kick* F copain *m*, copine *f*; *~light* mot. veilleuse *f*; *fig.* aperçu *m* indirect; *~line* *fig.* occupation *f* secondaire; *~long 1.* *adv.* de côté; obliquement; *2. adj.* de côté (*a. fig.*); *~step* éviter, éluder; *~stroke* nage *f* sur le côté; *~track 1.* problème *m* secondaire; **2.** faire (*q.*) dévier de son sujet; détourner; *~walk* trottoir *m*; *~ward(s)*, *~ways* de côté.

siding 🚂 voie *f* de garage.

sidle s'avancer *etc.* de guingois.

siege siège *m*; *lay ~ to* assiéger.

sieve 1. crible *m*; tamis *m*; passoire *f*; **2.** passer au crible (*a. fig.*), passer (au tamis), cribler, tamiser.

sift *see sieve 2*; *~ out* séparer (de, *from*); *~ through* examiner.

sigh 1. soupir *m*; **2.** soupirer.

sight 1. vue *f*; *fig.* spectacle *m*; portée *f* de la vue; visée *f*; mire *f* (*of a gun*); *~s pl.* monuments *m/pl.*, curiosités *f/pl.*; *at* (*or on*) *~* à vue (*a.* ✝, *a.* ♩); du premier coup; *catch ~ of* apercevoir; *lose ~ of* perdre de vue; *out of ~* hors de vue; *take ~* viser; *within ~* à portée de la vue; **2.** apercevoir; viser; *~ed* qui voit; *~ly* charmant, avenant; *~read* ♩ jouer *or* chanter à première vue; *~seeing* visite *f* (de la ville); *~seer* excursionniste *mf*.

sign 1. signe *m*; (*a. ~board*) écriteau *m*, panneau *m*; *inn etc.:* enseigne *f*; *in ~ of* en signe de; **2.** signer; *~ on* embaucher (*a worker*).

signal 1. signal *m*; **2.** insigne, remarquable; **3.** *vt/i.* signaler; transmettre par signaux (*a message etc.*); **~ to s.o.** donner un signal à q.; faire signe à q.; **~ize** signaler; marquer.

signat|ory signataire (*a. su./mf*); **~ure** signature *f*; **~ tune** *radio*: indicatif *m* musical.

signer signataire *mf.*

signet sceau *m*, cachet *m.*

signific|ance signification *f*; importance *f*; **~ant** important; significatif; **~ation** signification *f.*

signify signifier; vouloir dire.

signpost poteau *m* indicateur.

silence 1. silence *m*; **2.** faire taire; réduire au silence; **~r** ⊕ silencieux *m.*

silent silencieux; muet (*film*); ✝ **~ partner** commanditaire *m.*

silk 1. soie *f*; **2.** de soie; en soie; **~en** soyeux; **~worm** ver *m* à soie; **~y** soyeux.

sill seuil *m*; rebord *m* (de fenêtre).

silly sot; stupide.

silt 1 vase *f*; limon *m*; **2.** (*usu.* **~ up**) (s')envaser; (s')ensabler.

silver 1. argent *m*; (*a.* **~ware**) argenterie *f*; *money*: pièces *f/pl.* d'argent; **2.** d'argent, en argent **3.** (*or* ⊕ **~plate**) argenter; **~y** argenté; *fig.* argentin (*laughter, voice*).

similar semblable; pareil; **~ly** de la même façon; **~ity** ressemblance *f*; similarité.

simile comparaison *f.*

simmer *v/i.* (*v/t.* faire) mijoter.

simper minauder.

simple simple; **~minded** simple, naïf; **~ton** nigaud(e *f*) *m.*

simpli|city simplicité *f*; **~fication** simplification *f*, **~fy** simplifier.

simply *adv.* simplement.

simulat|e simuler, feindre; **~or** ⊕ simulateur *m.*

simultaneous simultané.

sin 1, péché *m*; **2.** pécher.

since 1. *prp.*, *adv.* depuis; **a short time ~** il y a peu de temps; **2.** *cj.* depuis que, *reason:* puisque.

sincer|e sincère; **~ity** sincérité *f.*

sinew tendon *m*; *fig. usu.* **~s** *pl.* nerf *m*, force *f*; **~y** musclé, nerveux.

sinful coupable; *fig.* scandaleux.

sing chanter; *sl.* se mettre à table, mou-

charder; F **~ another tune** changer de ton; F **~ small** déchanter, filer doux.

singe brûler légèrement; roussir.

singer chanteur (-euse *f*) *m*; cantatrice *f* (*by profession*).

singing 1. chant *m*; **2.** **~ bird** oiseau *m* chanteur.

single 1. seul; simple; unique; individuel; célibataire; pour une personne (*bed, room etc.*); **book-keeping by ~ entry** comptabilité *f* en partie simple; **in ~ file** en file indienne; **2.** *ticket:* aller *m* (simple); *thea. etc.* place *f* isolée; ♪ *record:* 45 tours *m/inv.*; *person:* célibataire *mf*; **~s** *sg. tennis:* (partie *f*) simple *m*; **3. ~ out** choisir; **~-breasted** droit (*coat etc.*); **~-handed** sans aide, seul; **~-hearted, ~-minded** résolu; immuable.

singlet tricot *m* (de corps).

singular 1. seul; singulier (*a. gramm.*); remarquable; **2.** *gramm.* (*a. ~ number*) singulier *m*; **~ity** singularité *f.*

sinister sinistre; menaçant.

sink 1. *v/i.* ⚓ couler; sombrer, s'enfoncer (dans, *into*); *give way:* s'affaisser; *fall:* tomber, baisser; **~ in** s'enfoncer; *v/t.* enfoncer; ⚓ couler; creuser (*a well*); **2.** évier *m*; *a. fig.* cloaque *m*; **~ing: ~ feeling** malaise *m*; **~ fund** caisse *f* d'amortissement.

sinless sans péché, pur.

sinner pécheur (-eresse *f*) *m.*

sinuous sinueux, onduleux; agile.

sip 1. petite gorgée *f*, F goutte *f*; **2.** boire à petits coups, siroter.

siphon 1. siphon *m*; **2.** (*a.* **~ off, ~ out**) siphonner.

sir monsieur (*pl.* messieurs) *m*; 2 *title:* Sir.

siren sirène *f.*

sirloin aloyau *m.*

sissy mou *m.*

sister sœur *f* (*a. eccl.*); *eccl.* religieuse *f*; infirmière *f* en chef; **~hood** communauté *f* religieuse; **~-in-law** belle-sœur (*pl.* belles-sœurs) *f*; **~ly** de sœur.

sit s'asseoir; être assis; siéger (*meeting*); (*a.* **~ for**) se présenter à (*an exam*); **~ back** se reposer; **~ down** s'asseoir; **~ up** rester debout, veiller tard; se redresser (*on a chair*).

sitcom F comédie *f* de situation.

sit-down (*a.* **~ strike**) grève *f* sur le tas.

site 1. emplacement *m*; site *m*; terrain *m* à bâtir; chantier *m*; **2.** placer.

sitting séance *f*; **~ room** salon *m*.

situat|ed situé; **~ion** situation *f*; emploi *m*.

six six; **~teen** seize; **~teenth** seizième; **~th** sixième; **~tieth** soixantième; **~ty** soixante (*a. su./m*).

size¹ colle *f*; apprêt *m*.

size² 1. dimensions *m/pl*.; grandeur *f*; grosseur *f*; *person*: taille *f*; *paper etc*.: format *m*; *shoes etc*.: pointure *f*; *shirt*: encolure *f*; numéro *m*; **2. ~ up** juger; **~able** assez grand; d'une belle taille.

sizzle 1. grésiller; **2.** grésillement *m*.

skate 1. patin *m*; **2.** patiner.

skedaddle F se sauver, décamper.

skein *wool etc*.: écheveau *m*.

skeleton 1. squelette *m*; *fig.* schéma *f*, esquisse *f*; *fig.* **~ in the cupboard** (*or* **closet**) secret *m* honteux; **2.** squelettique; réduit, minimum; esquissé, simplifié; **~ key** passe-partout *m/inv*.; rossignol *m* (*of a burglar*).

sketch 1. croquis *m*, esquisse *f*; *thea.* sketch *m*; *fig.* aperçu *m*; **2.** esquisser; faire un *or* des croquis de.

ski 1. *pl.* **ski(s)** ski *m*; **2.** de ski; à ski; **~ lift** remonte-pente *m*; **~ run** piste *f* de ski; **3.** faire du ski.

skid 1. ✈ patin *m*; *mot.* dérapage *m*; *mot.* **~ mark** trace *f* de dérapage; **~ row** quartier de(s) clochards; **go** (*or* **get**) **into a ~** faire un dérapage, déraper; **2.** *mot.* déraper.

ski|er skieur (-euse *f*) *m*; **~ing** ski *m*.

skilful adroit, habile.

skill adresse *f*, habileté *f*; **~ed** habile; spécialisé (*worker etc*.); expérimenté; **~ful** *see* **skilful**.

skim 1. *v/t.* (*oft.* **~ off**) écumer; dégraisser (*soup*); écrémer (*milk*); *fig.* effleurer; **~ through** parcourir (*a newspaper etc*.); *v/i.* glisser (sur, **over**); **2.:** **~ milk** lait *m* écrémé.

skimp lésiner (sur); être chiche (de); F bâcler; **~y** maigre, insuffisant.

skin 1. peau *f* (*a. of an animal, of a fruit*); F **have got s.o under one's ~** ne pouvoir oublier *or* se débarrasser de q.; **2.** *v/t.* dépouiller, écorcher (*an animal*); éplucher (*a fruit*); *v/i.* (*a. ~ over*) se recouvrir de peau; **~-deep** superficiel; **~-dive** faire de la plongée sousmarine;

~-diving plongée sousmarine; **~-flick** *sl.* film *m* porno; **~-flint** radin(e *f*) *m*; **~ny** maigre, maigrichon; **~-tight** collant.

skip 1. (petit) bond *m or* saut *m*; gambade *f*; **2.** *v/i.* sautiller, gambader; *v/t.* (*a. ~ over*) sauter.

skipper ♻ capitaine *m*.

skirmish ✗ escarmouche *f*.

skirt 1. jupe *f*; **2.** (*a. ~ round*) contourner; **~ing (board)** plinthe *f*.

skit sketch *m* satyrique; **~tish** frivole (*person*); ombrageux (*horse*).

skittle quille *f*; **~s** *pl.* (jeu *m* de) quilles *f/pl*.

skulduggery F maquignonnage *m*.

skulk se cacher; rôder furtivement.

skull crâne *m*.

sky ciel (*pl.* cieux, ciels) *m*; **~-blue** bleu ciel; **~-lark** alouette *f* des champs; **~-light** lucarne *f* (ligne *f* d')horizon *m*; **~-line** (ligne *f* d')horizon *m*; **~-rocket** F monter en flèche (*prices etc*.); **~-scraper** gratte-ciel *m/inv*.; **~-ward(s)** vers le ciel.

slab dalle *f*; plaque *f*.

slack 1. lâche; desserré; négligent (*person*); stagnant; peu vif; **2.** ♻ *rope etc*.: mou *m*; **~en** (se) relâcher; (se) ralentir; diminuer (de); *v/t.* détendre; *v/i.* devenir négligent; prendre du mou (*rope*); **~s** *pl.* pantalon *m*.

slag scories *f/pl*.

slake étancher (*one's thirst*); éteindre (*lime*); *fig.* assouvir.

slam *v/t.* (faire) claquer; fermer avec violence; *v/i.* claquer.

slander 1. calomnie *f*; **2.** calomnier, diffamer; **~ous** calomnieux.

slang 1. argot *m*; **2.** F réprimander vivement; injurier; **~ing match** prise *f* de bec.

slant 1. inclinaison *f*, pente *f*; *fig.* angle *m*, point *m* de vue; **2.** (faire) incliner; **~ing** *adj.*, **~wise** *adv.* incliné; oblique.

slap 1. coup *m*, tape *f*; (*a. ~ in the face*) gifle *f*; *fig.* affront *m*; **2.** gifler; donner une tape à; flanquer; **3.** tout droit; en plein; **~dash** insouciant; (fait) sans soin; **~stick: ~ comedy** farce *f* bouffonne.

slash 1. balafre *f*; entaille *f*; *cost.* taillade *f*; **2.** *v/t.* balafrer; taillader; *fig.* éreinter (*a book etc*.).

slate 1. ardoise *f*; *fig.* liste *f*; **2.** F éreinter; *fig.* mettre sur la liste.

slot

slattern souillon f.

slaughter 1. abattage m; fig. massacre m; **2.** abattre; fig. massacrer; **~house** abattoir m.

Slav 1. slave; **2.** Slave mf.

slave 1. esclave mf; **2.** d'esclaves; a. fig. **~ driver** négrier m; **3.** (a. **~ away**) trimer, bûcher.

slaver 1. bave f, salive f; **2.** baver.

slav|ery esclavage m; fig. asservissement m; **~ish** servile, d'esclave.

slay poet. tuer, mettre à mort.

sleazy usé, miteux, minable.

sled see **sledge¹**.

sledge¹ 1. traîneau m; **2.** aller en traîneau.

sledgehammer marteau m de forgeron.

sleek 1. lisse; luisant; brillant, fig. élégant; **2.** lisser; **~ness** luisant m; fig. douceur f.

sleep 1. dormir; coucher; **~ in** faire la grasse matinée; **2.** sommeil m; **get to ~, go to ~** s'endormir; **put** (or **send**) **to ~** endormir; (faire) piquer (an animal); **~er** dormeur (-euse f) m; 🚊 wagon-lit (pl. wagons-lits) m, rails: traverse f.

sleeping: **~ bag** sac m de couchage; **~ car, ~ carriage** 🚊 wagon-lit (pl. wagons-lits) m; **~ pill** somnifère m; **~ sickness** maladie f du sommeil.

sleepless sans sommeil; **~ night** nuit f blanche; **~ness** insomnie f.

sleepwalker somnambule mf.

sleepy somnolent; fig. endormi; **be ~** avoir sommeil.

sleet neige f fondue.

sleeve manche f; **~less** sans manches.

sleigh 1. traîneau m; **2.** transporter or aller en traîneau.

sleight: **~ of hand** tour m de passe-passe.

slender mince, ténu; svelte (person); faible (hope); maigre.

sleuth F détective m.

slice 1. tranche f; fig. **~ of life** tranche f de vie; **2.** découper en tranches; (a. **~ off**) trancher, couper.

slick habile; **2.** nappe f (d'huile); Am. F magazine m de luxe.

slid|e 1. (faire) glisser; **let things ~** laisser tout aller à vau-l'eau; **2.** glissade f; ⊕ coulisse f; toboggan m; fig. chute f, baisse f; phot. diapositive f; hair: barrette f; **~erule** règle f à calcul; **~ing** glissant; ⊕ a. coulissant; mot. **~ roof**

toit m décapotable; **~ rule** règle f à calcul; **~ scale** échelle f mobile.

slight 1. léger; mince; frêle; insignifiant, peu important; **2.** affront m; manque m d'égards; **3.** manquer d'égards pour; blesser (q.); **~ly** un peu, légèrement.

slim 1. svelte; mince; **2.** (a. **~ down**) maigrir; suivre un régime amaigrissant.

slim|e mucosité f; bave f; **~y** muqueux; a. fig. visqueux.

sling 1. 🏥 écharpe f; gun etc.: bretelle f; **2.** lancer, jeter.

slink: **~ in** (**out**) entrer (sortir) furtivement or en douce.

slip 1. v/i. glisser; se faufiler; se glisser (person, animal etc.); (oft. **~ away**) s'esquiver, F. s'écouler; v/t. (faire) glisser; couler; s'échapper de; **~ into** se glisser dans; **~ on** enfiler (a dress etc.); **~ off** enlever (a dress etc.); **2.** glissade f; erreur f; écart m de conduite, faux pas m; pillow: taie f; (a. **~ of paper**) fiche f; 🌱 rejeton m; cost. combinaison f; **give s.o. the ~** fausser compagnie à q., semer q.; **~per** pantoufle f; **~pery** glissant; **~shod** peu soigné, torché; **~up** bévue f.

slit 1. fente f; **2.** couper, trancher; **~ open** ouvrir, éventrer.

sliver éclat m, écharde f.

slobber baver; fig. s'attendrir (sur, **over**).

slogan pol. mot m d'ordre (a. fig.); ✝ devise f; slogan m.

slop 1. usu. **~s** lavasse; fond m de verre (or tasse); boissons f/pl. renversées; **2.** (a. **~ over**) v/t. répandre; v/i. se répandre, déborder.

slop|e 1. pente f, inclinaison f, mountain: versant m; **2.** v/i. être en pente; être incliné or penché; sl. **~ off** décamper; v/t. incliner; pencher; **~ing** incliné, penché.

sloppy mal soigné; négligé; trop grand (garment); mou (a. person), détrempé; fig. sentimental, larmoyant.

slosh v/t. répandre (liquid); F flanquer un coup à (q.); v/i. remuer, gargouiller (liquid); (a. **~ about** or **around**) patauger; **~ed** F soûl, bourrée f.

slot 1. fente f; entaille f, rainure f; **~ machine** distributeur m (automatique); gambling: machine f à sous; **2.** (s')insérer; (s')emboîter.

sloth paresse *f*; *zo.* paresseux *m*.

slouch 1. manquer de tenue; traîner en marchant; (*a.* ~ *about*) rôder; **2.** allure *f* mollasse; fainéant *m*; ~ *hat* chapeau *m* rabattu.

slough¹ bourbier *m* (*a. fig.*).

slough²: ~ *off* se dépouiller de.

slovenly malpropre; négligent.

slow 1. lent (à *of, to*); en retard; lourd (*mind*); petit (*speed*); **be** ~ retarder (*watch*); **be ...** ~ retarder de ...; *in* ~ *motion* au ralenti; **2.** *adv.* lentement; **3.** (*oft.* ~ *down, up, off*) ralentir; diminuer de vitesse; ~**coach** F lambin(e *f*) *m*; ~**ness** lenteur *f*; *clock:* retard *m*; ~**worm** *zo.* orvet *m*.

sludge fange *f*; ⊕ boue *f*; vase *f*.

slug 1. lingot *m*; F balle *f*; F *vending machine:* (faux) jeton *m*; F coup *m* (violent); F gnon *m*; F *drink:* coup *m*; **2.** F cogner, frapper.

sluggish lent; paresseux.

sluice 1. écluse *f*; **2.** *v/t.* laver à grande eau; *v/i.* ~ *out* couler à flots.

slum bas quartier *m*.

slumber 1. *a.* ~**s** *pl.* sommeil *m*; **2.** sommeiller.

slump 1. baisse *f* soudaine; crise *f*; **2.** baisser tout à coup; s'effondrer.

slur 1. tache *f*, *fig.* atteinte *f*; bredouillement *m*; ♪ liaison *f*; **2.** *v/t.* bredouiller; ♪ lier (*two notes*).

slush neige *f* à demi fondue; fange *f*; F lavasse *f*; F sensiblerie *f*, histoires *f/pl.* sentimentales; ~ *fund*, ~ *money* fonds *m/pl.* réservés à des pots à vin; ~**y** couvert de neige) à demi fondu(e); détrempe; *fig.* sentimental.

slut souillon *f*; F *co.* coquine *f*.

sly sournois, rusé, matois; *on the* ~ furtivement; en cachette.

smack¹ 1. léger goût *m*; soupçon *m* (*a. fig.*); **2.** ~ *of* avoir un goût de; sentir (*qch.*) (*a. fig.*).

smack² 1. tape *f*, claque *f*; F gros baiser *m*; F essai *m*, tour *m*; **2.** donner une tape *or* claque à (*q.*); frapper; ~ *one's lips* se lécher les babines; **3.** F en plein; ~**er** F gros baiser *m*; *money:* Br. livre *f*, Am. dollar *m*.

small 1. *usu.* petit; peu important; *make s.o. feel* ~ humilier q.; *in the* ~ *hours* au petit matin; **2.** partie *f* mince; *anat.* ~ *of the back* creux *m* des reins; ~**ish** assez

petit; ~**pox** ✚ *pl.* petite vérole *f*; ~**time** insignifiant, peu important.

smarmy F flagorneur, mielleux.

smart 1. *esp. Br.* chic, élégant; *esp. Am.* intelligent, habile, adroit, débrouillard; vif, violent; F ~ *aleck* je-sais-tout *mf/ inv.*; **2.** faire mal, brûler; **3.** douleur *f* (cuisante); ~**en** (*usu.* ~ *up*) *v/t.* donner du chic à, rendre plus beau; ~ *o.s. up* se faire beau; se (re)faire une beauté (*woman*); ~**ness** finesse *f*; intelligence *f*; élégance *f*, chic *m*; *mind:* vivacité *f*.

smash 1. *vt/i.* (se)briser, (se) fracasser (en morceaux, *to pieces*); (s')écraser (*a. fig.*); ~ *in* enfoncer; ~ *into* rentrer dans (*qch.*); **2.** fracassement *m*, fracas *m*; coup *m* (violent); collision *f*; *fig.* débâcle *f*; (*a.* ~ *hit*) succès *m* (fou); ~**er** F: *be a* (*real*) ~ être (vachement) épatant; ~**ing** F *fig.* formidable; ~**up** collision *f*, accident *m*.

smattering: *a* ~ (*of*) un peu (de); quelques connaissances *f/pl.* vagues (en *or* de).

smear 1. salir; barbouiller; enduire; **2.** tache *f*, salissure *f*.

smell 1. odeur *f*; (*a. sense of* ~) odorat *m*; **2.** *v/i.* sentir (*qch.*, *of s.th.*); *pej.* sentir mauvais; *v/t.* sentir; (*a.* ~ *at*) sentir (*a flower*).

smelt fondre; extraire par fusion.

smile 1. sourire *m*; **2.** sourire (à *at*).

smirk 1. sourire affecté; **2.** sourire d'un air satisfait.

smith forgeron *m*.

smithereens *pl.* miettes *f/pl.*

smithy forge *f*.

smitten (de, *with*) frappé, pris amoureux, épris.

smock blouse *f*, sarrau *m*.

smog smog *m*.

smoke 1. fumée *f*; *have a* ~ fumer; **2.** fumer; *no smoking!* défense de fumer; ~**ed** *cuis.* fumé; ~**er** fumeur (-euse *f*) *m*; ⚑ wagon *m* fumeurs; ~**y** fumeux; plein de fumée; noirci par la fumée.

smolder *Am.* couver.

smooth 1. lisse, uni, égale (*surface*); régulier (*movement etc.*); moelleux, doux (*taste*, *drink etc.*); onctueux (*cream etc.*); *fig.* calme, sans à-coups *or* secousses *or* heurts; **2.** aplanir, polir; (*a.* ~ *down*) lisser, (*a.* ~ *out*) défroisser; ~ *away* faire disparaître; ~ *s.th. into* faire pénétrer qch. dans; *fig.* **~ the way (to)** aplanir la route (de); **~ness** égalité *f*; douceur *f*; **~-tongued** mielleux, enjôleur.

smother (*fig. oft.* **~ up**) étouffer.

smoulder couver.

smudge 1. *v/t.* souiller; **2.** tache *f*.

smug suffisant, content de soi.

smuggl|e faire passer (*qch.*) en contrebande; **~er** contrebandier *m*; **~ing** contrebande *f*.

smut flocon *m or* tache *f* de suie; *coll.* saletés *f/pl.*; **~ty** sale, obscène.

snack casse-croûte *m/inv.*; **~bar** snack(bar) *m*.

snag *tree etc.*: chicot *m*; saillie *f*; *fig.* obstacle *m*, inconvenient *m*; *in cloth*: accroc *m*; **2.** faire un accroc à; F attraper, F pincer.

snail *zo.* limaçon *m*, escargot *m*.

snake *zo.* serpent *m*.

snap 1. claquement *m*; *fig.* énergie *f*; *suitcase*: fermoir *m*; rupture *f* soudaine; *phot.* instantané *m*; **cold ~** froid *m* soudain; **2.** *v/i.* (se) casser (net); claquer (*whip etc.*); **~ at** essayer de happer *or* de mordre; F *fig.* parler à (*q.*) d'un ton sec; F **~ out of it!** secouez-vous!; **~ open (shut)** s'ouvrir (se fermer) avec un bruit sec; *v/t.* happer; faire claquer; casser; *phot.* prendre un instantané de; **~ up** saisir; happer; *fig.* profiter de, sauter sur (*an opportunity*); **~ fastener** bouton-pression (*pl.* boutons-pression) *m*; **~pish** hargneux; irritable; **~py:** F **make it ~!** dépêchez-vous!; **~shot** *phot.* instantané *m*.

snare 1. piège *m*; lacet *m*; **2.** prendre au lacet *or* au piège; attraper.

snarl 1. *v/i.* grogner; (*a.* **~ up**) s'emmêler; **2.** grognement *m*; *a.* **~-up** enchevêtrement *m*; *traffic*: embouteillage *m*; F pagaïe *f*.

snatch 1. mouvement *m* pour saisir; morceau *m*; courte période *f*; **2.** saisir; **~ at** tâcher de saisir.

sneak 1. *v/i.* se glisser furtivement (dans, **in[to]**; hors de, **out of**); *school*: moucharder (*q.*, **on s.o.**); **2.** *school*: mouchard *m*; **~ers** *pl.* F (chaussures *f/pl.*) tennis *m/pl.*; **~y** F sournois.

sneer 1. ricanement *m*; **2.** ricaner; se moquer (de, **at**).

sneeze 1. éternuer; F **that's not to be ~d**

at ce n'est pas à dédaigner; **2.** éternuement *m*.

snicker *see* **snigger**; hennir (*horse*).

snide sarcastique.

sniff *v/i.* renifler (qch., [**at**] *s.th.*); *fig.* faire la grimace; *v/t.* renifler; humer; flairer.

sniffle 1. renifler; **2.** reniflement *m*; **~s** *pl.* petit rhume *m*.

snigger 1. rire sous cape (de, **at**); ricaner tout bas; **2.** ricanement *m*.

snip 1. coup *m* de ciseaux; petit bout *m*; petite entaille *f*; **2.** couper.

snipe bécassine *f*; **~r** canardeur *m*.

snivel pleurnicher.

snob snob *m*; **~bish** snob.

snog F se peloter.

snoop F **1.** fureter; **2.** fureteur (-euse *f*) *m*.

snooty F prétentieux, snob.

snooze F **1.** petit somme *m*; **2.** sommeiller; faire un petit somme.

snore ronfler; ronflement *m*.

snort s'ébrouer (*horse*); grogner.

snout museau *m*; *pig*: groin *m*.

snow 1. neige *f* (*a. sl.* cocaine); **2.** *v/i.* neiger; *v/t.:* **be ~ed in** être bloqué par la neige; *fig.* **be ~ed under** être accablé (de, **with**); **~ball** boule *f* de neige; **~bound** enneigé, bloqué par la neige; **~capped**, **~clad**, **~covered** couvert de neige; **~ drift** amas *m* de neige, congère *f*; **~drop** ♀ perce-neige *f/inv.*; **~flake** flocon *m* de neige; **~plough**, *Am.* **~plow** chasse-neige *m/inv.*; **~white** blanc comme la neige; **~y** neigeux, de neige.

snub 1. remettre (*q.*) à sa place; **2.** rebuffade *f*; **~-nosed** (au nez) camus.

snuff tabac *m* à priser.

snug douillet; confortable.

snuggle *v/i.* se blottir; *v/t.* serrer.

so ainsi; par conséquent; si, tellement; donc; **I hope ~** je l'espère bien; **are you tired?** ~ **I am** êtes-vous fatigué? je le suis en effet; **you are tired, ~ am I** vous êtes fatigué, (et) moi aussi; **a mile or ~** un mille à peu près; ~ **as to** pour (*inf.*), afin de (*inf.*), pour *or* afin que (*sbj.*); ~ **far** jusqu'ici.

soak *v/t.* (faire) tremper; ~ **up** (*or* **in**) absorber; **~ed through** trempé jusqu'aux os; *v/i.* tremper.

soap 1. savon *m*; ~ **bubble** bulle *f* de savon; ~ **opera** mélodrame *m* (télé-

S

visé); **~ powder** lessive f, détergent m;
2. savonner; **~box** caisse f à savon; **~
orator** orateur m de carrefour; **~stone**
stéatite f.

soar 1. planer; (a. **~ up**) monter (en flèche);
s'élever.

sob 1. sanglot m; **2.** sangloter.

sober 1. sobre, modéré; grave; sérieux;
pas ivre; rassis (mind); **2.** (oft. **~ down**)
(se) dégriser; **~ness, sobriety** sobriété
f; calme m.

sob-stuff F sensiblerie f, histoire(s) f/(pl.)
larmoyante(s).

so-called prétendu, soi-disant.

soccer sp. football m association.

sociable 1. sociable; zo. sociétaire; **2.**
Am. soirée f amicale.

social 1. social; **~ insurance** assurance f
sociale; (**be on**) **~ security** (recevoir
l'aide f sociale; **~ services** pl. institu-
tions f/pl. sociales; **2.** F réunion f; **~ism**
socialisme m; **~ work** assistance f sociale; **~ worker** assistant(e f) m social(e);
~ist socialiste (a. su.); **~istic** socialiste.

society société f; association f.

sock 1. chaussette f; F coup m (violent);
2. F flanquer un coup à.

socket douille f (a. ⚡); eye: orbite f;
tooth: alvéole m; ⚡ prise f (de courant);
cavité f.

sod gazon m; motte f; **2.** gazonner.

soda 🜔 soude f; **~ fountain** buvette f; **~
water** (eau f de) Seltz f.

sodden (dé)trempé; fig. abruti.

soft 1. mou; doux (a. voice, noise etc.);
tendre; flasque; facile (job etc.); sl. stupid: débile, bête; **~ drink** boisson f non
alcoolisée; F **~ soap** flatterie f; **2.** adv.
doucement; sans bruit; **3.** F niagud (-e
f) m; **~en** (s')amollir; (s')adoucir; fig.
(s')attendrir; v/t. atténuer (colours; a.
phot. the outlines); **~-boiled: ~ egg** œuf
m à la coque; **~-hearted** au cœur tendre; **~-soap** F flatter; **~-spoken** à la
voix douce; **~ware** data processing: lo-
giciel m.

soggy détrempé; lourd (weather).

soil 1. sol m, terre f; **2.** (se) salir; v/t.
souiller; **~ed** sale.

solace 1. consolation f; **2.** consoler.

solar solaire; **~ cell** cellule f photovol-
taïque; **~ eclipse** éclipse f du soleil; **~
plexus** plexus m solaire.

solder 1. soudure f; **2.** souder.

soldier soldat m; **~ly** de soldat.

sole¹ seul, unique; **~ly** uniquement, seulement; **~ agent** agent m exclusif.

sole² 1. semelle f; foot: plante f; **2.** ressemeler.

sole³ icht. sole f.

solemn solennel; sérieux; grave; **~ity** so-
lennité f (a. ceremony); gravité f; **~ize**
célébrer (a wedding).

solicit solliciter (qch. de q. **s.o. for s.th.,
s.th. from s.o.**); ⚖ racoler (prostitute);
~ation sollicitation f; **~or** ⚖ avoué m;
~ous préoccupé (de, **about**); soucieux
(de, **of**; de inf., **to** inf.).

solid 1. solide (a. fig., 🝆); plein (wall); vif
(rock); massif (gold); substantiel (meal
etc.); **a ~ hour** une bonne heure; **2.**
solide m; **~arity** solidarité f; **~ify** (se)
solidifier; v/i. se figer; **~ity** solidité f.

soliloquy monologue m.

solit|ary solitaire; isolé; ⚖ **~ confine-
ment** isolement m; **~ude** solitude f.

solo solo m; **~ist** soliste mf.

solstice solstice m.

solu|ble soluble; **~tion** solution f.

solve résoudre; **~nt 1.** dissolvant; 🜹
solvable; **2.** (dis)solvant m.

somb|re, Am. **~er** sombre; morne.

some 1. pron. certains; quelques-uns;
quelques-unes; un peu, en; **I need ~** j'en
ai besoin; **2.** adj. quelque; quelconque;
un certain; du, de la, des, quelques; **~
bread** du pain; **~ 20 miles** une vingtaine de milles; **3.** adv. quelque, environ;
~body, ~one quelqu'un; **~how** d'une
façon ou d'une autre; **~ or other** d'une
manière ou d'une autre.

somersault 1. culbute f; **turn a ~** faire
une culbute **2.** faire la ou des culbute(s);
mot. faire un tonneau.

some...: ~thing quelque chose m; **~ simple**
quelque chose de simple; **~ else** autre
chose; **~time 1.** adv. future: un de ces
jours; à un moment donné; past: autrefois; **2.** adj. ancien (before su.); **~times**
parfois, quelquefois; **~what** quelque
peu, un peu; **~where** quelque part.

somniferous somnifère, endormant.

son fils m.

sonata ♪ sonate f.

song chanson f; F **for a ~** pour une
bagatelle, pour rien; **~ bird** oiseau m
chanteur; **~book** recueil m de chan-
sons.

spade

sonic sonique (*speed etc.*); ~ **bang** (*or* **boom**) bang *m* (super)sonique; ~ **barrier** mur *m* du son.

son-in-law gendre *m*.

sonny F (mon) petit *m*.

sonorous sonore.

soon bientôt; tôt; vite, de bonne heure; *as* (*or* **so**) ~ *as* aussitôt que; **~er** plus tôt; plutôt; *no* ... ~ *than* à peine... que; *no* ~ *said than done* sitôt dit, sitôt fait.

soot 1. suie *f*; **2.** couvrir de suie.

soothe calmer, apaiser.

soothsayer devin(eresse *f*) *m*.

sooty couvert *or* noir de suie.

sop 1. concession *f*, petit cadeau *m*; **2.** ~ **up** éponger.

sophisticated sophistiqué; **~ry** sophistique *f*; sophismes *m/pl.*

sophomore *Am.* étudiant(e *f*) *m* de seconde année.

soporific soporifique (*a. su./m*).

sopping (*a.* ~ **wet**) (tout) trempé.

soppy F sentimental.

sorcer|er sorcier *m*; **~ess** sorcière *f*; **~y** sorcellerie *f*.

sordid sordide.

sore douloureux, sensible, *fig.* vexé, ulcéré; ~ **spot** point *m* délicat; ~ **throat** mal *m* de gorge; **2.** plaie *f*.

sorrel oseille *f*.

sorrow chagrin *m*; **~ful** triste.

sorry fâché (de *to*, *at*); *fig.* misérable; (*I am*) (**so**) ~! pardon! *I am ~ for you* je vous plains; *we are ~ to say* nous regrettons d'avoir à dire...

sort sorte *f*, genre *m*, espèce *f*; classe *f*; façon *f*; *out of* ~*s* indisposé; de mauvaise humeur; **2.** trier, assortir; classifier; ~ **out** séparer (de, *from*); mettre de l'ordre dans; (re)mettre en ordre; F régler.

so-so F comme ci comme ça.

sot ivrogne(sse *f*) *m*.

soul âme *f*.

sound¹ 1. en bon état; sain; bon; solide; sensé; **~ly** complètement; *sleep:* profondément; **2.** *be* ~ *asleep* être profondément endormi.

sound² 1. son *m*, bruit *m*; **2.** sonore (*film, wave etc.*); du son (*engineer, speed etc.*); ~ **barrier** mur *m* du son; ~ **effects** *pl.* bruitage *m*; **3.** *v/i.* sonner, retentir; *fig. seem:* sonner (juste, *right etc.*); (*a.* ~ *like*) sembler (être), avoir l'air de; *v/t.*

sonner (l'alarme, *the alarm etc.*); faire retentir; *mot.* ~ *one's horn* donner un coup de klaxon, klaxonner.

sound³ *geog.* détroit *m*; bras *m* de mer.

sound⁴ 1. ✶ *etc.* sonde *f*; **2.** sonder (*a. fig.* = ~ *out*); **~ings** *pl.* sondage(s) *m*(*pl.*) (*a. fig.*).

sound...: ~less muet; **~ness** bon état *m*; solidité *f* (*a. fig.*); **~proof 1.** insonorisé; **2.** insonoriser; **~track** *cin.* bande *f* sonore.

soup 1. potage *m*; soupe *f*; F *in the* ~ dans le pétrin; **2.** F ~ *up* mot. *etc.* gonfler.

sour 1. aigre, acide; tourné (*milk*); **2.** (s')aigrir; (faire) tourner (*milk*).

source source *f*; ~ **language** langue *f* de départ.

sour|ish aigrelet; **~ness** aigreur *f*.

souse tremper (d'eau, *with water*); *cuis.* mariner; **~d** *sl.* ivre.

south 1. *su.* sud *m*; midi *m*; **2.** *adj.* (du) sud; **3.** *adv.* au sud, vers le sud; **~east 1.** sud-est *m*; **2.** (*a.* **~ern**) (du) sud-est.

souther|ly; ~n (du) sud; du midi; méridional; **~ner** habitant(e *f*) *m* du sud; *Am.* ⹀ sudiste *mf*.

southpaw *sp.* gaucher *m*.

southward 1. *adj.* au *or* du sud; **2.** *adv.* (*a.* **~s**) vers le sud.

south...: ~west 1. *su.* sud-ouest *m*; **2.** *adv.* vers le sud-ouest; **3.** *adj.* (*a.* **~westerly**, **~western**) (du) sud-ouest.

souvenir souvenir *m*.

sovereign 1. souverain; **2.** souverain(e *f*) *m*; **~ty** souveraineté *f*.

soviet Soviet *m*; *attr.* soviétique.

sow¹ *zo.* truie *f*.

sow² semer, ensemencer (*a field*).

soy(a) soya *m*; **~bean** graine *f* de soya; ~ **sauce** sauce *f* de soya.

spa station *f* thermale.

space 1. espace *m*; *room a.* place *f*; *in time:* espace *m* (de temps), intervalle *m*; **2.** spatial (*flight, lab, weapon etc.*); ~ **shuttle** navette *f*; **3.** (*a.* ~ *out*) espacer; *typ.* **single** (**double**) **spacing** interligne *m* simple (double); **~craft**, **~ship** vaisseau *m* spatial; **~man**, **~woman** astronaute *fm*.

spacious spacieux, ample.

spade bêche *f*; *call a ~ a ~* appeler les choses par leur nom; *usu.* **~s** *pl. cards:* pique *m*.

span 1. *hand:* empan *m;* espace *m* de temps; △ portée *f; wings, a.* ✔ envergure *f;* **2.** franchir, enjamber; *fig.* embrasser.

spangle 1. paillette *f;* **2.** pailleter.

Spaniard Espagnol(e *f*) *m.*

Spanish 1. espagnol; d'Espagne; **2.** *ling.* espagnol *m; the ~ pl.* les Espagnols *m/pl.*

spank *v/t.* fesser; *v/i. ~ along* aller bon train; **~ing** fessée *f.*

spanner ⊕ clef *f* (à écrous).

spar|e 1. de réserve, ⊕ *etc. a.* de rechange; de trop, en trop; disponible; maigre; *~ part see* **2**; *~ room* chambre *f* d'ami; *~ time* temps *m* libre, loisir(s) *m/(pl.); mot. ~ wheel* roue *f* de secours; **2.** ⊕ pièce *f* de rechange; **3.** *v/t.* épargner, ménager (*a. fig.*); se passer de; donner, accorder, consacrer; *~ s.o. s.th.* épargner qch. à q., faire grâce à q. de qch.; *to ~* de trop; plus qu'il n'en faut; **~ing** restreint (*use etc.*); économe; *be ~ of (or in) sth.* être chiche de; *use ~ly* ménager, économiser.

spark 1. étincelle *f* (*a. fig.*); **2.** *v/i.* émettre des étincelles; *v/t.* susciter, éveiller; (*a. ~ off*) provoquer; **~(ing) plug** *mot.* bougie *f.*

sparkle 1. étincellement *m,* scintillement *m;* éclat *m* (*a. fig.*); **2.** étinceler, scintiller; chatoyer (*jewel*); pétiller (*wine*); *sparkling wine* vin *m* mousseux *or* pétillant.

sparrow moineau *m,* passereau *m.*

sparse épars, clairsemé.

spasm ⊹ spasme *m; fig.* accès *m;* **~odic(al)** spasmodique.

spastic paraplégique (spasmodique) (*adj., su./mf*).

spatial spatial.

spatter 1. *v/t.* éclabousser (de, *with*); *v/i.* gicler, jaillir; **2.** éclaboussure *f.*

spawn 1. *v/t. zo.* frai *m;* **2.** *v/i.* frayer; *pej.* se multiplier; *v/t.* pondre.

speak *v/i.* parler (à, *to, with;* de, *of, about*); *~ing of ...* à propos de ...; *so to ~* pour ainsi dire; *no ... to ~ of* pratiquement pas de ...; *be on ~ing terms* se parler; *fig. ~ for itself* se passer d'explication; *the facts ~ for themselves* les faits parlent d'eux-mêmes; *~ up* parler plus fort; *fig.* (*a. ~ out*) parler franchement; *~ up for* défendre; *v/t.* dire (qch.);

parler (*a language*); exprimer; *~easy* bar *m* clandestin; *~er* parleur (-euse *f*) *m;* orateur *m;* (*usu. loud.*) *radio:* haut-parleur *m; parl.* ♀ Président *m.*

spear 1. lance *f;* **2.** percer.

special 1. spécial; particulier; **2.** *restaurant:* spécialité *f* de la maison; *✝ on ~* en promotion (*article*); **~ist** spécialiste *mf;* **~ty** spécialité *f;* **~ize** se spécialiser (dans, *in*).

species *sg. or pl.* espèce *f.*

speci|fic particulier; précis; spécifique (*difference etc.*); *phys. ~ gravity* pesanteur *f* spécifique; **~fically** expressément; particulièrement; **~fy** spécifier; préciser; **~men** spécimen *m;* ✻prélèvement *m.*

specious spécieux; trompeur.

speck graine *f;* tache *f; fig.* brin *m;* **~le** tache(ture) *f;* **~led** tacheté; moucheté.

spectacle spectacle *m;* (*a pair of*) *~s pl.* (des) lunettes *f/pl.*

spectacular 1. spectaculaire; **2.** revue *f etc.* à grand spectacle.

spectator spectateur (-trice *f*) *m.*

spect|ral spectral (*a. opt.*); **~re,** *Am.* **~er** fantôme *m,* spectre *m.*

speculat|e spéculer (*a. ✝*); méditer (sur, [*up*]*on*); **~ion** spéculation *f* (*a. ✝*); conjecture(s) *f/(pl.);* **~ive** spéculatif.

speech parole(s) *f/(pl.);* langue *f;* discours *m; ~ day school:* distribution *f* des prix; **~less** muet.

speed 1. vitesse *f;* rapidité *f; ~ cop* motard *m; ~ limit* limitation *f* de vitesse; vitesse *f* maximale (permise); *at full (or top) ~* à toute vitesse; **2.** *v/i.* filer (à toute allure); *mot. a.* rouler trop vite; *~ up* aller (*or* marcher, rouler *etc.*) plus vite; se hâter; *mot.* accélérer; *v/t.* accélérer; faire marcher plus vite; **~iness** rapidité *f;* promptitude *f;* **~ing** *mot.* excès *m* de vitesse; **~ometer** *mot.* compteur *m* de vitesse; **~-up** accélération *f;* **~y** rapide, prompt.

spell 1. charme *m,* sortilège; période *f,* temps; tour *m; put under a ~, cast a ~ over* jeter un sort à, *fig. a.* envoûter; **2.** (*a. ~ out*) orthographier, écrire; épeler; *fig.* expliquer; **~bound** envoûté, fasciné; **~ing** épellation *f;* orthographe *f.*

spend dépenser (*money etc.*) (en, à, pour *on*); *pej.* dissiper (pour, *on*); passer (*one's time*); *~ o.s.* s'épuiser; **~ing**

sponsor

money argent *m* de poche; **~thrift** dépenser (-ère *f*) *m* (*a. attr.*).

spent épuisé.

sperm *physiol.* sperme *m.*

spew cracher; vomir.

spher|e sphère *f* (*a. fig. of activity, of influence etc.*); *fig. a.* domaine *m*; **~ical** sphérique.

spice 1. épice *f*; piquant *m*; **2.** épicer, *a. fig.* relever.

spick and span propre comme un sou neuf.

spicy épicé; aromatique; piquant.

spider *zo.* araignée *f.*

spiel *sl.* laïus *m*, baratin *m.*

spigot *barrel:* fausset *m.*

spike pointe *f*; ♀ *corn:* épi *m.*

spill *v/t.* répandre; renverser, *v/i.* se répandre; **~ over** déborder.

spin I. *v/t.* filer; faire tourner; *fig.* raconter *or* débiter (*a story*); **~ a coin** jouer à pile ou face; **~ out** faire durer; *v/i.* tourner; (*a.* **~ round**) tournoyer; **~ along** filer; **~ round** *a.* se retourner (brusquement); **2.** tournoiement *m*; ✈ vrille *f*; *fig.* chute *f*; F (petit) tour *m*, balade *f*; F **go for a ~** se balader; **go into a ~** tomber en vrille; se mettre à tournoyer; ⊢ *fig.* **got (o.s.) into a ~** s'affoler.

spinach ♀ épinard *m*; *cuis.* épinards *m/pl.*

spinal vertébral; **~ column** colonne *f* vertébrale; **~ cord** moelle *f* épinière.

spindle fuseau *m*; ⊕ arbre *m.*

spindly grêle.

spin-dry essorer à la machine.

spine épine *f*; *anat., geog.* épine *f* dorsale; *book:* dos *m.*

spinning...: **~ mill** filature *f*; **~ wheel** rouet *m.*

spin-off sous-produit *m*; avantage *m* supplémentaire.

spinster vieille fille *f.*

spiny épineux.

spiral 1. spiral; spiralé; en spirale; **~ staircase** escalier *m* en colimaçon; **2.** spirale *f*; *fig.* montée *f* en flèche; **3.** tourner en spirale; (*a.* **~ up**) monter en vrille, *suddenly* monter en flèche.

spire *church, tree:* flèche *f.*

spirit esprit *m*; humeur *f*; **~s** *pl.* spiritueux *m/pl.*; (**in** (**high**) **~s** en train; en verve; **in low ~s** abattu; accablé; **2.:** **~ away** (*or* **off**) enlever, faire disparaître;

~ed animé; plein d'entrain; fougueux; **~less** abattu; inanimé; sans vie (*a. fig.*); **~ual** spirituel; **~ualism** spiritisme *m*; **~uous** spiritueux.

spit¹ 1. *cuis.* broche *f*; *geog.* langue *f* de sable; **2.** embrocher.

spit² 1. crachat *m*; salive *f*; **2.** cracher; crépiter; **the ~ting image of ...** tout le portrait de ...

spite 1. dépit *m*; rancune *f*; **in ~ of** en dépit de, malgré; **2.** contrarier, vexer; **~ful** rancunier; méchant.

spittle salive *f*, crachat *m.*

spittoon crachoir *m.*

splash 1. éclaboussure *m*; éclaboussure *f*; *colour:* tache *f*; *sound:* plouf *m*; F *fig.* sensation *f*, bruit *m*; *v/t.* éclabousser; faire des éclaboussures de; **~ out** dépenser; *v/i.* patauger; barboter; **~ into** plonger avec un plouf dans (*the water*); **~ on** éclabousser (*qch.*).

splay *v/t.* faire tourner en dehors; *v/i.* se tourner en dehors; **~-footed** aux pieds plats.

spleen *anat.* rate *f*; *fig.* spleen *m.*

splend|id splendide, magnifique; **~o(u)r** splendeur *f*; éclat *m.*

splice ⊕ enter; épisser (*a cable*).

splint ✄ **1.** éclisse *f*; **2.** éclisser; **~er 1.** éclat *m*; écharde *f*; **2.** *v/t.* briser; *v/i.* voler en éclats; se fendre.

split 1. fente *f*, fissure *f*; *fig.* scission *f*; *sp.* **do the ~s** faire le grand écart; **2.** fendu; divisé; **~ ring** anneau *m* brisé; (**in**) **a ~ second** (en) un rien de temps; **3.** *v/t.* fendre; diviser; couper en deux; **~ one's sides with laughter** se tordre de rire; *v/i.* se fendre; se diviser; *fig.* rompre (avec, **with** *s.o.*); **~ up** se séparer; se disperser (*crowd etc.*); rompre (*couple*); **~ting 1.** fendage *m*; *atom:* fission *f*; **2.** **~ headache** mal *m* de tête atroce.

spoil 1. (se) gâter; (s')abîmer; **2.** **~s** *pl.* butin *m*; **~sport** trouble-fête *mf/inv.*

spoke *wheel:* rayon *m*; échelon *m.*

spokesman porte-parole *m/inv.*

sponge 1. éponge *f*; (*a.* **~ cake**) gâteau *m* de Savoie; **throw in the ~** abandonner (la partie), décrocher; **~ bag** sac *m* de toilette; **2.** *v/t.* nettoyer *or* laver avec une éponge; **~ up** éponger; *v/i.* **~ on** vivre aux crochets de; **~r** parasite *m.*

sponsor 1. garant *m*, caution *f*; *club:* parrain *m*; sponsor *m*; **2.** être le garant de; financer, sponsorer; **~ship** patronage *m*, parrainage *m*.

spontane|ity spontanéité *f*; **~ous** spontané.

spoof F **1.** parodie *f*; mystification *f*; **2.** parodier; mystifier.

spook F **1.** revenant *m*; **2.** spectral; de revenant; lugubre.

spool 1. bobine *f*; **2.** bobiner.

spoon 1. cuiller *f*, cuillère *f*; **2.** verser *or* mettre avec une cuiller; (*a.* **~ up**) manger avec une cuiller; *sl.* se peloter; **~feed** nourrir à la cuiller (*a baby*); *fig.* mâcher le travail à (*q.*), gâter; **~ful** cuillerée *f*.

sporadic sporadique.

spore ♀ spore *f*.

sport 1. sport *m*; jeu *m*; divertissement *m*; *fig.* jouet *m*; F (*a.* **good ~**) chic type *m*; **2.** *v/i.* jouer; se divertir; *v/t.* arborer; **~ive** folâtre, badin, enjoué; **~sman** sportif *m*; **~swoman** sportive *f*; **~y** sportif.

spot 1. tache *f*; *cloth:* pois *m*; lieu *m*, endroit *m*; *⚡* projecteur *m*; *radio:* spot *m*; F **a ~ of** un peu de; **on the ~** sur place; *adv.* immédiatement; **2.** (fait au hasard; *⛇* (au) comptant; (du) disponible; **~ check** contrôle *m* fait au hasard; **3.** *v/t.* tacher; tacheter; répérer, apercevoir; **~less** sans tache; immaculé; **~light 1.** projecteur *m*; *fig.* **in the ~** en vedette; **2.** mettre en vedette; attirer l'attention sur; **~ted** tacheté, moucheté; **~on** F exact(ement), précis(ement); **~ty** moucheté; couvert de boutons (*face*).

spouse époux (-ouse *f*) *m*.

spout 1. *teapot etc.:* bec *m*; *liquid:* jet *m*; **2.** (faire) jaillir.

sprain 1. entorse *f*, foulure *f*; **2.** se fouler (la cheville, *one's ankle*).

sprat *icht.* sprat *m*.

sprawl s'étendre, s'étaler.

spray 1. poussière *f* d'eau; spray *m*, aérosol *m*; *flowers etc.:* (petit) bouquet *m*; **2.** vaporiser (*a liquid*); arroser; **~er** atomiseur *m*, bombe *f*.

spread 1. (se) répandre; (*a.* **~ out**) (s') étaler, (s')étendre; (s')ouvrir; *v/t. a.* tartiner (*bread*); **2.** étendue *f*; *wings:* envergure *f*; propagation *f*; diffusion *f*; *Am.* dessus *m* de lit; *sandwich etc.:* pâte *f*; F festin *m*.

spree F bombe *f*, noce *f*; bringue *f*.

sprig brin *m*, rameau *m*.

sprightly alerte, vif.

spring 1. saut *m*, bond *m*; ⊕ ressort *m*; *car:* suspension *f*; *water, a. fig.:* source *f*; *season:* printemps *m*; **2.** *v/i.* sauter, bondir; jaillir (de, **from**); *fig.* sortir (de, **from**); **~ up** sauter en l'air; se former (*ideas*); **~ into existence** naître; *v/t.* franchir; faire sauter (*a mine*); **~board** tremplin *m*; **~time** printemps *m*; **~y** élastique; flexible.

sprinkl|e répandre; arroser; saupoudrer; **~d with** parsemé de; **~er** arroseur *m* automatique; **~ing** aspersion *f*; légère couche *f*; **a ~ of** quelques (bribes de).

sprint 1. sprint *m*; **2.** sprinter; **~er** sprinter (-euse *f*) *m*.

sprite lutin *m*; esprit *m*.

sprout 1. (laisser) pousser; **2.** ♀ pousse *f*; bourgeon *m*; **Brussels ~s** *pl.* choux *m*/ *pl.* de Bruxelles.

spruce¹ soigné; pimpant.

spruce² ♀ (*a.* **~ fir**) sapin *m*.

spry vif, alerte.

spur 1. éperon *m*; *fig.* aiguillon *m*; **on the ~ of the moment** sous l'inspiration du moment; **2.** (*a.* **~ on**) éperonner; *fig. a.* aiguillonner.

spurious faux.

spurn repousser avec mépris.

spurt 1. (faire) jaillir; *v/i. sp.* démarrer; **2.** jaillissement *m*; jet *m* (*of water etc.*); effort *m* soudain; *sp.* effort *m* de vitesse.

sputter bafouiller; crépiter.

spy 1. espion(ne *f*) *m*; **2.** *v/i.* espionner; **~ on s.o.** espionner q.; *v/t.* apercevoir; **~ out** explorer (*a country*); **~hole** *door:* judas *m*; **~ing** espionnage *m*.

squabble 1. querelle *f*; prise *f* de bec; chamaille *f*; **2.** se chamailler.

squad escouade *f*; peloton *m*; *police:* brigade *f*; *Am.* équipe *f*; *⚔* escadron *m*; *✈* escadrille *f*; *⚓* escadre *f*.

squalid sordide; misérable.

squall coup *m* de vent, rafale *f*.

squalor condition *f* sordide.

squander gaspiller; dissiper.

square 1. carré; *fig.* honnête, loyal; décent (*meal etc.*); catégorique (*refusal*); **~ measure** mesure *f* de surface; **~ mile** mille *m* carré; **2.** carré *m*; *town etc.:*

place *f*; *Am.* bloc *m* de maisons; **3.** *v/t.*
carrer; ⚔ élever au carré; *fig.* régler;
arranger; *v/i.* cadrer (avec, **with**); s'accorder (avec, **with**).

squash[1] **1.** cohue *f*; *sp.* squash *m*; **lemon ~** citronnade *f*; **orange ~** orangeade *f*; **2.** écraser; *fig.* (se) serrer; (se) tasser.

squat 1. s'accroupir; **2.** trapu.

squawk 1. pousser un cri rauque *or* des cris rauques; **2.** cri *m* rauque.

squeak 1. pousser des cris aigus; grincer; **2.** cri *m* aigu.

squeal pousser des cris aigus; F **~ on s.o.** dénoncer q.

squeamish sujet aux nausées; délicat, facilement dégoûté.

squeeze 1. *v/t.* serrer; presser; *fig.* extorquer (à, **from**); **~ out** exprimer; *v/i.* **~ together** (*or* **up**) se serrer; **2.** (com)pression *f*; *hand:* serrement *m*; **~r** presse-fruits *m/inv.*

squelch gargouiller; patauger.

squid *zo.* calmar *m*.

squiggle gribouillis *m*.

squint loucher.

squire propriétaire *m* terrien.

squirm F se tortiller; se tordre.

squirrel *zo.* écureuil *m*.

squirt 1. jet *m* (of water etc.); **2.** (faire) jaillir *or* gicler.

stab 1. coup *m* de poignard *or* de couteau etc.; **2.** poignarder.

stability stabilité *f*; fermeté *f*.

stable[1] stable; solide; ferme.

stable[2] écurie *f*.

stack tas *m*, pile *f*; *hay etc.:* meule *f*; *chimney:* souche *f*; ((tuyau *m* de) cheminée *f*; **~s** *pl.* magasin *m* de livres; F **~s of** un *or* des tas de, plein de; F **~s pl. blow one's ~** sortir de ses gonds, se mettre en rogne; **2.** (*a.* **~ up**) empiler.

stadium *sp.*, *pl.* **-dia** stade *m*.

staff 1. personnel *m*; bâton *m*; mât *m*; ⚔ état-major (*pl.* états-majors) *m*; ♪ (*pl.* **staves**) portée *f*; **2.** pourvoir en personnel.

stag *zo.* cerf *m*.

stage 1. estrade *f*; *thea.* scène *f*; *fig.* le théâtre *m*; période *f*; étape *f*; stade *m*, phase *f*; **in ~s** par étapes; *thea.* **on ~** sur scène; **2.** mettre en scène; monter; *fig.* organiser; **~coach** diligence *f*; **~ direction** indication *f* scénique; **~ fright** trac

m; **~ hand** machiniste *m*; **~ manager** régisseur *m*; **~ whisper** aparté *m*.

stagger 1. *v/i.* chanceler, tituber; *v/t.* faire chanceler; *fig.* renverser, bouleverser, stupéfier; *fig.* échelonner; **2.** allure *f* chancelante; *fig.* échelonnement *m*; **~ing** bouleversant, renversant.

stagna|nt stagnant; **~te** stagner.

stagy théâtral.

staid posé, sérieux.

stain 1. tache *f*; ⊕ colorant *m*, couleur *f*; **~ remover** détachant *m*; **2.** (se) tacher; ⊕ (se) teindre, (se) colorer; **~ed glass** verre *m* coloré; **~ed glass window** vitrail *m*; **~less** sans tache; immaculé; ⊕ inoxydable.

stair marche *f*; **~s** *pl.* escalier *m*; **~case** (cage *f* d')escalier *m*; **moving ~** escalier *m* mécanique, escalator *m*; **~way** see **staircase**.

stake 1. pieu *m*; poteau *m*; *gambling:* enjeu *m*; bûcher *m*; **~s** *pl.* *horse-race:* prix *m/pl.*; **be at ~** être en jeu; **2.** mettre en jeu; parier; hasarder; **~ out** (*or* **off**) jalonner.

stale rassis (bread etc.); éventé (beer etc.); *fig.* défraîchi (news); vicié (air); de renfermé (smell).

stalemate *chess:* pat *m*; impasse *f*.

stalk 1. tige *f*; *cabbage:* trognon *m*; **2.** *v/i.* marcher à grandes enjambées; traquer.

stall 1. *horse:* stalle *f*; *cattle:* box *m*; *market:* éventaire *m*, stand *m*; *thea.* fauteuil *m* d'orchestre; **2.** *v/t.* mettre à l'étable *or* à l'écurie; *mot.* (se) caler; essayer de gagner du temps.

stallion étalon *m*.

stalwart robuste, vigoureux, ferme.

stamina vigueur *f*, résistance *f*.

stammer 1. bégayer, balbutier; **2.** bégaiement *m*.

stamp 1. (postage **~** etc.) timbre *m*; on document: cachet *m*, timbre *m*; *implement:* timbre *m*; *fig.* empreinte *f*, marque *f*; **~ pad** tampon *m* (encreur); **date ~** timbre *m* dateur; **~ collecting** philatélie *f*; **2.** *v/t.* frapper (du pied, **one's foot**); ⊕ etc. estamper; marquer (*a.* *fig.*); timbrer (a letter, a document); **~ s.th. on** imprimer qch. sur; *v/t.* frapper *or* taper du pied; piétiner.

stampede 1. débandade *f*; ruée *f*; **2.** *v/t.* mettre en fuite; *v/i.* fuir en désordre; se précipiter.

stance position *f*.

stanch 1. étancher (*blood*); **2.** *adj.* ferme; loyal.

stand 1. *v/i.* se tenir (debout); être; se trouver; se lever, se mettre debout; ~ *against* s'adosser à; résister à; ~ *aside* se tenir à l'écart; *fig.* se désister (*in favour of s.o.*); ~ *back* se tenir en arrière; (se) reculer; ~ *by* se tenir prêt; se tenir à côté de; *fig.* soutenir; *fig.* rester fidèle à; ~ *for* représenter, signifier; se présenter comme candidat à; soutenir; tolérer; ~ *in for* remplacer; ~ *off* se tenir éloigne; s'éloigner; ~ *off!* tenez-vous à distance!; ~ *on* insister sur; ~ *out* être en or faire saillie; *fig.* se détacher (sur, *against*); résister (à, *against*); tenir bon (contre, *against*); ~ *over* rester en suspens; surveiller (*q.*); ~ *up* se lever; se dresser; ~ *up for* prendre le parti de; ~ *up to* résister à; ~ *upon* se tenir sur (*a. fig.*); insister sur; **2.** *v/t.* poser, mettre; supporter; soutenir (*a shock*); **3.** position *f*, place *f*; station(nement) *m*; *sp. etc.* tribune *f*, estrade *f*; ✝ *etc.* étalage *m*, stand *m*, étal *m*; support *m*, guéridon *m*; *Am.* 🚂 barre *f* des témoins; arrêt *m*; (*a.* wash-~) lavabo *m*; *fig.* résistance *f*; *make a* ~ *against* s'opposer résolument à.

standard 1. *measure:* étalon *m*; norme *f*; niveau *m*; qualité *f*; degré *m* (d'excellence); hauteur *f*; *gold, silver, etc.* 🔬: titre *m*; *flag:* ✗ étendard *m*, ♎ pavillon *m*; ~*s pl.* principes *m/pl.*; ~ *lamp* lampadaire *m*; *above* ~ au-dessus de la moyenne; ~ *of living* niveau *m* de vie; **2.** ordinaire, normal; courant; ~*ize* standardiser.

stand-by 1. remplaçant(e *f*) *m*; réserve *f*; *on* ~ en réserve; de garde (*person*); **2.** de réserve, de secours.

stand-in remplaçant(e *f*) *m*; *cin.* doublure *f*.

standing 1. debout; permanent; fixe; ✝ ~ *order* virement *m* automatique; ~ *room* place(s) *f/(pl.)* debout; **2.** réputation *f*, standing *m*; durée *f*; *of long* ~ d'ancienne date.

stand...: ~*offish* distant; raide; ~*point* point *m* de vue; ~*still* arrêt *m*; *come to a* ~ s'arrêter; ~*up* debout; droit (*collar*).

stanza strophe *f*, stance *f*.

staple¹ de base, principal.

staple² 1. agrafe *f*; **2.** agrafer.

star 1. étoile *f*; *thea.* vedette *f*, star *mf*; *Am.* ~*s and Stripes pl.* bannière *f* étoilée; **2.** *v/t. thea. etc.* avoir pour vedette; *v/i. thea. etc.* ~ *in* être la vedette de.

starboard ♎ tribord *m*.

starch 1. amidon *m*; **2.** empeser.

stardom célébrité *f*; *rise to* ~ devenir une vedette.

stare 1. regard *m* fixe; **2.** regarder (fixement *or* longuement); ~ *at* regarder (*qch.*, *q.*) fixement (*or* longuement); ~ *s.o. down* (*or* out) faire baisser les yeux à q.; *fig.* ~ *s.o. in the face* crever les yeux à q.; être imminent.

starfish *zo.* étoile *f* de mer.

stark 1. *adj. a. fig.* cru, nu, rude; pur, absolu, complet; désolé, morne; **2.** *adv.* complètement; ~ *naked* tout nu.

starling *orn.* étourneau *m*.

starlit étoilé.

starry étoilé; ~*eyed* rêveur; extasié; *fig.* peu réaliste.

star-spangled constellé d'étoiles; *Am.* *Star-Spangled Banner* bannière *f* étoilée.

start 1. départ *m* (*a. sp.*); commencement *m*; *sp.* avance *f*; *fig.* sursaut *m*; *get the* ~ *of s.o.* devancer q.; **2.** *v/i.* partir, se mettre en route; commencer; démarrer; ✈ décoller; *fig.* tressaillir (de, *with*; à *at*, *with*); *v/t.* faire partir (*a. game*); mettre (*an engine*) en marche; *sp.* donner le signal du départ; lancer; commencer (*one's work etc.*); entamer (*a conversation etc.*).

starter *sp.* starter *m*; *mot. etc.* démarreur *m*; *cuis.* entrée *f*.

starting de départ (*block, line, point etc.*); de début, initial (*phase, salary etc.*).

startle donner un choq à; alarmer.

starv|ation faim *f*; ✻ inanition *f*; *attr.* de famine; ~*e* (faire) mourir de faim; *fig.* *v/t.* priver (de, *of*).

state 1. état *m* (*a. pol.*); F *in a* ~ affolé, dans tous ses états; *Am.* the ~*s* les États-Unis; **2.** d'État; déclarer, affirmer; formuler; *at the* ~*d time* à l'heure dite; ♀ *Department Am. pol.* Ministère *m* des Affaires étrangères; ~*ly* majestueux; imposant; noble; ~*ment* déclaration *f*; affirmation *f*; 🚂 déposition;

✝ relevé *m* (de compte, *of account*);
~side *Am.* aux États-Unis; *Am.* F **go ~**
rentrer; **~sman** homme *m* d'État.

static 1. statique; **2.** ⚡ (*a.* **~s** *pl.*) parasites *m/pl.*

station 1. poste *m* (*a.* ⚔, ⚓, *radio*); 🚉
gare *f*; *underground*: station *f*; *fig.* situation *f*, condition *f*; rang *m*; **2.** placer; poster; **~ary** immobile; **~er** papetier *m*; **~ery** articles *m/pl.* de papeterie
f; **~ master** 🚉 chef *m* de gare; **~ wagon**
Am. mot. break *m*.

statistics *pl.* statistique *f*.

statue statue *f*.

stature taille *f*; stature *f*.

status situation *f*, état *m*; rang *m*, position *f*, standing *m*; ⚖ statut *m*; **~ seeker**
ambitieux (*euse f*) *m*; **~ symbol** marque *f* de standing.

statute loi *f*; **~s** *pl.* statuts *m/pl.*; **~ book**
code *m*; **~ law** droit *m* écrit.

staunch ferme; sûr; loyal.

stave 1. ♪ portée *f*; **2.** **~ in** enfoncer; **~ off**
écarter; parer; détourner.

stay 1. *v/i.* rester, demeurer; se tenir;
séjourner; **~ away** ne pas venir *or* arriver *or* assister; **~ behind** rester en
arrière; **~ in** rester à la maison; **~ put** ne
pas bouger; **~ up** veiller; rester debout;
~ing power résistance *f*; *v/t.* arrêter; **~**
the course tenir bon; **2.** séjour; ⚓ étai *m*; **~-at-home** casanier (*a. su.*).

stead: in his ~ à sa place; **stand s.o. in**
good ~ être très utile à q.; **~fast** ferme.

steady 1. être ferme; solide; constant; soutenu; sûr; régulier; **2.** *v/t.* (r)affermir; assurer; stabiliser; *v/i.* se raffermir; **3.** F
ami(e *f*) *m* attitrée *f*).

steak tranche *f*; bifteck *m*.

steal 1. voler, dérober; **2.** *v/i.* marcher à
pas furtifs; (se) glisser.

stealth: by ~ à la dérobée; furtivement;
~y furtif.

steam 1. vapeur *f*; buée *f*; *attr.* de *or* à
vapeur; **2.** *v/i.* fumer; jeter de la vapeur;
~ up (s')embuer; *v/t.* cuire à la vapeur;
~er ⚓ vapeur *m*; **~y** humide.

steel 1. acier *m*; **2.** aciérer; **~works**
aciérie *f*.

steep 1. raide, escarpé, abrupt; à pic; F
fort, exagéré; **2.** (faire) tremper; *fig.*
~ed in a. imprégné de.

steeple clocher *m*; **~chase** steeple
(-chase) *m*.

steer¹ jeune bœuf *m*; *Am.* bœuf *m*.

steer² diriger, conduire; **~ing** conduite *f*;
~ wheel *mot.* volant *m*; **~sman** timonier *m*.

stem¹ 1. *plant*: tige *f*; *fruit*: queue *f*; *tree*:
tronc *m*, souche *f*; *glass*: pied *m*; **2.** *v/i.*:
~ from provenir de.

stem² 1. ⚓ avant *m*; **2.** *v/t.* contenir;
résister à; refouler.

stench odeur *f* infecte; puanteur *f*.

stencil ⊕ pochoir *m*.

stenographer sténographe *mf*.

step¹ 1. pas *m*; *stair*: marche *f*; *fig.* mesure *f*, démarche *f*; (**a pair** *or* **set of**) **~s** *pl.*
(un) escabeau *m*; **in ~ with** au pas avec;
2. faire un pas; marcher; **~ down**
descendre; *fig.* se retirer, donner sa
démission; **~ in** entrer; **~ out** sortir; **~ off**
descendre; *v/t.* **~ up** augmenter.

step² *compounds*: beau-, demi-; **~broth-**
er demi-frère *m*; **~child** beau-fils *m*,
belle-fille *f*; **~daughter** belle-fille *f*;
~father beau-père *m*.

stepladder escabeau *m*.

stepmother belle-mère *f*.

steppe steppe *f*.

stepping-stone pierre *f* de gué; *fig.*
tremplin *m*.

step...: **~sister** demi-sœur *f*; **~son**
beau-fils *m*.

stereo 1. (*a.* **~ sound**) stéréophonie *f*,
stéréo *f*; (*a.* **~ set**) appareil *m* stéréo;
phonographe *m* stéréo; **2.** (*a.* **~ phoni-**
que) stéréophonique, stéréo; **~type 1.**
stéréotype *m*; **2.** stéréotyper.

steril|e stérile; **~ity** stérilité *f*; **~ization**
stérilisation *f*; **~ize** stériliser.

sterling de bon aloi (*a. fig.*); *fig. a.* excellent; ✝ sterling.

stern 1. sévère; **2.** ⚓ arrière *m*.

steward intendant *m*; steward *m*; **~ess**
hôtesse *f*.

stick¹ bâton *m*; canne *f*; baguette *f*;
broom: manche *m*; morceau *m*.

stick² *v/t.* enfoncer, planter; mettre,
fourrer; coller; F supporter; **~ up** monter, afficher; ⊢ **~ 'em up!** haut les
mains!; *v/i.* être collé, coller; tenir; rester; être coincé, être bloqué; être enlisé;
être enfoncé; **~ at nothing** ne pas reculer devant rien; **~ out** dépasser; *fig.* tenir
(bon); **~ to** rester fidèle à; **~ together**

rester ensemble; ~ **up for** défendre; ~**er** auto-collant m; ~**ing plaster** sparadrap m.

stickler: be a ~ **for** insister sur, être à cheval sur.

sticky adhésif; gluant; poisseux.

stiff 1. raide, rigide; fort (*drink, wind*); difficile; **2.** *sl.* cadavre m; *Am. sl.* nigaud m; ~**en** v/t. raidir; renforcer; v/i. (se) raidir; devenir ferme; *fig.* intraitable, obstiné.

stifl|**e** étouffer; ~**ing** suffocant.

stigma stigmate m; *fig. a.* flétrissure f; ~**tize** stigmatiser.

stile échalier m.

still 1. *adj.* tranquille; silencieux; calme; **2.** *adv.* encore; **3.** *cj.* cependant, pourtant; encore; **4.** calmer; apaiser; ~ silence f; **in the ~ of the night** dans le silence de la nuit; **6.** appareil m de distillation; ~**birth** enfant mf mort(e) à la naissance; ~**born** mort-né; ~**hunting** chasse f d'affût; ~ **life** nature f morte; ~**ness** calme m; silence m.

stilt échasse f; ~**ed** *fig.* guindé.

stimul|**ant** stimulant (*adj., su./m*); ~**ate** stimuler; ~**ation** stimulation f; ~**us,** *pl.* -**li** stimulant m; *physiol.* stimulus m.

sting 1. piquer; **2.** piqûre f; *insect:* dard m; ~**iness** mesquinerie f, ladrerie f; ~(**ing**)-**nettle** ~ ortie f brûlante; ~**y** mesquin, chiche.

stink 1. puanteur f; **2.** puer, empester (qch., **of** s.th.); ~**er F** vacherie f; ~**ing 1.** F *fig.* sale, vache; **2.** be ~ **rich** crever de fric.

stint 1. besogne f assignée; part f de travail; **without** ~ généreusement; **2.** ~ (**on**) lésiner sur; ~ **o.s.** (**of**) se priver (de).

stipend traitement m.

stipulat|**e** stipuler; ~**ion** stipulation f.

stir 1. remuement m; mouvement m; vt/i. remuer, bouger; v/t. *a.* tourner; agiter; ~ **up** éveiller, exciter.

stirrup étrier m.

stitch 1. point m; # suture f; # point m de côté; **2.** coudre; piquer; brocher (*a book*); # suturer.

stock 1. *tree:* tronc m; souche f; *tool:* manche m; *rifle:* fût m; *fig.* race f; provision f; # stock m; # *a.* ~**s** *pl.* fonds m/pl.; *fig.* actions f/pl.; (*a.* **live** ~) bétail m; (*a.* **dead** ~) matériel m; *cuis.* consommé m; ~**s** *pl.* ⚓ chantier m; ~ **ex-**

change, ~ market Bourse f; **take** ~ **of** # dresser l'inventaire de; *fig.* faire le point de; **2.** courant; de série; classique; consacré; ~**phrase** cliché m; **3.** v/t. (*a.* ~ **up**) approvisionner, fournir (de, **with**); # avoir en magasin; v/i. s'approvisionner (de, en **with**).

stockade palissade f; *Am.* prison f.

stock...: ~**broker** agent m de change; ~**holder** actionnaire mf.

stockinet jersey m.

stocking bas m.

stock...: ~**pile 1.** stock m, réserve f; **2.** accumuler, amasser; stocker; ~**still** (complètement) immobile; sans bouger; ~**taking** inventaire m; ~**y** trapu.

stodgy bourratif; lourd.

stoic stoïcien; stoïque; ~**al** stoïque.

stoke alimenter (*a fire*); charger (*a furnace*); ~**r** chauffeur m.

stolid impassible, lourd, lent.

stomach 1. estomac m; ventre m; **2.** *fig.* supporter, tolérer; ~**ache** mal m à l'estomac.

stomp marcher à pas bruyants.

stone 1. pierre f; *fruit:* noyau m; *a. measure:* 6,348 kg; **2.** de or en pierre; **3.** lapider; dénoyauter (*fruit*); ~**d** *sl.* soûl; drogué, enfoncé; ~**blind** complètement aveugle; ~**coal** anthracite m; ~**dead** raide mort; ~**mason** maçon m; ~**ware** (poterie f de) grès m.

stony pierreux; de pierre.

stool tabouret m; # selle f; ~ **pigeon** *sl.* mouchard m.

stoop se baisser; être voûté (*a.* = **have a** ~).

stop 1. v/t. arrêter; interrompre; suspendre (*payment*); mettre fin à; (*a.* ~ **up**) boucher; plomber (*a tooth*); ~ **doing** arrêter or cesser de faire; v/i. s'arrêter; cesser; demeurer; ~ **by, ~ in** faire une petite visite, s'arrêter un moment; ~ **off** faire étape; ~ **over** faire une halte, faire étape, *esp.* ✈ faire escale; descendre (à, **at**) (*a hotel*); **2.** arrêt m (*a.* ⊕); halte f; interruption f; ~**gap** bouche-trou m; ~**light** *traffic:* feu m rouge; *mot.* stop m; ~**over** halte f, étape f, *esp.* ✈ escale f; ~**page** obstruction f; arrêt m; *wages:* retenue f; *payment etc.:* suspension f; *work:* interruption f; ⊕ à-coup m; ~ ~ **of current** coupure f du courant; ~**per** bouchon m.

storage emmagasinage *m*; entrepôts *m*/ *pl.*; *computer*: (mise *f* en) mémoire *f*; **~ battery** accumulateur *m*.

store réserve *f*, provision *f*; magasin *m*; *fig.* fonds *m* (*of knowledge*); entrepôt *m*; **in ~** en réserve; *fig.* **set great (little) ~ by** faire grand (peu de) cas de; **2.** (*a.* **~ up**) amasser; emmagasiner; approvisionner (de, en **with**); **~house** magasin *m*; *fig.* mine *f*; **~keeper** garde-magasin (*pl.* gardes-magasin[s] *m*; *Am.* boutiquier (-ère *f*) *m*.

storey see **story²**, **~ed** see **storied**.

storied: **four-~** à quatre étages.

stork cigogne *f*.

storm 1. orage *m*, tempête *f*, **2.** *v/t.* prendre d'assaut; donner l'assaut à; *v/i. fig.* tempêter; **~ in (out)** entrer (sortir) en trombe; tempêter; s'emporter (contre, **at**); **~y** tempétueux; orageux; **~ petrel** *orn.* pétrel *m*; *fig.* enfant *mf* terrible.

story¹ histoire *f* (*a.* F lie).

story² étage *m*.

stout 1. gros; fort; intrépide; solide; **2.** bière *f* brune forte.

stove poêle *m*; ⊕ four *m*.

stow ranger; mettre, fourrer; **~away** ⬇ passager *m* clandestin.

straddle enjamber.

strafe ✗ mitrailler.

straggl|e rester en arrière, traîner; *fig.* s'égrener, s'éparpiller; **~ing** épars, éparpillé.

straight 1. *adj.* droit (*a. fig.*); en ordre; *fig.* honnête, franc; net (*refusal etc.*); sec (*whisky etc.*); **get** (*or* **put**) **~** rajuster; mettre de l'ordre dans; **put** (*or* **set**) **s.o. ~** (**about**) éclairer q. (sur); **2.** *adv.* (tout) droit; directement; **~ ahead** tout droit; **~ away**, **~ off** aussitôt; du premier coup; **~ on** tout droit; **~ out** carrément, franchement; **3.** *sp. la* ligne *f* droite; *fig.* (**keep to**) **the ~ and narrow** (rester dans *or* suivre) le droit chemin; **~en** (*a.* **~ up**) (se) redresser; *v/i. a.* devenir droit; **~ up** (se) redresser; *v/t. a.* mettre en ordre; **~forward** franc; honnête; loyal; **~out** direct, franc, vrai, véritable.

strain¹ 1. ⊕ tension *f* (*a. fig.*); effort *m*; ⊕ déformation *f*; ♫ entorse *f*; *fig.* ton *m*, accent *m*; **~s** *pl.* sons *m/pl.*; **2.** *v/t.* tendre; *fig.* forcer (*a.* ⊕, ♫); ⊕ déformer; ⊕ filtrer, passer; *fig.* fatiguer; ser-

rer; *v/i.* faire un (grand) effort (pour atteindre, **after**); peiner, tirer (sur, **at**).

strain² qualité *f* (héritée); élement *m*, trace *f*; tendance *f*; lignée *f*.

strained tendu; forcé; guindé.

strainer passoire *f*.

strait 1. *geog.* détroit *m*; **~s** *pl.* embarras *m*; **2.**: **~jacket** camisole *f* de force; **~en**: **in ~ed circumstances** dans la gêne; **~laced** col monté.

strand 1. plage *f*, rive *f*; brin *m*, fibre *f*, fil *f*; **2.** échouer (*a ship, a. fig.*); *fig.* **~ed** en plan, en rade.

strange étrange; singulier; inconnu; **~ly (enough)** curieusement, chose curieuse; **~r** inconnu(e *f*) *m*; étranger (-ère *f*) *m* (à, **to**).

strangle étrangler; **~hold** mainmise *f*.

strap lanière *f*, courroie *f*, bretelle *f*; **2.** attacher *or* lier avec une lanière *etc.*; **~less** sans bretelles.

strapping costaud.

stratagem stratagème *m*.

strateg|ic stratégique; **~y** stratégie *f*.

stratum, *pl.* **-ta** *geol.* strate *f*; couche *f* (*a. fig.*); *fig.* rang *m* social.

straw paille *f*; **~ man** homme *m* de paille; F **I don't care a ~** je m'en fiche (de, **for**); **~berry** fraise *f*; *plant*: fraisier *m*.

stray 1. s'égarer; **~ from** s'écarter de; **2.** égaré; errant; **3.** bête *f* perdue; enfant *m* abandonné.

streak 1. raie *f*, bande *f*; *fig.* tendance *f*; *fig.* période; (**like a**) **~ of lightning** (comme un) éclair *m*; **2.** filer; **~ed** strié, rayé, zébré (de, **with**).

stream 1. cours *m* d'eau, ruisseau *m*; courant *m*; flot *m* (*a. fig.*); **2.** ruisseler; couler; flotter (au vent) (*hair, flag etc.*); **~er** banderole *f*; *paper*: serpentin *m*; **~let** petit ruisseau *m*; **~line** *fig.* rationaliser; **~lined** ✈ fuselé; *mot.* aerodynamique.

street rue *f*; **~ floor** rez-de-chaussée *m*/ *inv.*; **the man in the ~** l'homme *m* moyen; F **not in the same ~** ne pas de taille (avec, **as**); **~car** *esp. Am.* tramway *m*.

strength force *f*; solidité *f*; **on the ~ of** sur la foi de; **~en** *v/t.* affermir, renforcer; fortifier; *v/i.* s'affermir *etc.*; (re)prendre des forces.

strenuous énergique, actif; fatigant; acharné (*effort*).

stress 1. pression *f*; *gramm.* accent *m*; ⊕ tension *f*; *psych.* stress *m*; **2.** insister sur; souligner; ⊕ fatiguer.

stretch 1. *v/t.* (*usu.* ~ *out*) tendre (*a. one's hand*); étendre; allonger; déployer (*its wings*); *fig.* exagérer; ~ *ones legs* se dégourdir les jambes; *v/i.* (*oft.* ~ *out*) s'étendre; s'élargir; *fig.* suffire; **2.** étendue *f*; extension *f*; élasticité *f*; *at a ~* (tout) d'un trait; sans arrêt; ~er brancard *m*.

strew éparpiller, répandre (*objects*); joncher, parsemer (de, *with*).

stricken frappé; accablé (de, *with*).

strict strict; ~*ly speaking* à proprement parler; ~*ness* rigueur *f*; exactitude *f*.

stride 1. marcher à grands pas; **2.** (grand) pas *m*; enjambée *f*; *take s.th. in one's* ~ se jouer de qch.

strident strident.

strife *poet.* conflit *m*, lutte *f*.

strike 1. coup *m*; grève *f*; ~ *ballot* référendum *m*; *be on* ~ être en ou faire grève; **2.** *v/t.* frapper (*a.* ♪, *a. fig.*) (de, *with*); heurter; porter (*a blow*); ⊕ rentrer (*the flag*); amener (*the sails*); plier (*a tent*); faire (*a bargain*); allumer (*a match*); prendre (*an attitude, root*); sonner (*the hour*); *fig.* impressionner; découvrir, trouver; ~ *a balance* dresser le bilan; ~ *up* commencer à jouer *or* à chanter; *v/i.* porter un coup, frapper (à, *at*); attaquer, faire grève; sonner (*clock*); prendre feu (*match*); prendre racine; ~ *home* frapper juste; ~*r* gréviste *mf*; *foot.* buteur *m*.

striking frappant, saisissant.

string 1. ficelle *f*; corde *f* (*a.* ♪); *beads, pearls*: rang *m*, *cars, people etc.*: file *f*; ⚛ fibre *f*; *eccl., onions, a. fig.* chapelet *m*; ~ *of pearls* collier *m*; ♪ ~s *pl.* instruments *m/pl.* à cordes; *pull the* ~s tirer les ficelles, tenir les fils; **2.** ♪ à cordes (*instrument, orchestra etc.*); pour cordes (*serenade etc.*); ~ *bag* filet *m* à provisions; ~ *bean* haricot *m* vert; **3.** enfiler (*beads, a. fig.*); monter (*a violin*); effiler (*beans*); corder (*a racket*); ~ *along* payer (*q.*) de promesses, F faire (*q.*) marcher; ~ *along with s.o.* suivre q., aller avec q.; *fig.* se ranger à l'avis de q.; ~ *out* échelonner; ~ *up* suspendre; pendre (*q.*).

stringent rigoureux, strict; convaincant; ✝ serré (*money*); tendu (*market*).

stringy filandreux; visqueux.

strip 1. *v/t.* dépouiller (de, *of*); dénuder (de, *of*); ⊕ démonter; déshabiller; (*a.* ~ *off*) ôter, enlever; *v/i.* se déshabiller; **2.** bande(lette) *f*.

stripe rayure *f*, raie *f*; ✗ galon *m*, chevron *m*; ~*d* rayé.

stripling adolescent *m*.

strive s'efforcer (de, *to*).

stroke 1. coup *m*; ✻ apoplexie *f*; ⊕ piston: course *f*; caresse *f*; trait *m* (de plume, *a. fig.*); *swimming*: brassée *f*; *at a* ~ d'un seul coup; *on the* ~ *of ...* à ... heures sonnantes; **2.** caresser.

stroll 1. flâner, F se balader; **2.** (petite) promenade *f*, F balade *f*.

strong *usu.* fort; vigoureux; puissant; solide; vif (*imagination*); bon (*memory*); robuste (*health*); ~ *language* propos *m/pl.* grossiers; ~*arm* brutal, de force; ~*box* coffre-fort (*pl.* coffresforts) *m*; ~*hold* bastion *m*; ~*minded* à l'esprit décidé.

strop cuir *m* (*for razor*).

stroppy F de mauvaise humeur.

structur|**al** structural; ~*e* **1.** structure *f*; édifice *m*; **2.** structurer.

struggle 1. lutter; **2.** lutte *f*.

strut 1. se pavaner; **2.** ⊕ étai *m*.

stub 1. *cigarette etc.*: bout *m*; *cheque*: talon *m*; **2.** ~ *out* écraser (*a cigarette*).

stubble chaume *m*; poil *m* raide.

stubborn obstiné, opiniâtre, entêté.

stuck-up hautain; prétentieux.

stud[1] **1.** clou *m* (à grosse tête); *shirt etc.*: bouton *m*; **2.** orner *or* parsemer (de, *with*).

stud[2] haras *m*; écurie *f*.

student étudiant(e) *f*(*m*); ~ *hostel* foyer *m* d'étudiants.

studied instruit; recherché; voulu.

studio studio *m*; ~ *couch* divan *m*.

studious studieux; attentif.

study 1. étude *f* (*a.* ♪, *a. paint.*); cabinet *m* de travail; bureau *m*; **2.** étudier.

stuff 1. choses *f/pl.*, F truc *m*; matière *f*; substance *f*; (rem)bourrer; *cuis.* farcir; ~*ing* (rem)bourrage *m*; *cuis.* farce *f*; ~*y* mal aéré; qui sent le renfermé; vieux jeu (*ideas etc.*).

stultify abrutir.

stumble trébucher; ~ *across*, ~ (*up*)*on* tomber sur; *stumbling block* pierre *f* d'achoppement.

stump souche *f*; *cigar*: bout *m*; *limb*: moignon *m*; *tooth*: chicot *m*; ~ **speaker** orateur *m* de carrefour *or* de réunion électorale; **2.** *v/t.* F faire sécher (*q.*); F ~ *the country* faire une tournée électorale; F *be* ~*ed* ne le savoir que répondre (à, *by*), F sécher (sur, *by*); *v/i.* clopiner; ~**y** écourté; trapu (*person*).

stun étourdir, abasourdir.

stunt tour *m* de force; ~ *man* cascadeur *m*; *publicity* ~ true *m* publicitaire.

stunted rabougri.

stup|efy *fig.* hébéter, abrutir; stupéfier, abasourdir; ~**endous** prodigieux; ~**id** stupide, bête; ~**idity** stupidité *f*, bêtise *f*.

stupor stupeur *f*.

sturdy vigoureux; robuste; hardi.

stutter 1. bégayer; **2.** bégaiement *m*; ~**er** bègue *mf*.

sty[1] étable *f* (à porcs); porcherie *f*.

sty[2] *eye*: orgelet *m*.

sty|le 1. style *m*; *cost.* mode *f*; allure *f*, chic *m*; **2.** appeler; façonner, modeler; ~**ish** élégant; chic; à la mode; ~**ize** styliser.

stylus pointe *f* de lecture.

suave suave; affable; doux (*wine*).

sub...: *usu.* sous-; sub-; presque.

subconscious subconscient (*psych. a. su./m.*).

subdivi|de (se) subdiviser; ~**sion** subdivision *f*.

subdue subjuguer; *fig.* contenir, réprimer; adoucir; ~**d** *a.* discret, peu voyant; tamisé (*light*).

subject 1. *su.* sujet *m*; *school*: matière *f*; ~ *matter* sujet *m*; **2.** *adj.* ~ *to* soumis à; sujet à (*diseases*); passible de; sauf; sous (la) réserve de; **3.** *v/t.* assujettir, subjuguer; ~ *to* soumettre à (*an examination etc.*); exposer à (*danger etc.*); ~**ion** sujétion *f*; ~**ive** subjectif.

subjugate subjuguer.

subjunctive subjonctif *m*.

sub|lease, ~let donner *or* prendre en sous-location; sous-louer.

sublime sublime.

subliminal subliminal; ~ *advertising* publicité *f* insidieuse.

sub-machine gun mitraillette *f*.

submarine sous-marin (*a. ♣ su./m.*).

submerge *v/t.* submerger; noyer, inonder; *v/i.* plonger.

submiss|ion soumission *f* (*a. fig.*); ~**ive** soumis; docile (*person*).

submit (se) soumettre.

subnormal au-dessous de la normale; faible d'esprit, arriéré.

subordinate 1. subordonné (*adj.; su.*); **2.** subordonner (à, *to*).

suborn suborner.

subpoena 1. citation *f*, assignation; **2.** citer, assigner.

subscribe (se) cotiser (pour, *towards*), souscrire (à *to, for*; pour une somme, *for a sum; u.* à une opinion, *to an opinion*); s'abonner (à, *to*) (*a newspaper*); ~**r** souscripteur (-trice *f*) *m*, signataire *mf* (de, *to*); *newspaper, teleph.*: abonné(e *f*) *m*.

subscription souscription *f*; *money*: cotisation *f*; *newspaper*: abonnement *m*.

subsequent ultérieur; suivant; ~**ly** plus tard.

subservient servile; subordonné.

subside baisser; s'affaisser (*building etc.*); s'apaiser (*storm, passion, fever etc.*); ~**nce** affaissement *m*; apaisement *m*.

subsid|iary 1. subsidiaire (à, *to*), auxiliaire; ~ *company* filiale *f*; **2.** filiale *f*; ~**ize** subventionner; ~**y** subvention *f*.

subsist subsister; vivre (de *on, by*); ~**ence** subsistance *f*.

substance substance *f* (*a. fig.*); *fig.* essentiel *m*; solidité *f*; fortune *f*, biens *m/pl.*

substandard de qualité inférieure; au-dessous de la moyenne.

substan|tial substantiel; considérable; ~**tiate** justifier; prouver, fournir des preuves à l'appui de; ~**tive** *gramm.* substantif *m*, nom *m*.

substitu|te 1. *v/t.* substituer (à, *for*); remplacer (par, *by*); *v/i.* ~ *for s.o.* remplacer q.; **2.** *person*: remplaçant(e *f*) *m* (*a. sp.*), *thing*: succédané *m*.

subterfuge subterfuge *m*.

subterranean souterrain.

sub-title *book, cin.*: sous-titre *m*.

subtle subtil; ~**ty** subtilité *f*.

subtract soustraire.

suburb faubourg *m*; *in the* ~**s** en banlieue; ~**an** de banlieue (*a. pej.*).

subvention subvention *f*.

subver|sion subversion *f*; ~**sive** subversif; ~**t** renverser.

S

subway (passage *m* or couloir *m*) souterrain *m*; *Am.* métro *m*.

succeed *v/i.* réussir; avoir du succès; ~ **in doing s.th.** réussir or arriver or parvenir à faire qch.; ~ **to** prendre la succession de; heriter (de); *v/t.* suivre.

success succès *m*, réussite *f*; (bonne) chance *f*; ~**ful** heureux, réussi; **be** ~ réussir; avoir du succès; ~**ion** succession *f*; **in** ~ successivement; de suite; ~**ive** successif, consécutif; ~**or** successeur *m*.

succinct succinct.

succulent succulent.

succumb succomber (à, *to*).

such *adj.* tel; pareil; semblable; ~ **a man** un tel homme; ~ **as** tel que; ~ **a naughty dog** un chien si méchant; **as** ~ à proprement parler.

suck (*a.* ~ **at**, ~ **out**) sucer; ~ **in**, ~ **up** engloutir; absorber; ~ **up to** faire de la lèche à; ~**er** ventouse *f*; F nigaud(e *f*) *m*; ~**le** *v/t.* allaiter; *v/i.* téter.

suction succion *f*; aspiration *f*; ~ **pump** pompe *f* aspirante.

sudden soudain, brusque; **on a** ~, (**all**) **of a** ~ = ~**ly** soudainement, subitement, tout à coup.

suds *pl.* eau *f* de savon; lessive *f*.

sue *v/t.* poursuivre; *v/i.* solliciter (de q., **to s.o.**); qch., **for s.th.**); demander (qch., **for s.th.**).

suede *f.* daim *m*; *imitation* ~ suédine *f*; **2.** de daim (*shoes*, *bag etc.*); de suède (*gloves*).

suet graisse *f* de rognon or de bœuf.

suffer *v/i.* souffrir (de, *from*); *v/t.* souffrir; subir (*pain, a defeat etc.*); tolérer; supporter; ~**ance**: **on** ~ par tolérance; ~**er** victime *f*; ✝ malade *mf*; ~**ing** souffrance *f*.

suffice suffire (à).

sufficient assez de; suffisant; ~**ly** assez, suffisamment.

suffix *gramm.* suffixe *m*.

suffocat|e *vt/i.* étouffer, suffoquer; ~**ion** étouffement *m*, suffocation *f*.

suffrage (droit *m* de) suffrage *m*.

suffuse inonder; se répandre sur.

sugar 1. sucre *m*; ~ **beet** betterave *f* sucrière; ~ **cane** canne *f* à sucre; **2.** sucrer; ~**coat** revêtir de sucre; *fig.* sucrer; ~**free** sans sucre; ~**y** sucré.

suggest suggérer (*a. psych.*); proposer;

insinuer; ~**ion** suggestion *f*; proposition *f*; *fig.* nuance *f*, soupçon *m*; ~**ive** suggestif.

suicid|al suicidaire; ~**e** suicide *m*; *person*: suicidé(e *f*) *m*.

suit 1. *cost.* man: complet *m*, woman: tailleur *m*, ensemble *m*; *cards*: couleur *f*; ✝ procès *m*; **2.** *v/t.* adapter, accommoder (à **to, with**); convenir à; être apte à; ~**ed** fait (pour **to, for**); apte (à, **to**); *v/i.* aller, convenir; ~**able** convenable, qui convient; bon, adapté (à **to, for**); ~**case** valise *f*; ~**e** *prince, a.* ♪: suite *f*; appartement *m*; mobilier *m*.

sulk bouder; ~**y** boudeur, maussade.

sullen maussade.

sulphur ✝ **1.** soufre *m*; **2.** soufrer; ~**ic**: ~ **acid** acide *m* sulfurique.

sultry étouffant, lourd; *fig.* chaud.

sum 1. somme *f*; **do** ~**s** faire du calcul; **2.** (*usu.* ~ **up**) additionner, faire la somme de; *fig.* résumer.

summar|ize résumer; ~**y 1.** sommaire (*a.* ✝); **2.** résumé *m*.

summer 1. été *m*; **2.** d'été; estival; ~**time** été *m*; *by clock:* heure *f* d'été.

summit sommet *m*; ~ **conference** (conférence *f* au) sommet *m*.

summon appeler; convoquer; ✝ citer, assigner; *fig.* (*usu.* ~ **up**) faire appel à, rassembler (*one's courage*); ~**s** appel *m*; ✝ citation *f*.

sumptuous somptueux.

sun 1. soleil *m*; **2.** du au or de soleil, par le soleil; **3.** *v/t.:* ~ **o.s.** prendre le soleil; ~**baked** brûlé par le soleil; ~**bath** bain *m* de soleil; ~**bathe** prendre un bain or des bains de soleil; ~**beam** rayon *m* de soleil; ~**burn** coup *m* de soleil; hâle *m*, bronzage *m*; ~**burnt** brûlé par le soleil; hâlé, bronzé.

Sunday dimanche *m*.

sun...: ~**dial** cadran *m* solaire; ~**down** coucher *m* du soleil.

sundry 1. divers; **all and** ~ tout le monde; **2.** *sundries pl.* articles *m/pl.* divers.

sunglasses *pl.* lunettes *f/pl.* de soleil.

sunken submergé; creux (*eyes*).

sun...: ~**light** lumière *f* du soleil; ~**lit** ensoleillé; ~**ny** ensoleillé; *fig.* radieux, heureux; ~**rise** lever *m* du soleil; ~**set** coucher *m* du soleil; ~**shade** ombrelle *f*; *phot., a. mot.* pare-soleil *m/inv.*; ~ **shine** (lumière *f* du) soleil *m*; ~**stroke**

⚲ coup *m* de soleil; **~up** lever *m* du soleil.

super F super.

super...: ~abundant surabondant; **~annuated** suranné, démodé; en retraite (*person*); **~annuation** pension *f* de retraite additionnelle.

superb superbe, magnifique.

super...: ~cilious hautain, dédaigneux; **~ficial** superficiel; **~fluous** superflu; **~highway** *Am.* autoroute *f*; **~human** surhumain; **~impose** superposer; **~intend** surveiller; diriger; **~intendent** surveillant(e *f*) *m*; directeur (-trice *f*) *m*.

superior supérieur (*adj.*, *su.*), **~ity** supériorité *f*.

super|lative 1. suprême; **2.** *gramm.* superlatif *m*; **~man** surhomme *m*; **~market** supermarché *m*; **~natural** surnaturel; **~numerary 1.** surnuméraire; **2.** *thea.* figurant(e *f*) *m*; **~power** superpuissance *f*; **~sede** remplacer, supplanter; **~sonic** supersonique; **~stition** superstition *f*; **~stitious** superstitieux; **~vene** survenir, **~vise** surveiller; diriger; **~vision** surveillance *f*; direction *f*; **~visor** surveillant(e *f*) *m*; directeur (-trice *f*) *m*.

supper souper *m*.

supplant supplanter; remplacer.

supple souple.

supplement 1. supplément *m*; **2.** ajouter à, compléter; **~ary** supplémentaire (de, *to*).

supplicate supplier.

supplier fournisseur (-euse *f*) *m*.

supply 1. fournir (*qch.*); approvisionner, munir (de, *with*); fournir (de, en *with*), alimenter, ravitailler (en, *with*); répondre à (*a need*); **2.** approvisionnement *m*; ravitaillement *m*; réserve *f*, provision *f*; service *m* de (*gas etc.*); **supplies** *pl. a.* vivres *m/pl.*

support 1. appui *m*, soutien *m* (*a.* ⊕, *a. fig.*); maintien *m*; ressources *f/pl.*; **2.** appuyer (*a. fig.*); supporter; soutenir (*a. purl. a. a theory*); maintenir; faire vivre (*a family*); tolérer; **~able** tolérable, supportable; **~ing** d'appui (*wall etc.*); *fig.* secondaire (*part, role etc.*); **~ program(me)** programme *m* supplémentaire.

suppose supposer, s'imaginer; **he is ~d to** (*inf.*) il est censé (*inf.*); **~ (that)**, **sup-**

posing (that) admettons que (*sbj.*), supposé que (*sbj.*).

supposed supposé, prétendu; soi-disant; **~ly** probablement.

supposition supposition *f*.

suppress supprimer; réprimer; **~ion** suppression *f*; répression *f*; **~ive** suppressif; répressif.

suppurate suppurer.

suprem|acy suprématie *f* (sur, *over*); **~e** suprême; souverain.

surcharge surcharge *f*; *letter:* surtaxe *f*.

sure sûr; certain; **~ (thing)!** bien sûr, mais oui!; **~ enough** vraiment, en effet!; **he is ~ to return** il reviendra sûrement *or* à coup sûr; **be ~ to** (*or and*) ... n'oublie(z) pas de ..., ne manque(z) pas de ...; **be ~ that** veille(z) à ce que ...; **it's a ~ thing** c'est une certitude, c'est sûr et certain; **make ~** s'assurer (de, *of*); **~ly** assurément; certainement, **~ty** caution *f*, garant(e *f*) *m*.

surf ressac *m*; brisants *m/pl.*

surface 1. surface *f*; **2.** ⊕ revêtir; apprêter, glacer; *v/i.* revenir à la surface; faire surface (*submarine*); *fig.* apparaître.

surfboard planche *f* de surf.

surfeit excès *m*, surabondance *f*.

surfing surf *m*.

surge 1. vague *f* (*u. fig.*); *fig.* accès *m*, poussée *f*; **2.** se déferler (*a. ~ up*) monter.

surg|eon chirurgien(ne *f*) *m*; **~ery** chirurgie *f*; cabinet *m* (de consultation); **~ical** chirurgical.

surly maussade; hargneux; bourru.

surmise 1. conjecture *f*, supposition *f*; **2.** conjecturer; soupçonner.

surmount surmonter.

surname nom *m* (de famille).

surpass surpasser; dépasser.

surplus 1. surplus *m*, excédent *m*; **2.** de *or* en surplus.

surprise 1. surprise *f*; étonnement *m*; ✗ coup *m* de main; **take by ~** surprendre; **2.** étonner; surprendre.

surrender 1. ✗ reddition *f*; capitulation *f*; **2.** (*a. ~ o.s.*) se rendre.

surround entourer; ✗ cerner; **~ing 1.** environnant; d'alentour; **2. ~s** *pl.* environs *m/pl.*, alentours *m/pl.*

survey 1. regarder, contempler, considérer; examiner; inspecter; enquêter sur; *surv.* arpenter (*a country*); **2.** vue *f* générale, aperçu *m*; inspection *f*, enquête *f*, étude *f*; (*a.* **~ing**) *land:* arpentage *m*; levé *m* (des plans); **~or** (arpenteur *m*) géomètre *m*; expert *m.*

surviv|al survie *f*; survivance *f*; **~e** *v/t.* survivre à; *v/i.* survivre; subsister; **~or** survivant(e *f*) *m.*

susceptible accessible (à, *to*); sensible (à *of, to*); susceptible (de, *of*).

suspect 1. soupçonner, suspecter; **2.** suspect (*adj., su.*).

suspend suspendre (*an official, a judgement, a payment, sp. a player etc.*); exclure temporairement; **~ers** *pl. Br.* jarretelles *f/pl.*, *Am.* bretelles *f/pl.*

suspens|e suspens *m*; incertitude *f*; **~ion** suspension *f*; *mot.* retrait *m* temporaire (*of licence*); **~ bridge** pont *m* suspendu.

suspici|on soupçon *m*; **~ous** suspect; (*suspecting*) méfiant, soupçonneux.

sustain soutenir; entretenir (*life*); supporter; essuyer, subir (*a loss*); **~ed** soutenu; continu.

sustenance nourriture *f*; valeur *f* nutritive.

swab 1. torchon *m*; ✻ tampon *m* d'ouate; ✻ prélèvement *m* (dans, *of*); **2.** (*a.* **~ down**) nettoyer.

swaddle emmailloter (de, *with*); **swaddling clothes** *pl.* maillot *m.*

swagger crâner; se pavaner.

swallow[1] *orn.* hirondelle *f.*

swallow[2] **1.** gorgée *f*; **2.** avaler, gober (*a. fig.*); **~ up** engloutir.

swamp 1. marais *m*, marécage *m*; **2.** inonder; submerger; déborder (de, *with work*); **~y** marécageux.

swan cygne *m.*

swank F esbroufe *f*; esbroufeur (-euse *f*) *m*; **2.** esbroufer.

swap 1. (contre, *for*) troquer, échanger; échange *m*, troc *m.*

swarm 1. essaim *m*; **2.** essaimer; *fig.* fourmiller (de, *with*).

swarthy basané, noiraud.

swat écraser (*a fly*); taper sur.

swath ⚘ andain *m*, fauchée *f.*

swathe emmailloter, envelopper.

sway 1. balancement *m*; oscillation *f*; empire *m*, domination *f*; **2.** *v/i.* osciller, se balancer; *v/t.* influencer.

swear *v/i.* jurer (de, *to*; par, *by*); *v/t.* **~ s.o. in** faire prêter serment à q.

sweat 1. sueur *f*, transpiration *f*; F corvée *f*; **2.** *v/i.* suer, transpirer; *v/t.* faire suer; exploiter (*a worker*); **~er** tricot *m*; pull *m*; **~y** en sueur; mouillé de sueur.

Swed|e Suédois(e *f*) *m*; **~ish 1.** suédois; **2.** *ling.* suédois *m.*

sweep 1. *v/t.* balayer (*a room, dust*); ramoner (*a chimney*); **~ away** emporter, entraîner; *v/i. fig.* (*usu. with adv.*) avancer rapidement; parcourir; entrer *etc.* d'un air majestueux; **2.** coup *m* de balai *or* de pinceau *or* de faux; geste *m* large; courbe *f*; mouvement *m* circulaire; étendue *f*, portée *f*; (*chimney* **~**) ramoneur *m*; **make a clean ~** faire table rase (de, *of*); *game:* faire rafle; *fig.* **at one ~** d'un seul coup; **~er** balayeur *m*; *machine:* balayeuse *f*; **~ing 1.** rapide; radical, complet; large (*gesture*); **2. ~s** *pl.* ordures *f/pl.*, balayures *f/pl.*

sweet 1. doux; gentil (*person*); *cuis.* **~ things** sucreries *f/pl.*; **have a ~ tooth** aimer les sucreries; **2.** bonbon *m*; *cuis.* dessert *m or* entremets *m* (sucré); **~s** *pl.* confiseries *f/pl.*; **~en** sucrer; adoucir (*a. fig.*); **~ener** édulcorant *m*; *fig.* pot-de-vin *m*; **~heart** bien-aimé(e *f*) *m*; chéri(e *f*) *m*; **~ish** assez doux *or* sucré; douceâtre; **~meat** bonbon *m*; **~ness** douceur *f* (*a. fig.*); *fig.* gentillesse *f*; **~shop** confiserie *f.*

swell 1. (se) gonfler, (s')enfler; *fig. a.* augmenter; **2.** bombement *m*; ⚓ houle *f*; **3.** F *esp. Am.* chic; **~ing** gonflement *m*; ✻ enflure *f*, grosseur *f.*

swelter étouffer (de chaleur).

swerve *v/i.* faire un écart; *mot.* faire une embardée; *fig.* dévier.

swift 1. rapide; prompt; **2.** *orn.* martinet *m*; **~ness** vitesse *f.*

swill 1. pâtée *f*; **2.** *v/t.* laver à grande eau; *v/i.* boire avidement.

swim 1. *v/i.* nager; *sp.* faire de la natation; **my head ~s** la tête me tourne; *v/t.* traverser à la nage; **2. go for a ~** aller nager; aller se baigner; *fig.* **be in the ~** être à la page; être lancé; **~ming 1.** nage *f*; natation *f*; *sp.* de natation; **~ bath(s** *pl.*) piscine *f* (publique); **~ cap** bonnet *m* de bain; **~ costume** maillot *m* (de bain); **~ pool** piscine *f*; **~ trunks** (**a pair**

of ~ un) caleçon *m* de bain; **~suit**
maillot *m* (de bain).
swindle 1. escroquer (qch. à q., *s.o. out
of s.th.*); **2.** escroquerie *f*.
swine *poet.*, *zo.*, *fig. pej.* cochon *m*; *sl.*
salaud *m*.
swing 1. *v/i.* se balancer; osciller; pivoter; ~ *round* tourner; virer; se retourner; *v/t.* (faire) balancer; faire osciller;
faire pivoter; ~ *round* tourner; faire
virer; **2.** balancement *m*; coup *m* balan-
cé; balançoire *f (for children)*; mouvement *m* rythmé; ♩ swing *m*; *in full* ~ en
pleine marche; **~ door** porte *f* battante,
porte *f* à bascule.
swipe 1. frapper à toute volée; chiper; **2.**
coup *m* (vehement); gifle *f*.
swirl 1. (faire) tournoyer *or* tourbillonner; **2.** tourbillon.
Swiss 1. suisse; **2.** Suisse(sse *f*) *m*.
switch 1. *apparatus*: bouton *m*, ∮ inter-
rupteur *m*; ⚙ aiguille *f*; *fig.* changement *m*, revirement; **2.** changer (de
qch.); passer; ⊕, ∮ *etc.* mettre; ⚙
aiguiller (*a. fig.*); manœuvrer (*a train*);
∮ *(oft. ~ over)* commuter; ∮ ~ *on* allumer; ~ *off* arrêter, éteindre; **~board** ∮
panneau *m or* tableau *m* de distribution.
swivel (*a.* ~ *round*) pivoter.
swoon se pâmer.
swoop 1. (*usu.* ~ *down*) s'abattre (sur,
[*up*]*on*); **2.** descente *f*.
swop F *see* **swap**.
sword épée *f*; **~sman** épéiste *m*.
swot F **1.** bûcher; **2.** bûcheur (-euse *f*) *m*.
sycophant flagerneur (-euse *f*) *m*.
syllable syllabe *f*.

syllabus *study*: programme *m*.
symbol symbole *m*; **~ic(al)** symbolique;
~ism symbolisme *m*; **~ize** symboliser.
symmetr|ical symétrique; **~y** symétrie *f*.
sympath|etic compatissant; compré-
hensif; ~ *to(wards)* bien disposé envers
or à l'égard de; ~ *strike* grève *f* de solidarité; **~ize** sympathiser (avec, *with*);
compatir (à, *with*); ~ *with a.* comprendre; **~y** compassion *f*; compréhension
f; *in* ~ *with* en accord avec; *my (deep-
est)* ~ (*or* *sympathies*) mes (sincères)
condoléances; *letter of* ~ lettre *f* de condoléances; *come out in* ~ faire grève de
or par solidarité.
symphony ♩ symphonie *f*.
symptom symptôme *m*; indice *m*.
sync(h) F: (*out of* ~ pas en) synchronis-
me *m*.
synchron|ize *v/i.* marquer la même heu-
re; se produire en même temps (que,
with); *v/t.* synchroniser; **~ous** synchro-
ne.
syndicate 1. syndicat *m*; **2.** (se) syndi-
quer.
syndrome syndrome *m*.
synonym synonyme *m*; **~ous** synonyme
(de, *with*).
synopsis, *pl.* **-ses** résumé *m*.
syntax *gramm.* syntaxe *f*.
synthe|sis, *pl.* **-ses** synthèse *f*; **~tic(al)**
synthétique.
Syrian 1. syrien; **2.** Syrien(ne *f*) *m*.
syringe 1. seringue *f*; **2.** seringuer.
syrup sirop *m*.
system système *m*; *pol.* régime *m*;
méthode *f*; **~atic** systématique.

T

tab étiquette *f*, *coat etc*: attache *f*; *keep
~s on* tenir à l'œil; *pick up the* ~ payer
(la note).
table 1. table *f*; A (*a.* *multiplication* ~)
table *f* (de multiplication); A *the three
times* ~ la table de trois; ~ *of contents*
table *f* des matières; *lay* (*or* *set*) *the* ~
mettre la table, mettre le couvert; **2.**

parl. etc. Br. présenter, *Am.* ajourner
(*usu. a bill*); **~cloth** nappe *f*; **~land**
geogr. plateau *m*; **~spoon** cuiller *f* (de
service); (*a.* **~ful**) cuillerée *f* à soupe
tablet *with inscription*: plaque *f*; *soap*:
pain *m*; *pharm.* comprimé *m*, pastille *f*.
table...: ~ *tennis* ping-pong *m*; **~top**
dessus *m* de table; **~ware** vaisselle *f*.

taboo 1. tabou (*adj.*, *su./m*); **2.** tabouer.

tabulate disposer en forme de tables *or* tableaux; classifier.

tacit tacite; **~urn** taciturne.

tack 1. petit clou *m*; (*a. tin ~*) semence *f*; *needlework*: point *m* de bâti; ♣ bord(ée *f*) *m*; *fig.* voie *f*; **2.** *v/t.* clouer, *fig.* attacher (à *to*, *on*); *v/i.* ♣ louvoyer; virer (*a. fig.*).

tackle 1. equipement *m*, matériel *m*, ustensiles *m/pl.*; ⊕ appareil *m* de levage; **2.** s'attaquer à.

tacky collant; *Am.* F minable.

tact tact *m*; **~ful** (plein) de tact; **~ly** avec tact.

tactic|al tactique; de tactique (*error*); **~s** *pl. or sg.* tactique *f*.

tactile tactile.

tactless (*a.* **~ly**) sans tact.

tadpole *zo.* têtard *m*.

taffy *Am. see* **toffee**; F flagornerie *f*.

tag 1. étiquette *f*; *cord etc.*: ferret *m*; *fig.* cliché *m*; **2.** étiqueter (*a. fig.* comme, *as*); **~ along** suivre, traîner derrière.

tail 1. queue *f*; F *shirt*: pan *m*; ✈ empennage *m*; **~s** *pl.* coin: (le côté *m*) pile *f*; habit *m* à queue (*q.*); **2.** *v/t.* suivre (*q.*) (de près), filer (*q.*); *v/i.* **~ away** (*or* **off**) diminuer (peu à peu); **~back** *traffic*: bouchon *m*, retenue *f*; **~coat** habit *m* à queue; **~gate** *mot.* **1.** hayon *m* (arrière); **2.** coller (*a car*); **~light** *mot.* feu *m* arrière *or* rouge.

tailor 1. tailleur *m*; **2.** *v/t.* faire, façonner (*a suit etc.*); *fig.* adapter (à, *to*); **~made** fait sur mesure; *fig.* spécialement conçu.cu.

tail...: **~ piece** appendice *m*; **~pipe** *mot.* tuyau *m* d'échappement; **~wind** vent *m* arrière.

taint 1. tache *f*; corruption *f*; infection *f*; **2.** *v/t.* infecter; (se) corrompre; (se) gâter.

take 1. *v/t. usu.* prendre (*a. time, food, a cold etc.*); (em)porter, (ap)porter (*qch.*); emmener (*s.o. somewhere*); *require*: demander, exiger; *hold*: contenir; *tolerate*: supporter; passer (*an examination*); tourner (*a film*); profiter de, saisir (*a chance*); comprendre; tenir, prendre (*pour, for*); *I* **~ it that** je suppose que; **~** (*a deep*) **breath** respirer (profondément); **~ comfort** se consoler; **~ compassion** avoir compassion *or* pitié

(de, *on*); **~ a drive** faire une promenade (en auto); **~ in hand** entreprendre; **~ s.o. about** faire visiter (*qch.*) à *q.*; **~ down** descendre (*qch.*); avaler; prendre note de, écrire; **~ for** prendre pour; **~ from** prendre à, enlever à; **~ in** recevoir (*lodgers*); comprendre; F tromper, F rouler; **~ off** enlever; ôter (*one's hat*); F imiter; **~ on** se charger de; accepter; engager (*workers*); prendre; s'attaquer à (*q.*); **~ out** sortir (*qch.*); arracher (*a tooth*); ôter (*a stain*); emmener (*a child*) en promenade; contracter (*an insurance*); **~ up** relever, ramasser; se mettre à (*an occupation*), embrasser (*a career*); occuper (*room etc.*); fixer (*one's residence*); adopter (*an idea*); **~ upon o.s.** prendre sur soi de, **✓** décoller; **2.** *v/i.* prendre; réussir, avoir du succès; **~ after** tenir de, ressembler à; **~ from** diminuer (*qch.*); **~ off** prendre son essor; **✓** décoller; **~ on** avoir du succès; F se désoler; F s'attaquer à; **~ over** prendre le pouvoir; assumer la responsabilité; **~ to** s'adonner à; prendre goût à; prendre (*flight*); **~ to** (*ger.*) se mettre à (*inf.*); **~ up with** se lier d'amitié avec; s'associer à; *that* **won't ~ with me** ça ne prend pas avec moi; **3.** prise *f*; *cin.* prise *f* de vues.

take...: ~away 1. à emporter (*food*); **2.** restaurant *m* qui vend des repas à emporter; **~home pay** gages *m/pl.* nets; salaire *m* net; **~in** pris; occupé; *be* **~up with** être occupé à; **~off ✓** décollage *m*; caricature *f*; **~over ✞** rachat *m*.

takings *pl.* ✞ recette *f*.

tale conte *m*, récit *m*, histoire *f*.

talent talent *m*; **~ed** doué.

talk 1. conversation *f*; causerie *f*; discours *m*; bavardage *m*; *small* **~** menus propos *m/pl.*; **2.** parler (de *of*, *about*); causer (avec, *to*); bavarder; **~ back** répondre d'une manière impertinente, répliquer; **~ down** faire taire; **~ down to s.o.** parler à *q.* avec condescendance; **~active** bavard; causeur; **~er** causeur (*-euse f*) *m*; **~ing** conversation *f*; bavardage *m*; **~ point** sujet *m* de conversation; **~ing-to** F attrapade *f*; *give s.o. a good* **~** bien attraper *q.*, passer un bon savon à *q.*

tall grand, de haute taille; haut, élevé (*building etc.*); *fig.* fort.

tallow suif *m*.

tally 1. (~ *with*) cadrer (avec), correspondre (à) (*a.* ~ *up*) compter; **2.** compte *m*.

talon *orn.* serre *f*; griffe *f*.

tame 1. apprivoisé; fade (*style*); **2.** apprivoiser; dompter.

tamper: ~ *with* toucher à.

tan 1. (*a.* sun ~) hâle *m*, bronzage *m*; **2.** couleur du tan, marron, brun-roux; **3.** *v/t.* tanner; ~ *s.o.'s hide* tanner le cuir à q.; *vt/i.* bronzer (*skin, person etc.*).

tandem tandem *m*; *a. fig. in* ~ en tandem.

tang goût *m* vif; saveur *f*; ~**y** âpre, piquant.

tangent A tangente *f*; *fig.* **fly off at a** ~ changer brusquement de sujet.

tangerine mandarine *f*.

tangible tangible, palpable; *fig.* réel.

tangle 1. enchevêtrement *m*; *a. fig.* **get into a** ~ s'embrouiller; **2.** (s')embrouiller, (s')emmêler.

tank réservoir *m*; X tank *m*.

tankard pot *m*; *of tin*: chope *f*.

tanker ♣ pétrolier *m*, *mot.* camion-citerne *m*.

tanne|d bronzé; ~**r** tanneur *m*.

tannoy (*TM*) (système *m* de) haut-parleurs *m/pl.*

tantalize tourmenter.

tantamount équivalent (à, *to*).

tantrum F accès *m* de colère.

tap¹ 1. *barrel*: fausset *m*; *water*: robinet *m*; **on** ~ en fût (*beer*); *fig.* disponible, à notre *etc.* disposition; ~ *water* eau *f* du robinet; **2.** percer, mettre en perce (*a barrel*); *fig.* exploiter (*resources etc.*); *fig.* mettre sur écoute (*a telephone*).

tap² 1. petit coup *m*; **2.** frapper doucement; ~ *dance* claquettes *f/pl.*

tape ruban *m*; *sp.* bande *f* d'arrivée; **re-cording** ~ ruban *m* magnétique; *fig.* **red** ~ bureaucratie *f*; ~ *measure* mètre *m* à ruban; centimètre *m*; ~-**record** enregistrer sur bande; ~ *recorder* magnétophone *m*.

taper 1. bougie *f* filée; *eccl.* cierge *m*; **2.** (s')effiler; (*a.* ~ *off*) diminuer (peu à peu).

tapestry tapisserie *f*.

tapeworm ver *m* solitaire.

taproom buvette *f*, estaminet *m*.

taps *Am.* X *pl.* extinction *f* des feux.

tar 1. goudron *m*; **2.** goudronner.

tardy lent; tardif; *Am.* en retard.

tare ♥ **1.** tare *f*; **2.** tarer.

target cible *f*; *fig.* objectif *m*, but *m*; ~ *date* date *f* limite; ~ *language* langue *f* d'arrivée; ~ *practice* tir *m* à la cible.

tariff tarif *m* (*oft.* douanier).

tarmac 1. macadam *m*; ✈ aire *f* d'envol; **2.** macadamiser.

tarnish 1. (se) ternir (*a. fig.*); **2.** ternissure *f*.

tarragon estragon *m*.

tarry¹ *poet.* tarder; attendre; rester.

tarry² goudronneux.

tart 1. âpre, aigre; *fig.* mordant; **2.** *cuis.* tarte *f*; *sl.* poule *f*.

tartan tartan *m*; **2.** écossais.

task 1. tâche *f*; *school:* devoir *m*, **take to** ~ réprimander; X ~ *force* détachement *m* spécial.

tassel gland *m*; pompon *m*.

taste 1. goût *m* (de *of, for*); **have a** ~ **of** goûter (à) (*a. fig.*), goûter (le; **to** ~ selon son goût; **2.** *v/t.* goûter (de); déguster; *v/i.* avoir un goût (de, *of*); ~**ful** de bon goût; de goût (*person*); ~**less** insipide, fade.

tasty savoureux.

tatter|ed déguenillé (*person*); en lambeaux (*clothes etc.*); en miettes (*reputation etc.*); ~**s** *pl.* lambeaux *m/pl.*; **in** ~ **see tattered**.

tattle 1. cancaner; **2.** cancans *m/pl.*

tattoo¹ 1. X retraite *f* du soir; **2.** *fig.* tambouriner.

tattoo² 1. *v/t.* tatouer; **2.** tatouage *m*.

tatty F miteux.

taunt 1. railler; **2.** raillerie *f*.

Taurus *astr.* le Taureau *m*.

taut ♣ raide, tendu; étarque (*sail*).

tavern taverne *f*.

tawdry d'un mauvais goût; voyant.

tawny fauve; basané (*skin*).

tax 1. *income:* impôts *m/pl.*; *goods, services:* taxe *f*; ~ *allowances pl.* sommes *f/pl.* déductibles; ~ *evasion* fraude *f* fiscale; ~ *haven* refuge *m* fiscal; ~ *return* déclaration *f* d'impôts; **2.** imposer; taxer; *fig.* mettre à l'épreuve; *fig.* ~ *with* accuser de; ~**ation** imposition *f*; impôts *m/pl.*; ~-**deductible** déductible; ~-**free** exempt d'impôts.

taxi 1. (*or* ~-**cab**) taxi *m*; ~ *driver* chauffeur *m* de taxi; ~ *rank or stand* station *f* de taxis; **2.** aller en taxi; ✈ rouler au sol.

taxpayer contribuable *mf.*

tea thé *m*; *high* ~ goûter *m*; ~ *bag* sachet *m* de thé; ~ *break* pause-thé *f*; ~ *caddy* boîte *f* à thé; ~ *towel* torchon *m* (à vaisselle); ~ *urn* fontaine *f* à thé.

teach apprendre (qch. à q., *s.o. s.th.*; à *inf.*, *to inf.*); *in school etc.*: enseigner; **~able** enseignable; à l'intelligence ouverte (*person*); **~er** instituteur (-trice *f*) *m*; maître(sse *f*) *m*; professeur *mf*; **~ing** *school*: enseignement *m*; *phls. etc.* doctrine *f.*

teacup tasse *f* à thé; *fig. storm in a* ~ tempête *f* dans un verre d'eau.

team équipe *f*; *animals*: attelage *m*; ~ *spirit* esprit *m* d'équipe; **~work** travail *m* d'équipe.

teapot théière *f.*

tear[1] *v/t.* déchirer; arracher; *v/i.* se déchirer; **2.** déchirure *f.*

tear[2] larme *f*; **~drop** larme *f*; **~ful** larmoyant.

tearoom salon *m* de thé.

tease 1. taquiner; **2.** taquin(e *f*) *m.*

teaspoon petite cuiller *f*; (*a.* **~ful**) cuillerée *f* à café.

teat tétine *f.*

teatime l'heure *f* du thé.

technic|al technique; **~ality** détail *m* technique; **~ian** technicien *m.*

technique technique *f.*

technology technologie *f.*

tedious ennuyeux; fatigant.

tee *sp. curling*: but *m*; *golf*: tee *m.*

teem (*with*) abonder (en), fourmiller (de), grouiller (de).

teenager adolescent(e *f*) *m.*

teens *pl.* années *f/pl.* entre 13 et 19 ans; adolescence *f.*

teeny F tout petit, minuscule.

teeth *pl. of* tooth.

teethe faire ses dents.

teetotal(l)er abstinent(e *f*) *m.*

telecast téléviser.

telecommunications *pl.* télécommunication *f.*

telegram télégramme *m.*

telegraph 1. télégraphe *m*; **2.** télégraphier; **~ic** télégraphique; **~y** télégraphie *f.*

telephon|e 1. téléphone *m*; ~ *booth* (*or box*) cabine *f* téléphonique; ~ *call* appel *m* téléphonique, coup *m* de téléphone *or* de fil; ~ *directory* annuaire *m*; ~ *exchange* central *m* (téléphonique); ~ *number* numéro *m* de téléphone; ~ *subscriber* abonné(e *f*) *m* au téléphone; *be on the* ~ avoir le téléphone; **2.** téléphoner (à q., [*to*] *s.o.*); **~ic** téléphonique; **~ist** téléphoniste *mf.*

telephoto: ~ *lens* téléobjectif *m.*

teleprinter téléscripteur *m.*

telescope 1. *opt.* télescope *m*; **2.** (se) télescoper.

televiewer téléspectateur *m.*

televis|e téléviser; **~ion** télévision *f* (*a.* =) ~ *set* poste *m* de télévision.

telex 1. télex *m*; **2.** télexer.

tell *v/t.* dire; raconter; savoir; reconnaître (à, *by*); distinguer (de, *from*); ~ *s.o. to do s.th.* dire *or* ordonner à q. de faire qch.; *I have been told that* on m'a dit que; j'ai appris que; ~ *off* gronder, réprimander; *v/i.* se faire sentir (chez q., *on s.o.*); ~ *against* nuire à; ~ *of* parler de; F ~ *on s.o.* cafarder q.; **~er** *bank*: caissier (-ière *f*) *m*; **~ing** efficace; décisif; **~ing-off** F attrapade *f*; *give s.o. a* (*good*) ~ passer un (bon) savon à q.; **~tale 1.** indicateur; révélateur; **2.** rapporteur (-euse *f*) *m.*

telly F télé *f.*

temerity témérité *f*, audace *f.*

temp intermédiaize *m/f.*

temper 1. tempérer; modérer; adoucir; **2.** humeur *f*; colère *f*; tempérament *m*; *lose one's* ~ se mettre en colère; **~ament** tempérament *m*; **~amental** du tempérament; capricieux (*person*); **~ance** tempérance *f*; antialcoolisme *m*; **~ate** tempéré; modéré; **~ature** température *f*; ♂ *have* (*or run*) *a* ~ avoir de la fièvre.

tempest tempête *f.*

temple temple *m*; *anat.* tempe *f.*

tempor|al temporel; **~ary** temporaire; provisoire; passager.

tempt tenter; inspirer (q. à *inf.*, *s.o. to inf.*); **~ation** tentation *f*; **~ing** tentant; séduisant, attrayant.

ten dix (*a. su./m*).

tenable soutenable, défendable.

tenaci|ous tenace; **~ty** ténacité *f.*

tenan|cy location *f*; **~t** locataire *mf.*

tend[1]: ~ *to* avoir tendance à.

tend[2] s'occuper de; *Am.* tenir (*a shop*).

tendency tendance *f.*

tender[1] *usu.* tendre, sensible; délicat (*subject*); affectueux; soigneux.

tender² **1.** offre *f*; *contract*: soumission *f*; *legal* ~ cours *m* légal; **2.** offrir.

tender|foot F nouveau venu *m*; **~ize** *cuis.* attendrir (*meat*); **~loin** *cuis.* filet *m*; **~ness** tendresse *f*; douceur *f*.

tendon *anat.* tendon *m*.

tendril ♣ vrille *f*.

tenement appartement *m*; (*a.* ~ *house*) maison *f* de rapport.

tenfold (*adv.* au) décuple.

tennis tennis *m*; ~ *court* tennis *m*.

tenor sens *m* général; ♪ ténor *m*.

tens|e 1. *gramm.* temps *m*; **2.** tendu; crispé; **~ed up** tendu (et nerveux); **~ion** tension *f*.

tent tente *f*.

tentacle *zo.* tentacule *m*; cir(r)e *m*.

tentative expérimental, sujet à révision; hésitant; **~ly** à titre d'essai.

tenterhooks: on ~ sur des charbons ardentes.

tenth dixième (*a. su./m*).

tenuous ténu; mince.

tenure ♣♣ bail *m*; jouissance *f*.

tepid tiède.

term 1. temps *m*, durée *f*, limite *f*; terme *m* (*a.* ♣, *phls.*, *ling.*); ♣♣ session *f*; *univ.*, *school:* trimestre *m*; ♥ échéance *f*; **~s** *pl.* conditions *f/pl.*; relations *f/pl.*; rapports *m/pl.*; **in ~s of** en ce qui concerne; **be on good** (**bad**) **~s** être bien (mal) (avec, **with**); **come to** (*or* **make**) **~s with** s'arranger avec; **2.** appeler, nommer.

termagant mégère *f*, virago *f*.

termina|l 1. terminal, dernier; ✈ en phase terminale; **2.** *traffic:* terminus *m*; ✈ borne *f*; *computer:* terminal *m*; (*a.* **air** ~) aérogare *f*; (*a.* **coach** ~) gare *f* routière; **~te** (se) terminer; finir; **~tion** fin *f*, conclusion *f*; terminaison *f* (*a.* *gramm.*); ♣♣ *etc.* résiliation *f*; ✈ ~ *of pregnancy* interruption *f* de grossesse.

terminus, *pl.* **~ni** terminus *m* (*a.* ♠).

terrace terrasse *f*; rangée *f* de maisons; **~d** en terrasse; en rangée.

terrestrial terrestre.

terrible terrible; affreux.

terri|fic énorme; formidable; terrible; **~fy** terrifier.

territor|ial territorial; **~y** territoire *m*.

terror terreur *f*; **~ism** terrorisme *m*; **~ist** terroriste *mf*; **~ize** terroriser.

terry(cloth) tissu *m* éponge.

terse concis; brusque.

test 1. examen *m*; essai *m*; analyse *f*; *psych.*, *phys.*, ⊕ *etc.* test *m*; *school:* interrogation *f*; *trial*, *a. fig.:* épreuve *f*; **put to the** ~ mettre à l'épreuve; **2.** examiner; essayer; analyser; tester (*a.* *students*); *a. fig.* mettre à l'épreuve; **3.** ... d'essai (*flight*, *pilot etc.*), ... -test; ~ *ban* (*treaty* traité *m* d')interdiction *f* d'essais nucleaires; ~ *case* affaire-test *f*; ~ *paper* interrogation *f* écrite, test *m* (scolaire) (écrit); ~ *run* essai *m* (de bon fonctionnement), ~ *tube* éprouvette; **~tube baby** bébé-éprouvette *m*.

testament *bibl.*, ♣♣ testament *m*.

testicle *anat.* testicule *m*.

testify témoigner (*a. fig.* **de**, **to**).

testimon|ial attestation *f*; témoignage *m* d'estime, **~y** témoignage *m*, déposition *f*.

testy irritable; bilieux.

tether 1. attache *f*, longe *f*; *fig.* **at the end of one's** ~ à bout; **2.** attacher.

text texte *m*; **~book** manuel *m*.

textile textile (*adj.*, *su./m*).

texture (con)texture *f*.

than *after comp.*: que; *before numerals:* de.

thank 1. remercier (de *inf.*, **for** *ger.*); ~ *you* merci; **2.** **~s** *pl.* remerciements *m/pl.*; **~s!** merci!; **~s to** grâce à; **~ful** reconnaissant; **~less** ingrat; **~sgiving** action *f* de grâce(s).

that 1. *cj.* que; **2.** *dem./pron.* (*pl.* **those**) celui-là (*pl.* ceux-là), celle-là (*pl.* celles-là); celui (*pl.* ceux), celle (*pl.* celles); cela, F ça; ce; **3.** *rel./pron.* qui, que, lequel, laquelle, lesquels, lesquelles; **4.** *adj.* (*pl.* **those**) ce (cet *before a vowel or a voiceless* h; *pl.* ces), cette (*pl.* ces); ce (cet, cette, *pl.* ces) ...-là; **5.** *adv.* (aus)si.

thatch 1. chaume *m*; **2.** couvrir de chaume.

thaw 1. dégel *m*; *v/i.* fondre; *v/t.* (faire) dégeler.

the 1. *art.* le, la, les; **2.** *adv.*... **richer he is** ~ **more arrogant he seems** plus il est riche, plus il semble arrogant.

theat|re, *Am.* **~er** théâtre *m*; **~rical** théâtral; de théâtre.

thee *poet.* accusative: te; *dative:* toi.

theft vol *m*.

their leur, leurs; **~s** le (la) leur, les leurs; à eux, à elles.

them *accusative*: les; *dative*: leur; à eux, à elles.

theme thème *m*; ~ **song** chanson *f* principale.

themselves eux-mêmes, elles-mêmes, *rfl.* se.

then 1. *adv.* alors; dans ce temps-là; puis; ensuite; aussi; d'ailleurs; *every now and* ~ de temps en temps; *there and* ~ sur le champ; *from* ~ *on* dès lors; **2.** *cj.* donc, alors, dans ce cas; **3.** *adj.* de ce temps-là.

thence de là.

theolog|ian théologien *m*; ~**y** théologie *f*.

theor|etic(al) théorique; ~**ist**, ~**etician** théoricien(ne *f*) *m*; ~**ize** théoriser; ~**y** théorie *f*.

therap|eutics *usu. sg.* thérapeutique *f*; ~**y** thérapie *f*.

there là; y; là-bas; ~ *is*, ~ *are* il y a; ~ *you are!* vous voilà!; ça y est!; ~**after** après cela, ensuite; ~**by** par là, de cette façon; ~**fore** donc, par conséquent; aussi (*with inversion*); ~**upon** là-dessus.

thermal thermal; thermique.

thermo|meter thermomètre *m*; ~**nuclear** *phys.* thermonucléaire; ~**s** (*a.* ~ *flask*) (*TM*) bouteille *f* Thermos; ~**stat** thermostat *m*.

these *see this*; ~ *three years* depuis trois ans; *in* ~ *days* à notre époque.

thesis, *pl.* **-ses** thèse.

they ils, *stressed*: eux; elles; on.

thick 1. épais (*fog, liquid etc.*); dense (*fog, crowd*); empâté (*voice*); F *stupid*: bête, bouché; F *that's a bit* ~! ça c'est un peu fort!; **2.** partie *f* épaisse; *in the* ~ *of* au beau milieu de; ~**en** (s')épaissir; ~**et** fourré *m*; ~**headed** obtus; ~**ness** épaisseur *f*; ~**set** trapu; ~**skinned** *fig.* peu sensible.

thief, *pl.* **thieves** voleur (-euse *f*) *m*.

thieve voler.

thigh cuisse *f*; ~**bone** fémur *m*.

thimble dé *m*; ⊕ bague *f*; ⚓ cosse *f*.

thin 1. mince; peu épais; maigre (*person*); clairsemé (*hair etc.*); grêle (*voice*); **2.** (s')amincir; (s')éclaircir; (*a.* ~ *down*) (se) délayer.

thine *bibl.*, *poet.* le tien, la tienne, les tiens, les tiennes; à toi.

thing chose *f*; objet *m*; ~**s** *pl. a.* affaires *f*/*pl.*; F *be the* ~ être ce qu'il faut; F *how*

are ~*s?* comment ça va?; *the best* ~ *would be to* (*inf.*) le mieux serait de (*inf.*).

think *v/i.* penser; réfléchir; ~ *of* penser à; considérer; *v/t.* croire; penser; s'imaginer; juger; trouver; tenir pour; ~ *much etc. of* avoir une bonne *etc.* opinion de; ~ *s.th. over* réfléchir à qch.; ~ *up* inventer.

third 1. troisième; *date, king*: trois; **2.** tiers *m*; troisième *mf*; *the* ♀ *World* le Tiers-Monde *m*; ~**ly** en troisième lieu; ~**party insurance** assurance *f* aux tiers; ~**rate** (de qualité) assez médiocre.

thirst 1. soif *f*; **2.** avoir soif (de *for, after*); ~**y** assoiffé; *be* ~ avoir soif (de, *for*).

thirt|een treize; ~**eenth** treizième; ~**ieth** trentième; ~**y** trente.

this 1. *pron.* (*pl.* **these**) celui-ci (*pl.* ceux-ci), celle-ci (*pl.* celles-ci); celui (*pl.* ceux), celle (*pl.* celles); ceci; ce; **2.** *adj.* (*pl.* **these**) ce (cet *before a vowel or a voiceless h*; *pl.* ces), cette (*pl.* ces); ce (cet, cette, *pl.* ces) ...-ci.

thistle ♀ chardon *m*.

thong lanière *f* (de cuir).

thorn ♀ épine *f*; ~**y** épineux (*a. fig.*).

thorough complet; profond, approfondi; à fond; minutieux; parfait, vrai; ~**ly** *a.* à fond; *a.* tout à fait; ~**bred** pur sang; ~**fare** voie *f* de communication; passage *m*; ~**ness** minutie *f*.

those *pl.* of *that* 2,4.

thou *poet.* tu, *stressed*: toi.

though quoique, bien que (*sbj.*); (*usu. at the end of a sentence*) pourtant, cependant; *as* ~ comme si.

thought pensée *f*; idée *f*; avis *m*, opinion *f*; *on second* ~*s* réflexion faite; ~**ful** pensif; réfléchi; soucieux, prévenant; ~**less** étourdi, irréfléchi.

thousand mille; ~**th** millième (*a. su.*/*m*).

thrash *v/t.* battre; rosser; F *fig.* battre (*an opponent*) à plate(s) couture(s); *v/i.*: ~ *about* se débattre; *see a.* **thresh**; ~**ing** battage *m*; rossée *f*; F défaite *f*.

thread fil *m*; ⊕ *screw*: pas *m*, filet *m*; **2.** enfiler; *fig.* se faufiler; ~**bare** râpé; *fig.* usé.

threat menace *f*; ~**en** *vt*/*i.* menacer (de, *with*).

three trois (*a. su.*/*m*); ~**dimensional** à trois dimensions; *cin. etc.* en relief *(film)*; *fig.* qui a du relief; **~fold** triple; *adv.* trois fois autant; ***increase* ~** tripler; **~-piece** en trois pièces; **~ *suit*** trois-pièces *m/inv.*; **~score** soixante.

thresh battre *(corn)*; *see* **thrash**; *fig.* **~ out** discuter *(a question)* à fond; **~ing machine** batteuse *f*; **~old** seuil *m*.

thrift économie *f*; **~y** économe.

thrill 1. *(v/t.* faire) frissonner, frémir (de, *with)*; *v/t. a.* électriser; *be* **~ed** *a.* être ravi; **2.** frisson *m*, émotion *f*; **~er** thriller *m*; **~ing** émouvant; sensationnel.

thrive se développer bien; pousser bien *(plants)*; *fig.* prospérer.

throat gorge *f*.

throb 1. battre *(heart etc.)*; lanciner *(wound)*; palpiter; vibrer *(engine)*; **2.** battement *m*; pulsation *f*, vibration *f*.

throes *pl.* tourments *m/pl.*; *in* **~** *of death* à l'agonie; *in* **~** *of* au beau milieu de.

throne trône *m*.

throng 1. foule *f*; **2.** (se) presser.

throttle 1. étrangler; ⊕ *(a.* **~** *back,* **~** *down)* mettre *(an engine)* au ralenti; **2.** *mot.* accélérateur *m*.

through 1. *prp.* à travers; au travers de; au moyen de, par; à cause de; pendant *(a period)*; **2.** *adj.* direct *(flight, train etc.)*; **~ *street*** rue *f* prioritaire; **~ *traffic*** transit *m*; **~out 1.** *prp.* d'un bout à l'autre de; dans tout; pendant tout *(a period)*; **2.** *adv.* partout, d'un bout à l'autre.

throw 1. *v/t.* jeter; lancer; projeter; terrasser *(an opponent)*; désarçonner *(a rider, a. fig.)*; *fig. a.* déconcerter, décontenancer; **~ *away*** jeter; gaspiller; **~ *off*** jeter; se dépouiller de; **~ *out*** jeter dehors; émettre; **~ *over*** abandonner; **~ *up*** jeter en l'air; vomir; *v/i. zo.* mettre bas des petits; **~ *up*** vomir; **2.** jet *m*; coup *m*.

thru *Am. see* **through**.

thrush *orn.* grive *f*.

thrust 1. poussée *f(a.* ⊕*)*; **2.** *v/t.* pousser; enfoncer; *fig.* imposer (à, *upon)*; *v/i.:* **~** *at* donner un coup à.

thruway autoroute *f* (à péage).

thud bruit *m* sourd.

thug thug *m*; *fig.* bandit *m*.

thumb 1. pouce *m*; *book:* **~ *index*** onglets *m/pl.*; **2.** feuilleter *(a book)*; manier; **~ *a lift* (*or ride*)** faire de l'auto-stop; arrêter une voiture, un pouce en l'air (pour se faire emmener); **~** *one's nose* faire un pied de nez (à q., *to s.o.)*; **~nail** ongle *m* du pouce; **~** *sketch* petit croquis (hâtif); **~tack** punaise *f*.

thump 1. coup *m* (fort); bruit *m* sourd; **2.** *v/t.* cogner (sur, *on)*; donner un coup de poing à; *v/i.* battre fort *(heart)*; **~ing** F énorme.

thunder 1. tonnerre *m*; **2.** tonner; **~bolt** foudre *f*; *fig.* coup *m* de tonnerre; **~ous** orageux; **~storm** orage *m*; **~struck** foudroyé.

Thursday jeudi *m*.

thus ainsi; de cette manière; donc.

thwart contrarier, contrecarrer.

thy *poet.* ton, ta, tes.

tick¹ *zo.* tique *f*.

tick² 1. tic-tac *m/inv.*; F moment *m*; F *on* **~** à crédit; **2.** *v/i.* faire tic-tac; battre; *mot., a. fig.* **~** *over* tourner au ralenti; *v/t.:* **~** *off* cocher; F réprimander, attraper.

tickertape serpentin *m*.

ticket 1. 🚆, *thea., lottery:* billet *m*; *tram, ship etc.:* ticket *m*; coupon *m*; *(a price* **~)** étiquette *f*; bon *m*; *mot.* contravention *f*; *parl. Am.* liste *f* des candidats; F programme *m*; **2.** étiqueter; marquer; destiner (à, *for)*; *Am. mot.* donner une contravention à; **~ *agency*** 🚆 agence *f* de voyages; *thea.* agence *f* de spectacles; **~ *collector*** 🚆 contrôleur *m* des billets; **~ *office,* ~ *window*** guichet *m*.

tickle 1. chatouiller; amuser, faire rire; plaire à, flatter; **2.** chatouillement *m*; **~ish** chatouilleux; délicat.

tidal à marée; **~ *wave*** raz *m* de marée; *fig.* vague *f*.

tidbit *see* **titbit**

tide 1. marée *f*; *fig.* vague *f*; ⚓ flot *m*; *low* *(high)* **~** marée *f* basse (haute); *in compounds:* temps *m*; **2.** **~** *s.o. over* dépanner q., tirer q. d'embarras; **~mark** F ligne sale *(round the neck etc.)*.

tidings *pl. or sg.* nouvelle(s) *f(pl.)*.

tidy 1. bien rangé; ordonné; net; soigné *(a person)*; **2.** *(a.* **~** *up)* ranger; mettre en ordre dans.

tie 1. lien *m (a. fig.)*; attache *f*; *(a. neck~)* cravate *f*; *fig.* entrave *f*; *shoe:* cordon *m*; *sp. etc.* égalité *f*; *sp.* match *m* nul; *Am.* 🚆 traverse *f*; **2.** *v/t.* lier; nouer *(a ribbon etc.)*; faire un nœud à; **~ *down***

immobiliser; obliger (*q.*) à se décider (à, pour **to**); **~ up** attacher; ficeler; *fig.* immobiliser; *fig.* occuper; *v/i.*: **~ in (with)** cadrer (avec), correspondre (à).

tier gradin *m*; étage *m*.

tie-up rapport *m*, lien *m*; ✝ *etc.* fusion *f*; *Am.* arrêt *m* (*of traffic etc.*).

tiff petite querelle *f*.

tiger tigre *m*.

tight 1. *adj.* serré; tendu, raide; étroit (*shoes*); bien fermé, étanche; rare (*money*); strict (*control etc.*); *fig.* **in a ~ corner** (*or* **squeeze** *or* **spot**) dans une mauvaise passe, dans l'embarras; **2.** *adv.* bien; (très) fort; **~en** (se) tendre; (se) (re)serrer; **~ ones belt** se serrer la ceinture; **~ up** (se) renforcer; devenir plus strict; **~-fisted** F dur à la détente, serré; **~-lipped** taciturne; à l'air pincé; **~ness** tension *f*; raideur *f*; étroitesse *f*; **~s** *pl. thea.* maillot *m*.

tile carreau *m*; *roof*: tuile *f*.

till¹ caisse *f* (enregistreuse).

till² **1.** *prp.* jusqu'(à); **2.** *cj.* jusqu'à ce que (*sbj.*).

till³ 🖉 labourer; cultiver.

tilt 1. inclinaison *f*; (*at*) **full ~** en plein; **2.** (faire) pencher.

timber bois *m* (*for building*); poutre *f*.

time 1. temps *m*; fois *f*; heure *f*; moment *m*; saison *f*; époque *f*; terme *m*; *sp. etc.* pas *m*; ♪ mesure *f*; **~ bomb** bombe *f* à retardement; **~ lag** décalage *m* (horaire); **~ limit** délai *m*; **~ signal** signal *m* horaire; **~ switch** minuteur *m*; *lighting*: minuterie *f*; **~ zone** fuseau *m* horaire; **~ and again** à maintes reprises; **at ~s** de temps en temps; parfois; **at a ~** à la fois; **at the same ~** en même temps; **behind (one's) ~** en retard; **for the ~ being** pour le moment; provisoirement; **have a good ~** s'amuser (bien); **in ~** à temps; avec le temps; ♪ en mesure; **in good ~** de bonne heure; **on ~** à l'heure; **2.** *v/t.* *sp. etc.* chronométrer; choisir le moment de; minuter (*a process, activity etc.*); fixer l'heure de; régler (sur, **by**); calculer la durée de; **~-and-motion study** étude *f* des cadences; **~-consuming** qui prend beaucoup de temps; **~less** éternel; **~-saving** qui fait gagner du temps; **~ly** opportun, à propos; **~-sharing** *data processing*: travail *m* en partage de temps; **~table** horaire *m*; 🚂

indicateur *m*; *school*: emploi *m* du temps.

timid timide, peureux.

timing ⊕ *mot.* réglage *m*; *sp.* chronométrage *m*; *activity*: minutage *m*; moment choisi.

tin 1. étain *m*; fer-blanc (*pl.* fers-blancs) *m*; boîte *f* (de conserve); **~ opener** ouvre-boîtes *m/inv.*; **2.** en *or* d'étain; en fer-blanc; de plomb (*soldier*); **3.** étamer; mettre en boîtes; **~ned meat** viande *f* de conserve.

tincture teinture *f*.

tinfoil papier *m* (d')étain.

tinge teinte *f*, nuance *f*; **~d: ~ with** teinté de.

tingle 1. picoter; **2.** picotement *m*.

tinker bricoler; **~ with** tripoter (*qch.*).

tinkle 1. (faire) tinter; **2.** F coup *m* de fil.

tin|plate fer-blanc (*pl.* fers-blancs) *m*; **~ny** métallique (*sound*); *cheap*: de camelote.

tinsel clinquant *m* (*a. fig.*).

tint 1. teinte *f*; shampooing *m* colorant; **2.** teinter, colorer.

tiny tout petit, minuscule.

tip 1. pointe *f*; bout *m*; (*cap*) embout *m*; pourboire *m*; conseil *m*, F tuyau *m*; *rubbish*: décharge *f*; **2.** (dé)verser; toucher; donner un pourboire à; (*guess*) pronostiquer; (*oft.* **~ over**) (faire) pencher; (*a.* **~ up**) (faire) basculer; **~ off** avertir (*q.*), F donner un tuyau à (*q.*); **~ out** vider; **~ over** *a.* renverser; **~ up** a. remonter; **~-off** F tuyau *m*; **...-ped** à (em)bout...; **filter-~** (bout) filtre (*cigarettes*).

tipple se livrer à la boisson.

tipsy gris, ivre; F pompette.

tiptoe 1. on ~ sur la pointe des pieds; **2.** marcher sur la pointe de pieds.

tip-top F excellent.

tire¹ pneu(matique) *m*.

tire² (se) fatiguer, *fig. a.* (se) lasser; **~d** fatigué, *fig. a.* las (de, **of**); **~less** infatigable; **~some** ennuyeux, F exaspérant.

tissue tissu *m*; mouchoir *m* (en) papier; **~ paper** papier *m* de soie.

tit¹: **~ for tat** un prêté un rendu.

tit² *orn.* mésange *f*.

titbit friandise *f*; bon morceau *m*; *fig.* quelque chose de piquant.

titillate chatouiller.

title titre *m*; ⚖ **~ deed** titre *m* de propriété; ~ **page** page *f* de titre; ~ **rôle** rôle *m* principal.

titmouse *orn.*, *pl.* -**mice** mésange *f.*

titter rire bêtement.

tittle-tattle bavardage *m.*

to 1. *prp. direction:* à; vers (*Paris*); en (*France*); chez (*me, my aunt*); *feelings:* envers, pour; *distance:* jusqu'à; ~ *me stressed:* à moi, *not stressed:* me; *it happened* ~ *me* cela m'arriva; *I bet* 10 ~ 1 je parie 10 contre 1; *the train* (*road*) ~ *London* le train (la route) de Londres; *a quarter* (*ten*) ~ *six* six heures moins le quart (dix); *here's* ~ *you!* à votre santé!; **2.** *adv.:* ~ *and fro* de long en large; *push the window* ~ fermer la fenêtre; *go* ~ *and fro* aller et venir; **3.** *indicating the infinitive:* ~ *take* prendre; *I am going* ~ (*inf.*) je vais (*inf.*); *he came* ~ *see it* il vint le voir.

toad *zo.* crapaud *m*; ~**stool** champignon *m* vénéneux; ~**y 1.** flagorneur (-euse *f*) *m*; **2.** ~ *to* lécher les bottes à (*q.*), flagorner (*q.*).

to-and-fro allées et venues *f/pl.*

toast 1. toast *m* (*a. fig.*); (faire) griller; *fig.* porter un toast à.

tobacco tabac *m*; ~**nist** marchand *m* de tabac.

toboggan toboggan *m*; *child:* luge *f.*

tod F: *on one's* ~ tout(e) seul(e).

today aujourd'hui.

toddle marcher à pas hésitants; F ~ *off* se trotter; ~**r** enfant *mf* qui commence juste à marcher.

toddy grog *m* chaud.

to-do F affaire, histoire(s) *f/(pl.).*

toe 1. *anat.* doigt *m* de pied, orteil *m*; bout *m* (*of shoe*); **2.** ~ *the line* se conformer; ~**hold** prise *f* (pour le pied); ~**nail** ongle *m* de l'orteil.

toffee, **~y** caramel *m*; ~ *apple* pomme *f* caramélisée; F *not for* ~ pas du tout; ~**nosed** F bêcheur.

together ensemble; en même temps.

togs F fringues *f/pl.*

toil 1. travail *m*, peine *f*; **2.** peiner.

toilet *les* toilettes *f/pl.*, les cabinets *m/pl.*; **2.** de toilette (*bag, soap, water etc.*); ~ *paper* papier *m* hygiénique.

toilsome fatigant.

token 1. signe *m*, marque *f*; bon *m*, coupon *m*, chèque *m*; (*a. gift* ~) bon-cadeau *m*; *book* ~ chèque-livre *m*; **2.** *in* ~ *of* en

---

signe *or* témoignage de; **3.** symbolique (*payment etc.*).

tolera|ble tolérable; assez bon; ~**nce** tolérance *f* (*a.* ⊕, ⊕); ~**nt** tolérant (à l'égard de, *of*); ~**te** tolérer; supporter; ~**tion** tolérance *f.*

toll¹ péage *m*; *fig.* **take a heavy** ~ faire un grand nombre de victimes (*accident, disaster etc.*).

toll² tinter; sonner (*oft.* le glas).

toll...: ~ *bar*, ~**gate** barrière *f* de péage; ~ *road* route *f* à péage.

tom F matou *m.*

tomato ♀, *pl.* -**toes** tomate *f.*

tomb tombe(au *m*) *f.*

tomboy fille *f* d'allures garçonnières, garçon *m* manqué.

tombstone pierre *f* tombale.

tomcat matou *m.*

tome tome *m*, (gros) livre *m.*

tomfool nigaud (*adj., su.*); ~**ery** bêtise(s) *f/(pl.).*

tomorrow demain; ~ *week* demain en huit; *the day after* ~ après-demain; ~ *night* demain soir.

ton tonne *f*; ⚓ (*a. register* ~) tonneau *m*; F ~**s** *pl.* tas *m/pl.*

tone 1. ton *m* (*a. ling.*, ♪, *paint., fig.*); ♪ *instrument:* sonorité *f*; ♪ tonus *m*; **2.** ~ *down* adoucir, atténuer; ~ *in with* aller avec, s'harmoniser avec; ~ *up* tonifier; ~**deaf** qui n'a pas d'oreille.

tongs *pl.:* (*a pair of*) ~ (des) pinces *f/pl.*; (des) pincettes *f/pl.*

tongue langue *f* (*a. fig., ling.*); *shoe:* languette *f*; (*with one's*) ~ *in* (*one's*) *cheek* ironiquement; *hold one's* ~ se taire; ~**tied** muet.

tonic 1. ♪, ♂, tonique; **2.** ♪ tonique *f*; ♂ tonique *m*, réconfortant *m.*

tonight ce soir; cette nuit.

tonnage ⚓ tonnage *m.*

tonsil *anat.* amygdale *f*; ~**itis** amygdalite *f.*

too trop; aussi; ~ *much* trop (de).

tool 1. outil *m*; **2.** travailler; façonner; ouvrager; ~**bag**, ~**kit** trousse *f* à outils.

toot 1. *mot.* (*a. one's horn*) klaxonner; **2.** coup *m* de klaxon.

tooth dent *f*; ~**ache** mal *m* de dents; ~**brush** brosse *f* à dents; ~**less** sans dents; ~**paste** (pâte *f*) dentifrice *m*; ~**pick** cure-dent *m*; ~**some** savoureux.

top[1] toupie *f*; *sleep like a ~* dormir comme un loir.

top[2] **1.** sommet *m*, cime *f*; haut *m*, dessus *m*; *tree, roof*: faîte *m*; *house*: toit *m*; *page*: tête *f*; *water*: surface *f*; *table*: dessus *m*; *box*: couvercle *m*; *bus etc.*: impériale *f*; *fig.* chef *m*, tête *f* (*in degree*); *fig.* comble *m*; *mot. Am.* capote *f*; *at the ~* (*of*) au sommet (de), en haut (de); *fig.* en tête (de) (*the list etc.*); *at the ~ of one's voice* à pleine gorge; *on ~* sur le dessus; en haut; *on ~ of* sur; *fig.* en plus de; *F blow one's ~* sortir de ses gonds, piquer une crise; **2.** supérieur; du haut; maximum; meilleur; *the ~ floor* le plus haut étage; **3.** surmonter, couronner; dépasser; être en *or* à la tête de (*a class, a list etc.*); *~ off* compléter, finir.

top...: *~ coat* pardessus *m*, manteau *m*; *~ dog* celui (celle *f*) *m* qui commande; *~ earners* les gros salaires *m/pl.*; *~ flight* de premier ordre; *~ hat* haut-de-forme (*pl.* hauts-de-forme); *~-heavy* trop lourd du haut; *fig.* pléthorique au sommet.

topic sujet *m*, thème *m*; question *f*; matière *f*; *~al* d'actualité.

top...: *~less* aux seins nus; *~ swimsuit* monokini *m*; *~-level* au niveau le plus élevé; *~most* le plus haut *or* élevé; *~-notch* F de premier ordre.

topple (*usu. ~ over or down*) (faire) tomber, culbuter.

topsyturvy sens dessus dessous; en désarroi.

torch troche *f*, flambeau *m*; *Br.* lampe *f* de poche.

torment 1. tourment *m*; **2.** tourmenter; harceler; *fig.* taquiner.

tornado, *pl.* **-does** tornade *f*.

torpedo 1. *pl.* **-does** torpille *f*; **2.** torpiller (*a. fig. a project etc.*).

torp|id inerte; *~idity*, *~or* torpeur *f*.

torque ⊕ moment *m* de torsion.

torrent torrent *m*; *in ~s* à torrents; *~ial* torrentiel.

torrid torride.

torsion torsion *f*.

tortoise *zo.* tortue *f*.

tortuous tortueux; sinueux.

torture 1. torture *f*; supplice *m*; **2.** torturer.

toss 1. jet *m*, lancement *m*; coup *m*;

mouvement *m* brusque; coup *m* de pile ou face; **2.** lancer, jeter; rejeter en arrière (*one's head*); faire sauter (*a. a pancake*); jeter en l'air; (*a. ~ about*) agiter, secouer; *v/i.* s'agiter, tanguer (*ship*); (*a. ~ up*) jouer à pile ou face (*qch., for s.th.*).

tot F tout(e) petit(e) enfant *mf*; petit verre *m*.

total 1. total (*adj., su./m*); **2.** *v/t.* (*a. ~ up*) additionner; *v/i.* s'élever (à, *up to*); *~itarian* totalitaire; *~ity* totalité *f*.

totter chanceler, vaciller.

touch 1. *v/t.* toucher; (*interfere with*) toucher à; *F a bit ~ed* un peu toqué; *sl. ~ s.o. for a pound* taper q. d'une livre; *~ off* faire partir; *a. fig.* déclencher; *~ up* retoucher; *v/i.* se toucher; ⚓ *~ at* toucher à; *~ down* atterrir; *~ on* effleurer, toucher (*a topic etc.*); **2.** toucher *m* (*a. ♪*); contact *m*; attouchement *m*; léger coup *m*; *cuis., illness etc.*: soupçon *m*; *paint.* (coup *m* de) pinceau *m*; *fig.* nuance *f*; *in ~* en contact; *get in(to) ~* (avec, *with*) prendre contact; *lose ~* se perdre de vue (*persons*); *~-and--go* incertain; hasardeux; *~down* atterrissage *m*; amerrissage *m*; *~ing* touchant, émouvant; *~stone* pierre *f* de touche (*a. fig.*); *~y* susceptible; *see testy*.

tough dur, coriace (*meat*); résistant; fort; rude; inflexible (*person*); ténace, acharné (*efforts, resistance etc.*); *~ luck!* pas de veine!; **2.** dur *m*; *~en v/t.* durcir; (s')endurcir (*person*); *~ness* dureté *f*; résistance *f*; *fig.* difficulté *f*.

tour 1. voyage *m*; tour *m*; tournée *f* (*artist etc.*); *~ operator* organisateur *m* de voyages; **2.** *v/i.* voyager, faire du tourisme; *v/t.* voyager en; visiter en touriste; *~ism* tourisme *m*; *~ist* touriste *mf*; voyageur (-euse *f*) *m*; *~ agency* (*or office or bureau*) bureau *m* de tourisme; *~ season* la saison *f*.

tournament tournoi *m*.

tousle ébouriffer (*hair*).

tow ⚓ **1.** (câble *m* de) remorque *f*; *take in ~* prendre en remorque; **2.** remorquer.

toward(s) *place*: vers; *person*: envers, à l'égard de; *purpose*: pour.

towel 1. serviette *f*; essuie-mains *m/inv.*; **2.** frotter avec une serviette; *~(l)ing* tissu-éponge *m*.

tower 1. tour *f*; *church*: clocher *m*; ~ **block** tour *f* (d'habitation); **2.** (*a. ~ over*) dominer; monter très haut; **~ing** très haut; éminent.

towline câble *m* de remorquage, remorque *f*.

town 1. ville *f*; *county* ~ chef-lieu *m* (*pl.* chefs-lieux); *go to* ~ aller en ville; *fig.* mettre le paquet; **2.** municipal; de la ville; à la ville; ~ **council** conseil *m* municipal; ~ **hall** hôtel *m* de ville; mairie *f*; ~ **planning** urbanisme *m*; **~sfolk** *pl.* citadins *m/pl.*; **~ship** commune *f*, **~speople** *pl.* citadins *m/pl.*

toxic toxique; **~in** toxine *f*.

toy 1. jouet *m*; *attr.* de jouets; tout petit; **2.** jouer (avec, *with*); **~shop** magasin *m* de jouets.

trace 1. trace *f*; vestige *m* (*a. fig.*); trait *m*; **2.** tracer (*a. a plan*); calquer (*a design*); *fig.* esquisser; suivre à la trace; retrouver; **~ back** faire remonter (à, *to*).

track 1. trace *f*; piste *f* (*a. sp., hunt.* ⊕); voie *f* (*a.* 🚂); sentier *m*; chemin *m* (*a.* ⊕); 🚂, 🚋 rail *m*; *esp. Am.* ~ **athletics** *pl.* l'athlétisme *m* (sur piste); la course, le saut, et le lancement du poids; *keep* ~ *of* suivre; *lose* ~ *of* perdre (de vue); *be on the wrong* ~ faire fausse route; **2.** *v/t.* suivre la trace *or* la piste de; ~ **down** trouver, dénicher.

tract étendue *f*, région *f*; 🔬 système *m*, appareil *m*; *brochure*: tract *m*; **~able** docile, traitable.

traction traction *f*; ~ **engine** remorqueur *m*; **~or** tracteur *m*.

trade 1. commerce *m*; affaires *f/pl.*; métier *m*; *free* ~ libre échange *m*; **2.** *v/i.* faire des affaires (avec, *with*); faire commerce (de, *in*); échanger (contre, *for*); ~ *in* faire reprendre; **~-in** reprise *f*; objet *m* donné en reprise; ~ **price** (*value*) prix *m* (valeur *f*) à la reprise; **~mark** marque *f* de fabrique; *registered* ~ marque *f* déposée; ~ **name** appellation *f*; marque *f* déposée; ~ **price** prix *m* marchand; **~r** commerçant(e *f*) *m*, négociant(e *f*) *m*; marchand(e *f*) *m*; ~ **relations** *pl.* relations *f/pl.* commerciales; **~sman** marchand *m*; **~union** syndicat *m* ouvrier; **~unionist 1.** syndiqué(e *f*) *m*; **2.** syndical; ~ **war** guerre *f* économique; **~wind** ⚓ (vent *m*) alizé *m*.

tradition tradition *f* (*a.* 🏛); **~al** traditionnel; de tradition.

traffic 1. *street*: circulation *f*; ✈ trafic *m* (de, *in*); ~ **jam** embouteillage *m*; ~ **lights** *pl.* feux *m/pl.* (de circulation); ~ **sign** poteau *m* de signalisation; **~warden** contractuel(le *f*) *m*; *v/i.*: ~ *in* faire le trafic de.

trag|edy tragédie *f*; **~ic** tragique.

trail 1. piste *f*; chemin *m*; *smoke etc.*: trainée *f*; **2.** *v/t.* traîner; suivre la piste de; *v/i.* traîner; 🌿 grimper, ramper; ~ **behind** être à la traîne; **~blazer** pionnier *m*; précurseur *m*, **~er** *vehicle*: remorque *f*; *mot. Am.* caravane *f*; *cin.* film-annonce *m*.

train 1. train *m* (*a.* ⊕), rame *f*; file; suite *f* (*a. attendants etc.*); *cost.* traîne *f*; ~ *of thought* fil *m* de pensée(s); **2.** *v/t.* former, dresser (*an animal*); exercer (*a faculty etc.*); diriger (*a plant*); *sp.* entraîner; ~ **s.th. on** braquer qch. sur; *v/i.* s'exercer; *sp.* s'entraîner; **~ee** apprenti(e *f*) *m*; stagiaire *fm*; **~er** *sp.* entraîneur (-euse *f*) *m*; *animals*: dresseur (-euse *f*) *m*; **~ing** formation *f* (professionnelle); *sp.* entraînement *m*; *sp. in* ~ en cours d'entraînement; en bonne forme.

traipse F se traîner; cheminer.

trait trait *m* (*of character etc.*).

traitor traître *m*.

trajectory *phys.* trajectoire *f*.

tram(car) tramway *m*.

tramp 1. promenade *f* à pied; pas lourd; *person*: chemineau *m*, vagabond(e *f*) *m*; *Am.* ~ a. coureuse *f*; **2.** *v/i.* marcher lourdement; voyager à pied; *v/t.* parcourir (à pied).

trample (*a. ~ on*, *fig.* ~ **underfoot**) piétiner.

trance transe *f*.

tranquil tranquille; **~(l)ity** tranquillité *f*, **~(l)izer** 🔬 tranquillisant *m*.

transact traiter, faire; **~ion** transaction *f*, 📋 ~s *pl.* actes *m/pl.*

transatlantic transatlantique.

transcend transcender; dépasser; **~ence, ~ency** transcendance *f*.

transcribe transcrire (*a.* 🎵).

transcript, ~ion transcription *f*.

transfer 1. *v/t.* transférer; passer; décalquer (*a drawing etc.*); *v/i.* changer de train *etc.*; **2.** transfert *m*; passation *f*;

picture: décalcomanie *f*; **~ ticket** *Am.* billet *m* de correspondance; **~able** transmissible.

transfix transpercer; *fig.* **~ed** cloué au sol (par, **with**).

transform transformer; **~ation** transformation *f*; **~er** ⚡ transformateur *m*.

transfusion transfusion *f*.

transgress *v/t.* transgresser; *v/i.* pécher; **~ion** transgression *f*; péché *m*; **~or** transgresseur *m*.

transient 1. passager, transitoire; **2.** voyageur *m* de passage; personne *f* sans domicile fixe.

transistor (*a.* **~ radio**) transistor *m*; **~ize** transistoriser.

transit transit *m*; passage *m*.

transition transition *f*; passage *m*.

transitive *gramm.* transitif.

transitory transitoire, passager.

translat|e traduire; **~ion** traduction *f*; *school*: version *f*; **~or** traducteur (-trice *f*) *m*.

translucent translucide.

transmission transmission *f*; *radio, TV a.* émission *f*.

transmit transmettre; *radio, TV a.* émettre; **~ter** émetteur *m*.

transmute transmu(t)er.

transparen|cy transparence *f*; *phot.* diapositive *f*; **~t** transparent.

transpire transpirer (*a.* = *become known*); F arriver, se passer.

transplant transplanter; **~ation** transplantation *f*.

transport 1. transporter; **2.** transport *m*; **~ café** relais *m* des routiers; **~ undertaking** entreprise *f* de transport; **Minister of** ⚹ ministre *m* des transports; **~able** transportable; **~ation** (moyen *m* de) transport *f*; ⚹⚹ déportation *f*.

transpose transposer (*a.* ♪).

transverse transversal; en travers.

transvestite travesti(e *f*) *m*.

trap 1. piège *m*; *vehicle*: cabriolet *m*; **2.** prendre au piège; **~door** trappe *f*.

trapeze trapèze *f*.

trapez|ium, **~oid** Ⱥ trapèze *m*.

trapper trappeur *m*.

trappings *pl.* ornements *m/pl.*; signes *m/pl.* (extérieurs).

traps F *pl.* effets *m/pl.* (personnels).

trash *surt. Am.* ordures *f/pl.*; déchets *m/pl.*; rebut *m*; camelote *f*; *fig.* sottises

f/pl.; **~ can** boîte *f* à ordures; poubelle *f*; **~y** sans valeur, de rebut.

trauma trauma *m*; **~tic** traumatique; **~ experience** traumatisme *m*.

travel 1. *v/i.* voyager; faire des voyages; aller, se déplacer; *v/t.* parcourir (*a country, a distance etc.*); **~ agency** (*or agent's, bureau*) agence *f* de voyages; **~ allowance** indemnité *f* de déplacement; **2.** voyage *m*, -s *m/pl.*; **~(l)er** voyageur (-euse *f*) *m* (*a.* ✝); **~'s cheque** (*Am.* **check**) chèque *m* de voyage; **~(l)ing 1.** voyage(s) *m/pl.*); **2.** ambulant (*circus etc.*); de voyage (*bag, alarm clock, etc.*); **~ expenses** *pl.* frais *m/pl.* de déplacement; **~ salesman** voyageur *m* de commerce.

traverse 1. traversée *f* (*a.* mount.); ⊕ traverse *f*; **2.** traverser.

travesty 1. parodie *f*; travestissement *m*; **2.** parodier; travestir.

trawler ⚓ chalutier *m*.

tray plateau *m*; corbeille *f*.

treacher|ous traître; **~y** traîtrise *f*.

treacle mélasse *f*.

tread 1. *v/i.* marcher (sur, [up]on); *v/t.* marcher sur; fouler, parcourir, suivre (*a path*); **2.** pas *m*; bruit *m* des pas; *tire*: chape *f*; *stair*: marche *f*; **~mill** *fig.* besogne *f* ingrate quotidienne.

treason trahison *f*; **~able** de trahison.

treasure 1. trésor *m*; **~ hunt** chasse *f* au trésor; ⚹⚹ **~ trove** trésor *m*; **2.** estimer, priser; (*usu.* **~ up**) conserver précieusement.

treasury trésorerie *f*; ⚹ **Department** ministère *m* des Finances.

treat 1. traiter; **~ s.o. to s.th.** offrir qch. à q.; **2.** plaisir *m*; (petit) cadeau *m*, surprise *f*; **~ise** traité *m*; **~ment** traitement *m*; **~y** traité *m*.

treble 1. triple; **2.** triple *m*; ♪ **voice**: soprano *m*; ♪ **~ clef** clef *f* de sol; **3.** *adv.* trois fois autant; **4.** *vt/i.* tripler.

tree arbre *m*; **~ trunk** tronc *m* d'arbre; F **be up a (gum) ~** être dans la nasse.

trefoil ♣ trèfle *m*.

trek 1. voyage *m*; randonnée *f*; (bout *m* de) chemin *m*; **2.** faire une randonnée; cheminer; se traîner.

trellis treillis *m*, treillage *m*.

tremble 1. trembler (devant, **at**; de, **with**); **2.** trembl(ot)ement *m*.

tremendous énorme; F fantastique.

T

tremor tremblement *m*.

tremulous trembl(ot)ant.

trench tranchée *f* (*a.* ⚔); fossé *m*.

trend tendance *f*; *fashion*: mode *f*; **up-ward** (**downward**) ~ tendance à la hausse (baisse); **~setter** lanceur (-euse *f*) *m* de modes; personne *or* chose qui donne le ton; **~y** à la (dernière) mode, dernier cri; dans le vent (*person, idea etc.*).

trepidation inquiétude *f*.

trespass 1. s'introduire sans permission (dans, **on**); *fig.* ~ (**up**)**on** abuser de; empiéter sur; '*no* ~*ing!*' 'défense d'entrer'; **2.** offense *f*; **~er** intrus(e *f*) *m*; *bibl.* pécheur (-eresse *f*) *m*.

tress boucle *f* (*of hair*).

trestle tréteau *m*, chevalet *m*.

trial essai *m*; ⚖ procès *m*, jugement; *fig.* épreuve *f*, affliction *f*; **~ period** période *f* d'essai; ⚖ **stand** ~ passer en jugement, on ~ à l'essai; en jugement.

triang|le triangle *m* (*a.* ♪); **~ular** triangulaire; en triangle.

tribe tribu *f* (*a. zo.*); **~sman** membre *m* de (la) tribu.

tribulation tribulation *f*.

tribunal tribunal *m*.

tribut|ary 1. tributaire; **2.** *geog.* affluent *m*; **~e** tribut *m*; *fig. a.* hommage *m*; **pay** ~ **to** rendre hommage à.

trice: *In a* ~ en un clin d'œil.

trick 1. tour *m*; tour *m* d'adresse; ruse *f*; truc *m*; habitude *f*; *cards*: levée *f*; **2.** duper, attraper; ~ *s.o.* **out of** *s.th.* escroquer qch. à q.; **~ery** tromperie *f*.

trickle 1. couler (goutte à goutte); suinter; ~ **in** (**out**) entrer (sortir) les un(e)s après les autres; **2.** filet *m*.

trick|ster escroc *m*; **~y** difficile, épineux, délicat (*problem etc.*); rusé (*person*).

tricycle tricycle *m*.

trif|le 1. bagatelle *f*; **a** ~ un tout petit peu; **2.** *v/i.* jouer, badiner (avec, **with**); *v/t.* ~ **away** gaspiller (*son argent*), **~ing** insignifiant.

trigger 1. *gun*: détente *f*, gâchette *f*, *phot.* déclencheur *m*; **2.** (*a.* ~ **off**) déclencher.

trill 1. trille *m*; **2.** triller.

trillion trillion *m*, *Am.* billion *m*.

trim 1. bien tenu, net, soigné; coquet; bien tourné; **2.** (légère) coupe *f*; garniture *f*, ornement *m*; **in** (**good**) ~ en bon état; en (bonne) forme; **3.** garnir, orner

(de, **with**); tailler; émonder; ⚓ gréer; ~ **down** réduire; ~ **off** enlever; **~mings** *pl.* garniture(s) *f*(*pl.*); accessoires *m*/*pl.*

trinket colifichet *m*; bibelot *m*.

trip 1. excursion *f*; voyage *m*; faux pas *m*; **2.** *v/i.* trébucher, faire un faux pas; marcher à petits pas; *v/t.* (*usu.* ~ **up**) faire un croc-en-jambe à, faire trébucher (*q.*).

tripartite tripartite; triple.

tripe *cuis.* tripes *f*/*pl.*; F idioties *f*/*pl.*

triple triple, **~ts** *pl.* triplets *m*/*pl.*

triplicate (*a. in* ~) en trois exemplaires.

tripod trépied *m*.

tripper excursionniste *mf*.

trite banal; rebattu.

triumph 1. triomphe *m* (sur, **over**); **2.** triompher (de, **over**); **~al** triomphal; **~ant** triomphant.

trivial insignifiant; banal; **~ity** insignifiance *f*; banalité *f*.

troll(e)y chariot *m*; **~bus** trolleybus *m*.

trollop putain *f*.

troop 1. troupe *f*, bande *f*; ⚔ **~s** *pl.* troupes *f*/*pl.*, soldats *m*/*pl.*; **2.** s'assembler; ~ **away**, ~ **off** partir en bande; **~er** *Br.* soldat *m* de cavalerie; *Am.* membre *m* de la police montée.

trophy trophée *m*.

tropic 1. trophique; **2.** *a.* **~al** tropique; tropical.

trot 1. trot *m*; **on the** ~ de suite; d'affilée; **2.** (faire) trotter.

trouble 1. ennuis *m*/*pl.*, difficulté(s) *f*(*pl.*); souci *m*; inquiétude *f*; mal *m*, peine *f*; ✚, *pol. etc.* troubles *m*/*pl.*; ~ **spot** point *m* de conflit, foyer *m* de troubles; ✚ **stomach** (**heart**) ~ troubles *m*/*pl.* gastriques (cardiaques); **be in** ~ avoir des ennuis, être en difficulté; **go to the** ~ **of, take the** ~ **of** (*ger.*) se donner la peine *or* le mal de, prendre la peine de (*inf.*); **what's the** ~ qu'est-ce qui ne va pas?; **2.** *v/t.* inquiéter; déranger, gêner, ennuyer; donner de la peine à; **may I** ~ **you for the salt?** voudriez-vous bien me passer le sel?; *v/i.* ~ **to** (*inf.*) se donner la peine de (*inf.*); s'inquiéter de (*inf.*); ~ **about** s'enquiéter, se soucier de; **~d** préoccupé, inquiet (*look, person etc.*); troublé (*period, area etc.*), trouble (*water*); **~-free** sans ennuis, sans difficulté(s); **~man**, **~shooter** F dépanneur *m*; **~some** ennuyeux; gênant.

T

trough *phys.* creux (*of a wave*); *meteor.* dépression *f.*

trounce F rosser (*q.*).

troupe *thea. etc.*: troupe *f.*

trouser de pantalon (*pocket, leg etc.*); **~ suit** tailleur-pantalon *m* (*pl.* tailleurs-pantalons); **~s** *pl.* (**a pair of** un) pantalon *m.*

trout *icht.* truite *f.*

trowel truelle *f.*; 🖉 déplantoir *m.*

truant élève *mf* qui manque l'école; **play ~** faire l'école buissonnière.

truce trêve *f.*

truck¹ 1. camion *m*; chariot *m* (à bagages); 🚃 wagon *m* à marchandises ouvert; **~-driver** camionneur *m*, routier *m*; **~ stop** relais *m* des routiers; **2.** transporter par camion, camionner.

truck² relations *f/pl.*, rapports *m/pl.*; troc *m*, échange *m*; (*usu.* **~ system**) paiement *m* des ouvriers en nature; *Am.* produits *m/pl.* maraîchers; **~ farm**, **~ garden** jardin *m* maraîcher; **~ farmer** maraîcher *m.*

trucker camionneur *m*, routier *m.*

truckle s'abaisser (devant, **to**).

truculent agressif; brutal.

trudge marcher lourdement *or* péniblement, se traîner.

true vrai; véritable; exact; juste; fidèle; ⊕ droit; **come ~** se réaliser; **~ to life** (*or* **nature**) tout à fait naturel; **prove ~** se vérifier; se réaliser.

truism truisme *m.*

truly vraiment; sincèrement; **yours ~** agréez, Monsieur (Madame), l'expression de mes sentiments les plus distingués.

trump 1. *cards*: atout *m*; **2.** *v/i.* jouer atout; **~ up** couper (*a card*); **~ up** inventer; **~ery** friperie *f*, camelote *f.*

trumpet 1. trompette *f*; **2.** (*a.* **~ forth**) proclamer.

truncheon bâton *m* (*of a policeman*); casse-tête *m/inv.*

trundle (faire) rouler; *v/t.* passer.

trunk tronc *m* (*of tree, a. of body*); *elephant*: trompe *f*; *suitcase*: malle *f*; **~s** *pl.* caleçon *m* court; slip *m* de bain; *teleph.* **~ call** communication *f* interurbaine; **~ road** route *f* nationale.

truss 1. 🧵 bandage *m* herniaire; 🏛 ferme *f*; *cuis.* trousser (*a. chicken etc.*); 🏛 renforcer; ligoter (*q.*).

trust 1. confiance *f* (en, **in**); 🏛 fidéicommis *m*; ✝ trust *m*, syndicat *m*; **in ~** par fidéicommis; **have ~ in** avoir confiance en; **place** (*or* **put**) **one's ~ in** faire confiance à, avoir confiance en; **position of ~** poste *m* de confiance; **2.** *v/t.* se fier à, avoir confiance en; croire; espérer; **~ s.th. to s.o.**, **~ s.o. with s.th.** confier qch. à q.; **~ s.o. to do s.th.** se fier à q. pour qu'il fasse qch.; *v/i.*: **~ in** avoir confiance en, faire confiance à; **~ to** se fier à, s'en remettre à; **~ee** *admin.* administrateur *m*; 🏛 fiduciaire *m*; **~ful** confiant; **~worthy** loyal; digne de foi.

truth vérité *f*; **~ful** vrai; fidèle.

try 1. *v/t.* essayer; ⊕ *etc.* mettre à l'essai; 🏛 juger; *strain*: éprouver; **~ one's best** faire de son mieux (pour, **to**); **~ to** (*inf.*), F **~ and** essayer de (*inf.*); chercher à (*inf.*); **~ on, ~ out** essayer; **~ one's hand at** s'essayer à; *v/i.* essayer; **~ hard** s'efforcer (de, **to**), faire un effort (pour, **to**); **~ for** essayer d'obtenir; **2.** essai *m*; tentative *f*; **~ing** pénible, ennuyeux.

tub cuve *f*; baquet *m*; (*a.* **bath~**) baignoire *f.*

tubby boulot, dodu.

tube tube *m* (*a. radio*); tuyau *m*; *mot.* chambre *f* à air; F métro *m* (*in London*); **~less** sans chambre à air.

tuberculosis tuberculose *f.*

tubular tubulaire.

tuck 1. petit pli *m*, rempli *m*; *sl.* mangeaille *f*; **2.** mettre, fourrer; (*a.* **~ away**) cacher; **~ in** rentrer; F manger de bon appétit; **~ into a meal** attaquer un repas; **~ up** border (dans son lit, **in bed**); **~-in** F (grande) bouffe *f.*

Tuesday mardi *m.*

tuft touffe *f*; *bird*: huppe *f.*

tug 1. ⚓ remorqueur *m*; **give s.th. a ~** tirer sur qch.; **2.** tirer (sur, **at**); ⚓ remorquer.

tuition cours *m/pl.*, leçons *f/pl.*

tulip 🌷 tulipe *f.*

tumble 1. *v/i.* tomber; rouler; **~ down** s'écrouler (*building*); *v/t.* bouleverser; déranger; **2.** chute *f*; désordre *m*; **~down** délabré; croulant; **~r** acrobate *mf*; verre *m* sans pied; gobelet *m.*

tumid 🧵 enflé, gonflé.

tummy F estomac *m*, ventre *m.*

tumo(u)r 🧵 tumeur *f.*

tumult tumulte *m*; **~uous** tumultueux.

tuna *icht.* thon *m.*

tune 1. ♪ air *m; fig.* ton *m; fig.* humeur *f;* **in ~** ♪ accordé; *fig.* en bon accord (avec, **with**); **out of ~** ♪ désaccordé; *fig.* en désaccord (avec, **with**); **sing in (out of) ~** chanter juste (faux); **2.** *v/t.* ♪ accorder; ⊕ *etc.* mettre au point; régler; **~ in** *radio.* capter (un poste, to **a station**); *v/i.* **~ up** accorder son ou ses instrument(s); **~ful** mélodieux, harmonieux; **~less** discordant; **~r** *radio:* tuner *m.*

tunnel 1. tunnel *m,* ⚒ galerie *f;* **2.** percer un tunnel (à travers, dans, sous).

tunny *icht.* thon *m.*

turbid trouble; bourbeux.

turbine ⊕ turbine *f.*

turbojet turboréacteur *m*

turbot *icht.* turbot *m.*

turbulent turbulent; agité (*sea*).

tureen soupière *f;* saucière *f.*

turf 1. gazon *m;* motte *f* (de gazon); courses *f/pl.* de chevaux; **2.** gazonner; *sl.* **~ out** flanquer (*q.*) dehors.

turgid turgide, *fig.* boursouflé.

Turk Turc (Turque *f*) *m.*

turkey *orn.* dindon *m,* dinde *f; cuis.* dindonneau *m; thea., cin. Am. sl.* navet *m.*

Turkish turc, de Turquie

turmoil trouble *m;* émoi *m.*

turn 1. *v/t.* tourner; faire tourner; retourner; rendre; changer (en, **into**); diriger; ⊕ tourner; *fig.* tourner (*phrases etc.*); **~ colo(u)r** pâlir *or* rougir; changer de couleur; **he can ~ his hand to anything** c'est un homme à tout main; **~ away** détourner; **~ down** rabattre; retourner (*a card*); baisser (*the gas etc.*); ouvrir (*the bed*); *fig.* refuser (*an invitation etc.*); **~ off** (**on**) fermer, (ouvrir) (*a tap*); **~ out** faire sortir; mettre dehors; fabriquer, produire (*goods*); éteindre (*the light*); **~ over** renverser; feuilleter, tourner (*pages*); *fig.* transférer; ♦ faire; **~ up** retourner (*cards, a ♠*); relever (*one's trousers*); retrousser (*one's sleeve*); donner (*the gas etc.*); **2.** *v/i.* tourner; se (re)tourner; se diriger; se transformer (en, **into**); changer (*weather*); devenir (*Christian, soldier, pale etc.*); (*a.* **~ sour**) tourner (*milk*); **~ about** se (re)tourner; **~ away** se détourner (de, **from**); **~ back** faire demi-tour; revenir; **~ in** se tourner en dedans; F se coucher; **~ off** *mot.* tourner

(à gauche, **to the left**); **~ on** se retourner contre, attaquer; **~ out** sortir; se mettre en grève; (+ *adj.*) se révéler, s'avérer, devenir; se lever; **~ over** se (re)tourner; *mot. etc.* capoter; se renverser; **~ to** se mettre à; tourner à; devenir; F **~ to** *adv.* se mettre au travail; **~ up** se relever; se présenter; **3.** *su.* tour *m* (*a. walk*); *tendency etc., disposition of mind:* tournure *f; wheel:* révolution *f; fig.* changement *m* de direction, *mot.* virage *m; road:* tournant *m; thea.* numéro *m; ✆* attaque *f,* crise *f; fig.* service *m;* **at every ~** à tout moment; **at the ~ of the century** en fin (*or* en début) de siècle; **by** (*or* **in**) **~s** tour à tour; **in my ~** à mon tour; **it is my ~** c'est à mon tour, c'est à moi (de, **to**); **take ~s** se relayer (pour *inf.* **at,** in *ger.*); **do s.o. a good ~** rendre service à q.; **does it serve your ~?** est-ce que cela fera votre affaire?; **~about,** **~(a)round** revirement *m,* volte-face *f;* **~coat** renégat *m;* apostat (*e f*) *m;* **~ed-up** retroussé (*nose*); **~er** tourneur *m.*

turning *road, street:* tournant *m; mot.* **~ circle** rayon *m* de braquage; **~ point** tournant *m,* point *m* décisif.

turnip 🌱 navet *m.*

turn...: **~out** assistance *f,* (nombre *m* de) gens *m/pl.;* tenue *f* (*of a person*); ♦ production *f;* **~over** ♦ chiffre *m* d'affaires; **~pike** *hist.* barrière *f* de péage; *Am.* autoroute *f* à péage; **~stile** tourniquet *m* (*of entrance*); **~table** 🎦 plaque *f* tournante; *record player:* tourne-disque *m;* **~up** *trousers:* revers *m.*

turpentine 🌲 térébenthine *f.*

turquoise turquoise (*su./f, adj.*).

turret tourelle *f* (*a.* ✕, ⚓, ⊕).

turtle *zo.* tortue *f* de mer; *orn.* (*usu.* **~dove**) tourterelle *f;* **turn ~** capoter; **~neck** (pullover *m* à) col *m* roulé.

tusk *elephant:* défense *f;* **~s** *pl. boar:* broches *f/pl.*

tussle 1. mêlée *f,* lutte *f;* **2.** se bagarrer, lutter.

tussock touffe *f* d'herbe.

tut allons donc!; zut!

tutelage tutelle *f.*

tutor 1. (*a.* **private ~**) précepteur (-trice *f*) *m; school, univ.:* directeur (-trice *f*) *m* d'études; *Am. univ.* chargé *m* de cours; **2.** instruire; donner des leçons particulières à; **~ial 1.** d'instruction; **2.** cours *m* individuel.

tuxedo *Am.* smoking *m*.

TV télé(vision) *f*.

twaddle 1. fadaises *f/pl.*; **2.** dire des sottises.

twang 1. bruit *m* vibrant; (*usu.* **nasal ~**) accent *m* nasillard; **2.** (faire) résonner; nasiller (*person*).

tweak pincer (et tordre) (*s.o.'s ear etc.*).

tweed tweed *m*.

tweezers *pl.*: (**a pair of**) **~** (une) petite pince *f*; (une) pince *f* à épiler.

twelfth douzième; **~-night** veille *f* des Rois.

twelve douze; **~o'clock** midi *m*; minuit *m*.

twent|ieth vingtième; **~y** vingt.

twice deux fois; **~ as much** deux fois autant; **~ as many books** deux fois plus de livres.

twiddle (*a.* **~ with**) jouer avec; tripoter; **~ one's thumbs** se tourner les pouces.

twig 1. brindille *f*; **2.** F piger, entraver.

twilight crépuscule *m* (*a. fig.*).

twin 1. jumeau; jumelé; **~ beds** *pl.* lits *m/pl.* jumeaux; **~ town** ville *f* jumelée; **2.** jumeau (-elle *f*) *m*; **3.** jumeler.

twine ficelle *f*; fil *m* retors; **2.** *v/t.* tordre, tresser; enrouler; *v/i.* (*a.* **~ o.s.**) s'enrouler.

twinge élancement *m* (*of pain*); *fig.* remords *m* (*of conscience*).

twinkle 1. scintiller, pétiller; **2.** scintillement *m*, pétillement *m*; clignotement *m* (*of the eyes*); **in a ~** en un clin d'œil.

twirl 1. tournoiement *m*; *smoke*: volute *f*; **2.** (faire) tourn(oy)er.

twit F idiot(e *f*) *m*.

twist 1. fil *m* retors; torsion *f*; *path*: coude *m*; contorsion *f* (*of the face*); *fig.* déformation *f*; *fig.* tournure *f* (*of mind*); **2.** *v/t.* tordre (*a. one's face etc.*), tortiller; entortiller; enrouler; déformer; *v/i.* se tordre, se tortiller; *fig.* tourner, serpenter; **~er** *Am.* tornade *f*.

twitch 1. *v/t.* tirer brusquement; *v/i.* se convulser; **2.** saccade *f*; contraction *f*, tic *m* (*of the face*).

twitter 1. gazouiller; F jacasser (*person*); **2.** gazouillement *m*.

two deux (*a. su./m*); **in ~** en deux; *fig.* **put ~ and ~ together** raisonner juste; **~-bit** F sans importance; bon marché; **~-dimensional** à deux dimensions; **~-edged** à deux tranchants (*a. fig.*); **~-faced** faux, hypocrite; **~-fisted** costaud; **~-fold** double; *increase ~* doubler; **~-penny** à *or* de deux pence; *fig.* de quatre sous, bon marché; **~-piece** *cost.* (en) deux pièces; **~-seater** *mot.* voiture *f* à deux places; **~some** couple *m*; **~-stroke** *mot.* à deux temps; **~-time** F doubler (*q.*); **~-way** *road:* à double sens; *traffic:* dans les deux sens; *fig.* bilatéral.

tycoon magnat *m* de l'industrie.

type 1. type *m*; genre *m*; modèle *m*; *typ.* caractère *m*, type *m*, *coll.* caractères *m/pl.*; *typ.* **set in ~** composer; **2.** taper (à la machine); **~script** texte *m* dactylographié; **~write** écrire à la machine; **~writer** machine *f* à écrire; **~ ribbon** ruban *m* encreur.

typhoid ℞ (*a.* **~ fever** fièvre *f*) typhoïde *f*.

typhoon *meteor.* typhon *m*.

typhus ℞ typhus *m*.

typ|ical typique; caractéristique (de, *of*); *it's ~ of him* c'est bien lui; **~fy** être caractéristique de; **~ing** dactylo(graphie) *f*; **~pool** bureau *m* des dactylos, F dactylo *f*; *be good at ~* taper bien; **~st** dactylographe *f*, F dactylo *f*; *shorthand ~* sténodactylographe *mf*, F sténodactylo *mf*.

tyrann|ic(al) tyrannique; **~ize** (*a.* **over**) tyranniser; **~y** tyrannie *f*.

tyrant tyran *m* (*a. orn.*).

tyre pneu(matique) *m*.

Tyrolese 1. tyrolien; **2.** Tyrolien (-ne *f*) *m*.

U

ubiquitous qui se trouve *or* que l'on rencontre partout.

udder pis *m*, mamelle *f*.

ugly laid; vilain (*wound, word etc.*); mauvais (*weather*); *fig.* répugnant.

ulcer ⚕ ulcère *m*; ~**ate** (s')ulcérer; ~**ous** ulcéreux.

ulterior ultérieur; *fig.* caché, secret; ~ **motive** arrière-pensée *f*.

ultimate final; dernier; fondamental; ~**ly** à la fin; en fin de compte; finalement; par la suite.

ultimatum, *pl. a.* **-ta** ultimatum *m*.

ultimo ✝ du mois dernier.

ultra- ultra-; extrêmement.

ultra...: ~**marine** (bleu *m*) d'outre-mer; ~**-short wave** onde *f* ultracourte; ~**violet** ultraviolet.

umbilical: ~ **cord** cordon *m* ombilical.

umbrage ~ ressentiment *m*; ombrage *m*; **take** ~ (**at**) porter ombrage (de).

umbrella parapluie *m*, *fig.* protection *f*; ~ **organization** organisation *f* de tête.

umpire 1. arbitre *m*; 2. arbitrer

umpteen F je ne sais combien de; infiniment de.

un- non; in-; dé(s)-; peu; sans.

unabashed nullement décontenancé.

unable incapable (de, *to*); **be** ~ **to** (*inf.*) *a.* ne pas pouvoir *or* savoir (*inf.*).

unabridged non abrégé, intégral.

unaccompanied non accompagné.

unaccommodating peu accommodant (*person*).

unaccountable inexplicable.

unaccustomed inaccoutumé; peu habitué (à, *to*); **be** ~ **to** *a.* ne pas avoir l'habitude de.

unacquainted: **be** ~ **with** ne pas connaître (*q.*); ignorer (*qch.*).

unadulterated pur.

unadvised imprudent; sans prendre conseil.

unaffected qui n'est pas atteint; *fig.* sincère; sans affectation.

unaided sans aide; (tout) seul.

unalloyed sans mélange (*happiness*).

unalterable invariable, immuable.

unambiguous non équivoque, sans ambiguïté.

unanim|ity unanimité *f*; ~**ous** unanime; ~**ously** à l'unanimité.

unanswerable qu'on ne peut pas résoudre; où il n'y a pas de réponse; incontestable.

unapproachable inabordable.

unashamed impudent; sans honte.

unasked non invité; spontané.

unassisted tout seul, sans aide.

unassuming sans prétentions; modeste.

unattached indépendant; libre.

unattended (tout) seul; sans surveillance.

unattractive déplaisant; peu attrayant.

unauthorized sans autorisation; non autorisé.

unavail|able indisponible; ~**ing** vain; inutile.

unavoidable inévitable.

unaware peu conscient (de, *of*); **be** ~ *a.* ignorer (qch., *of s.th.*; que, *that*); ~**s** au dépourvu; sans s'en rendre compte.

unbalanced mal équilibré.

unbearable insupportable.

unbeaten invaincu.

unbecoming peu seyant (*dress*); peu convenable; déplacé.

unbeknown(st): ~ **to** à l'insu de.

unbelie|f incrédulité *f*; *eccl.* incroyance *f*; ~**vable** incroyable; ~**ving** incrédule.

unbend *v/t.* détendre (*a. fig.*); redresser (*q., a* ⊕); *v/i.* se détendre; *fig.* se déraidir; ~**ing** intransigeant; irréductible.

unbias(s)ed *fig.* impartial, sans parti pris.

unbid(den) non invité; spontané.

unbind dénouer (*one's hair*); délier (*a. fig.*).

unblushing sans vergogne.

unborn à naître; qui n'est pas encore né; *fig.* futur.

unbounded sans bornes; illimité.

unbowed invaincu.

unbreakable incassable.

unbridled débridé; déchaîné

unbroken intact; non brisé; inviolé; imbattu (*record*); *fig.* insoumis.

unburden décharger; *a. fig.* soulager; *fig.* ~ **o.s.,** ~ **one's heart** s'épancher (auprès de q., **to s.o.**).

unbutton déboutonner.

uncalled-for injustifié; déplacé (*remark*).

uncanny étrange, mystérieux.

uncap décapsuler.

uncared-for mal *or* peu soigné; abandonné; négligé.

unceasing incessant; continu; soutenu; **~ly** continuellement, sans cesse.

unceremonious brusque.

uncertain incertain; peu sûr; **~ty** incertitude *f*.

unchain déchaîner.

unchallenged incontesté.

unchang|eable, **~ing** invariable.

uncharitable peu charitable.

unchecked non réprimé.

uncivil impoli; **~ized** barbare, incivilisé.

unclaimed non réclamé.

unclasp défaire, dégrafer; desserrer (*one's hand*).

unclassified non classé; non secret (*information*).

uncle oncle *m*.

unclean sale, malpropre; *fig.*, *eccl.* impur.

uncomfortable peu confortable; désagréable; mal à l'aise.

uncommon peu commun, singulier; rare.

uncommunicative taciturne; peu communicatif.

uncompromising intransigeant; inflexible.

unconcern indifférence *f*; insouciance *f*; **~ed** insouciant; indifférent (à, *about*); étranger (à *with*, *in*).

unconditional sans condition (*surrender*); inconditionnel, absolu; sans réserve.

unconquerable invincible; irrépressible (*emotion etc.*).

unconscionable déraisonnable.

unconscious 1. inconscient (de, *of*); ✝ sans connaissance; **~ly** inconsciemment; 2. *psych.* **the ~** l'inconscient *m*; **~ness** inconscience *f*; évanouissement *m*.

uncontrollable ingouvernable; irrésistible, irrépressible (*emotion etc.*).

unconventional peu conventionnel; original.

unconvinc|ed sceptique (à l'égard de, *of*); **~ing** peu convaincant.

uncork déboucher.

uncountable innombrable.

uncouple découpler.

uncouth grossier.

uncover découvrir.

unct|ion onction *f* (*a. fig.*); **~uous** onctueux (*a. fig.*).

uncultivated inculte (*soil*, *fig. person*); sans raffinement.

undamaged intact, non endommagé.

undaunted intrépide; non intimidé.

undeceive désabuser; détromper.

undecided indécis.

undecipherable indéchiffrable.

undefined *adv.* non défini; vague.

undeniable incontestable.

undenominational non confessionnel, laïque (*school*).

under 1. *adv.* (au)dessous; **2.** *prp.* sous; au-dessous de; *from* **~** de sous; de dessous; **3.** *compounds*: trop peu; insuffisamment; inférieur; sous-; **~age** mineur; de mineurs; **~bid** demander moins cher que; **~brush** broussailles *f/pl.*; **~carriage** ✈ train *m* d'atterrissage; **~clothes** *pl.* **~clothing** sous-vêtements *m/pl.*; *ladies*: dessous *m/pl.*; **~cover** secret; **~current** courant sous-marin; *fig.* courant sous-jacent; **~cut** vendre moins cher que; **~developed** sous-développé; **~dog** perdant *m*; *fig.* **the ~(s** *pl.*) les opprimés *m/pl.*; **~done** pas assez cuit; saignant (*meat*); **~employment** sous-emploi *m*; **~estimate** sous-estimer; **~fed** sous-alimenté; **~go** subir; suivre (*treatment*); **~graduate** étudiant(e *f*) *m*; **~ground 1.** souterrain; *art etc.*: (d')avant-garde; **2.** (*~ railway*) métro *m*; *fig.* clandestinité *f*; *pol. etc.* résistance; *art etc.*: avant-garde *f*, underground *m*; **~growth** broussailles *f/pl.*; **~hand(ed)** peu honnête; **~ly** *a.* en dessous, sournoisement; **~lie** être en dessous *or* au-dessous *or* *fig.* à la base de; **~line** souligner.

underling subordonné(e *f*) *m*, sous-ordre *m*.

under|mentioned (cité) ci-dessous; **~mine** miner, saper (*a. fig.*); **~most 1.** *adj.* le plus bas; le plus en dessous; **2.** *adv.* au-dessous; en dessous; **~neath 1.** *prp.* au-dessous de, sous; **2.** *adv.* au-dessous; par-dessous; **~paid** sous-payé; **~pants**

slip *m*; **~pass** passage *m* souterrain; *motorway*: passage *m* inférieur; **~pin** étayer (*a wall*); *fig.* soutenir; **~play** minimiser; **~ ones hand** cacher son jeu; **~plot** intrigue *f* secondaire; **~privileged** déshérité (*a. su.*); **~rate** sous-estimer; mésestimer; **~score** souligner; **~secretary** sous-secrétaire *mf*; **~sell ✝** vendre moins cher que; vendre (*qch.*) au-dessous de sa valeur; **~shorts** slip *m*; **~side** dessous *m*; **~signed** sous-signé(o *f*) *m*; **~sized** trop petit; rabougri; **~staffed** à court de personnel.

understand comprendre; **make o.s. understood** se faire comprendre; **~able** compréhensible; **~ing 1.** compréhension *f*; entente *f*, accord *m*; **2.** compréhensif

under|statement affirmation *f* qui reste au-dessous de la vérité; amoindrissement *m* (*of facts*); **~take** entreprendre; se charger de; **~taker** entrepreneur *m* de pompes funèbres; **~taking** entreprise *f* (*a. ✝*); promesse *f*, entreprise *f* de pompes funèbres; **~tenant** sous-locataire *mf*; **~-the-counter** clandestin(ement); **~tone** fond *m*; **in an ~** parler à mi-voix; **~value** sous-estimer; mésestimer; **~water** sousmarin; **~wear** *see* **underclothes**; **~weight** trop léger; **~wood** broussailles *f/pl.*; sous-bois *m*; **~world** pègre *f*, milieu *m*; **~write** souscrire à; **~writer** souscripteur *m*.

undeserv|ed immérité; **~ly** indûment; *punish*. etc. à tort; **~ing** peu méritoire; sans mérite.

undesirable peu désirable; *pol.*, *admin.* etc. indésirable (*a. su.*).

undeviating constant; droit.

undies *pl.* F dessous *m/pl.*

undigested mal digéré.

undignified qui manque de dignité.

undisciplined indiscipliné.

undiscriminating sans discernement.

undisputed incontesté.

undivided indivisé; entier.

undo défaire; détruire; **~ing** ruine *f*, perte *f*; **~ne** défait *etc.*; inachevé, non accompli; **come ~** se défaire.

undoubted indubitable, certain; **~ly** sans aucun doute.

undreamt-of inattendu; imaginé.

undress 1. (se) déshabiller; **2.** déshabillé *m*, négligé *m*; **~ed** déshabillé; en déshabillé; **get ~** se déshabiller.

undue exagéré, excessif.

undulat|e *vt/i.* onduler; *v/i.* ondoyer; **~ing** onduleux, ondoyant; **~ion** ondulation *f*.

unduly excessivement, trop; outre mesure (*worried*).

undying qui ne meurt pas, éternel.

unearth déterrer; *fig.* découvrir, F dénicher; **~ly** sublime; surnaturel.

uneas|iness gêne *f*; inquiétude *f*; **~y** gêné; mal à l'aise; inquiet.

uneconomic peu rentable; *a.* **~al** peu économique.

uneducated sans éducation; ignorant; vulgaire (*language*).

unemploy|ed 1. désœuvré; sans travail; ✝ inemployé; **the ~** les chômeurs *m/pl.*; **~ment** chômage *m*; **~ benefit, ~ compensation** allocation *f* de chômage.

unending sans fin; interminable.

unenviable peu enviable.

unequal inégal; irrégulier; **be ~ to** ne pas être à la hauteur de (*a task etc.*); **~(l)ed** sans égal.

unequivocal clair; franc; sans équivoque.

unerring infaillible.

unessential non essentiel.

uneven inégal (*a. fig.*); accidenté (*land*); raboteux; impair (*number*).

uneventful peu mouvementé; sans incidents.

unexampled unique; sans pareil.

unexceptionable irréprochable.

unexceptional ordinaire, banal, qui ne sort pas de l'ordinaire.

unexpected imprévu; inattendu.

unexpressed inexprimé.

unfailing infaillible; inépuisable.

unfair injuste; déloyal (*play*, *competition*).

unfaithful infidèle (à, *to*).

unfamiliar étrange; peu connu *or* familier.

unfasten délier; détacher; défaire.

unfavo(u)rable défavorable; inopportun (*moment etc.*).

unfeeling insensible; impitoyable, dur, cruel.

unfinished inachevé; ⊕ brut.

unfit (*not well*) pas bien, mal en forme; **~**

U

for inapte à, impropre à; ~ **to** (*inf.*) inapte *or* impropre à, ne pas en état de (*inf.*).

unflagging inlassable.

unflappable F imperturbable.

unflinching ferme, qui ne bronche pas; stoïque; impassible; ~**ly** sans broncher; impassiblement.

unfold *vt/i.* (se) déplier; (se) déployer; *v/i.* s'épanouir; *fig.* se dérouler; *v/t.* révéler; développer.

unforced libre; volontaire; naturel.

unforeseeable imprévisible.

unforeseen imprévu, inattendu.

unforgettable inoubliable.

unforgiv|able impardonnable; ~**ing** implacable; rancunier.

unfortunate malheureux; fâcheux, regrettable; ~**ly** malheureusement.

unfounded sans fondement (*rumour etc.*); injustifié.

unfriendly inamical; hostile.

unfurl (se) déployer.

unfurnished non meublé.

ungainly gauche; dégingandé.

ungentle rude, dur.

ungodly impie; F impossible; indu (*hour etc.*).

ungraceful gauche; disgracieux.

ungracious peu aimable.

ungrateful ingrat (*a. fig., job etc.*); peu reconnaissant.

ungrudging généreux.

unguarded non gardé; *fig.* irréfléchi; **in an ~ moment** dans un moment d'inattention.

unguent onguent *m.*

unhandy incommode; maladroit.

unhappy malheureux (*a. fig. remark etc.*); ~ **at** (*or about*) peu content de.

unharmed sain et sauf.

unhealthy malsain (*a. fig.*); maladif (*person*).

unheard-of sans précédent, inouï.

unhinge enlever (*a door*) de ses gonds; *fig.* déranger (*the mind*), désaxer (*q.*).

unholy F impossible.

unhook (se) décrocher; (se) dégrafer.

unhoped-for inespéré; inattendu.

unhurt sans blessure (*person*), indemne; intact (*thing*).

unidentified non identifié; ~ **flying object** objet *m* volant non identifié, ovni *m.*

unification unification *f.*

uniform 1. uniforme; **2.** uniforme *m*; ~**ed** en uniforme (*person*); *fig.* uniformisé; ~**ity** uniformité *f.*

unify unifier.

unilateral unilatéral.

unimagina|ble inimaginable; ~**tive** peu imaginatif.

unimpaired intact; non diminué.

unimpeachable inattaquable; irréprochable.

unimportant peu important, sans importance.

uninformed ignorant; non averti.

uninhabit|able inhabitable; ~**ed** inhabité; désert.

uninhibited sans inhibitions (*person*); sans retenu (*laughter etc.*).

uninjured indemne.

unintelligible inintelligible.

unintentional involontaire.

uninteresting peu intéressant.

uninterrupted ininterrompu.

union union *f*; association *f*; (*a. trade ~*) syndicat; *attr.* syndical; de *or* du syndicat; ~ **member** syndiqué(e *f*) *m*; ~ **shop** atelier *m* d'ouvriers syndiqués; ~**ism** unionisme *m*; syndicalisme *m*; ~**ist** unioniste *mf*; syndiqué(e *f*) *m*; syndicaliste *mf.*

unique unique; seul en son genre.

unison ♪, *a. fig.* unisson *m*; **in ~** à l'unisson.

unit unité *f* (*a.* ✂, ✈, ✝, *measure*); élément *m*; ⊕ bloc *m*; ~**e** (s')unir; **2d Nations Organisation** Organisation *f* des Nations Unies; **2d States** *pl.* États-Unis *m/pl.* (d'Amérique); ~**y** unité *f.*

univers|al universel; ⊕ ~ **joint** (joint *m* de) cardan *m*; ~**e** univers *m*; ~**ity** université *f.*

unjust injuste (avec, envers, pour **to**); ~**ifiable** injustifiable.

unkempt mal peigné; *fig.* mal *or* peu soigné; mal tenu.

unkind peu aimable, peu gentil.

unknow|ing ignorant; inconscient (de, **of**); ~**n 1.** *adj.* inconnu (de, à **to**); ✕, *fig.* ~ **quantity** inconnue *f*; **2.** *adv.*: ~ **to me** à mon insu; **3.** inconnu(e *f*) *m.*

unlace délacer, défaire.

unlatch lever le loquet de; ouvrir.

unlawful illégal; illicite.

unlearn désapprendre.

unless 1. *cj.* à moins que (*sbj.*); à moins de (*inf.*); si ... ne ... pas; **2.** *prp.* sauf, excepté.

unlike 1. *adj.* différent (de q., [**to**] *s.o.*); dissemblable; **2.** *prp.* à la différence de; ~**ly** invraisemblable, improbable.

unlimited illimité; sans bornes.

unload décharger.

unlock ouvrir; *fig.* débloquer (*emotions etc.*); *fig.* révéler (*s.th. secret*), résoudre.

unlooked-for inattendu.

unloose(n) (re)lâcher; défaire.

unlucky malchanceux (*person*), malheureux (*moment, remark etc.*); qui porte malheur (*omen etc.*).

unmanageable difficile à manier.

unmanned inhabité (*spacecraft*), sans équipage.

unmannerly impoli; mal élevé (*person*).

unmarried célibataire; non marié.

unmask démasquer.

unmatched sans égal.

unmentionable dont il ne faut pas parler; qu'il ne faut pas prononcer.

unmerited immérité.

unmindful négligent (*person*); ~ **of** oublieux de; sans penser à.

unmistakable indubitable; dont on ne peut se tromper; facilement reconnaissable.

unmitigated non mitigé; *fig.* parfait, pur, véritable.

unmolested sans être molesté; sans empêchement.

unmoved indifférent (à, **by**); impassible.

unnamed anonyme.

unnatural non naturel; anormal; contre nature; *fig.* forcé, guindé, affecté.

unnecessary inutile; superflu.

unnerve faire perdre courage à, démonter.

unnoticed (**go** ~ passer) inaperçu.

unnumbered sans numéro.

unobjectionable irréprochable.

unobserved inaperçu, inobservé.

unobtrusive discret.

unoccupied inoccupé; libre.

unofficial officieux; non officiel; privé.

unopposed sans opposition.

unorthodox hétérodox; peu orthodoxe.

unostentatious discret; simple.

unpack déballer; défaire (*v/i.* sa valise *etc.*).

unpaid impayé; non rétribué (*work, worker*); ✝ non acquitté (*debt*); non affranchi (*letter*).

unpalatable désagréable.

unparalleled incomparable; sans égal; sans précédent.

unpardonable impardonnable.

unpleasant désagréable; déplaisant.

unplug ⚡ débrancher.

unpolished non poli (*diamond etc.*); *fig.* qui manque de raffinement; mal éduqué (*person*).

unpolluted non pollué (*environment etc.*); *fig.* non contaminé.

unpopular impopulaire; mal vu; ~**ity** impopularité *f.*

unpractical peu pratique; ~**sed**, *Am.* ~**ced** peu versé, inexpérimenté.

unprecedented sans précédent.

unpredictable imprévisible (*thing*); **she's quite** ~ on ne sait jamais ce qu'elle va faire *or* comment elle va réagir.

unprejudiced sans préjugé; impartial.

unprepossessing peu avenant.

unprepared non préparé; au dépourvu; improvisé (*speech*).

unpretentious sans prétention.

unprincipled peu scrupuleux.

unproductive improductif.

unprompted spontané.

unprofitable improfitable; inutile.

unproved non prouvé.

unprovided-for (laissé) sans ressources.

unpunctual peu ponctuel; ~**ity** manque *f* de ponctualité.

unqualified non qualifié; non diplômé; *fig.* total, absolu; ~ **to** (*inf.*) (ne) pas compétent pour (*inf.*).

unquenchable inassouvissable.

unquestionable indubitable; indiscutable; ~**ing** inconditionnel, total.

unquote fermer les guillemets.

unravel (s')effiler; (se) défaire; (se) démêler; *fig.* (s')éclaircir.

unreal irréel; ~**istic** peu réaliste.

unreasonable déraisonnable, peu raisonnable, absurde; excessif, exagéré; ~**ing** irraisonné.

unrecognizable méconnaissable.

unredeemed non racheté *or* récompensé (par, **by**); inaccompli (*promise*); ✝ non remboursé.

unrelated sans rapport (avec, **to**); non apparenté (*person*).

unrelenting implacable; acharné.

unreliable sur lequel on ne peut pas compter; peu fiable (*car etc.*); douteux (*source, information, firm etc.*).

unrelieved constant, non (inter)rompu; uniforme, monotone.

unremitting inlassable.

unrequited non partagé (*love*).

unreserved sans réserve (*a. ~ly*); entier; non réservé (*seat*).

unresponsive peu sensible.

unrest troubles *m/pl.*, agitation *f.*

unrestrained non restreint; effréné.

unrestricted sans restriction(s).

unripe vert; *fig.* pas encore mûr.

unrival(l)ed sans pareil; incomparable.

unroll (se) dérouler.

unruffled calme (*person, sea*).

unruly indiscipliné, mutin.

unsafe dangereux; peu sûr.

unsaid inexprimé; *leave ~* passer sous silence, ne pas parler de.

unsalaried non rémunéré.

unsal(e)able invendable.

unsatisfactory peu satisfaisant, qui laisse à désirer; *~fied* insatisfait; mécontent; *fig.* non convaincu.

unsavo(u)ry désagréable, répugnant; *fig.* peu recommandable, louche.

unscathed indemne.

unscrew (se) dévisser.

unscrupulous sans scrupules.

unseason|able hors de saison; *~ed* vert (*wood*); *cuis.* non assaisonné.

unseat desarçonner; *parl.* faire perdre son siège à.

unseeing aveugle.

unseemly inconvenant.

unseen inaperçu; invisible.

unselfish sans égoïsme; désintéressé; *~ly* sans égoïsme; *give etc.* généreusement.

unsettle déranger; troubler le repos de (*q.*); ébranler (*s. o.'s convictions*); *~d* troublé, perturbé; incertain (*a. weather*); † impayé; indécis (*question*); sans domicile fixe; non colonisé (*country*).

unshak|(e)able, *~en* inébranlable, ferme.

unshaven non rasé.

unsightly laid.

unshrink|able *tex.* irrétrécissable.

unskil(l)ful maladroit; malhabile; *~led* inexpérimenté (à, *in*); *~ worker* ouvrier

(*-ère f*) *m* specialisé(e) *or* sans qualification.

unsoci|able insociable; *~al* insocial.

unsolv|able insoluble; *~ed* non résolu.

unsophisticated simple.

unsound peu solide; malsain (*person, conditions etc.*); en mauvais état.

unsparing libéral; prodigue (de, *of, in*); impitoyable.

unspeakable indicible; ineffable (*bad*) abominable.

unspoil|ed, *~t* intact; naturel.

unspoken inexprimé (*a. ~-of*) dont on ne fait pas mention.

unstable instable.

unsteady instable; peu solide; mal assuré; *fig.* déréglé (*person, work etc.*); irrégulier.

unstint|ed sans réserve; *~ing* généreux; prodigue (de, *of*).

unstop déboucher.

unstressed inaccentué; atone.

unstuck: *come ~* se décoller; *fig.* faire fiasco.

unstudied naturel.

unsubmissive insoumis, indocile.

unsuccessful sans succès (*a. ~y*); raté; *be ~* ne pas avoir de succès, échouer; ne pas réussir (à *inf.*, *in ger.*).

unsuit|able qui ne convient pas (à, *for*) inopportun; peu approprié; *~ed* impropre (à *for, to*); inapte (à, *to*); peu fait (pour *for, to*).

unsung méconnu.

unsurpassed non surpassé, sans égal.

unsuspecting qui ne se méfie pas; qui ne se doute de rien; *~ly* sans se méfier; sans se douter de rien.

unsuspicious qui ne suscite pas de soupçons; *see a.* **unsuspecting**.

unswerving inébranlable.

untam(e)able inapprivoisable; *fig.* indomptable.

untangle démêler.

untapped inexploité.

untarnished non terni (*a. fig.*).

untaught ignorant; naturel.

unteachable incapable d'apprendre (*person*); non enseignable (*thing*).

untenable intenable.

unthink|able impensable, inconcevable; *~ing* irréfléchi; étourdi.

unthought-of inattendu.

untidy en désordre (*room, desk etc.*);

débraillé (*person, clothes, appearance etc.*), mal soigné (*a. piece of work*), (*dirty*) sale.

untie défaire (*a knot etc.*); (*set free*) délier.

until 1. *prp.* jusqu'à; **2.** *cj.* jusqu'à ce que; jusqu'au moment où.

untimely prématuré; inopportun; mal à propos.

untiring infatigable.

untold non raconté; indicible; incalculable; immense.

untouched *fig.* intact; *fig.* indifférent (à, *by*).

untoward malencontreux, ennuyeux.

untrammel(l)ed (*by*) libre (de); non entravé (par).

untranslatable intraduisible.

untried jamais mis à l'épreuve.

untroubled non troublé; calme.

untrue faux; infidèle (*person*).

untrustworthy indigne de confiance (*person*); douteux, peu sûr.

unus|ed inutilisé; neuf; ~ **to** peu habitué à; **~ual** rare; extraordinaire.

unutterable indicible.

unvarying invariable.

unveil (se) dévoiler.

unverified non vérifié.

unversed versé (dans, *in*).

unwanted non souhaité; superflu.

unwarrant|able, **~ed** injustifié.

unwary imprudent.

unwavering inébranlable.

unwelcome importun, fâcheux.

unwell souffrant, indisposé.

unwholesome malsain (*a. fig.*); insalubre.

unwieldy peu maniable; lourd (*person*).

unwilling de mauvaise volonté; fait *etc.* à contre-cœur; **be ~ to** (*inf.*) ne pas vouloir (*inf.*); **~ly** à contrecœur.

unwind *v/t.* dérouler, débobiner; *v/i.* se détendre, se relaxer.

unwise imprudent; peu sage.

unwitting involontaire.

unwonted inaccoutumé.

unworkable impraticable.

unworthy indigne.

unwrap désenvelopper, défaire (*a parcel*).

unwritten tacite; **it is an ~ law** (*or* **rule**) **that** il est tacitement admis que.

unyielding qui ne cède pas; ferme.

unzip ouvrir la fermeture éclair de (*a garment*).

up 1. *adv.* vers le haut; en montant; haut; en haut; en dessus; en l'air; debout; levé (*a. sun etc.*); fini (*time*); fermé (*window etc.*); *Am. baseball:* à la batte; **be ~ against a task** être aux prises avec une tâche; **~ to** jusque, jusqu'à; **be ~ to s.th.** être à la hauteur de qch., être capable de qch.; (*do*) fricoter *or* fabriquer qch.; **it is ~ to me to** (*inf.*) c'est à moi de (*inf.*); F **what's ~?** qu'est-ce qu'il y a?; **2.** *int.* en haut!; **3.** *prp.* en haut de; dans *or* vers le haut de; **~ the hill** en montant (*or* en haut de) la colline; **4.** *adj.*: **~ train** train *m* en direction de la capitale; F **train** *m* de retour; **5.** *su.*: F **on the ~ and ~** *Br.* en bonne voie, en train de monter *or* de s'améliorer; **~s and downs** *pl.* hauts et bas *m/pl.*; vicissitudes *f/pl.* (*of life*); **6.** F *v/i.* se lever; *v/t.* (*a.* **~ with**) augmenter.

up|-and-coming qui promet; qui a de l'avenir; **~braid** reprocher (qch. à q., *s.o.* with *or* for s.th.); **~bringing** éducation *f*; **~coming** imminent; **~date** mettre à jour; **~end** mettre debout; renverser (*an opponent*); **~grade** revaloriser; **~heaval** bouleversement *m*; branlebas *m*; **~hill** qui monte; *fig.* pénible; **go ~** monter, aller en montant; **~hold** soutenir; maintenir.

upholster capitonner; rembourrer; **~er** tapissier *m*; *y trade.* tapisserie *f*; **material** capitonnage *m*, rembourrage *m*, *car:* garniture *f*

up|keep entretien *m*; **~land** *usu.* **~s** *pl.* hautes terres *f/pl.*; **~lift 1.** élever; **2.** élévation *f*.

upon *see* **on**.

upper plus haut; supérieur; **the ~ class(es** *pl.*) la haute société *f*; F **the ~ crust** le gratin *m*; **get (have) the ~ hand** prendre (avoir) le dessus; **get the ~ hand of** venir à bout de, triompher de; **~class** aristocratique; **~most** le plus haut; en dessus; *fig.* (le) premier.

uppish F suffisant; arrogant.

up|raise (sou)lever; élever; **~rear** dresser; **~right 1.** vertical; droit (*a. fig.*); **2.** montant *m*; piano *m* droit; **~rising** insurrection *f*.

uproar tapage *m*, vacarme *m*; tumulte *m*; **~ious** tapageur.

U

up|root déraciner; **~set 1.** *v/t.* renverser; bouleverser (*a. fig.*); déranger, dérégler; vexer, fâcher; rendre malade (*food*); **2.** *adj.* fâché, vexé; dérangé, déréglé; **3.** *su.* dérangement *m*, dérèglement; désordre *m*; **~shot** résultat *m*; **~side** *adv.*: **~ down** sens dessus dessous; *fig.* en désordre; *turn* **~ down** retourner; *a. fig.* mettre sens dessus dessous; **~stage** F **1.** hautain, arrogant; **2.** éclipser (*q.*); **~stairs** *adv.* en haut; *adj.* d'en haut, du dessus (*room etc.*); **~start** parvenu *m*; **~state** *Am.* région éloignée; **~stream** *adv.* en amont; en remontant le courant; **~tight** crispé, tendu; nerveux; **~to-date** moderne; au courant, à jour; à la page (*person*); **~to-the-minute** le plus moderne; dernier, de dernière heure; **~town** *adv. Am.* dans le quartier résidentiel de la ville; **~turn** lever; retourner; **~ward 1.** *adj.* montant; **2.** *adv.* (*or* **~s**) de bas en haut; vers le haut; *and* **~** et au-dessus; **~ of** ... et plus.

uranium 🜨 uranium *m*.

urban urbain; **~e** urbain; **~ization** urbanisation *f*.

urchin gosse *mf*.

urge 1. pousser (*q. à inf.*; *s.o. to inf.*; *qch.*); recommander (vivement) (qch. à q., *s.th. on s.o.*); inister (sur qch., *s.th.*; pour que *sbj.*, *that*); **~ on** pousser, presser, aiguillonner; **2.** impulsion *f*; forte envie *f*; **~ncy** urgence *f*; *tone*: insistence *f*; **~nt** urgent; pressant; **~ntly** (*immediately*) d'urgence; *ask etc.*: instamment.

urin|al urinoir *m*; ⚕ urinal *m*; **~ate** uriner; **~e** urine *f*.

urn urne *f*; (*tea* **~**) fontaine *f* à thé.

us *accusative, dative*: nous.

usage usage *m*; emploi *m*.

usance 🜨 usance *f*.

use 1. emploi *m* (*a.* ⚕); usage *m*; utilité *f*; service *m*; *be of* **~** servir, être utile (*à* for, *to*); *it is* (*of*) *no* **~** (*ger.*, *to inf.*) il (*or* cela) ne sert à rien de (*inf.*), inutile (de *inf.*); *what's the* **~** *of* (*ger.*)? à quoi sert de (*inf.*)?; *have no* **~** *for* ne savoir que faire de (*qch.*); F ne pas pouvoir voir (*q.*); **2.** se servir de, employer, utiliser; **~ up** finir; consommer; épuiser; *I* **~d** *to go* j'allais; j'avais l'habitude d'aller; **~d** usagé, qui a servi; d'occasion (*car etc.*); *be* **~** *to* (*s.th.*, *inf.*) être habitué à (qch., *inf.*), avoir l'habitude de (qch., *inf.*); **~ful** utile (*a.* ⊕); pratique; **~ load** charge *f* utile; **~fulness** utilité *f*; **~less** inutile; inefficace; vain; **~r** utilisateur (-trice *f*) *m*; *public service etc.*: usager *m*.

usher 1. ⚖ huissier *m*; *cinema etc.*: placeur *m*; **2.** conduire; **~ in** faire entrer, introduire; *fig.* inaugurer; **~ette** *cin.* ouvreuse *f*.

usual habituel; *it is* **~** *for him to* (*inf.*) d'habitude il ...; *as* **~** comme d'habitude; **~ly** d'habitude.

usurp usurper; **~ation** usurpation *f*; **~er** usurpateur (-trice *f*) *m*.

usurer usurier (-ière *f*) *m*.

utensil ustensil *m*.

uterus *anat.* utérus *m*, matrice *f*.

utility 1. utilité *f*; *public* **~** service *m* public; **2.** utilitaire.

utiliz|ation utilisation *f*; exploitation *f*; **~e** utiliser; profiter de.

utmost extrême; *le plus grand*; *do one's* **~** faire de son mieux; *at the* **~** tout au plus.

Utopian 1. utopique; **2.** utopiste *mf*.

utter 1. *fig.* absolu; extrême; complet; **2.** dire, exprimer; pousser (*a sigh etc.*); **~ance** expression *f*; émission *f*; prononciation *f*; **~most** extrême; dernier.

U-turn *mot.* demi-tour *m*; *fig.* revirement *m*, volte-face *f/inv.*; *mot.* „*no* **~s**' ,défense de faire demi-tour!'

uvula *anat.* luette *f*, uvule *f*.

uxorious (extrêmement) dévoué à sa femme (*husband*).

V

vacan|cy chambre *f or* appartement *m* libre; poste *m* vacant; *fig.* vide *m*; **~ for** on cherche (*an employee, worker etc.*); **no vacancies** hotel: complet, job: pas d'embauche; **~t** vacant, libre; inoccupé (*mind*).

vacate quitter.

vacation 1. *esp. Am.* vacances *f|pl.*; 🏫 vacations *f|pl.*; **2.** *esp. Am.* prendre des *or* être en vacances; **~ist** *Am.* vacancier (*-ière f*) *m.*

vaccin|ate vacciner; **~ation** vaccination *f*; **~e** vaccin *m.*

vacillate vaciller; hésiter.

vacu|ous vide (*de sens or d'expression*); **~um** *phys.* vide *m*, vacuum *m*; **~ cleaner** aspirateur *m*; **~ flask, ~ bottle** (bouteille *f*) Thermos *f* (*TM*); **~-packed** emballé sous vide.

vagabond 1. vagabond, errant; **2.** chemineau *m*; vagabond(e *f*) *m*; F vaurien *m.*

vagary caprice *m*; fantaisie *f.*

vagina *anat.* vagin *m.*

vagrant 1. errant, vagabond (*a. fig.*); **2.** *see* **vagabond** 2.

vague vague; imprécis; indécis.

vain vain; vaniteux (*person*); **in ~** en vain; **do s.th. in ~** avoir beau faire qch.; **~glorious** vaniteux.

vale *poet.* val *m*; vallée *f.*

valediction adieu(x) *m|(pl.).*

valentine carte *f* de la Saint-Valentin; bien-aimé(e *f*) *m.*

valerian ❦ valériane *f.*

valet valet *m* de chambre; **~ing (service)** pressing *m.*

valetudinarian valétudinaire.

valiant vaillant.

valid valable; valide; **~ity** validité *f*

valise sac *m* de voyage.

valley vallée *f*; vallon *m.*

valo(u)r *poet.* vaillance *f.*

valuable 1. précieux; **2.** **~s** *pl.* objets *m|pl.* de valeur.

valuation évaluation *f*; expertise *f*; appréciation *f.*

value 1. valeur *f*; **~ judgment** jugement *m* de valeur; **get good ~ (for one's money)** en avoir pour son argent; **2.**

évaluer; estimer; priser (*a. fig.*); **~-added tax** taxe *f* à la valeur ajoutée; **~r** expert *m* (en estimations).

valve soupape *f*; *mot. tyre*: valve *f*; *anat.* valvule *f*; *radio*: lampe *f.*

vamoose *Am. sl.* filer; ficher le camp; décamper.

vamp vamp *f.*

van camionnette *f*; 🚃 fourgon *m.*

vandal vandale *m*; **~ism** vandalisme *m*; **~ize** saccager, mutiler.

vane girouette *f.*

vanguard avant-garde *f*

vanilla ❦ vanille *f.*

vanish disparaître; s'évanouir; **~ing cream** crème *f* de jour.

vanity vanité *f*; **~ bag** sac *m* de soirée; **~ case** sac *m* de toilette.

vanquish vaincre; triompher de

vantage *tennis*: avantage *m*; **~ point** point *m* stratégique; *fig.* point *m* de vue.

vapid insipide; fade.

vapor|ize (se) vaporiser; **~ous** vaporeux.

vapo(u)r vapeur *f*; **~ trail** trainée *f* de condensation.

varia|ble variable; *weather etc.*: changeant; **~nce** divergence *f*; discorde *f*; **be at ~** être en désaccord; **set at ~** mettre en désaccord; **~nt 1.** différent (de, *from*); **2.** variante *f*; **~tion** variation *f* (*a. ♪*); changement *m.*

varicose 🩺 **~ vein** varice *f.*

varie|d varié, divers; **~gated** bigarré, **~ty** diversité *f*; variété *f* (*a. biol.*); ✝ assortiment *m*; **~ show** (spectacle *m* de) music-hall *m.*

various divers, différent; plusieurs.

varnish 1. vernis *m*; **2.** vernir.

vary varier; changer.

vase vase *m.*

vassal vassal *m.*

vast vaste; immense; énorme.

vat cuve *f*; (*small*) cuveau *m.*

vault 1. cave *f*; △ voûte *f*; tombeau *m*; *sp.*: saut *m*; *bank*: chambre *f* forte; **2.** (se) voûter; *sp.* sauter; **~ing-horse** cheval *m* de bois.

vaunt *poet.* (se) vanter (de).

veal veau *m*; *roast* ~ rôti *m* de veau.

veer (faire) virer *or* tourner.

vegeta|ble 1. végétal; 2. légume *m*; ~ *garden* potager *m*; ~**rian** végétarien (*a. su.*); ~**rianism** végétarisme *m*; ~**te** végéter; ~**tive** végétatif.

vehemen|ce véhémence *f*; ~**t** véhément.

vehicle véhicule *m* (*a. fig.*).

veil 1. voile *m*; 2. (se) voiler.

vein veine *f*; ~ nervure *f*; *fig.* esprit *m*; *fig.* élément *m*.

velocity vélocité *f*; vitesse *f*.

velvet velours *m*; ~**y** velouté.

venal vénal.

vend vendre; ~**ing machine** distributeur *m* automatique; ~**or** vendeur (-euse *f*) *m*.

veneer 1. placage *m*; *fig.* vernis *m*; 2. plaquer; *fig.* cacher.

venera|ble vénérable; ~**te** vénérer; ~**tion** vénération *f*.

venereal vénérien.

Venetian 1. vénitien; ~ *blind* jalousie *f*; 2. Vénitien(ne *f*) *m*.

vengeance vengeance *f*; *take* ~ se venger (de, *for*; de, sur q., *on s.o.*); *fig.* *with a* ~ pour de bon; furieusement.

venial pardonnable; véniel (*sin*).

venison venaison *f*.

venom venin *m*; ~**ous** venimeux (*animal*); vénéneux (*plant*).

vent 1. trou *m*, orifice *m*; *cost.* fente *f*; *fig.* *give* ~ to donner libre cours à (*one's anger etc.*); 2. *fig.* décharger (sur, *on*); ~ *one's anger on s.o.* passer sa colère sur q.

ventilat|e ventiler, aérer; *fig.* mettre en discussion (*a question*); ~**ion** ventilation *f*; *fig.* mise *f* en discussion; ~**or** ventilateur *m*.

ventriloquist ventriloque *mf*.

ventur|e 1. entreprise *f* (hasardeuse); *at a* ~ au hasard; 2. *v/t.* risquer, hasarder; *v/i.* se risquer (à *inf.*, *to inf.*); s'aventurer (*sur etc.*, *on etc.*); ~**esome**, ~**ous** risqué, hasardeux; aventureux (*person*).

venue lieu *m* de rencontre.

veracious véridique.

verb *gramm.* verbe *m*; ~**al** verbal; de mots; littéral (*translation*); ~**alize** verbaliser; rendre par des mots; ~**iage** verbiage *m*; ~**ose** verbeux, prolixe.

verdict verdict *m*; *bring in* (*or return*) *a* ~

of (*not*) *guilty* rendre un verdict de (non-)culpabilité.

verdigris vert-de-gris *m*.

verdure verdure *f*.

verge 1. *usu. fig.* bord *m*; *on the* ~ au seuil (de, *of*); sur le point (de *inf.*, *of ger.*); *mot.* **soft** ~**s** accotements non stabilisés; 2. *fig.* ~ (*up*)*on* côtoyer, frôler, être voisin de.

veri|fication vérification *f*; ~**fy** vérifier; ~**similitude** vraisemblance *f*; ~**table** véritable.

vermilion vermillon (*a. su./m*).

vermin vermine *f* (*a. fig.*); animaux *m/pl.* nuisibles; ~**ous** pouilleux.

verm(o)uth vermouth *m*.

vernacular 1. indigène; du pays; 2. langue *f* du pays.

versatile aux talents variés; souple (*mind*); universel, aux usages multiples.

verse vers *m*; strophe *f*.

versed: (*on* *the* *well*) ~ *in* (bien) versé dans.

version version *f*.

verso: (*on the* ~ au) verso *m*.

versus *esp.* 🕭 contre.

vertebra *anat.*, *pl.* ~**brae** vertèbre *f*.

vertical 1. vertical; ~ *take-off aircraft* avion *m* à décollage vertical; 2. verticale *f*.

vertig|inous vertigineux; ~**o** vertige *m*.

verve verve *f*.

very 1. *adv.* très, fort, bien; *the* ~ *best* tout ce qu'il y a de mieux; 2. *adj.*: *the* ~ *same* le (la *etc.*) ... même(s *pl.*); *in the* ~ *act* sur le fait; *the* ~ *thing* ce qu'il faut; *the* ~ *thought* la seule pensée.

vessel vaisseau *m* (*a.* ⚓, *anat.*, *fig.*); récipient *m*.

vest 1. *Br.* tricot *m* de corps; *Am.* gilet *m*; 2. ~ *s.o. with s.th.*, ~ *s.th. in s.o.* investir q. de qch.; ~**ed rights** *pl.* droits *m/pl.* acquis.

vestibule vestibule *m*.

vestige vestige *m*.

vestry sacristie *f*.

vet F 1. vétérinaire *m*; *Am.* ancien combattant *m*; 2. traiter (*an animal*); *fig.* examiner (minutieusement).

veteran 1. vétéran *m*; ✕ ancien combattant *m*; 2. expérimenté; vieux ~ *car* voiture *f* d'époque.

veterinar|ian *Am.* vétérinaire *m*; ~**y** 1. vétérinaire; 2. (*a.* ~ *surgeon*) vétérinaire *m*.

veto 1. pl. **-toes** veto m; **put a** (or one's) ~ = **2.** mettre son veto à.

vex fâcher, contrarier; **~atious** fâcheux; **~ed** controversé (question).

via par (la voie de).

viable viable.

viaduct viaduc m.

vibes F sg. ♪ vibraphone m; pl. vibrations f/pl.

vibrant vibrant.

vibraphone vibraphone m.

vibrat|e (faire) vibrer; **~ion** vibration f.

vicar eccl. pasteur m, curé m; **~age** presbytère m; cure f.

vice[1] vice m; ⊕ étau m; ~ **squad** la (brigade) mondaine f.

vice[2] vice m; sous-; **~-president** viceprésident m.

vice versa vice versa.

vicinity environs m/pl. (de, of); proximité f (de to, with).

vicious vicieux; méchant.

vicissitudes pl. vicissitudes f/pl.

victim victime f.; **~ization** représailles f/pl.; brimades f/pl.; **~ize** exercer des représailles à l'égard de (q.); brimer.

victor vainqueur m; **~ian** victorien; **~ious** victorieux; **~y** victoire f.

victual 1. (s')approvisionner; (se) ravitailler; **2.** **~s** pl. vivres m/pl.

video vidéo f, adj. **~ recorder** magnetoscope m; ~ **tape** bande f vidéo; **~phone** vidéotéléphone m; **~tape** magnétoscoper.

vie rivaliser (avec, with).

Viennese viennois.

view 1. vue f, aperçu m; fig. intention f; fig. avis m; **in** ~ en vue, sous les regards; **in** ~ **of** en vue de; fig. en raison de; **in my** ~ à mon avis; **on** ~ exposé; **with a** ~ **to** (ger.), **with the** ~ **of** (ger.) dans le but de (inf.), en vue de (inf.); dans l'intention de (inf.); **keep in** ~ ne pas perdre de vue; **2.** regarder; considérer; inspecter; apercevoir; fig. envisager; **~er** (telev. télé)spectateur (-trice f) m; phot. **~finder** viseur m; **~point** point m de vue.

vigil veille f; **~ance** vigilance f; **~ant** vigilant.

vigo|rous vigoureux; **~(u)r** vigueur f.

vile vil; infâme; infect.

vilify diffamer, dénigrer; médire de.

villa villa f.

village village m; **~r** villageois(e f) m.

villain scélérat m; bandit m; traître m; coquin(e f) m; **~ous** infâme, vil; **~y** infamie f.

vim F énergie f, vigueur f.

vindicat|e justifier; **~ion** justification f.

vindictive vindicatif, rancunier.

vine ♀ vigne f; plante f grimpante; **~gar** vinaigre m; **~-growing 1.** viticulture f; **2.** viticole; **~yard** vignoble m.

vintage 1. vendange(s) f/(pl.); année f; **2.** de grand cru (wine); fig. d'époque (car etc.).

viola ♪ alto m.

violat|e violer; **~ion** violation f.

violen|ce violence f; **~t** violent.

violet 1. ♀ violette f; colour: violet m; **2.** violet.

violin ♪ violon m.

VIP V.I.P. m.

viper zo. vipère f (a. fig.).

virgin 1. vierge f; **2.** vierge (a. fig.); **~la:** ♀ ~ **creeper** vigne f vierge; **~ tobacco** virginie m; **~ity** virginité f.

Virgo astr. la Vierge.

viril|e viril; **~ity** virilité f.

virtual vrai, de fait; **~ly** pratiquement.

virtue vertu f; avantage m, mérite m; pouvoir m, propriété f; **in** (or **by**) ~ **of** en vertu de.

virtuos|ity virtuosité f; **~o** virtuose fm.

virtuous vertueux.

virulent virulent.

virus virus m.

visa 1. visa m; **entrance** (**exit**) ~ visa m d'entrée (de sortie); **2.** viser

viscount vicomte m; **~ess** vicomtesse f.

viscous visqueux; gluant; pâteux.

visib|ility visibilité f; **~le** visible.

vision vision f; vue f, **~ary** visionnaire (a. su.).

visit 1. v/t. rendre visite à, faire (une) visite à; aller voir; visiter (a place); v/i. séjourner, faire un séjour (à, en **in**); ~ **with** être en visite chez, séjourner chez (a person); F bavarder avec; **2.** visite f; séjour m; **~ation** visite f or tournée f d'inspection; fig. affliction f; **~ing** en visite; ~ **card** carte f de visite; ~ **hours** heures f/pl. de visite; sp. ~ **team** les visiteurs m/pl.; **~or** visiteur (-euse f) m (de, **to**); hotel: client(e f) m; **~s' book** hotel: registre m; place of interest: livre m d'or.

visor visière f; pare-soleil m/inv.

vista perspective *f*, vue.

visual visuel; *anat.* optique; **~ize** se représenter, (s')imaginer; envisager.

vital 1. vital; essentiel; mortel (*wound*); F **~ statistics** *pl.* mensurations *f/pl.*; **~ly** énormément; **~ parts** *pl.* = **2.** **~s** *pl.* organes *m/pl.* vitaux; **~ity** vitalité *f*; **~ize** vivifier; *fig.* animer.

vitamin(e) vitamine *f*.

vitiate vicier.

vitreous vitreux; *anat.* vitré.

vituperat|e vitupérer (*v/t.* contre); **~ion** vitupération *f*.

vivaci|ous animé, vif; **~ty** vivacité *f*; verve *f*.

vivi|d vif; éclatant (*colour*); **~ly** vivement, intensément; *describe* d'une manière colorée, *remember:* de façon précise; **~fy** (s')animer; **~section** vivisection *f*.

vixen renarde *f*; F mégère *f*.

V-neck décolleté *m* en V.

vocabulary vocabulaire *m*.

vocal vocal; *fig.* qui se fait entendre, qui fait du bruit; *anat.* **~ c(h)ords** *pl.* cordes *f/pl.* vocales; **~ist** chanteur (-euse *f*) *m*; **~ize** vocaliser; *fig.* exprimer.

vocation vocation *f*; **~al** professionnel.

vociferate *vt/i.* vociférer, crier.

vogue vogue *f*; mode *f*.

voice 1. voix *f*; *gramm.* **active ~** actif *m*; **passive ~** passif *m*; **give ~ to** = **2.** exprimer, formuler, verbaliser; **~d** *gramm.* sonore, voisé.

void 1. vide (de, *of*); ⚖ nul; **~ of** *a.* dépourvu *or* libre de; **2.** vide *m*.

volatile ⚗ volatil; *fig.* instable, versatile; *fig.* explosif.

volcano, *pl.* **-noes** volcan *m*.

volition volonté *f*, volition *f*; **on one's own ~** de son propre gré.

volley 1. volée *f* (*a.* tennis), salve *f*; **2.** lancer; **~ball** volley-ball *m*.

volt ⚡ volt *m*; **~age** ⚡ voltage *m*, tension *f*; **~meter** voltmètre *m*.

volub|ility volubilité *f*; **~le** volubile.

volum|e volume *m* (*a.* book; *a.* phys., voice, fig. etc.); **~ control** (bouton *m*) de réglage *m* de volume; **~inous** volumineux.

volunt|ary volontaire; bénévole (*work, service etc.*); **~eer 1.** volontaire *m*; *attr.* de volontaires; **2.** *v/i.* s'offrir; ✗ s'engager comme volontaire; *v/t.* offrir spontanément; **~ to** (*inf.*) s'offrir pour (*inf.*).

voluptuous voluptueux.

vomit 1. vomir; **2.** vomissure *f*.

voraci|ous vorace; **~ty** voracité *f*.

vortex, *pl.* *usu.* **-tices** tourbillon *m*.

vote 1. vote *m*; scrutin *m*; voix *f*; suffrage *m*; **~ of (no) confidence** vote *m* de confiance (censure); **cast a ~** donner sa voix *or* son vote; **take a ~** procéder au scrutin; **2.** *v/t.* voter (*a bill, motion etc.*); élire (*q.*); F déclarer; *v/i.* voter, donner sa voix (pour, **for**); **~r** votant(e *f*) *m*; électeur (-trice *f*) *m*.

voting vote *m*; scrutin *m*; **~ booth** isoloir *m*; **~ box** urne *f* de scrutin; **~ paper** bulletin *m* de vote.

vouch: ~ for garantir, se porter garant de; répondre de; **~er** *ticket:* bon *m*; ⚖ *etc.* reçu *m*; **~safe** *v/t.* accorder; *v/i.:* **~ to** (*inf.*) daigner (*inf.*).

vow 1. vœu *m*; serment *m*; **2.** *v/t.* vouer; jurer.

vowel voyelle *f*.

voyage 1. voyage *m* (par mer); traversée *f*; **2.** *v/i.* voyager (par mer); *v/t.* parcourir (*the sea*).

vulgar vulgaire; **~ity** vulgarité *f*.

vulnerable vulnérable.

vulture *orn.* vautour *m*.

W

wacky *Am. sl.* fou; toqué.

wad tampon *m*; *banknotes etc.*: liasse *f*; **~ding** rembourrage *m*; ouate *f*; bourre *f*.

waddle se dandiner.

wade *v/i.* marcher (dans l'eau, **in the water**); *fig.* (s')avancer péniblement; **~ through** passer; F **~ into** attaquer, se ruer sur; *v/t.* (faire) passer à gué (*a brook*).

wafer gaufrette *f*; *eccl.* hostie *f*.

waffle *v/i.* parler *or* écrire dans le vague.

waft 1. *v/t.* porter; faire avancer; *v/i.* flotter; 2. bouffée *f*, souffle *m*.

wag 1. *v/t.* agiter, remuer (*one's tail etc.*); *v/i.* remuer; 2. remuement *m*; *person*: plaisantin *m*.

wage 1. *a.* **~s** *pl.* salaire *m*, paye *f*; 2. de salaire, de paye; **~(s) claim**, **~ demands** *pl.* revendications *f/pl.* de salaire(s); **~ dispute** conflit *m* social; **~ earner** salarié(e *f*) *m*; soutien de (la) famille; **~ packet** enveloppe *f* de paye; **~ slip** bulletin *m* de salaire; fiche *f* de paye; **~ war (on)** faire la guerre (à *or* contre).

waggish facétieux.

wager 1. pari *m*; 2. parier.

waggle remuer.

wag(g)on chariot; *Br.* 🚃 wagon *m* de marchandises; F **be (go) on the ~** s'abstenir de boissons alcooliques; **~er** roulier *m*; camionneur *m*.

wagtail *orn.* bergeronnette *f*.

waif: ~s and strays enfants *m/pl.* *or* animaux *m/pl.* abandonnés.

wail 1. gémir; se lamenter; hurler; 2. gémissement *m*; hurlement *m*.

wainscot lambris *m*; boiserie *f*.

waist taille *f*; ceinture *f*; **~coat** gilet *m*; **~ed** *cost.* cintré; **high-~ (low-~)** à taille haute (basse); **slim-~** à la taille fine; **~line** (tour *m* de) taille *f*.

wait 1. *v/i.* attendre; (*oft.* **~ at table**) servir; **~ behind** rester (à attendre); **~ for** attendre (*qch., q.*); **~ (up)on** servir (*q.*); être aux ordres de (*q.*); **~ and see** attendre voir; voir venir; *v/t.* attendre; différer (*a meal*) (jusqu'à l'arrivée de *q.*, **for s.o.**); 2. attente *f*; **lie in ~** être à l'affût (de, **for**); **~er** restaurant: garçon *m*, serveur *m*.

waiting attente *f*; **~ list** liste *f* d'attente; **~ room** salle *f* d'attente; *mot.* **,no ~' **,stationnement interdit'; **play a ~ game** attendre son heure, (se mettre à) voir venir.

waitress serveuse *f*; **~!** Mademoiselle!

waive ✝ renoncer à.

wake¹ ⚓ sillage *m* (*a. fig.*); *fig.* **in the ~ of** après, à la suite de; **in its ~** dans son sillage.

wake² 1. (*a.* **~ up**) (se) réveiller; 2. veillée *f*; **~ful** éveillé; sans sommeil; **~n** (se) réveiller.

walk 1. *v/i.* marcher; se promener; aller à pied; cheminer; aller au pas (*horse*); **~ about** se promener, circuler; **~ out** se mettre en grève; Γ **~ out on** laisser là (*q.*); *v/t.* faire marcher; courir (*the streets*); faire (*a distance*); promener (*a dog*); **~ s.o. off** emmener (*q.*); 2. marche *f*; promenade *f*; allée *f*; démarche *f*; *pace*: pas *m*; **~ of life** position *f* sociale; métier *m*; **~about: (go on a ~** prendre un) bain *m* de foule; **~away** victoire *f* (*etc.*) facile; **~er** marcheur (-euse *f*) *m*; piéton *m*.

walkie-talkie walkie-talkie *m*.

walking 1. marche *f*; promenade *f* à pied; *sp.* footing *m*; 2. ambulant; de marche; *Am.* F **~ papers** *pl.* congé *m*; **~ tour** excursion *f* à pied; **~ stick** canne *f*.

walk...: ~out grève *f*; **~over** *sp.* walk-over *m*; *fig.* victoire *f* facile; **~up** (maison *f* *or* appartement *m*) sans ascenseur.

wall 1. mur *m*; muraille *f*; (*a.* **side..**) paroi *f* (*a.* ⊕); *fig.* **go to the ~** être ruiné *or* mis à l'écart; 2. mural; **~ chart** planche *f* murale; **~ cupboard** placard mural *or* suspendu; 3. (*a.* **~ in**, **~ up**) entourer de murs; murer; *fig. a.* emmurer; **~ off** séparer par un mur, *a. fig.* isoler.

wallet portefeuille *m*.

wallflower ♣ giroflée *f*; *fig.* **be a ~** faire tapisserie.

wallop Γ battre (*q.*) à plate(s) couture(s); cogner.

wallow se vautrer.

wall...: ~paper 1. papier *m* peint; 2. tapisser; **~to-~: ~ carpet(ing)** moquette *f*.

walnut ♀ noix *f*; *tree*: noyer *m*; (bois *m* de) noyer *m*.

walrus *zo.* morse *m*.

waltz 1. valse *f*; **2.** valser.

wan blême, pâle; blafard.

wand baguette *f*; bâton *m*.

wander errer; *a. fig.* vagabonder (*thoughts etc.*); (*a.* ~ *about*) se promener au hasard; *fig.* s'écarter (de, *from*); ~**er** promeneur (-euse *f*) *m*; vagabond(e *f*) *m*; ~**lust** envie *f* de voyager.

wane 1. décroître (*moon*); *fig.* s'affaiblir, diminuer, baisser; **2. on the** ~ sur son déclin.

wangle *sl. v/i.* employer le système D; *v/t.* carotter (*qch.*).

want 1. *v/t.* vouloir, désirer; avoir besoin de; demander; exiger, réclamer (*good care etc.*); *not to have*: manquer de; ~ *s.o. to do s.th.* vouloir que q. fasse qch.; ~**ed** (*for*) recherché (pour) (*criminal*); *v/i.*: ~ *for* manquer de; **2.** manque *m*; ~**s** *pl.* besoins *m/pl.*; *for* ~ *of* faute de; par manque de; ~ *ad* demande *f* d'emploi; ~**ing** qui manque; insuffisant; *be* ~ manquer, faire défaut; *be* ~ *in s.th.* manquer de qch.

wanton injustifié, gratuit (*act*).

war 1. guerre *f*; *attr.* de guerre; guerrier; *at* ~ en guerre (avec, contre *with*); *go to* ~ se mettre en guerre (contre, *against*); *make* ~ faire la guerre (à, contre [*up*]*on*); **2.** de guerre.

warble *vt/i.* chanter (en gazouillant); *v/i.* gazouiller.

ward 1. *person*: pupille *mf*; *hospital*: salle *f*; *Br.* circonscription *f* électorale; **2.** ~ *off* éviter; prévenir (*a disease etc.*); ~**en** directeur (-trice *f*) *m*; gardien(ne *f*) *m*; ~**er** gardien *m* de prison; ~**robe** garde-robe *f*; *furniture*: armoire *f*.

ware|house 1. entrepôt *m*; magasin *m*; **2.** emmagasiner; ~**s** *pl.* marchandises *f/pl.*

war...: ~**fare** guerre *f*; ~**head** ogive *f*; *nuclear* ~ tête *f* nucléaire; ~**horse** cheval *m* de bataille; *fig.* vétéran *m*.

wariness circonspection *f*; prudence *f*; défiance *f*.

warlike guerrier; martial.

warm 1. chaud (*a. fig.*); *fig.* chaleureux, vif; F riche; *be* ~ avoir chaud (*person*); être chaud (*thing*); **2.** *v/t.* chauffer; *fig.* (r)échauffer; ~ *up* (ré)chauffer; *v/i.* (*a.* ~

up) s'échauffer; s'animer; ~**hearted** affectueux, chaleureux; ~**th** chaleur *f*; ~**up** mise *f* en train.

warn avertir (de *of*, *against*); prévenir; (*a.* ~ *off*) détourner; ~ *not to* conseiller de ne pas *inf.*; ~**ing** avertissement *m*; avis *m*.

warp *vt/i.* gauchir, (se) voiler; *v/t. fig.* fausser; pervertir.

warrant 1. justification *f*; ⚖ mandat *m*; ~ *of arrest* mandat *m* d'arrêt; **2.** garantir (*a.* ♥); répondre de (*qch.*); justifier; ~**y** garantie *f*.

warrior guerrier *m*.

wart verrue *f*; ♀ excroissance *f*.

wary circonspect; prudent; défiant.

was: *he* ~ *to have come* il devait venir.

wash 1. *v/t.* laver; ~ *away* enlever, faire partir au lavage (*a stain etc.*) (*a.* ~ *off*, ~ *out*); emporter (*water, rain etc.*); ~ *down* laver (à grande eau); ~ *out* laver; rincer (*the mouth*); *see a.* ~ *away*; ~ *up* faire la vaisselle; *v/i.* se laver; ~ *against the cliff* baigner la falaise; **2.** lessive *f*; *paint*: badigeon *m*, blanchissage *m*; toilette *f*; ♣ sillage *m*; *give s.th. a* ~ laver qch.; *have a* ~ se laver; **3.** = ~**able** lavable; ~**basin** cuvette *f*, lavabo *m*; ~**cloth** torchon *m*; ~**ed-out** délavé; décoloré; F *fig.* épuisé, F lessivé; ~**ed-up** F fichu, ruiné; F lessivé; ~**er** laveur (-euse *f*) *m*; *machine*: laveuse *f*; ⊕ rondelle *f*; ~**erwoman** blanchisseuse *f*; ~**ing 1.** lavage *m*; lessive *f*; **2.** lessive; ~ *machine* machine *f* à laver; ~ *powder* lessive *f*; ~**ing-up** (lavage *m* de la) vaisselle *f*; ~**out** F fiasco *m*, F four *m*; déception *f*; ~**rag** lavette *f*; ~**y** délavé (*colour*); *fig.* fade.

wasp guêpe *f*.

wastage gaspillage *m*; *coll.* déchets *m/pl.*

waste 1. désert, inculte (*land etc.*); perdu (*energy, heat etc.*); ⊕ de rebut; *lay* ~ dévaster, ravager; ~ *paper* vieux papiers *m/pl.*; ~ *products* F déchets *m/pl.*; **2.** perte *f*; gaspillage *m*; rebut *m*; ⊕ déchets *m/pl.*; (*household* ~) ordures *f/pl.*; région *f* inculte; *go* (*or run*) *to* ~ se gaspiller; se perdre; **3.** *v/t.* gaspiller; perdre (*one's time*); *v/i.* se gaspiller; ~ *away* dépérir; ~ *bin* boîte *f* à ordures; ~**ful** gaspilleur; prodigue; inutile; ruineux; (~**paper**) *basket* corbeille *f* à papier; **~pipe** trop-plein *m*; écoulement *m*.

watch 1. montre *f*; garde *f*; ♱ quart *m*; **be on the ~ for** épier; **keep (a) close ~ on** surveiller de près; **2.** *v/t.* regarder, observer; faire attention à; surveiller; *v/i.* regarder; veiller; **~ for** attendre; guetter; **~ out (for)** faire attention (à), prendre garde (à); **~ over** surveiller; s'occuper de; **~dog** chien *m* de garde; **~ful** vigilant, attentif; **~maker** horloger *m*; **~man** gardien *m*; veilleur *m* (de nuit); **~strap** bracelet *m* de montre; **~word** mot *m* d'ordre.

water 1. eau *f*; **by ~** en bateau, par eau; F **be in hot ~** être dans le pétrin; avoir des ennuis; F **be in deep ~(s)** être dans la gêne; **2.** *v/t.* arroser (*the soil, the street, plants etc.*); abreuver (*animals*); **~ down** couper (d'eau) (*wine etc.*); *fig.* édulcorer (*a story*); atténuer; *v/i.* pleurer (*eyes*); **make s.o.'s mouth ~** faire venir l'eau à la bouche de q.; **~ cannon** lance-eau *m/inv.*; **~closet** (*usu. written* **W.C.**) cabinets *m/pl.*, F waters *m/pl.*; **~colo(u)r** *paint:* couleur *f* à l'eau; *painting:* aquarelle *f*; **~course** cours *m* d'eau; conduit *m*; conduite *f* d'eau; **~cress** ♱ cresson *m* (de fontaine); **~fall** chute *f* d'eau; **~front** *esp. Am.* quai *m*, port *m*; **~gauge** ⊕ hydromètre *m*; (indicateur *m* de) niveau *m* d'eau.

watering: ~ can arrosoir *m*; **~ place** abreuvoir *m*; ville *f* d'eau, station *f* thermale; station *f* balnéaire.

water...: ~level niveau *m* d'eau; **~ lily** nénuphar *m*; **~logged** détrempé; **~ main** conduite *f* (principale) d'eau; **~mark** *on paper:* filigrane *m*; **~ melon** pastèque *f*; **~plane** hydravion *m*; **~proof 1.** imperméable (*a. su./m*); étanche (*watch, shoes etc.*); **2.** imperméabiliser; **~shed** *geog.* ligne *f* de partage des eaux; **~side 1.** riverain; **2.** bord *m* de l'eau; **~skiing** *m* nautique; **~tight** étanche; *fig.* inattaquable, *fig.* **in ~ compartments** séparés par des cloisons étanches; **~way** voie *f* d'eau; **~works** *pl.* usine *f* de distribution d'eau; **~y** aqueux; larmoyant (*eyes*).

watt ⚡ watt *m*.

wattle clayonnage *m*; claie *f*.

wave 1. vague *f* (*a. fig.*); *phys.* onde *f*; *hair:* ondulation *f*; geste *m*, signe *m* (de

la main); **2.** *v/t.* agiter; brandir; onduler (*one's hair*); faire signe de; *v/i.* s'agiter; flotter (au vent) (*flag etc.*); onduler; faire signe (de la main) (à q., **to s.o.**); **~length** ⚡, *radio:* longueur *f* d'onde; F *fig.* **be on the same ~** être sur la même longueur d'onde(s).

waver vaciller (*a. fig.*); hésiter.

wavy onduleux; ondulé.

wax¹ 1. cire *f*; *ears:* cérumen *m*; **2.** cirer; lustrer.

wax² croître (*moon*).

wax|en de cire; *fig.* **~ = ~y** cireux.

way 1. chemin *m*, voie *f*; direction *f*, sens *m*; façon *f*, manière *f*; genre *m*; moyen *m*; progrès *m*, habitude *f*, coutume *f*; état *m* (*physique etc.*); **~s and means** *pl.* moyens *m/pl.*; ressources *f/pl.* (*necessaires*); **~ in** entrée *f*; **~ out** sortie *f*; **this ~** par ici; **in some** (*or* **a**) **~** en quelque sorte; **in no ~** ne ... aucunement; **by the ~** en passant, à propos; **by ~ of** *place:* par, via; *fig.* en guise de (*s.th. else*); *fig.* pour (*inf.*), afin de (*inf.*); **on the** (*or* **one's**) **~** en route (pour, **to**); chemin faisant; **out of the ~** écarté, isolé; *fig.* peu ordinaire, extravagant; **under ~** en marche (*a.* ♱); **give ~** céder; faire place; **have one's ~** agir à sa guise; **go out of one's ~** (**to** *inf.*) se donner du mal (pour *inf.*); **if I had my ~** si on me laissait faire; **have a ~ with** savoir (comment) s'y prendre avec; **lead the ~** marcher en tête; montrer le chemin; *Am.* **~ station** petite gare *f*; *Am.* **~ train** train *m* omnibus; *see a.* **right 3** *etc.*; **2.** *adv.* (très) loin; là-bas; du côté de, près de; **~bill** bordereau *m* d'expédition; **~farer** voyageur (-euse *f*) *m*; **~lay** guetter (au passage); **~side 1.** bord *m* de la route; **by the ~** au bord de la route; **2.** au bord de la route; **~ward** capricieux; entêté.

we nous (*a. stressed*).

weak faible; léger (*tea*); peu solide; **~en** (s')affaiblir; (faire) faiblir; **~ling** faible *mf*, mou *m*; **~ly 1.** *adj.* faible, chétif; **2.** *adv.* faiblement; sans force; **~minded** faible d'esprit; **~ness** faiblesse *f*.

weal¹ bien(-être) *m*.

weal² marque *f* (*d'un coup*).

wealth richesse(s) *f/(pl.)*; **~y** riche.

wean sevrer (*a baby*); *fig.* détourner (*q.*) (de **from, of**).

weapon arme *f.*

wear 1. *v/t.* porter (*clothes, shoes etc.*); (*a. ~ away, down, off, out*) user (*a. one's patience*): ronger; *v/i.* faire de l'usage; (*a. ~ well*) résister à l'usure; se conserver; tenir le coup (*person*); (*a. ~ away, down, out, thin*) s'user; *~ away* s'user; s'effacer; passer; *~ off* disparaître (*a. fig.*); *~ on* passer, avancer (*time*); durer, se poursuivre; *~ out* s'user; s'épuiser; **2.** usage *m*; usure *f*; vêtements *m/pl.*; *~ and tear* usure *f*; *for hard ~* d'un bon usage; *sports* vêtements *m/pl.* de sport; *town* (*evening*) *~* tenue *f* de ville (*de soirée*); *the worse for ~* usé; *~ing* fatigant.

wear|iness fatigue *f*; lassitude *f*; *~i-some* ennuyeux; *~y 1.* las, fatigué (*de, with*); fatigant; **2.** (se) lasser.

weasel 1. *zo.* belette *f*; **2.** se faufiler; F *~ out* se retirer, se raviser.

weather 1. temps *m*; **2.** météorologique; *~forecast* prévisions *f/pl.* météorologiques, météo *f*; *~ report* bulletin *m* météorologique, météo *f*; **3.** *v/t.* désagréger, altérer (*rock etc.*); faire mûrir (*wood*); *fig.* survivre à, résister à (*a crisis etc.*); *v/i.* se désagréger, s'altérer (*rock etc.*); mûrir (*wood*); *~-beaten* basané (*face*); dégradé par le temps; *~cock* girouette *f*; *~proof, ~tight* imperméable; étanche.

weave 1. tisser; entrelacer (*strands*); tresser (*a basket, garland etc.*); **2.** tissage *m*; *~r* tisserand(e *f*) *m*.

web tissu *m*; *spider:* toile *f*; *orn.* palmure *f*; *~bing* sangles *f/pl.*

wed épouser; *the newly-~s* les jeunes mariés; *fig. ~ded to* attaché à; *~ding 1.* mariage *m*; noce *f*, -s *f/pl.*; **2.** de noce(s); de mariage; *~ anniversary* anniversaire *m* de mariage; *~ ring* alliance *f*.

wedge 1. coin *m*; *for fixing:* cale *f*; *piece:* part *f*, morceau; **2.** caler; (*a. ~ in*) coincer; *push, force:* enfoncer.

wedlock mariage *m*.

Wednesday mercredi *m*.

weed 1. mauvaise herbe *f*; F tabac *m*; **2.** désherber, sarcler; (*a. ~ out*) arracher (*weeds*); *fig.* éliminer; *~ killer* herbicide *m*; *~s* (*usu. widow's ~*) (*vêtements m/pl.* de) deuil *m*; *~y* plein de mauvaises herbes; F malingre (*person*).

week semaine *f*; *this day ~* (d')aujourd'hui en huit; *~day* jour *m* de semaine; jour *m* ouvrable; *~end 1.* week-end *m*; **2.** passer le weekend; *~ly 1.* hebdomadaire (*a. su./m = ~ paper*) **2.** *adv.* chaque semaine.

weeny F tout petit, minuscule.

weep pleurer (*de for* [*joy etc.*], *over* [*qch.*]); *~ing willow* saule *m* pleureur.

weigh *v/t.* peser; ♣ *~ anchor* lever l'ancre; *~ down* faire plier; *fig. a.* accabler; *~ in, ~ out, ~ up* (*a. fig.*) peser; *v/i.* peser; *fig. ~ on* peser à or sur; accabler (*burden etc.*); *~bridge* pont-bascule *m*.

weight 1. poids *m* (*a. fig.*); pesanteur *f*; *atomic* ~ poids *m* atomique; **2.** lester; *~ed down* lourdement chargé; *a. fig.* accablé, écrasé; *~less* qui ne pèse rien; en état d'apesanteur; *~lessness* apesanteur *f*; *~y* lourd; pesant.

weir barrage *m*; *pond:* déversoir *m.*

weird étrange; mystérieux; surnaturel; F singulier.

welcome 1. bienvenu; *you are ~ to* (*inf.*) libre à vous de (*inf.*); *you are ~ to it* c'est à votre service; (*you are*) *~!* de rien!, il n'y a pas de quoi!; **2.** bienvenue *f*, *a. fig.* accueil *m*; **3.** souhaiter la bienvenue à; accueillir (*a. fig.*).

weld 1. souder; **2.** soudure *f.*

welfare bien-être *m*; *~ state* État-providence *m*; *~ work* assistance *f* sociale; *~ worker* assistant(-e *f*) social(e).

well¹ 1. puits *m*; **2.** jaillir, sourdre (*a. out, ~ up*).

well² 1. *adv.* bien; *do ~ in* bien réussir dans; **2.** *pred./adj.* en bonne santé; bon; bien; *I am not ~* je ne me porte pas bien; *all's ~* tout va bien; F *be ~ in with* s'entendre bien avec; **3.** *int.* eh bien!; F ça alors!; *~-being* bien-être *m*; *~-advised* prudent, sage; *you would be ~ to* (*inf.*) vous feriez bien de (*inf.*); *~-behaved* sage; obéissant (*a. animal*); *~-bred* bien élevé; *~-disposed* disposé (envers, *to*[*wards*]); *~-done cuis.* bien cuit; *~-earned* bien mérité; *~-groomed* bien soigné de sa personne; *~-heeled* F (assez) riche, F friqué; *~-intentioned* bien intentionné; *~-known* bien connu; célèbre; *~-mannered* bien élevé; *~-meaning* bien intentionné; *~-meant* fait avec de bonnes intentions; amical (*advise etc.*); *~-off*

bien; (*a.* **~ for money**) aisé, assez riche, bien nanti; **~ for** bien fourni de; **~-nigh** presque; **~-read** littré; instruit; **~-thought-of** (bien) considéré; **~-timed** opportun; bien calculé; **~-to-do** aisé, riche; **~-tried** éprouvé; **~-wisher** ami(e *f*) *m* sincère, partisan *m*; **~-worn** usé; *fig.* rebattu (*cliché etc.*).

Welsh 1. gallois; 2. *ling.* gallois *m*; **the ~** les Gallois *m/pl.*; **~man** (**~woman**) Gallois(e *f*) *m*.

welter se rouler, se vautrer; *fig.* **~ in** nager dans (*blood etc.*).

wench jeune fille *f* ou femme *f*.

wend: **~ one's way** aller son chemin.

west 1. *su.* ouest *m*; 2. *adj.* de l'ouest; occidental; 3. *adv.* à *or* vers l'ouest; **~erly** *see* **western** 1; **~ern** 1. de l'ouest; occidental; 2. *cin.* western *m*, **~orner** occidental *m*.

westward 1. *adj.* à *or* de l'ouest; 2. *adv.* (*a.* **~s**) vers l'ouest.

wet 1. mouillé; humide; *soaked:* trempé; *rainy:* pluvieux; **~ through** trempé jusqu'aux os; **get ~** se mouiller; 2. pluie *f*; humidité *f*; 3. (*a.* **~ through**) mouiller, tremper.

wether bélier *m* châtré; mouton *m*.

wet-nurse 1. nourrice *f*; 2. chouchouter (*q.*).

whack F 1. cogner; taper sur; 2. coup *m*; (grand) morceau *m*; **~er** F chose *f* *or* personne *f* énorme.

whale baleine *f*; F **a ~ of a ...** un(e) ... sensass; **~bone** baleine *f*; **~r** baleinier *m*.

wharf (*pl. a.* **wharves**) quai *m*.

what 1. *interr./pron.* que, quoi; qu'est-ce qui; qu'est-ce que ...? et ...?; **~ about ...?** et ...?; **~ about** (*ger.*)? que pensez-vous de (*inf.*)?; **~ for?** pourquoi donc?; **~ of it?** et alors?; **~ next?** et ensuite?; *iro.* par exemple!; et quoi encore?; 2. *rel./pron.* ce qui, ce que; **know ~'s ~** en savoir long; savoir son affaire, s'y connaître; **and ~ not** et ainsi de suite; 3. *interr./adj.* quel, quelle, quels, quelles; **~ time is it?** quelle heure est-il?; **~ a blessing!** quel bonheur!; **~ impudence!** quelle impertinence!; 4. *rel./adj.* que, qui; 5. *int.* **~!** quoi!; **~(so)ever** 1. *pron.* tout ce qui, tout ce que; quoi qui (*sbj.*), quoi que (*sbj.*); 2. *adj.* quelque ... qui *or* que (*sbj.*); **~not**, **~sit** F truc *m*, machin *m*.

wheat & froment *m*; blé *m*.

wheedle cajoler; **~ s.o. into** (*ger.*) amener q. à (*inf.*) à force de cajoleries; **~ s.th. out of s.o.** cajoler q. pour en obtenir qch.

wheel 1. roue *f*; (*a.* **steering-~**) volant *m*; & gouvernail *m*; F bicyclette *f*; 2. *v/t.* rouler, pousser; 2. **~ (a)round**, **about** tourner; se retourner (*person*); F aller à bicyclette; **~ and deal** se livrer à des manigances; **~barrow** brouette *f*; **~chair** fauteuil *m* roulant; **~ed** à roues; roulant; **~ing and dealing** manigances *f/pl.*, affaires *f/pl.* louches.

wheeze 1. respirer péniblement; 2. respiration *f* pénible; **~y** poussif, asthmatique.

whelp 1. *zo.* petit *m* (d'un fauve); *see* **puppy**; 2. mettre bas.

when 1. *adv.* quand?; 2. *cj.* quand, lorsque; alors que; (*the day*) où; (*one day*) que.

whence d'où.

when(so)ever chaque fois que, toutes les fois que; quand.

where 1. *adv.* où?; 2. *cj.* (là) où; **~about** 1. où (donc); 2. (*usu.* **~abouts**); **the ~ of** le lieu *m* où (*q.*, *qch.*) se trouve; **~as** puisque, attendu que; tandis que, alors que; **~by** par où; par quoi; par lequel (*etc.*); **~fore** (C'est) pourquoi; pourquoi; **~in** en quoi; où; dans lequel (*etc.*); **~of** dont, de quoi; duquel (*etc.*); **~upon** sur quoi; sur lequel (*etc.*).

wherever où que (*sbj.*).

wherewithal moyens *m/pl.*

whet aiguiser.

whether si; **~ ... or no** que ... (*sbj.*) ou non.

whetstone pierre *f* à aiguiser.

whey petit lait *m*.

which 1. *interr./pron.* lequel, laquelle, lesquels, lesquelles; 2. *rel./pron.* qui, que; 3. *interr./adj.* quel, quelle, quels, quelles; 4. *rel./adj.* lequel, laquelle, lesquels, lesquelles; **~ever** 1. *pron.* celui qui, celui que; n'importe lequel (*etc.*); 2. *adj.* le ... que, n'importe quel (*etc.*); quelque ... que (*sbj.*).

whiff *wind, smoke etc.:* bouffée *f*.

while 1. *a.* **~** quelque temps, un moment; **for a ~** pendant quelque temps; **be worth one's ~** (en) valoir la peine; 2. (*usu.* **~ away**) faire passer, tuer (*the*

time); **3.** (*a.* **whilst**) pendant que; tant que; alors que, tandis que.

whim caprice *m*, lubie *f*.

whimper 1. gémir, geindre; pleurnicher; **2.** gémissement *m*.

whimsical bizarre; capricieux (*person*); fantasque.

whims(e)y caprice *m*.

whine 1. gémir; se lamenter; **2.** gémissement *m* (prolongé); lamentation(s) *f*/(*pl.*).

whinny hennir.

whip 1. fouet *m*; (*riding ~*) cravache *f*; *parl.* chef *m* de file, whip *m*; appel *m* aux membres du parti; convocation *f*; *fig.* **have the ~ hand** être (le) maître; **2.** *v/t.* fouetter; enlever *or* saisir (brusquement); F battre (à plates coutures) (= *defeat*); F faucher (= *steal*); **~ up** fouetter (*an emotion etc.*), stimuler, donner un coup de fouet à; F faire *or* préparer en vitesse (*a meal etc.*); *cuis.* **~ped cream** crème *f* Chantilly; *v/i.* filer, aller *or* venir à toute vitesse; **~ back** revenir brusquement; **~lash** coup de fouet; (*a.* **~ injury**) syndrome *m* cervical traumatique; **~ping boy** tête *f* de Turc; **~round** F (**have a ~** faire une) collecte *f*.

whirl 1. (faire) tournoyer; *v/i.* tourbillonner; **2.** tourbillon(nement) *m*; **~pool** tourbillon *m*; **~wind** trombe *f*, tornade *f*.

whir(r) tourner en ronronnant; vrombir; siffler.

whisk 1. verge(tte) *f*; *cuis.* fouet *m*; **2.** *v/t.* agiter; *cuis.* fouetter, battre; **~ away**, **~ off** enlever (*qch.*) *or* emmener (*q.*) rapidement; *v/i.* aller comme un trait *or* à toute vitesse; **~er** *zo.* moustache *f*; *usu.* (**a pair of**) **~s** *pl.* (des) favoris *m/pl.*

whisk(e)y whisky *m*.

whisper 1. *vt/i.* chuchoter; **2.** chuchotement *m*; *fig.* bruit *m*.

whistle 1. siffler; **2.** sifflement *m*; sifflet *m*; F gorge *f*.

white 1. blanc; *face etc.*: blême, pâle; **~ coffee** café *m* crème *or* au lait; **~ lie** pieux mensonge; *admin.* **~ paper** livre *m* blanc; **2.** blanc *m*; *person*: blanc *m*, blanche *f*; **~collar** d'employé de bureau; **~ worker** col *m* blanc; **~hot** chauffé à blanc; **~n** blanchir (*a. fig.*); *v/i.* pâlir (*person*); **~ness** blancheur *f*;

pâleur *f*; **~ning** blanchiment *m*; *hair*: blanchissement *m*; **~wash 1.** blanc *m* de chaux, badigeon *m* blanc; **2.** blanchir à la chaux; *fig.* faire apparaître innocent (*a person*) *or* anodin (*s.th.*).

whither *poet.* où.

whitish blanchâtre.

Whitsun de la Pentecôte; **~tide** (fête *f* de) la Pentecôte *f*.

whittle tailler (au couteau); *fig.* **~ away**, **~ down** rogner, réduire petit à petit.

whiz(z) siffler; **~ by**, **~ past** passer à toute vitesse.

who 1. *interr./pron.* qui (est-ce qui); quelle personne; lequel, laquelle, lesquels, lesquelles; **2.** *rel./pron.* qui; lequel, laquelle, lesquels, lesquelles; celui (celle, ceux *pl.*) qui.

whodun(n)it *sl.* polar *m*.

whoever celui qui; quiconque.

whole 1. entier; complet; tout; **2.** tout *m*; totalité *f*; ensemble *m*; **the ~ of London** le tout Londres; **on the ~** à tout prendre; somme toute; **~-hearted** sincère, qui vient du cœur; **~hog** F total, à fond; **~meal** complet (*bread*); **~sale 1.** (*usu.* ~ **trade**) (vente *f* en) gros *m*; **2.** en gros; de gros; *fig.* en bloc, en masse; **~saler** grossiste *m/f*; **~some** sain, salubre; *fig.* salutaire.

wholly *adv.* entièrement, tout à fait, complètement.

whom *acc.* of **who**.

whoop 1. cri *m*; **2.** crier, pousser des cris; F **~ it up** faire la noce; **~ing cough** coqueluche *f*; **~ee:** F **make ~** faire la noce.

whopp|er *sl.* personne *f* or chose *f* énorme; *esp.* gros mensonge *m*; **~ing** *sl.* colossal, énorme.

whore *pej.* prostituée *f*, putain *f*.

whose *genitive* of **who**.

why 1. pourquoi?; **~ so?** pourquoi cela?; **2.** tiens!; eh bien.

wick *lamp:* mèche *f*.

wicked mauvais, méchant; *co.* fripon; **~ness** méchanceté *f*.

wicker: **~ basket** panier *m* d'osier; **~work** vannerie *f*.

wicket guichet *m* (*a.* cricket); barrière *f* (*of a garden*).

wide 1. *adj.* large; étendu, vaste; répandu (*influence*); grand (*difference etc.*); loin (*de*, **of**); **3 feet ~** large de 3 pieds; **2.**

adv. loin; à de grands intervalles; largement; **~ awake** tout éveillé; **~ open** grand ouvert; **open ~** ouvrir tout grand; **go (shoot) ~ (of the target)** passer (tirer) à côté; **~-angle** *phot.*: **~ lense** (objectif *m*) grand angulaire *m*; **~-awake** F averti, malin; **~n** (s')élargir; (s')agrandir; **~ness** largeur *f*; **~-open** grand ouvert; **~spread** répandu.

widow veuve *f*; **~er** veuf *m*.

width largeur *f*; ampleur *f*.

wield *poet.* manier (*a sword*); *fig.* exercer (*control etc.*).

wife (*pl. wives*) femme *f*, épouse *f*.

wig perruque *f*; postiche *m*.

wigging F attrapade *f*.

wild 1. sauvage; farouche (*look, appearance etc.*); excited, *unrestrained etc.*: fou (de *about, over, with*); frénétique (*applause etc.*); fait au hasard (*guess etc.*); **go ~** devenir (comme) fou; ne plus se tenir (de joie, *with joy*); s'emballer (pour, *about*); **run ~** courir en liberté; *fig.* **allow to run ~** donner libre cours à; **talk ~** divaguer, déraisonner; **2.** nature *f*, **~(s** *pl.*) région(s) *f*/(*pl.*) sauvages; **~ cat** *zo.* chat *m* sauvage; **~ strike** grève *f* sauvage; **~erness** région(s) *f*/(*pl.*) sauvages; *usu. fig.* désert *m*; **~fire: spread like ~** se répandre comme une traînée de poudre; **~-goose chase** fausse piste *f*; **~life** animaux *m*/*pl.* (et plantes *f*/*pl.*) sauvages.

wile artifice *m*, ruse *f*.

wilful obstiné, entêté; délibéré (*act*).

will 1. volonté *f*; ⚖ testament *m*; **at ~** à volonté; **free ~** libre arbitre *m*; **2.** *defective verb*: **he ~ come** il viendra; il veut bien venir; **3.** *v/i.* ⚖ léguer; **~ful** *see* **wilful**.

willing de bonne volonté; prêt (à, **to**); **I am ~ to believe** je veux bien croire; **~ly** volontiers; de bon cœur; **~ness** bonne volonté *f*.

will-o'-the-wisp feu *m* follet.

willow ♀ saule *m*; ⊦ *cricket*: batte *f*.

willpower volonté *f*.

willy-nilly bon gré mal gré.

wilt (se) flétrir; *v/i.* se faner; *fig.* languir; *sl.* se dégonfler.

wily astucieux, rusé.

win 1. *v/t.* gagner; remporter (*a prize, a victory*); acquérir, parvenir *or* arriver à (*fame, recognition etc.*); **~over, ~round**

convaincre (de, **to**); **~ s.o. over** *or* **round to s.th.** *a.* faire q. accepter qch.; *v/i.* gagner; **2.** *sp.* victoire *f*.

wince 1. grimacer (de douleur *etc.*); sourciller; tressaillir; **2.** grimace *f*; tressaillissement *m*.

winch manivelle *f*; treuil *m*.

wind¹ 1. vent *m* (*a.* ⚓); *fig.* haleine *f*; ♪ instruments *m*/*pl.* à vent; *fig.* **throw to the ~s** abandonner; F **get (or put) the ~ up s.o.** flanquer la trouille à q.; **2.** *hunt.* flairer (*game*); faire perdre le souffle à (*q.*); essouffler.

wind² 1. *v/t.* tourner; enrouler; **~ up** enrouler; remonter (*a watch*); *fig.* terminer, finir; conclure; ♥ liquider; *v/i.* (*a.* **~ o.s., ~ one's way**) serpenter; *fig.* **~ up** terminer; **2.** tournant *m*; tour *m* (de manivelle *etc.*).

wind...: **~bag** *pej.* hâbleur (-euse *f*) *m*; **~fall** fruit *m* abattu par le vent; *fig.* aubaine *f*.

winding 1. mouvement *m or* cours *m* sinueux; ⚡ enroulement *m*; **2.** sinueux; **~ staircase** (*or* **stairs** *pl.*) escalier *m* tournant.

wind...: **~instrument** ♪ instrument *m* à vent; **~jammer** ⚓ (grand) voilier *m*.

windlass ⊕ treuil *m*.

windmill moulin *m* à vent.

window fenêtre *f*; *shop etc.*: vitrine *f*, *car, train etc.*: glace *f*, vitre *f*, *ticket office*: guichet *m*; **~box** jardinière *f*; **~ dresser** étalagiste *mf*; **~ dressing** composition *f* de l'étalage; arrangement *m* de la vitrine; *fig.* façade *f*; trompe-l'œil *m*/*inv.*; **~ frame** châssis *m* de fenêtre; **~pane** vitre *f*, carreau *m*; **~ shade** store *m*; **~shop = go ~ping** faire du lèche-vitrines; **~sill** *outside*: rebord *m* (*inside*: appui *m*) de la fenêtre.

wind...: **~pipe** *anat.* trachée-artère (*pl.* trachées-artères) *f*; **~screen**, *Am.* **~shield** pare-brise *m*/*inv.*; **~ wiper** essuie-glace *m*; **~ tunnel** tunnel *m* aérodynamique.

windy venteux; verbeux.

wine vin *m*; **~ grower** viticulteur *m*; vigneron *m*; **~ merchant** négociant *m* en vins; **~ press** pressoir *m*.

wing 1. aile *f* (*a.* *fig.*, ✕, ⚓, △, ✈, *mot.*, *sp.*); *door*: battant *m*; **~s** *pl.* coulisse *f*; **take ~** s'envoler; prendre son vol; **be on the ~** voler; **2.** *v/t.* blesser à l'aile *or fig.*

au bras; *v/i.* voler; **~span**, **~spread** envergure *f*.

wink 1. clignement *m* (d'œil); clin *m* d'œil; F *not get a ~ of sleep* ne pas fermer l'œil de toute la nuit; **2.** *v/i.* cligner les yeux; clignoter (*light*); **~ at** cligner de l'œil à (*q.*); fermer les yeux sur (*qch.*).

winner gagnant(e) *f m*; *sp.* vainqueur *m*.

winning 1. gagnant; *fig.* engageant; **2.**: **~s** *pl.* gains *m/pl.* (*at game etc.*).

wint|er 1. hiver *m*; **2.** hiverner; **3.** d'hiver (*sports etc.*); **~erize** préparer pour l'hiver; **~ry** d'hiver; *fig.* glacial.

wipe essuyer (*a.* = ~ *off*, ~ *up*); ~ *out* essuyer; *fig.* effacer; exterminer.

wire 1. fil *m* (de fer); *⚡* fil *m* électrique; télégramme *m*; **2.** en *or* de fil de fer; **3.** *v/t.* munir d'un fil métallique; (*a.* ~ *up*) (r)attacher avec du fil de fer (à, *to*); *⚡* brancher (sur, *to*); *vt/i.* *tel.* télégraphier; **~less 1.** sans fil; de T.S.F., de radio; **2.** (~ *set* poste *m* de) radio *f*; **~ netting** treillis *m* métallique; grillage *m*; **~-puller** *fig.* intrigant(e *f*) *m*; **~-pulling** intrigues *f/pl.*, manigances *f/pl.*; **~tap(ping)** *tel.* mise *f* sur écoute.

wir|ing installation *f* électrique, câblage *m*; **~y** raide (*hair*); sec et nerveux (*person*).

wisdom sagesse *f*; ~ *tooth* dent *f* de sagesse.

wise sage; prudent; F ~ *guy* malin *m*; F *put s.o.* ~ mettre *q.* à la page.

wisecrack F **1.** remarque *f* ironique; **2.** faire de l'esprit.

wish 1. vouloir, désirer; souhaiter (qch. à *q.*, *s.o. s.th.*); ~ *for* désirer, souhaiter (*qch.*); ~ *s.o. well* (*ill*) vouloir du bien (mal) à *q.*; **2.** vœu *m*, souhait *m*; désir *m*; **~ful** désireux (de *of*, *to*); *that is* ~ *thinking* c'est confondre ses désirs avec la réalité.

wisp *hair*: mèche *f* (fine), *grass etc.*: poignée *f*; *smoke etc.*: ruban *m*; *a* ~ *of ...* un petit bout de ...

wistful pensif; d'envie.

wit 1. (*a.* ~ *s pl.*) esprit *m*; intelligence *f*; *person*: homme *m* d'esprit; *be at one's* ~'*s end* ne plus savoir que faire; *live by one's* ~ *s* vivre d'expédients; *be out of one's* ~ *s* avoir perdu la raison; **2.**: *to* ~ à savoir.

witch sorcière *f*; **~craft** sorcellerie *f*; **~hunt** *pol.* chasse *f* aux sorcières.

with avec; de; à; par; malgré; *sl.* ~ *it* dans le vent.

withdraw (se) retirer (de, *from*); **~al** retraite *f*; retrait *m* (*of money*); *⚕* manque *m*; *⚕* ~ *symptom* symptôme(s) *m(/pl.)* de manque.

wither (*oft.* ~ *up*, *away*) (se) faner; (se) dessécher; *v/i.* dépérir (*person*).

with|hold retenir; refuser (à *q.*, *from s.o.*); différer (*payment etc.*); cacher, taire (*information etc.*); **~ing tax** impôt *m* retenu à la source; **~in 1.** *adv.* à l'intérieur, au dedans; à la maison; **2.** *prp.* à l'intérieur de, en dedans de; ~ *doors* à la maison; ~ *10 minutes* en moins de dix minutes; ~ *call* à (la) portée de la voix; **~out 1.** *adv.* à l'extérieur, au dehors; **2.** *prp.* sans; *poet.* en dehors de; **~stand** résister à; supporter.

witness 1. témoignage *m*; *person*: témoin *m*; *bear* ~ témoigner, porter témoignage (de *to*, *of*); **2.** *v/t.* être témoin de; assister à; témoigner de; attester l'authenticité de (*a document*); *v/i.* témoigner; ~ *box*, *Am.* ~ *stand* barre *f* des témoins.

wit|ticism trait *m* d'esprit, bon mot *m*; **~ty** spirituel.

wives *pl. of wife*.

wizard sorcier *m*, magicien *m*; **~ry** sorcellerie *f*.

wizen(ed) ratatiné; parcheminé.

wobble trembler; branler; chanceler, osciller.

woe malheur *m*; ~ *is me!* pauvre de moi!; **~begone** triste, désolé; **~ful** triste.

wog *sl.* métèque *mf*.

wolf 1. (*pl. wolves*) loup *m*; F tombeur *m*, coureur *m*; **2.** dévorer; **~ish** de loup.

woman (*pl. women*) femme *f*; *attr.* femme ... (de femme)(s; ~ *doctor* femme *f* médecin; ~ *student* étudiante *f*; **~hood** état *m* de femme; **~ish** féminin; efféminé (*man*); **~kind** les femmes *f/pl.*; **~ly** féminin.

womb *anat.* utérus *m*; *fig.* sein *m*.

women *pl. of woman*; **~'s lib** mouvement *m* de libération de la femme; **~folk** *pl.*, **~kind** les femmes *f/pl.* (*esp. of a family*).

wonder 1. merveille *f*, miracle *m*; étonnement *m*; **2.** s'étonner, s'émerveiller (de, **at**); se demander (si *whether*, *if*); **~ful** merveilleux, étonnant; **~ing** émerveillé, étonne.

wondrous merveilleux.

wonky F chancelant; peu solide.

wont 1.: *be ~ to* (*inf.*) avoir l'habitude de (*inf.*); **2.** habitude *f*; **~ed** accoutumé.

woo faire la cour à.

wood bois *m*; F *touch ~!* touchez du bois!; **~ carving** sculpture *f* sur bois; **~cock** *orn.* (*pl. usu. ~*) bécasse *f*; **~cut** gravure *f* sur bois; **~cutter** bûcheron *m*; graveur *m* sur bois; **~ed** boisé; **~en** en bois; de bois; **~land(s** *pl.*) bois, pays *m* boisé; **~pecker** *orn.* pic *m*, **~wind** ♩ bois *m/pl.*; **~work** *esp.* △ boiserie *f*; menuiserie *f*; travail *m* sur bois; **~worm** ver *m* du bois; **~y** boisé; ♀ ligneux; *fig.* sourd, mat.

wool laine *f*, **~gathering 1.** rêvasserie *f*; *go ~* avoir l'esprit absent, rêvasser, rêver; **~(l)en 1.** de laine; lainière (*industry etc.*); **2.: ~s** *pl.* lainages *m/pl.*; **~(l)y 1.** laineux; de laine; cotonneux (*fruit*); *fig.* flou, imprécis (*idea*); **2.** **wool(l)ies** *pl.* lainages *m/pl.*

word 1. *usu.* mot *m*; parole *f* (*u. fig.*); **~s** *pl.* of a song: paroles *f/pl.*; *by ~ of mouth* de vive voix; *have ~s* se disputer (avec, *with*); *in other ~s* autrement dit; *take s.o. at his ~* prendre q. au mot; **2.** formuler; **~ing** langage *m*, termes *m/pl.*; **~splitting** ergotage *m*; **~y** verbeux.

work 1. travail *m*; ouvrage *m*, œuvre *f* (*a. literature etc.*); ⊕ **~s** *usu. sg.* usine *f*; *clock*: mouvement *m*; **~ of art** œuvre *f* d'art; *at ~* au travail; en marche; *fig.* en jeu; *be in ~* avoir du travail; *be out of ~* chômer, être sans travail; *set to ~* se mettre au travail; **~s council** comité *m* d'entreprise; **2.** *v/i.* travailler; fonctionner, aller (*machine*); *fig.* faire son effet, réussir; *~ at* travailler (à); *~ out* sortir peu à peu; s'élever (à, *at*); aboutir; *v/t.* faire travailler; faire fonctionner *or* marcher (*a machine*); diriger (*a project*); opérer, façonner; faire (*a calculation*); résoudre (*a problem*); exploiter (*a mine*); *~ loose* se défaire; se détacher; se desserrer (*screw etc.*); *~ off* se dégager (de); cuver (*one's anger*); ♥ écouler (*stock*); *~ one's way* se frayer un che-

min; *~ out* mener à bien; élaborer, développer; résoudre; *~ up* développer; exciter, émouvoir; élaborer (*an idea*).

work|able réalisable (*project*); ouvrable (*wood etc.*); exploitable (*mine*); **~aday** de tous les jours; *fig.* prosaïque; **~day** jour *m* ouvrable; **~ed-up** énervé; *be* (*get*) *~* a. être (se mettre) dans tous ses états; **~er** travailleur (-euse *f*) *m*; ouvrier (-ère *f*) *m*; **~s** *pl.* classes *f/pl.* laborieuses; ouvriers *m/pl.*; *social ~* assistant *f* sociale; **~force** main-d'œuvre *f*, *les ouvriers m/pl.*; **~ing 1.** fonctionnement *m*; manœuvre *f*; exploitation *f*; **2.** qui travaille; qui fonctionne; de travail; ♥ *~ capital* capital *m* d'exploitation; *~ class* classe *f* ouvrière; *~ day* jour *m* ouvrable; journée *f* (de travail); (*in*) *~ order* (en) état *m* de marche *or* de fonctionnement; *~ process* mode *m* d'opération; **~load** travail *m*.

workman ouvrier *m*, artisan *m*; **~like** bien travaillé, bien fait; compétent; **~ship** exécution *f*; habileté *f* (professionnelle); travail *m*.

work...: ~out entraînement *m* (préliminaire); **~shop** atelier *m*; **~-to-rule** grève *f* du zèle.

world 1. monde *m*; *fig. a. ~ of* beaucoup de; *in the ~* au monde; *what in the ~?* que diable?; *bring* (*come*) *into the ~* mettre (venir) au monde; *think the ~ of* avoir une très haute opinion de; *man of the ~* homme *m* qui connaît la vie; mondain *m*; **~('s** *Am*) *record* record *m* mondial; **2.** du monde (*champion[ship]* *etc.*); mondial.

worldly du monde, de ce monde; **~wise** qui connaît la vie.

world...: ~-power *pol.* puissance *f* mondiale; **~-weary** las du monde; **~-wide** universel; mondial.

worm 1. ver *m* (*a. fig.*); vis *f* sans fin; **2.: ~** *a secret out of s.o.* tirer un secret de q.; *~ one's way, ~ o.s.* se glisser; *fig.* s'insinuer (dans, *into*); **~-eaten** rongé par les vers; vermoulu (*bois*).

worn-out usé, râpé (*clothes*); épuisé.

worry 1. (s')inquiéter; *v/i. a.* se soucier; **2.** ennui *m*; souci *m*.

worse 1. *adj.* pire; plus mauvais; *adv.* plus mal; pis; (*all*) *the ~ adv.* encore pis; *adj.* (encore) pire; *the ~ for wear* épuisé; maltraité; *get ~* empirer; se détério-

rer, se dégrader; **2.** *su.* pire *m*; *change*
for the ~ dégradation *f*, détérioriation
f; F ~ *luck* pas de veine!; **~n** empirer;
(s')aggraver.

worship 1. adoration *f*, culte *m*; **2.** adorer; **~(p)er** adorateur (-trice *f*) *m*; *eccl.*
fidèle *mf*.

worst 1. *adj.* (le) pire; (le) plus mauvais;
2. *adv.* le pis, le plus mal; **3.** *su.* le pire
m; *at (the)* ~ au pis aller; **4.** *v/t.* vaincre,
battre.

worsted laine *f* peignée.

worth 1.: *be* ~ valoir (*qch.*); mériter de
(*inf.*); *be* ~ *it* (en) valoir la peine; *for all*
one is ~ de toutes ses forces; **2.** valeur *f*;
money: ... ~ *of s.th.* pour ... de *qch.*;
~less sans valeur; **~while:** *be* ~ (en)
valoir la peine; **~y** digne (*of*, **of**).

would-be prétendu; soi-disant.

wound 1. blessure *f*; **2.** blesser (à, *in the*
arm etc.).

wow *sl.* grand succès *m*.

wrangle 1. se chamailler, se quereller; **2.**
querelle *f*, chamaille(rie) *f*; **~r** querelleur (-euse *f*) *m*; (*a.* *horse* ~) cowboy *m*.

wrap 1. *v/t.* (*oft.* ~ *up*) envelopper (de,
in) (*a. fig.*); *fig.* **be ~ped up in** être
plongé dans; *v/i.* ~ *up* s'envelopper,
s'emmitoufler (dans, *in*); **2.** couverture
f; *cost.* pélerine *f*, écharpe *f*; **~per** couverture *f*; (*a.* *postal* ~) bande *f*; **~ping**
enveloppe(ment) *f*; (*a.* ~ *paper*) papier *m* d'emballage; *for gift:* papier *m*
cadeau; **~-up** F résumé *m*.

wrath courroux *m*.

wreak assouvir (*one's hatred, one's fury,*
one's vengeance) (sur, [*up*]on).

wreath, *pl.* **~s** *flowers:* couronne *f*; guirlande *f*; panache *m*, volute *f* (*of smoke*).

wreathe *v/t.* couronner; enguirlander;
fig. enrouler; envelopper; *v/i.* s'enrouler.

wreck 1. ♠ naufrage *m* (*a. fig.*); ♠ épave
f (*a. fig.*); *fig.* ruine *f*; navire *m* naufragé; **2.** causer le naufrage de; *fig.* faire
échouer, démolir, ruiner; ♠ **be ~ed** faire naufrage; **~age** ♠ épave *f*; *fig.* décombres *m/pl.*, débris *m/pl.*; *fig.* anéantisse-
ment *m*, ruine *f*; **~ed** naufragé; *fig.* dé-
moli, ruiné; **~er** démolisseur *m* (*a.* de
bâtiments); ♠ sauveteur *m* (d'épaves);
mot. Am. dépanneuse *f*; *Am.* marchand
m de voitures délabrées, marchand *m*
de ferraille.

wren *orn.* roitelet *m*.

wrench 1. tordre; arracher (violemment) (à, *from*); tourner (violemment)
sur; ~ *open* forcer (*a door etc.*); ~ *out*
arracher; **2.** mouvement *m or* effort *m*
de torsion; effort *m* violent; *fig.* violente douleur *f*; ⊕ clef *f* à écrous.

wrest arracher (à, *from*).

wrestle 1. *v/i.* lutter; *v/t.* lutter avec *or*
contre; **2.** (*a.* *wrestling*) lutte *f*.

wretch malheureux (-euse *f*) *m*; *poor* ~
pauvre diable *m*; **~ed** misérable; F
diable de ..., sacré.

wriggle (se) tortiller, (s')agiter, (se) remuer; ~ *out of* se tirer de.

wring tordre; essorer (*wet clothes*).

wrinkle 1. ride *f*; *dress:* pli *m*; **2.** (se)
rider; (se) plisser; (se) froisser.

wrist poignet *m*; ~ *watch* montre-brace-
let (*pl.* montres-bracelets) *f*; **~band**
poignet *m*; bracelet *m*.

writ mandat *m*, ordonnance *f*; acte *m*
judiciaire; assignation *f*; *Holy* ⩔ Écriture *f* sainte.

write *v/t.* écrire; rédiger (*an article*); F
it's nothing to ~ *home about* ça ne
casse pas les vitres; ~ *back* répondre
(par écrit); ~ *down* noter; mettre (*qch.*)
par écrit; ~ *off* ♥ passer aux profits et
pertes, annuler; *fig.* abandonner, faire
son deuil de; regarder comme perdu;
fig. car etc. abîmer complètement; ~
out écrire (en toutes lettres, *in full*);
rédiger (*a report etc.*); (re)copier,
mettre au net (*notes etc.*); remplir (*a
cheque*); ~ *up* (re)copier, mettre au net
(*notes etc.*); rédiger (*an article, report
etc.*); écrire un article élogieux sur;
~off perte *f* totale *or* sèche; *v/i.* écrire;
être écrivain; **~r** écrivain *m*; auteur *m*;
~-up critique *f*; compte rendu *m*; éloge
m.

writhe se tordre.

writing écriture *f*; art *m* d'écrire; métier
m d'écrivain; (**~s** *pl.*) écrits *m/pl.*,
œuvre(s) *f*(*pl.*); *in* ~ par écrit; ~ *desk*
secrétaire *m*, bureau *m*; ~ *pad*
sous-main *m*; bloc-notes *m*; ~ *paper* papier *m* à écrire.

written (fait par) écrit.

wrong 1. mauvais; faux; inexact; erroné; *be* ~ être faux; être mal (de *inf.*, *to*
inf.); ne pas être à l'heure (*watch*); avoir
tort (*person*); *go* ~ se tromper (*a.* de

chemin); ***there is something*** ~ il y a quelque chose qui ne va pas *or* qui cloche; ***what's ~?*** qu'est-ce qui ne va pas?; F ***what's ~ with him?*** qu'est-ce qu'il a?; ***be on the ~ side of sixty*** avoir dépassé la soixantaine; **2.** mal *m*; tort *m*; ⚖ dommage *m*; ***be in the ~*** avoir tort; **3.** faire tort à; être injuste envers; **~doer** malfaiteur (-trice *f*) *m*; **~doing** méfaits *m/pl.*; **~ful** injuste; injustifié; **~ly** à tort.

wrought: ⊕ ~ ***iron*** fer *m* forgé.

wry tordu; *fig.* désabusé (*smile, expression etc.*); ***pull a ~ face*** faire la grimace.

X

xenophobia xénophobie *f*

xerox (*TM*) **1.** photocopie *f*; **2.** photocopier.

Xmas F Noël *m*; *see a.* ***Christmas***.

X-ray 1.: **~s** *pl.* rayons *m/pl.* X; **2.** radiologique; **3.** radiographier.

xylophone ♪ xylophone *m*.

Y

yacht ⚓ **1.** yacht *m*; **2.** faire du yachting; **~ing** yachting *m*.

Yankee F Amerlot *m*.

yap japper; F criailler.

yard[1] *measure*: yard *m*; ⚓ vergue *f*.

yard[2] cour *f*; chantier *m* (*of work*); dépôt *m* (*of coal, a.* 🚂).

yardstick *fig.* étalon *m*, critère *m*.

yarn fil *m*; F (longue) histoire *f*.

yawl ⚓ yole *f*.

yawn 1. bâiller; **2.** bâillement *m*; **~ing** *fig.* béant (*opening etc.*).

yea oui.

year an *m*; année *f*; **~book** annuaire *m*, almanach *m*; **~long** qui dure un an, d'un an, d'une année; **~ly 1.** *adj.* annuel; **2.** *adv.* tous les ans; une fois par an.

yearn languir (pour, ***for***; après, ***after***); aspirer (à, ***for***; à *inf.*; ***to*** *inf.*); **~ing 1.** envie *f* (de, ***for***); désir *m* ardent; **2.** ardent; plein d'envie.

yeast levure *f*; levain *m*.

yell 1. *vt/i.* hurler; *v/i.* crier à tue-tête; **2.** hurlement *m*; cri *m*.

yellow 1. jaune; ***~ press*** presse *f* à sensation; **2.** jaune *m*; **3.** jaunir; **~ish** jaunâtre.

yelp 1. jappement *m*; **2.** japper.

yen désir *m* (ardent).

yes 1. oui; *after negative question*: si; **2.** oui *m*.

yesterday hier (*a. su./m*).

yet 1. *adv.* encore; jusqu'ici; jusque-là; déjà; malgré tout; ***as ~*** jusqu'à présent; ***not ~*** pas encore; **2.** *cj.* (et) cependant; tout de même.

yew ♀ if *m*.

Yiddish yiddish *m*, *adj*.

yield 1. *v/t.* rendre; donner; produire; céder (*ground, a town etc.*); rapporter (*a.* † *a profit*); *v/i. esp.* ✓ rendre; céder (à ***to, beneath***); **2.** rapport *m*; rendement *m*; **~ing** peu résistant; *fig.* accommodant.

yodel 1. tyrolienne *f*; **2.** faire des tyroliennes.

yoga yoga *m*.

yoghourt, yog(h)urt yaourt *m*.

yoke 1. joug *m*; **2.** accoupler; atteler; *fig.* unir.

yokel F rustre *m*.

yolk jaune *m* (d'œuf).

yonder là-bas.

yore: *of ~* (d')autrefois.

you 1. tu; *stressed and dative*: toi; *accusative*: te; *a*. on; 2. vous.

young 1. jeune; petit (*animal*); 2. petit *m* (*of animals*); *the ~ pl.* les jeunes gens *m/pl.*; *~ish* assez jeune; *~ster* F jeune homme *m*; petit(e *f*) *m*.

your 1. ton, ta, tes; 2. votre, vos; *~s* 1. le tien, la tienne, les tiens, les tiennes; à toi; 2. le (la) vôtre, les vôtres; à vous; *~self* toi-même; *rfl.* te, *stressed*: toi; *~selves pl.* vous-mêmes; *rfl.* vous (*a. stressed*).

youth jeunesse *f*; (*pl. ~s*) jeune homme *m*, adolescent *m*; *~ hostel* auberge *f* de la jeunesse; *~ful* juvénile; de jeunesse; jeune (*look etc.*).

Yugoslav 1. yougoslave; 2. Yougoslave *mf*.

Yule Noël; *~tide* Noël *f*.

Z

zany loufoque; burlesque.

zap F 1. *v/t.* attaquer, agresser; assommer; détruire, abîmer; faire à la hâte; *v/i.* filer (à toute allure); 2. vigueur *f*, énergie *f*, entrain *m*.

zeal zèle *m*; *~ot* zélateur (-trice *f*) *m*; *~otry* fanatisme *m*; *~ous* zélé; zélateur.

zebra *zo.* zèbre *m*; *~ crossing* passage *m* clouté.

zenith zénith *m*; *fig. a.* apogée *m*.

zero 1. zéro *m*; 2. zéro *inv.*, nul; *~ growth* (**option, point**) croissance *f* (option *f*, point *m*) zéro; *~ hour* l'heure *f* H; 3. *~ in on* ✗ régler le tir sur; *fig.* diriger son attention sur.

zest 1. saveur *f*, goût *m*; enthousiasme *m* (pour, *for*); élan *m*; verve *f*; *lemon etc.*: zeste *m*; 2. épicer.

zigzag 1. zigzag *m*; 2. zigzaguer.

zinc 1. *min.* zinc *m*; 2. zinguer.

zip 1. F entrain *m*, énergie *f*; (*a. ~ fastener, ~per*) fermeture *f* éclair (*TM*); *Am. ~ code* code *m* postal; 2. filer (à toute allure); siffler; (*a. ~ up, ~ shut*) fermer (avec une fermeture éclair).

zodiac *astr.* zodiaque *m*.

zone 1. zone *f*; secteur *m*; 2. diviser en zones *or* secteurs; *~ as, ~ for* réserver à.

zoo zoo *m*.

zoolog|ical zoologique; *~y* zoologie *f*.

zoom 1. filer (à toute vitesse); vrombir, bourdonner; (*a. ~ up*) monter en flèche; *~ past* passer en trombe; 2. vrombissement *m*, bourdonnement *m*; *phot.* (*a. ~ lens*) zoom *m*.

French Proper Names

A

Açores [aˈsɔːr] *f/pl. the* Azores.
Adriatique [adriaˈtik] *f* Adriatic (Sea).
Afrique [aˈfrik] *f: l'~* Africa.
Albanie [albaˈni] *f: l'~* Albania.
Alger [alˈʒe] Algiers.
Algérie [alʒeˈri] *f: l'~* Algeria.
Allemagne [alˈmaɲ] *f: l'~* Germany.
Alpes [alp] *f/pl.* Alps.
Alsace [alˈzas] *f: l'~* Alsace, Alsatia.
Amérique [ameˈrik] *f. l'~* America
Andorre [ãˈdɔːr] *f* Andorra
Angleterre [ãgləˈtɛːr] *f: l'~* England.
Anglo-Normand [ãglɔnɔrˈmã]: *les îles f/pl. ~es* the Channel Islands.
Antarctique [ãtar(k)ˈtik] *m: l'~* the Antarctic.
Anvers [ãˈvɛːr, ~ˈvɛrs] Antwerp.
Arabie [araˈbi] *f: l'~* Arabia; *l'~ Saoudite* Saudi Arabia.
Arctique [arkˈtik] *m: l'~* the Arctic.
Argentine [arʒãˈtin] *f: l'~* Argentina, the Argentine.
Asie [aˈzi] *f: l'~* Asia; *l'~ Mineure* Asia Minor.
Athènes [aˈtɛn] *f* Athens.
Atlantique [atlãˈtik] *m* Atlantic (Ocean).
Aurigny [ɔriˈɲi] Alderney.
Australie [ɔstraˈli] *f: l'~* Australia.
Autriche [oˈtriʃ] *f: l'~* Austria.

B

Bahamas [baaˈmas] *f/pl.: les (îles f/pl.) ~* the Bahamas, the Bahama Islands.
Balkans [balˈkã] *m/pl.: les ~* the Balkan Peninsula *sg.*
Baltique [balˈtik] *f: la ~* the Baltic (Sea).
Basque [bask]: *le pays ~* the Basque Provinces *pl. (in Spain);* the Basque Region *(in France).*
Belgique [bɛlˈʒik] *f: la ~* Belgium.
Belgrade [bɛlˈgrad] Belgrade.
Bermudes [bɛrˈmyd] *f/pl. the* Bermudas.

Berne [bɛrn] Bern(e).
Beyrouth [bɛˈrut] Beirut.
Bolivie [bɔliˈvi] *f: la ~* Bolivia.
Bourget [burˈʒɛ]: *lac m du ~* French *lake;* **Le ~** [laburˈʒɛ] *airport of Paris.*
Bourgogne [burˈgɔɲ] *f: la ~* Burgundy *(old province of France).*
Brésil [breˈzil] *m: le ~* Brazil.
Bretagne [brəˈtaɲ] *f: la ~* Brittany.
Bruxelles [bryˈsɛl] Brussels.
Bucarest [bykaˈrɛst] Bucharest.
Bulgarie [bylgaˈri] *f: la ~* Bulgaria

C

Caire, Le [ləˈkɛːr] Cairo.
Cambodge [kãˈbɔdʒ] *m: le ~* Cambodia.
Canada [kanaˈda] *m: le ~* Canada.
Canaries [kanaˈri] *f/pl · les (îles f/pl.) ~* the Canary Islands.
Caucase [koˈkaːz] *m* Caucasus.
Centre [ˈsãtr(ə)] *m: le ~* Central France.
Cervin [sɛrˈvɛ̃]: *le mont m ~* the Matterhorn.
Chili [ʃiˈli] *m: le ~* Chile, Chili.
Chine [ʃin] *f: la ~* China.
Chypre [ʃipr] *f* Cyprus.
Colombie [kɔlɔ̃ˈbi] *f: la ~* Colombia.
Copenhague [kɔpəˈnag] Copenhagen.
Corée [kɔˈre] *f: la ~* Korea.
Corse [kɔrs] *f: la ~* Corsica *(French island; department of France).*
Côte d'Azur [kotdaˈzyːr] *f the* French Riviera.
Crète [krɛt] *f: la ~* Crete.
Crimée [kriˈme] *f: la ~* the Crimea.
Croatie [krɔaˈsi]: *la ~* Croatia.
Cuba [kyˈba]: *(île f de ~)* Cuba.

D

Danemark [danˈmark] *m: le ~* Denmark.
Douvres [duːvr] Dover.
Dunkerque [dœ̃ˈkɛrk] Dunkirk.

E

Écosse [e'kɔs] *f* Scotland.
Édimbourg [edɛ̃'buːr] Edinburgh.
Égypte [e'ʒipt] *f:* *l'~* Egypt.
Elbe [ɛlb] *f:* *l'île d'~* Elba.
Équateur [ekwa'tœːr] Ecuador.
Espagne [ɛs'paɲ] *f* Spain.
États-Unis d'Amérique [etazynidame-̩'rik] *m/pl.* the U.S.A.
Éthiopie [etjɔ'pi] *f* Ethiopia.
Europe [ø'rɔp] *f:* *l'~* Europe.

F

Finlande [fɛ̃'lãːd] *f* Finland.
Flandre [flãːdr] *f:* *la ~* Flanders.
France [frãːs] *f:* *la ~* France.

G

Galles [gal] *f:* *le pays m de ~* Wales.
Gand [gã] Ghent.
Gange [gãːʒ] *m* the Ganges.
Gascogne [gas'kɔɲ] *f:* *la ~* Gascony; *le golfe de ~* the Bay of Biscay.
Gênes [ʒɛn] *f* Genoa.
Genève [ʒə'nɛːv] Geneva.
Grande-Bretagne [grãdbrə'taɲ] *f:* *la ~* Great Britain.
Grèce [grɛs] *f:* *la ~* Greece.
Groenland [grɔɛn'lãːd] *m:* *le ~* Greenland.
Guatémala [gwatema'la] *m:* *le ~* Guatemala.
Guinée [gi'ne] *f:* *la ~* Guinea.
Guyane [gɥi'jan] *f:* *la ~* Guiana.

H

Haïti [ai'ti] *f* Haiti.
Haye, La [la'*ɛ] the Hague.
Hollande [*ɔ'lãːd] *f:* *la ~* Holland.
Honduras [*ɔndu'rɑːs] *m:* *le ~* Honduras.
Hongrie [*ɔ̃'gri] *f:* *la ~* Hungary.

I

Inde [ɛ̃ːd] *f:* *l'~* India.
Indien [ɛ̃'djɛ̃]: *océan m ~* Indian Ocean.
Indochine [ɛ̃dɔ'ʃin] *f:* *l'~* Indochina.
Indonésie [ɛ̃dɔne'zi] *f:* *l'~* Indonesia.
Irak, Iraq [i'rak] *m:* *l'~* Irak, Iraq.

Iran [i'rã] *m:* *l'~* Iran.
Irlande [ir'lãːd] *f:* *l'~* Ireland.
Islande [is'lãːd] *f:* *l'~* Iceland.
Israël [isra'ɛl] *m* Israel.
Italie [ita'li] *f:* *l'~* Italy.

J

Jamaïque [ʒama'ik] *f:* *la ~* Jamaica.
Japon [ʒa'põ] *m:* *le ~* Japan.
Jérusalem [ʒeryza'lɛm] Jerusalem.
Jordanie [ʒɔrda'ni] *f:* *la ~* Jordan.

K

Karpates [kar'pat] *f/pl.* Carpathians.
Kremlin [krɛm'lɛ̃] *m* the Kremlin.
Koweït [kɔ'wɛjt] Kuweit.

L

Laos [la'oːs] *m:* *le ~* Laos.
Léman [le'mã] *m:* *le lac m ~* the lake of Geneva, Lake Leman.
Liban [li'bã] *m:* *le ~* Lebanon.
Lisbonne [liz'bɔn] Lisbon.
Londres [lõːdr] London.
Luxembourg [luksã'buːr] *m* Luxemb(o)urg; *gardens in Paris.*

M

Madère [ma'dɛːr] *f* Madeira.
Malaisie [male'zi] *f:* *la ~* Malaysia.
Malte [malt] *f* Malta.
Manche [mãːʃ] *f:* *la ~* the English Channel; *department of France.*
Maroc [ma'rɔk] *m:* *le ~* Morocco.
Marseille [mar'sɛːj] Marseilles.
Maurice [mɔ'ris]: *l'île f ~* Mauritius.
Méditerranée [meditɛra'ne] *f:* *la ~* the Mediterranean.
Mexico [mɛksi'ko] Mexico City.
Mexique [mɛk'sik] *m:* *le ~* Mexico.
Monaco [mɔna'ko] *m* Monaco.
Mongolie [mõgɔ'li] *f:* *la ~* Mongolia.
Montréal [mõre'al] Montreal.
Moscou [mɔs'ku] Moscow.
Moyen-Orient [mwaɛnɔr'jã] *m:* *le ~* the Middle East.

N

Nil [nil] *m* Nile.
Nord [nɔːr] *m*; *la mer f du ~* the North Sea.

Normandie [nɔrmɑ̃'di] *f: la ~* Normandy (*old province of France*).
Norvège [nɔr'vɛːʒ] *f: la ~* Norway.
Nouvelle-Zélande [nuvɛlze'lɑ̃:d] *f* New Zealand.

O

Océanie [ɔsea'ni] *f: l'~* Oceania.
Orcades [ɔr'kad] *f/pl.* the Orkneys.
Orléans [ɔrle'ɑ̃]; *la Nouvelle ~* New Orleans.
Orly [ɔr'li] *airport of Paris.*
Ostende [ɔs'tɑ̃:d] *f* Ostend.
Oural [u'ral] Ural.

P

Pacifique [pasi'fik] *m. le ~* the Pacific (Ocean).
Pakistan [pakis'tɑ̃] *m: le ~* Pakistan.
Palestine [palɛs'tin] *f: la ~* Palestine.
Panamá [pana'ma] *m: le ~* Panama.
Paraguay [para'gɛ] *m: le ~* Paraguay.
Pas de Calais [padka'lɛ] *m* Straits *pl.* of Dover.
Pays-Bas [pei'bɑ] *m/pl.: les ~* the Netherlands.
Pékin [pe'kɛ̃] Peki(n)g.
Pérou [pe'ru] *m: le ~* Peru.
Persique [pɛr'sik]: *le golfe ~* Persian Gulf.
Philippines [fili'pin] *f/pl.: les ~* the Philippines.
Pologne [pɔ'lɔɲ] *f: la ~* Poland.
Polynésie [pɔline'zi] *f: la ~* Polynesia.
Portugal [pɔrty'gal] *m: le ~* Portugal.
Proche-Orient [prɔʃɔr'jɑ̃] *m: le ~* the Near East.
Pyrénées [pire'ne] *f/pl.* Pyrenees.

Q

Québec [ke'bɛk] Quebec.

R

Reims [rɛ̃s] Rheims (*French town*).
Rhin [rɛ̃] *m* Rhine.
Roumanie [ruma'ni] *f: la ~* Rumania.
Royaume Uni [rwajo:my'ni] *m* the United Kingdom.
Russie [ru'si] *f: la ~* Russia.

S

Saint-Laurent [sɛ̃lo'rɑ̃] *m* the St. Lawrence.

Saint-Marin [sɛ̃ma'rɛ̃] *m* San Marino.
Sardaigne [sar'dɛɲ] *f: la ~* Sardinia.
Sarre [sar] *f: la ~* the Saar.
Savoie [sa'vwa] *f: la ~* Savoy (*department of France*).
Scandinavie [skãdina'vi] *f: la ~* Scandinavia.
Serbie [sɛr'bi] *f: la ~* Serbia.
Sibérie [sibe'ri] *f: la ~* Siberia.
Sicile [si'sil] *f: la ~* Sicily.
Slovaquie [slɔva'ki] *f: la ~* Slovakia.
Strasbourg [straz'buːr] Strasb(o)urg.
Suède [sɥɛd] *f: la ~* Sweden.
Suez [sɥɛz] *m* Suez.
Suisse [sɥis] *f: la ~* Switzerland.
Syrie [si'ri] *f: la ~* Syria.

T

Tamise [ta'miːz] *f: la ~* the Thames.
Tanger [tɑ̃'ʒe] Tangier.
Tchécoslovaquie [tʃekɔslɔva'ki] *f: la ~* Czechoslovakia.
Terre-Neuve [tɛr'nœːv] *f* Newfoundland.
Tibet [ti'bɛ] *m: le ~* Tibet.
Thaïlande [taj'lɑ̃:d] *f: la ~* Thailand.
Tunisie [tyni'zi] *f: la ~* Tunisia.
Turquie [tyr'ki] *f: la ~* Turkey.

U

Uruguay [yry'gɛ] *m: l'~* Uruguay.

V

Varsovie [varsɔ'vi] Warsaw.
Vatican [vati'kɑ̃] *m: le ~* the Vatican.
Venezuela [venezɥe'la] *m: le ~* Venezuela.
Venise [və'niz] *f* Venice.
Vienne [vjɛn] *f* Vienna (*capital of Austria*).
Viêt-nam [vjɛt'nam] *m: le ~* Vietnam.

Y

Yémen [je'mɛn] *m: le ~* Yemen.

Z

Zurich [zy'rik] *m* Zurich.

Common French Abbreviations

A

A *ampère* ampere.

A.C.F. *Automobile Club de France* Automobile Association of France.

act. *action* share.

à dr. *à droite* on *or* to the right.

AELE *Association européenne de libre échange* EFTA, European Free Trade Association.

A.F. *Allocations familiales* family allowance.

A.F.P. *Agence France-Presse* French press agency.

à g. *à gauche* on *or* to the left.

A.O.C. *appellation d'origine contrôlée* guaranteed vintage.

ap. J.-C. *après Jésus-Christ* A.D., anno Domini.

arr. *arrondissement* district.

av. *avenue* avenue; *avoir* credit.

av. J.-C. *avant Jésus-Christ* B.C., before Jesus Christ.

B

B.D. *bande dessinée* cartoon; comic.

Bd. *boulevard* boulevard.

BENELUX *Belgique-Nederland-Luxembourg* BENELUX, Belgium, Netherlands, Luxemb(o)urg.

B.P. *boîte postale* POB, Post Office Box.

C

C *degré Celsius* degree centigrade.

c. *centime* (*hundredth part of a franc*).

c.-à-d. *c'est-à-dire* i.e., that is to say.

C.A.F. *coût, assurance, fret* c.i.f., cost, insurance, freight.

C.C. *corps consulaire* consular corps.

CCI *Chambre de Commerce internationale* ICC, International Chamber of Commerce.

C.C.P. *compte chèques postaux* postal cheque account.

C.D. *corps diplomatique* diplomatic corps.

CE *Conseil de l'Europe* Council of Europe.

CEE *Communauté économique européenne* E.E.C., European Economic Community.

CERN *Organisation européenne pour la recherche nucléaire* European Organization for Nuclear Research.

C.E.S. *collège d'enseignement secondaire* (*Secondary School*).

C.E.T. *collège d'enseignement technique* (*a technical college*).

Cf. *conférez* cf., compare.

C.G.T. *Confédération générale du travail* General confederation of Labour.

ch *cheval*(*-vapeur*) H.P., h.p., horsepower.

ch.-l. *chef-lieu* capital.

Cie., *Cie. Compagnie* Co., Company.

CIO *Comité international olympique* IOC, International Olympic Committee.

cl *centilitre* centiliter.

cm *centimètre* centimeter.

C.N.P.F. *Conseil national du patronat français* (*employers' association*).

C.N.R.S. *Centre national de la recherche scientifique* (*approx.*) S.R.C., Scientific Research Centre.

ct. *courant* inst., instant.

C.V. *cheval-vapeur* H.P., h.p., horsepower; *cette ville* this town.

D

dép. *départ* departure.

dépt. *département* administrative department.

D.E.U.G. [døg] *diplôme d'études universitaires générales* certificate of general studies at university level.

D.O.M.-T.O.M., *Dom-Tom* [dɔm'tɔm] *départements, territoires d'outre-mer* overseas administrative departments and territories.

D.P.L.G. *Diplômé par le gouvernement* state certificated.
Dr *Docteur* Dr., Doctor.

E

E. *est* E., east.
E.N.A. *École nationale d'administration* national administrative school.
env. *environ* about.
etc. *et cætera* etc., etcetera.
Éts *établissements* establishments.
É.-U. *États-Unis* U.S.A,, United States.
ex. *exemple* example.
exp. *expéditeur* consigner.

F

F *franc* franc; **°F** *degré Fahrenheit* degree Fahrenheit.
FB *franc(s) belge(s)* Belgian franc(s).
F.E.N. *Fédération de l'éducation nationale* National Education Federation.
FF *franc(s) français* French franc(s).
fig. *figure* figure.
FMI *Fond monétaire international* IMF, International Monetary Fund.
F.N.A.C. *Fédération nationale d'achats des cadres* (*department store [chain] for high-quality goods*).
F.O. *Force Ouvrière* (*a Socialist trade union*).
FR 3 *France trois* channel three (*on French television*).
FS *franc(s) suisse(s)* Swiss franc(s).
F.S. *faire suivre* please forward.

G

g *gramme* gram(me).
G.O. *grandes ondes* L.W., long wave(s).

H

h *heure* hour, o'clock.
ha *hectare* hectare.
H.E.C. (*École des*) *Hautes Etudes commerciales* School of Advanced Commercial and Management Studies, Paris.
H.L.M. *habitations à loyer modéré* property to let at moderate rents.

I

I.F.O.P. [iˈfɔp] *Institut français d'opinion publique* (*state institute monitoring public opinion*).
I.U.T. *Institut universitaire de technologie* (*a technical college*).
I.V.G. *interruption volontaire de grossesse* voluntary termination of pregnancy.

J

J.-C. *Jésus-Christ* J.C., Jesus (Christ).
J.O. *Journal officiel* Official Gazette.

K

kg *kilogramme* kilogram(me).
km *kilomètre* kilometer.
km/h *kilomètres par heure* kilometers per hour.
kW *kilowatt* k.w., kilowatt.
kWh *kilowatt-heure* kilowatt-hour.

L

l *litre* liter.
loc. cit. *loco citato* at the place cited.

M

M. *Monsieur* Mr., Mister.
m *mètre* meter.
mb *millibar* millibar.
Me *Maître* (*barrister's title*).
mg *milligramme* milligram(me).
M.L.F. *Mouvement de libération des femmes* Women's Liberation Movement.
Mlle *Mademoiselle* Miss.
Mlles *Mesdemoiselles* the Misses.
MM. *Messieurs* Messrs.
mm *millimètre* millimeter.
Mme *Madame* Mrs., Mistress.
Mmes *Mesdames* Mesdames.
mn *minute* minute.
ms *manuscrit* MS., manuscript.

N

N. *nord* N., North, *nom* name.
N.B. *notez bien* N.B., note well.
N.D.L.R. *note de la rédaction* editor's note.
N.E. *nord-est* N.E., north-east.

N°., n° numéro number.
N.O., N.W. nord-ouest N.W., Northwest.

O

O. ouest W., west.
OAS Organisation de l'Armée Secrète Secret Army Organization.
O.C. ondes courtes s.w., short wave(s).
OCDE Organisation de coopération et de développement économiques O.E.C.D., Organization for Economic Co-operation and Development.
OIT Organisation internationale du travail ILO, International Labour Organization.
O.L.P. Organisation de libération de la Palestine PLO, Palestine Liberation Organization.
OMS Organisation mondiale de la santé WHO, World Health Organization.
ONU Organisation des Nations Unies UNO, United Nations Organization.
O.P.E.P. [ɔˈpep] **Organisation des pays exportateurs de pétrole** OPEC, Organization of Petroleum Exporting Countries.
O.S. ouvrier spécialisé semi-skilled worker.
OTAN Organisation du Traité de l'Atlantique Nord NATO, North Atlantic Treaty Organization.
OTASE Organisation du Traité de défense collective pur l'Asie du Sud-Est SEATO, Southeast Asia Treaty Organization.

P

P. Père Fr., Father.
p. pour per; **par** per; **page** page.
P.C. Parti Communiste Communist Party.
p.c.c. pour copie conforme true copy.
P.D.G. président-directeur général chairman (of the board).
p.ex. par exemple e.g., for example.
P.J. Police judiciaire (approx.) C.I.D., Criminal Investigation Department.
P.M.E. petites et moyennes entreprises small businesses.
P.N.B. produit national brut gross national product.
P.O. par ordre by order.
P.-S. post-scriptum P.S., postscript.

P.T.T. Postes, Télégraphes, Téléphones (French) G.P.O., General Post Office.
P.V. petite vitesse per goods train; **procès-verbal** (see main dictionary).

Q

q. carré square; **quintal** quintal.
Q.G. Quartier général H.Q., Headquarters.
Q.I. quotient intellectuel I.Q., intelligence quotient.

R

R, r. rue Rd., road, street.
R.A.T.P. régie autonome des transports parisiens (Paris Public Transport Board).
R.C. registre du commerce register of trade.
Rem. remarque annotation.
R.E.R. Réseau express régional (commuter-train network).
R.F. République française French Republic.
R.F.A. République fédérale d'Allemagne F.R.G., Federal Republic of Germany.
R.N. route nationale (approx.) National Highway.
R.P. réponse payée R.P., reply paid.
R.S.V.P. répondez, s'il vous plaît the favour of an answer is requested.

S

S. sud S., south; **Saint** St., Saint.
s. seconde s., second.
S.A. Société anonyme Co Ltd., limited company; Am. Inc., Incorporated.
S.A.R.L. société à responsabilité limitée limited liability company.
S.-E. sud-est S.E., southeast.
S.I. Syndicat d'initiative Travel and Tourist Bureau or Association.
S.I.D.A. [siˈda] **syndrome immunodéficitaire acquis** AIDS, Acquired Immunity Deficiency Syndrome.
S.M.E. Système monétaire européen E.M.S., European Monetary System.
S.M.I.G. salaire minimum interprofessionnel garanti guaranteed minimum professional salary.
S.N.C.F. Société nationale des che-

mins de fer français French National Railways.

S.-O. *sud-ouest* S.W., southwest.

S.O.F.R.S. [sɔ'frɛs] *Société française d'enquêtes par sondage* (*a French institute for opinion-polling and market research*).

S.S. *sécurité sociale* Social Security.

st *stère* cubic meter.

S^{t(e)} *Saint(e)* St., Saint.

Sté *société* company.

S.V.P., s.v.p. *s'il vous plaît* please.

T

t *tonne* ton.

T.C.F. *Touring Club de France* Touring Club of France.

tél. *téléphone* telephone.

TF 1 *Télévision française un* channel one (*on French television*).

t.p.m *tours par minute* r.p.m., revolutions per minute.

T.S.F. *Télégraphie sans fil f* wireless; *m* wireless operator.

T.S.V.P. *tournez, s'il vous plaît* P.T.O., please turn over.

T.V. *télévision* TV, television.

T.V.A. *taxe à la valeur ajoutée* V.A.T., value-added tax.

U

UEFA *Union européenne de football association* European Union of Football Associations.

UEO *Union européenne occidentale* WEU, Western European Union.

UIT *Union internationale des télécommunications* ITU, International Telecommunication Union.

U.N.E.F. *Union nationale des étudiants de France* French National Union of Students.

V

V *volt* V, volt.

v. *votre, vos* your; *voir, voyez* see.

V.D.Q.S. *vin délimité de qualité supérieure* (*medium-quality wine*).

vol. *volume* volume.

V(v)e *veuve* widow.

W

W *watt* watt.

W.C. *water-closet* W.C., water-closet.

Z

Z.U.P. *zone à urbaniser en priorité* priority development area *or* zone.

English Geographical Names

Africa l'Afrique *f.*
Alderney Aurigny *f.*
Algeria l'Algérie *f.*
Algiers Alger *m.*
America l'Amérique *f.*
Argentina l'Argentine *f.*
Asia l'Asie *f.*
Athens Athènes *f.*
Atlantic (*l'océan m*) Atlantique *m.*
Australia l'Australie *f.*
Austria l'Autriche *f.*

Belgium la Belgique *f.*
Brazil le Brésil *m.*
Brittany la Bretagne *f.*
Brussels Bruxelles.
Bucharest Bucarest.
Bulgaria la Bulgarie *f.*

Cairo Le Caire *m.*
Canada le Canada *m.*
Channel: the English ~ la Manche *f.*
China la Chine *f.*
Copenhagen Copenhague.
Corsica la Corse *f.*
Cyprus Chypre *f.*
Czecho-Slovakia la Tchécoslovaquie *f.*

Denmark le Danemark *m.*
Dover Douvres.

Ecuador Équateur *m.*
Edinburgh Édimbourg.
Egypt l'Égypte *f.*
England l'Angleterre *f.*
Europe l'Europe *f.*

Flanders la Flandre *f.*
France la France *f.*

Geneva Genève.
Genoa Gènes *f.*
Germany l'Allemagne *f.*
Great Britain la Grande-Bretagne *f.*
Greece la Grèce *f.*

Hague: the ~ La Haye.
Hungary la Hongrie *f.*
Iceland l'Islande *f.*

Indies *pl.* les Indes *f/pl.*
Ireland l'Irlande *f.*
Israel l'Israël *m.*
Italy l'Italie *f.*

Japan le Japon *m.*

London Londres.

Madeira Madère *f.*
Mexico le Mexique *m.*
Montreal Montréal *m.*
Morocco le Maroc *m.*
Moscow Moscou.

Netherlands *pl.* les Pays-Bas *m/pl.*
Newfoundland Terre-Neuve *f.*
New Zealand la Nouvelle-Zélande *f.*
North Sea *la* mer *f* du Nord.
Norway la Norvège *f.*

Orkney Islands *pl.* les Orcades *f/pl.*

Pacific *le* Pacifique *m.*
Poland la Pologne *f.*

Quebec Québec *m.*

Rhine le Rhin *m.*
Romania, Rumania la Roumanie *f.*
Russia la Russie *f.*

Scandinavia la Scandinavie *f.*
Scotland l'Écosse *f.*
Sicily la Sicile *f.*
Spain l'Espagne *f.*
St. Lawrence *le* Saint-Laurent *m.*
Sweden la Suède *f.*
Switzerland la Suisse *f.*

Tangier Tanger *f.*
Thames *la* Tamise *f.*
Tunisia la Tunisie *f.*
Turkey la Turquie *f.*

United States (of America) les
État-Unis *m/pl.* (d'Amérique).

Wales le Pays *m* de Galles.
Warsaw Varsovie.

Common British and American Abbreviations

A.C. *alternating current* C.A., courant *m* alternatif.
AIDS *acquired immunity deficiency syndrome* S.I.D.A., syndrome *m* immuno-déficitaire acquis.
a.m. *ante meridiem* avant midi.

B.A. *Bachelor of Arts* (*approx.*) L. ès L., licencié(e *f*) *m* ès lettres.

C. *Celsius, centigrade* C. Celsius, *agr.* centigrade.
CET *Central European Time* H.E.C., heure *f* de l'Europe Centrale.
c/o *care of* aux bons soins de, chez.
C.O.D. *cash* (*Am. a. collect*) *on delivery* RB, (envoi *m*) contre remboursement.

D.C. *direct current* C.C., courant *m* continu.
Dr. *Doctor* Dr., docteur *m.*

EEC *European Economic Community* CEE, Communauté *f* économique européenne.

F. *Fahrenheit* F, Fahrenheit.

G.M.T. *Greenwich mean time* T.U., temps *m* universel.

H.P., h.p. *horse-power* ch, c.v., cheval-vapeur *m.*

i.e. *id est* c.-à-d., c'est-à-dire.
Inc. *Incorporated* associés *m/pl.*
I.O.U, I owe you reconnaissance *f* de dette.
IRC *International Red Cross* CRI, Croix-Rouge *f* internationale.

Ltd. *Limited* à responsabilité limitée.

M.A. *Master of Arts* Maître *m* ès Arts.
m.p.h. *miles per hour* milles *m/pl.* à l'heure.
Mr. *Mister* M., Monsieur *m.*

Mrs. *Mistress* Mme, Madame *f.*

NATO *North Atlantic Treaty Organization* OTAN, Organisation *f* du traité de l'Atlantique Nord.

p.m. *post meridiem* de l'après-midi.
P.T.O., p.t.o. *please turn over* T.S.V.P., tournez, s'il vous plaît.

R. *Réaumur* R, Réaumur.
R.C. *Red Cross* C.R., Croix-Rouge *f.*
Rd. *Road* r., rue *f*
r.p.m. *revolutions per minute* t.p.m., tours *m/pl.* par minute.

SEATO *South East Asia Treaty Organization* OTASE, Organisation *f* du traité de l'Asie du Sud-Est.

U.K. *United Kingdom* Royaume-Uni *m.*
U.N. *United Nations* O.N.U., Organisation *f* des Nations Unies.
UNESCO *United Nations Educational, Scientific, and Cultural Organization* UNESCO, Organisation *f* des Nations Unies pour l'Éducation, la Science et la Culture.
UNO *United Nations Organization* O.N.U., Organisation *f* des Nations Unies.
U.N.S.C. *United Nations Security Council* Conseil *m* de Sécurité des Nations Unies.
UPI *United Press International* (*agence d'informations américaine*).
U.S.(A.) *United States* (*of America*) É.-U., États-Unis *m/pl.* (d'Amérique).
U.S.S.R. *Union of Socialist Soviet Republics* U.R.S.S., Union *f* des Républiques Socialistes Soviétiques.

V.A.T. *value-added tax* T.V.A., taxe *f* à la valeur ajoutée.
VHF *very high frequency* OTC, onde *f* très courte.

French Weights and Measures

Linear Measures

km	*kilomètre*	=	1 000 m	=	0.6214 mi.
m	*mètre*	=	1 m	=	3.281 ft.
dm	*décimètre*	=	$^1/_{10}$ m	=	3.937 in.
cm	*centimètre*	=	$^1/_{100}$ m	=	0.394 in.
mm	*millimètre*	=	$^1/_{1000}$ m	=	0.039 in.
	mille marin	=	1 852 m	=	6080 ft.

Square Measures

km²	*kilomètre carré*	=	1 000 000 m²	=	0.3861 sq. mi.
m²	*mètre carré*	=	1 m²	=	1.196 sq. yd.
dm²	*décimètre carré*	=	$^1/_{100}$ m²	=	15.5 sq. in.
cm²	*centimètre carré*	=	$^1/_{10000}$ m²	=	0.155 sq. in.
mm²	*millimètre carré*	=	$^1/_{1000000}$ m²	=	0.002 sq. in.

Land Measures

ha	*hectare*	=	100 a *or* 10 000 m²	=	2.471 acres
a	*are*	=	100 m²	=	119.599 sq. yd.

Cubic Measures

m³	*mètre cube*	=	1 m³	=	35.32 cu. ft.
dm³	*décimètre cube*	=	$^1/_{1000}$ m³	=	61.023 cu. in.
cm³	*centimètre cube*	=	$^1/_{1000000}$ m³	=	0.061 cu. in.
mm³	*millimètre cube*	=	$^1/_{1000000000}$ m³	=	0.00006 cu. in.

Measures of Capacity

hl	*hectolitre*	=	100 l	=	22.01 gals.
l	*litre*	=	1 l	=	1.76 pt.
dl	*décilitre*	=	$^1/_{10}$ l	=	0.176 pt.
cl	*centilitre*	=	$^1/_{100}$ l	=	0.018 pt.
st	*stère*	=	1 m³	=	35.32 cu. ft. (*of wood*)

Weights

t	*tonne*	=	1 t *or* 1 000 kg	=	19.68 cwt.
q	*quintal*	=	$^1/_{10}$ t *or* 100 kg	=	1.968 cwt.
kg	*kilogramme*	=	1 000 g	=	2.205 lb.
g	*gramme*	=	1 g	=	15.432 gr.
mg	*milligramme*	=	$^1/_{1000}$ g	=	0.015 gr.

Temperature Conversion Tables
Tables de conversion des températures
1. FROM −273 °C TO + 1000 °C
1. DE −273 °C À + 1000 °C

Celsius °C	Kelvin K	Fahrenheit °F	Réaumur °R
1000	1273	1832	800
950	1223	1742	760
900	1173	1652	720
850	1123	1562	680
800	1073	1472	640
750	1023	1382	600
700	973	1292	560
650	923	1202	520
600	873	1112	480
550	823	1022	440
500	773	932	400
450	723	842	360
400	673	752	320
350	623	662	280
300	573	572	240
250	523	482	200
200	473	392	160
150	423	302	120
100	373	212	80
95	368	203	76
90	363	194	72
85	358	185	68
80	353	176	64
75	348	167	60
70	343	158	56
65	338	149	52
60	333	140	48
55	328	131	44
50	323	122	40
45	318	113	36
40	313	104	32
35	308	95	28
30	303	86	24
25	298	77	20
20	293	68	16
15	288	59	12
10	283	50	8
+ 5	278	41	+ 4
0	273.15	32	0
− 5	268	23	4
− 10	263	14	− 8
− 15	258	+ 5	− 12
− 17.8	255.4	0	− 14.2
− 20	253	− 4	− 16

Celsius °C	Kelvin K	Fahrenheit °F	Réaumur °R
– 25	248	– 13	– 20
– 30	243	22	– 24
– 35	238	– 31	– 28
– 40	233	– 40	– 32
– 45	228	– 49	– 36
– 50	223	– 58	– 40
– 100	173	– 148	– 80
– 150	123	– 238	– 120
– 200	73	– 328	– 160
– 250	23	– 418	– 200
– 273.15	0	– 459.4	– 218.4

2. CLINICAL THERMOMETER
2. THERMOMÈTRE MÉDICAL

Celsius °C	Fahrenheit °F	Réaumur °R
42.0	107.6	33.6
41.8	107.2	33.4
41.6	106.9	33.3
41.4	106.5	33.1
41.2	106.2	33.0
41.0	105.8	32.8
40.8	105.4	32.6
40.6	105.1	32.5
40.4	104.7	32.3
40.2	104.4	32.2
40.0	104.0	32.0
39.8	103.6	31.8
39.6	103.3	31.7
39.4	102.9	31.5
39.2	102.6	31.4
39.0	102.2	31.2
38.8	101.8	31.0
38.6	101.5	30.9
38.4	101.1	30.7
38.2	100.8	30.6
38.0	100.4	30.4
37.8	100.0	30.2
37.6	99.7	30.1
37.4	99.3	29.9
37.2	99.0	29.8
37.0	98.6	29.6
36.8	98.2	29.4
36.6	97.9	29.3

Conjugations of French Verbs

In this section specimen verb tables are set out. Within the body of the dictionary every infinitive is followed by a number in brackets, e.g. (1 a), (2 b), (3 c), etc. This number refers to the appropriate model or type in the following pages. (1 a), (2 a), (3 a), (4 a) are the **regular** verbs of their conjugation. Others have some irregularity or other special feature.

The Roman numerals indicate the following forms of the verb in question:
I *Présent de l'indicatif*, **II** *Présent du subjonctif*, **III** *Passé simple*, **IV** *Futur simple*, **V** *Impératif*, **VI** *Participe passé*.

How to Form the Tenses

Impératif. Take the 2nd person singular and the 1st and 2nd persons plural of the *Indicatif présent*. In verbs of the 1st Conjugation the singular imperative has no final **s** unless followed by *en* or *y*.

Imparfait. From the 1st person plural of the *Indicatif présent*: replace **-ons** by **-ais** etc.

Participe présent. From the 1st person plural of the *Indicatif présent*: replace **-ons** by **-ant.**

Subjonctif présent. From the 3rd person plural of the *Indicatif présent*: replace **-ent** by **-e** etc.

Subjonctif imparfait. To the 2nd person singular of the *Passé simple* add **-se** etc.

Futur simple. To the *Infinitif présent* add **-ai** etc.

Conditionnel présent. To the *Infinitif présent* add **-ais** etc.

Auxiliary Verbs

(1) avoir

A. Indicatif

I. Simple Tenses

Présent

sg.	j'ai	
	tu as	
	il a[1]	
pl.	nous avons	
	vous avez	
	ils ont	

Imparfait

sg.	j'avais
	tu avais
	il avait
pl.	nous avions
	vous aviez
	ils avaient

Passé simple

sg.	j'eus
	tu eus
	il eut
pl.	nous eûmes
	vous eûtes
	ils eurent

Futur simple

sg.	j'aurai
	tu auras
	il aura
pl.	nous aurons
	vous aurez
	ils auront

Conditionnel présent

sg.	j'aurais
	tu aurais
	il aurait
pl.	nous aurions
	vous auriez
	ils auraient

Participe présent

ayant

Participe passé

eu

II. Compound Tenses

Passé composé

j'ai eu

Plus-que-parfait

j'avais eu

Passé antérieur

j'eus eu

Futur antérieur

j'aurai eu

Conditionnel passé

j'aurais eu

Participe composé

ayant eu

Infinitif passé

avoir eu

B. Subjonctif

I. Simple Tenses

Présent

sg.	que j'aie
	que tu aies
	qu'il ait
pl.	que nous ayons
	que vous ayez
	qu'ils aient

Imparfait

sg.	que j'eusse
	que tu eusses
	qu'il eût
pl.	que nous eussions
	que vous eussiez
	qu'ils eussent

Impératif

aie – ayons – ayez

II. Compound Tenses

Passé

que j'aie eu

Plus-que-parfait

que j'eusse eu

---

[1] a-t-il?

Auxiliary Verbs

(1) être

A. Indicatif

I. Simple Tenses

Présent

sg.	je suis tu es il est
pl.	nous sommes vous êtes ils sont

Imparfait

sg.	j'étais tu étais il était
pl.	nous étions vous étiez ils étaient

Passé simple

sg.	je fus tu fus il fut
pl.	nous fûmes vous fûtes ils furent

Futur simple

sg.	je serai tu seras il sera
pl.	nous serons vous serez ils seront

Conditionnel présent

sg.	je serais tu serais il serait
pl.	nous serions vous seriez ils seraient

Participe présent

étant

Participe passé

été

II. Compound Tenses

Passé composé

j'ai été

Plus-que-parfait

j'avais été

Passé antérieur

j'eus été

Futur antérieur

j'aurai été

Conditionnel passé

j'aurais été

Participe composé

ayant été

Infinitif passé

avoir été

B. Subjonctif

I. Simple Tenses

Présent

sg.	que je sois que tu sois qu'il soit
pl.	que nous soyons que vous soyez qu'ils soient

Imparfait

sg.	que je fusse que tu fusses qu'il fût
pl.	que nous fussions que vous fussiez qu'ils fussent

Impératif

sois – soyons – soyez

II. Compound Tenses

Passé

que j'aie été

Plus-que-parfait

que j'eusse été

First Conjugation

(1 a) blâmer

I. Simple Tenses

Présent

sg. je blâme
tu blâmes
il blâme[1]

pl. nous blâmons
vous blâmez
ils blâment

Passé simple

sg. je blâmai
tu blâmas
il blâma

pl. nous blâmâmes
vous blâmâtes
ils blâmèrent

Participe passé

blâmé

Infinitif présent

blâmer

Impératif

blâme[2]
blâmons
blâmez

Imparfait

sg. je blâmais
tu blâmais
il blâmait

pl. nous blâmions
vous blâmiez
ils blâmaient

Participe présent

blâmant

Futur simple

sg. je blâmerai
tu blâmeras
il blâmera

pl. nous blâmerons
vous blâmerez
ils blâmeront

[1] blâme-t-il?

[2] blâmes-en
blâmes-y

Conditionnel présent

sg. je blâmerais
tu blâmerais
il blâmerait

pl. nous blâmerions
vous blâmeriez
ils blâmeraient

Subjonctif présent

sg. que je blâme
que tu blâmes
qu'il blâme

pl. que nous blâmions
que vous blâmiez
qu'ils blâment

Subjonctif imparfait

sg. que je blâmasse
que tu blâmasses
qu'il blâmât

pl. que nous blâmassions
que vous blâmassiez
qu'ils blâmassent

II. Compound Tenses

(*Participe passé* with the help of **avoir** and **être**)

1. Actif

Passé composé: j'ai blâmé
Plus-que-parfait: j'avais blâmé
Passé antérieur: j'eus blâmé
Futur antérieur: j'aurai blâmé
Conditionnel passé: j'aurais blâmé

2. Passif

Présent: je suis blâmé
Imparfait: j'étais blâmé
Passé simple: je fus blâmé
Passé composé: j'ai été blâmé
Plus-que-parf.: j'avais été blâmé
Passé antérieur: j'eus été blâmé
Futur simple: je serai blâmé
Futur antérieur: j'aurai été blâmé
Conditionnel présent: je serais blâmé
Conditionnel passé: j'aurais été blâmé
Impératif: sois blâmé
Participe présent: étant blâmé
Participe composé: ayant été blâmé
Infinitif présent: être blâmé
Infinitif passé: avoir été blâmé

Second Conjugation

Note the cases in which the verb stem is lengthened by ...iss...

I. Simple Tenses

Présent

sg. je punis
tu punis
il punit

pl. nous punissons
vous punissez
ils punissent

Passé simple

sg. je punis
tu punis
il punit

pl. nous punîmes
vous punîtes
ils punirent

Participe passé

puni

Infinitif présent

punir

Impératif

punis
punissons
punissez

Imparfait

sg. je punissais
tu punissais
il punissait

pl. nous punissions
vous punissiez
ils punissaient

Participe présent

punissant

Futur simple

sg. je punirai
tu puniras
il punira

pl. nous punirons
vous punirez
ils puniront

Conditionnel présent

sg. je punirais
tu punirais
il punirait

pl. nous punirions
vous puniriez
ils puniraient

Subjonctif présent

sg. que je punisse
que tu punisses
qu'il punisse

pl. que nous punissions
que vous punissiez
qu'ils punissent

Subjonctif imparfait

sg. que je punisse
que tu punisses
qu'il punît

pl. que nous punissions
que vous punissiez
qu'ils punissent

II. Compound Tenses

Participe passé with the help of **avoir** and **être**; *see* (1 a)

---

1) **saillir** is used only in the 3rd persons of the simple tenses. *P.pr.* saillant

Third Conjugation

(3 a) recevoir

I. Simple Tenses

Présent

sg. je reçois
tu reçois
il reçoit

pl. nous recevons
vous recevez
ils reçoivent

Imparfait

sg. je recevais
tu recevais
il recevait

pl. nous recevions
vous receviez
ils recevaient

Passé simple

sg. je reçus
tu reçus
il reçut

pl. nous reçûmes
vous reçûtes
ils reçurent

Futur simple

sg. je recevrai
tu recevras
il recevra

pl. nous recevrons
vous recevrez
ils recevront

Conditionnel présent

sg. je recevrais
tu recevrais
il recevrait

pl. nous recevrions
vous recevriez
ils recevraient

Subjonctif présent

sg. que je reçoive
que tu reçoives
qu'il reçoive

pl. que nous recevions
que vous receviez
qu'ils reçoivent

Subjonctif imparfait

sg. que je reçusse
que tu reçusses
qu'il reçût

pl. que nous reçussions
que vous reçussiez
qu'ils reçussent

Impératif

reçois
recevons
recevez

Participe présent

recevant

Participe passé [1]

reçu

Infinitif présent

recevoir

II. Compound Tenses

Participe passé with the help of **avoir** and **être**; *see* (1 a)

---

[1] **devoir** and its derivative **redevoir** have **dû, due,** m/pl. **dus** and **redû, redue,** m/pl. **redus**

Fourth Conjugation

(4 a) vendre

In the regular 4th Conjugation verbs, the stem does not change

I. Simple Tenses

Présent[1]

sg.
- je vends
- tu vends
- il vend[2]

pl.
- nous vendons
- vous vendez
- ils vendent

Passé simple

sg.
- je vendis
- tu vendis
- il vendit

pl.
- nous vendîmes
- vous vendîtes
- ils vendirent

Participe passé

vendu

Infinitif présent

vendre

Impératif

- vends
- vendons
- vendez

Imparfait

sg.
- je vendais
- tu vendais
- il vendait

pl.
- nous vendions
- vous vendiez
- ils vendaient

Participe présent

vendant

Futur simple

sg.
- je vendrai
- tu vendras
- il vendra

pl.
- nous vendrons
- vous vendrez
- ils vendront

Conditionnel présent

sg.
- je vendrais
- tu vendrais
- il vendrait

pl.
- nous vendrions
- vous vendriez
- ils vendraient

Subjonctif présent

sg.
- que je vende
- que tu vendes
- qu'il vende

pl.
- que nous vendions
- que vous vendiez
- qu'ils vendent

Subjonctif imparfait

sg.
- que je vendisse
- que tu vendisses
- qu'il vendît

pl.
- que nous vendissions
- que vous vendissiez
- qu'ils vendissent

II. Compound Tenses

Participe passé with the help of **avoir** and **être**; see (1 a)

---

[1] **battre** and its derivatives have **bats, bats, bat** in the sg.; the pl. is regular: **battons**, etc.

[2] **rompre** and its derivatives have **il rompt.**

(1b) aimer I aime, aimes, aime, aimons, aimez, aiment; **II** aime, aimes, aime, aimions, aimiez, aiment; **III** aimai, aimas, aima, aimâmes, aimâtes, aimèrent; **IV** aimerai, aimeras, aimera, aimerons, aimerez, aimeront; **V** aime, aimons, aimez; **VI** aimé.

(1c) appeler I appelle, appelles, appelle, appelons, appelez, appellent; **II** appelle, appelles, appelle, appelions, appeliez, appellent; **III** appelai, appelas, appela, appelâmes, appelâtes, appelèrent; **IV** appellerai, appelleras, appellera, appellerons, appellerez, appelleront; **V** appelle, appelons, appelez; **VI** appelé.
Note: [ə] becomes [ɛ] before a mute syllable.

(1d) amener I amène, amènes, amène, amenons, amenez; amènent; **II** amène, amènes, amène, amenions, ameniez, amènent; **III** amenai, amenas, amena, amenâmes, amenâtes, amenèrent; **IV** amènerai, amèneras, amènera, amènerons, amènerez, amèneront; **V** amène, amenons, amenez; **VI** amené.

(1e) arguer I arguë, arguës, arguë, arguons, arguez, arguënt; **II** arguë, arguës, arguë, arguïons, arguïez, arguënt; **III** arguai, arguas, argua, arguâmes, arguâtes, arguèrent; **IV** arguërai, arguëras, arguëra, arguërons, arguërez, arguëront; **V** arguë, arguons, arguez; **VI** argué.

(1f) céder I cède, cèdes, cède, cédons, cédez, cèdent; **II** cède, cèdes, cède, cédions, cédiez, cèdent; **III** cédai, cédas, céda, cédâmes, cédâtes, cédèrent; **IV** céderai, céderas, cédera, céderons, céderez, céderont; **V** cède, cédons, cédez; **VI** cédé.

(1g) abréger I abrège, abrèges, abrège, abrégeons, abrégez, abrègent; **II** abrège, abrèges, abrège, abrégions, abrégiez, abrègent; **III** abrégeai, abrégeas, abrégea, abrégeâmes, abrégeâtes, abrégèrent; **IV** abrégerai, abrégeras, abrégera, abrégerons, abrégerez, abrégeront; **V** abrège, abrégeons, abrégez; **VI** abrégé.

(1h) employer I emploie, emploies, emploie, employons, employez, emploient; **II** emploie, emploies, emploie, employions, employiez, emploient; **III** employai, employas, employa, employâmes, employâtes, employèrent; **IV** emploierai, emploieras, emploiera, emploierons, emploierez, emploieront; **V** emploie, employons, employez; **VI** employé.

(1i) payer I paye (paie), payes (paies), paye (paie), payons, payez, payent (paient); **II** paye (paie), payes (paies), paye (paie), payions, payiez, payent (paient); **III** payai, payas, paya, payâmes, payâtes, payèrent; **IV** payerai (paierai), payeras (paieras), payera (paiera), payerons (paierons), payerez (paierez), payeront (paieront); **V** paye (paie), payons, payez; **VI** payé.

(1k) menacer I menace, menaces, menace, menaçons, menacez, menacent; **II** menace, menaces, menace, menacions, menaciez, menacent; **III** menaçai, menaças, menaça, menaçâmes, menaçâtes, menacèrent; **IV** menacerai, menaceras, menacera, menacerons, menacerez, menaceront; **VI** menacé.

(1l) manger I mange, manges, mange, mangeons, mangez, mangent; **II** mange, manges, mange, mangions, mangiez, mangent; **III** mangeai, mangeas, mangea, mangeâmes, mangeâtes, mangèrent; **IV** mangerai, mangeras, mangera, mangerons, mangerez, mangeront; **V** mange, mangeons, mangez; **VI** mangé.

(1m) conjuguer I conjugue, conjugues, conjugue, conjuguons, conjuguez, conjuguent; **II** conjugue, conjugues, conjugue, conjuguions, conjuguiez, conjuguent; **III** conjuguai, conjuguas, conjugua, conjuguâmes, conjuguâtes, conjuguèrent; **IV** conjuguerai, conjugueras, conjuguera, conjuguerons, conjuguerez, conjugueront; **V** conjugue, conjuguons, conjuguez; **VI** conjugué.

(1n) saluer I salue, salues, salue, saluons, saluez, saluent; **II** salue, salues, salue, saluions, saluiez, saluent; **III** saluai, saluas, salua, saluâmes, saluâtes, saluèrent; **IV** saluerai, salueras, saluera, saluerons, saluerez, salueront; **V** salue, saluons, saluez; **VI** salué.

(1o) châtier I châtie, châties, châtie, châtions, châtiez, châtient; **II** châtie, châties, châtie, châtiions, châtiiez, châtient; **III** châtiai, châtias, châtia, châtiâmes, châtiâtes, châtièrent; **IV** châtierai, châtieras, châtiera, châtierons, châtierez, châtieront; **V** châtie, châtions, châtiez; **VI** châtié.

(1p) allouer I alloue, alloues, alloue, allouons, allouez, allouent; **II** alloue, alloues, alloue, allouions, allouiez, allouent; **III** allouai, allouas, alloua, allouâmes, allouâtes, allouèrent; **IV** allouerai, alloueras, allouera, allouerons, allouerez, alloueront; **V** alloue, allouons, allouez; **VI** alloué.

(1q) aller I vais, vas, va, allons, allez, vont; **II** aille, ailles, aille, allions, alliez, aillent; **III** allai, allas, alla, allâmes, allâtes, allèrent; **IV** irai, iras, ira, irons, irez, iront; **V** va (vas-y), allons, allez; **VI** allé.

(1r) envoyer I envoie, envoies, envoie, envoyons, envoyez, envoient; **II** envoie, envoies, envoie, envoyions, envoyiez, envoient; **III** envoyai, envoyas, envoya, envoyâmes, envoyâtes, envoyèrent; **IV** enverrai, enverras, enverra, enverrons, enverrez, enverront; **V** envoie, envoyons, envoyez; **VI** envoyé.

(1s) léguer I lègue, lègues, lègue, léguons, léguez, lèguent; **II** lègue, lègues, lègue, léguions, léguiez, lèguent; **III** léguai, léguas, légua, léguâmes, léguâtes, léguèrent; **IV** léguerai, légueras, léguera, léguerons, léguerez, légueront; **V** lègue, léguons, léguez; **VI** légué.

(2b) sentir I sens, sens, sent, sentons, sentez, sentent; **II** sente, sentes, sente, sentions, sentiez, sentent; **III** sentis, sentis, sentit, sentîmes, sentîtes, sentirent; **IV** sentirai, sentiras, sentira, sentirons, sentirez, sentiront; **V** sens, sentons, sentez; **VI** senti.

(2c) cueillir I cueille, cueilles, cueille, cueillons, cueillez, cueillent; **II** cueille, cueilles, cueille, cueillions, cueilliez, cueillent; **III** cueillis, cueillis, cueillit, cueillîmes, cueillîtes, cueillirent; **IV** cueillerai, cueilleras, cueillera, cueillerons, cueillerez, cueilleront; **V** cueille, cueillons, cueillez; **VI** cueilli.

(2d) fuir I fuis, fuis, fuit, fuyons, fuyez, fuient; **II** fuie, fuies, fuie, fuyions, fuyiez, fuient; **III** fuis, fuis, fuit, fuîmes, fuîtes, fuirent; **IV** fuirai, fuiras, fuira, fuirons, fuirez, fuiront; **V** fuis, fuyons, fuyez; **VI** fui.

(2e) bouillir I bous, bous, bout, bouillons, bouillez, bouillent; **II** bouille, bouilles, bouille, bouillions, bouilliez, bouillent; **III** bouillis, bouillis, bouillit, bouillîmes, bouillîtes, bouillirent; **IV** bouillirai, bouilliras, bouillira, bouillirons, bouillirez, bouilliront; **V** bous, bouillons, bouillez; **VI** bouilli.

(2f) couvrir I couvre, couvres, couvre, couvrons, couvrez, couvrent; **II** couvre, couvres, couvre, couvrions, couvriez, couvrent; **III** couvris, couvris, couvrit, couvrîmes, couvrîtes, couvrirent; **IV** couvrirai, couvriras, couvrira, couvrirons, couvrirez, couvriront; **V** couvre, couvrons, couvrez; **VI** couvert.

(2g) vêtir I vêts, vêts, vêt, vêtons, vêtez, vêtent; **II** vête, vêtes, vête, vêtions, vêtiez, vêtent; **III** vêtis, vêtis, vêtit, vêtîmes, vêtîtes, vêtirent; **IV** vêtirai, vêtiras, vêtira, vêtirons, vêtirez, vêtiront; **V** vêts, vêtons, vêtez; **VI** vêtu.

(2h) venir **I** viens, viens, vient, venons, venez, viennent; **II** vienne, viennes, vienne, venions, veniez, viennent; **III** vins, vins, vint, vînmes, vîntes, vinrent; **IV** viendrai, viendras, viendra, viendrons, viendrez, viendront; **V** viens, venons, venez; **VI** venu.

(2i) courir **I** cours, cours, court, courons, courez, courent; **II** coure, coures, coure, courions, couriez, courent; **III** courus, courus, courut, courûmes, courûtes, coururent; **IV** courrai, courras, courra, courrons, courrez, courront; **V** cours, courons, courez; **VI** couru.

(2k) mourir **I** meurs, meurs, meurt, mourons, mourez, meurent; **II** meure, meures, meure, mourions, mouriez, meurent; **III** mourus, mourus, mourut, mourûmes, mourûtes, moururent; **IV** mourrai, mourras, mourra, mourrons, mourrez, mourront; **V** meurs, mourons, mourez; **VI** mort.

(2l) acquérir **I** acquiers, acquiers, acquiert, acquérons, acquérez, acquièrent; **II** acquière, acquières, acquière, acquérions, acquériez, acquièrent; **III** acquis, acquis, acquit, acquîmes, acquîtes, acquirent; **IV** acquerrai, acquerras, acquerra, acquerrons, acquerrez, acquerront; **V** acquiers, acquérons, acquérez; **VI** acquis.

(2m) haïr **I** hais [ɛ], hais, hait, haïssons, haïssez, haïssent; **II** haïsse, haïsses, haïsse, haïssions, haïssiez, haïssent; **III** haïs [aˈi], haïs, haït, haïmes, haïtes, haïrent; **IV** haïrai, haïras, haïra, haïrons, haïrez, haïront; **V** hais [ɛ], haïssons, haïssez; **V** haï.

(2n) faillir **III** faillis, faillis, faillit, faillîmes, faillîtes, faillirent; **IV** faillirai, failliras, faillira, faillirons, faillirez, failliront; **VI** failli.
Note: No other forms extant.

(2o) fleurir **I** fleuris, fleuris, fleurit, fleurissons, fleurissez, fleurissent; **II** fleurisse, fleurisses, fleurisse, fleurissions, fleurissiez, fleurissent; **III** fleuris, fleuris, fleurit, fleurîmes, fleurîtes, fleurirent; **IV** fleurirai, fleuriras, fleurira, fleurirons, fleurirez, fleuriront; **V** fleuris, fleurissons, fleurissez; **VI** fleuri.
Note: In the sense of prosper has *p.pr.* florissant and *impf.ind.* florissais, etc.

(2p) saillir **I** saille, saillent; **II** saille, saillent; **IV** saillera, sailleront; **VI** sailli.
Note: No other forms extant.

(2q) gésir **I** gît, gisons, gisez, gisent.
Note: No other forms extant.

(2r) ouïr **VI** ouï.
Note: No other forms extant.

(2s) assaillir **I** assaille, assailles, assaille, assaillons, assaillez, assaillent; **II** assaille, assailles, assaille, assaillions, assailliez, assaillent; **III** assaillis, assaillis, assaillit, assaillîmes, assaillîtes, assaillirent; **IV** assaillirai, assailliras, assaillira, assaillirons, assaillirez, assailliront; **V** assaille, assaillons, assaillez; **VI** assailli.

(2t) défaillir **I** défaille, défailles, défaille, défaillons, défaillez, défaillent; **II** défaille, défailles, défaille, défaillions, défailliez, défaillent; **III** défaillis, défaillis, défaillit, défaillîmes, défaillîtes, défaillirent; **IV** défaillirai, défailliras, défaillira, défaillirons, défaillirez, défailliront; **VI** défailli.

(2u) férir VI féru.
Note: No other forms extant.

(2v) quérir
Note: No other forms extant.

(3b) apparoir I il appert.
Note: No other forms extant.

(3c) asseoir I assieds, assieds, assied, asseyons, asseyez, asseyent; **II** asseye, asseyes, asseye, asseyions, asseyiez, asseyent; **III** assis, assis, assit, assîmes, assîtes, assirent; **IV** assiérai, assiéras, assiéra, assiérons, assiérez, assiéront; **V** assieds, asseyons, asseyez; **VI** assis.
Note: Alternative forms: assois etc.

surseoir I sursois, sursois, sursoit, sursoyons, sursoyez, sursoient; **II** sursoie, sursoies, sursoie, sursoyions, sursoyiez, sursoient; **III** sursis, sursis, sursit, sursîmes, sursîtes, sursirent; **IV** surseoirai, surseoiras, surseoira, surseoirons, surseoirez, surseoiront; **V** sursois, sursoyons, sursoyez; **VI** sursis.

(3d) choir I chois, chois, choit; **III** chus, chus, chut, chûmes, chûtes, churent; **IV** choirai, choiras, choira, choirons, choirez, choiront; **VI** chu.
Note: No other forms extant. There are alternative forms: *fut.* cherrai etc.

déchoir I déchois, déchois, déchoit, déchoyons, déchoyez, déchoient; **II** déchoie, déchoies, déchoie, déchoyions, déchoyiez, déchoient; **III** déchus, déchus, déchut, déchûmes, déchûtes, déchurent; **IV** déchoirai, déchoiras, déchoira, déchoirons, déchoirez, déchoiront; **VI** déchu.
Note: No *impf.ind.* and no *p.pr.*

échoir I il échoit, ils échoient; **II** qu'il échoie; **III** il échut, ils échurent; **IV** il échoira, ils échoiront; **VI** échu.
Note: *P.pr.* échéant. *Impf.ind.* il échoyait or échéait. Alternative forms: *fut.* il écherra, ils écherront.

(3e) falloir I il faut; **II** qu'il faille; **III** il fallut; **IV** il faudra; **VI** fallu *inv*.

(3f) mouvoir I meus, meus, meut, mouvons, mouvez, meuvent; **II** meuve, meuves, meuve, mouvions, mouviez, meuvent; **III** mus, mus, mut, mûmes, mûtes, murent; **IV** mouvrai, mouvras, mouvra, mouvrons, mouvrez, mouvront; **V** meus, mouvons, mouvez; **VI** mû, mue.
Note: **émouvoir** has *p.p.* ému.

(3g) pleuvoir I il pleut; **II** qu'il pleuve; **III** il plut; **IV** pleuvra; **VI** plu *inv*.

(3h) pouvoir I peux, peux, peut, pouvons, pouvez, peuvent; **II** puisse, puisses, puisse, puissions, puissiez, puissent; **III** pus, pus, put, pûmes, pûtes, purent; **IV** pourrai, pourras, pourra, pourrons, pourrez, pourront; **VI** pu *inv*.
Note: In the *pres.ind.* the 1st person can also be je puis and the interrogative is puis-je not peux-je.

(3i) savoir I sais, sais, sait, savons, savez, savent; **II** sache, saches, sache, sachions, sachiez, sachent; **III** sus, sus, sut, sûmes, sûtes, surent; **IV** saurai, sauras, saura, saurons, saurez, sauront; **V** sache, sachons, sachez; **VI** su.
Note: *P.pr.* sachant.

(3k) seoir I il sied, ils siéent; **II** il siée, ils siéent; **IV** il siéra, ils siéront; **VI** sis.
Note: *P.pr.* seyant or séant; *Impf.ind.* is il seyait, ils seyaient.

(3l) valoir I vaux, vaux, vaut, valons, valez, valent; **II** vaille, vailles, vaille, valions, valiez, vaillent; **III** valus, valus, valut, valûmes, valûtes, valurent; **IV** vaudrai, vaudras, vaudra, vaudrons, vaudrez, vaudront; **VI** valu.
Note: **Prévaloir** forms its *pres.sbj.* regularly: que je prévale etc.

(3m) voir I vois, vois, voit, voyons, voyez, voient; **II** voie, voies, voie, voyions, voyiez, voient; **III** vis, vis, vit, vîmes, vîtes, virent; **IV** verrai, verras, verra, verrons, verrez, verront; **V** vois, voyons, voyez; **VI** vu.
Note: **Pourvoir** and **prévoir** have *fut.* and *cond.* in ...oir...; **pourvoir** has *p.s.* pourvus.

(3n) vouloir I veux, veux, veut, voulons, voulez, veulent; **II** veuille, veuilles, veuille, voulions, vouliez, veuillent; **III** voulus, voulous, voulut, voulûmes, voulûtes, voulurent; **IV** voudrai, voudras, voudra, voudrons, voudrez, voudront; **V** veuille, veuillons, veuillez; **VI** voulu.

(4b) boire I bois, bois, boit, buvons, buvez, boivent; **II** boive, boives, boive, buvions, buviez, boivent; **III** bus, bus, but, bûmes, bûtes, burent; **IV** boirai, boiras, boira, boirons, boirez, boiront; **V** bois, buvons, buvez; **VI** bu.

(4c) braire I il brait, ils braient; **IV** il braira, ils brairont; **VI** brait.
Note: No other forms extant. *Impf.ind.* is il brayait.

(4d) bruire I il bruit, ils bruissent; **IV** il bruira.
Note: No other forms extant. *Impf.ind.* is also bruyait.

(4e) circoncire I circoncis, circoncis, circoncit, circoncisons, circoncisez, circoncisent; **II** circoncise, circoncises, circoncise, circoncisions, circoncisiez, circoncisent; **III** circoncis, circoncis, circoncit, circoncîmes, circoncîtes, circoncirent; **IV** circoncirai, circonciras, circoncira, circoncirons, circoncirez, circonciront; **V** circoncis, circoncisons, circoncisez; **VI** circoncis.

(4f) clore I je clos, tu clos, il clôt; **II** close, closes, close, closions, closiez, closent; **IV** clorai, cloras, clora, clorons, clorez, cloront; **V** clos; **VI** clos.
Note: No other forms extant. **Enclore** has all forms of the *pres.ind.*
éclore I il éclôt, ils éclosent; **II** qu'il éclose, qu'ils éclosent; **IV** il éclora, ils écloront; **VI** éclos.

(4g) conclure I conclus, conclus, conclut, concluons, concluez, concluent; **II** conclue, conclues, conclue, concluions, concluiez, concluent; **III** conclus, conclus, conclut, conclûmes, conclûtes, conclurent; **IV** conclurai, concluras, conclura, conclurons, conclurez, concluront; **V** conclus, concluons, concluez; **VI** conclu.

(4h) conduire I conduis, conduis, conduit, conduisons, conduisez, conduisent; **II** conduise, conduises, conduise, conduisions, conduisiez, conduisent; **III** conduisis, conduisis, conduisit, conduisîmes, conduisîtes, conduisirent; **IV** conduirai, conduiras, conduira, conduirons, conduirez, conduiront; **V** conduis, conduisons, conduisez; **VI** conduit.
Note: **Luire, reluire, nuire** have no t in the *p.p.*

(4i) suffire I suffis, suffis, suffit, suffisons, suffisez, suffisent; **II** suffise, suffises, suffise, suffisions, suffisiez, suffisent; **III** suffis, suffis, suffit, suffîmes, suffîtes, suffirent; **IV** suffirai, suffiras, suffira, suffirons, suffirez, suffiront; **V** suffis, suffisons, suffisez; **VI** suffi *inv*.
Note: **Confire** has *p.p.* confit.

(4k) connaître I connais, connais, connaît, connaissons, connaissez, connaissent; II connaisse, connaisses, connaisse, connaissions, connaissiez, connaissent; III connus, connus, connut, connûmes, connûtes, connurent; IV connaîtrai, connaîtras, connaîtra, connaîtrons, connaîtrez, connaîtront; V connais, connaissons, connaissez; VI connu.

Note: **Repaître** goes like **connaître, paître** has no *p.s.* and no *p.p.*

(4l) coudre I couds, couds, coud, cousons, cousez, cousent; II couse, couses, couse, cousions, cousiez, cousent; III cousis, cousis, cousit, cousîmes, cousîtes, cousirent; IV coudrai, coudras, coudra, coudrons, coudrez, coudront; V couds, cousons, cousez; VI cousu.

(4m) craindre I crains, crains, craint, craignons, craignez, craignent; II craigne, craignes, craigne, craignions, craigniez, craignent; III craignis, craignis, craignit, craignîmes, craignîtes, craignirent; IV craindrai, craindras, craindra, craindrons, craindrez, craindront; V crains, craignons, craignez; VI craint.

Note: **Oindre** has only *inf.* and *p.p.*; **poindre** has only *inf., 3rd person sg.pres. ind., fut.* and *cond.*, and the compound tenses.

(4n) croire I crois, crois, croit, croyons, croyez, croient; II croie, croies, croie, croyions, croyiez, croient; III crus, crus, crut, crûmes, crûtes, crurent; IV croirai, croiras, croira, croirons, croirez, croiront; V crois, croyons, croyez; VI cru.

Note: **Accroire** occurs only in the *inf.*

(4o) croître I croîs, croîs, croît, croissons, croissez, croissent; II croisse, croisses, croisse, croissions, croissiez, croissent; III crûs, crûs, crût, crûmes, crûtes, crûrent; IV croîtrai, croîtras, croîtra, croîtrons, croîtrez, croîtront; V croîs, croissons, croissez; VI crû, crue, *m/pl.* crus.

Note: **Décroître** and **accroître** have no circumflex in *p.s.* or *p.p.*

(4p) dire I dis, dis, dit, disons, dites, disent; II dise, dises, dise, disions, disiez, disent; III dis, dis, dit, dîmes, dîtes, dirent; IV dirai, diras, dira, dirons, direz, diront; V dis, disons, dites; VI dit.

Note: **Redire** goes like **dire**. The other derivatives of **dire** have ...disez in the *2nd person pl pres. ind.* and *imper.*, except **maudire** which goes like (2a) but has *p.p.* maudit.

(4q) écrire I écris, écris, écrit, écrivons, écrivez, écrivent; II écrive, écrives, écrive, écrivions, écriviez, écrivent; III écrivis, écrivis, écrivit, écrivîmes, écrivîtes, écrivirent; IV écrirai, écriras, écrira, écrirons, écrirez, écriront; V écris, écrivons, écrivez; VI écrit.

(4r) faire I fais, fais, fait, faisons, faites, font; II fasse, fasses, fasse, fassions, fassiez, fassent; III fis, fis, fit, fîmes, fîtes, firent; IV ferai, feras, fera, ferons, ferez, feront; V fais, faisons, faites; VI fait.

Note: **Malfaire** is used only in the *inf.* and **forfaire** and **parfaire** only in the *inf., p.p.* and compound tenses.

(4s) frire I fris, fris, frit; IV frirai, friras, frira, frirons, frirez, friront; V fris; VI frit.

Note: No other forms extant.

(4t) lire I lis, lis, lit, lisons, lisez, lisent; II lise, lises, lise, lisions, lisiez, lisent; III lus, lus, lut, lûmes, lûtes, lurent; IV lirai, liras, lira, lirons, lirez, liront; V lis, lisons, lisez; VI lu.

624

(4u) luire
Note: See (4h). *P.s.* and *impf.sbj.* are rarely used.

(4v) mettre I mets, mets, met, mettons, mettez, mettent; **II** mette, mettes, mette, mettions, mettiez, mettent; **III** mis, mis, mit, mîmes, mîtes, mirent; **IV** mettrai, mettras, mettra, mettrons, mettrez, mettront; **V** mets, mettons, mettez; **VI** mis.

(4w) moudre I mouds, mouds, moud, moulons, moulez, moulent; **II** moule, moules, moule, moulions, mouliez, moulent; **III** moulus, moulus, moulut, moulûmes, moulûtes, moulurent; **IV** moudrai, moudras, moudra, moudrons, moudrez, moudront; **V** mouds, moulons, moulez; **VI** moulu.

(4x) naître I nais, nais, naît, naissons, naissez, naissent; **II** naisse, naisses, naisse, naissions, naissiez, naissent; **III** naquis, naquis, naquit, naquîmes, naquîtes, naquirent; **IV** naîtrai, naîtras, naîtra, naîtrons, naîtrez, naîtront; **V** nais, naissons, naissez; **VI** né.

(4z) plaire I plais, plais, plaît, plaisons, plaisez, plaisent; **II** plaise, plaises, plaise, plaisions, plaisiez, plaisent; **III** plus, plus, plut, plûmes, plûtes, plurent; **IV** plairai, plairas, plaira, plairons, plairez, plairont; **V** plais, plaisons, plaisez; **VI** plu *inv.*
Note: **Taire** has no circumflex in il tait; *p.p.* tu.

(4aa) prendre I prends, prends, prend, prenons, prenez, prennent; **II** prenne, prennes, prenne, prenions, preniez, prennent; **III** pris, pris, prit, prîmes, prîtes, prirent; **IV** prendrai, prendras, prendra, prendrons, prendrez, prendront; **V** prends, prenons, prenez; **VI** pris.

(4bb) résoudre I résous, résous, résout, résolvons, résolvez, résolvent; **II** résolve, résolves, résolve, résolvions, résolviez, résolvent; **III** résolus, résolus, résolut, résolûmes, résolûtes, résolurent; **IV** résoudrai, résoudras, résoudra, résoudrons, résoudrez, résoudront; **V** résous, résolvons, résolvez; **VI** résolu; in 🥕 résous.
Note: **Absoudre** has *p.p.* absous, absoute. **Dissoudre** goes like **absoudre.**

(4cc) rire I ris, ris, rit, rions, riez, rient; **II** rie, ries, rie, riions, riiez, rient; **III** ris, ris, rit, rîmes, rîtes, rirent; **IV** rirai, riras, rira, rirons, rirez, riront; **V** ris, rions, riez; **VI** ri *inv.*

(4dd) sourdre I il sourd, ils sourdent; **II** qu'il sourde, qu'ils sourdent; **III** il sourdit, ils sourdirent; **IV** il sourdra, ils sourdront.
Note: No other forms extant.

(4ee) suivre I suis, suis, suit, suivons, suivez, suivent; **II** suive, suives, suive, suivions, suiviez, suivent; **III** suivis, suivis, suivit, suivîmes, suivîtes, suivirent; **IV** suivrai, suivras, suivra, suivrons, suivrez, suivront; **V** suis, suivons, suivez; **VI** suivi.

(4gg) vaincre I vaincs, vaincs, vainc, vainquons, vainquez, vainquent; **II** vainque, vainques, vainque, vainquions, vainquiez, vainquent; **III** vainquis, vainquis, vainquit, vainquîmes, vainquîtes, vainquirent; **IV** vaincrai, vaincras, vaincra, vaincrons, vaincrez, vaincront; **V** vaincs, vainquons, vainquez; **VI** vaincu.

(4hh) vivre I vis, vis, vit, vivons, vivez, vivent; **II** vive, vives, vive, vivions, viviez, vivent; **III** vécus, vécus, vécut, vécûmes, vécûtes, vécurent; **IV** vivrai, vivras, vivra, vivrons, vivrez, vivront; **V** vis, vivons, vivez; **VI** vécu.

Abbreviations

a.	*aussi*, also.		*gramm.*	*grammaire*, grammar.
abbr.	abbreviation, *abréviation.*			
adj.	*adjectif*, adjective.		*hist.*	*histoire*, history.
admin.	*administration*, administration.		*hunt.*	hunting, *chasse.*
adv.	*adverbe*, adverb; *locution adverbiale*, adverbial phrase.		*icht.*	*ichtyologie*, ichthyology.
Am.	Americanism, *américanisme.*		*imper.*	imperative, *impératif.*
anat.	*anatomie*, anatomy.		*impers.*	*impersonnel*, impersonal.
approx.	*approximativement*, approximately.		*impf.*	*imparfait*, imperfect.
archeol.	archeology, *archéologie.*		*ind.*	*indicatif*, indicative.
art.	*article*, article.		*indef.*	indefinite, *indéfini.*
astr.	*astronomie*, astronomy.		*inf.*	*infinitif*, infinitive.
attr.	*attribut*, attributively.		*int.*	*interjection*, interjection.
			interr.	*interrogatif*, interrogative.
bibl.	*biblique*, biblical.		*inv.*	*invariable*, invariable.
biol.	*biologie*, biology.		*iro.*	*ironiquement*, ironically.
box.	*boxe*, boxing.		*irr.*	*irrégulier*, irregular.
Br.	British, *britannique.*			
			journ.	*journalisme*, journalism.
ch.sp.	childish speech, *langage enfantin.*		*ling.*	*linguistique*, linguistics.
cin.	*cinéma*, cinema.			
cj.	*conjonction*, conjunction.		*m*	*masculin*, masculine.
co.	*comique*, comical.		*metall.*	metallurgy, *métallurgie.*
coll.	*collectif*, collective.		*meteor.*	meteorology, *météorologie.*
comp.	*comparatif*, comparative.		*min.*	*minéralogie*, mineralogy.
cond.	*conditionnel*, conditional.		*mot.*	motoring, *automobilisme.*
cost.	*costume*, costume.		*mount.*	mountaineering, *alpinisme.*
cuis.	*cuisine*, culinary art.		*myth.*	*mythologie*, mythology.
			n	*neutre*, neuter.
def.	definite, *défini.*		*neg.*	negative, *négatif.*
dem.	demonstrative, *démonstratif.*		*npr.*	*nom propre*, proper name.
dial.	*dialectal*, dialectal.		*num.*	*numéral*, numeral.
dimin.	*diminutif*, diminutive.			
			oft.	often, *souvent.*
eccl.	*ecclésiastique*, ecclesiastical.		*opt.*	*optique*, optics.
e.g.	exempli gratia, for example, *par exemple.*		*orn.*	*ornithologie*, ornithology.
esp.	especially, *surtout.*		*o.s., o.s.*	oneself, *soi-même.*
etc.	et cetera, and so on.		*p.*	*personne*, person.
f	*féminin*, feminine.		*paint.*	painting, *peinture.*
fig.	figuratively, *sens figuré.*		*parl.*	*parlement*, parliament.
foot.	football, football.		*pej.*	pejoratively, *sens péjoratif.*
Fr.	French, *français.*		*pers.*	*personnel*, personal.
fut.	*futur*, future.		*phls.*	*philosophie*, philosophy.
			phot.	*photographie*, photography.
geog.	geography, *géographie.*		*phys.*	*physique*, physics.
geol.	geology, *géologie.*		*physiol.*	*physiologie*, physiology.
ger.	gerund, *gérondif.*		*pl.*	*pluriel*, plural.
			poet.	poetic, *poétique.*
			pol.	*politique*, politics.